KEY TO WORLD MAP PAGES

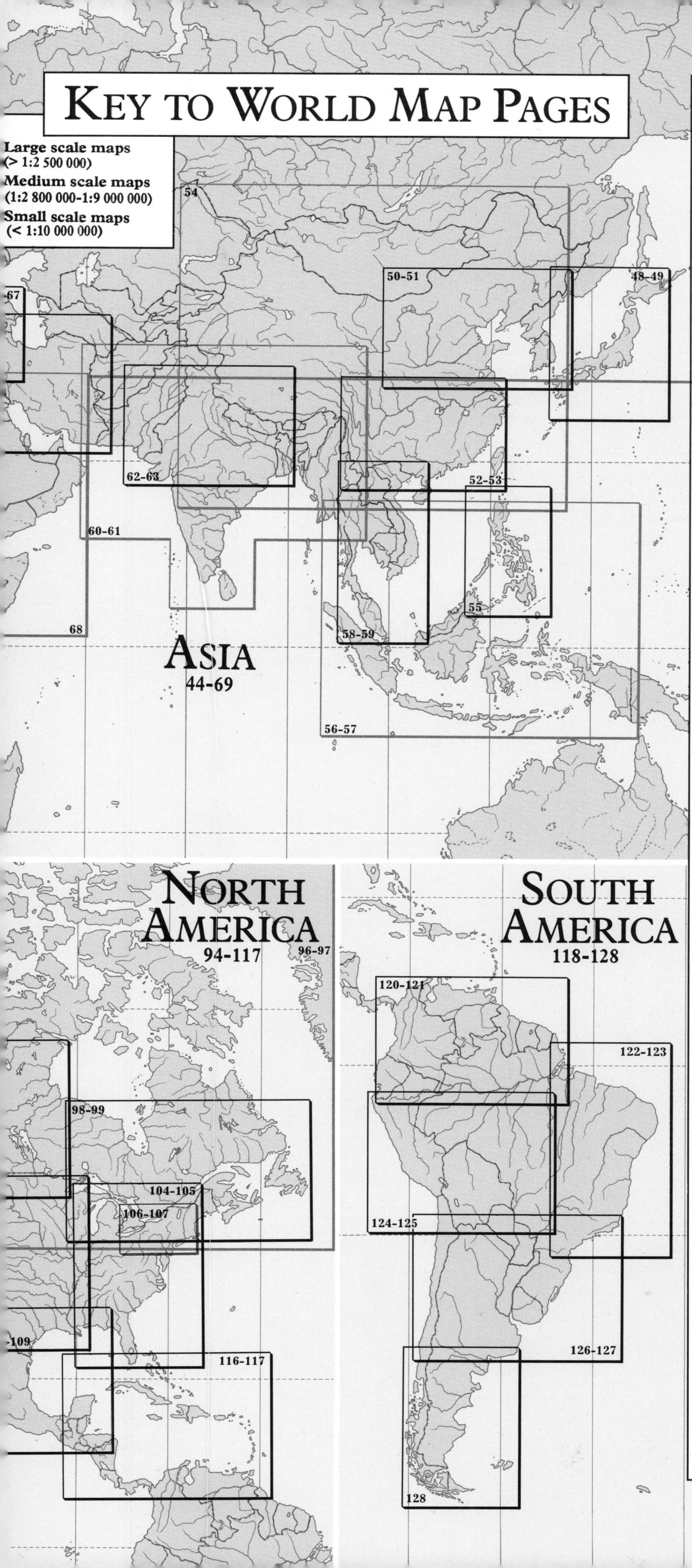

COUNTRY INDEX

Country	Page
Afghanistan	60
Albania	38–39
[illegible]	[illegible]
Bahamas	[illegible]
Bahrain	65
Bangladesh	61
Barbados	117
Belarus	40
Belgium	17
Belize	116
Benin	79
Bhutan	61
Bolivia	124–125
Bosnia-Herzegovina	21
Botswana	84–85
Brazil	120–127
Brunei	56
Bulgaria	38–39
Burkina Faso	78–79
Burma	61
Burundi	82
Cambodia	58–59
Cameroon	82
Canada	96–101
Central African Republic	82
Chad	73
Chile	126, 128
China	50–54
Colombia	120
Congo	80
Costa Rica	116
Croatia	21
Cuba	116–117
Cyprus	37
Czech Republic	20–21
Denmark	11
Djibouti	68
Dominican Republic	117
Ecuador	120
Egypt	76
El Salvador	116
England	12–13
Equatorial Guinea	80
Eritrea	76–77
Estonia	40
Ethiopia	68, 77
Fiji	87
Finland	8–9
France	24–27
French Guiana	121
Gabon	80
Gambia	78
Georgia	43
Germany	18–19
Ghana	78–79
Greece	39
Greenland	4
Guatemala	116
Guinea	78
Guinea-Bissau	78
Guyana	121
Haiti	117
Honduras	116
Hong Kong	53
Hungary	21
Iceland	8
India	60–63
Indonesia	56–57
Iran	64–65
Iraq	64–65
Irish Republic	15
Israel	69
Italy	32–35
Ivory Coast	78
Jamaica	116
Japan	48–49
Jordan	69
Kazakstan	44
Kenya	82
Korea, North	51
Korea, South	51
Kuwait	64–65
Kyrgyzstan	44
[illegible]	58
[illegible]	40
[illegible]	69
[illegible]	85
[illegible]	78
[illegible]	73
[illegible]	40
[illegible]urg	17
Macedonia	38–39
Madagascar	85
Malawi	83
Malaysia	55–56
Mali	78–79
Malta	37
Mauritania	78
Mauritius	71
Mexico	114–115
Moldova	41
Mongolia	54
Morocco	74
Mozambique	83
Namibia	84
Nepal	63
Netherlands	16–17
New Zealand	87
Nicaragua	116
Niger	79
Nigeria	79
Northern Ireland	15
Norway	8–9
Oman	68
Pakistan	62
Panama	116
Papua New Guinea	86
Paraguay	126–127
Peru	124
Philippines	55
Poland	20
Portugal	30–31
Puerto Rico	117
Qatar	65
Romania	38
Russia	40–45
Rwanda	82
Saudi Arabia	68
Scotland	14
Senegal	78
Sierra Leone	78
Singapore	59
Slovak Republic	20–21
Slovenia	33
Somali Republic	68
South Africa	84–85
Spain	28–31
Sri Lanka	60
Sudan	77
Surinam	121
Swaziland	85
Sweden	8–9
Switzerland	22–23
Syria	67
Taiwan	53
Tajikistan	44
Tanzania	82–83
Thailand	58–59
Togo	79
Trinidad and Tobago	117
Tunisia	75
Turkey	66–67
Turkmenistan	44
Uganda	82
Ukraine	41
United Arab Emirates	65
United Kingdom	12–15
USA	102–113
Uruguay	126–127
Uzbekistan	44
Venezuela	120–121
Vietnam	58–59
Wales	12–13
Yemen	68
Yugoslavia	38–39
Zaïre	80–81
Zambia	83
Zimbabwe	83

Enzo Falò

PHILIP'S

CONCISE WORLD ATLAS

PHILIP'S

CONCISE WORLD ATLAS

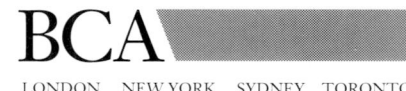

BCA
LONDON NEW YORK SYDNEY TORONTO

THE EARTH IN SPACE
Cartography by Philip's

Text
Keith Lye

Executive Editor
Caroline Rayner

Executive Art Editor
Alison Myer

Editor
Kara Turner

Production
Claudette Morris

Picture Research
Liz Fowler

Illustrations
Stefan Chabluk

Star Charts
John Cox
Richard Monkhouse

PICTURE ACKNOWLEDGEMENTS
Zefa Picture Library /Tom V. Sant /Geosphere Project front cover, spine, main title page
Robert Harding Picture Library /PHOTRI 13, /Bill Ross 41, /Adam Woolfitt 43
Hutchison Library /Melanie Friend 47, /John Hatt 46
Image Bank /Peter Hendrie 20, /Daniel Hummel 34, /Image Makers 8 top, /Pete Turner 39
Images Colour Library Limited 15
Japan National Tourist Organisation 45
Panos Pictures /Howard Davies 35
Chris Rayner 19 top
Rex Features /SIPA Press /Scott Andrews 12
Science Photo Library /Martin Bond 14, /CNES, 1992 Distribution Spot Image 27 top, /Luke Dodd 3, 6, /Earth Satellite Corporation 25 bottom, /NASA 9 centre right, 9 top, 22, 23, 24, /David Parker 26, /Peter Ryan 27 below, /Jerry Schad 4, /Space Telescope Science Institute /NASA 9 centre left, 9 bottom right, /US Geological Survey 8 centre right
Space Telescope Science Institute /R. Williams /NASA 2 top
Starland Picture Library /NASA 8 centre left
Still Pictures /Francois Pierrel 28, /Heine Pedersen 31, 40
Tony Stone Images 33, /Glen Allison 38, /James Balog 16, /John Beatty 21, /Neil Beer 30, /Kristin Finnegan 11, /Jeremy Horner 42, /Kevin Kelley 8 bottom, /Gary Norman 36, /Frank Oberle 25 top, /Dennis Oda 17, /Nigel Press 37, /Donovan Reese 18, 19, /Hugh Sitton 32, /Richard Surman 44, /Michael Townsend 29, /World Perspectives 10
Telegraph Colour Library /Space Frontiers 9 bottom left

This edition published 1996
by BCA by arrangement with
George Philip Limited,
an imprint of Reed Books.

Cartography by Philip's

CN 3515

Printed in China

Philip's World Maps

The reference maps which form the main body of this atlas have been prepared in accordance with the highest standards of international cartography to provide an accurate and detailed representation of the Earth. The scales and projections used have been carefully chosen to give balanced coverage of the world, while emphasizing the most densely populated and economically significant regions. A hallmark of Philip's mapping is the use of hill shading and relief colouring to create a graphic impression of landforms: this makes the maps exceptionally easy to read. However, knowledge of the key features employed in the construction and presentation of the maps will enable the reader to derive the fullest benefit from the atlas.

MAP SEQUENCE

The atlas covers the Earth continent by continent: first Europe; then its land neighbour Asia (mapped north before south, in a clockwise sequence), then Africa, Australia and Oceania, North America and South America. This is the classic arrangement adopted by most cartographers since the 16th century. For each continent, there are maps at a variety of scales. First, physical relief and political maps of the whole continent; then a series of larger-scale maps

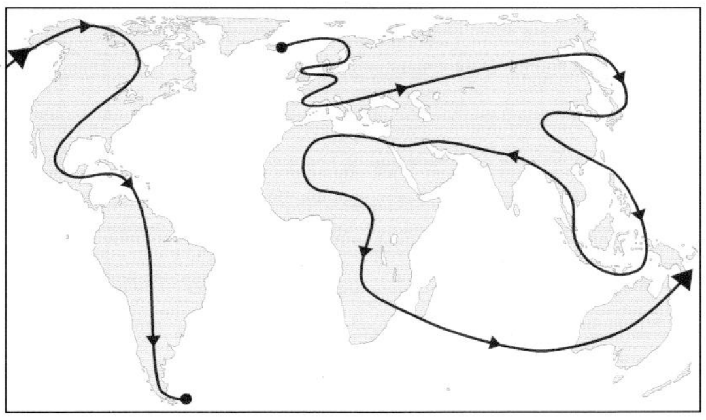

of the regions within the continent, each followed, where required, by still larger-scale maps of the most important or densely populated areas. The governing principle is that by turning the pages of the atlas, the reader moves steadily from north to south through each continent, with each map overlapping its neighbours. A key map showing this sequence, and the area covered by each map, can be found on the endpapers of the atlas.

MAP PRESENTATION

With very few exceptions (e.g. for the Arctic and Antarctic), the maps are drawn with north at the top, regardless of whether they are presented upright or sideways on the page. In the borders will be found the map title; a locator diagram showing the area covered and the page numbers for maps of adjacent areas; the scale; the projection used; the degrees of latitude and longitude; and the letters and figures used in the index for locating place names and geographical features. Physical relief maps also have a height reference panel identifying the colours used for each layer of contouring.

MAP SYMBOLS

Each map contains a vast amount of detail which can only be conveyed clearly and accurately by the use of symbols. Points and circles of varying sizes locate and identify the relative importance of towns and cities; different styles of type are employed for administrative, geographical and regional place names to aid identification. A variety of pictorial symbols denote landscape features such as glaciers, marshes and coral reefs, and man-made structures including roads, railways, airports, canals and dams. International borders are shown by red lines. Where neighbouring countries are in dispute, for example in parts of the Middle East, the maps show the *de facto* boundary between nations, regardless of the legal or historical situation. The symbols are explained on the first page of the World Maps section of the atlas.

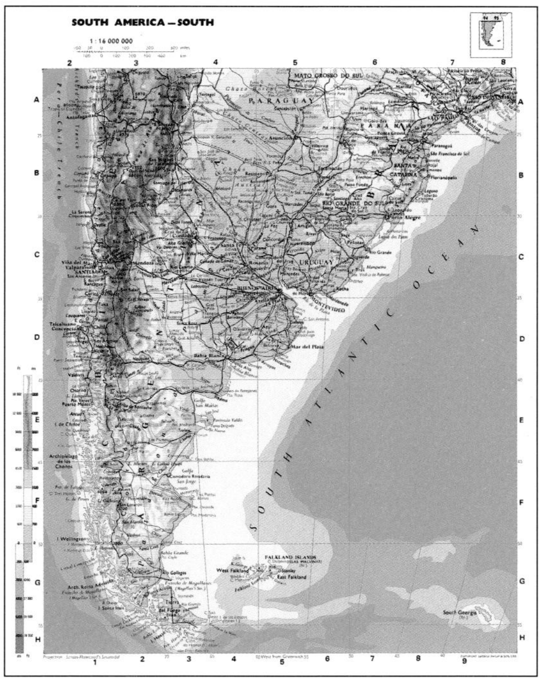

MAP SCALES

1:16 000 000
1 inch = 252 statute miles

The scale of each map is given in the numerical form known as the 'representative fraction'. The first figure is always one, signifying one unit of distance on the map; the second figure, usually in millions, is the number by which the map unit must be multiplied to give the equivalent distance on the Earth's surface. Calculations can easily be made in centimetres and kilometres, by dividing the Earth units figure by 100 000 (i.e. deleting the last five 0s). Thus 1:1 000 000 means 1 cm = 10 km. The calculation for inches and miles is more laborious, but 1 000 000 divided by 63 360 (the number of inches in a mile) shows that 1:1 000 000 means approximately 1 inch = 16 miles. The table below provides distance equivalents for scales down to 1:50 000 000.

LARGE SCALE

1:1 000 000	1 cm = 10 km	1 inch = 16 miles
1:2 500 000	1 cm = 25 km	1 inch = 39.5 miles
1:5 000 000	1 cm = 50 km	1 inch = 79 miles
1:6 000 000	1 cm = 60 km	1 inch = 95 miles
1:8 000 000	1 cm = 80 km	1 inch = 126 miles
1:10 000 000	1 cm = 100km	1 inch = 158 miles
1:15 000 000	1 cm = 150 km	1 inch = 237 miles
1:20 000 000	1 cm = 200 km	1 inch = 316 miles
1:50 000 000	1 cm = 500 km	1 inch = 790 miles

SMALL SCALE

MEASURING DISTANCES

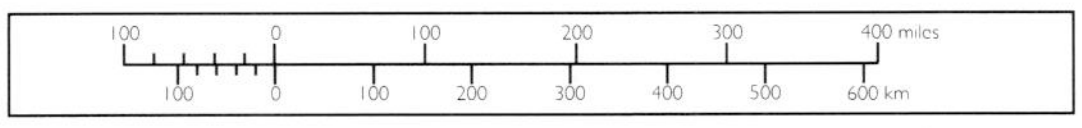

Although each map is accompanied by a scale bar, distances cannot always be measured with confidence because of the distortions involved in portraying the curved surface of the Earth on a flat page. As a general rule, the larger the map scale (i.e. the lower the number of Earth units in the representative fraction), the more accurate and reliable will be the distance measured. On small-scale maps such as those of the world and of entire continents, measurement may only be accurate along the 'standard parallels', or central axes, and should not be attempted without considering the map projection.

MAP PROJECTIONS

Unlike a globe, no flat map can give a true scale representation of the world in terms of area, shape and position of every region. Each of the numerous systems that have been devised for projecting the curved surface of the Earth on to a flat page involves the sacrifice of accuracy in one or more of these elements. The variations in shape and position of landmasses such as Alaska, Greenland and Australia, for example, can be quite dramatic when different projections are compared.

For this atlas, the guiding principle has been to select projections that involve the least distortion of size and distance. The projection used for each map is noted in the border. Most fall into one of three categories – conic, cylindrical or azimuthal – whose basic concepts are shown above. Each involves plotting the forms of the Earth's surface on a grid of latitude and longitude lines, which may be shown as parallels, curves or radiating spokes.

LATITUDE AND LONGITUDE

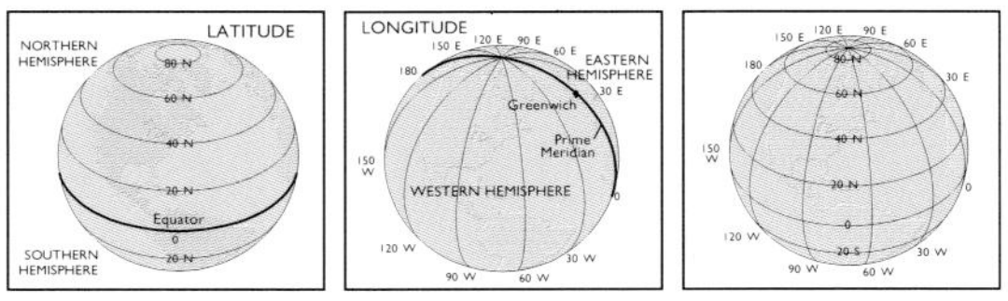

Accurate positioning of individual points on the Earth's surface is made possible by reference to the geometrical system of latitude and longitude. Latitude *parallels* are drawn west–east around the Earth and numbered by degrees north and south of the Equator, which is designated 0° of latitude. Longitude *meridians* are drawn north–south and numbered by degrees east and west of the *prime meridian*, 0° of longitude, which passes through Greenwich in England. By referring to these co-ordinates and their subdivisions of minutes (1/60th of a degree) and seconds (1/60th of a minute), any place on Earth can be located to within a few hundred yards. Latitude and longitude are indicated by blue lines on the maps; they are straight or curved according to the projection employed. Reference to these lines is the easiest way of determining the relative positions of places on different maps, and for plotting compass directions.

NAME FORMS

For ease of reference, both English and local name forms appear in the atlas. Oceans, seas and countries are shown in English throughout the atlas; country names may be abbreviated to their commonly accepted form (e.g. Germany, not The Federal Republic of Germany). Conventional English forms are also used for place names on the smaller-scale maps of the continents. However, local name forms are used on all large-scale and regional maps, with the English form given in brackets only for important cities – the large-scale map of Russia and Central Asia thus shows Moskva (Moscow). For countries which do not use a Roman script, place names have been transcribed according to the systems adopted by the British and US Geographic Names Authorities. For China, the Pin Yin system has been used, with some more widely known forms appearing in brackets, as with Beijing (Peking). Both English and local names appear in the index, the English form being cross-referenced to the local form.

Contents

ASIA

NORTH AMERICA

SOUTH AMERICA

INDEX TO WORLD MAPS

World Statistics: Countries

This alphabetical list includes all the countries and territories of the world. If a territory is not completely independent, then the country it is associated with is named. The area figures give the total area of land, inland water and ice. Units for areas and populations are thousands. The population figures are 1995 estimates. The annual income is the Gross National Product per capita in US dollars. The figures are the latest available, usually 1994.

Country/Territory	Area km² Thousands	Area miles² Thousands	Population Thousands	Capital	Annual Income US $
Afghanistan	652	252	19,509	Kabul	220
Albania	28.8	11.1	3,458	Tirana	340
Algeria	2,382	920	25,012	Algiers	1,650
American Samoa (US)	0.20	0.08	58	Pago Pago	2,600
Andorra	0.45	0.17	65	Andorra La Vella	14,000
Angola	1,247	481	10,020	Luanda	600
Anguilla (UK)	0.1	0.04	8	The Valley	6,800
Antigua & Barbuda	0.44	0.17	67	St John's	6,390
Argentina	2,767	1,068	34,663	Buenos Aires	7,290
Armenia	29.8	11.5	3,603	Yerevan	660
Aruba (Neths)	0.19	0.07	71	Oranjestad	17,500
Australia	7,687	2,968	18,107	Canberra	17,510
Austria	83.9	32.4	8,004	Vienna	23,120
Azerbaijan	86.6	33.4	7,559	Baku	730
Azores (Port.)	2.2	0.87	238	Ponta Delgada	–
Bahamas	13.9	5.4	277	Nassau	11,500
Bahrain	0.68	0.26	558	Manama	7,870
Bangladesh	144	56	118,342	Dhaka	220
Barbados	0.43	0.17	263	Bridgetown	6,240
Belarus	207.6	80.1	10,500	Minsk	2,930
Belgium	30.5	11.8	10,140	Brussels	21,210
Belize	23	8.9	216	Belmopan	2,440
Benin	113	43	5,381	Porto-Novo	420
Bermuda (UK)	0.05	0.02	64	Hamilton	27,000
Bhutan	47	18.1	1,639	Thimphu	170
Bolivia	1,099	424	7,900	La Paz/Sucre	770
Bosnia-Herzegovina	51	20	3,800	Sarajevo	2,500
Botswana	582	225	1,481	Gaborone	2,590
Brazil	8,512	3,286	161,416	Brasília	3,020
Brunei	5.8	2.2	284	Bandar Seri Begawan	9,000
Bulgaria	111	43	8,771	Sofia	1,160
Burkina Faso	274	106	10,326	Ouagadougou	300
Burma (Myanmar)	677	261	46,580	Rangoon	950
Burundi	27.8	10.7	6,412	Bujumbura	180
Cambodia	181	70	10,452	Phnom Penh	600
Cameroon	475	184	13,232	Yaoundé	770
Canada	9,976	3,852	29,972	Ottawa	20,670
Canary Is. (Spain)	7.3	2.8	1,494	Las Palmas/Santa Cruz	–
Cape Verde Is.	4	1.6	386	Praia	870
Cayman Is. (UK)	0.26	0.10	31	George Town	20,000
Central African Republic	623	241	3,294	Bangui	390
Chad	1,284	496	6,314	Ndjaména	200
Chile	757	292	14,271	Santiago	3,070
China	9,597	3,705	1,226,944	Beijing	490
Colombia	1,139	440	34,948	Bogotá	1,400
Comoros	2.2	0.86	654	Moroni	520
Congo	342	132	2,593	Brazzaville	920
Cook Is. (NZ)	0.24	0.09	19	Avarua	900
Costa Rica	51.1	19.7	3,436	San José	2,160
Croatia	56.5	21.8	4,900	Zagreb	4,500
Cuba	111	43	11,050	Havana	1,250
Cyprus	9.3	3.6	742	Nicosia	10,380
Czech Republic	78.9	30.4	10,500	Prague	2,730
Denmark	43.1	16.6	5,229	Copenhagen	26,510
Djibouti	23.2	9	603	Djibouti	780
Dominica	0.75	0.29	89	Roseau	2,680
Dominican Republic	48.7	18.8	7,818	Santo Domingo	1,080
Ecuador	284	109	11,384	Quito	1,170
Egypt	1,001	387	64,100	Cairo	660
El Salvador	21	8.1	5,743	San Salvador	1,320
Equatorial Guinea	28.1	10.8	400	Malabo	360
Eritrea	94	36	3,850	Asmara	500
Estonia	44.7	17.3	1,531	Tallinn	3,040
Ethiopia	1,128	436	51,600	Addis Ababa	100
Faroe Is. (Den.)	1.4	0.54	47	Tórshavn	23,660
Fiji	18.3	7.1	773	Suva	2,140
Finland	338	131	5,125	Helsinki	18,970
France	552	213	58,286	Paris	22,360
French Guiana (Fr.)	90	34.7	154	Cayenne	5,000
French Polynesia (Fr.)	4	1.5	217	Papeete	7,000
Gabon	268	103	1,316	Libreville	4,050
Gambia, The	11.3	4.4	1,144	Banjul	360
Georgia	69.7	26.9	5,448	Tbilisi	560
Germany	357	138	82,000	Berlin/Bonn	23,560
Ghana	239	92	17,462	Accra	430
Gibraltar (UK)	0.007	0.003	28	Gibraltar Town	5,000
Greece	132	51	10,510	Athens	7,390
Greenland (Den.)	2,176	840	59	Godthåb (Nuuk)	9,000
Grenada	0.34	0.13	94	St George's	2,410
Guadeloupe (Fr.)	1.7	0.66	443	Basse-Terre	9,000
Guam (US)	0.55	0.21	155	Agana	6,000
Guatemala	109	42	10,624	Guatemala City	1,110
Guinea	246	95	6,702	Conakry	510
Guinea-Bissau	36.1	13.9	1,073	Bissau	220
Guyana	215	83	832	Georgetown	350
Haiti	27.8	10.7	7,180	Port-au-Prince	800
Honduras	112	43	5,940	Tegucigalpa	580
Hong Kong (UK)	1.1	0.40	6,000	–	17,860
Hungary	93	35.9	10,500	Budapest	3,330
Iceland	103	40	269	Reykjavik	23,620
India	3,288	1,269	942,989	New Delhi	290
Indonesia	1,905	735	198,644	Jakarta	730
Iran	1,648	636	68,885	Tehran	4,750
Iraq	438	169	20,184	Baghdad	2,000
Ireland	70.3	27.1	3,589	Dublin	12,580
Israel	27	10.3	5,696	Jerusalem	13,760
Italy	301	116	57,181	Rome	19,620
Ivory Coast	322	125	14,271	Yamoussoukro	630
Jamaica	11	4.2	2,700	Kingston	1,390
Japan	378	146	125,156	Tokyo	31,450
Jordan	89.2	34.4	5,547	Amman	1,190
Kazakstan	2,717	1,049	17,099	Alma-Ata	1,540
Kenya	580	224	28,240	Nairobi	270
Kiribati	0.72	0.28	80	Tarawa	710
Korea, North	121	47	23,931	Pyŏngyang	1,100
Korea, South	99	38.2	45,088	Seoul	7,670
Kuwait	17.8	6.9	1,668	Kuwait City	23,350
Kyrgyzstan	198.5	76.6	4,738	Bishkek	830
Laos	237	91	4,906	Vientiane	290
Latvia	65	25	2,558	Riga	2,030
Lebanon	10.4	4	2,971	Beirut	1,750
Lesotho	30.4	11.7	2,064	Maseru	660
Liberia	111	43	3,092	Monrovia	800
Libya	1,760	679	5,410	Tripoli	6,500
Liechtenstein	0.16	0.06	31	Vaduz	33,510
Lithuania	65.2	25.2	3,735	Vilnius	1,310
Luxembourg	2.6	1	408	Luxembourg	35,850
Macau (Port.)	0.02	0.006	490	Macau	7,500
Macedonia	25.7	9.9	2,173	Skopje	730
Madagascar	587	227	15,206	Antananarivo	240
Madeira (Port.)	0.81	0.31	253	Funchal	–
Malawi	118	46	9,800	Lilongwe	220
Malaysia	330	127	20,174	Kuala Lumpur	3,160
Maldives	0.30	0.12	254	Malé	820
Mali	1,240	479	10,700	Bamako	300
Malta	0.32	0.12	367	Valletta	6,800
Marshall Is.	0.18	0.07	55	Dalap-Uliga-Darrit	1,500
Martinique (Fr.)	1.1	0.42	384	Fort-de-France	3,500
Mauritania	1,025	396	2,268	Nouakchott	510
Mauritius	2.0	0.72	1,112	Port Louis	2,980
Mayotte (Fr.)	0.37	0.14	101	Mamoundzou	1,430
Mexico	1,958	756	93,342	Mexico City	3,750
Micronesia, Fed. States of	0.70	0.27	125	Palikir	1,560
Moldova	33.7	13	4,434	Chişinău	1,180
Monaco	0.002	0.0001	32	Monaco	16,000
Mongolia	1,567	605	2,408	Ulan Bator	400
Montserrat (UK)	0.10	0.04	11	Plymouth	4,500
Morocco	447	172	26,857	Rabat	1,030
Mozambique	802	309	17,800	Maputo	80
Namibia	825	318	1,610	Windhoek	1,660
Nauru	0.02	0.008	12	Yaren District	10,000
Nepal	141	54	21,953	Katmandu	160
Netherlands	41.5	16	15,495	Amsterdam/The Hague	20,710
Neths Antilles (Neths)	0.99	0.38	199	Willemstad	9,700
New Caledonia (Fr.)	19	7.3	181	Nouméa	6,000
New Zealand	269	104	3,567	Wellington	12,900
Nicaragua	130	50	4,544	Managua	360
Niger	1,267	489	9,149	Niamey	270
Nigeria	924	357	88,515	Abuja	310
Northern Mariana Is. (US)	0.48	0.18	47	Saipan	11,500
Norway	324	125	4,361	Oslo	26,340
Oman	212	82	2,252	Muscat	5,600
Pakistan	796	307	143,595	Islamabad	430
Palau	0.46	0.18	17	Koror	2,260
Panama	77.1	29.8	2,629	Panama City	2,580
Papua New Guinea	463	179	4,292	Port Moresby	1,120
Paraguay	407	157	4,979	Asunción	1,500
Peru	1,285	496	23,588	Lima	1,490
Philippines	300	116	67,167	Manila	830
Poland	313	121	38,587	Warsaw	2,270
Portugal	92.4	35.7	10,600	Lisbon	7,890
Puerto Rico (US)	9	3.5	3,689	San Juan	7,020
Qatar	11	4.2	594	Doha	15,140
Réunion (Fr.)	2.5	0.97	655	Saint-Denis	3,900
Romania	238	92	22,863	Bucharest	1,120
Russia	17,075	6,592	148,385	Moscow	2,350
Rwanda	26.3	10.2	7,899	Kigali	200
St Kitts & Nevis	0.36	0.14	45	Basseterre	4,470
St Lucia	0.62	0.24	147	Castries	3,040
St Vincent & Grenadines	0.39	0.15	111	Kingstown	1,730
San Marino	0.06	0.02	26	San Marino	20,000
São Tomé & Príncipe	0.96	0.37	133	São Tomé	330
Saudi Arabia	2,150	830	18,395	Riyadh	8,000
Senegal	197	76	8,308	Dakar	730
Seychelles	0.46	0.18	75	Victoria	6,370
Sierra Leone	71.7	27.7	4,467	Freetown	140
Singapore	0.62	0.24	2,990	Singapore	19,310
Slovak Republic	49	18.9	5,400	Bratislava	1,900
Slovenia	20.3	7.8	2,000	Ljubljana	6,310
Solomon Is.	28.9	11.2	378	Honiara	750
Somalia	638	246	9,180	Mogadishu	500
South Africa	1,220	471	44,000	C. Town/Pretoria/Bloemfontein	2,900
Spain	505	195	39,664	Madrid	13,650
Sri Lanka	65.6	25.3	18,359	Colombo	600
Sudan	2,506	967	29,980	Khartoum	750
Surinam	163	63	421	Paramaribo	1,210
Swaziland	17.4	6.7	849	Mbabane	1,050
Sweden	450	174	8,893	Stockholm	24,830
Switzerland	41.3	15.9	7,268	Bern	36,410
Syria	185	71	14,614	Damascus	5,700
Taiwan	36	13.9	21,100	Taipei	11,000
Tajikistan	143.1	55.2	6,102	Dushanbe	470
Tanzania	945	365	29,710	Dodoma	100
Thailand	513	198	58,432	Bangkok	2,040
Togo	56.8	21.9	4,140	Lomé	330
Tonga	0.75	0.29	107	Nuku'alofa	1,610
Trinidad & Tobago	5.1	2	1,295	Port of Spain	3,730
Tunisia	164	63	8,906	Tunis	1,780
Turkey	779	301	61,303	Ankara	2,120
Turkmenistan	488.1	188.5	4,100	Ashkhabad	1,400
Turks & Caicos Is. (UK)	0.43	0.17	15	Cockburn Town	5,000
Tuvalu	0.03	0.01	10	Fongafale	600
Uganda	236	91	21,466	Kampala	190
Ukraine	603.7	233.1	52,027	Kiev	1,910
United Arab Emirates	83.6	32.3	2,800	Abu Dhabi	22,470
United Kingdom	243.3	94	58,306	London	17,970
United States of America	9,373	3,619	263,563	Washington, DC	24,750
Uruguay	177	68	3,186	Montevideo	3,910
Uzbekistan	447.4	172.7	22,833	Tashkent	960
Vanuatu	12.2	4.7	167	Port-Vila	1,230
Venezuela	912	352	21,800	Caracas	2,840
Vietnam	332	127	74,580	Hanoi	170
Virgin Is. (UK)	0.15	0.06	20	Road Town	–
Virgin Is. (US)	0.34	0.13	105	Charlotte Amalie	12,000
Wallis & Futuna Is. (Fr.)	0.20	0.08	13	Mata-Utu	–
Western Sahara	266	103	220	El Aaiún	300
Western Samoa	2.8	1.1	169	Apia	980
Yemen	528	204	14,609	Sana	800
Yugoslavia	102.3	39.5	10,881	Belgrade	1,000
Zaire	2,345	905	44,504	Kinshasa	500
Zambia	753	291	9,500	Lusaka	370
Zimbabwe	391	151	11,453	Harare	540

World Statistics: Cities

This list shows the principal cities with more than 500,000 inhabitants (for China and India only cities with more than 1 million inhabitants are included). The figures are taken from the most recent census or population estimate available, and as far as possible are the population of the metropolitan area, e.g. greater New York, Mexico or London. All the figures are in thousands. Local name forms have been used for the smaller cities (e.g. Kraków).

AFGHANISTAN	
Kabul	1,424
ALGERIA	
Algiers	1,722
Oran	664
ANGOLA	
Luanda	1,544
ARGENTINA	
Buenos Aires	11,256
Córdoba	1,198
Rosario	1,096
Mendoza	775
La Plata	640
San Miguel de Tucumán	622
Mar del Plata	520
ARMENIA	
Yerevan	1,254
AUSTRALIA	
Sydney	3,657
Melbourne	3,081
Perth	1,193
Adelaide	1,050
Brisbane	777
AUSTRIA	
Vienna	1,560
AZERBAIJAN	
Baku	1,149
BANGLADESH	
Dhaka	6,105
Chittagong	2,041
Khulna	877
Rajshahi	517
BELARUS	
Minsk	1,613
Gomel	506
BELGIUM	
Brussels	952
BOLIVIA	
La Paz	1,126
Santa Cruz	695
BOSNIA-HERZEGOVINA	
Sarajevo	526
BRAZIL	
São Paulo	9,480
Rio de Janeiro	5,336
Salvador	2,056
Belo Horizonte	2,049
Fortaleza	1,758
Brasília	1,596
Curitiba	1,290
Recife	1,290
Nova Iguaçu	1,286
Pôrto Alegre	1,263
Belém	1,246
Manaus	1,011
Goiânia	921
Campinas	846
Guarulhos	781
São Gonçalo	748
São Luís	696
Duque de Caxias	665
Maceió	628
Santo André	614
Natal	607
Teresina	598
São Bernado de Campo	565
Osasco	563
Campo Grande	526
BULGARIA	
Sofia	1,221
BURKINA FASO	
Ouagadougou	634
BURMA (MYANMAR)	
Rangoon	2,513
Mandalay	533
CAMBODIA	
Phnom Penh	900
CAMEROON	
Douala	884
Yaoundé	750
CANADA	
Toronto	3,893
Montréal	3,127
Vancouver	1,603
Ottawa–Hull	921
Edmonton	840
Calgary	754
Winnipeg	652
Québec	646
Hamilton	600
CENTRAL AFRICAN REP.	
Bangui	597
CHAD	
Ndjaména	530
CHILE	
Santiago	5,343
CHINA	
Shanghai	8,930
Beijing	6,690
Tianjin	5,000
Shenyang	4,050
Chongqing	3,870
Wuhan	3,870
Guangzhou	3,750
Harbin	3,120
Chengdu	2,760
Nanjing	2,490
Changchun	2,470
Xi'an	2,410
Dalian	2,400
Zibo	2,400
Qingdao	2,300
Jinan	2,150
Hangzhou	1,790
Taiyuan	1,720
Zhengzhou	1,690
Shijiazhuang	1,610
Changsha	1,510
Kunming	1,500
Nanchang	1,440
Fuzhou, Fujian	1,380
Lanzhou	1,340
Anshan	1,204
Fushun	1,202
Ürümqi	1,130
Hefei	1,110
Ningbo	1,100
Guiyang	1,080
Qiqihar	1,070
Tangshan	1,044
Jilin	1,037
Linhai	1,012
Macheng	1,010
COLOMBIA	
Bogotá	5,132
Cali	1,687
Medellín	1,608
Barranquilla	1,049
Cartagena	726
CONGO	
Brazzaville	938
Pointe-Noire	576
CROATIA	
Zagreb	931
CUBA	
Havana	2,119
CZECH REPUBLIC	
Prague	1,216
DENMARK	
Copenhagen	1,337
DOMINICAN REPUBLIC	
Santo Domingo	2,200
ECUADOR	
Guayaquil	1,508
Quito	1,101
EGYPT	
Cairo	6,800
Alexandria	3,380
El Gîza	2,144
Shubra el Kheima	834
EL SALVADOR	
San Salvador	1,522
ETHIOPIA	
Addis Ababa	2,213
FINLAND	
Helsinki	516
FRANCE	
Paris	9,319
Lyons	1,262
Marseilles	1,087
Lille	959
Bordeaux	696
Toulouse	650
Nice	516
GEORGIA	
Tbilisi	1,279
GERMANY	
Berlin	3,475
Hamburg	1,703
Munich	1,256
Cologne	693
Frankfurt	660
Essen	622
Dortmund	602
Stuttgart	594
Düsseldorf	575
Bremen	552
Duisburg	537
Hanover	525
GHANA	
Accra	965
GREECE	
Athens	3,097
GUATEMALA	
Guatemala	2,000
GUINEA	
Conakry	810
HAITI	
Port-au-Prince	1,402
HONDURAS	
Tegucigalpa	679
HONG KONG	
Kowloon	2,031
Hong Kong	1,251
HUNGARY	
Budapest	2,009
INDIA	
Bombay (Mumbai)	12,572
Calcutta	10,916
Delhi	7,207
Madras	5,361
Hyderabad	4,280
Bangalore	4,087
Ahmadabad	3,298
Pune	2,485
Kanpur	2,111
Nagpur	1,661
Lucknow	1,642
Surat	1,517
Jaipur	1,514
Coimbatore	1,136
Vadodara	1,115
Indore	1,104
Patna	1,099
Madurai	1,094
Bhopal	1,064
Vishakhapatnam	1,052
Varanasi	1,026
Ludhiana	1,012
INDONESIA	
Jakarta	8,259
Surabaya	2,421
Medan	1,686
Bandung	2,027
Palembang	1,084
Semarang	1,005
Ujung Pandang	913
Malang	650
Surakarta	504
IRAN	
Tehran	6,476
Mashhad	1,759
Esfahan	1,127
Tabriz	1,089
Shiraz	965
Ahvaz	725
Qom	681
Bakhtaran	624
IRAQ	
Baghdad	3,841
Diyala	961
As Sulaymaniyah	952
Arbil	770
Al Mawsil	644
Kadhimain	521
IRELAND	
Dublin	1,024
ISRAEL	
Jerusalem	544
ITALY	
Rome	2,723
Milan	1,359
Naples	1,072
Turin	953
Palermo	697
Genoa	668
IVORY COAST	
Abidjan	1,929
JAMAICA	
Kingston	644
JAPAN	
Tokyo	11,927
Yokohama	3,288
Osaka	2,589
Nagoya	2,159
Sapporo	1,732
Kobe	1,509
Kyoto	1,452
Fukuoka	1,269
Kawasaki	1,200
Hiroshima	1,102
Kitakyushu	1,020
Sendai	951
Chiba	851
Sakai	806
Kumamoto	640
Okayama	605
Hamamatsu	561
Sagamihara	560
Funabashi	540
Kagoshima	540
Higashiosaka	515
JORDAN	
Amman	1,272
Az-Zarqā	605
KAZAKSTAN	
Alma-Ata (Almaty)	1,147
Qaraghandy	613
KENYA	
Nairobi	1,429
KOREA, NORTH	
Pyŏngyang	2,639
Hamhung	775
Chŏngjin	754
Chinnampo	691
Sinŭiju	500
KOREA, SOUTH	
Seoul	10,628
Pusan	3,798
Taegu	2,229
Inchon	1,818
Kwangju	1,145
Taejŏn	1,062
Ulsan	683
Puch'on	668
Suwŏn	645
Sŏngnam	541
Chŏnju	517
KYRGYZSTAN	
Bishkek	628
LATVIA	
Riga	840
LEBANON	
Beirut	1,500
Tripoli	500
LIBYA	
Tripoli	990
LITHUANIA	
Vilnius	576
MACEDONIA	
Skopje	563
MADAGASCAR	
Antananarivo	1,053
MALAYSIA	
Kuala Lumpur	1,145
MALI	
Bamako	746
MAURITANIA	
Nouakchott	600
MEXICO	
Mexico City	15,048
Guadalajara	2,847
Monterrey	2,522
Puebla	1,055
León	872
Ciudad Juárez	798
Tijuana	743
Culiacán Rosales	602
Mexicali	602
Acapulco de Juárez	592
Mérida	557
Chihuahua	530
San Luis Potosí	526
Aguascalientés	506
MOLDOVA	
Chişinău (Kishinev)	667
MONGOLIA	
Ulan Bator	601
MOROCCO	
Casablanca	3,079
Rabat-Salé	1,344
Fès	735
Marrakesh	665
Oujda	661
MOZAMBIQUE	
Maputo	1,070
NETHERLANDS	
Amsterdam	1,091
Rotterdam	1,069
The Hague	694
Utrecht	543
NEW ZEALAND	
Auckland	896
NICARAGUA	
Managua	974
NIGERIA	
Lagos	1,347
Ibadan	1,295
Kano	700
Ogbomosho	661
NORWAY	
Oslo	714
PAKISTAN	
Karachi	5,181
Lahore	2,953
Faisalabad	1,104
Rawalpindi	795
Hyderabad	752
Multan	722
Gujranwala	659
Peshawar	556
PANAMA	
Panama City	584
PARAGUAY	
Asunción	945
PERU	
Lima–Callao	6,601
Callao	638
Arequipa	620
Trujillo	509
PHILIPPINES	
Manila	6,720
Quezon City	1,667
Davao	868
Cebu	641
Caloocan	629
POLAND	
Warsaw	1,655
Lódz	847
Kraków	751
Wroclaw	643
Poznań	590
PORTUGAL	
Lisbon	2,561
Oporto	1,174
PUERTO RICO	
San Juan	1,816
ROMANIA	
Bucharest	2,067
RUSSIA	
Moscow	8,957
Petersburg	5,004
Novosibirsk	1,472
Nizhniy Novgorod	1,451
Yekaterinburg	1,413
Samara	1,271
Omsk	1,193
Chelyabinsk	1,170
Perm	1,108
Kazan	1,107
Ufa	1,100
Volgograd	1,031
Rostov	1,027
Voronezh	958
Krasnoyarsk	925
Saratov	916
Krasnodar	751
Togliatti	677
Vladivostok	675
Barnaul	665
Izhevsk	651
Irkutsk	644
Simbirsk	638
Yaroslavl	637
Khabarovsk	626
Novokuznetsk	614
Tula	591
Orenburg	574
Kemerovo	559
Penza	553
Tyumen	550
Ryazan	533
Naberezhnyye-Chelny	517
Astrakhan	512
Tomsk	506
Lipetsk	504
SAUDI ARABIA	
Riyadh	2,000
Jedda	1,400
Mecca	618
Medina	500
SENEGAL	
Dakar	1,730
SIERRA LEONE	
Freetown	505
SINGAPORE	
Singapore	2,874
SOMALIA	
Mogadishu	1,000
SOUTH AFRICA	
Cape Town	1,912
Johannesburg	1,196
East Rand	1,379
Durban	1,137
Pretoria	1,080
Port Elizabeth	853
West Rand	870
Vanderbijlpark–Vereeniging	774
Soweto	597
Sasolburg	540
SPAIN	
Madrid	3,041
Barcelona	1,631
Valencia	764
Sevilla	714
Zaragoza	607
Málaga	531
SRI LANKA	
Colombo	1,863
SUDAN	
Khartoum	561
Omdurman	526
SWEDEN	
Stockholm	1,539
Göteburg	783
SWITZERLAND	
Zürich	840
SYRIA	
Damascus	1,451
Aleppo	1,445
Homs	518
TAIWAN	
Taipei	2,653
Kaohsiung	1,405
Taichung	817
Tainan	700
Panchiao	544
TAJIKISTAN	
Dushanbe	602
TANZANIA	
Dar-es-Salaam	1,361
THAILAND	
Bangkok	5,876
TOGO	
Lomé	590
TUNISIA	
Tunis	1,395
TURKEY	
Istanbul	6,620
Ankara	2,559
Izmir	1,757
Adana	916
Bursa	835
Gaziantep	603
Konya	513
UGANDA	
Kampala	773
UKRAINE	
Kiev	2,643
Kharkiv	1,622
Dnipropetrovsk	1,190
Donetsk	1,121
Odesa	1,096
Zaporizhzhya	898
Lviv	807
Kryvyy Rih	729
Mariupol	523
Mykolayiv	515
Luhansk	505
UNITED KINGDOM	
London	6,967
Birmingham	1,220
Manchester	981
Glasgow	720
Liverpool	664
Leeds	529
Newcastle	525
UNITED STATES	
New York	19,670
Los Angeles	15,048
Chicago	8,410
San Francisco	6,410
Philadelphia	5,939
Boston	5,439
Detroit	5,246
Washington, DC	4,360
Dallas	4,215
Houston	3,962
Miami	3,309
Atlanta	3,153
Seattle	3,131
Cleveland	2,890
Minneapolis–St Paul	2,618
San Diego	2,601
St Louis	2,519
Baltimore	2,434
Pittsburgh	2,406
Phoenix	2,330
Tampa	2,107
Denver	2,089
Portland (Or.)	1,897
Cincinnati	1,865
Milwaukee	1,629
Kansas City (Mo.)	1,617
Sacramento	1,563
Norfolk	1,497
Indianapolis	1,424
Columbus (Oh.)	1,394
San Antonio	1,379
New Orleans	1,303
Charlotte	1,212
Buffalo	1,194
Hartford	1,156
Salt Lake City	1,128
Oklahoma	984
San Jose	801
Jacksonville	661
Omaha	656
Memphis	610
El Paso	544
URUGUAY	
Montevideo	1,384
UZBEKISTAN	
Tashkent	2,094
VENEZUELA	
Caracas	2,784
Maracaibo	1,364
Valencia	1,032
Maracay	800
Barquisimeto	745
Ciudad Guayana	524
VIETNAM	
Ho Chi Minh City	3,924
Hanoi	3,056
Haiphong	1,448
YUGOSLAVIA	
Belgrade	1,137
ZAÏRE	
Kinshasa	3,804
Lubumbashi	739
Mbuji-Mayi	613
Kolwezi	544
ZAMBIA	
Lusaka	982
ZIMBABWE	
Harare	1,189
Bulawayo	622

World Statistics: Climate

Rainfall and temperature figures are provided for more than 70 cities around the world. As climate is affected by altitude, the height of each city is shown in metres beneath its name. For each location, the top row of figures shows the average temperature in degrees Celsius, and the bottom row the total rainfall or snow in millimetres; the average annual temperature and total annual rainfall are at the end of the rows. The map opposite shows the city locations.

CITY	JAN.	FEB.	MAR.	APR.	MAY	JUNE	JULY	AUG.	SEPT.	OCT.	NOV.	DEC.	YEAR
EUROPE													
Athens, Greece	62	37	37	23	23	14	6	7	15	51	56	71	402
107 m	10	10	12	16	20	25	28	28	24	20	15	11	18
Berlin, Germany	46	40	33	42	49	65	73	69	48	49	46	43	603
55 m	–1	0	4	9	14	17	19	18	15	9	5	1	9
Istanbul, Turkey	109	92	72	46	38	34	34	30	58	81	103	119	816
14 m	5	6	7	11	16	20	23	23	20	16	12	8	14
Lisbon, Portugal	111	76	109	54	44	16	3	4	33	62	93	103	708
77 m	11	12	14	16	17	20	22	23	21	18	14	12	17
London, UK	54	40	37	37	46	45	57	59	49	57	64	48	593
5 m	4	5	7	9	12	16	18	17	15	11	8	5	11
Málaga, Spain	61	51	62	46	26	5	1	3	29	64	64	62	474
33 m	12	13	16	17	19	29	25	26	23	20	16	13	18
Moscow, Russia	39	38	36	37	53	58	88	71	58	45	47	54	624
156 m	13	–10	–4	6	13	16	18	17	12	6	–1	–7	4
Odesa, Ukraine	57	62	30	21	34	34	42	37	37	13	35	71	473
64 m	–3	–1	2	9	15	20	22	22	18	12	9	1	10
Paris, France	56	46	35	42	57	54	59	64	55	50	51	50	619
75 m	3	4	8	11	15	18	20	19	17	12	7	4	12
Rome, Italy	71	62	57	51	46	37	15	21	63	99	129	93	744
17 m	8	9	11	14	18	22	25	25	22	17	13	10	16
Shannon, Ireland	94	67	56	53	61	57	77	79	86	86	96	117	929
2 m	5	5	7	9	12	14	16	16	14	11	8	6	10
Stockholm, Sweden	43	30	25	31	34	45	61	76	60	48	53	48	554
44 m	–3	–3	–1	5	10	15	18	17	12	7	3	0	7
ASIA													
Bahrain	8	18	13	8	<3	0	0	0	0	0	18	18	81
5 m	17	18	21	25	29	32	33	34	31	28	24	19	26
Bangkok, Thailand	8	20	36	58	198	160	160	175	305	206	66	5	1,397
2 m	26	28	29	30	29	29	28	28	28	28	26	25	28
Beirut, Lebanon	191	158	94	53	18	3	<3	<3	5	51	132	185	892
34 m	14	14	16	18	22	24	27	28	26	24	19	16	21
Bombay, India	3	3	3	<3	18	485	617	340	264	64	13	3	1,809
11 m	24	24	26	28	30	29	27	27	27	28	27	26	27
Calcutta, India	10	31	36	43	140	297	325	328	252	114	20	5	1,600
6 m	20	22	27	30	30	30	29	29	29	28	23	19	26
Colombo, Sri Lanka	89	69	147	231	371	224	135	109	160	348	315	147	2,365
7 m	26	26	27	28	28	27	27	27	27	27	26	26	27
Harbin, China	6	5	10	23	43	94	112	104	46	33	8	5	488
160 m	–18	–15	–5	6	13	19	22	21	14	4	–6	–16	3

CITY	JAN.	FEB.	MAR.	APR.	MAY	JUNE	JULY	AUG.	SEPT.	OCT.	NOV.	DEC.	YEAR
ASIA (continued)													
Ho Chi Minh, Vietnam	15	3	13	43	221	330	315	269	335	269	114	56	1,984
9 m	26	27	29	30	29	28	28	28	27	27	27	26	28
Hong Kong	33	46	74	137	292	394	381	361	257	114	43	31	2,162
33 m	16	15	18	22	26	28	28	28	27	25	21	18	23
Jakarta, Indonesia	300	300	211	147	114	97	64	43	66	112	142	203	1,798
8 m	26	26	27	27	27	27	27	27	27	27	27	26	27
Kabul, Afghanistan	31	36	94	102	20	5	3	3	<3	15	20	10	338
1,815 m	–3	–1	6	13	18	22	25	24	20	14	7	3	12
Karachi, Pakistan	13	10	8	3	3	18	81	41	13	<3	3	5	196
4 m	19	20	24	28	30	31	30	29	28	28	24	20	26
Kazalinsk, Kazakstan	10	10	13	13	15	5	5	8	8	10	13	15	125
63 m	–12	–11	–3	6	18	23	25	23	16	8	–1	–7	7
New Delhi, India	23	18	13	8	13	74	180	172	117	10	3	10	640
218 m	14	17	23	28	33	34	31	30	29	26	20	15	25
Omsk, Russia	15	8	8	13	31	51	51	51	28	25	18	20	318
85 m	–22	–19	–12	–1	10	16	18	16	10	1	–11	–18	–1
Shanghai, China	48	58	84	94	94	180	147	142	130	71	51	36	1,135
7 m	4	5	9	14	20	24	28	28	23	19	12	7	16
Singapore	252	173	193	188	173	173	170	196	178	208	254	257	2,413
10 m	26	27	28	28	28	28	28	27	27	27	27	27	27
Tehran, Iran	46	38	46	36	13	3	3	3	3	8	20	31	246
1,220 m	2	5	9	16	21	26	30	29	25	18	12	6	17
Tokyo, Japan	48	74	107	135	147	165	142	152	234	208	97	56	1,565
6 m	3	4	7	13	17	21	25	26	23	17	11	6	14
Ulan Bator, Mongolia	<3	<3	3	5	10	28	76	51	23	5	5	3	208
1,325 m	–26	–21	–13	–1	6	14	16	14	8	–1	–13	–22	–3
Verkhoyansk, Russia	5	5	3	5	8	23	28	25	13	8	8	5	134
100 m	–50	–45	–32	–15	0	12	14	9	2	–15	–38	–48	–17
AFRICA													
Addis Ababa, Ethiopia	<3	3	25	135	213	201	206	239	102	28	<3	0	1,151
2,450 m	19	20	20	20	19	18	18	19	21	22	21	20	20
Antananarivo, Madag.	300	279	178	53	18	8	8	10	18	61	135	287	1,356
1,372 m	21	21	21	19	18	15	14	15	17	19	21	21	19
Cairo, Egypt	5	5	5	3	3	<3	0	0	<3	<3	3	5	28
116 m	13	15	18	21	25	28	28	28	26	24	20	15	22
Cape Town, S. Africa	15	8	18	48	79	84	89	66	43	31	18	10	508
17 m	21	21	20	17	14	13	12	13	14	16	18	19	17
Jo'burg, S. Africa	114	109	89	38	25	8	8	8	23	56	107	125	709
1,665 m	20	20	18	16	13	10	11	13	16	18	19	20	16

CITY	JAN.	FEB.	MAR.	APR.	MAY	JUNE	JULY	AUG.	SEPT.	OCT.	NOV.	DEC.	YEAR
AFRICA (continued)													
Khartoum, Sudan	<3	<3	<3	<3	3	8	53	71	18	5	<3	0	158
390 m	24	25	28	31	33	34	32	31	32	32	28	25	29
Kinshasa, Zaïre	135	145	196	196	158	8	3	3	31	119	221	142	1,354
325 m	26	26	27	27	26	24	23	24	25	26	26	26	25
Lagos, Nigeria	28	46	102	150	269	460	279	64	140	206	69	25	1,836
3 m	27	28	29	28	28	26	26	25	26	26	28	28	27
Lusaka, Zambia	231	191	142	18	3	<3	<3	0	<3	10	91	150	836
1,277 m	21	22	21	21	19	16	16	18	22	24	23	22	21
Monrovia, Liberia	31	56	97	216	516	973	996	373	744	772	236	130	5,138
23 m	26	26	27	27	26	25	24	25	25	25	26	26	26
Nairobi, Kenya	38	64	125	211	158	46	15	23	31	53	109	86	958
820 m	19	19	19	19	18	16	16	16	18	19	18	18	18
Timbuktu, Mali	<3	<3	3	<3	5	23	79	81	38	3	<3	<3	231
301 m	22	24	28	32	34	35	32	30	32	31	28	23	29
Tunis, Tunisia	64	51	41	36	18	8	3	8	33	51	48	61	419
66 m	10	11	13	16	19	23	26	27	25	20	16	11	18
Walvis Bay, Namibia	<3	5	8	3	3	<3	<3	3	<3	<3	<3	<3	23
7 m	19	19	19	18	17	16	15	14	14	15	17	18	18
AUSTRALIA, NEW ZEALAND AND ANTARCTICA													
Alice Springs, Aust.	43	33	28	10	15	13	8	8	8	18	31	38	252
579 m	29	28	25	20	15	12	12	14	18	23	26	28	21
Christchurch, N.Z.	56	43	48	48	66	66	69	48	46	43	48	56	638
10 m	16	16	14	12	9	6	6	7	9	12	14	16	11
Darwin, Australia	386	312	254	97	15	3	<3	3	13	51	119	239	1,491
30 m	29	29	29	29	28	26	25	26	28	29	30	29	28
Mawson, Antarctica	11	30	20	10	44	180	4	40	3	20	0	0	362
14 m	0	–5	–10	–14	–15	–16	–18	–18	–19	–13	–5	–1	–11
Perth, Australia	8	10	20	43	130	180	170	149	86	56	20	13	881
60 m	23	23	22	19	16	14	13	13	15	16	19	22	18
Sydney, Australia	89	102	127	135	127	117	117	76	73	71	73	73	1,181
42 m	22	22	21	18	15	13	12	13	15	18	19	21	17
NORTH AMERICA													
Anchorage, USA	20	18	15	10	13	18	41	66	66	56	25	23	371
40 m	–11	–8	–5	2	7	12	14	13	9	2	–5	–11	2
Chicago, USA	51	51	66	71	86	89	84	81	79	66	61	51	836
251 m	–4	–3	2	9	14	20	23	22	19	12	5	–1	10
Churchill, Canada	15	13	18	23	32	44	46	58	51	43	39	21	402
13 m	–28	–26	–20	–10	–2	6	12	11	5	–2	–12	–22	–7
Edmonton, Canada	25	19	19	22	43	77	89	78	39	17	16	25	466
676 m	–15	–10	–5	4	11	15	17	16	11	6	–4	–10	3
Honolulu, USA	104	66	79	48	25	18	23	28	36	48	64	104	643
12 m	23	18	19	20	22	24	25	26	26	24	22	19	22
Houston, USA	89	76	84	91	119	117	99	99	104	94	89	109	1,171
12 m	12	13	17	21	24	27	28	29	26	22	16	12	21

CITY	JAN.	FEB.	MAR.	APR.	MAY	JUNE	JULY	AUG.	SEPT.	OCT.	NOV.	DEC.	YEAR
NORTH AMERICA (continued)													
Kingston, Jamaica	23	15	23	31	102	89	38	91	99	180	74	36	800
34 m	25	25	25	26	26	28	28	28	27	27	26	26	26
Los Angeles, USA	79	76	71	25	10	3	<3	<3	5	15	31	66	381
95 m	13	14	14	16	17	19	21	22	21	18	16	14	17
Mexico City, Mexico	13	5	10	20	53	119	170	152	130	51	18	8	747
2,309 m	12	13	16	18	19	19	17	18	18	16	14	13	16
Miami, USA	71	53	64	81	173	178	155	160	203	234	71	51	1,516
8 m	20	20	22	23	25	27	28	28	27	25	22	21	24
Montréal, Canada	72	65	74	74	66	82	90	92	88	76	81	87	946
57 m	–10	–9	–3	–6	13	18	21	20	15	9	2	–7	6
New York, USA	94	97	91	81	81	84	107	109	86	89	76	91	1,092
96 m	–1	–1	3	10	16	20	23	23	21	15	7	2	11
St Louis, USA	58	64	89	97	114	114	89	86	81	74	71	64	1,001
173 m	0	1	7	13	19	24	26	26	22	15	8	2	14
San José, Costa Rica	15	5	20	46	229	241	211	241	305	300	145	41	1,798
1,146 m	19	19	21	21	22	21	21	21	21	20	20	19	20
Vancouver, Canada	154	115	101	60	52	45	32	41	67	114	150	182	1,113
14 m	3	5	6	9	12	15	17	17	14	10	6	4	10
Washington, DC, USA	86	76	91	84	94	99	112	109	94	74	66	79	1,064
22 m	1	2	7	12	18	23	25	24	20	14	8	3	13
SOUTH AMERICA													
Antofagasta, Chile	0	0	0	<3	<3	3	5	3	<3	3	<3	0	13
94 m	21	21	20	18	16	15	14	14	15	16	18	19	17
Buenos Aires, Arg.	79	71	109	89	76	61	56	61	79	86	84	99	950
27 m	23	23	21	17	13	9	10	11	13	15	19	22	16
Lima, Peru	3	<3	<3	<3	5	5	8	8	8	3	3	<3	41
120 m	23	24	24	22	19	17	17	16	17	18	19	21	20
Manaus, Brazil	249	231	262	221	170	84	58	38	46	107	142	203	1,811
44 m	28	28	28	27	28	28	28	28	29	29	29	28	28
Paraná, Brazil	287	236	239	102	13	<3	3	5	28	127	231	310	1,582
260 m	23	23	23	23	23	21	21	22	24	24	24	23	23
Rio de Janeiro, Brazil	125	122	130	107	79	53	41	43	66	79	104	137	1,082
61 m	26	26	25	24	22	21	21	21	21	22	23	25	23

World Statistics: Physical Dimensions

Each topic list is divided into continents and within a continent the items are listed in order of size. The order of the continents is as in the atlas, Europe through to South America. The lists down to this mark > are complete; below they are selective. The world top ten are shown in square brackets; in the case of mountains this has not been done because the world top 30 are all in Asia. The figures are rounded as appropriate.

WORLD, CONTINENTS, OCEANS

THE WORLD	km²	miles²	%
The World	509,450,000	196,672,000	–
Land	149,450,000	57,688,000	29.3
Water	360,000,000	138,984,000	70.7
Asia	44,500,000	17,177,000	29.8
Africa	30,302,000	11,697,000	20.3
North America	24,241,000	9,357,000	16.2
South America	17,793,000	6,868,000	11.9
Antarctica	14,100,000	5,443,000	9.4
Europe	9,957,000	3,843,000	6.7
Australia & Oceania	8,557,000	3,303,000	5.7
Pacific Ocean	179,679,000	69,356,000	49.9
Atlantic Ocean	92,373,000	35,657,000	25.7
Indian Ocean	73,917,000	28,532,000	20.5
Arctic Ocean	14,090,000	5,439,000	3.9

SEAS

PACIFIC	km²	miles²
South China Sea	2,974,600	1,148,500
Bering Sea	2,268,000	875,000
Sea of Okhotsk	1,528,000	590,000
East China & Yellow	1,249,000	482,000
Sea of Japan	1,008,000	389,000
Gulf of California	162,000	62,500
Bass Strait	75,000	29,000

ATLANTIC	km²	miles²
Caribbean Sea	2,766,000	1,068,000
Mediterranean Sea	2,516,000	971,000
Gulf of Mexico	1,543,000	596,000
Hudson Bay	1,232,000	476,000
North Sea	575,000	223,000
Black Sea	462,000	178,000
Baltic Sea	422,170	163,000
Gulf of St Lawrence	238,000	92,000

INDIAN	km²	miles²
Red Sea	438,000	169,000
The Gulf	239,000	92,000

MOUNTAINS

EUROPE		m	ft
Mont Blanc	France/Italy	4,807	15,771
Monte Rosa	Italy/Switzerland	4,634	15,203
Dom	Switzerland	4,545	14,911
Liskamm	Switzerland	4,527	14,852
Weisshorn	Switzerland	4,505	14,780
Taschorn	Switzerland	4,490	14,730
Matterhorn/Cervino	Italy/Switz.	4,478	14,691
Mont Maudit	France/Italy	4,465	14,649
Dent Blanche	Switzerland	4,356	14,291
Nadelhorn	Switzerland	4,327	14,196
>			
Grandes Jorasses	France/Italy	4,208	13,806
Jungfrau	Switzerland	4,158	13,642
Barre des Ecrins	France	4,103	13,461
Gran Paradiso	Italy	4,061	13,323
Piz Bernina	Italy/Switzerland	4,049	13,284
Eiger	Switzerland	3,970	13,025
Monte Viso	Italy	3,841	12,602
Grossglockner	Austria	3,797	12,457
Wildspitze	Austria	3,772	12,382
Monte Disgrazia	Italy	3,678	12,066
Mulhacén	Spain	3,478	11,411
Pico de Aneto	Spain	3,404	11,168
Marmolada	Italy	3,342	10,964
Etna	Italy	3,340	10,958
Zugspitze	Germany	2,962	9,718
Musala	Bulgaria	2,925	9,596
Olympus	Greece	2,917	9,570
Triglav	Slovenia	2,863	9,393
Monte Cinto	France (Corsica)	2,710	8,891
Gerlachovka	Slovak Republic	2,655	8,711
Galdhöpiggen	Norway	2,468	8,100
Hvannadalshnúkur	Iceland	2,119	6,952
Kebnekaise	Sweden	2,117	6,946
Ben Nevis	UK	1,343	4,406

ASIA		m	ft
Everest	China/Nepal	8,848	29,029
K2 (Godwin Austen)	China/Kashmir	8,611	28,251
Kanchenjunga	India/Nepal	8,598	28,208
Lhotse	China/Nepal	8,516	27,939
Makalu	China/Nepal	8,481	27,824
Cho Oyu	China/Nepal	8,201	26,906
Dhaulagiri	Nepal	8,172	26,811
Manaslu	Nepal	8,156	26,758
Nanga Parbat	Kashmir	8,126	26,660
Annapurna	Nepal	8,078	26,502
Gasherbrum	China/Kashmir	8,068	26,469
Broad Peak	China/Kashmir	8,051	26,414
Xixabangma	China	8,012	26,286
Kangbachen	India/Nepal	7,902	25,925
Jannu	India/Nepal	7,902	25,925
Gayachung Kang	Nepal	7,897	25,909
Himalchuli	Nepal	7,893	25,896
Disteghil Sar	Kashmir	7,885	25,869
Nuptse	Nepal	7,879	25,849
Khunyang Chhish	Kashmir	7,852	25,761
Masherbrum	Kashmir	7,821	25,659
Nanda Devi	India	7,817	25,646
Rakaposhi	Kashmir	7,788	25,551
Batura	Kashmir	7,785	25,541
Namche Barwa	China	7,756	25,446
Kamet	India	7,756	25,446
Soltoro Kangri	Kashmir	7,742	25,400
Gurla Mandhata	China	7,728	25,354
Trivor	Pakistan	7,720	25,328
>			
Kongur Shan	China	7,719	25,324
Tirich Mir	Pakistan	7,690	25,229
K'ula Shan	Bhutan/China	7,543	24,747
Pik Kommunizma	Tajikistan	7,495	24,590
Elbrus	Russia	5,642	18,510
Demavend	Iran	5,604	18,386
Ararat	Turkey	5,165	16,945
Gunong Kinabalu	Malaysia (Borneo)	4,101	13,455
Yu Shan	Taiwan	3,997	13,113
Fuji-San	Japan	3,776	12,388

AFRICA		m	ft
Kilimanjaro	Tanzania	5,895	19,340
Mt Kenya	Kenya	5,199	17,057
Ruwenzori (Margherita)	Uganda/Zaïre	5,109	16,762
Ras Dashan	Ethiopia	4,620	15,157
Meru	Tanzania	4,565	14,977
Karisimbi	Rwanda/Zaïre	4,507	14,787
Mt Elgon	Kenya/Uganda	4,321	14,176
Batu	Ethiopia	4,307	14,130
Guna	Ethiopia	4,231	13,882
Toubkal	Morocco	4,165	13,665
Irhil Mgoun	Morocco	4,071	13,356
Mt Cameroon	Cameroon	4,070	13,353
Amba Ferit	Ethiopia	3,875	13,042
Pico del Teide	Spain (Tenerife)	3,718	12,198
Thabana Ntlenyana	Lesotho	3,482	11,424
Emi Koussi	Chad	3,415	11,204
>			
Mt aux Sources	Lesotho/S. Africa	3,282	10,768
Mt Piton	Réunion	3,069	10,069

OCEANIA		m	ft
Puncak Jaya	Indonesia	5,029	16,499
Puncak Trikora	Indonesia	4,750	15,584
Puncak Mandala	Indonesia	4,702	15,427
Mt Wilhelm	Papua NG	4,508	14,790
>			
Mauna Kea	USA (Hawaii)	4,205	13,796
Mauna Loa	USA (Hawaii)	4,170	13,681
Mt Cook	New Zealand	3,753	12,313
Mt Balbi	Solomon Is.	2,439	8,002
Orohena	Tahiti	2,241	7,352
Mt Kosciusko	Australia	2,237	7,339

NORTH AMERICA		m	ft
Mt McKinley (Denali)	USA (Alaska)	6,194	20,321
Mt Logan	Canada	5,959	19,551
Citlaltepetl	Mexico	5,700	18,701
Mt St Elias	USA/Canada	5,489	18,008
Popocatepetl	Mexico	5,452	17,887

NORTH AMERICA (continued)		m	ft
Mt Foraker	USA (Alaska)	5,304	17,401
Ixtaccihuatl	Mexico	5,286	17,342
Lucania	Canada	5,227	17,149
Mt Steele	Canada	5,073	16,644
Mt Bona	USA (Alaska)	5,005	16,420
Mt Blackburn	USA (Alaska)	4,996	16,391
Mt Sanford	USA (Alaska)	4,940	16,207
Mt Wood	Canada	4,848	15,905
Nevado de Toluca	Mexico	4,670	15,321
Mt Fairweather	USA (Alaska)	4,663	15,298
Mt Hunter	USA (Alaska)	4,442	15,573
Mt Whitney	USA	4,418	14,495
Mt Elbert	USA	4,399	14,432
Mt Harvard	USA	4,395	14,419
Mt Rainier	USA	4,392	14,409
Blanca Peak	USA	4,372	14,344
>			
Longs Peak	USA	4,345	14,255
Tajumulco	Guatemala	4,220	13,845
Grand Teton	USA	4,197	13,770
Mt Waddington	Canada	3,994	13,104
Mt Robson	Canada	3,954	12,972
Chirripó Grande	Costa Rica	3,837	12,589
Pico Duarte	Dominican Rep.	3,175	10,417

SOUTH AMERICA		m	ft
Aconcagua	Argentina	6,960	22,834
Bonete	Argentina	6,872	22,546
Ojos del Salado	Argentina/Chile	6,863	22,516
Pissis	Argentina	6,779	22,241
Mercedario	Argentina/Chile	6,770	22,211
Huascaran	Peru	6,768	22,204
Llullaillaco	Argentina/Chile	6,723	22,057
Nudo de Cachi	Argentina	6,720	22,047
Yerupaja	Peru	6,632	21,758
N. de Tres Cruces	Argentina/Chile	6,620	21,719
Incahuasi	Argentina/Chile	6,601	21,654
Cerro Galan	Argentina	6,600	21,654
Tupungato	Argentina/Chile	6,570	21,555
Sajama	Bolivia	6,542	21,463
>			
Illimani	Bolivia	6,485	21,276
Coropuna	Peru	6,425	21,079
Ausangate	Peru	6,384	20,945
Cerro del Toro	Argentina	6,380	20,932
Siula Grande	Peru	6,356	20,853
Chimborazo	Ecuador	6,267	20,561
Alpamayo	Peru	5,947	19,511
Cotapaxi	Ecuador	5,896	19,344
Pico Colon	Colombia	5,800	19,029
Pico Bolivar	Venezuela	5,007	16,427

ANTARCTICA	m	ft
Vinson Massif	4,897	16,066
Mt Kirkpatrick	4,528	14,855
Mt Markham	4,349	14,268

OCEAN DEPTHS

ATLANTIC OCEAN	m	ft	
Puerto Rico (Milwaukee) Deep	9,220	30,249	[7]
Cayman Trench	7,680	25,197	[10]
Gulf of Mexico	5,203	17,070	
Mediterranean Sea	5,121	16,801	
Black Sea	2,211	7,254	
North Sea	660	2,165	
Baltic Sea	463	1,519	
Hudson Bay	258	846	

INDIAN OCEAN	m	ft
Java Trench	7,450	24,442
Red Sea	2,635	8,454
Persian Gulf	73	239

PACIFIC OCEAN	m	ft	
Mariana Trench	11,022	36,161	[1]
Tonga Trench	10,882	35,702	[2]
Japan Trench	10,554	34,626	[3]
Kuril Trench	10,542	34,587	[4]
Mindanao Trench	10,497	34,439	[5]
Kermadec Trench	10,047	32,962	[6]

PACIFIC OCEAN (continued)	m	ft	
Peru–Chile Trench	8,050	26,410	[8]
Aleutian Trench	7,822	25,662	[9]

ARCTIC OCEAN	m	ft
Molloy Deep	5,608	18,399

LAND LOWS

		m	ft
Caspian Sea	Europe	–28	–92
Dead Sea	Asia	–403	–1,322
Lake Asale	Africa	–116	–381
Lake Eyre North	Oceania	–16	–52
Death Valley	N. America	–86	–282
Valdés Peninsula	S. America	–40	–131

RIVERS

EUROPE		km	miles	
Volga	Caspian Sea	3,700	2,300	
Danube	Black Sea	2,850	1,770	
Ural	Caspian Sea	2,535	1,575	
Dnepr (Dnipro)	Volga	2,285	1,420	
Kama	Volga	2,030	1,260	
Don	Volga	1,990	1,240	
Petchora	Arctic Ocean	1,790	1,110	
Oka	Volga	1,480	920	
Belaya	Kama	1,420	880	
Dnister (Dniester)	Black Sea	1,400	870	
Vyatka	Kama	1,370	850	
Rhine	North Sea	1,320	820	
N. Dvina	Arctic Ocean	1,290	800	
Desna	Dnepr (Dnipro)	1,190	740	
Elbe	North Sea	1,145	710	
Wisla	Baltic Sea	1,090	675	
Loire	Atlantic Ocean	1,020	635	

ASIA		km	miles	
Yangtze	Pacific Ocean	6,380	3,960	[3]
Yenisey–Angara	Arctic Ocean	5,550	3,445	[5]
Huang He	Pacific Ocean	5,464	3,395	[6]
Ob–Irtysh	Arctic Ocean	5,410	3,360	[7]
Mekong	Pacific Ocean	4,500	2,795	[9]
Amur	Pacific Ocean	4,400	2,730	[10]
Lena	Arctic Ocean	4,400	2,730	
Irtysh	Ob	4,250	2,640	
Yenisey	Arctic Ocean	4,090	2,540	
Ob	Arctic Ocean	3,680	2,285	
Indus	Indian Ocean	3,100	1,925	
Brahmaputra	Indian Ocean	2,900	1,800	
Syrdarya	Aral Sea	2,860	1,775	
Salween	Indian Ocean	2,800	1,740	
Euphrates	Indian Ocean	2,700	1,675	
Vilyuy	Lena	2,650	1,645	
Kolyma	Arctic Ocean	2,600	1,615	
Amudarya	Aral Sea	2,540	1,575	
Ural	Caspian Sea	2,535	1,575	
Ganges	Indian Ocean	2,510	1,560	
Si Kiang	Pacific Ocean	2,100	1,305	
Irrawaddy	Indian Ocean	2,010	1,250	
Tarim–Yarkand	Lop Nor	2,000	1,240	
Tigris	Indian Ocean	1,900	1,180	

AFRICA		km	miles	
Nile	Mediterranean	6,670	4,140	[1]
Zaïre/Congo	Atlantic Ocean	4,670	2,900	[8]
Niger	Atlantic Ocean	4,180	2,595	
Zambezi	Indian Ocean	3,540	2,200	
Oubangi/Uele	Zaïre	2,250	1,400	
Kasai	Zaïre	1,950	1,210	
Shaballe	Indian Ocean	1,930	1,200	
Orange	Atlantic Ocean	1,860	1,155	
Cubango	Okavango Swamps	1,800	1,120	
Limpopo	Indian Ocean	1,600	995	
Senegal	Atlantic Ocean	1,600	995	
Volta	Atlantic Ocean	1,500	930	

AUSTRALIA		km	miles
Murray–Darling	Indian Ocean	3,750	2,330
Darling	Murray	3,070	1,905
Murray	Indian Ocean	2,575	1,600
Murrumbidgee	Murray	1,690	1,050

NORTH AMERICA		km	miles	
Mississippi–Missouri	Gulf of Mexico	6,020	3,740	[4]
Mackenzie	Arctic Ocean	4,240	2,630	
Mississippi	Gulf of Mexico	3,780	2,350	
Missouri	Mississippi	3,780	2,350	
Yukon	Pacific Ocean	3,185	1,980	
Rio Grande	Gulf of Mexico	3,030	1,880	

NORTH AMERICA (continued)		km	miles
Arkansas	Mississippi	2,340	1,450
Colorado	Pacific Ocean	2,330	1,445
Red	Mississippi	2,040	1,270
Columbia	Pacific Ocean	1,950	1,210
Saskatchewan	Lake Winnipeg	1,940	1,205
Snake	Columbia	1,670	1,040
Churchill	Hudson Bay	1,600	990
Ohio	Mississippi	1,580	980
Brazos	Gulf of Mexico	1,400	870
St Lawrence	Atlantic Ocean	1,170	730

SOUTH AMERICA		km	miles	
Amazon	Atlantic Ocean	6,450	4,010	[2]
Paraná–Plate	Atlantic Ocean	4,500	2,800	
Purus	Amazon	3,350	2,080	
Madeira	Amazon	3,200	1,990	
São Francisco	Atlantic Ocean	2,900	1,800	
Paraná	Plate	2,800	1,740	
Tocantins	Atlantic Ocean	2,750	1,710	
Paraguay	Paraná	2,550	1,580	
Orinoco	Atlantic Ocean	2,500	1,550	
Pilcomayo	Paraná	2,500	1,550	
Araguaia	Tocantins	2,250	1,400	
Juruá	Amazon	2,000	1,240	
Xingu	Amazon	1,980	1,230	
Ucayali	Amazon	1,900	1,180	
Maranón	Amazon	1,600	990	
Uruguay	Plate	1,600	990	

LAKES

EUROPE		km^2	$miles^2$
Lake Ladoga	Russia	17,700	6,800
Lake Onega	Russia	9,700	3,700
Saimaa system	Finland	8,000	3,100
Vänern	Sweden	5,500	2,100
Rybinskoye Res.	Russia	4,700	1,800

ASIA		km^2	$miles^2$	
Caspian Sea	Asia	371,800	143,550	[1]
Aral Sea	Kazakstan/Uzbekistan	33,640	13,000	[6]
Lake Baykal	Russia	30,500	11,780	[9]
Tonlé Sap	Cambodia	20,000	7,700	
Lake Balqash	Kazakstan	18,500	7,100	
Lake Dongting	China	12,000	4,600	
Lake Ysyk	Kyrgyzstan	6,200	2,400	
Lake Orumiyeh	Iran	5,900	2,300	
Lake Koko	China	5,700	2,200	
Lake Poyang	China	5,000	1,900	
Lake Khanka	China/Russia	4,400	1,700	
Lake Van	Turkey	3,500	1,400	

AFRICA		km^2	$miles^2$	
Lake Victoria	E. Africa	68,000	26,000	[3]
Lake Tanganyika	C. Africa	33,000	13,000	[7]
Lake Malawi/Nyasa	E. Africa	29,600	11,430	[10]
Lake Chad	C. Africa	25,000	9,700	
Lake Turkana	Ethiopia/Kenya	8,500	3,300	
Lake Volta	Ghana	8,500	3,300	
Lake Bangweulu	Zambia	8,000	3,100	
Lake Rukwa	Tanzania	7,000	2,700	
Lake Mai-Ndombe	Zaïre	6,500	2,500	
Lake Kariba	Zambia/Zimbabwe	5,300	2,000	
Lake Albert	Uganda/Zaïre	5,300	2,000	
Lake Nasser	Egypt/Sudan	5,200	2,000	
Lake Mweru	Zambia/Zaïre	4,900	1,900	
Lake Cabora Bassa	Mozambique	4,500	1,700	
Lake Kyoga	Uganda	4,400	1,700	
Lake Tana	Ethiopia	3,630	1,400	

AUSTRALIA		km^2	$miles^2$
Lake Eyre	Australia	8,900	3,400
Lake Torrens	Australia	5,800	2,200
Lake Gairdner	Australia	4,800	1,900

NORTH AMERICA		km^2	$miles^2$	
Lake Superior	Canada/USA	82,350	31,800	[2]
Lake Huron	Canada/USA	59,600	23,010	[4]
Lake Michigan	USA	58,000	22,400	[5]
Great Bear Lake	Canada	31,800	12,280	[8]
Great Slave Lake	Canada	28,500	11,000	
Lake Erie	Canada/USA	25,700	9,900	
Lake Winnipeg	Canada	24,400	9,400	
Lake Ontario	Canada/USA	19,500	7,500	
Lake Nicaragua	Nicaragua	8,200	3,200	
Lake Athabasca	Canada	8,100	3,100	
Smallwood Reservoir	Canada	6,530	2,520	
Reindeer Lake	Canada	6,400	2,500	
Lake Winnipegosis	Canada	5,400	2,100	
Nettilling Lake	Canada	5,500	2,100	

SOUTH AMERICA		km^2	$miles^2$
Lake Titicaca	Bolivia/Peru	8,300	3,200
Lake Poopo	Peru	2,800	1,100

ISLANDS

EUROPE		km^2	$miles^2$	
Great Britain	UK	229,880	88,700	[8]
Iceland	Atlantic Ocean	103,000	39,800	
Ireland	Ireland/UK	84,400	32,600	
Novaya Zemlya (N.)	Russia	48,200	18,600	
W. Spitzbergen	Norway	39,000	15,100	
Novaya Zemlya (S.)	Russia	33,200	12,800	
Sicily	Italy	25,500	9,800	
Sardinia	Italy	24,000	9,300	
N.E. Spitzbergen	Norway	15,000	5,600	
Corsica	France	8,700	3,400	
Crete	Greece	8,350	3,200	
Zealand	Denmark	6,850	2,600	

ASIA		km^2	$miles^2$	
Borneo	S. E. Asia	744,360	287,400	[3]
Sumatra	Indonesia	473,600	182,860	[6]
Honshu	Japan	230,500	88,980	[7]
Celebes	Indonesia	189,000	73,000	
Java	Indonesia	126,700	48,900	
Luzon	Philippines	104,700	40,400	
Mindanao	Philippines	101,500	39,200	
Hokkaido	Japan	78,400	30,300	
Sakhalin	Russia	74,060	28,600	
Sri Lanka	Indian Ocean	65,600	25,300	
Taiwan	Pacific Ocean	36,000	13,900	
Kyushu	Japan	35,700	13,800	
Hainan	China	34,000	13,100	
Timor	Indonesia	33,600	13,000	
Shikoku	Japan	18,800	7,300	
Halmahera	Indonesia	18,000	6,900	
Ceram	Indonesia	17,150	6,600	
Sumbawa	Indonesia	15,450	6,000	
Flores	Indonesia	15,200	5,900	
Samar	Philippines	13,100	5,100	
Negros	Philippines	12,700	4,900	
Bangka	Indonesia	12,000	4,600	
Palawan	Philippines	12,000	4,600	
Panay	Philippines	11,500	4,400	
Sumba	Indonesia	11,100	4,300	
Mindoro	Philippines	9,750	3,800	

AFRICA		km^2	$miles^2$	
Madagascar	Indian Ocean	587,040	226,660	[4]
Socotra	Indian Ocean	3,600	1,400	
Réunion	Indian Ocean	2,500	965	
Tenerife	Atlantic Ocean	2,350	900	
Mauritius	Indian Ocean	1,865	720	

OCEANIA		km^2	$miles^2$	
New Guinea	Indon./Papua NG	821,030	317,000	[2]
New Zealand (S.)	Pacific Ocean	150,500	58,100	
New Zealand (N.)	Pacific Ocean	114,700	44,300	
Tasmania	Australia	67,800	26,200	
New Britain	Papua NG	37,800	14,600	
New Caledonia	Pacific Ocean	19,100	7,400	
Viti Levu	Fiji	10,500	4,100	
Hawaii	Pacific Ocean	10,450	4,000	
Bougainville	Papua NG	9,600	3,700	
Guadalcanal	Solomon Is.	6,500	2,500	
Vanua Levu	Fiji	5,550	2,100	
New Ireland	Papua NG	3,200	1,200	

NORTH AMERICA		km^2	$miles^2$	
Greenland	Atlantic Ocean	2,175,600	839,800	[1]
Baffin Is.	Canada	508,000	196,100	[5]
Victoria Is.	Canada	212,200	81,900	[9]
Ellesmere Is.	Canada	212,000	81,800	[10]
Cuba	Caribbean Sea	110,860	42,800	
Newfoundland	Canada	110,680	42,700	
Hispaniola	Dom. Rep./Haiti	76,200	29,400	
Banks Is.	Canada	67,000	25,900	
Devon Is.	Canada	54,500	21,000	
Melville Is.	Canada	42,400	16,400	
Vancouver Is.	Canada	32,150	12,400	
Somerset Is.	Canada	24,300	9,400	
Jamaica	Caribbean Sea	11,400	4,400	
Puerto Rico	Atlantic Ocean	8,900	3,400	
Cape Breton Is.	Canada	4,000	1,500	

SOUTH AMERICA		km^2	$miles^2$
Tierra del Fuego	Argentina/Chile	47,000	18,100
Falkland Is. (East)	Atlantic Ocean	6,800	2,600
South Georgia	Atlantic Ocean	4,200	1,600
Galapagos (Isabela)	Pacific Ocean	2,250	870

WORLD : REGIONS IN THE NEWS

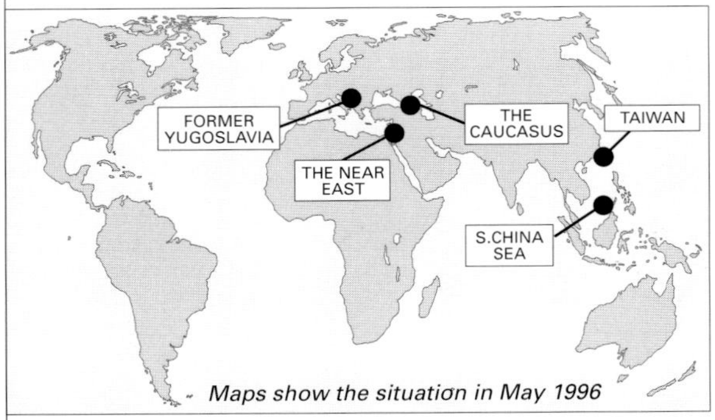

THE BREAK UP OF YUGOSLAVIA
The former country of Yugoslavia comprised six republics. In 1991 Slovenia and Croatia declared independence. Bosnia-Herzegovina followed in 1992 and Macedonia in 1993. Yugoslavia now comprises the remaining two republics, Serbia and Montenegro.

YUGOSLAVIA
Population : 10,763,000 (Serb 62.6%, Albanian 16.5%, Montenegrin 5%, Hungarian 3.3%, Muslim 3.2%)
Serbia
Population : 5,824,211 (Serb 87.7%) excluding the former autonomous provinces of Kosovo and Vojvodina
Kosovo
Population : 1,956,196 (Albanian 81.6%, Serb 9.9%)
Vojvodina
Population : 2,014,000 (Serb 56.8%, Hungarian 16.9%)
Montenegro Population : 615,035 (Montenegrin 61.9%, Muslim 14.6%, Albanian 6.6%)
CROATIA
Population : 4,504,000 (Croat 78.1%, Serb 12.2%)
SLOVENIA
Population : 1,942,000 (Slovene 88%, Croat 3%, Serb 2%)
MACEDONIA (F.Y.R.O.M.)
Population : 2,142,000 (Macedonian 64%, Albanian 21.7%, Turkish 5%, Romanian 3%, Serb 2%)
BOSNIA - HERZEGOVINA
Population : 3,527,000 (Muslim 49%, Serb 31.2%, Croat 17.2%)

The large scale map on the left shows the situation in Bosnia-Herzegovina in early 1996.

ISRAEL Population : 5,458,000 (inc. East Jerusalem and Jewish settlers in the areas under Israeli administration. (Jewish 82%, Arab Muslim 13.8%, Arab Christian 2.5%, Druze 1.7%)
West Bank Population : 973,500 (Palestinian Arabs 97% [of whom Arab Muslim 85%, Jewish 7%, Christian 8%])
Gaza Strip Population : 658,200 (Arab Muslim 98%)
JORDAN Population : 5,198,000 (Arab 99% [of whom about 50% are Palestinian Arab])

1949 Armistice Line
1974 Cease-fire Lines
Efrata ● Main Jewish settlements in the West Bank and Gaza Strip
Halhul □ Main Palestinian Arab towns in the West Bank and Gaza Strip

Georgia, Armenia and Azerbaijan achieved independence in 1991. Abkhazia, Ajaria and South Ossetia seek independence from Georgia. Chechenia has been trying to break away from Russia since 1991, but Russia has resisted with military force. Hostility also continues between Armenia and Azerbaijan over the enclave of Nagorno-Karabakh.

RUSSIA
North Ossetia
Population : 695,000 (Ossetian 53%, Russian 29%, Chechen 5.2%, Ingush 5% [expelled in 1992])
Chechenia
Population : 1,308,000 (Chechen and Ingush 70.7%, Russian 23.1%)
Neighbouring **Ingushetia** (now split from Chechenia)
Population : 250,000 (mainly Ingush)
GEORGIA
Population : 5,450,000 (Georgian 70.1%, Armenian 8.1%, Russian 6.3%, Azerbaijani 5.7%, Ossetian 3%, Greek 2%, Abkhazian 2%)
Abkhazia
Population : 537,500 (Georgian 45.7%, Abkhazian 17.8%, Armenian 14.6%, Russian 14.3%)
Ajaria
Population : 382,000 (Georgian 82.8%, Russian 7.7%, Armenian 4%
South Ossetia
Population : 99,800 (Ossetian 66.2% Georgian 29%)
ARMENIA
Population : 3,548,000 (Armenian 93.3%, Azerbaijani 2.6%)
Nagorno-Karabakh
Population : 192,400 (Armenian 76.9%, Azerbaijani 21.5%)
AZERBAIJAN
Population : 7,472,000 (Azerbaijan 82.7%, Russian 5.6%, Armenian 5.6%, Lezgin 2.4%)
Naxçivan
Population : 300,400 (Azerbaijani 95.9%)

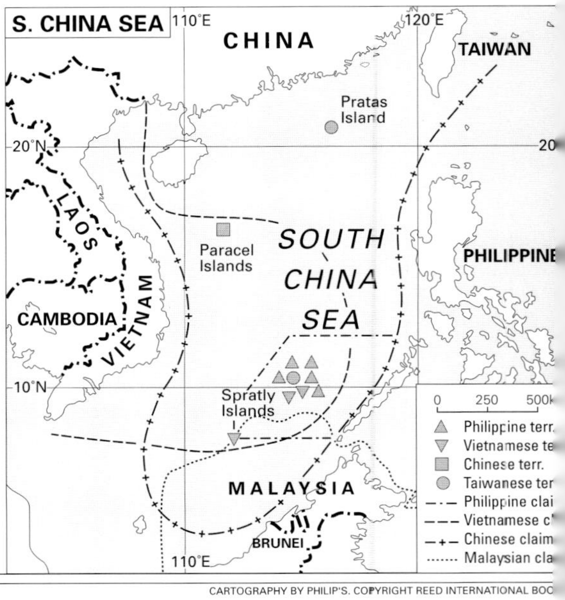

The Earth in Space

The Universe 2
Star Charts and Constellations 4
The Solar System 8
The Earth: Time and Motion 10
The Earth from Space 12
The Dynamic Earth 14
Earthquakes and Volcanoes 16
Forces of Nature 18
Oceans and Ice 20
The Earth's Atmosphere 22
Climate and Weather 24
Water and Land Use 26
The Natural World 28
The Human World 30
Languages and Religions 32
International Organizations 34
Agriculture 36
Energy and Minerals 38
World Economies 40
Trade and Commerce 42
Travel and Communications 44
The World Today 46
Glossary of Terms 48

The Universe

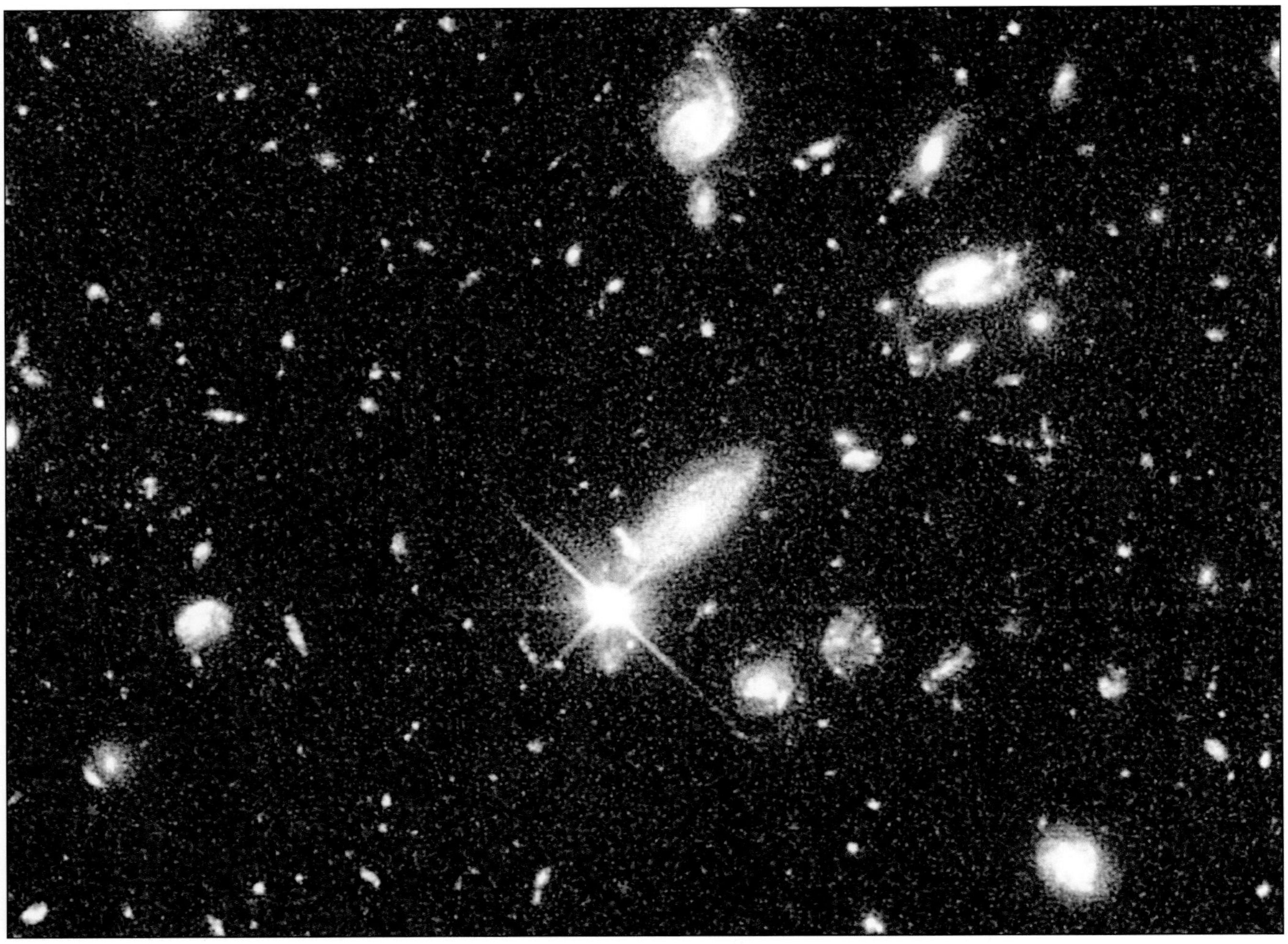

The depths of the Universe
This photograph shows some of the 1,500 or more galaxies that were recorded in the montage of photographs taken by the Hubble Space Telescope in 1995.

THE NEAREST STARS

The 20 nearest stars, excluding the Sun, with their distance from the Earth in light-years.*

Proxima Centauri	4.2
Alpha Centauri A	4.3
Alpha Centauri B	4.3
Barnard's Star	6.0
Wolf 359	7.8
Lalande 21185	8.3
Sirius A	8.7
Sirius B	8.7
UV Ceti A	8.7
UV Ceti B	8.7
Ross 154	9.4
Ross 248	10.3
Epsilon Eridani	10.7
Ross 128	10.9
61 Cygni A	11.1
61 Cygni B	11.1
Epsilon Indi	11.2
Groombridge 34 A	11.2
Groombridge 34 B	11.2
L789-6	11.2

* A light-year equals approximately 9,500 billion km [5,900 billion miles]

Just before Christmas 1995, the Hubble Space Telescope, which is in orbit about 580 km [360 miles] above the Earth, focused on a tiny area in distant space. Over a ten-day period, photographs taken by the telescope revealed unknown galaxies billions of times fainter than the human eye can see.

Because the light from these distant objects has taken so long to reach us, the photographs transmitted from the telescope and released to the media were the deepest look into space that astronomers have ever seen. The features they revealed were in existence when the Universe was less than a billion years old.

The Hubble Space Telescope is operated by the Space Telescope Science Institute in America and was launched in April 1990. The photographs it took of the Hubble Deep Field have been described by NASA as the biggest advance in astronomy since the work of the Italian scientist Galileo in the early 17th century. US scientists have graphically described the astonishing photographs received from the Telescope as 'postcards from the edge of space and time'.

The Big Bang

According to the latest theories, the Universe was created, and 'time' began, about 15,000 million (or 15 billion) years ago, though other estimates range from 8 to 24 billion years. Following a colossal explosion, called the 'Big Bang', the Universe expanded in the first millionth of a

The End of the Universe
The diagram shows two theories concerning the fate of the Universe. One theory, top, suggests that the Universe will expand indefinitely, moving into an immense dark graveyard. Another theory, bottom, suggests that the galaxies will fall back until everything is again concentrated in one point in a so-called 'Big Crunch'. This might then be followed by a new 'Big Bang'.

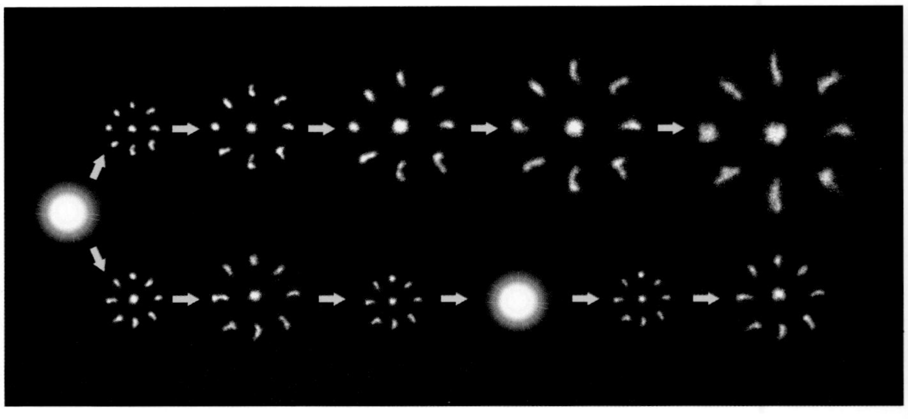

second of its existence from a dimensionless point of infinite mass and density into a fireball, about 30 billion km [19 billion miles] across. The Universe has been expanding ever since, as demonstrated in the 1920s by Edwin Hubble, the American astronomer after whom the Hubble Space Telescope was named.

The temperature at the end of the first second was perhaps 10 billion degrees – far too hot for composite atomic nuclei to exist. As a result, the fireball consisted mainly of radiation mixed with microscopic particles of matter. Almost a million years passed before the Universe was cool enough for atoms to form.

A few billion years later, atoms in regions where matter was relatively dense began, under the influence of gravity, to move together to form proto-galaxies – masses of gas separated by empty space. The proto-galaxies were dark, because the Universe had cooled. But a few billion years later, stars began to form within the proto-galaxies as particles were drawn together. The internal pressure produced as matter condensed created the high temperatures required to cause nuclear fusion. Stars were born and later destroyed. Each generation of stars fed on the debris of extinct ones. Each generation produced larger atoms, increasing the number of different chemical elements.

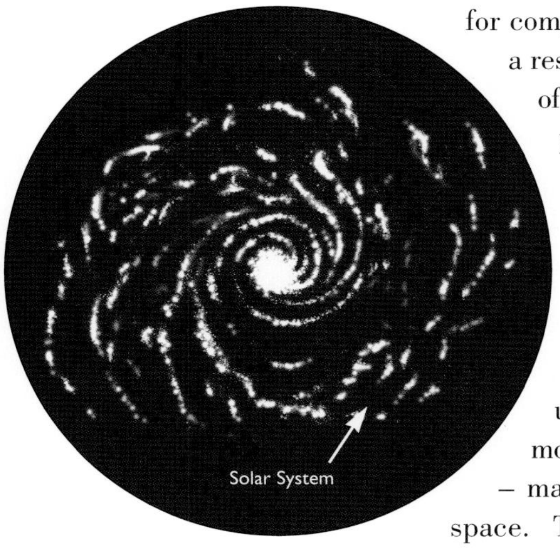

The Home Galaxy

This schematic plan shows that our Solar System is located in one of the spiral arms of the Milky Way galaxy, a little less than 30,000 light-years from its centre. The centre of the Milky Way galaxy is not visible from Earth. Instead, it is masked by light-absorbing clouds of interstellar dust.

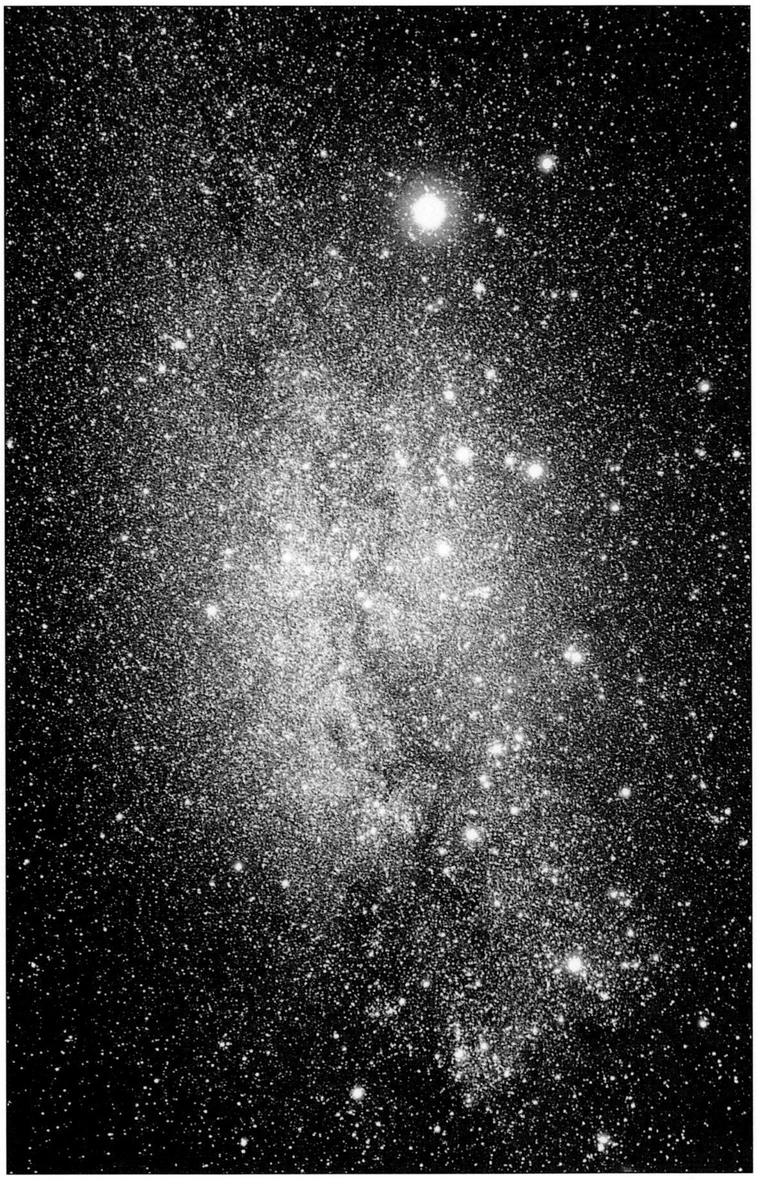

The Milky Way

This section of the Milky Way is dominated by Sirius, the Dog Star, top centre, in the constellation of Canis Major. Sirius is the brightest star in the sky.

The Galaxies

At least a billion galaxies are scattered through the Universe, though the discoveries made by the Hubble Space Telescope suggest that there may be far more than once thought, and some estimates are as high as 50 billion. The largest galaxies contain trillions of stars, while small ones contain less than a billion.

Galaxies tend to occur in groups or clusters, while some clusters appear to be grouped in vast superclusters. Our Local Cluster includes the spiral Milky Way galaxy, whose diameter is about 100,000 light-years; one light-year, the distance that light travels in one year, measures about 9,500 billion km [5,900 billion miles]. The Milky Way is a huge galaxy, shaped like a disk with a bulge at the centre. It is larger, brighter and more massive than many other known galaxies. It contains about 100 billion stars which rotate around the centre of the galaxy in the same direction as the Sun does.

One medium-sized star in the Milky Way galaxy is the Sun. After its formation, about 5 billion years ago, there was enough leftover matter around it to create the planets, asteroids, moons and other bodies that together form our Solar System. The Solar System rotates around the centre of the Milky Way galaxy approximately every 225 million years.

Recent discoveries suggest that other stars similar to our Sun have planets orbiting around them, while evidence from the Hubble Space Telescope suggests that the raw materials from which planets are formed is common in dusty disks around many stars. This provokes one of the most intriguing of all the questions that has ever faced humanity. If there are other planets in the Universe, then do living organisms exist elsewhere?

Before the time of Galileo, people thought that the Earth lay at the centre of the Universe. But we now know that our Solar System and even the Milky Way galaxy are tiny specks in the Universe as a whole. Perhaps our planet is also not unique in being the only one to support intelligent life.

Star Charts and Constellations

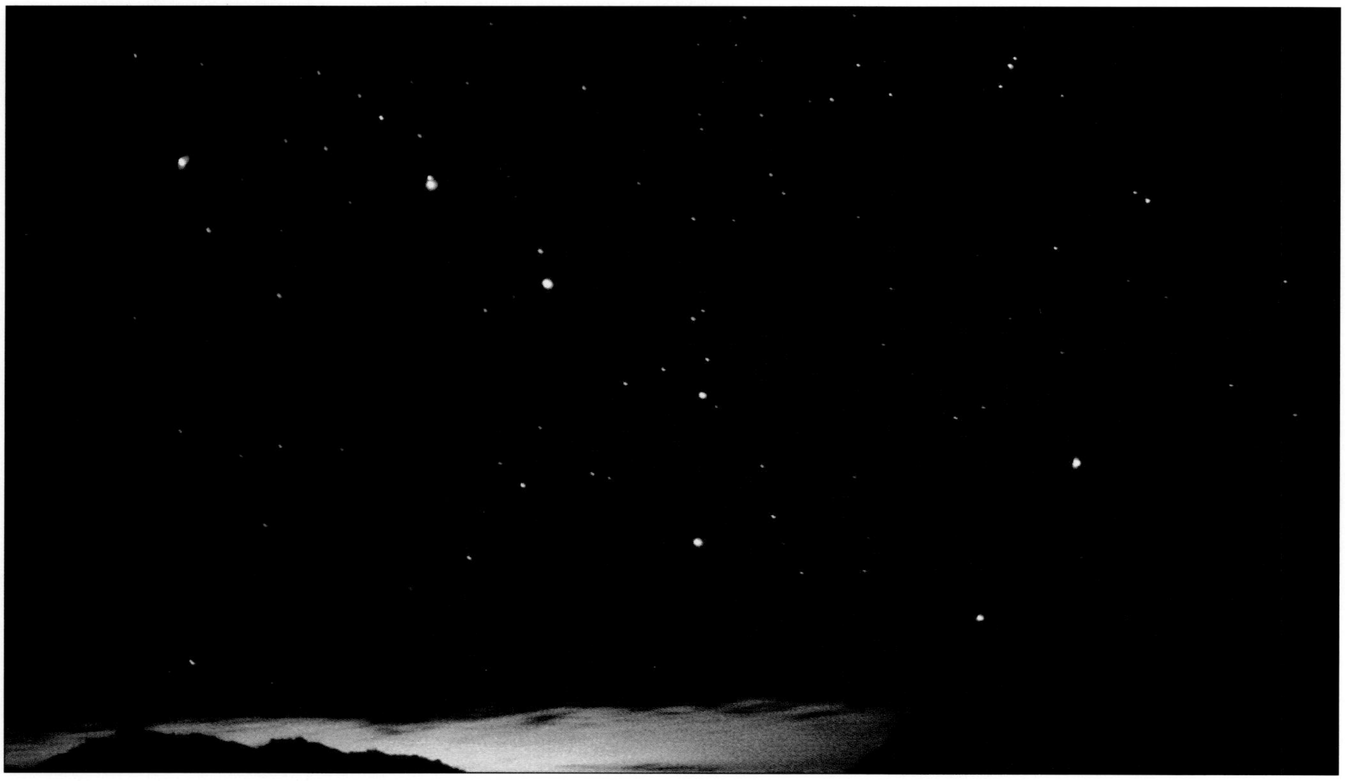

The Plough

The Plough, or Big Dipper, above glowing yellow clouds lit by city lights. It is part of a larger group called Ursa Major one of the best-known constellations of the northern hemisphere. The two bright stars to the lower right of the photograph (Merak and Dubhe) are known as the Pointers because they show the way to the Pole Star.

On a clear night, under the best conditions and far away from the glare of city lights, a person in northern Europe can look up and see about 2,500 stars. In a town, however, light pollution can reduce visibility to 200 stars or less. Over the whole celestial sphere it is possible to see about 8,500 stars with the naked eye and it is only when you look through a telescope that you begin to realize that the number of stars is countless.

Small and Large Stars

Stars come in several sizes. Some, called neutron stars, are compact, with the same mass as the Sun but with diameters of only about 20 km [12 miles]. Larger than neutron stars are the small white dwarfs. Our Sun is a medium-sized star, but many visible stars in the night sky are giants with diameters between 10 and 100 times that of the Sun, or supergiants with diameters over 100 times that of the Sun.

Two bright stars in the constellation Orion are Betelgeuse (also known as Alpha Orionis) and Rigel (or Beta Orionis). Betelgeuse is an orange-red supergiant, whose diameter is about 400 times that of the Sun. Rigel is also a supergiant. Its diameter is about 50 times that of the Sun, but its luminosity is estimated to be over 100,000 times that of the Sun.

The stars we see in the night sky all belong to our home galaxy, the Milky Way. This name is also used for the faint, silvery band that arches across the sky. This band, a slice through our

THE BRIGHTEST STARS

The 15 brightest stars visible from northern Europe. Magnitudes are given to the nearest tenth.

Sirius	−1.5
Arcturus	0.0
Vega	0.0
Capella	0.1
Rigel	0.1
Procyon	0.4
Betelgeuse	0.4
Altair	0.8
Aldebaran	0.8
Antares	1.0
Spica	1.0
Pollux	1.1
Fomalhaut	1.2
Deneb	1.2
Regulus	1.3

THE CONSTELLATIONS

The constellations and their English names. Constellations visible from both hemispheres are listed.

Andromeda	Andromeda	Delphinus	Dolphin	Perseus	Perseus
Antlia	Air Pump	Dorado	Swordfish	Phoenix	Phoenix
Apus	Bird of Paradise	Draco	Dragon	Pictor	Easel
Aquarius	Water Carrier	Equuleus	Little Horse	Pisces	Fishes
Aquila	Eagle	Eridanus	River Eridanus	Piscis Austrinus	Southern Fish
Ara	Altar	Fornax	Furnace	Puppis	Ship's Stern
Aries	Ram	Gemini	Twins	Pyxis	Mariner's Compass
Auriga	Charioteer	Grus	Crane	Reticulum	Net
Boötes	Herdsman	Hercules	Hercules	Sagitta	Arrow
Caelum	Chisel	Horologium	Clock	Sagittarius	Archer
Camelopardalis	Giraffe	Hydra	Water Snake	Scorpius	Scorpion
Cancer	Crab	Hydrus	Sea Serpent	Sculptor	Sculptor
Canes Venatici	Hunting Dogs	Indus	Indian	Scutum	Shield
Canis Major	Great Dog	Lacerta	Lizard	Serpens*	Serpent
Canis Minor	Little Dog	Leo	Lion	Sextans	Sextant
Capricornus	Sea Goat	Leo Minor	Little Lion	Taurus	Bull
Carina	Ship's Keel	Lepus	Hare	Telescopium	Telescope
Cassiopeia	Cassiopeia	Libra	Scales	Triangulum	Triangle
Centaurus	Centaur	Lupus	Wolf	Triangulum Australe	Southern Triangle
Cepheus	Cepheus	Lynx	Lynx		
Cetus	Whale	Lyra	Harp	Tucana	Toucan
Chamaeleon	Chameleon	Mensa	Table	Ursa Major	Great Bear
Circinus	Compasses	Microscopium	Microscope	Ursa Minor	Little Bear
Columba	Dove	Monoceros	Unicorn	Vela	Ship's Sails
Coma Berenices	Berenice's Hair	Musca	Fly	Virgo	Virgin
Corona Australis	Southern Crown	Norma	Level	Volans	Flying Fish
Corona Borealis	Northern Crown	Octans	Octant	Vulpecula	Fox
Corvus	Crow	Ophiuchus	Serpent Bearer		
Crater	Cup	Orion	Hunter		
Crux	Southern Cross	Pavo	Peacock		
Cygnus	Swan	Pegasus	Winged Horse		

** In two halves: Serpens Caput, the head, and Serpens Cauda, the tail.*

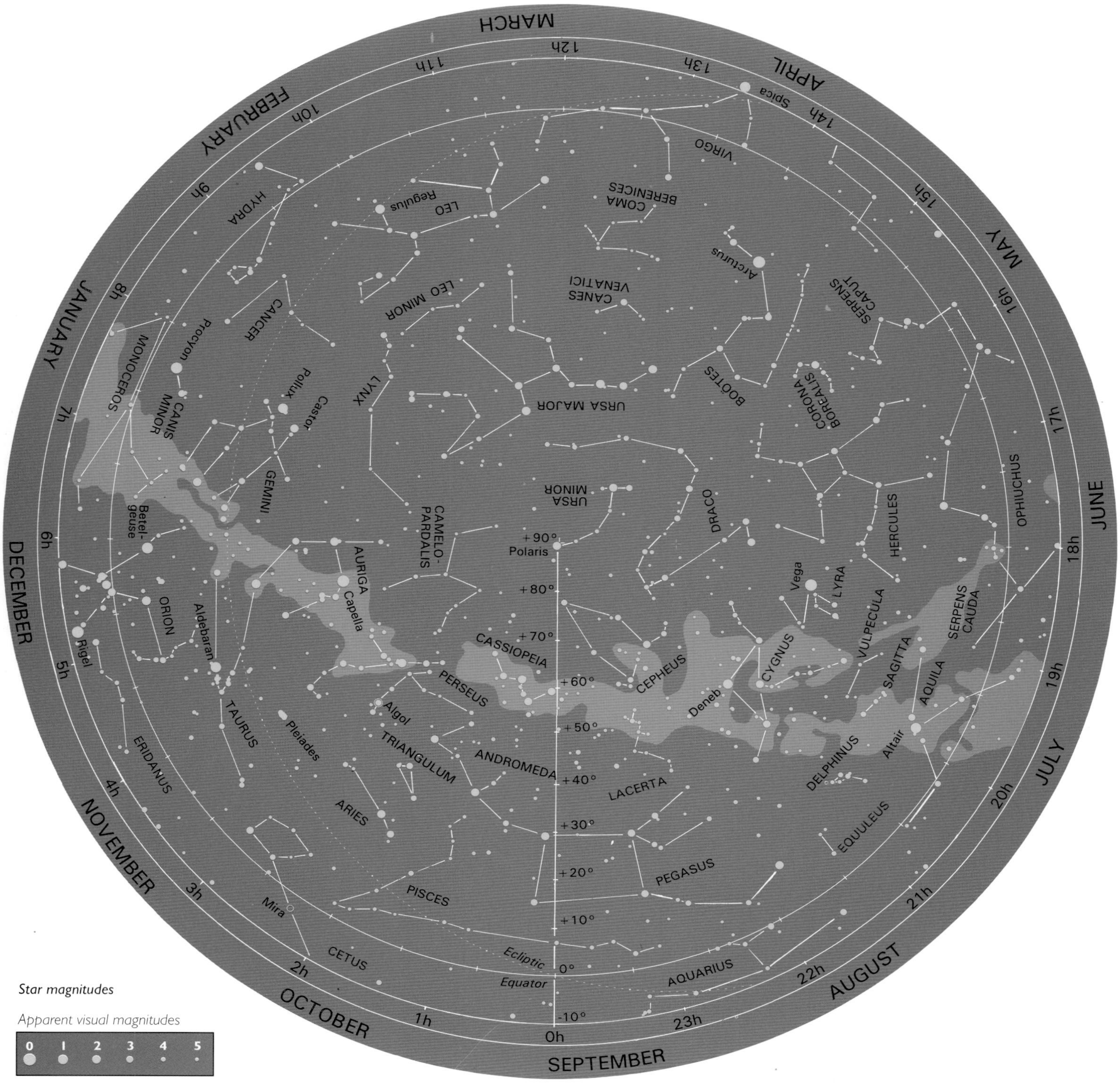

Star magnitudes

Apparent visual magnitudes

0 1 2 3 4 5

The Milky Way is shown in light blue on the above chart.

Star chart of the northern hemisphere

When you look into the sky, the stars seem to be on the inside of a huge dome. This gives astronomers a way of mapping them. This chart shows the sky as it would appear from the North Pole. To use the star chart above, an observer in the northern hemisphere should face south and turn the chart so that the current month appears at the bottom. The chart will then show the constellations on view at approximately 11pm Greenwich Mean Time. The map should be rotated clockwise 15° for each hour before 11pm and anticlockwise for each hour after 11pm.

galaxy, contains an enormous number of stars. The nucleus of the Milky Way galaxy cannot be seen from Earth. Lying in the direction of the constellation Sagittarius in the southern hemisphere, it is masked by clouds of dust.

The Brightness of Stars

Astronomers use a scale of magnitudes to measure the brightness of stars. The brightest visible to the naked eye were originally known as first-magnitude stars, ones not so bright were second-magnitude, down to the faintest visible, which were rated as sixth-magnitude. The brighter the star, the lower the magnitude. With the advent of telescopes and the development of accurate instruments for measuring birightnesses, the magnitude scale has been refined and extended. Very bright bodies such as Sirius, Venus and the Sun have negative magnitudes. The nearest star is Proxima Centauri, part of a multiple star system, which is 4.2 light-years away. Proxima Centauri is very faint and has a magnitude of 11.3. Alpha Centauri A, one of the two brighter members of the system, is the nearest visible star to Earth. It has a magnitude of 1.7.

These magnitudes are what are called apparent magnitudes – measures of the brightnesses of the stars as they appear to us. These are the magnitudes shown on the charts on these pages. But the stars are at very different distances. The star Deneb, in the constellation Cygnus, for example, is over 1,200 light-years away. So astronomers also use absolute magnitudes – measures of how bright the stars really are. A star's absolute magnitude is the apparent magnitude it would have if it could be placed 32.6 light-years away. So Deneb, with an apparent magnitude of 1.2, has an absolute magnitude of –7.2.

The brightest star in the night sky is Sirius, the Dog Star, with a magnitude of –1.5. This medium-sized star is 8.64 light-years distant but it gives out about 20 times as much light as the Sun. After the Sun and the Moon, the brightest objects in the sky are the planets Venus, Mars and Jupiter. For example, Venus has a magnitude of up to –4. The planets have no light of their own however, and shine only because they reflect the Sun's rays. But whilst stars have fixed positions, the planets shift nightly in relation to the constellations, following a path called the Ecliptic (shown on the star charts). As they follow their orbits around the Sun, their distances from the Earth vary, and therefore so also do their magnitudes.

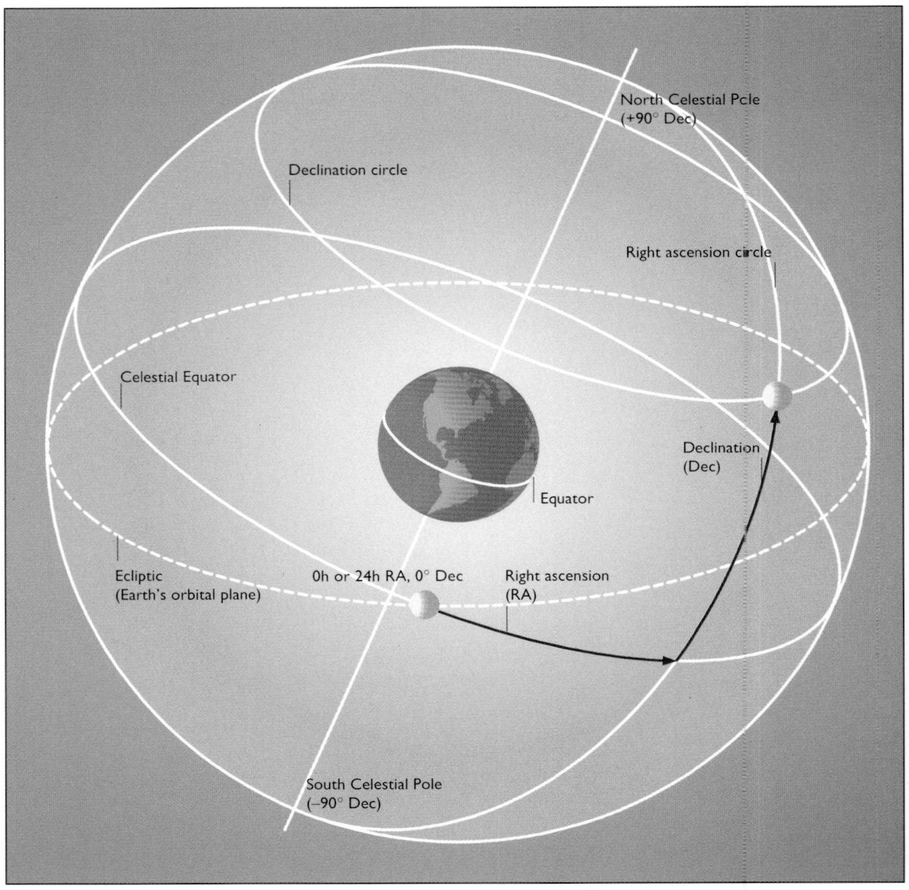

Celestial sphere
The diagram shows the imaginary surface on which astronomical positions are measured. The celestial sphere appears to rotate about the celestial poles, as though an extension of the Earth's own axis. The Earth's axis points towards the celestial poles.

The Southern Cross
The Southern Cross, or Crux, in the southern hemisphere, was classified as a constellation in the 17th century. It is as familiar to Australians and New Zealanders as the Plough is to people in the northern hemisphere. The vertical axis of the Southern Cross points towards the South Celestial Pole.

While atlas maps record the details of the Earth's surface, star charts are a guide to the heavens. An observer at the Equator can see the entire sky at some time during the year, but an observer at the poles can see only the stars in a single hemisphere. As a result, star charts of both hemispheres are produced. The northern hemisphere chart is centred on the North Celestial Pole, while the southern hemisphere chart is centred on the South Celestial Pole.

In the northern hemisphere, the North Pole is marked by the star Polaris, or North Star. Polaris lies within a degree of the point where an extension of the Earth's axis meets the sky. Polaris appears to be stationary and navigators throughout history have used it as a guide. Unfortunately, the South Pole has no convenient reference point.

Star charts of the two hemispheres are bounded by the Celestial Equator, an imaginary line in the sky directly above the terrestrial Equator. Astronomical co-ordinates, which give the location of stars, are normally stated in terms of right ascension (the equivalent of longitude) and declination (the equivalent of latitude). Because the stars appear to rotate around the Earth every 24 hours, right ascension is measured eastwards in hours and minutes. Declination is measured in degrees north or south of the Celestial Equator.

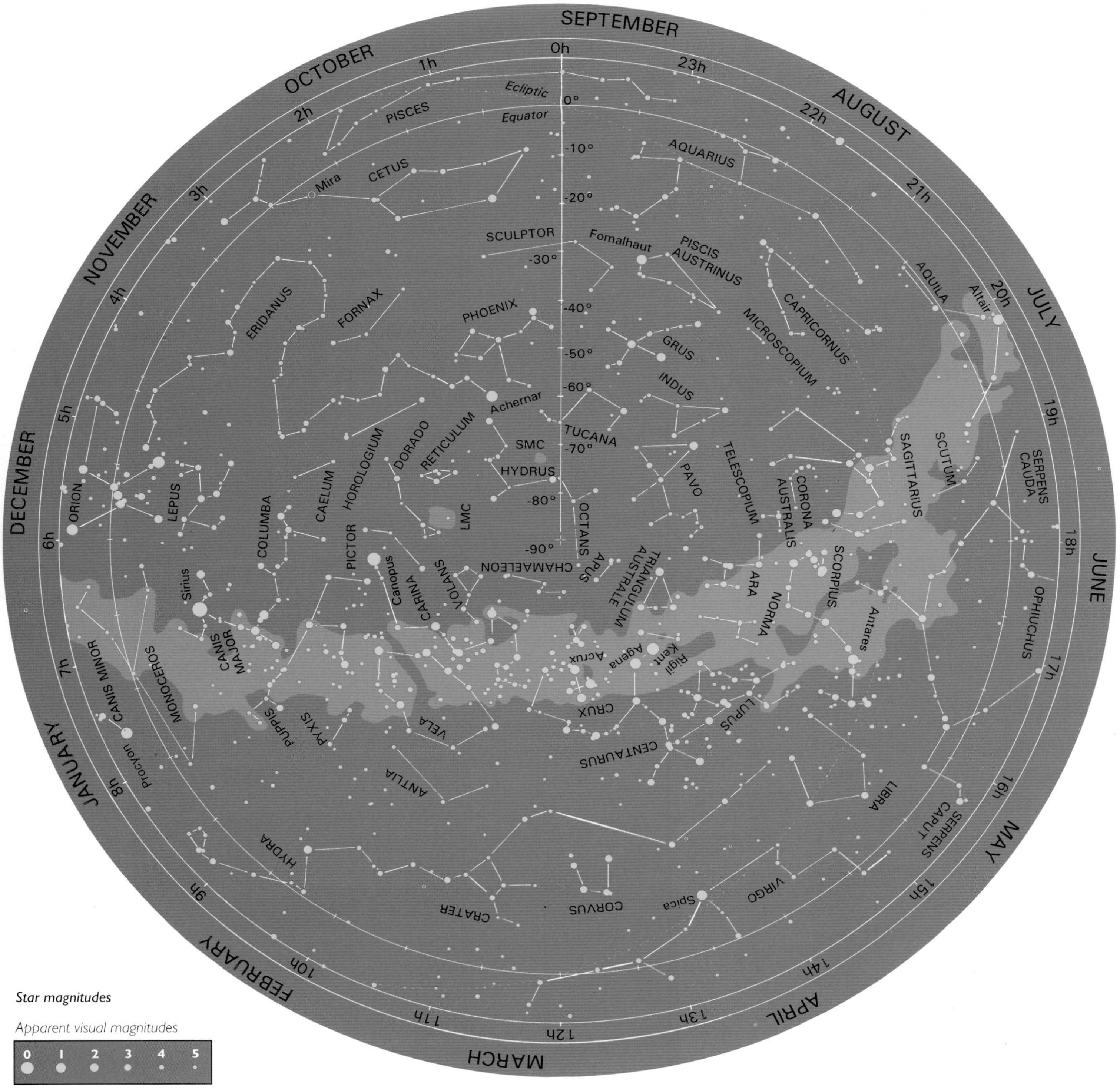

Star magnitudes

Apparent visual magnitudes

0	1	2	3	4	5

The Milky Way is shown in light blue on the above chart.

Star chart of the southern hemisphere

Many constellations in the southern hemisphere were named not by the ancients but by later astronomers. Some, including Antila (Air Pump) and Microscopium (Microscope), have modern names. The Large and Small Magellanic Clouds (LMC, SMC) are small 'satellite' galaxies of the Milky Way. To use the chart, an observer in the southern hemisphere should face north and turn the chart so that the current month appears at the bottom. The map will then show the constellations on view at approximately 11pm Greenwich Mean Time. The chart should be rotated clockwise 15° for each hour before 11pm and anticlockwise for each hour after 11pm.

Constellations

Every star is identifiable as a member of a constellation. The night sky contains 88 constellations, many of which were named by the ancient Greeks, Romans and other early peoples after animals and mythological characters, such as Orion and Perseus. More recently, astronomers invented names for constellations seen in the southern hemisphere, in areas not visible around the Mediterranean Sea.

Some groups of easily recognizable stars form parts of a constellation. For example, seven stars form the shape of the Plough or Big Dipper within the constellation Ursa Major. Such groups are called asterisms.

The stars in constellations lie in the same direction in space, but normally at vastly different distances. Hence, there is no real connection between them. The positions of stars seem fixed, but in fact the shapes of the constellations are changing slowly over very long periods of time. This is because the stars have their own 'proper motions', which because of the huge distances involved are imperceptible to the naked eye.

The Solar System

Although the origins of the Solar System are still a matter of debate, many scientists believe that it was formed from a cloud of gas and dust, the debris from some long-lost, exploded star. Around 5 billion years ago, material was drawn towards the hub of the rotating disk of gas and dust, where it was compressed to thermonuclear fusion temperatures. A new star, the Sun, was born, containing 99.8% of the mass of the Solar System. The remaining material was later drawn together to form the planets and the other bodies in the Solar System. Spacecraft, manned and unmanned, have greatly increased our knowledge of the Solar System since the start of the Space Age in 1957, when the Soviet Union launched the satellite Sputnik I.

The Planets

Mercury is the closest planet to the Sun and the fastest moving. Space probes have revealed that its surface is covered by craters, and looks much like our Moon. Mercury is a hostile place, with no significant atmosphere and temperatures ranging between 400°C [750°F] by day and –170°C [–275°F] by night. It seems unlikely that anyone will ever want to visit this planet.

Venus is much the same size as Earth. But it is the hottest of the planets, with temperatures reaching 475°C [885°F], even at night. The reason for this scorching heat is the atmosphere, which consists mainly of carbon dioxide, a gas that traps heat thus creating a greenhouse effect. The density of the atmosphere is about 90 times that of Earth and dense clouds permanently mask the surface. Active volcanic regions discharging sulphur dioxide may account for the haze of sulphuric acid droplets in the upper atmosphere.

From planet Earth, Venus is brighter than any other star or planet and is easy to spot. It is often the first object to be seen in the evening sky and the last to be seen in the morning sky. It can even be seen in daylight.

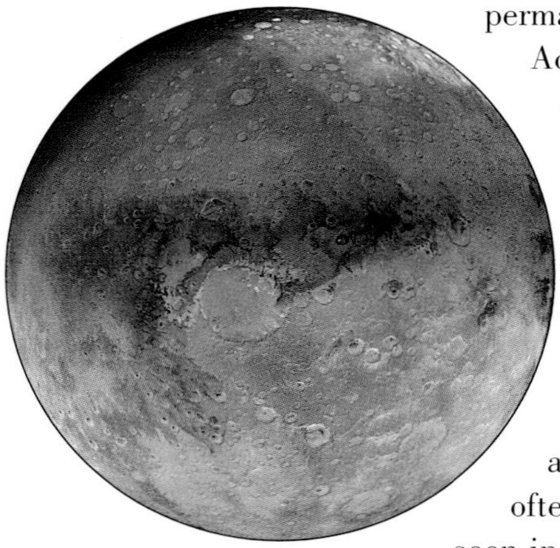

Earth, seen from space, looks blue (because of the oceans which cover more than 70% of the planet) and white (a result of clouds in the atmosphere). The atmosphere and water make Earth the only planet known to support life. The Earth's hard outer layers, including the crust and the top of the mantle, are divided into rigid plates. Forces inside the Earth move the plates, modifying the landscape and causing earthquakes and volcanic activity. Weathering and erosion also change the surface.

Mars has many features in common with Earth, including an atmosphere with clouds and polar caps that partly melt in summer. Scientists once considered that it was the most likely planet on which other life might exist, but the two Viking space probes that went there in the 1970s found only a barren rocky surface with no trace of water. But Mars did have flowing water at one time and there are many dry channels – but these are not the fictitious 'canals'. There are also giant, dormant volcanoes.

PLANETARY DATA

Planet	Mean distance from Sun (million km)	Mass (Earth=1)	Period of orbit (Earth yrs)	Period of rotation (Earth days)	Equatorial diameter (km)	Average density (water=1)	Surface gravity (Earth=1)	Number of known satellites
Sun	–	333,000	–	25.38	1,392,000	1.41	28	–
Mercury	57.91	0.055	0.2406	58.67	4,878	5.43	0.38	0
Venus	108.2	0.815	0.6152	243.0	12,104	5.25	0.90	0
Earth	149.6	1.0	1.00	1.00	12,756	5.52	1.00	1
Mars	227.9	0.107	1.88	1.028	6,787	3.94	0.38	2
Jupiter	778.3	317.8	11.86	0.411	142,800	1.33	2.69	16
Saturn	1,427	95.2	29.46	0.427	120,000	0.69	1.19	20
Uranus	2,871	14.5	84.01	0.748	51,118	1.29	0.79	15
Neptune	4,497	17.1	164.8	0.800	49,528	1.64	0.98	8
Pluto	5,914	0.002	248.5	6.39	2,320	2.0	0.03	1

Asteroids are small, rocky bodies. Most of them orbit the Sun between Mars and Jupiter, but some small ones can approach the Earth. The largest is Ceres, 913 km [567 miles] in diameter. There may be around a million asteroids bigger than 1 km [0.6 miles].

Jupiter, the giant planet, lies beyond Mars and the asteroid belt. Its mass is almost three times as much as all the other planets combined and, because of its size, it shines more brightly than any other planet apart from Venus and, occasionally, Mars. The four largest moons of Jupiter were discovered by Galileo. Jupiter is made up mostly of hydrogen and helium, covered by a layer of clouds. Its Great Red Spot is a high-pressure storm. Jupiter made headline news when it was struck by fragments of Comet Shoemaker–Levy 9 in July 1994. This was the greatest collision ever seen by scientists between a planet and another heavenly body. The fragments of the comet that crashed into Jupiter created huge fireballs that caused scars on the planet that remained visible for months after the event.

Saturn is structurally similar to Jupiter but it is best known for its rings. The rings measure about 270,000 km [170,000 miles] across, yet they are no more than a few hundred metres thick. Seen from Earth, the rings seem divided into three main bands of varying brightness, but photographs sent back by the *Voyager* space probes in 1980 and 1981 showed that they are broken up into thousands of thin ringlets composed of ice particles ranging in size from a snowball to an iceberg. The origin of the rings is still a matter of debate.

Uranus was discovered in 1781 by William Herschel who first thought it was a comet. It is broadly similar to Jupiter and Saturn in composition, though its distance from the Sun makes its surface even colder. Uranus is circled by thin rings which were discovered in 1977. Unlike the rings of Saturn, the rings of Uranus are black, which explains why they cannot be seen from Earth.

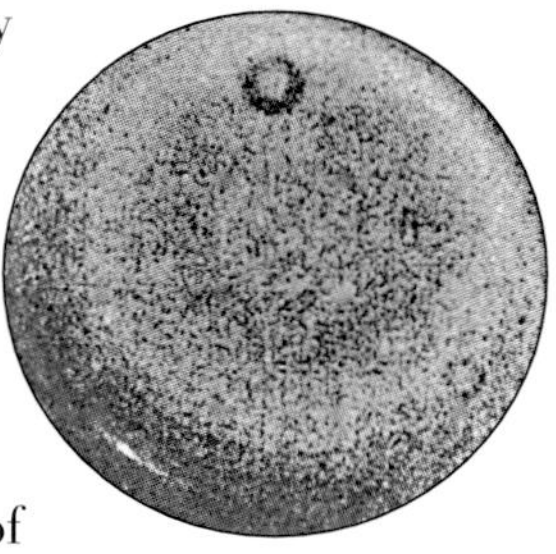

Neptune, named after the mythological sea god, was discovered in 1846 as the result of mathematical predictions made by astronomers to explain irregularities in the orbit of Uranus, its near twin. Little was known about this distant body until *Voyager 2* came close to it in 1989. Neptune has thin rings, like those of Uranus. Among its blue-green clouds is a prominent dark spot, which rotates anticlockwise every 18 hours or so.

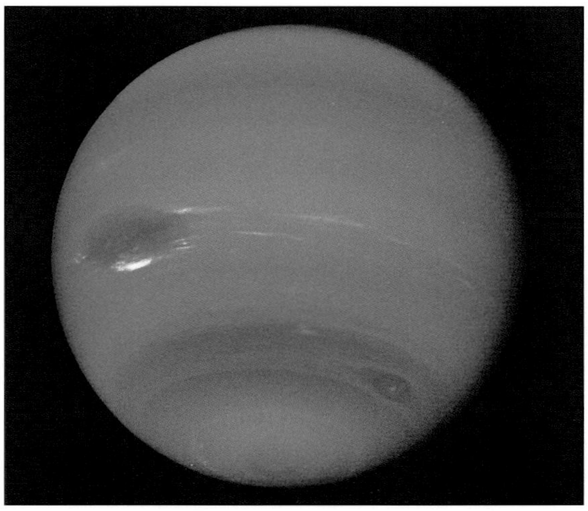

Pluto is the smallest planet in the Solar System, even smaller than our Moon. The American astronomer Clyde Tombaugh discovered Pluto in 1930. Its orbit is odd and it sometimes comes closer to the Sun than Neptune. The nature of Pluto, a gloomy planet appropriately named after the Greek and Roman god of the underworld, is uncertain. At Pluto's distance and beyond are many small, asteroid-like bodies the first of which was found in 1992.

Comets are small icy bodies that orbit the Sun in highly elliptical orbits. When a comet swings in towards the Sun some of its ice evaporates, and the comet brightens and may become visible from Earth. The best known is Halley's Comet, which takes 76 years to orbit the Sun.

The Earth: Time and Motion

The Earth is constantly moving through space like a huge, self-sufficient spaceship. First, with the rest of the Solar System, it moves around the centre of the Milky Way galaxy. Second, it rotates around the Sun at a speed of more than 100,000 km/h [more than 60,000 mph], covering a distance of nearly 1,000 million km [600 million miles] in a little over 365 days. The Earth also spins on its axis, an imaginary line joining the North and South Poles, via the centre of the Earth, completing one turn in a day. The Earth's movements around the Sun determine our calendar, though accurate observations of the stars made by astronomers help to keep our clocks in step with the rotation of the Earth around the Sun.

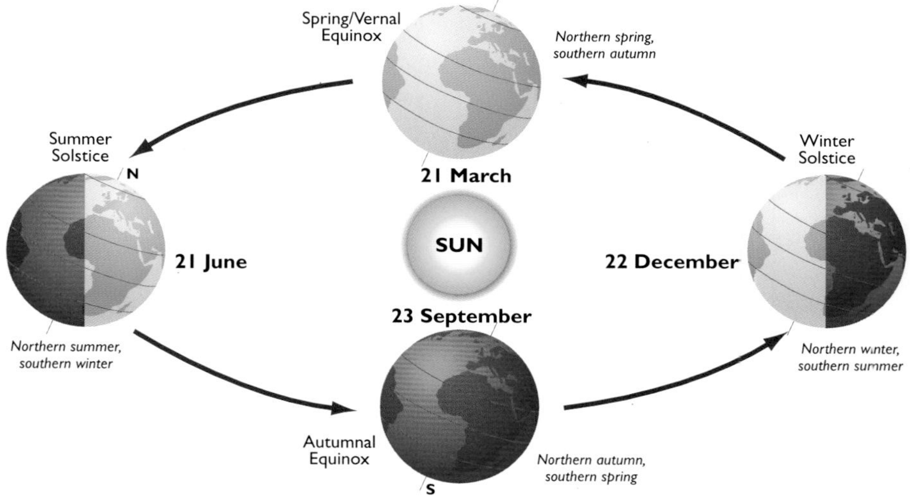

The Seasons

The 23½° tilt of the Earth's axis remains constant as the Earth orbits around the Sun. As a result, first the northern and then the southern hemispheres lean towards the Sun. Annual variations in the amount of sunlight received in turn by each hemisphere are responsible for the four seasons experienced in the middle latitudes.

The Earth from the Moon

In 1969, Neil Armstrong and Edwin 'Buzz' Aldrin Junior were the first people to set foot on the Moon. This superb view of the Earth was taken by the crew of Apollo 11.

The Changing Year

The Earth takes 365 days, 6 hours, 9 minutes and 9.54 seconds to complete one orbit around the Sun. We have a calendar year of 365 days, so allowance has to be made for the extra time over and above the 365 days. This is allowed for by introducing leap years of 366 days. Leap years are generally those, such as 1992 and 1996, which are divisible by four. Century years, however, are not leap years unless they are divisible by 400. Hence, 1700, 1800 and 1900 were not leap years, but the year 2000 will be one. Leap years help to make the calendar conform with the solar year.

Because the Earth's axis is tilted by 23½°, the middle latitudes enjoy four distinct seasons. On 21 March, the vernal or spring equinox in the northern hemisphere, the Sun is directly overhead at the Equator and everywhere on Earth has about 12 hours of daylight and 12 hours of darkness. But as the Sun continues on its journey around the Sun, the northern hemisphere tilts more and more towards the Sun. Finally, on 21 June, the Sun is overhead at the Tropic of Cancer (latitude 23½° North). This is

Tides

The daily rises and falls of the ocean's waters are caused by the gravitational pull of the Moon and the Sun. The effect is greatest on the hemisphere facing the Moon, causing a 'tidal bulge'. The diagram below shows that the Sun, Moon and Earth are in line when the spring tides occur. This causes the greatest tidal ranges. On the other hand, the neap tides occur when the pull of the Moon and the Sun are opposed. Neap tides, when tidal ranges are at their lowest, occur near the Moon's first and third quarters.

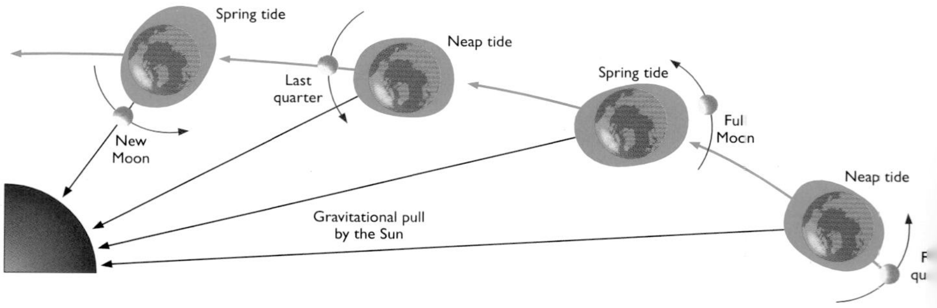

SUN DATA

DIAMETER	1.392×10^{6} km
VOLUME	1.412×10^{18} km^3
VOLUME (EARTH = 1)	1.303×10^{6}
MASS	1.989×10^{30} kg
MASS (EARTH = 1)	3.329×10^{6}
MEAN DENSITY (WATER = 1)	1.409
ROTATION PERIOD	
AT EQUATOR	24.25 days
AT POLES	about 35 days
SURFACE GRAVITY (EARTH = 1)	27.9
MAGNITUDE	
APPARENT	–26.9
ABSOLUTE	+4.71
TEMPERATURE	
AT SURFACE	5,400°C [5,700 K]
AT CORE	14×10^{16} K

MOON DATA

DIAMETER	3,476 km
MASS (EARTH = 1)	0.0123
DENSITY (WATER = 1)	3.34
MEAN DISTANCE FROM EARTH	384,402 km
MAXIMUM DISTANCE (APOGEE)	406,740 km
MINIMUM DISTANCE (PERIGEE)	356,410 km
SIDERIAL ROTATION AND REVOLUTION PERIOD	27.322 days
SYNODIC MONTH (NEW MOON TO NEW MOON)	29.531 days
SURFACE GRAVITY (EARTH = 1)	0.165
MAXIMUM SURFACE TEMPERATURE	+130°C [403 K]
MINIMUM SURFACE TEMPERATURE	–158°C [115 K]

the summer solstice in the northern hemisphere.

The overhead Sun then moves south again until on 23 September, the autumn equinox in the northern hemisphere, the Sun is again overhead at the Equator. The overhead Sun then moves south until, on around 22 December, it is overhead at the Tropic of Capricorn. This is the winter solstice in the northern hemisphere, and the summer solstice in the southern, where the seasons are reversed.

At the poles, there are two seasons. During half of the year, one of the poles leans towards the Sun and has continuous sunlight. For the other six months, the pole leans away from the Sun and is in continuous darkness.

Regions around the Equator do not have marked seasons. Because the Sun is high in the sky throughout the year, it is always hot or warm. When people talk of seasons in the tropics, they are usually referring to other factors, such as rainy and dry periods.

Day, Night and Tides

As the Earth rotates on its axis every 24 hours, first one side of the planet and then the other faces the Sun and enjoys daylight, while the opposite side is in darkness.

The length of daylight varies throughout the year. The longest day in the northern hemisphere falls on the summer solstice, 21 June, while the longest day in the southern hemisphere is on 22 December. At 40° latitude, the length of daylight on the longest day is 14 hours, 30 minutes. At 60° latitude, daylight on that day lasts 18 hours, 30 minutes. On the shortest day, 22 December in the northern hemisphere and 21 June in the southern, daylight hours at 40° latitude total 9 hours and 9 minutes. At latitude 60°, daylight lasts only 5 hours, 30 minutes in the 24-hour period.

Tides are caused by the gravitational pull of the Moon and, to a lesser extent, the Sun on the waters in the world's oceans. Tides occur twice every 24 hours, 50 minutes – one complete orbit of the Moon around the Earth.

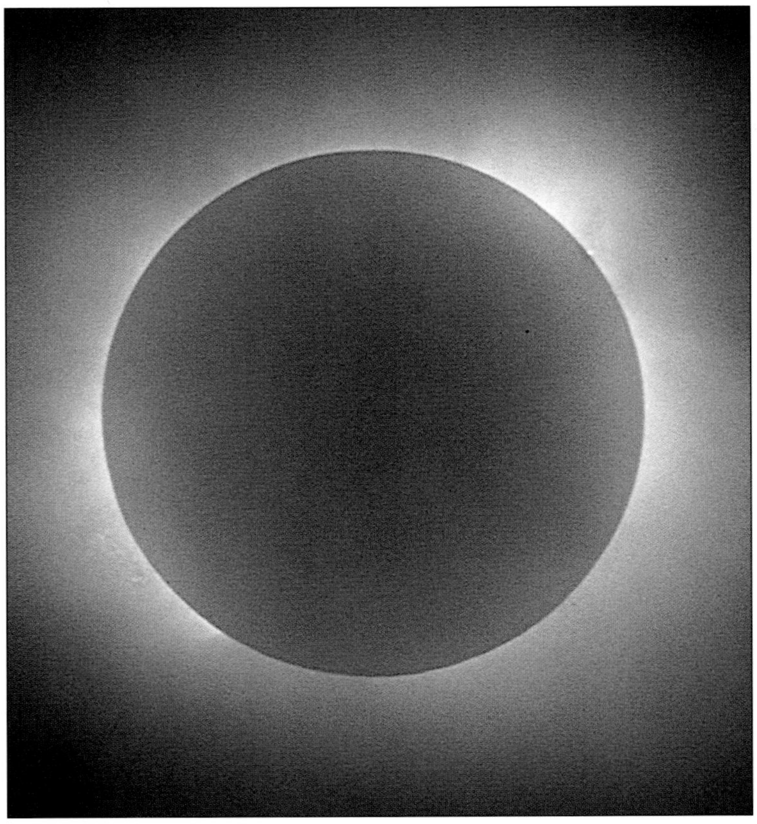

Total eclipse of the Sun

A total eclipse is caused when the Moon passes between the Sun and the Earth. With the Sun's bright disk completely obscured, the Sun's corona, or outer atmosphere, can be viewed.

The highest tides, the spring tides, occur when the Earth, Moon and Sun are in a straight line, so that the gravitational pulls of the Moon and Sun are combined. The lowest, or neap, tides occur when the Moon, Earth and Sun form a right angle. The gravitational pull of the Moon is then opposed by the gravitational pull of the Sun. The greatest tidal ranges occur in the Bay of Fundy in North America. The greatest mean spring range is 14.5 m [47.5 ft].

The speed at which the Earth is spinning on its axis is gradually slowing down, because of the movement of tides. As a result, experts have calculated that, in about about 200 million years, the day will be 25 hours long.

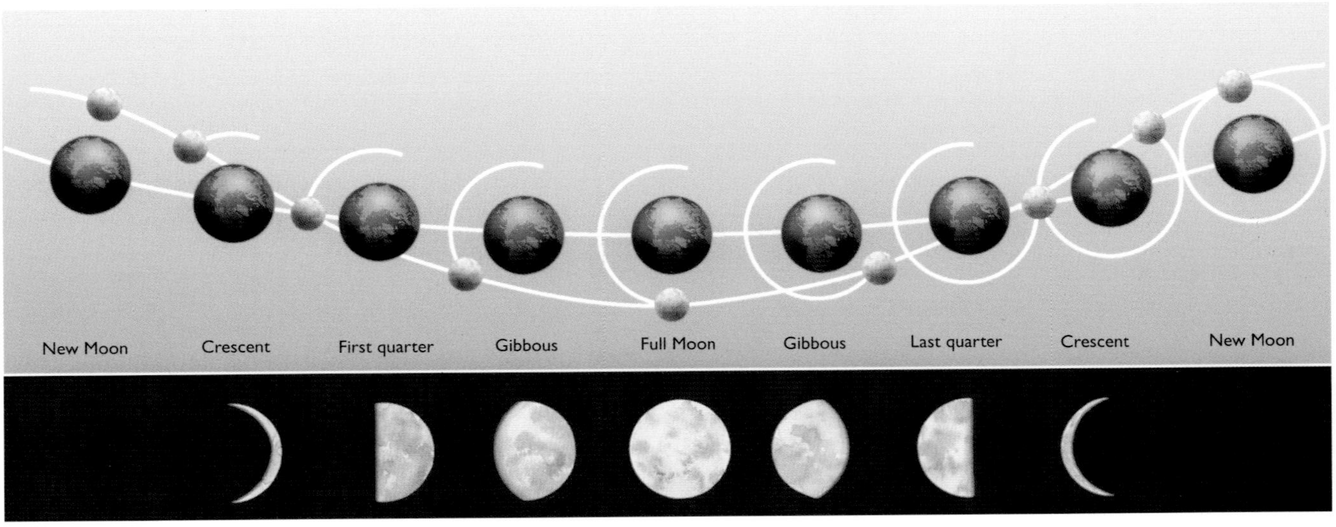

Phases of the Moon

The Moon rotates more slowly than the Earth, making one complete turn on its axis in just over 27 days. This corresponds to its period of revolution around the Earth and, hence, the same hemisphere always faces us. The interval between one full Moon and the next (and also between new Moons) is about 29½ days, or one lunar month. The apparent changes in the appearance of the Moon are caused by its changing position in relation to Earth. Like the planets, the Moon produces no light of its own. It shines by reflecting the Sun's rays, varying from a slim crescent to a full circle and back again.

The Earth from Space

Any last doubts about whether the Earth was round or flat were finally resolved by the appearance of the first photographs of our planet taken at the start of the Space Age. Satellite images also confirmed that map- and globe-makers had correctly worked out the shapes of the continents and the oceans.

More importantly, images of our beautiful, blue, white and brown planet from space impressed on many people that the Earth and its resources are finite. They made people realize that if we allow our planet to be damaged by such factors as overpopulation, pollution and irresponsible over-use of resources, then its future and the survival of all the living things upon it may be threatened.

Views from Above

The first aerial photographs were taken from balloons in the mid-19th century and their importance in military reconnaissance was recognized as early as the 1860s during the American Civil War.

Since the end of World War II, photographs taken by aircraft have been widely used in map-making. The use of air photographs has greatly speeded up the laborious process of mapping land details and they have enabled cartographers to produce maps of the most remote parts of the world.

Aerial photographs have also proved useful because they reveal features that are not visible at ground level. For example, circles that appear on many air photographs do not correspond to visible features on the ground. Many of these mysterious shapes have turned out to be the sites of ancient settlements previously unknown to archaeologists.

Images from Space

Space probes equipped with cameras and a variety of remote sensing instruments have sent back images of distant planets and moons. From these images, detailed maps have been produced, rapidly expanding our knowledge of the Solar System.

Photographs from space are also proving invaluable in the study of the Earth. One of the best known uses of space imagery is the study of the atmosphere. Polar-orbiting weather satellites that circle the Earth, together with geostationary satellites, whose motion is synchronized with the Earth's rotation, now regularly transmit images showing the changing patterns of weather systems from above. Forecasters use these images to track the development and the paths taken by hurricanes, enabling them to issue storm warnings to endangered areas, saving lives and reducing damage to property.

Remote sensing devices are now monitoring changes in temperatures over the land and sea, while photographs indicate the melting of ice sheets. Such evidence is vital in the study of global warming. Other devices reveal polluted areas, patterns of vegetation growth, and areas suffering deforestation.

In recent years, remote sensing devices have been used to monitor the damage being done to the ozone layer in the stratosphere, which prevents most of the Sun's harmful ultraviolet radiation from reaching the surface. The discovery of 'ozone holes', where the protective layer of ozone is being thinned by chlorofluorocarbons (CFCs), chemicals used in the manufacture of such things as air conditioners and refrigerators, has enabled governments to take concerted action to save our planet from imminent danger.

Launch of the Space Shuttle Atlantis

Space Shuttles transport astronauts and equipment into orbit around the Earth. The American Space Shuttle Atlantis*, shown below, launched the Magellan probe, which undertook a radar mapping programme of the surface of Venus in the early 1990s.*

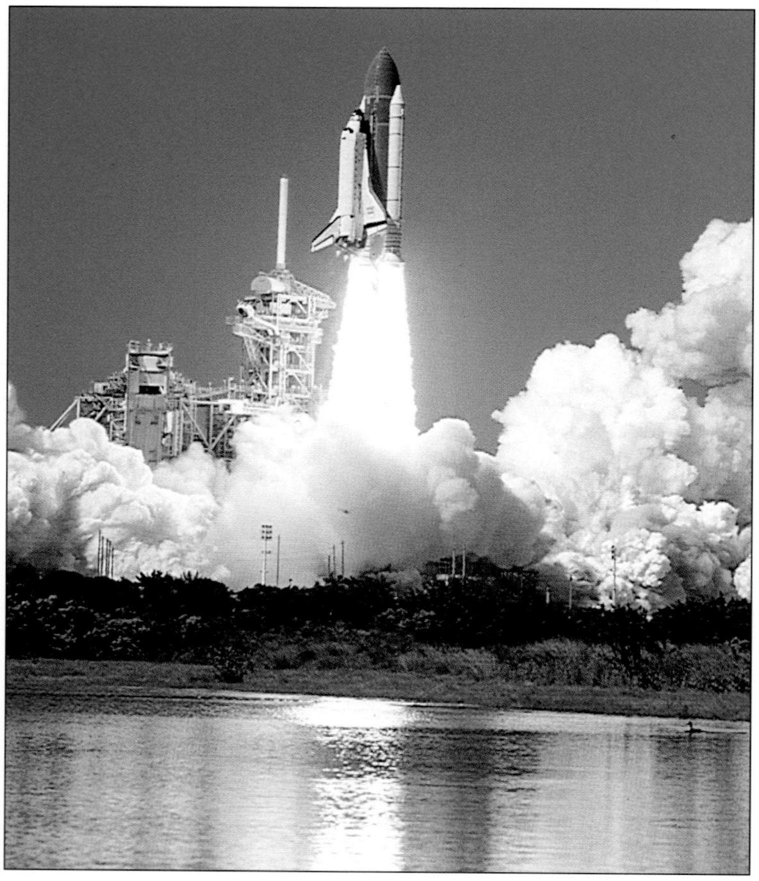

Earth Data

MAXIMUM DISTANCE FROM SUN (APHELION)
152,007,016 km

MINIMUM DISTANCE FROM SUN (PERIHELION)
147,000,830 km

LENGTH OF YEAR – SOLAR TROPICAL (EQUINOX TO EQUINOX)
365.24 days

LENGTH OF YEAR – SIDEREAL (FIXED STAR TO FIXED STAR)
365.26 days

LENGTH OF DAY – MEAN SOLAR DAY
24 hours, 03 minutes, 56 seconds

LENGTH OF DAY – MEAN SIDEREAL DAY
23 hours, 56 minutes, 4 seconds

SUPERFICIAL AREA
510,000,000 km²

LAND SURFACE
149,000,000 km² (29.3%)

WATER SURFACE
361,000,000 km² (70.7%)

EQUATORIAL CIRCUMFERENCE
40,077 km

POLAR CIRCUMFERENCE
40,009 km

EQUATORIAL DIAMETER
12,756.8 km

POLAR DIAMETER
12,713.8 km

EQUATORIAL RADIUS
6,378.4 km

POLAR RADIUS
6,356.9 km

VOLUME OF THE EARTH
1,083,230 x 10^6 km³

MASS OF THE EARTH
5.9 x 10^{21} tonnes

Satellite image of San Francisco Bay

Unmanned scientific satellites called ERTS (Earth Resources Technology Satellites), *or* Landsats, *were designed to collect information about the Earth's resources. The satellites transmitted images of the land using different wavelengths of light in order to identify, in false colours, such subtle features as areas that contain minerals or areas covered with growing crops, that are not identifiable on simple photographs using the visible range of the spectrum. They were also equipped to monitor conditions in the atmosphere and oceans, and also to detect pollution levels. This* Landsat *image of San Francisco Bay covers an area of great interest to geologists because it lies in an earthquake zone in the path of the San Andreas fault.*

The Dynamic Earth

The Earth was formed about 4.6 billion years ago from the ring of gas and dust left over after the formation of the Sun. As the Earth took shape, lighter elements, such as silicon, rose to the surface, while heavy elements, notably iron, sank towards the centre.

Gradually, the outer layers cooled to form a hard crust. The crust enclosed the dense mantle which, in turn, surrounded the even denser liquid outer and solid inner core. Around the Earth was an atmosphere, which contained abundant water vapour. When the surface cooled, rainwater began to fill hollows, forming the first lakes and seas. Since that time, our planet has been subject to constant change – the result of powerful internal and external forces that still operate today.

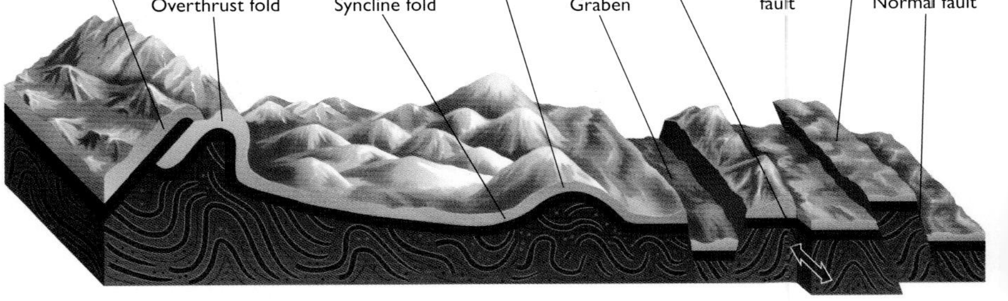
Nappe fold
Overthrust fold
Syncline fold
Symmetrical anticline fold
Graben
Strike-slip fault
Reverse fault
Horst
Normal fault

Mountain building

Lateral pressure, which occurs when plates collide, squeezes and compresses rocks into folds. Simple symmetrical upfolds are called anticlines, while downfolds are synclines. As the pressure builds up, strata become asymmetrical and they may be tilted over to form recumbent folds. The rocks often crack under the intense pressure and the folds are sheared away and pushed forward over other rocks. These features are called overthrust folds or nappes. Plate movements also create faults along which rocks move upwards, downwards and sideways. The diagram shows a downfaulted graben, or rift valley, and an uplifted horst, or block mountain.

Lulworth Cove, southern England

When undisturbed by earth movements, sedimentary rock strata are generally horizontal. But lateral pressure has squeezed the Jurassic strata at Lulworth Cove into complex folds.

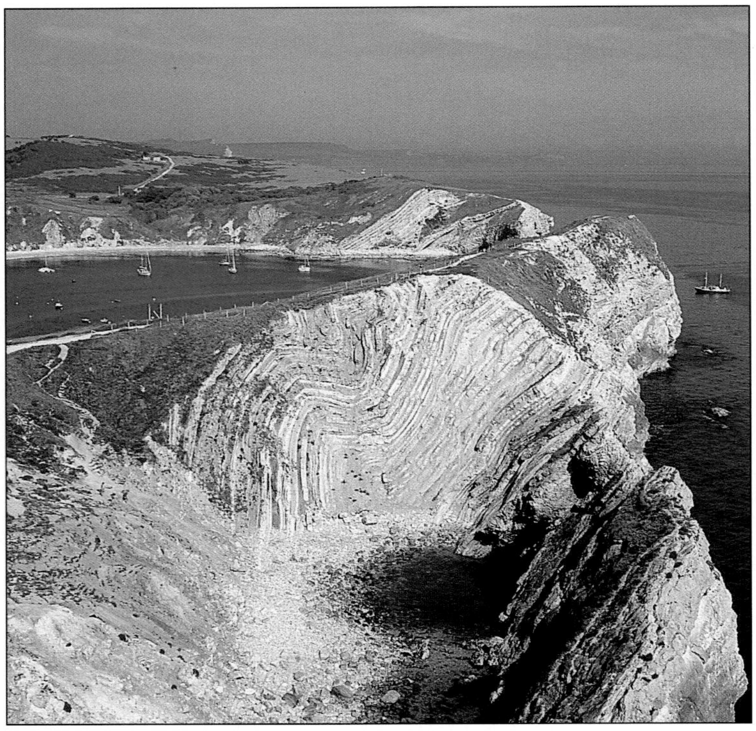

THE HISTORY OF THE EARTH

From their study of rocks, geologists have pieced together the history of our planet and the life forms that evolved upon it. They have dated the oldest known crystals, composed of the mineral zircon, at 4.2 billion years. But the oldest rocks are younger, less than 4 billion years old. This is because older rocks have been weathered away by natural processes.

The oldest rocks that contain fossils, which are evidence of once-living organisms, are around 3.5 billion years old. But fossils are rare in rocks formed in the first 4 billion years of Earth history. This vast expanse of time is called the Precambrian. This is because it precedes the Cambrian period, at the start of which, about 590 million years ago, life was abundant in the seas.

The Cambrian is the first period in the Paleozoic (or ancient life) era. The Paleozoic era is followed by the Mesozoic (middle life) era, which witnessed the spectacular rise and fall of the dinosaurs, and the Cenozoic (recent life) era, which was dominated by the evolution of mammals. Each of the eras is divided into periods, and the periods in the Cenozoic era, covering the last 65 million years, are further divided into epochs.

THE EARTH'S CHANGING FACE

While life was gradually evolving, the face of the Earth was constantly changing. By piecing together evidence of rock structures and fossils, geologists have demonstrated that around 250 million years ago, all the world's land areas were grouped together in one huge landmass called Pangaea. Around 180 million years ago, the supercontinent Pangaea, began to break up. New oceans opened up as the continents began to move towards their present positions.

Evidence of how continents drift came from studies of the ocean floor in the 1950s and 1960s. Scientists discovered that the oceans are young features. By contrast with the continents, no part of the ocean floor is more than 200 million years old. The floors of oceans older than 200 million years have completely vanished.

Studies of long undersea ranges, called ocean ridges, revealed that the youngest rocks occur along their centres, which are the edges of huge plates – rigid blocks of the Earth's lithosphere, which is made up of the crust and the solid upper layer of the mantle. The Earth's lithosphere is split into six large and several smaller

The Himalayas seen from Nepal
The Himalayas are a young fold mountain range formed by a collision between two plates. The earthquakes felt in the region testify that the plate movements are still continuing.

plates. The ocean ridges are 'constructive' plate margins, because new crustal rock is being formed there from magma that wells up from the mantle as the plates gradually move apart. By contrast, the deep ocean trenches are 'destructive' plate edges. Here, two plates are pushing against each other and one plate is descending beneath the other into the mantle where it is melted and destroyed. Geologists call these areas subduction zones.

A third type of plate edge is called a transform fault. Here two plates are moving alongside each other. The best known of these plate edges is the San Andreas fault in California, which separates the Pacific plate from the North American plate.

Slow-moving currents in the partly molten asthenosphere, which underlies the solid lithosphere, are responsible for moving the plates, a process called plate tectonics.

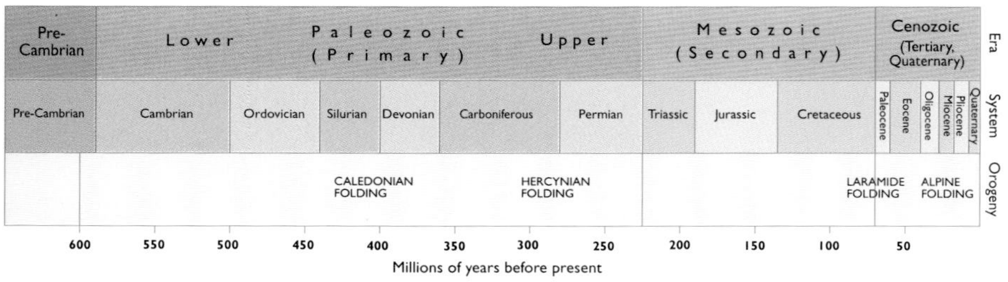

MOUNTAIN BUILDING

The study of plate tectonics has helped geologists to understand the mechanisms that are responsible for the creation of mountains. Many of the world's greatest ranges were created by the collision of two plates and the bending of the intervening strata into huge loops, or folds. For example, the Himalayas began to rise around 50 million years ago, when a plate supporting India collided with the huge Eurasian plate. Rocks on the floor of the intervening and long-vanished Tethys Sea were squeezed up to form the Himalayan Mountain Range.

Plate movements also create tension that cracks rocks, producing long faults along which rocks move upwards, downwards or sideways. Block mountains are formed when blocks of rock are pushed upwards along faults. Steep-sided rift valleys are formed when blocks of land sink down between faults. For example, the basin and range region of the south-western United States has both block mountains and down-faulted basins, such as Death Valley.

Geological time scale
The geological time scale was first constructed by a study of the stratigraphic, or relative, ages of layers of rock. But the absolute ages of rock strata could not be fixed until the discovery of radioactivity in the early 20th century. Some names of periods, such as Cambrian (Latin for Wales), come from places where the rocks were first studied. Others, such as Carboniferous, refer to the nature of the rocks formed during the period. For example, coal seams (containing carbon) were formed from decayed plant matter during the Carboniferous period.

Pre-Cambrian	Lower		Paleozoic (Primary)				Upper		Mesozoic (Secondary)			Cenozoic (Tertiary, Quaternary)				Era
Pre-Cambrian	Cambrian	Ordovician	Silurian	Devonian	Carboniferous		Permian	Triassic	Jurassic	Cretaceous	Paleocene	Eocene	Oligocene	Miocene Pliocene Pleistocene Quaternary		System
			CALEDONIAN FOLDING		HERCYNIAN FOLDING						LARAMIDE FOLDING	ALPINE FOLDING				Orogeny
600	550	500	450	400	350	300	250	200	150	100	50					

Millions of years before present

Earthquakes and Volcanoes

At 5.46 AM on 17 January 1995, when most people were asleep, an earthquake with a magnitude of 7.2 struck the Japanese city of Kobe. More than 5,400 people died, more than 30,000 were injured and nearly 200,000 buildings were destroyed. It was Japan's worst earthquake since 1923, when Tokyo was destroyed.

The Restless Earth

Earthquakes can occur anywhere, whenever rocks move along faults. But the most severe and most numerous earthquakes occur near the edges of the plates that make up the Earth's lithosphere. Japan lies in a particularly unstable region above subduction zones, where plates are descending into the Earth's mantle. It lies in a zone encircling the Pacific Ocean, called the 'Pacific ring of fire'.

Plates do not move smoothly. Their edges are jagged and for most of the time they are locked together. However, pressure gradually builds up until the rocks break and the plates lurch forwards, setting off vibrations ranging from tremors that are recorded only by sensitive instruments to terrifying earthquakes. The greater the pressure released, the more destructive the earthquake.

Earthquakes are also common along the ocean trenches where plates are moving apart, but they mostly occur so far from land that they do little damage. Far more destructive are the earthquakes that occur where plates are moving alongside each other. For example, the earthquakes that periodically rock south-western California are caused by movements along the San Andreas Fault.

The spot where an earthquake originates is called the focus, while the point on the Earth's surface directly above the focus is called the epicentre. Two kinds of waves, P-waves or compressional waves and S-waves or shear waves, travel from the focus to the surface where they make the ground shake. P-waves travel faster than S-waves and the time difference between their arrival at recording stations enables scientists to calculate the distance from a station to the epicentre.

Earthquakes are measured on the Richter scale, which indicates the magnitude of the shock. The most destructive earthquakes are shallow-focus, that is, the focus is within 60 km [37 miles] of the surface. A magnitude of 7.0 is a major earthquake, but earthquakes with a somewhat lower magnitude can cause tremendous damage if their epicentres are on or close to densely populated areas.

NOTABLE EARTHQUAKES *(since 1900)*

Year	Location	Mag.
1906	San Francisco, USA	8.3
1906	Valparaiso, Chile	8.6
1908	Messina, Italy	7.5
1915	Avezzano, Italy	7.5
1920	Gansu, China	8.6
1923	Yokohama, Japan	8.3
1927	Nan Shan, China	8.3
1932	Gansu, China	7.6
1934	Bihar, India/Nepal	8.4
1935	Quetta, India[1]	7.5
1939	Chillan, Chile	8.3
1939	Erzincan, Turkey	7.9
1964	Anchorage, Alaska	8.4
1968	N. E. Iran	7.4
1970	N. Peru	7.7
1976	Guatemala	7.5
1976	Tangshan, China	8.2
1978	Tabas, Iran	7.7
1980	El Asnam, Algeria	7.3
1980	S. Italy	7.2
1985	Mexico City, Mexico	8.1
1988	N. W. Armenia	6.8
1990	N. Iran	7.7
1993	Maharashtra India	6.4
1994	Los Angeles, USA	6.4
1995	Kobe, Japan	7.2
1995	Sakhalin Is., Russia	7.5
1996	Yunnan, China	7.0

[1] now Pakistan

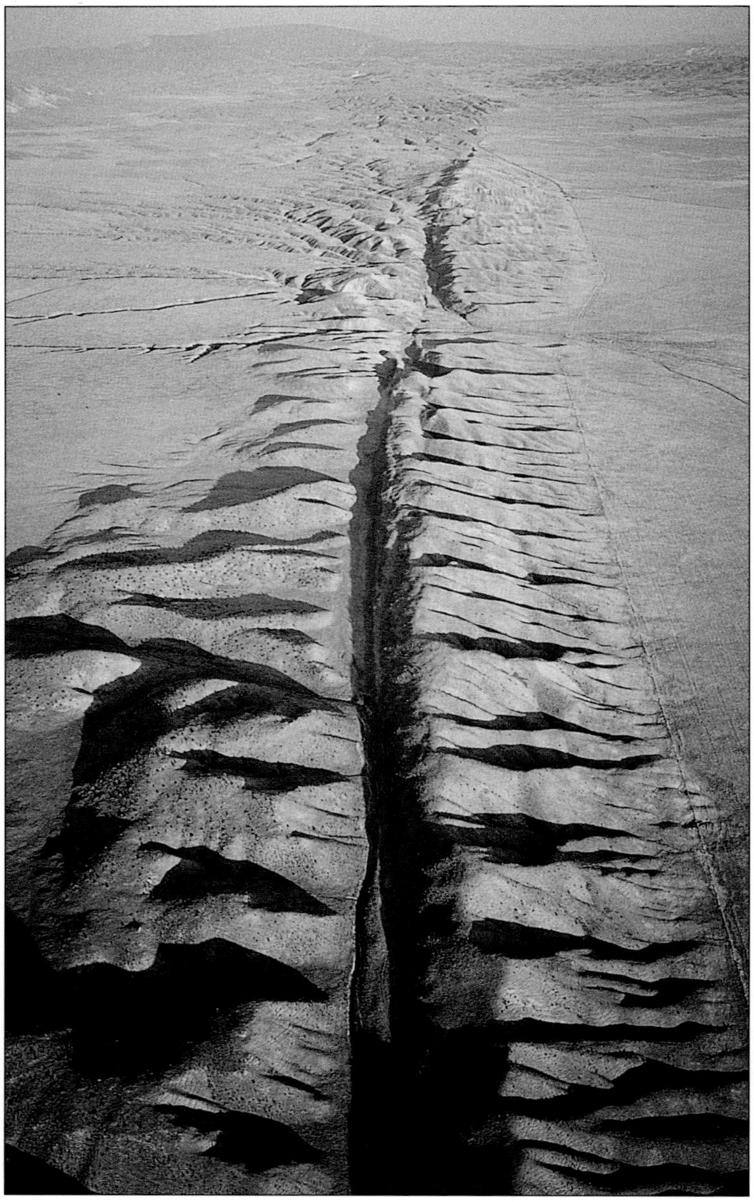

San Andreas Fault, United States

Geologists call the San Andreas fault in south-western California a transform, or strike-slip, fault. Sudden movements along it cause earthquakes. In 1906, shifts of about 4.5 metres [15 ft] occurred near San Francisco, causing a massive earthquake.

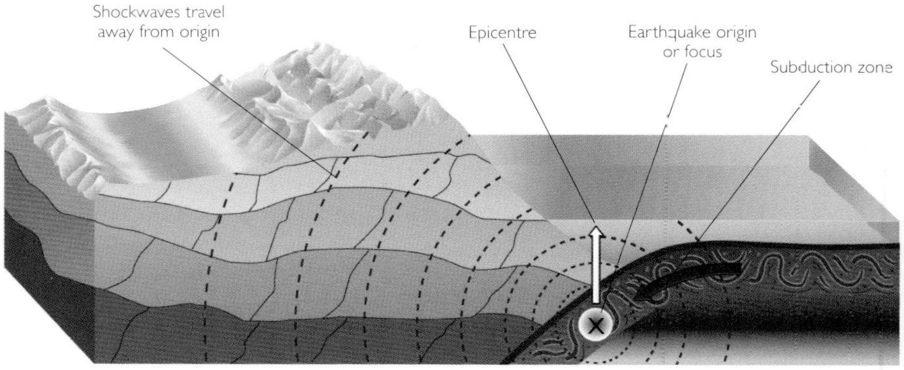
Shockwaves travel away from origin
Epicentre
Earthquake origin or focus
Subduction zone

Earthquakes in subduction zones

Along subduction zones, one plate is descending beneath another. The plates are locked together until the rocks break and the descending plate lurches forwards. From the point where the plate moves – the origin – seismic waves spread through the lithosphere, making the ground shake. The earthquake in Mexico City in 1985 occurred in this way.

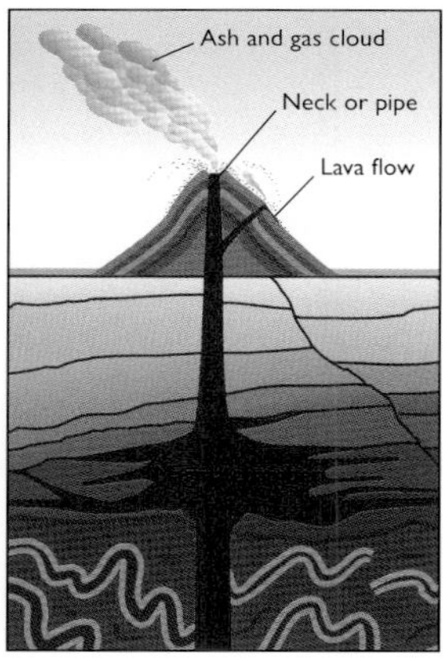

Cross-section of a volcano

Volcanoes are vents in the ground, through which magma reaches the surface. The term volcano is also used for the mountains formed from volcanic rocks. Beneath volcanoes are pockets of magma derived from the semi-molten asthenosphere in the mantle. The magma rises under pressure through the overlying rocks until it reaches the surface. There it emerges through vents as pyroclasts, ranging in size from large lumps of magma, called volcanic bombs, to fine volcanic ash and dust. In quiet eruptions, streams of liquid lava run down the side of the mountain. Side vents sometimes appear on the flanks of existing volcanoes.

Scientists have been working for years to find effective ways of forecasting earthquakes but with very limited success. Following the Kobe earthquake in 1995, many experts argued that they would be better employed developing techniques of reducing the damage caused by earthquakes, rather than pursuing an apparently vain attempt to predict them.

Volcanic Eruptions

Most active volcanoes also occur on or near plate edges. Many undersea volcanoes along the ocean ridges are formed from magma that wells up from the asthenosphere to fill the gaps created as the plates, on the opposite sides of the ridges, move apart. Some of these volcanoes reach the surface to form islands. Iceland is a country which straddles the Mid-Atlantic Ocean Ridge. It is gradually becoming wider as magma rises to the surface through faults and vents. Other volcanoes lie alongside subduction zones. The magma that fuels them comes from the melted edges of the descending plates.

A few volcanoes lie far from plate edges. For example, Mauna Loa and Kilauea on Hawaii are situated near the centre of the huge Pacific plate. The molten magma that reaches the surface is created by a source of heat, called a 'hot spot', in the Earth's mantle.

Magma is molten rock at temperatures of about 1,100°C to 1,200°C [2,012°F to 2,192°F]. It contains gases and superheated steam. The chemical composition of magma varies. Viscous magma is rich in silica and superheated steam, while runny magma contains less silica and steam. The chemical composition of the magma affects the nature of volcanic eruptions.

Explosive volcanoes contain thick, viscous magma. When they erupt, they usually hurl clouds of ash (shattered fragments of cooled magma) into the air. By contrast, quiet volcanoes emit long streams of runny magma, or lava. However, many volcanoes are intermediate in type, sometimes erupting explosively and sometimes emitting streams of fluid lava. Explosive and intermediate volcanoes usually have a conical shape, while quiet volcanoes are flattened, resembling upturned saucers. They are often called shield volcanoes.

One dangerous type of eruption is called a *nuée ardente*, or 'glowing cloud'. It occurs when a cloud of intensely hot volcanic gases and dust particles and superheated steam are exploded from a volcano. They move rapidly downhill, burning everything in their path and choking animals and people. The blast that creates the *nuée ardente* may release the pressure inside the volcano, resulting in a tremendous explosion that hurls tall columns of ash into the air.

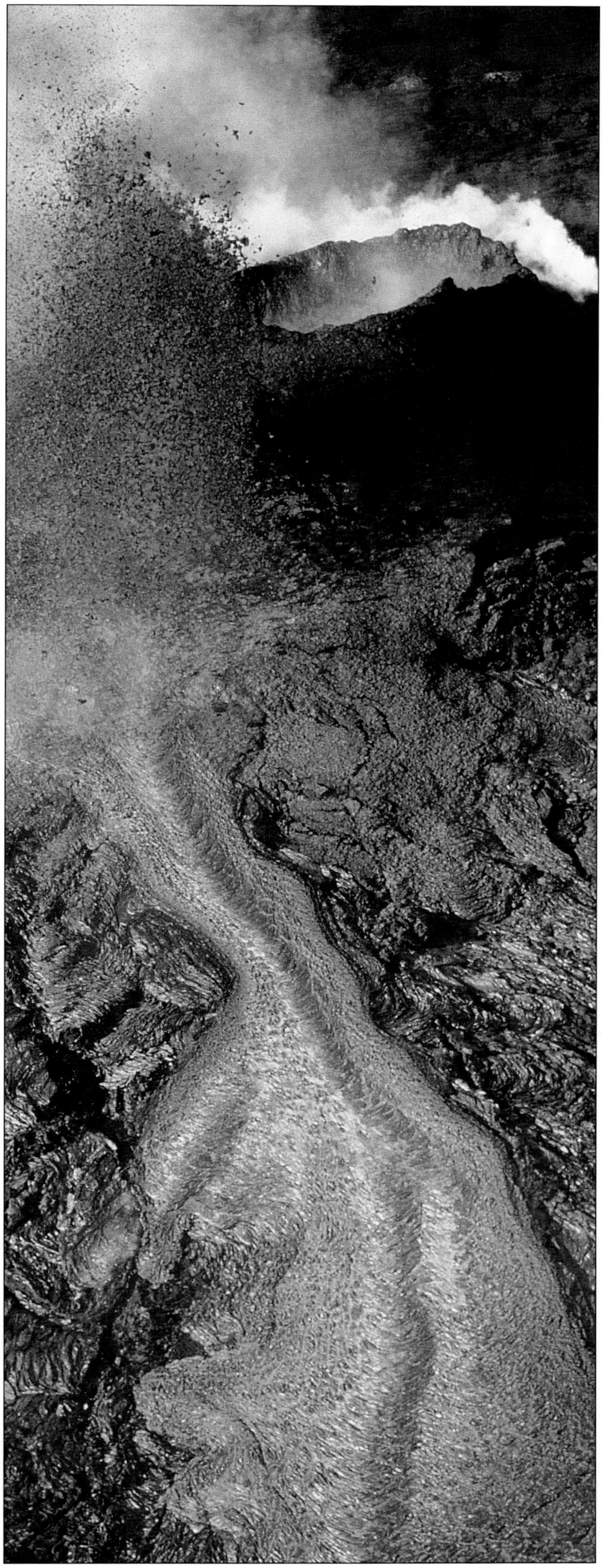

Kilauea Volcano, Hawaii

The volcanic Hawaiian islands in the North Pacific Ocean were formed as the Pacific plate moved over a 'hot spot' in the Earth's mantle. Kilauea on Hawaii emits blazing streams of liquid lava.

Forces of Nature

When the volcano Mount Pinatubo erupted in the Philippines in 1991, large areas around the mountain were covered by ash. Later, rainwater mixed with the loose ash on sloping land, created lahars, or mudflows, which swept down river valleys burying many areas. Such incidents are not only reminders of the great forces that operate inside our planet but also of those natural forces operating on the surface, which can have dramatic effects on the land.

The chief forces acting on the surface of the Earth are weathering, running water, ice and winds. The forces of erosion seem to act slowly. One estimate suggests that an average of only 3.5 cm [1.4 in] of land is removed by natural processes every 1,000 years. This may not sound much, but over millions of years, it can reduce mountains to almost flat surfaces.

RATES OF EROSION

	SLOW	WEATHERING RATE	FAST
Mineral solubility	low (e.g. quartz)	moderate (e.g. feldspar)	high (e.g. calcite)
Rainfall	low	moderate	heavy
Temperature	cold	temperate	hot
Vegetation	sparse	moderate	lush
Soil cover	bare rock	thin to moderate soil	thick soil

Weathering is the breakdown and decay of rocks in situ. It may be mechanical (physical), chemical or biological.

Rates of erosion
The chart shows that the rates at which weathering takes place depend on the chemistry and hardness of rocks, climatic factors, especially rainfall and temperature, the vegetation and the nature of the soil cover in any area. The effects of weathering are increased by human action, particularly the removal of vegetation and the exposure of soils to the rain and wind.

Weathering

Weathering occurs in all parts of the world, but the most effective type of weathering in any area depends on the climate and the nature of the rocks. For example, in cold mountain areas, when water freezes in cracks in rocks, the ice occupies 9% more space than the water. This exerts a force which, when repeated over and over again, can split boulders apart. By contrast, in hot deserts, intense heating by day and cooling by night causes the outer layers of rocks to expand and contract until they break up and peel away like layers of an onion. These are examples of what is called mechanical weathering.

Other kinds of weathering include chemical reactions usually involving water. Rainwater containing carbon dioxide dissolved from the air or the soil is a weak acid which reacts with limestone, wearing out pits, tunnels and networks of caves in layers of limestone rock. Water also combines with some minerals, such as the feldspars in granite, to create kaolin, a white

Grand Canyon, Arizona, at dusk
The Grand Canyon in the United States is one of the world's natural wonders. Eroded by the Colorado River and its tributaries, it is up to 1.6 km [1 mile] deep and 29 km [18 miles] wide.

clay. These are examples of chemical weathering which constantly wears away rock.

Running Water, Ice and Wind

In moist regions, rivers are effective in shaping the land. They transport material worn away by weathering and erode the land. They wear out V-shaped valleys in upland regions, while vigorous meanders widen their middle courses. The work of rivers is at its most spectacular when earth movements lift up flat areas and rejuvenate the rivers, giving them a new erosive power capable of wearing out such features as the Grand Canyon. Rivers also have a constructive role. Some of the world's most fertile regions are deltas and flood plains composed of sediments periodically dumped there by such rivers as the Ganges, Mississippi and Nile.

Running water in the form of sea waves and currents shapes coastlines, wearing out caves, natural arches, and stacks. The sea also transports and deposits worn material to form such features as spits and bars.

Glaciers in cold mountain regions flow downhill, gradually deepening valleys and shaping dramatic landscapes. They erode steep-sided U-shaped valleys, into which rivers plunge in huge waterfalls. Other features include cirques, armchair-shaped basins bounded by knife-edged ridges called *arêtes*, and, when several *arêtes* form back to back, they erode pyramidal peaks called horns. Deposits of moraine, rock material dumped by the glacier, are further evidence that ice once covered large areas. The work of glaciers, like other agents of erosion, varies with the climate. In recent years, global warming has been making glaciers retreat in many areas, while several of the ice shelves in Antarctica have been breaking up.

Many land features in deserts were formed by running water at a time when the climate was much rainier than it is today. Water erosion also occurs when flash floods are caused by rare thunderstorms. But the chief agent of erosion in dry areas is wind-blown sand, which can strip the paint from cars, and undercut boulders to create mushroom-shaped rocks.

Glaciers
During Ice Ages, ice spreads over large areas and the effect of glacial erosion on landscapes is enormous. However, during warm periods, the world's ice sheets and glaciers retreat. The chart shows that in recent years, the volumes of many glaciers around the world have been decreasing, possibly as a result of global warming.

ANNUAL FLUCTUATIONS FOR SELECTED GLACIERS

Glacier name and location	Changes in the annual mass balance† 1970–1	1990–1	Cumulative total 1970–90
Alfotbreen, Norway	+940	+790	+12,110
Wolverine, USA	+770	–410	+2,320
Storglaciaren, Sweden	–190	+170	–120
Djankuat, Russia	–230	–310	–1,890
Grasubreen, Norway	+470	–520	–2,530
Ürümqi, China	+102	–706	–3,828
Golubin, Kyrgyzstan	–90	–722	–7,105
Hintereisferner, Austria	–600	–1,325	–9,081
Gries, Switzerland	–970	–1,480	–10,600
Careser, Italy	–650	–1,730	–11,610
Abramov, Tajikistan	–890	–420	–13,700
Sarennes, France	–1,100	–1,360	–15,020
Place, Canada	–343	–990	–15,175

† The annual mass balance is defined as the difference between glacier accumulation and ablation (melting) averaged over the whole glacier. Balances are expressed as water equivalent in millimetres. A plus indicates an increase in the depth or length of the glacier; a minus indicates a reduction.

Juneau Glacier, Alaska
Like huge conveyor belts, glaciers transport weathered debris from mountain regions. Rocks frozen in the ice give the glaciers teeth, enabling them to wear out typical glaciated land features.

Oceans and Ice

Since the 1970s, oceanographers have found numerous hot vents on the ocean ridges. Called black smokers, the vents emit dark, mineral-rich water reaching 350°C [662°F]. Around the vents are chimney-like structures formed from minerals deposited from the hot water. The discovery of black smokers did not surprise scientists who already knew that the ridges were plate edges, where new crustal rock was being formed as molten magma welled up to the surface. But what was astonishing was that the hot water contained vast numbers of bacteria, which provided the base of a food chain that included many strange creatures, such as giant worms, eyeless shrimps and white clams. Many species were unknown to science.

Little was known about the dark world beneath the waves until about 50 years ago. But through the use of modern technology such as echo-sounders, magnetometers, research ships equipped with huge drills, submersibles that can carry scientists down to the ocean floor, and satellites, the secrets of the oceans have been gradually revealed.

The study of the ocean floor led to the discovery that the oceans are geologically young features – no more than 200 million years old. It also revealed evidence as to how oceans form and continents drift because of the action of plate tectonics.

Vava'u Island, Tonga

This small coral atoll in northern Tonga consists of a central island covered by rainforest. Low coral reefs washed by the waves surround a shallow central lagoon.

The Blue Planet

Water covers almost 71% of the Earth, which makes it look blue when viewed from space. Although the oceans are interconnected, geographers divide them into four main areas: the Pacific, Atlantic, Indian and Arctic oceans. The average depth of the oceans is 3,370 m [12,238 ft], but they are divided into several zones.

Around most continents are gently sloping continental shelves, which are flooded parts of the continents. The shelves end at the continental slope, at a depth of about 200 m [656 ft]. This slope leads steeply down to the abyss. The deepest parts of the oceans are the trenches, which reach a maximum depth of 11,033 m [36,198 ft] in the Mariana Trench in the western Pacific.

Most marine life is found in the top 200 m [656 ft], where there is sufficient sunlight for plants, called phytoplankton, to grow. Below this zone, life becomes more and more scarce, though no part of the ocean, even at the bottom of the deepest trenches, is completely without living things.

Continental islands, such as the British Isles, are high parts of the continental shelves. For example, until about 7,500 years ago, when the ice sheets formed during the Ice Ages were melting, raising the sea level and filling the North Sea and the Strait of Dover, Britain was linked to mainland Europe.

By contrast, oceanic islands, such as the Hawaiian chain in the North Pacific Ocean, rise from the ocean floor. All oceanic islands are of volcanic origin, although many of them in warm parts of the oceans have sunk and are capped by layers of coral to form ring- or horseshoe-shaped atolls and coral reefs.

Ocean Water

The oceans contain about 97% of the world's water. Seawater contains more than 70 dissolved elements, but chloride and sodium make up 85% of the total. Sodium chloride is common salt and it makes seawater salty. The salinity of the oceans is mostly between 3.3–3.7%. Ocean water fed by icebergs or large rivers is less saline than shallow seas in the tropics, where the evaporation rate is high. Seawater is a source of salt but the water is useless for agriculture or drinking unless it is desalinated. However, land

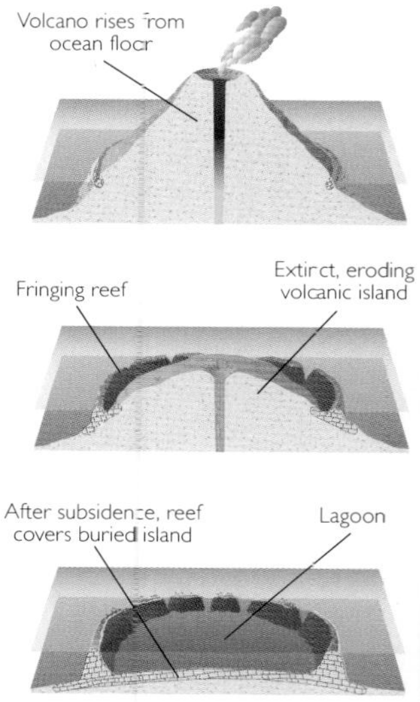

Development of an atoll

Some of the volcanoes that rise from the ocean floor reach the surface to form islands. Some of these islands subside and become submerged. As an island sinks, coral starts to grow around the rim of the volcano, building up layer upon layer of limestone deposits to form fringing reefs. Sometimes coral grows on the tip of a central cone to form an island in the middle of the atoll.

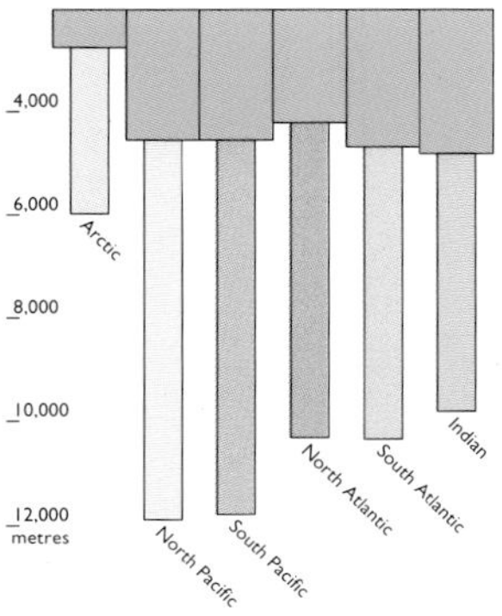

The ocean depths

The diagram shows the average depths (in dark blue) and the greatest depths in the four oceans. The North Pacific Ocean contains the world's deepest trenches, including the Mariana Trench, where the deepest manned descent was made by the bathyscaphe Trieste in 1960. It reached a depth of 10,916 metres [35,813 ft].

Relative sizes of the world's oceans:

PACIFIC	49%	ATLANTIC	26%
INDIAN	21%	ARCTIC	4%

Some geographers distinguish a fifth ocean, the Southern or Antarctic Ocean, but most authorities regard these waters as the southern extension of the Pacific, Atlantic and Indian oceans.

areas get a regular supply of fresh water through the hydrological cycle (see page 26).

The density of seawater depends on its salinity and temperature. Temperatures vary from –2°C [28°F], the freezing point of seawater at the poles, to around 30°C [86°F] in parts of the tropics. Density differences help to maintain the circulation of the world's oceans, especially deep-sea currents. But the main cause of currents within 350 m [1,148 ft] of the surface is the wind. Because of the Earth's rotation, currents are deflected, creating huge circular motions of surface water – clockwise in the northern hemisphere and anticlockwise in the southern hemisphere.

Ocean currents transport heat from the tropics to the polar regions and thus form part of the heat engine that drives the Earth's climates. Ocean currents have an especially marked effect on coastal climates, such as north-western Europe. In the mid-1990s, scientists warned that global warming may be weakening currents, including the warm Gulf Stream which is responsible for the mild winters experienced in north-western Europe.

Ice Sheets, Ice Caps and Glaciers

Global warming is also a threat to the world's ice sheets, ice caps and glaciers that together account for about 2% of the world's water. There are two ice sheets in the world, the largest covers most of Antarctica. With the ice reaching maximum depths of 4,800 m [15,748 ft], the Antarctic ice sheet contains about 70% of the world's fresh water, with a total volume about nine times greater than the Greenland ice sheet. Smaller bodies of ice include ice caps in northern Canada, Iceland and Scandinavia. Also throughout the world in high ranges are many valley glaciers, which help to shape dramatic mountain scenery.

Only about 11,000 years ago, during the final phase of the Pleistocene Ice Age, ice covered much of the northern hemisphere. The Ice Age, which began about 1.8 million years ago, was not a continuous period of cold. Instead, it consisted of glacial periods when the ice advanced and warmer interglacial periods when temperatures rose and the ice retreated.

Some scientists believe that we are now living in an inter-glacial period, and that glacial conditions will recur at some time in the future. Others fear the opposite, that global warming, caused mainly by pollution, may melt the world's ice, raising sea levels by up to 55 m [180 ft]. Many fertile and densely populated coastal plains, islands and great cities would vanish from the map.

Weddell Sea, Antarctica

Antarctica contains two huge bays, occupied by the Ross and Weddell seas. Ice shelves extend from the ice sheet across parts of these seas. Pack ice covers the open sea in winter.

The Earth's Atmosphere

Since the discovery in 1985 of a thinning of the ozone layer, creating a so-called 'ozone hole', over Antarctica, many governments have worked to reduce the emissions of ozone-eating substances, notably the chlorofluorocarbons (CFCs) used in aerosols, refrigeration, air conditioning and dry cleaning.

Following forecasts that the ozone layer would rapidly repair itself as a result of controls on these emissions, scientists were surprised in early 1996 when a marked thinning of the ozone layer occurred over the Arctic, northern Europe, Russia and Canada. The damage, which was recorded as far south as southern Britain, was due to pollution combined with intense cold in the stratosphere. It was another sharp reminder of the dangers humanity faces when it interferes with and harms the environment.

The ozone layer in the stratosphere blocks out most of the dangerous ultraviolet B radiation in the Sun's rays. This radiation causes skin cancer and cataracts, as well as harming plants on the land and plankton in the oceans. The ozone layer is only one way in which the atmosphere protects life on Earth. The atmosphere also provides the air we breathe and the carbon dioxide required by plants. It is also a shield against meteors and it acts as a blanket to prevent heat radiated from the Earth escaping into space.

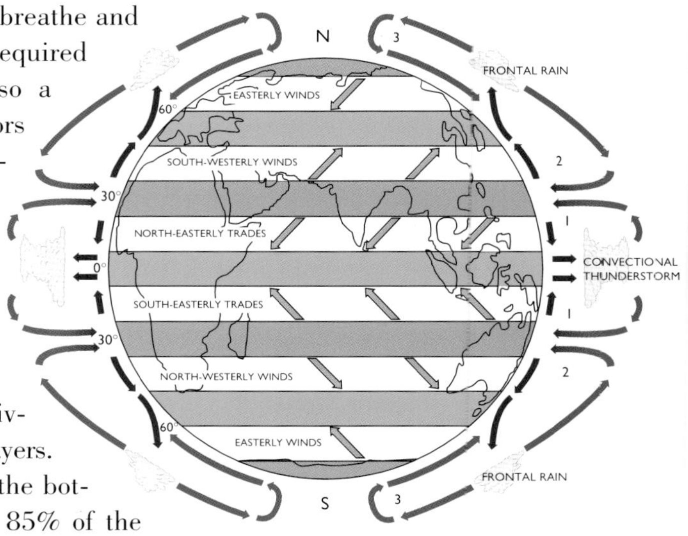

The circulation of the atmosphere can be divided into three rotating but interconnected air systems, or cells. The Hadley cell (figure 1 on the above diagram) is in the tropics; the Ferrel cell (2) lies between the sub-tropics and the mid-latitudes, and the Polar cell (3) is in the high latitudes.

Layers of Air

The atmosphere is divided into four main layers. The troposphere at the bottom contains about 85% of the atmosphere's total mass, where most weather conditions occur. The troposphere is about 15 km [9 miles] thick over the Equator and 8 km [5 miles] thick at the poles. Temperatures decrease with height by approximately 1°C [2°F] for every 100 m [328 ft]. At the top of the troposphere is a level called the tropopause where temperatures are stable at around –55°C [–67°F]. Above the tropopause is the stratosphere, which contains the ozone layer. Here, at about 50 km [31 miles] above the Earth's surface, temperatures rise to about 0°C [32°F].

The ionosphere extends from the stratopause to about 600 km [373 miles] above the surface. Here temperatures fall up to about 80 km

Moonrise seen from orbit

This photograph taken by an orbiting Shuttle shows the crescent of the Moon. Silhouetted at the horizon is a dense cloud layer. The reddish-brown band is the tropopause, which separates the blue-white stratosphere from the yellow troposphere.

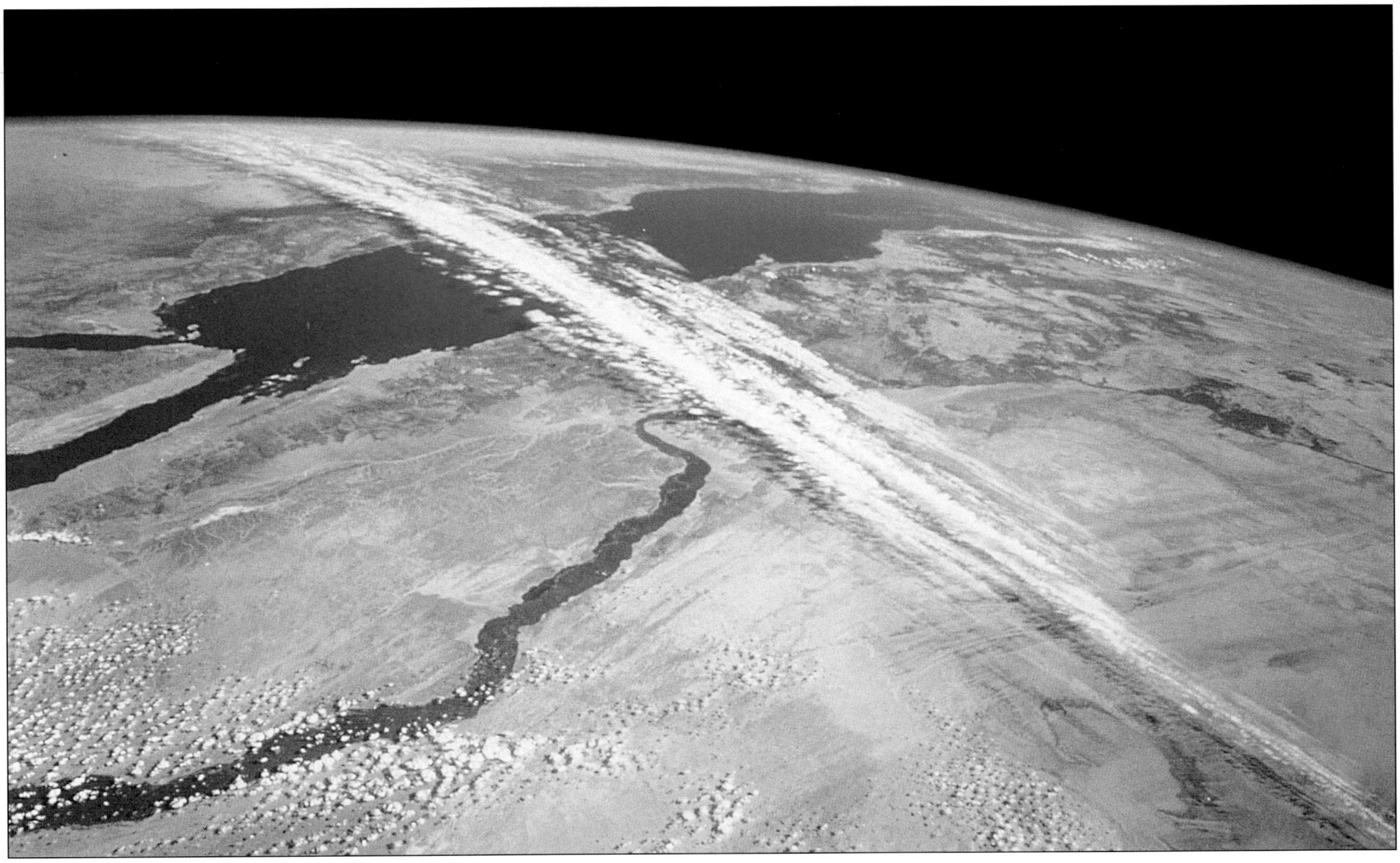

Jetstream from space

Jetstreams are strong winds that normally blow near the tropopause. Cirrus clouds mark the route of the jet stream in this photograph, which shows the Red Sea, North Africa and the Nile valley, which appears as a dark band crossing the desert.

[50 miles], but then rise. The aurorae, which occur in the ionosphere when charged particles from the Sun interact with the Earth's magnetic field, are strongest near the poles. In the exosphere, the outermost layer, the atmosphere merges into space.

Circulation of the Atmosphere

The heating of the Earth is most intense around the Equator where the Sun is high in the sky. Here warm, moist air rises in strong currents, creating a zone of low air pressure: the doldrums. The rising air eventually cools and spreads out north and south until it sinks back to the ground around latitudes 30° North and 30° South. This forms two zones of high air pressure called the horse latitudes.

From the horse latitudes, trade winds blow back across the surface towards the Equator, while westerly winds blow towards the poles. The warm westerlies finally meet the polar easterlies (cold dense air flowing from the poles). The line along which the warm and cold air streams meet is called the polar front. Depressions (or cyclones) are low air pressure frontal systems that form along the polar front.

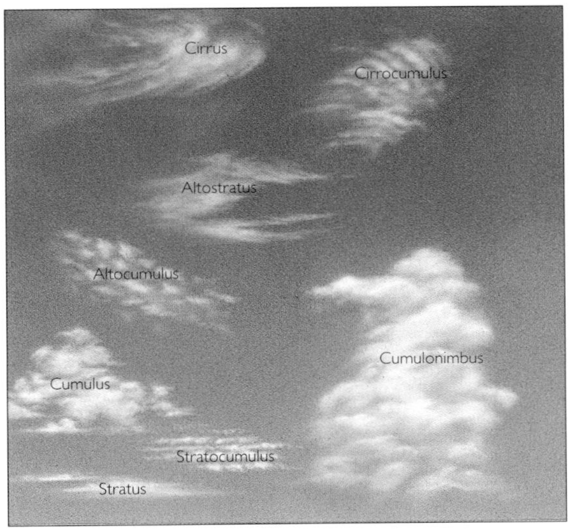

Classification of clouds

Clouds are classified broadly into cumuliform, or 'heap' clouds, and stratiform, or 'layer' clouds. Both types occur at all levels. The highest clouds, composed of ice crystals, are cirrus, cirrostratus and cirrocumulus. Medium-height clouds include altostratus, a grey cloud that often indicates the approach of a depression, and altocumulus, a thicker and fluffier version of cirrocumulus. Low clouds include stratus, which forms dull, overcast skies; nimbostratus, a dark grey layer cloud which brings almost continuous rain and snow; cumulus, a brilliant white heap cloud; and stratocumulus, a layer cloud arranged in globular masses or rolls. Cumulonimbus, a cloud associated with thunderstorms, lightning and heavy rain, often extends from low to medium altitudes. It has a flat base, a fluffy outline and often an anvil-shaped top.

Composition of the Atmosphere

The air in the troposphere is made up mainly of nitrogen (78%) and oxygen (21%). Argon makes up more than 0.9% and there are also minute amounts of carbon dioxide, helium, hydrogen, krypton, methane, ozone and xenon. The atmosphere also contains water vapour, the gaseous form of water, which, when it condenses around minute specks of dust and salt, forms tiny water droplets or ice crystals. Large masses of water droplets or ice crystals form clouds.

Climate and Weather

In April 1989, a tornado destroyed the town of Shaturia in Bangladesh, killing 1,300 people. In April 1991, at least 139,000 people died when a tropical cyclone (known also as a hurricane, a typhoon or a willy-willy) struck Bangladesh. In June and July 1993, record floods in the North American Midwest did enormous damage. And in June and July 1995, a heat wave in the north-eastern and central United States, with temperatures soaring above 32°C [90°F], led to more than 600 deaths.

Every year, exceptional weather conditions cause disasters around the world. Modern forecasting techniques now give people warning of advancing storms, but the toll of human deaths continues as people are powerless in the face of the awesome forces of nature.

Weather is the day-to-day condition of the atmosphere. In some places, the weather is nomally stable, but in other areas, especially the middle latitudes, it is highly variable, changing from hour to hour with the passing of a depression. By contrast, climate is the average, or usual weather of a place, based on data obtained over a long period.

Hurricane Elena, 1995

Hurricanes form over warm oceans north and south of the Equator. Their movements are tracked by satellites, enabling forecasters to issue storm warnings as they approach land. In North America, forecasters identify them with boys' and girls' names.

Climatic Factors

Climate depends basically on the unequal heating of the Sun between the Equator and the poles. But ocean currents and terrain also affect climate. For example, despite their northerly positions, Norway's ports remain ice-free in winter. This is because of the warming effect of the North Atlantic Drift, an extension of the Gulf Stream which flows across the Atlantic Ocean from the Gulf of Mexico.

By contrast, the cold Benguela current which flows up the coast of south-western Africa cools the coast and causes arid conditions. This is because the cold onshore winds are warmed as they pass over the land. The warm air can hold more water vapour than cold air, giving the winds a drying effect.

The terrain affects climate in several ways. Because temperatures fall with altitude, highlands are cooler than lowlands in the same

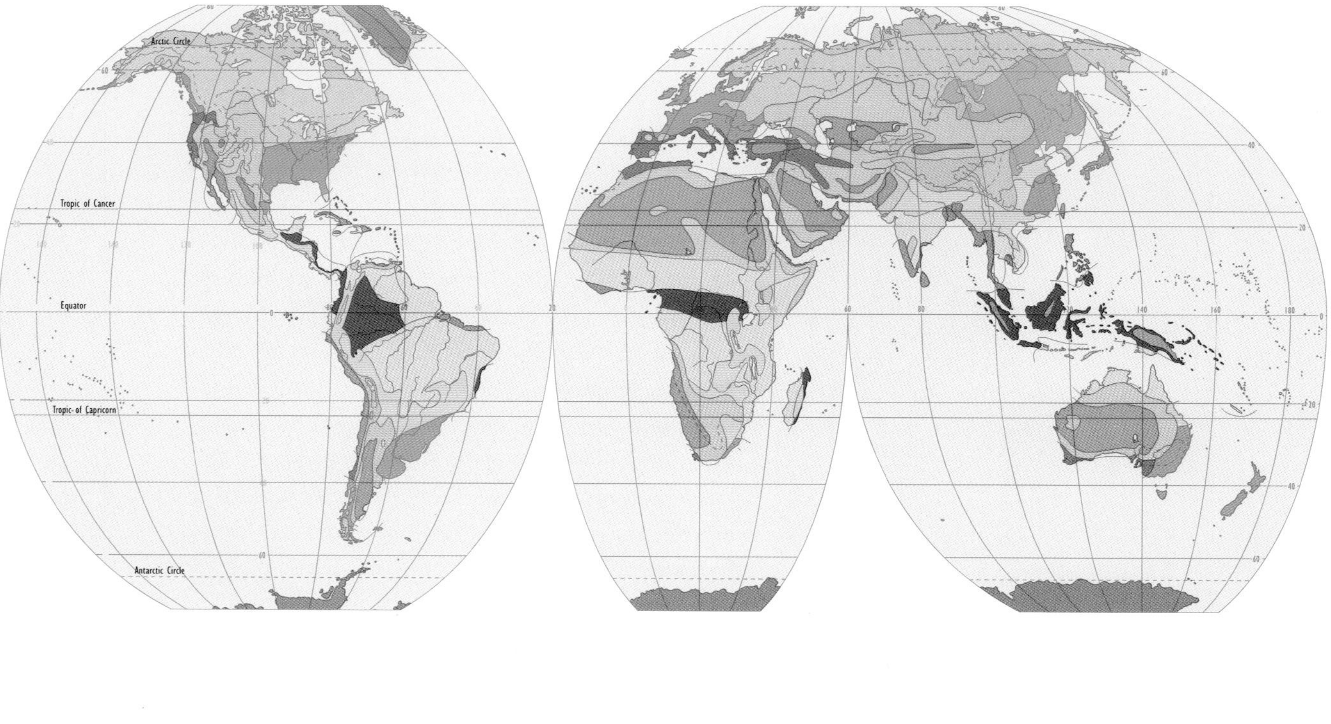

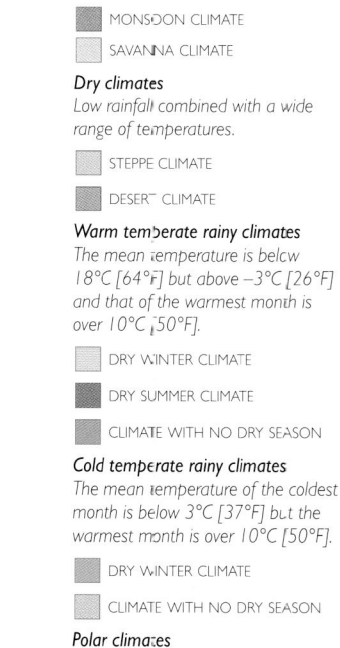

CLIMATIC REGIONS

Tropical rainy climates
All mean monthly temperatures above 18°C [64°F].

- RAINFOREST CLIMATE
- MONSOON CLIMATE
- SAVANNA CLIMATE

Dry climates
Low rainfall combined with a wide range of temperatures.

- STEPPE CLIMATE
- DESERT CLIMATE

Warm temperate rainy climates
The mean temperature is below 18°C [64°F] but above –3°C [26°F] and that of the warmest month is over 10°C [50°F].

- DRY WINTER CLIMATE
- DRY SUMMER CLIMATE
- CLIMATE WITH NO DRY SEASON

Cold temperate rainy climates
The mean temperature of the coldest month is below 3°C [37°F] but the warmest month is over 10°C [50°F].

- DRY WINTER CLIMATE
- CLIMATE WITH NO DRY SEASON

Polar climates
The temperature of the warmest month is below 10°C [50°F], giving permanently frozen subsoil.

- TUNDRA CLIMATE
- POLAR CLIMATE

Flood damage in the United States

In June and July 1993, the Mississippi River basin suffered record floods. The photograph shows a sunken church in Illinois. The flooding along the Mississippi, Missouri and other rivers caused great damage, amounting to about $12 billion. At least 48 people died in the floods.

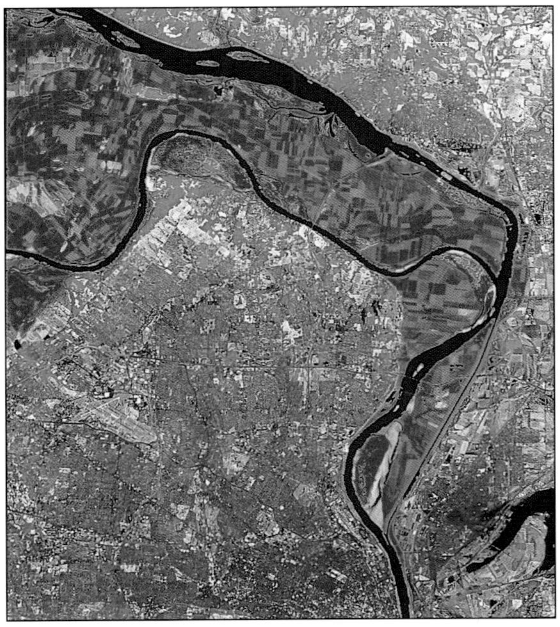

Floods in St Louis, United States

The satellite image, right, shows the extent of the floods at St Louis at the confluence of the Mississippi and the Missouri rivers in June and July 1993. The floods, which finally subsided in August, occurred when the heaviest rains in 20 years raised river levels by up to about 14 m [46 ft]. The floods reached their greatest extent between Minneapolis in the north and a point approximately 150 km [93 miles] south of St Louis. In places, the width of the Mississippi increased to nearly 11 km [7 miles], while the Missouri reached widths of 32 km [20 miles]. In all, more than 28,000 sq km [10,800 sq miles] were inundated and hundreds of towns and cities were flooded. Damage to crops was estimated at $8 billion, while the repairs to rail lines and bridges were estimated at $200 million. South of the devastated region, the virtually continuous levées (artificial river banks) contained the flood water.

latitude. Terrain also affects rainfall. When moist onshore winds pass over mountain ranges, they are chilled as they are forced to rise and the water vapour they contain condenses to form clouds which bring rain and snow. After the winds have crossed the mountains, the air descends and is warmed. These warm, dry winds create rain shadow (arid) regions on the lee side of the mountains.

Climatic Regions

The two major factors that affect climate are temperature and precipitation, including rain and snow. In addition, seasonal variations and other climatic features are also taken into account. Climatic classifications vary because of the weighting given to various features. Yet most classifications are based on five main climatic types: tropical rainy climates; dry climates; warm temperate rainy climates; cold temperate rainy climates; and very cold polar climates. Some classifications also allow for the effect of altitude. The main climatic regions are subdivided according to seasonal variations and also to the kind of vegetation associated with the climatic conditions. Thus, the rainforest climate, with rain throughout the year, differs from monsoon and savanna climates, which have marked dry seasons. Similarly, parched desert climates differ from steppe climates which have enough moisture for grasses to grow.

Water and Land Use

All life on land depends on fresh water. Yet about 80 countries now face acute water shortages. The world demand for fresh water is increasing by about 2.3% a year and this demand will double every 21 years. About a billion people, mainly in developing countries, do not have access to clean drinking water and around 10 million die every year from drinking dirty water. This problem is made worse in many countries by the pollution of rivers and lakes.

In 1995, a World Bank report suggested that wars will be fought over water in the 21st century. Relations between several countries are already soured by disputes over water resources. Egypt fears that Sudan and Ethiopia will appropriate the waters of the Nile, while Syria and Iraq are concerned that Turkish dams will hold back the waters of the Euphrates.

However, experts stress that while individual countries face water crises, there is no global crisis. The chief global problems are the uneven distribution of water and its inefficient and wasteful use.

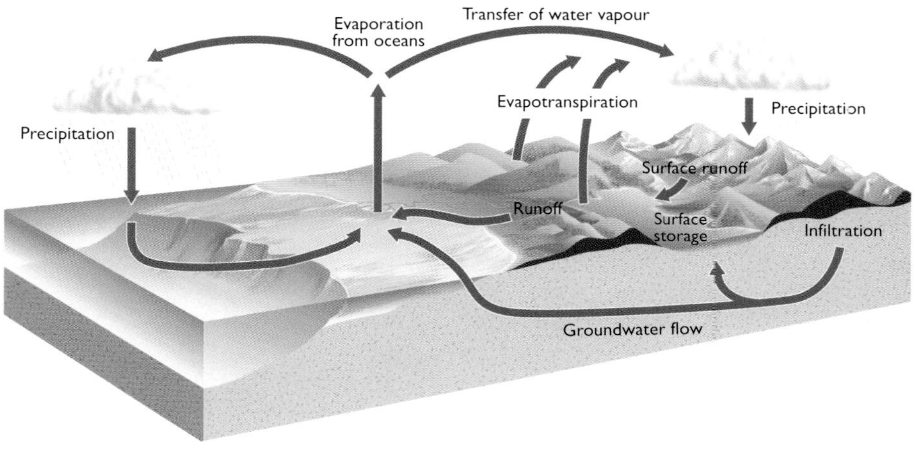

The hydrological cycle

The hydrological cycle is responsible for the continuous circulation of water around the planet. Water vapour contains and transports latent heat, or latent energy. When the water vapour condenses back into water (and falls as rain, hail or snow), the heat is released. When condensation takes place on cold nights, the cooling effect associated with nightfall is offset by the liberation of latent heat.

Hoover Dam, United States

The Hoover Dam in Arizona controls the Colorado River's flood waters. Its reservoir supplies domestic and irrigation water to the south-west, while a hydroelectric plant produces electricity.

The World's Water Supply

Of the world's total water supply, 99.4% is in the oceans or frozen in bodies of ice. Most of the rest circulates through the rocks beneath our feet as ground water. Water in rivers and lakes, in the soil and in the atmosphere together make up only 0.013% of the world's water.

The freshwater supply on land is dependent on the hydrological, or water cycle which is driven by the Sun's heat. Water is evaporated from the oceans and carried into the air as invisible water vapour. Although this vapour averages less than 2% of the total mass of the atmosphere, it is the chief component from the standpoint of weather.

When air rises, water vapour condenses into visible water droplets or ice crystals, which eventually fall to earth as rain, snow, sleet, hail or frost. Some of the precipitation that reaches the ground returns directly to the atmosphere through evaporation or transpiration via plants. Much of the rest of the water flows into the rocks to become ground water or across the surface into rivers and, eventually, back to the oceans, so completing the hydrological cycle.

Water and Agriculture

Only about a third of the world's land area is used for growing crops, while another two-thirds

WATER DISTRIBUTION

The distribution of planetary water, by percentage.

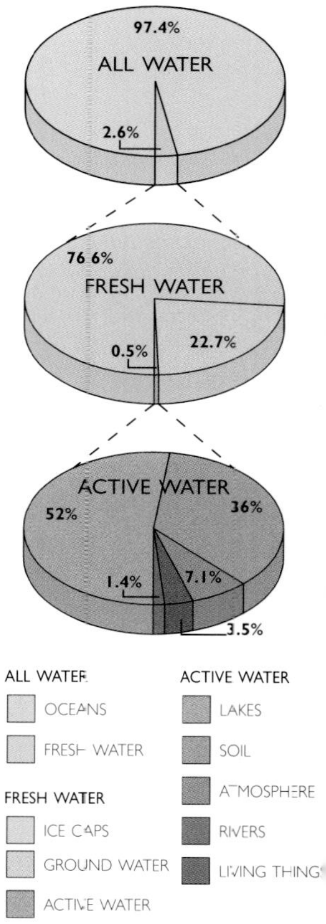

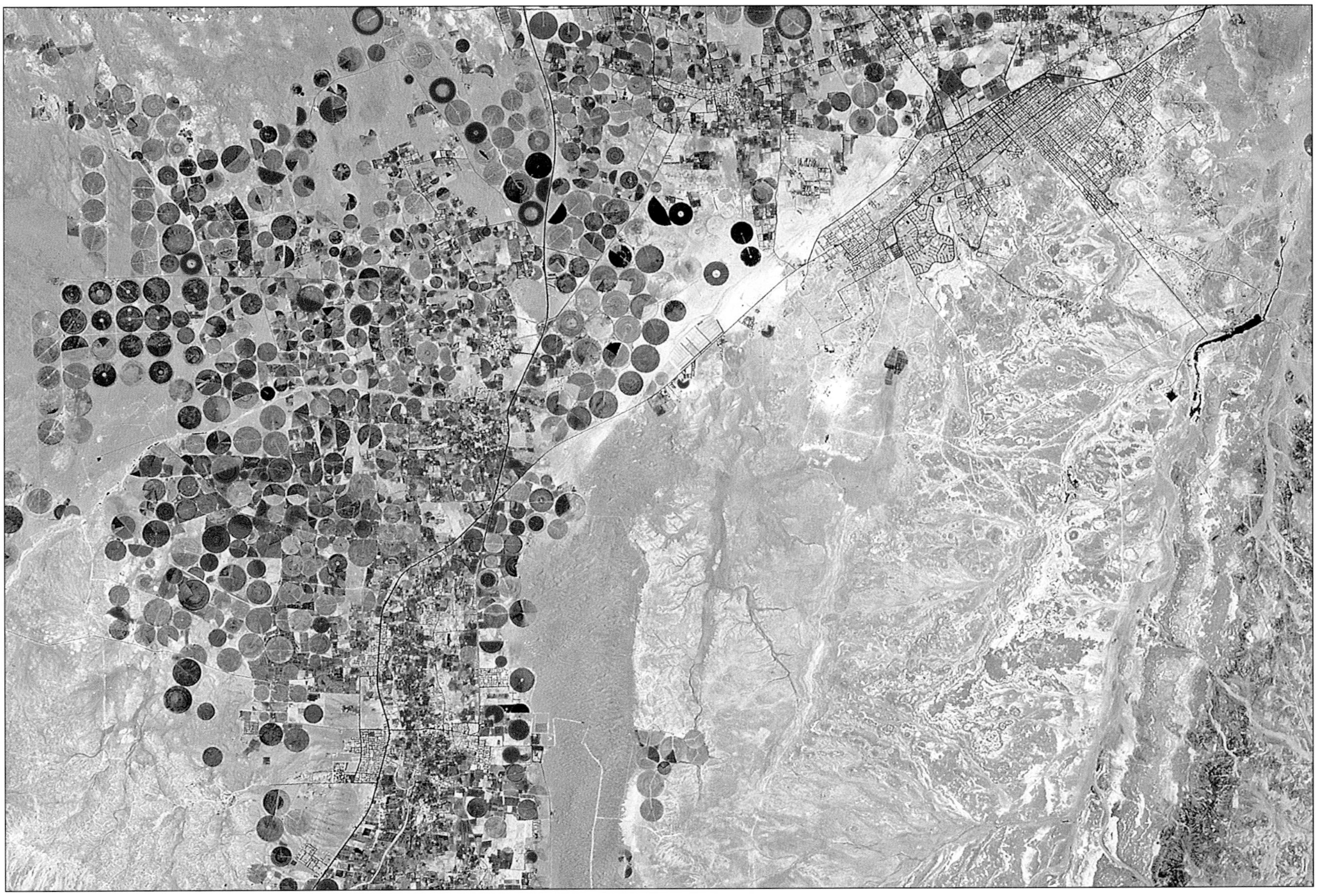

Irrigation in Saudi Arabia

Saudi Arabia is a desert country which gets its water from oases, which tap ground water supplies, and desalination plants. The sale of oil has enabled the arid countries of south-western Asia to develop their agriculture. In the above satellite image, vegetation appears brown and red.

Irrigation boom

The photograph shows a pivotal irrigation boom used to sprinkle water over a wheat field in Saudi Arabia. Irrigation in hot countries often takes place at night so that water loss through evaporation is reduced. Irrigation techniques vary from place to place. In monsoon areas with abundant water, the fields are often flooded, or the water is led to the crops along straight furrows. Sprinkler irrigation has become important since the 1940s. In other types of irrigation, the water is led through pipes which are on or under the ground. Underground pipes supply water directly to the plant roots and, as a result, water loss through evaporation is minimized.

consists of meadows and pasture. The rest of the world is unsuitable for farming, being too dry, too cold, too mountainous, or covered by dense forests. Although the demand for food increases every year, problems arise when attempts are made to increase the existing area of farmland. For example, the soils and climates of tropical forest and semi-arid regions of Africa and South America are not ideal for farming. Attempts to work such areas usually end in failure. To increase the world's food supply, scientists now concentrate on making existing farmland more productive rather than farming marginal land.

To grow crops, farmers need fertile, workable land, an equable climate, including a frost-free growing period, and an adequate supply of fresh water. In some areas, the water falls directly as rain. But many other regions depend on irrigation.

Irrigation involves water conservation through the building of dams which hold back storage reservoirs. In some areas, irrigation water comes from underground aquifers, layers of permeable and porous rocks through which ground water percolates. But in many cases, the water in the aquifers has been there for thousands of years, having accumulated at a time when the rainfall was much greater than it is today. As a result, these aquifers are not being renewed and will, one day, dry up.

Other sources of irrigation water are desalination plants, which remove salt from seawater and pump it to farms. This is a highly expensive process and is employed in areas where water supplies are extremely low, such as the island of Malta, or in the oil-rich desert countries around the Gulf, which can afford to build huge desalination plants.

LAND USE BY CONTINENT

	Forest	Permanent pasture	Permanent crops	Arable	Non-productive
North America	32.2%	17.3%	0.3%	12.6%	37.6%
South America	51.8%	26.7%	1.5%	6.6%	13.4%
Europe	33.4%	17.5%	3.0%	26.8%	19.3%
Africa	23.2%	26.6%	0.6%	5.6%	44.0%
Asia	20.2%	25.0%	1.2%	16.0%	37.8%
Oceania	23.5%	52.2%	0.1%	5.7%	18.5%

The Natural World

In 1995, a United Nations Environment Programme report stated that 11% of all mammal species, 18% of birds and 5% of fish are now threatened with extinction. Furthermore, it predicted that half of all bird and mammal species will become extinct within 300 years, or sooner if current trends continue. This will greatly reduce the biodiversity of our planet, causing the disappearance of unique combinations of genes that could be vital in improving food yields on farms or in the production of drugs to combat diseases.

Extinctions of species have occurred throughout Earth history, but today the extinction rate is estimated to be about 10,000 times the natural average. Some scientists have even compared it with the mass extinction that wiped out the dinosaurs 65 million years ago. However, the main cause of today's high extinction rate is not some natural disaster, such as the impact of an asteroid a few kilometres across, but it is the result of human actions, most notably the destruction of natural habitats for farming and other purposes. In some densely populated areas, such as Western Europe, the natural habitats were destroyed long ago. Today, the greatest damage is occurring in tropical rainforests, which contain more than half of the world's known species.

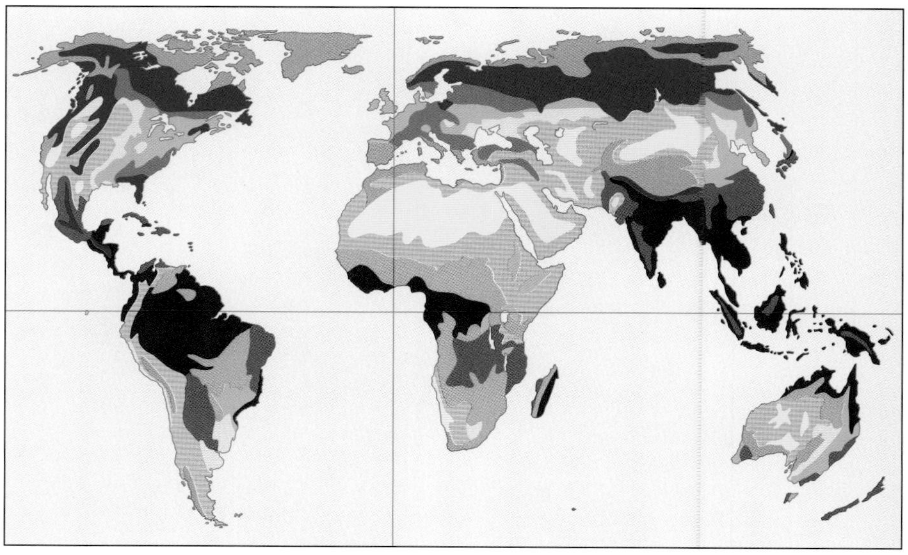

NATURAL VEGETATION

- TUNDRA & MOUNTAIN VEGETATION
- NEEDLELEAF EVERGREEN FOREST
- MIXED NEEDLELEAF EVERGREEN & BROADLEAF DECIDUOUS TREES
- BROADLEAF DECIDUOUS WOODLAND
- MID-LATITUDE GRASSLAND
- EVERGREEN BROADLEAF & DECIDUOUS TREES & SHRUBS
- SEMI-DESERT SCRUB
- DESERT
- TROPICAL GRASSLAND (SAVANNA)
- TROPICAL BROADLEAF RAINFOREST & MONSOON FOREST
- SUBTROPICAL BROADLEAF & NEEDLELEAF FOREST

The map shows the world's main biomes. The classification is based on the natural 'climax' vegetation of regions a result of the climate and the terrain. But human activities have greatly modified this basic division. For example, the original deciduous forests of Western Europe and the eastern United States have largely disappeared. In recent times, human development of some semi-arid areas has turned former dry grasslands into barren desert.

Modern technology has enabled people to live comfortably almost anywhere on Earth. But most plants and many animals are adapted to particular climatic conditions, and they live in association with and dependent on each other. Plant and animal communities that cover large areas are called biomes.

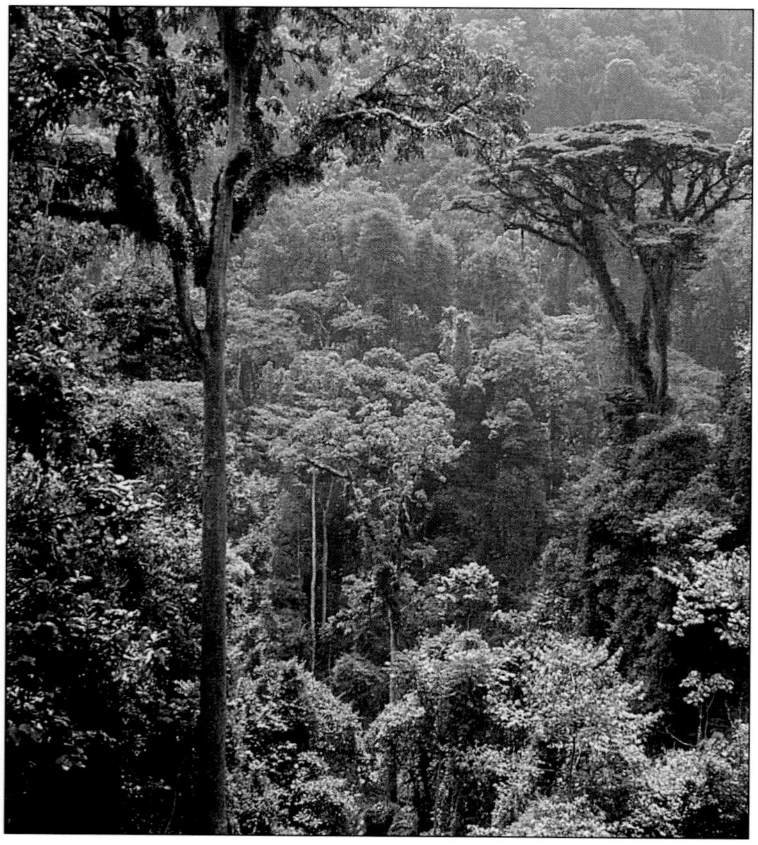

Rainforest in Rwanda

Rainforests are the most threatened of the world's biomes. Effective conservation policies must demonstrate to poor local people that they can benefit from the survival of the forests.

The World's Biomes

The world's biomes are defined mainly by climate and vegetation. They range from the tundra, in polar regions and high mountain regions, to the lush equatorial rainforests.

The Arctic tundra covers large areas in the polar regions of the northern hemisphere. Snow covers the land for more than half of the year and the subsoil, called permafrost, is permanently frozen. Comparatively few species can survive in this harsh, treeless environment. The main plants are hardy mosses, lichens, grasses, sedges and low shrubs. However, in summer, the tundra plays an important part in world animal geography, when its growing plants and swarms of insects provide food for migrating animals and birds that arrive from the south.

The tundra of the northern hemisphere merges in the south into a vast region of needleleaf evergreen forest, called the boreal forest or taiga. Such trees as fir, larch, pine and spruce are adapted to survive the long, bitterly cold winters of this region, but the number of plant and animal species is again small. South of the boreal forests is a zone of mixed needleleaf evergreens and broadleaf deciduous trees, which

Tundra in subarctic Alaska
The Denali National Park, Alaska, contains magnificent mountain scenery and tundra vegetation which flourishes during the brief summer. The park is open between 1 June and 15 September.

shed their leaves in winter. In warmer areas, this mixed forest merges into broadleaf deciduous forest, where the number and diversity of plant species is much greater.

Deciduous forests are adapted to temperate, humid regions. Evergreen broadleaf and deciduous trees grow in Mediterranean regions, with their hot, dry summers. But much of the original deciduous forest has been cut down and has given way to scrub and heathland. Grasslands occupy large areas in the middle latitudes, where the rainfall is insufficient to support forest growth. The moister grasslands are often called prairies, while drier areas are called steppe.

The tropics also contain vast dry areas of semi-desert scrub which merges into desert, as well as large areas of savanna, which is grassland with scattered trees. Savanna regions, with their marked dry season, support a wide range of mammals.

Tropical and subtropical regions contain three types of forest biomes. The tropical rainforest, the world's richest biome measured by its plant and animal species, experiences rain and high temperatures throughout the year. Similar forests occur in monsoon regions, which have a season of very heavy rainfall. They, too, are rich in plant species, though less so than the tropical rainforest. A third type of forest is the subtropical broadleaf and needleleaf forest, found in such places as south-eastern China, south-central Africa and eastern Brazil.

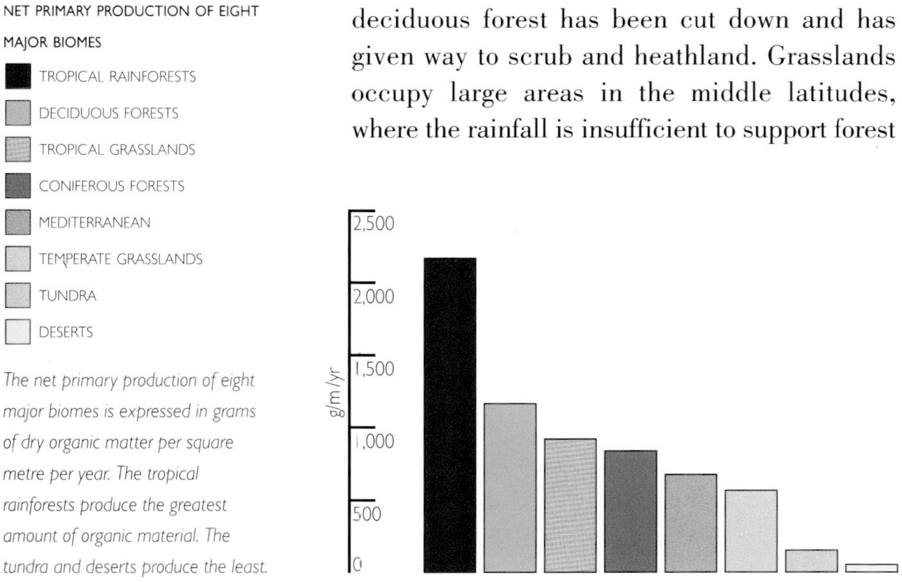

The net primary production of eight major biomes is expressed in grams of dry organic matter per square metre per year. The tropical rainforests produce the greatest amount of organic material. The tundra and deserts produce the least.

The Human World

Every minute, the world's population increases by between 160 and 170. While forecasts of future growth are difficult to make, most demographers are in agreement that the world's population is likely to increase from around 5.75 billion in 1996 to 10 billion by 2050, reaching a peak of around 11 billion by 2075. It is then expected to level out or even decline a little towards the year 2100. The fastest rates of increase will take place in the developing countries of Africa, Asia and Latin America – the places least able to afford the costs incurred by such a rapidly expanding population.

Average world population growth rates have declined from about 2% a year in the early 1960s to 1.6% in 1994. This was partly due to a decline in fertility rates – that is, the number of births to the number of women of child-bearing age – especially in developed countries where, as income has risen, the average size of families has fallen.

Declining fertility rates were also evident in many developing countries. Even Africa shows signs of such change, though its population is expected to triple before it begins to fall. Population growth is also dependent on death rates, which are affected by such factors as famine, disease and the quality of medical care.

Elevated view of Ki Lung Street, Hong Kong

Urban areas of Hong Kong, a territory on the southern coast of China, contain busy streets overlooked by crowded apartments. They reflect the early days of urbanization in China.

The Population Explosion

The world's population has grown steadily throughout most of human history, though certain events triggered periods of population growth. The invention of agriculture around 10,000 years ago, led to great changes in human society. Before then, most people had obtained food by hunting animals and gathering plants. Average life expectancies were probably no more than 20 years and life was hard. However, when farmers began to produce food surpluses, people began to live settled lives. This major milestone in human history led to the development of the first cities and the emergence of the early civilizations.

From an estimated 8 million in 8000 BC, the world population rose to about 300 million by AD 1000. Between 1000 and 1750, the rate of world population increase was around 0.1% per year, but another period of major economic and social change – the Industrial Revolution – began in the late 18th century. The Industrial Revolution led to improvements in farm technology and increases in food production. The world population began to increase quickly as industrialization spread across Europe and into North America. By 1850, it had reached 1.2 billion. The 2 billion mark was passed in the 1920s, and then the population rapidly doubled to 4 billion by the 1970s.

Population Features

Population growth affects the structure of societies. In developing countries with high annual rates of population increase, the large majority of the people are young and soon to become parents themselves. For example, in Kenya, which had until recently an annual rate of population growth of around 4%, just over half

Largest Cities

Within 10 years, for the first time ever, the majority of the world's population will live in urban areas. Almost all the urban growth will be in developing countries. Below is a list of cities with their estimated populations in the year 2015, in millions.

1	Tokyo	28.7
2	Bombay (Mumbai)	27.4
3	Lagos	24.1
4	Shanghai	23.2
5	Jakarta	21.5
6	São Paulo	21.0
7	Karachi	20.6
8	Beijing	19.6
9	Dhaka	19.2
10	Mexico City	19.1
11	Calcutta	17.6
12	Delhi	17.5
13	New York City	17.4
14	Tianjin	17.1
15	Metro Manila	14.9
16	Cairo	14.7
17	Los Angeles	14.5
18	Seoul	13.1
19	Buenos Aires	12.5
20	Istanbul	12.1

These city populations are based on figures for urban agglomerations rather than actual city limits.

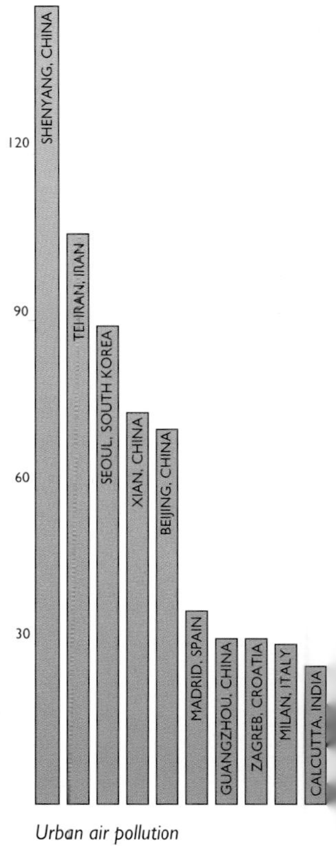

Urban air pollution

This diagram of the world's most polluted cities indicates the number of days per year when sulphur dioxide levels exceed the WHO threshold of 150 micrograms per cubic metre.

Hong Kong's business district

By contrast with the picturesque old streets of Hong Kong, the business district of Hong Kong City, on the northern shore of Hong Kong Island, is a cluster of modern high-rise buildings. The glittering skyscrapers reflect the success of this tiny territory, which has one of the strongest economies in Asia.

of the population is under 15 years of age. On the other hand, the populations of developed countries, with low population growth rates, have a fairly even spread across age groups.

Such differences are reflected in average life expectancies at birth. In rich countries, such as Australia and the United States, the average life expectancy is 77 years (74 years for men and 80 for women; women live longer, on average, than their male counterparts). As a result, an increasing proportion of the people are elderly and retired, contributing little to the economy. The reverse applies in many of the poorer countries, where average life expectancies are below 60 years. In more than a dozen countries in Africa, the average life expectancy is less than 50.

Paralleling the population explosion has been a rapid growth in the number and size of cities and towns, which contained nearly half of the world's people by the 1990s. This proportion is expected to rise to nearly two-thirds by 2025.

Urbanization occurred first in areas undergoing the industrialization of their economies, but today it is also a feature of the developing world. In developing countries, people are leaving impoverished rural areas hoping to gain access to the education, health and other services available in cities. But many cities are unable to provide the housing and other facilities necessitated by rapid population growth. As a result, slums grow up around the cities. Pollution, crime and disease become features of everyday life.

The population explosion poses another probem for the entire world. No one knows how many people the world can support or how consumer demand will damage the fragile environments on our planet. The British economist Thomas Malthus argued in the late 18th century that overpopulation would lead to famine and war. But an increase in farm technology in the 19th and 20th centuries, combined with a green revolution, in which scientists developed high-yield crop varieties, has greatly increased food production since Malthus' time.

However, some modern scientists argue that overpopulation may become a problem in the 21st century. They argue that food shortages leading to disastrous famines will result unless population growth can be halted. Such people argue in favour of birth control programmes. China, the only country with more than a billion people, has introduced a one-child family policy. Their action has slowed the growth of China's huge population, though rising living standards seem to be the most effective brakes on rapid population growth.

POPULATION CHANGE 1990–2000

The predicted population change for the years 1990–2000.

- OVER 40% POPULATION GAIN
- 30–40% POPULATION GAIN
- 20–30% POPULATION GAIN
- 10–20% POPULATION GAIN
- 0–10% POPULATION GAIN
- NO CHANGE OR LOSS

TOP 5 COUNTRIES	
Kuwait	+75.0%
Namibia	+62.5%
Afghanistan	+60.1%
Mali	+55.5%
Tanzania	+54.6%

BOTTOM 5 COUNTRIES	
Belgium	–0.1%
Hungary	–0.2%
Grenada	–2.4%
Germany	–3.2%
Tonga	–3.2%

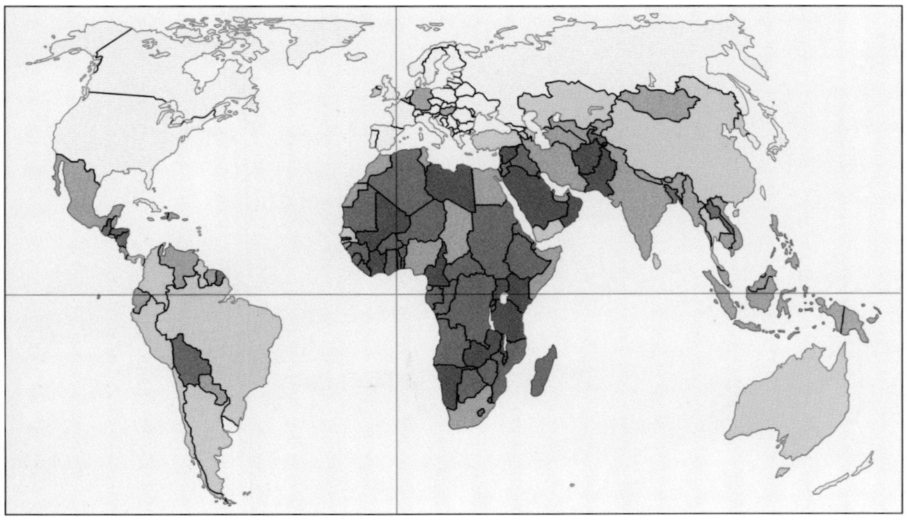

Languages and Religions

In 1995, 90-year-old Edna Guerro died in northern California. She was the last person able to speak Northern Pomo, one of about 50 Native American languages spoken in the state. Her death marked the extinction of one of the world's languages.

This event is not an isolated incident. Language experts regularly report the disappearance of languages and some of them predict that between 20 to 50% of the world's languages will no longer exist by the end of the next century. Improved transport and communications are partly to blame, because they bring people from various cultures into closer and closer contact. Many children no longer speak the language of their parents, preferring instead to learn the language used at their schools. The pressures on children to speak dominant rather than minority languages are often great. In the first part of the 20th century, Native American children were punished if they spoke their native language.

The disappearance of a language represents the extinction of a way of thinking, a unique expression of the experiences and knowledge of a group of people. Language and religion together give people an identity and a sense of belonging. However, there are others who argue that the disappearance of minority languages is a step towards international understanding and economic efficiency.

The World's Languages

Definitions of what is a language or a dialect vary and, hence, estimates of the number of languages spoken around the world range from about 3,000 to 6,000. But whatever the figure, it is clear that the number of languages far exceeds the number of countries.

Religious Adherents

The number of adherents to the world's major religions, in millions.

Christian	1,667
Roman Catholic	952
Protestant	337
Orthodox	162
Anglican	70
Other Christian	148
Muslim	881
Sunni	841
Shia	40
Hindu	663
Buddhist	312
Chinese Folk	172
Tribal	92
Jewish	18
Sikhs	17

Buddhist monks in Katmandu, Nepal

Hinduism is Nepal's official religion, but the Nepalese observe the festivals of both Hinduism and Buddhism. They also regard Buddhist shrines and Hindu temples as equally sacred.

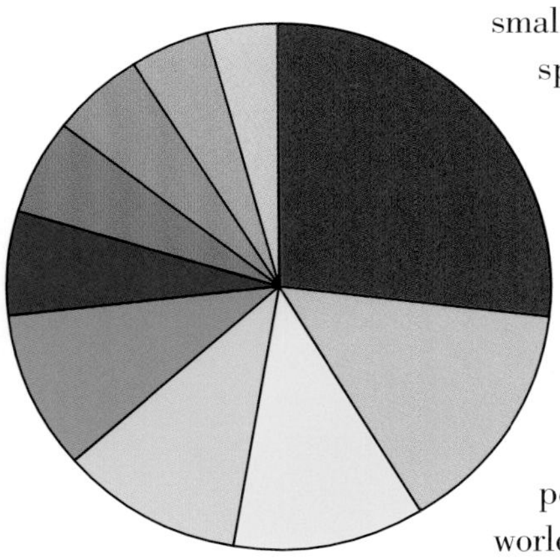

MOTHER TONGUES

Native speakers of the major languages, in millions (1990).

- MANDARIN CHINESE 834M
- ENGLISH 443M
- HINDI 352M
- SPANISH 341M
- RUSSIAN 293M
- ARABIC 197M
- BENGALI 184M
- PORTUGUESE 173M
- MALAY 142M
- JAPANESE 125M

Countries with only one language tend to be small. For example, in Liechtenstein, everyone speaks German. By contrast, more than 860 languages have been identified in Papua New Guinea, whose population is only about 4.3 million people. Hence, many of its languages are spoken by only small groups of people. In fact, scientists have estimated that about a third of the world's languages are now spoken by less than 1,000 people. By contrast, more than half of the world's population speak just seven languages.

The world's languages are grouped into families. The Indo-European family consists of languages spoken between Europe and the Indian subcontinent. The growth of European empires over the last 300 years led several Indo-European languages, most notably English, French, Portuguese and Spanish, to spread throughout much of North and South America, Africa, Australia and New Zealand.

English has become the official language in many countries which together contain more than a quarter of the world's population. It is now a major international language, surpassing in importance Mandarin Chinese, a member of the Sino-Tibetan family, which is the world's leading first language. Without a knowledge of English, businessmen face many problems when conducting international trade, especially with the United States or other English-speaking countries. But proposals that English, French, Russian or some other language should become a world language seem unlikely to be acceptable to a majority of the world's peoples.

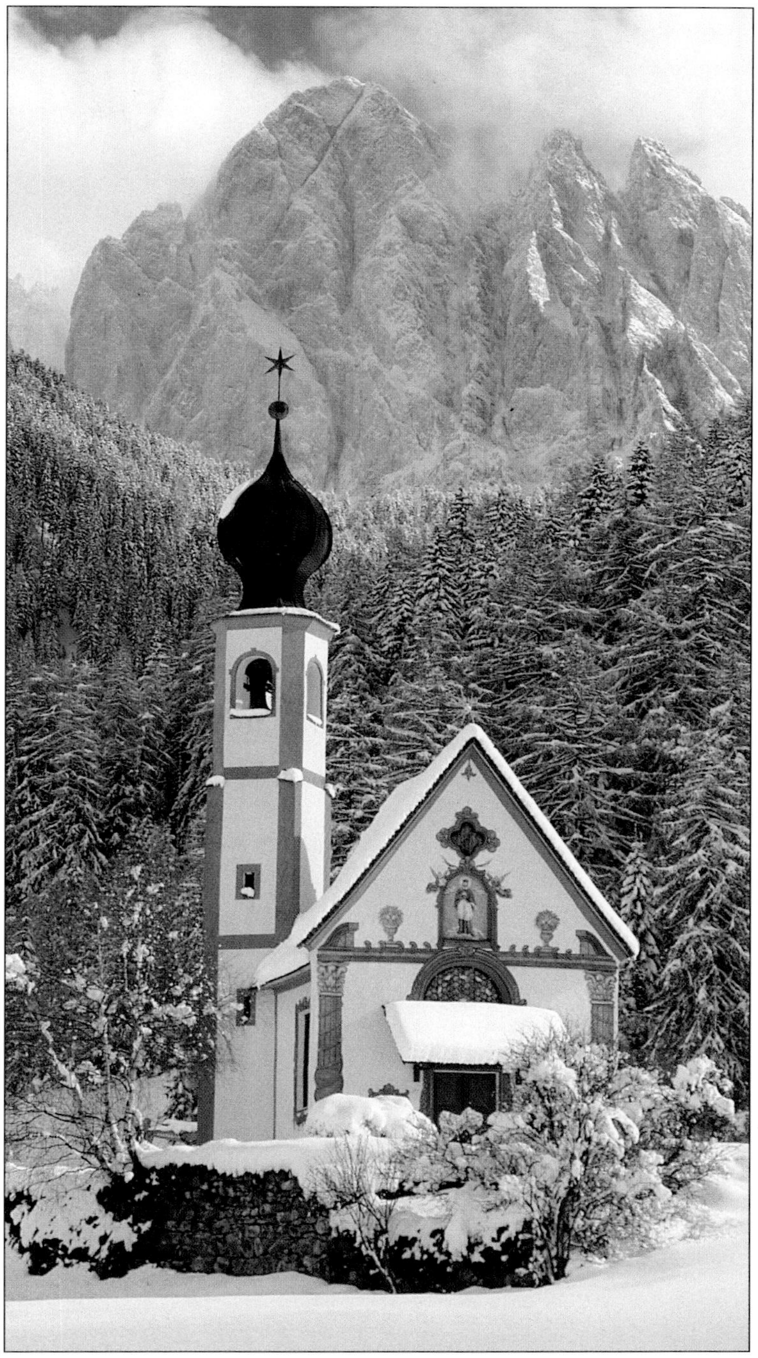

The Church of San Giovanni, Dolomites, Italy

Christianity has done much to shape Western civilization. Christian churches were built as places of worship, but many of them are among the finest achievements of world architecture.

World Religions

Religion is another fundamental aspect of human culture. It has inspired much of the world's finest architecture, literature, music and painting. It has also helped to shape human cultures since prehistoric times and is responsible for the codes of ethics by which most people live.

The world's major religions were all founded in Asia. Judaism, one of the first faiths to teach that there is only one god, is one of the world's oldest. Founded in south-western Asia, it influenced the more recent Christianity and Islam, two other monotheistic religions which now have the greatest number of followers. Hinduism, the third leading faith in terms of the numbers of followers, originated in the Indian subcontinent and most Hindus are now found in India. Another major religion, Buddhism, was founded in the subcontinent partly as a reaction to certain aspects of Hinduism. But unlike Hinduism, it has spread from India throughout much of eastern Asia.

Religion and language are powerful creative forces. They are also essential features of nationalism, which gives people a sense of belonging and pride. But nationalism is often also a cause of rivalry and tension. Cultural differences have led to racial hatred, the persecution of minorities, and to war between national groups.

OFFICIAL LANGUAGES: % OF WORLD POPULATION	
English	27.0%
Chinese	19.0%
Hindi	13.5%
Spanish	5.4%
Russian	5.2%
French	4.2%
Arabic	3.3%
Portuguese	3.0%
Malay	3.0%
Bengali	2.9%
Japanese	2.3%

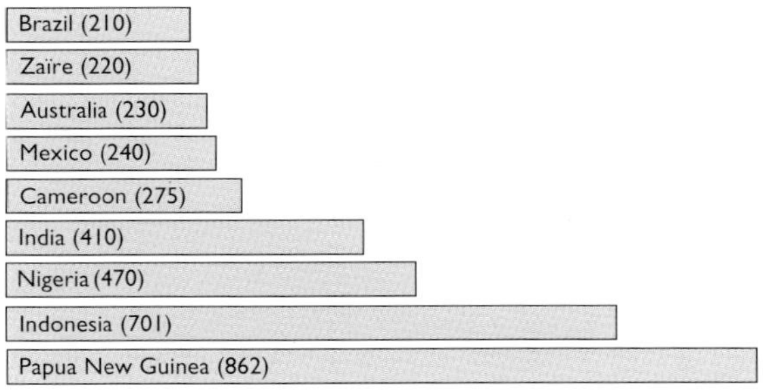
Brazil (210)
Zaïre (220)
Australia (230)
Mexico (240)
Cameroon (275)
India (410)
Nigeria (470)
Indonesia (701)
Papua New Guinea (862)

Polyglot nations

The graph, right, shows countries of the world with more than 200 languages. Although it has only about 4.3 million people, Papua New Guinea holds the record for the number of languages spoken.

International Organizations

Twelve days before the surrender of Germany and four months before the final end of World War II, representatives of 50 nations met in San Francisco to create a plan to set up a peace-keeping organization, the United Nations. Since its birth on 24 October 1945, its membership has grown from 51 to 185.

Its first 50 years have been marked by failures as well as successes. While it has helped to prevent some disputes from flaring up into full-scale wars, the Blue Berets, as the UN troops are called, have been forced, because of their policy of neutrality, to stand by when atrocities are committed by rival warring groups.

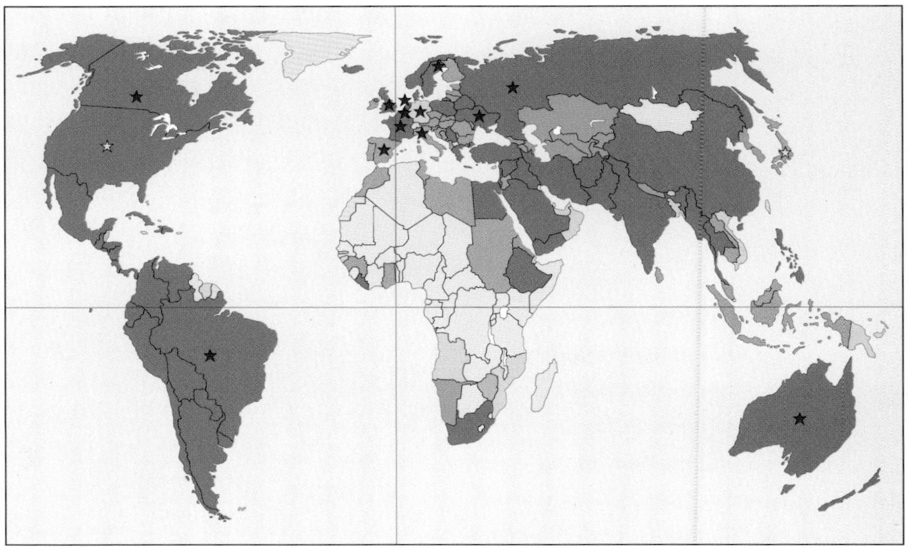

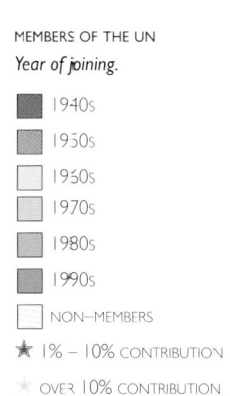

MEMBERS OF THE UN

Year of joining.

- 1940s
- 1950s
- 1960s
- 1970s
- 1980s
- 1990s
- NON-MEMBERS
- ★ 1% – 10% CONTRIBUTION
- ☆ OVER 10% CONTRIBUTION

The Work of the UN

The United Nations has six main organs. They include the General Assembly, where member states meet to discuss issues concerned with peace, security and development. The Security Council, containing 15 members, is concerned with maintaining world peace. The Secretariat, under the Secretary-General, helps the other organs to do their jobs effectively, while the Economic and Social Council works with specialized agencies to implement policies concerned with such matters as development, education and health. The International Court of Justice, or World Court, helps to settle disputes between member nations. The sixth organ of the UN, the Trusteeship Council, was designed to bring 11 UN trust territories to independence. Its task has now been completed.

The specialized agencies do much important work. For example, UNICEF (United Nations International Children's Fund) has provided health care and aid for children in many parts of the world. The ILO (International Labour Organization) has improved working conditions in many areas, while the FAO (Food and Agricultural Organization) has worked to improve the production and distribution of food. Among the other agencies are organizations to help refugees, to further human rights and to control the environment. The latest agency, set up in 1995, is the WTO (World Trade Organization), which took over the work of GATT (General Agreement on Tariffs and Trade).

Other Organizations

In a world in which nations have become increasingly interdependent, many other organizations have been set up to deal with a variety of problems. Some, such as NATO (the North Atlantic Treaty Organization), are defence alliances. In the early 1990s, the end of the Cold War suggested that NATO's role might be finished, but the civil war in the former Yugoslavia showed that it still has a role in maintaining peace and security.

Other organizations encourage social and economic co-operation in various regions. Some are NGOs (non-governmental organizations), such as the Red Cross and its Muslim equivalent, the Red Crescent. Other NGOs raise funds to provide aid to countries facing major crises, such as famine.

Some major international organizations aim at economic co-operation and the removal of trade barriers. The best known of these organizations is the European Union, which has 15 members. Its

Food aid to Bosnia-Herzegovina

International organizations supply aid to people living in areas suffering from war or famine. In Bosnia-Herzegovina, the UN Protection Force supervised the movements of food aid.

INTERNATIONAL AID AND GNP

Aid provided as a percentage of GNP, with total aid in brackets (1993).

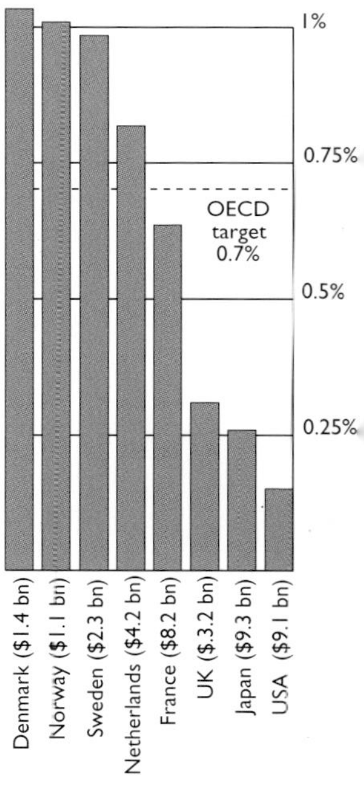
1%
0.75%
OECD target 0.7%
0.5%
0.25%
Denmark ($1.4 bn)
Norway ($1.1 bn)
Sweden ($2.3 bn)
Netherlands ($4.2 bn)
France ($8.2 bn)
UK ($3.2 bn)
Japan ($9.3 bn)
USA ($9.1 bn)

UNHCR-funded jetty, Sri Lanka

In 1994, the UN High Commission for Refugees was responsible for 23 million people. Sometimes, it has to provide transport facilities, such as this jetty, to get aid to the refugees.

economic success has led some people to support the idea of setting up a federal Europe. Others oppose such developments, they fear that a 'United States of Europe' would lead to a loss of national identity among the member states.

Other groupings include ASEAN (the Association of South-east Asian Nations) which aims at reducing trade barriers between its members (Brunei, Indonesia, Malaysia, the Philippines, Singapore, Thailand and Vietnam). APEC (the Asia-Pacific Co-operation Group) was founded in 1989 with the aim of creating a free trade zone between the countries of eastern Asia, North America, Australia and New Zealand by 2020. Meanwhile, Canada, Mexico and the United States have formed NAFTA (the North American Free Trade Agreement), while other economic groupings link most of the countries in Latin America. Another grouping with a more limited but important objective is OPEC (the Organization of Oil-Exporting Countries). OPEC works to unify policies concerning trade in oil on the world markets.

Some organizations exist to discuss matters of common interest between groups of nations. The Commonwealth of Nations, for example, initially developed from links created by the British Empire. In North and South America, the OAS (Organization of American States) aims at increasing understanding in the Western hemisphere. The OAU (Organization of African Unity) has a similar role in Africa, while the Arab League represents the Arab nations of North Africa and the Middle East.

COUNTRIES OF THE EUROPEAN UNION

	Total land area (sq km)	Total population (1995)	GNP per capita, US$ (1994)	Unemployment rate, % (1994)	Year of accession to the EU	Seats in EU parliament (1996)
Austria	83,850	8,004,000	24,950	4.3%	1995	21
Belgium	30,510	10,140,000	22,920	9.7%	1958	25
Denmark	43,070	5,229,000	28,110	10.7%	1973	16
Finland	338,130	5,125,000	18,850	18.4%	1995	16
France	551,500	58,286,000	23,470	12.2%	1958	87
Germany	356,910	82,000,000	25,580	8.6%	1958	99
Greece	131,990	10,510,000	7,390	9.4%	1981	25
Ireland	70,280	3,589,000	12,580	15.2%	1973	15
Italy	301,270	57,181,000	19,270	11.4%	1958	87
Luxembourg	2,590	408,000	39,850	3.4%	1958	6
Netherlands	41,526	15,495,000	21,970	7.6%	1958	31
Portugal	92,390	10,600,000	7,890	6.7%	1986	25
Spain	504,780	39,664,000	13,650	24.4%	1986	64
Sweden	449,960	8,893,000	23,630	7.4%	1995	22
United Kingdom	243,368	58,306,000	18,410	9.7%	1973	87

Agriculture

In 1995, the world production of grains was lower than average – the result mainly of a wet spring in the United States, and bad weather combined with economic turmoil in the former Soviet Union. Downward trends in world food production in the 1990s reopened an old debate – whether food production will be able to keep pace with a rapidly rising world population in the 21st century.

Some experts argue that the lower than expected production figures in the 1990s herald a period of relative scarcity and high prices of food, which will be felt most in the poorer developing countries. Others are more optimistic. They point to the successes of the 'green revolution' which, through the use of new crop varieties produced by scientists, irrigation and the extensive use of fertilizers and pesticides, has revolutionized food production since the 1950s and 1960s.

The green revolution has led to a great expansion in the production of many crops, including such basic foods as rice, maize and wheat. In India, its effects have been spectacular. Between 1955 and 1995, grain production trebled, giving the country sufficient food reserves to prevent famine in years when droughts or floods reduce the harvest. While once India had to import food, it is now self-sufficient.

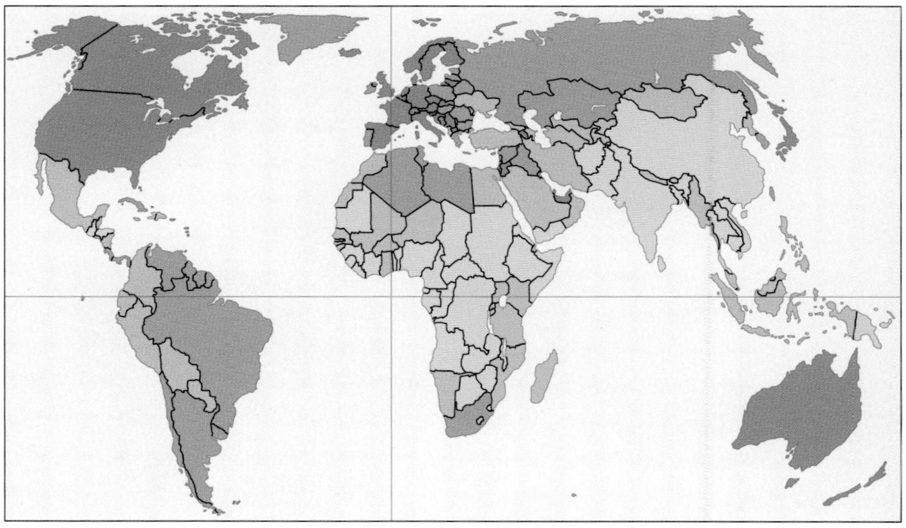

IMPORTANCE OF AGRICULTURE
Percentage of the population dependent on agriculture (1994).

- OVER 75% DEPENDENT
- 50–75% DEPENDENT
- 25–50% DEPENDENT
- 10–25% DEPENDENT
- UNDER 10% DEPENDENT

Rice harvest, Bali, Indonesia
More than half of the world's people eat rice as their basic food. Rice grows well in tropical and subtropical regions, such as in Indonesia, India and south-eastern China.

Food Production

Agriculture, which supplies most of our food, together with materials to make clothes and other products, is the world's most important economic activity. But its relative importance has declined in comparison with manufacturing and service industries. As a result, the end of the 20th century marked the first time for 10,000 years when the vast majority of the people no longer had to depend for their living on growing crops and herding animals.

However, agriculture remains the dominant economic activity in many developing countries in Africa and Asia. For example, in the early 1990s, 90% or more of the people of Benin, Bhutan, Burundi and Nepal depended on farming for their living.

Many people in developing countries eke out the barest of livings by nomadic herding or shifting cultivation, combined with hunting, fishing and gathering plant foods. A large proportion of farmers live at subsistence level, producing little more than they require to provide the basic needs of their families.

The world's largest food producer and exporter is the United States, although agriculture employs

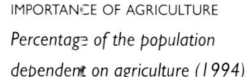

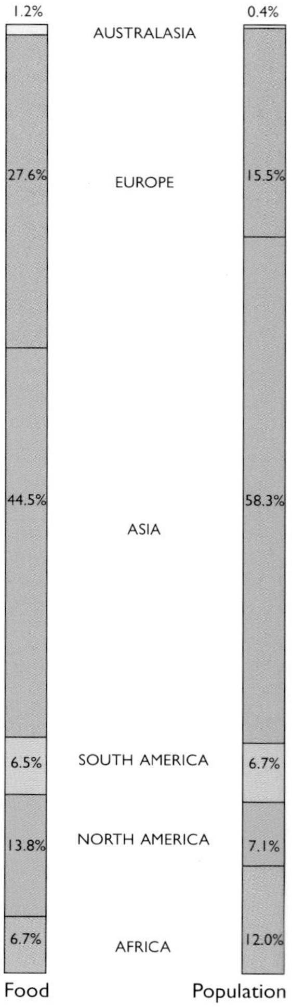

A comparison of world food production and population by continent.

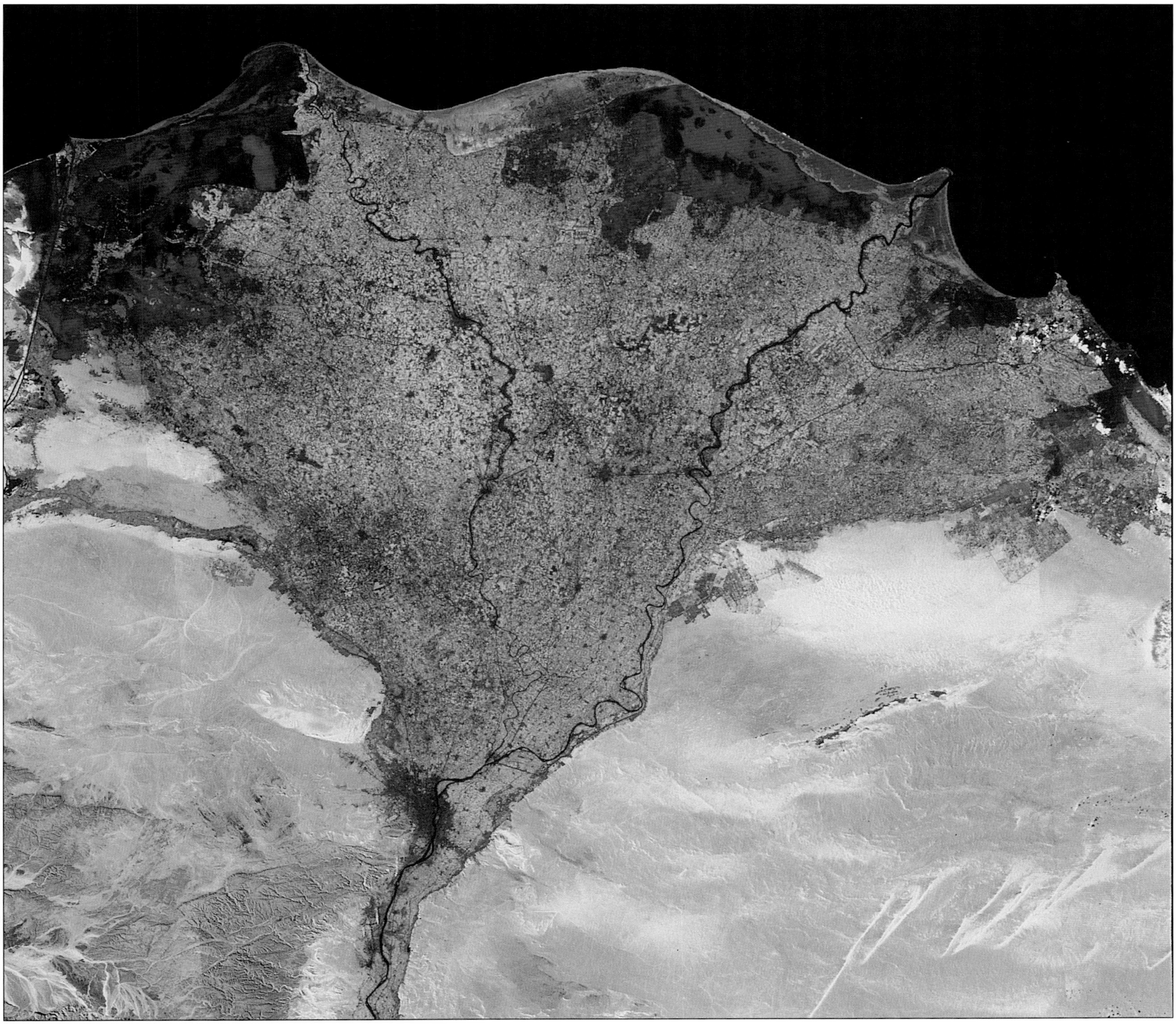

Landsat *image of the Nile delta, Egypt*

Most Egyptians live in the Nile valley and on its delta. Because much of the silt carried by the Nile now ends up on the floor of Lake Nasser, upstream of the Aswan Dam, the delta is now retreating and seawater is seeping inland. This eventuality was not foreseen when the Aswan High Dam was built in the 1960s.

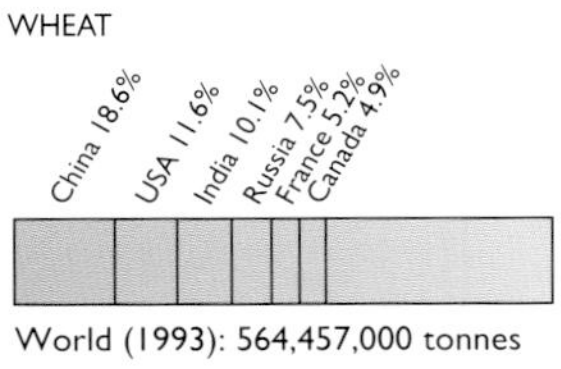
WHEAT
China 18.6%
USA 11.6%
India 10.1%
Russia 7.5%
France 5.2%
Canada 4.9%
World (1993): 564,457,000 tonnes

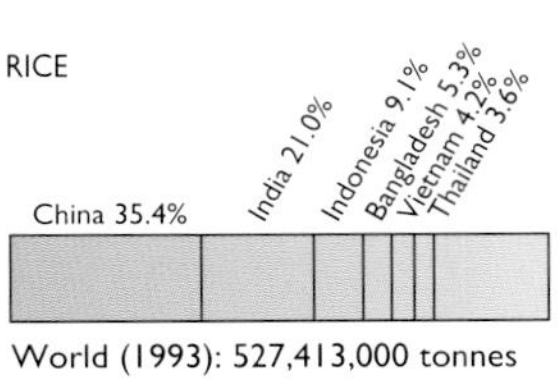
RICE
China 35.4%
India 21.0%
Indonesia 9.1%
Bangladesh 5.3%
Vietnam 4.2%
Thailand 3.6%
World (1993): 527,413,000 tonnes

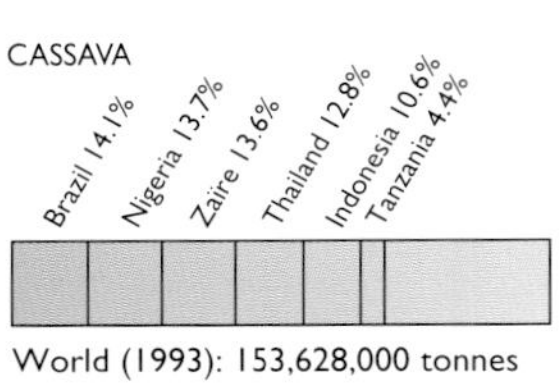
CASSAVA
Brazil 14.1%
Nigeria 13.7%
Zaïre 13.6%
Thailand 12.8%
Indonesia 10.6%
Tanzania 4.4%
World (1993): 153,628,000 tonnes

less than 3% of its total workforce. The high production of the United States is explained by its use of scientific methods and mechanization, which are features of agriculture throughout the developed world.

Intensive or Organic Farming

By the late 20th century, some people were beginning to question the dependence of farmers on chemical fertilizers and pesticides. Many people became concerned that the widespread use of chemicals was seriously polluting and damaging the environment.

Others objected to the intensive farming of animals to raise production and lower prices. For example, the suggestion in Britain in 1996 that BSE, or 'mad cow disease', might be passed on to people causing CJD (Creuzfeldt-Jakob Disease) caused widespread alarm.

Such problems have led some farmers to return to organic farming, which is based on animal-welfare principles and the banning of chemical fertilizers and pesticides. The costs of organic foods are certainly higher than those produced by intensive farming, but an increasing number of consumers in the Western world are beginning to demand organic products from their retailers.

Energy and Minerals

In March 1996, floods in Ukraine carried radioactive waste dumped near Chernobyl hundreds of kilometres downstream. This was the latest chapter in the disaster caused by the explosion at the Chernobyl nuclear power station in 1986, the worst nuclear accident in history. Nuclear power now provides about 17% of the world's electricity and experts once thought that it would eventually supply much of the world's energy supply. But concern about safety and worries about the high costs involved make this seem unlikely. Several developed countries have already abandoned their nuclear programmes.

Fossil Fuels

Huge amounts of energy are needed for heating, generating electricity and for transport. In the early years of the Industrial Revolution, coal formed from organic matter buried beneath the Earth's surface, was the leading source of energy. It remains important as a raw material in the manufacture of drugs and other products and also as a fuel, despite the fact that burning coal causes air pollution and gives off carbon dioxide, an important greenhouse gas.

However, oil and natural gas, which came into wide use in the 20th century, are cheaper to produce and easier to handle than coal, while, kilogram for kilogram, they give out more heat. Oil is especially important in moving transport, supplying about 97% of the fuel required.

In 1995, proven reserves of oil were sufficient to supply the world, at current rates of production, for 43 years, while supplies of natural gas stood at about 66 years. Coal reserves are more abundant and known reserves would last 200 years at present rates of use. Although these figures must be regarded with caution, because they do not allow for future discoveries, it is clear that fossil fuel reserves will one day run out.

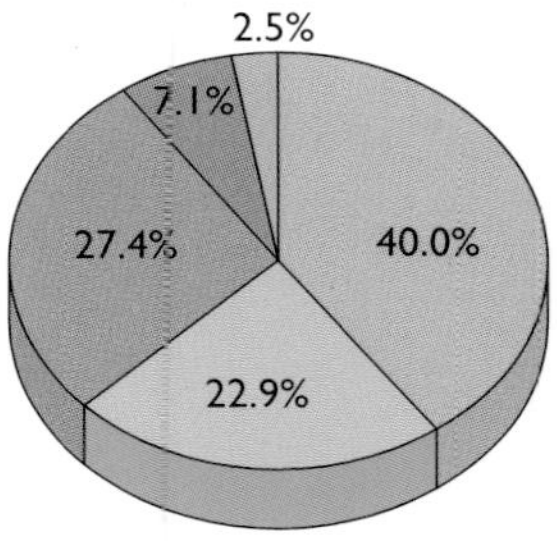
2.5%
7.1%
27.4%
40.0%
22.9%
WORLD ENERGY CONSUMPTION
OIL
GAS
COAL
NUCLEAR
HYDRO

The diagram shows the proportion of world energy consumption in 1993 by type. Total energy consumption was 7,804 million tonnes of oil equivalent. Such fuels as wood, peat and animal wastes, together with renewable forms of energy, such as wind and geothermal power, are not included, although they are important in some areas.

Wind farms in California, United States

Wind farms using giant turbines can produce electricity at a lower cost than conventional power stations. But in many areas, winds are too light or too strong for wind farms to be effective.

SELECTED MINERAL PRODUCTION STATISTICS (1993)

Bauxite		Diamonds	
Australia	36%	Australia	41%
Guinea	15%	Zaïre	16%
Jamaica	10%	Botswana	15%
Brazil	8%	Russia	11%
Russia	7%	South Africa	10%
Gold		**Iron ore**	
South Africa	27%	China	25%
USA	3%	Brazil	16%
Australia	11%	Australia	12%
Canada	7%	Ukraine	7%
Russia	7%	India	6%
Potash		**Zinc**	
Canada	36%	China	11%
Germany	17%	Japan	11%
Russia	17%	USA	8%
Belarus	16%	Canada	8%
USA	8%	Germany	7%

Potash mines in Utah, United States

Potash is a mineral used mainly to make fertilizers. Much of it comes from mines where deposits formed when ancient seas dried up are exploited. Potash is also extracted from salt lakes.

Alternative Energy

Other sources of energy are therefore required. Besides nuclear energy, the main alternative to fossil fuels is water power. The costs of building dams and hydroelectric power stations is high, though hydroelectric production is comparatively cheap and it does not cause pollution. But the creation of reservoirs uproots people and, in tropical rainforests, it destroys natural habitats. Hydroelectricity is also suitable only in areas with plenty of rivers and steep slopes, such as Norway, while it is unsuitable in flat areas, such as the Netherlands.

In Brazil, alcohol made from sugar has been used to fuel cars. Initially, this government-backed policy met with great success, but it has proved to be extremely expensive. Battery-run, electric cars have also been developed in the United States, but they appear to have limited use, because of the problems involved in regular and time-consuming recharging.

Other forms of energy, which are renewable and cleaner than fossil fuels, are winds, sea waves, the rise and fall of tides, and geothermal power. These forms of energy are already used to some extent. However, their contribution in global terms seems likely to remain small in the immediate future.

Minerals for Industry

In addition to energy, manufacturing industries need raw materials, including minerals, and these natural resources, like fossil fuels, are being used in such huge quantities that some experts have predicted shortages of some of them before long.

Manufacturers depend on supplies of about 80 minerals. Some, such as bauxite (aluminium ore) and iron, are abundant, but others are scarce or are found only in deposits that are uneconomical to mine. Many experts advocate a policy of recycling scrap metal, including aluminium, chromium, copper, lead, nickel and zinc. This practice would reduce pollution and conserve the energy required for extracting and refining mineral ores.

MINERAL DISTRIBUTION

Location of the principal mines and deposits.

IRON & FERRO-ALLOYS
- IRON
- CHROME
- MANGANESE
- NICKEL

PRECIOUS METALS
- GOLD
- SILVER

PRECIOUS STONES
- DIAMONDS

LIGHT METALS
- BAUXITE

BASE METALS
- COPPER
- LEAD
- MERCURY
- TIN
- ZINC

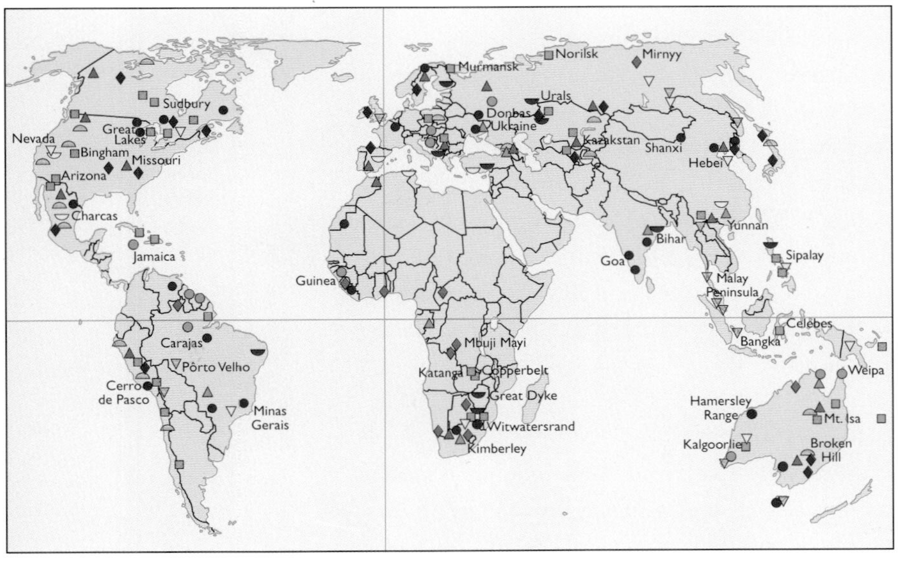

World Economies

In 1994, Tanzania had a per capita GNP (Gross National Product) of US$90, as compared with Switzerland, whose per capita GNP stood at $37,180. These figures indicate the vast gap between the economies and standards of living of the two countries.

The GNP includes the GDP (Gross Domestic Product), which consists of the total output of goods and services in a country in a given year, plus net exports – that is, the value of goods and services sold abroad less the value of foreign goods and services used in the country in the same year. The GNP divided by the population gives a country's GNP per capita. In low-income developing countries, agriculture makes a high contribution to the GNP. For example, in Tanzania, 56% of the GDP in 1993 came from agriculture. On the other hand, manufacturing was small-scale and contributed only 5% of the GDP. By comparison, in high-income economies, the percentage contribution of manufacturing far exceeds that of agriculture.

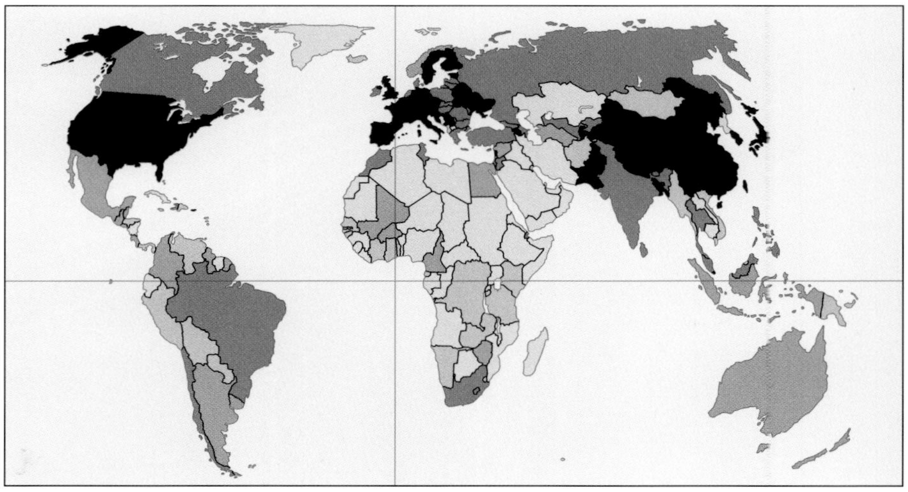

INDUSTRY AND TRADE

Manufactured goods (including machinery and transport) as a percentage of total exports.

- OVER 75%
- 50–75%
- 25–50%
- 10–25%
- UNDER 10%

Eastern Asia, including Japan (98.3%), Taiwan (92.7%) and Hong Kong (93.0%), contains countries whose exports are most dominated by manufactures. But some countries in Europe, such as Slovenia (92.5%), are also heavily dependent on manufacturing.

Microchip production, Taiwan

Despite its lack of resources, Taiwan is one of eastern Asia's 'tiger' economies. Its high-tech industies have helped it to achieve fast economic growth and to compete on the world market.

Industrialization

The Industrial Revolution began in Britain in the late 18th century. Before that time, most people worked on farms. But with the Industrial Revolution came factories, using machines that could manufacture goods much faster and more cheaply than those made by cottage industries which already existed.

The Industrial Revolution soon spread to several countries in mainland Europe and the United States and, by the late 19th century, it had reached Canada, Japan and Russia. At first, industrial development was based on such areas as coalfields or ironfields. But in the 20th century, the use of oil, which is easy to transport along pipelines, made it possible for industries to be set up anywhere.

Some nations, such as Switzerland, became industrialized even though they lacked natural resources. They depended instead on the specialized skills of their workers. This same pattern applies today. Some countries with rich natural resources, such as Mexico (with a per capita GNP in 1994 of $4,010), lag far behind Japan ($34,630) and South Korea ($8,220), which lack resources and have to import many of the materials they need for their manufacturing industries.

Service Industries

Experts often refer to high-income countries as industrial economies. But manufacturing employs only one in six workers in the United

GROSS NATIONAL PRODUCT PER CAPITA US$ (1994)

1	Luxembourg	39,850
2	Switzerland	37,180
3	Japan	34,630
4	Denmark	28,110
5	Norway	26,480
6	USA	25,860
7	Germany	25,580
8	Austria	24,950
9	Iceland	24,590
10	Sweden	23,630
11	France	23,470
12	Singapore	23,360
13	Belgium	22,920
14	Netherlands	21,970
15	Hong Kong	21,650
16	Canada	19,570
17	Italy	19,270
18	Kuwait	19,040
19	Finland	18,850
20	UK	18,410

New cars awaiting transportation, Los Angeles, United States
Cars are the most important single manufactured item in world trade, followed by vehicle parts and engines. The world's leading car producers are Japan, the United States, Germany and France.

States, one in five in Britain, and one in three in Germany and Japan.

In most developed economies, the percentage of manufacturing jobs has fallen in recent years, while jobs in service industries have risen. For example, in Britain, the proportion of jobs in manufacturing fell from 37% in 1970 to 20% in 1993, while jobs in the service sector rose from just under 50% to 73%. While change in Britain was especially rapid, similar changes were taking place in most industrial economies. By 1993, service industries accounted for well over half the jobs in the generally prosperous countries that made up the OECD (Organization for Economic Co-operation and Development). Instead of being called the 'industrial' economies, these countries might be better named the 'service' economies.

Service industries offer a wide range of jobs and many of them require high educational qualifications. These include finance, insurance and high-tech industries, such as computer programming, entertainment and telecommunications. Service industries also include marketing and advertising, which are essential if the cars and television sets made by manufacturers are to be sold. Another valuable service industry is tourism; in some countries, such as the Gambia, it is the major foreign exchange earner. Trade in services now plays an important part in world economics. The share of services in world trade rose from 17% in 1980 to 22% in 1992.

THE WORKFORCE
Percentage of men and women between 15 and 64 years old in employment, selected countries (latest available year).

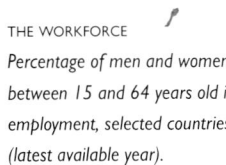

MEN
WOMEN

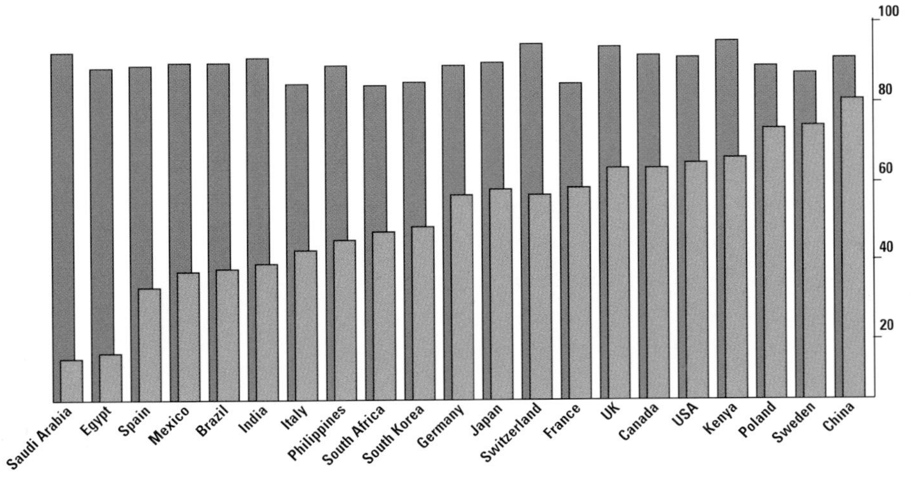

Trade and Commerce

The establishment of the WTO (World Trade Organization) on 1 January 1995 was the latest step in the long history of world trade. The WTO was set up by the eighth round of negotiations, popularly called the 'Uruguay round', conducted by the General Agreement on Tariffs and Trade (GATT). This treaty was signed by representatives of 125 governments in April 1994 after many difficulties.

GATT was first established in 1948. Its initial aim was to produce a charter to create a body called the International Trade Organization. This body never came into being. Instead, GATT, acting as an *ad hoc* agency, pioneered a series of agreements aimed at liberalizing world trade by reducing tariffs on imports and other obstacles to free trade.

GATT's objectives were based on the belief that international trade creates wealth. Trade occurs because the world's resources are not distributed evenly between countries, and, in theory, free trade means that every country should concentrate on what it can do best and purchase from others goods and services that they can supply more cheaply. In practice, however, free trade may cause unemployment when imported goods are cheaper than those produced within the country.

Trade is sometimes an important factor in world politics, especially when trade sanctions are applied against countries whose actions incur the disapproval of the international community. For example, in the 1990s, worldwide trade sanctions were imposed on Serbia because of its involvement in the civil war in Bosnia-Herzegovina.

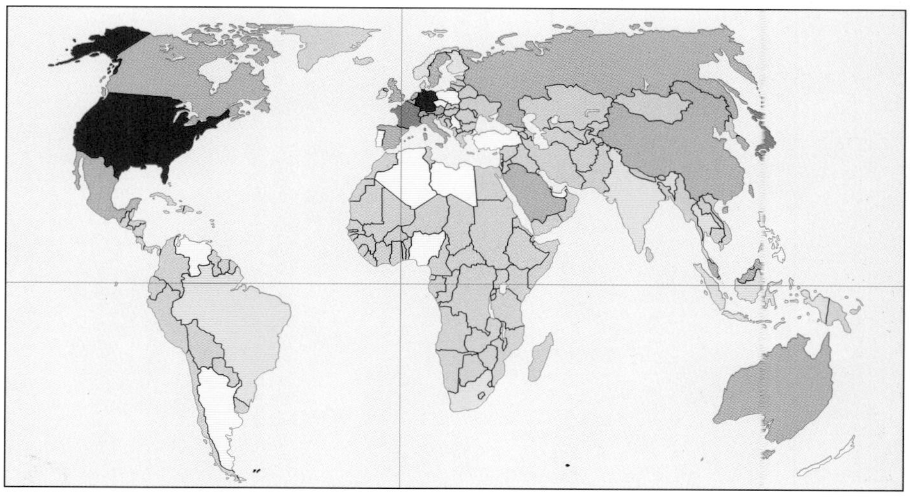

WORLD TRADE

Percentage share of total world exports by value (1993).

- OVER 10% OF WORLD TRADE
- 5–10% OF WORLD TRADE
- 1–5% OF WORLD TRADE
- 0.5–1% OF WORLD TRADE
- 0.25–0.5% OF WORLD TRADE
- UNDER 0.25% OF WORLD TRADE

The world's leading trading nations, according to the combined value of their exports and imports, are the United States, Germany, Japan, France and the United Kingdom.

New York City Stock Exchange, United States

Stock exchanges, where stocks and shares are sold and bought, are important in channelling savings and investments to companies and governments. The world's largest stock exchange is in Tokyo, Japan.

Changing Trade Patterns

The early 16th century, when Europeans began to divide the world into huge empires, opened up a new era in international trade. By the 19th century, the colonial powers, who were among the first industrial powers, promoted trade with their colonies, from which they obtained unprocessed raw materials, such as food, natural fibres, minerals and timber. In return, they shipped clothes, shoes and other cheap items to the colonies.

From the late 19th century until the early 1950s, primary products dominated world trade, with oil becoming the leading item in the later part of this period. Many developing countries still depend heavily on the export of one or two primary products, such as coffee or iron ore, but overall the proportion of primary products in world trade has fallen since the 1950s. Today the most important elements in world trade are

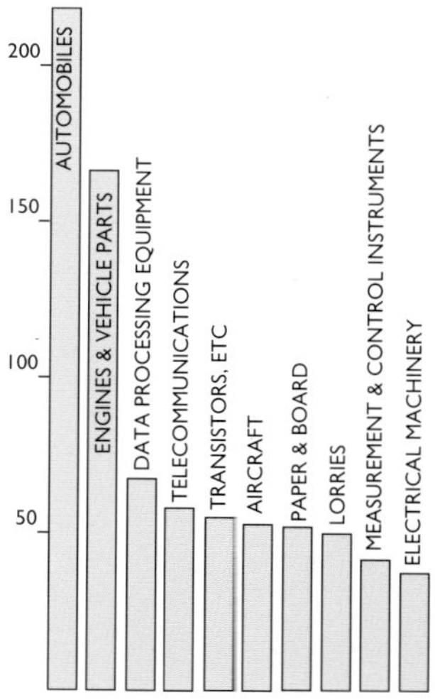

Traded products

Top ten manufactures traded by value in billions of US$ (latest available year).

Rotterdam, Netherlands

World trade depends on transport. Rotterdam, the world's largest port, serves not only the Netherlands, but also industrial areas in parts of Germany, France and Switzerland.

manufactures and semi-manufactures, exchanged mainly between the industrialized nations.

The World's Markets

Private companies conduct most of world trade, but government policies affect it. Governments which believe that certain industries are strategic, or essential for the country's future, may impose tariffs on imports, or import quotas to limit the volume of imports, if they are thought to be undercutting the domestic industries.

For example, the United States has argued that Japan has greater access to its markets than the United States has to Japan's. This might have led the United States to resort to protectionism, but instead the United States remains committed to free trade.

Other problems in international trade occur when governments give subsidies to its producers, who can then export products at low prices. Another difficulty, called 'dumping', occurs when products are sold at below the market price in order to gain a market share. One of the aims of the newly-created WTO is the phasing out of government subsidies for agricultural products, though the world's poorest countries will be exempt from many of the WTO's most severe regulations.

Governments are also concerned about the volume of imports and exports and most countries keep records of international transactions. When the total value of goods and services imported exceeds the value of goods and services exported, then the country has a deficit in its balance of payments. Large deficits can weaken a country's economy.

BALANCE OF TRADE

Value of exports in proportion to the value of imports (1993).

- OVER 50% GDP FROM EXPORTS
- 40–50% GDP FROM EXPORTS
- 30–40% GDP FROM EXPORTS
- 20–30% GDP FROM EXPORTS
- 10–20% GDP FROM EXPORTS
- UNDER 10% GDP FROM EXPORTS
- MOST DEPENDENT ON INDUSTRIAL EXPORTS (OVER 75% OF TOTAL)
- MOST DEPENDENT ON FUEL EXPORTS (OVER 75% OF TOTAL)
- MOST DEPENDENT ON MINERAL EXPORTS (OVER 75% OF TOTAL)

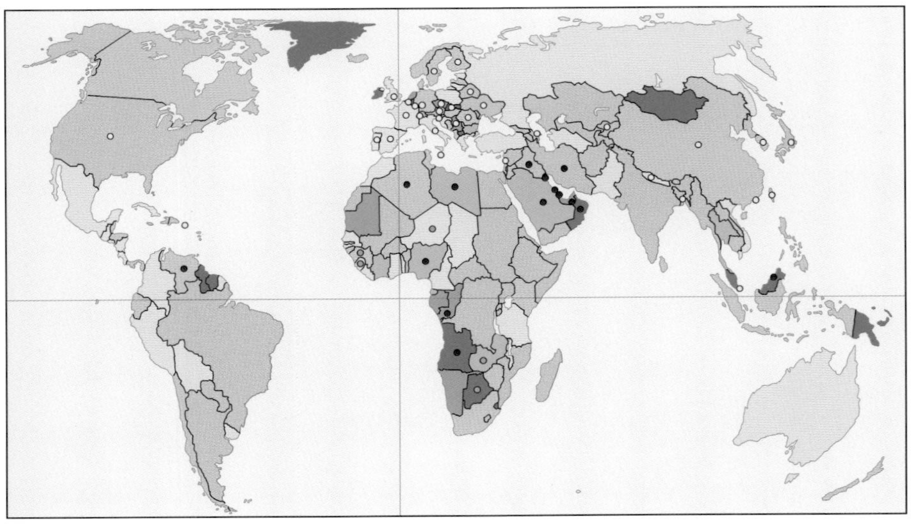

Travel and Communications

In the 1990s, millions of people became linked into an 'information superhighway' called the Internet. Equipped with a personal computer, an electricity supply, a telephone and a modem, people are able to communicate with others all over the world. People can now send messages by e-mail (electronic mail), they can engage in electronic discussions, contacting people with similar interests, and engage in 'chat lines', which are the latest equivalent of telephone conferences.

These new developments are likely to affect the working lives of people everywhere, enabling them to work at home whilst having many of the facilities that are available in an office. The Internet is part of an ongoing and astonishingly rapid evolution in the fields of communications and transport.

Transport

Around 200 years ago, most people never travelled far from their birthplace, but today we are much more mobile. Cars and buses now provide convenient forms of transport for many millions of people, huge ships transport massive cargoes around the world, and jet airliners, some travelling faster than the speed of sound, can transport high-value goods as well as holidaymakers to almost any part of the world.

Land transport of freight has developed greatly since the start of the Industrial Revolution. Canals, which became important in the 18th century, could not compete with rail transport in the 19th century. Rail transport remains important, but, in the 20th century, it has suffered from competition with road transport (especially in the United Kingdom), which is cheaper and has the advantage of carrying materials and goods from door to door.

Road transport causes pollution and the burning of fuels creates greenhouse gases that contribute to global warming. Yet privately owned cars are now the leading form of passenger traffic in developed nations, especially for journeys of less than about 400 km [250 miles]. Car owners do not have to suffer the inconvenience of waiting for public transport, such as buses, though they often have to endure traffic jams at peak travel times.

Ocean passenger traffic is now modest, but ships carry the bulk of international trade. Huge oil tankers and bulk grain carriers now ply the oceans with their cargoes, while container ships

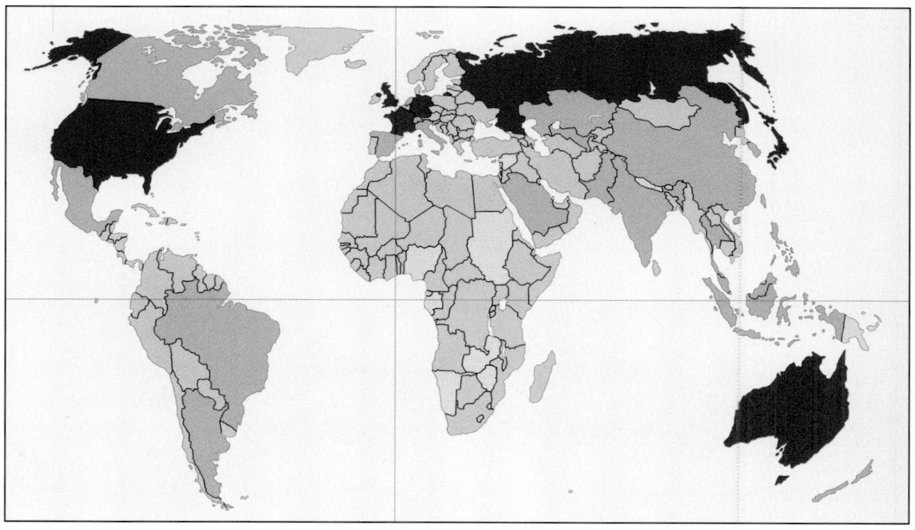

PASSENGER KILOMETRES* FLOWN
In millions (1992).

- Over 100,000
- 50,000–100,000
- 10,000–50,000
- 1,000–10,000
- 500–1,000
- Under 500

** Passenger kilometres are the number of passengers multiplied by the distance flown by each passenger from airport of origin.*

Jodrell Bank Observatory, Cheshire, England
The world's first giant radio telescope began operations at Jodrell Bank in 1957. Radio telescopes can explore the Universe as far as 16 billion light-years away.

SELECTED NEWSPAPER CIRCULATION FIGURES (1995)

Country	Newspaper	Edition	Circulation
France			
	Le Monde		357,362
	Le Figaro		350,000
Germany			
	Bild		4,500,000
	Süddeutsche Zeitung		402,866
Italy			
	Corriera Della Sella		676,904
	La Republica		655,321
	La Stampa		436,047
Japan			
	Yomiuri Shimbun	(a.m. edition)	9,800,000
		(p.m. edition)	4,400,000
	Manichi Shimbun	(a.m. edition)	3,200,000
		(p.m. edition)	1,900,000
Russia			
	Pravda		1,373,795
	Ivestia		700,000
Spain			
	El Pais		407,629
United Kingdom			
	The Sun		4,061,253
	Daily Mirror		2,525,000
	Daily Express		1,270,642
	The Times		672,802
	The Guardian		402,214
United States			
	New York Times		1,724,705
	Chicago Tribune		1,110,552
	Houston Chronicle		605,343

Kansai International Airport, Japan
The new airport, opened in September 1994, is built on an artificial island in Osaka Bay. The island holds the world's biggest airport terminal at nearly 2 km [1.2 miles] long.

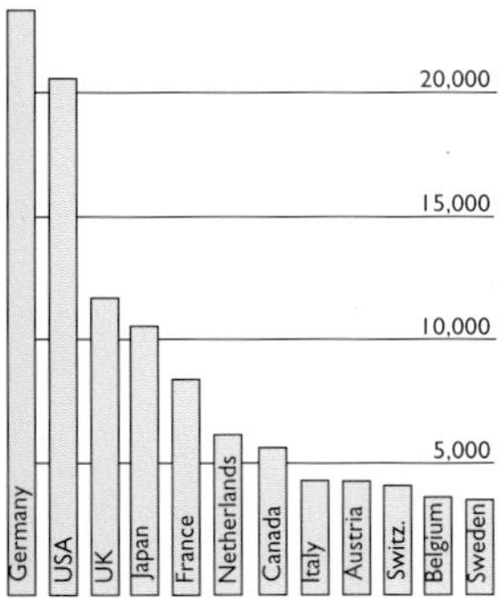

Spending on tourism
Countries spending the most on overseas tourism, US$ million (latest available year).

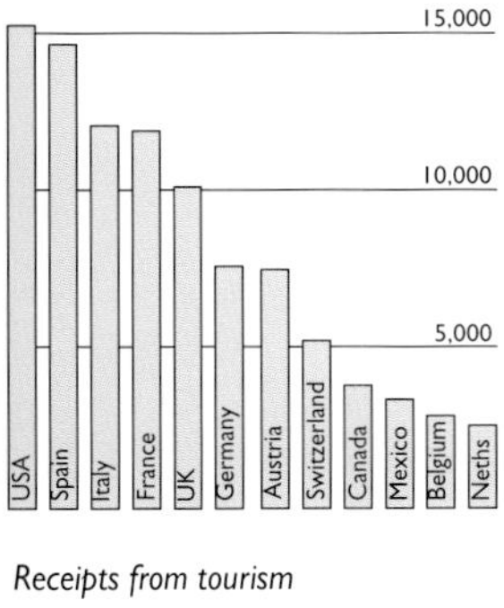

Receipts from tourism
Countries receiving the most from overseas tourism, US$ million (latest available year).

carry mixed cargoes. Containers are boxes built to international standards that contain cargo. Containers are easy to handle, and so they reduce shipping costs, speed up deliveries and cut losses caused by breakages. Most large ports now have the facilities to handle containers.

Air transport is suitable for carrying goods that are expensive, light and compact, or perishable. However, because of the high costs of air freight, it is most suitable for carrying passengers along long-distance routes around the world. Through air travel, international tourism, with people sometimes flying considerable distances, has become a major and rapidly expanding industry.

Communications

After humans first began to communicate by using the spoken word, the next great stage in the development of communications was the invention of writing around 5,500 years ago.

The invention of movable type in the mid 15th century led to the mass production of books and, in the early 17th century, the first newspapers. Newspapers now play an important part in the mass communication of information, although today radio and, even more important, television have led to a decline in the circulation of newspapers in many parts of the world.

The most recent developments have occurred in the field of electronics. Artificial communications satellites now circle the planet, relaying radio, television, telegraph and telephone signals. This enables people to watch events on the far side of the globe as they are happening. Electronic equipment is also used in many other ways, such as in navigation systems used in air, sea and space, and also in modern weaponry, as shown vividly in the television coverage of the 1991 Gulf War.

The Age of Computers

One of the most remarkable applications of electronics is in the field of computers. Computers are now making a huge contribution to communications. They are able to process data at incredibly high speeds and can store vast quantities of information. For example, the work of weather forecasters has been greatly improved now that computers can process the enormous amount of data required for a single weather forecast. They also have many other applications in such fields as business, government, science and medicine.

Through the Internet, computers provide a free interchange of news and views around the world. But the dangers of misuse, such as the exchange of pornographic images, have led to calls for censorship. Censorship, however, is a blunt weapon, which can be used by authoritarian governments to suppress the free exchange of information that the new information superhighway makes possible.

The World Today

The early years of the 20th century witnessed the exploration of Antarctica, the last uncharted continent. Today, less than 100 years later, tourists are able to take cruises to the icy southern continent, while almost no part of the globe is inaccessible to the determined traveller. Improved transport and images from space have made our world seem smaller.

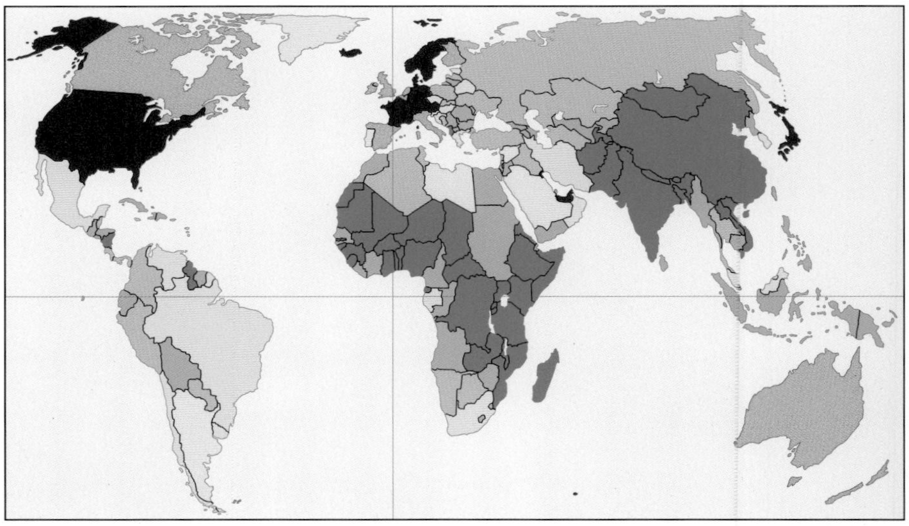

GROSS NATIONAL PRODUCT PER CAPITA

The value of total production divided by the population (1994).

- OVER 400% OF WORLD AVERAGE
- 200–400%
- 100–200%

[WORLD AVERAGE WEALTH PER PERSON US$5,359]

- 50–100%
- 25–50%
- 10–25%
- UNDER 10% OF WORLD AVERAGE

RICHEST COUNTRIES	
Luxembourg	$39,850
Switzerland	$37,180
Japan	$34,630
Denmark	$28,110

POOREST COUNTRIES	
Mozambique	$80
Tanzania	$90
Ethiopia	$130
Malawi	$140

A Divided World

Between the end of World War II in 1945 and the late 1980s, the world was divided, politically and economically, into three main groups: the developed countries or Western democracies, with their free enterprise or mixed economies; the centrally planned or Communist countries; and the developing countries or Third World.

This division became obsolete when the former Soviet Union and its old European allies, together with the 'special economic zones' in eastern China, began the transition from centrally planned to free enterprise economies. This left the world divided into two broad camps: the prosperous developed countries and the poorer developing countries. The simplest way of distinguishing between the groups is with reference to their per capita Gross National Products (per capita GNPs).

The World Bank divides the developing countries into three main groups. At the bottom are the low-income economies, which include China, India and most of sub-Saharan Africa. This group contains about 56% of the world's population but its average per capita GNP in 1994 was only US$390. The other two groups are the lower-middle-income economies with an average GNP per capita of $1,650, and the upper-middle-income economies, with an average GNP per capita of $4,640. By contrast, the high-income economies, also called the developed countries, contain less than 15% of the world's population but have the high (and rising) average GNP per capita of $24,170.

Economic and Social Contrasts

Economic differences are coupled with other factors, such as rates of population growth. For example, in 1980–93, the low-income economies had a high rate of population growth of 2% per year, while the populations of the middle-income economies were increasing by 1.7%. By contrast, the populations of countries in the high-income category were increasing by only 0.6%.

Stark contrasts exist worldwide in the quality

Porters carrying luggage for tourists, Selous Park, Tanzania
Improved and cheaper transport has led to a boom in tourism in many developing countries. Tourism provides jobs and foreign exchange, though it can undermine local cultures.

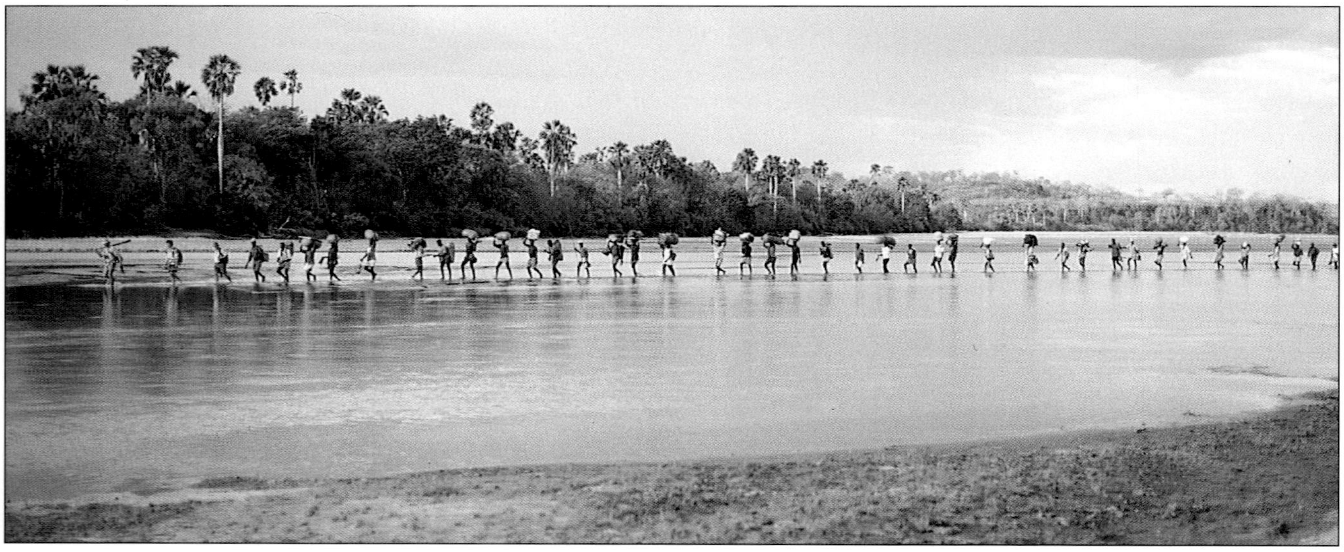

Birth control poster, China

China is the only country with more than a billion people. Central to its economic development policies is population control. Posters exhort the advantages of one-child families.

of life. Generally, the people in Western Europe and North America are better fed, healthier and have more cars and better homes than the people in low- and middle-income economies.

The average life expectancy at birth in low-income economies in 1993 was 62 years, 15 years less than in the high-income economies. Illiteracy in countries in the low-income category is high, at 42% in 1992, while for women, who get fewer opportunities, the percentage of those who could not read and write stood at 54%. By contrast, illiteracy is relatively rare in the high-income economies.

Future Development

In the last 50 years, despite all the aid supplied to developing countries, much of the world still suffers from poverty and economic backwardness. Some countries are even poorer now than they were a generation ago while others have become substantially richer.

The most remarkable success has been achieved in eastern Asia. Japan and the 'tiger economies' of Hong Kong, Indonesia, Malaysia, Singapore, South Korea, Thailand and Taiwan had an average annual economic growth rate of 5.5% between 1965 and 1993, while their share in the exports of manufactured goods more than doubled in the same period. Their success has led some to predict that the new centre of power in the 21st century will be the Pacific region.

Reasons advanced to explain the success of the eastern Asian countries include low wage scales, strong family structures, low state expenditure on welfare and large investment in education for both sexes. Some of the arguments are contradictory. For example, while some argue that the success of Hong Kong is due to free enterporise, the governments of Japan and South Korea have intervened substantially in the development of their economies.

Eastern Asia's economic growth is exceptional and probably cannot be regarded as a model for the developing world. But several factors suggest that poor countries may find progress easier in the 21st century. For example, technology is now more readily transferable between countries, while improved transport and communications make it easier for countries to take part in the world economy. But industrial development and rising living standards could lead to an increase in global pollution. Hence, any strategy for global economic expansion must also take account of environmental factors.

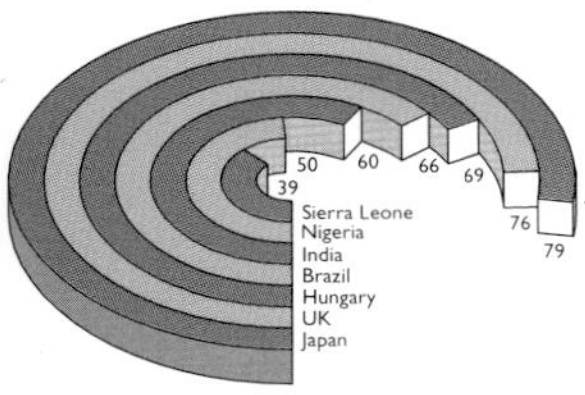

Years of life expectancy at birth, selected countries (1990–95).

The chart shows the contrasting range of average life expectancies at birth for a range of countries, including both low-income and high-income economies. Generally, improved health services are raising life expectancies. On average, women live longer than men, even in the poorer developing countries.

Glossary

Abyss The lowest part of the oceans, at the foot of the continental slope, which forms the true edge of the continents.

Apparent magnitude The magnitude of a star as seen from Earth; it depends on the absolute magnitude (the apparent magnitude if the star was observed from a standard distance of 32.6 light-years) and the distance of the star from the Earth.

Aquifer A layer of rock which contains water and allows water to percolate through it. It may be porous, as in sandstone, or fissured, as in limestone.

Atmosphere The layer of air which surrounds the Earth, which includes gases, such as nitrogen and oxygen, and water vapour.

Biome A major type of plant and animal community, such as tundra, taiga (boreal forest) or tropical rainforest.

Comet A body in the Solar System consisting of a nucleus and a tail. It is composed of ice particles, gases and dust.

Declination How far north or south a star is above the Celestial Equator, an imaginary line in the sky directly above the Equator. It is measured in degrees.

Delta An area of land at the mouths of some rivers which is made up of sediment deposited there by the river. It gets its name from the triangular Greek letter delta (Δ), though some deltas are not triangular.

Demographers People who study human populations, such as their numbers and distribution.

Developed country A country with a balanced economy, including a major manufacturing sector.

Developing country A poor country in which agriculture (often at subsistence level) is usually the mainstay of the economy.

Element A basic chemical substance which cannot be broken down into other substances by chemical means.

Equinox Two days during the year when the Sun is overhead at the Equator and everywhere on Earth has 12 hours of darkness. The equinoxes occur on or around 21 March and 23 September.

Erosion The processes by which natural forces, including weathering, running water, ice and winds, constantly modify the land.

Fault A crack or fracture in the Earth's crust along along which the rocks have moved so that the rocks on either side are displaced.

Fold Bends in rock strata caused by enormous lateral pressure.

Fossil fuel Any non-renewable fuel formed from once-living plant or animal matter, including peat and coal, oil and natural gas.

Glacier A body of ice which flows down a valley. It is composed of compacted snow.

Ice Age A period in history when global temperatures fell and ice covered large areas that are now ice-free.

Ice sheet A huge body of ice covering a large area. The world's two ice sheets cover Antarctica and Greenland. Small ice sheets are called ice caps.

Internet A global network of interconnected computer networks. Until the late 1980s the Internet was used only by governments and universities. By the mid-1990s, millions of home computers were connected.

Lithosphere The hard outer layer of the Earth, consisting of the crust and the hard upper layer of the mantle.

Monsoon A seasonal wind, especially in southern Asia, where the prevailing north-easterly trade winds in winter are replaced in summer by moist south-westerly winds which bring heavy rain.

Moraine Eroded rock ranging from clay to large boulders, that is transported and deposited by glaciers and other bodies of ice.

Neutron star A star made up almost entirely of atomic particles called neutrons.

Nuclear fision The process in stars by which hydrogen nuclei change into helium nuclei, creating energy which escapes in the form of light.

Ozone layer A layer of the gas ozone in the stratosphere that blocks out most of the Sun's harmful ultraviolet radiation.

Population growth A change in human population caused by natural increase (the difference between births and deaths) and migration.

Primary products Raw materials, such as crops, minerals or timber, that have not been processed.

Pyroclasts Fragments of magma thrown out by explosions during volcanic activity.

Porous rock A rock, such as sandstone, that contains pores through which water can percolate.

Right ascension A measure in hours of the position of a star east of the place where the Sun crosses the Celestial Equator on 21 March. One hour represents 15 degrees.

Solstice Two days during the year when the overhead Sun reaches either its northernmost point (the Tropic of Cancer) or its southernmost point (the Tropic of Capricorn).

Special economic zones Areas in eastern China where the government has encouraged foreign investment and where economic growth has been exceptionally rapid.

'Tiger' economies The name given to the developing economies of rapidly industrializing countries of eastern Asia, including Hong Kong, South Korea, Singapore and Taiwan.

Tornado A small, but violent whirlwind which occurs over land areas.

Trade wind A prevailing wind that blows from the high-pressure horse latitudes towards the low-pressure doldrums around the Equator.

Tropical cyclone A large storm which forms over warm seas north and south of the Equator. It may cause great damage to coastal areas, but it dies out quickly when it reaches land. Other names for this kind of storm are hurricane (in North America), typhoon (in Asia) and willy-willy (in Australia).

WORLD MAPS

MAP SYMBOLS

SETTLEMENTS

PARIS Berne Livorno Brugge *Algeciras* *Fréjus* *Oberammergau* *Thira*

Settlement symbols and type styles vary according to the scale of each map and indicate the importance of towns on the map rather than specific population figures

∴ Ruins or Archæological Sites

Wells in Desert

ADMINISTRATION

International Boundaries

International Boundaries (Undefined or Disputed)

Internal Boundaries

National Parks

Country Names

NICARAGUA

Administrative Area Names

KENT

CALABRIA

International boundaries show the *de facto* situation where there are rival claims to territory

COMMUNICATIONS

Principal Roads

Other Roads

Trails and Seasonal Roads

Passes

Airfields

Principal Railways

Railways Under Construction

Other Railways

Railway Tunnels

Principal Canals

PHYSICAL FEATURES

Perennial Streams

Intermittent Streams

Perennial Lakes

Intermittent Lakes

Swamps and Marshes

Permanent Ice and Glaciers

▲ 8848 Elevations in metres

▼ 8050 Sea Depths in metres

1134 Height of Lake Surface Above Sea Level in metres

1 2 3 4 5 6 7 8
A B C D E F G H
Beaufort Sea
Banks I.
Parry Is.
Queen Elizabeth Is.
Ellesmere I.
Devon I.
Victoria I.
GREENLAND
(Denmark)
Baffin Bay
Baffin I.
Davis Str.
Godthåb
Denmark Str.
ICELAND
Reykjavík
Bering Strait
St. Lawrence I.
Yukon
Fairbanks
ALASKA
(U.S.A.)
Anchorage
G. of Alaska
Kodiak I.
Aleutian Is. (U.S.A.)
Great Bear L.
Yellowknife
Great Slave L.
Hudson Bay
Churchill
Nelson
Queen Charlotte Is.
Edmonton
Calgary
C A N A D A
Schefferville
Vancouver
Vancouver I.
Winnipeg
L. Winnipeg
Missouri
Seattle
Portland
UNITED STATES OF AMERICA
L. Superior
Newfoundland
St. John's
Québec
Ottawa
Montréal
Minneapolis
Michigan
L. Huron
Toronto
Milwaukee
Detroit
Boston
Halifax
Salt Lake City
CHICAGO
Cleveland
Denver
Pittsburgh
NEW YORK
SAN FRANCISCO
Sacramento
PHILADELPHIA
Kansas City
St. Louis
Cincinnati
Baltimore
Washington D.C.
Colorado
LOS ANGELES
San Diego
Phoenix
Memphis
Atlanta
Dallas
El Paso
Ciudad Juárez
Rio Grande
Houston
New Orleans
Jacksonville
Bermuda
(U.K.)
Azores
(Port.)
NORTH ATLANTIC OCEAN
Guadalupe I.
(Mexico)
Monterrey
G. of California
Gulf of Mexico
Miami
BAHAMAS
Midway Is.
Hawaiian Is.
(U.S.A.)
Tropic of Cancer
Honolulu
Oahu
Hawaii
International Date Line
MEXICO
León
Guadalajara
MÉXICO
Puebla
Havana
CUBA
Turks & Caicos Is.
(U.K.)
Cayman Is. (U.K.)
Port-au-Prince
HAITI
DOMINICAN REP.
JAMAICA
Kingston
Santo Domingo
PUERTO RICO
Virgin Is. (U.S.A.) & (U.K.)
ANTIGUA & BARBUDA
ST. KITTS & NEVIS
GUADELOUPE (Fr.)
MARTINIQUE (Fr.)
DOMINICA
ST. LUCIA
ST. VINCENT & THE GRENADINES
BARBADOS
GRENADA
NETH. ANTILLES
TRINIDAD & TOBAGO
Revilla Gigedo Is.
(Mexico)
Belmopan
BELIZE
GUATEMALA
Guatemala
HONDURAS
San Salvador
Tegucigalpa
EL SALVADOR
NICARAGUA
Managua
Caribbean Sea
Barranquilla
San José
COSTA RICA
Panamá
PANAMA
Caracas
Orinoco
VENEZUELA
Georgetown
Paramaribo
Cayenne
GUYANA
SURINAM
FRENCH GUIANA
Clipperton I.
(Fr.)
Cocos I.
(C.Rica)
Malpelo
(Colombia)
Medellín
Cali
BOGOTÁ
COLOMBIA
Palmyra Is.
(U.S.A.)
P A C I F I C
Kiritimati
Howland I. (U.S.A.)
Baker I. (U.S.A.)
Jarvis I.
(U.S.A.)
Equator
Galápagos
(Ecuador)
Quito
ECUADOR
Guayaquil
Negro
Japurá
Manaus
Amazon
Belém
Iquitos
Fortaleza
Fernando de Noronha
(Brazil)
Natal
Recife
Abariringa
K I R I B A T I
Phoenix Is.
Malden I.
Starbuck I.
Tokelau Is.
(N.Z.)
Penrhyn Is.
Manihiki
Marquesas Is.
B R A Z I L
Xingu
Madeira
Tocantins
São Francisco
Ucayali
Marañón
PERU
LIMA
Callao
Flint I.
FRENCH
Wallis & Futuna
(Fr.)
WESTERN SAMOA
AMERICAN SAMOA
O C E A N
Salvador
Brasília
L. Titicaca
La Paz
BOLIVIA
Sucre
Arequipa
Tuamotu Is.
Society Is.
Tahiti
FIJI
TONGA
Niue
(N.Z.)
Cook Is.
(N.Z.)
POLYNESIA
Tubuai Is.
Belo Horizonte
SÃO PAULO
RIO DE JANEIRO
Santos
Tropic of Capricorn
Antofagasta
PARAGUAY
Asunción
Curitiba
Pitcairn I.
(U.K.)
Ducie I.
Sala-y-Gómez
(Chile)
San Felix
(Chile)
San Ambrosio
(Chile)
Tucumán
Easter I.
(Chile)
Rapa
Paraná
Uruguay
Pôrto Alegre
Córdoba
Rio Grande
Valparaíso
Rosario
URUGUAY
Montevideo
SANTIAGO
BUENOS AIRES
ARGENTINA
Juan Fernández
(Chile)
Talcahuano
Bahía Blanca
C H I L E
Kermadec Is. (N.Z.)
Chiloé I.
Chatham Is.
(N.Z.)
Falkland Is.
(U.K.)
Punta Arenas
Tierra del Fuego
C. Horn
Scotia Sea
South Georgia
(U.K.)
South Sandwich Is.
(U.K.)
Drake Passage
South Shetland Is.
(U.K.)
South Orkney Is.
(U.K.)
Antarctic Circle
Bellingshausen Sea
Weddell Sea
Amundsen Sea
A n t a
West from G
Arctic
Faroe Is.
(Den.)
UNITED KINGDOM
Glasg
Dublin
IRELAND
LON
PORTUGAL
Lisbon
Tangier
Rabat
Casablanca
Madeira
(Port.)
Marrakesh
MOROCCO
Canary Is.
(Sp.)
El Aaiun
WESTERN SAHARA
MAURITANIA
Nouakchott
Timb
CAPE VERDE IS.
Dakar
SENEGAL
GAMBIA
Bamako
GUINEA-BISSAU
Bissau
GUINEA
Conakry
Freetown
SIERRA LEONE
Monrovia
LIBERIA
Abidj
São Paulo
(Brazil)
Ascension I.
(U.K.)
St. Helena
(U.K.)
Trindade
(Brazil)
SOUTH ATLANTIC OCEAN
Tristan da
180 160 140 120 100 80 60 40 20
80 60 40 20 0 20 40 60 80

Projection: Hammer Equal Area

ARCTIC OCEAN
Barents Sea
Kara Sea
Laptev Sea
East Siberian Sea
New Siberian Is.
Wrangel I.
Severnaya Zemlya
Novaya Zemlya
Arctic Circle
RUSSIA
Murmansk
Arkhangelsk
Norilsk
Verkhoyansk
Salekhard
Yakutsk
Okhotsk
Magadan
Sea of Okhotsk
Bering Sea
Petropavlovsk-Kamchatskiy
International Date Line
Sakhalin
Komsomolsk
Khabarovsk
Kuril Is.
FINLAND
Helsinki
SWEDEN
Stockholm
EST.
LATVIA
LITH.
Copenhagen
POLAND
Berlin
Warsaw
BELARUS
Minsk
Prague
Vienna
Budapest
UKRAINE
Kiev
Odessa
ROMANIA
Bucharest
Belgrade
BULGARIA
Sofia
Milan
ITALY
Rome
Naples
ALB.
GREECE
Athens
MALTA
Crete
Tunis
TUNISIA
Tripoli
Benghazi
Mediterranean Sea
ST.PETERSBURG
MOSCOW
Perm
Yekaterinburg
Kazan
Chelyabinsk
Samara
Saratov
Volgograd
Astrakhan
Omsk
Tomsk
Novosibirsk
Krasnoyarsk
Barnaul
Irkutsk
Ulan Ude
L. Baikal
KAZAKSTAN
Karaganda
L. Balkhash
Aral Sea
Caspian Sea
Black Sea
GEORGIA
Tbilisi
Yerevan
Baku
TURKEY
ISTANBUL
Ankara
Izmir
CYPRUS
SYRIA
LEB.
Beirut
Damascus
ISR.
Jerusalem
Amman
JORDAN
Alexandria
CAIRO
Nile
EGYPT
Aswân
LIBYA
UZBEKISTAN
TURKMENISTAN
Tashkent
Samarkand
Ashkhabad
Bishkek
Alma Ata
KYRGYZSTAN
Dushanbe
TAJIKISTAN
Tabriz
TEHRAN
Mashhad
Esfahân
Shîrâz
IRAQ
IRAN
Baghdad
KUWAIT
The Gulf
BAHRAIN
QATAR
U.A.E.
Abu Dhabi
Muscat
OMAN
Riyadh
Mecca
SAUDI ARABIA
Red Sea
Kâbul
AFGHANISTAN
PAKISTAN
Islamabad
Lahore
KARACHI
Indus
Arabian Sea
DELHI
New Delhi
NEPAL
Katmandu
BHUTAN
Kanpur
INDIA
Ganges
Ahmadabad
CALCUTTA
BANGLADESH
DACCA
Nagpur
BOMBAY
Hyderabad
Bay of Bengal
Bangalore
MADRAS
Lakshadweep Is. (India)
Andaman Is. (India)
SRI LANKA
Colombo
Nicobar Is. (India)
MALDIVES
Ulan Bator
MONGOLIA
Ürümqi
CHINA
TIBET
Lhasa
Lanzhou
Taiyuan
Xi'an
Hwang Ho
Chengdu
Wuhan
CHONGQING
Yangtze
Nanjing
SHANGHAI
Kunming
Fuzhou
GUANGZHOU
HONG KONG (U.K.)
TAIWAN
Taipei
East China Sea
Harbin
Changchun
SHENYANG
BEIJING
TIANJIN
Dalian
Vladivostok
NORTH KOREA
Pyŏngyang
SEOUL
SOUTH KOREA
Sapporo
JAPAN
TŌKYŌ
Ōsaka
Kitakyūshū
Ryukyu Is.
BURMA MYANMAR
Rangoon
Hanoi
Hainan
LAOS
Vientiane
THAILAND
BANGKOK
VIETNAM
CAMBODIA
Phnom Penh
Ho Chi Minh City
South China Sea
MANILA
PHILIPPINES
MALAYSIA
Kuala Lumpur
PEN. MALAYSIA
SABAH
BRUNEI
SARAWAK
SINGAPORE
Medan
Sumatra
Borneo
Palembang
Banjarmasin
INDONESIA
JAKARTA
Bandung
Java
Surabaya
Ujung Pandang
Timor
IRIAN JAYA
Arafura Sea
PAPUA NEW GUINEA
Port Moresby
New Ireland
New Britain
SOLOMON IS.
PACIFIC OCEAN
Bonin Is. (Japan)
Volcano Is. (Japan)
Marcus I. (Japan)
Tropic of Cancer
NORTHERN MARIANAS (U.S.A.)
Wake I. (U.S.A.)
GUAM (U.S.A.)
Yap
PALAU
FEDERATED STATES OF MICRONESIA
Truk
Caroline Is.
Pohnpei
MARSHALL IS.
Gilbert Is.
NAURU
KIRIBATI
TUVALU
Santa Cruz I.
VANUATU
FIJI
Suva
NEW CALEDONIA (Fr.)
NIGER
CHAD
L. Chad
Kano
NIGERIA
Abuja
Ndjamena
CAMEROON
Douala
Yaoundé
CENTRAL AFRICAN REP.
Bangui
Omdurmân
Khartoum
SUDAN
Blue Nile
White Nile
ERITREA
Asmara
DJIBOUTI
Addis Ababa
ETHIOPIA
SOMALI REP.
Mogadishu
Sana
YEMEN
Aden
G. of Aden
Socotra (Yemen)
EQUATORIAL GUINEA
Libreville
GABON
CONGO
Brazzaville
Kinshasa
Kisangani
ZAÏRE
Zaïre
Kasai
UGANDA
Kampala
L. Turkana
KENYA
L. Victoria
Nairobi
RWANDA
Kigali
BURUNDI
Bujumbura
Kananga
L. Tanganyika
Mombasa
Zanzibar
TANZANIA
Dar es Salaam
CABINDA (Angola)
Luanda
ANGOLA
Benguela
Lubumbashi
ZAMBIA
Lusaka
L. Malawi
Lilongwe
MALAWI
Harare
ZIMBABWE
MOZAMBIQUE
Bulawayo
Mozambique Channel
NAMIBIA
Windhoek
BOTSWANA
Gaborone
Pretoria
Johannesburg
Maputo
SWAZILAND
SOUTH AFRICA
LESOTHO
Durban
Cape Town
C. of Good Hope
Port Elizabeth
SEYCHELLES
Amirante Is.
Aldabra Is.
COMOROS
Mayotte (Fr.)
Agalega Is.
MADAGASCAR
Antananarivo
Cargados Carajos
Rodriguez
MAURITIUS
RÉUNION (Fr.)
Diego Garcia
Chagos Arch. (U.K.)
Equator
INDIAN OCEAN
Cocos Is. (Austral.)
Christmas I. (Austral.)
Tropic of Capricorn
C. York
Darwin
Cairns
Townsville
Port Hedland
Alice Springs
AUSTRALIA
Rockhampton
Geraldton
Brisbane
Perth
Fremantle
Kalgoorlie-Boulder
Darling
Great Australian Bight
Adelaide
Newcastle
Sydney
Canberra
Melbourne
Tasmania
Hobart
Lord Howe I. (Austral.)
Norfolk I. (Austral.)
Tasman Sea
Auckland
North I.
NEW ZEALAND
Wellington
Christchurch
South I.
Stewart I.
Dunedin
Bounty Is. (N.Z.)
Antipodes Is.
Auckland Is. (N.Z.)
Campbell I. (N.Z.)
Macquarie Is. (Austral.)
Amsterdam I. (Fr.)
St. Paul (Fr.)
Prince Edward Is. (S.Africa)
Crozet Is. (Fr.)
Kerguelen (Fr.)
McDonald Is. (Austral.)
Heard I. (Austral.)
SOUTHERN OCEAN
Antarctic Circle
Antarctica
Ross Sea
Greenwich
A
B
C
D
E
F
G
H
11 12 13 14 15 16 17 18
20 40 60 80 100 120 140 160 180

Hanoi ● Capital Cities

ARCTIC OCEAN

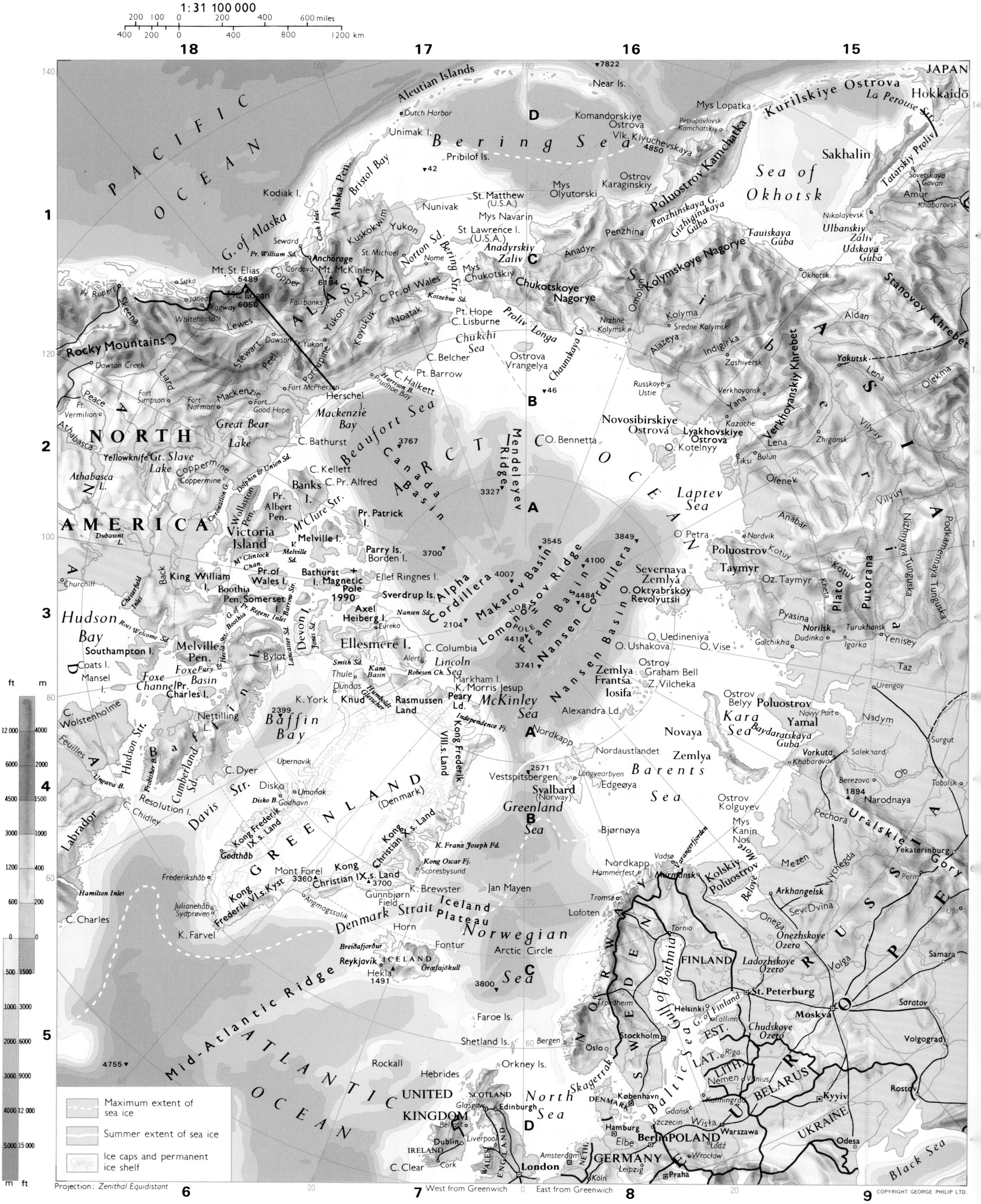
1:31 100 000
200 100 0 200 400 600 miles
400 200 0 400 800 1200 km
18
17
16
15
1
2
3
4
5
6
7
8
9
PACIFIC OCEAN
Aleutian Islands
Near Is.
JAPAN
Hokkaido
Kurilskiye Ostrova
La Perouse Str.
Mys Lopatka
Komandorskiye Ostrova
Petropavlovsk Kamchatskiy
Vlk. Klyuchevskaya 4850
Poluostrov Kamchatka
Bering Sea
Dutch Harbor
Unimak I.
Pribilof Is.
Sakhalin
Tatarskiy Proliv
Sovetskaya Gavan
Sea of Okhotsk
Amur
Khabarovsk
Kodiak I.
Alaska Pen.
Bristol Bay
St. Matthew (U.S.A.)
Mys Olyutorski
Ostrov Karaginskiy
Nunivak
Mys Navarin
Penzhinskaya G.
Gizhiginskaya Guba
Nikolayevsk
G. of Alaska
Cook Inlet
Kuskokwim
Yukon
St. Lawrence I. (U.S.A.)
Penzhina
Tauiskaya Guba
Ulbanskiy Zaliv
Udskaya Guba
Seward
Pr. William Sd.
Anchorage
St. Michael
Norton Sd.
Nome
Bering Str.
Anadyrskiy Zaliv
Anadyr
Kolymskoye Nagorye
Okhotsk
Mt. St. Elias 5489
Cordova
Copper
Mt. McKinley 6194
ALASKA
Mys Chukotskiy
Chukotskoye Nagorye
Omolon
Stanovoy Khrebet
Sitka
Pr. Rupert
Juneau
Skagway
Mt. Logan 6050
Fairbanks
Yukon (U.S.A.)
C. Pr. of Wales
Kotzebue Sd.
Noatak
Koyukuk
Pt. Hope
C. Lisburne
Proliv Longa
Chaunskaya G.
Nizhne Kolymsk
Kolyma
Sredne Kolymsk
Aldan
Skeena
Whitehorse
Lewes
Dawson
Ft. Yukon
Porcupine
Chukchi Sea
Ostrova Vrangelya
Alazeya
Indigirka
Zashiversk
Rocky Mountains
Stewart
Peel
C. Belcher
Pt. Barrow
Yakutsk
Lena
Dawson Creek
Liard
C. Halkett
Harrison B.
Prudhoe Bay
Russkoye Ustie
Verkhoyansk
Verkhoyanskiy Khrebet
Olekma
Peace
Fort Simpson
Fort Norman
Mackenzie
Fort McPherson
Fort Good Hope
Herschel I.
Mackenzie Bay
Beaufort Sea
Yana
Ft. Vermilion
Great Bear Lake
Novosibirskiye Ostrova
Lyakhovskiye Ostrova
Kazache
Vilyuy
Athabasca
NORTH AMERICA
C. Bathurst
3767
Canada Basin
ARCTIC OCEAN
Mendeleyev Ridge
O. Bennetta
O. Kotelnyy
Lena
Zhigansk
Yellowknife
Gt. Slave Lake
Coppermine
Dolphin & Union Sd.
C. Kellett
C. Pr. Alfred
Tiksi
Bulun
Athabasca L.
Banks I.
3327
Olenek
Laptev Sea
Coronation G.
Wollaston Pen.
Pr. Albert Pen.
M'Clure Str.
Pr. Patrick I.
Anabar
Victoria Island
Melville I.
Petra
Nordvik
Poluostrov Taymyr
Kotuy
Dubawnt L.
M'Clintock Chan.
Viscount Melville Sd.
Parry Is.
Borden I.
3700
3545
3849
4100
Makarov Basin
Lomonosov Ridge
Fram Basin
Nansen Cordillera
Severnaya Zemlya
Oz. Taymyr
Plato Putorana
Podkamennaya Tunguska
Nizhnyaya Tunguska
Churchill
Chesterfield Inlet
Back
King William I.
Pr. of Wales I.
Boothia Pen.
Somerset I.
Bathurst I.
Magnetic Pole 1990
Ellef Ringnes I.
Sverdrup Is.
Alpha Cordillera
4007
4484
O. Oktyabrskoy Revolyutsii
Kheta
Hudson Bay
Roes Welcome Sd.
G. of Boothia
Pr. Regent Inlet
Barrow Str.
Lancaster Sd.
Devon I.
Jones Sd.
Axel Heiberg I.
Nansen Sd.
Eureka
2104
NORTH POLE
4418
Nansen Basin
Pyasina
Norilsk
Dudinka
Turukhansk
Igarka
Yenisey
Southampton I.
Melville Pen.
Hecla Str.
Fury
Bylot I.
Ellesmere I.
C. Columbia
Alert
Lincoln Sea
O. Uedineniya
O. Ushakova
O. Vise
Golchikha
Coats I.
Mansel I.
Foxe Channel
Foxe Basin
Pr. Charles I.
Smith Sd.
Thule
Kane Basin
Robeson Ch.
Markham I.
K. Morris Jesup
3741
Zemlya Frantsa Iosifa
Ostrov Graham Bell
Z. Vilcheka
Taz
Urengoy
Dundas
Humboldt Gletscher
K. York
Knud Rasmussen Land
Peary Ld.
McKinley Sea
Ostrov Belyy
Poluostrov Yamal
C. Wolstenholme
2399
Baffin Bay
Nettilling L.
Independence Fj.
Kong Frederik VIII.s. Land
Alexandra Ld.
A
Nordkapp
Kara Sea
Novaya Zemlya
Novy Port
Nadym
Baydaratskaya Guba
Surgut
Feuilles
Hudson Str.
Frobisher B.
Cumberland Sd.
C. Dyer
Upernavik
Nordaustlandet
Barents Sea
Vorkuta
Salekhard
Khabarovo
Ob
Ungava B.
Resolution I.
Davis Str.
Disko
Disko B.
Umanak
Godhavn
GREENLAND (Denmark)
2571
Vestspitsbergen
Longyearbyen
Edgeøya
Svalbard (Norway)
Berezovo
Tobolsk
1894
Narodnaya
C. Chidley
Labrador
Kong Frederik IX.s. Land
Kong Christian X.s. Land
Greenland Sea
Bjørnøya
Ostrov Kolguyev
Pechora
Uralskiye Gory
Mys Kanin Nos
Godthåb
K. Franz Joseph Fd.
Kong Oscar Fj.
Scoresbysund
Nordkapp
Hammerfest
Vadsø
Varangerfjorden
Murmansk
Kolskiy Poluostrov
Beloye More
Mezen
Yekaterinburg
Perm
Frederikshåb
Mont Forel 3360
Kong Christian IX.s. Land
3700
K. Brewster
Gunnbjørn Field
Jan Mayen
Vychegda
Arkhangelsk
Hamilton Inlet
Julianehåb
Sydprøven
Kong Frederik VI.s. Kyst
Angmagssalik
Denmark Strait
Iceland Plateau
Tromsø
Lofoten
Onega
Sev. Dvina
Ufa
C. Charles
K. Farvel
Horn
Norwegian Sea
Tornio
Onezhskoye Ozero
Samara
Breidafjördur
Fontur
Arctic Circle
NORWAY
SWEDEN
FINLAND
Ladozhskoye Ozero
Reykjavík
ICELAND
Öræfajökull
Hekla 1491
3800
Trondheim
Gulf of Bothnia
Helsinki
St. Peterburg
Volga
Mid-Atlantic Ridge
Faroe Is.
Tallinn
G. of Finland
EST.
Chudskoye Ozero
Moskva
Saratov
Volgograd
Shetland Is.
Bergen
Oslo
Stockholm
Riga
LAT.
LITH.
RUSSIA
EUROPE
4755
Rockall
Hebrides
Orkney Is.
Skagerrak
Baltic Sea
Nemen
Vilnius
BELARUS
ATLANTIC OCEAN
UNITED KINGDOM
SCOTLAND
Glasgow
Edinburgh
North Sea
København
DENMARK
Kaliningrad
Gdańsk
Kyyiv
Rostov
Belfast
Dublin
Liverpool
IRELAND
Cork
WALES
ENGLAND
Hamburg
Berlin
Elbe
Szczecin
Wisla
POLAND
Warszawa
UKRAINE
Odesa
Black Sea
Amsterdam
NETH.
GERMANY
Leipzig
Wrocław
Łódź
Praha
Köln
C. Clear
London
Maximum extent of sea ice
Summer extent of sea ice
Ice caps and permanent ice shelf
ft m
12 000 4000
6000 2000
4500 1500
3000 1000
1200 400
600 200
0 0
500 1500
1000 3000
2000 6000
3000 9000
4000 12 000
5000 15 000
m ft
Projection: Zenithal Equidistant
West from Greenwich
East from Greenwich
COPYRIGHT GEORGE PHILIP LTD.

1 : 31 100 000

Ice cap

Permanent ice shelf

Maximum extent of sea ice

March (Summer) extent of sea ice

▲3488 Surface elevation and 3700 depth of ice (in metres)

• Stanley (U.K.) Permanent bases

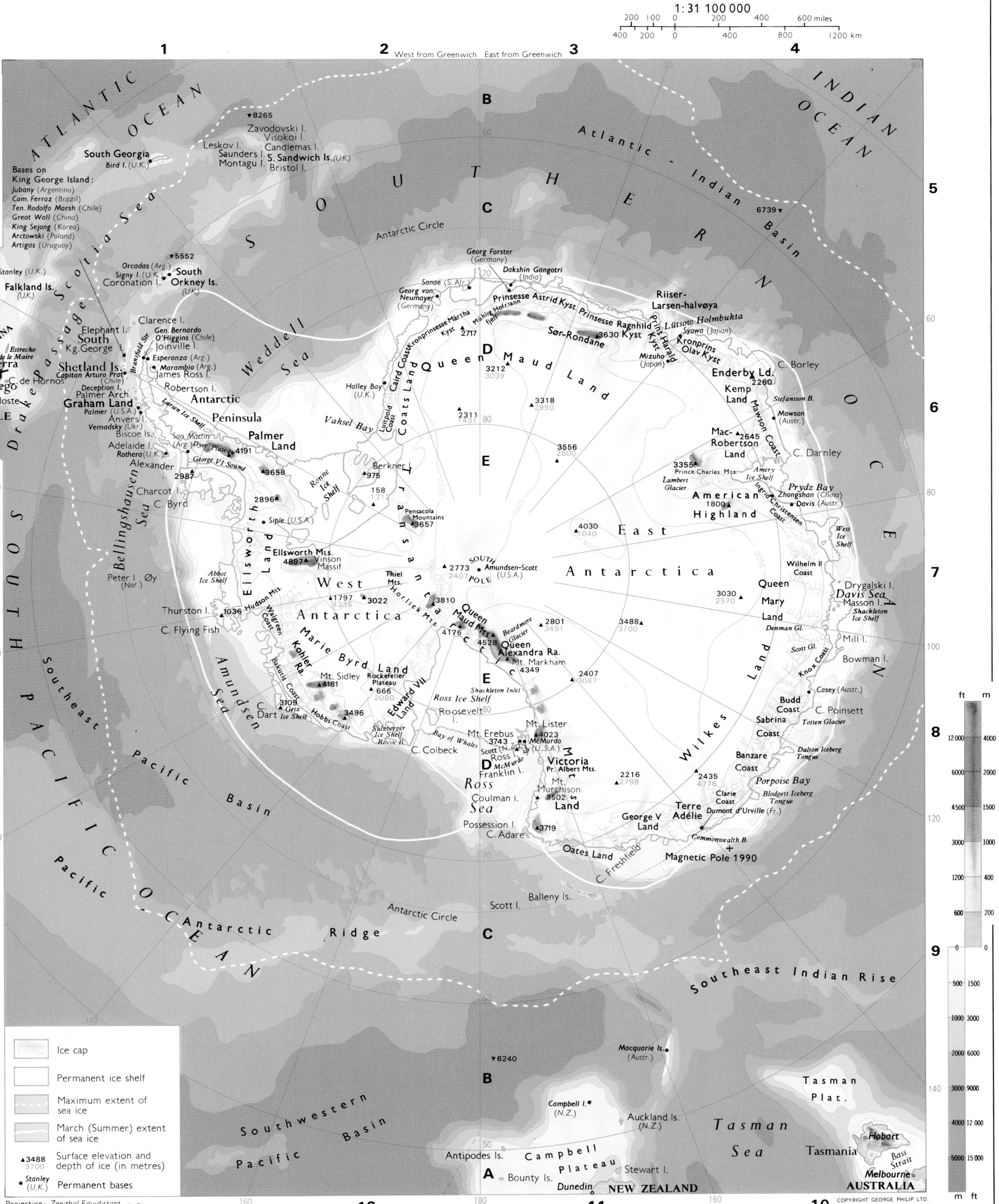

Projection: Zenithal Equidistant

The Antarctic Treaty was signed in Washington in 1959 so that scientific and technical research could continue unhampered by international politics.

All territorial claims covering land areas south of latitude 60°S have been suspended. Those claims were:

Norwegian claim	45°E – 20°W	French claim	136°E – 142°E	British claim	80°W – 20°W
Australian claims	45°E – 136°E	New Zealand claim	160°E – 150°W	Argentine claim	74°W – 53°W
	142°E – 160°E	Chilean claim	90°W – 53°W		

COPYRIGHT GEORGE PHILIP LTD.

1: 17 800 000

100 0 100 200 300 400 miles

100 0 100 200 300 400 500 600 km

Ural Mountains
Obshchi Syrt
Caspian Depression
Caspian Sea
Volga Hts.
Central Russian Uplands
Ukraine
Sea of Azov
Black Sea
Caucasus
Elbrus 5642
Pontine Mts.
Armenia
Ararat 5165
L. Van
L. Urmia
Kurdistan
Mesopotamia
Tigris
Euphrates
Anatolia (Asia Minor)
Taurus Mts.
Cyprus
Rhodes
Sea of Marmara
Bosporus
Dardanelles
Mt. Ida 1766
Ægean Sea
Olympus 2917
Pindus
Morea
C. Matapan
Ionian Is.
Ionian Sea
Str. of Otranto
Balkans
Rhodope
Walachia
Transylvanian Alps
Carpathians
Tatra 2655
Plain of Hungary
Tisza
Danube
Dinaric Alps
Adriatic Sea
Apennines
Gran Sasso d'Italia 2914
Vesuvius 1277
Etna 3340
Sicily
Str. of Messina
Calabria
Tyrrhenian Sea
Malta
Pantelleria
C. Bon
Sardinia
Corsica
Str. of Bonifacio
Ligurian Sea
G. of Lions
Alps
Mont Blanc 4807
Jura
Vosges
Black Forest
Bohemian Forest
Erzgebirge
Moravian Hts.
Sudeten
Harz
Taunus
Hunsrück
Ardennes
Rhine
Elbe
Oder
Vistula
North European Plain
Baltic Sea
Gotland
Öland
Bornholm
Saaremaa
G. of Riga
G. of Finland
Åland
G. of Bothnia
Finland
Lapland
Scandinavia
Kebnekaise 2117
Galdhøpiggen 2469
Kattegat
Skagerrak
Jutland
Lindesnes
North Sea
Helgoland
Norwegian Sea
Lofoten
Vesterålen
North Cape
Nordkinn
Kola Pen.
White Sea
Kanin Pen.
L. Ladoga
L. Onega
Pechora
Kama
Volga
Don
Dnieper
Dniester
Pripet
Iceland
Hekla 1491
Öræfajökull 2119
Arctic Circle
Faroe Is.
Shetland Is.
Orkney Is.
Hebrides
Great Britain
Ben Nevis 1344
Snowdon 1085
Ireland
Irish Sea
British Isles
English Channel
Channel Is.
Land's End
Celtic Sea
C. Clear
Rockall
ATLANTIC OCEAN
Bay of Biscay
Brittany
Ushant
Seine
Loire
Garonne
Massif Central
Puy de Sancy 1886
Pyrenees
Pico de Aneto 3404
Cantabrian Mts.
Iberian Peninsula
Old Castile
New Castile
Sierra Morena
Sierra Nevada
Mulhacén 3478
Andalusia
Guadalquivir
Ebro
Tagus
Douro
Serra da Estrêla
C. Finisterre
C. da Roca
C. de São Vicente
C. Trafalgar
Str. of Gibraltar
Balearic Is.
Majorca
Minorca
Ibiza
Mediterranean Sea
Plateau of the Shotts
Africa
Er Rif
CARTOGRAPHY BY PHILIP'S COPYRIGHT REED INTERNATIONAL BOOKS LTD

1 : 17 800 000

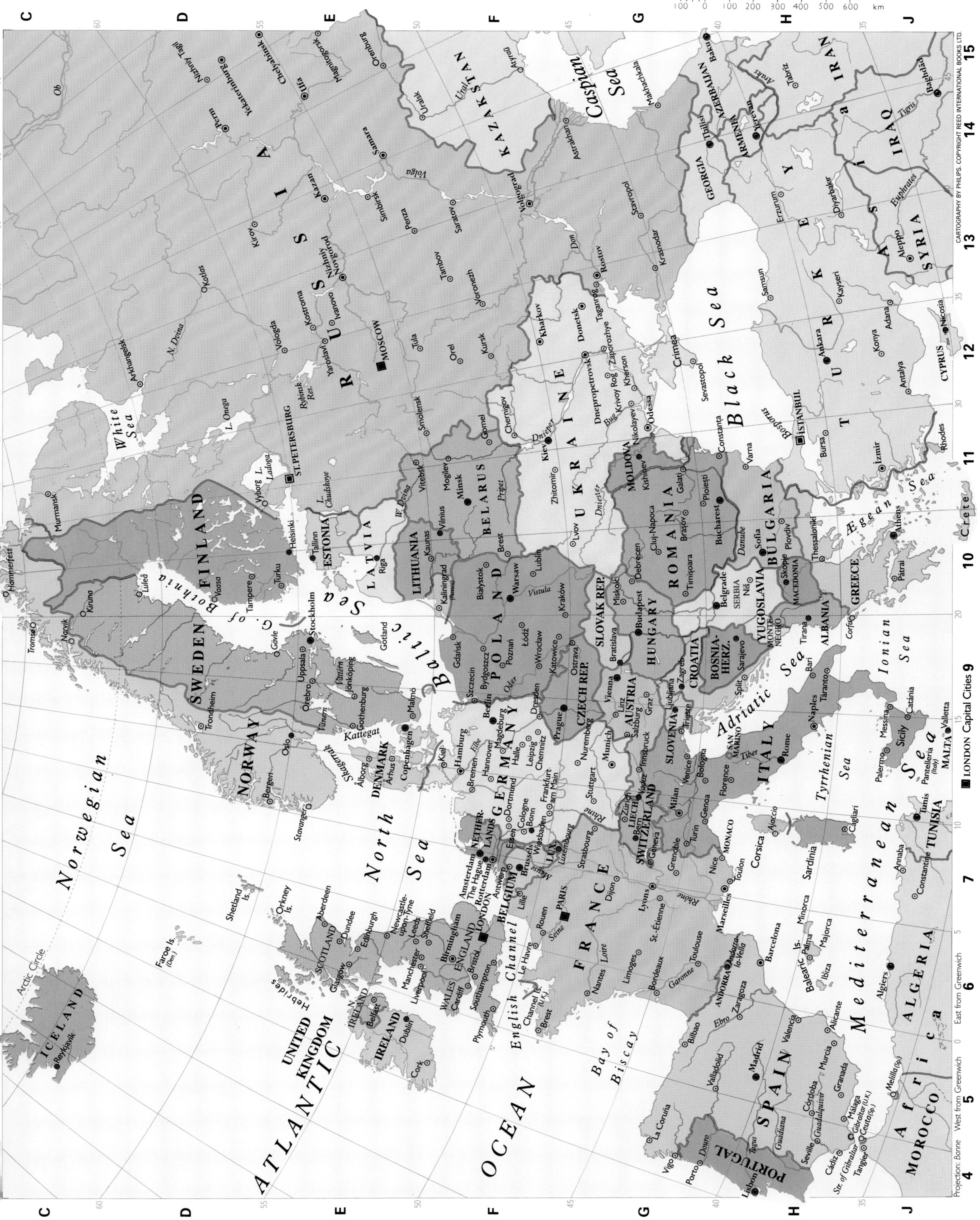

100 0 100 200 300 400 miles
100 0 100 200 300 400 500 600 km
ICELAND
Reykjavik
Arctic Circle
Faroe Is. (Den.)
Norwegian Sea
NORWAY
SWEDEN
FINLAND
DENMARK
UNITED KINGDOM
IRELAND
ATLANTIC OCEAN
North Sea
Baltic Sea
G. of Bothnia
White Sea
ESTONIA
LATVIA
LITHUANIA
BELARUS
RUSSIA
KAZAKSTAN
UKRAINE
MOLDOVA
ROMANIA
BULGARIA
POLAND
GERMANY
NETHER-LANDS
BELGIUM
LUX.
FRANCE
SWITZERLAND
AUSTRIA
CZECH REP.
SLOVAK REP.
HUNGARY
SLOVENIA
CROATIA
BOSNIA-HERZ.
YUGOSLAVIA
MACEDONIA
ALBANIA
GREECE
ITALY
SPAIN
PORTUGAL
ANDORRA
MONACO
SAN MARINO
MALTA
TUNISIA
ALGERIA
MOROCCO
Africa
TURKEY
SYRIA
IRAQ
IRAN
CYPRUS
GEORGIA
ARMENIA
AZERBAIJAN
Black Sea
Caspian Sea
Ægean Sea
Ionian Sea
Adriatic Sea
Tyrrhenian Sea
Mediterranean Sea
Bay of Biscay
English Channel
MOSCOW
ST. PETERSBURG
LONDON
PARIS
Projection: Bonne
West from Greenwich
East from Greenwich
LONDON Capital Cities

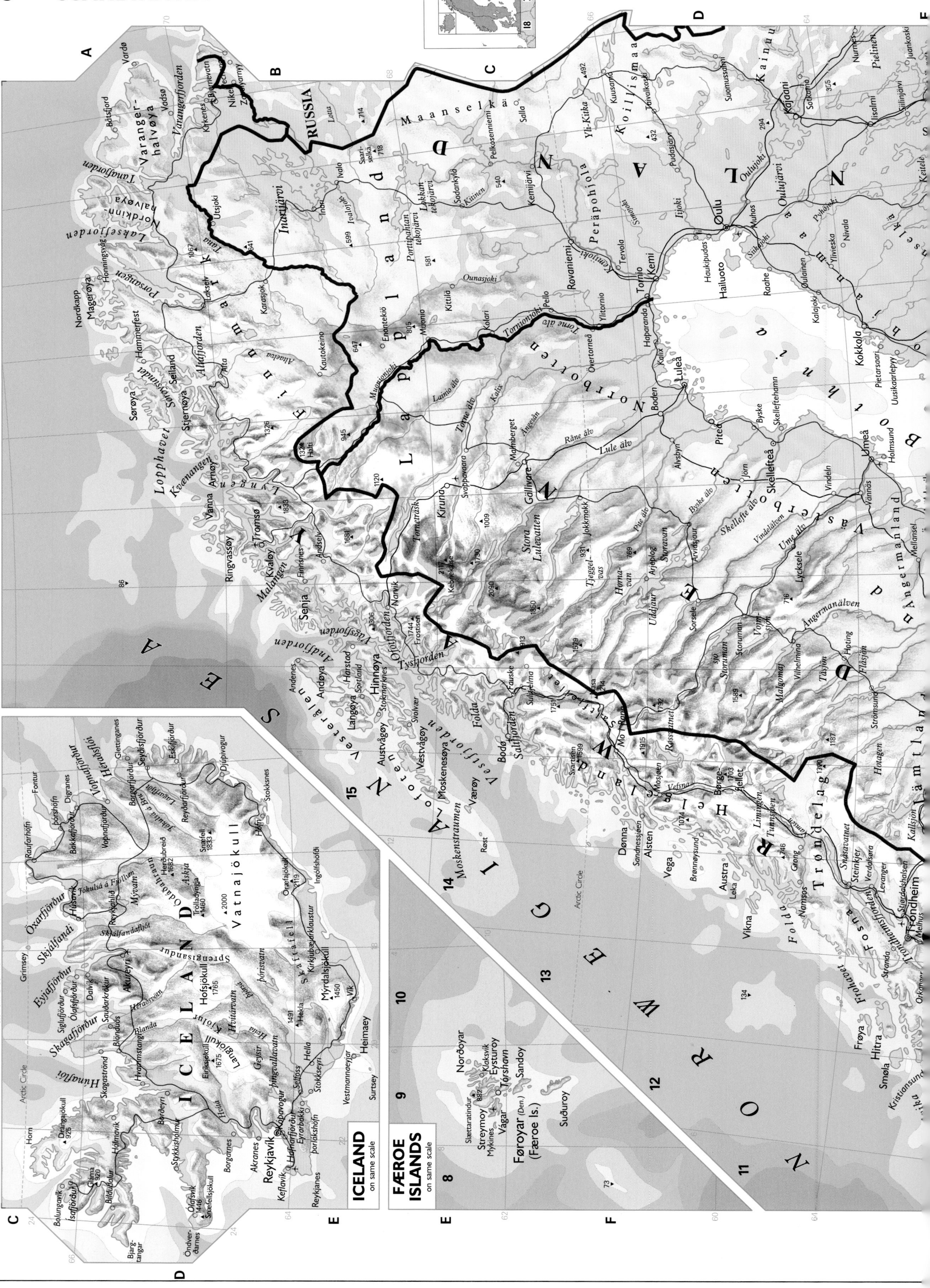
RUSSIA
Finnmark
Lappland
Norrbotten
Västerbotten
Ångermanland
Jämtland
Trøndelag
Helgeland
NORWEGIAN SEA
Lofoten
Vesterålen
Vestfjorden
Senja
Tromsø
Hammerfest
Nordkapp
Vardø
Vadsø
Varangerfjorden
Porsangen
Laksefjorden
Tanafjorden
Altafjorden
Lopphavet
Inarijärvi
Maanselkä
Oulu
Oulujärvi
Kajaani
Kemi
Tornio
Haparanda
Luleå
Boden
Piteå
Skellefteå
Umeå
Kiruna
Gällivare
Narvik
Bodø
Mo i Rana
Mosjøen
Trondheim
Steinkjer
Namsos
Kokkola
Raahe
Kautokeino
Karasjok
Kittilä
Ivalo
Inari
Sodankylä
Rovaniemi
Kemijärvi
Stora Lulevatten
Tjeggelvas
Hornavan
Uddjaur
Storavan
Storuman
Vojmsjön
Malgomaj
Vilhelmina
Lycksele
Arvidsjaur
Arjeplog
Jokkmokk
Sorsele
Hoting
Strömsund
Snåsavatnet
Frøya
Hitra
Smøla
Kristiansund
Vikna
Vega
Dønna
Alsten
Austvågøy
Vestvågøy
Moskenesøya
Værøy
Røst
Hinnøya
Andøya
Langøya
Ringvassøy
Kvaløy
Sørøya
Seiland
Magerøya
Arctic Circle
ICELAND
on same scale
Reykjavík
Akureyri
Vatnajökull
Hofsjökull
Langjökull
Mýrdalsjökull
Heimaey
Vestmannaeyjar
Surtsey
Faxaflói
Skagafjörður
Eyjafjörður
Húnaflói
Vopnafjörður
Seyðisfjörður
Ísafjörður
Keflavík
Akranes
Borgarnes
Selfoss
Hella
Vík
Höfn
Húsavík
Grímsey
Stykkishólmur
Snæfellsjökull
Hvannadalshnúkur 2119
FÆROE ISLANDS
on same scale
Føroyar (Færoe Is.)
Streymoy
Eysturoy
Norðoyar
Sandoy
Suðuroy
Vágar
Tórshavn
Mykines

1 : 4 400 000
50 0 50 100 miles
50 0 50 100 150 km
9
Gulf of Finland
Gulf of Riga
Ålands hav
BALTIC SEA
Kattegat
Skagerrak
ESTONIA
LATVIA
LITHUANIA
POLAND
GERMANY
DENMARK
NORWAY
SWEDEN
BELARUS
STOCKHOLM
Oslo
KØBENHAVN (Copenhagen)
Helsinki (Helsingfors)
Tallinn
Riga
Vilnius
Kaunas
Gotland
Öland
Bornholm
Kaliningrad (Russia)
Göteborg (Gothenburg)
Svealand
Götaland
Projection: Conical with two standard parallels
East from Greenwich
CARTOGRAPHY BY PHILIP'S. COPYRIGHT REED INTERNATIONAL BOOKS LTD

Gulf of Bothnia
Trondheim
Kristiansund
Östersund
Sundsvall
Härnösand
Hudiksvall
Söderhamn
Gävle
Uppsala
STOCKHOLM
Västerås
Örebro
Karlstad
Falun
Borlänge
Mora
Oslo
Drammen
Lillehammer
Hamar
Gjøvik
Kongsberg
Skien
Porsgrunn
Larvik
Tønsberg
Moss
Fredrikstad
Sarpsborg
Halden
Jotunheimen
Dovrefjell
Snøhetta 2286
Galdhøpiggen 2469
Glittertind 2470
Sylarna 1766
Helagsfjället 1796
JÄMTLANDS LÄN
VÄSTERNORRLANDS LÄN
GÄVLEBORGS LÄN
KOPPARBERGS LÄN
VÄRMLANDS LÄN
ÖREBRO LÄN
VÄSTMANLANDS LÄN
UPPSALA LÄN
STOCKHOLMS LÄN
SÖDERMANLANDS LÄN
MØRE OG ROMSDAL FYLKE
SØR-TRØNDELAG FYLKE
HEDMARK
OPPLAND FYLKE
BUSKERUD
AKERSHUS FYLKE
ØSTFOLD
VESTFOLD
TELEMARK

Skagerrak
Norskerenna
Kattegat
BALTIC SEA
Jammerbugt
Ålborg Bugt
Kieler Bucht
Fehmarn Bælt
Femer Bælt
Store Bælt
Lille Bælt
Hanöbukten
Kalmarsund
Bornholmsgattet
GERMANY
POLAND
JYLLAND
SJÆLLAND
FYN
FALSTER
LOLLAND
Gotland
Öland
Bornholm
Anholt
Læsø
Rugen
Fehmarn
KØBENHAVN (COPENHAGEN)
Göteborg
Malmö
Århus
Ålborg
Odense
Helsingborg
Helsingør
Jönköping
Norrköping
Linköping
Kalmar
Karlskrona
Flensburg
Kiel
Visby
SKARABORGS LÄN
ÖSTERGÖTLAND
JÖNKÖPINGS LÄN
KALMAR LÄN
KRONOBERGS LÄN
BLEKINGE LÄN
KRISTIANSTADS LÄN
MALMÖHUS
HALLANDS LÄN
ÄLVSBORGS LÄN
GÖTEBORGS OCH BOHUS
Götaland
Vättern
DENMARK
1 : 2 200 000
Projection: Conical with two standard parallels
East from Greenwich
COPYRIGHT, GEORGE PHILIP & SON, LTD.

11

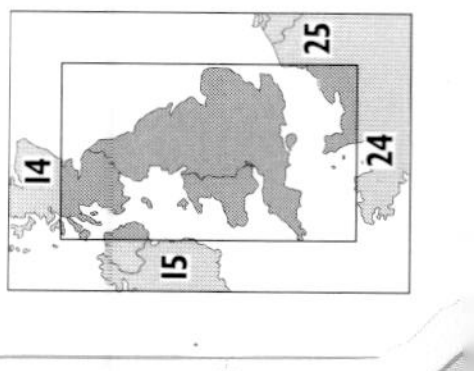
14
15
24
25

NORTH SEA
IRISH SEA
North Channel
Firth of Clyde
Solway Firth
Firth of Forth
SCOTLAND
Southern Uplands
Pennines
Cheviot Hills
Cumbrian Mts.
N. York Moors
ISLE OF MAN
English Unitary Authorities
(from April 1996)
12. Hartlepool
13. Stockton-on-Tees
14. Middlesbrough
15. Redcar and Cleveland
16. Kingston upon Hull
17. York
18. South Gloucester
19. Bristol
20. North Somerset
21. Bath and N.E. Somerset
Welsh Unitary Authorities
(from April 1996)
1. Neath Port Talbot
2. Rhondda Cynon Taff
3. Bridgend
4. Merthyr Tydfil
5. Caerphilly
6. Vale of Glamorgan
7. Cardiff
8. Blaenau Gwent
9. Torfaen
10. Newport
11. Monmouthshire

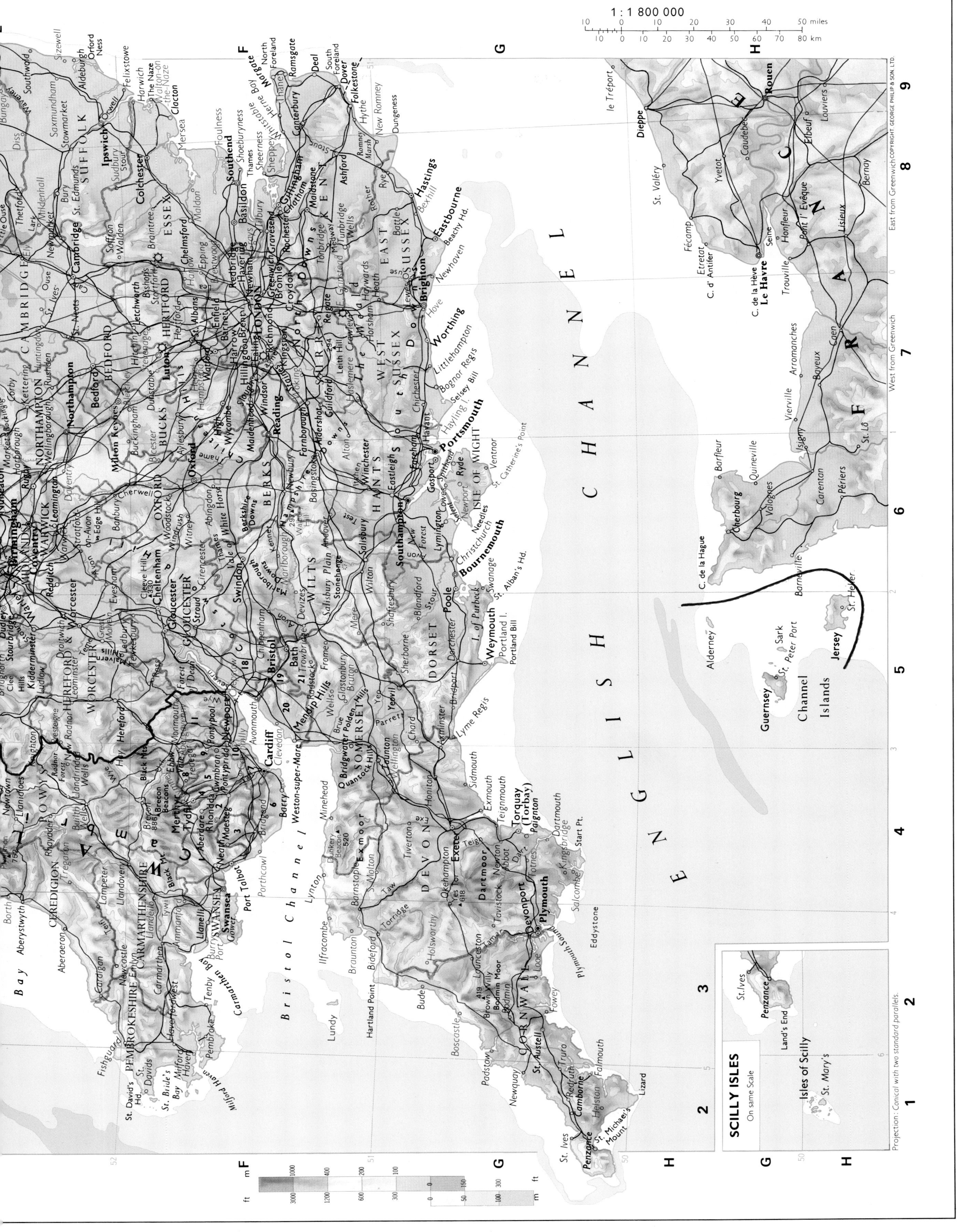
1 : 1 800 000
50 miles
80 km
ENGLISH CHANNEL
FRANCE
Bristol Channel
Bay
SCILLY ISLES
On same Scale
Isles of Scilly
St. Mary's
Land's End
Penzance
St. Ives
Channel Islands
Guernsey
Jersey
Alderney
Sark
St. Peter Port
St. Helier
C. de la Hague
Cherbourg
Le Havre
Rouen
Dieppe
Caen
London
Birmingham
Bristol
Cardiff
Swansea
Plymouth
Exeter
Southampton
Portsmouth
Bournemouth
Brighton
Hastings
Dover
Oxford
Reading
Cambridge
Ipswich
Colchester
Southend
Gloucester
Worcester
Hereford
Northampton
Bedford
Luton
Weymouth
Torquay (Torbay)
Dartmoor
Exmoor
CORNWALL
DEVON
DORSET
SOMERSET
WILTS
HANTS
BERKS
SURREY
KENT
EAST SUSSEX
WEST SUSSEX
ESSEX
SUFFOLK
HERTFORD
BUCKS
OXFORD
GLOUCESTER
WARWICK
NORTHAMPTON
BEDFORD
CAMBRIDGE
WORCESTER
HEREFORD
POWYS
CEREDIGION
CARMARTHENSHIRE
PEMBROKESHIRE
ISLE OF WIGHT
East from Greenwich
West from Greenwich
Projection: Conical with two standard parallels.
COPYRIGHT GEORGE PHILIP & SON, LTD.

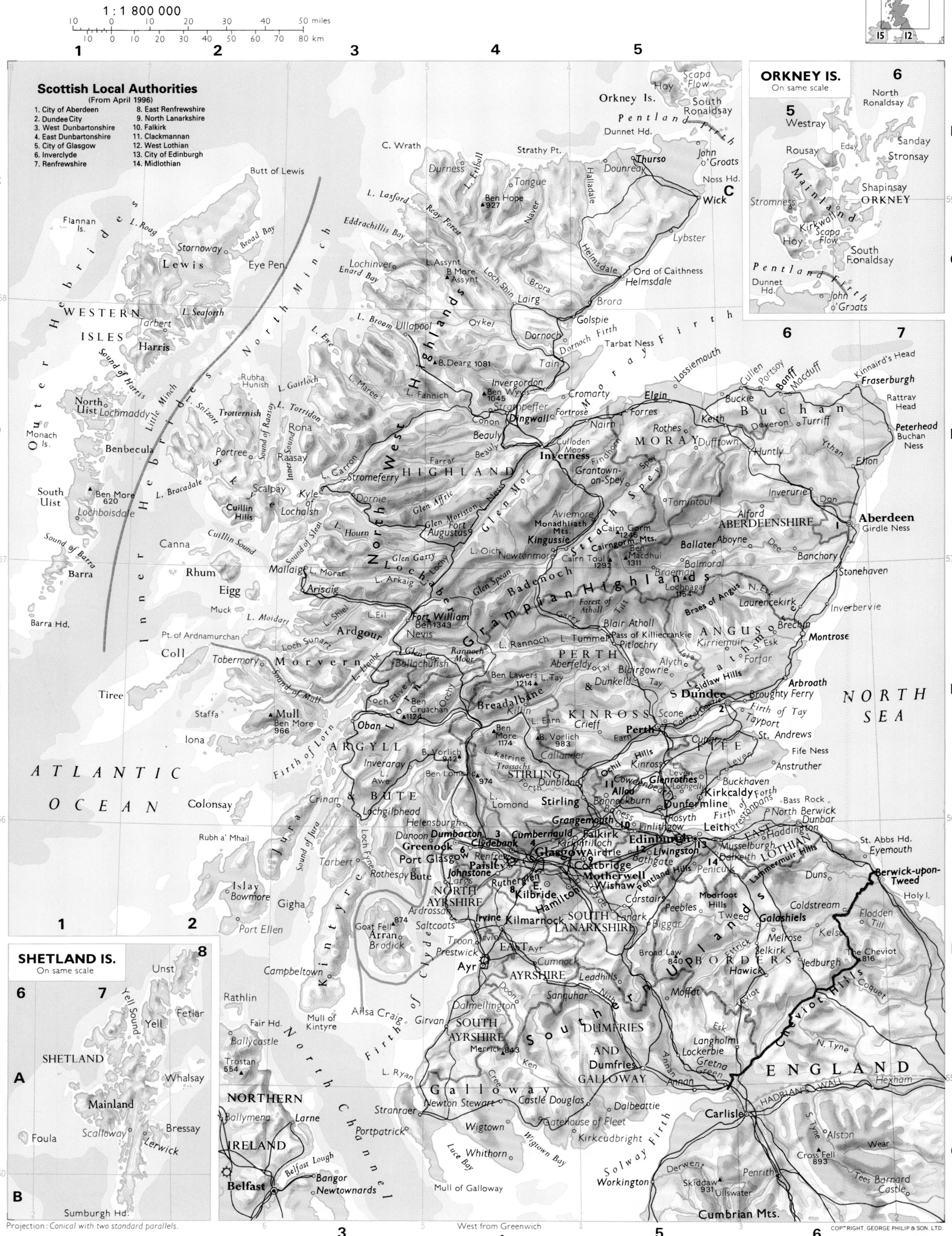
1 : 1 800 000
10 0 10 20 30 40 50 miles
10 0 10 20 30 40 50 60 70 80 km
15
12
1 2 3 4 5
6 7
C
D
E
F
Scottish Local Authorities
(From April 1996)
1. City of Aberdeen
2. Dundee City
3. West Dunbartonshire
4. East Dunbartonshire
5. City of Glasgow
6. Inverclyde
7. Renfrewshire
8. East Renfrewshire
9. North Lanarkshire
10. Falkirk
11. Clackmannan
12. West Lothian
13. City of Edinburgh
14. Midlothian
ORKNEY IS.
On same scale
North Ronaldsay
Westray
Rousay
Eday
Sanday
Stronsay
Mainland
Shapinsay
ORKNEY
Stromness
Kirkwall
Scapa Flow
Hoy
South Ronaldsay
Pentland Firth
Dunnet Hd.
John o'Groats
Orkney Is.
Scapa Flow
Pentland Firth
Dunnet Hd.
C. Wrath
Strathy Pt.
Thurso
Dounreay
John o'Groats
Noss Hd.
Wick
Lybster
Halladale
Helmsdale
Ord of Caithness
Durness
L. Eriboll
Tongue
Ben Hope 927
Naver
L. Laxford
Reay Forest
Eddrachillis Bay
Butt of Lewis
Flannan Is.
L. Roag
Broad Bay
Stornoway
Lewis
Eye Pen.
Lochinver
Enard Bay
L. Assynt
B. More Assynt
Loch Shin
Lairg
Brora
Golspie
Dornoch
Dornoch Firth
Tarbat Ness
Moray Firth
Tain
WESTERN ISLES
Tarbert
L. Seaforth
Harris
Outer Hebrides
North Minch
Little Minch
Sound of Harris
North Uist
Lochmaddy
Monach Is.
Benbecula
South Uist
Ben More 620
Lochboisdale
Sound of Barra
Barra
Barra Hd.
Canna
Rhum
Eigg
Muck
Coll
Tiree
Inner Hebrides
L. Broom
Ullapool
Oykel
L. Ewe
B. Dearg 1081
Rubha Hunish
L. Gairloch
L. Maree
L. Fannich
Ben Wyvis 1045
Invergordon
Cromarty
Strathpeffer
Dingwall
Fortrose
Conon
Beauly
Nairn
Forres
Elgin
Lossiemouth
Cullen
Portsoy
Banff
Macduff
Fraserburgh
Kinnaird's Head
Rattray Head
Buckie
Keith
Buchan
Deveron
Turriff
Peterhead
Buchan Ness
Rothes
Dufftown
MORAY
Huntly
Ythan
Ellon
Trotternish
L. Snizort
Sound of Raasay
L. Torridon
Rona
Raasay
Inner Sound
Portree
Skye
L. Bracadale
Cuillin Hills
Scalpay
L. Carron
Stromeferry
Kyle of Lochalsh
Dornie
Glen Affric
HIGHLAND
North West Highlands
Farrar
Culloden Moor
Inverness
Findhorn
Grantown-on-Spey
Spey
Glen Moriston
Fort Augustus
Loch Ness
Glen Mor
Aviemore
Monadhliath Mts.
Kingussie
Cairn Gorm 1245
Cairngorm Mts.
Ben Macdhui 1311
Cairn Toul 1293
Tomintoul
Inverurie
Don
Alford
ABERDEENSHIRE
Aberdeen
Girdle Ness
Ballater
Aboyne
Dee
Banchory
Stonehaven
Balmoral
Braemar
Lochnagar 1154
Grampian Highlands
Cuillin Sound
Sound of Sleat
L. Hourn
Glen Garry
L. Oich
Newtonmore
Badenoch
Mallaig
L. Morar
L. Arkaig
Lochaber
Glen Spean
Arisaig
L. Moidart
L. Shiel
L. Eil
Fort William
Ben Nevis 1343
Forest of Atholl
Garry
Tilt
Blair Atholl
Pass of Killiecrankie
Pitlochry
Braes of Angus
N. Esk
Laurencekirk
Inverbervie
Brechin
Montrose
ANGUS
Kirriemuir
S. Esk
Forfar
Strathmore
Pt. of Ardnamurchan
Ardgour
Loch Sunart
Glen Coe
Ballachulish
Rannoch Moor
L. Rannoch
L. Tummel
PERTH
Aberfeldy
Tay
Blairgowrie
Alyth
Isla
Tobermory
Morvern
L. Linnhe
Sound of Mull
Loch Etive
Ben Cruachan 1124
Orchy
Ben Lawers 1214
L. Tay
Dunkeld
Sidlaw Hills
Dundee
Broughty Ferry
Arbroath
NORTH SEA
Mull
Ben More 966
Staffa
Iona
Oban
Breadalbane
Killin
L. Earn
Crieff
KINROSS
Scone
Firth of Tay
Tayport
Perth
Earn
Cupar
FIFE
St. Andrews
Fife Ness
Anstruther
Ben More 1174
B. Vorlich 983
Callander
ARGYLL
B. Vorlich 942
L. Katrine
Trossachs
Ochil Hills
Kinross
Leven
Glenrothes
Lochgelly
Buckhaven
Kirkcaldy
Firth of Forth
Bass Rock
North Berwick
Dunbar
ATLANTIC OCEAN
Firth of Lorn
Inveraray
L. Awe
Ben Lomond 974
STIRLING
Forth
Dunblane
Cowdenbeath
Alloa
Dunfermline
Colonsay
Crinan
ARGYLL & BUTE
Lochgilphead
L. Lomond
Stirling
Bannockburn
Bo'ness
Rosyth
Grangemouth
Linlithgow
Leith
Prestonpans
Haddington
EAST LOTHIAN
Helensburgh
Dunoon
Dumbarton
Clydebank
Cumbernauld
Kirkintilloch
Falkirk
Edinburgh
Musselburgh
St. Abbs Hd.
Eyemouth
Rubh a' Mhail
Jura
Sound of Jura
Loch Fyne
Greenock
Port Glasgow
Renfrew
Glasgow
Airdrie
Livingston
Bathgate
Dalkeith
Penicuik
Lammermuir Hills
Pentland Hills
Tarbert
Paisley
Coatbridge
Motherwell
Wishaw
Rothesay
Bute
Johnstone
Largs
Rutherglen
E. Kilbride
Hamilton
Clyde
Carstairs
Duns
Berwick-upon-Tweed
Holy I.
Islay
Bowmore
Gigha
NORTH AYRSHIRE
Ardrossan
Saltcoats
Irvine
Kilmarnock
SOUTH LANARKSHIRE
Lanark
Peebles
Moorfoot Hills
Tweed
Galashiels
Coldstream
Flodden
Till
Port Ellen
Kintyre
Goat Fell 874
Arran
Brodick
Troon
Prestwick
EAST AYRSHIRE
Biggar
Melrose
Kelso
Selkirk
Ettrick
Broad Law 840
BORDERS
Hawick
Jedburgh
The Cheviot 816
Southern Uplands
Campbeltown
Ayr
Cumnock
Leadhills
Cheviot Hills
Coquet
Rathlin
Firth of Clyde
Sanquhar
Nith
Moffat
Teviot
Fair Hd.
Ballycastle
Mull of Kintyre
Ailsa Craig
Girvan
Dalmellington
Doon
SOUTH AYRSHIRE
Merrick 843
DUMFRIES AND GALLOWAY
Esk
Langholm
Lockerbie
Gretna Green
N. Tyne
Trostan 554
North Channel
L. Ryan
Ken
Dumfries
Annan
ENGLAND
Hexham
Galloway
NORTHERN IRELAND
Newton Stewart
Castle Douglas
Dalbeattie
Hadrian's Wall
Stranraer
Ballymena
Larne
Portpatrick
Cree
Wigtown
Gatehouse of Fleet
Kirkcudbright
Carlisle
S. Tyne
Alston
Wear
Belfast Lough
Whithorn
Luce Bay
Wigtown Bay
Solway Firth
Derwent
Penrith
Cross Fell 893
Bangor
Newtownards
Belfast
Mull of Galloway
Workington
Skiddaw 931
Ullswater
Tees
Barnard Castle
Cumbrian Mts.
SHETLAND IS.
On same scale
Unst
Yell Sound
Yell
Fetlar
SHETLAND
Whalsay
Mainland
Bressay
Foula
Scalloway
Lerwick
Sumburgh Hd.
A
B
8
ft m
3000 1000
1200 400
600 200
300 100
0 0
50 150
100 300
m ft
Projection: Conical with two standard parallels.
West from Greenwich
COPYRIGHT, GEORGE PHILIP & SON, LTD.

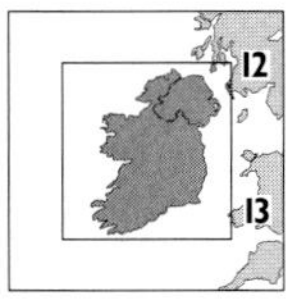
12
13

1 : 1 800 000
10 0 10 20 30 40 50 miles
10 0 10 20 30 40 50 60 70 80 km
1 2 3 4 5 6
A B C D E
ATLANTIC OCEAN
IRISH SEA
North Channel
St. George's Channel
NORTHERN IRELAND
IRELAND
ULSTER
CONNACHT
LEINSTER
MUNSTER
Kintyre
Arran
Campbeltown
Ailsa Craig
Mull of Kintyre
Stranraer
Portpatrick
Malin Hd.
Lough Swilly
Sheep Haven
Tory I.
Horn Hd.
Bloody Foreland
Gweedore
Derryveagh Mts.
Errigal 752
Aran I.
Letterkenny
DONEGAL
Gweebarra B.
Glenties
Loughros More B.
Bluestack 676
Finn
Lifford
Rossan Pt.
Rathlin O Birne I.
Killybegs
Donegal
Donegal Bay
Bundoran
Ballyshannon
Inishowen Pen.
Carndonagh
Moville
Buncrana
Giant's Causeway
Portrush
Rathlin I.
Fair Hd.
Ballycastle
Coleraine
Ballymoney
Limavady
Roe
Londonderry
Mts. of Antrim
554 Trostan
Bann
Main
Ballymena
Larne
I. Magee
Sperrin Mts.
Strabane
Sawel 683
Magherafelt
Carrickfergus
Antrim
Belfast L.
Donaghadee
Bangor
Newtownards
Cookstown
Lough Neagh 16
Belfast
Ards Pen.
Strangford L.
Deel
Mourne
Derg
Omagh
Dungannon
Lurgan (Craigavon)
Lisburn
Lagan
Erne
Lower L. Erne
Irvinestown
Blackwater
Portadown
Armagh
Banbridge
Downpatrick
Dundrum
Enniskillen
Upper L. Erne
Monaghan
Newry
Slieve Donard 852
Newcastle
Mourne Mts.
Dundrum Bay
St. Gullion 577
Warrenpoint
Clones
Castleblayney
Carlingford L.
Greenore
Dundalk
Dundalk Bay
Downpatrick Hd.
Killala B.
Broad Haven
Erris Hd.
Belmullet
Mullet Peninsula
Blacksod Bay
Killala
Ballina
Moy
Ox Mts.
Sligo B.
Sligo
Collooney
SLIGO
LEITRIM
L. Allen
L. Arrow
MONAGHAN
L. Conn
Nephin 806
Achill Hd.
Achill I.
Achill
MAYO
Leitrim
Belturbet
Annalee
Cootehill
CAVAN
Cavan
Carrickmacross
Boyle
Carrick-on-Shannon
Kingscourt
Louth
LOUTH
Castlebar
Clew Bay
Clare I.
Westport
Croagh Patrick 765
Claremorris
ROSCOMMON
Castlerea
L. Gowna
Granard
L. Sheelin
Ardee
Longford
Oldcastle
Ceanannas Mor (Kells)
Killary Harbour
Mweelrea 819
L. Mask
Inishbofin
Robe
LONGFORD
An Uaimh (Navan)
Drogheda
Balbriggan
Ballinrobe
Roscommon
L. Ree
Inny
Athboy
Trim
MEATH
Boyne
Clifden
Twelve Pins
Connemara
Tuam
Suck
Mullingar
Lambay I.
Swords
Slyne Hd.
L. Corrib
Athlone
WESTMEATH
DUBLIN
Ireland's Eye
Howth Head
GALWAY
Ballinasloe
Clara
Edenderry
Maynooth
Dublin (Baile Atha Cliath)
Clare
Brosna
Tullamore
Celbridge
Dublin Bay
Galway
Athenry
Daingean
Bog of Allen
Droichead Nua
Liffey
Naas
Dun Laoghaire
Kilkieran B.
Loughrea
OFFALY
Kippure 754
Bray
Galway Bay
Inishmore
Shannon
Portarlington
KILDARE
Kildare
Poulaphouca Res.
Aran Is.
Slieve Aughty
Gort
Portumna
Birr
Sl. Bloom
Mountmellick
Port Laoise
Wicklow Mts.
Wicklow
Wicklow Hd.
Hags Hd.
Ennistymon
L. Derg
LAOIS
Athy
Barrow
WICKLOW
Lugnaquilla 923
Liscannor Bay
Roscrea
Rathdrum
Mal Bay
CLARE
Miltown Malbay
Ennis
Ballina
Nenagh
Mizen Hd.
Carlow
Avoca
Killaloe
Keeper 694
Templemore
Nore
Tullow
Shillelagh
Arklow
Kilkee
Rineanna
Ardnacrusha
CARLOW
Kilrush
Thurles
Muine Bheag
Gorey
Limerick
TIPPERARY
Kilkenny
Mt. Leinster 796
Loop Hd.
Foynes
Vale
Cashel
KILKENNY
Slaney
Cahore Pt.
Rathkeale
Suir
R. Shannon
LIMERICK
Golden
Tipperary
Callan
Enniscorthy
Listowel
Newcastle
WEXFORD
Kerry Hd.
Feale
Rath Luirc (Charleville)
Slievenamon 721
Tralee Bay
Fenit
Galtymore 920
Galty Mts.
Caher
Carrick-on-Suir
New Ross
Brandon Bay
Wexford Harbour
Tralee
Clonmel
Wexford
Rosslare
953 Brandon Mt.
Newmarket
Mitchelstown
Comeragh Mts.
Waterford
Greenore Pt.
Sl. Mish
Knockmealdown Mts.
Tuscar Rock
Dingle
Maine
KERRY
Kanturk
Mallow
Blackwater
WATERFORD
Tramore
Carnsore Pt
Gt. Blasket I.
Laune
Fermoy
Lismore
Hook Hd.
Saltee Is.
Dunmore Hd.
Dingle Bay
Killarney
Macgillycuddy's Reeks
Boggeragh Mts.
Dungarvan
Waterford Harbour
Carrauntuohill 1040
Lakes of Killarney
Dungarvan Bay
Valentia Harbour
Valencia I.
Cahirciveen
CORK
Blarney
Youghal
Kenmare
Macroom
Lee
Cork
Midleton
Youghal Harbour
St. David's Hd.
Skellig Rocks
Passage West
Cobh
Ballinskelligs B.
Caha Mts.
Kenmare River
Glengariff
Bandon
Crosshaven
Cork Harbour
Castletown Bearhaven
Bantry
Kinsale
Bear I.
Clonakilty
Old Head of Kinsale
Crow Hd.
Bantry Bay
Skibbereen
Clonakilty Bay
Dunmanus Bay
Skull
Galley Hd
Mizen Hd.
Clear I.
Baltimore
Fastnet Rock
C. Clear
Towns underlined in Northern Ireland give their names to the Districts in which they stand
The remaining Districts are:—
1 Fermanagh
2 Moyle
3 Newtownabbey
4 North Down
5 Castlereagh
6 Ards
7 Down
8 Newry & Mourne
ft m
3000 1000
1200 400
600 200
300 100
0 0
100 300
200 600
m ft
Projection: Conical with two standard parallels.
West from Greenwich

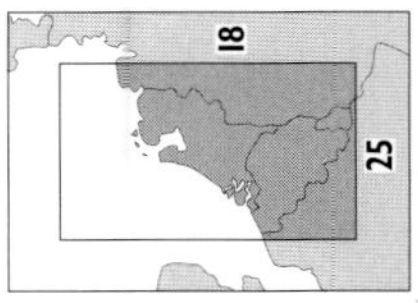
18
25

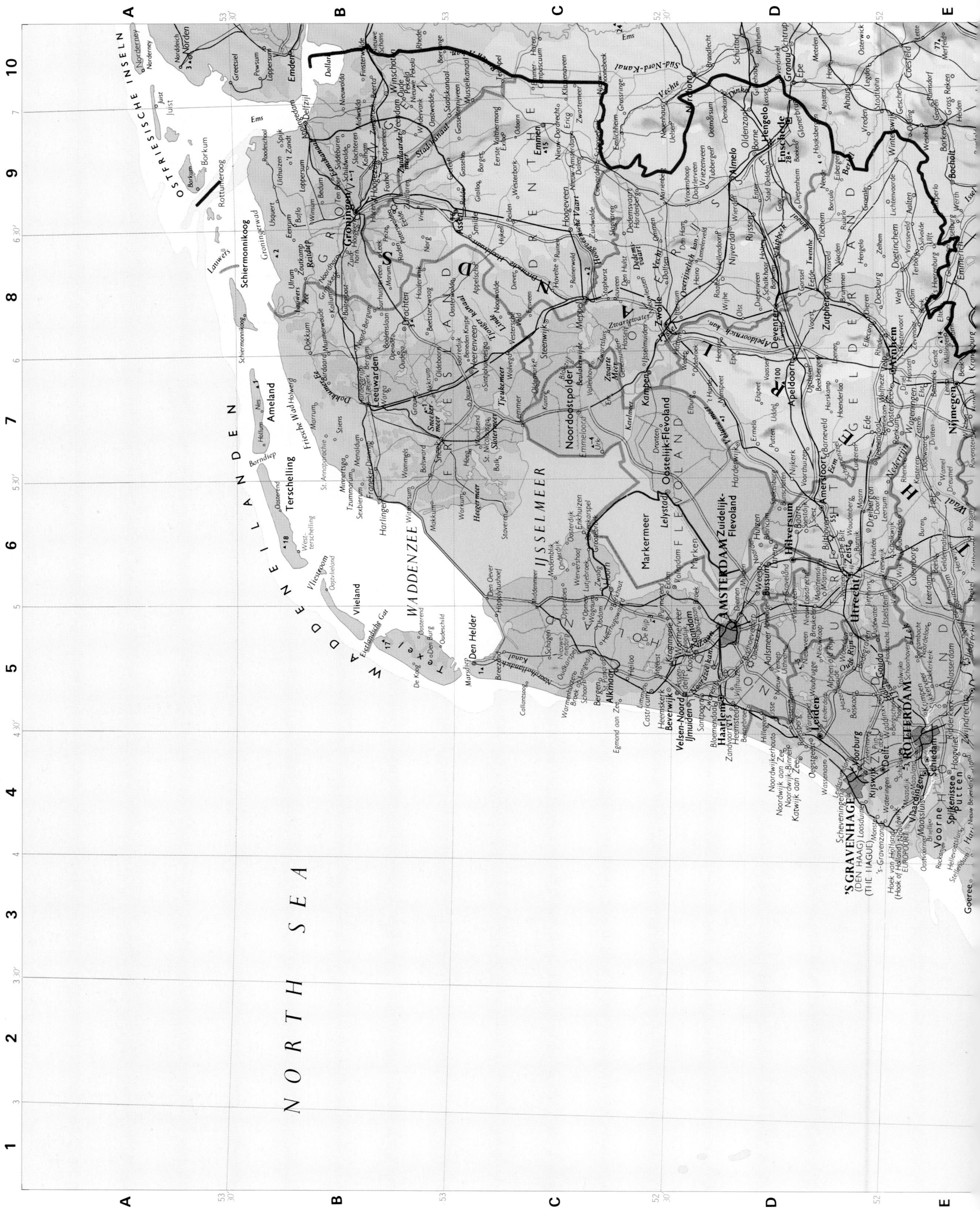
A
B
C
D
E
1
2
3
4
5
6
7
8
9
10
NORTH SEA
WADDENZEE
IJSSELMEER
OSTFRIESISCHE INSELN
WADDENEILANDEN
Markermeer
Noordoostpolder
AMSTERDAM
ROTTERDAM
'S GRAVENHAGE
(DEN HAAG)
(THE HAGUE)
Groningen
Leeuwarden
Utrecht
Arnhem
Nijmegen
Zwolle
Deventer
Apeldoorn
Enschede
Hengelo
Haarlem
Leiden
Delft
Den Helder
Texel
Vlieland
Terschelling
Ameland
Schiermonnikoog
Borkum
Emden

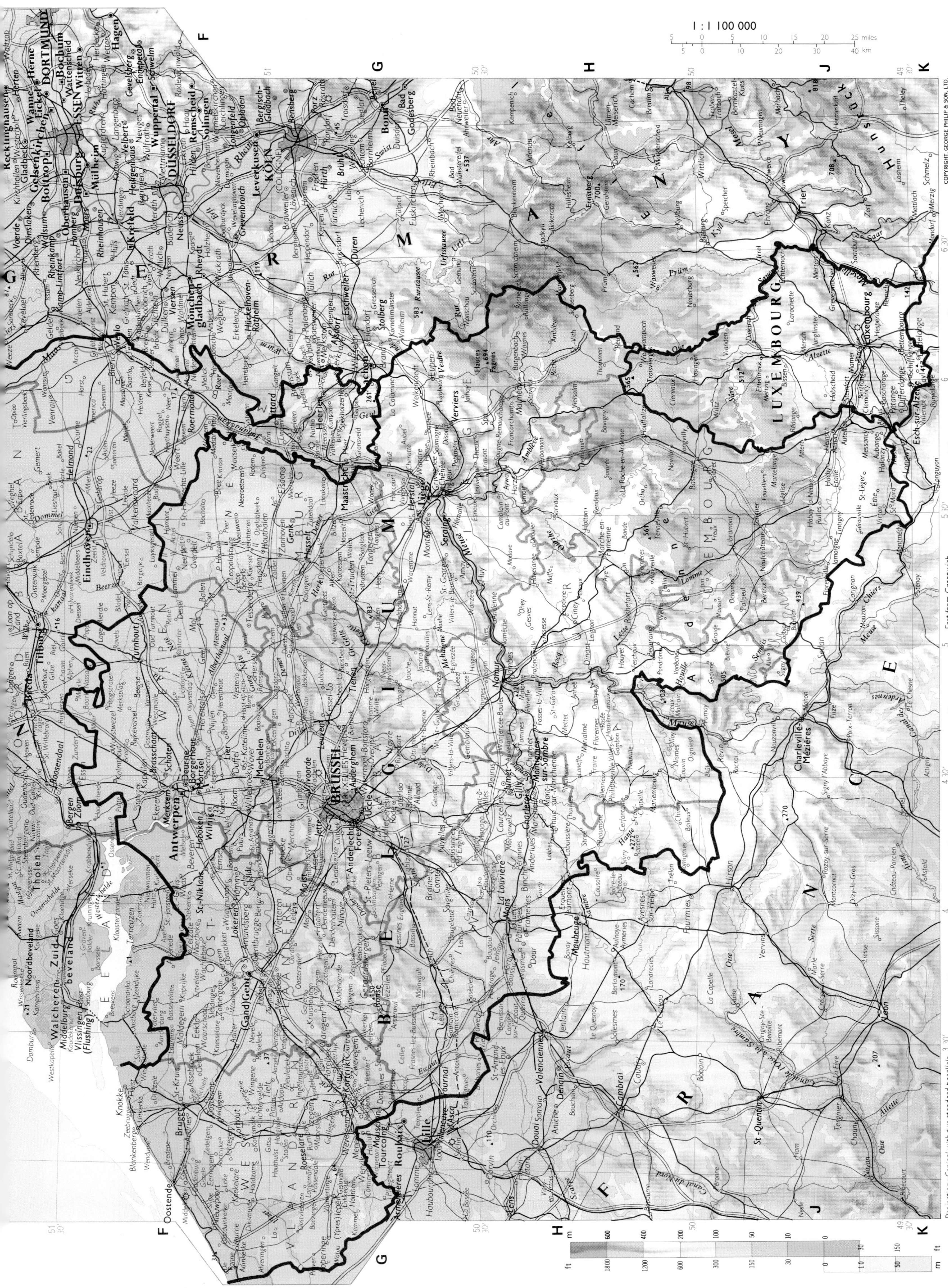
1 : 1 100 000
25 miles
40 km
BELGIUM
NEDERLAND
GERMANY
FRANCE
LUXEMBOURG
BRUSSEL (BRUXELLES)
Antwerpen
Gent
Brugge
Oostende
Liège
Namur
Charleroi
Mons
Lille
Luxembourg
Maastricht
Eindhoven
KÖLN (COLOGNE)
DÜSSELDORF
Aachen
Trier
Ardennes
East from Greenwich
Projection: Conical with two standard parallels
COPYRIGHT, GEORGE PHILIP & SON, LTD.

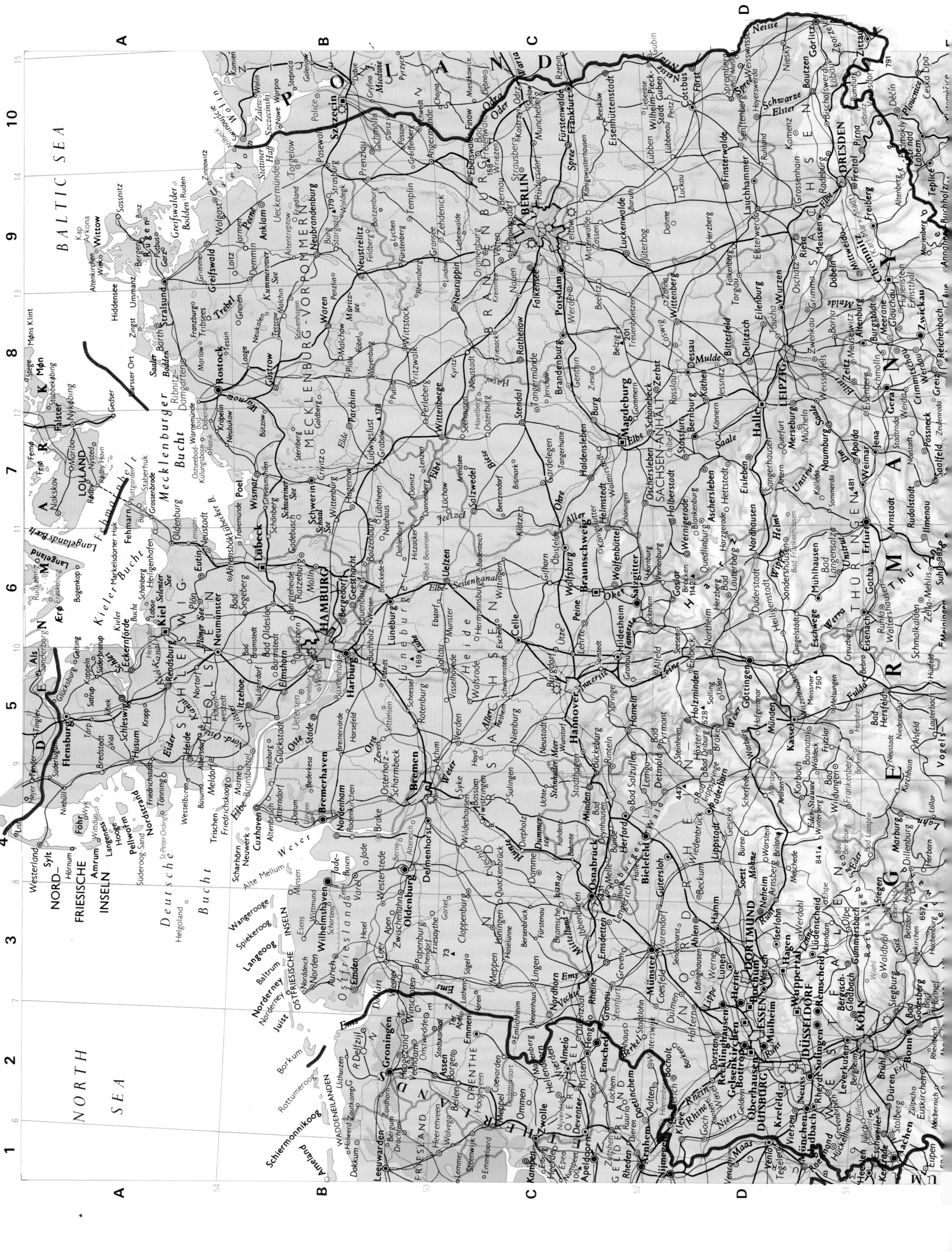
BALTIC SEA
NORTH SEA
POLAND
BERLIN
HAMBURG
DRESDEN
LEIPZIG
HANNOVER
BREMEN
MAGDEBURG
DÜSSELDORF
KÖLN
DORTMUND
ESSEN
DUISBURG
MECKLENBURG-VORPOMMERN
SCHLESWIG-HOLSTEIN
SACHSEN-ANHALT
NORDFRIESISCHE INSELN
OSTFRIESISCHE INSELN
WADDENEILANDEN

CZECH REP.
SWITZERLAND
AUSTRIA
BAYERN
BADEN WÜRTTEMBERG
SAARLAND
SLOVENIA
LUXEMBOURG
FRANKFURT
STUTTGART
MÜNCHEN
Nürnberg
Regensburg
Augsburg
Ulm
Karlsruhe
Mannheim
Heidelberg
Wiesbaden
Mainz
Darmstadt
Würzburg
Saarbrücken
Strasbourg
Mulhouse
Basel
Zürich
Bern
Luzern
Lausanne
Genève
Innsbruck
Salzburg
Linz
Plzeň
PRAHA
Bolzano
Trento
Udine
Klagenfurt
Como
Nancy
Metz
Freiburg
Konstanz
Bodensee
Donau
Rhein
Inn
Vltava
ft
m
12000
9000
6000
4500
3000
1200
600
0
4000
3000
2000
1500
1000
400
200
0
1 : 2 200 000
10 0 10 20 30 40 50 miles
10 0 10 20 30 40 50 60 70 80 km
Projection: Conical with two standard parallels.
East from Greenwich
COPYRIGHT GEORGE PHILIP & SON LTD.
F
G
H
J
K
2
3
4
5
6
7
8
9

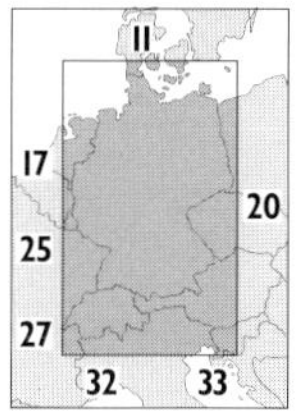

11
17
20
25
27
32
33

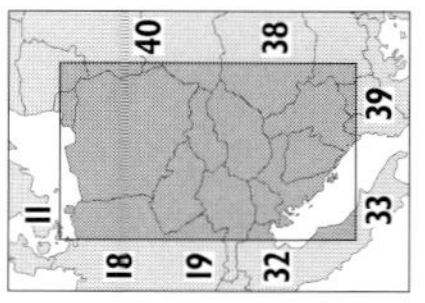
11
18
19
32
33
39
38
40

BALTIC SEA
LITHUANIA
BELARUS
UKRAINE
POLAND
GERMANY
CZECH REP.
SLOVAKIA
DENMARK
Kaliningrad (Russia)
Hrodna
Brest
Lviv
WARSZAWA (Warsaw)
BERLIN
PRAHA
DRESDEN
LEIPZIG
KRAKÓW
KATOWICE
ŁÓDŹ
WROCŁAW
Poznań
Gdańsk
Gdynia
Szczecin (Stettin)
Bydgoszcz
Toruń
Białystok
Lublin
Olsztyn
Rzeszów
Ostrava
Brno
Plzeň
Košice
Rostock
Potsdam
Frankfurt
Chemnitz
Wisła (Vistula)
Odra
Oder
Warta
Bug
San
Labe (Elbe)
Vltava
Sudety
Mazurskie
Karpaty
Beskydy
Nízke Tatry
Bayerischer Wald

1 : 3 100 000
miles
km
HUNGARY
ROMANIA
YUGOSLAVIA
CROATIA
SLOVENIA
BOSNIA-
HERZEGOVINA
MONTENEGRO
MACEDONIA
ALBANIA
BULGARIA
ITALY
ADRIATIC SEA
BUDAPEST
BEOGRAD
Zagreb
Ljubljana
Sarajevo
WIEN
Bratislava
Inter-entity boundaries as agreed at the 1995 Dayton Peace Agreement
East from Greenwich
Projection: Conical with two standard parallels
COPYRIGHT GEORGE PHILIP & SON, LTD
m
ft

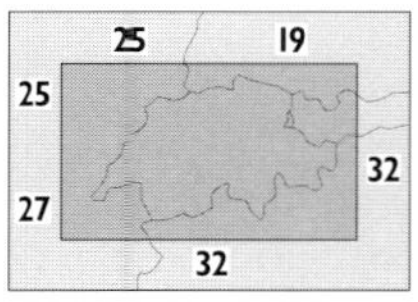

25
19
25
32
27
32

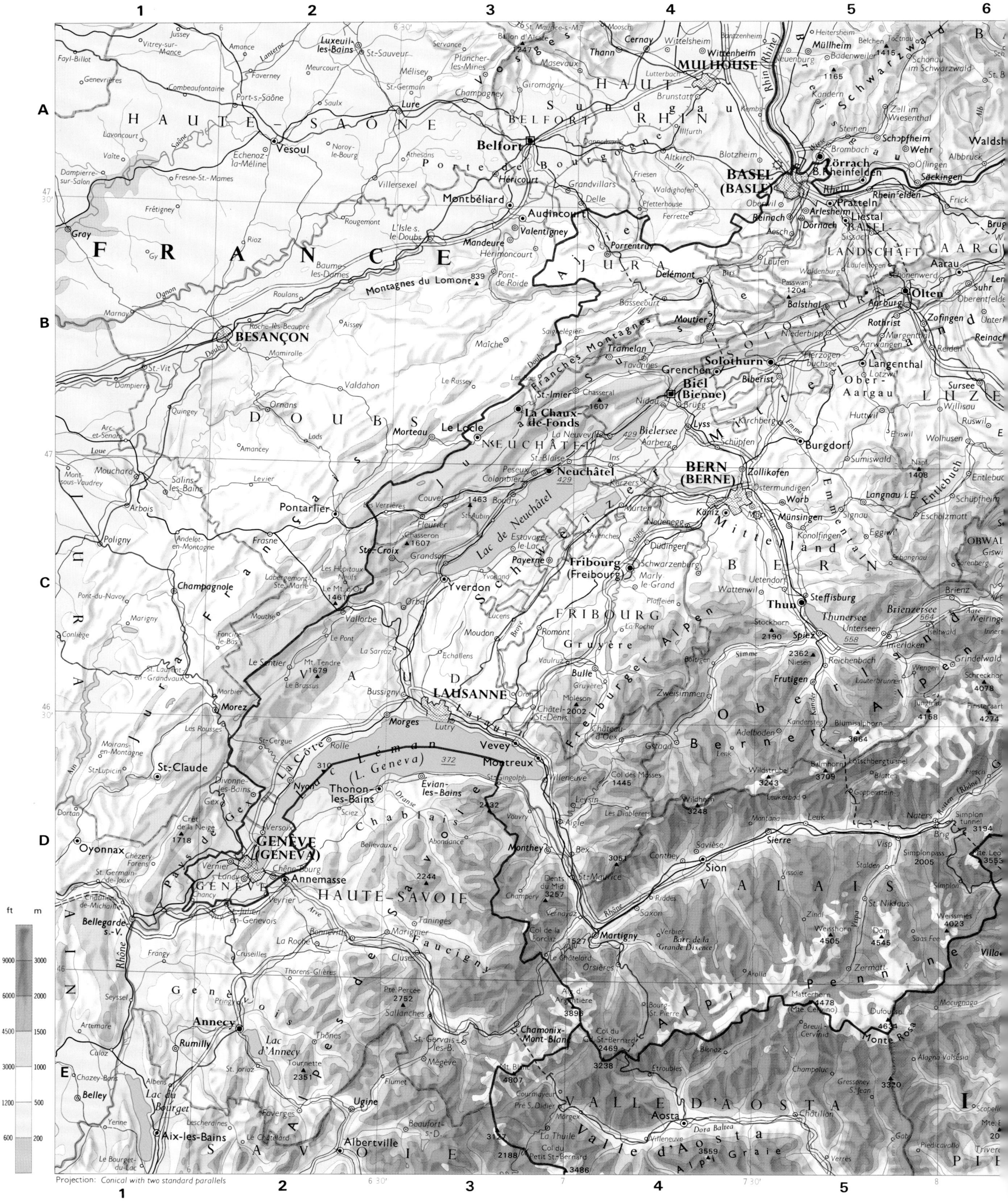

1
2
3
4
5
6
A
B
C
D
E
FRANCE
HAUTE-SAÔNE
DOUBS
JURA
HAUTE-SAVOIE
SAVOIE
VALLE D'AOSTA
HAUT-RHIN
BELFORT
NEUCHÂTEL
VAUD
FRIBOURG
BERN
SOLOTHURN
BASEL-LANDSCHAFT
VALAIS
GENÈVE
Vesoul
Belfort
Montbéliard
Audincourt
Valentigney
Hericourt
BESANÇON
Pontarlier
Morteau
Le Locle
La Chaux-de-Fonds
Neuchâtel
BERN (BERNE)
Biel (Bienne)
Solothurn
Grenchen
Burgdorf
Langenthal
Olten
Aarau
Delémont
Porrentruy
BASEL (BASLE)
MULHOUSE
Lörrach
Fribourg (Freiburg)
Thun
Spiez
Interlaken
LAUSANNE
Yverdon
Morges
Vevey
Montreux
Nyon
GENÈVE (GENEVA)
Annemasse
Thonon-les-Bains
Évian-les-Bains
Monthey
Aigle
Martigny
Sion
Sierre
Brig
Visp
Zermatt
Chamonix-Mont-Blanc
Annecy
Aix-les-Bains
Albertville
Aosta
St.-Claude
Oyonnax
Morez
Champagnole
Gray
Lac Léman (L. Geneva)
Lac de Neuchâtel
Bielersee
Thunersee
Brienzersee
Lac d'Annecy
Lac du Bourget
Montagnes du Lomont
Franches Montagnes
Schweizer Mittelland
Freiburger Alpen
Berner Alpen
Alpi Pennine
Alpi Graie
Schwarzwald
Sundgau
Porte de Bourgogne
Chablais
Faucigny
Genevois
Mt. Blanc 4807
Matterhorn (Mte. Cervino) 4478
Dufourspitze 4634
Monte Rosa
Dom 4545
Weisshorn 4505
Jungfrau 4158
Finsteraarhorn 4274
Schreckhorn 4078
Weissmies 4023
Chasseron 1607
Chasseral 1607
Mt. Tendre 1679
Le Mt. d'Or 1461
Dents du Midi 3257
Wildstrubel 3243
Balmhorn 3709
Blümlisalphorn 3664
Wildhorn 3248
Col du Gd. St.-Bernard 2469
Simplonpass 2005
Simplon tunnel
Lötschbergtunnel
Col des Mosses 1445
Col de la Forclaz 1527
Crêt de la Neige 1718
Rhône
Rhein (Rhine)
Doubs
Saône
Aare
Emme
Dora Baltea
ft m
9000 3000
6000 2000
4500 1500
3000 1000
1200 500
600 200
Projection: Conical with two standard parallels

1 : 900 000
miles
km
GERMANY
AUSTRIA
BAYERN
VORARLBERG
TIROL
THURGAU
ZÜRICH
SCHWYZ
GLARUS
APPENZELL
GRAUBÜNDEN
TICINO
LOMBARDIA
LIECHTENSTEIN
ZÜRICH
Winterthur
Schaffhausen
Konstanz
Friedrichshafen
Lindau
Bregenz
Dornbirn
Feldkirch
Vaduz
St. Gallen
Chur
Davos
St. Moritz
Zug
Schwyz
Altdorf
Glarus
Landeck
Imst
Kempten
Füssen
Ravensburg
Weingarten
Bellinzona
Locarno
Lugano
Como
Lecco
Varese
Verbania
Gallarate
BÉRGAMO
Sóndrio
Tirano
Chiavenna
Bodensee (L. Constance)
Zürichsee
Walensee
Lago Maggiore
Lago di Lugano
Lago di Como
Lago d'Iseo
Lago d'Idro
Lago di Garda
Allgäuer Alpen
Lechtaler Alpen
Ötztaler Alpen
Glarner Alpen
Urner Alpen
Lepontine Alpen
Adula-Gruppe
Silvretta-Gruppe
Rätikon
Montafon
Prätigau
Oberland
Unter Engadin
Ober Engadin
National-Park
Alpi Retiche
Alpi Orobie
Valtellina
Val Camonica
Brianza
Bregenzer Wald
Vinschgau
Giudicarie
East from Greenwich
COPYRIGHT, GEORGE PHILIP & SON, LTD.

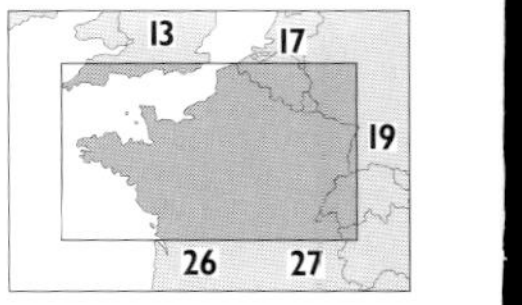

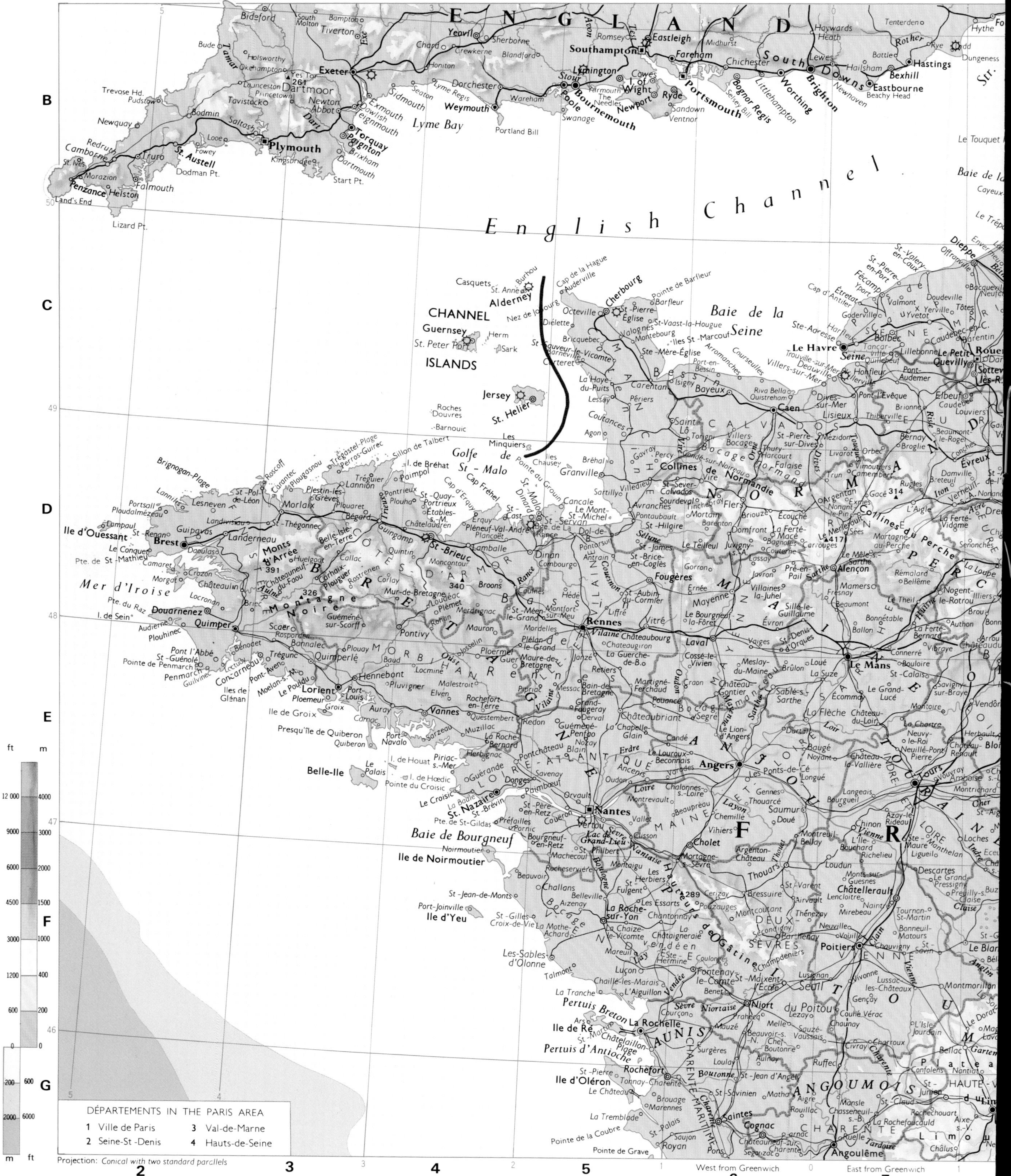

Projection: *Conical with two standard parallels*

ENGLAND

English Channel

CHANNEL
ISLANDS

Guernsey
St. Peter Port
Alderney
Jersey
St. Helier

Mer d'Iroise

Baie de la Seine

Golfe de St-Malo

NORMANDIE

BRETAGNE

MORBIHAN

Baie de Bourgneuf

Ile de Noirmoutier

Ile d'Yeu

Les-Sables-d'Olonne

Pertuis Breton
Ile de Ré
La Rochelle
Pertuis d'Antioche
Ile d'Oléron

FRANCE

ANJOU

MAINE

POITOU

AUNIS

ANGOUMOIS

CHARENTE

Brest
Quimper
Lorient
Vannes
St. Nazaire
Nantes
Rennes
Le Mans
Angers
Cholet
La Roche-sur-Yon
Niort
Poitiers
Rochefort
Cognac
Angoulême
Saintes

Plymouth
Exeter
Torquay
Penzance
Southampton
Portsmouth
Bournemouth
Weymouth
Hastings
Eastbourne
Brighton

Le Havre
Cherbourg
Caen
Bayeux
Avranches
Le Mont-St-Michel
Granville
St-Brieuc
Morlaix
Lannion
Dinan
Fougères
Laval
Alençon

DÉPARTEMENTS IN THE PARIS AREA
1 Ville de Paris 3 Val-de-Marne
2 Seine-St-Denis 4 Hauts-de-Seine

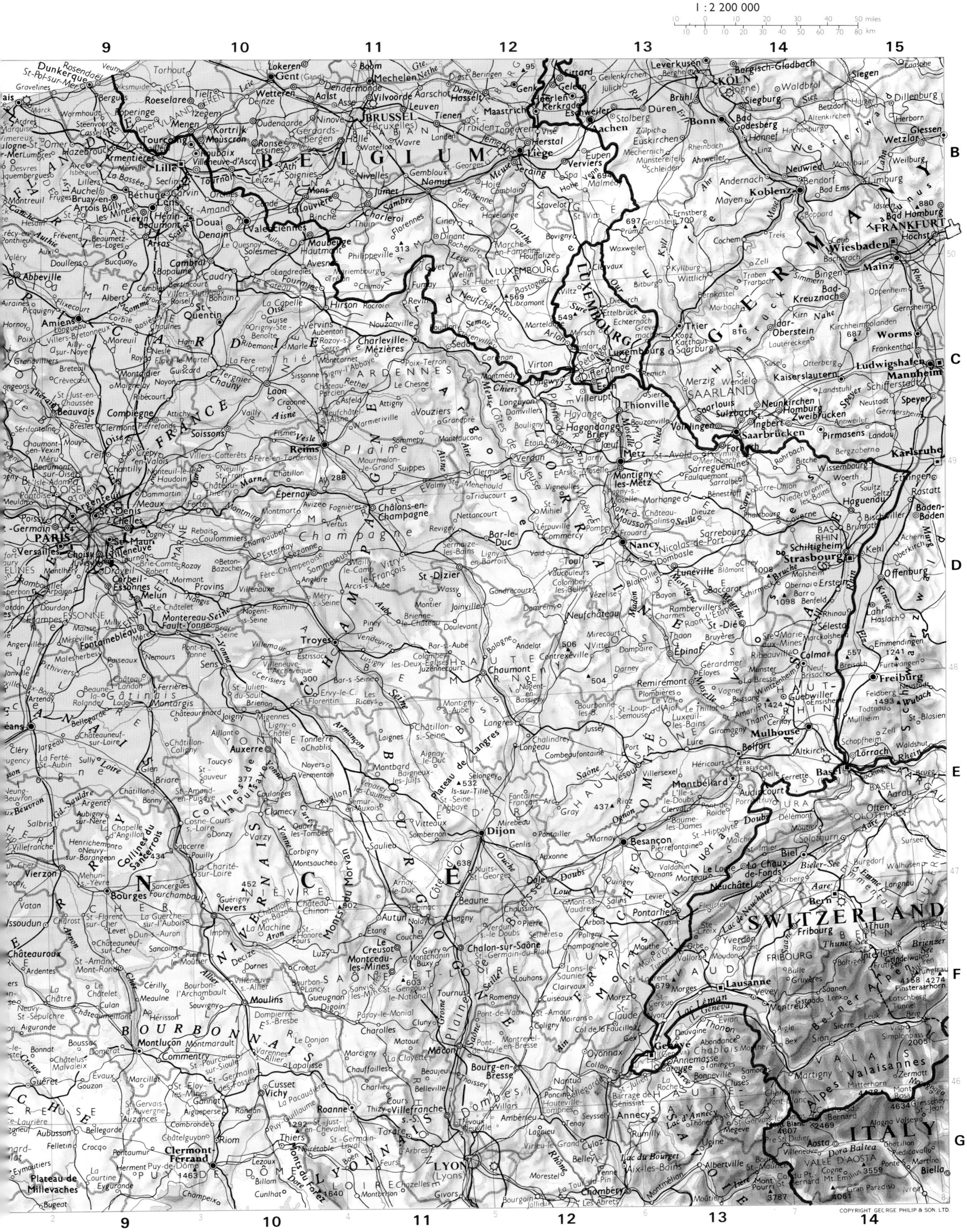
1 : 2 200 000
10 0 10 20 30 40 50 miles
10 0 10 20 30 40 50 60 70 80 km
9
10
11
12
13
14
15
B
C
D
E
F
G
BELGIUM
FRANCE
LUXEMBOURG
GERMANY
SWITZERLAND
ITALY
BRUSSEL
(Bruxelles)
PARIS
LUXEMBOURG
Lille
Gent
Liège
Aachen
Köln
Bonn
Koblenz
FRANKFURT
Wiesbaden
Mainz
Reims
Metz
Nancy
Strasbourg
Mannheim
Karlsruhe
Saarbrücken
Trier
Dijon
Besançon
Mulhouse
Basel
Freiburg
Bern
Lausanne
Genève
LYON
(Lyons)
Clermont-Ferrand
Troyes
Orléans
Bourges
Nevers
Amiens
Dunkerque
Valenciennes
Charleville-Mézières
Épernay
Châlons-en-Champagne
Chaumont
Épinal
Colmar
Belfort
Neuchâtel
Annecy
Chambéry
Aosta
Champagne
ARDENNES
Plateau de Langres
Côte d'Or
Monts du Morvan
Dombes
SAARLAND
BOURBONNAIS
Plateau de Millevaches
Lac Léman
(L. Geneva)
Alpes Valaisannes
Berner Alpen
Mont Blanc
4807
Matterhorn
4478
COPYRIGHT GEORGE PHILIP & SON. LTD.

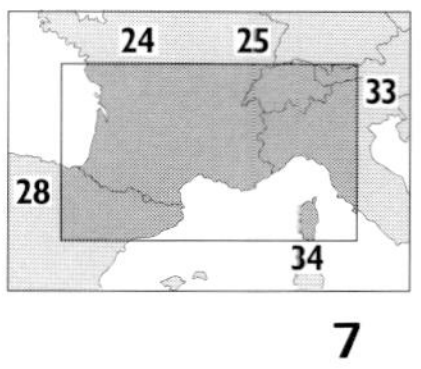
24
25
33
28
34

1
2
3
4
5
6
7
B
C
D
E
F
G
ATLANTIC
OCEAN
Golfe de
Gascogne
Ile de Noirmoutier
Ile d'Yeu
Ile de Ré
Ile d'Oléron
Pertuis Breton
Pertuis d'Antioche
Bassin d'Arcachon
Étang d'Hourtin et de Carcans
Étang de Lacanau
Étang de Cazaux et de Sanguinet
Étang de Biscarrosse et de Parentis
Cholet
La Roche-sur-Yon
Les Sables-d'Olonne
Poitiers
Châtellerault
Niort
La Rochelle
Rochefort
Saintes
Cognac
Angoulême
Limoges
Châteauroux
Bourges
Nevers
Montluçon
Moulins
Vichy
Clermont-Ferrand
Périgueux
Brive-la-Gaillarde
Tulle
Aurillac
Bordeaux
Bègles
Libourne
Bergerac
Agen
Cahors
Rodez
Millau
Montauban
Albi
Castres
Toulouse
Carcassonne
Narbonne
Béziers
Perpignan
Pau
Tarbes
Lourdes
Bayonne
Biarritz
Dax
Auch
Foix
Pamplona
Huesca
Zaragoza (Saragossa)
Lérida
Manresa
Gerona
Figueras
San Sebastián
ANDORRA
POITOU
ANGOUMOIS
LIMOUSIN
MARCHE
BERRY
BOURBONNAIS
AUVERGNE
SAINTONGE
AUNIS
GASCOGNE
GUYENNE
LANGUEDOC
ROUSSILLON
BÉARN
NAVARRE
NAVARRA
ARAGON
CATALUÑA
SPAIN
FRANCE
Plateau de Millevaches
Puy de Sancy 1885
Plomb du Cantal 1858
Pic de Vignemale 3303
Pico de Aneto 3404
Pic d'Estats 3141
Pic de Montcalm 3080
Pic Carlit 2921
Sierra de la Peña
Sierra de Guara 2077
Sierra del Cadi 2557
Causse Méjean
Mts de Lacaune
Monts Dore
PYRÉNÉES-ATLANTIQUES
HAUTES-PYRÉNÉES
PYRÉNÉES-ORIENTALES
Golfe
Cabo de Creus
Cap Béar
ft
m
12,000
4000
9000
3000
6000
2000
4500
1500
3000
1000
1200
400
600
200
0
0
200
600
2000
6000
Projection: Conical with two standard parallels
West from Greenwich
East from Greenwich
47
46
45
44
42

1 : 2 200 000
10 0 10 20 30 40 50 miles
10 0 10 20 30 40 50 60 70 80 km
8 9 10 11 12 13 14
B
C
D
E
F
G
SWITZERLAND
FRANCHE COMTÉ
BOURGOGNE
RHÔNE
ALPES
HAUTE-SAVOIE
SAVOIE
ISÈRE
DAUPHINÉ
DRÔME
HAUTES-ALPES
ALPES-DE-HAUTE-PROVENCE
ALPES-MARITIMES
VAUCLUSE
BOUCHES-DU-RHÔNE
PROVENCE
VAR
VALAIS
VAUD
FRIBOURG
BERN
GRAUBÜNDEN
TICINO
ITALY
PIEMONTE
LIGURIA
VALLE D'AOSTA
LOMBARDIA
Alpes Valaisannes
Alpi Orobie
Alpi Apuane
Alpes Maritimes
Appennino Ligure
Riviera
Côte d'Azur
Golfo di Génova
LIGURIAN SEA
MEDITERRANEAN SEA
Lion
ILES D'HYÈRES
CORSE (CORSICA)
HAUTE CORSE
CORSE DU SUD
Lac Léman (Lake Geneva)
Lac de Neuchâtel
Lac d'Annecy
Lac du Bourget
Lago Maggiore
L. di Como
L. d'Iseo
L. d'Orta
L. di Lugano
Thuner See
Brienzer See
Vierwaldstätter See
Zuger See
Bieler-See
Rhône
Rhein
Isère
Durance
Verdon
Po
Ticino
Adda
Sesia
Tanaro
Var
LYON
Genève
Lausanne
Bern
Luzern
Fribourg
Neuchâtel
Grenoble
Chambéry
Annecy
Valence
Avignon
Arles
Aix-en-Provence
MARSEILLE
Toulon
Hyères
Fréjus
Cannes
Antibes
Grasse
Nice
MONACO
Menton
San Remo
Impéria
Savona
GENOVA (Genoa)
Rapallo
La Spezia
Carrara
Massa
Livorno
Pietrasanta
Viareggio
TORINO (Turin)
MILANO (Milan)
Bergamo
Brescia
Cremona
Piacenza
Parma
Pavia
Novara
Vercelli
Biella
Asti
Alessandria
Cuneo
Aosta
Mont Blanc 4807
Matterhorn 4478
Monte Rosa 4634
Gran Paradiso 4061
Barre des Écrins 4103
Bastia
Ajaccio
Calvi
Corte
Porto-Vecchio
Bonifacio
Sartène
Monte Cinto 2710
Elba
Capraia
Gorgona
Pianosa
C. Corse
▼ 2940
COPYRIGHT, GEORGE PHILIP & SON, LTD.

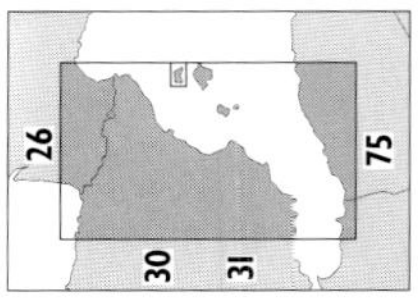
26
75
30
31

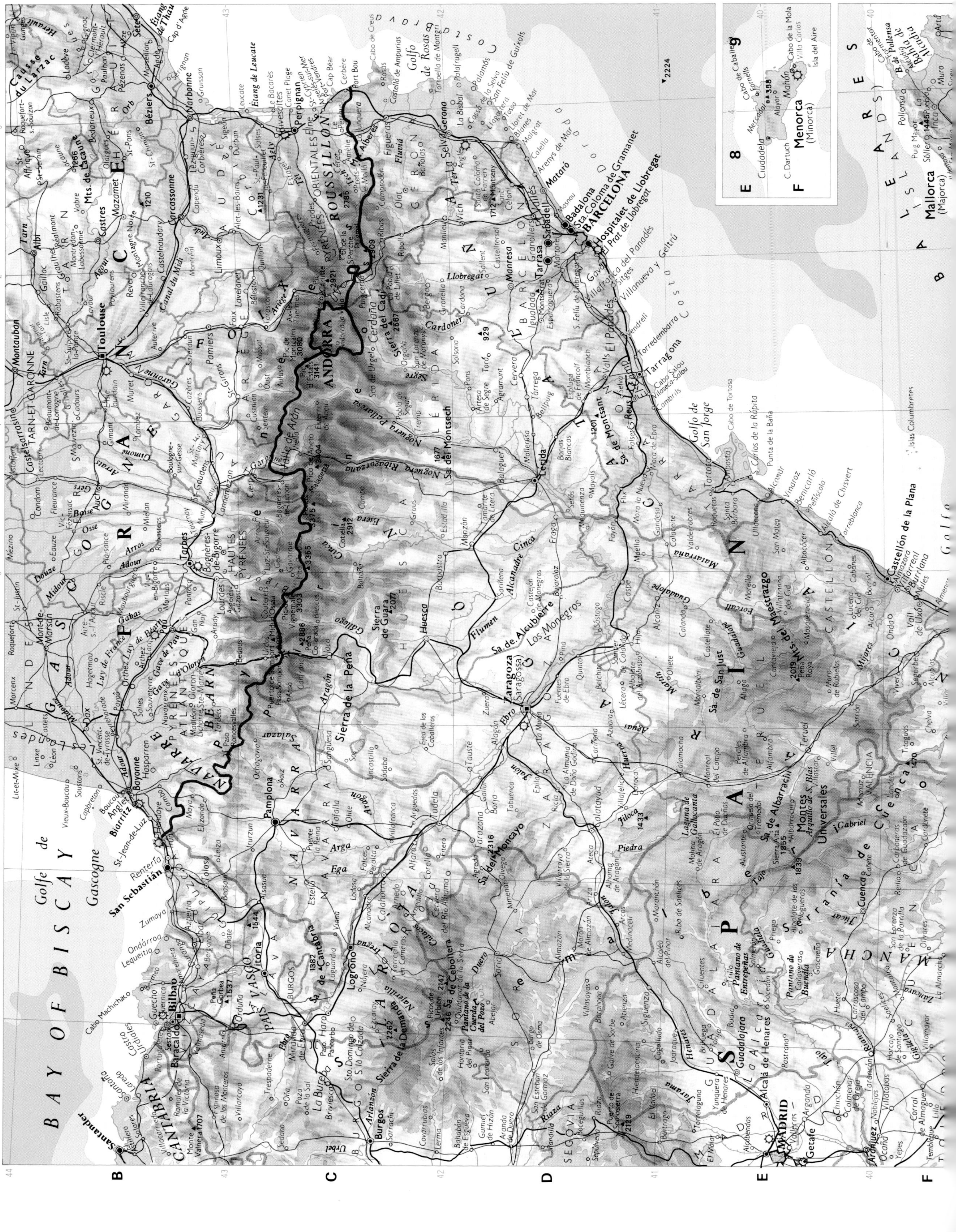
BAY OF BISCAY
Golfe de Gascogne
PAÍS VASCO
NAVARRA
LA RIOJA
CANTABRIA
ARAGÓN
CATALUÑA
ANDORRA
PYRÉNÉES ORIENTALES
ROUSSILLON
HAUTES PYRÉNÉES
PYRÉNÉES ATLANTIQUES
ISLAS BALEARES
Menorca (Minorca)
Mallorca (Majorca)
Golfo de San Jorge
Golfo de Rosas
Zaragoza
Pamplona
San Sebastián
Bilbao
Vitoria
Logroño
Burgos
Santander
Huesca
Lérida
Tarragona
BARCELONA
Gerona
Toulouse
Perpignan
Carcassonne
Narbonne
Béziers
Bayonne
Biarritz
Tarbes
Lourdes
Madrid
Guadalajara
Teruel
Cuenca
Castellón de la Plana
Sierra de la Peña
Sa. de Alcubierre
Los Monegros
Montes Universales
Serranía de Cuenca
Sierra de la Demanda
Sa. del Moncayo
Sa. de Cebollera
Sierra de Guara
MANCHA
Sierra del Cadí
Mts. de Lacaune
Montagne Noire

1 : 2 200 000
miles
km
MEDITERRANEAN SEA
ALGERIA
MOROCCO
Valencia
ALGER (Algiers)
ORAN
Mostaganem
Sidi-Bel-Abbès
Mascara
Tiaret
Blida
Boufarik
Koléa
Médéa
Berrouaghia
Ech Cheliff
Khemis Miliana
Miliana
Ighil Izane
Mohammadia
Sig
Aïn Témouchent
Melilla (Sp.)
Nador
Alborán (Sp.)
Murcia
Cartagena
Alicante
Elche
Albacete
Almería
Granada
Guadix
Lorca
Benidorm
Alcoy
Orihuela
Linares
Ubeda
Valdepeñas
Manzanares
Tomelloso
Daimiel
Sierra Nevada
Sierra Morena
Sierra de Segura
Sierra de Alcaraz
Sa. de los Filabres
Sierra de Gádor
Las Alpujarras
Golfo de Mazarrón
Golfo de Almería
Mar Menor
Ibiza (Iviza)
Formentera
Cabrera
C. Tres Forcas
C. Falcon
C. Caxine
C. Kramis
Cabo de Gata
Cabo de Palos
Cabo de la Nao
Cabo de San Antonio
Cabo Sacratif
2850
ft
m
9000
6000
4500
3000
1200
600
0
200
2000
3000
2000
1500
1000
400
200
0
200
600
2000
6000
F
G
H
J
K
1
2
3
4
5
6
7
8
West from Greenwich
East from Greenwich
Projection: Conical with two standard parallels
COPYRIGHT, GEORGE PHILIP & SON, LTD.

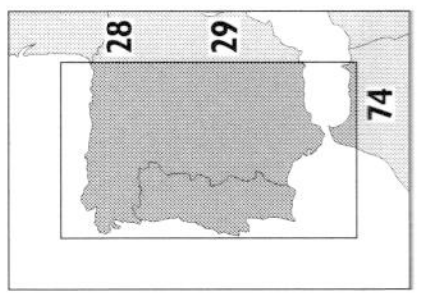
28
29
74

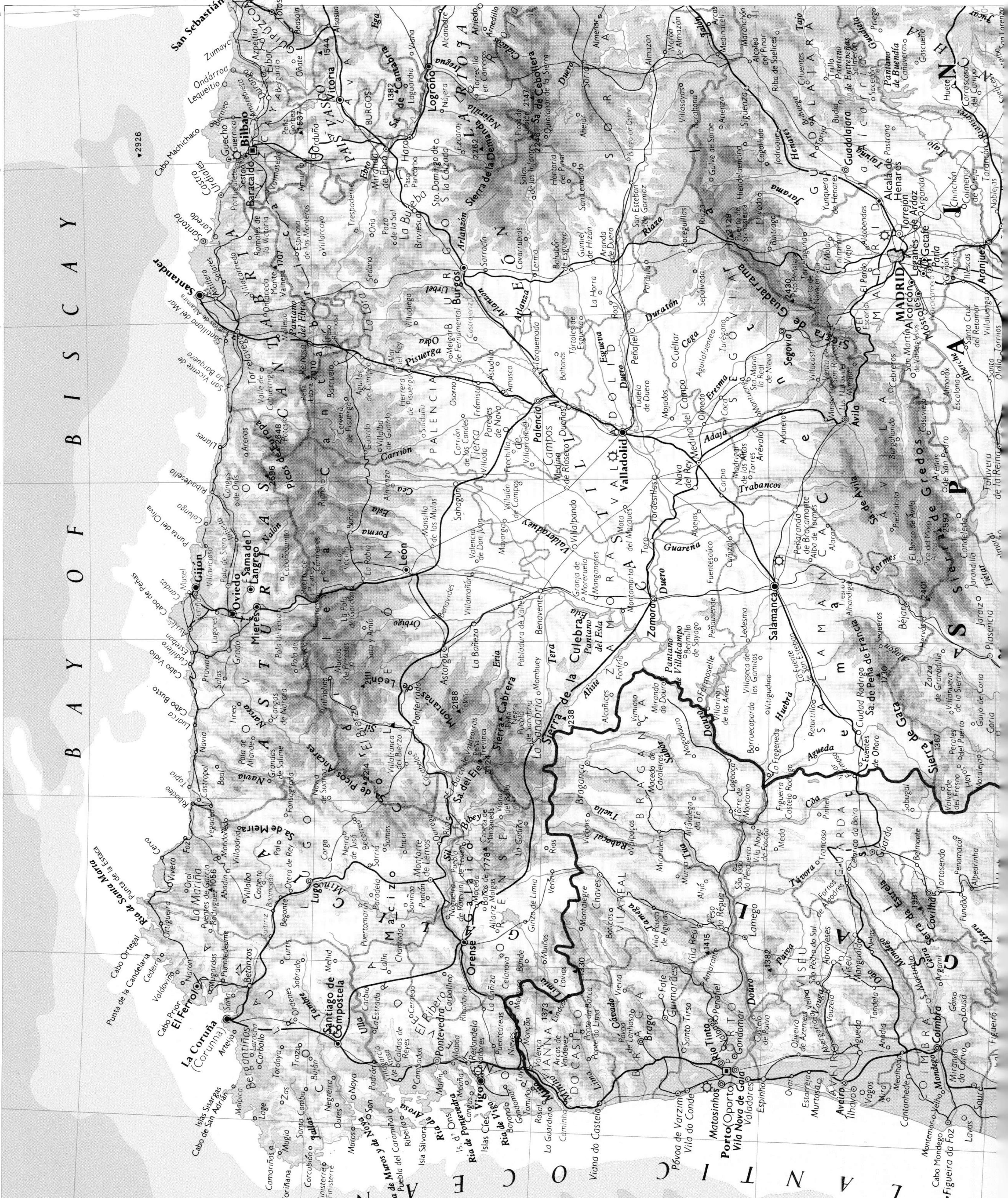
BAY OF BISCAY
ATLANTIC OCEAN
San Sebastián
Bilbao
Santander
Gijón
Oviedo
La Coruña
El Ferrol
Santiago de Compostela
Lugo
Orense
Vigo
Porto (Oporto)
Vila Nova de Gaia
Braga
Coimbra
Aveiro
León
Burgos
Valladolid
Salamanca
Zamora
Segovia
Ávila
MADRID
Vitoria
Logroño
Palencia

1 : 2 200 000

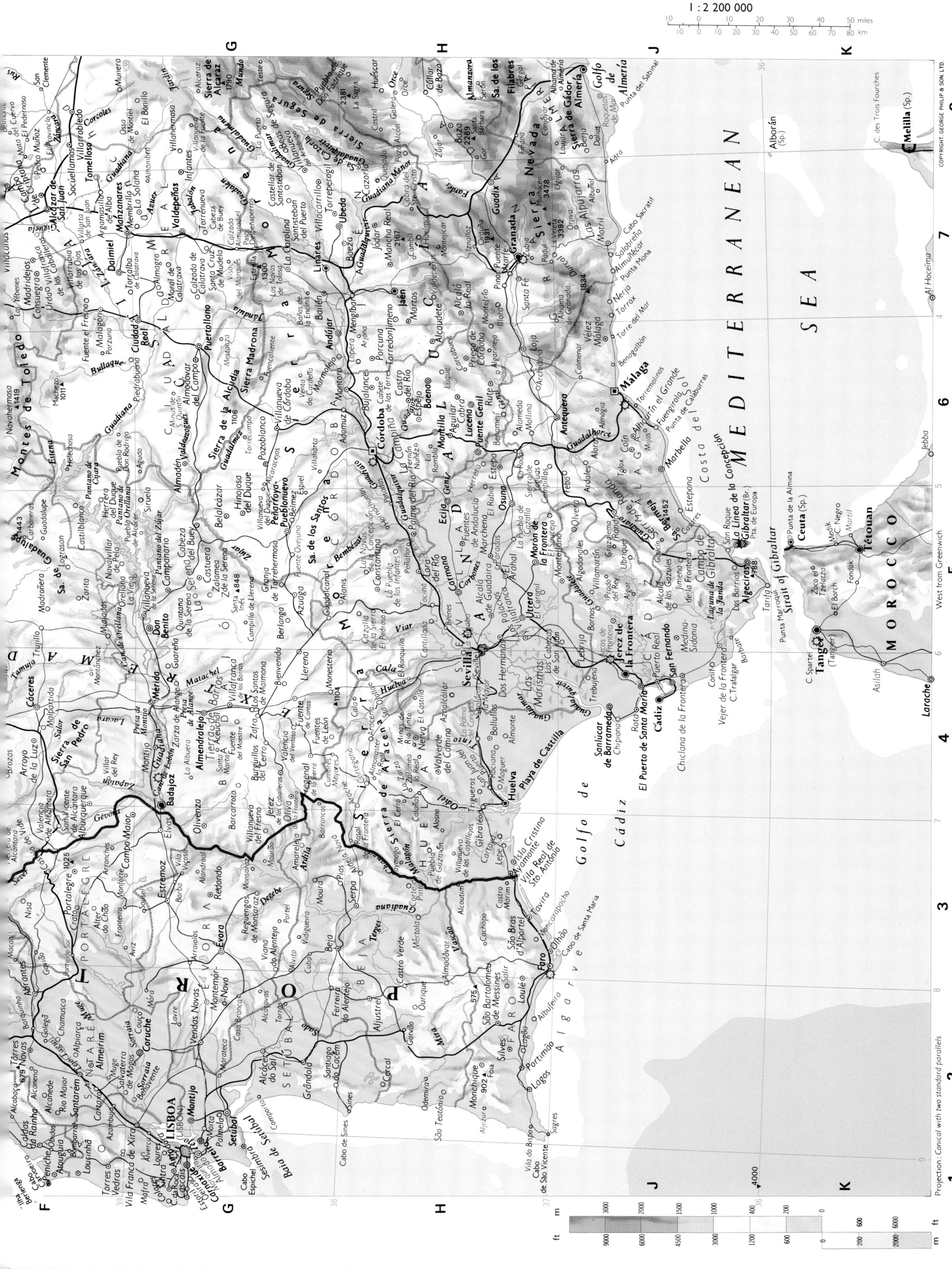

MEDITERRANEAN SEA
Golfo de Cádiz
MOROCCO
Strait of Gibraltar
Costa del Sol
Sierra Nevada
Sierra Morena
Montes de Toledo
LISBOA (LISBON)
Sevilla
Córdoba
Granada
Málaga
Cádiz
Huelva
Badajoz
Almería
Gibraltar (Br.)
Ceuta (Sp.)
Melilla (Sp.)
Tanger (Tangier)
Tétouan
Faro
Évora
Setúbal
Mérida
Cáceres
Ciudad Real
Jaén
Algarve
ALENTEJO
West from Greenwich
Projection: Conical with two standard parallels
COPYRIGHT, GEORGE PHILIP & SON, LTD.

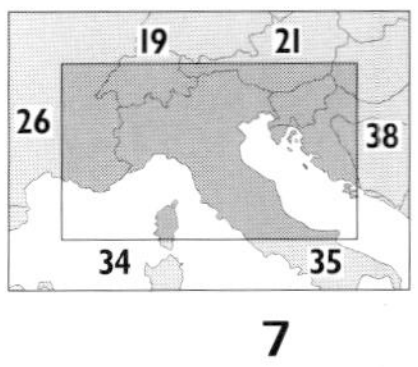
19
21
26
38
34
35

SWITZERLAND
FRANCE
LIGURIAN SEA
Golfo di Génova
CORSE
(CORSICA)
Riviera di Ponente
Riviera di Levante
Côte d'Azur
ILES D'HYERES
Arcipelago Toscano
Bern
Lausanne
Genève
Luzern
Lyon (Lyons)
Grenoble
Chambéry
Annecy
TORINO (Turin)
MILANO (Milan)
GENOVA (Genoa)
Nice
MONACO
Marseille (Marseilles)
Toulon
Avignon
Aix-en-Provence
Bastia
Ajaccio
Livorno (Leghorn)
La Spezia
Parma
Bergamo
Brescia
Cremona
Piacenza
Pavia
Novara
Alessándria
Asti
Cúneo
Savona
San Remo
Aosta
Lago Maggiore
L. di Como
L. d'Orta
Lac du Bourget
Lac d'Annecy
Lac Léman (L. Genève)
Mont Blanc 4807
Matterhorn
Monte Rosa 4634
Gran Paradiso 4061
VALAIS
TICINO
GRAUBÜNDEN
SAVOIE
HAUTE-SAVOIE
PIEMONTE
LOMBARDIA
EMILIA
TOSCANA
HAUTE-CORSE
CORSE-DU-SUD
PROVENCE
VAUCLUSE
BOUCHES-DU-RHÔNE
ALPES-DE-HAUTE-PROVENCE
ALPES MARITIMES
HAUTES ALPES
DRÔME
ISÈRE
Rhône
Po
Durance
Elba
Capraia
Gorgona
Pianosa
Montecristo
Giglio
2650
A
B
C
D
E
F
G
1
2
3
4
5
6
7
m
ft
12 000
9000
6000
4500
3000
1200
600
0
4000
3000
2000
1500
1000
400
200
200
2000
600
6000
Projection: Conical with two standard parallels
East from Greenwich

---- Inter-entity boundaries as agreed at the 1995 Dayton Peace Agreement

SOUTHERN ITALY

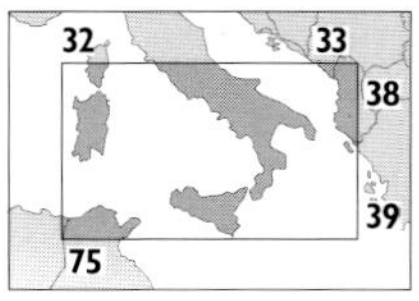

1
2
3
4
5
6
A
B
C
D
E
Iles Sanguinaires
G. d'Ajaccio
C. di Muro
Petreto
Taravo
Incudine
2136
Zonza
Levie
Solenzara
Favone
CORSE
CORSICA
G. de Valinco
Propriano
Sartène
Porto-Vecchio
CORSE-DU-SUD
Iles Cerbicales
Bonifacio
I. de Cavallo
Bouches de Bonifacio
Maddalena
Santa Teresa Gallura
La Maddalena
Caprera
Asinara
Punta dello Scorno
Golfo dell' Asinara
Pto. Cervo
Arzachena
Costa Smeralda
Coghinas
Àggius
Tèmpio Pausania
Calangianus
Golfo Aranci
G. di Ólbia
Ólbia
Tavolara
Porto Tórres
Sorso
Sennori
1362
M. Limbara
Sássari
Ósilo
C. dell'Argentiera
Óschiri
L. di Coghinas
Tanaunella
Fertilia
Ittiri
Alghero
Ozieri
Posada
Villanova Monteleone
Pattada
Buddusò
Siniscola
1259
Bonorva
Tirso
Bitti
C. Comino
Orune
Bosa
Temo
Núoro
Dorgali
Macomer
Oliena
Golfo di Orosei
SARDEGNA
Cedrino
Ghilarza
L. del Tirso
Fonni
C. Mannu
Sorgono
Monti del Gennargentu
1834
Baunei
C. di Monte Santu
Cabras
Oristano
SARDEGNA
Golfo di Oristano
Láconi
M. Arci
812
Arbatax
Lanusei
Arborea
Terralba
Nurri
Jerzu
Campidano
S. Gavino Monreale
Mannu
Mándas
Flumendosa
SARDINIA
Gúspini
Arbus
Sanluri
C. Pécora
1236
Gonnosfanádiga
Villacidro
Senorbì
Fluminimaggiore
M. Linas
Serramanna
S. Vito
Villaputzu
Iglésias
Cixerri
Dolianova
Muravera
Sestu
Pta. Serpeddi
1069
Portoscuso
Gonnesa
Assemini
Sinnai
Siliqua
Selárgius
C. Ferrato
Carloforte
Carbonia
1116
Quartu Sant'Elena
San Pietro
Santadi
Cágliari
Golfo di Cágliari
Sant'Antioco
Porto Botte
Serpentara
C. Carbonara
Sant' Antíoco
Pula
Teulada
G. di Pálmas
C. Spartivento
TYRRHENIAN
SEA
3719
3589
Vatican City
ROMA
(Rome)
Tívoli
Subiaco
Trasacco
Fregene
Palestrina
Valmontone
Tevere
Tiber
Frascati
Anagni
Alatri
Véroli
Sora
Lido di Óstia
(Lido di Roma)
Pomezia
Albano Laziale
Velletri
Cori
Ferentino
Frosinone
Isola del Liri
Arpino
Monte S. Giovanni
Aprilia
Cisterna di Latina
Ceccano
Ceprano
Cassino
Latina
Sezze
Priverno
Ánzio
Nettuno
Sonnino
Fondi
533
Pontínia
Terracina
Fórmia
Sabáudia
Monte Circeo
541
Gaeta
Minturno
Garigliano
Golfo di Gaeta
Zannone
Palmarola
Ponza
283
Ísole Ponziane
Ventotene
Ustica
C. San Vito
Golfo di Castellammare
Terrasini Favarotta
C. Gallo
PALERMO
Bagheria
Levanzo
Trápani
Érice
1110
Cárini
Monreale
Partinico
Misilmeri
Maréttimo
Ísole Égadi
Alcamo
S. Giuseppe Jato
Favignana
Paceco
Calatafimi
Marineo
Stagnone
Salemi
Camporeale
Corleone
1613
Marsala
Gibellina
Lercara Friddi
Castelvetrano
Partanna
Bisacquino
Prizzi
Mazara del Vallo
Sambuca di Sicilia
Campobello di Mazara
Menfi
Burgio
Mussomeli
Belice
Sciacca
Caltabellotta
Ribera
Platani
Racalmuto
Cattólica Eraclea
Raffadali
Siculiana
Aragona
Porto Empédocle
Agrigento
Favara
Palma di Montechiaro
Campobello
Sicilian Channel
Iles de la Galite
C. Serrat
Bizerte (Binzert)
C. Blanc
Cani
Menzel-Bourguiba
Plane
Zembra
Mateur
Golfe de Tunis
C. Bon
El Kala
Tabarka
ALGERIA
Tébourba
TUNIS
Halq el Oued
Kelibia
Medjerda
Menzel-Temime
Bou Salem
Béja
Soliman
TUNISIA
Téboursouk
Mellègue
Nabeul
Zaghouan
Hammamet
Pantelleria
836
(It.)
1319
MEDITERRANEAN
ft
m
9000
3000
6000
2000
4500
1500
3000
1000
1200
400
600
200
37
0
200
600
2000
6000
4000
12,000
Projection: Conical with two standard parallels
East from Greenwich

1 : 2 200 000

10 0 10 20 30 40 50 miles
10 0 20 40 60 80 km

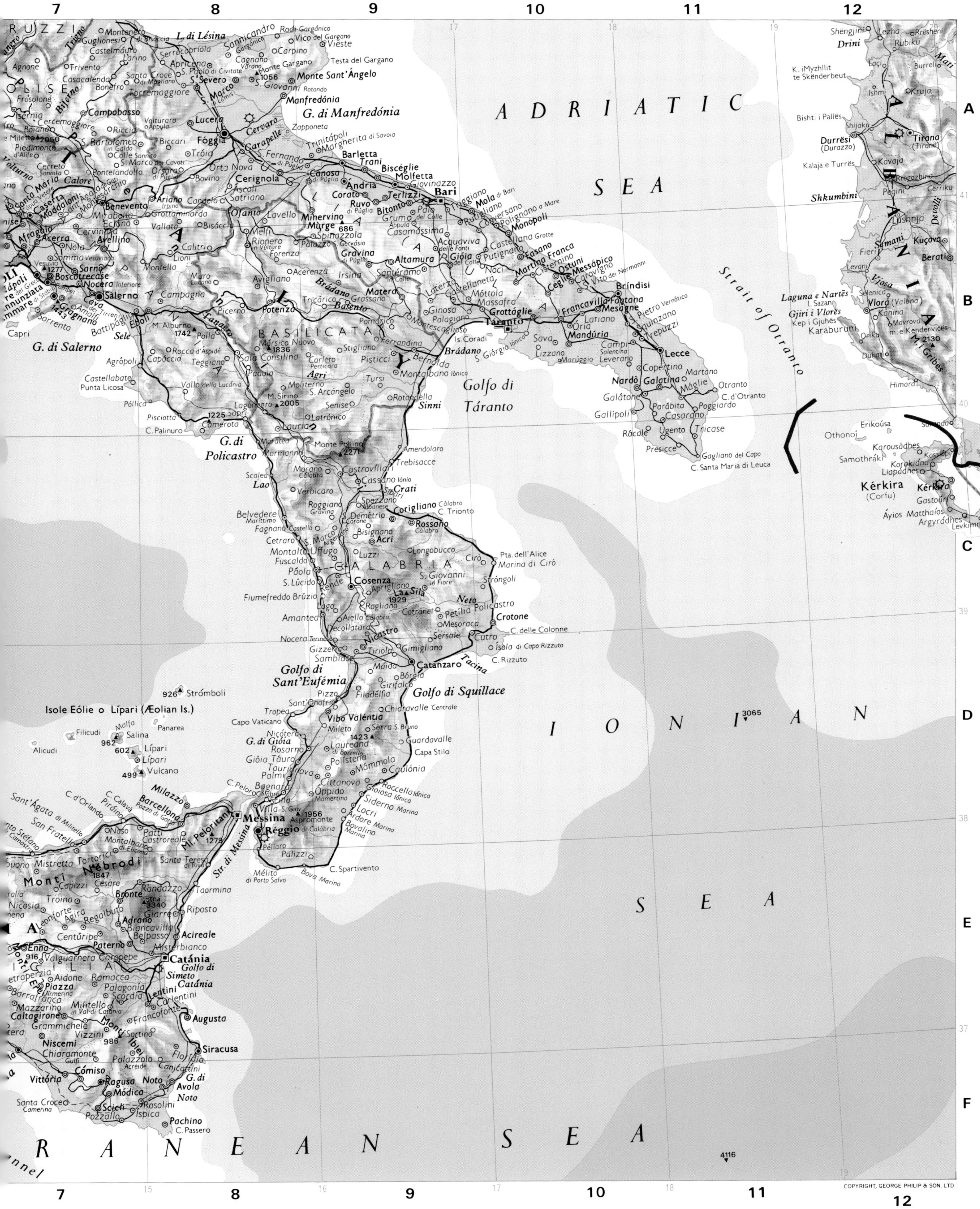

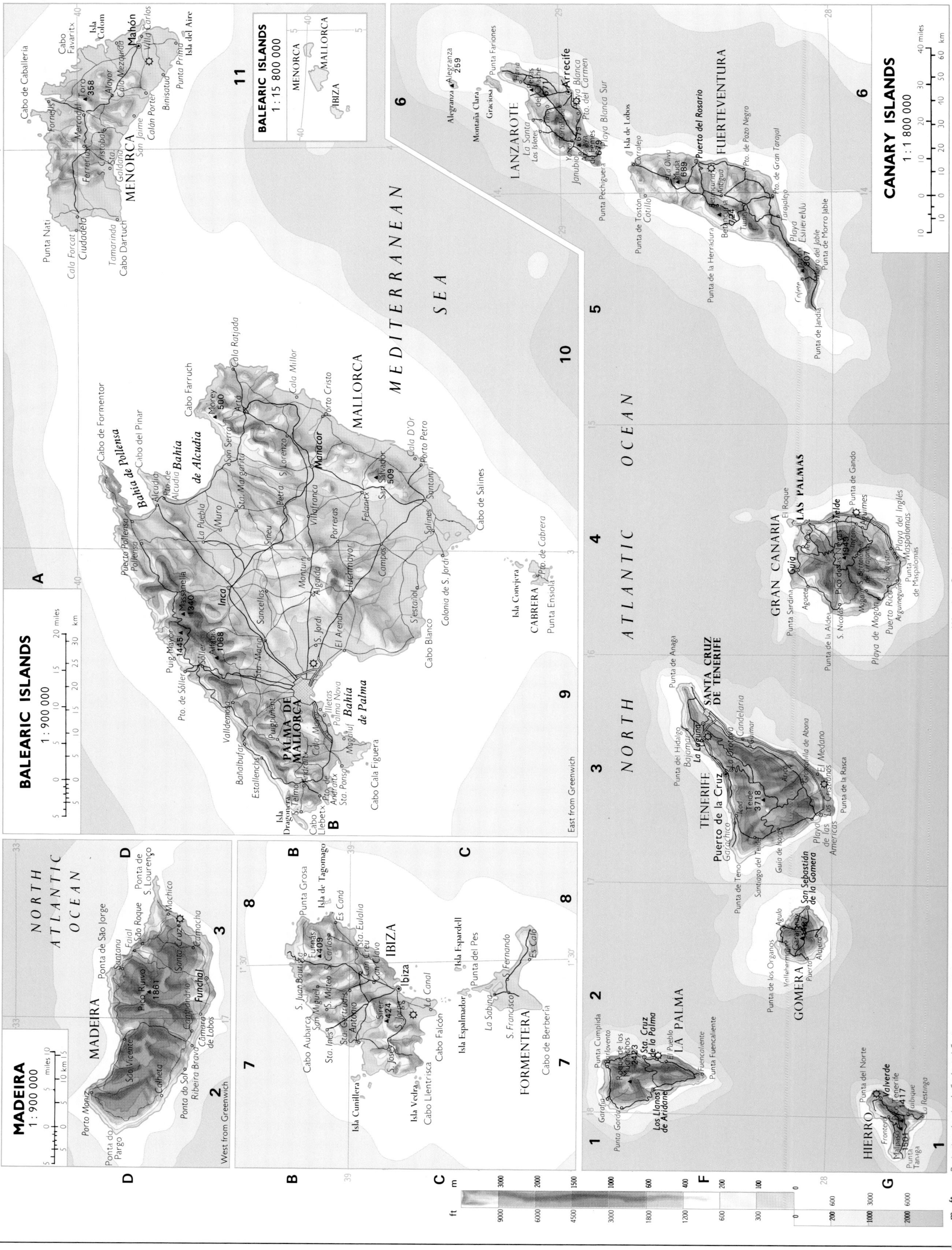

BALEARIC ISLANDS
1 : 900 000
BALEARIC ISLANDS
1 : 15 800 000
MENORCA
MALLORCA
IBIZA
CANARY ISLANDS
1 : 1 800 000
MADEIRA
1 : 900 000
MEDITERRANEAN SEA
NORTH ATLANTIC OCEAN
PALMA DE MALLORCA
Bahía de Palma
Bahía de Pollensa
Bahía de Alcudia
CABRERA
FORMENTERA
LANZAROTE
FUERTEVENTURA
GRAN CANARIA
LAS PALMAS
TENERIFE
SANTA CRUZ DE TENERIFE
GOMERA
LA PALMA
HIERRO
Funchal
Mahón
Ibiza
Arrecife
Puerto del Rosario
East from Greenwich
West from Greenwich
COPYRIGHT GEORGE PHILIP & SON LTD.

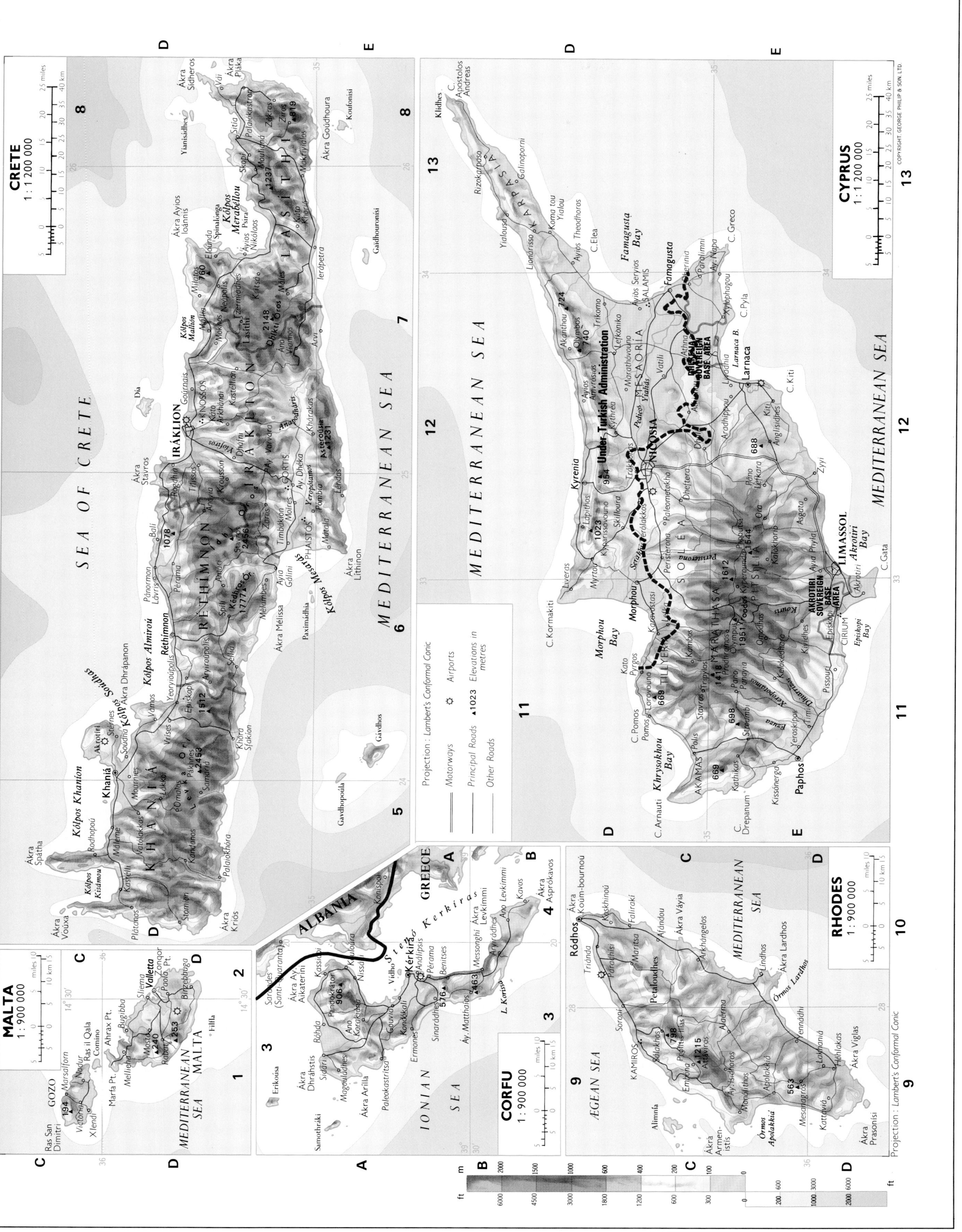
CRETE
1 : 1 200 000
SEA OF CRETE
MEDITERRANEAN SEA
CYPRUS
1 : 1 200 000
MEDITERRANEAN SEA
Under Turkish Administration
MALTA
1 : 900 000
CORFU
1 : 900 000
IONIAN SEA
RHODES
1 : 900 000
AEGEAN SEA
Projection : Lambert's Conformal Conic
Motorways
Principal Roads
Other Roads
Airports
▲1023 Elevations in metres
COPYRIGHT GEORGE PHILIP & SON, LTD.

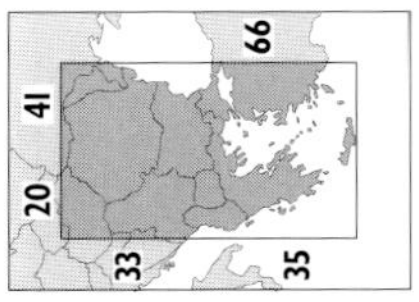
20
41
66
33
35

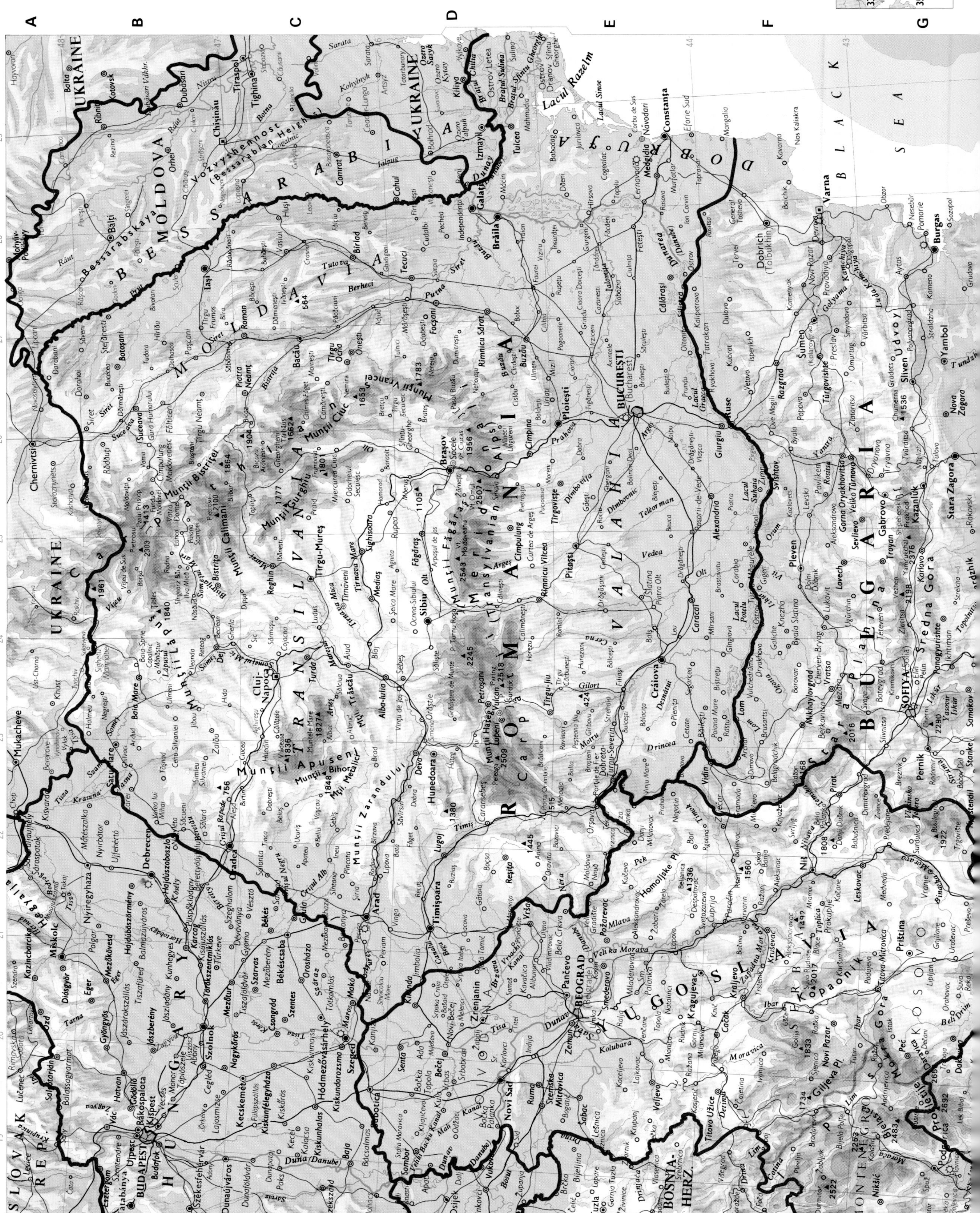
UKRAINE
MOLDOVA
ROMANIA
BULGARIA
YUGOSLAVIA
HUNGARY
SLOVAK REP.
BOSNIA-HERZ.
MONTENEGRO
SERBIA
KOSOVO
BLACK SEA
BESSARABIA
MOLDAVIA
TRANSILVANIA
DOBRUJA
BUCUREŞTI (Bucharest)
SOFIYA (Sofia)
BEOGRAD (Belgrade)
BUDAPEST
Chişinău
Constanţa
Varna
Burgas
Cluj-Napoca
Timişoara
Iaşi
Braşov
Craiova
Galaţi
Brăila
Ploieşti
Debrecen
Szeged
Novi Sad
Niš
Priština
Munţii Apuseni
Dunav
Duna (Danube)

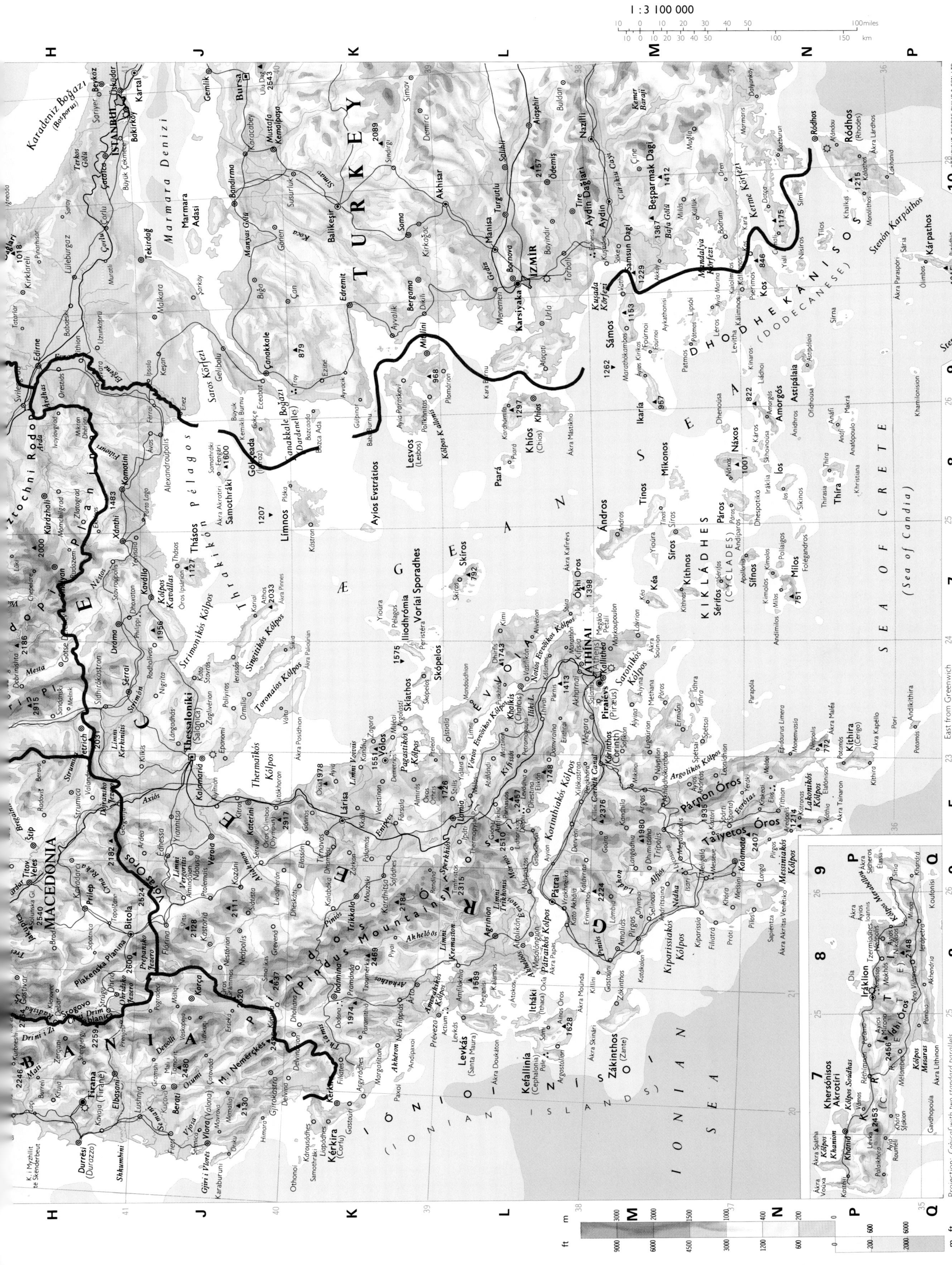
1 : 3 100 000
miles
km
TURKEY
MACEDONIA
ALBANIA
GREECE
AEGEAN SEA
IONIAN SEA
IONIAN ISLANDS
SEA OF CRETE
(Sea of Candia)
KIKLÁDHES
(CYCLADES)
DHODHEKÁNISOS
(DODECANESE)
Marmara Denizi
Thrakikón Pélagos
Pindus Mountains
İSTANBUL
İZMİR
ATHINAI
Thessaloniki
(Salonica)
Tirana
Kríti
East from Greenwich
Projection: Conical with two standard parallels
COPYRIGHT, GEORGE PHILIP & SON, LTD.
m
ft

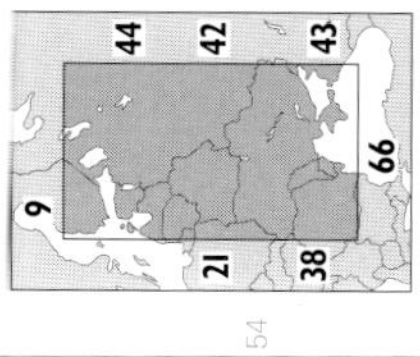
9
21
38
44
42
43
66

1 : 4 400 000

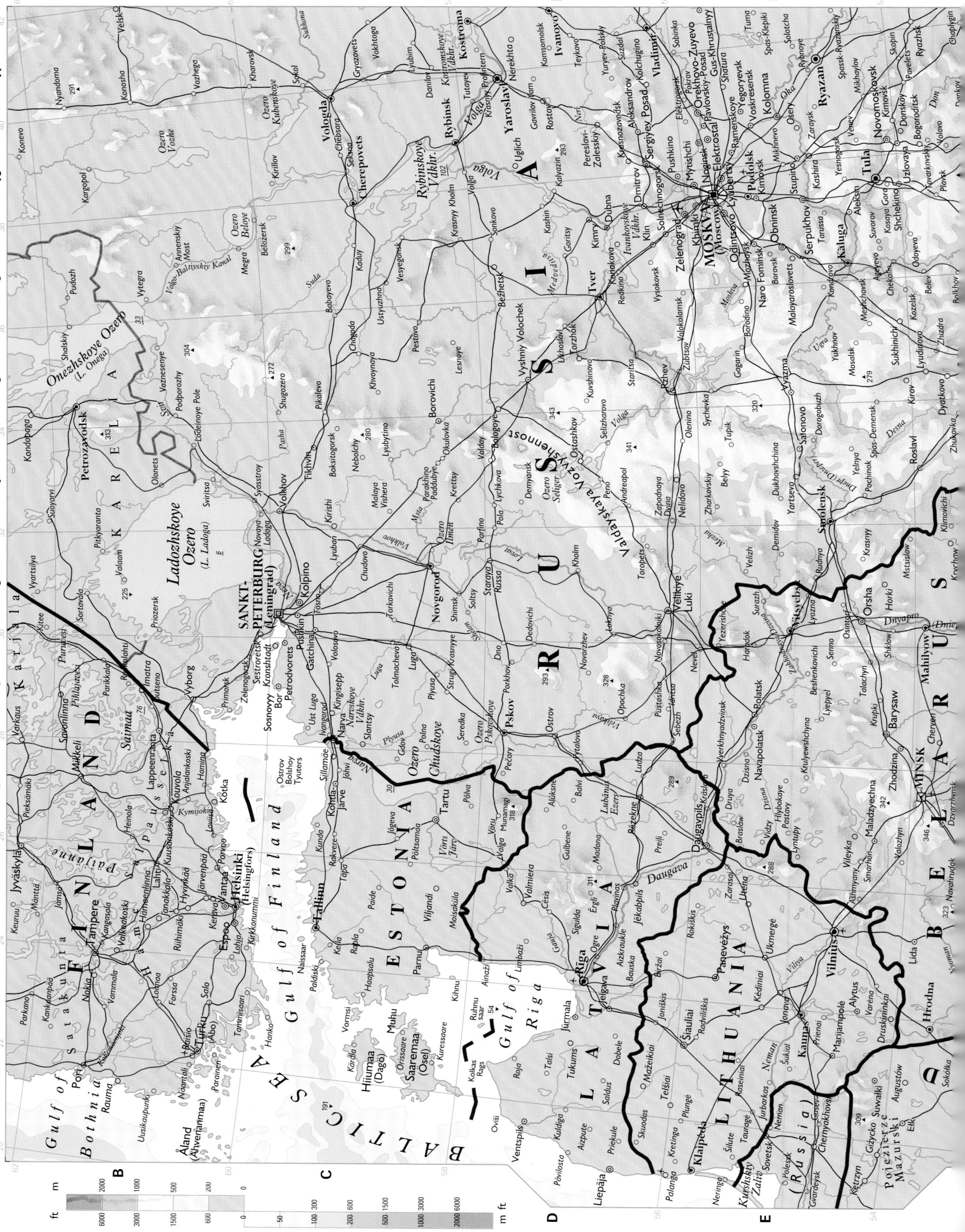
50 0 50 100 miles
50 0 50 100 150 km
FINLAND
ESTONIA
LATVIA
LITHUANIA
BELARUS
RUSSIA
KARELIA
BALTIC SEA
Gulf of Finland
Gulf of Riga
Gulf of Bothnia
Ladozhskoye Ozero (L. Ladoga)
Onezhskoye Ozero (L. Onega)
Ozero Chudskoye
Rybinskoye Vdkhr.
Valdayskaya Vozvyshennost
SANKT-PETERBURG (Leningrad)
MOSKVA (Moscow)
Helsinki (Helsingfors)
Tallinn
Riga
Vilnius
MINSK
Tampere
Turku (Åbo)
Tartu
Pskov
Novgorod
Tver
Smolensk
Vologda
Yaroslavl
Kaunas
Daugavpils
Klaipeda
Hrodna
Vitsyebsk
Mahilyow
Kaliningrad (Russia)
Ivanovo
Vladimir
Kostroma
Ryazan
Tula
Kaluga
ft m
6000 2000
3000 1000
1500 500
600 200
0 0
m ft
50
100 300
200 600
500 1500
1000 3000
2000 6000

CARTOGRAPHY BY PHILIP'S. COPYRIGHT REED INTERNATIONAL BOOKS LTD

Projection: *Conical with two standard parallels*

1 : 4 400 000

0 50 100 miles
0 50 100 150 km

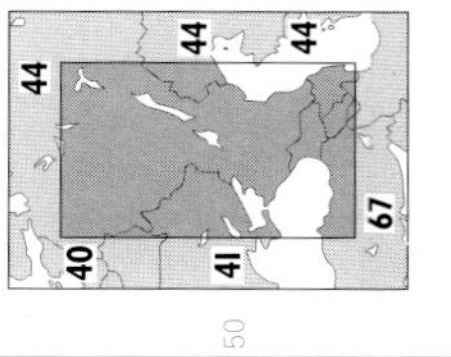

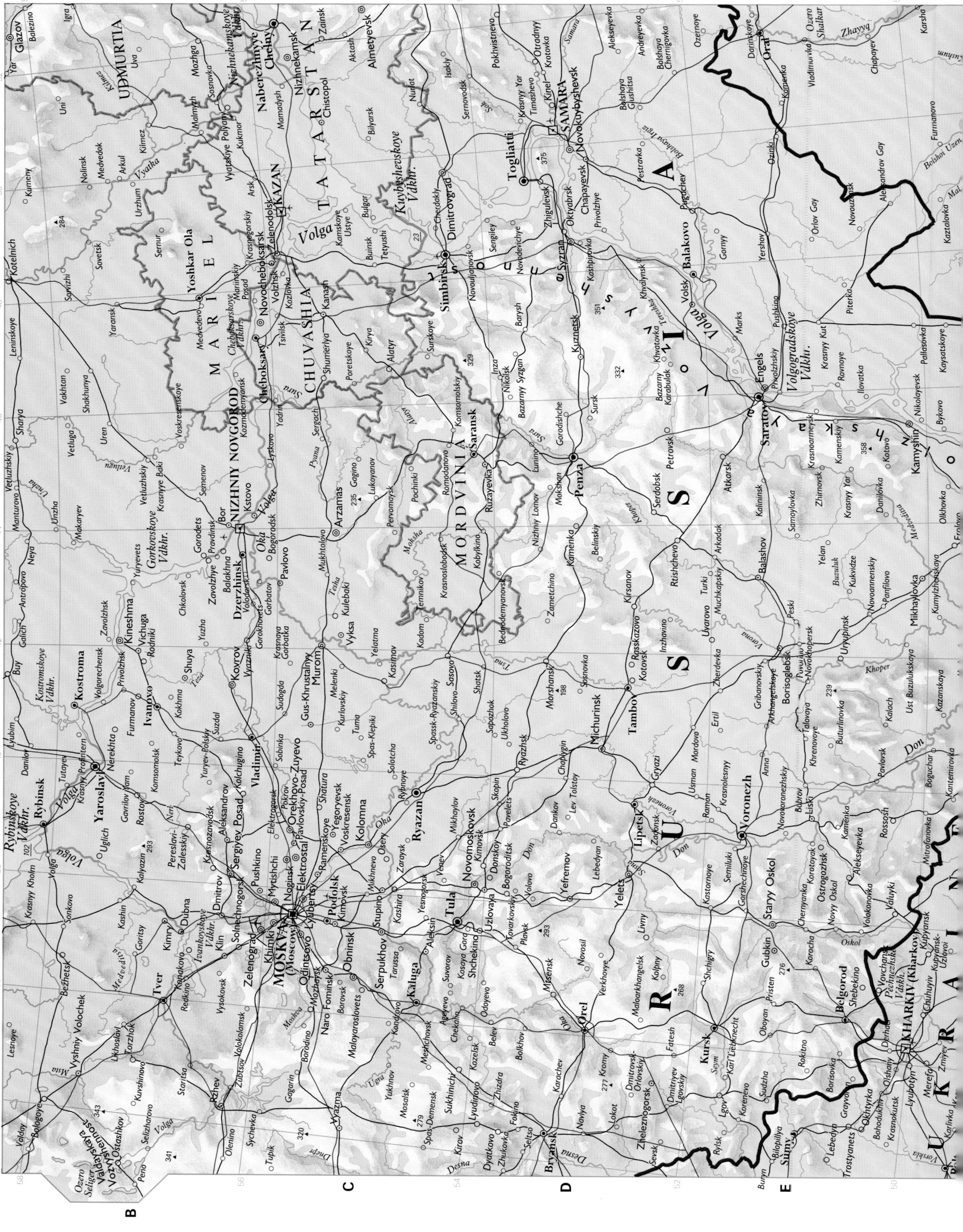

B C D E
1 2 3 4 5 6 7 8 9 10 11

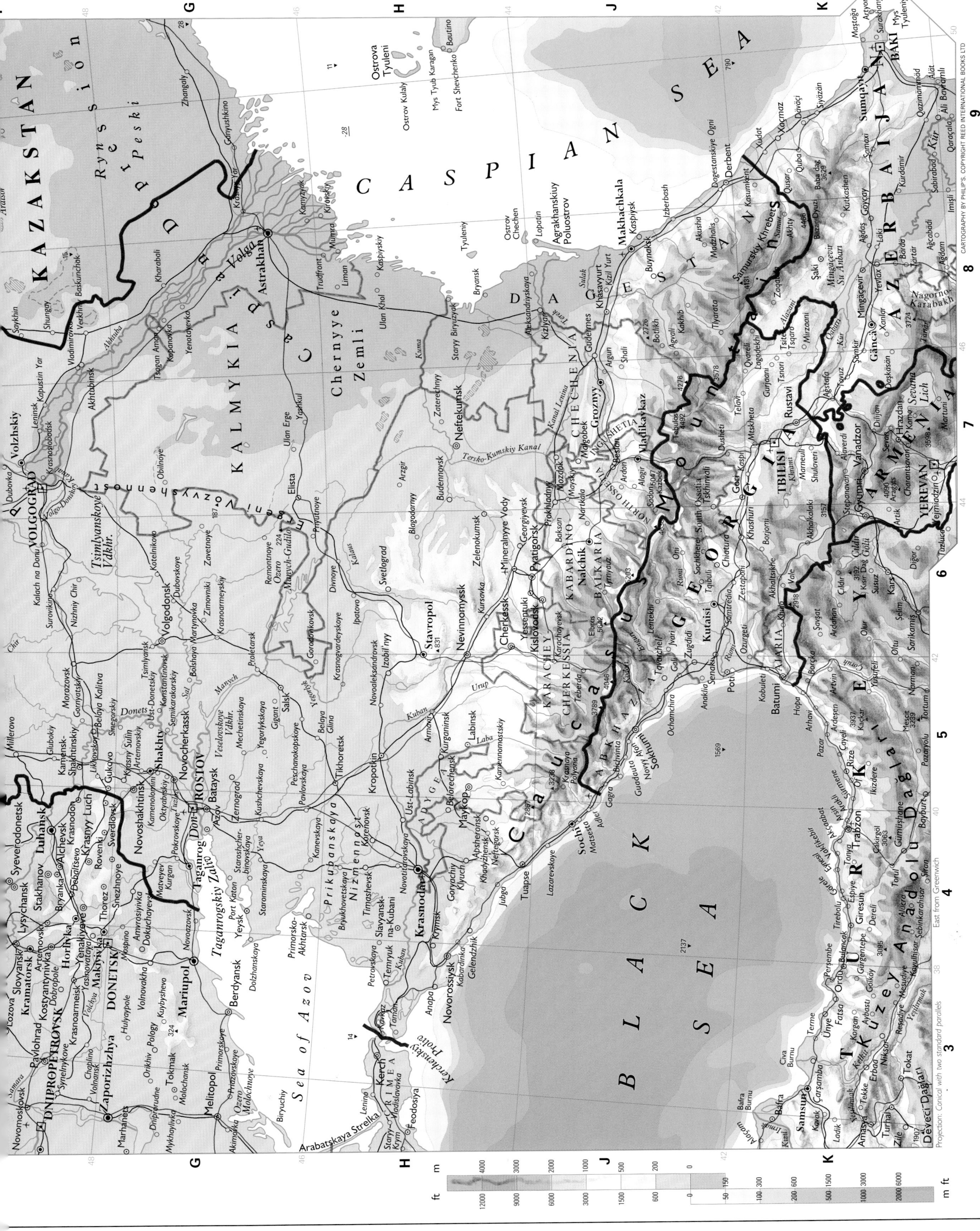
KAZAKSTAN
CASPIAN SEA
BLACK SEA
Sea of Azov
Taganrogskiy Zaliv
KALMYKIA
Chernyye Zemli
DAGESTAN
CHECHENIA
INGUSHETIA
NORTH OSSETIA
KABARDINO BALKARIA
KARACHEY CHERKESSIA
ADYGEA
ABKHAZIA
AJARIA
GEORGIA
ARMENIA
AZERBAIJAN
TURKEY
CRIMEA
Caucasus Mountains
Kuzey Anadolu Dağları
Prikubanskaya Nizmennost
Ryn Peski
VOLGOGRAD
ROSTOV
DONETSK
DNIPROPETROVSK
Astrakhan
Stavropol
Krasnodar
Makhachkala
Grozny
Vladikavkaz
Nalchik
Elista
Sochi
Novorossiysk
TBILISI
YEREVAN
BAKI
Kutaisi
Batumi
Trabzon
Samsun
Luhansk
Zaporizhzhya
Mariupol
Taganrog
Kerch
Volga
Kuban
Manych
Donets
Elbrus 5642
Kazbek
Projection: Conical with two standard parallels
East from Greenwich
m ft

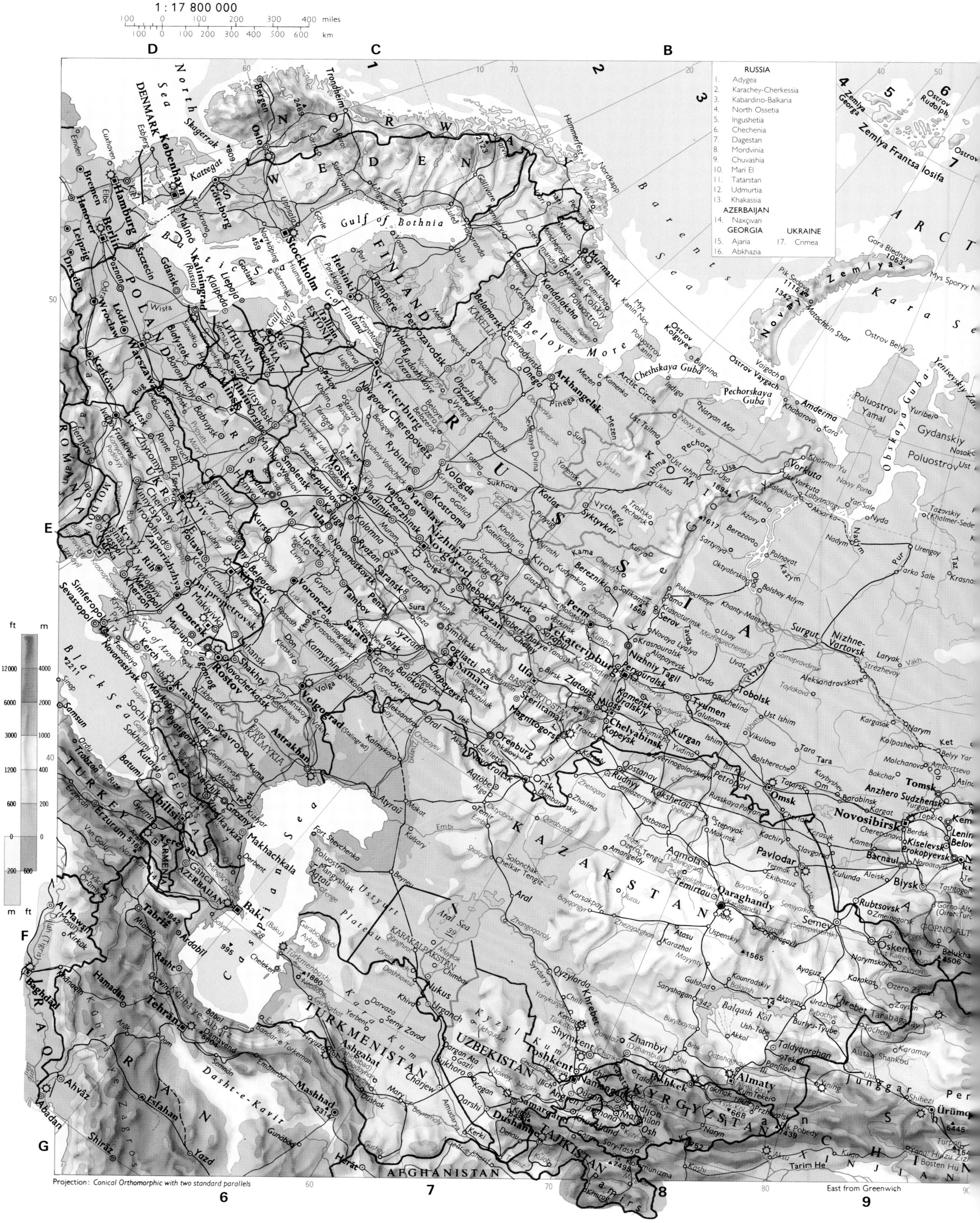

Projection: *Conical Orthomorphic with two standard parallels*

A B C

19

D

E

F

OCEAN

Lapte v Novosibirskiye Ostrova

East Siberian Sea

Laptev Sea

Bering Sea

Chukchi Sea

Mys Dezhneva (East C.)

St. Lawrence I. (U.S.A.)

Ostrov Vrangelya

Mys Arkticheskiy

Ostrov Komsomolets

Ostrov Pioner

Ostrov Shmidta

Ostrov Oktyabrskoy Revolyutsii

965

Severnaya Zemlya

Ostrov Bolshevik

Proliv Vilkitskogo

Poluostrov Taymyr

Gory Byrranga

Oz. Taymyr

No-dvik

Ostrov Bolshoy Begichev

Novorybnoye

Khatanga

Pepigay

Anabar

Ust Olenek

Tit-Ary

Tiksi

Bulun

Kyusyur

Verkhoyansk

2389

Mys Buorkhaya

Nizhneyansk

Yana

Kazachye

Chokurdakh

Indigirka

Srednekolymsk

Ostrova Zhokhova

Ostrov Novaya Sibir

Ostrov Faddeyevskiy

Ostrov Maly Lyakhovskiy

Ostrov Bolshoy Lyakhovskiy

Lyakhovskiye Ostrova

Proliv Dmitriya Lapteva

Ostrova Medvezhi

Ostrov Ayon

Nizhne Kolymsk

Kolyma

1853

Bolshoy Anyuy

Omolon

Khrebet Cherskogo

Pobeda 3147

Anadyrskoye Nagorye

Anadyrskiy Zaliv

1843

Providniya

2562

1742

Poluostrov Kamchatka

Sredinnyy Khrebet

Petropavlovsk-Kamchatskiy

Sea of Okhotsk

Komandorskiye Ostrova

Magadan

2959

Okhotsk

Zaliv Shelikhova

Gizhiginskaya Guba

Penzhinskaya Guba

Gizhiga

Koryakskoye Nagorye

Kurilskiye Ostrova

Sakhalin

Yuzhno-Sakhalinsk

Sovetskaya Gavan

Khrebet Sikhote Alin

Khabarovsk

Komsomolsk

2078

Nikolayevsk-na-Am.

Ostrov Bolshoy Shantar

Sakhalinskiy Zaliv

Hokkaidō

Sapporo

Hakodate

RUSSIA

Krasnoyarsk

Bratsk

Kirensk

Irkutsk

Ulan Ude

Angarsk

Cheremkhovo

Usolye Sibirskoye

Vostochnyy Sayan

Chita

Shilka

Nerchinsk

Blagoveshchensk

Amur

Birobidzhan

Ussuriysk

Vladivostok

Nakhodka

Sea of JAPAN

Honshū

Niigata

Toyama

Kanazawa

Akita

Stanovoy Khrebet

Yakutsk

Olekminsk

Aldan

Tommot

Yablonovyy Khrebet

Ulan Ude

Ulaanbaatar (Ulan Bator)

Hangayn Nuruu

Hentiyn Nuruu

Hövsgöl Nuur

MONGOLIA

Hyargas Nuur

Har Nuur

Edrengiyn Nuruu

3957

GOBI

Baotou

Hohhot

Zhangjiakou

Beijing

Qiqihar

Harbin

Changchun

Jilin

Shenyang

Fushun

Anshan

Dalian

Dandong

Yingkou

Dongbei

NORTH KOREA

Pyongyang

Nampo

Wŏnsan

Chŏngjin

Sŏul

Inch'on

SOUTH KOREA

Taejŏn

Taegu

Pusan

JAPAN

Sea of Japan

Boundaries of Republics

COPYRIGHT. GEORGE PHILIP & SON, LTD.

10 11 12 13 14

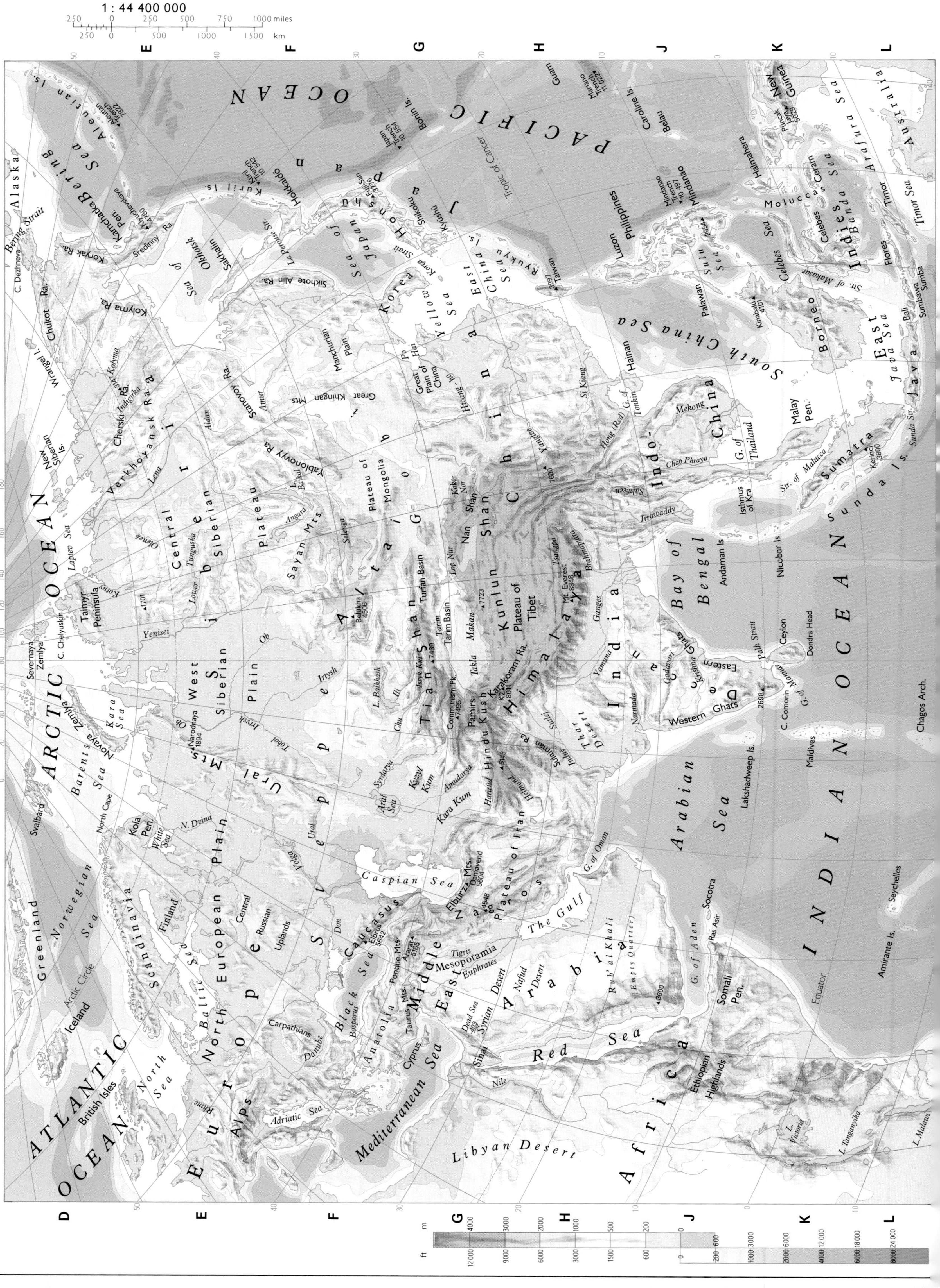
1 : 44 400 000
250 0 250 500 750 1000 miles
250 0 500 1000 1500 km
ARCTIC OCEAN
PACIFIC OCEAN
INDIAN OCEAN
ATLANTIC OCEAN
Europe
Africa
Siberia
Japan
China
Gobi
Altai
Steppe
India
Arabia
Indo-China
East Indies
West Siberian Plain
Central Siberian Plateau
North European Plain
Central Russian Uplands
Plateau of Tibet
Plateau of Mongolia
Plateau of Iran
Great Plain of China
Manchurian Plain
Middle East
Mesopotamia
Himalaya
Kunlun Shan
Tian Shan
Nan Shan
Hindu Kush
Karakoram Ra.
Pamirs
Ural Mts.
Caucasus
Elburz Mts.
Zagros Mts.
Sayan Mts.
Yablonovy Ra.
Stanovoy Ra.
Verkhoyansk Ra.
Cherski Ra.
Kolyma Ra.
Great Khingan Mts.
Sikhote Alin Ra.
Western Ghats
Eastern Ghats
Deccan
Thar Desert
Takla Makan
Kara Kum
Kyzyl Kum
Rub' al Khali (Empty Quarter)
Nafud Desert
Syrian Desert
Libyan Desert
Caspian Sea
Aral Sea
Black Sea
Mediterranean Sea
Red Sea
Arabian Sea
Bay of Bengal
South China Sea
East China Sea
Yellow Sea
Sea of Japan
Sea of Okhotsk
Bering Sea
Barents Sea
Kara Sea
Laptev Sea
Norwegian Sea
North Sea
Baltic Sea
The Gulf
G. of Oman
G. of Aden
G. of Thailand
G. of Tonkin
Java Sea
Banda Sea
Celebes Sea
Sulu Sea
Molucca Sea
Arafura Sea
Timor Sea
Mt. Everest 8848
Elbrus 5642
Ararat 5165
Damavand 5604
Communism Pk. 7495
Belukha 4506
Kinabalu 4101
Puncak Jaya 5029
Kerinci 3800
Narodnaya 1894
Kamchatka Pen.
Taimyr Peninsula
Kola Pen.
Malay Pen.
Somali Pen.
Arabian Pen.
Anatolia
Scandinavia
Greenland
Iceland
British Isles
Svalbard
Novaya Zemlya
Severnaya Zemlya
New Siberian Is.
Wrangel I.
Sakhalin
Hokkaido
Honshu
Kyushu
Shikoku
Ryukyu Is.
Taiwan
Hainan
Luzon
Philippines
Mindanao
Borneo
Sumatra
Java
Celebes
New Guinea
Ceylon
Maldives
Lakshadweep Is.
Andaman Is.
Nicobar Is.
Socotra
Seychelles
Chagos Arch.
Cyprus
Bering Strait
Alaska
Aleutian Is.
Kuril Is.
Yenisei
Ob
Irtysh
Lena
Amur
Ganges
Indus
Brahmaputra
Mekong
Yangtze
Hwang-ho
Tigris
Euphrates
Nile
Volga
Danube
L. Balkhash
Baikal
Tropic of Cancer
Equator
Arctic Circle
m
4000 3000 2000 1000 500 200 0
200 1000 2000 4000 6000 8000
ft
12 000 9000 6000 3000 1500 600 0
600 3000 6000 12 000 18 000 24 000

1 : 44 400 000

250 0 250 500 750 1000 miles

250 0 500 1000 1500 km

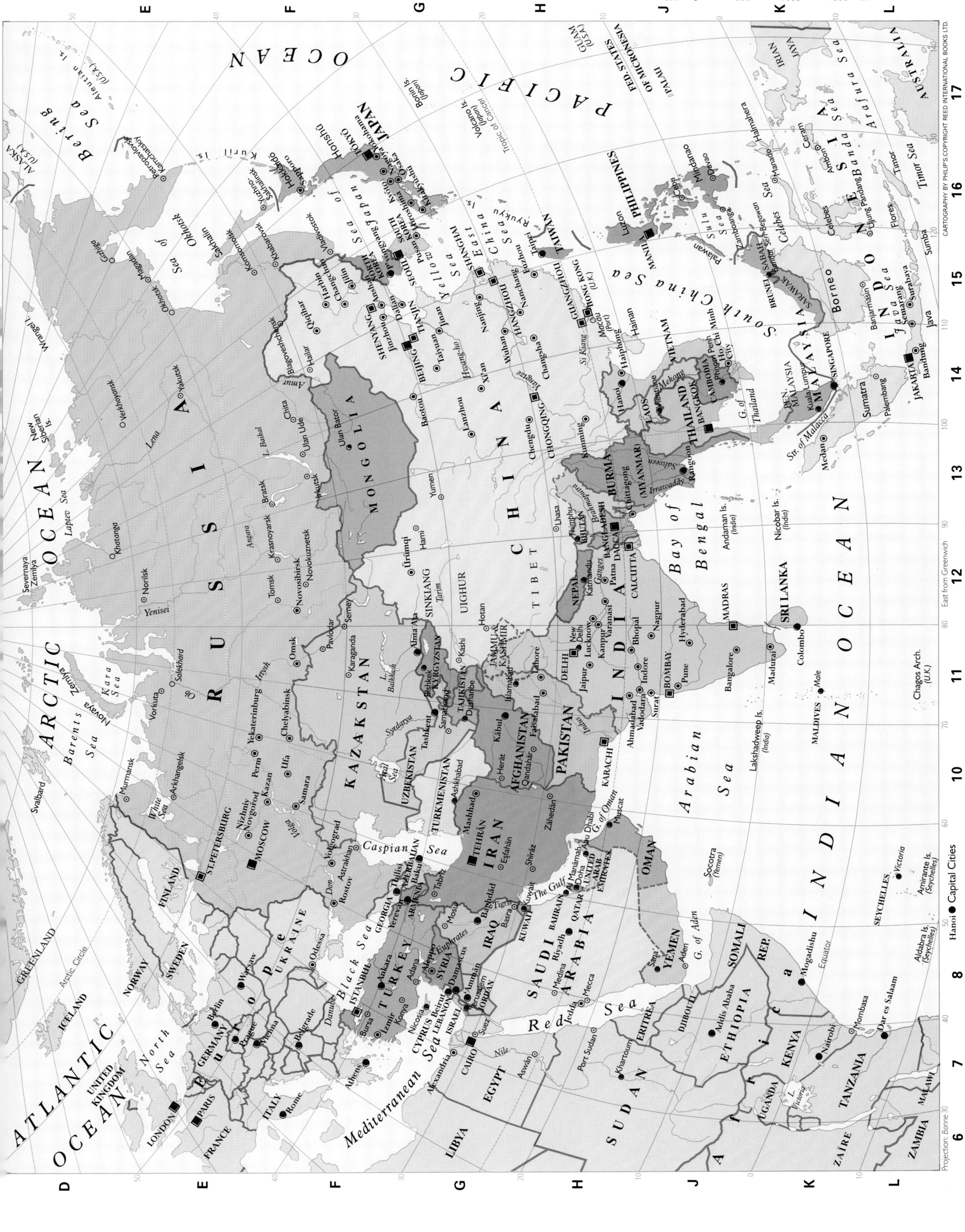

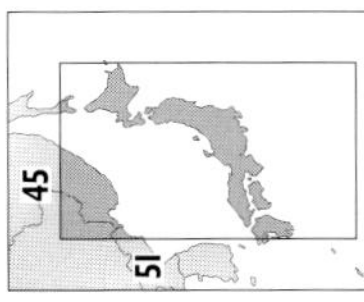
45
51

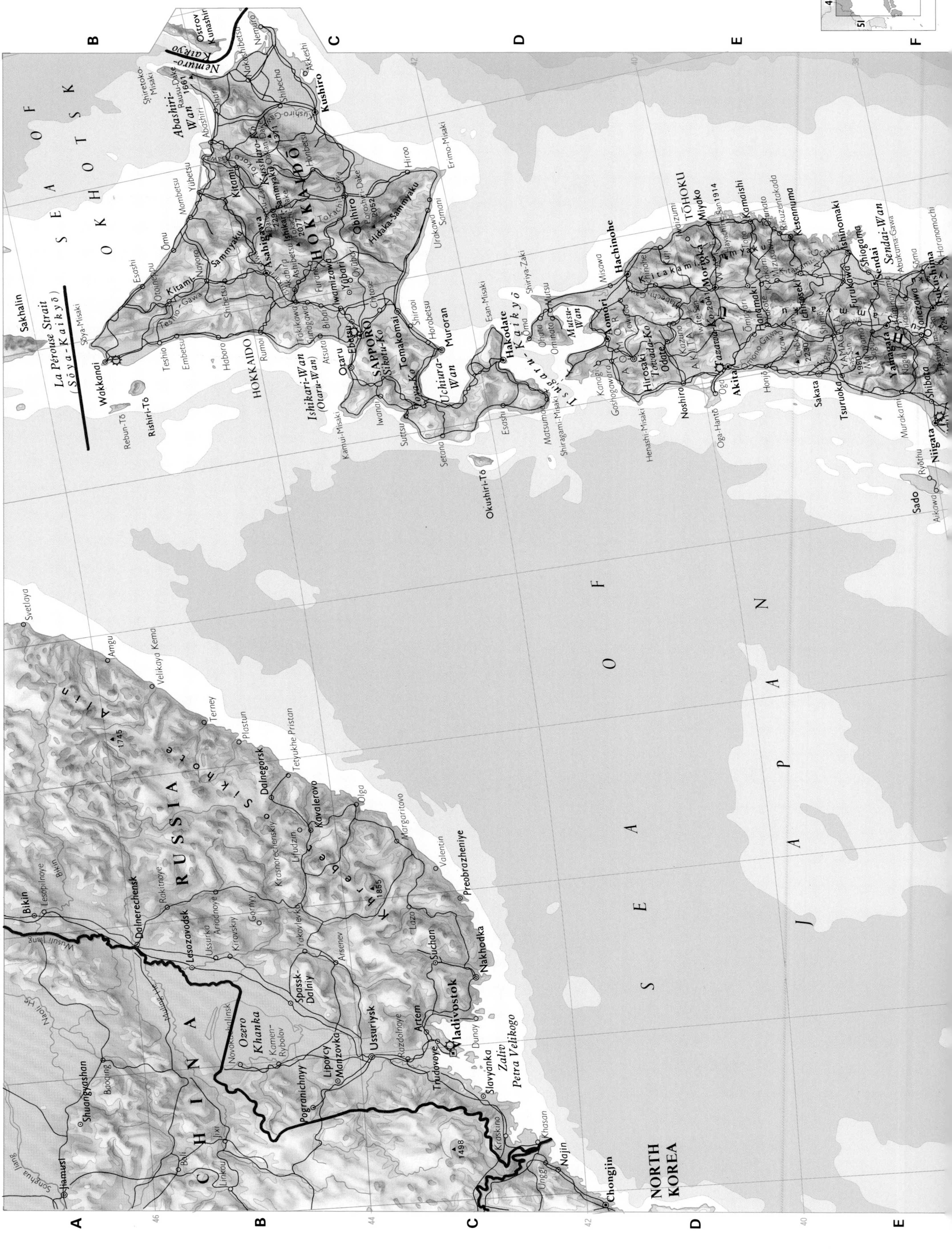
SEA OF OKHOTSK
SEA OF JAPAN
RUSSIA
CHINA
NORTH KOREA
HOKKAIDO
TŌHOKU
La Pérouse Strait
(Sōya-Kaikyō)
Sakhalin
Ostrov Kunashir
Nemuro-Kaikyō
Abashiri-Wan
Ishikari-Wan
(Otaru-Wan)
Uchiura-Wan
Tsugaru-Kaikyō
Mutsu-Wan
Sendai-Wan
Zaliv Petra Velikogo
Ozero Khanka
Wakkanai
Rishiri-Tō
Rebun-Tō
Okushiri-Tō
Sado
Sapporo
Otaru
Asahikawa
Kitami
Kushiro
Obihiro
Muroran
Tomakomai
Hakodate
Aomori
Hachinohe
Hirosaki
Akita
Morioka
Miyako
Kamaishi
Kesennuma
Ishinomaki
Shiogama
Sendai
Yamagata
Yonezawa
Fukushima
Niigata
Shibata
Sakata
Tsuruoka
Noshiro
Vladivostok
Nakhodka
Ussuriysk
Artem
Spassk-Dalniy
Lesozavodsk
Dalnerechensk
Bikin
Dalnegorsk
Kavalerovo
Preobrazheniye
Terney
Plastun
Svetlaya
Amgu
Chongjin
Najin
Khasan
Kraskino
Slavyanka
Pogranichnyy
Jiamusi
Shuangyashan
Jixi
Sikhote Alin
1745
1855
1498
A
B
C
D
E
F
5
6
7
8
9
10
11
12
132
134
136
138
140
142
144
38
40
42
44
46

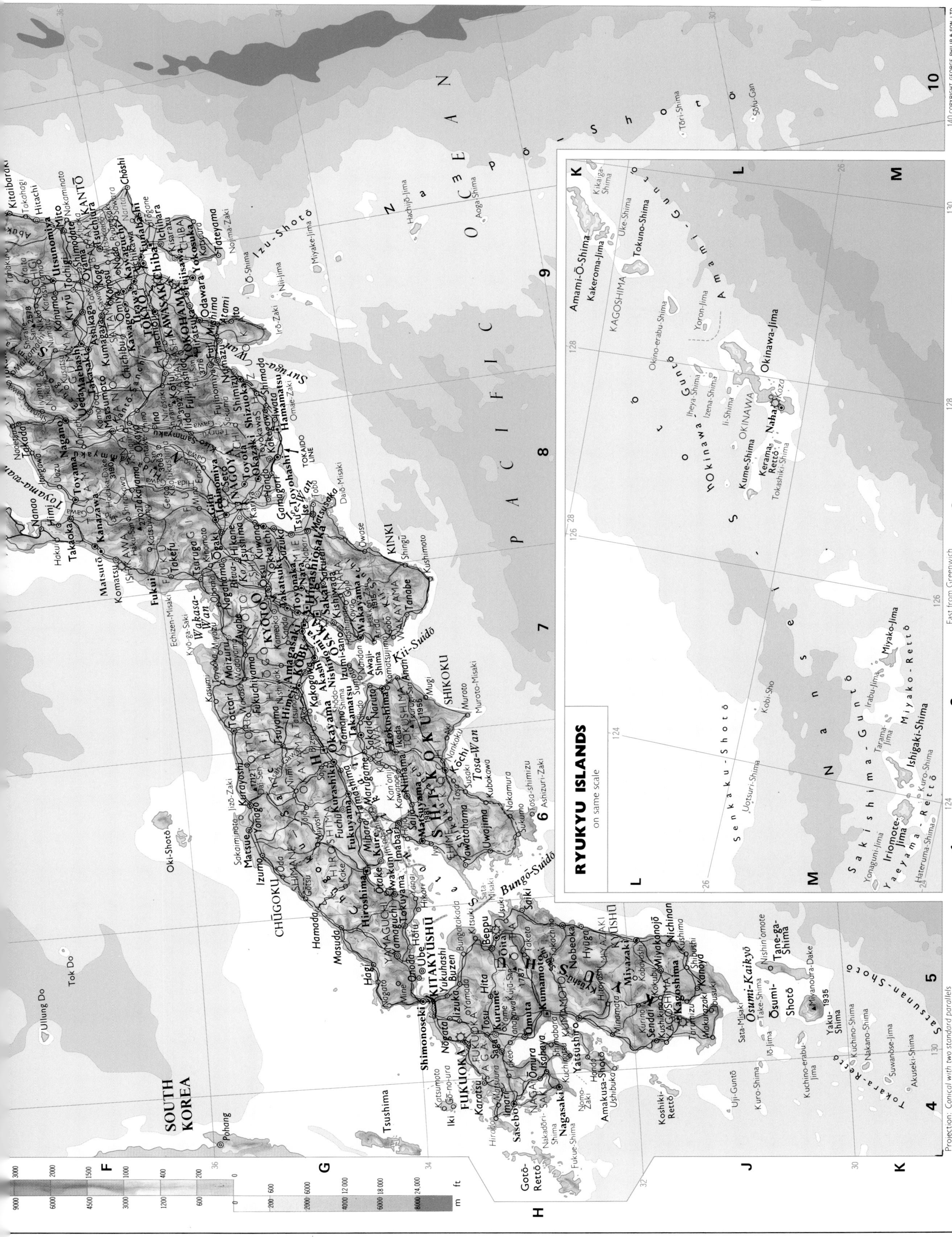
SOUTH KOREA
Pohang
Ullung Do
Tok Do
Tsushima
Oki-Shotō
CHŪGOKU
SHIKOKU
KYŪSHŪ
KINKI
KANTŌ
TŌKYŌ
YOKOHAMA
KAWASAKI
NAGOYA
KYŌTO
ŌSAKA
KŌBE
Hiroshima
FUKUOKA
KITAKYŪSHŪ
Shimonoseki
Nagasaki
Kagoshima
Kumamoto
Ōita
Miyazaki
Okayama
Takamatsu
Matsuyama
Kōchi
Tokushima
Wakayama
Nara
Kanazawa
Toyama
Fukui
Gifu
Shizuoka
Hamamatsu
Chiba
Mito
Utsunomiya
Maebashi
Kōfu
Nagano
Tottori
Matsue
Yamaguchi
Saga
Chōshi
Kii-Suidō
Bungo-Suidō
Tosa-Wan
Suruga-Wan
Ise-Wan
Wakasa-Wan
Izu-Shotō
Nampō-Shotō
PACIFIC OCEAN
Ōsumi-Kaikyō
Ōsumi-Shotō
Tane-ga-Shima
Yaku-Shima
Tokara-Rettō
Satsunan-Shotō
TOKAIDO LINE
RYUKYU ISLANDS
on same scale
Amami-Ō-Shima
Kakeroma-Jima
Tokuno-Shima
Okinawa-Jima
Naha
Okinawa-Guntō
Amami-Guntō
Nansei-Shotō
Senkaku-Shotō
Sakishima-Guntō
Miyako-Jima
Miyako-Rettō
Ishigaki-Shima
Iriomote-Jima
Yaeyama-Rettō
Hachijō-Jima
Miyake-Jima
Tōri-Shima
1 : 4 400 000
50 0 50 100 miles
50 0 50 100 150 km
m ft
East from Greenwich
Projection: Conical with two standard parallels

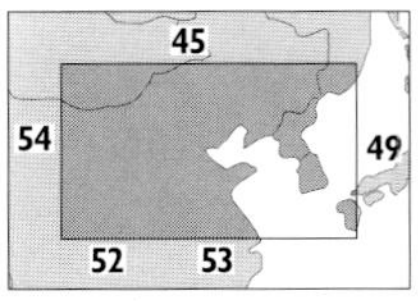

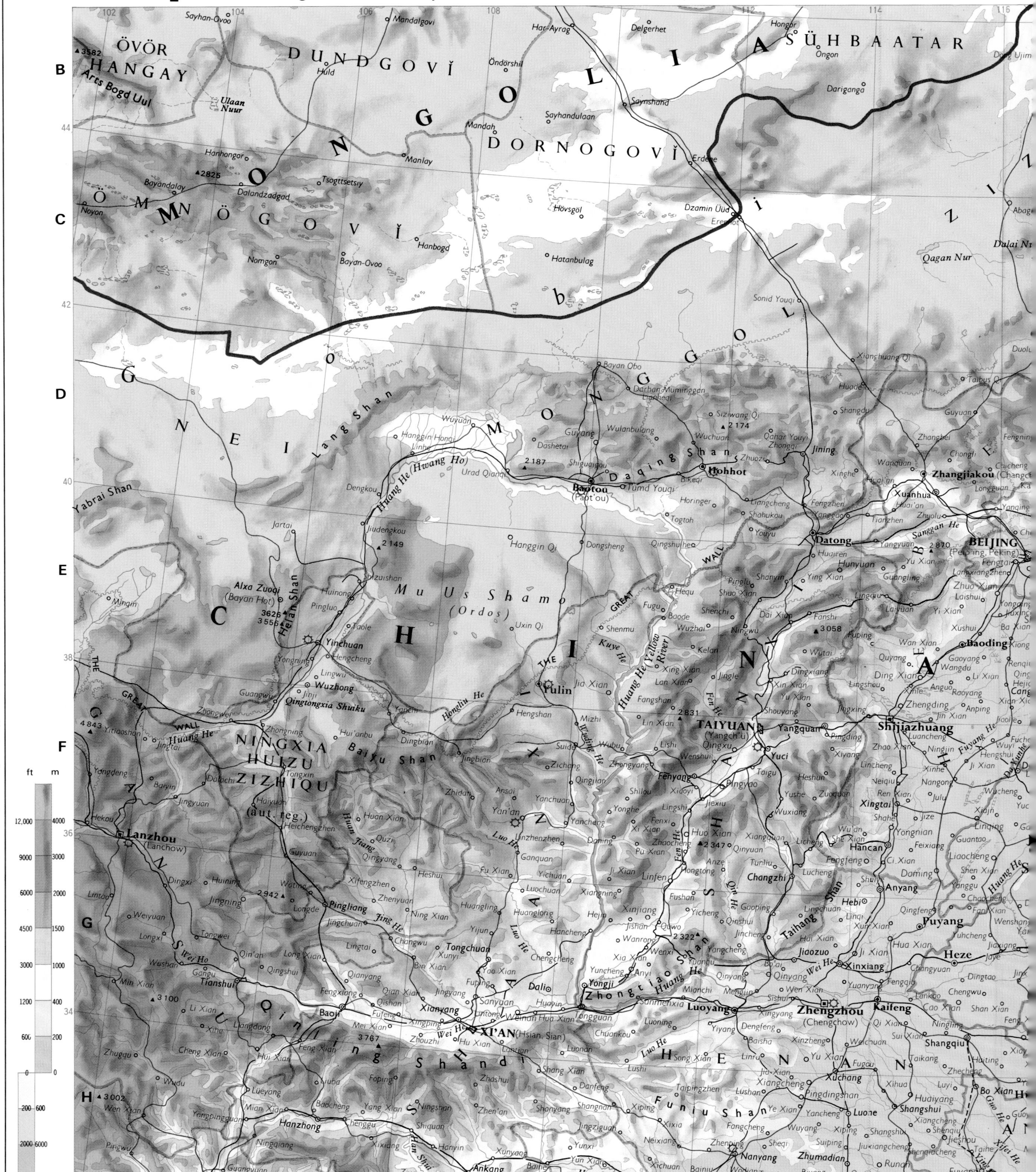

Projection: Conical with two standard parallels

3
4
5
6
7
8

1 : 5 300 000
50 0 50 100 150 miles
50 0 50 100 150 200 km
East from Greenwich
HARBIN (Haerhpin)
Changchun
Jilin (Kirin, Chilin)
Shuangliao
Siping
SHENYANG (Mukden)
Fushun
Anshan
Benxi
Liaoyang
Jinzhou
Yingkou
Dandong
DALIAN (Lüda)
Lüshun
Liaodong Wan
Liaodong Bandao
Korea Bay
Bo Hai
(Gulf of Chihli)
TIANJIN (Tientsin, T'ienching)
Tanggu
Tangshan
Qinhuangdao
Chifeng
Tongliao
Zhangguangcai Ling
Changbai Shan
Mudanjiang
Vladivostok
Ussuriysk (Voroshilov)
Ozero Khanka
RUSSIA
NORTH KOREA
P'YONGYANG
Hamhung
Hungnam
Chongjin
Kimchaek (Songjin)
Wonsan
Tongjoson Man
Kaesong
Cease Fire Line
SOUTH KOREA
SOUL
INCH'ON
Suwon
Taejon
TAEGU
PUSAN
Kwangju
Chonju
Mokpo
Ulsan
Pohang
Kangnung
Ulleung-do
Cheju-do
Cheju
SEA OF JAPAN
Korea Strait
Tsushima
Tsushima-kaikyo
JAPAN
Sasebo
Nagasaki
HUANG HAI
(Yellow Sea)
Shandong Bandao
Laizhou Wan
Yantai
Weihai
Weifang
Zibo
QINGDAO (Ch'ingtao)
Jiaozhou Wan
Linyi
Lianyungang
Yancheng
JIANGSU
Bengbu
Haizhou Wan
Liaoning
Jilin
Heilongjiang
Manchuria
Yalu Jiang
Songhua Jiang
Liao He
Xiliao He
Paektu-san
1677
2541
2522
1638
1578
1915
1950
923
1108
1949
2020
1885
845
1690
9 10 11 12 13 14 15 16
B C D E F G H

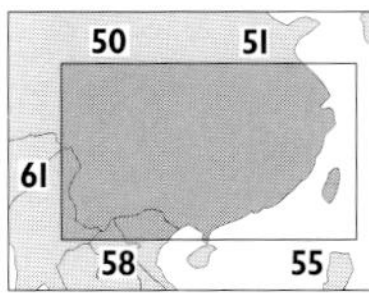
50
51
61
58
55

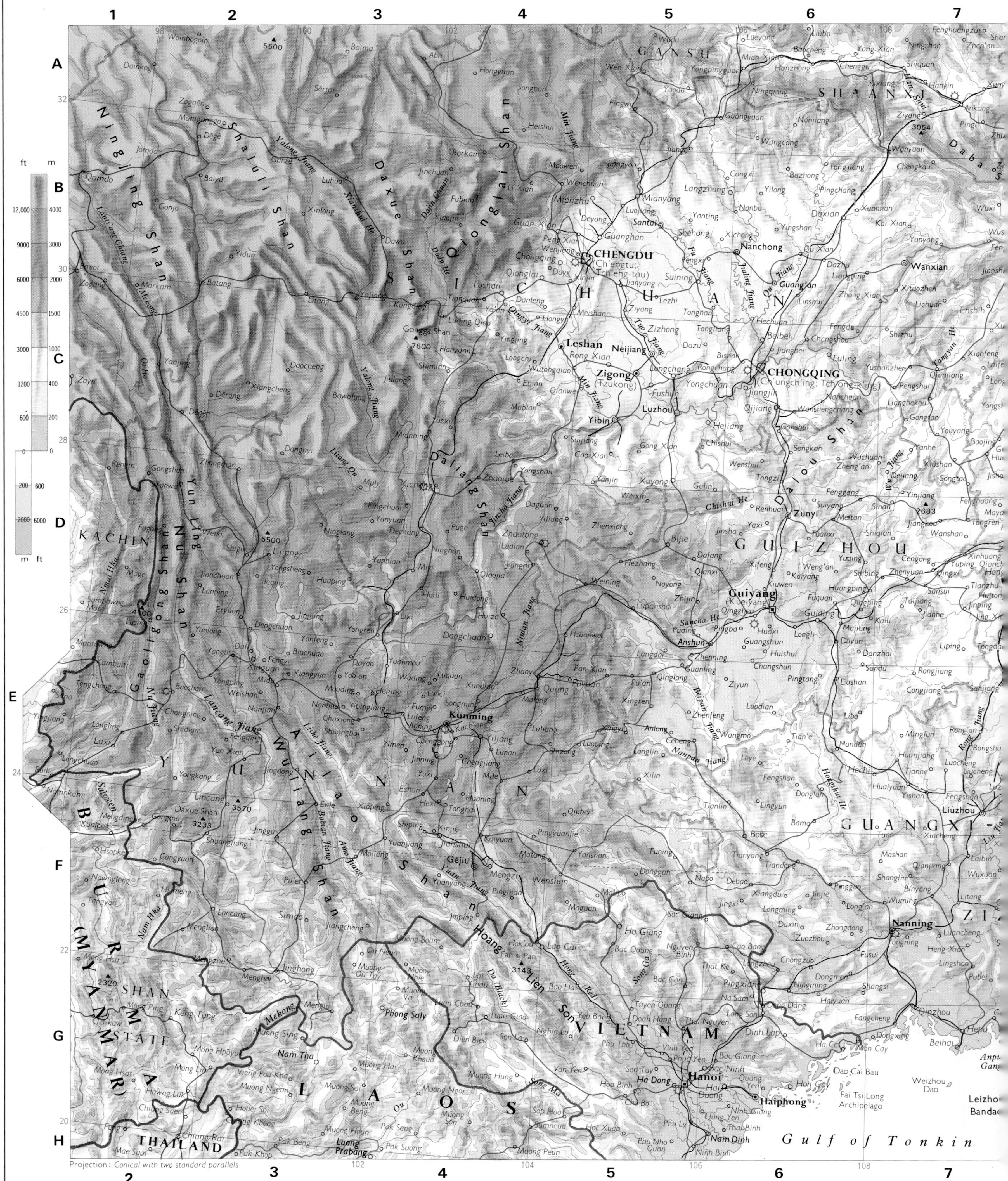
1 2 3 4 5 6 7
A B C D E F G H
ft m
12,000 4000
9000 3000
6000 2000
4500 1500
3000 1000
1200 400
600 200
0 0
200 600
2000 6000
m ft
GANSU
SHAANXI
SICHUAN
GUIZHOU
YUNNAN
GUANGXI
KACHIN
BURMA (MYANMAR)
SHAN STATE
LAOS
VIETNAM
THAILAND
CHENGDU
(Ch'engtu; Tch'eng-tou)
CHONGQING
(Ch'ungch'ing; Tch'ong-k'ing)
Kunming
Guiyang
(Kueiyang)
Nanning
Hanoi
Haiphong
Leshan
Zigong
(Tzukong)
Neijiang
Yibin
Luzhou
Nanchong
Wanxian
Zunyi
Liuzhou
Gejiu
Anshun
Ningjing Shan
Shaluli Shan
Daxue Shan
Qionglai Shan
Daliang Shan
Dalou Shan
Daba Shan
Nu Shan
Yun Ling
Gaoligong Shan
Ailao Shan
Wuliang Shan
Hoang Lien Son
Gongga Shan
7600
5500
3054
2683
3570
3233
3143
2320
4100
Min Jiang
Yalong Jiang
Jinsha Jiang
Lancang Jiang
Nu Jiang
Yuan Jiang
Hong (Red)
Da (Black)
Mekong
Salween
Wujiang
Chishui He
Beipan Jiang
Nanpan Jiang
Hongshui He
Jialing Jiang
Qu Jiang
Tuo Jiang
Gulf of Tonkin
Fai Tsi Long Archipelago
Weizhou Dao
Leizhou Bandao
Projection: Conical with two standard parallels

1 : 5 300 000

50 0 50 100 miles
50 0 50 100 150 km
8 9 10 11 12 13 14
A B C D E F G H
HENAN
HUBEI
ANHUI
JIANGSU
ZHEJIANG
JIANGXI
HUNAN
FUJIAN
GUANGDONG
TAIWAN
SOUTH CHINA SEA
Formosa Strait
Luzon Strait
Tropic of Cancer
SHANGHAI
(Changhai)
NANJING
(Nanking; Nanching)
WUHAN
(Wou-han)
GUANGZHOU
(Kuangchou; Canton)
HONG KONG (U.K.)
Kowloon
Macau (Macao) (Port.)
T'AIPEI
Chilung
Kaohsiung
T'ainan
T'aichung
Hsinchu
Hualien
Changhua
Chiai
P'ingtung
Nanyang
Xiangfan
Yichang
(Ich'ang)
Shashi
Hankou
Xinyang
Hefei
Bengbu
Huainan
Yangzhou
Zhenjiang
(Chenchiang)
Changzhou
(Ch'angchou)
Wuxi
(Wuhsi)
Suzhou
(Suchou)
Nantong
Hangzhou
(Hangchou; Hangchow)
Shaoxing
Ningbo
(Ningpo)
Wenzhou
(Wenchow)
Linhai
Jinhua
Wuhu
Anqing
Huangshi
Jiujiang
Jingdezhen
Nanchang
Changsha
Xiangtan
Zhuzhou
Hengyang
Shaoyang
Changde
Yiyang
Shangrao
Linchuan
Ganzhou
Shaoguan
Fuzhou
(Foochow; Fuchou)
Nanping
Sanming
Quanzhou
(Ch'uanchou)
Zhangzhou
Xiamen
(Hsiamen; Amoy)
Shantou
(Swatow)
Chao'an
Foshan
Jiangmen
Shenzhen
Wuzhou
Zhaoqing
Zhanjiang
Macheng
Tunxi
Dabie Shan
Mufu Shan
Jiuling Shan
Wugong Shan
Wuyi Shan
Chungyang Shanmo
Poyang Hu
Chao Hu
Hongze Hu
Gaoyou Hu
Dongting Hu
Chang Jiang (Yangtze)
Han Shui
Huai He
Gan Jiang
Xiang Jiang
Min Jiang
Xi Jiang
Bei Jiang
Dong Jiang
Yuan Jiang
Zi Shui
Hangzhou Wan
Chongming Dao
Zhoushan Dao
Daishan Dao
Xuefeng Shan
Chinmen Tao
Matsu Tao
Hainan
Xinghua Wan
Honghai Wan
Dangan Liedao
Gaolan Dao
Shangchuan Dao
Xiachuan Dao
Hailing Dao
Donghai Dao
Naozhou Dao
Tungsha Tao
Nanji Shan
Yuhuan Dao
Taizhou Liedao
Fuying Dao
Nanri Dao
Lü Tao
Hungt'ou Hsu
1834
1810
1725
2120
1629
2164
1703
3931
3997
East from Greenwich
112 114 116 118 120 122
32 30 28 26 24 22 20

1 : 17 800 000

100 0 100 200 300 400 miles
100 0 100 200 300 400 500 600 km

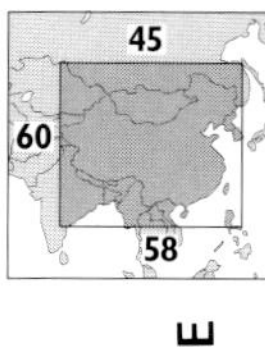

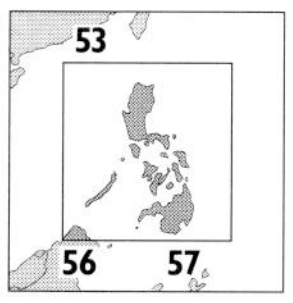

1 : 6 700 000

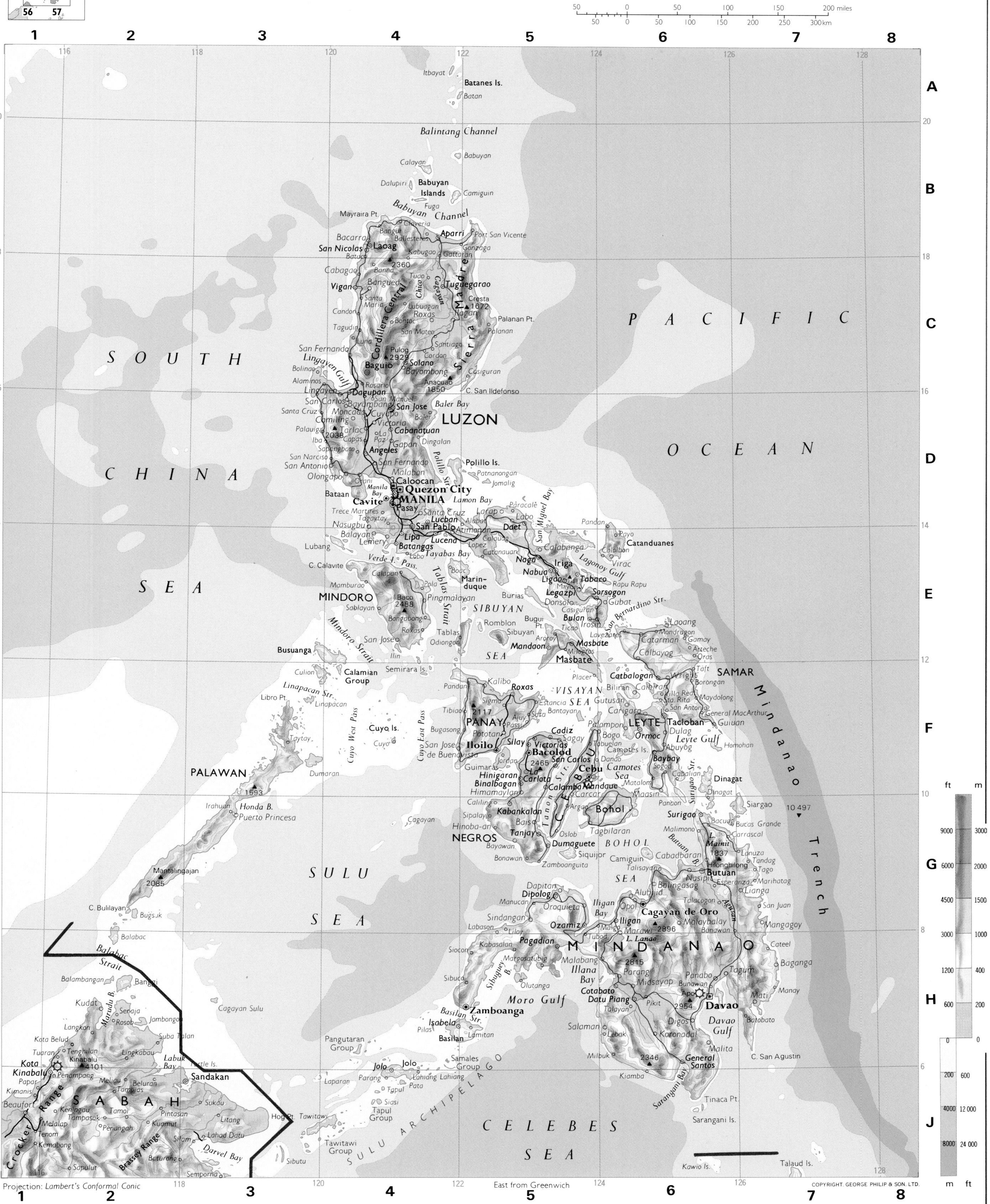

Projection: Lambert's Conformal Conic

East from Greenwich

58
88
90

1 2 3 4 5

A B C D E F

THAILAND
BURMA (MYANMAR)
LAOS
CAMBODIA
VIETNAM
PENINSULAR MALAYSIA
MALAYSIA
SINGAPORE
BRUNEI
SARAWAK
SABAH
BORNEO
KALIMANTAN
INDONESIA
SUMATERA
JAWA (JAVA)
BALI
NUSA TENGG...

ANDAMAN SEA
Gulf of Thailand
SOUTH CHINA SEA
Strait of Malacca
Selat Karimata
JAVA SEA
Greater Sunda Isla...
INDIAN OCEAN
Java Trench
G. of Martaban
Paracel Is.
Spratly Is.

RANGOON
BANGKOK
Vientiane
PHNOM PENH
THANH PHO HO CHI MINH (Saigon)
Da Nang
Hue
Nha Trang
Kuala Lumpur
George Town
Medan
Padang
Palembang
Pontianak
Kuching
Bandar Seri Begawan
Kota Kinabalu
Banjarmasin
JAKARTA
Bandung
Semarang
Surabaya
Yogyakarta
Malang
Bangka
Belitung
Kepulauan Natuna Besar
Kepulauan Anambas
Kepulauan Riau
Kepulauan Lingga
Kepulauan Mentawai
Nias
Siberut
Simeulue
Enggano
Madura
Lombok

ft m
12 000 4000
9000 3000
6000 2000
4500 1500
3000 1000
1200 400
600 200
0 0
200 600
2000 6000
4000 12 000
6000 18 000
8000 24 000
m ft

Projection: Mercator

100 105 110 115

East from Greenwich

1 2 3 4

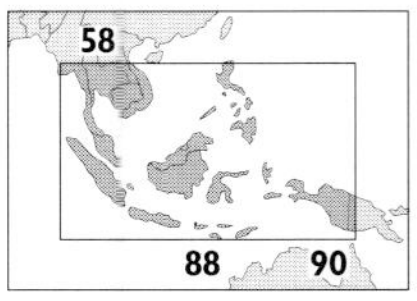

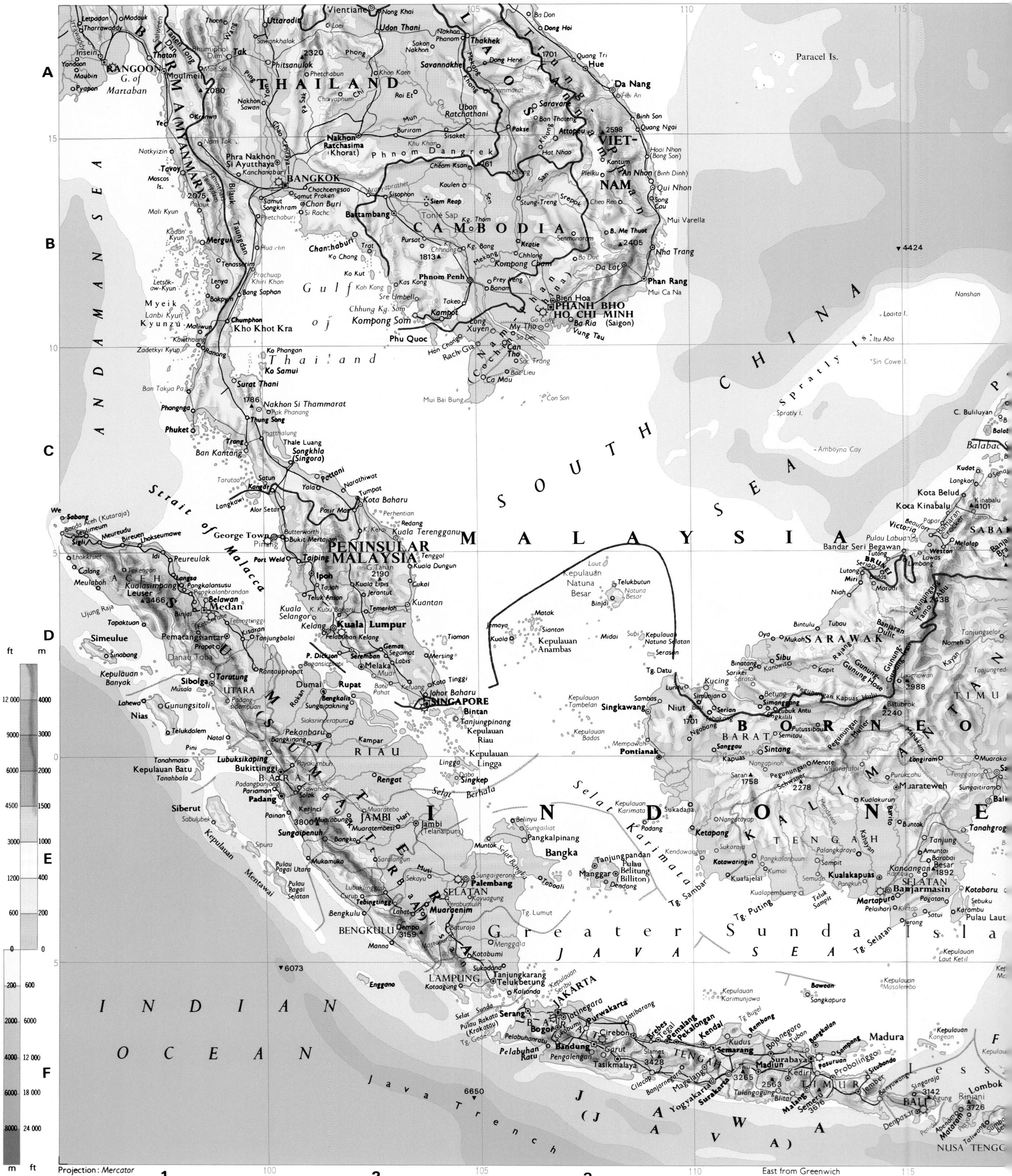

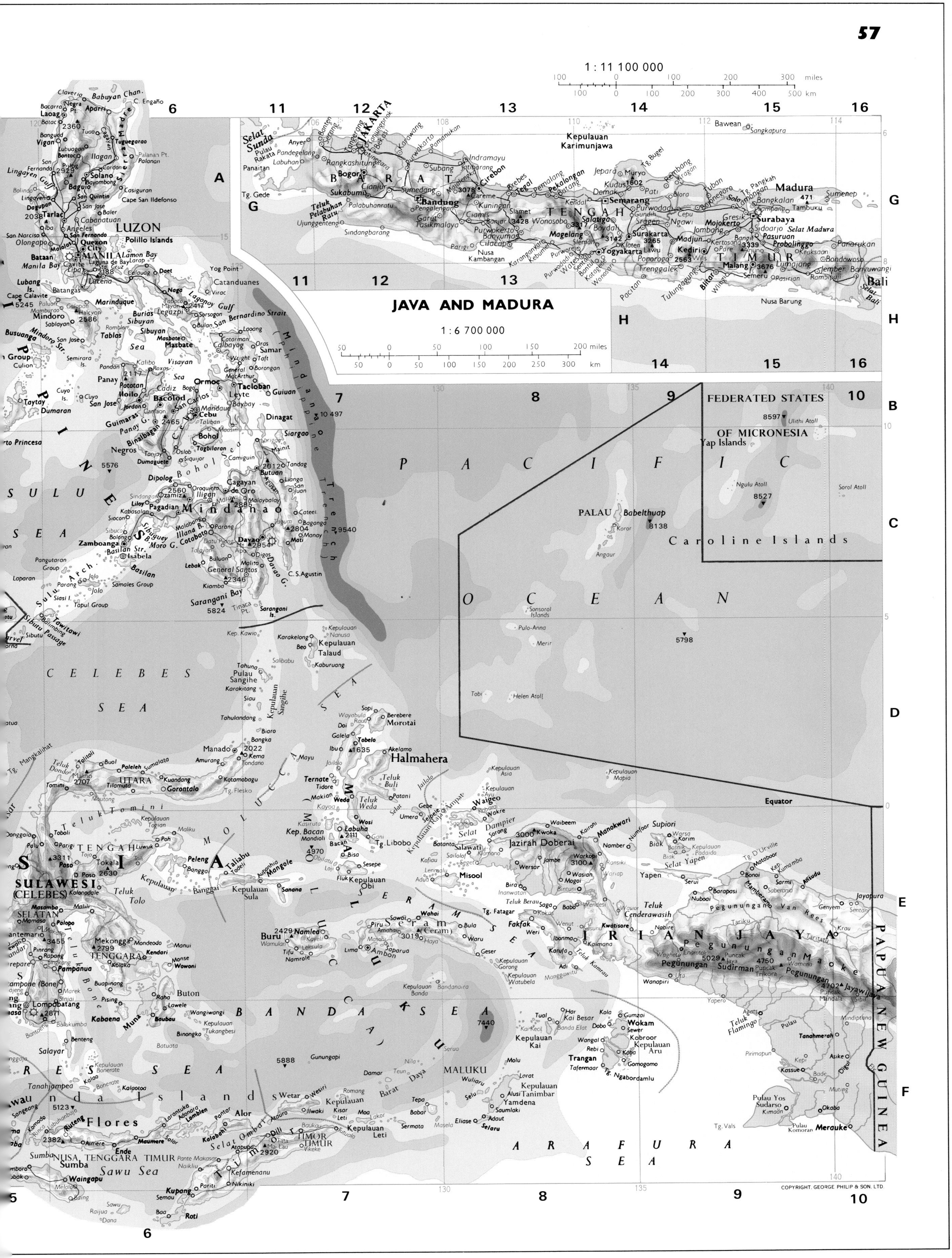
1 : 11 100 000
100 0 100 200 300 miles
100 0 100 200 300 400 500 km
JAVA AND MADURA
1 : 6 700 000
50 0 50 100 150 200 miles
50 0 50 100 150 200 250 300 km
JAKARTA
Selat Sunda
Bogor
Bandung
Cirebon
Sukabumi
Tasikmalaya
Pekalongan
Tegal
Semarang
Magelang
Yogyakarta
Surakarta
Madiun
Kediri
Malang
Surabaya
Madura
Bawean
Kepulauan Karimunjawa
Probolinggo
Pasuruan
Mojokerto
Jember
Banyuwangi
Bali
Nusa Kambangan
Nusa Barung
Tg. Gede
BARAT
TENGAH
TIMUR
LUZON
MANILA
Quezon City
Manila Bay
Polillo Islands
Lamon Bay
Babuyan Chan.
C. Engaño
Aparri
Laoag
Vigan
Baguio
Lingayen Gulf
Tarlac
San Fernando
Olongapo
Batangas
Lucena
Mindoro
Marinduque
Tablas
Sibuyan
Masbate
Samar
Catanduanes
Legazpi
San Bernardino Strait
Sibuyan Sea
Visayan Sea
Panay
Iloilo
Negros
Bacolod
Cebu
Bohol
Leyte
Tacloban
Ormoc
Dinagat
Siargao
Bohol Sea
Mindanao
Iligan
Cagayan de Oro
Butuan
Pagadian
Dipolog
Zamboanga
Basilan
Basilan Str.
Isabela
Cotabato
Moro G.
Davao
Davao G.
General Santos
Sarangani Bay
C. S.Agustin
Sulu Arch.
Jolo
Tawitawi
Sibutu Passage
SULU SEA
PHILIPPINES
Mindanao Trench
Philippine Trench
10 497
9540
PACIFIC OCEAN
FEDERATED STATES OF MICRONESIA
Yap Islands
Ulithi Atoll
Ngulu Atoll
Sorol Atoll
Caroline Islands
PALAU
Babelthuap
Koror
Angaur
Sonsorol Islands
Pulo-Anna
Merir
Tobi
Helen Atoll
5798
8138
8527
8597
CELEBES SEA
Kepulauan Talaud
Kepulauan Sangihe
Pulau Sangihe
Manado
Morotai
Halmahera
Ternate
Tidore
Kep. Bacan
Kepulauan Obi
Kepulauan Sula
Mangole
Taliabu
Peleng
Banggai
MOLUCCA SEA
MALUKU
Gorontalo
Teluk Tomini
UTARA
TENGAH
SULAWESI (CELEBES)
SELATAN
TENGGARA
Kendari
Teluk Bone
Buton
Muna
Kabaena
Salayar
Lompobatang
Buru
Seram (Ceram)
Ambon
Seram Sea
BANDA SEA
Kepulauan Banda
Kepulauan Kai
Kepulauan Aru
Kepulauan Tanimbar
Yamdena
Wetar
Alor
Flores
Sumba
Sawu Sea
Timor
Dili
Kupang
Roti
NUSA TENGGARA TIMUR
TIMOR TIMUR
Sunda Island
Flores Sea
ARAFURA SEA
Waigeo
Misool
Salawati
Sorong
Jazirah Doberai
Manokwari
Biak
Supiori
Yapen
Selat Yapen
Teluk Cenderawasih
Fakfak
Kaimana
IRIAN JAYA
Pegunungan Sudirman
Pegunungan Jayawijaya
Puncak Jaya 5029
Puncak Trikora 4750
4702
Jayapura
Merauke
Pulau Yos Sudarso
Teluk Flamingo
PAPUA NEW GUINEA
Equator
7440
5888
COPYRIGHT. GEORGE PHILIP & SON, LTD.

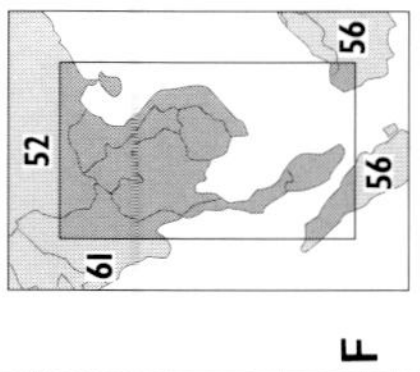
52
56
56
61

Gulf of Tonkin
Gulf of Martaban
HAINAN
GUANGXI ZHUANGZU ZIZHIQU AUTONOMOUS REGION
YUNNAN
BURMA
(MYANMAR)
SHAN STATE
KAYAH
LAOS
THAILAND
CAMBODIA
Mekong
Khorat
Phnom Dangrek
Central Highlands
Dawna Range
Taungnyo Taung
Mandalay
Rangoon
Moulmein
Vientiane
Luang Prabang
HANOI
Haiphong
Hue
Da Nang
Haikou
Zhanjiang
Nanning
BANGKOK
Chiang Mai
Udon Thani
Ubon Ratchathani
Nakhon Ratchasima (Khorat)
Battambang
Tonle Sap
Pakse
Vinh
Thanh Hoa
Red River Delta
Lancang Jiang
Salween
Sittang
Qiongzhou Haixia (Hainan Strait)
Leizhou Bandao
Tran Ninh
Boloven
Cao Nguyen
Qui Nhon

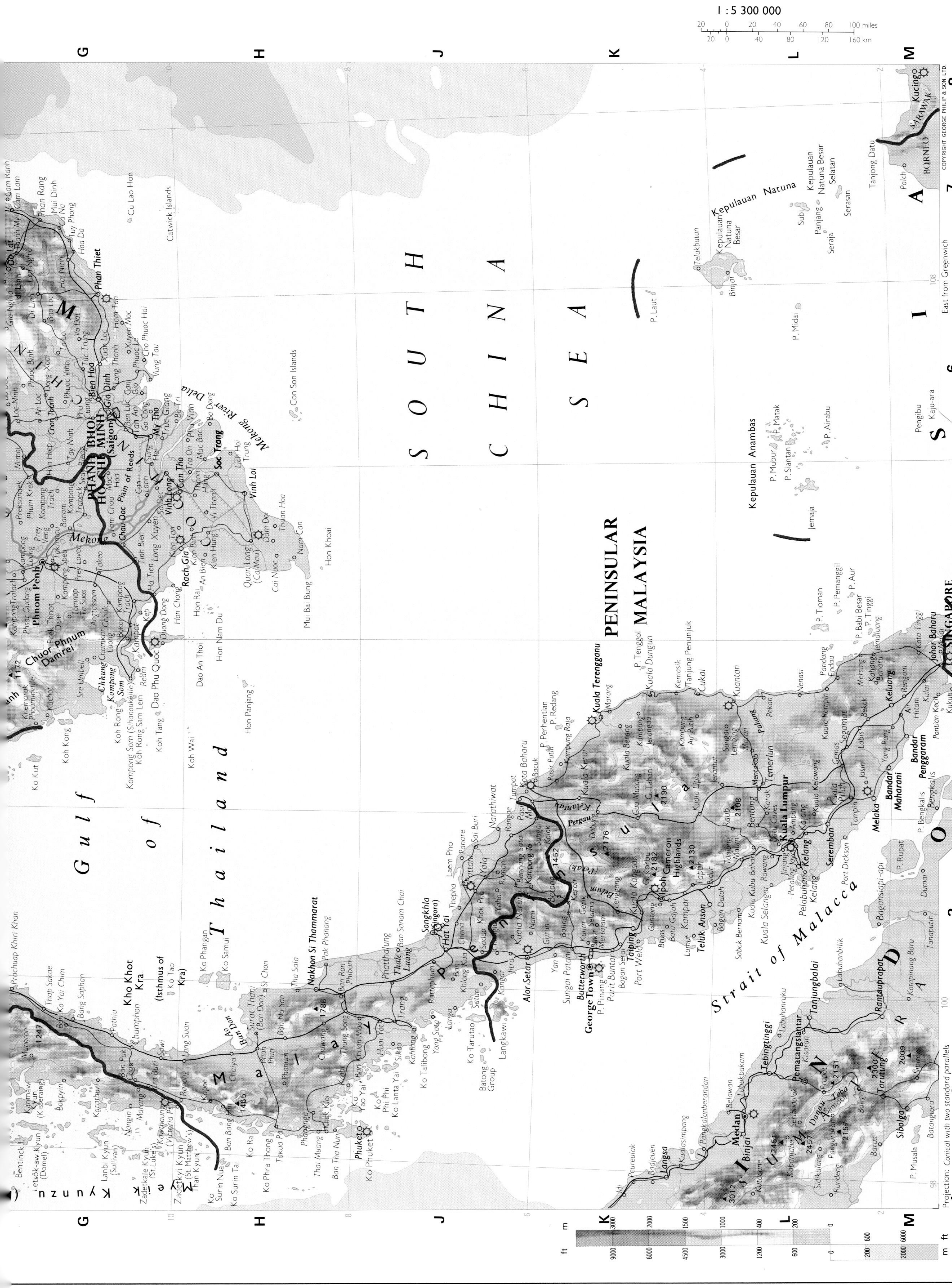
1 : 5 300 000
20 0 20 40 60 80 100 miles
20 0 40 80 120 160 km
SOUTH CHINA SEA
Gulf of Thailand
PENINSULAR MALAYSIA
Strait of Malacca
INDONESIA
SUMATERA
Kepulauan Natuna
Kepulauan Anambas
Mekong River Delta
PHANH BHO HO CHI MINH (Saigon)
Phnom Penh
Kuala Lumpur
SINGAPORE
George Town
Medan
Kuala Terengganu
Kota Baharu
Ipoh
Melaka
Johor Baharu
Alor Setar
Songkhla
Hat Yai
Nakhon Si Thammarat
Surat Thani
Phuket
Kuantan
Seremban
Kelang
Taiping
Kuching
SARAWAK
BORNEO
Cameron Highlands
Kho Khot Kra (Isthmus of Kra)
Con Son Islands
Plain of Reeds
Projection: Conical with two standard parallels
East from Greenwich
COPYRIGHT GEORGE PHILIP & SON LTD.
m ft
3000 9000
2000 6000
1500 4500
1000 3000
400 1200
200 600
0 0
200 600
2000 6000

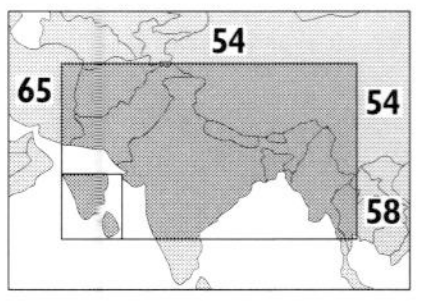
54
65
54
58

TURKMEN.
HERAT
Safīd Kūh
AFGHANISTAN
Hindu Kush
Kābul
Peshawar
Rawalpindi
Islamabad
NORTH WEST FRONTIER
JAMMU AND KASHMIR
Karakoram Range
Srinagar
Lahore
Faisalabad
Amritsar
Multan
Quetta
Toba Kakar
Sulaiman Range
Kirthar Range
Siahan Range
Central Makran Range
Makran Coast Range
PAKISTAN
IRAN
Sukkur
Hyderabad
KARACHI
Mouths of the Indus
ARABIAN SEA
Tropic of Cancer
Thar Desert (Great Indian Desert)
RAJASTHAN
Jodhpur
Jaipur
Ajmer
Bikaner
DELHI
Agra
PUNJAB
Ludhiana
HARYANA
Meerut
Aligarh
Gwalior
Rann of Kachchh
Gulf of Kachchh
GUJARAT
Ahmadabad
Vadodara (Baroda)
Rajkot
Jamnagar
Surat
Gulf of Khambhat
Daman
DADRA & NAGAR HAVELI
BOMBAY
MAHARASHTRA
Pune (Poona)
Nasik
Aurangabad
Solapur
Kolhapur
Belgaum
Panaji (Panjim)
MADHYA PRADESH
Indore
Bhopal
Ujjain
Nagpur
Satpura Range
ANDHRA PRADESH
Hyderabad
Western Ghats
KARNATAKA
Bangalore
Mysore
Mangalore
TAMIL NADU
Madras
Salem
Coimbatore
Tiruchchirappalli
Madurai
Pondicherry
KERALA
Calicut (Kozhikode)
Cochin
Trivandrum
Cape Comorin
Malabar Coast
Coromandel Coast
Palk Strait
Palk Bay
Gulf of Mannar
SRI LANKA (CEYLON)
Jaffna
Trincomalee
Kandy
Colombo
Galle
Dondra Head
Continuation Southwards on same scale
Projection: Conical with two standard parallels
ft m
18 000 6000
12 000 4000
9000 3000
6000 2000
4500 1500
3000 1000
1200 400
600 200
0 0
200 600
m ft

1 : 8 900 000

100 50 0 50 100 150 200 miles

100 0 100 200 300 km

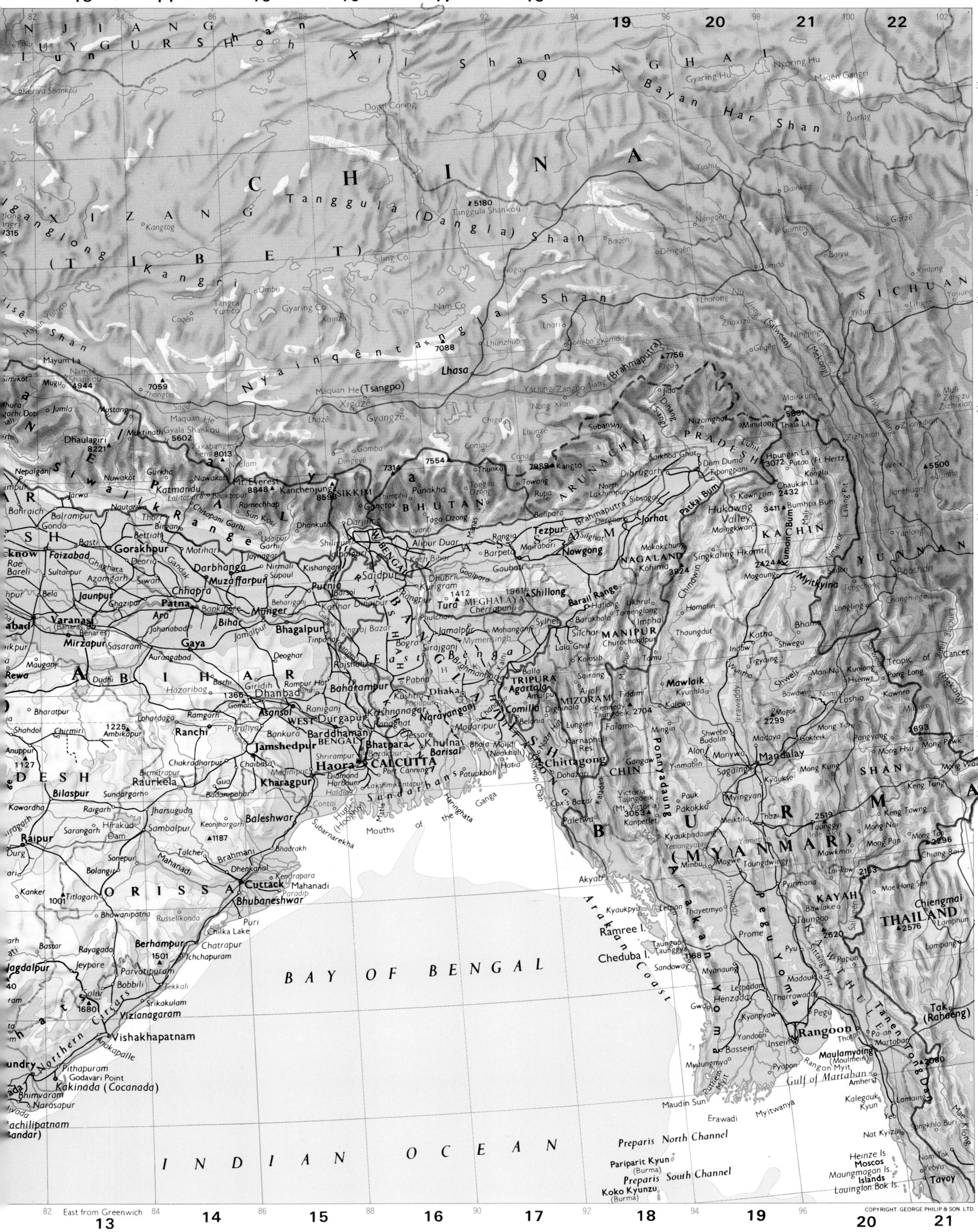

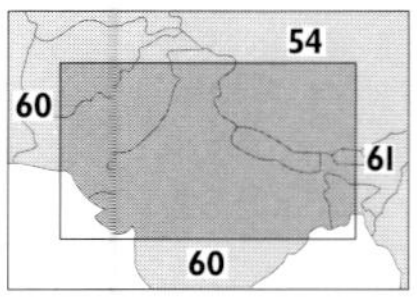
54
60
61
60

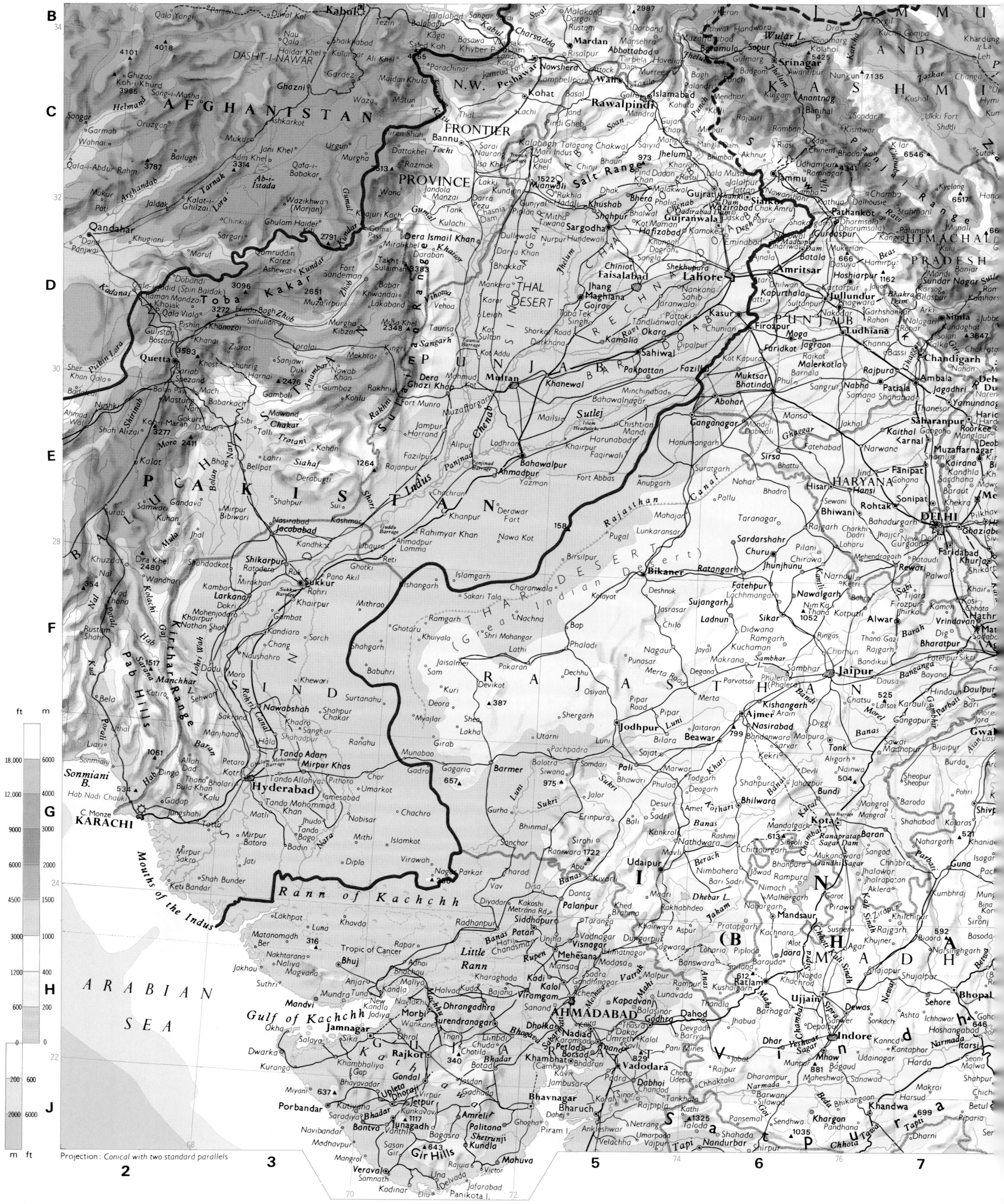
1
2
3
4
5
6
7
B
C
D
E
F
G
H
J
AFGHANISTAN
Kabul
Ghazni
Qandahar
DASHT-I-NAWAR
Helmand
Arghandab
N.W. FRONTIER PROVINCE
Peshawar
Mardan
Kohat
Bannu
Dera Ismail Khan
Islamabad
Rawalpindi
Jhelum
Salt Range
Sargodha
Gujranwala
Sialkot
Faisalabad
Lahore
Amritsar
Jammu
Srinagar
Wular L.
JAMMU AND KASHMIR
HIMACHAL PRADESH
Simla
Chandigarh
Ludhiana
Jullundur
PUNJAB
Quetta
Toba Kakar
Sulaiman Range
THAL DESERT
Multan
Bahawalpur
Sutlej
Chenab
Ravi
Indus
PAKISTAN
BALUCHISTAN
Kalat
Jacobabad
Sukkur
Larkana
Kirthar Range
Pab Hills
SIND
Nawabshah
Hyderabad
KARACHI
C. Monze
Sonmiani B.
Mouths of the Indus
Rann of Kachchh
ARABIAN SEA
Gulf of Kachchh
Bhuj
Jamnagar
Rajkot
Junagadh
Porbandar
Gir Hills
Bhavnagar
GUJARAT
AHMADABAD
Vadodara
THAR DESERT (Great Indian Desert)
Rajasthan Canal
RAJASTHAN
Bikaner
Jodhpur
Jaipur
Ajmer
Udaipur
HARYANA
DELHI
Hisar
Rohtak
Alwar
MADHYA PRADESH
Indore
Ujjain
Bhopal
Narmada
Tapti
Vindhya Range
Satpura Range
Tropic of Cancer
Projection: Conical with two standard parallels
ft
m
18,000
12,000
9000
6000
4500
3000
1200
600
0
200
2000
6000
4000
3000
2000
1500
1000
400
200
0
600
6000

1 : 5 300 000
50 0 50 100 150 miles
50 0 50 100 150 200 km
JAMMU AND KASHMIR
On same scale as Main Map
CHINA
Karakoram Range
Kunlun Shan
N.W. FRONTIER PROVINCE
PUNJAB
JAMMU AND KASHMIR
Zaskar Mountains
Ladakh Range
HIMACHAL PRADESH
Srinagar
Rawalpindi
Islamabad
Gilgit
Leh
Jammu
Nganglong Kangri
Gangdisê Shan
CHINA
XIZANG (TIBET)
NEPAL
Katmandu
Mt. Everest 8848
Kanchenjunga
SIKKIM
BHUTAN
ASSAM
BANGLADESH
DHAKA
UTTAR PRADESH
MADHYA PRADESH
BIHAR
WEST BENGAL
Lucknow
Kanpur
Allahabad
Varanasi
Patna
Calcutta
Mouths of the Ganga
The Sandheads
East from Greenwich
COPYRIGHT. GEORGE PHILIP & SON. LTD.

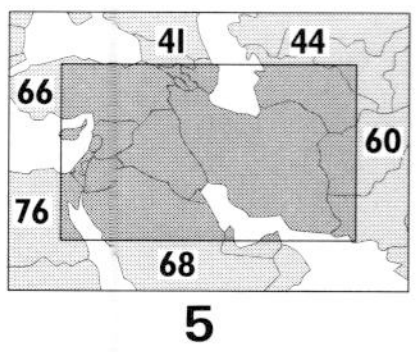

Projection: Conical with two standard parallels

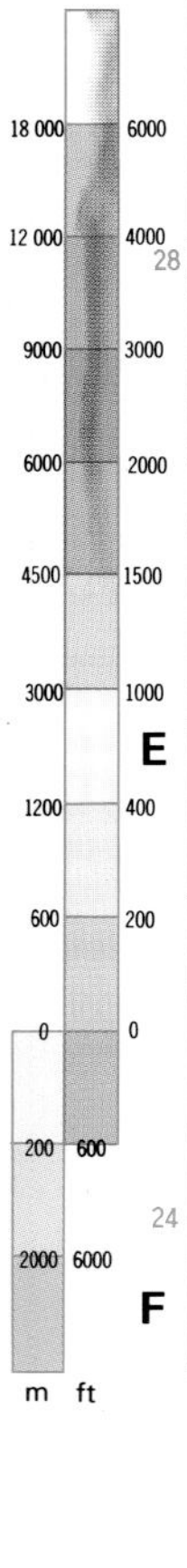

1 : 6 200 000

50 0 50 100 150 200 miles
50 0 50 100 150 200 250 300 km

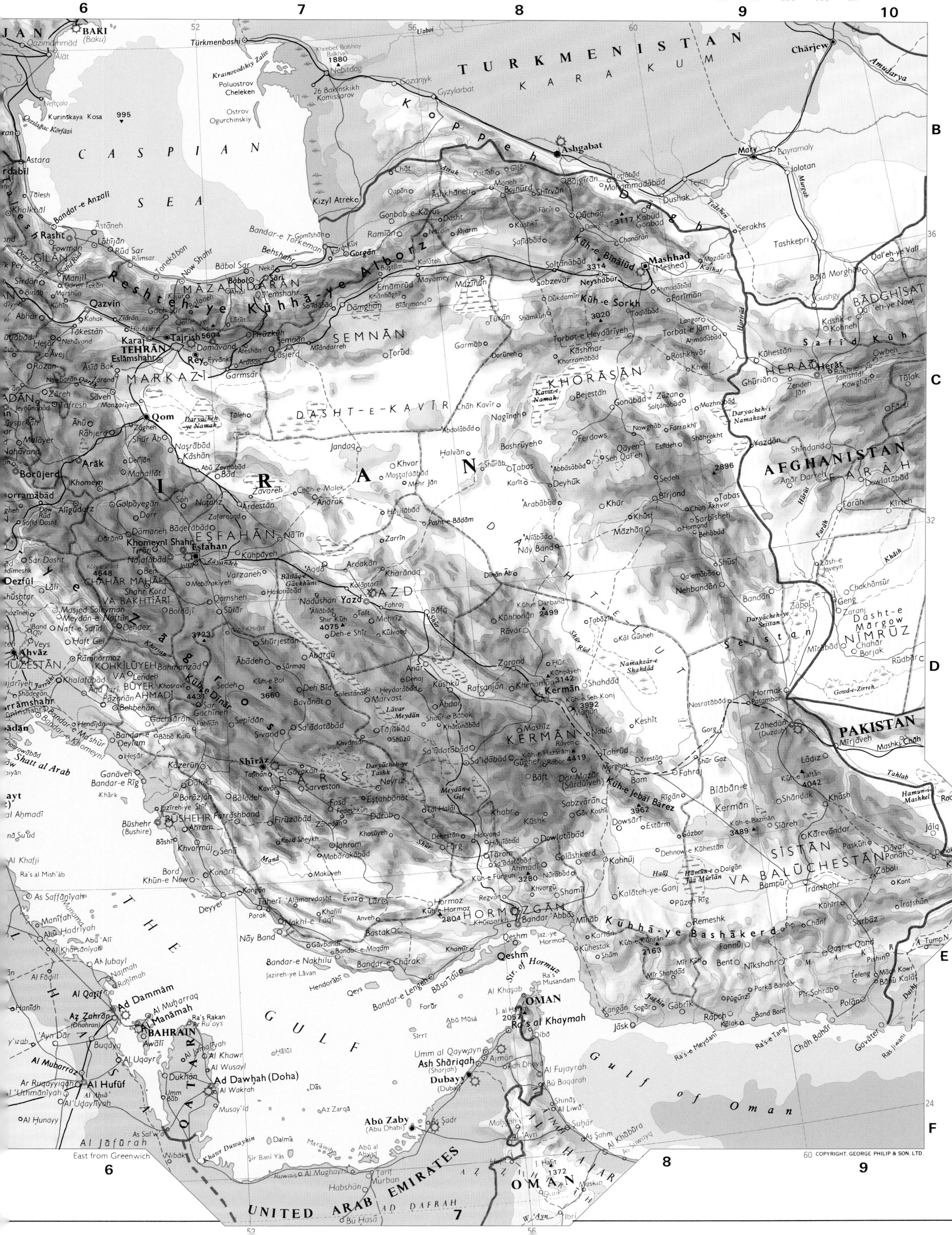

1 : 4 400 000

50 0 50 100 miles
50 0 50 100 150 km

Projection: *Conical with two standard parallels*

Division between Greeks and Turks in Cyprus; Turks to the North.

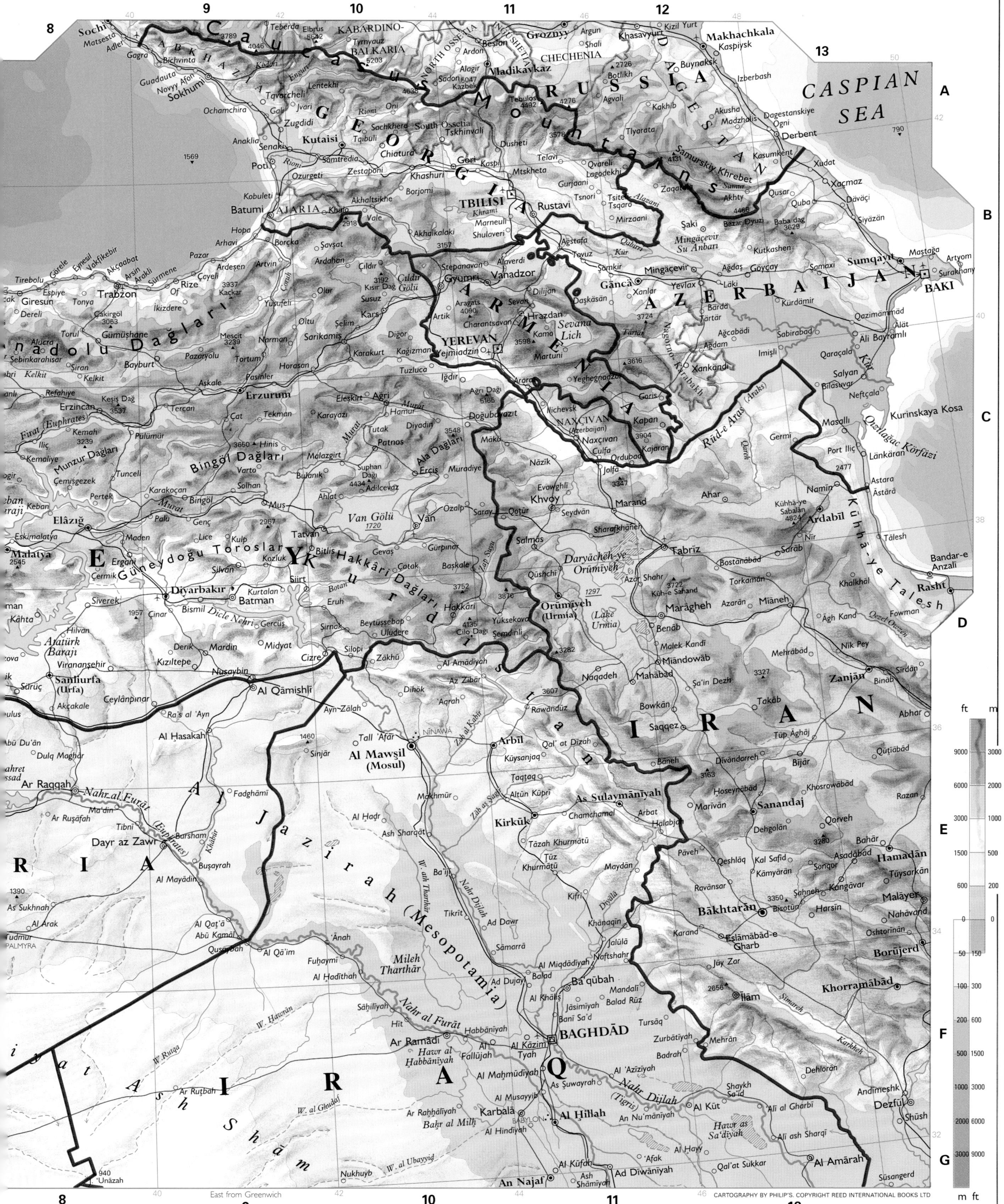
Caucasus Mountains
RUSSIA
DAGESTAN
CHECHENIA
NORTH OSSETIA
INGUSHETIA
KABARDINO-BALKARIA
ABKHAZIA
GEORGIA
AJARIA
South Ossetia
ARMENIA
AZERBAIJAN
NAXÇIVAN (Azerbaijan)
Nagorno Karabakh
CASPIAN SEA
TURKEY
IRAN
IRAQ
SYRIA
Anadolu Dağları
Güneydoğu Toroslar
Hakkâri Dağları
Kurdistan
Al Jazirah (Mesopotamia)
Ash Shām
Kühhā-ye Talesh
Samursky Khrebet
Bingöl Dağları
Munzur Dağları
Ala Dağları
Van Gölü
Daryācheh-ye Orūmīyeh (Lake Urmia)
Sevana Lich
Mingäçevir Su Anbarı
Qızılağac Körfäzi
Mileh Tharthār
Hawr al Habbānīyah
Hawr as Sa'dīyah
Nahr al Furāt (Euphrates)
Nahr Dijlah (Tigris)
Firat (Euphrates)
Rūd-e Aras (Araks)
Kür
TBILISI
YEREVAN
BAKI
BAGHDĀD
Sochi
Sokhumi
Kutaisi
Batumi
Poti
Rustavi
Gyumri
Vanadzor
Gäncä
Sumqayıt
Makhachkala
Derbent
Groznyy
Vladikavkaz
Trabzon
Rize
Giresun
Erzurum
Erzincan
Kars
Ağrı
Van
Elâzığ
Malatya
Diyarbakır
Batman
Siirt
Şanlıurfa (Urfa)
Mardin
Cizre
Al Qāmishlī
Al Hasakah
Ar Raqqah
Dayr az Zawr
Al Mawşil (Mosul)
Arbil
Kirkūk
As Sulaymānīyah
Ar Ramādī
Karbalā
Al Hillah
An Najaf
Al Kūt
Al 'Amārah
Tabrīz
Ardabīl
Rasht
Orūmīyeh (Urmia)
Marāgheh
Zanjān
Sanandaj
Bākhtarān
Hamadān
Khorramābād
Dezfūl
Ilām
Borūjerd
Malāyer
CARTOGRAPHY BY PHILIP'S. COPYRIGHT REED INTERNATIONAL BOOKS LTD
East from Greenwich

ARABIA AND THE HORN OF AFRICA

1 : 13 300 000

100 0 100 200 300 400 miles

100 0 100 200 300 400 500 600 km

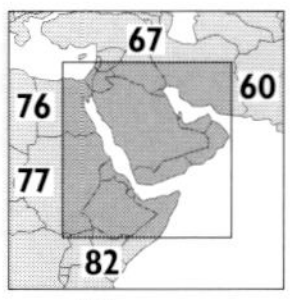

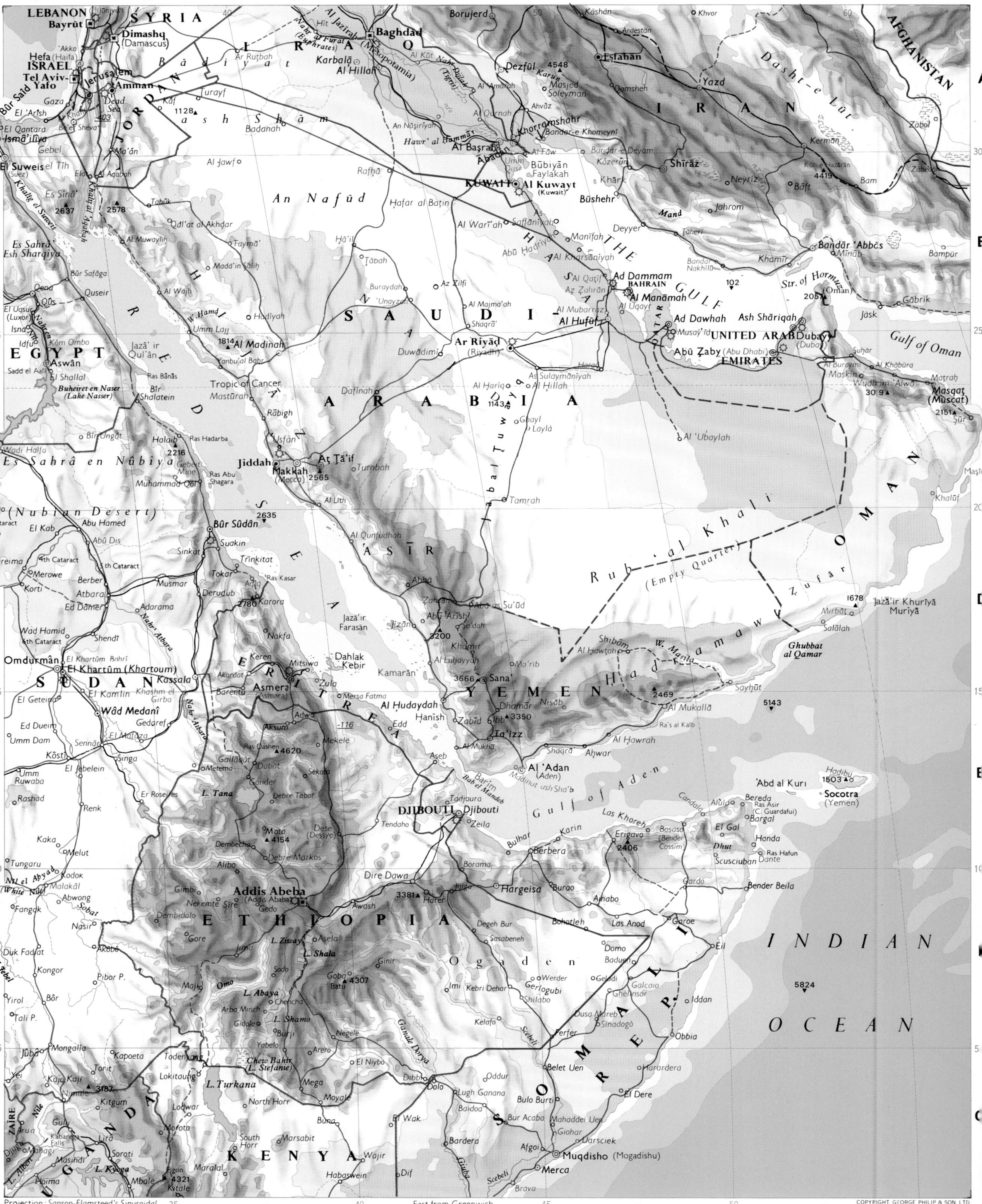

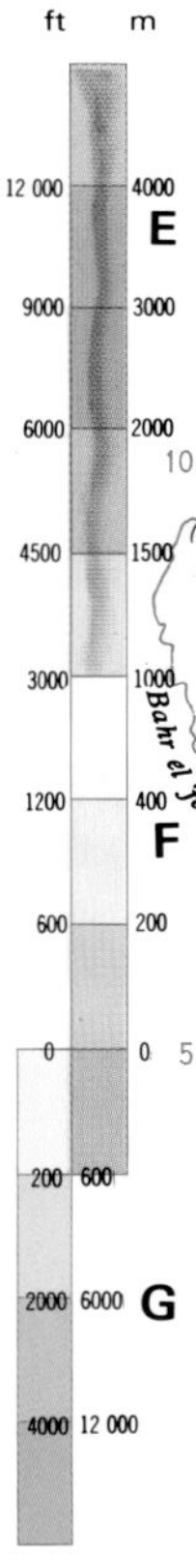

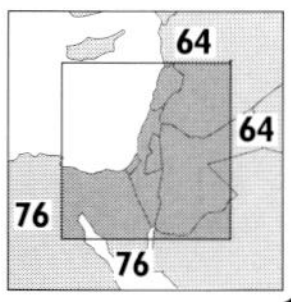

1 : 2 200 000

10 0 10 20 30 40 50 miles
10 0 10 20 30 40 50 60 70 80 km

CYPRUS

Paphos
Episkopi Limassol Akrotiri
Bay C. Gata Bay

MEDITERRANEAN

SEA

Al Hamidiyah Tall Kalakh Hims
(Homs) Furqlus
Al Mina' ASH Shinshār
Tarābulus SHAMĀL Al Qusayr
(Tripoli) Zgharta Al Hirmil Al Qaryatayn
Al Batrūn Dūma Qurnat as Sawdā' An Nabk
3088 Al Buray Tā'r Ghadir
Jubayl Qortāba 2616 J. az Zubaydiyah
Ibrāhim 2628 Ba'labakk 1406 SYRIA
BAYRŪT Al Labwah
(Beirut) 2420 DIMASHQ
Ash Shuwayfāt Zaḥlah Az Zabdānī Al Qutaylah Khān Abū Shāmāt
LEBANON Khirbat Hawsh Jabal Dūma
An Nabatiyah Qanawāt DIMASHQ
Saydā at Tahta 1942 (Damascus) Al Hījānah
(Sidon) 2814 Al Kiswah Burāq
Jazzin Hermon Al Kiswah AD BADAS
Sūr AL Al Qunaytirah DARĀ As Sanamayn AS SAFA
(Tyre) JANŪB 1197 Golan Ra'id
Qiryat Shemona Heights Shahba
Nahariyya Me'ona HAZOR Fiq Sahnāyā As Suwaydā SUWAYDĀ
Akko Zefat Dar'ā 1800 Salah
(Acre) Hagalil Yam Ṭafas Busrā ash Shām Salkhad
Mifraz Sakhnin Kinneret Yarmūk Ar Ramthā DURŪZ
Hefa Qiryat Yam Tverya Umm
Hefa Qiryat Ata (Tiberias) Ramtha IRBID Umm al Qittayn
(Haifa) Nazerat Irbid
Tirat Karmel (Nazareth) Ajlūn Al Mafraq
Dāliyat el Karmil HAZAFON Afula 'ad Dam
TEL MEGIDDO 1247
CAESAREA Shomron Al Jarash
Hadera Janin Zarqā'
ISRAEL Samaria Az Zarqā'
Netanya Tübás AMMĀN
HAMERKAZ Tulkarm W. al Fari'ah As Salt
Herzliyya Nābulus AL BALQĀ AL ʿĀSIMAH
Benē Beraq Azzūn
Tel Aviv-Yafo Petah Tiqwa SHILO
Ramat Gan West As Salt
Bat Yam 1016 Bank 259 Nā'ūr
Rishon le Ziyyon Ramla El Arod At Tunayb
N. Soreq Rehovot Rām Allāh Jericho Ma'daba
Ashdod Yavne
Jerusalem MĀ'ĪN
Qiryat Mal'akhi (Yerushalayim) Bayt Lahm
Ashqelon Bet Shemesh (Al Quds) Bethlehem W. al Haydān 1065
TEL Al Khalil Dhībān W. al
Qiryat Gat LAKHISH (Hebron) Yam Ha Melah Mawjib
Gaza N. Shiqma Az Zāhiriya (Al Bahr al Mayyit) 981
Strip Sederot W. al Ghadaf W. al Makhrūq
Khān Yūnis Be'er Sheva 'Ar'ad AL KARAK J. ash Shawmarī
Bûr Sa'îd Rafah Al Qatrānah 1072
(Port Said) Al Karak
Bûr Fu'ad Rās Burūn El Daheiriya 1305 Al Mazār SAUDI
Khalîg el Tîna Sabkhet el El 'Arîsh Bor Mashash 1682 W. al Hasā
Bardawîl El Daheir Dimona At Tafilah J. ash Shawmarī
Romani Bîr Qatia Bîr el Abd Bîr el Garārāt 333 W. Bā'ir
DEI Qantara Bîr el Jafir HADAROM Bā'ir ARABIA
Wâhid Bîr Madkūr Qezi'ot 127 JORDAN
Bîr el Duweidar Birein Mahattat Unayzah
Ismâ'iliya Muweilih Mizpe Ramon Nijila
Krafāta ET Qusaima 892 Ruim Tal'at 952
Khamsa Bîr Hasana al Jamā'āh 1735 Qa' el Jafr
El Buheirat Hanegev PETRA Aṭ Ṭubaiq
el Murrat G. Yi 'Allaq (Negev Desert) Ma'ān
el Kubra 1094 Bîr Beida Bîr-ad Dabbaghāt W. Abu Safāt
(Gt. Bitter L.) Bîr el Thamāda W. Qiratya El 'Agrūd N. Paran Mahattat ash Shidīyah
Ginīfa EL W. el Brūk N. Hiyyon
EL SUWEIS W. Malhasham Ras'an Naqb
E G Y P T W. Girāfi 'En 'Avrona 1435
El Suweis Bîr Gebel Husn Nakhl El Kuntilla Yotvata Ra's an Naqb
(Suez) 875 W. el 'Aqaba Mahattat ash Shidīyah
Bir Taufiq Ūyûn Mūsa W. el Tamabhi Bîr al Butayyinah
Bîr Bad 'Ain Sukr G. el Kabrit Bîr Abu Muhammad El Thamad Bir al Mōri SAUDI
Ghubbet 948 948 1592 Al 'Aqabah ARABIA
el Bûs El Wabeira Gebel el Tîh El Thamad 952
Bîr Abu Sanūiq Sinai Peninsula W. el Biarāt Khalîg el Aṭ Ṭubaiq
Rās W. Abu Ga'da Bîr el Hsei 'Aqaba ARABIA
Matarma 1272 W. Abu el Gari W. an Nuwaybi
1165 Haql

Projection: Polyconic

East from Greenwich

=== 1974 Cease Fire Lines

COPYRIGHT. GEORGE PHILIP & SON. LTD.

ft m
9000 3000
6000 2000
4500 1500
3000 1000
1200 400
600 200
0 0
200 600
2000 6000
m ft

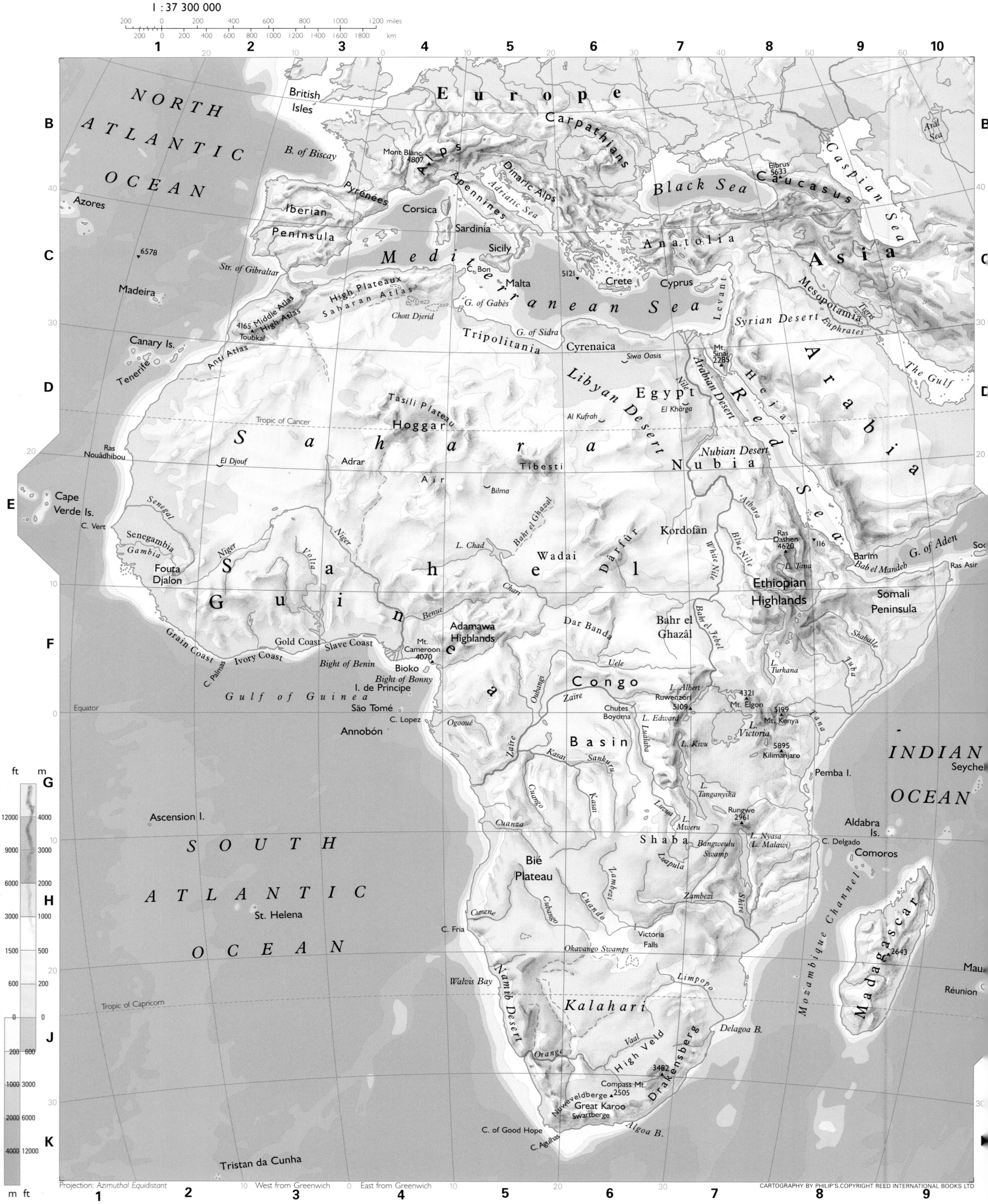
1 : 37 300 000
miles
km
Europe
British Isles
NORTH ATLANTIC OCEAN
B. of Biscay
Mont Blanc 4807
Alps
Carpathians
Dinaric Alps
Apennines
Adriatic Sea
Black Sea
Elbrus 5633
Caucasus
Caspian Sea
Aral Sea
Azores
Pyrénées
Iberian Peninsula
Corsica
Sardinia
Sicily
Anatolia
Asia
6578
Str. of Gibraltar
Mediterranean Sea
C. Bon
Malta
5121
Crete
Cyprus
Levant
Mesopotamia
Tigris
Madeira
High Plateaux
Saharan Atlas
Middle Atlas
High Atlas
4165
Toubkal
G. of Gabès
Chott Djerid
Syrian Desert
Euphrates
Canary Is.
Anti Atlas
Tenerife
Tripolitania
G. of Sidra
Cyrenaica
Siwa Oasis
Mt. Sinai 2285
The Gulf
Libyan Desert
Egypt
Nile
Arabian Desert
Hejaz
Red Sea
Arabia
Tasili Plateau
Hoggar
Al Kufrah
El Khârga
Tropic of Cancer
Ras Nouâdhibou
Sahara
El Djouf
Adrar
Tibesti
Nubian Desert
Nubia
Aïr
Bilma
Cape Verde Is.
C. Vert
Senegal
Senegambia
Gambia
Niger
Volta
Bahr el Ghazal
Atbara
Kordofân
L. Chad
Darfûr
Wadai
White Nile
Blue Nile
Ras Dashen 4620
116
L. Tana
Barim
G. of Aden
Bab el Mandeb
Ras Asir
Fouta Djalon
Sahel
Chari
Ethiopian Highlands
Somali Peninsula
Guinea
Benue
Adamawa Highlands
Dar Banda
Bahr el Ghazâl
Bahr el Jebel
Shaballe
Grain Coast
Gold Coast
Slave Coast
Ivory Coast
C. Palmas
Mt. Cameroon 4070
Bight of Benin
Bioko
Bight of Bonny
Uele
L. Turkana
Juba
Gulf of Guinea
I. de Principe
São Tomé
Equator
Congo
Oubangi
Zaïre
L. Albert
Ruwenzori 5109
4321
Mt. Elgon
5199
Mt. Kenya
Tana
C. Lopez
Annobón
Ogooué
Chutes Boyoma
L. Edward
Lualaba
L. Victoria
Basin
L. Kivu
5895
Kilimanjaro
INDIAN OCEAN
Seyche
Kasai
Sankuru
Cuango
L. Tanganyika
Pemba I.
Ascension I.
Lucuya
L. Mweru
Rungwe 2961
Cuanza
Aldabra Is.
SOUTH ATLANTIC OCEAN
Shaba
Bangweulu Swamp
L. Nyasa (L. Malawi)
C. Delgado
Comoros
Luapula
Bié Plateau
Lambezi
Zambezi
Shire
Mozambique Channel
Madagascar
St. Helena
Cunene
Cubango
Cuando
C. Fria
Victoria Falls
Okavango Swamps
2643
Namib Desert
Walvis Bay
Limpopo
Mau
Réunion
Tropic of Capricorn
Kalahari
Delagoa B.
Vaal
Orange
High Veld
Drakensberg
3482
Compass Mt. 2505
Nuweveldberge
Great Karoo
Swartberge
C. of Good Hope
C. Agulhas
Algoa B.
Tristan da Cunha
ft m
12000 4000
9000 3000
6000 2000
3000 1000
1500 500
600 200
0 0
200 600
1000 3000
2000 6000
4000 12000
m ft
Projection: Azimuthal Equidistant
West from Greenwich
East from Greenwich
CARTOGRAPHY BY PHILIP'S.COPYRIGHT REED INTERNATIONAL BOOKS LTD

1 : 37 300 000
200 0 200 400 600 800 1000 1200 miles
200 0 200 400 600 800 1000 1200 1400 1600 1800 km
1 2 3 4 5 6 7 8 9 10
B C D E F G H J K
NORTH ATLANTIC OCEAN
Azores (Port.)
B. of Biscay
UNITED KINGDOM
LONDON
NETH.
BELG.
GERMANY
POLAND
Warsaw
RUSSIA
KAZAKSTAN
Kiev
Volgograd
Prague
CZECH REP.
UKRAINE
PARIS
FRANCE
Vienna
SLOVAK REP.
AUSTRIA
HUNGARY
SWITZ.
ROMANIA
Odessa
Caspian Sea
Aral Sea
CROATIA
BOS.-HERZ.
YUG.
Adriatic Sea
ITALY
Black Sea
GEORGIA
AZER.
ARM.
Baku
TURKMEN.
BULGARIA
Corsica
Rome
ALB.
MAC.
Madrid
SPAIN
PORTUGAL
Lisbon
Sardinia
Ankara
TURKEY
GREECE
Athens
Sicily
Mosul
TEHRĀN
Algiers
Annaba
Constantine
Tunis
Mediterranean Sea
Aleppo
SYRIA
Tigris
Euphrates
Baghdād
IRAQ
IRAN
Eşfahān
Madeira (Port.)
Rabat
Tétouan
Casablanca
Fès
TUNISIA
Sfax
MALTA
Crete
CYPRUS
LEB.
Damascus
Tel Aviv-Jaffa
Jerusalem
ISRAEL
JORDAN
Syrian Desert
Basra
KUWAIT
Chott Djerid
Tripoli
Misrātah
MOROCCO
Marrakesh
Benghazi
Alexandria
Port Said
Suez
CAIRO
El Faiyûm
Canary Is. (Sp.)
ALGERIA
LIBYA
Nile
Asyût
EGYPT
The Gulf
BAHRAIN
QATAR
SAUDI ARABIA
Riyadh
El Aaiún
In Salah
Marzūq
Aswân
Red Sea
Medina
Dakhla
WESTERN SAHARA
Fdérik
Tropic of Cancer
Sahara
Al Jawf
Jedda
Mecca
Ras Nouâdhibou
Wadi Halfa
Port Sudan
MAURITANIA
NIGER
Agadès
CHAD
Atbara
Athara
Mesewa
ERITREA
Asmera
YEMEN
Nouakchott
Tombouctou
Omdurmân
Khartoum
Wad Medani
St-Louis
Senegal
C. Vert
Dakar
SENEGAL
MALI
Niger
Niamey
L. Chad
Abéché
SUDAN
White Nile
Blue Nile
G. of Aden
Socotra (Yemen)
Ras Asir
GAMBIA
Banjul
GUINEA-BISSAU
Bissau
Bamako
BURKINA FASO
Ouagadougou
Kano
Maiduguri
Ndjamena
El Fâsher
El Obeid
L. Tana
DJIBOUTI
Djibouti
GUINEA
Bobo-Dioulasso
BENIN
NIGERIA
Abuja
Chari
Malakâl
Addis Ababa
Harer
Berbera
Conakry
Freetown
SIERRA LEONE
IVORY COAST
GHANA
TOGO
Benue
Wau
Bahr el Jebel
ETHIOPIA
SOMALI REP.
Shabelle
Monrovia
LIBERIA
Yamoussoukro
Bouaké
Kumasi
Lomé
Ibadan
Lagos
Enugu
CENTRAL AFRICAN REP.
Abidjan
Sekondi-Takoradi
Accra
Porto Novo
CAMEROON
Port Harcourt
Douala
Yaoundé
Bangui
Malabo
Bight of Benin
L. Turkana
Gulf of Guinea
EQUATORIAL GUINEA
Oubangi
L. Albert
Mogadishu
SÃO TOMÉ & PRINCIPE
Libreville
Zaïre
Kisangani
UGANDA
KENYA
Juba
Equator
C. Lopez
GABON
Mbandaka
Kampala
Kisumu
Kismayu
Annobón
CONGO
ZAÏRE
L. Edward
RWANDA
Kigali
L. Victoria
Nairobi
Tana
Lualaba
L. Kivu
BURUNDI
Bujumbura
INDIAN OCEAN
Brazzaville
Kasai
Mombasa
Pointe Noire
Kinshasa
SEYCHELLES
CABINDA (Angola)
Matadi
TANZANIA
Zanzibar
Kananga
Dodoma
Dar es Salaam
Cuango
L. Tanganyika
Ascension I. (U.K.)
Luanda
Aldabra Is.
L. Mweru
Likasi
Lubumbashi
L. Malawi
C. Delgado
COMOROS
SOUTH ATLANTIC OCEAN
Lobito
ANGOLA
Huambo
MALAWI
Antsiranana
Ndola
Lilongwe
Mayotte (Fr.)
Namibe
ZAMBIA
Moçambique
Lusaka
Zambezi
Mahajanga
Cunene
Cubango
Blantyre
Mozambique Channel
St. Helena (U.K.)
C. Fria
Livingstone
Harare
Toamasina
ZIMBABWE
Antananarivo
Beira
Bulawayo
MOZAMBIQUE
NAMIBIA
MADAGASCAR
MAURITIUS
BOTSWANA
Limpopo
Windhoek
Fianarantsoa
Réunion (Fr.)
Tropic of Capricorn
Gaborone
Pretoria
Johannesburg
Maputo
Mbabane
SWAZ.
Vaal
Orange
Kimberley
Maseru
LESOTHO
Durban
SOUTH AFRICA
East London
Cape Town
C. of Good Hope
Port Elizabeth
C. Agulhas
Tristan da Cunha (U.K.)
Projection: Azimuthal Equidistant
West from Greenwich
East from Greenwich
● Dakar Capital Cities
CARTOGRAPHY BY PHILIP'S.COPYRIGHT REED INTERNATIONAL BOOKS LTD

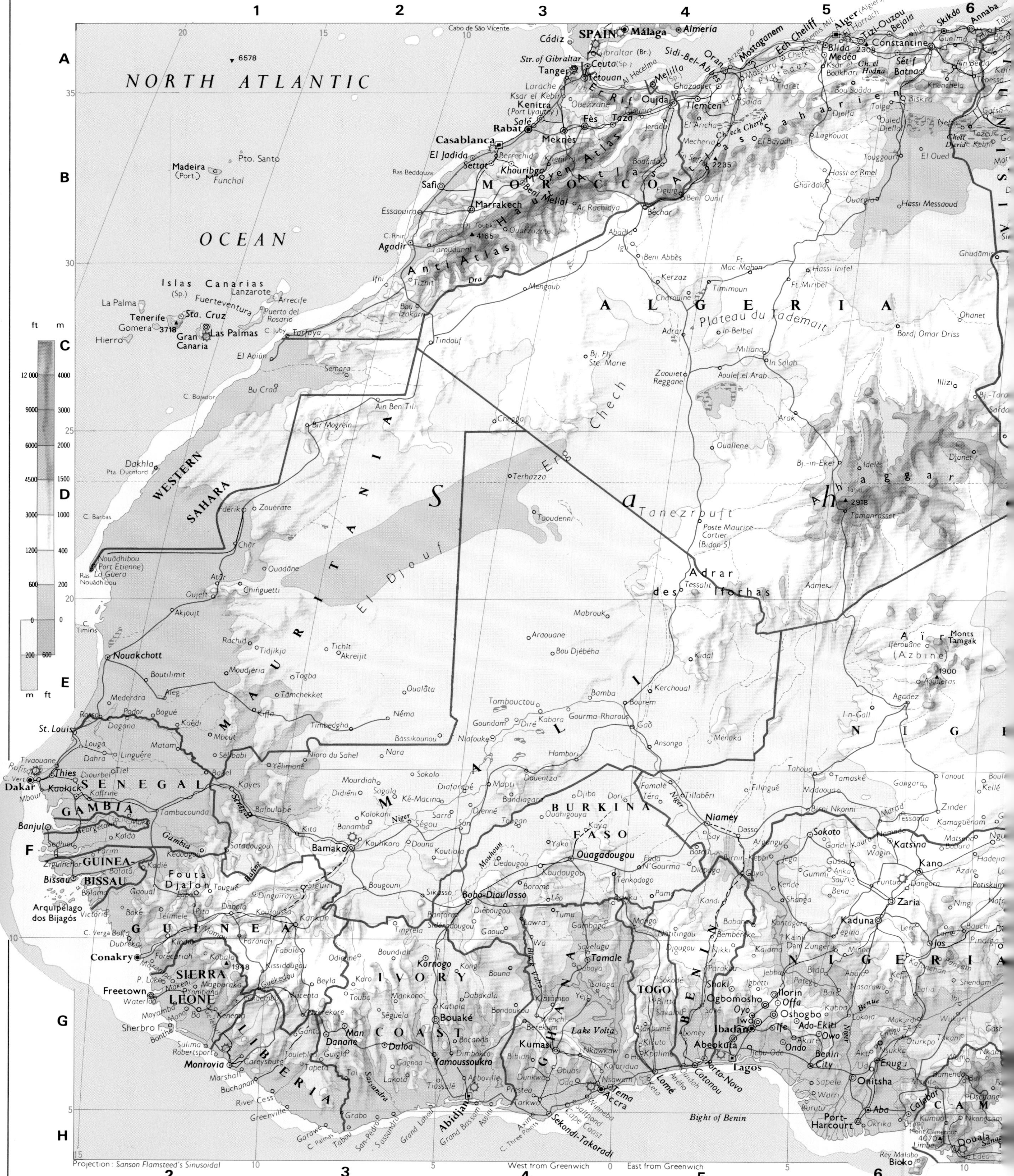
NORTH ATLANTIC
OCEAN
SPAIN
Cádiz
Málaga
Almería
Str. of Gibraltar
Gibraltar (Br.)
Tanger
Ceuta (Sp.)
Tétouan
Melilla (Sp.)
Oujda
Oran
Sidi-Bel-Abbès
Mostaganem
Ech Cheliff
Alger (Algiers)
Tizi-Ouzou
Bejaia
Skikda
Annaba
Blida
Medea
Constantine
Sétif
Batna
Biskra
Larache
Ksar el Kebir
Kenitra (Port Lyautey)
Rabat
Salé
Fès
Taza
Meknès
Casablanca
El Jadida
Settat
Khouribga
Beni Mellal
Safi
Marrakech
Essaouira
Agadir
Ouarzazate
Ar Rachidya
Béchar
Tlemcen
Saïda
Tiaret
Laghouat
Ghardaïa
Ouargla
Touggourt
El Oued
Hassi Messaoud
Hassi er Rmel
Madeira (Port.)
Pto. Santo
Funchal
Islas Canarias (Sp.)
Lanzarote
Fuerteventura
Arrecife
Puerto del Rosario
La Palma
Tenerife
Sta. Cruz
Gomera
Hierro
Gran Canaria
Las Palmas
C. Juby
Tarfaya
El Aaiún
Semara
Bu Craa
C. Bojador
Dakhla
WESTERN SAHARA
C. Barbas
Nouâdhibou (Port Etienne)
La Güera
MOROCCO
Moyen Atlas
Haut Atlas
Anti Atlas
Er Rif
Tiznit
Ifni
Dra
Tindouf
Mengoub
ALGERIA
Plateau du Tademaït
Béni Abbès
Kerzaz
Timimoun
Adrar
In Belbel
In Salah
Aoulef el Arab
Zaouiet Reggane
Bj. Fly Ste. Marie
Erg Chech
Arak
Ouallene
Illizi
Djanet
Idelès
Ahaggar
Tahat 2918
Tamanrasset
Tanezrouft
Poste Maurice Cortier (Bidon 5)
Adrar des Iforhas
Tessalit
Admer
Ghudamis
Ohanet
Bordj Omar Driss
Hassi Inifel
Ft. Miribel
Ft. Mac-Mahon
MAURITANIA
Zouérate
Fdérik
Bir Mogrein
Aïn Ben Tili
Chegga
Terhazza
Taoudenni
El Djouf
Ouadâne
Chinguetti
Atâr
Choûm
Akjoujt
Nouakchott
Tidjikja
Rachid
Moudjéria
Tichit
Akreijit
Tâmchekket
Aleg
Kiffa
Oualâta
Néma
Timbedgha
Boutilimit
Rosso
Kaédi
Mbout
Sélibabi
SAHARA
MALI
Araouane
Mabrouk
Bou Djébéha
Kidal
Kerchoual
Bamba
Bourem
Tombouctou
Goundam
Diré
Gourma-Rharous
Gao
Ansongo
Ménaka
Hombori
Douentza
Mopti
Bandiagara
Niafounké
Nara
Nioro du Sahel
Kayes
Bafoulabé
Kita
Bamako
Ségou
San
Koutiala
Sikasso
Bougouni
Aïr (Azbine)
Monts Tamgak
Agadez
I-n-Gall
NIGER
Tahoua
Niamey
Dosso
Tillabéri
Zinder
Maradi
St. Louis
Louga
Thiès
Dakar
Kaolack
SENEGAL
Tambacounda
GAMBIA
Banjul
Ziguinchor
GUINEA-BISSAU
Bissau
Arquipélago dos Bijagós
GUINEA
Fouta Djalon
Conakry
Kindia
Kankan
Siguiri
SIERRA LEONE
Freetown
Sherbro I.
LIBERIA
Monrovia
Buchanan
River Cess
Greenville
IVORY COAST
Korhogo
Bouaké
Man
Danané
Daloa
Yamoussoukro
Abidjan
Grand Bassam
Sassandra
San-Pédro
Tabou
BURKINA FASO
Ouagadougou
Bobo-Dioulasso
Koudougou
Tenkodogo
Fada N'Gourma
Dori
Djibo
GHANA
Tamale
Lake Volta
Kumasi
Accra
Tema
Sekondi-Takoradi
Cape Coast
C. Three Points
TOGO
Lomé
BENIN
Cotonou
Porto-Novo
Abomey
Parakou
Natitingou
Kandi
NIGERIA
Sokoto
Katsina
Kano
Zaria
Kaduna
Jos
Bauchi
Ilorin
Ogbomosho
Oshogbo
Ibadan
Abeokuta
Lagos
Oyo
Ado-Ekiti
Ondo
Benin City
Onitsha
Enugu
Aba
Port-Harcourt
Calabar
Benue
Niger
Bight of Benin
Biokpo
Douala
Mont Cameroun 4070
Limbe
Projection: Sanson Flamsteed's Sinusoidal
West from Greenwich
East from Greenwich

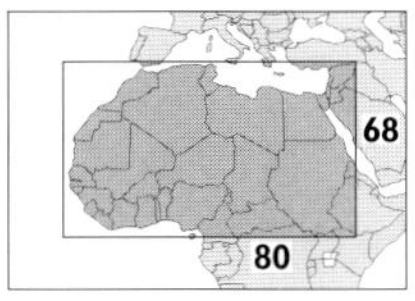
68
80

1 : 13 300 000

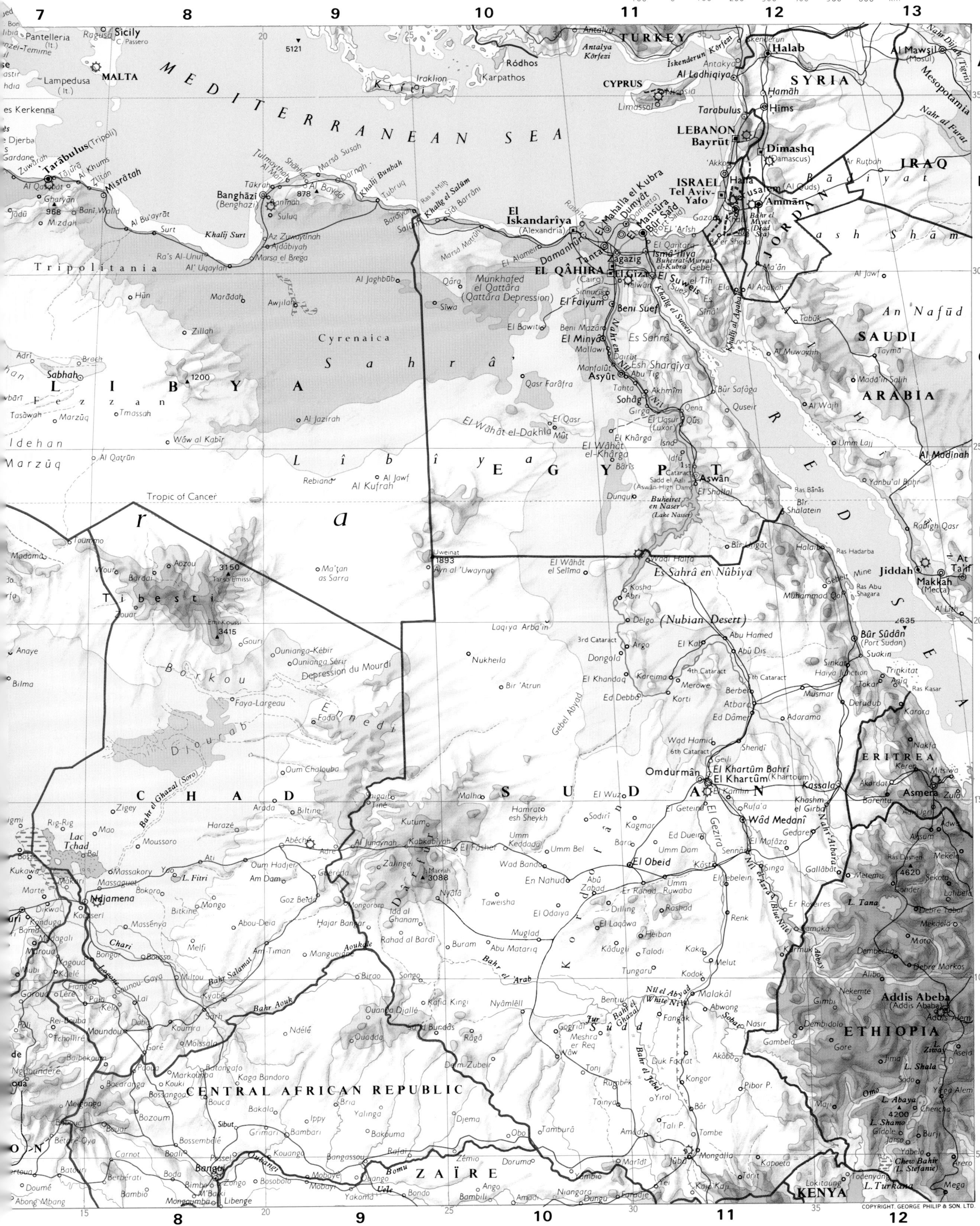
100 0 100 200 300 400 miles
100 0 100 200 300 400 500 600 km
7
8
9
10
11
12
13
A
B
C
D
E
F
G
H
MEDITERRANEAN SEA
Sicily
Pantelleria (It.)
MALTA
Lampedusa (It.)
Kerkenna
Djerba
Tarābulus (Tripoli)
Mişrātah
Banghāzi (Benghazi)
Khalīj Surt
Tripolitania
Cyrenaica
Sahrâ'
Lîbîya
LIBYA
Fezzan
Sabhah
Idehan Marzūq
Tropic of Cancer
Tibesti
Emi Koussi 3415
3150
Borkou
Ennedi
Djourab
Faya-Largeau
Ouniangа-Kébir
Depression du Mourdi
CHAD
Lac Tchad
Ndjamena
Abéché
Bahr el Ghazal (Soro)
Chari
Logone
Bahr Salamat
Bahr Aouk
CENTRAL AFRICAN REPUBLIC
Bangui
Oubangui
Bomu
Uele
ZAÏRE
Kríti
Iraklion
Karpathos
Ródhos
Antalya Körfezi
TURKEY
CYPRUS
Lefkosia
Limassol
İskenderun Körfezi
Halab
SYRIA
Hamāh
Hims
Tarabulus
LEBANON
Bayrūt
Dimashq (Damascus)
ISRAEL
Tel Aviv-Yafo
Haifa
Jerusalem (Al Quds)
'Ammān
JORDAN
Bahr el Miyet (Dead Sea)
IRAQ
Bādiyat ash Shām
Nahr Dijlah (Tigris)
Al Mawşil (Mosul)
Mesopotamia
Nahr al Furat
An Nafūd
SAUDI ARABIA
Tabūk
Al Madinah
Jiddah
Makkah (Mecca)
RED SEA
El Iskandarîya (Alexandria)
EL QÂHIRA (Cairo)
El Gîza
Bûr Sa'îd (Port Said)
El Suweis (Suez)
El Mansûra
Dumyât
Tanta
Zagazig
Munkhafed el Qattâra (Qattâra Depression)
Sîwa
El Faiyûm
Beni Suef
El Minyâ
Asyût
Sohâg
Qena
El Uqsur (Luxor)
Aswân
Sadd el Aali (Aswan High Dam)
Buheiret en Naser (Lake Nasser)
EGYPT
Es Sahrâ esh Sharqîya
El Wâhât el-Dakhla
El Wâhât el-Khârga
Nahr en Nîl
Es Sahrâ en Nûbiya
(Nubian Desert)
Wadi Halfa
Uweinat 1893
Gebel Abyad
SUDAN
Dongola
Atbara
Abu Hamed
Bûr Sûdân (Port Sudan)
Suakin
Kassala
Omdurmân
El Khartûm Bahrî
El Khartûm (Khartoum)
Wâd Medanî
El Gezira
El Obeid
Kordofân
El Fasher
Jebel Marra 3088
Dârfur
Nyala
Nahr Atbara
Nîl el Azraq (Blue Nile)
Nîl el Abyad (White Nile)
Malakâl
Sobat
Bahr el Ghazal
Bahr el Jebel
Bahr el 'Arab
Sudd
Jûba
ERITREA
Asmera
Mitsiwa
ETHIOPIA
L. Tana
Addis Abeba
Ras Dashen 4620
Gonder
Abay
L. Ziway
L. Abaya
L. Shamo
Chew Bahir (L. Stefanie)
L. Turkana
KENYA
COPYRIGHT GEORGE PHILIP & SON. LTD.
15
20
25
30
35
40

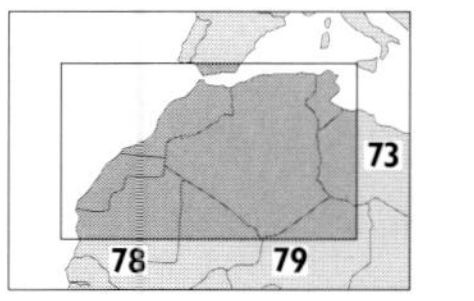
73
78
79

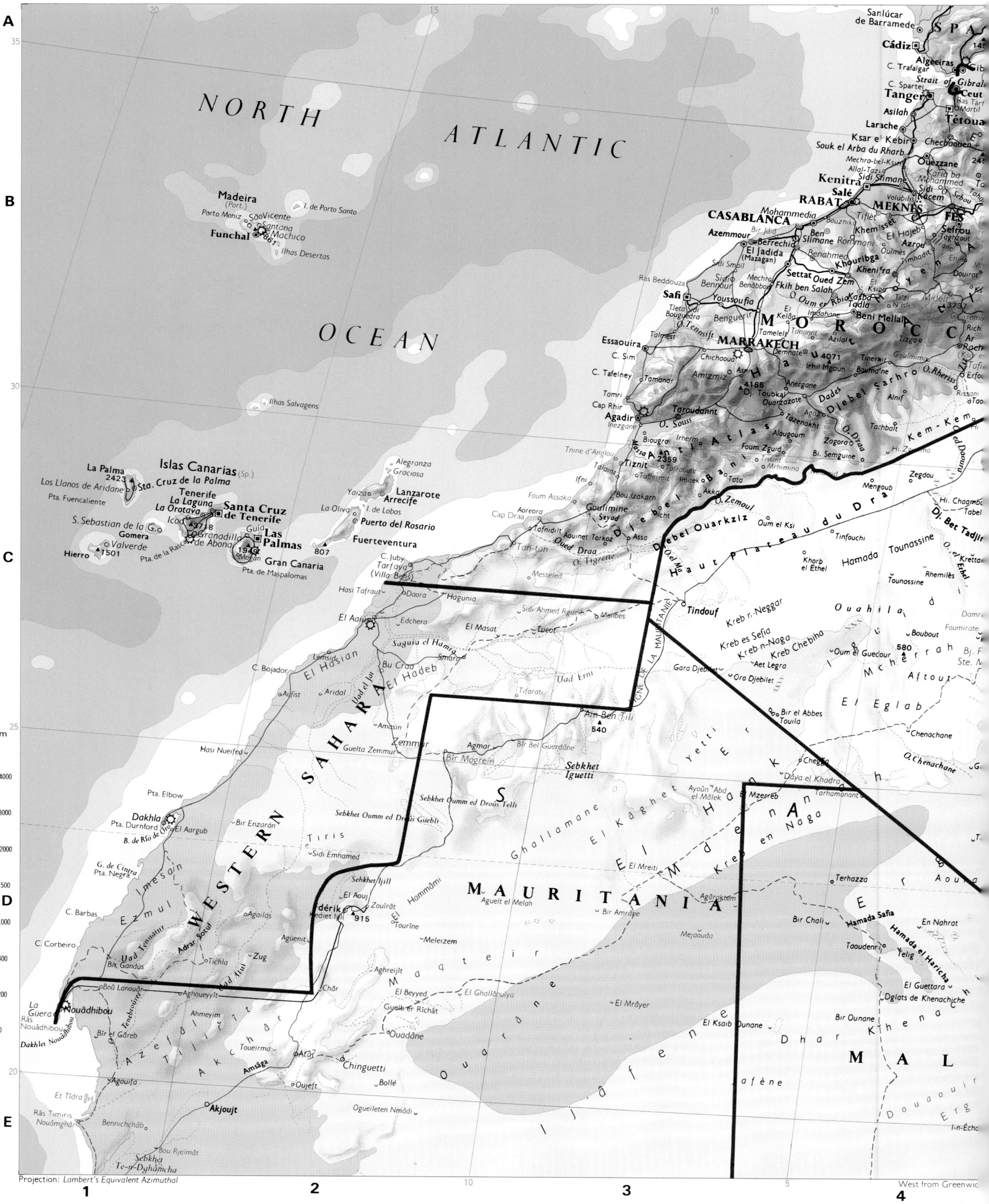
1
2
3
A
B
C
D
E
NORTH ATLANTIC OCEAN
Madeira
(Port.)
I. de Porto Santo
Porto Moniz
São Vicente
Santana
Machico
Funchal
1861
Ilhas Desertas
Ilhas Salvagens
Islas Canarias (Sp.)
La Palma
2423
Sta. Cruz de la Palma
Los Llanos de Aridane
Pta. Fuencaliente
Tenerife
La Laguna
La Orotava
Santa Cruz de Tenerife
Icod
3718
S. Sebastian de la G.
Gomera
Granadilla de Abona
Valverde
Hierro
1501
Pta. de la Rasca
Guía
Las Palmas
1949
Mogán
Gran Canaria
Pta. de Maspalomas
Alegranza
Graciosa
Yaiza
Lanzarote
Arrecife
La Oliva
I. de Lobos
Puerto del Rosario
Fuerteventura
807
Sanlúcar de Barrameda
Cádiz
C. Trafalgar
Algeciras
Strait of Gibraltar
C. Spartel
Tanger
Ceuta
Asilah
Tétouan
Larache
Ksar el Kebir
Chechaouen
Souk el Arba du Rharb
Ouezzane
Kenitra
Sidi Slimane
Salé
RABAT
MEKNES
FES
CASABLANCA
Mohammedia
Azemmour
El Jadida (Mazagan)
Berrechid
Ben Slimane
Khemisset
Sefrou
Azrou
Khouribga
Khenifra
Ras Beddouza
Safi
Settat
Oued Zem
Fkih ben Salah
Youssoufia
Kasba Tadla
Beni Mellal
Benguerir
MOROCCO
Essaouira
C. Sim
MARRAKECH
Demnate
4071
C. Tafelney
Chichaoua
Amizmiz
4165
Dj. Toubkal
Ouarzazate
Tamri
Cap Rhir
Agadir
Inezgane
Taroudannt
O. Souss
Djebel Sarhro
Tazenakht
Zagora
Anti Atlas
2359
Tiznit
Ifni
Tata
Akka
Foum Assaka
Goulimine
Bou Izakarn
Cap Draa
Aoreora
Tan-tan
Assa
Oued Draa
Djebel Ouarkziz
Oum el Ksi
Haut Plateau du Dra
Kem-Kem
Zegdou
Mengoub
Tinfouchi
Hamada Tounassine
Tounassine
C. Juby
Tarfaya (Villa Bens)
Hasi Tafraut
Daora
Hagunia
El Aaiún
Edchera
Sidi Ahmed Reguebi
Mahbes
El Masat
Tuicot
Saguia el Hamra
Smara
Bu Craa
El Hadeb
C. Bojador
El Hasian
Uad Erni
Tifariti
Tindouf
Kreb en Neggar
Kreb es Sefia
Kreb n-Naga
Kreb Chebiha
Gara Djebilet
Ora Djebilet
Oum el Guecour
580
Aftout
El Eglab
Bir el Abbes
Touila
Chenachane
O. Chenachane
Ouahila
Boubout
Aïn Ben Tili
540
Hasi Nueifed
Amasin
Guelta Zemmur
Zemmur
Agmar
Bir Bel Guerdâne
Bir Mogrein
Sebkhet Iguetti
WESTERN SAHARA
Pta. Elbow
Dakhla
Pta. Durnford
El Aargub
B. de Río de Oro
Bir Enzarân
Sebkhet Oumm ed Drous Guebli
Sebkhet Oumm ed Drous Telli
Tiris
Sidi Emhamed
G. de Cintra
Pta. Negra
Imesan
Ezmul
C. Barbas
Sebkhet Ijill
Fdérik
Kediet Ijill
915
Zouîrât
El Hammâmi
MAURITANIA
Aguelt el Melah
Bir Amrâne
El Mreiti
Agâraktem
Tourine
Meleizem
C. Corbeiro
Uad Tenuatur
Adrar Sotuf
Tichla
Zug
Agaiids
Aguenit
Bir Gandús
Boû Lanouâr
Aghoueyyît
Aghreijît
Chôr
El Beyyed
El Ghallâouîya
Guelb er Richât
El Mrâyer
Ouadâne
La Guera
Nouâdhibou
Râs Nouâdhibou
Dakhlet Nouâdhibou
Ahmeyim
Bir el Gâreb
Azefal
Touerma
Akchar
Atâr
Chinguetti
Amsâga
Ouarane
Maqteïr
El Khnachich
Agouîfa
Oujeft
Bollé
Et Tîdra
Râs Timiris
Nouâmghâr
Bennichchâb
Akjoujt
Ogueileten Nmâdi
Bou Rjeimât
Sebkhet Te-n-Dghâmcha
Ijâfene
Ouâfène
El Ksaïb Ounane
Dhar
El Hank
Ghallamane
El Kâghet
Yetti
Ayoûn Abd el Mâlek
Chegga
Dâya el Khadra
Tarhamanant
Mzereb
El Mdena
Kreb en Naga
Terhazza
Bir Chali
Hamada Safia
En Nahrat
Taoudenni
Telig
Hamada el Haricha
Mejaouda
El Guettara
Dglats de Khenachiche
Bir Ounane
Khenachich
MALI
Erg Iguidi
Erg Chech
I-n-Echaï
ft m
12,000 4000
9000 3000
6000 2000
4500 1500
3000 1000
1200 400
600 200
0 0
200 600
2000 6000
4000 12,000
m ft
Projection: Lambert's Equivalent Azimuthal
West from Greenwich
35
30
25
20
20
15
10
10
5
4

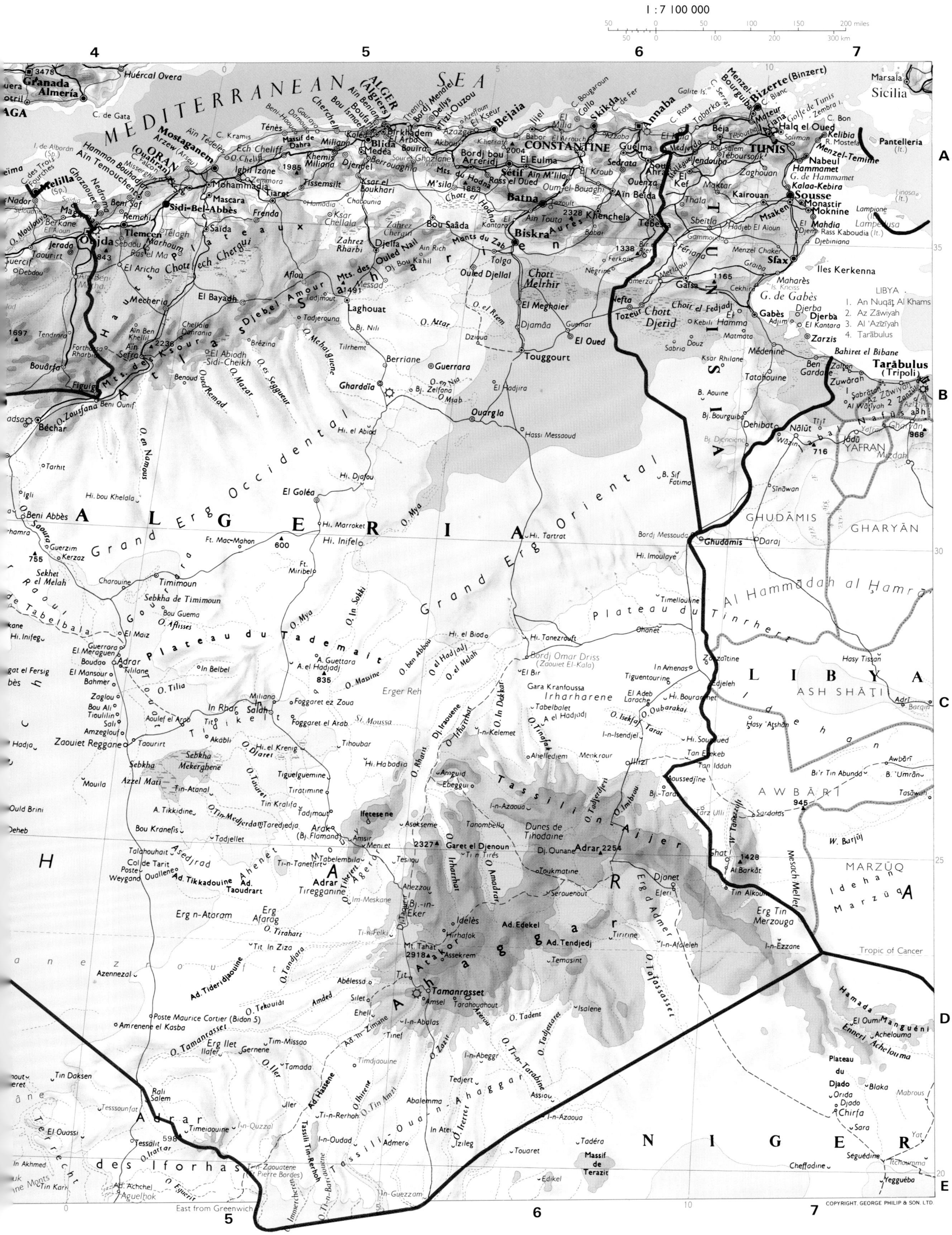

1 : 7 100 000
50 0 50 100 150 200 miles
50 0 100 200 300 km
4
5
6
7
A
B
C
D
E
MEDITERRANEAN SEA
Granada
Almería
Huércal Overa
C. de Gata
Melilla (Sp.)
Nador
Oujda
Tlemcen
Sidi-Bel-Abbès
ORAN (Ouahran)
Mostaganem
Arzew
Mascara
Saïda
Tiaret
Mohammadia
Relizane
Tissemsilt
Ténès
Cherchell
Miliana
Blida
Médéa
ALGER (Algiers)
Dellys
Tizi-Ouzou
Bejaia
Jijel
Skikda
Collo
Annaba
Guelma
Souk Ahras
CONSTANTINE
Sétif
Bordj bou Arreridj
El Eulma
M'sila
Batna
Biskra
Khenchela
Tebessa
Aïn Beida
Oum el Bouaghi
Bou Saâda
Djelfa
Ksar Chellala
Aflou
Laghouat
El Bayadh
Mecheria
Aïn Sefra
Figuig
Béchar
Beni Abbès
Monts du Zab
Mts. des Ouled Nail
Djebel Amour
Mts. des Ksour
Atlas Saharien
Hauts Plateaux
Chott ech Chergui
Chott el Hodna
Chott Melrhir
Chott Djerid
Chott el Fedjadj
Touggourt
El Oued
Djamâa
El Meghaier
Ghardaïa
Berriane
Guerrara
Ouargla
Hassi Messaoud
El Goléa
Timimoun
Adrar
Reggane
Zaouiet Reggane
In Salah
Grand Erg Occidental
Grand Erg Oriental
Plateau du Tademait
Plateau du Tinrhert
Tidikelt
Erg Chech
Tanezrouft
Adrar des Iforhas
Tassili n Ajjer
Tassili-Oua-n-Ahaggar
Ahaggar
Tamanrasset
Assekrem
Mt. Tahat 2918
Djanet
Illizi
In Amenas
Bordj Omar Driss
Adrar 2254
Idelès
Erg d'Admer
Erg Tin Merzouga
Tin Alkoum
Ghat
ALGERIA
TUNISIA
TUNIS
Bizerte (Binzert)
Béja
Jendouba
Le Kef
Kairouan
Sousse
Monastir
Mahdia
Sfax
Gafsa
Tozeur
Nefta
Gabès
Médenine
Zarzis
Djerba
Iles Kerkenna
G. de Gabès
Kelibia
Nabeul
Hammamet
Pantelleria (It.)
Lampedusa
Sicilia
Marsala
LIBYA
1. An Nuqāţ Al Khams
2. Az Zāwiyah
3. Al 'Azīzīyah
4. Ţarābulus
Tarābulus (Tripoli)
Zuwārah
Ghudāmis
Darāj
GHUDĀMIS
GHARYĀN
YAFRAN
Nālūt
Al Ḩammādah al Ḩamrā'
ASH SHĀŢI
AWBĀRĪ
MARZŪQ
Idehan Marzūq
Tropic of Cancer
Hamada Manguéni
Plateau du Djado
Djado
NIGER
Massif de Terazit
Tin Zaouatene
In Guezzam
MALI
Tessalit
Bordj Mokhtar
East from Greenwich
COPYRIGHT, GEORGE PHILIP & SON, LTD.

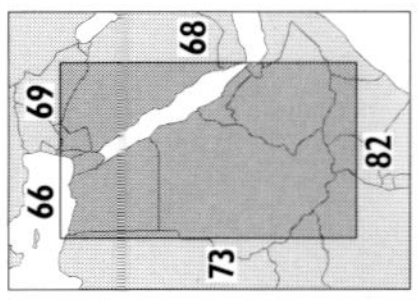
68
69
66
73
82

THE NILE DELTA
1: 3 600 000
MEDITERRANEAN SEA
EGYPT
SAUDI ARABIA
JORDAN
ISRAEL
EL ISKANDARÎYA (Alexandria)
EL QÂHIRA (Cairo)
Bûr Sa'îd (Port Said)
Dumyât (Damietta)
Rashîd (Rosetta)
El Suweis (Suez)
Ismâ'ilîya
Heliopolis
El Mansûra
Tanta
Zagazig
El Faiyûm
Beni Suef
El Minyâ
Asyût
Sohâg
Qena
El Uqsur (Luxor)
Aswân
Kôm Ombo
Buheiret en Naser (Lake Nasser)
Bûr Sûdân (Port Sudan)
Jiddah
Makkah (Mecca)
Al Madînah (Medina)
Yanbu' al Bahr
Jerusalem (Al Quds)
'Ammân
Tel Aviv-Yafo
Gaza
Es Sahrâ' el Gharbîya (Western Desert)
Sahrâ en Nûbîya (Nubian Desert)
El Bahr el Ahmar
Khalîg el Suweis
Tropic of Cancer
East from Greenwich

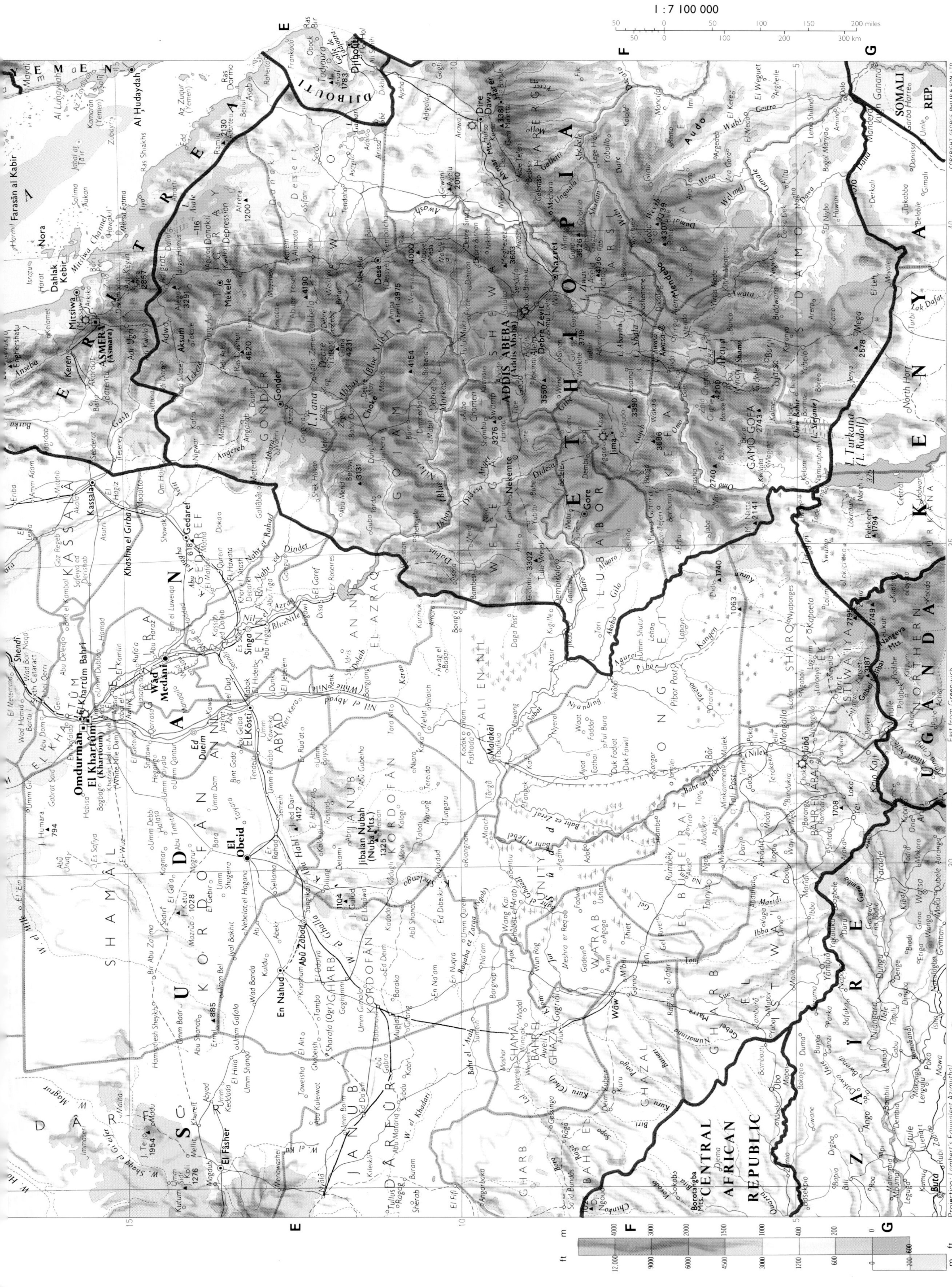
1 : 7 100 000
SUDAN
ETHIOPIA
ERITREA
DJIBOUTI
YEMEN
KENYA
UGANDA
ZAÏRE
CENTRAL AFRICAN REPUBLIC
SOMALI REP.
El Kharṭûm (Khartoum)
Omdurman
ADDIS ABEBA (Addis Ababa)
ASMERA (Asmara)
Djibouti
Projection: Lambert's Equivalent Azimuthal
East from Greenwich
COPYRIGHT GEORGE PHILIP & SON LTD

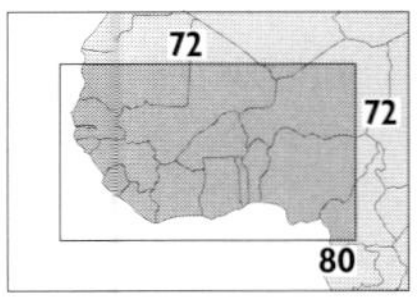
72
72
80

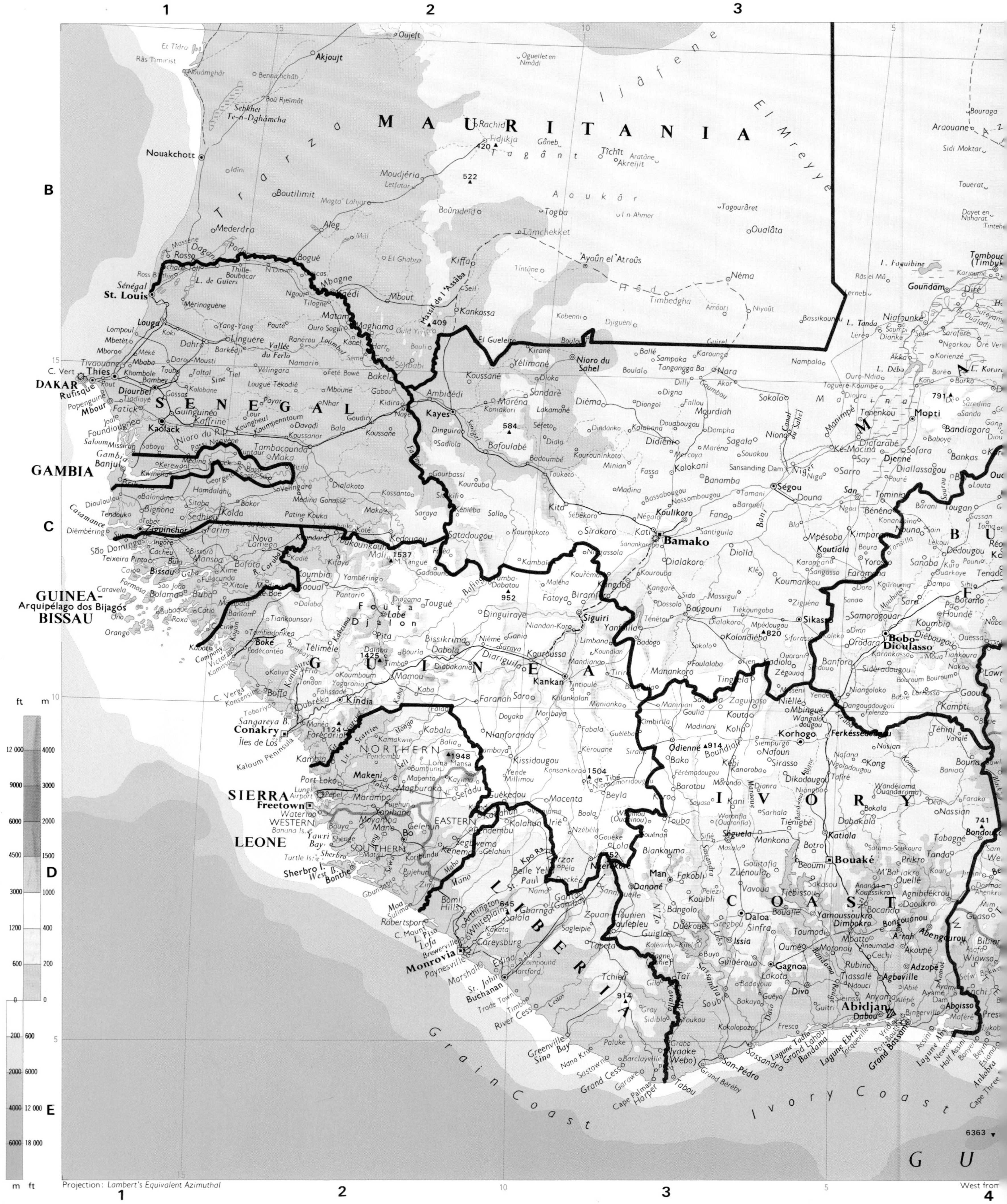
1
2
3
4
B
C
D
E
MAURITANIA
SENEGAL
GAMBIA
GUINEA-BISSAU
GUINEA
SIERRA LEONE
LIBERIA
IVORY COAST
Nouakchott
Akjoujt
Ouadâne
Tidjikja
Tîchît
Aleg
Boutilimit
Rosso
Kiffa
Ayoûn el 'Atroûs
Néma
Oualâta
Tombouctou (Timbuktu)
St. Louis
Louga
Thies
DAKAR
Rufisque
Mbour
Diourbel
Kaolack
Tambacounda
Banjul
Ziguinchor
Bissau
Arquipélago dos Bijagós
Kayes
Nioro du Sahel
Bamako
Koulikoro
Ségou
Sikasso
Mopti
Bobo-Dioulasso
Labé
Boké
Kindia
Conakry
Îles de Los
Kankan
Siguiri
Faranah
Kissidougou
Freetown
Bo
Makeni
Monrovia
Buchanan
Harper
Korhogo
Odienné
Man
Bouaké
Daloa
Gagnoa
Yamoussoukro
Abidjan
Grand Bassam
San-Pédro
Sassandra
Tabou
Grain Coast
Ivory Coast
Fouta Djalon
Massif de l'Assaba
Aoukâr
Tagânt
Trarza
Ijâfene
El Mreyyé
NORTHERN
EASTERN
SOUTHERN
WESTERN
Projection: Lambert's Equivalent Azimuthal
ft
m
12 000
9000
6000
4500
3000
1200
600
4000
3000
2000
1500
1000
400
200
0
200
2000
4000
6000
600
6000
12 000
18 000
West from

1 : 7 100 000
50 0 50 100 150 200 miles
50 0 100 200 300 km
ALGERIA
Adrar des Iforhas
NIGER
Aïr (Azbine)
Ténéré
Massif de Terazit
Monts Bagzane 2022
Agadez (Agadès)
Niamey
Zinder
Maradi
Tahoua
Gao
Manga
NIGERIA
SOKOTO
KATSINA
KANO
JIGAWA
BAUCHI
KADUNA
NIGER
PLATEAU
FED. CAP. TERR.
OYO
OSUN
KWARA
KOGI
BENUE
TARABA
ADAMAWA
EDO
DELTA
ENUGU
ANAMBRA
IMO
ABIA
AKWA IBOM
CROSS RIVER
RIVERS
LAGOS
IBADAN
Abeokuta
Ilorin
Ogbomosho
Oshogbo
Benin City
Onitsha
Enugu
Port-Harcourt
Calabar
Kaduna
Zaria
Kano
Sokoto
Jos
Abuja
Minna
Makurdi
Maiduguri
Yola
BENIN
Cotonou
Porto-Novo
TOGO
Lomé
GHANA
ACCRA
Tema
CAMEROON
DOUALA
Yaoundé
Mts. Manengouba
EQUATORIAL GUINEA
Bioko (Fernando Poo)
Rey Malabo
Slave Coast
Bight of Benin
Niger Delta
Bight of Bonny
GULF OF GUINEA
N. E. NIGERIA
on same scale as general map
Lac Tchad
CHAD
East from Greenwich
4
5
6
7
A
B
C
D
E

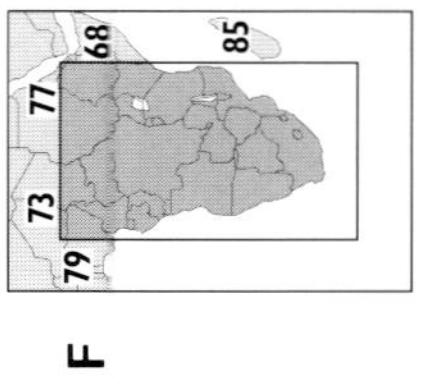
77
68
85
73
79

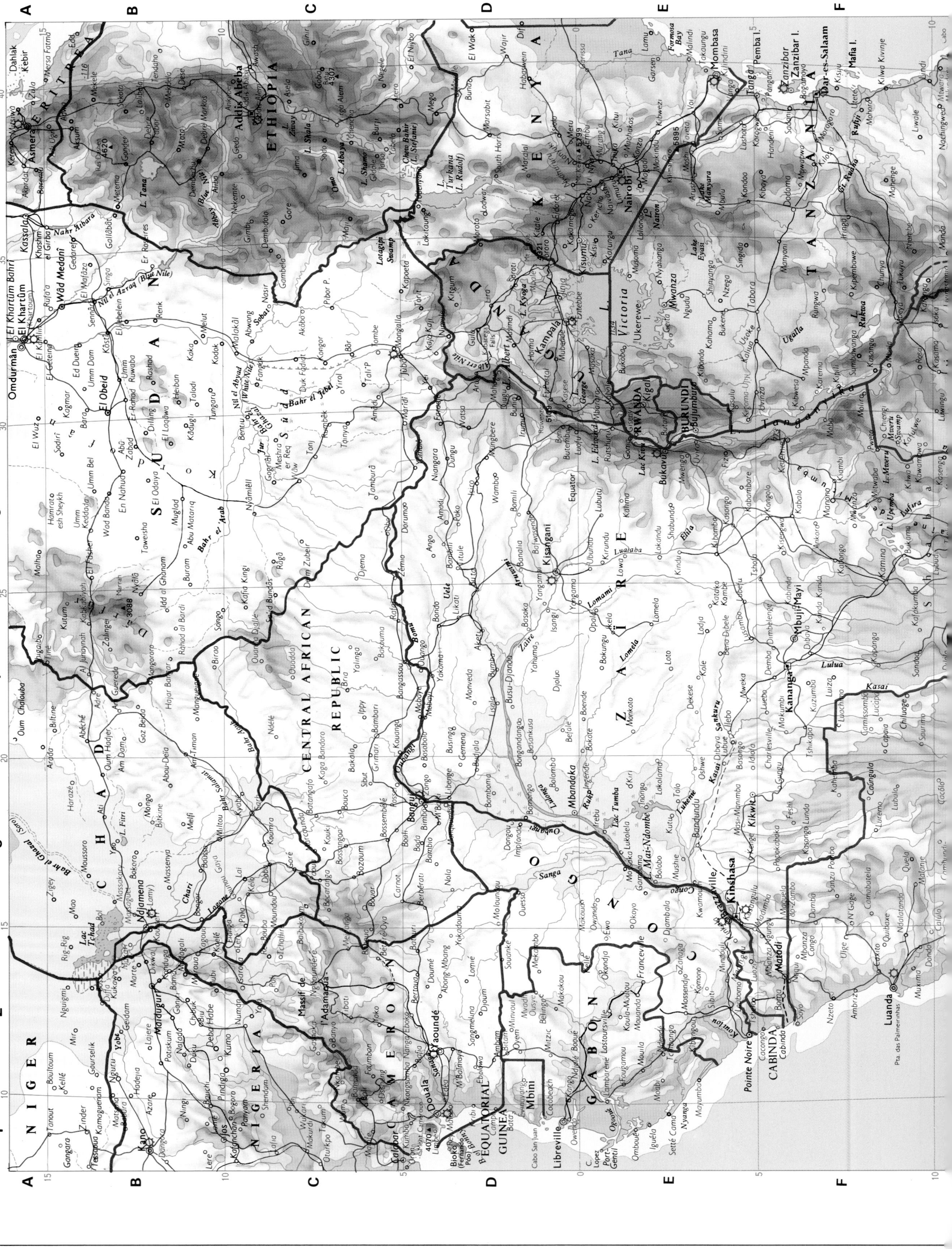
NIGER
CHAD
SUDAN
ETHIOPIA
ERITREA
KENYA
UGANDA
TANZANIA
RWANDA
BURUNDI
ZAÏRE
CONGO
GABON
CAMEROON
NIGERIA
CENTRAL AFRICAN REPUBLIC
EQUATORIAL GUINEA
CABINDA
Omdurman
El Khartûm
Wad Medanî
Kassala
Asmera
Addis Abeba
Nairobi
Mombasa
Dar-es-Salaam
Zanzibar
Kampala
Kigali
Bujumbura
Kisangani
Kinshasa
Brazzaville
Pointe Noire
Luanda
Libreville
Douala
Yaoundé
Bangui
Ndjamena
Kano
Maiduguri
El Obeid
Mbandaka
Kananga
Mbuji-Mayi
Lac Tchad
L. Victoria
L. Tana
L. Turkana
L. Albert
L. Tanganyika
Lake Eyasi
Lualaba
Congo
Kasai
Ubangi
Bahr el Ghazal
Nil el Abyad (White Nile)
Nil el Azraq (Blue Nile)
Massif de l'Adamaoua
Formosa Bay
Pemba I.
Mafia I.

1 : 13 300 000

ZIMBABWE
BOTSWANA
NAMIBIA
SOUTH AFRICA
LESOTHO
SWAZILAND
INDIAN OCEAN
ATLANTIC OCEAN
Kalahari
Damaraland
Ovamboland
Namaland
Caprivi Strip
Okavango Swamps
Makgadikgadi Salt Pans
Ngami Depression
Mozambique Channel
Tropic of Capricorn
Windhoek
Harare
Lusaka
Bulawayo
Gaborone
Pretoria
Johannesburg
Maputo
Beira
Durban
Bloemfontein
Kimberley
Cape Town (Kaapstad)
Port Elizabeth
East London
Pietermaritzburg
Antananarivo
Bassas da India (Réunion)
Île Europa (Réunion)
Îles Glorieuses (Réunion)
MADAGASCAR
On same scale as General Map
Projection: Sanson Flamsteed's Sinusoidal
East from Greenwich

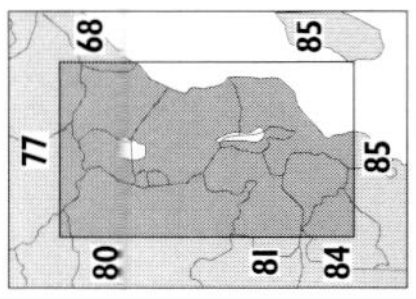
68
85
77
80
81
84
85

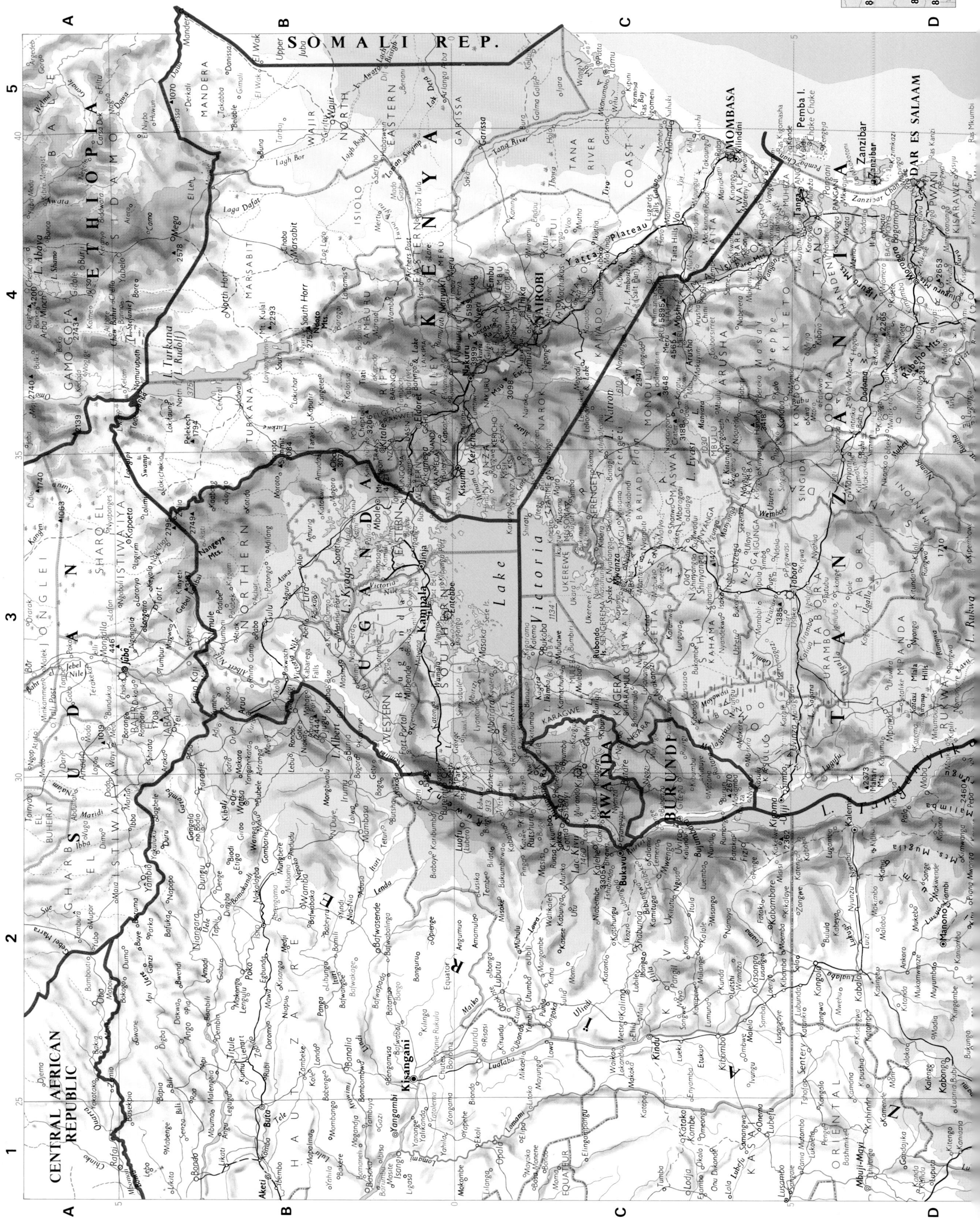
SOMALI REP.
ETHIOPIA
SUDAN
KENYA
UGANDA
TANZANIA
RWANDA
BURUNDI
ZAIRE
CENTRAL AFRICAN REPUBLIC
Lake Victoria
NAIROBI
MOMBASA
DAR ES SALAAM
Zanzibar
Pemba I.
Kampala
Kisangani
L. Turkana (L. Rudolf)
L. Tanganyika

1 : 7 100 000

50 0 50 100 150 200 miles
50 0 100 200 300 km

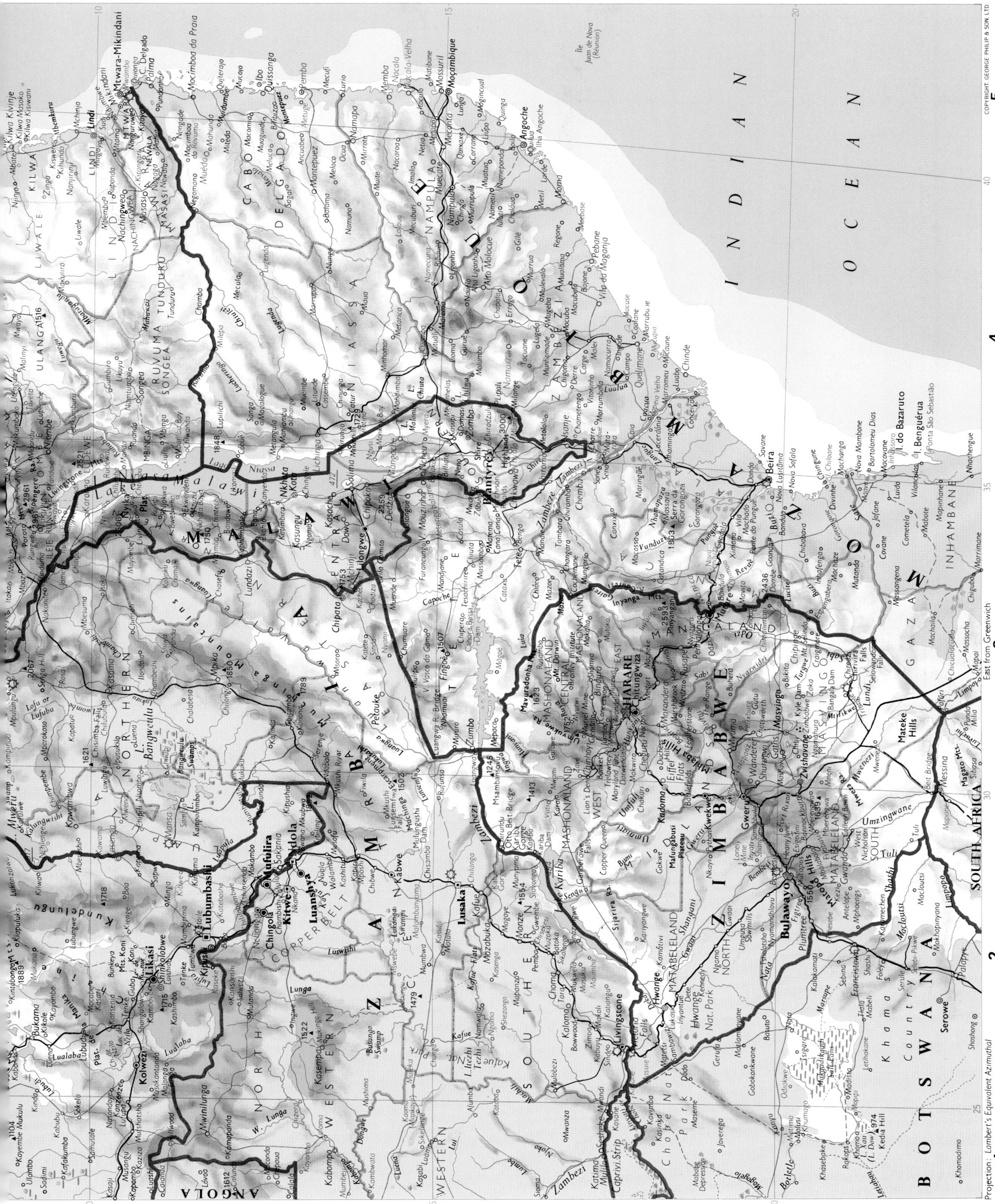

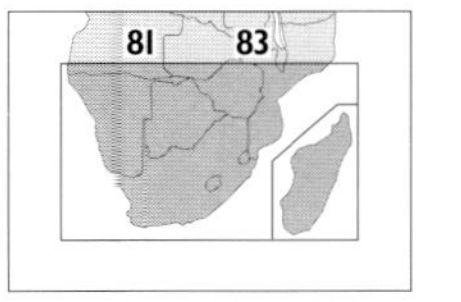

1 2 3

ANGOLA

Ponta Albina
Pta. da Marca
Ba. dos Tigres
NAMIBE
Namibe
Iona
Foz do Cunene
C. Fria
Rocky Point
Hoarusib

Tombua
Cahama
Chanhanga
Caraculo
Otchinjau
Humbe
Cafu
Evale
Mupa
Ondjiva
Chibemba
Mucula
Djamba
Xangongo
Ruacana
Namacunde
Enana
Chiede
Tandaua
Chiquelequele
Cuito
Catuala
Mussuco
L. do Lépo
Cavelo
Marungo
Capuça
Didimbo
Calai
Cuangar
Macusse
Dirico
Mucusso
Nkurenkuru
Rundu
Andara
Bagani
Shakawe

ZAMBIA
SOUTH
Mulonga Plain Sioma
Senanga
Kwando
Nangweshi
Mwanza
Mulobezi
Kaloma
Sesheke
Mwandi
Livingstone
Victoria Falls
Kazungula
Kasane

CUANDO CUBANGO

Caprivi Strip
Katima Mulilo
Linyanti
Chobe Nat. Park
Mababe Depression
Okavango Swamps
Maun

BOTSWANA

Tsodilo Hill ▲1300
Nxau Nxau
Tsau
Sehitwa
Ngami Depression
Nokaneng
L. Xau (L. Dow) ▲974
Kedia Hill
Makgadikgadi Salt Pan
Rakops
Letlhakane
Mopipi
Orapa

NAMIBIA

Sesfontein
Opuwo
Etanga
Joubertberge
Kaokoveld (Namib)
Baynes Mts. 2195
Steilrandberge
Hartmannberge
Ovamboland
Oshigambo
Ondangua
Oponono L.
Ekuma
Etosha Pan
Namutoni
Tsumeb 2148
Grootfontein
Otavi
Uchab
Kamanjab
Fransfontein
Khorixas
Outjo
Okaputa
Otjiwarongo
Kalkfeld
Omaruru
Brandberg ▲2606
Uis
Anichab
Ugab
Huab
Otjohorongo
Okombahe
Erongo 2350
Usakos
Karibib
Wilhelmstal
Okahandja
Steinhausen
Swartmossob
Omitara
Witvlei
Gobabis
Sandfontein
Epukiro
Steinhausen
Damaraland
Khomas Hochland
Windhoek 2483
Brakwater
Auasberge
Dordabis
Rehoboth
Hakos 2351
Tsumis
Uhlenhorst
Leonardville
Aminuis
Aranos
Stampriet
Mariental
Hardap Dam
Gibeon
Maltahöhe
Namaland
Helmeringhausen
Bersebo
Tses
Gochas
Koës
Kalahari Gemsbok National Park

Swakopmund
Walvisbaai (Walvis Bay)
Sandwich B.
Conception B.
Meob B.
Sossus Vlei
Spencer B.
Hottentotsbaai
Lüderitzbaai
Halifax I.
Lüderitz
Namib Desert
Kuisib
Tropic of Capricorn

ATLANTIC OCEAN

Oranjemund
Alexander Bay
Port Nolloth
Steinkopf
Springbok
Nababeep
Okiep
Namaqualand
Kamieskroon
Garies
Hondeklipbaai
Bitterfontein
Biesiesfontein

SOUTH AFRICA
NORTHERN CAPE
Upington
Keimoes
Kakamas
Kenhardt
Groblershoop
Prieska
Carnarvon
Victoria West
De Aar
Hanover
Richmond
Middelburg
Colesberg
Britstown
Williston
Calvinia
Vanrhynsdorp
Clanwilliam
Citrusdal
Piketberg

WESTERN CAPE
EASTERN CAPE
Cradock
Graaff-Reinet
Beaufort West
Murraysburg
Aberdeen
Great Karoo
Little Karoo
Swellendam
Oudtshoorn
George
Mossel Bay
Knysna
Plettenbergbaai

CAPE TOWN (Kaapstad)
Table Mt. 1086
Simonstown
Kaap die Goeie Hoop (Cape of Good Hope)
Stellenbosch
Somerset West
Strand
Hermanus
Danger Pt.
C. Agulhas
Bredasdorp
Caledon
Worcester
Paarl
Malmesbury
Saldanha
Vredenburg
St. Helena B.
Lambert's Bay

PORT ELIZABETH
Algoa Bay
Uitenhage
Humansdorp

FREE STATE
Bloemfontein
Kimberley
Welkom
Virginia
Vryburg
Kuruman
Mafikeng
Gaborone
Lobatse
Molepolole
Kanye
Mochudi
Zeerust

NORTH-WEST
Klerksdorp
Potchefstroom

Projection : Lambert's Equivalent Azimuthal

ft m
9000 3000
6000 2000
4500 1500
3000 1000
1200 400
600 200
0 0
m ft
200 600
2000 6000
4000 12,000
m ft

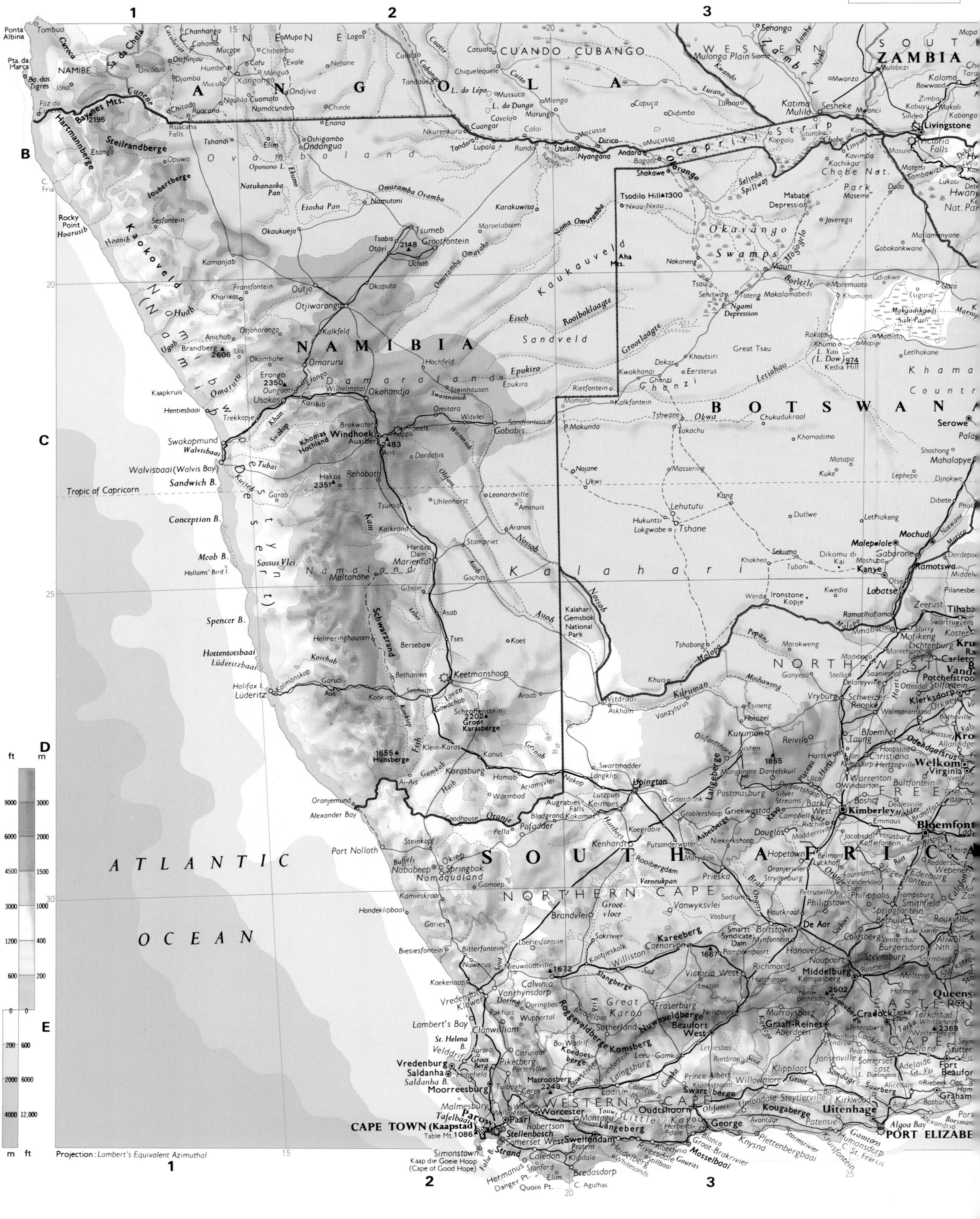

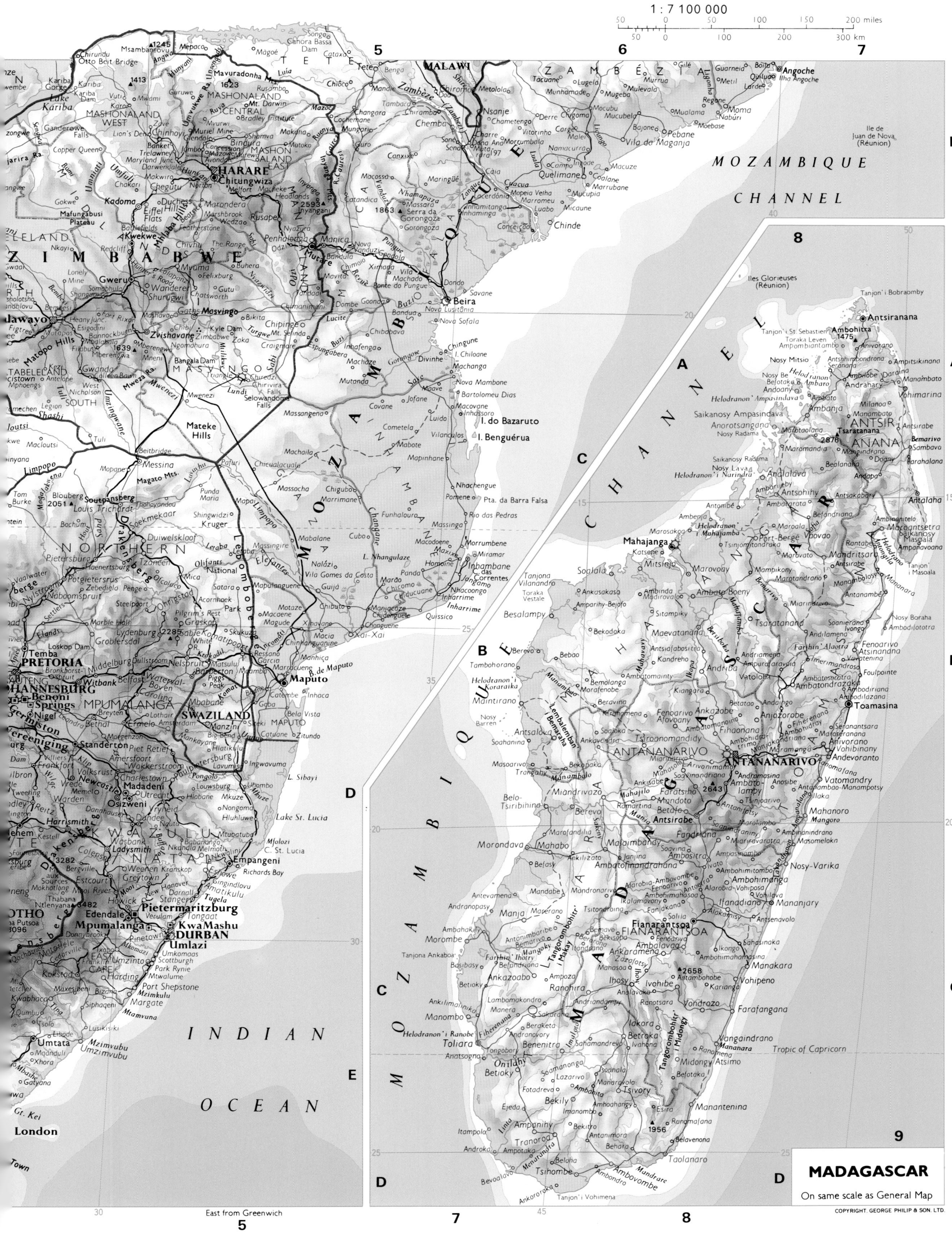
1 : 7 100 000
50 0 50 100 150 200 miles
50 0 100 200 300 km
5
6
7
8
9
A
B
C
D
E
MADAGASCAR
On same scale as General Map
East from Greenwich
MOZAMBIQUE CHANNEL
INDIAN OCEAN
MOZAMBIQUE
ZIMBABWE
MALAWI
SWAZILAND
MADAGASCAR
ZAMBÉZIA
TETE
MASHONALAND CENTRAL
MASHONALAND WEST
MASHONALAND EAST
MANICALAND
MASVINGO
MIDLANDS
GAZA
INHAMBANE
SOFALA
MAPUTO
NORTHERN
MPUMALANGA
KWAZULU NATAL
ANTANANARIVO
FIANARANTSOA
ANTSIRANANA
MAHAJANGA
TOAMASINA
TOLIARA
HARARE
Chitungwiza
Mutare
Beira
Maputo
PRETORIA
Pietermaritzburg
DURBAN
Umlazi
KwaMashu
Antsiranana
Mahajanga
Toamasina
Antananarivo
Antsirabe
Fianarantsoa
Toliara
Taolanaro
Chinde
Quelimane
Angoche
Inhambane
Xai-Xai
Limpopo
Tropic of Capricorn
Iles Glorieuses (Réunion)
Ile de Juan de Nova (Réunion)
I. do Bazaruto
Tanjon' i Vohimena
London

1 : 44 400 000

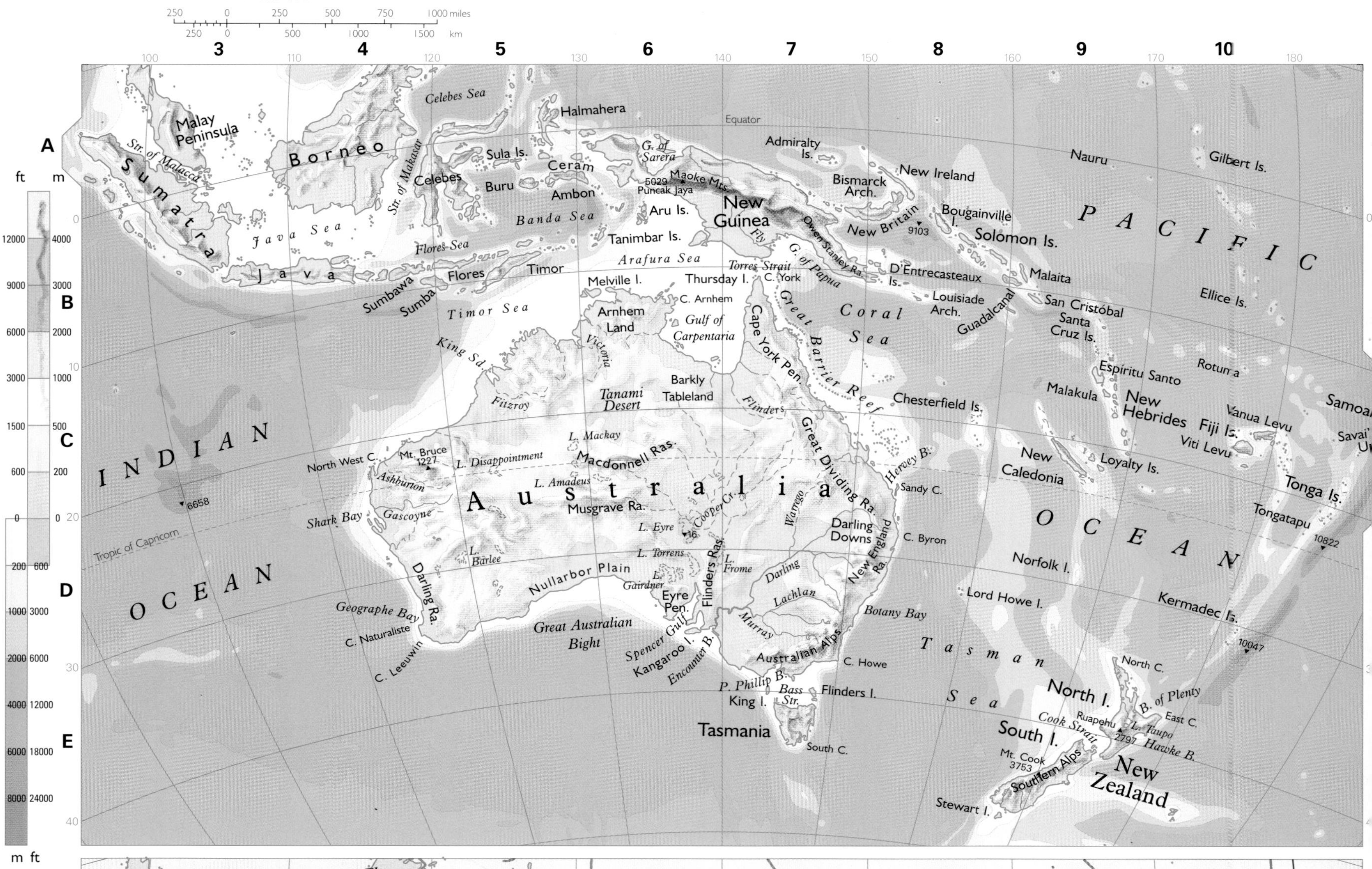

250 0 250 500 750 1000 miles
250 0 500 1000 1500 km
ft m
12000 4000
9000 3000
6000 2000
3000 1000
1500 500
600 200
0 0
200 600
1000 3000
2000 6000
4000 12000
6000 18000
8000 24000
m ft
Malay Peninsula
Str. of Malacca
Sumatra
Borneo
Celebes Sea
Halmahera
Celebes
Str. of Makasar
Sula Is.
Ceram
Buru
Ambon
Banda Sea
Java Sea
Java
Flores Sea
Sumbawa
Sumba
Flores
Timor
Timor Sea
G. of Sarera
5029 Puncak Jaya
Maoke Mts.
Aru Is.
New Guinea
Tanimbar Is.
Arafura Sea
Equator
Admiralty Is.
Bismarck Arch.
New Ireland
New Britain
9103
Bougainville I.
Solomon Is.
Nauru
Gilbert Is.
PACIFIC
Owen Stanley Ra.
G. of Papua
Torres Strait
Thursday I.
C. York
Melville I.
C. Arnhem
Arnhem Land
Gulf of Carpentaria
D'Entrecasteaux Is.
Louisiade Arch.
Malaita
Guadalcanal
San Cristóbal
Santa Cruz Is.
Ellice Is.
Coral Sea
Great Barrier Reef
Cape York Pen.
King Sd.
Victoria
Barkly Tableland
Tanami Desert
Fitzroy
Flinders
Espíritu Santo
Rotuma
Malakula
New Hebrides
Fiji Is.
Vanua Levu
Viti Levu
Samoa
Savai'i
Chesterfield Is.
INDIAN
OCEAN
6658
North West C.
Mt. Bruce 1227
L. Disappointment
L. Mackay
Macdonnell Ras.
L. Amadeus
Ashburton
Gascoyne
Shark Bay
Australia
Musgrave Ra.
Great Dividing Ra.
Warrego
Cooper Cr.
Hervey B.
Sandy C.
New Caledonia
Loyalty Is.
Tonga Is.
Tongatapu
10822
Tropic of Capricorn
L. Eyre
-16
L. Torrens
L. Barlee
Darling Downs
C. Byron
New England Ra.
Norfolk I.
OCEAN
Darling Ra.
Nullarbor Plain
L. Gairdner
Flinders Ras.
L. Frome
Darling
Lachlan
Lord Howe I.
Kermadec Is.
Geographe Bay
C. Naturaliste
C. Leeuwin
Great Australian Bight
Eyre Pen.
Spencer Gulf
Kangaroo I.
Encounter B.
Murray
Botany Bay
Australian Alps
C. Howe
Tasman Sea
10047
North C.
P. Phillip B.
Bass Str.
King I.
Flinders I.
Tasmania
South C.
North I.
B. of Plenty
East C.
Ruapehu
L. Taupo
2797
Hawke B.
Cook Strait
South I.
Mt. Cook 3753
Southern Alps
New Zealand
Stewart I.

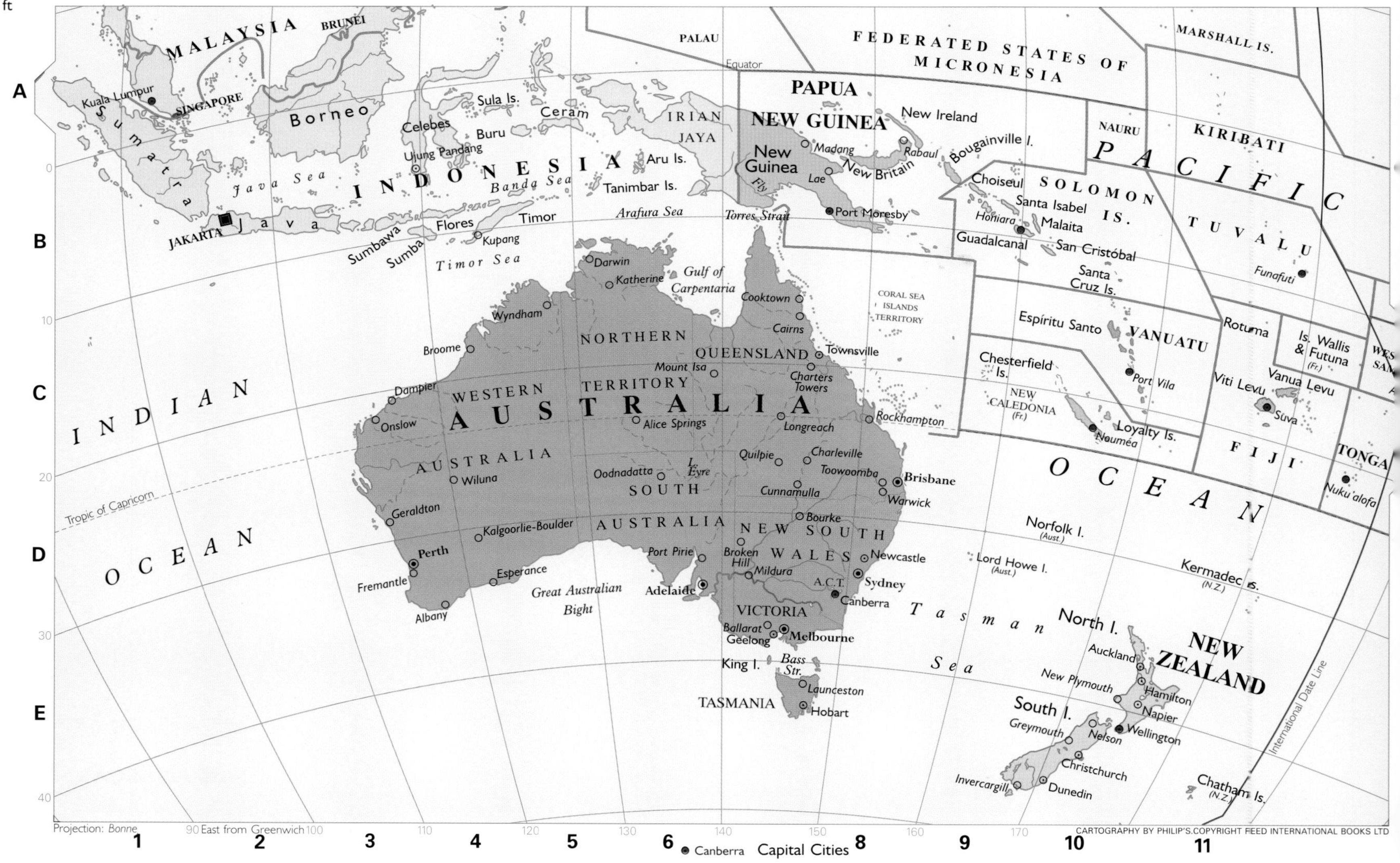

MALAYSIA
BRUNEI
PALAU
FEDERATED STATES OF MICRONESIA
MARSHALL IS.
Equator
Kuala Lumpur
SINGAPORE
Sumatra
Borneo
Sula Is.
Celebes
Ceram
Buru
Ujung Pandang
IRIAN JAYA
PAPUA NEW GUINEA
New Ireland
Madang
Rabaul
New Guinea
Lae
New Britain
Bougainville I.
NAURU
KIRIBATI
Java Sea
INDONESIA
Banda Sea
Aru Is.
Tanimbar Is.
Fly
Choiseul
SOLOMON IS.
Santa Isabel
Malaita
Honiara
PACIFIC
Port Moresby
JAKARTA
Java
Sumbawa
Sumba
Flores
Timor
Kupang
Arafura Sea
Torres Strait
Guadalcanal
San Cristóbal
Santa Cruz Is.
TUVALU
Funafuti
Timor Sea
Darwin
Katherine
Gulf of Carpentaria
Cooktown
CORAL SEA ISLANDS TERRITORY
Wyndham
Cairns
Espíritu Santo
VANUATU
Rotuma
Is. Wallis & Futuna (Fr.)
Broome
NORTHERN TERRITORY
QUEENSLAND
Townsville
Mount Isa
Charters Towers
Chesterfield Is.
Port Vila
Vanua Levu
Viti Levu
INDIAN
Dampier
WESTERN AUSTRALIA
AUSTRALIA
Onslow
Alice Springs
Longreach
Rockhampton
NEW CALEDONIA (Fr.)
Nouméa
Loyalty Is.
Suva
FIJI
TONGA
Nuku'alofa
Wiluna
Oodnadatta
L. Eyre
SOUTH AUSTRALIA
Quilpie
Charleville
Toowoomba
Brisbane
Warwick
Cunnamulla
OCEAN
Tropic of Capricorn
Geraldton
Kalgoorlie-Boulder
Bourke
NEW SOUTH WALES
Norfolk I. (Aust.)
OCEAN
Perth
Fremantle
Esperance
Port Pirie
Broken Hill
Mildura
Newcastle
Sydney
Lord Howe I. (Aust.)
Kermadec Is. (N.Z.)
Albany
Great Australian Bight
Adelaide
A.C.T.
Canberra
Tasman Sea
VICTORIA
Ballarat
Geelong
Melbourne
North I.
Auckland
NEW ZEALAND
King I.
Bass Str.
New Plymouth
Hamilton
Launceston
TASMANIA
Hobart
South I.
Greymouth
Napier
Nelson
Wellington
International Date Line
Christchurch
Invercargill
Dunedin
Chatham Is. (N.Z.)
Projection: Bonne
East from Greenwich
Canberra Capital Cities

92
92
92
92

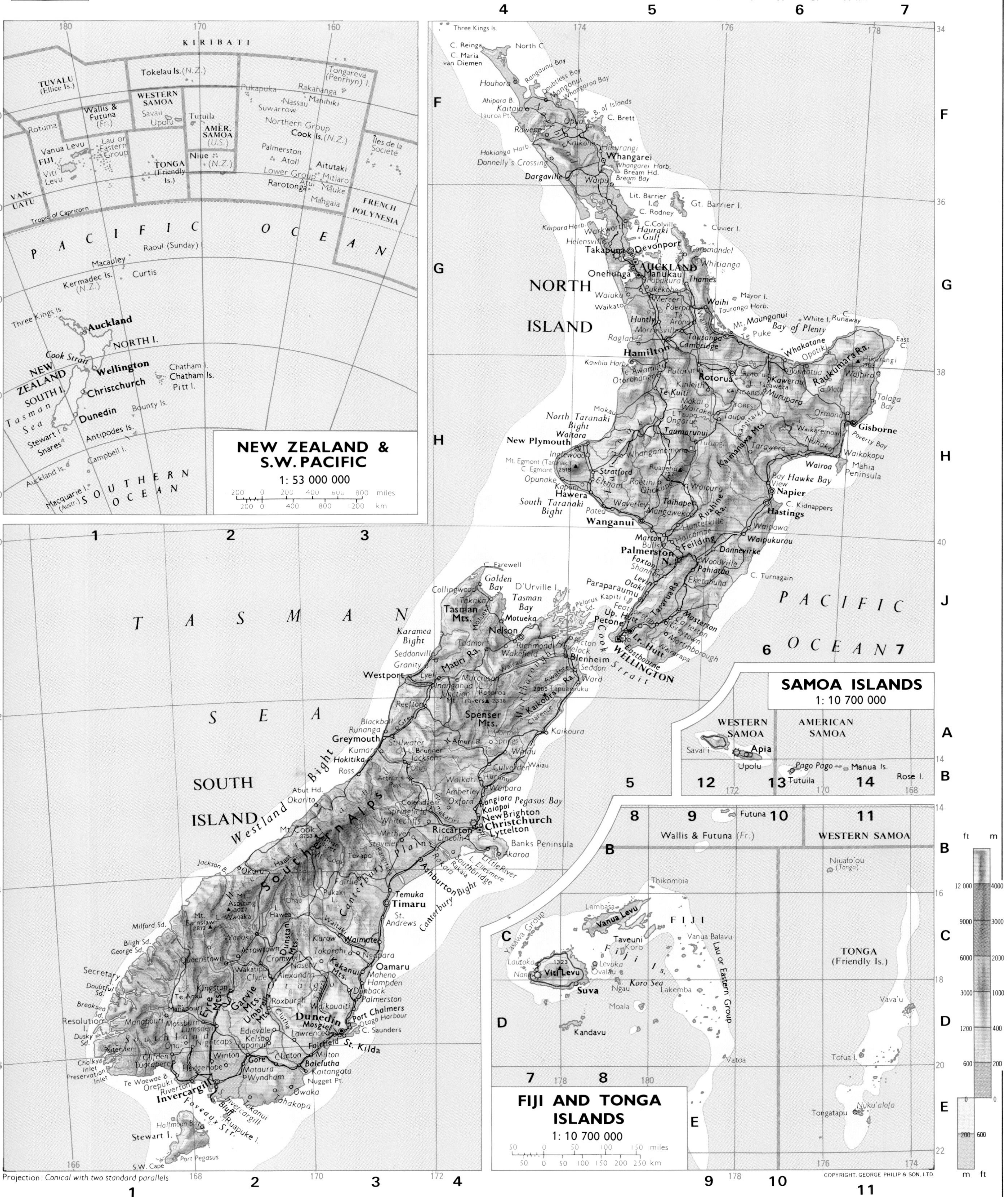
1 : 5 300 000
20 0 20 40 60 80 100 miles
20 0 40 80 120 160 km
NEW ZEALAND & S.W. PACIFIC
1: 53 000 000
KIRIBATI
TUVALU (Ellice Is.)
Tokelau Is. (N.Z.)
WESTERN SAMOA
Savaii
Upolu
Tutuila
AMER. SAMOA (U.S.)
Wallis & Futuna (Fr.)
Rotuma
Vanua Levu
FIJI
Viti Levu
Lau or Eastern Group
TONGA (Friendly Is.)
Niue (N.Z.)
Tongareva (Penrhyn) I.
Pukapuka
Rakahanga
Nassau
Manihiki
Suwarrow
Northern Group
Cook Is. (N.Z.)
Palmerston Atoll
Lower Group
Aitutaki
Mitiaro
Atiu
Mauke
Rarotonga
Mangaia
Îles de la Société
FRENCH POLYNESIA
VAN-UATU
Tropic of Capricorn
PACIFIC OCEAN
Raoul (Sunday) I.
Macauley
Kermadec Is. (N.Z.)
Curtis
Three Kings Is.
Auckland
NORTH I.
Cook Strait
NEW ZEALAND
Wellington
SOUTH I.
Christchurch
Chatham I.
Chatham Is.
Pitt I.
Tasman Sea
Dunedin
Bounty Is.
Stewart I.
Snares
Antipodes Is.
Campbell I.
Auckland Is.
Macquarie I. (Austr.)
SOUTHERN OCEAN
NORTH ISLAND
SOUTH ISLAND
TASMAN SEA
PACIFIC OCEAN
Three Kings Is.
C. Reinga
North C.
C. Maria van Diemen
Houhora
Rangaunu Bay
Doubtless Bay
Mangonui
Whangaroa Bay
B. of Islands
Ahipara B.
Kaitaia
Tauroa Pt.
C. Brett
Rawene
Opua
Hokianga Harb.
Kaikohe
Hikurangi
Whangarei
Whangarei Harb.
Bream Hd.
Bream Bay
Donnelly's Crossing
Dargaville
Waipu
Lit. Barrier I.
Gt. Barrier I.
C. Rodney
C. Colville
Cuvier I.
Kaipara Harb.
Warkworth
Hauraki Gulf
Helensville
Takapuna
Devonport
Coromandel
AUCKLAND
Onehunga
Manukau
Whitianga
Thames
Papakura
Pukekohe
Waiuku
Waikato
Mercer
Waihi
Mayor I.
Tauranga Harb.
Paeroa
Te Aroha
Mt. Maunganui
Te Puke
White I.
C. Runaway
Bay of Plenty
Huntly
Morrinsville
Raglan
Hamilton
Cambridge
Tauranga
Whakatane
Opotiki
Raukumara Ra.
East C.
Hikurangi
Kawhia Harb.
Te Awamutu
Putaruru
Rotorua
Otorohanga
Kawerau
L. Tarawera
Waipiro
Te Kuiti
Kinleith
Murupara
Tolaga Bay
Mokau
Mokai
Wairakei
L. Taupo
Taupo
Ongarue
Ormond
North Taranaki Bight
Waitara
New Plymouth
Taumarunui
Gisborne
Waikaremoana
Nuhaka
Poverty Bay
Inglewood
Mt. Egmont (Taranaki)
C. Egmont
Stratford
Whangamomona
Ruapehu
Kaimanawa Mts.
Tarawera
Waikokopu
Mahia Peninsula
Wairoa
Opunake
Eltham
Raetihi
Ohakune
Waiouru
Hawke Bay
Bay View
Kaponga
Hawera
Napier
South Taranaki Bight
Patea
Waverley
Taihape
Mangaweka
Ruahine Ra.
C. Kidnappers
Hastings
Wanganui
Hunterville
Waipawa
Marton
Bulls
Feilding
Waipukurau
Palmerston N.
Dannevirke
Foxton
Shannon
Woodville
Pahiatua
Eketahuna
C. Turnagain
Levin
Otaki
Paraparaumu
Kapiti I.
Tararua Ra.
Masterton
Carterton
Greytown
Martinborough
Up. Hutt
Petone
Lr. Hutt
WELLINGTON
Eastbourne
Cook Strait
C. Farewell
Golden Bay
Collingwood
Takaka
D'Urville I.
Tasman Bay
Tasman Mts.
Motueka
Karamea Bight
Nelson
Pelorus Sd.
Picton
Havelock
Richmond
Tadmor
Wakefield
Blenheim
Seddon
Ward
Seddonville
Granity
Westport
Lyell
Matiri Ra.
Murchison
Inangahua Junction
Rotoroa
Mt. Travers
Tapuaenuku
Kaikoura Ra.
Reefton
Spenser Mts.
Kaikoura
Blackball
Runanga
Greymouth
Stillwater
Kumara
L. Brunner
Jacksons
Hokitika
Ross
Hanmer Springs
Culverden
Waiau
Arthur's Pass
Waikari
Hurunui
Amberley
Waipara
Abut Hd.
Okarito
Oxford
Rangiora
Kaiapoi
Pegasus Bay
New Brighton
Christchurch
Lyttelton
Riccarton
Lincoln
Banks Peninsula
Akaroa
Coleridge
Springfield
Whitecliffs
Methven
Westland Bight
Mt. Cook
Southern Alps
Canterbury Plains
L. Ellesmere
Little River
Rakaia
Southbridge
Ashburton
Tekapo
Fairlie
Jackson B.
Haast
Okuru
Pukaki
Temuka
Timaru
Canterbury Bight
Mt. Aspiring
Ohau
Hawea
Wanaka
St. Andrews
Milford Sd.
Mt. Earnslaw
Waimate
Bligh Sd.
George Sd.
Kurow
Arrowtown
Queenstown
Cromwell
Dunstan Mts.
Kakanui Mts.
Oamaru
Secretary I.
Wakatipu
Alexandra
Maheno
Hampden
Doubtful Sd.
Kingston
Clyde
Te Anau
Garvie Mts.
Eyre Mts.
Dunback
Palmerston
Breaksea Sd.
Manapouri
Roxburgh
Umbrella Mts.
Waikouaiti
Port Chalmers
Otago Harbour
Resolution I.
Dusky Sd.
Mossburn
Lumsden
Mosgiel
Dunedin
C. Saunders
Lawrence
Edievale
Kelso
Nightcaps
Tapanui
St. Kilda
Chalky Inlet
Preservation Inlet
Clifden
Tuatapere
Otautau
Winton
Gore
Clinton
Milton
Balclutha
Kaitangata
Nugget Pt.
Hedgehope
Mataura
Wyndham
Te Waewae B.
Orepuki
Riverton
Invercargill
Owaka
Mahakopa
Bluff
Foveaux Str.
Ruapuke I.
Halfmoon Bay
Stewart I.
Port Pegasus
S.W. Cape
SAMOA ISLANDS
1: 10 700 000
WESTERN SAMOA
AMERICAN SAMOA
Savai'i
Apia
Upolu
Pago Pago
Tutuila
Manua Is.
Rose I.
Futuna
Wallis & Futuna (Fr.)
WESTERN SAMOA
Niuafo'ou (Tonga)
Thikombia
Lambasa
Vanua Levu
FIJI
Taveuni
Koro
Vanua Balavu
Yasawa Group
Lautoka
Viti Levu
Levuka
Ovalau
Nandi
Suva
Ngau
Koro Sea
Lakemba
Lau or Eastern Group
Moala
Kandavu
Vatoa
TONGA (Friendly Is.)
Vava'u
Tofua I.
Tongatapu
Nuku'alofa
FIJI AND TONGA ISLANDS
1: 10 700 000
50 0 50 100 150 miles
50 0 50 100 150 200 250 km
ft m
12 000 4000
9000 3000
6000 2000
3000 1000
1200 400
600 200
0 0
200 600
m ft
Projection: Conical with two standard parallels
COPYRIGHT, GEORGE PHILIP & SON, LTD.

INDONESIA
TIMOR SEA
INDIAN OCEAN
NORTHERN TERRITORY
Timor
Roti
Sawa
Sumba
Sumbawa
Lombok
Semau
Raidjoea
Danu
Melville I.
Bathurst I.
Darwin
Port Darwin
Clarence Str.
Van Diemen Gulf
Cobourg Pen.
Dundas Str.
C. Van Diemen
Gordan B.
Pt. Fawcett
C. Gambier
C. Hotham
Field I.
Croker I.
C. Croker
C. Don
P. Essington
Goulburn I.
Oenpelli
Jabiru
Noonamah
Rum Jungle
Batchelor
Adelaide River
Pine Creek
Katherine
Tindal
Mataranka
Maranboy
Larrimah
Birdum
Birdum Creek
Willeroo
Top Springs
Montejinnie
Daly River
Daly
Mt. Greenwood
Fitzmaurice
Victoria
Victoria River Downs
Humbert River
Timber Creek
Auvergne
Newcastle Ra.
Stokes Ra.
West Baines
Wave Hill
Hooker Creek
Limbunya
Inverway
Pt. Blaze
Peron Is.
Anson B.
C. Scott
C. Hay
Queens Chan.
Joseph Bonaparte Gulf
Cambridge Gulf
C. Dussejour
Buckle Hd.
Wyndham
Ivanhoe
Kununurra
Ord
L. Argyle
Rosewood
Carr Boyd Ra.
Cockburn Ra.
Turkey Creek
Nicholson
Gordon Downs
Sturt Creek
Durack Range
Chamberlain
Bedford Downs
Alice Downs
Springvale
Halls Creek
Albert Edward Ra.
McClintock Ra.
Mueller Ra.
Margaret River
Bohemia Downs
Christmas Creek
Billiluna
Gregory Lake
Tanami
Tanami Desert
Horden Hills
Lewis Ra.
L. White
L. Hazlett
Lake Mackay
Stansmore Ra.
Angas Hills
Baron Ra.
Willowra
Lander
Anningie
Reynolds Ra.
Stuart Bluff Ra.
Mt. Singleton 808
Yuendumu
Mt. Liebig 1524
Papunya
Mt. Zeil 1510
Macdonnell Ranges
Hermannsburg Mission
Haast Bluff
Mt. Leisler 901
Kintore Ra.
L. Macdonald
Bonython Ra.
Lesueur I.
Rulhieres
Londonderry
Napier Broome B.
Vansittart B.
Kalumburu
Drysdale
King Edward
Mt. Hann 776
Mount Elizabeth
Gibb River
Tableland
Mornington
Mt. Ord 1007
King Leopold Ranges
Fitzroy Crossing
Margaret
C. Bougainville
Admiralty Gulf
C. Voltaire
Montague Sd.
Long Reef
Princess May Ras.
Harding Ra.
Synnot Ra.
Bonaparte Archipelago
York Sd.
Brunswick B.
St. George Basin
Coronation Is.
Camden Sd.
Augustus I.
Adieu Pt.
Collier B.
Hall Pt.
Raft Pt.
Eagle Pt.
Browse I.
Hibernia Reef
Ashmore Reef
Cartier I.
Seringapatam Reef
Scott Reef
Adele I.
Buccaneer Archipelago
Yampi Sd.
King Sound
C. Leveque
Lombadina
Beagle Bay
Pender B.
Derby
Yeeda
Meda
Kimberley Downs
Napier Downs
Ellendale
Fitzroy
Liveringa
Myroodah
Noonkanbah
St. George Ra.
Geegully
Roebuck Plains
Thangoo
Broome
Roebuck B.
Carnot B.
Lacepede Is.
C. Boileau
Lagrange
Lagrange B.
Frazier Downs
Anna Plains
Eighty Mile Beach
Wallal Downs
C. Latouche Treville
Lynner Reef
Great Sandy Desert
Percival Lakes
L. Tobin
L. Auld
L. George
L. Dora
L. Blanche
L. Waukarlycarly
Paterson Ra.
Broadhurst Ra.
Throssell Ra.
Poisonbush Ra.
McKay Ra.
Rudall
Runton
Tropic of Capricorn
Gregory Ra.
Isabella Ra.
Oakover
Nullagine
Shay Gap
Goldsworthy
De Grey
Warrawagine
Marble Bar
Shaw
Woodstock
Hillside
Bonnie Downs
Roy Hill
Ethel Creek
Newman
Ophthalmia Ra.
Chichester Ra.
Mt. Bruce 1235
Mt. Meharry 1251
Tom Price
Wittenoom
Hamersley Range
Robertson Ra.
Talawana
Jigalong
C. Keraudren
Poissonnier Pt.
Port Hedland
C. Thouin
Pippingarra
Yule
Roebourne
Dampier
Karratha
Dampier Archipelago
Legendre I.
Delambre I.
Enderby I.
Fortescue
Yandeearra
Mardie
Yarraloola
Pannawonica
Duck Cr.
Wyloo
Nanutarra
Hardey
Ashburton
Robe
Onslow
C. Preston
Barrow I.
Pasco I.
Monte Bello Is.
Exmouth Gulf
Exmouth
North West C.
Learmonth
Bullara
Rowley Shoals
Mermaid Reef
Clerke Reef
Imperieuse Reef
Lake

1 : 7 100 000
miles
km
WESTERN AUSTRALIA
SOUTH AUSTRALIA
SOUTHERN OCEAN
Great Australian Bight
Nullarbor Plain
Great Victoria Desert
Hampton Tableland
PERTH
Fremantle
Kalgoorlie-Boulder
Geraldton
Carnarvon
Albany
Bunbury
Esperance
Norseman
Northam
Kwinana
Rockingham
Mandurah
Busselton
Collie
Narrogin
Katanning
Merredin
Wiluna
Meekatharra
Cue
Mount Magnet
Laverton
Leonora
Warburton
Eucla Motel
Cook
Hughes
Forrest
Ooldea
Nullarbor
Shark Bay
Dirk Hartog I.
Houtman Abrolhos
Archipelago of the Recherche
Ayers Rock 868
Mt. Olga 1069
Musgrave Ranges
Mt. Woodroffe 1549
Everard Ranges
L. Carnegie
L. Wells
L. Carey
L. Barlee
L. Moore
L. Dundas
L. Cowan
Dividing Ra.
Tallering Peak 439
Mt. Augustus 1105
Peak Eleanora 503
Mt. Ragged 585
Stirling Ra. 1073
C. Leeuwin
Pt. D'Entrecasteaux
East from Greenwich
Projection: Bonne
COPYRIGHT GEORGE PHILIP & SON, LTD.

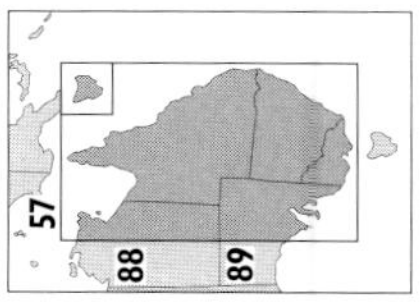

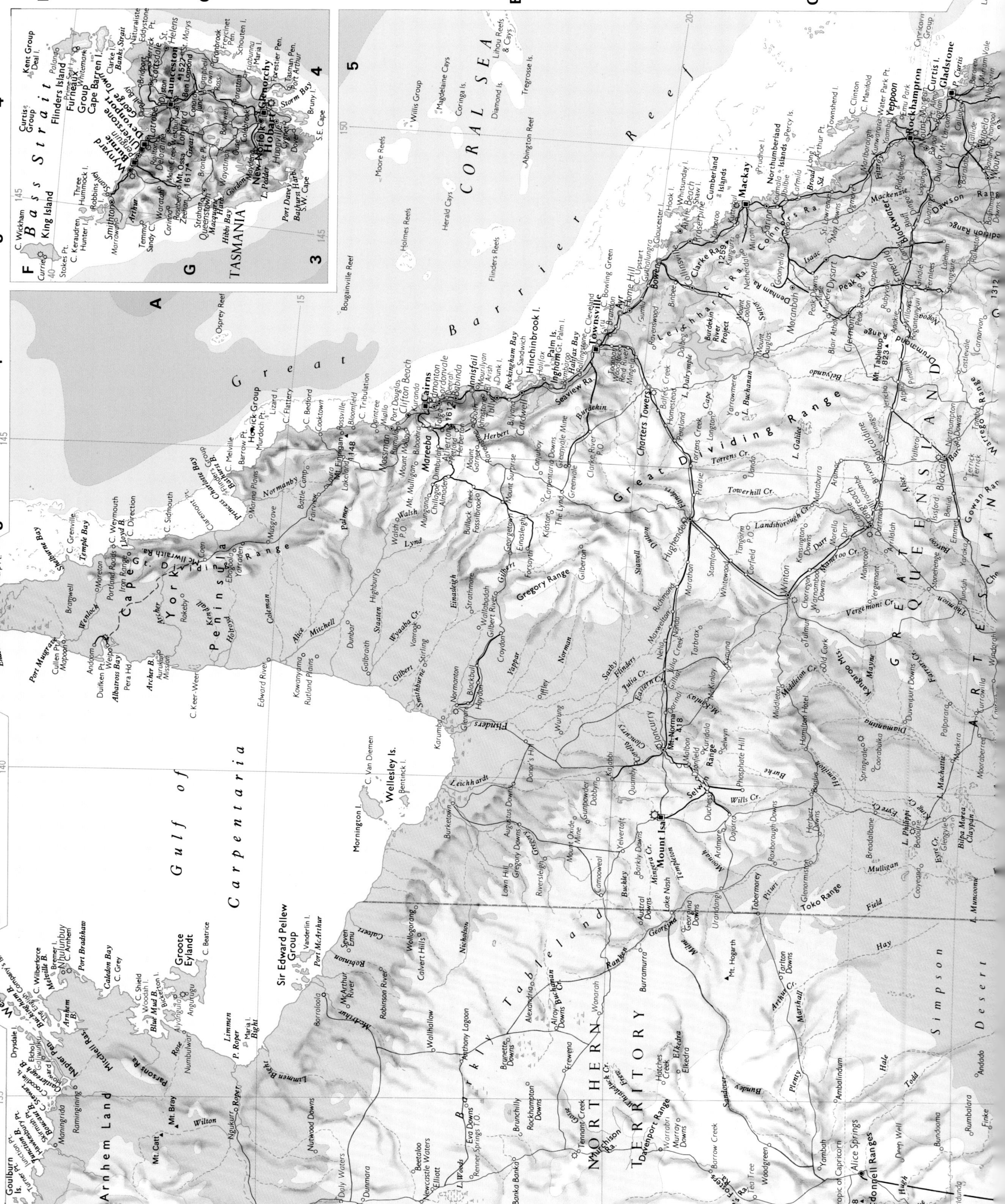

CORAL SEA
Great Barrier Reef
Gulf of Carpentaria
Cape York Peninsula
Great Dividing Range
QUEENSLAND
NORTHERN TERRITORY
Barkly Tableland
Arnhem Land
Simpson Desert
Bass Strait
TASMANIA
Hobart
Launceston
Flinders Island
King Island
Cairns
Townsville
Mackay
Rockhampton
Gladstone
Mount Isa
Alice Springs
Macdonnell Ranges
Groote Eylandt
Wellesley Is.
Tropic of Capricorn

1 : 7 100 000
50 0 50 100 150 200 miles
50 0 100 200 300 km
SOUTH AUSTRALIA
NEW SOUTH WALES
VICTORIA
TASMAN SEA
Bass Strait
Flinders Ranges
Grey Range
Barrier Range
Lake Eyre (North)
Lake Torrens
Lake Gairdner
Lake Frome
Darling
Murray
SYDNEY
MELBOURNE
ADELAIDE
BRISBANE
CANBERRA
AUSTRALIAN CAPITAL TERR.
COMMONWEALTH TERR.
Newcastle
Wollongong
Geelong
Ballarat
Bendigo
Broken Hill
Port Augusta
Port Pirie
Whyalla
Port Lincoln
Mount Gambier
Mildura
Wagga Wagga
Albury
Dubbo
Orange
Bathurst
Tamworth
Armidale
Toowoomba
Ipswich
Maryborough
Bourke
Charleville
Kangaroo I.
King Island
Flinders Island
Furneaux Group
Cape Barren I.
Spencer Gulf
Eyre Peninsula
Projection: Bonne
East from Greenwich
COPYRIGHT. GEORGE PHILIP & SON. LTD.
D
E
F
G
1
2
3
4
5
135
140
145
150
30
35
40
ft
m
4500
3000
1200
600
0
200
6000
12 000
1500
1000
400
200
0
600
2000
4000

St. Peterburg
EUROPE
Moskva
Volga
Yekaterinburg
RUSSIA
Ob
Tomsk
Novosibirsk
Irkutsk
Ozero Baykal
Chita
Lena
Okhotsk
Sea of Okhotsk
P-ov. Kamchatka
Komandorskiye O. (Russia)
Petropavlovsk
Sakhalin
G. of Sakhalin
Amur
Blagoveshchensk
Khabarovsk
Kurilskiye Ostrova
(Kuril Is.)
La Perouse Strait
10,542
Kuril Trench
7822
Aleutian
Aleutian Trench
Emperor Seamount Chain
7168
KAZAKSTAN
Semey
Balqash Köl
Aral Sea
Almaty
Toshkent
Ulaanbaatar
MONGOLIA
Altai
ASIA
Urumqi
Manchuria
Harbin
Changchun
Shenyang
Vladivostok
Hakodate
Beijing
Tianjin
Taiyuan
Dalian
KOREA
N.
S.
Sea of Japan
Sendai
JAPAN
Kyōto
TŌKYŌ
Yokohama
8412
Fujisan 3776
Nagoya
Ōsaka
Shikoku
Kyūshū
Japan Trench
10,554
South Honshū Ridge
AFGHANISTAN
Kabul
Srinagar
Indus
Lahore
PAKISTAN
Delhi
Kunlun
TIBET
Lanzhou
Huang
Xi'an
Qingdao
Kitakyūshū
CHINA
Nanjing
Yellow Sea
SHANGHAI
Chongqing
Wuhan
Mt. Everest 8848
Lhasa
Himalaya
NEPAL
Brahmaputra
Kanpur
Ganga
Chang J.
Changsha
Fuzhou
East China Sea
Ryūkyū-retto
Kunming
Taipei
TAIWAN
BANGLADESH
Dhaka
Irrawaddy
Salween
Calcutta
INDIA
Mandalay
Guangzhou
MACAU (Port.)
HONG KONG (U.K.)
BURMA
Hanoi
Hainan
Hyderabad
Bay of Bengal
Rangoon
LAOS
VIETNAM
THAILAND
Mekong
Bangkok
CAMBODIA
Madras
Andaman Is.
Gulf of Thailand
Phnom Penh
Phanh-Bho Ho Chi Minh
South China Sea
SRI LANKA
Colombo
Nicobar Is.
C. Engano
Manila
PHILIPPINES
Mindoro
Palawan
Samar
10,497
Sulu Sea
Mindanao
Mindanao Trench
4101
SABAH
BRUNEI
PEN. MALAYSIA
Kuala Lumpur
MALAYSIA
SARAWAK
SINGAPORE
Celebes Sea
Moluccas
Halmahera
Borneo
Celebes
Sumatra
INDONESIA
Palembang
Java Sea
Ujung Pandang
Buru
Ceram
Banda Sea
Flores Sea
Jakarta
Surabaya
Java
Sunda Strait
Bali
Flores
Sumbawa
Sumba
Timor
7440
Java Trench
7450
Sunda Islands
Christmas I. (Austral.)
Cocos (Keeling) Is. (Austral.)
Okhotsk
Ogasawara Gunto (Bonin Is.)
Kazan Retto (Volcano Is.)
Minami-Tori-Shima (Marcus I.)
Midway Is.
Lisia
6603
Marcus Necker Ridge
Wake I. (U.S.)
NORTHERN MARIANAS (U.S.)
Saipan
GUAM (U.S.)
11,022
Mariana Trench
Yap
PALAU
PACIFIC
Bikini Atoll
MARSHALL IS.
Enewetak Atoll
International Date Line
FEDERATED STATES OF MICRONESIA
Truk
Pohnpei
Micronesia
Caroline Islands
Jaluit
Butaritari
Gilbert Is.
Howland
Baker
OCEAN
Melanesia
Admiralty Is.
NAURU
Banaba
Abarin
Bismarck Arch.
New Ireland
IRIAN JAYA
5029
PAPUA NEW GUINEA
New Guinea
Rabaul
New Britain
9103
Lae
SOLOMON IS.
Honiara
Guadalcanal
TUVALU
Port Moresby
Arafura Sea
Torres Strait
C. York
C. Arnhem
Darwin
G. of Carpentaria
Sta. Cruz I.
9165
Rotuma
Wallis & Futuna (Fr.)
Louisiade Arch. (Austral.)
VANUATU
FIJI
Vanua Levu
Viti Levu
Suva
Coral Sea
Is. Chesterfield
Cairns
Townsville
NORTHERN TERRITORY
Mt. Isa
7570
Is. Loyauté
NEW CALEDONIA (Fr.)
Nouméa
N.W. Cape
AUSTRALIA
Great Dividing Range
Rockhampton
Alice Springs
QUEENSLAND
WESTERN AUSTRALIA
Brisbane
Lord Howe Ridge
Norfolk I. (Aust.)
Kermadec Is. (N.Z.)
Kermadec Trench
10,047
L. Eyre
SOUTH AUSTRALIA
Darling
Perth
NEW SOUTH WALES
Lord Howe I. (Aust.)
Sydney
Great Australian Bight
Adelaide
Murray
Canberra
Mt. Kosciusko 2230
VICTORIA
Melbourne
Tasman Sea
Auckland
NEW ZEALAND
Cook Strait
Wellington
Bass Strait
TASMANIA
Hobart
Mt. Cook 3753
Christchurch
Chatham
Dunedin
Invercargill
Bounty Is.
Antipodes
Auckland Is. (N.Z.)
Macquarie Is. (Aust.)
Campbell I. (N.Z.)
INDIAN OCEAN
Mid-Indian Ridge
Î. Amsterdam (Fr.)
Î. St. Paul (Fr.)
Îs. Crozet (Fr.)
Kerguelen (Fr.)
Heard I. (Aust.)
ft m
18,000 6000
12 000 4000
6000 2000
3000 1000
600 200
0 0
200 600
2000 6000
4000 12 000
6000 18,000
8000 24,000
m ft
Projection: Mollweide's Homolographic
East from Greenwich

1 : 48 000 000

12 13 14 15 16 17 18 19 20

ALASKA
(U.S.)

GREENLAND

A

C. Farewell

60

Gulf of Alaska

6959

Juneau

Hudson
Bay

B

Prince of Wales I.

Prince Rupert
Kitimat
Edmonton

R O C K Y

C A N A D A

NORTH AMERICA

Labrador

NORTH

Queen Charlotte Is.

Vancouver
Vancouver I.
Victoria
Seattle

Calgary

Regina

Winnipeg
L. Winnipeg

Montréal
Quebec
St. Lawrence

Newfoundland

50

C

Portland

Boise
Snake

Minneapolis

L. Superior

Ottawa
Toronto
L. Ontario

Saint John
Pr. Edward I.

ATLANTIC

CHICAGO
L. Huron
Michigan
Detroit
Erie
Buffalo
Pittsburgh
Boston
C. Sable

C. Mendocino

Salt Lake
City

Denver
Kansas
City St. Louis
Cincinnati

NEW YORK
Philadelphia
Baltimore
Washington

40

D

San Francisco

4418

M o u n t a i n s

Colorado

UNITED STATES

Memphis

Appalachian Mts.

Atlanta

C. Hatteras

6741

Los Angeles
San Diego

Ciudad
Juarez

Dallas
Mississippi

Jacksonville

Bermuda (U.K.)

30

E

Hawaiian Is.
(U.S.)
Honolulu
Oahu

Tropic of Cancer

6225

I. Guadalupe
(Mexico)

Sierra Madre

M E X I C O

San Antonio

Houston
New
Orleans

Gulf of Mexico

Monterrey

Miami

Florida
Strait

BAHAMAS

OCEAN

4205
Hawaii

Gulf of California

La Habana

Yucatan Channel

CUBA

West Indies

Hispaniola
DOM.
REP.
9200

20

I. (U.S.)

Is. Revilla Gigedo
(Mexico)

México
Guadalajara
Puebla 5700
Acapulco

7680
JAMAICA

Mérida
C.

HAITI
Kingston

PUERTO
RICO
(U.S.)

Leeward
Is.

F

P A C I F I C

Ridge

I.Clipperton (Fr.)

GUATEMALA
Guatemala
San Salvador
EL SALVADOR
CENTRAL
AMERICA
COSTA RICA

BELIZE

HONDURAS

NICARAGUA
Managua

San José
Colón
PANAMA

Caribbean Sea

Barranquilla
Maracaibo

Panama
Canal

Caracas

BARBADOS
Windward
Is.
TRINIDAD &
TOBAGO

VENEZUELA

10

Palmyra Is. (U.S.)
Teraina
Tabuaeran
Kiritimati

I. del Coco
(Costa Rica)

I. de Malpelo
(Colombia)

Medellín
Bogota

Cali
COLOMBIA

G

Jarvis I.
(U.S.)

Equator

Galápagos
(Ecuador)

Quito
ECUADOR

Orinoco

0

I.
Is.
B A T I

Malden I.
Starbuck I.

Guayaquil

Iquitos

C. Pariñas

Amazonas

Manaus

BRAZIL

H

Îs. Marquises

SOUTH

Tongareva
Penrhyn Is.

Vostok
Caroline I.

Trujillo

Manihiki
Suwarrow Is.

Flint I.

6369

PERU
Lima

AMERICA

10

Cook
Islands
(N.Z.)

Îs. de la
Société

Îs. Tuamotu

Cuzco

L.Titicaca
Illampu & Ancohuma
6550

J

Manuae

Tahiti

FRENCH POLYNESIA

Arequipa

La Paz
BOLIVIA

Austral

Tuamotu Ridge

6866
Peru

20

Rarotonga

Îs. Tubuai
(Îs. Australes)

Seamount Chain

Tropic of Capricorn

Pitcairn I. (U.K.)

Ducie I.
(U.K.)

Iquique
Chile

8050
Antofagasta
Trench

PARAGUAY

Asunción

K

Rapa

I. de Pascua
(Easter I.)
(Chile)

Sala-y-Gomez
(Chile)

San Félix (Chile)
San Ambrosio (Chile)

A n d e s

Tucumán

Pto. Alegre

30

Arch. de Juan Fernández
(Chile)

6960
Valparaíso
Santiago
Concepción

Córdoba
Rosario
Buenos Aires

URUGUAY
Montevideo
Rio de la Plata

L

Pacific – Antarctic Ridge

Chile Rise

ARGENTINA

SOUTH

40

ATLANTIC

M

East Pacific Ridge

P a t a g o n i a

6212

Falkland Is. (U.K.)

OCEAN

50

N

Punta Arenas
Str. of Magellan
Tierra del Fuego
C. Horn

South Georgia (U.K.)

1 : 31 100 000
200 0 200 400 600 800 miles
400 0 400 800 1200 km
ARCTIC OCEAN
Beaufort Sea
Asia
Bering Strait
Bering Sea
Alaska
Alaska Range
Alaska Peninsula
Brooks Ra.
Mt. McKinley 6194
Mt. Logan 5959
Mt. St. Elias 5489
Gulf of Alaska
Kodiak I.
Greenland
Baffin Bay
Baffin Island
Queen Elizabeth Is.
Ellesmere I.
Axel Heiberg I.
Victoria I.
Banks I.
Hudson Bay
Hudson Strait
Southampton I.
Ungava Peninsula
Coast of Labrador
Newfoundland
Iceland
Denmark Strait
Davis Strait
Cape Farewell
Mackenzie Mts.
Great Bear L.
Great Slave L.
L. Athabasca
Reindeer L.
L. Winnipeg
Rocky Mountains
Coast Mountains
Mt. Waddington 3994
Mt. Robson 3954
Great Plains
Laurentian Plateau
Gulf of St. Lawrence
Nova Scotia
Vancouver I.
Queen Charlotte Islands
Alexander Archipelago
Mt. Rainier 4392
Cascade Range
Coast Ranges
Mt. Shasta 4317
Sierra Nevada
Mt. Whitney 4418
Great Basin
Great Salt Lake
Wasatch Ra.
Mt. Elbert 4399
Blanca Peak 4378
Colorado Plateau
Grand Canyon
Death Valley -86
L. Superior
L. Michigan
L. Huron
L. Erie
L. Ontario
Niagara Falls
Mt. Washington 1917
Appalachian Mts.
Allegheny Mts.
Blue Ridge Mts.
Cumberland Plateau
Ozark Plateau
Mississippi
Missouri
Mississippi River Delta
Florida
Bermuda
NORTH ATLANTIC OCEAN
PACIFIC OCEAN
Lower California
Gulf of California
Western Sierra Madre
Mexican Plateau
Eastern Sierra Madre
Gulf of Mexico
Gulf of Campeche
Yucatán Peninsula
Popocatepetl 5452
Citlaltépetl 5700
Isthmus of Tehuantepec
Cuba
Bahamas
Hispaniola
Jamaica
Greater Antilles
Caribbean Sea
Clarion Fracture Zone
Guatemala Trench
Tropic of Cancer
Revilla Gigedo Is.
G. of Panamá
Andes
Sierra Nevada de Santa Marta 5800
Projection: Bonne
West from Greenwich

1 : 31 100 000

200 0 200 400 600 800 miles
400 0 400 800 1200 km
A
B
C
D
E
F
G
H
J
7
8
9
10
11
12
RUSSIA
Asia
International Date Line
ARCTIC OCEAN
Beaufort Sea
Bering Sea
Bering Strait
St. Lawrence I.
Queen Elizabeth Is.
Ellesmere I.
GREENLAND (Denmark)
ICELAND
Reykjavik
Denmark Strait
Baffin Bay
Baffin Island
Davis Strait
Godthaab
Cape Farewell
Victoria I.
ALASKA (U.S.A.)
Yukon
Porcupine
Fairbanks
Anchorage
Kodiak I.
Gulf of Alaska
YUKON TERRITORY
Arctic Circle
Mackenzie
NORTHWEST TERRITORIES
Great Bear L.
Back
Whitehorse
Juneau
Liard
Yellowknife
Great Slave L.
Dubawnt
Hudson Strait
Hudson Bay
CANADA
BRITISH COLUMBIA
Skeena
Peace
L. Athabasca
Athabasca
ALBERTA
Fraser
Edmonton
Churchill
Nelson
MANITOBA
SASKATCHEWAN
Saskatchewan
Calgary
L. Winnipeg
ONTARIO
Eastmain
QUÉBEC
Labrador
NEWFOUNDLAND
St. John's
St. Lawrence
PRINCE EDWARD I.
Charlottetown
St.-Pierre Et Miquelon (Fr.)
NEW BRUNSWICK
NOVA SCOTIA
Halifax
C. Sable
Fredericton
Québec
Victoria
Vancouver
Regina
Winnipeg
Montréal
Ottawa
WASHINGTON
Olympia
Seattle
Portland
Salem
Columbia
OREGON
MONTANA
Missouri
Helena
NORTH DAKOTA
Bismarck
MINNESOTA
L. Superior
MAINE
Augusta
VER.
N.H.
Concord
Boston
MASS.
Providence
IDAHO
Boise
Snake
SOUTH DAKOTA
Minneapolis
WISCONSIN
Madison
L. Michigan
MICHIGAN
Lansing
Huron
Toronto
L. Ontario
Buffalo
NEW YORK
Hartford
NEW YORK CITY
PHILADELPHIA
WYOMING
IOWA
Milwaukee
Detroit
L. Erie
Toledo
Cleveland
PA.
Pittsburgh
N.J.
Sacramento
SAN FRANCISCO
San Jose
Carson City
NEVADA
Salt Lake City
Cheyenne
NEBRASKA
CHICAGO
OHIO
Baltimore
DE.
MD.
UNITED STATES
Lincoln
ILLINOIS
INDIANA
Indianapolis
Columbus
Washington D.C.
Richmond
UTAH
Denver
Kansas City
Springfield
Cincinnati
W.V.
VIRGINIA
CALIFORNIA
COLORADO
Topeka
St. Louis
KENTUCKY
Raleigh
Las Vegas
KANSAS
MISSOURI
Nashville
NORTH CAROLINA
TENNESSEE
Charlotte
LOS ANGELES
Santa Fe
OKLAHOMA
Oklahoma City
ARKANSAS
Memphis
Columbia
SOUTH CAROLINA
San Diego
Colorado
ARIZONA
Albuquerque
NEW MEXICO
Little Rock
Birmingham
Atlanta
GEORGIA
Charleston
Phoenix
Mississippi
MISSISSIPPI
Montgomery
Tucson
El Paso
Dallas
Jackson
ALABAMA
Jacksonville
Tallahassee
TEXAS
Baton Rouge
LOUISIANA
New Orleans
Austin
Houston
FLORIDA
Tampa
Miami
Bermuda (U.K.)
NORTH ATLANTIC OCEAN
PACIFIC OCEAN
Guadalupe (Mex.)
Hermosillo
Rio Grande
MEXICO
Nassau
BAHAMAS
Florida Str.
Turks & Caicos Is. (U.K.)
Tropic of Cancer
Culiacan
Monterrey
Gulf of Mexico
Havana
CUBA
DOMINICAN REP.
San Juan
HAITI
Port-au-Prince
Santo Domingo
PUERTO RICO (U.S.A.)
Cayman Is. (U.K.)
JAMAICA
Kingston
Mérida
Guadalajara
MÉXICO
Puebla
Revilla Gigedo Is. (Mex.)
Caribbean Sea
Belmopan
BELIZE
Acapulco
GUATEMALA
Guatemala
HONDURAS
Tegucigalpa
San Salvador
EL SALVADOR
NICARAGUA
L. Nicaragua
Managua
Barranquilla
Maracaibo
VENEZUELA
COSTA RICA
San José
Panamá
PANAMA
South America
COLOMBIA
Medellín
Projection: Bonne
West from Greenwich

■ MÉXICO Capital Cities

CARTOGRAPHY BY PHILIP'S.

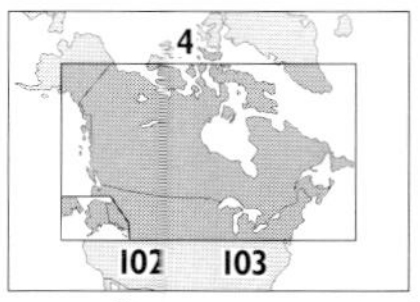
4
102
103

PACIFIC OCEAN
ALASKA
YUKON TERRITORY
BRITISH COLUMBIA
ALBERTA
SASKATCHEWAN
MANITOBA
NORTHWEST TERRITORIES
INUVIK
KITIKMEOT
KEEWATIN
FORT SMITH
MONTANA
NORTH DAKOTA
SOUTH DAKOTA
WYOMING
NEBRASKA
MINNESOTA
WASHINGTON
UNITED STATES
Anchorage
Fairbanks
Whitehorse
Dawson
Juneau
Vancouver
Victoria
Seattle
Tacoma
Spokane
Calgary
Edmonton
Lethbridge
Medicine Hat
Saskatoon
Regina
Moose Jaw
Prince Albert
Winnipeg
Yellowknife
Great Slave L.
Gt. Bear Lake
Lake Athabasca
Amundsen Gulf
Victoria Island
Banks Island
Prince Albert Pen.
Coronation Gulf
Queen Maud Gulf
Viscount Melville Sound
Prince of Wales Island
M'Clintock Channel
Rocky Mountains
Mackenzie Mountains
Coast Mountains
Cassiar Mountains
Columbia Mountains
Queen Charlotte Is.
Vancouver I.
L. Manitoba
Minneapolis
Omaha
Projection: Bonne
ALASKA
1:26 700 000
100 0 100 200 300 miles
100 0 200 400 km
BERING SEA
GULF OF ALASKA
PACIFIC OCEAN
Aleutian Is.
Brooks Range
RUSSIA
CANADA
West from Greenwich
ft m
9000 3000
6000 2000
4500 1500
3000 1000
1200 400
600 200
0 0
200 600
2000 6000
m ft

1 : 13 300 000
100 0 100 200 300 400 miles
100 0 100 200 300 400 500 600 km
11 12 13 14 15 16
B C D E
Baffin Bay
Lancaster Sound
Bylot I.
Arctic Bay
Pond Inlet
Milne Inlet
Scott I.
Clyde
C. Hewett
Svartenhuk Halvø
Disko
Disko B.
Christianshåb
GREENLAND
Angmagssalik
Søndre Strømfjord
Holsteinsborg
Sukkertoppen
Godthåb
Fiskenæsset
Frederikshåb
Ivigtut
Julianehåb
Sydprøven
Nanortalik
Kap Farvel
Kong Frederik VI's Kyst
Davis Strait
ATLANTIC OCEAN
Baffin Island
Home B.
Broughton Island
Padloping Island
C. Dyer
Cape Dyer
Cumberland Peninsula
Pangnirtung
Hoare B.
C. Mercy
Cumberland Sd.
Fury & Hecla Str.
Igloolik Island
Hall Lake
Melville Peninsula
Committee B.
Foxe Basin
Prince Charles I.
Nettilling L.
Amadjuak L.
Foxe Penin.
Repulse Bay
Wager B.
Roes Welcome Sd.
C. Dorchester
Foxe Channel
Southampton I.
Coral Harbour
Bell Pen.
Cape Dorset
Amadjuak
Iqaluit
Kimmirut
Frobisher Bay
Resolution I.
Hudson Strait
Coats I.
Digges Is.
Mansel I.
Ivujivik
Salluit
Kangiqsujuaq
Quaqtaq (Notre Dame de Koartac)
Akpatok I.
C. Chidley
Arnaud
Kangirsuk
Ungava Bay
Ungava Peninsula
Kangiqsualujjuaq
Hebron
Nutak
Nain
Kuujjuaq
George
Whale
Koksoak
Feuilles
Mélèzes
Kaniapiskau
L. Minto
Portland Promontory
Inukjuak
Hudson Bay
Ottawa Is.
Sleeper Is.
King George Is.
Baker's Dozen Is.
Belcher Is.
L. à L'Eau Claire
Kuujjuarapik
Grand Baleine
Lac Bienville
C. Henrietta Maria
Pte. Louis-XIV
Winisk
Kanaaupscow
La Grande
Chisasibi
James Bay
Akimiski I.
Wemindji
Attawapiskat
Eastmain
Charlton I.
Waskaganish
Ft. Albany
Albany
Moosonee
Rupert
Nottaway
Mistassini L.
L. Albanel
Péribonca
Manicouagan
Gagnon
Schefferville
Petitsikapau L.
Ashuanipi
Moisie
Sept Îles
Port-Cartier
Coast of Labrador
C. Harrison
Indian Harbour
Hopedale
Rigolet
L. Melville
Cartwright
Battle Harb.
Belle Isle
Str. of Belle Isle
Churchill Falls
Churchill
North West R.
Happy Valley
Goose Bay
Natashquan
St.-Augustin-Saguenay
Romaine
Mingon
Notoshquan
Î. d'Anticosti
QUEBEC
NEWFOUNDLAND
Notre Dame B.
Twillingate
Lewisporte
Gander
Bonavista
Trinity B.
Carbonear
St. John's
Grand Falls
Corner Brook
Buchans
Newfoundland
Harbour Grace
Placentia B.
Placentia
Trepassey
C. Race
C. Ray
Channel-Port aux Basques
ST.-PIERRE et MIQUELON (Fr.)
Cabot Str.
Gulf of St. Lawrence
C. de Gaspé
Gaspé
Pén. de Gaspé
Matane
Campbellton
Îs. de la Madeleine
PR. EDWARD I.
Summerside
Charlottetown
C. North
Cape Breton I.
Glace Bay
Sydney
Port Hawkesbury
Mulgrave
NOVA SCOTIA
New Glasgow
Truro
Windsor
Dartmouth
Halifax
Kentville
Digby
Bridgewater
Liverpool
Shelburne
C. Sable
Yarmouth
Sable I. (Nova Scotia)
Northumberland Str.
Pictou
Springhill
Amherst
Moncton
Bathurst
Chatham
Tignish
Dalhousie
Newcastle
NEW BRUNSWICK
Fredericton
Saint John
Woodstock
Edmundston
St. Leonard
B. of Fundy
R. St. Lawrence
Rimouski
Rivière-du-Loup
Baie-Comeau
Betsiamites
Saguenay
Chicoutimi
Jonquière
Tadoussac
Roberval
Dolbeau
St.-Jean
Chibougamau
Rés. de Gouin
Senneterre
Val d'Or
Taschereau
L. Abitibi
Rouyn
Noranda
Matagami
Harricana
Missinaibi
Kirkland Lake
Cochrane
Timmins
Mattagami
Hearst
Kenogami
Nakina
Longlac
Heron Bay
Oba
Franz
Michipicoten
Thunder Bay
L. Superior
Sault Ste. Marie
Copper Cliff
Sudbury
North Bay
Haileybury
Cobalt
L. Témiscamingue
Rés. de Cabonga
La Tuque
Shawinigan
Trois-Rivières
Québec
Lévis
Thetford Mines
Joliette
Sorel
St. Hyacinthe
MONTREAL
Lachine
Granby
Sherbrooke
Hull
Ottawa
Pembroke
Parry Sound
Georgian Bay
Lake Huron
Orillia
Peterboro'
Owen Sound
Oshawa
Cobourg
Kingston
Cornwall
Arnprior
Belleville
TORONTO
Guelph
Kitchener
Stratford
Brantford
Hamilton
St. Catharines
Niagara Falls
London
Sarnia
Windsor
Chatham
DETROIT
Toledo
Cleveland
Youngstown
Akron
Erie
Buffalo
Rochester
Syracuse
Utica
Albany
Watertown
Glens Falls
Burlington
L. Champlain
Rutland
Concord
VERMONT
NEW HAMPSHIRE
MAINE
Augusta
Bangor
Lewiston
Portland
Manchester
Lowell
Boston
C. Cod
Worcester
MASS.
Springfield
Providence
Waterbury
New Haven
Bridgeport
CONN.
DEL.
NEW YORK
Jersey City
Newark
NEW JERSEY
Trenton
Reading
Allentown
Scranton
Binghamton
Elmira
Williamsport
Jamestown
PENNSYLVANIA
OHIO
INDIANA
South Bend
Gary
CHICAGO
Evanston
Kenosha
Racine
Milwaukee
L. Michigan
Kalamazoo
Grand Rapids
Muskegon
Saginaw
Saginaw B.
Ludington
Cadillac
Traverse City
Petoskey
Cheboygan
Manistique
Sault Ste. Marie
North Chan.
Calumet
Keweenaw Bay
Marquette
Escanaba
Iron Mt.
Menominee
Green Bay
Appleton
Manitowoc
Antigo
Wausau
Sheboygan
1890
2136
2591
2850
3809
1676
257
1128
814
1190
1917
6309
80 70 60 50 40 30
West from Greenwich
COPYRIGHT. GEORGE PHILIP & SON, LTD.
11 12 13 14

97
101
108
104
1
2
3
4
5
A
B
C
D
N. W. TERRITORIES
MANITOBA
ONTARIO
HUDSON BAY
JAMES BAY
Belcher Islands
North Belcher Is.
Baker's Dozen Is.
Akimiski I.
Polar Bear Provincial Park
C. Henrietta Maria
Winisk
Attawapiskat
Albany
Fort Albany
Moosonee
Moose Factory
Chisasibi
Grand Baleine
Lac Bienville
Eastmain
L. Mistassini
Q
Lake Nipigon
Thunder Bay
LAKE SUPERIOR
Isle Royale
Duluth
Superior
Marquette
Sault Ste. Marie
Pukaskwa Nat. Park
Michipicoten I.
Kapuskasing
Timmins
Kirkland Lake
Rouyn
Val-d'Or
Amos
Sudbury
North Bay
Elliot Lake
Manitoulin I.
Georgian Bay
Parry Sound
LAKE HURON
LAKE MICHIGAN
WISCONSIN
Green Bay
Milwaukee
Madison
Chicago
Rockford
Kenosha
Racine
Grand Rapids
Flint
Lansing
Saginaw
Bay City
Detroit
Windsor
Toledo
Cleveland
Port Huron
Sarnia
London
Kitchener
Guelph
Hamilton
Toronto
LAKE ONTARIO
St. Catharines
Niagara Falls
Buffalo
LAKE ERIE
Erie
Rochester
Syracuse
Utica
Binghamton
Elmira
Ithaca
Albany
Ottawa
Hull
Kingston
Peterborough
Barrie
Owen Sound
Pembroke
Algonquin Prov. Park
Adirondack Mountains
Trois-Rivières
Montreal
Joliette
Watertown
Ogdensburg
NEW YORK
INDIANA
OHIO
PENNSYLVANIA
ILLINOIS
South Bend
Elkhart
Kalamazoo
Lambert's Equivalent Azimuthal
ft
m
4500
3000
1200
600
1500
1000
400
200
0
200
2000
4000
600
6000
12 000

1 : 6 200 000

50 0 50 100 150 200 miles
50 0 50 100 150 200 250 300 km

6
7
8
9
A
B
C
D
NEWFOUNDLAND
COAST OF LABRADOR
LABRADOR
QUEBEC
NEW BRUNSWICK
NOVA SCOTIA
MAINE
PRINCE EDWARD ISLAND
NEWFOUNDLAND
GULF OF ST. LAWRENCE
ATLANTIC OCEAN
St. Lawrence
Cabot Strait
Str. of Belle Isle
Dét. de Jacques-Cartier
Dét. d'Honguedo
Î. d'Anticosti
Bay of Fundy
Northumberland Str.
Mealy Mts.
Long Range Mts.
Mts. Chic-Chocs
Pén. de Gaspé
South Aulatsivik I.
Nain
Hopedale
Makkovik
Kaipokok B.
Holton
Cartwright
Sandwich B.
Table B.
Island of Ponds
Square Islands
Battle Harbour
Mary's Harbour
St. Lewis
Red Bay
Belle I.
L'Anse-au-Loup
Forteau
Bradore Bay
Lourdes-de-Blanc-Sablon
St. Anthony
Hare B.
Flower's Cove
Roddickton
Conche
Englee
Groais I.
Bell I.
Horse Is.
White B.
Great Harbour Deep
Port Saunders
Daniel's Harbour
Seal Cove
Baie Verte
La Scie
C. St. John
Notre Dame B.
Fogo I.
Twillingate
Carmanville
C. Freels
Wesleyville
Bonavista B.
C. Bonavista
Bonavista
Catalina
Trinity B.
Trinity
Lewisporte
Gander
Glenwood
Botwood
Grand Falls
Bishop's Falls
Windsor
Buchans
Red Indian L.
Howley
Deer Lake
Springdale
Corner Brook
Bay of Islands
Trout River
GROS MORNE NAT. PARK
Stephenville
Port au Port B.
Long Pt.
C. St. George
St. George's B.
St. George's
South Branch
St. Andrew's
C. Ray
Channel-Port aux Basques
Burgeo
Ramea
Harbour Breton
Grand Bank
Fortune B.
Marystown
Burin
St. Lawrence
Placentia
Placentia B.
Argentia
St. Mary's B.
St. Bride's
C. St. Mary's
Trepassey
C. Race
Ferryland
Avalon Peninsula
Holyrood
St. John's
Conception B.
Carbonear
Harbour Grace
Torbay
Pearl
Bay Bulls
Clarenville
Port Blandford
Terrenceville
Glovertown
Dark Cove
Grey Res.
Salmon Res.
Victoria Res.
White Bear Res.
Miquelon
Langlade
St. Pierre
SAINT-PIERRE ET MIQUELON (Fr.)
Happy Valley-Goose Bay
North-West River
L. Melville
Hamilton Inlet
Rigolet
Churchill Falls
Smallwood Res.
Schefferville
Labrador City
Wabush
Gagnon
Rés. Manicouagan
Sept-Îles
Port-Cartier
Rivière-Pentecôte
Godbout
Baie-Trinité
Pte. des Monts
Baie-Comeau
Forestville
Mingan
Havre-St-Pierre
Natashquan
Kegaska
Gethsémani
Harrington Harbour
Étamamu
St-Augustin
Port-Menier
Heath Pt.
Gaspé
Percé
Chandler
Grande-Rivière
Matane
Mont-Joli
Rimouski
Rivière-du-Loup
Trois-Pistoles
Dalhousie
Campbellton
Bathurst
Chaleur Bay
Miscou I.
Shippegan
Lamèque
Tracadie
Miramichi B.
Chatham
Newcastle
Edmundston
St. Leonard
Grand Falls
Woodstock
Fredericton
Moncton
Saint John
St. Stephen
Campobello
Grand Manan I.
Îs. de la Madeleine (Quebec)
Cap-aux-Meules
Havre-Aubert
Î. Brion
Grande-Entrée
Summerside
Charlottetown
Souris
Amherst
Springhill
Truro
New Glasgow
Stellarton
Pictou
Antigonish
Halifax
Dartmouth
Windsor
Kentville
Middleton
Annapolis Royal
Bridgetown
Digby
Yarmouth
Shelburne
Lockeport
Liverpool
Port Mouton
Bridgewater
Lunenburg
Mahone Bay
Musquodoboit Hr.
Sheet Hr.
Sherbrooke
Canso
Chedabucto B.
Port Hawkesbury
Inverness
Chéticamp
Pleasant Bay
Ingonish
CAPE BRETON NAT. PARK
Sydney Mines
New Waterford
Glace Bay
Sydney
N. Sydney
Louisbourg
Cape Breton Island
Bras d'Or L.
St. Peters
I. Madame
Fourchu
Sable I. (Nova Scotia)
Clark's Harbour
C. Sable
Wedgeport
Bangor
Augusta
Waterville
Skowhegan
Millinocket
Houlton
Presque Isle
Caribou
Calais
Machias
Eastport
Ellsworth
Bar Harbor
Mt. Desert I.
Belfast
Camden
Rockland
Bath
Brunswick
Portland
Lewiston
Auburn
Biddeford
Saco
Sanford
Portsmouth
Dover
Concord
Manchester
Nashua
Haverhill
Lawrence
Lowell
Lynn
Gloucester
C. Ann
BOSTON
Brockton
Thetford Mines
Lac-Mégantic
Plessisville
Montmagny
Lauzon
Lévis
Chicoutimi
Arvida
Tadoussac
West from Greenwich

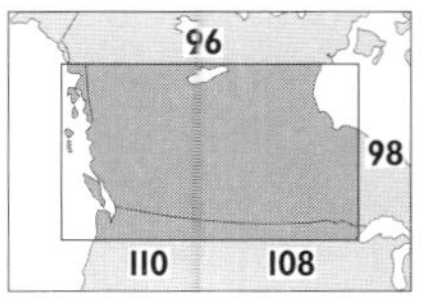
96
98
110
108

1
2
3
4
5
6
A
B
C
D
YUKON TERRITORY
NORTHWEST TERRITORIES
BRITISH COLUMBIA
ALBERTA
ALASKA
WASHINGTON
IDAHO
PACIFIC OCEAN
VANCOUVER ISLAND
QUEEN CHARLOTTE ISLANDS
ALEXANDER ARCH.
GREAT SLAVE LAKE
Coast Mountains
Skeena Mountains
Rocky Mountains
Cariboo Mountains
Selkirk Mountains
Cassiar Mountains
Caribou Mts.
Buffalo Head Hills
Birch Mountains
Whitehorse
Yellowknife
Fort Nelson
Fort St. John
Dawson Creek
Grande Prairie
Peace River
Prince Rupert
Prince George
Kitimat
Kamloops
Kelowna
Penticton
Vernon
Nelson
Cranbrook
Lethbridge
Calgary
Red Deer
EDMONTON
St. Albert
VANCOUVER
New Westminster
North Vancouver
Victoria
Nanaimo
Port Alberni
Bellingham
SEATTLE
Everett
Bremerton
Port Angeles
Juneau
Sitka
Petersburg
Ketchikan
Wrangell
Skagway
Haines
Stewart
Hay River
Fort Simpson
Fort Smith
Jasper
Banff
Golden
Revelstoke
Mt. Robson 3954
Mt. Waddington 3994
Mt. Columbia 3747
JASPER NATIONAL PARK
WELLS GRAY PROV. PARK
TWEEDSMUIR PROV. PARK
STRATHCONA PROV. PARK
GLACIER BAY NAT. MONUMENT
OLYMPIC NATIONAL PARK
Kootenay L.
Okanagan L.
Williston Lake
Lesser Slave L.
Queen Charlotte Str.
Dixon Entrance
Hecate Strait
Juan de Fuca Str.
Chichagof I.
Baranof I.
Admiralty I.
Prince of Wales I.
Graham I.
Moresby I.
ft
m
12 000
9000
6000
4500
3000
1200
600
0
200
2000
4000
3000
2000
1500
1000
400
200
0
600
6000
Projection: Lambert's Equivalent Azimuthal
West from Greenwich
135
130
125
120
115
55
50

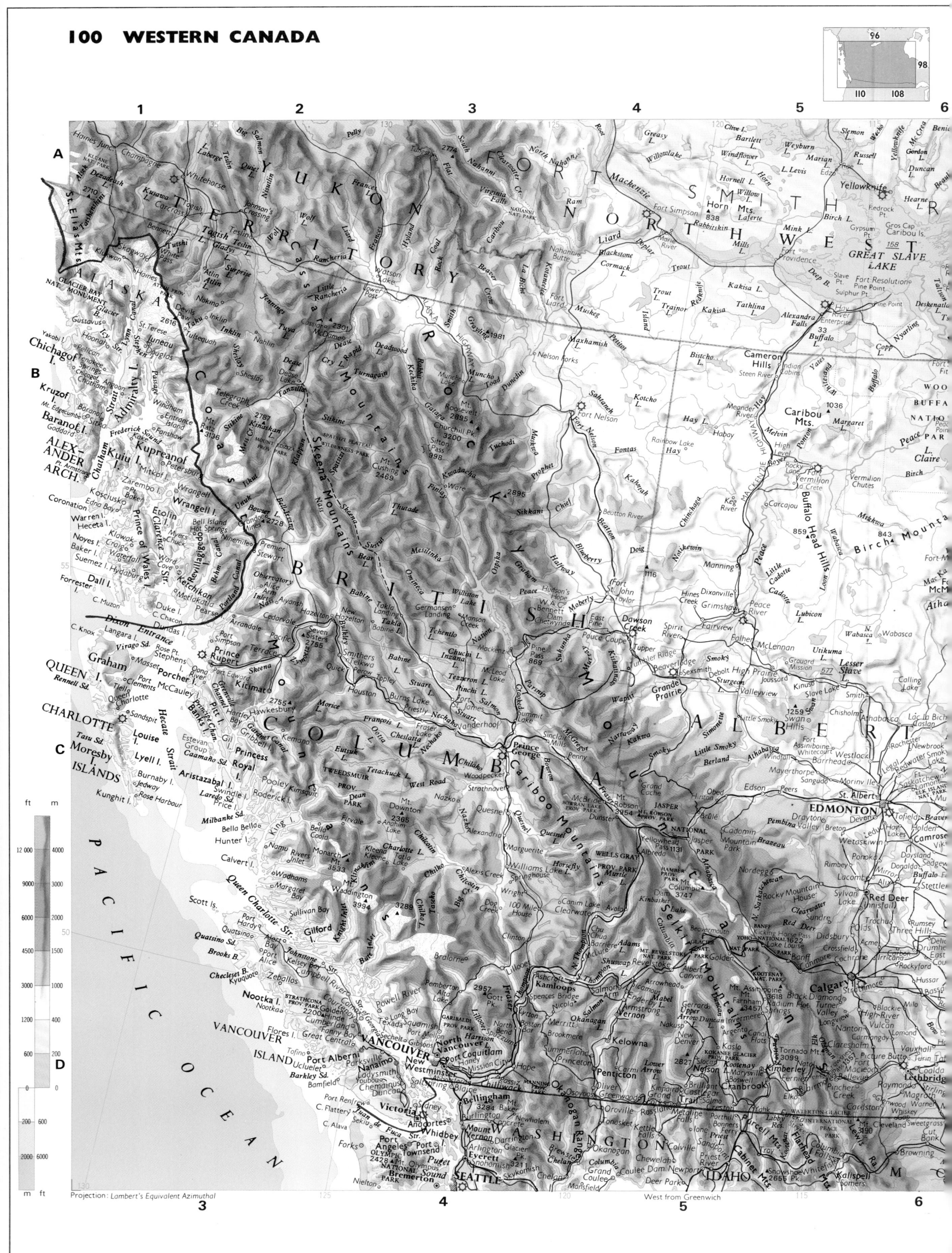

1 : 6 200 000

miles 50 0 50 100 150 200
km 50 0 50 100 150 200 250 300
7
8
9
10
11
A
B
C
D
KEEWATIN REGION
TERRITORIES
HUDSON BAY
MANITOBA
SASKATCHEWAN
ONTARIO
NORTH DAKOTA
MINNESOTA
MONTANA
LAKE WINNIPEG
Lake Winnipegosis
Lake Manitoba
Lake Athabasca
Reindeer L.
Wollaston L.
Southern Indian L.
Cedar Lake
Lake of the Woods
Dubawnt L.
Yathkyed L.
Nueltin L.
Kasba L.
Churchill
C. Churchill
Port Nelson
Nelson
Hayes
Flin Flon
The Pas
Thompson
Lynn Lake
Uranium City
Prince Albert
North Battleford
Saskatoon
Yorkton
Regina
Moose Jaw
Swift Current
Weyburn
Estevan
Brandon
Portage la Prairie
WINNIPEG
St. Boniface
Transcona
Selkirk
Dauphin
Kenora
Fort Frances
International Falls
Minot
Williston
Grand Forks
Devils Lake
Bemidji
Duluth
Hibbing
Virginia
Grand Rapids
Havre
Glasgow
Cypress Hills
Lac la Ronge
La Ronge
Athabasca
Red Deer
Qu'Appelle
Assiniboine
Souris
Churchill
Moose Jaw Cr.
Saskatchewan
S. Saskatchewan
N. Saskatchewan
Red Lake
Island L.
Gods L.
Severn L.
Big Trout L.
Lac Seul
Sakakawea
TRANS CANADA HIGHWAY
110
105
100
95
90
60
55
50
7
8
9
10

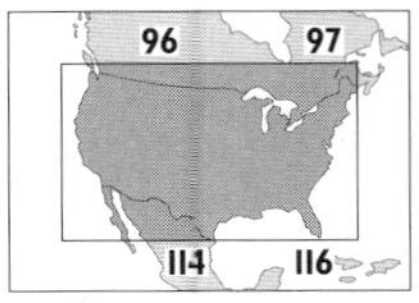
96
97
114
116

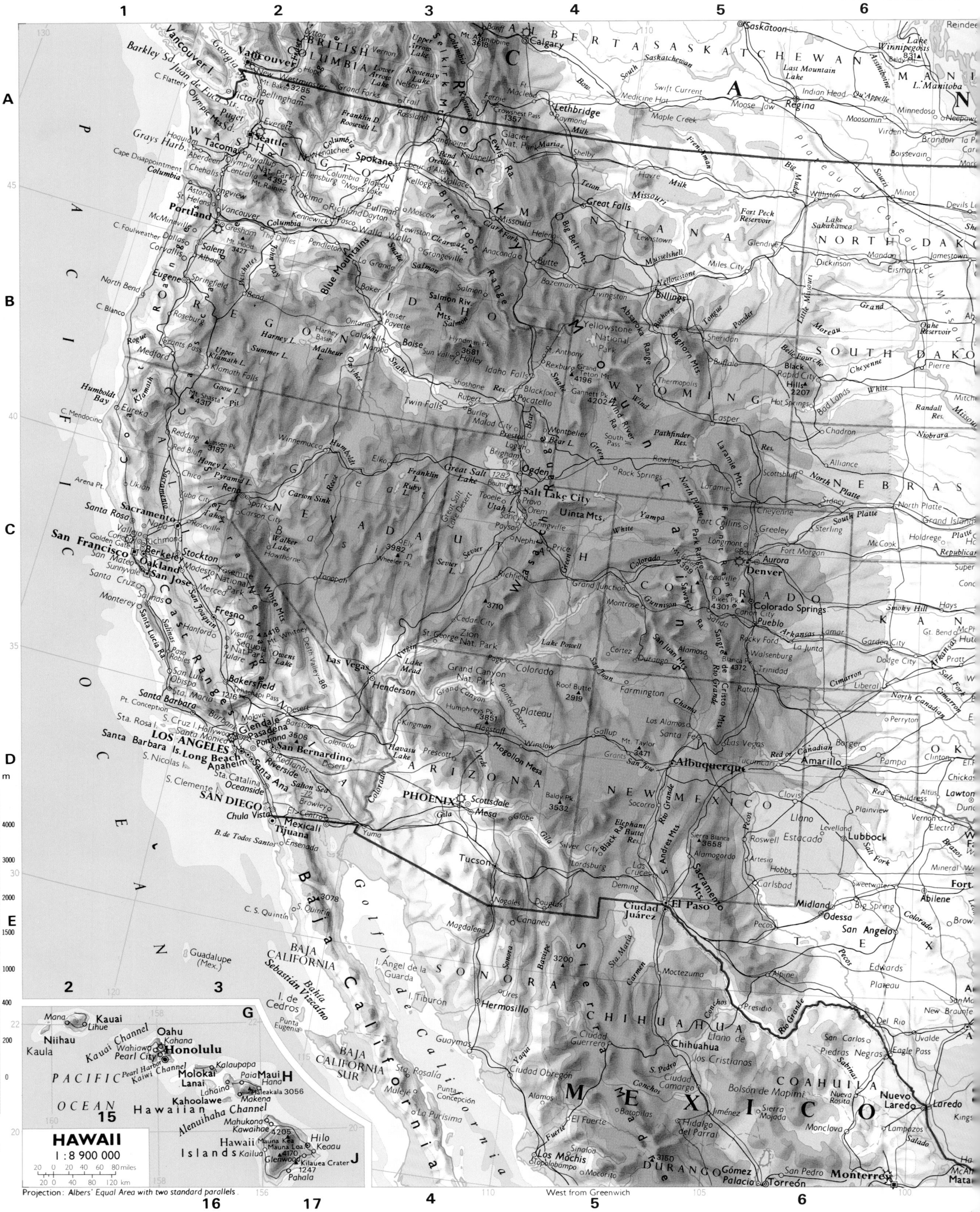
1
2
3
4
5
6
A
B
C
D
E
BRITISH COLUMBIA
ALBERTA
SASKATCHEWAN
MANITOBA
CANADA
Vancouver I.
Vancouver
Victoria
Calgary
Saskatoon
Regina
Lethbridge
Medicine Hat
Seattle
Tacoma
Spokane
Portland
Salem
Eugene
WASHINGTON
OREGON
IDAHO
MONTANA
WYOMING
NORTH DAKOTA
SOUTH DAKOTA
NEBRASKA
KANSAS
OKLAHOMA
TEXAS
NEVADA
UTAH
COLORADO
ARIZONA
NEW MEXICO
CALIFORNIA
ROCKY MTS.
PACIFIC OCEAN
Great Falls
Missoula
Helena
Butte
Billings
Boise
Idaho Falls
Pocatello
Twin Falls
Yellowstone National Park
Casper
Cheyenne
Ogden
Great Salt Lake
Salt Lake City
Provo
Uinta Mts.
Reno
Carson City
Sacramento
San Francisco
Oakland
San Jose
Stockton
Fresno
Bakersfield
Las Vegas
Henderson
Santa Barbara
LOS ANGELES
Long Beach
Pasadena
San Bernardino
Anaheim
Santa Ana
SAN DIEGO
Tijuana
Mexicali
PHOENIX
Scottsdale
Mesa
Tucson
Flagstaff
Grand Canyon Nat. Park
Albuquerque
Santa Fe
Denver
Aurora
Colorado Springs
Pueblo
El Paso
Ciudad Juárez
Amarillo
Lubbock
Midland
Odessa
San Angelo
Abilene
Nuevo Laredo
Laredo
Monterrey
Torreón
Chihuahua
Hermosillo
MEXICO
SONORA
CHIHUAHUA
COAHUILA
DURANGO
BAJA CALIFORNIA
BAJA CALIFORNIA SUR
Golfo de California
Sierra Madre Occidental
Great Basin
Rio Grande
Colorado
Snake
Columbia
Missouri
Yellowstone
Lake Powell
Mt. Rainier 4392
Mt. Hood 3427
Mt. Shasta 4317
Lassen Pk. 3187
Mt. Whitney 4418
Death Valley -86
Pikes Pk. 4301
Grand Teton Mt. 4196
Projection: Albers' Equal Area with two standard parallels
West from Greenwich
ft
m
12 000
9000
6000
4500
3000
1200
600
0
200
2000
4000
3000
2000
1500
1000
400
200
0
600
6000
HAWAII
1 : 8 900 000
Kauai
Niihau
Oahu
Honolulu
Pearl City
Molokai
Lanai
Maui
Kahoolawe
Hawaii
Hilo
Mauna Kea 4205
Mauna Loa 4170
Haleakala 3056
PACIFIC OCEAN
Hawaiian Islands
15
16
17
G
H
J

1 : 10 700 000

50 0 50 100 150 200 250 300 miles
50 0 50 100 150 200 250 300 350 400 450 km

8 9 10 11 12 13

8 9 10 11 12

LAKE SUPERIOR
LAKE HURON
LAKE ONTARIO
LAKE ERIE
Georgian Bay
CHICAGO
MILWAUKEE
DETROIT
CLEVELAND
PITTSBURGH
TORONTO
MONTREAL
BOSTON
NEW YORK
PHILADELPHIA
BALTIMORE
WASHINGTON D.C.
INDIANAPOLIS
COLUMBUS

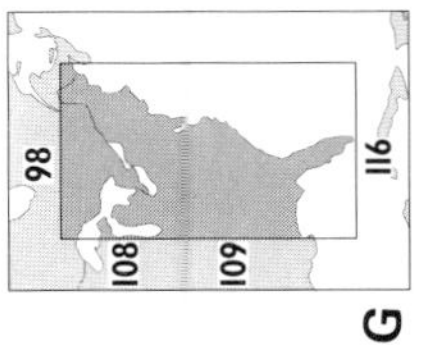
98
108
109
116

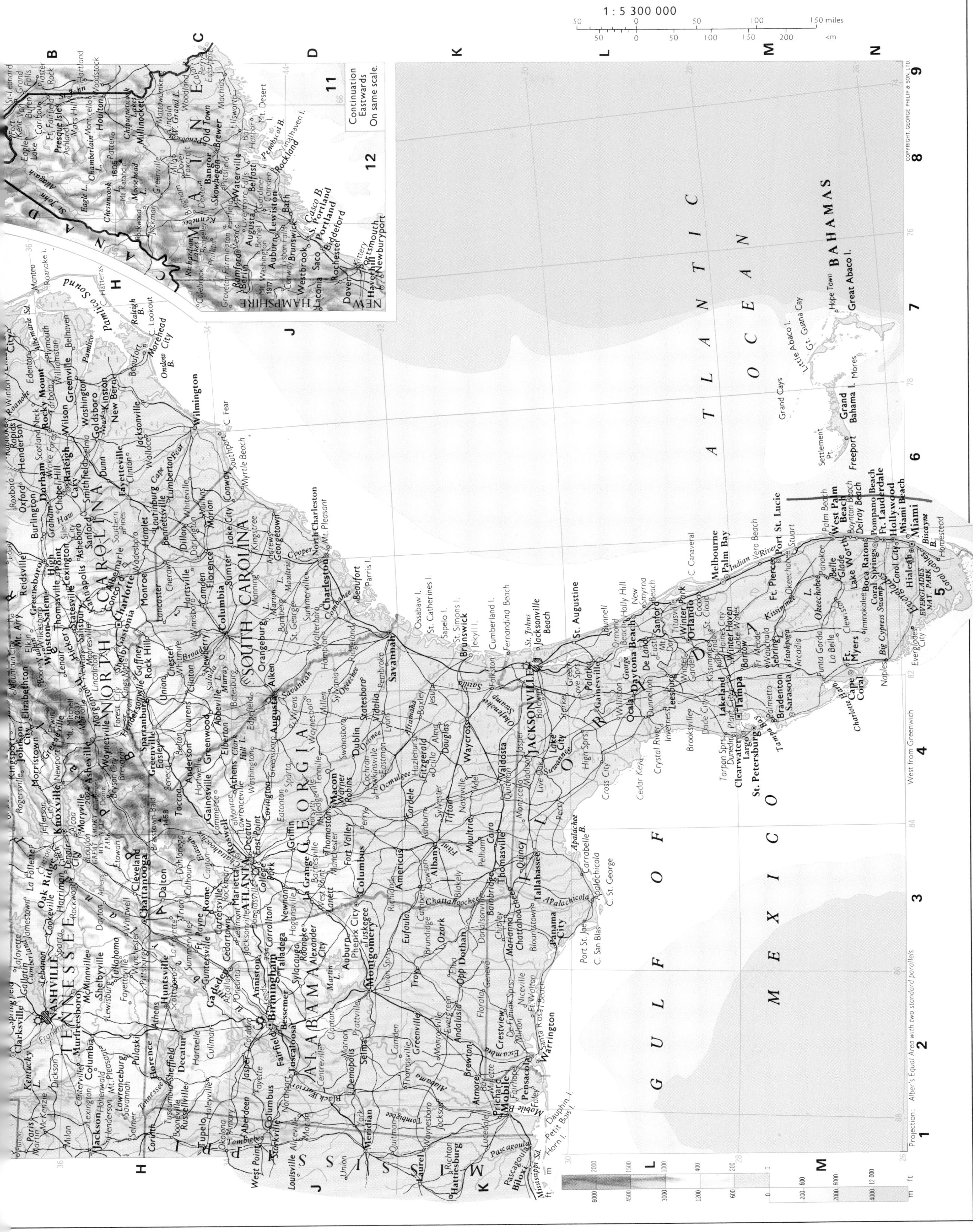

1 : 5 300 000

50 0 50 100 150 miles

50 0 50 100 150 200 km

N

9

Continuation
Eastwards
On same scale.

11

12

COPYRIGHT GEORGE PHILIP & SON, LTD

B A H A M A S

Great Abaco I.
Hope Town
Little Abaco I.
Gt. Guana Cay
Grand Cays
Grand
Bahama I. Mores
Settlement
Pt.
Freeport
Biscayne
B.

A T L A N T I C O C E A N

Projection: Alber's Equal Area with two standard parallels West from Greenwich

M A I N E

N E W H A M P S H I R E

C A N A D A

Pamlico Sound

J

H

K

D

C

B

E

ft. m
6000
4500
3000
1500
1200 400
600 200
0 0
200 600
2000 6000
4000 12 000
m ft.

A L A B A M A

M I S S I S S I P P I

T E N N E S S E E

G E O R G I A

F L O R I D A

N O R T H C A R O L I N A

S O U T H C A R O L I N A

G U L F O F M E X I C O

Miami
Hialeah
Hollywood
Ft. Lauderdale
Pompano Beach
Boca Raton
Delray Beach
Boynton Beach
West Palm
Beach
Palm Beach
Lake Worth
Belle
Glade
Pahokee
L.
Okeechobee
Port St. Lucie
Stuart
Ft. Pierce
Vero Beach
Indian R.
Melbourne
Palm Bay
C. Canaveral
Cocoa Beach
Titusville
Orlando
Winter Park
Sanford
De Land
Daytona Beach
Ormond
Beach
St. Augustine
Jacksonville
Beach
Jacksonville
EVERGLADES
NAT. PARK
Homestead
Coral Gables
Big Cypress Swamp
Everglades
Immokalee
Naples
Ft. Myers
Cape
Coral
Punta Gorda
Arcadia
Sebring
La Belle
Clewiston
Bartow
Winter Haven
Lakeland
Plant City
Tampa
St. Petersburg
Clearwater
Dunedin
Tarpon Sprs.
Largo
Sarasota
Bradenton
Palmetto
Crystal River
Cedar Keys
Cross City
Inverness
Brooksville
Dade City
Wauchula
Mt. Dora
Kissimmee
St. Cloud
Gainesville
Ocala
Leesburg
High Sprs.
Lake
City
Live Oak
Palatka
St. Johns R.
L. George
Fernandina Beach
Cumberland I.
St. Simons I.
Brunswick
Jekyll I.
Sapelo I.
St. Catherines I.
Ossabaw I.
Savannah
Beaufort
Parris I.
Charleston
North Charleston
Mt. Pleasant
Georgetown
Kingstree
Andrews
Lake City
Conway
Myrtle Beach
C. Fear
Southport
Wilmington
Wallace
Whiteville
Lumberton
Laurinburg
Hamlet
Rockingham
Bennettsville
Marlboro
Florence
Darlington
Dillon
Marion
Sumter
Manning
Moncks Corner
Summerville
Walterboro
Hampton
Ridgeland
Columbia
Orangeburg
Bamberg
St. George
Aiken
Augusta
Barnwell
Millen
Statesboro
Sylvania
Pembroke
Swainsboro
Dublin
Vidalia
Lyons
Waycross
Folkston
Brunswick
Jesup
Baxley
Hazlehurst
Douglas
Fitzgerald
Alma
Ocilla
Tifton
Sylvester
Adel
Nashville
Valdosta
Quitman
Madison
Monticello
Live Oak
Perry
Quincy
Tallahassee
Cairo
Thomasville
Quitman
Moultrie
Ashburn
Cordele
Americus
Dawson
Albany
Cuthbert
Richland
Eufaula
Blakely
Bainbridge
Donalsonville
Chattahoochee
Marianna
Apalachicola
Blountstown
Apalachee B.
Port St. Joe
C. San Blas
C. St. George
St. George
Panama
City
Chipley
Bonifay
De Funiak Sprs.
Crestview
Niceville
Ft. Walton Beach
Valparaiso
Santa Rosa I.
Pensacola
Warrington
Milton
Mobile
B.
Mobile
Pascagoula
Biloxi
Gulfport
Pass Christian
Mississippi Sd.
Dauphin I.
Petit Bois I.
Horn I.
Gautier
Pascagoula R.

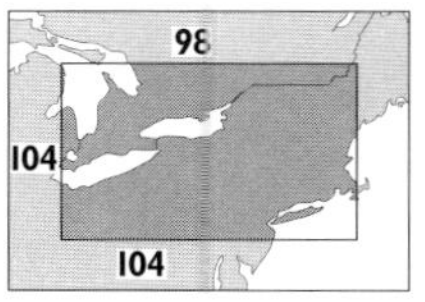

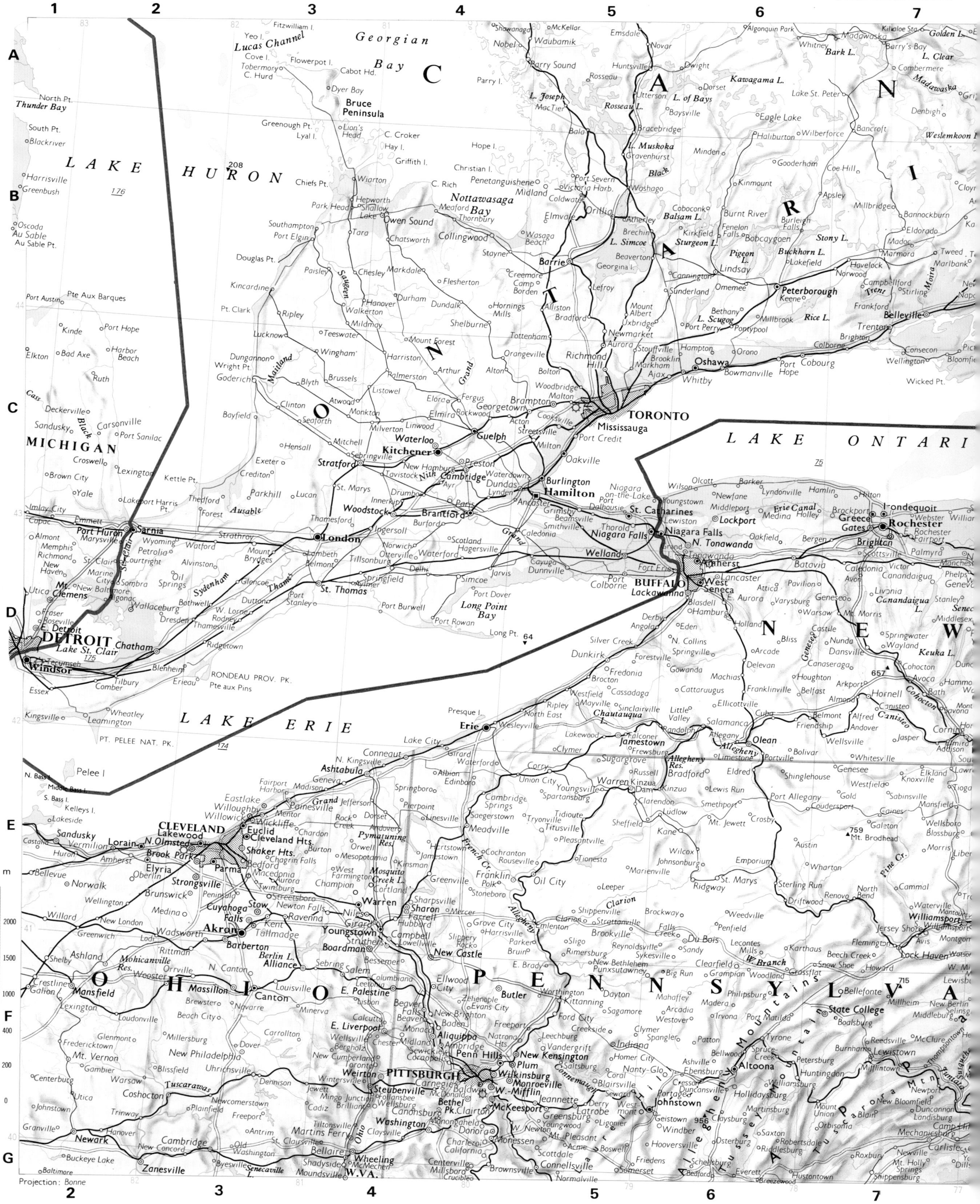

Projection: Bonne

LAKE HURON

Georgian Bay

ONTARIO

Bruce Peninsula

MICHIGAN

TORONTO

LAKE ONTARIO

DETROIT

Windsor

LAKE ERIE

Buffalo

Rochester

Niagara Falls

NEW

Erie

Cleveland

OHIO

PENNSYLVANIA

Akron

Youngstown

PITTSBURGH

W.VA.

1 : 2 200 000

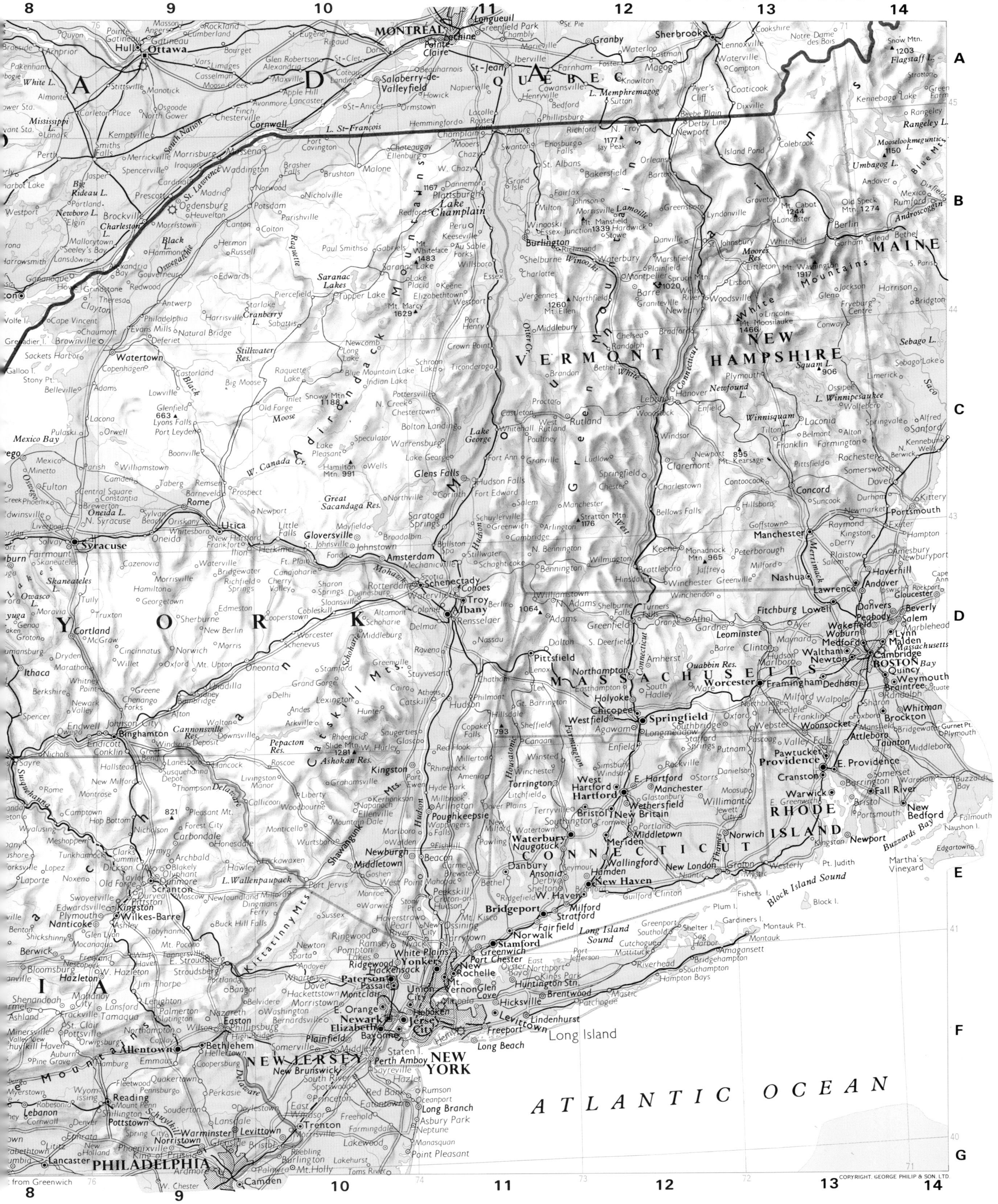

8
9
10
11
12
13
14
A
B
C
D
E
F
G
QUEBEC
MAINE
NEW HAMPSHIRE
VERMONT
MASSACHUSETTS
RHODE ISLAND
CONNECTICUT
NEW YORK
NEW JERSEY
ATLANTIC OCEAN
Long Island
Long Island Sound
Block Island Sound
L. Champlain
Adirondack Mountains
Green Mountains
White Mountains
Catskill Mts.
MONTREAL
Ottawa
Sherbrooke
Burlington
Syracuse
Utica
Schenectady
Albany
Troy
Concord
Manchester
Portsmouth
Springfield
Worcester
BOSTON
Providence
Hartford
New Haven
Bridgeport
Stamford
Yonkers
Paterson
Newark
Jersey City
NEW YORK
Trenton
PHILADELPHIA
Allentown
Bethlehem
Scranton
Wilkes-Barre
Binghamton
Poughkeepsie
Kingston
from Greenwich

1 : 5 300 000
50 0 50 100 150 miles
50 0 50 100 150 200 km
CANADA
NORTH DAKOTA
SOUTH DAKOTA
NEBRASKA
MINNESOTA
WISCONSIN
IOWA
ILLINOIS
MICHIGAN
COLORADO
WYOMING
MONTANA
LAKE SUPERIOR
LAKE MICHIGAN
CHICAGO
MILWAUKEE
Minneapolis
St. Paul
Des Moines
Omaha
Lincoln
Denver
Cheyenne
Bismarck
Pierre
Madison
Duluth
Sand Hills
Laramie Mountains

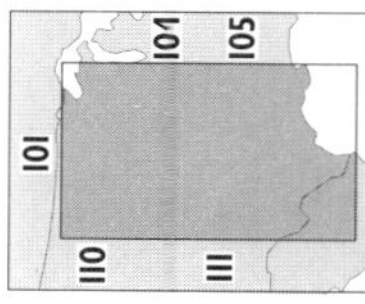

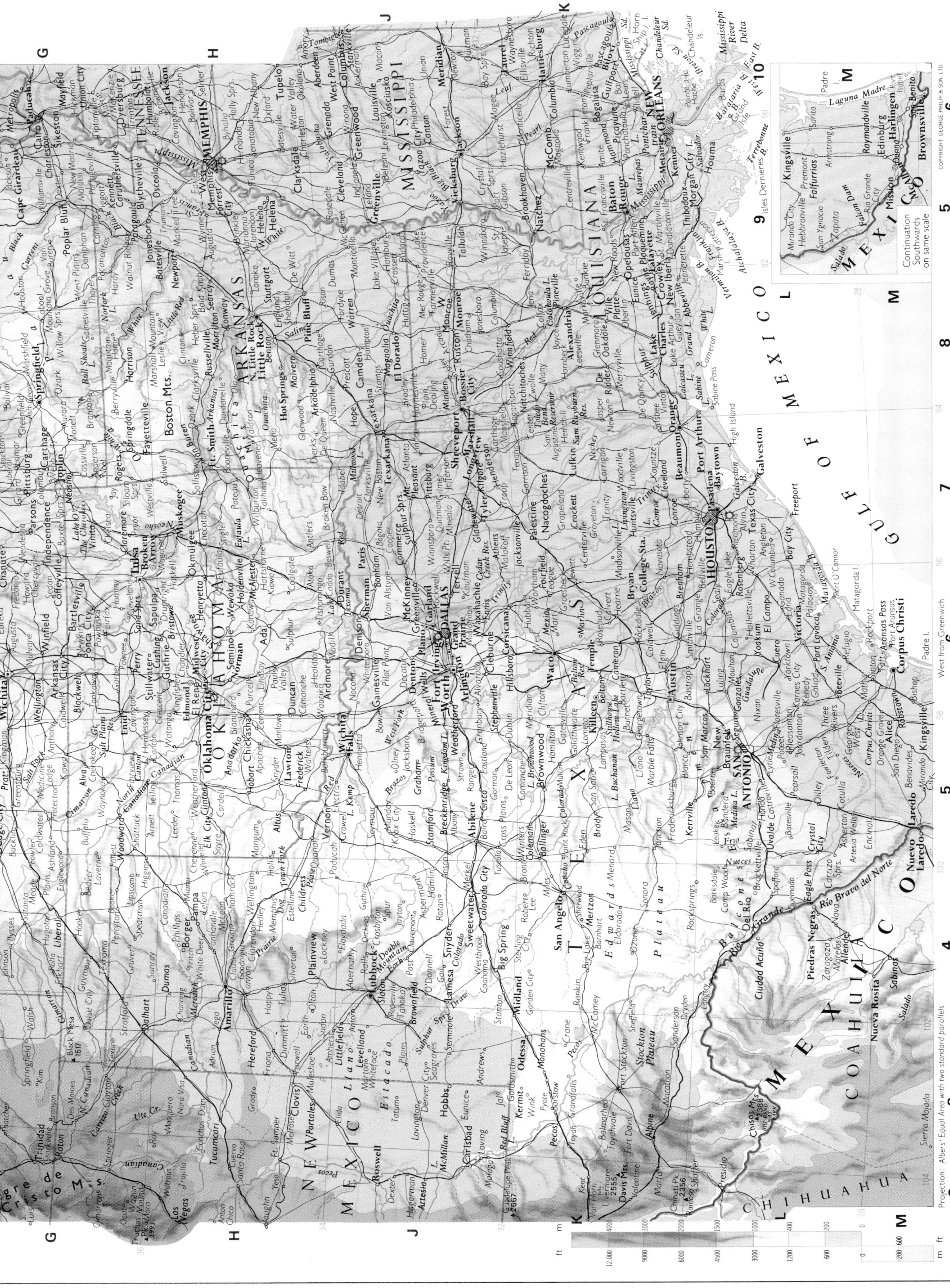
OKLAHOMA
TEXAS
ARKANSAS
LOUISIANA
MISSISSIPPI
TENNESSEE
NEW MEXICO
MEXICO
COAHUILA
CHIHUAHUA
GULF OF MEXICO
Continuation Southwards on same scale
West from Greenwich
Projection: Albers' Equal Area with two standard parallels
COPYRIGHT GEORGE PHILIP & SON, LTD

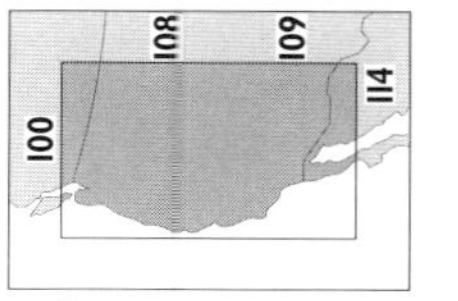
100
108
109
114

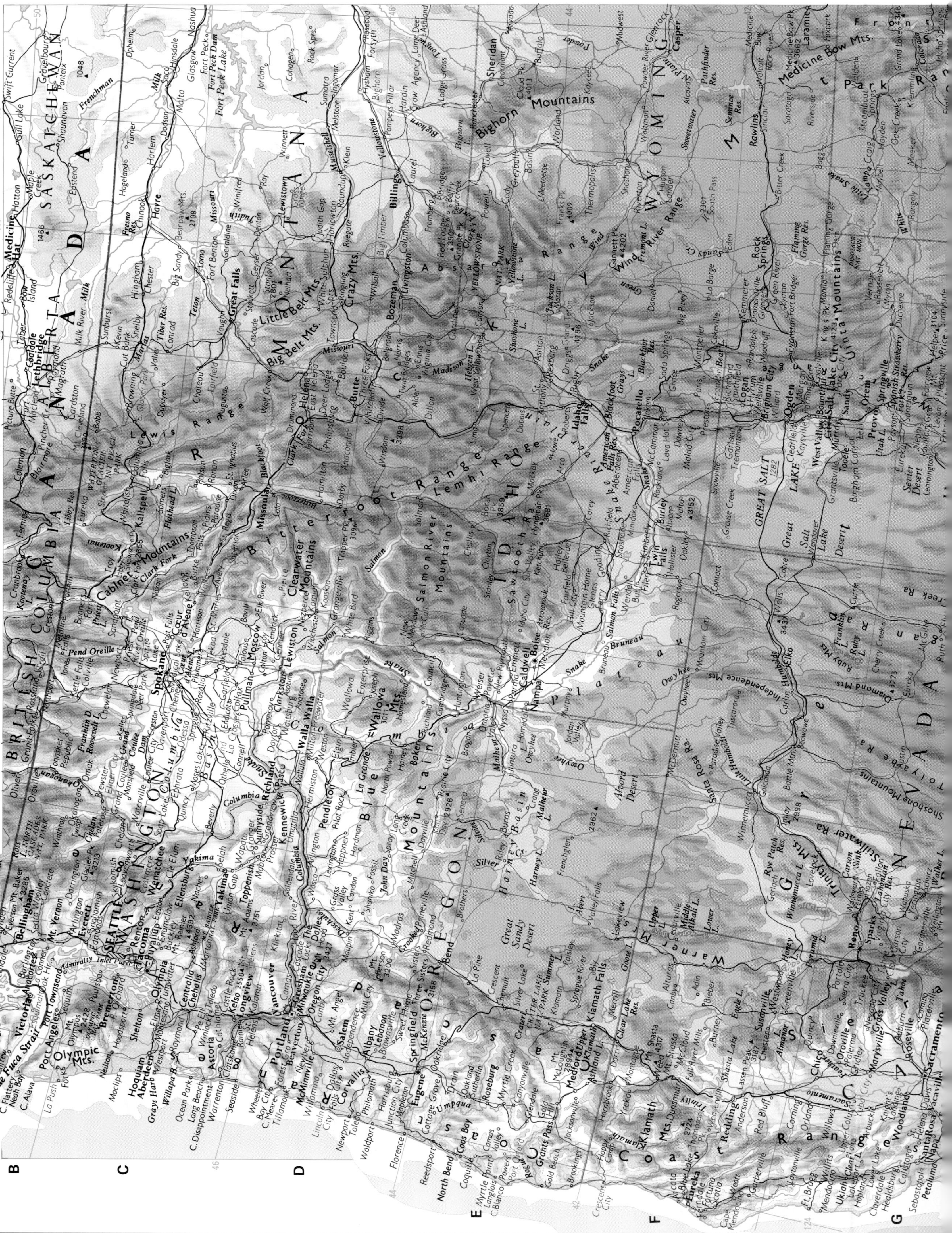
BRITISH COLUMBIA
ALBERTA
SASKATCHEWAN
MONTANA
IDAHO
WASHINGTON
OREGON
WYOMING
NEVADA
UTAH
CALIFORNIA
Bighorn Mountains
Bitterroot Range
Salmon River Mountains
Blue Mountains
Great Sandy Desert
Great Salt Lake Desert
SEATTLE
Spokane
Portland
Boise
Salt Lake City
Sacramento
VANCOUVER
Olympic Mts.
Cascade Range

III

1 : 5 300 000

50 0 50 100 miles
50 0 50 100 150 km

COLORADO

NEW MEXICO

ARIZONA

CALIFORNIA

Nevada

TEXAS

CHIHUAHUA

SONORA

MEXICO

BAJA CALIFORNIA

PACIFIC OCEAN

Golfo de California

Desierto de Altar

LOS ANGELES
SAN DIEGO
SAN JOSE
PHOENIX
Tucson
Albuquerque
Santa Fe
EL PASO
CIUDAD JUAREZ
Las Vegas
Hermosillo
Chihuahua
Bakersfield
Fresno
Tijuana
Mexicali
Nogales
Yuma
Flagstaff
Gallup
Douglas
Aquiles Serdán

Sangre de Cristo Mts.
San Juan Mts.
Sacramento Mts.
Santa Lucia Range
Grand Canyon
Death Valley
Mogollon Rim
Sonora Desert
Painted Desert
Colorado Plateau
Rio Grande
Rio Bravo del Norte
Colorado
Salton Sea
L. Mead
L. Powell

Projection: Albers' Equal Area with two standard parallels
West from Greenwich
COPYRIGHT. GEORGE PHILIP & SON, LTD.

ft m
12,000 4000
9000 3000
6000 2000
4500 1500
3000 1000
1200 400
600 200
0
200 600
6000 2000
12,000 4000
m ft

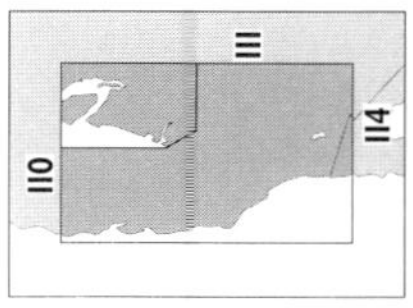
110
111
114

SEATTLE-PORTLAND REGION
On same scale
VANCOUVER
CANADA
Vancouver Island
Strait of Georgia
Juan de Fuca Strait
PACIFIC OCEAN
WASHINGTON
OREGON
SEATTLE
Tacoma
Olympia
Everett
Bellingham
Victoria
Vancouver
PORTLAND
Longview
Olympic Mountains
Cascade Range
Mt. Rainier 4392
Mt. St. Helens 2550
Mt. Adams 3751
Columbia
Sierra Nevada
Sacramento
Stockton
Modesto
Merced
Fresno
Clovis
Visalia
Reno
Sparks
Carson City
L. Tahoe
Mono L.
Yosemite
SAN FRANCISCO
Oakland
Berkeley
SAN JOSE
Santa Rosa
Napa
Salinas
Monterey
Monterey Bay
Santa Cruz
Santa Lucia Range
San Joaquin
Sacramento
White Mts.
Inyo Mts.
Pahute Mesa

1 : 2 200 000
miles
km
N E V A D A
A R I Z O N A
C A L I F O R N I A
M E X I C O
P A C I F I C
O C E A N
Las Vegas
North Las Vegas
Henderson
Lake Mead
L. Mohave
L. Havasu
Death Valley
Amargosa Range
Providence Mts.
Chocolate Mts.
Coachella Canal
Salton Sea
Imperial Valley
El Centro
Mexicali
Tijuana
SAN DIEGO
Chula Vista
Escondido
Oceanside
Gulf of Santa Catalina
San Pedro Channel
Santa Barbara Channel
Channel Islands
LOS ANGELES
Long Beach
Santa Ana
Anaheim
Riverside
SAN BERNARDINO
Palm Springs
Lancaster
Palmdale
Bakersfield
Tehachapi Mts.
Santa Barbara
Ventura
Oxnard
Santa Maria
Lompoc
Pt. Conception
San Clemente I.
Santa Catalina I.
Santa Cruz I.
Santa Rosa I.
San Miguel I.
San Nicolas I.
Santa Barbara I.
Blythe
Needles
Barstow
Victorville
Hesperia
Apple Valley
Yuma
West from Greenwich
Projection: Bonne
COPYRIGHT GEORGE PHILIP & SON, LTD.

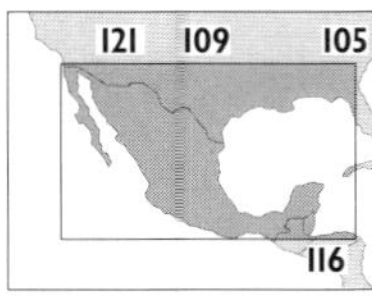
121
109
105
116

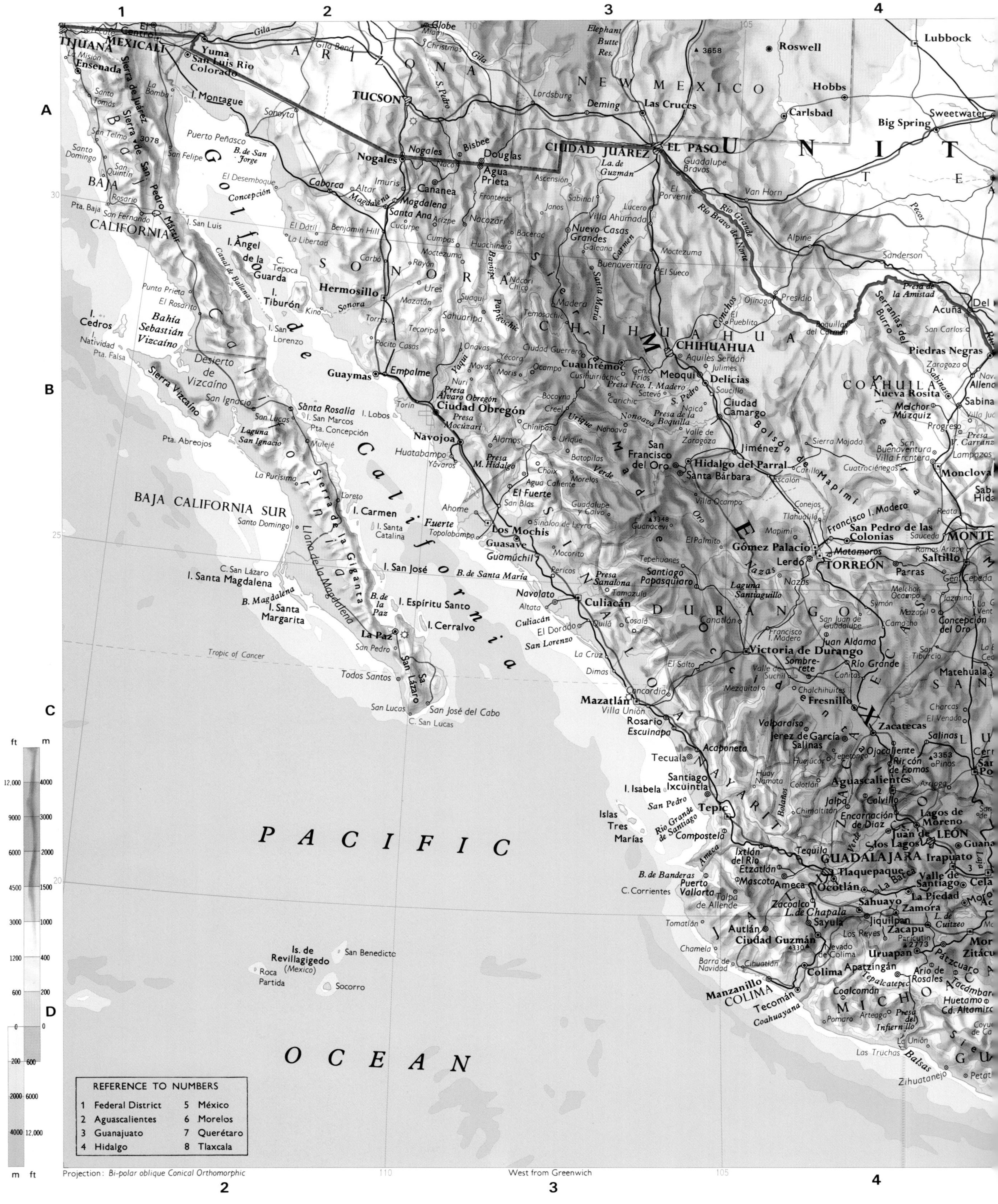
1
2
3
4
A
B
C
D
TIJUANA
MEXICALI
Ensenada
Yuma
San Luis Rio Colorado
Sierra de Juárez
Sierra de San Pedro Mártir
3078
I. Montague
Puerto Peñasco
B. de San Jorge
San Felipe
Santo Domingo
San Quintín
BAJA CALIFORNIA
El Rosario
Pta. Baja
San Fernando
Golfo de California
I. San Luis
I. Ángel de la Guarda
Canal de Ballenas
C. Tepoca
I. Tiburón
Kino
Punta Prieta
El Rosarito
Bahía Sebastián Vizcaíno
I. Cedros
Natividad
Pta. Falsa
Desierto de Vizcaíno
Sierra Vizcaíno
San Ignacio
Laguna San Ignacio
Pta. Abreojos
Santa Rosalía
I. San Marcos
Pta. Concepción
Mulejé
La Purísima
Loreto
I. Carmen
BAJA CALIFORNIA SUR
Santo Domingo
Sierra de la Giganta
Llano de la Magdalena
C. San Lázaro
I. Santa Magdalena
B. Magdalena
I. Santa Margarita
I. San José
I. Espíritu Santo
B. de la Paz
La Paz
I. Cerralvo
San Pedro
Tropic of Cancer
Todos Santos
San Lázaro
San Lucas
San José del Cabo
C. San Lucas
I. Santa Catalina
ARIZONA
Gila
Gila Bend
Globe
Miami
Christmas
TUCSON
Sonoyta
S. Pedro
Nogales
Bisbee
Douglas
Agua Prieta
Naco
Cananea
Caborca
Altar
Magdalena
Imuris
Santa Ana
Arizpe
Cucurpe
Benjamin Hill
El Desemboque
Concepción
El Dátil
La Libertad
SONORA
Hermosillo
Mazatán
Ures
Torres
Pocito Casas
Guaymas
Empalme
Ciudad Obregón
Navojoa
Huatabampo
Yávaros
Presa Álvaro Obregón
Presa Mocúzari
Yaqui
Fronteras
Nacozari
Huachinera
Bacerac
Bavispe
Sahuaripa
Tecoripa
Onavas
Yécora
Movas
Moris
I. Lobos
Torín
NEW MEXICO
Elephant Butte Res.
▲3658
Roswell
Lordsburg
Deming
Las Cruces
Carlsbad
Hobbs
Lubbock
Big Spring
Sweetwater
CIUDAD JUÁREZ
EL PASO
UNITED
TE
La. de Guzmán
Guadalupe Bravos
Ascensión
Janos
Sabinal
El Porvenir
Van Horn
Río Bravo del Norte
Río Grande
Pecos
Alpine
Sanderson
Presidio
Ojinaga
Villa Ahumada
Lucero
Nuevo Casas Grandes
Galeana
Carmen
Buenaventura
El Sueco
Moctezuma
Madera
Sierra Madre Occidental
Santa María
Temosachic
CHIHUAHUA
Cuauhtémoc
Ciudad Guerrero
Ocampo
Gen. Trías
Cusihuiriáchic
Presa Fco. I. Madero
Meoqui
Delicias
Aquiles Serdán
Julimes
Saucillo
Ciudad Camargo
Satevó
S. Pedro
Carichic
Bocoyna
Creel
Nonoava
Presa de la Boquilla
Nuevo
Conchos
El Pueblito
Boquillas del Carmen
Presa de la Amistad
Serranías del Burro
Acuña
San Carlos
Piedras Negras
Zaragoza
COAHUILA
Nueva Rosita
Melchor Múzquiz
Sabinas
Allende
Progreso
Sierra Mojada
Bolsón de Mapimí
Jiménez
Hidalgo del Parral
Santa Bárbara
San Francisco del Oro
Valle de Zaragoza
Buenaventura
Villa Frontera
Cuatrociénegas
Monclova
Lampazos
Urique
Chínipas
Batopilas
Álamos
Presa M. Hidalgo
Choix
Agua Caliente
Morelos
El Fuerte
San Blas
Fuerte
Ahome
Topolobampo
Los Mochis
Guasave
Guamúchil
Mocorito
Sinaloa de Leyva
Guadalupe y Calvo
▲3348
Guanaceví
El Palmito
Villa Ocampo
Escalón
Conejos
Tlahualilo
Francisco I. Madero
San Pedro de las Colonias
Mapimí
Gómez Palacio
Lerdo
TORREÓN
Matamoros
Nazas
Parras
Saltillo
Ramos Arizpe
MONTE
B. de Santa María
Pericos
Presa Sanalona
Tamazula
Santiago Papasquiaro
Tepehuanes
Navolato
Culiacán
Altata
Cosalá
Quilá
El Dorado
San Lorenzo
La Cruz
Dimas
SINALOA
DURANGO
Laguna Santiaguillo
Canatlán
Victoria de Durango
Francisco I. Madero
San Juan de Guadalupe
Juan Aldama
Sombrerete
Río Grande
El Salto
Concepción del Oro
Mazapil
Simón
Melchor Ocampo
Matehuala
Cañitas
Valle de Súchil
Mezquital
Chalchihuites
Fresnillo
Zacatecas
Concordia
Mazatlán
Villa Unión
Rosario
Escuinapa
Acaponeta
Tecuala
Santiago Ixcuintla
NAYARIT
I. Isabela
San Pedro
Tepic
Islas Tres Marías
Río Grande de Santiago
Compostela
Valparaíso
Jerez de García Salinas
Huejúcar
Tepetongo
Ojocaliente
Rincón de Romos
Aguascalientes
Salinas
▲3353
Pinos
Charcas
El Venado
Huay Namota
Colotlán
Bolaños
Jalpa
Calvillo
Chimaltitán
Encarnación de Díaz
Lagos de Moreno
Juan de los Lagos
LEÓN
Irapuato
Ameca
Ixtlán del Río
Etzatlán
Tequila
GUADALAJARA
Tlaquepaque
La Barca
Valle de Santiago
B. de Banderas
Puerto Vallarta
C. Corrientes
Mascota
Talpa de Allende
Ocotlán
Sahuayo
La Piedad
Zamora
Zacoalco
L. de Chapala
Sayula
Jiquilpan
L. de Cuitzeo
Tomatlán
JALISCO
Autlán
Ciudad Guzmán
4330
Nevado de Colima
Los Reyes
Zacapu
Paricutín
▲2773
Uruapan
Pátzcuaro
Chamela
Barra de Navidad
Cihuatlán
Colima
Apatzingán
Tepalcatepec
Ario de Rosales
Manzanillo
COLIMA
Tecomán
Coahuayana
Coalcomán
MICHOACÁN
Arteaga
Presa del Infiernillo
Pomaro
La Unión
Huetamo
Cd. Altamirano
Las Truchas
Balsas
Zihuatanejo
Petatlán
PACIFIC OCEAN
Is. de Revillagigedo (Mexico)
San Benedicto
Roca Partida
Socorro
ft
m
12,000
9000
6000
4500
3000
1200
600
0
200
2000
4000
4000
3000
2000
1500
1000
400
200
600
6000
12,000
m
ft
115
110
105
30
25
20
REFERENCE TO NUMBERS
1 Federal District
2 Aguascalientes
3 Guanajuato
4 Hidalgo
5 México
6 Morelos
7 Querétaro
8 Tlaxcala
Projection: Bi-polar oblique Conical Orthomorphic
West from Greenwich

1 : 7 100 000
50 0 50 100 150 200 miles
50 0 100 200 300 km
5
6
7
8
A
B
C
D
E
UNITED STATES
ARKANSAS
MISSISSIPPI
ALABAMA
GEORGIA
LOUISIANA
FLORIDA
TEXAS
Wichita Falls
Denison
Sherman
Paris
Texarkana
Hope
Camden
El Dorado
Greenville
Tuscaloosa
Opelika
Columbus
McRae
Possum Kingdom Res.
Brazos
Denton
Greenville
FORT WORTH
DALLAS
Marshall
Monroe
Vicksburg
Meridian
Selma
Montgomery
Phenix City
Americus
Cordele
Albany
Tifton
Ranger
Longview
Tyler
Shreveport
Tallulah
Jackson
Troy
Waycross
Cleburne
Corsicana
Toledo Bend Res.
Natchez
Laurel
Alabama
Dothan
Jim Woodruff Res.
Valdosta
Hillsboro
Palestine
Nacogdoches
Pearl
Hattiesburg
Flomaton
Chattahoochee
Brownwood
Waco
Alexandria
McComb
Tallahassee
Lufkin
Sam Rayburn Res.
Bogalusa
MOBILE
Pensacola
Panama City
Lake City
Temple
Jewett
Sabine
Baton Rouge
Hammond
Biloxi
Gulfport
Apalachee Bay
Colorado
Huntsville
Bryan
Trinity
L. Pontchartrain
Mobile Bay
Austin
Navasota
Lake Charles
Lafayette
NEW ORLEANS
C. San Blas
Suwannee
Beaumont
Breton Sound
HOUSTON
Port Arthur
Atchafalaya Bay
Mississippi Delta
Terrebonne B.
SAN ANTONIO
Rosenberg
Guadalupe
Galveston
Clearwater
Victoria
Dilley
Nueces
Alice
Corpus Christi
Laredo
Kingsville
Nuevo Laredo
Zapata
GULF OF MEXICO
Laguna Madre
Camargo
Mc Allen
Harlingen
Brownsville
Presa M.R. Gomez
Reynosa
Matamoros
Valle Hermoso
China
Santa Teresa
Montemorelos
Conchos
Mendez
Laguna Madre
Linares
San Fernando
Villagrán
Santander-Jiménez
TAMAULIPAS
Sierra de Tamaulipas
La Pesca
Soto la Marina
Tropic of Cancer
La Esperanza
CUBA
Guane
La Fé
Ciudad Victoria
Llera
Aldama
Pta. Jerez
Isla Desterrada
Isla Pérez
Canal de Yucatán
C. San Antonio
C. Corrientes
Ciudad Mante
Ciudad Madero
Tampico
Altamira
Ciudad de Valles
Pánuco
Pta. Yalkubul
Rio Lagartos
C. Catoche
El Cuyo
Cancun
Pto. Juárez
Dzilam de Bravo
Progreso
Temax
Tizimín
Motul
Izamal
Espita
Puerto Morelos
Mérida
YUCATAN
Valladolid
Isla Cozumel
Cozumel
Laguna de Tamiahua
Ozuluama
C. Rojo
Tempoal
Tantoyuca
Tamazunchale
Maxcanú
Sotuta
Ticul
Uxmal
Tekax
Peto
Chicontepec
Tuxpan
Golfo de Campeche
Tenabo
Bolonchenticul
Vigia Chico
B. de la Ascensión
Zimapán
Zacualtipán
Poza Rica
Papantla
Campeche
Hopelchén
Felipe Carrillo Puerto
B. del Espíritu Santo
Nautla
QUINTANA ROO
Huichapan
Pachuca
Huauchinango
Misantla
Champotón
Banco Chinchorro
Tulancingo
Teziutlán
Jalapa Enríquez
Chenkán
Bacalar
Zumpango
Zempoala
Laguna de Términos
Chetumal
B. de Chetumal
MEXICO
Tlaxcala
Apizaco
Coatepec
Veracruz Llave
Ciudad del Carmen
Corozal
PUEBLA
4282
Citlaltépetl
5700
Matamoros
Amecameca
5452
Popocatépetl
Orizaba
Alvarado
Tlacotalpan
Frontera
Pital
CAMPECHE
Ambergris Cay
Cuernavaca
Córdoba
San Andrés Tuxtla
Coatzacoalcos
Paraíso
Comalcalco
Palizada
Concepción
Orange Walk
Hondo
Tehuacán
Cosamaloapan
1879
La Venta
TABASCO
Turneffe Is.
Tres Valles
Villahermosa
Balancán
Belize City
BELIZE
Jojutla
San Gabriel Chilac
Presa Miguel Alemán
Cárdenas
Chiautla
Acatlán
Acayucan
Minatitlán
Macuspana
Tenosique
Uaxactún
Tikal
San Ignacio
Belmopan
Dangriga
Iguala
Huajuapan de León
Istme de Tehuantepec
Jesús Carranza
Presa de Netzahualcoyotl
Teapa
Palenque
Usumacinta
L. Petén Itza
La Libertad
Flores
Benque Viejo
Islas de la Bahía
Golfo de Honduras
Roatán
Chilapa
Chilpancingo
Asunción Nochixtlán
Silacayoapan
San Juan Bautista Valle Nacional
Copainalá
Simojovel
Chiapa de Corzo
Ocosingo
San Cristóbal de las Casas
Maya Mts.
Monkey River
Puerto Castilla
Iriona
Tlaxiaco
Oaxaca
Monte Albán
Trinidad
Tuxtla Gutiérrez
La Independencia
Lacantún
San Luis
San Antonio
Puerto Barrios
Puerto Cortés
Tela
La Ceiba
Trujillo
Tierra Colorada
Ayutla
Ocotlán
Matías Romero
Juchitán
Ixtepec
Comitán
Punta Gorda
Livingston
Balfate
Sava
Olanchito
Acapulco
Ometepec
San Jerónimo
Tavichi
Ejutla
Tehuantepec
Arriaga
Tonalá
La Concordia
Sebol
GUATEMALA
L. de Izabal
Cobán
San Pedro Sula
El Progreso
Arenal
Yoro
Catacamas
Papagayo
Pinotepa Nacional
Salina Cruz
Puerto Arista
3993
Cuchumatanes
HONDURAS
Santa Bárbara
Sulaco
Pta. Maldonado
Jamiltepec
Tututepec
Miahuatlán
3139
Golfo de Tehuantepec
Mar Muerto
Pijijiapan
Mapastepec
Motozintla
Cuilco
Huehuetenango
Utatlán
Sa. de las Minas
Zacapa
Santa Rosa de Copán
El Jaral
L. de Yojoa
Comayagua
Juticalpa
Patuca
Verde
San Pedro Mixtepec
Puerto Escondido
Pochutla
Puerto Ángel
Huixtla
4220
San Marcos
Totonicapán
Sololá
Jalapa
Chiquimula
Copán
Tegucigalpa
Danlí
Tapachula
Coatepeque
Quez.
Antigua
Mazatenango
GUATEMALA
La Esperanza
La Paz
Yuscarán
Ocos
Retalhuleu
Amatitlán
95
90
85
30
25
20
15

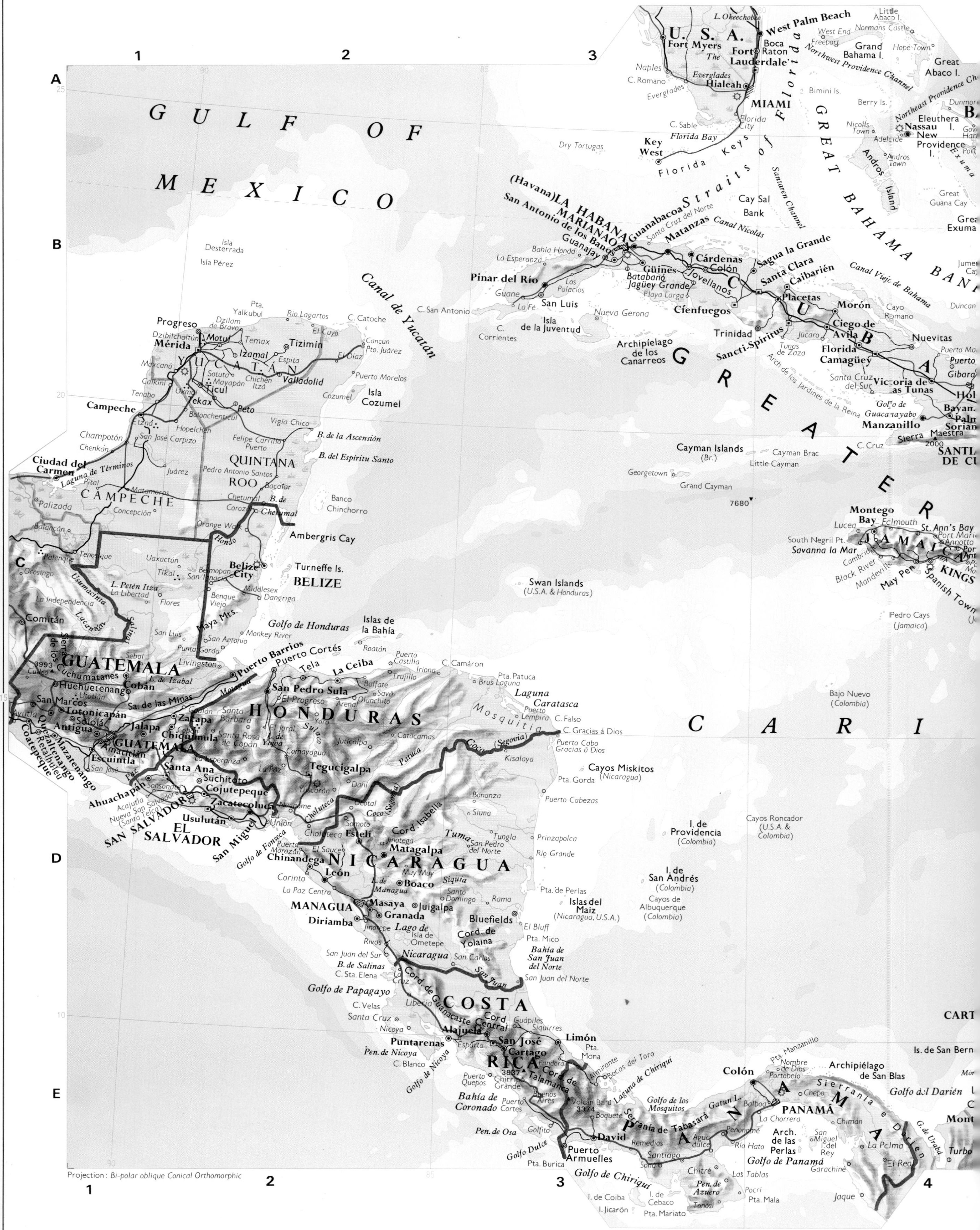

Projection: *Bi-polar oblique Conical Orthomorphic*

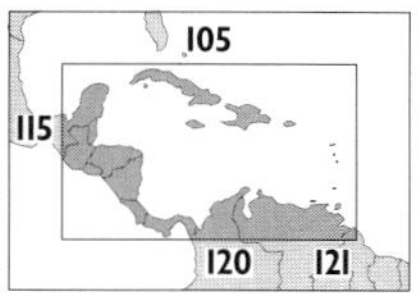

1 : 7 100 000

50 0 50 100 150 200 miles
50 0 100 200 300 km

1 : 31 100 000

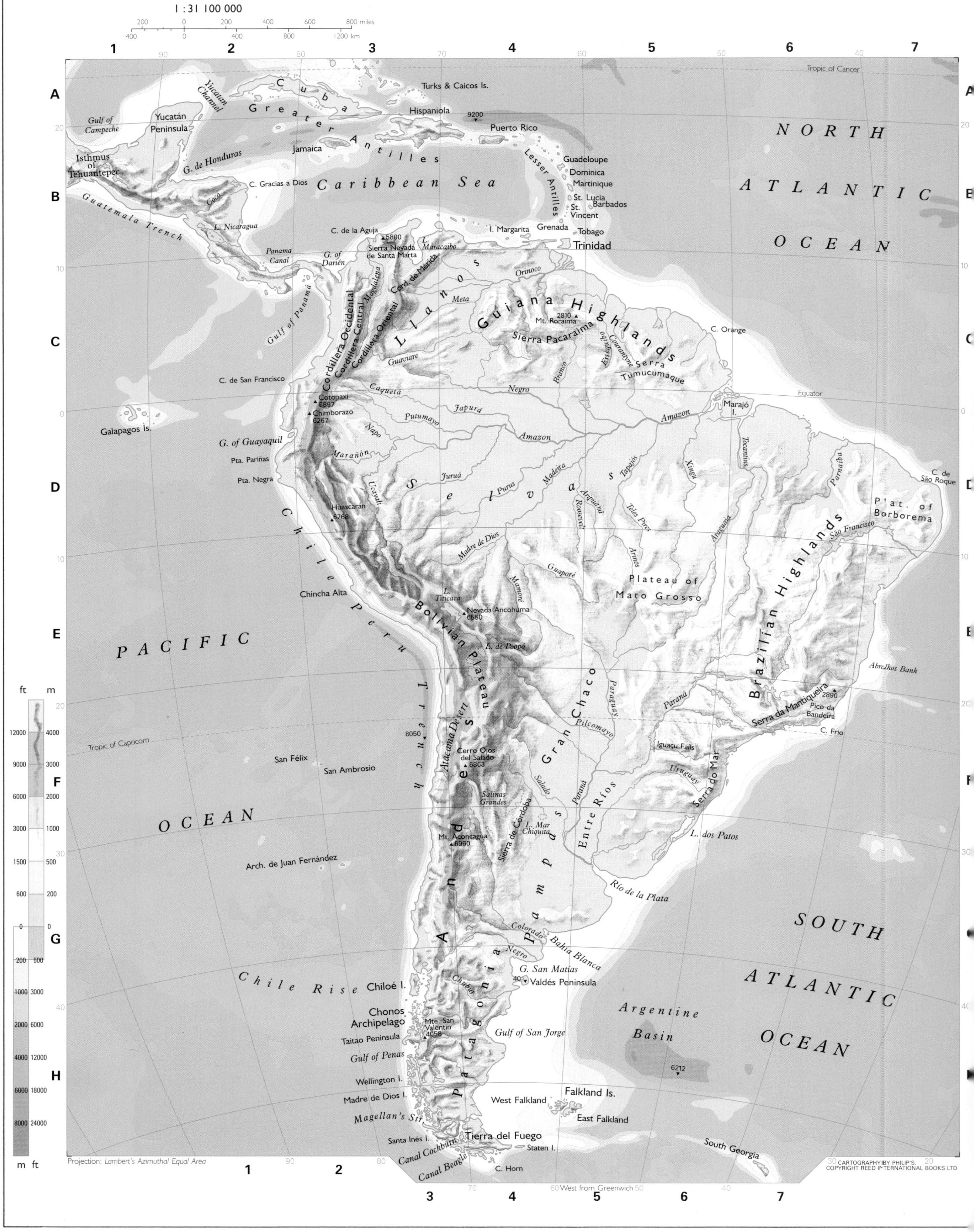

Tropic of Cancer
Turks & Caicos Is.
Cuba
Yucatan Channel
Greater Antilles
Hispaniola
9200
Gulf of Campeche
Yucatán Peninsula
Puerto Rico
NORTH ATLANTIC OCEAN
Jamaica
Lesser Antilles
Isthmus of Tehuantepec
G. de Honduras
Guadeloupe
Dominica
Martinique
C. Gracias a Dios
Caribbean Sea
St. Lucia
St. Vincent
Barbados
Guatemala Trench
Coco
L. Nicaragua
C. de la Aguja
5800
I. Margarita
Grenada
Tobago
Trinidad
Panama Canal
G. of Darién
Sierra Nevada de Santa Marta
L. Maracaibo
Cord. de Mérida
Llanos
Orinoco
Magdalena
Meta
Guiana Highlands
2810
Mt. Roraima
Sierra Pacaraima
C. Orange
Gulf of Panamá
Cordillera Occidental
Cordillera Central
Cordillera Oriental
Essequibo
Courantyne
Serra Tumucumaque
Guaviare
Branco
C. de San Francisco
Caquetá
Negro
Equator
Cotopaxi 5897
Chimborazo 6267
Japurá
Marajó I.
Putumayo
Amazon
Galapagos Is.
Napo
G. of Guayaquil
Pta. Pariñas
Marañón
Tocantins
Parnaíba
Pta. Negra
Juruá
Purus
Madeira
Tapajós
Xingu
C. de São Roque
Selvas
Ucayali
Aripuanã
Roosevelt
Teles Pires
Plat. of Borborema
Huascarán 6768
Araguaia
São Francisco
Brazilian Highlands
Madre de Dios
Arinos
Chile Peru Trench
Guaporé
Plateau of Mato Grosso
Mamoré
Chincha Alta
L. Titicaca
Nevada Ancohuma 6550
PACIFIC OCEAN
Bolivian Plateau
L. de Poopó
Abrolhos Bank
Paraguay
Gran Chaco
Paraná
2890
Serra da Mantiqueira
Pico da Bandeira
Pilcomayo
C. Frio
8050
Tropic of Capricorn
Atacama Desert
Cerro Ojos del Salado 6863
Iguaçu Falls
San Félix
San Ambrosio
Uruguay
Serra do Mar
Salado
Salinas Grandes
Entre Ríos
Sierra de Córdoba
L. Mar Chiquita
L. dos Patos
Mt. Aconcagua 6960
Andes
Arch. de Juan Fernández
Pampas
Río de la Plata
SOUTH ATLANTIC OCEAN
Colorado
Bahía Blanca
Negro
G. San Matías
40
Valdés Peninsula
Chile Rise
Chiloé I.
Patagonia
Chubut
Argentine Basin
Chonos Archipelago
Mte. San Valentín 4058
Gulf of San Jorge
Taitao Peninsula
Gulf of Penas
6212
Wellington I.
Madre de Dios I.
West Falkland
Falkland Is.
East Falkland
Magellan's Str.
Santa Inés I.
Tierra del Fuego
Staten I.
South Georgia
Canal Cockburn
Canal Beagle
C. Horn
Projection: Lambert's Azimuthal Equal Area
West from Greenwich
CARTOGRAPHY BY PHILIP'S.
COPYRIGHT REED INTERNATIONAL BOOKS LTD

1 : 31 100 000
200 0 200 400 600 800 miles
400 0 400 800 1200 km
Tropic of Cancer
Havana
CUBA
BAHAMAS
Turks & Caicos Is. (U.K.)
MEXICO
BELIZE
GUATEMALA
Guatemala
HONDURAS
Tegucigalpa
San Salvador
EL SALVADOR
NICARAGUA
Managua
COSTA RICA
San José
Panamá
PANAMA
JAMAICA
Kingston
HAITI
Port-au-Prince
DOMINICAN REP.
San Juan
PUERTO RICO (U.S.A.)
Virgin Is. (U.K.)
ST. KITTS-NEVIS
Basse-Terre
ANTIGUA & BARBUDA
GUADELOUPE (Fr.)
DOMINICA
Fort-de-France
MARTINIQUE (Fr.)
Castries
ST. LUCIA
ST. VINCENT
Kingstown
BARBADOS
Bridgetown
GRENADA
St. George's
Port of Spain
TRINIDAD & TOBAGO
Caribbean Sea
NORTH ATLANTIC OCEAN
Aruba
Curaçao
C. de la Aguja
Barranquilla
Cartagena
G. of Darién
Maracaibo
Barquisimeto
Caracas
Valencia
Cúcuta
San Cristóbal
Orinoco
Ciudad Guayana
VENEZUELA
Georgetown
GUYANA
Paramaribo
SURINAM
Cayenne
C. Orange
FRENCH GUIANA
Essequibo
Bucaramanga
Medellín
Magdalena
Bogotá
Cali
Gulf of Panamá
COLOMBIA
RORAIMA
Branco
AMAPÁ
Equator
Galapagos Is. (Ecuador)
Quito
ECUADOR
Guayaquil
G. of Guayaquil
Putumayo
Japurá
Napo
Iquitos
Marañón
Amazon
Manaus
Santarém
Marajó I.
Belém
São Luís
AMAZONAS
Juruá
Purus
Madeira
Tapajós
Xingu
Tocantins
PARÁ
MARANHÃO
Teresina
Fortaleza
C. de São Roque
CEARÁ
RIO G. DO NORTE
Natal
PARAÍBA
Campina Grande
Recife
PERNAMBUCO
ALAGOAS
Maceió
SERGIPE
Aracaju
Parnaíba
PIAUÍ
Chiclayo
Trujillo
Chimbote
Ucayali
ACRE
Pôrto Velho
RONDÔNIA
Araguaia
TOCANTINS
PERU
Callao
LIMA
Madre de Dios
Cuzco
L. Titicaca
Arequipa
La Paz
BOLIVIA
Mamoré
Cochabamba
Santa Cruz
Sucre
BRAZIL
MATO GROSSO
Cuiabá
GOIÁS
DIS. FED.
Brasília
Goiânia
São Francisco
BAHIA
Salvador
MINAS GERAIS
Belo Horizonte
ESPIRITO SANTO
Vitória
PACIFIC OCEAN
Iquique
Paraguay
MATO GROSSO DO SUL
Ribeirão Prêto
Juiz de Fora
Campos
SÃO PAULO
Campinas
R. DE J.
Niterói
RIO DE JANEIRO
Paraná
PARAGUAY
Antofagasta
Pilcomayo
Asunción
PARANÁ
Curitiba
Tropic of Capricorn
Salta
San Félix (Chile)
San Ambrosio (Chile)
San Miguel de Tucumán
Resistencia
Corrientes
SANTA CATARINA
Uruguay
RIO GRANDE DO SUL
Pôrto Alegre
Salado
Córdoba
San Juan
Santa Fe
Paraná
Pelotas
URUGUAY
Viña del Mar
Valparaiso
SANTIAGO
Mendoza
Rosario
BUENOS AIRES
La Plata
Montevideo
Río de la Plata
Arch. de Juan Fernández (Chile)
Talca
Concepción
Bahía Blanca
Mar del Plata
Colorado
ARGENTINA
CHILE
Valdivia
Negro
Viedma
Puerto Montt
Chubut
SOUTH ATLANTIC OCEAN
Comodoro Rivadavia
Gulf of San Jorge
Gulf of Penas
West Falkland
FALKLAND IS. (U.K.)
Stanley
East Falkland
Magellan's Str.
Punta Arenas
Tierra del Fuego
C. Horn
South Georgia (U.K.)
Projection: Lambert's Azimuthal Equal Area
LIMA Capital Cities
West from Greenwich
CARTOGRAPHY BY PHILIP'S. COPYRIGHT REED INTERNATIONAL BOOKS LTD

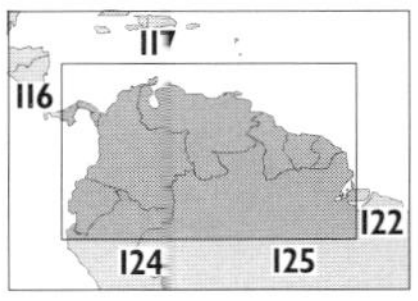

Projection: Lambert's Equivalent Azimuthal

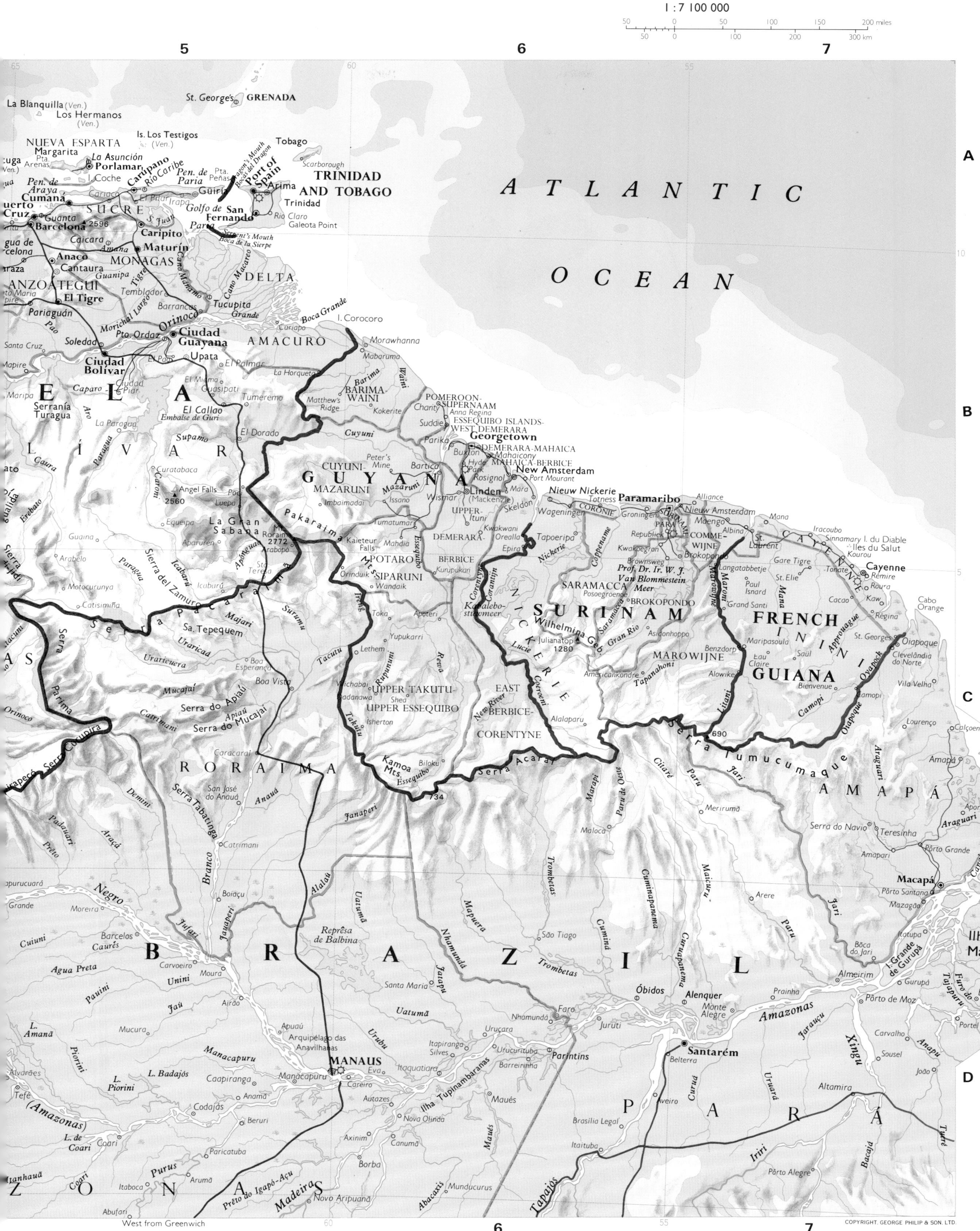
1 : 7 100 000
50 0 50 100 150 200 miles
50 0 100 200 300 km
5
6
7
A
B
C
D
ATLANTIC
OCEAN
La Blanquilla (Ven.)
Los Hermanos (Ven.)
St. George's GRENADA
NUEVA ESPARTA
Margarita
Is. Los Testigos (Ven.)
Tobago
Scarborough
La Asunción
Porlamar
Pta. Arenas
I. Coche
Carúpano
Río Caribe
Pen. de Paria
Pta. Peñas
Dragon's Mouth
Boca del Dragón
Port of Spain
Arima
TRINIDAD AND TOBAGO
Trinidad
Pen. de Araya
Cumaná
SUCRE
Güiria
Golfo de Paria
San Fernando
Rio Claro
Galeota Point
Serpent's Mouth
Boca de la Sierpe
Barcelona
2596
Caripito
Maturín
MONAGAS
Caicara
Anaco
Cantaura
ANZOATEGUI
El Tigre
Guanipa
Temblador
DELTA
Tucupita
Barrancas
Pariaguán
Soledad
Pto. Ordaz
Ciudad Guayana
AMACURO
Boca Grande
I. Corocoro
Curiapo
Ciudad Bolívar
Upata
El Palmar
La Horqueta
Morawhanna
Mabaruma
BARIMA-WAINI
Barima
Waini
Matthew's Ridge
Kokerite
POMEROON-SUPERNAAM
Anna Regina
Charity
Suddie
ESSEQUIBO ISLANDS-WEST DEMERARA
Georgetown
DEMERARA-MAHAICA
Mahaicony
MAHAICA-BERBICE
New Amsterdam
Port Mourant
Parika
Buxton
Rosignol
Cuyuni
El Callao
Guasipati
Tumeremo
El Dorado
Embalse de Guri
Serranía Turagua
La Paragua
Supamo
Caparo
Caroní
Curatabaca
Angel Falls
2560
Luepa
La Gran Sabana
Roraima
2772
CUYUNI-MAZARUNI
GUYANA
Mazaruni
Imbaimadai
Issano
Bartica
Peter's Mine
Linden
(Mackenzie)
Skeldon
Wismar
Tumatumari
Kaieteur Falls
Mahdia
Pakaraima Mts.
UPPER DEMERARA-BERBICE
Kwakwani
Orealla
Epira
POTARO-SIPARUNI
Kurupukari
Orinduik
Wandaik
Apoteri
Toka
Yupukarri
Lethem
Rupununi
Rewa
Tacutu
UPPER TAKUTU-UPPER ESSEQUIBO
Shea
Isherton
Aishalton
Dadanawa
Kamoa Mts.
Biloku
Esseguibo
734
Serra Acaraí
EAST BERBICE-CORENTYNE
New River
Coeroeni
Alalaparu
Corantijn
Kabalebo-stuwmeer
NICKERIE
Nieuw Nickerie
Totness
CORONIE
Wageningen
Paramaribo
Groningen
Alliance
Nieuw Amsterdam
Moengo
Albina
PARA
COMMEWIJNE
Republiek
Kwakoegron
Brownsweg
Brokopondo
Coppename
Tapoeripa
SARAMACCA
Posoegroenoe
Prof. Dr. Ir. W. J. Van Blommestein Meer
BROKOPONDO
SURINAM
Wilhelmina Geb.
Julianatop
1280
Gran Rio
Asindonhopo
MAROWIJNE
Tapanahoni
Americankondre
Lucie
Marowijne
Langatabbetje
Grand Santi
Benzdorp
Maripasoula
Alowike
Litani
690
Maroni
Lawa
St. Laurent
Mana
Iracoubo
Sinnamary
I. du Diable
Îles du Salut
Kourou
CAYENNE
Cayenne
Rémire
Roura
Gare Tigre
St. Elie
Paul Isnard
Tonate
Cacao
Kaw
FRENCH GUIANA
INNINI
Saül
Approuague
Régina
St. Georges
Oiapoque
Cabo Orange
Clevelândia do Norte
Camopi
Oyapock
Bienvenue
Vila Velha
Serra Tumucumaque
Lourenço
Calçoene
Amapá
I. de Maracá
Sucuriju
Aporema
Araguari
AMAPÁ
Serra do Navio
Teresinha
Amapari
Pôrto Grande
Canal do Norte
Macapá
Pôrto Santana
Mazagão
I. Janaucu
I. Caviana
Chaves
Afuá
Ilha de Marajó
Anajás
Breves
Furo do Tajapuru
Pôrto de Moz
Gurupá
I. Grande de Gurupá
Almeirim
Bôca do Jari
Jari
Paru
Arere
Merirumã
Citaré
Paru de Oeste
Marapi
Maloca
Trombetas
Cuminapanema
Curuapanema
Cuminá
Maicuru
Óbidos
Alenquer
Monte Alegre
Prainha
Faro
Juruti
Nhamundá
Santarém
Belterra
Amazonas
Jarauçu
Xingu
Curuá
Uruará
Carvalho
Souzel
Portel
Araticu
Anapu
Jôão
Altamira
Tucuruí
PARÁ
Aveiro
Brasília Legal
Itaituba
Iriri
Bacajá
Pôrto Alegre
Tapajós
Mundurucus
Abacaxis
Maués
Ilha Tupinambaranas
Parintins
Barreirinha
Urucurituba
Itapiranga
Silves
Itaquatiara
Urucara
Uatumã
Urubu
Nhamundá
Mapuera
São Tiago
Jatapu
Santa Maria
Represa de Balbina
Alalaú
Janaperi
Uatumã
Manaus
Careiro
Autazes
Nova Olinda
Axinim
Canumã
Borba
Novo Aripuanã
Madeira
Manacapuru
Caapiranga
Anamã
Codajás
Beruri
Arquipélago das Anavilhanas
Apuaú
Airão
Mucura
Manacapuru
L. Badajós
L. Piorini
Piorini
L. Amanã
Alvarães
Tefé
(Amazonas)
L. de Coari
Coari
Paricatuba
Purus
Arumã
Itaboca
Abufari
Prêto do Igapó-Açu
AMAZONAS
BRAZIL
Negro
Moreira
Barcelos
Caurés
Carvoeiro
Moura
Unini
Jaú
Pauini
Cuiuni
Agua Preta
Jufari
Jauaperi
Boiaçu
Branco
Catrimani
Serra Tabatinga
San José do Anauá
Anauá
Caracaraí
RORAIMA
Demini
Padauari
Araçá
Preto
Serra do Apiaú
Serra do Mucajaí
Mucajaí
Apiaú
Catrimani
Boa Vista
Boa Esperança
Uraricoera
Uraricaá
Sa. Tepequem
Surumu
Majari
Serra Pacaraima
Serra Parima
Serra Curupira
Orinoco
Icabarú
Sta. Teresa
Sierra del Zamuro
Paragua
Guaina
Arabelo
Motocurunya
Catisimiña
Caura
Maripa
Santa Cruz
Mapire
ELA
BOLÍVAR
West from Greenwich
COPYRIGHT, GEORGE PHILIP & SON, LTD.

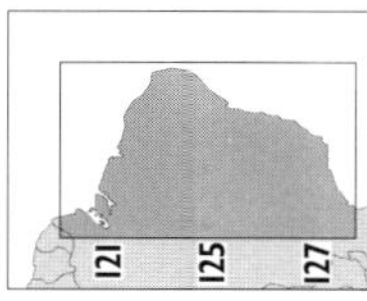
121
125
127

ATLANTIC OCEAN
AMAPÁ
PARÁ
MARANHÃO
CEARÁ
PIAUÍ
RIO GRANDE DO NORTE
PERNAMBUCO
ALAGOAS
TOCANTINS
BRAZIL
FORTALEZA (Ceará)
NATAL
RECIFE (Pernambuco)
João Pessoa (Paraíba)
MACEIÓ
BELÉM (Pará)
SÃO LUÍS (Maranhão)
Teresina
Macapá
Ilha de Marajó
Tocantins
Xingu
Serra do Gurupi
Serra dos Carajás
Serra dos Gradaús
Chapada das Mangabeiras
Serra do Penitente
Sa. do Tiracambu
Represa de Tucuruí
Represa de Sobradinho
São Francisco
Parnaíba
A
B
C
1
2
3
4
5

1 : 7 100 000

ATLANTIC OCEAN
BAHIA
GOIÁS
MINAS GERAIS
ESPÍRITO SANTO
RIO DE JANEIRO
SÃO PAULO
PARANÁ
DISTRITO FEDERAL
SALVADOR (Bahia)
BRASÍLIA
BELO HORIZONTE
RIO DE JANEIRO
NITERÓI
SÃO PAULO
SANTO ANDRÉ
SANTOS
CAMPINAS
CURITIBA
GOIÂNIA
CAMPOS
VITÓRIA
DUQUE DE CAXIAS
SÃO GONÇALO
Feira de Santana
Vitória da Conquista
Montes Claros
Teófilo Otoni
Uberlândia
Uberaba
Anápolis
Juiz de Fora
Ribeirão Prêto
Londrina
Ponta Grossa
Tropic of Capricorn
West from Greenwich
Projection: Lambert's Equivalent Azimuthal
COPYRIGHT, GEORGE PHILIP & SON, LTD.

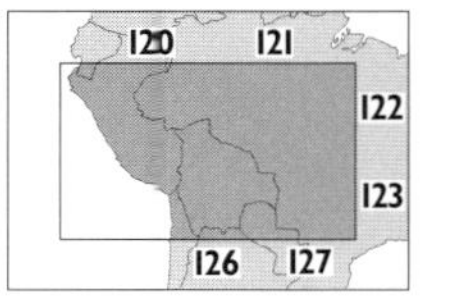
120
121
122
123
126
127

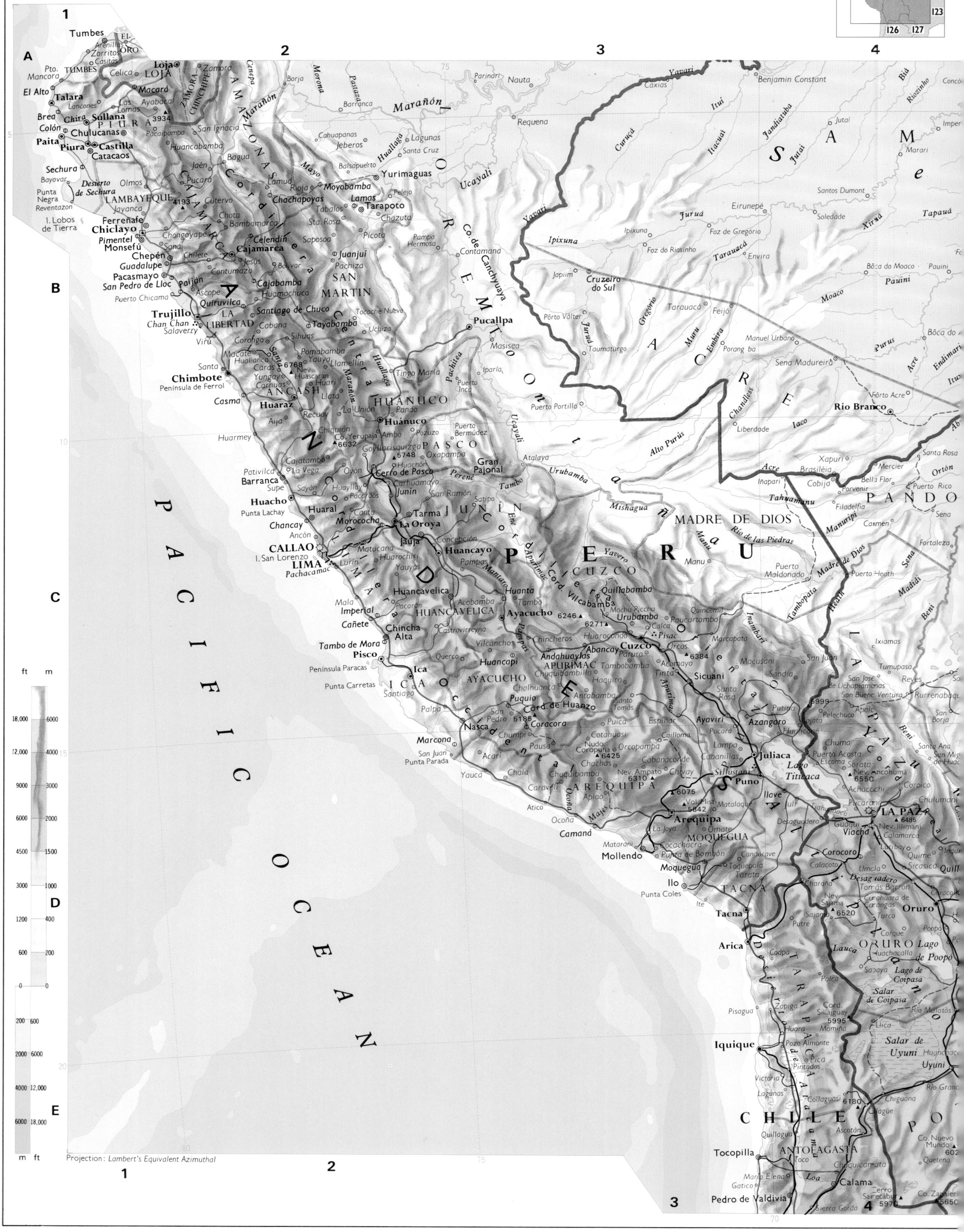
1
2
3
4
A
B
C
D
E
PACIFIC OCEAN
P E R U
A N D E S
C H I L E
P A N D O
A C R E
Cordillera Central
Cordillera Occidental
Cordillera Oriental
Tumbes
Talara
Sullana
Piura
Paita
Castilla
Catacaos
Chulucanas
Sechura
Desierto de Sechura
LAMBAYEQUE
Chiclayo
Ferreñafe
Pimentel
Monsefú
Chepén
Guadalupe
Pacasmayo
San Pedro de Lloc
Trujillo
Chan Chan
Salaverry
Chimbote
Casma
Huarmey
Barranca
Huacho
Huaral
Chancay
Callao
Lima
Pachacamac
Cañete
Chincha Alta
Pisco
Ica
Nasca
Marcona
Camaná
Mollendo
Ilo
Moquegua
Tacna
Arica
Iquique
Tocopilla
Calama
Pedro de Valdivia
Loja
Cajamarca
Celendín
Chachapoyas
Moyobamba
Tarapoto
Yurimaguas
Jaén
Huaraz
Huánuco
Cerro de Pasco
Tarma
La Oroya
Jauja
Huancayo
Huancavelica
Ayacucho
Andahuaylas
Abancay
Cuzco
Urubamba
Quillabamba
Sicuani
Juliaca
Puno
Arequipa
Lago Titicaca
La Paz
Oruro
Lago de Poopó
Salar de Uyuni
Uyuni
Pucallpa
Tingo María
Iquitos
Requena
Nauta
Marañón
Ucayali
Urubamba
Madre de Dios
Puerto Maldonado
Rio Branco
Cruzeiro do Sul
Benjamin Constant
Eirunepé
HUANUCO
PASCO
JUNIN
LIMA
ICA
AYACUCHO
HUANCAVELICA
APURIMAC
CUZCO
AREQUIPA
MOQUEGUA
TACNA
ANCASH
LA LIBERTAD
SAN MARTIN
AMAZONAS
CAJAMARCA
PIURA
TUMBES
MADRE DE DIOS
ORURO
ANTOFAGASTA
TARAPACA
Desierto de Atacama
Projection: Lambert's Equivalent Azimuthal
ft
m

1 : 7 100 000

50 0 50 100 150 200 miles

50 0 100 200 300 km

5 6 7

A B C D E

West from Greenwich

5 6 7

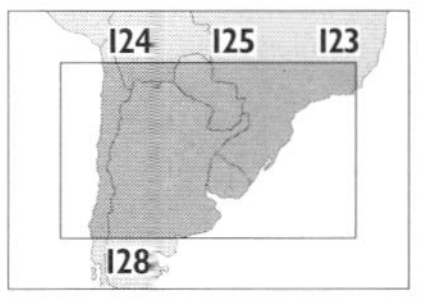
124
125
123
128

1
2
3
4
A
B
C
D
PACIFIC OCEAN
BOLIVIA
PARAGUAY
CHILE
ARGENTINA
Gran Chaco
POTOSÍ
TARIJA
NUEVA ASUNCIÓN
ALTO PARAGUAY
BOQUERÓN
PRESIDENTE HAYES
TARAPACÁ
ANTOFAGASTA
ATACAMA
COQUIMBO
JUJUY
SALTA
TUCUMÁN
CATAMARCA
SANTIAGO DEL ESTERO
FORMOSA
CHACO
CORRIENTES
LA RIOJA
SAN JUAN
CÓRDOBA
SANTA FE
ENTRE RÍOS
MENDOZA
SAN LUIS
LA PAMPA
BUENOS AIRES
NEUQUÉN
Iquique
Tocopilla
Calama
Antofagasta
Taltal
Chañaral
Copiapó
Vallenar
La Serena
Coquimbo
Ovalle
Illapel
Viña del Mar
VALPARAÍSO
SANTIAGO
Rancagua
San Fernando
Curicó
Talca
Linares
Chillán
Talcahuano
Concepción
Los Angeles
Tarija
Villazón
La Quiaca
S. Salvador de Jujuy
Salta
SAN MIGUEL DE TUCUMÁN
Santiago del Estero
Catamarca
La Rioja
San Juan
Mendoza
San Luis
CÓRDOBA
Río Cuarto
San Rafael
Santa Rosa
Bahía Blanca
ASUNCIÓN
Concepción
Formosa
Resistencia
Corrientes
Reconquista
Santa Fe
Paraná
ROSARIO
BUENOS AIRES
La Plata
Mar del Plata
Salto
Paysandú
Aconcagua 6960
Ojos del Salado 6863
Projection: Lambert's Equivalent Azimuthal
ft
m
18 000
12 000
9000
6000
4500
3000
1200
600
0
200
2000
4000
6000
6000
4000
3000
2000
1500
1000
400
200
0
600
6000
12 000
18 000

1 : 7 100 000
50 0 50 100 150 200 miles
50 0 100 200 300 km
5
6
7
A
B
C
D
West from Greenwich
COPYRIGHT. GEORGE PHILIP & SON. LTD
BRAZIL
SÃO PAULO
PARANÁ
SANTA CATARINA
RIO GRANDE DO SUL
MATO GROSSO DO SUL
RIO DE JANEIRO
MISIONES
ALTO PARANÁ
URUGUAY
ATLANTIC
OCEAN
Tropic of Capricorn
BELO HORIZONTE
Vitória
Vila Velha
CAMPOS
RIO DE JANEIRO
NITERÓI
SÃO GONÇALO
DUQUE DE CAXIAS
Nova Iguaçu
Petrópolis
Volta Redonda
Juiz de Fora
SÃO PAULO
SANTO ANDRÉ
SANTOS
São Vicente
Guarujá
São Bernardo do Campo
CAMPINAS
Jundiaí
Sorocaba
S. J. dos Campos
Taubaté
Mogi das Cruzes
Ribeirão Prêto
S. José do Rio Prêto
Araçatuba
Bauru
Marília
Presidente Prudente
Londrina
Maringá
Ponta Grossa
CURITIBA
Paranaguá
Joinvile
Blumenau
Itajaí
Florianópolis
Lajes
Tubarão
Criciúma
Caxias do Sul
PÔRTO ALEGRE
Canoas
São Leopoldo
Nôvo Hamburgo
Santa Maria
Pelotas
Rio Grande
Lagoa dos Patos
Bagé
Passo Fundo
Guarapuava
Foz do Iguaçu
Ciudad del Este
Posadas
Rivera
Melo
Treinta y Tres
Rocha
Maldonado
San Carlos
MONTEVIDEO
Lagoa Mirim
Lagoa Mangueira
Ilha de São Sebastião
Ilha Grande
Ilha de Santa Catarina
Cabo Frio
Cabo de São Tomé
Cabo Santa Marta Grande
Represa de Itaipú
Serra do Mar
Serra Geral
1889
1808
2787
2890
5304
25
30
35
40
45
50
55

CENTRAL & SOUTHERN CHILE AND ARGENTINA

126 127
1:7 100 000
50 0 50 100 150 200 miles
50 0 100 200 300 km
LA PAMPA
BUENOS AIRES
NEUQUÉN
RÍO NEGRO
CHUBUT
SANTA CRUZ
ARAUCANIA
LOS LAGOS
ARGENTINA
CHILE
MAGALLANES
Patagonia
Cordillera de los Andes
TIERRA DEL FUEGO
Golfo San Matías
Golfo San Jorge
Bahía Grande
SOUTH ATLANTIC OCEAN
PACIFIC OCEAN
FALKLAND ISLANDS
(ISLAS MALVINAS)
Jason Is.
Pebble I.
C. Dolphin
King George B.
Queen Charlotte B.
Mt. Adam
700
Mt. Usborne
705
Falkland Sound
Weddell I.
West Falkland
C. Meredith
Port Darwin
Stanley
East Falkland
Beauchêne I.
Arauco
Cañete
Angol
Mulchén
Collipulli
Victoria
Capitán Pastene
I. Mocha
Traiguén
Curacautín
Galvarino
Temuco
Lautaro
Carahue
Puerto Saavedra
Nueva Imperial
Freire
Cunco
Pitrufquén
Toltén
Villarrica
Lanco
Loncoche
Valdivia
Los Lagos
Panguipulli
Corral
Pta. Galera
La Unión
L. Ranco
Futrono
Osorno
Río Bueno
Puyehue
Río Negro
Vol. Osorno
2660
L. Llanquihue
Puerto Varas
La Ensenada
Mte. Tronador
3554
Puerto Montt
Maullín
G. de los Coronados
Pta. Huechucuicui
Ancud
G. de Ancud
820
Isla de Chiloé
Castro
Achao
Chaitén
2470
Puerto Quellón
C. Quilán
Golfo Corcovado
2300
Yelcho
2440
Boca del Guafo
I. Guafo
Islas Guaitecas
Palena
Canal Moraleda
Archipiélago de los Chonos
I. Guamblin
Magdalena
Puerto Aisén
Coihaique
Balmaceda
C. Taitao
1372
Península de Taitao
Mte. San Valentín
4058
L. Gral. Carrera
Chile Chico
C. Tres Montes
I. Javier
Golfo de Penas
Archipiélago Guayaneco
Co. Arenales
3437
Cochrane
Co. San Lorenzo
3700
Canal Baker
I. Campana
Canal Messier
Co. Mellizo Sur
3050
I. Patricio Lynch
I. Esmeralda
I. Wellington
G. Ladrillero
I. Mornington
G. Trinidad
Canal Ancho
I. Madre de Dios
Co. Murallón
3600
I. Duque de York
Chatham
C. Santiago
B. Salvación
I. Hanover
C. Jorge
Estrecho Nelson
Arch. Reina Adelaida
Puerto Natales
Pen. Muñoz Gamero
Estrecho de Magallanes
C. Deseado
I. Desolación
I. Riesco
Seno de Otway
Punta Arenas
B. Otway
I. Santa Inés
Pen. Brunswick
Clarence I.
Capt. Aracena
Pen. Brecknock
2469
Mte. Darwin
Canal Cockburn
I. Stewart
I. Londonderry
Gordon
B. Cook
I. Hoste
Pen. Hardy
B. Nassau
I. Navarino
Canal Beagle
Ushuaia
Is. Hermite
Islas Wollaston
Cabo de Hornos
(Cape Horn)
Islas Diego Ramírez
I. Picton
Nueva
I. Lennox
Est. de Le Maire
I. de los Estados
(Staten I.)
C. San Diego
Misión Fagnano
L. Fagnano
Isla Grande de Tierra del Fuego
Porvenir
B. Inútil
Dawson
Canal Whiteside
Río Grande
San Sebastián
Cerro Sombrero
Strait of Magellan
C. Vírgenes
Monte Dinero
Río Gallegos
Güer Aike
El Turbio
Gallegos
Seno Skyring
G. Almirante Montt
Puerto Coig
Coig
Esperanza
Calafate
Lago Argentino
Santa Cruz
Mte. Fitzroy
3375
L. Viedma
Tres Lagos
Shehuen
Cmte. Luis Piedrabuena
Chico
San Julián
Gran Altiplanicie Central
L. Cardiel
Gob. Gregores
Mt. Inés
1120
L. San Martín
2280
Las Horquetas
Lago Posadas
L. Pueyrredón
2726
Los Antiguos
Perito Moreno
L. Buenos Aires
Los Monos
Colonia Las Heras
Pico Truncado
1335
Fitz Roy
Jaramillo
Deseado
Puerto Deseado
Pta. Medanosa
Bahía Laura
Mazarredo
C. Tres Puntas
C. Blanco
Caleta Olivia
Comodoro Rivadavia
Holdich
Sarmiento
L. Colhué Huapi
L. Musters
Senguerr
Alto Río Senguerr
Facundo
Mayo
Río Mayo
L. Fontana
La Plata
2020
Río Pico
L. Gral. Vintter
José de San Martín
1245
Genoa
2075
El Corcovado
Tecka
Pampa de Agnia
Esquel
L. Menéndez
Gualjaina
Leleque
El Maitén
El Bolsón
Norquinco
2185
Gastre
Gan Gan
Telsen
Paso de Indios
Las Plumas
Perdido
Gran Laguna Salada
Chico
Meseta de Montemayor
Chubut
Gaimán
Rawson
Trelew
C. Raso
Camarones
B. Camarones
C. Dos Bahías
B. Bustamante
Puerto Madryn
G. Nuevo
Pen. Valdés
Puerto Pirámides
Punta Delgada
Pta. Norte
G. San José
Puerto Lobos
Sierra Grande
Meseta de Somuncurá
Cona Niyeu
Verde
1879
El Caín
Quetrequile
Ingeniero Jacobacci
Maquinchao
Los Menucos
Comallo
Paso Flores
San Carlos de Bariloche
L. Nahuel Huapi
San Martín de los Andes
Junín de los Andes
Piedra del Aguila
Limay
1314
La Esperanza
Sa. Colorada
El Cuy
Valcheta
Aguada Cecilio
San Antonio Oeste
Salado
Salina Gualicho
Gen. Lorenzo Vintter
Gral. Conesa
Negro
Viedma
Carmen de Patagones
Pta. Rasa
Stroeder
B. Anegada
Choele Choel
Lamarque
Río Colorado
Colorado
Fortín Uno
Chelforó
Gral. Roca
Allen
Neuquén
Cipolletti
Barda del Medio
Cutral-Có
Zapala
Plaza Huincul
Picún Leufú
Las Lajas
Paso Pino Hachado
1824
Loncopué
Paso Copahue
2980
3124
Paso de los Indios
Añelo
Colonia 25 de Mayo
Puelches
Bernasconi
Cuchillo-Có
Tornquist
Villa Iris
1243
Coronel Pringles
Tres Arroyos
Gonzáles Chaves
Juárez
Balcarce
Lobería
Quequén
Necochea
Oriente
Coronel Dorrego
Bahía Blanca
Médanos
Punta Alta
B. Blanca
I. Trinidad
Mayor Buratovich
Paso Mamuil Malal
1253
3776
Lonquimay
Cherquenco
Projection: Lambert's Equivalent Azimuthal
West from Greenwich
ft m
9000 3000
6000 2000
4500 1500
3000 1000
1200 400
600 200
0 0
200 600
2000 6000
4000 12,000
m ft
40
45
50
55
75
70
65
60
1 2 3 4 5
A B C D

INDEX

The index contains the names of all the principal places and features shown on the World Maps. Each name is followed by an additional entry in italics giving the country or region within which it is located. The alphabetical order of names composed of two or more words is governed primarily by the first word and then by the second. This is an example of the rule:

Mīr Kūh, *Iran* **65 E8**
Mīr Shahdād, *Iran* **65 E8**
Miraj, *India* **60 L9**
Miram Shah, *Pakistan* **62 C4**
Miramar, *Mozam.* **85 C6**

Physical features composed of a proper name (Erie) and a description (Lake) are positioned alphabetically by the proper name. The description is positioned after the proper name and is usually abbreviated:

Erie, L., *N. Amer.* **106 D3**

Where a description forms part of a settlement or administrative name however, it is always written in full and put in its true alphabetic position:

Mount Morris, *U.S.A.* **106 D7**

Names beginning with M' and Mc are indexed as if they were spelt Mac. Names beginning St. are alphabetised under Saint, but Sankt, Sint, Sant', Santa and San are all spelt in full and are alphabetised accordingly. If the same place name occurs two or more times in the index and all are in the same country, each is followed by the name of the administrative subdivision in which it is located. The names are placed in the alphabetical order of the subdivisions. For example:

Jackson, *Ky., U.S.A.* **104 G4**
Jackson, *Mich., U.S.A.* **104 D3**
Jackson, *Minn., U.S.A.* **108 D7**

The number in bold type which follows each name in the index refers to the number of the map page where that feature or place will be found. This is usually the largest scale at which the place or feature appears. The letter and figure which are in bold type immediately after the page number give the grid square on the map page, within which the feature is situated. The letter represents the latitude and the figure the longitude.

In some cases the feature itself may fall within the specified square, while the name is outside. This is usually the case only with features which are larger than a grid square. Rivers are indexed to their mouths or confluences, and carry the symbol → after their names. A solid square ■ follows the name of a country while, an open square □ refers to a first order administrative area.

ABBREVIATIONS USED IN THE INDEX

A.C.T. — Australian Capital Territory
Afghan. — Afghanistan
Ala. — Alabama
Alta. — Alberta
Amer. — America(n)
Arch. — Archipelago
Ariz. — Arizona
Ark. — Arkansas
Atl. Oc. — Atlantic Ocean
B. — Baie, Bahía, Bay, Bucht, Bugt
B.C. — British Columbia
Bangla. — Bangladesh
Barr. — Barrage
Bos.-H. — Bosnia-Herzegovina
C. — Cabo, Cap, Cape, Coast
C.A.R. — Central African Republic
C. Prov. — Cape Province
Calif. — California
Cent. — Central
Chan. — Channel
Colo. — Colorado
Conn. — Connecticut
Cord. — Cordillera
Cr. — Creek
Czech. — Czech Republic
D.C. — District of Columbia
Del. — Delaware
Dep. — Dependency
Des. — Desert
Dist. — District
Dj. — Djebel
Domin. — Dominica
Dom. Rep. — Dominican Republic
E. — East
El Salv. — El Salvador
Eq. Guin. — Equatorial Guinea
Fla. — Florida
Falk. Is. — Falkland Is.
G. — Golfe, Golfo, Gulf, Guba, Gebel
Ga. — Georgia
Gt. — Great, Greater
Guinea-Biss. — Guinea-Bissau
H.K. — Hong Kong
H.P. — Himachal Pradesh
Hants. — Hampshire
Harb. — Harbor, Harbour
Hd. — Head
Hts. — Heights
I.(s). — Île, Ilha, Insel, Isla, Island, Isle
Ill. — Illinois
Ind. — Indiana
Ind. Oc. — Indian Ocean
Ivory C. — Ivory Coast
J. — Jabal, Jebel, Jazira
Junc. — Junction
K. — Kap, Kapp
Kans. — Kansas
Kep. — Kepulauan
Ky. — Kentucky
L. — Lac, Lacul, Lago, Lagoa, Lake, Limni, Loch, Lough
La. — Louisiana
Liech. — Liechtenstein
Lux. — Luxembourg
Mad. P. — Madhya Pradesh
Madag. — Madagascar
Man. — Manitoba
Mass. — Massachusetts
Md. — Maryland
Me. — Maine
Medit. S. — Mediterranean Sea
Mich. — Michigan
Minn. — Minnesota
Miss. — Mississippi
Mo. — Missouri
Mont. — Montana
Moza. — Mozambique
Mt.(e). — Mont, Monte, Monti, Montaña, Mountain
N. — Nord, Norte, North, Northern, Nouveau
N.B. — New Brunswick
N.C. — North Carolina
N. Cal. — New Caledonia
N. Dak. — North Dakota
N.H. — New Hampshire
N.I. — North Island
N.J. — New Jersey
N. Mex. — New Mexico
N.S. — Nova Scotia
N.S.W. — New South Wales
N.W.T. — North West Territory
N.Y. — New York
N.Z. — New Zealand
Nebr. — Nebraska
Neths. — Netherlands
Nev. — Nevada
Nfld. — Newfoundland
Nic. — Nicaragua
O. — Oued, Ouadi
Occ. — Occidentale
Okla. — Oklahoma
Ont. — Ontario
Or. — Orientale
Oreg. — Oregon
Os. — Ostrov
Oz. — Ozero
P. — Pass, Passo, Pasul, Pulau
P.E.I. — Prince Edward Island
Pa. — Pennsylvania
Pac. Oc. — Pacific Ocean
Papua N.G. — Papua New Guinea
Pass. — Passage
Pen. — Peninsula, Péninsule
Phil. — Philippines
Pk. — Park, Peak
Plat. — Plateau
P-ov. — Poluostrov
Prov. — Province, Provincial
Pt. — Point
Pta. — Ponta, Punta
Pte. — Pointe
Qué. — Québec
Queens. — Queensland
R. — Rio, River
R.I. — Rhode Island
Ra.(s). — Range(s)
Raj. — Rajasthan
Reg. — Region
Rep. — Republic
Res. — Reserve, Reservoir
S. — San, South, Sea
Si. Arabia — Saudi Arabia
S.C. — South Carolina
S. Dak. — South Dakota
S.I. — South Island
S. Leone — Sierra Leone
Sa. — Serra, Sierra
Sask. — Saskatchewan
Scot. — Scotland
Sd. — Sound
Sev. — Severnaya
Sib. — Siberia
Sprs. — Springs
St. — Saint, Sankt, Sint
Sta. — Santa, Station
Ste. — Sainte
Sto. — Santo
Str. — Strait, Stretto
Switz. — Switzerland
Tas. — Tasmania
Tenn. — Tennessee
Tex. — Texas
Tg. — Tanjung
Trin. & Tob. — Trinidad & Tobago
U.A.E. — United Arab Emirates
U.K. — United Kingdom
U.S.A. — United States of America
Ut. P. — Uttar Pradesh
Va. — Virginia
Vdkhr. — Vodokhranilishche
Vf. — Vîrful
Vic. — Victoria
Vol. — Volcano
Vt. — Vermont
W. — Wadi, West
W. Va. — West Virginia
Wash. — Washington
Wis. — Wisconsin
Wlkp. — Wielkopolski
Wyo. — Wyoming
Yorks. — Yorkshire
Yug. — Yugoslavia

A

A Coruña = La Coruña, *Spain* 30 B2
Aachen, *Germany* 18 E2
Aadorf, *Switz.* 23 B7
Aalborg = Ålborg, *Denmark* 11 G3
Aalen, *Germany* 19 G6
A'âli en Nîl □, *Sudan* 77 F3
Aalsmeer, *Neths.* 16 D5
Aalst, *Belgium* 17 G4
Aalst, *Neths.* 17 F6
Aalten, *Neths.* 16 E9
Aalter, *Belgium* 17 F2
Äänekoski, *Finland* 9 E21
Aarau, *Switz.* 22 B6
Aarberg, *Switz.* 22 B4
Aardenburg, *Belgium* 17 F2
Aare →, *Switz.* 22 A6
Aargau □, *Switz.* 22 B6
Aarhus = Århus, *Denmark* 11 H4
Aarle, *Neths.* 17 E7
Aarschot, *Belgium* 17 G5
Aarsele, *Belgium* 17 G2
Aartrijke, *Belgium* 17 F2
Aarwangen, *Switz.* 22 B5
Aba, *China* 52 A3
Aba, *Nigeria* 79 D6
Aba, *Zaïre* 82 B3
Âbâ, Jazîrat, *Sudan* 77 E3
Abacaxis →, *Brazil* 121 D6
Ābādān, *Iran* 65 D6
Abade, *Ethiopia* 77 F4
Ābādeh, *Iran* 65 D7
Abadin, *Spain* 30 B3
Abadla, *Algeria* 75 B4
Abaeté, *Brazil* 123 E2
Abaeté →, *Brazil* 123 E2
Abaetetuba, *Brazil* 122 B2
Abagnar Qi, *China* 50 C9
Abai, *Paraguay* 127 B4
Abak, *Nigeria* 79 E6
Abakaliki, *Nigeria* 79 D6
Abakan, *Russia* 45 D10
Abalemma, *Niger* 79 B6
Abana, *Turkey* 66 B6
Abancay, *Peru* 124 C3
Abanilla, *Spain* 29 G3
Abano Terme, *Italy* 33 C8
Abapó, *Bolivia* 125 D5
Abarán, *Spain* 29 G3
Abariringa, *Kiribati* 92 H10
Abarqū, *Iran* 65 D7
Abashiri, *Japan* 48 B12
Abashiri-Wan, *Japan* 48 B12
Abaújszántó, *Hungary* 21 G11
Abay, *Kazakstan* 44 E8
Abaya, L., *Ethiopia* 77 F4
Abaza, *Russia* 44 D10
Abbadia San Salvatore, *Italy* 33 F8
'Abbāsābād, *Iran* 65 C8
Abbay = Nîl el Azraq →, *Sudan* 77 D3
Abbaye, Pt., *U.S.A.* 104 B1
Abbé, L., *Ethiopia* 77 E5
Abbeville, *France* 25 B8
Abbeville, *La., U.S.A.* 109 K8
Abbeville, *S.C., U.S.A.* 105 H4
Abbiategrasso, *Italy* 32 C5
Abbieglassie, *Australia* 91 D4
Abbot Ice Shelf, *Antarctica* 5 D16
Abbotsford, *Canada* 100 D4
Abbotsford, *U.S.A.* 108 C9
Abbottabad, *Pakistan* 62 B5
Abcoude, *Neths.* 16 D5
Abd al Kūrī, *Ind. Oc.* 68 E5
Ābdar, *Iran* 65 D7
'Abdolābād, *Iran* 65 C8
Abéché, *Chad* 73 F9
Abejar, *Spain* 28 D2
Abekr, *Sudan* 77 E2
Abêlessa, *Algeria* 75 D5
Abengourou, *Ivory C.* 78 D4
Åbenrå, *Denmark* 11 J3
Abensberg, *Germany* 19 G7
Abeokuta, *Nigeria* 79 D5
Aber, *Uganda* 82 B3
Aberaeron, *U.K.* 13 E3
Aberayron = Aberaeron, *U.K.* 13 E3
Aberconwy & Colwyn □, *U.K.* 12 D4
Abercorn = Mbala, *Zambia* 83 D3
Abercorn, *Australia* 91 D5
Aberdare, *U.K.* 13 F4
Aberdare Ra., *Kenya* 82 C4
Aberdeen, *Australia* 91 E5
Aberdeen, *Canada* 101 C7
Aberdeen, *S. Africa* 84 E3
Aberdeen, *U.K.* 14 D6
Aberdeen, *Ala., U.S.A.* 105 J1
Aberdeen, *Idaho, U.S.A.* 110 E7
Aberdeen, *S. Dak., U.S.A.* 108 C5
Aberdeen, *Wash., U.S.A.* 112 D3
Aberdeenshire □, *U.K.* 14 D6
Aberdovey = Aberdyfi, *U.K.* 13 E3
Aberdyfi, *U.K.* 13 E3
Aberfeldy, *U.K.* 14 E5
Abergaria-a-Velha, *Portugal* 30 E2
Abergavenny, *U.K.* 13 F4
Abernathy, *U.S.A.* 109 J4
Abert, L., *U.S.A.* 110 E3
Aberystwyth, *U.K.* 13 E3
Abha, *Si. Arabia* 76 D5
Abhar, *Iran* 67 D13
Abhayapuri, *India* 63 F14
Abia □, *Nigeria* 79 D6
Abidiya, *Sudan* 76 D3
Abidjan, *Ivory C.* 78 D4
Abilene, *Kans., U.S.A.* 108 F6
Abilene, *Tex., U.S.A.* 109 J5
Abingdon, *U.K.* 13 F6
Abingdon, *Ill., U.S.A.* 108 E9
Abingdon, *Va., U.S.A.* 105 G5
Abington Reef, *Australia* 90 B4
Abitau →, *Canada* 101 B7
Abitau L., *Canada* 101 A7
Abitibi L., *Canada* 98 C4
Abiy Adi, *Ethiopia* 77 E4
Abkhaz Republic □ = Abkhazia □, *Georgia* 43 J5
Abkhazia □, *Georgia* 43 J5
Abkit, *Russia* 45 C16
Abminga, *Australia* 91 D1
Abnûb, *Egypt* 76 B3
Åbo = Turku, *Finland* 9 F20
Abocho, *Nigeria* 79 D6
Abohar, *India* 62 D6
Aboisso, *Ivory C.* 78 D4
Aboméy, *Benin* 79 D5
Abondance, *France* 27 B10
Abong-Mbang, *Cameroon* 80 D2
Abonnema, *Nigeria* 79 E6
Abony, *Hungary* 21 H10
Aboso, *Ghana* 78 D4
Abou-Deïa, *Chad* 73 F8
Aboyne, *U.K.* 14 D6
Abra Pampa, *Argentina* 126 A2
Abrantes, *Portugal* 31 F2
Abraveses, *Portugal* 30 E3
Abreojos, Pta., *Mexico* 114 B2
Abreschviller, *France* 25 D14
Abri, *Esh Shamâliya, Sudan* 76 C3
Abri, *Janub Kordofân, Sudan* 77 E3
Abrolhos, Banka, *Brazil* 123 E4
Abruzzi □, *Italy* 33 F10
Absaroka Range, *U.S.A.* 110 D9
Abū al Khaṣīb, *Iraq* 65 D6
Abū 'Alī, *Si. Arabia* 65 E6
Abū 'Alī →, *Lebanon* 69 A4
Abu 'Arīsh, *Si. Arabia* 68 D3
Abû Ballas, *Egypt* 76 C2
Abu Deleiq, *Sudan* 77 D3
Abu Dhabi = Abū Ẓāby, *U.A.E.* 65 E7
Abû Dis, *Sudan* 76 D3
Abû Dom, *Sudan* 77 D3
Abū Du'ān, *Syria* 67 D8
Abu el Gairi, W. →, *Egypt* 69 F2
Abû Gabra, *Sudan* 77 E2
Abu Ga'da, W. →, *Egypt* 69 F1
Abû Gubeiha, *Sudan* 77 E3
Abu Habl, Khawr →, *Sudan* 77 E3
Abū Ḥadrīyah, *Si. Arabia* 65 E6
Abu Hamed, *Sudan* 76 D3
Abu Haraz, *An Nîl el Azraq, Sudan* 77 E3
Abû Haraz, *Esh Shamâliya, Sudan* 76 D3
Abû Higar, *Sudan* 77 E3
Abū Kamāl, *Syria* 67 E9
Abū Madd, Ra's, *Si. Arabia* 64 E3
Abu Matariq, *Sudan* 77 E2
Abu Qir, *Egypt* 76 H7
Abu Qireiya, *Egypt* 76 C4
Abu Qurqâs, *Egypt* 76 J7
Abu Şafāt, W. →, *Jordan* 69 E5
Abû Simbel, *Egypt* 76 C3
Abū Şukhayr, *Iraq* 67 G11
Abu Tig, *Egypt* 76 B3
Abu Tiga, *Sudan* 77 E3
Abû Zabad, *Sudan* 77 E2
Abū Ẓāby, *U.A.E.* 65 E7
Abū Zeydābād, *Iran* 65 C6
Abufari, *Brazil* 125 B5
Abuja, *Nigeria* 79 D6
Abukuma-Gawa →, *Japan* 48 E10
Abukuma-Sammyaku, *Japan* 48 F10
Abunã, *Brazil* 125 B4
Abunã →, *Brazil* 125 B4
Aburo, *Zaïre* 82 B3
Abut Hd., *N.Z.* 87 K3
Abwong, *Sudan* 77 F3
Åby, *Sweden* 11 F10
Aby, Lagune, *Ivory C.* 78 D4
Acacías, *Colombia* 120 C3
Acajutla, *El Salv.* 116 D2
Açailândia, *Brazil* 122 C2
Acámbaro, *Mexico* 114 C4
Acaponeta, *Mexico* 114 C3
Acapulco, *Mexico* 115 D5
Acarai, Serra, *Brazil* 121 C6
Acaraú, *Brazil* 122 B3
Acari, *Brazil* 122 C4
Acarí, *Peru* 124 D3
Acarigua, *Venezuela* 120 B4
Acatlán, *Mexico* 115 D5
Acayucan, *Mexico* 115 D6
Accéglio, *Italy* 32 D3
Accomac, *U.S.A.* 104 G8
Accous, *France* 26 E3
Accra, *Ghana* 79 D4
Accrington, *U.K.* 12 D5
Acebal, *Argentina* 126 C3
Aceh □, *Indonesia* 56 D1
Acerenza, *Italy* 35 B8
Acerra, *Italy* 35 B7
Aceuchal, *Spain* 31 G4
Achacachi, *Bolivia* 124 D4
Achaguas, *Venezuela* 120 B4
Achalpur, *India* 60 J10
Achao, *Chile* 128 B2
Achel, *Belgium* 17 F6
Acheng, *China* 51 B14
Achenkirch, *Austria* 19 H7
Achensee, *Austria* 19 H7
Acher, *India* 62 H5
Achern, *Germany* 19 G4
Achill, *Ireland* 15 C2
Achill Hd., *Ireland* 15 C1
Achill I., *Ireland* 15 C1
Achill Sd., *Ireland* 15 C2
Achim, *Germany* 18 B5
Achinsk, *Russia* 45 D10
Achol, *Sudan* 77 F3
Acıgöl, *Turkey* 66 D3
Acireale, *Italy* 35 E8
Ackerman, *U.S.A.* 109 J10
Acklins I., *Bahamas* 117 B5
Acme, *Canada* 100 C6
Acobamba, *Peru* 124 C3
Acomayo, *Peru* 124 C3
Aconcagua, Cerro, *Argentina* 126 C2
Aconquija, Mt., *Argentina* 126 B2
Acopiara, *Brazil* 122 C4
Açores, Is. dos = Azores, *Atl. Oc.* 70 C1
Acorizal, *Brazil* 125 D6
Acquapendente, *Italy* 33 F8
Acquasanta Terme, *Italy* 33 F10
Acquaviva delle Fonti, *Italy* 35 B9
Acqui Terme, *Italy* 32 D5
Acraman, L., *Australia* 91 E2
Acre = 'Akko, *Israel* 69 C4
Acre □, *Brazil* 124 B3
Acre →, *Brazil* 124 B4
Acri, *Italy* 35 C9
Acs, *Hungary* 21 H8
Acton, *Canada* 106 C4
Açu, *Brazil* 122 C4
Ad Dammām, *Si. Arabia* 65 E6
Ad Dawhah, *Qatar* 65 E6
Ad Dawr, *Iraq* 67 E10
Ad Dir'īyah, *Si. Arabia* 64 E5
Ad Dīwānīyah, *Iraq* 67 F11
Ad Dujayl, *Iraq* 67 F11
Ad Durūz, J., *Jordan* 69 C5
Ada, *Ghana* 79 D5
Ada, *Serbia, Yug.* 21 K10
Ada, *Minn., U.S.A.* 108 B6
Ada, *Okla., U.S.A.* 109 H6
Adaja →, *Spain* 30 D6
Ådalsliden, *Sweden* 10 A10
Adam, Mt., *Falk. Is.* 128 D4
Adamantina, *Brazil* 123 F1
Adamaoua, Massif de l', *Cameroon* 79 D7
Adamawa □, *Nigeria* 79 D7
Adamawa Highlands = Adamaoua, Massif de l', *Cameroon* 79 D7
Adamello, Mte., *Italy* 32 B7
Adami Tulu, *Ethiopia* 77 F4
Adaminaby, *Australia* 91 F4
Adams, *Mass., U.S.A.* 107 D11
Adams, *N.Y., U.S.A.* 107 C8
Adams, *Wis., U.S.A.* 108 D10
Adam's Bridge, *Sri Lanka* 60 Q11
Adams L., *Canada* 100 C5
Adams Mt., *U.S.A.* 112 D5
Adam's Peak, *Sri Lanka* 60 R12
Adamuz, *Spain* 31 G6
Adana, *Turkey* 66 D6
Adanero, *Spain* 30 E6
Adapazarı, *Turkey* 66 B4
Adarama, *Sudan* 77 D3
Adare, C., *Antarctica* 5 D11
Adaut, *Indonesia* 57 F8
Adavale, *Australia* 91 D3
Adda →, *Italy* 32 C6
Addis Ababa = Addis Abeba, *Ethiopia* 77 F4
Addis Abeba, *Ethiopia* 77 F4
Addis Alem, *Ethiopia* 77 F4
Addison, *U.S.A.* 106 D7
Addo, *S. Africa* 84 E4
Adebour, *Niger* 79 C7
Ādeh, *Iran* 64 B5
Adel, *U.S.A.* 105 K4
Adelaide, *Australia* 91 E2
Adelaide, *Bahamas* 116 A4
Adelaide, *S. Africa* 84 E4
Adelaide I., *Antarctica* 5 C17
Adelaide Pen., *Canada* 96 B10
Adelaide River, *Australia* 88 B5
Adelanto, *U.S.A.* 113 L9
Adelboden, *Switz.* 22 D5
Adele I., *Australia* 88 C3
Adélie, Terre, *Antarctica* 5 C10
Adélie Land = Adélie, Terre, *Antarctica* 5 C10
Ademuz, *Spain* 28 E3
Aden = Al 'Adan, *Yemen* 68 E4
Aden, G. of, *Asia* 68 E4
Adendorp, *S. Africa* 84 E3
Adh Dhayd, *U.A.E.* 65 E7
Adhoi, *India* 62 H4
Adi, *Indonesia* 57 E8
Adi Daro, *Ethiopia* 77 E4
Adi Keyih, *Eritrea* 77 E4
Adi Kwala, *Eritrea* 77 E4
Adi Ugri, *Eritrea* 77 E4
Adieu, C., *Australia* 89 F5
Adieu Pt., *Australia* 88 C3
Adigala, *Ethiopia* 77 E5
Adige →, *Italy* 33 C9
Adigrat, *Ethiopia* 77 E4
Adilabad, *India* 60 K11
Adilcevaz, *Turkey* 67 C10
Adin, *U.S.A.* 110 F3
Adin Khel, *Afghan.* 60 C6
Adinkerke, *Belgium* 17 F1
Adirondack Mts., *U.S.A.* 107 C10
Adıyaman, *Turkey* 67 D8
Adjim, *Tunisia* 75 B7
Adjohon, *Benin* 79 D5
Adjud, *Romania* 38 C10
Adjumani, *Uganda* 82 B3
Adlavik Is., *Canada* 99 B8
Adler, *Russia* 43 J4
Adliswil, *Switz.* 23 B7
Admer, *Algeria* 75 D6
Admer, Erg d', *Algeria* 75 D6
Admiralty G., *Australia* 88 B4
Admiralty I., *U.S.A.* 96 C6
Admiralty Inlet, *U.S.A.* 110 C2
Admiralty Is., *Papua N. G.* 92 H6
Ado, *Nigeria* 79 D5
Ado-Ekiti, *Nigeria* 79 D6
Adok, *Sudan* 77 F3
Adola, *Ethiopia* 77 E5
Adonara, *Indonesia* 57 F6
Adoni, *India* 60 M10
Adony, *Hungary* 21 H8
Adour →, *France* 26 E2
Adra, *India* 63 H12
Adra, *Spain* 29 J1
Adrano, *Italy* 35 E7
Adrar, *Algeria* 75 C4
Adré, *Chad* 73 F9
Adrī, *Libya* 75 C7
Ádria, *Italy* 33 C9
Adrian, *Mich., U.S.A.* 104 E3
Adrian, *Tex., U.S.A.* 109 H3
Adriatic Sea, *Medit. S.* 6 G9
Adua, *Indonesia* 57 E7
Adula, *Switz.* 23 D8
Adwa, *Ethiopia* 77 E4
Adygea □, *Russia* 43 H5
Adzhar Republic □ = Ajaria □, *Georgia* 43 K6
Adzopé, *Ivory C.* 78 D4
Ægean Sea, *Medit. S.* 39 L8
Aerhtai Shan, *Mongolia* 54 B4
Ærø, *Denmark* 11 K4
Ærøskøbing, *Denmark* 11 K4
Aesch, *Switz.* 22 B5
'Afak, *Iraq* 67 F11
Afándou, *Greece* 37 C10
Afarag, Erg, *Algeria* 75 D5
Affreville = Khemis Miliana, *Algeria* 75 A5
Afghanistan ■, *Asia* 60 C4
Afgoi, *Somali Rep.* 68 G3
Afikpo, *Nigeria* 79 D6
Aflou, *Algeria* 75 B5
Afogados da Ingàzeira, *Brazil* 122 C4
Afognak I., *U.S.A.* 96 C4
Afragola, *Italy* 35 B7
Afrera, *Ethiopia* 77 E5
'Afrīn, *Syria* 66 D7
Afşin, *Turkey* 66 C7
Afton, *U.S.A.* 107 D9
Aftout, *Algeria* 74 C4
Afuá, *Brazil* 121 D7
Afula, *Israel* 69 C4
Afyonkarahisar, *Turkey* 66 C4
Aga, *Egypt* 76 H7
Agadès = Agadez, *Niger* 79 B6
Agadez, *Niger* 79 B6
Agadir, *Morocco* 74 B3
Agaete, *Canary Is.* 36 F4
Agailás, *Mauritania* 74 D2
Agapa, *Russia* 45 B9
Agar, *India* 62 H7
Agaro, *Ethiopia* 77 F4
Agartala, *India* 61 H17
Agassiz, *Canada* 100 D4
Agats, *Indonesia* 57 F9
Agbélouvé, *Togo* 79 D5
Agboville, *Ivory C.* 78 D4
Ağcabädi, *Azerbaijan* 43 K8
Ağdam, *Azerbaijan* 43 L8
Ağdaş, *Azerbaijan* 43 K8
Agde, *France* 26 E7
Agde, C. d', *France* 26 E7
Agdz, *Morocco* 74 B3
Agdzhabedi = Ağcabädi, *Azerbaijan* 43 K8
Agen, *France* 26 D4
Agersø, *Denmark* 11 J5
Ageyevo, *Russia* 42 C3
Agger, *Denmark* 11 H2
Äggius, *Italy* 34 B2
Āgh Kand, *Iran* 67 D13
Aghoueyyît, *Mauritania* 74 D1
Aginskoye, *Russia* 45 D12
Agira, *Italy* 35 E7
Ağlasun, *Turkey* 66 D4
Agly →, *France* 26 F7
Agnibilékrou, *Ivory C.* 78 D4
Agnita, *Romania* 38 D7
Agnone, *Italy* 35 A7
Agofie, *Ghana* 79 D5
Agogna →, *Italy* 32 C5
Agogo, *Sudan* 77 F2
Agon, *France* 24 C5
Agön, *Sweden* 10 C11
Ágordo, *Italy* 33 B9
Agout →, *France* 26 E5
Agra, *India* 62 F7
Agrakhanskiy Poluostrov, *Russia* 43 J8
Agramunt, *Spain* 28 D6
Agreda, *Spain* 28 D3
Ağri, *Turkey* 67 C10
Agri →, *Italy* 35 B9
Ağrı Dağı, *Turkey* 67 C11
Agrigento, *Italy* 34 E6
Agrinion, *Greece* 39 L4
Agrópoli, *Italy* 35 B7
Ağstafa, *Azerbaijan* 43 K7
Agua Branca, *Brazil* 122 C3
Agua Caliente, *Baja Calif., Mexico* 113 N10
Agua Caliente, *Sinaloa, Mexico* 114 B3
Agua Caliente Springs, *U.S.A.* 113 N10
Água Clara, *Brazil* 125 E7
Agua Hechicero, *Mexico* 113 N10
Agua Preta →, *Brazil* 121 D5
Agua Prieta, *Mexico* 114 A3
Aguachica, *Colombia* 120 B3
Aguada Cecilio, *Argentina* 128 B3
Aguadas, *Colombia* 120 B2
Aguadilla, *Puerto Rico* 117 C6
Aguadulce, *Panama* 116 E3
Aguanga, *U.S.A.* 113 M10
Aguanish, *Canada* 99 B7
Aguanus →, *Canada* 99 B7
Aguapeí, *Brazil* 125 D6
Aguapeí →, *Brazil* 123 F1
Aguapey →, *Argentina* 126 B4
Aguaray Guazú →, *Paraguay* 126 A4
Aguarico →, *Ecuador* 120 D2
Aguas →, *Spain* 28 D4
Aguas Blancas, *Chile* 126 A2
Aguas Calientes, Sierra de, *Argentina* 126 B2
Águas Formosas, *Brazil* 123 E3
Aguascalientes, *Mexico* 114 C4
Aguascalientes □, *Mexico* 114 C4
Agudo, *Spain* 31 G6
Águeda, *Portugal* 30 E2
Águeda →, *Spain* 30 D4
Aguié, *Niger* 79 C6
Aguilafuente, *Spain* 30 D6
Aguilar, *Spain* 31 H6
Aguilar de Campóo, *Spain* 30 C6
Aguilares, *Argentina* 126 B2
Aguilas, *Spain* 29 H3
Agüimes, *Canary Is.* 36 G4
Aguja, C. de la, *Colombia* 120 A3
Agulaa, *Ethiopia* 77 E4
Agulhas, C., *S. Africa* 84 E3
Agulo, *Canary Is.* 36 F2
Agung, *Indonesia* 56 F5
Agur, *Uganda* 82 B3
Agusan →, *Phil.* 55 G6
Agustín Codazzi, *Colombia* 120 A3
Agvali, *Russia* 43 J8
Aha Mts., *Botswana* 84 B3
Ahaggar, *Algeria* 75 D6
Ahamansu, *Ghana* 79 D5
Ahar, *Iran* 67 C12
Ahaus, *Germany* 18 C3
Ahelledjem, *Algeria* 75 C6
Ahipara B., *N.Z.* 87 F4
Ahiri, *India* 60 K12
Ahlat, *Turkey* 67 C10
Ahlen, *Germany* 18 D3
Ahmad Wal, *Pakistan* 62 E1
Ahmadabad, *India* 62 H5
Aḥmadābād, *Khorāsān, Iran* 65 C9
Aḥmadābād, *Khorāsān, Iran* 65 C8
Aḥmadī, *Iran* 65 E8
Ahmadnagar, *India* 60 K9
Ahmadpur, *Pakistan* 62 E4
Ahmar, *Ethiopia* 77 F5
Ahmedabad = Ahmadabad, *India* 62 H5
Ahmednagar = Ahmadnagar, *India* 60 K9
Ahoada, *Nigeria* 79 D6
Ahome, *Mexico* 114 B3
Ahr →, *Germany* 18 E3
Ahram, *Iran* 65 D6
Ahrax Pt., *Malta* 37 D1
Ahrensbök, *Germany* 18 A6
Ahrweiler, *Germany* 18 E3
Āhū, *Iran* 65 C6
Ahuachapán, *El Salv.* 116 D2
Ahvāz, *Iran* 65 D6
Ahvenanmaa = Åland, *Finland* 9 F19
Aḥwar, *Yemen* 68 E4
Ahzar, *Mali* 79 B5
Aiari →, *Brazil* 120 C4
Aichach, *Germany* 19 G7
Aichi □, *Japan* 49 G8
Aidone, *Italy* 35 E7
Aiello Calabro, *Italy* 35 C9
Aigle, *Switz.* 22 D3
Aignay-le-Duc, *France* 25 E11
Aigoual, Mt., *France* 26 D7
Aigre, *France* 26 C4
Aigua, *Uruguay* 127 C5
Aigueperse, *France* 26 B7
Aigues →, *France* 27 D8
Aigues-Mortes, *France* 27 E8
Aigues-Mortes, G. d', *France* 27 E8

Aiguilles, *France* 27 D10
Aiguillon, *France* 26 D4
Aigurande, *France* 26 B5
Aihui, *China* 54 A7
Aija, *Peru* 124 B2
Aikawa, *Japan* 48 E9
Aiken, *U.S.A.* 105 J5
Ailao Shan, *China* 52 F3
Aillant-sur-Tholon, *France* 25 E10
Aillik, *Canada* 99 A8
Ailly-sur-Noye, *France* 25 C9
Ailsa Craig, *U.K.* 14 F3
'Ailūn, *Jordan* 69 C4
Aim, *Russia* 45 D14
Aimere, *Indonesia* 57 F6
Aimogasta, *Argentina* 126 B2
Aimorés, *Brazil* 123 E3
Ain □, *France* 27 B9
Ain →, *France* 27 C9
Aïn Beïda, *Algeria* 75 A6
Aïn Ben Khellil, *Algeria* 75 B4
Aïn Ben Tili, *Mauritania* 74 C3
Aïn Beni Mathar, *Morocco* 75 B4
Aïn Benian, *Algeria* 75 A5
Ain Dalla, *Egypt* 76 B2
Ain el Mafki, *Egypt* 76 B2
Ain Girba, *Egypt* 76 B2
Aïn M'lila, *Algeria* 75 A6
Ain Qeiqab, *Egypt* 76 B1
Aïn-Sefra, *Algeria* 75 B4
Ain Sheikh Murzûk, *Egypt* 76 B2
'Ain Sudr, *Egypt* 69 F2
Ain Sukhna, *Egypt* 76 J8
Aïn Tédelès, *Algeria* 75 A5
Aïn-Témouchent, *Algeria* 75 A4
Aïn Touta, *Algeria* 75 A6
Ain Zeitûn, *Egypt* 76 B2
Aïn Zorah, *Morocco* 75 B4
Ainabo, *Somali Rep.* 68 F4
Ainaži, *Latvia* 9 H21
Aínos Óros, *Greece* 39 L3
Ainsworth, *U.S.A.* 108 D5
Aipe, *Colombia* 120 C2
Aiquile, *Bolivia* 125 D4
Aïr, *Niger* 79 B6
Air Hitam, *Malaysia* 59 M4
Airaines, *France* 25 C8
Airão, *Brazil* 121 D5
Airdrie, *U.K.* 14 F5
Aire →, *France* 25 C11
Aire →, *U.K.* 12 D7
Aire, I. del, *Spain* 36 B11
Aire-sur-la-Lys, *France* 25 B9
Aire-sur-l'Adour, *France* 26 E3
Airlie Beach, *Australia* 90 C4
Airolo, *Switz.* 23 C7
Airvault, *France* 24 F6
Aisch →, *Germany* 19 F7
Aisen □, *Chile* 128 C2
Aisne □, *France* 25 C10
Aisne →, *France* 25 C9
Aitana, Sierra de, *Spain* 29 G4
Aitkin, *U.S.A.* 108 B8
Aitolikón, *Greece* 39 L4
Aiuaba, *Brazil* 122 C3
Aiud, *Romania* 38 C6
Aix-en-Provence, *France* 27 E9
Aix-la-Chapelle = Aachen, *Germany* 18 E2
Aix-les-Bains, *France* 27 C9
Aixe-sur-Vienne, *France* 26 C5
Aiyansh, *Canada* 100 B3
Áíyina, *Greece* 39 M6
Aiyínion, *Greece* 39 J5
Aiyion, *Greece* 39 L5
Aizawl, *India* 61 H18
Aizenay, *France* 24 F5
Aizkraukle, *Latvia* 9 H21
Aizpute, *Latvia* 9 H19
Aizuwakamatsu, *Japan* 48 F9
Ajaccio, *France* 27 G12
Ajaccio, G. d', *France* 27 G12
Ajaju →, *Colombia* 120 C3
Ajalpan, *Mexico* 115 D5
Ajanta Ra., *India* 60 J9
Ajari Rep. = Ajaria □, *Georgia* 43 K6
Ajaria □, *Georgia* 43 K6
Ajax, *Canada* 106 C5
Ajdâbiyah, *Libya* 73 B9
Ajdovščina, *Slovenia* 33 C10
Ajibar, *Ethiopia* 77 E4
Ajka, *Hungary* 21 H7
'Ajmān, *U.A.E.* 65 E7
Ajmer, *India* 62 F6
Ajo, *U.S.A.* 111 K7
Ajoie, *Switz.* 22 B4
Ajok, *Sudan* 77 F2
Ajuy, *Phil.* 55 F5
Ak Dağ, *Turkey* 66 D3
Ak Dağlar, *Turkey* 66 C7
Akaba, *Togo* 79 D5
Akabira, *Japan* 48 C11
Akabli, *Algeria* 75 C5
Akaki Beseka, *Ethiopia* 77 F4
Akala, *Sudan* 77 D4
Akamas □, *Cyprus* 37 D11
Akanthou, *Cyprus* 37 D12
Akaroa, *N.Z.* 87 K4
Akasha, *Sudan* 76 C3
Akashi, *Japan* 49 G7
Akbou, *Algeria* 75 A5
Akçaabat, *Turkey* 67 B8
Akçadağ, *Turkey* 66 C7
Akçakale, *Turkey* 67 D8
Akçakoca, *Turkey* 66 B4
Akchâr, *Mauritania* 74 D2
Akdağmadeni, *Turkey* 66 C6
Akelamo, *Indonesia* 57 D7
Akershus fylke □, *Norway* 10 E5
Aketi, *Zaïre* 80 D4
Akhalkalaki, *Georgia* 43 K6
Akhaltsikhe, *Georgia* 43 K6
Akharnaí, *Greece* 39 L6
Akhelóös →, *Greece* 39 L4
Akhendria, *Greece* 39 Q8
Akhéron →, *Greece* 39 K3
Akhisar, *Turkey* 66 C2
Akhladhókambos, *Greece* 39 M5
Akhmîm, *Egypt* 76 B3
Akhnur, *India* 63 C6
Akhtuba →, *Russia* 43 G8
Akhtubinsk, *Russia* 43 F8
Akhty, *Russia* 43 K8
Akhtyrka = Okhtyrka, *Ukraine* 41 G8
Aki, *Japan* 49 H6
Akimiski I., *Canada* 98 B3
Akimovka, *Ukraine* 41 J8
Akita, *Japan* 48 E10
Akita □, *Japan* 48 E10
Akjoujt, *Mauritania* 78 B2
Akka, *Morocco* 74 C3
Akkeshi, *Japan* 48 C12
'Akko, *Israel* 69 C4
Akkol, *Kazakstan* 44 E8
Akkrum, *Neths.* 16 B7
Aklampa, *Benin* 79 D5
Aklavik, *Canada* 96 B6
Akmolinsk = Aqmola, *Kazakstan* 44 D8
Akmonte, *Spain* 31 H4
Aknoul, *Morocco* 75 B4
Akō, *Japan* 49 G7
Ako, *Nigeria* 79 C7
Akobo →, *Ethiopia* 77 F3
Akola, *India* 60 J10
Akonolinga, *Cameroon* 79 E7
Akordat, *Eritrea* 77 D4
Akosombo Dam, *Ghana* 79 D5
Akot, *Sudan* 77 F3
Akpatok I., *Canada* 97 B13
Åkrahamn, *Norway* 9 G11
Akranes, *Iceland* 8 D2
Akreïjit, *Mauritania* 78 B3
Akrítas Venétiko, Ákra, *Greece* 39 N4
Akron, *Colo., U.S.A.* 108 E3
Akron, *Ohio, U.S.A.* 106 E3
Akrotiri, *Cyprus* 66 E5
Akrotíri, Ákra, *Greece* 39 J8
Akrotiri Bay, *Cyprus* 37 E12
Aksai Chin, *India* 63 B8
Aksaray, *Turkey* 66 C6
Aksarka, *Russia* 44 C7
Aksay, *Kazakstan* 44 D6
Akşehir, *Turkey* 66 C4
Akşehir Gölü, *Turkey* 66 C4
Aksenovo Zilovskoye, *Russia* 45 D12
Akstafa = Ağstafa, *Azerbaijan* 43 K7
Aksu, *China* 54 B3
Aksu →, *Turkey* 66 D4
Aksum, *Ethiopia* 77 E4
Aktash, *Russia* 42 C11
Aktogay, *Kazakstan* 44 E8
Aktsyabrski, *Belarus* 41 F5
Aktyubinsk = Aqtöbe, *Kazakstan* 44 D6
Aku, *Nigeria* 79 D6
Akure, *Nigeria* 79 D6
Akureyri, *Iceland* 8 D4
Akuseki-Shima, *Japan* 49 K4
Akusha, *Russia* 43 J8
Akwa-Ibom □, *Nigeria* 79 E6
Akyab = Sittwe, *Burma* 61 J18
Akyazı, *Turkey* 66 B4
Al 'Adan, *Yemen* 68 E4
Al Aḩsā, *Si. Arabia* 65 E6
Al Ajfar, *Si. Arabia* 64 E4
Al Amādīyah, *Iraq* 67 D10
Al Amārah, *Iraq* 67 G12
Al 'Aqabah, *Jordan* 69 F4
Al Arak, *Syria* 67 E8
Al 'Aramah, *Si. Arabia* 64 E5
Al Arṭāwīyah, *Si. Arabia* 64 E5
Al 'Āṣimah □, *Jordan* 69 D5
Al' Assāfīyah, *Si. Arabia* 64 D3
Al 'Ayn, *Oman* 65 E7
Al 'Ayn, *Si. Arabia* 64 E3
Al A'ẓamīyah, *Iraq* 64 C5
Al 'Azīzīyah, *Iraq* 67 F11
Al 'Azīzīyah, *Libya* 75 B7
Al Bāb, *Syria* 66 D7
Al Bad', *Si. Arabia* 64 D2
Al Bādī, *Iraq* 64 C4
Al Baḩrah, *Kuwait* 64 D5
Al Balqā' □, *Jordan* 69 C4
Al Barkāt, *Libya* 75 D7
Al Bārūk, J., *Lebanon* 69 B4
Al Baṣrah, *Iraq* 64 D5
Al Baṭḩā, *Iraq* 64 D5
Al Batrūn, *Lebanon* 69 A4
Al Bayḍā, *Libya* 73 B9
Al Biqā □, *Lebanon* 69 A5
Al Bi'r, *Si. Arabia* 64 D3
Al Bu'ayrāt al Ḩasūn, *Libya* 73 B8
Al Burayj, *Syria* 69 A5
Al Fallūjah, *Iraq* 67 F10
Al Fāw, *Iraq* 65 D6
Al Fujayrah, *U.A.E.* 65 E8
Al Ghadaf, W. →, *Jordan* 69 D5
Al Ghammās, *Iraq* 64 D5
Al Hābah, *Si. Arabia* 64 E5
Al Ḩadīthah, *Iraq* 67 E10
Al Ḩadīthah, *Si. Arabia* 64 D3
Al Ḩaḍr, *Iraq* 67 E10
Al Hājānah, *Syria* 69 B5
Al Ḩāmad, *Si. Arabia* 64 D3
Al Hamdānīyah, *Syria* 64 C3
Al Ḩamīdīyah, *Syria* 69 A4
Al Ḩammādah al Ḩamrā', *Libya* 75 C7
Al Ḩammār, *Iraq* 64 D5
Al Ḩarīr, W. →, *Syria* 69 C4
Al Ḩasā, W. →, *Jordan* 69 D4
Al Ḩasakah, *Syria* 67 D9
Al Ḩawrah, *Yemen* 68 E4
Al Ḩaydān, W. →, *Jordan* 69 D4
Al Ḩayy, *Iraq* 67 F12
Al Ḩijāz, *Si. Arabia* 68 B2
Al Ḩillah, *Iraq* 67 F11
Al Ḩillah, *Si. Arabia* 68 C4
Al Hindīyah, *Iraq* 67 F11
Al Hirmil, *Lebanon* 69 A5
Al Hoceïma, *Morocco* 74 A4
Al Ḩudaydah, *Yemen* 68 E3
Al Hufūf, *Si. Arabia* 65 E6
Al Ḩumaydah, *Si. Arabia* 64 D2
Al Ḩunayy, *Si. Arabia* 65 E6
Al Īsāwīyah, *Si. Arabia* 64 D3
Al Ittihad = Madīnat ash Sha'b, *Yemen* 68 E3
Al Jafr, *Jordan* 69 E5
Al Jaghbūb, *Libya* 73 C9
Al Jahrah, *Kuwait* 64 D5
Al Jalāmīd, *Si. Arabia* 64 D3
Al Jamalīyah, *Qatar* 65 E6
Al Janūb □, *Lebanon* 69 B4
Al Jawf, *Libya* 73 D9
Al Jawf, *Si. Arabia* 64 D3
Al Jazirah, *Iraq* 67 E10
Al Jazirah, *Libya* 73 C9
Al Jithāmīyah, *Si. Arabia* 64 E4
Al Jubayl, *Si. Arabia* 65 E6
Al Jubaylah, *Si. Arabia* 64 E5
Al Jubb, *Si. Arabia* 64 E4
Al Junaynah, *Sudan* 73 F9
Al Kabā'ish, *Iraq* 64 D5
Al Karak, *Jordan* 69 D4
Al Karak □, *Jordan* 69 E5
Al Kāzim Tyah, *Iraq* 67 F11
Al Khalīl, *West Bank* 69 D4
Al Khāliş, *Iraq* 67 F11
Al Khawr, *Qatar* 65 E6
Al Khiḍr, *Iraq* 64 D5
Al Khiyām, *Lebanon* 69 B4
Al Kiswah, *Syria* 69 B5
Al Kūfah, *Iraq* 67 F11
Al Kufrah, *Libya* 73 D9
Al Kuhayfīyah, *Si. Arabia* 64 E4
Al Kūt, *Iraq* 67 F11
Al Kuwayt, *Kuwait* 64 D5
Al Labwah, *Lebanon* 69 A5
Al Lādhiqīyah, *Syria* 66 E6
Al Līth, *Si. Arabia* 76 C5
Al Liwā', *Oman* 65 E8
Al Luḩayyah, *Yemen* 68 D3
Al Madīnah, *Iraq* 64 D5
Al Madīnah, *Si. Arabia* 64 E3
Al-Mafraq, *Jordan* 69 C5
Al Maḩmūdīyah, *Iraq* 67 F11
Al Majma'ah, *Si. Arabia* 64 E5
Al Makhruq, W. →, *Jordan* 69 D6
Al Makḩūl, *Si. Arabia* 64 E4
Al Manāmah, *Bahrain* 65 E6
Al Maqwa', *Kuwait* 64 D5
Al Marj, *Libya* 73 B9
Al Maṭlā, *Kuwait* 64 D5
Al Mawjib, W. →, *Jordan* 69 D4
Al Mawşil, *Iraq* 67 D10
Al Mayādin, *Syria* 67 E9
Al Mazār, *Jordan* 69 D4
Al Midhnab, *Si. Arabia* 64 E5
Al Mīnā', *Lebanon* 69 A4
Al Miqdādīyah, *Iraq* 67 E11
Al Mubarraz, *Si. Arabia* 65 E6
Al Mughayrā', *U.A.E.* 65 E7
Al Muḩarraq, *Bahrain* 65 E6
Al Mukallā, *Yemen* 68 E4
Al Mukhā, *Yemen* 68 E3
Al Musayjīd, *Si. Arabia* 64 E3
Al Musayyib, *Iraq* 67 F11
Al Muwayliḩ, *Si. Arabia* 64 E2
Al Owuho = Otukpa, *Nigeria* 79 D6
Al Qā'im, *Iraq* 67 E9
Al Qalībah, *Si. Arabia* 64 D3
Al Qāmishlī, *Syria* 67 D9
Al Qaryatayn, *Syria* 69 A6
Al Qaşabát, *Libya* 73 B7
Al Qaţ'ā, *Syria* 67 E9
Al Qaţīf, *Si. Arabia* 65 E6
Al Qatrānah, *Jordan* 69 D5
Al Qaţrūn, *Libya* 73 D8
Al Qayşūmah, *Si. Arabia* 64 D5
Al Quds = Jerusalem, *Israel* 69 D4
Al Qunaytirah, *Syria* 69 C4
Al Qunfudhah, *Si. Arabia* 76 D5
Al Qurnah, *Iraq* 64 D5
Al Quşayr, *Iraq* 64 D5
Al Quşayr, *Syria* 69 A5
Al Qutayfah, *Syria* 69 B5
Al' Uḍaylīyah, *Si. Arabia* 65 E6
Al 'Ulā, *Si. Arabia* 64 E3
Al Uqaylah ash Sharqīgah, *Libya* 73 B8
Al Uqayr, *Si. Arabia* 65 E6
Al 'Uwaynid, *Si. Arabia* 64 E5
Al 'Uwayqīlah, *Si. Arabia* 64 D4
Al 'Uyūn, *Si. Arabia* 64 E4
Al 'Uyūn, *Si. Arabia* 64 E3
Al Wajh, *Si. Arabia* 64 E3
Al Wakrah, *Qatar* 65 E6
Al Wannān, *Si. Arabia* 65 E6
Al Waqbah, *Si. Arabia* 64 D5
Al Wari'āh, *Si. Arabia* 64 E5
Al Wātīyah, *Libya* 75 B7
Al Wusayl, *Qatar* 65 E6
Ala, *Italy* 32 C8
Ala Dağları, *Turkey* 67 C10
Alabama □, *U.S.A.* 105 J2
Alabama →, *U.S.A.* 105 K2
Alaca, *Turkey* 66 B6
Alaçam, *Turkey* 66 B6
Alaçam Dağları, *Turkey* 66 C3
Alaejos, *Spain* 30 D5
Alaérma, *Greece* 37 C9
Alagir, *Russia* 43 J7
Alagna Valsésia, *Italy* 32 C4
Alagoa Grande, *Brazil* 122 C4
Alagoas □, *Brazil* 122 C4
Alagoinhas, *Brazil* 123 D4
Alagón, *Spain* 28 D3
Alagón →, *Spain* 31 F4
Alajero, *Canary Is.* 36 F2
Alajuela, *Costa Rica* 116 D3
Alakamisy, *Madag.* 85 C8
Alalapura, *Surinam* 121 C6
Alalaú →, *Brazil* 121 D5
Alameda, *Spain* 31 H6
Alameda, *Calif., U.S.A.* 112 H4
Alameda, *N. Mex., U.S.A.* 111 J10
Alaminos, *Phil.* 55 C3
Alamo, *U.S.A.* 113 J11
Alamo Crossing, *U.S.A.* 113 L13
Alamogordo, *U.S.A.* 111 K11
Alamos, *Mexico* 114 B3
Alamosa, *U.S.A.* 111 H11
Åland, *Finland* 9 F19
Alandroal, *Portugal* 31 G3
Ålands hav, *Sweden* 9 F18
Alandur, *India* 60 N12
Alange, Presa de, *Spain* 31 G4
Alania = North Ossetia □, *Russia* 43 J7
Alanis, *Spain* 31 G5
Alanya, *Turkey* 66 D5
Alaotra, Farihin', *Madag.* 85 B8
Alapayevsk, *Russia* 44 D7
Alar del Rey, *Spain* 30 C6
Alaraz, *Spain* 30 E5
Alaşehir, *Turkey* 66 C3
Alaska □, *U.S.A.* 96 B5
Alaska, G. of, *Pac. Oc.* 96 C5
Alaska Highway, *Canada* 100 B3
Alaska Peninsula, *U.S.A.* 96 C4
Alaska Range, *U.S.A.* 96 B4
Alássio, *Italy* 32 D5
Älät, *Azerbaijan* 43 L9
Alataw Shankou, *China* 54 B3
Alatri, *Italy* 34 A6
Alatyr, *Russia* 42 C8
Alatyr →, *Russia* 42 C8
Alausi, *Ecuador* 120 D2
Álava □, *Spain* 28 C2
Alava, C., *U.S.A.* 110 B1
Alaverdi, *Armenia* 43 K7
Alavus, *Finland* 9 E20
Alawoona, *Australia* 91 E3
'Alayh, *Lebanon* 69 B4
Alayor, *Spain* 36 B11
Alazani →, *Azerbaijan* 43 K8
Alba, *Italy* 32 D5
Alba de Tormes, *Spain* 30 E5
Alba-Iulia, *Romania* 38 C6
Albac, *Romania* 38 C6
Albacete, *Spain* 29 G3
Albacete □, *Spain* 29 G3
Albacutya, L., *Australia* 91 F3
Ålbæk, *Denmark* 11 G4
Ålbæk Bugt, *Denmark* 11 G4
Albaida, *Spain* 29 G4
Albalate de las Nogueras, *Spain* 28 E2
Albalate del Arzobispo, *Spain* 28 D4
Albania ■, *Europe* 39 J3
Albano Laziale, *Italy* 34 A5
Albany, *Australia* 89 G2
Albany, *Ga., U.S.A.* 105 K3
Albany, *Minn., U.S.A.* 108 C7
Albany, *N.Y., U.S.A.* 107 D11
Albany, *Oreg., U.S.A.* 110 D2
Albany, *Tex., U.S.A.* 109 J5
Albany →, *Canada* 98 B3
Albardón, *Argentina* 126 C2
Albarracín, *Spain* 28 E3
Albarracín, Sierra de, *Spain* 28 E3
Albatross B., *Australia* 90 A3
Albegna →, *Italy* 33 F8
Albemarle, *U.S.A.* 105 H5
Albemarle Sd., *U.S.A.* 105 H7
Albenga, *Italy* 32 D5
Alberche →, *Spain* 30 F6
Alberdi, *Paraguay* 126 B4
Alberes, Mts., *Spain* 28 C7
Alberique, *Spain* 29 F4
Albersdorf, *Germany* 18 A5
Albert, *France* 25 B9
Albert, L., *Australia* 91 F2
Albert Canyon, *Canada* 100 C5
Albert Edward Ra., *Australia* 88 C4
Albert L., *Africa* 82 B3
Albert Lea, *U.S.A.* 108 D8
Albert Nile →, *Uganda* 82 B3
Albert Town, *Bahamas* 117 B5
Alberta □, *Canada* 100 C6
Alberti, *Argentina* 126 D3
Albertinia, *S. Africa* 84 E3
Albertkanaal →, *Belgium* 17 F4
Alberton, *Canada* 99 C7
Albertville = Kalemie, *Zaïre* 82 D2
Albertville, *France* 27 C10
Albi, *France* 26 E6
Albia, *U.S.A.* 108 E8
Albina, *Surinam* 121 B7
Albina, Ponta, *Angola* 84 B1
Albino, *Italy* 32 C6
Albion, *Idaho, U.S.A.* 110 E7
Albion, *Mich., U.S.A.* 104 D3
Albion, *Nebr., U.S.A.* 108 E5
Albion, *Pa., U.S.A.* 106 E4
Alblasserdam, *Neths.* 16 E5
Albocácer, *Spain* 28 E5
Alborán, *Medit. S.* 31 K7
Alborea, *Spain* 29 F3
Ålborg, *Denmark* 11 G3
Ålborg Bugt, *Denmark* 11 H4
Alborz, Reshteh-ye Kūhhā-ye, *Iran* 65 C7
Albox, *Spain* 29 H2
Albreda, *Canada* 100 C5
Albufeira, *Portugal* 31 H2
Albula →, *Switz.* 23 C8
Albuñol, *Spain* 29 J1
Albuquerque, *Brazil* 125 D6
Albuquerque, *U.S.A.* 111 J10
Albuquerque, Cayos de, *Caribbean* 116 D3
Alburg, *U.S.A.* 107 B11
Alburno, Mte., *Italy* 35 B8
Alburquerque, *Spain* 31 F4
Albury, *Australia* 91 F4
Alby, *Sweden* 10 B9
Alcácer do Sal, *Portugal* 31 G2
Alcaçovas, *Portugal* 31 G2
Alcalá de Chisvert, *Spain* 28 E5
Alcalá de Guadaira, *Spain* 31 H5
Alcalá de Henares, *Spain* 28 E1
Alcalá de los Gazules, *Spain* 31 J5
Alcalá la Real, *Spain* 31 H7
Alcamo, *Italy* 34 E5
Alcanadre, *Spain* 28 C2
Alcanadre →, *Spain* 28 D4
Alcanar, *Spain* 28 E5
Alcanede, *Portugal* 31 F2
Alcanena, *Portugal* 31 F2
Alcañices, *Spain* 30 D4
Alcaníz, *Spain* 28 D4
Alcântara, *Brazil* 122 B3
Alcántara, *Spain* 31 F4
Alcantara L., *Canada* 101 A7
Alcantarilla, *Spain* 29 H3
Alcaracejos, *Spain* 31 G6
Alcaraz, *Spain* 29 G2
Alcaraz, Sierra de, *Spain* 29 G2
Alcaudete, *Spain* 31 H6
Alcázar de San Juan, *Spain* 29 F1
Alchevsk, *Ukraine* 41 H10
Alcira, *Spain* 29 F4
Alcoa, *U.S.A.* 105 H4
Alcobaça, *Portugal* 31 F2
Alcobendas, *Spain* 28 E1
Alcolea del Pinar, *Spain* 28 D2
Alcora, *Spain* 28 E4
Alcorcón, *Spain* 30 E7
Alcoutim, *Portugal* 31 H3
Alcova, *U.S.A.* 110 E10
Alcoy, *Spain* 29 G4
Alcubierre, Sierra de, *Spain* 28 D4
Alcublas, *Spain* 28 F4
Alcudia, *Spain* 36 B10
Alcudia, B. de, *Spain* 36 B10
Alcudia, Sierra de la, *Spain* 31 G6
Aldabra Is., *Seychelles* 70 G8
Aldama, *Mexico* 115 C5
Aldan, *Russia* 45 D13
Aldan →, *Russia* 45 C13
Aldea, Pta. de la, *Canary Is.* 36 G4
Aldeburgh, *U.K.* 13 E9
Aldeia Nova, *Portugal* 31 H3
Alder, *U.S.A.* 110 D7
Alder Pk., *U.S.A.* 112 K5
Alderney, *U.K.* 13 H5
Aldershot, *U.K.* 13 F7
Aledo, *U.S.A.* 108 E9
Alefa, *Ethiopia* 77 E4
Aleg, *Mauritania* 78 B2
Alegranza, *Canary Is.* 36 E6
Alegranza, I., *Canary Is.* 36 E6
Alegre, *Brazil* 123 F3
Alegrete, *Brazil* 127 B4
Aleisk, *Russia* 44 D9
Aleksandriya = Oleksandriya, *Ukraine* 41 H7
Aleksandriya = Oleksandriya, *Ukraine* 41 G4
Aleksandriyskaya, *Russia* 43 J8
Aleksandrov, *Russia* 42 B4
Aleksandrov Gay, *Russia* 42 E9
Aleksandrovac, *Serbia, Yug.* 21 L11
Aleksandrovka = Oleksandrovka, *Ukraine* 41 H7
Aleksandrovo, *Bulgaria* 38 F7
Aleksandrovsk-Sakhalinskiy, *Russia* 45 D15
Aleksandrovskiy Zavod, *Russia* 45 D12
Aleksandrovskoye, *Russia* 44 C8

Aleksandrów Kujawski, *Poland* 20 C8
Aleksandrów Łódźki, *Poland* 20 D9
Alekseyevka, *Russia* 42 D10
Alekseyevka, *Russia* 42 E4
Aleksin, *Russia* 42 C3
Aleksinac, *Serbia, Yug.* 21 M11
Além Paraíba, *Brazil* 123 F3
Alemania, *Argentina* 126 B2
Alemania, *Chile* 126 B2
Ålen, *Norway* 10 B5
Alençon, *France* 24 D7
Alenuihaha Channel, *U.S.A.* 102 H17
Aleppo = Ḥalab, *Syria* 66 D7
Aléria, *France* 27 F13
Alert Bay, *Canada* 100 C3
Alès, *France* 27 D8
Aleşd, *Romania* 38 B5
Alessándria, *Italy* 32 D5
Ålestrup, *Denmark* 11 H3
Ålesund, *Norway* 9 E12
Alet-les-Bains, *France* 26 F6
Aletschhorn, *Switz.* 22 D6
Aleutian Is., *Pac. Oc.* 96 C2
Aleutian Trench, *Pac. Oc.* 92 B10
Alexander, *U.S.A.* 108 B3
Alexander, Mt., *Australia* 89 E3
Alexander Arch., *U.S.A.* 100 B2
Alexander Bay, *S. Africa* 84 D2
Alexander City, *U.S.A.* 105 J3
Alexander I., *Antarctica* 5 C17
Alexandra, *Australia* 91 F4
Alexandra, *N.Z.* 87 L2
Alexandra Falls, *Canada* 100 A5
Alexandria = El Iskandarîya, *Egypt* 76 H6
Alexandria, *Australia* 90 B2
Alexandria, *B.C., Canada* 100 C4
Alexandria, *Ont., Canada* 98 C5
Alexandria, *Romania* 38 F8
Alexandria, *S. Africa* 84 E4
Alexandria, *Ind., U.S.A.* 104 E3
Alexandria, *La., U.S.A.* 109 K8
Alexandria, *Minn., U.S.A.* 108 C7
Alexandria, *S. Dak., U.S.A.* 108 D6
Alexandria, *Va., U.S.A.* 104 F7
Alexandria Bay, *U.S.A.* 107 B9
Alexandrina, L., *Australia* 91 F2
Alexandroúpolis, *Greece* 39 J8
Alexis →, *Canada* 99 B8
Alexis Creek, *Canada* 100 C4
Alfabia, *Spain* 36 B9
Alfambra, *Spain* 28 E3
Alfândega da Fé, *Portugal* 30 D4
Alfaro, *Spain* 28 C3
Alfeld, *Germany* 18 D5
Alfenas, *Brazil* 127 A6
Alfiós →, *Greece* 39 M4
Alfonsine, *Italy* 33 D9
Alford, *U.K.* 14 D6
Alfred, *Maine, U.S.A.* 107 C14
Alfred, *N.Y., U.S.A.* 106 D7
Alfreton, *U.K.* 12 D6
Alga, *Kazakstan* 44 E6
Algaida, *Spain* 36 B9
Algar, *Spain* 31 J5
Algård, *Norway* 9 G11
Algarinejo, *Spain* 31 H6
Algarve, *Portugal* 31 J2
Algeciras, *Spain* 31 J5
Algemesí, *Spain* 29 F4
Alger, *Algeria* 75 A5
Algeria ■, *Africa* 75 C5
Alghero, *Italy* 34 B1
Algiers = Alger, *Algeria* 75 A5
Algoa B., *S. Africa* 84 E4
Algodonales, *Spain* 31 J5
Algodor →, *Spain* 30 F7
Algoma, *U.S.A.* 104 C2
Algona, *U.S.A.* 108 D7
Algonac, *U.S.A.* 106 D2
Alhama de Almería, *Spain* 29 J2
Alhama de Aragón, *Spain* 28 D3
Alhama de Granada, *Spain* 31 J7
Alhama de Murcia, *Spain* 29 H3
Alhambra, *Spain* 29 G1
Alhambra, *U.S.A.* 102 D3
Alhaurín el Grande, *Spain* 31 J6
Alhucemas = Al Hoceïma, *Morocco* 74 A4
'Alī al Gharbī, *Iraq* 67 F12
Alī ash Sharqī, *Iraq* 67 F12
Äli Bayramlı, *Azerbaijan* 43 L9
'Alī Khēl, *Afghan.* 62 C3
Ali Sahīh, *Djibouti* 77 E5
Alī Shāh, *Iran* 64 B5
Ália, *Italy* 34 E6
'Alīābād, *Khorāsān, Iran* 65 C8
'Alīābād, *Kordestān, Iran* 65 C5
'Alīābād, *Yazd, Iran* 65 D7
Aliaga, *Spain* 28 E4
Aliağa, *Turkey* 66 C2
Aliákmon →, *Greece* 39 J5
Alibo, *Ethiopia* 77 F4
Alibunar, *Serbia, Yug.* 21 K10
Alicante, *Spain* 29 G4
Alicante □, *Spain* 29 G4
Alice, *S. Africa* 84 E4
Alice, *U.S.A.* 109 M5
Alice →, *Queens., Australia* 90 C3
Alice →, *Queens., Australia* 90 B3
Alice, Punta dell', *Italy* 35 C10
Alice Arm, *Canada* 100 B3
Alice Downs, *Australia* 88 C4
Alice Springs, *Australia* 90 C1
Alicedale, *S. Africa* 84 E4
Aliceville, *U.S.A.* 105 J1
Alick Cr. →, *Australia* 90 C3
Alicudi, I., *Italy* 35 D7
Alida, *Canada* 101 D8
Aligarh, *Raj., India* 62 G7
Aligarh, *Ut. P., India* 62 F8
Alīgūdarz, *Iran* 65 C6
Alijó, *Portugal* 30 D3
Alimena, *Italy* 35 E7
Alimnía, *Greece* 37 C9
Alingsås, *Sweden* 11 G6
Alipur, *Pakistan* 62 E4
Alipur Duar, *India* 61 F16
Aliquippa, *U.S.A.* 106 F4
Aliste →, *Spain* 30 D5
Alitus = Alytus, *Lithuania* 9 J21
Alivérion, *Greece* 39 L7
Aliwal North, *S. Africa* 84 E4
Alix, *Canada* 100 C6
Aljezur, *Portugal* 31 H2
Aljustrel, *Portugal* 31 H2
Alkamari, *Niger* 79 C7
Alken, *Belgium* 17 G6
Alkmaar, *Neths.* 16 C5
All American Canal, *U.S.A.* 111 K6
Allada, *Benin* 79 D5
Allah Dad, *Pakistan* 62 G2
Allahabad, *India* 63 G9
Allakh-Yun, *Russia* 45 C14
Allal Tazi, *Morocco* 74 B3
Allan, *Canada* 101 C7
Allanche, *France* 26 C6
Allanmyo, *Burma* 61 K19
Allanridge, *S. Africa* 84 D4
Allanwater, *Canada* 98 B1
Allaqi, Wadi →, *Egypt* 76 C3
Allariz, *Spain* 30 C3
Allassac, *France* 26 C5
Alle, *Belgium* 17 J5
Allegan, *U.S.A.* 104 D3
Allegany, *U.S.A.* 106 D6
Allegheny →, *U.S.A.* 106 F5
Allegheny Mts., *U.S.A.* 94 F11
Allegheny Plateau, *U.S.A.* 104 G6
Allegheny Reservoir, *U.S.A.* 106 E6
Allègre, *France* 26 C7
Allen, *Argentina* 128 A3
Allen, Bog of, *Ireland* 15 C4
Allen, L., *Ireland* 15 B3
Allende, *Mexico* 114 B4
Allentown, *U.S.A.* 107 F9
Alleppey, *India* 60 Q10
Aller →, *Germany* 18 C5
Alleur, *Belgium* 17 G7
Allevard, *France* 27 C10
Alliance, *Surinam* 121 B7
Alliance, *Nebr., U.S.A.* 108 D3
Alliance, *Ohio, U.S.A.* 106 F3
Allier □, *France* 26 B6
Allier →, *France* 25 F10
Allingåbro, *Denmark* 11 H4
Alliston, *Canada* 98 D4
Alloa, *U.K.* 14 E5
Allora, *Australia* 91 D5
Allos, *France* 27 D10
Alluitsup Paa = Sydprøven, *Greenland* 4 C5
Alma, *Canada* 99 C5
Alma, *Ga., U.S.A.* 105 K4
Alma, *Kans., U.S.A.* 108 F6
Alma, *Mich., U.S.A.* 104 D3
Alma, *Nebr., U.S.A.* 108 E5
Alma, *Wis., U.S.A.* 108 C9
Alma Ata = Almaty, *Kazakstan* 44 E8
Almada, *Portugal* 31 G1
Almaden, *Australia* 90 B3
Almadén, *Spain* 31 G6
Almagro, *Spain* 31 G7
Almanor, L., *U.S.A.* 110 F3
Almansa, *Spain* 29 G3
Almanza, *Spain* 30 C5
Almanzor, Pico del Moro, *Spain* 30 E5
Almanzora →, *Spain* 29 H3
Almas, *Brazil* 123 D2
Almaty, *Kazakstan* 44 E8
Almazán, *Spain* 28 D2
Almazora, *Spain* 28 F4
Almeirim, *Brazil* 121 D7
Almeirim, *Portugal* 31 F2
Almelo, *Neths.* 16 D9
Almenar, *Spain* 28 D2
Almenara, *Brazil* 123 E3
Almenara, *Spain* 28 F4
Almenara, Sierra de, *Spain* 29 H3
Almendralejo, *Spain* 31 G4
Almería, *Spain* 29 J2
Almería □, *Spain* 29 H2
Almería, G. de, *Spain* 29 J2
Almetyevsk, *Russia* 42 C11
Almirante, *Panama* 116 E3
Almirante Montt, G., *Chile* 128 D2
Almirós, *Greece* 39 K5
Almiroú, Kólpos, *Greece* 37 D6
Almodôvar, *Portugal* 31 H2
Almodóvar del Campo, *Spain* 31 G6
Almogia, *Spain* 31 J6
Almonaster la Real, *Spain* 31 H4
Almont, *U.S.A.* 106 D1
Almonte, *Canada* 107 A8
Almonte →, *Spain* 31 F4
Almora, *India* 63 E8
Almoradi, *Spain* 29 G4
Almorox, *Spain* 30 E6
Almoustarat, *Mali* 79 B5
Almuñécar, *Spain* 31 J7
Alnif, *Morocco* 74 B3
Alnwick, *U.K.* 12 B6
Aloi, *Uganda* 82 B3
Alon, *Burma* 61 H19
Alor, *Indonesia* 57 F6
Alor Setar, *Malaysia* 59 J3
Alora, *Spain* 31 J6
Alosno, *Spain* 31 H3
Alougoum, *Morocco* 74 B3
Aloysius, Mt., *Australia* 89 E4
Alpaugh, *U.S.A.* 112 K7
Alpedrinha, *Portugal* 30 E3
Alpena, *U.S.A.* 104 C4
Alpercatas →, *Brazil* 122 C3
Alpes-de-Haute-Provence □, *France* 27 D10
Alpes-Maritimes □, *France* 27 E11
Alpha, *Australia* 90 C4
Alphen, *Neths.* 17 F5
Alphen aan den Rijn, *Neths.* 16 D5
Alpiarça, *Portugal* 31 F2
Alpine, *Ariz., U.S.A.* 111 K9
Alpine, *Calif., U.S.A.* 113 N10
Alpine, *Tex., U.S.A.* 109 K3
Alpnach, *Switz.* 23 C6
Alps, *Europe* 6 F7
Alpu, *Turkey* 66 C4
Alrø, *Denmark* 11 J4
Alroy Downs, *Australia* 90 B2
Alsace, *France* 25 D14
Alsask, *Canada* 101 C7
Alsásua, *Spain* 28 C2
Alsdorf, *Germany* 18 E2
Alsen, *Sweden* 10 A7
Alsfeld, *Germany* 18 E5
Alsten, *Norway* 8 D15
Alta, *Norway* 8 B20
Alta, Sierra, *Spain* 28 E3
Alta Gracia, *Argentina* 126 C3
Alta Lake, *Canada* 100 C4
Alta Sierra, *U.S.A.* 113 K8
Altaelva →, *Norway* 8 B20
Altafjorden, *Norway* 8 A20
Altagracia, *Venezuela* 120 A3
Altagracia de Orituco, *Venezuela* 120 B4
Altai = Aerhtai Shan, *Mongolia* 54 B4
Altamachi →, *Bolivia* 124 D4
Altamaha →, *U.S.A.* 105 K5
Altamira, *Brazil* 121 D7
Altamira, *Chile* 126 B2
Altamira, *Colombia* 120 C2
Altamira, *Mexico* 115 C5
Altamira, Cuevas de, *Spain* 30 B6
Altamont, *U.S.A.* 107 D10
Altamura, *Italy* 35 B9
Altanbulag, *Mongolia* 54 A5
Altar, *Mexico* 114 A2
Altata, *Mexico* 114 C3
Altavista, *U.S.A.* 104 G6
Altay, *China* 54 B3
Altdorf, *Switz.* 23 C7
Alte Mellum, *Germany* 18 B4
Altea, *Spain* 29 G4
Altenberg, *Germany* 18 E9
Altenbruch, *Germany* 18 B4
Altenburg, *Germany* 18 E8
Altenkirchen, *Mecklenburg-Vorpommern, Germany* 18 A9
Altenkirchen, *Rhld-Pfz., Germany* 18 E3
Altentreptow, *Germany* 18 B9
Alter do Chão, *Portugal* 31 F3
Altıntas, *Turkey* 66 C4
Altiplano, *Bolivia* 124 D4
Altkirch, *France* 25 E14
Altmühl →, *Germany* 19 G7
Alto Adige = Trentino-Alto Adige □, *Italy* 32 B8
Alto Araguaia, *Brazil* 125 D7
Alto Cuchumatanes = Cuchumatanes, Sierra de los, *Guatemala* 116 C1
Alto del Inca, *Chile* 126 A2
Alto Garças, *Brazil* 125 D7
Alto Iriri →, *Brazil* 125 B7
Alto Ligonha, *Mozam.* 83 F4
Alto Molocue, *Mozam.* 83 F4
Alto Paraguai, *Brazil* 125 C6
Alto Paraguay □, *Paraguay* 126 A4
Alto Paraná □, *Paraguay* 127 B5
Alto Parnaíba, *Brazil* 122 C2
Alto Purús →, *Peru* 124 B3
Alto Río Senguerr, *Argentina* 128 C2
Alto Santo, *Brazil* 122 C4
Alto Sucuriú, *Brazil* 125 D7
Alto Turi, *Brazil* 122 B2
Alton, *Canada* 106 C4
Alton, *U.S.A.* 108 F9
Alton Downs, *Australia* 91 D2
Altoona, *U.S.A.* 106 F6
Altopáscio, *Italy* 32 E7
Altos, *Brazil* 122 C3
Altötting, *Germany* 19 G8
Altstätten, *Switz.* 23 B9
Altūn Kūprī, *Iraq* 67 E11
Altun Shan, *China* 54 C3
Alturas, *U.S.A.* 110 F3
Altus, *U.S.A.* 109 H5
Alubijid, *Phil.* 55 G6
Alucra, *Turkey* 67 B8
Alūksne, *Latvia* 9 H22
Alùla, *Somali Rep.* 68 E5
Alunite, *U.S.A.* 113 K12
Alupka, *Ukraine* 41 K8
Alushta, *Ukraine* 41 K8
Alusi, *Indonesia* 57 F8
Alustante, *Spain* 28 E3
Al'Uzayr, *Iraq* 64 D5
Alva, *U.S.A.* 109 G5
Alvaiázere, *Portugal* 30 F2
Älvängen, *Sweden* 11 G6
Alvarado, *Mexico* 115 D5
Alvarado, *U.S.A.* 109 J6
Alvarães, *Brazil* 121 D5
Alvaro Obregón, Presa, *Mexico* 114 B3
Alvdal, *Norway* 10 B4
Alvear, *Argentina* 126 B4
Alverca, *Portugal* 31 G1
Alveringen, *Belgium* 17 F1
Alvesta, *Sweden* 9 H16
Alvie, *Australia* 91 F3
Alvin, *U.S.A.* 109 L7
Alvinston, *Canada* 106 D3
Alvito, *Portugal* 31 G3
Älvkarleby, *Sweden* 9 F17
Älvros, *Sweden* 10 B8
Älvsborgs län □, *Sweden* 11 F6
Älvsbyn, *Sweden* 8 D19
Älvsered, *Sweden* 11 G6
Alwar, *India* 62 F7
Alxa Zuoqi, *China* 50 E3
Alyaskitovyy, *Russia* 45 C15
Alyata = Älät, *Azerbaijan* 43 L9
Alyth, *U.K.* 14 E5
Alytus, *Lithuania* 9 J21
Alzada, *U.S.A.* 108 C2
Alzano Lombardo, *Italy* 32 C6
Alzette →, *Lux.* 17 J8
Alzey, *Germany* 19 F4
Am Dam, *Chad* 73 F9
Am-Timan, *Chad* 73 F9
Amacuro □, *Venezuela* 121 B5
Amadeus, L., *Australia* 89 D5
Amâdi, *Sudan* 77 F3
Amadi, *Zaïre* 82 B2
Amadjuak, *Canada* 97 B12
Amadjuak L., *Canada* 97 B12
Amadora, *Portugal* 31 G1
Amagasaki, *Japan* 49 G7
Amager, *Denmark* 11 J6
Amakusa-Shotō, *Japan* 49 H5
Åmål, *Sweden* 9 G15
Amalfi, *Colombia* 120 B2
Amalfi, *Italy* 35 B7
Amaliás, *Greece* 39 M4
Amalner, *India* 60 J9
Amambaí, *Brazil* 127 A4
Amambaí →, *Brazil* 127 A5
Amambay □, *Paraguay* 127 A4
Amambay, Cordillera de, *S. Amer.* 127 A4
Amami-Guntō, *Japan* 49 L4
Amami-Ō-Shima, *Japan* 49 L4
Amana →, *Venezuela* 121 B5
Amaná, L., *Brazil* 121 D5
Amanda Park, *U.S.A.* 112 C3
Amándola, *Italy* 33 F10
Amangeldy, *Kazakstan* 44 D7
Amantea, *Italy* 35 C9
Amapá, *Brazil* 121 C7
Amapá □, *Brazil* 121 C7
Amapari, *Brazil* 121 C7
Amara, *Sudan* 77 E3
Amarante, *Brazil* 122 C3
Amarante, *Portugal* 30 D2
Amarante do Maranhão, *Brazil* 122 C2
Amaranth, *Canada* 101 C9
Amareleja, *Portugal* 31 G3
Amargosa, *Brazil* 123 D4
Amargosa →, *U.S.A.* 113 J10
Amargosa Range, *U.S.A.* 113 J10
Amári, *Greece* 37 D6
Amarillo, *U.S.A.* 109 H4
Amaro, Mte., *Italy* 33 F11
Amaro Leite, *Brazil* 123 D2
Amarpur, *India* 63 G12
Amasra, *Turkey* 66 B5
Amassama, *Nigeria* 79 D6
Amasya, *Turkey* 66 B6
Amataurá, *Brazil* 120 D4
Amatikulu, *S. Africa* 85 D5
Amatitlán, *Guatemala* 116 D1
Amatrice, *Italy* 33 F10
Amay, *Belgium* 17 G6
Amazon = Amazonas →, *S. Amer.* 121 D7
Amazonas □, *Brazil* 125 B5
Amazonas □, *Peru* 124 B2
Amazonas □, *Venezuela* 120 C4
Amazonas →, *S. Amer.* 121 D7
Ambahakily, *Madag.* 85 C7
Ambala, *India* 62 D7
Ambalavao, *Madag.* 85 C8
Ambalindum, *Australia* 90 C2
Ambam, *Cameroon* 80 D2
Ambanja, *Madag.* 85 A8
Ambarchik, *Russia* 45 C17
Ambarijeby, *Madag.* 85 A8
Ambaro, Helodranon', *Madag.* 85 A8
Ambartsevo, *Russia* 44 D9
Ambato, *Ecuador* 120 D2
Ambato, Sierra de, *Argentina* 126 B2
Ambato Boeny, *Madag.* 85 B8
Ambatofinandrahana, *Madag.* 85 C8
Ambatolampy, *Madag.* 85 B8
Ambatondrazaka, *Madag.* 85 B8
Ambatosoratra, *Madag.* 85 B8
Ambenja, *Madag.* 85 B8
Amberg, *Germany* 19 F7
Ambergris Cay, *Belize* 115 D7
Ambérieu-en-Bugey, *France* 27 C9
Amberley, *N.Z.* 87 K4
Ambert, *France* 26 C7
Ambidédi, *Mali* 78 C2
Ambikapur, *India* 63 H10
Ambikol, *Sudan* 76 C3
Ambilobé, *Madag.* 85 A8
Ambinanindrano, *Madag.* 85 C8
Ambjörnarp, *Sweden* 11 G7
Ambleside, *U.K.* 12 C5
Amblève, *Belgium* 17 H8
Amblève →, *Belgium* 17 H7
Ambo, *Ethiopia* 77 E4
Ambo, *Peru* 124 C2
Ambodifototra, *Madag.* 85 B8
Ambodilazana, *Madag.* 85 B8
Ambohimahasoa, *Madag.* 85 C8
Ambohimanga, *Madag.* 85 C8
Ambohitra, *Madag.* 85 A8
Amboise, *France* 24 E8
Ambon, *Indonesia* 57 E7
Amboseli L., *Kenya* 82 C4
Ambositra, *Madag.* 85 C8
Ambovombé, *Madag.* 85 D8
Amboy, *U.S.A.* 113 L11
Amboyna Cay, *S. China Sea* 56 C4
Ambridge, *U.S.A.* 106 F4
Ambriz, *Angola* 80 F2
Amby, *Australia* 91 D4
Amchitka I., *U.S.A.* 96 C1
Amderma, *Russia* 44 C7
Ameca, *Mexico* 114 C4
Ameca →, *Mexico* 114 C3
Amecameca, *Mexico* 115 D5
Ameland, *Neths.* 16 B7
Amélia, *Italy* 33 F9
Amélie-les-Bains-Palalda, *France* 26 F6
Amen, *Russia* 45 C18
Amendolara, *Italy* 35 C9
America, *Neths.* 17 F7
American Falls, *U.S.A.* 110 E7
American Falls Reservoir, *U.S.A.* 110 E7
American Highland, *Antarctica* 5 D6
American Samoa ■, *Pac. Oc.* 87 B13
Americana, *Brazil* 127 A6
Americus, *U.S.A.* 105 J3
Amersfoort, *Neths* 16 D6
Amersfoort, *S. Africa* 85 D4
Amery, *Australia* 89 F2
Amery, *Canada* 101 B10
Amery Ice Shelf, *Antarctica* 5 C6
Ames, *U.S.A.* 108 E8
Amesbury, *U.S.A.* 107 D14
Amfíklia, *Greece* 39 L5
Amfilokhía, *Greece* 39 L4
Amga, *Russia* 45 C14
Amga →, *Russia* 45 C14
Amgu, *Russia* 45 E14
Amgun →, *Russia* 45 D14
Amherst, *Burma* 61 L20
Amherst, *Canada* 99 C7
Amherst, *Mass., U.S.A.* 107 D12
Amherst, *N.Y., U.S.A.* 106 D6
Amherst, *Ohio, U.S.A.* 106 E2
Amherst, *Tex., U.S.A.* 109 H3
Amherst I., *Canada* 107 B8
Amherstburg, *Canada* 98 D3
Amiata, Mte., *Italy* 33 F8
Amiens, *France* 25 C9
Amindaion, *Greece* 39 J4
Amīrābād, *Iran* 64 C5
Amirante Is., *Seychelles* 46 K9
Amisk L., *Canada* 101 C8
Amistad, Presa de la, *Mexico* 114 B4
Amite, *U.S.A.* 109 K9
Amizmiz, *Morocco* 74 B3
Åmli, *Norway* 11 F2
Amlwch, *U.K.* 12 D3
Amm Adam, *Sudan* 77 D4
'Ammān, *Jordan* 69 D4
Ammanford, *U.K.* 13 F3
Ammassalik = Angmagssalik, *Greenland* 4 C6
Ammerån, *Sweden* 10 A10
Ammerån →, *Sweden* 10 A10
Ammersee, *Germany* 19 G7
Ammerzoden, *Neths.* 16 E6
Amnat Charoen, *Thailand* 58 E5
Amo Jiang →, *China* 52 F3
Āmol, *Iran* 65 B7
Amorebieta, *Spain* 28 B2
Amorgós, *Greece* 39 N8
Amory, *U.S.A.* 105 J1
Amos, *Canada* 98 C4
Åmot, *Buskerud, Norway* 10 E3
Åmot, *Telemark, Norway* 10 E2
Åmotsdal, *Norway* 10 E2
Amour, Djebel, *Algeria* 75 B5
Amoy = Xiamen, *China* 53 E12
Ampang, *Malaysia* 59 L3
Ampanihy, *Madag.* 85 C7

Ampasindava, Helodranon', *Madag.* 85 A8
Ampasindava, Saikanosy, *Madag.* 85 A8
Ampato, Nevado, *Peru* 124 D3
Ampenan, *Indonesia* 56 F5
Amper, *Nigeria* 79 D6
Amper →, *Germany* 19 G7
Ampezzo, *Italy* 33 B9
Amposta, *Spain* 28 E5
Ampotaka, *Madag.* 85 D7
Ampoza, *Madag.* 85 C7
Amqui, *Canada* 99 C6
Amravati, *India* 60 J10
Amreli, *India* 62 J4
Amrenene el Kasba, *Algeria* 75 D5
Amriswil, *Switz.* 23 A8
Amritsar, *India* 62 D6
Amroha, *India* 63 E8
Amrum, *Germany* 18 A4
Amsel, *Algeria* 75 D6
Amsterdam, *Neths.* 16 D5
Amsterdam, *U.S.A.* 107 D10
Amsterdam, I., *Ind. Oc.* 3 F13
Amstetten, *Austria* 21 G4
Amudarya →, *Uzbekistan* 44 E6
Amundsen Gulf, *Canada* 96 A7
Amundsen Sea, *Antarctica* 5 D15
Amuntai, *Indonesia* 56 E5
Amur →, *Russia* 45 D15
Amurang, *Indonesia* 57 D6
Amuri Pass, *N.Z.* 87 K4
Amurrio, *Spain* 28 B1
Amursk, *Russia* 45 D14
Amurzet, *Russia* 45 E14
Amusco, *Spain* 30 C6
Amvrakikós Kólpos, *Greece* 39 L4
Amvrosiyivka, *Ukraine* 41 J10
Amyderya = Amudarya →, *Uzbekistan* 44 E6
Amzeglouf, *Algeria* 75 C5
An Bien, *Vietnam* 59 H5
An Hoa, *Vietnam* 58 E7
An Khe, *Vietnam* 58 F7
An Nabatīyah at Tahta, *Lebanon* 69 B4
An Nabk, *Si. Arabia* 64 D3
An Nabk, *Syria* 69 A5
An Nabk Abū Qaşr, *Si. Arabia* 64 D3
An Nafūd, *Si. Arabia* 64 D4
An Najaf, *Iraq* 67 G11
An Nāşirīyah, *Iraq* 64 D5
An Nhon, *Vietnam* 58 F7
An Nîl □, *Sudan* 76 D3
An Nîl el Abyad □, *Sudan* 77 E3
An Nîl el Azraq □, *Sudan* 77 E3
An Nu'ayrīyah, *Si. Arabia* 65 E6
An Nu'mānīyah, *Iraq* 67 F11
An Nuwayb'ī, W. →, *Si. Arabia* 69 F3
An Thoi, Dao, *Vietnam* 59 H4
An Uaimh, *Ireland* 15 C5
Anabar →, *Russia* 45 B12
'Anabtā, *West Bank* 69 C4
Anaco, *Venezuela* 121 B5
Anaconda, *U.S.A.* 110 C7
Anacortes, *U.S.A.* 112 B4
Anacuao, Mt., *Phil.* 55 C4
Anadarko, *U.S.A.* 109 H5
Anadia, *Brazil* 122 C4
Anadia, *Portugal* 30 E2
Anadolu, *Turkey* 66 C5
Anadyr, *Russia* 45 C18
Anadyr →, *Russia* 45 C18
Anadyrskiy Zaliv, *Russia* 45 C19
Anáfi, *Greece* 39 N8
Anafópoulo, *Greece* 39 N8
Anaga, Pta. de, *Canary Is.* 36 F3
Anagni, *Italy* 34 A6
'Ānah, *Iraq* 67 E10
Anaheim, *U.S.A.* 113 M9
Anahim Lake, *Canada* 100 C3
Anáhuac, *Mexico* 114 B4
Anajás, *Brazil* 122 B2
Anajatuba, *Brazil* 122 B3
Anakapalle, *India* 61 L13
Anakie, *Australia* 90 C4
Anaklia, *Georgia* 43 J5
Analalava, *Madag.* 85 A8
Análipsis, *Greece* 37 A3
Anamã, *Brazil* 121 D5
Anambar →, *Pakistan* 62 D3
Anambas, Kepulauan, *Indonesia* 56 D3
Anambas Is. = Anambas, Kepulauan, *Indonesia* 56 D3
Anambra □, *Nigeria* 79 D6
Anamoose, *U.S.A.* 108 B4
Anamosa, *U.S.A.* 108 D9
Anamur, *Turkey* 66 D5
Anamur Burnu, *Turkey* 66 D5
Anan, *Japan* 49 H7
Anand, *India* 62 H5
Anantnag, *India* 63 C6
Ananyiv, *Ukraine* 41 J5
Anapa, *Russia* 43 H3
Anapodháris →, *Greece* 37 E7
Anápolis, *Brazil* 123 E2
Anapu →, *Brazil* 121 D7
Anār, *Iran* 65 D7
Anārak, *Iran* 65 C7
Anatolia = Anadolu, *Turkey* 66 C5
Anatone, *U.S.A.* 110 C5
Anatsogno, *Madag.* 85 C7
Añatuya, *Argentina* 126 B3
Anauá →, *Brazil* 121 C5
Anaunethad L., *Canada* 101 A8
Anavilhanas, Arquipélago das, *Brazil* 121 D5
Anaye, *Niger* 73 E7
Anbyŏn, *N. Korea* 51 E14
Ancash □, *Peru* 124 B2
Ancenis, *France* 24 E5
Ancho, Canal, *Chile* 128 D2
Anchor Bay, *U.S.A.* 112 G3
Anchorage, *U.S.A.* 96 B5
Anci, *China* 50 E9
Ancohuma, Nevada, *Bolivia* 124 D4
Ancón, *Peru* 124 C2
Ancona, *Italy* 33 E10
Ancud, *Chile* 128 B2
Ancud, G. de, *Chile* 128 B2
Andacollo, *Argentina* 126 D1
Andacollo, *Chile* 126 C1
Andado, *Australia* 90 D2
Andahuaylas, *Peru* 124 C3
Andalgalá, *Argentina* 126 B2
Åndalsnes, *Norway* 10 B1
Andalucía □, *Spain* 31 H6
Andalusia, *U.S.A.* 105 K2
Andalusia □ = Andalucía □, *Spain* 31 H6
Andaman Is., *Ind. Oc.* 46 H13
Andaman Sea, *Ind. Oc.* 56 B1
Andara, *Namibia* 84 B3
Andaraí, *Brazil* 123 D3
Andeer, *Switz.* 23 C8
Andelfingen, *Switz.* 23 A7
Andelot, *France* 25 D12
Andenes, *Norway* 8 B17
Andenne, *Belgium* 17 H6
Andéranboukane, *Mali* 79 B5
Anderlecht, *Belgium* 17 G4
Anderlues, *Belgium* 17 H4
Andermatt, *Switz.* 23 C7
Andernach, *Germany* 18 E3
Andernos-les-Bains, *France* 26 D2
Anderslöv, *Sweden* 11 J7
Anderson, *Calif., U.S.A.* 110 F2
Anderson, *Ind., U.S.A.* 104 E3
Anderson, *Mo., U.S.A.* 109 G7
Anderson, *S.C., U.S.A.* 105 H4
Anderson →, *Canada* 96 B7
Andes = Andes, Cord. de los, *S. Amer.* 124 C3
Andes, *S. Amer.* 124 C2
Andes, Cord. de los, *S. Amer.* 124 C3
Andfjorden, *Norway* 8 B17
Andhra Pradesh □, *India* 60 L11
Andijon, *Uzbekistan* 44 E8
Andikíthira, *Greece* 39 P6
Andīmeshk, *Iran* 67 F13
Andímilos, *Greece* 39 N7
Andípaxoi, *Greece* 39 K3
Andizhan = Andijon, *Uzbekistan* 44 E8
Andoany, *Madag.* 85 A8
Andoas, *Peru* 120 D2
Andong, *S. Korea* 51 F15
Andongwei, *China* 51 G10
Andorra ■, *Europe* 28 C6
Andorra La Vella, *Andorra* 28 C6
Andover, *U.K.* 13 F6
Andover, *Mass., U.S.A.* 107 D13
Andover, *N.Y., U.S.A.* 106 D7
Andover, *Ohio, U.S.A.* 106 E4
Andøya, *Norway* 8 B16
Andradina, *Brazil* 123 F1
Andrahary, Mt., *Madag.* 85 A8
Andraitx, *Spain* 36 B9
Andramasina, *Madag.* 85 B8
Andranopasy, *Madag.* 85 C7
Andreanof Is., *U.S.A.* 96 C2
Andreapol, *Russia* 40 D7
Andrespol, *Poland* 20 D9
Andrewilla, *Australia* 91 D2
Andrews, *S.C., U.S.A.* 105 J6
Andrews, *Tex., U.S.A.* 109 J3
Andreyevka, *Russia* 42 D10
Ándria, *Italy* 35 A9
Andriba, *Madag.* 85 B8
Andrijevica, *Montenegro, Yug.* 21 N9
Andrítsaina, *Greece* 39 M4
Androka, *Madag.* 85 C7
Andropov = Rybinsk, *Russia* 42 A4
Ándros, *Greece* 39 M7
Andros I., *Bahamas* 116 B4
Andros Town, *Bahamas* 116 B4
Andselv, *Norway* 8 B18
Andújar, *Spain* 31 G6
Andulo, *Angola* 80 G3
Anegada, B., *Argentina* 128 B4
Anegada I., *Virgin Is.* 117 C7
Anegada Passage, *W. Indies* 117 C7
Aného, *Togo* 79 D5
Añelo, *Argentina* 128 A3
Anergane, *Morocco* 74 B3
Aneto, Pico de, *Spain* 28 C5
Añez, *Bolivia* 125 D5
Anfu, *China* 53 D10
Ang Thong, *Thailand* 58 E3
Angamos, Punta, *Chile* 126 A1
Ang'angxi, *China* 54 B7
Angara →, *Russia* 45 D10
Angarab, *Ethiopia* 77 E4
Angarsk, *Russia* 45 D11
Angas Downs, *Australia* 89 E5
Angas Hills, *Australia* 88 D4
Angaston, *Australia* 91 E2
Ånge, *Sweden* 10 B9
Ángel, Salto = Angel Falls, *Venezuela* 121 B5
Ángel de la Guarda, I., *Mexico* 114 B2
Angel Falls, *Venezuela* 121 B5
Angeles, *Phil.* 55 D4
Ängelholm, *Sweden* 11 H6
Angellala, *Australia* 91 D4
Angels Camp, *U.S.A.* 111 G3
Anger →, *Ethiopia* 77 F4
Angereb →, *Ethiopia* 77 E4
Ångermanälven →, *Sweden* 10 B12
Ångermanland, *Sweden* 8 E18
Angermünde, *Germany* 18 B10
Angers, *Canada* 107 A9
Angers, *France* 24 E6
Angerville, *France* 25 D8
Ängesån →, *Sweden* 8 C20
Anghiari, *Italy* 33 E9
Angical, *Brazil* 123 D3
Angikuni L., *Canada* 101 A9
Angkor, *Cambodia* 58 F4
Anglés, *Spain* 28 D7
Anglesey, *U.K.* 12 D3
Anglesey □, *U.K.* 12 D3
Anglet, *France* 26 E2
Angleton, *U.S.A.* 109 L7
Angleur, *Belgium* 17 G7
Anglin →, *France* 26 B4
Anglisidhes, *Cyprus* 37 E12
Anglure, *France* 25 D10
Angmagssalik, *Greenland* 4 C6
Ango, *Zaïre* 82 B2
Angoche, *Mozam.* 83 F4
Angoche, I., *Mozam.* 83 F4
Angol, *Chile* 126 D1
Angola, *Ind., U.S.A.* 104 E3
Angola, *N.Y., U.S.A.* 106 D5
Angola ■, *Africa* 81 G3
Angoon, *U.S.A.* 100 B2
Angoulême, *France* 26 C4
Angoumois, *France* 26 C4
Angra dos Reis, *Brazil* 127 A7
Angren, *Uzbekistan* 44 E8
Angtassom, *Cambodia* 59 G5
Angu, *Zaïre* 82 B1
Anguang, *China* 51 B12
Anguilla ■, *W. Indies* 117 C7
Anguo, *China* 50 E8
Angurugu, *Australia* 90 A2
Angus □, *U.K.* 14 E6
Angus, Braes of, *U.K.* 14 E5
Anhanduí →, *Brazil* 127 A5
Anhée, *Belgium* 17 H5
Anholt, *Denmark* 11 H5
Anhua, *China* 53 C8
Anhui □, *China* 53 B11
Anhwei □ = Anhui □, *China* 53 B11
Anichab, *Namibia* 84 C1
Anicuns, *Brazil* 123 E2
Ánidhros, *Greece* 39 N8
Anie, *Togo* 79 D5
Animas, *U.S.A.* 111 L9
Ånimskog, *Sweden* 11 F6
Anina, *Romania* 38 D4
Anivorano, *Madag.* 85 B8
Anjalankoski, *Finland* 9 F22
Anjar, *India* 62 H4
Anjidiv I., *India* 60 M9
Anjou, *France* 24 E6
Anjozorobe, *Madag.* 85 B8
Anju, *N. Korea* 51 E13
Anka, *Nigeria* 79 C6
Ankaboa, Tanjona, *Madag.* 85 C7
Ankang, *China* 50 H5
Ankara, *Turkey* 66 C5
Ankaramena, *Madag.* 85 C8
Ankazoabo, *Madag.* 85 C7
Ankazobe, *Madag.* 85 B8
Ankisabe, *Madag.* 85 B8
Anklam, *Germany* 18 B9
Ankober, *Ethiopia* 77 F4
Ankoro, *Zaïre* 82 D2
Anlong, *China* 52 E5
Anlu, *China* 53 B9
Anmyŏn-do, *S. Korea* 51 F14
Ånn, *Sweden* 10 A6
Ann, C., *U.S.A.* 107 D14
Ann Arbor, *U.S.A.* 104 D4
Anna, *Russia* 42 E5
Anna, *U.S.A.* 109 G10
Anna Plains, *Australia* 88 C3
Anna Regina, *Guyana* 121 B6
Annaba, *Algeria* 75 A6
Annaberg-Buchholz, *Germany* 18 E8
Annalee →, *Ireland* 15 B4
Annam = Trung-Phan, *Vietnam* 58 E7
Annamitique, Chaîne, *Asia* 58 D6
Annan, *U.K.* 14 G5
Annan →, *U.K.* 14 G5
Annapolis, *U.S.A.* 104 F7
Annapolis Royal, *Canada* 99 D6
Annapurna, *Nepal* 63 E10
Annean, L., *Australia* 89 E2
Anneberg, *Sweden* 11 G6
Annecy, *France* 27 C10
Annecy, L. d', *France* 27 C10
Annemasse, *France* 27 B10
Annenskiy Most, *Russia* 40 B9
Anning, *China* 52 E4
Anningie, *Australia* 88 D5
Anniston, *U.S.A.* 105 J3
Annobón, *Atl. Oc.* 70 G4
Annonay, *France* 27 C8
Annot, *France* 27 E10
Annotto Bay, *Jamaica* 116 C4
Annuello, *Australia* 91 E3
Annville, *U.S.A.* 107 F8
Annweiler, *Germany* 19 F3
Áno Viánnos, *Greece* 37 D7
Anoka, *U.S.A.* 103 A8
Anorotsangana, *Madag.* 85 A8
Anóyia, *Greece* 37 D6
Anping, *Hebei, China* 50 E8
Anping, *Liaoning, China* 51 D12
Anpu Gang, *China* 52 G7
Anqing, *China* 53 B11
Anqiu, *China* 51 F10
Anren, *China* 53 D9
Ans, *Belgium* 17 G7
Ansai, *China* 50 F5
Ansbach, *Germany* 19 F6
Anseba →, *Eritrea* 77 D4
Anserma, *Colombia* 120 B2
Anseroeul, *Belgium* 17 G3
Anshan, *China* 51 D12
Anshun, *China* 52 D5
Ansião, *Portugal* 30 F2
Ansirabe, *Madag.* 85 B8
Ansley, *U.S.A.* 108 E5
Ansó, *Spain* 28 C4
Anson, *U.S.A.* 109 J5
Anson B., *Australia* 88 B5
Ansongo, *Mali* 79 B5
Ansonia, *U.S.A.* 107 E11
Anstruther, *U.K.* 14 E6
Ansudu, *Indonesia* 57 E9
Antabamba, *Peru* 124 C3
Antakya, *Turkey* 66 D7
Antalaha, *Madag.* 85 A9
Antalya, *Turkey* 66 D4
Antalya Körfezi, *Turkey* 66 D4
Antananarivo, *Madag.* 85 B8
Antananarivo □, *Madag.* 85 B8
Antanimbaribe, *Madag.* 85 C7
Antarctic Pen., *Antarctica* 5 C18
Antarctica 5 E3
Antelope, *Zimbabwe* 83 G2
Antenor Navarro, *Brazil* 122 C4
Antequera, *Paraguay* 126 A4
Antequera, *Spain* 31 H6
Antero, Mt., *U.S.A.* 111 G10
Anthony, *Kans., U.S.A.* 109 G5
Anthony, *N. Mex., U.S.A.* 111 K10
Anthony Lagoon, *Australia* 90 B2
Anti Atlas, *Morocco* 74 C2
Anti-Lebanon = Ash Sharqi, Al Jabal, *Lebanon* 69 B5
Antibes, *France* 27 E11
Antibes, C. d', *France* 27 E11
Anticosti, I. d', *Canada* 99 C7
Antifer, C. d', *France* 24 C7
Antigo, *U.S.A.* 108 C10
Antigonish, *Canada* 99 C7
Antigua, *Canary Is.* 36 F5
Antigua, *Guatemala* 116 D1
Antigua, *W. Indies* 117 C7
Antigua & Barbuda ■, *W. Indies* 117 C7
Antilla, *Cuba* 116 B4
Antimony, *U.S.A.* 111 G8
Antioch, *U.S.A.* 112 G5
Antioche, Pertuis d', *France* 26 B2
Antioquia, *Colombia* 120 B2
Antioquia □, *Colombia* 120 B2
Antipodes Is., *Pac. Oc.* 92 M9
Antler, *U.S.A.* 108 A4
Antler →, *Canada* 101 D8
Antlers, *U.S.A.* 109 H7
Antofagasta, *Chile* 126 A1
Antofagasta □, *Chile* 126 A2
Antofagasta de la Sierra, *Argentina* 126 B2
Antofalla, *Argentina* 126 B2
Antofalla, Salar de, *Argentina* 126 B2
Antoing, *Belgium* 17 G2
Anton, *U.S.A.* 109 J3
Anton Chico, *U.S.A.* 111 J11
Antongila, Helodrano, *Madag.* 85 B8
Antonibé, *Madag.* 85 B8
Antonibé, Presqu'île d', *Madag.* 85 A8
Antonina, *Brazil* 127 B6
Antonito, *U.S.A.* 111 H10
Antrain, *France* 24 D5
Antrim, *U.K.* 15 B5
Antrim □, *U.K.* 15 B5
Antrim, Mts. of, *U.K.* 15 B5
Antrim Plateau, *Australia* 88 C4
Antrodoco, *Italy* 33 F10
Antropovo, *Russia* 42 A6
Antsalova, *Madag.* 85 B7
Antsiranana, *Madag.* 85 A8
Antsohihy, *Madag.* 85 A8
Antsohimbondrona Seranana, *Madag.* 85 A8
Antu, *China* 51 C15
Antwerp = Antwerpen, *Belgium* 17 F4
Antwerp, *U.S.A.* 107 B9
Antwerpen, *Belgium* 17 F4
Antwerpen □, *Belgium* 17 F5
Anupgarh, *India* 62 E5
Anuradhapura, *Sri Lanka* 60 Q12
Anveh, *Iran* 65 E7
Anvers = Antwerpen, *Belgium* 17 F4
Anvers I., *Antarctica* 5 C17
Anxi, *Fujian, China* 53 E12
Anxi, *Gansu, China* 54 B4
Anxiang, *China* 53 C9
Anxious B., *Australia* 91 E1
Anyama, *Ivory C.* 78 D4
Anyang, *China* 50 F8
Anyi, *Jiangxi, China* 53 C10
Anyi, *Shanxi, China* 50 G6
Anyuan, *China* 53 E10
Anza, *U.S.A.* 113 M10
Anze, *China* 50 F7
Anzhero-Sudzhensk, *Russia* 44 D9
Ánzio, *Italy* 34 A5
Anzoátegui □, *Venezuela* 121 B5
Aoga-Shima, *Japan* 49 H9
Aoiz, *Spain* 28 C3
Aomori, *Japan* 48 D10
Aomori □, *Japan* 48 D10
Aonla, *India* 63 E8
Aosta, *Italy* 32 C4
Aoudéras, *Niger* 79 B6
Aouinet Torkoz, *Morocco* 74 C3
Aoukar, *Mali* 74 D4
Aouker, *Mauritania* 78 B3
Aoulef el Arab, *Algeria* 75 C5
Apa →, *S. Amer.* 126 A4
Apache, *U.S.A.* 109 H5
Apalachee B., *U.S.A.* 105 L3
Apalachicola, *U.S.A.* 105 L3
Apalachicola →, *U.S.A.* 105 L3
Apapa, *Nigeria* 79 D5
Apaporis →, *Colombia* 120 D4
Aparecida do Taboado, *Brazil* 123 F1
Aparri, *Phil.* 55 B4
Apararén, *Venezuela* 121 B5
Apateu, *Romania* 38 C4
Apatin, *Serbia, Yug.* 21 K8
Apatzingán, *Mexico* 114 D4
Apeldoorn, *Neths.* 16 D7
Apeldoornsch Kanal →, *Neths.* 16 D8
Apen, *Germany* 18 B3
Apennines = Appennini, *Italy* 32 D7
Apere →, *Bolivia* 125 C4
Apia, *W. Samoa* 87 A13
Apiacás, Serra dos, *Brazil* 125 B6
Apiaú →, *Brazil* 121 C5
Apiaú, Serra do, *Brazil* 121 C5
Apidiá →, *Brazil* 125 C5
Apinajé, *Brazil* 123 D2
Apizaco, *Mexico* 115 D5
Aplao, *Peru* 124 D3
Apo, Mt., *Phil.* 57 C7
Apodi, *Brazil* 122 C4
Apolakkiá, *Greece* 37 C9
Apolakkiá, Órmos, *Greece* 37 C9
Apolda, *Germany* 18 D7
Apollonia = Marsá Susah, *Libya* 73 B9
Apollonia, *Greece* 39 N7
Apolo, *Bolivia* 124 C4
Apónguao →, *Venezuela* 121 C5
Aporé, *Brazil* 125 D7
Aporé →, *Brazil* 123 E1
Aporema, *Brazil* 122 A1
Apostle Is., *U.S.A.* 108 B9
Apóstoles, *Argentina* 127 B4
Apostolos Andreas, C., *Cyprus* 66 E6
Apostolovo, *Ukraine* 41 J7
Apoteri, *Guyana* 121 C6
Appalachian Mts., *U.S.A.* 104 G6
Appelscha, *Neths.* 16 C8
Appennini, *Italy* 32 D7
Appennino Ligure, *Italy* 32 D5
Appenzell, *Switz.* 23 B8
Appenzell-Ausser Rhoden □, *Switz.* 23 B8
Appenzell-Inner Rhoden □, *Switz.* 23 B8
Appiano, *Italy* 33 B8
Appingedam, *Neths.* 16 B9
Apple Hill, *Canada* 107 A10
Apple Valley, *U.S.A.* 113 L9
Appleby-in-Westmorland, *U.K.* 12 C5
Appleton, *U.S.A.* 104 C1
Approuague, *Fr. Guiana* 121 C7
Approuague →, *Fr. Guiana* 121 C7
Apricena, *Italy* 35 A8
Aprigliano, *Italy* 35 C9
Aprília, *Italy* 34 A5
Apsheronsk, *Russia* 43 H4
Apt, *France* 27 E9
Apuane, Alpi, *Italy* 32 D7
Apuaú, *Brazil* 121 D5
Apucarana, *Brazil* 127 A5
Apulia = Púglia □, *Italy* 35 B9
Apure □, *Venezuela* 120 B4
Apure →, *Venezuela* 120 B4
Apurímac □, *Peru* 124 C3
Apurimac →, *Peru* 124 C3
Apuseni, Munţii, *Romania* 38 C5
Aqabah = Al 'Aqabah, *Jordan* 69 F4
'Aqabah, Khalīj al, *Red Sea* 64 D2
'Aqdā, *Iran* 65 C7
Aqiq, *Sudan* 76 D4
Aqiq, Khalīg, *Sudan* 76 D4
Aqmola, *Kazakstan* 44 D8
Aqrah, *Iraq* 67 D10
Aqtöbe, *Kazakstan* 44 D6

Aquidauana, *Brazil* 125 E6
Aquidauana →, *Brazil* 125 D6
Aquiles Serdán, *Mexico* 114 B3
Aquin, *Haiti* 117 C5
Ar Rachidiya, *Morocco* 74 B4
Ar Rafid, *Syria* 69 C4
Ar Raḩḩālīyah, *Iraq* 67 F10
Ar Ramādī, *Iraq* 67 F10
Ar Ramthā, *Jordan* 69 C5
Ar Raqqah, *Syria* 67 E8
Ar Rass, *Si. Arabia* 64 E4
Ar Rifā'ī, *Iraq* 64 D5
Ar Riyāḑ, *Si. Arabia* 64 E5
Ar Ru'ays, *Qatar* 65 E6
Ar Rukhaymīyah, *Iraq* 64 D5
Ar Ruqayyidah, *Si. Arabia* 65 E6
Ar Ruṣāfah, *Syria* 67 E8
Ar Ruṭbah, *Iraq* 67 F9
Ara, *India* 63 G11
'Arab, Bahr el →, *Sudan* 77 F2
Arab, Khalîg el, *Egypt* 76 H6
'Arabābād, *Iran* 65 C8
Araban, *Turkey* 66 D7
Arabatskaya Strelka, *Ukraine* 41 K8
Arabba, *Italy* 33 B8
Arabelo, *Venezuela* 121 C5
Arabia, *Asia* 68 C4
Arabian Desert = Es Sahrâ' Esh Sharqîya, *Egypt* 76 B3
Arabian Gulf = Gulf, The, *Asia* 65 E6
Arabian Sea, *Ind. Oc.* 47 H10
Araç, *Turkey* 66 B5
Aracaju, *Brazil* 122 D4
Aracataca, *Colombia* 120 A3
Aracati, *Brazil* 122 B4
Araçatuba, *Brazil* 127 A5
Aracena, *Spain* 31 H4
Aracena, Sierra de, *Spain* 31 H4
Araçuaí, *Brazil* 123 E3
Araçuaí →, *Brazil* 123 E3
'Arad, *Israel* 69 D4
Arad, *Romania* 38 C4
Arada, *Chad* 73 F9
Aradhippou, *Cyprus* 37 E12
Arafura Sea, *E. Indies* 57 F8
Aragarças, *Brazil* 125 D7
Aragats, *Armenia* 43 K7
Aragón □, *Spain* 28 D4
Aragón →, *Spain* 28 C3
Aragona, *Italy* 34 E6
Aragua □, *Venezuela* 120 B4
Aragua de Barcelona, *Venezuela* 121 B5
Araguacema, *Brazil* 122 C2
Araguaçu, *Brazil* 123 D2
Araguaia →, *Brazil* 122 C2
Araguaiana, *Brazil* 125 D7
Araguaína, *Brazil* 122 C2
Araguari, *Brazil* 123 E2
Araguari →, *Brazil* 121 C8
Araguatins, *Brazil* 122 C2
Araioses, *Brazil* 122 B3
Arak, *Algeria* 75 C5
Arāk, *Iran* 65 C6
Arakan Coast, *Burma* 61 K19
Arakan Yoma, *Burma* 61 K19
Arakli, *Turkey* 67 B8
Araks = Aras, Rūd-e →, *Azerbaijan* 43 K9
Aral, *Kazakstan* 44 E7
Aral Sea, *Asia* 44 E7
Aral Tengizi = Aral Sea, *Asia* 44 E7
Aralsk = Aral, *Kazakstan* 44 E7
Aralskoye More = Aral Sea, *Asia* 44 E7
Aralsor, Ozero, *Kazakstan* 43 F9
Aramac, *Australia* 90 C4
Arambag, *India* 63 H12
Aran I., *Ireland* 15 B3
Aran Is., *Ireland* 15 C2
Aranda de Duero, *Spain* 28 D1
Arandān, *Iran* 64 C5
Aranjuez, *Spain* 30 E7
Aranos, *Namibia* 84 C2
Aransas Pass, *U.S.A.* 109 M6
Aranzazu, *Colombia* 120 B2
Araouane, *Mali* 78 B4
Arapahoe, *U.S.A.* 108 E5
Arapari, *Brazil* 122 C2
Arapey Grande →, *Uruguay* 126 C4
Arapgir, *Turkey* 67 C8
Arapiraca, *Brazil* 122 C4
Arapongas, *Brazil* 127 A5
Ar'ar, *Si. Arabia* 64 D4
Araracuara, *Colombia* 120 D3
Araranguá, *Brazil* 127 B6
Araraquara, *Brazil* 123 F2
Ararás, Serra das, *Brazil* 127 B5
Ararat, *Armenia* 67 C11
Ararat, *Australia* 91 F3
Ararat, Mt. = Ağrı Dağı, *Turkey* 67 C11
Arari, *Brazil* 122 B3
Araria, *India* 63 F12
Araripe, Chapada do, *Brazil* 122 C3
Araripina, *Brazil* 122 C3
Araruama, L. de, *Brazil* 123 F3
Araruna, *Brazil* 122 C4
Aras, Rūd-e →, *Azerbaijan* 43 K9
Araticu, *Brazil* 122 B2
Arauca, *Colombia* 120 B3
Arauca □, *Colombia* 120 B3
Arauca →, *Venezuela* 120 B4
Arauco, *Chile* 126 D1
Arauco □, *Chile* 126 D1
Araújos, *Brazil* 123 E2
Arauquita, *Colombia* 120 B3
Araure, *Venezuela* 120 B4
Arawa, *Ethiopia* 77 F5
Araxá, *Brazil* 123 E2
Araya, Pen. de, *Venezuela* 121 A5
Arba Minch, *Ethiopia* 77 F4
Arbat, *Iraq* 67 E11
Arbatax, *Italy* 34 C2
Arbedo, *Switz.* 23 D8
Arbīl, *Iraq* 67 D11
Arbois, *France* 25 F12
Arboletes, *Colombia* 120 B2
Arbon, *Switz.* 23 A8
Arbore, *Ethiopia* 77 F4
Arboréa, *Italy* 34 C1
Arborfield, *Canada* 101 C8
Arborg, *Canada* 101 C9
Arbrå, *Sweden* 10 C10
Arbroath, *U.K.* 14 E6
Arbuckle, *U.S.A.* 112 F4
Arbus, *Italy* 34 C1
Arc, *France* 25 E12
Arc →, *France* 27 C10
Arcachon, *France* 26 D2
Arcachon, Bassin d', *France* 26 D2
Arcade, *U.S.A.* 106 D6
Arcadia, *Fla., U.S.A.* 105 M5
Arcadia, *La., U.S.A.* 109 J8
Arcadia, *Nebr., U.S.A.* 108 E5
Arcadia, *Pa., U.S.A.* 106 F6
Arcadia, *Wis., U.S.A.* 108 C9
Arcata, *U.S.A.* 110 F1
Arcévia, *Italy* 33 E9
Archangel = Arkhangelsk, *Russia* 44 C5
Archar, *Bulgaria* 38 F5
Archbald, *U.S.A.* 107 E9
Archena, *Spain* 29 G3
Archer →, *Australia* 90 A3
Archer B., *Australia* 90 A3
Archers Post, *Kenya* 82 B4
Archidona, *Spain* 31 H6
Arci, Mte., *Italy* 34 C1
Arcidosso, *Italy* 33 F8
Arcila = Asilah, *Morocco* 74 A3
Arcis-sur-Aube, *France* 25 D11
Arckaringa, *Australia* 91 D1
Arckaringa Cr. →, *Australia* 91 D2
Arco, *Italy* 32 C7
Arco, *U.S.A.* 110 E7
Arcola, *Canada* 101 D8
Arcos, *Spain* 28 D2
Arcos de la Frontera, *Spain* 31 J5
Arcos de Valdevez, *Portugal* 30 D2
Arcot, *India* 60 N11
Arcoverde, *Brazil* 122 C4
Arctic Bay, *Canada* 97 A11
Arctic Ocean, *Arctic* 4 B18
Arctic Red River, *Canada* 96 B6
Arda →, *Bulgaria* 39 H9
Arda →, *Italy* 32 D6
Ardabīl, *Iran* 67 C13
Ardahan, *Turkey* 67 B10
Ardakān = Sepīdān, *Iran* 65 D7
Ardales, *Spain* 31 J6
Årdalstangen, *Norway* 10 C1
Ardea, *Greece* 39 J5
Ardèche □, *France* 27 D8
Ardèche →, *France* 27 D8
Ardee, *Ireland* 15 C5
Arden, *Canada* 106 B8
Arden, *Denmark* 11 H3
Arden, *Calif., U.S.A.* 112 G5
Arden, *Nev., U.S.A.* 113 J11
Ardenne, *Belgium* 25 C12
Ardennes = Ardenne, *Belgium* 25 C12
Ardennes □, *France* 25 C11
Ardentes, *France* 25 F8
Ardeşen, *Turkey* 67 B9
Ardestān, *Iran* 65 C7
Ardgour, *U.K.* 14 E3
Árdhas →, *Greece* 39 H9
Ardila →, *Portugal* 31 G3
Ardlethan, *Australia* 91 E4
Ardmore, *Australia* 90 C2
Ardmore, *Okla., U.S.A.* 109 H6
Ardmore, *Pa., U.S.A.* 107 G9
Ardmore, *S. Dak., U.S.A.* 108 D3
Ardnacrusha, *Ireland* 15 D3
Ardnamurchan, Pt. of, *U.K.* 14 E2
Ardon, *Russia* 43 J7
Ardooie, *Belgium* 17 G2
Ardore, *Italy* 35 D9
Ardres, *France* 25 B8
Ardrossan, *Australia* 91 E2
Ardrossan, *U.K.* 14 F4
Ards □, *U.K.* 15 B6
Ards Pen., *U.K.* 15 B6
Ardud, *Romania* 38 B5
Åre, *Sweden* 10 A7
Arecibo, *Puerto Rico* 117 C6
Areia Branca, *Brazil* 122 B4
Arena, Pt., *U.S.A.* 112 G3
Arenales, Cerro, *Chile* 128 C2
Arenápolis, *Brazil* 125 C6
Arenas, *Spain* 30 B6
Arenas de San Pedro, *Spain* 30 E5
Arendal, *Norway* 11 F2
Arendonk, *Belgium* 17 F6
Arendsee, *Germany* 18 C7
Arenillas, *Ecuador* 120 D1
Arenys de Mar, *Spain* 28 D7
Arenzano, *Italy* 32 D5
Areópolis, *Greece* 39 N5
Arequipa, *Peru* 124 D3
Arequipa □, *Peru* 124 D3
Arere, *Brazil* 121 D7
Arero, *Ethiopia* 77 G4
Arès, *France* 26 D2
Arévalo, *Spain* 30 D6
Arezzo, *Italy* 33 E8
Arga →, *Spain* 28 C3
Argalastí, *Greece* 39 K6
Argamakmur, *Indonesia* 56 E2
Argamasilla de Alba, *Spain* 29 F1
Arganda, *Spain* 28 E1
Arganil, *Portugal* 30 E2
Argelès-Gazost, *France* 26 F3
Argelès-sur-Mer, *France* 26 F7
Argens →, *France* 27 E10
Argent-sur-Sauldre, *France* 25 E9
Argenta, *Italy* 33 D8
Argentan, *France* 24 D6
Argentário, Mte., *Italy* 33 F8
Argentat, *France* 26 C5
Argentera, *Italy* 32 D3
Argentera, Monte del, *Italy* 32 D4
Argenteuil, *France* 25 D9
Argentia, *Canada* 99 C9
Argentiera, C. dell', *Italy* 34 B1
Argentière, Aiguilles d', *Switz.* 22 E4
Argentina ■, *S. Amer.* 128 B3
Argentina Is., *Antarctica* 5 C17
Argentino, L., *Argentina* 128 D2
Argenton-Château, *France* 24 F6
Argenton-sur-Creuse, *France* 26 B5
Argeş →, *Romania* 38 E9
Arghandab →, *Afghan.* 62 D1
Argo, *Sudan* 76 D3
Argolikós Kólpos, *Greece* 39 M5
Argonne, *France* 25 C12
Árgos, *Greece* 39 M5
Argostólion, *Greece* 39 L3
Arguedas, *Spain* 28 C3
Arguello, Pt., *U.S.A.* 113 L6
Arguineguín, *Canary Is.* 36 G4
Argun, *Russia* 43 J7
Argun →, *Russia* 45 D13
Argungu, *Nigeria* 79 C5
Argus Pk., *U.S.A.* 113 K9
Argyle, *U.S.A.* 108 A6
Argyle, L., *Australia* 88 C4
Argyll & Bute □, *U.K.* 14 E3
Arhavi, *Turkey* 67 B9
Århus, *Denmark* 11 H4
Århus Amtskommune □, *Denmark* 11 H4
Ariadnoye, *Russia* 48 B7
Ariamsvlei, *Namibia* 84 D2
Ariana, *Tunisia* 75 A7
Ariano Irpino, *Italy* 35 A8
Ariano nel Polèsine, *Italy* 33 D9
Ariari →, *Colombia* 120 C3
Aribinda, *Burkina Faso* 79 C4
Arica, *Chile* 124 D3
Arica, *Colombia* 120 D3
Arico, *Canary Is.* 36 F3
Arid, C., *Australia* 89 F3
Arida, *Japan* 49 G7
Ariège □, *France* 26 F5
Ariège →, *France* 26 E5
Arieş →, *Romania* 38 C6
Arīḩā, *Syria* 64 C3
Arílla, Ákra, *Greece* 37 A3
Arima, *Trin. & Tob.* 117 D7
Arinos →, *Brazil* 125 C6
Ario de Rosales, *Mexico* 114 D4
Aripuanã, *Brazil* 125 B5
Aripuanã →, *Brazil* 125 B5
Ariquemes, *Brazil* 125 B5
Arisaig, *U.K.* 14 E3
Arîsh, W. el →, *Egypt* 76 H8
Arismendi, *Venezuela* 120 B4
Arissa, *Ethiopia* 77 E5
Aristazabal I., *Canada* 100 C3
Arivaca, *U.S.A.* 111 L8
Arivonimamo, *Madag.* 85 B8
Ariza, *Spain* 28 D2
Arizaro, Salar de, *Argentina* 126 A2
Arizona, *Argentina* 126 D2
Arizona □, *U.S.A.* 111 J8
Arizpe, *Mexico* 114 A2
Arjeplog, *Sweden* 8 D18
Arjona, *Colombia* 120 A2
Arjona, *Spain* 31 H6
Arjuno, *Indonesia* 57 G15
Arka, *Russia* 45 C15
Arkadak, *Russia* 42 E6
Arkadelphia, *U.S.A.* 109 H8
Arkaig, L., *U.K.* 14 E3
Arkalyk = Arqalyk, *Kazakstan* 44 D7
Arkansas □, *U.S.A.* 109 H8
Arkansas →, *U.S.A.* 109 J9
Arkansas City, *U.S.A.* 109 G6
Árkathos →, *Greece* 39 K4
Arkhángelos, *Greece* 37 C10
Arkhangelsk, *Russia* 44 C5
Arkhangelskoye, *Russia* 42 E5
Arkiko, *Eritrea* 77 D4
Arklow, *Ireland* 15 D5
Arkona, Kap, *Germany* 18 A9
Arkösund, *Sweden* 11 F10
Arkticheskiy, Mys, *Russia* 45 A10
Arkul, *Russia* 42 B10
Arlanc, *France* 26 C7
Arlanza →, *Spain* 30 C6
Arlanzón →, *Spain* 30 C6
Arlberg P., *Austria* 19 H6
Arlee, *U.S.A.* 110 C6
Arles, *France* 27 E8
Arlesheim, *Switz.* 22 B5
Arlington, *S. Africa* 85 D4
Arlington, *Oreg., U.S.A.* 110 D3
Arlington, *S. Dak., U.S.A.* 108 C6
Arlington, *Va., U.S.A.* 104 F7
Arlington, *Wash., U.S.A.* 112 B4
Arlington Heights, *U.S.A.* 104 D2
Arlon, *Belgium* 17 J7
Arlöv, *Sweden* 11 J7
Arly, *Burkina Faso* 79 C5
Armagh, *U.K.* 15 B5
Armagh □, *U.K.* 15 B5
Armagnac, *France* 26 E4
Armançon →, *France* 25 E10
Armavir, *Russia* 43 H5
Armenia, *Colombia* 120 C2
Armenia ■, *Asia* 43 K7
Armenistís, Ákra, *Greece* 37 C9
Armentières, *France* 25 B9
Armidale, *Australia* 91 E5
Armour, *U.S.A.* 108 D5
Armstrong, *B.C., Canada* 100 C5
Armstrong, *Ont., Canada* 98 B2
Armstrong, *U.S.A.* 109 M6
Armstrong →, *Australia* 88 C5
Arnarfjörður, *Iceland* 8 D2
Arnaud →, *Canada* 97 B12
Arnauti, C., *Cyprus* 37 D11
Arnay-le-Duc, *France* 25 E11
Arnedillo, *Spain* 28 C2
Arnedo, *Spain* 28 C2
Arnemuiden, *Neths.* 17 F3
Årnes, *Norway* 10 D5
Arnett, *U.S.A.* 109 G5
Arnhem, *Neths.* 16 E7
Arnhem, C., *Australia* 90 A2
Arnhem B., *Australia* 90 A2
Arnhem Land, *Australia* 90 A1
Arno →, *Italy* 32 E7
Arno Bay, *Australia* 91 E2
Arnold, *Calif., U.S.A.* 112 G6
Arnold, *Nebr., U.S.A.* 108 E4
Arnoldstein, *Austria* 21 J3
Arnon →, *France* 25 E9
Arnot, *Canada* 101 B9
Arnøy, *Norway* 8 A19
Arnprior, *Canada* 98 C4
Arnsberg, *Germany* 18 D4
Arnstadt, *Germany* 18 E6
Aro →, *Venezuela* 121 B5
Aroab, *Namibia* 84 D2
Aroche, *Spain* 31 H4
Aroeiras, *Brazil* 122 C4
Arolla, *Switz.* 22 D4
Arolsen, *Germany* 18 D5
Aron →, *France* 26 B7
Arona, *Italy* 32 C5
Aroroy, *Phil.* 55 E5
Arosa, *Switz.* 23 C9
Arosa, Ria de, *Spain* 30 C2
Arpajon, *France* 25 D9
Arpajon-sur-Cère, *France* 26 D6
Arpino, *Italy* 34 A6
Arqalyk, *Kazakstan* 44 D7
Arque, *Bolivia* 124 D4
Arrabury, *Australia* 91 D3
Arrah = Ara, *India* 63 G11
Arraias, *Brazil* 123 D2
Arraias →, *Mato Grosso, Brazil* 125 C7
Arraias →, *Pará, Brazil* 122 C2
Arraiolos, *Portugal* 31 G3
Arran, *U.K.* 14 F3
Arrandale, *Canada* 100 C3
Arras, *France* 25 B9
Arrats →, *France* 26 D4
Arreau, *France* 26 F4
Arrecife, *Canary Is.* 36 F6
Arrecifes, *Argentina* 126 C3
Arrée, Mts. d', *France* 24 D3
Arriaga, *Chiapas, Mexico* 115 D6
Arriaga, *San Luis Potosí, Mexico* 114 C4
Arrilalah P.O., *Australia* 90 C3
Arrino, *Australia* 89 E2
Arrojado →, *Brazil* 123 D3
Arromanches-les-Bains, *France* 24 C6
Arronches, *Portugal* 31 F3
Arros →, *France* 26 E3
Arrou, *France* 24 D8
Arrow, L., *Ireland* 15 B3
Arrow Rock Res., *U.S.A.* 110 E6
Arrowhead, *Canada* 100 C5
Arrowhead, L., *U.S.A.* 113 L9
Arrowtown, *N.Z.* 87 L2
Arroyo de la Luz, *Spain* 31 F4
Arroyo Grande, *U.S.A.* 113 K6
Års, *Denmark* 11 H3
Ars, *Iran* 64 B5
Ars-en-Ré, *France* 26 B2
Ars-sur-Moselle, *France* 25 C13
Arsenault L., *Canada* 101 B7
Arsenev, *Russia* 48 B6
Arsi □, *Ethiopia* 77 F4
Arsiero, *Italy* 33 C8
Arsin, *Turkey* 67 B8
Arsk, *Russia* 42 B9
Árta, *Greece* 39 K4
Artá, *Spain* 36 B10
Arteaga, *Mexico* 114 D4
Arteche, *Phil.* 55 E6
Arteijo, *Spain* 30 B2
Artem = Artyom, *Azerbaijan* 43 K10
Artem, *Russia* 48 C6
Artemovsk, *Russia* 45 D10
Artemovsk, *Ukraine* 41 H9
Artemovskiy, *Russia* 43 G5
Artenay, *France* 25 D8
Artern, *Germany* 18 D7
Artesa de Segre, *Spain* 28 D6
Artesia = Mosomane, *Botswana* 84 C4
Artesia, *U.S.A.* 109 J2
Artesia Wells, *U.S.A.* 109 L5
Artesian, *U.S.A.* 108 C6
Arth, *Switz.* 23 B7
Arthez-de-Béarn, *France* 26 E3
Arthington, *Liberia* 78 D2
Arthur →, *Australia* 90 G3
Arthur Cr. →, *Australia* 90 C2
Arthur Pt., *Australia* 90 C5
Arthur's Pass, *N.Z.* 87 K3
Arthur's Town, *Bahamas* 117 B4
Artigas, *Uruguay* 126 C4
Artik, *Armenia* 43 K6
Artillery L., *Canada* 101 A7
Artois, *France* 25 B9
Artsyz, *Ukraine* 41 J5
Artvin, *Turkey* 67 B9
Artyom, *Azerbaijan* 43 K10
Aru, Kepulauan, *Indonesia* 57 F8
Aru Is. = Aru, Kepulauan, *Indonesia* 57 F8
Aru Meru □, *Tanzania* 82 C4
Arua, *Uganda* 82 B3
Aruanã, *Brazil* 123 D1
Aruba ■, *W. Indies* 117 D6
Arucas, *Canary Is.* 36 F4
Arudy, *France* 26 E3
Arumã, *Brazil* 121 D5
Arumpo, *Australia* 91 E3
Arun →, *Nepal* 63 F12
Arunachal Pradesh □, *India* 61 E19
Arusha, *Tanzania* 82 C4
Arusha □, *Tanzania* 82 C4
Arusha Chini, *Tanzania* 82 C4
Aruwimi →, *Zaïre* 82 B1
Arvada, *U.S.A.* 110 D10
Arvayheer, *Mongolia* 54 B5
Arve →, *France* 27 B10
Árvi, *Greece* 37 E7
Arvida, *Canada* 99 C5
Arvidsjaur, *Sweden* 8 D18
Arvika, *Sweden* 9 G15
Arvin, *U.S.A.* 113 K8
Arxan, *China* 54 B6
Aryirádhes, *Greece* 37 B3
Aryiroúpolis, *Greece* 37 D6
Arys, *Kazakstan* 44 E7
Arzachena, *Italy* 34 A2
Arzamas, *Russia* 42 C6
Arzew, *Algeria* 75 A4
Arzgir, *Russia* 43 H7
Arzignano, *Italy* 33 C8
As, *Belgium* 17 F7
Aş Şadr, *U.A.E.* 65 E7
Aş Şafā, *Syria* 69 B6
'As Saffānīyah, *Si. Arabia* 65 D6
As Safīrah, *Syria* 66 D7
Aş Şahm, *Oman* 65 E8
As Sājir, *Si. Arabia* 64 E5
As Salamīyah, *Syria* 66 E7
As Salṭ, *Jordan* 69 C4
As Sal'w'a, *Qatar* 65 E6
As Samāwah, *Iraq* 64 D5
As Sanamayn, *Syria* 69 B5
As Sukhnah, *Syria* 67 E8
As Sulaymānīyah, *Iraq* 67 E11
As Sulaymī, *Si. Arabia* 64 E4
As Summān, *Si. Arabia* 64 E5
As Suwaydā', *Syria* 69 C5
As Suwaydā' □, *Syria* 69 C5
As Şuwayrah, *Iraq* 67 F11
Asab, *Namibia* 84 D2
Asaba, *Nigeria* 79 D6
Asadābād, *Iran* 67 E13
Asafo, *Ghana* 78 D4
Asahi-Gawa →, *Japan* 49 G6
Asahigawa, *Japan* 48 C11
Asale, L., *Ethiopia* 77 E5
Asamankese, *Ghana* 79 D4
Asansol, *India* 63 H12
Åsarna, *Sweden* 10 B8
Asbe Teferi, *Ethiopia* 77 F5
Asbesberge, *S. Africa* 84 D3
Asbestos, *Canada* 99 C5
Asbury Park, *U.S.A.* 107 F10
Ascensión, *Mexico* 114 A3
Ascensión, B. de la, *Mexico* 115 D7
Ascension I., *Atl. Oc.* 70 G2
Aschaffenburg, *Germany* 19 F5
Aschendorf, *Germany* 18 B3
Aschersleben, *Germany* 18 D7
Asciano, *Italy* 33 E8
Áscoli Piceno, *Italy* 33 F10
Áscoli Satriano, *Italy* 35 A8
Ascona, *Switz.* 23 D7
Ascope, *Peru* 124 B2
Ascotán, *Chile* 126 A2
Aseb, *Eritrea* 68 E3
Asedjrad, *Algeria* 75 D5
Asela, *Ethiopia* 77 F4
Asenovgrad, *Bulgaria* 39 G7

Asfeld, *France* 25 C11
Asfûn el Matâ'na, *Egypt* 76 B3
Åsgårdstrand, *Norway* 10 E4
Asgata, *Cyprus* 37 E12
Ash Fork, *U.S.A.* 111 J7
Ash Grove, *U.S.A.* 109 G8
Ash Shām, Bādiyat, *Asia* 46 F7
Ash Shamāl □, *Lebanon* 69 A5
Ash Shāmīyah, *Iraq* 67 G11
Ash Shāriqah, *U.A.E.* 65 E7
Ash Sharmah, *Si. Arabia* 64 D2
Ash Sharqāt, *Iraq* 67 E10
Ash Sharqi, Al Jabal, *Lebanon* 69 B5
Ash Shaṭrah, *Iraq* 64 D5
Ash Shawbak, *Jordan* 64 D2
Ash Shawmari, J., *Jordan* 69 E5
Ash Shaykh, J., *Lebanon* 69 B4
Ash Shināfīyah, *Iraq* 64 D5
Ash Shu'aybah, *Si. Arabia* 64 E5
Ash Shumlūl, *Si. Arabia* 64 E5
Ash Shūr'a, *Iraq* 64 C4
Ash Shurayf, *Si. Arabia* 64 E3
Ash Shuwayfāt, *Lebanon* 69 B4
Ashanti □, *Ghana* 79 D4
Ashau, *Vietnam* 58 D6
Ashburn, *U.S.A.* 105 K4
Ashburton, *N.Z.* 87 K3
Ashburton →, *Australia* 88 D1
Ashburton Downs, *Australia* 88 D2
Ashby de la Zouch, *U.K.* 12 E6
Ashcroft, *Canada* 100 C4
Ashdod, *Israel* 69 D3
Asheboro, *U.S.A.* 105 H6
Asherton, *U.S.A.* 109 L5
Asheville, *U.S.A.* 105 H4
Asheweig →, *Canada* 98 B2
Ashford, *Australia* 91 D5
Ashford, *U.K.* 13 F8
Ashford, *U.S.A.* 110 C2
Ashgabat, *Turkmenistan* 44 F6
Ashibetsu, *Japan* 48 C11
Ashikaga, *Japan* 49 F9
Ashizuri-Zaki, *Japan* 49 H6
Ashkarkot, *Afghan.* 62 C2
Ashkhabad = Ashgabat, *Turkmenistan* 44 F6
Ashland, *Kans., U.S.A.* 109 G5
Ashland, *Ky., U.S.A.* 104 F4
Ashland, *Maine, U.S.A.* 99 C6
Ashland, *Mont., U.S.A.* 110 D10
Ashland, *Nebr., U.S.A.* 108 E6
Ashland, *Ohio, U.S.A.* 106 F2
Ashland, *Oreg., U.S.A.* 110 E2
Ashland, *Pa., U.S.A.* 107 F8
Ashland, *Va., U.S.A.* 104 G7
Ashland, *Wis., U.S.A.* 108 B9
Ashley, *N. Dak., U.S.A.* 108 B5
Ashley, *Pa., U.S.A.* 107 E9
Ashmont, *Canada* 100 C6
Ashmore Reef, *Australia* 88 B3
Ashmûn, *Egypt* 76 H7
Ashmyany, *Belarus* 9 J21
Ashqelon, *Israel* 69 D3
Ashtabula, *U.S.A.* 106 E4
Ashton, *S. Africa* 84 E3
Ashton, *U.S.A.* 110 D8
Ashton under Lyne, *U.K.* 12 D5
Ashuanipi, L., *Canada* 99 B6
'Āṣī →, *Asia* 66 D6
Asia, Kepulauan, *Indonesia* 57 D8
Āsīā Bak, *Iran* 65 C6
Asiago, *Italy* 33 C8
Asidonhoppo, *Surinam* 121 C6
Asifabad, *India* 60 K11
Asike, *Indonesia* 57 F10
Asilah, *Morocco* 74 A3
Asinara, *Italy* 34 A1
Asinara, G. dell', *Italy* 34 B1
Asino, *Russia* 44 D9
Asipovichy, *Belarus* 40 F5
'Asīr □, *Si. Arabia* 68 D3
Asir, Ras, *Somali Rep.* 68 E5
Aşkale, *Turkey* 67 C9
Asker, *Norway* 10 E4
Askersund, *Sweden* 11 F8
Askham, *S. Africa* 84 D3
Askim, *Norway* 10 E5
Askja, *Iceland* 8 D5
Askøy, *Norway* 9 F11
Asl, *Egypt* 76 J8
Asmara = Asmera, *Eritrea* 77 D4
Asmera, *Eritrea* 77 D4
Asnæs, *Denmark* 11 J5
Åsnen, *Sweden* 9 H16
Asni, *Morocco* 74 B3
Ásola, *Italy* 32 C7
Asoteriba, Jebel, *Sudan* 76 C4
Asotin, *U.S.A.* 110 C5
Aspe, *Spain* 29 G4
Aspen, *U.S.A.* 111 G10
Aspendos, *Turkey* 66 D4
Aspermont, *U.S.A.* 109 J4
Aspiring, Mt., *N.Z.* 87 L2
Aspres-sur-Buëch, *France* 27 D9
Asprókavos, Ákra, *Greece* 37 B4
Aspromonte, *Italy* 35 D8
Aspur, *India* 62 H6
Asquith, *Canada* 101 C7
Assa, *Morocco* 74 C3
Assâba, *Mauritania* 78 B2
Assad, Bahret, *Syria* 67 D8
Assam □, *India* 61 F18
Assamakka, *Niger* 79 B6
Asse, *Belgium* 17 H4
Assebroek, *Belgium* 17 F2
Assekrem, *Algeria* 75 D6
Assémini, *Italy* 34 C2
Assen, *Neths.* 16 C9
Assendelft, *Neths.* 16 D5
Assenede, *Belgium* 17 F3
Assens, *Århus, Denmark* 11 H4
Assens, *Fyn, Denmark* 11 J3
Assesse, *Belgium* 17 H6
Assini, *Ivory C.* 78 D4
Assiniboia, *Canada* 101 D7
Assiniboine →, *Canada* 101 D9
Assis, *Brazil* 127 A5
Assisi, *Italy* 33 E9
Assynt, L., *U.K.* 14 C3
Astaffort, *France* 26 D4
Astara, *Azerbaijan* 67 C13
Āstārā, *Iran* 67 C13
Asten, *Neths.* 17 F7
Asteroúsia, *Greece* 37 E7
Asti, *Italy* 32 D5
Astipálaia, *Greece* 39 N9
Astorga, *Spain* 30 C4
Astoria, *U.S.A.* 112 D3
Åstorp, *Sweden* 11 H6
Astrakhan, *Russia* 43 G9
Astudillo, *Spain* 30 C6
Asturias □, *Spain* 30 B5
Asunción, *Paraguay* 126 B4
Asunción Nochixtlán, *Mexico* 115 D5
Asutri, *Sudan* 77 D4
Aswa →, *Uganda* 82 B3
Aswad, Ras al, *Si. Arabia* 76 C4
Aswân, *Egypt* 76 C3
Aswân High Dam = Sadd el Aali, *Egypt* 76 C3
Asyût, *Egypt* 76 B3
Asyûti, Wadi →, *Egypt* 76 B3
Aszód, *Hungary* 21 H9
At Ṭafīlah, *Jordan* 69 E4
At Ṭā'if, *Si. Arabia* 68 C3
Aṯ Ṯirāq, *Si. Arabia* 64 E5
Atacama □, *Chile* 126 B2
Atacama, Desierto de, *Chile* 126 A2
Atacama, Salar de, *Chile* 126 A2
Ataco, *Colombia* 120 C2
Atakor, *Algeria* 75 D6
Atakpamé, *Togo* 79 D5
Atalándi, *Greece* 39 L5
Atalaya, *Peru* 124 C3
Atalaya de Femes, *Canary Is.* 36 F6
Ataléia, *Brazil* 123 E3
Atami, *Japan* 49 G9
Atapupu, *Indonesia* 57 F6
Atâr, *Mauritania* 74 D2
Ataram, Erg n-, *Algeria* 75 D5
Atarfe, *Spain* 31 H7
Atascadero, *U.S.A.* 111 J3
Atasu, *Kazakstan* 44 E8
Atatürk Barajı, *Turkey* 67 D8
Atauro, *Indonesia* 57 F7
Atbara, *Sudan* 76 D3
'Atbara →, *Sudan* 76 D3
Atbasar, *Kazakstan* 44 D7
Atchafalaya B., *U.S.A.* 109 L9
Atchison, *U.S.A.* 108 F7
Atebubu, *Ghana* 79 D4
Ateca, *Spain* 28 D3
Aterno →, *Italy* 33 F10
Atesine, Alpi, *Italy* 32 B8
Atessa, *Italy* 33 F11
Ath, *Belgium* 17 G3
Athabasca, *Canada* 100 C6
Athabasca →, *Canada* 101 B6
Athabasca, L., *Canada* 101 B7
Athboy, *Ireland* 15 C5
Athenry, *Ireland* 15 C3
Athens = Athínai, *Greece* 39 M6
Athens, *Ala., U.S.A.* 105 H2
Athens, *Ga., U.S.A.* 105 J4
Athens, *N.Y., U.S.A.* 107 D11
Athens, *Ohio, U.S.A.* 104 F4
Athens, *Pa., U.S.A.* 107 E8
Athens, *Tenn., U.S.A.* 105 H3
Athens, *Tex., U.S.A.* 109 J7
Atherley, *Canada* 106 B5
Atherton, *Australia* 90 B4
Athiéme, *Benin* 79 D5
Athienou, *Cyprus* 37 D12
Athínai, *Greece* 39 M6
Athlone, *Ireland* 15 C4
Athna, *Cyprus* 37 D12
Atholl, Forest of, *U.K.* 14 E5
Atholville, *Canada* 99 C6
Áthos, *Greece* 39 J7
Athus, *Belgium* 17 J7
Athy, *Ireland* 15 D5
Ati, *Chad* 73 F8
Ati, *Sudan* 77 E2
Atiak, *Uganda* 82 B3
Atico, *Peru* 124 D3
Atienza, *Spain* 28 D2
Atikokan, *Canada* 98 C1
Atikonak L., *Canada* 99 B7
Atimonan, *Phil.* 55 E4
Atka, *Russia* 45 C16
Atkarsk, *Russia* 42 E7
Atkinson, *U.S.A.* 108 D5
Atlanta, *Ga., U.S.A.* 105 J3
Atlanta, *Tex., U.S.A.* 109 J7
Atlantic, *U.S.A.* 108 E7
Atlantic City, *U.S.A.* 104 F8
Atlantic Ocean 2 E9
Atlántico □, *Colombia* 120 A2
Atlas Mts. = Haut Atlas, *Morocco* 74 B3
Atlin, *Canada* 100 B2
Atlin, L., *Canada* 100 B2
Atmore, *U.S.A.* 105 K2
Atoka, *U.S.A.* 109 H6
Átokos, *Greece* 39 L3
Atolia, *U.S.A.* 113 K9
Atouguia, *Portugal* 31 F1
Atoyac →, *Mexico* 115 D5
Atrak = Atrek →, *Turkmenistan* 65 B8
Ätran, *Sweden* 11 G6
Atrato →, *Colombia* 120 B2
Atrauli, *India* 62 E8
Atrek →, *Turkmenistan* 65 B8
Atri, *Italy* 33 F10
Atsbi, *Ethiopia* 77 E4
Atsoum, Mts., *Cameroon* 79 D7
Atsuta, *Japan* 48 C10
Attalla, *U.S.A.* 105 H2
Attáviros, *Greece* 37 C9
Attawapiskat, *Canada* 98 B3
Attawapiskat →, *Canada* 98 B3
Attawapiskat, L., *Canada* 98 B2
Attendorn, *Germany* 18 D3
Attert, *Belgium* 17 J7
Attica, *U.S.A.* 104 E2
Attichy, *France* 25 C10
Attigny, *France* 25 C11
Attikamagen L., *Canada* 99 A6
Attleboro, *U.S.A.* 107 E13
Attock, *Pakistan* 62 C5
Attopeu, *Laos* 58 E6
Attur, *India* 60 P11
Atuel →, *Argentina* 126 D2
Åtvidaberg, *Sweden* 11 F10
Atwater, *U.S.A.* 111 H3
Atwood, *Canada* 106 C3
Atwood, *U.S.A.* 108 F4
Atyraū, *Kazakstan* 44 E6
Au Sable →, *U.S.A.* 104 C4
Au Sable Pt., *U.S.A.* 98 C2
Aubagne, *France* 27 E9
Aubange, *Belgium* 17 J7
Aubarca, C., *Spain* 36 B7
Aube □, *France* 25 D11
Aube →, *France* 25 D10
Aubel, *Belgium* 17 G7
Aubenas, *France* 27 D8
Aubenton, *France* 25 C11
Auberry, *U.S.A.* 112 H7
Aubigny-sur-Nère, *France* 25 E9
Aubin, *France* 26 D6
Aubrac, Mts. d', *France* 26 D7
Auburn, *Ala., U.S.A.* 105 J3
Auburn, *Calif., U.S.A.* 112 G5
Auburn, *Ind., U.S.A.* 104 E3
Auburn, *N.Y., U.S.A.* 107 D8
Auburn, *Nebr., U.S.A.* 108 E7
Auburn, *Wash., U.S.A.* 112 C4
Auburn Ra., *Australia* 91 D5
Auburndale, *U.S.A.* 105 L5
Aubusson, *France* 26 C6
Auch, *France* 26 E4
Auchel, *France* 25 B9
Auchi, *Nigeria* 79 D6
Auckland, *N.Z.* 87 G5
Auckland Is., *Pac. Oc.* 92 N8
Aude □, *France* 26 E6
Aude →, *France* 26 E7
Auden, *Canada* 98 B2
Auderghem, *Belgium* 17 G4
Auderville, *France* 24 C5
Audierne, *France* 24 D2
Audincourt, *France* 25 E13
Audo, *Ethiopia* 77 F5
Audubon, *U.S.A.* 108 E7
Aue, *Germany* 18 E8
Auer = Ora, *Italy* 33 B8
Auerbach, *Germany* 18 E8
Aueti Paraná →, *Brazil* 120 D4
Aufist, *W. Sahara* 74 C2
Augathella, *Australia* 91 D4
Augrabies Falls, *S. Africa* 84 D3
Augsburg, *Germany* 19 G6
Augusta, *Italy* 35 E8
Augusta, *Ark., U.S.A.* 109 H9
Augusta, *Ga., U.S.A.* 105 J5
Augusta, *Kans., U.S.A.* 109 G6
Augusta, *Maine, U.S.A.* 99 D6
Augusta, *Mont., U.S.A.* 110 C7
Augusta, *Wis., U.S.A.* 108 C9
Augustenborg, *Denmark* 11 K3
Augustów, *Poland* 20 B12
Augustus, Mt., *Australia* 88 D2
Augustus Downs, *Australia* 90 B2
Augustus I., *Australia* 88 C3
Aukan, *Eritrea* 77 D5
Aukum, *U.S.A.* 112 G6
Auld, L., *Australia* 88 D3
Aulla, *Italy* 32 D6
Aulnay, *France* 26 B3
Aulne →, *France* 24 D2
Aulnoye-Aymeries, *France* 25 B10
Ault, *France* 24 B8
Ault, *U.S.A.* 108 E2
Aulus-les-Bains, *France* 26 F5
Aumale, *France* 25 C8
Aumont-Aubrac, *France* 26 D7
Auna, *Nigeria* 79 C5
Aunis, *France* 26 B3
Auponhia, *Indonesia* 57 E7
Aups, *France* 27 E10
Aur, P., *Malaysia* 59 L5
Auraiya, *India* 63 F8
Aurangabad, *Bihar, India* 63 G11
Aurangabad, *Maharashtra, India* 60 K9
Auray, *France* 24 E4
Aurès, *Algeria* 75 A6
Aurich, *Germany* 18 B3
Aurilândia, *Brazil* 123 E1
Aurillac, *France* 26 D6
Auronzo di Cadore, *Italy* 33 B9
Aurora, *Canada* 106 C5
Aurora, *S. Africa* 84 E2
Aurora, *Colo., U.S.A.* 108 F2
Aurora, *Ill., U.S.A.* 104 E1
Aurora, *Mo., U.S.A.* 109 G8
Aurora, *Nebr., U.S.A.* 108 E6
Aurora, *Ohio, U.S.A.* 106 E3
Aursmoen, *Norway* 10 E5
Aurukun Mission, *Australia* 90 A3
Aus, *Namibia* 84 D2
Auschwitz = Oświęcim, *Poland* 20 E9
Austin, *Minn., U.S.A.* 108 D8
Austin, *Nev., U.S.A.* 110 G5
Austin, *Pa., U.S.A.* 106 E6
Austin, *Tex., U.S.A.* 109 K6
Austin, L., *Australia* 89 E2
Austra, *Norway* 8 D14
Austral Downs, *Australia* 90 C2
Austral Is. = Tubuai Is., *Pac. Oc.* 93 K12
Austral Seamount Chain, *Pac. Oc.* 93 K13
Australia ■, *Oceania* 92 K5
Australian Alps, *Australia* 91 F4
Australian Capital Territory □, *Australia* 91 F4
Austria ■, *Europe* 21 H4
Austvågøy, *Norway* 8 B16
Autazes, *Brazil* 121 D6
Autelbas, *Belgium* 17 J7
Auterive, *France* 26 E5
Authie →, *France* 25 B8
Authon-du-Perche, *France* 24 D7
Autlán, *Mexico* 114 D4
Autun, *France* 25 F11
Auvelais, *Belgium* 17 H5
Auvergne, *Australia* 88 C5
Auvergne, *France* 26 C7
Auvergne, Mts. d', *France* 26 C6
Auvézère →, *France* 26 C4
Auxerre, *France* 25 E10
Auxi-le-Château, *France* 25 B9
Auxonne, *France* 25 E12
Auzances, *France* 26 B6
Auzat-sur-Allier, *France* 26 C7
Avallon, *France* 25 E10
Avalon, *U.S.A.* 113 M8
Avalon Pen., *Canada* 99 C9
Avaré, *Brazil* 127 A6
Ávas, *Greece* 39 J8
Avawatz Mts., *U.S.A.* 113 K10
Aveiro, *Brazil* 121 D6
Aveiro, *Portugal* 30 E2
Aveiro □, *Portugal* 30 E2
Āvej, *Iran* 65 C6
Avelgem, *Belgium* 17 G2
Avellaneda, *Argentina* 126 C4
Avellino, *Italy* 35 B7
Avenal, *U.S.A.* 112 K6
Avenches, *Switz.* 22 C4
Averøya, *Norway* 10 A1
Aversa, *Italy* 35 B7
Avery, *U.S.A.* 110 C6
Aves, I. de, *W. Indies* 117 C7
Aves, Is. de, *Venezuela* 117 D6
Avesnes-sur-Helpe, *France* 25 B10
Avesta, *Sweden* 9 F17
Aveyron □, *France* 26 D6
Aveyron →, *France* 26 D5
Avezzano, *Italy* 33 F10
Aviá Terai, *Argentina* 126 B3
Aviano, *Italy* 33 B9
Avigliana, *Italy* 32 C4
Avigliano, *Italy* 35 B8
Avignon, *France* 27 E8
Ávila, *Spain* 30 E6
Ávila □, *Spain* 30 E6
Ávila, Sierra de, *Spain* 30 E5
Avila Beach, *U.S.A.* 113 K6
Avilés, *Spain* 30 B5
Avísio →, *Italy* 33 B8
Aviz, *Portugal* 31 F3
Avize, *France* 25 D11
Avoca, *Ireland* 15 D5
Avoca, *U.S.A.* 106 D7
Avoca →, *Australia* 91 F3
Avola, *Canada* 100 C5
Avola, *Italy* 35 F8
Avon, *N.Y., U.S.A.* 106 D7
Avon, *S. Dak., U.S.A.* 108 D5
Avon →, *Australia* 89 F2
Avon →, *Bristol, U.K.* 13 F5
Avon →, *Dorset, U.K.* 13 G6
Avon →, *Warks., U.K.* 13 F5
Avondale, *Zimbabwe* 83 F3
Avonlea, *Canada* 101 D7
Avonmore, *Canada* 107 A10
Avonmouth, *U.K.* 13 F5
Avranches, *France* 24 D5
Avre →, *France* 24 D8
Awag el Baqar, *Sudan* 77 E3
A'waj →, *Syria* 69 B5
Awaji-Shima, *Japan* 49 G7
'Awālī, *Bahrain* 65 E6
Awantipur, *India* 63 C6
Awasa, L., *Ethiopia* 77 F4
Awash, *Ethiopia* 68 F3
Awash →, *Ethiopia* 77 E5
Awaso, *Ghana* 78 D4
Awatere →, *N.Z.* 87 J5
Awbārī, *Libya* 75 C7
Awbārī □, *Libya* 75 C7
Awe, L., *U.K.* 14 E3
Aweil, *Sudan* 77 F2
Awgu, *Nigeria* 79 D6
Awjilah, *Libya* 73 C9
Ax-les-Thermes, *France* 26 F5
Axel, *Neths.* 17 F3
Axel Heiberg I., *Canada* 4 B3
Axim, *Ghana* 78 E4
Axinim, *Brazil* 121 D6
Axintele, *Romania* 38 E9
Axioma, *Brazil* 125 B5
Axiós →, *Greece* 39 J5
Axminster, *U.K.* 13 G4
Axvall, *Sweden* 11 F7
Aÿ, *France* 25 C11
Ayabaca, *Peru* 124 A2
Ayabe, *Japan* 49 G7
Ayacucho, *Argentina* 126 D4
Ayacucho, *Peru* 124 C3
Ayaguz, *Kazakstan* 44 E9
Ayamonte, *Spain* 31 H3
Ayan, *Russia* 45 D14
Ayancık, *Turkey* 66 B6
Ayapel, *Colombia* 120 B2
Ayas, *Turkey* 66 B5
Ayaviri, *Peru* 124 C3
Aybastı, *Turkey* 66 B7
Aydın, *Turkey* 66 D2
Aye, *Belgium* 17 H6
Ayenngré, *Togo* 79 D5
Ayer's Cliff, *Canada* 107 A12
Ayers Rock, *Australia* 89 E5
Ayiá, *Greece* 39 K5
Ayia Aikateríni, Ákra, *Greece* 37 A3
Ayia Dhéka, *Greece* 37 D6
Ayia Gálini, *Greece* 37 D6
Ayía Marína, *Greece* 39 M9
Ayia Napa, *Cyprus* 37 E13
Ayía Paraskeví, *Greece* 39 K9
Ayia Phyla, *Cyprus* 37 E12
Ayía Rouméli, *Greece* 39 P6
Ayia Varvára, *Greece* 37 D7
Áyios Amvrósios, *Cyprus* 37 D12
Áyios Andréas, *Greece* 39 M5
Áyios Evstrátios, *Greece* 39 K7
Áyios Ioánnis, Ákra, *Greece* 37 D7
Áyios Isidhoros, *Greece* 37 C9
Áyios Kiríkos, *Greece* 39 M9
Áyios Matthaíos, *Greece* 37 B3
Áyios Mírono, *Greece* 39 P8
Áyios Nikólaos, *Greece* 37 D7
Áyios Seryios, *Cyprus* 37 D12
Ayios Theodhoros, *Cyprus* 37 D13
Aykathonisi, *Greece* 39 M9
Aylesbury, *U.K.* 13 F7
Aylmer, *Canada* 106 D4
Aylmer, L., *Canada* 96 B8
Ayn Zālah, *Iraq* 67 D10
Ayna, *Spain* 29 G2
Ayolas, *Paraguay* 126 B4
Ayom, *Sudan* 77 F2
Ayon, Ostrov, *Russia* 45 C17
Ayora, *Spain* 29 F3
Ayr, *Australia* 90 B4
Ayr, *U.K.* 14 F4
Ayr →, *U.K.* 14 F4
Ayrancı, *Turkey* 66 D5
Ayre, Pt. of, *U.K.* 12 C3
Aysha, *Ethiopia* 77 E5
Aytos, *Bulgaria* 38 G10
Ayu, Kepulauan, *Indonesia* 57 D8
Ayutla, *Guatemala* 116 D1
Ayutla, *Mexico* 115 D5
Ayvacık, *Turkey* 66 C2
Ayvalık, *Turkey* 66 C2
Aywaille, *Belgium* 17 H7
Az Zabdānī, *Syria* 69 B5
Aẓ Ẓāhirīyah, *West Bank* 69 D3
Aẓ Ẓahrān, *Si. Arabia* 65 E6
Az Zarqā, *Jordan* 69 C5
Az Zāwiyah, *Libya* 75 B7
Az Zībār, *Iraq* 67 D11
Az-Zilfī, *Si. Arabia* 64 E5
Az Zubayr, *Iraq* 64 D5
Az Zuwaytīnah, *Libya* 73 B9
Azambuja, *Portugal* 31 F2
Azamgarh, *India* 63 F10
Azangaro, *Peru* 124 C3
Azaouak, Vallée de l', *Mali* 79 B5
Āzār Shahr, *Iran* 67 D11
Azarān, *Iran* 67 D12
Azärbayjan = Azerbaijan ■, *Asia* 43 K9
Āzarbāyjān-e Gharbī □, *Iran* 64 B5
Āzarbāyjān-e Sharqī □, *Iran* 64 B5
Azare, *Nigeria* 79 C7
Azay-le-Rideau, *France* 24 E7
A'zāz, *Syria* 66 D7
Azazga, *Algeria* 75 A5
Azbine = Aïr, *Niger* 79 B6
Azefal, *Mauritania* 74 D2
Azeffoun, *Algeria* 75 A5
Azemmour, *Morocco* 74 B3
Azerbaijan ■, *Asia* 43 K9
Azerbaijchan = Azerbaijan ■, *Asia* 43 K9
Azezo, *Ethiopia* 77 E4
Azimganj, *India* 63 G13
Aznalcóllar, *Spain* 31 H4
Azogues, *Ecuador* 120 D2
Azores, *Atl. Oc.* 70 C1
Azov, *Russia* 43 G4
Azov, Sea of, *Europe* 43 H3
Azovskoye More = Azov, Sea of, *Europe* 43 H3

Azovy, *Russia* 44 C7
Azpeitia, *Spain* 28 B2
Azrou, *Morocco* 74 B3
Aztec, *U.S.A.* 111 H10
Azúa, *Dom. Rep.* 117 C5
Azuaga, *Spain* 31 G5
Azuara, *Spain* 28 D4
Azuay □, *Ecuador* 120 D2
Azuer →, *Spain* 31 F7
Azuero, Pen. de, *Panama* 116 E3
Azul, *Argentina* 126 D4
Azul, Serra, *Brazil* 125 C7
Azurduy, *Bolivia* 125 D5
Azusa, *U.S.A.* 113 L9
Azzaba, *Algeria* 75 A6
Azzano Décimo, *Italy* 33 C9
'Azzūn, *West Bank* 69 C4

B

Ba Don, *Vietnam* 58 D6
Ba Dong, *Vietnam* 59 H6
Ba Ngoi = Cam Lam, *Vietnam* 59 G7
Ba Ria, *Vietnam* 59 G6
Ba Tri, *Vietnam* 59 G6
Ba Xian, *China* 50 E9
Baa, *Indonesia* 57 F6
Baamonde, *Spain* 30 B3
Baar, *Switz.* 23 B7
Baarle Nassau, *Belgium* 17 F5
Baarlo, *Neths.* 17 F8
Baarn, *Neths.* 16 D6
Bab el Mandeb, *Red Sea* 68 E3
Baba Burnu, *Turkey* 66 C2
Baba dag, *Azerbaijan* 43 K9
Bābā Kalū, *Iran* 65 D6
Babaçulândia, *Brazil* 122 C2
Babadag, *Romania* 38 E11
Babadayhan, *Turkmenistan* 44 F7
Babaeski, *Turkey* 66 B2
Babahoyo, *Ecuador* 120 D2
Babakin, *Australia* 89 F2
Babana, *Nigeria* 79 C5
Babar, *Algeria* 75 A6
Babar, *Indonesia* 57 F7
Babar, *Pakistan* 62 D3
Babarkach, *Pakistan* 62 E2
Babayevo, *Russia* 40 C8
Babb, *U.S.A.* 110 B7
Babenhausen, *Germany* 19 F4
Babi Besar, P., *Malaysia* 59 L4
Babian Jiang →, *China* 52 F3
Babile, *Ethiopia* 77 F5
Babinda, *Australia* 90 B4
Babine, *Canada* 100 B3
Babine →, *Canada* 100 B3
Babine L., *Canada* 100 C3
Babo, *Indonesia* 57 E8
Bābol, *Iran* 65 B7
Bābol Sar, *Iran* 65 B7
Baboua, *C.A.R.* 80 C2
Babruysk, *Belarus* 41 F5
Babura, *Nigeria* 79 C6
Babusar Pass, *Pakistan* 63 B5
Babušnica, *Serbia, Yug.* 21 M12
Babuyan Chan., *Phil.* 55 B4
Babuyan Is., *Phil.* 55 B4
Babylon, *Iraq* 67 F11
Bac Can, *Vietnam* 58 A5
Bac Giang, *Vietnam* 58 B6
Bac Ninh, *Vietnam* 58 B6
Bac Phan, *Vietnam* 58 B5
Bac Quang, *Vietnam* 58 A5
Bacabal, *Brazil* 122 B3
Bacajá →, *Brazil* 121 D7
Bacalar, *Mexico* 115 D7
Bacan, Kepulauan, *Indonesia* 57 E7
Bacan, Pulau, *Indonesia* 57 E7
Bacarra, *Phil.* 55 B4
Bacău, *Romania* 38 C9
Baccarat, *France* 25 D13
Bacerac, *Mexico* 114 A3
Băceşti, *Romania* 38 C10
Bach Long Vi, Dao, *Vietnam* 58 B6
Bachaquero, *Venezuela* 120 B3
Bacharach, *Germany* 19 E3
Bachelina, *Russia* 44 D7
Bachuma, *Ethiopia* 77 F4
Bačina, *Serbia, Yug.* 21 M11
Back →, *Canada* 96 B9
Bačka Palanka, *Serbia, Yug.* 21 K9
Bačka Topola, *Serbia, Yug.* 21 K9
Bäckefors, *Sweden* 11 F6
Backnang, *Germany* 19 G5
Backstairs Passage, *Australia* 91 F2
Baco, Mt., *Phil.* 55 E4
Bacolod, *Phil.* 55 F5
Bacqueville-en-Caux, *France* 24 C8
Bácsalmás, *Hungary* 21 J9
Bacuag, *Phil.* 55 G6
Bacuk, *Malaysia* 59 J4
Bād, *Iran* 65 C7
Bad →, *U.S.A.* 108 C4
Bad Axe, *U.S.A.* 106 C2
Bad Bergzabern, *Germany* 19 F4
Bad Berleburg, *Germany* 18 D4
Bad Bevensen, *Germany* 18 B6
Bad Bramstedt, *Germany* 18 B5
Bad Brückenau, *Germany* 19 E5
Bad Doberan, *Germany* 18 A7
Bad Driburg, *Germany* 18 D5
Bad Ems, *Germany* 19 E3
Bad Frankenhausen, *Germany* 18 D7
Bad Freienwalde, *Germany* 18 C10
Bad Godesberg, *Germany* 18 E3
Bad Hersfeld, *Germany* 18 E5
Bad Hofgastein, *Austria* 21 H3
Bad Homburg, *Germany* 19 E4
Bad Honnef, *Germany* 18 E3
Bad Ischl, *Austria* 21 H3
Bad Kissingen, *Germany* 19 E6
Bad Königshofen, *Germany* 19 E6
Bad Kreuznach, *Germany* 19 F3
Bad Laasphe, *Germany* 18 E4
Bad Lands, *U.S.A.* 108 D3
Bad Langensalza, *Germany* 18 D6
Bad Lauterberg, *Germany* 18 D6
Bad Lippspringe, *Germany* 18 D4
Bad Mergentheim, *Germany* 19 F5
Bad Münstereifel, *Germany* 18 E2
Bad Muskau, *Germany* 18 D10
Bad Nauheim, *Germany* 19 E4
Bad Oeynhausen, *Germany* 18 C4
Bad Oldesloe, *Germany* 18 B6
Bad Orb, *Germany* 19 E5
Bad Pyrmont, *Germany* 18 D5
Bad Ragaz, *Switz.* 23 B9
Bad Reichenhall, *Germany* 19 H8
Bad Säckingen, *Germany* 19 H3
Bad Salzuflen, *Germany* 18 C4
Bad Segeberg, *Germany* 18 B6
Bad Tölz, *Germany* 19 H7
Bad Urach, *Germany* 19 G5
Bad Waldsee, *Germany* 19 H5
Bad Wildungen, *Germany* 18 D5
Bad Wimpfen, *Germany* 19 F5
Bad Windsheim, *Germany* 19 F6
Badagara, *India* 60 P9
Badagri, *Nigeria* 79 D5
Badajós, L., *Brazil* 121 D5
Badajoz, *Spain* 31 G4
Badajoz □, *Spain* 31 G4
Badalona, *Spain* 28 D7
Badalzai, *Afghan.* 62 E1
Badampahar, *India* 61 H15
Badanah, *Si. Arabia* 64 D4
Badarinath, *India* 63 D8
Badas, *Brunei* 56 D4
Badas, Kepulauan, *Indonesia* 56 D3
Baddo →, *Pakistan* 60 F4
Bade, *Indonesia* 57 F9
Baden, *Austria* 21 G6
Baden, *Switz.* 23 B6
Baden-Baden, *Germany* 19 G4
Baden-Württemberg □, *Germany* 19 G5
Badenoch, *U.K.* 14 E4
Badger, *Canada* 99 C8
Badger, *U.S.A.* 112 J7
Bādghīsāt □, *Afghan.* 60 B3
Badgom, *India* 63 B6
Badhoevedorp, *Neths.* 16 D5
Badia Polésine, *Italy* 33 C8
Badin, *Pakistan* 62 G3
Badogo, *Mali* 78 C3
Badong, *China* 53 B8
Badrah, *Iraq* 67 F11
Baduen, *Somali Rep.* 68 F4
Badulla, *Sri Lanka* 60 R12
Baena, *Spain* 31 H6
Baexem, *Neths.* 17 F7
Baeza, *Ecuador* 120 D2
Baeza, *Spain* 29 H1
Bafang, *Cameroon* 79 D7
Bafatá, *Guinea-Biss.* 78 C2
Baffin B., *Canada* 4 B4
Baffin I., *Canada* 97 B12
Bafia, *Cameroon* 79 E7
Bafilo, *Togo* 79 D5
Bafing →, *Mali* 78 C2
Bafliyūn, *Syria* 64 B3
Baflo, *Neths.* 16 B9
Bafoulabé, *Mali* 78 C2
Bafoussam, *Cameroon* 79 D7
Bāfq, *Iran* 65 D7
Bafra, *Turkey* 66 B6
Bafra Burnu, *Turkey* 66 B7
Bāft, *Iran* 65 D8
Bafut, *Cameroon* 79 D7
Bafwasende, *Zaïre* 82 B2
Bagamoyo, *Tanzania* 82 D4
Bagamoyo □, *Tanzania* 82 D4
Bagan Datoh, *Malaysia* 59 L3
Bagan Serai, *Malaysia* 59 K3
Baganga, *Phil.* 55 H7
Bagani, *Namibia* 84 B3
Bagansiapiapi, *Indonesia* 56 D2
Bagasra, *India* 62 J4
Bagawi, *Sudan* 77 E3
Bagdad, *U.S.A.* 113 L11
Bagdarin, *Russia* 45 D12
Bagé, *Brazil* 127 C5
Bagenalstown = Muine Bheag, *Ireland* 15 D5
Baggs, *U.S.A.* 110 F10
Bagh, *Pakistan* 63 C5
Baghdād, *Iraq* 67 F11
Bagheria, *Italy* 34 D6
Baghlān, *Afghan.* 60 A6
Bagley, *U.S.A.* 108 B7
Bagnacavallo, *Italy* 33 D8
Bagnara Cálabra, *Italy* 35 D8
Bagnères-de-Bigorre, *France* 26 E4
Bagnères-de-Luchon, *France* 26 F4
Bagni di Lucca, *Italy* 32 D7
Bagno di Romagna, *Italy* 33 E8
Bagnoles-de-l'Orne, *France* 24 D6
Bagnoli di Sopra, *Italy* 33 C8
Bagnolo Mella, *Italy* 32 C7
Bagnols-sur-Cèze, *France* 27 D8
Bagnorégio, *Italy* 33 F9
Bagolino, *Italy* 32 C7
Bagotville, *Canada* 99 C5
Bagrationovsk, *Russia* 9 J19
Bagua, *Peru* 124 B2
Baguio, *Phil.* 55 C4
Bahabón de Esgueva, *Spain* 28 D1
Bahadurgarh, *India* 62 E7
Bahama, Canal Viejo de, *W. Indies* 116 B4
Bahamas ■, *N. Amer.* 117 B5
Bahār, *Iran* 67 E13
Baharampur, *India* 63 G13
Baharîya, El Wâhât al, *Egypt* 76 J6
Bahau, *Malaysia* 59 L4
Bahawalnagar, *Pakistan* 62 D5
Bahawalpur, *Pakistan* 62 E4
Bahçe, *Turkey* 66 D7
Baheri, *India* 63 E8
Bahi, *Tanzania* 82 D4
Bahi Swamp, *Tanzania* 82 D4
Bahía = Salvador, *Brazil* 123 D4
Bahía □, *Brazil* 123 D3
Bahía, Is. de la, *Honduras* 116 C2
Bahía Blanca, *Argentina* 126 D3
Bahía de Caráquez, *Ecuador* 120 D1
Bahía Honda, *Cuba* 116 B3
Bahía Laura, *Argentina* 128 C3
Bahía Negra, *Paraguay* 125 E6
Bahir Dar, *Ethiopia* 77 E4
Bahmanzād, *Iran* 65 D6
Bahmer, *Algeria* 75 C4
Bahönye, *Hungary* 21 J7
Bahr Aouk →, *C.A.R.* 80 C3
Bahr el Ahmar □, *Sudan* 76 C3
Bahr el Ghazâl □, *Sudan* 77 F2
Bahr Salamat →, *Chad* 73 G8
Bahr Yûsef →, *Egypt* 76 J7
Bahra el Burullus, *Egypt* 76 H7
Bahraich, *India* 63 F9
Bahrain ■, *Asia* 65 E6
Bahror, *India* 62 F7
Bāhū Kalāt, *Iran* 65 E9
Bai, *Mali* 78 C4
Bai Bung, Mui, *Vietnam* 59 H5
Bai Duc, *Vietnam* 58 C5
Bai Thuong, *Vietnam* 58 C5
Baia Mare, *Romania* 38 B6
Baia-Sprie, *Romania* 38 B6
Baião, *Brazil* 122 B2
Baïbokoum, *Chad* 73 G8
Baicheng, *China* 51 B12
Baidoa, *Somali Rep.* 68 G3
Baie Comeau, *Canada* 99 C6
Baie-St-Paul, *Canada* 99 C5
Baie Trinité, *Canada* 99 C6
Baie Verte, *Canada* 99 C8
Baignes-Ste.-Radegonde, *France* 26 C3
Baigneux-les-Juifs, *France* 25 E11
Baihe, *China* 50 H6
Ba'ījī, *Iraq* 67 E10
Baikal, L. = Baykal, Oz., *Russia* 45 D11
Baile Atha Cliath = Dublin, *Ireland* 15 C5
Bailei, *Ethiopia* 77 F5
Bailén, *Spain* 31 G7
Băileşti, *Romania* 38 E6
Baileux, *Belgium* 17 H4
Bailique, Ilha, *Brazil* 122 A2
Bailleul, *France* 25 B9
Bailundo, *Angola* 81 G3
Baima, *China* 52 A3
Bain-de-Bretagne, *France* 24 E5
Bainbridge, *Ga., U.S.A.* 105 K3
Bainbridge, *N.Y., U.S.A.* 107 D9
Baing, *Indonesia* 57 F6
Bainiu, *China* 50 H7
Bainville, *U.S.A.* 108 A2
Bā'ir, *Jordan* 69 E5
Baird, *U.S.A.* 109 J5
Baird Mts., *U.S.A.* 96 B3
Bairin Youqi, *China* 51 C10
Bairin Zuoqi, *China* 51 C10
Bairnsdale, *Australia* 91 F4
Bais, *Phil.* 55 G5
Baisha, *China* 50 G7
Baïsole →, *France* 26 E4
Baissa, *Nigeria* 79 D7
Baitadi, *Nepal* 63 E9
Baixa Grande, *Brazil* 123 D3
Baiyin, *China* 50 F3
Baiyü, *China* 52 B2
Baiyu Shan, *China* 50 F4
Baiyuda, *Sudan* 76 D3
Baj Baj, *India* 63 H13
Baja, *Hungary* 21 J8
Baja, Pta., *Mexico* 114 B1
Baja California, *Mexico* 114 A1
Baja California □, *Mexico* 114 B2
Baja California Sur □, *Mexico* 114 B2
Bajamar, *Canary Is.* 36 F3
Bajana, *India* 62 H4
Bājgīrān, *Iran* 65 B8
Bajimba, Mt., *Australia* 91 D5
Bajo Nuevo, *Caribbean* 116 C4
Bajoga, *Nigeria* 79 C7
Bajool, *Australia* 90 C5
Bakala, *C.A.R.* 73 G9
Bakar, *Croatia* 33 C11
Bakchar, *Russia* 44 D9
Bakel, *Neths.* 17 E7
Bakel, *Senegal* 78 C2
Baker, *Calif., U.S.A.* 113 K10
Baker, *Mont., U.S.A.* 108 B2
Baker, *Oreg., U.S.A.* 110 D5
Baker, Canal, *Chile* 128 C2
Baker, L., *Canada* 96 B10
Baker I., *Pac. Oc.* 92 G10
Baker L., *Australia* 89 E4
Baker Lake, *Canada* 96 B10
Baker Mt., *U.S.A.* 110 B3
Bakers Creek, *Australia* 90 C4
Baker's Dozen Is., *Canada* 98 A4
Bakersfield, *Calif., U.S.A.* 113 K7
Bakersfield, *Vt., U.S.A.* 107 B12
Bakhchysaray, *Ukraine* 41 K7
Bakhmach, *Ukraine* 41 G7
Bākhtarān, *Iran* 67 E12
Bākhtarān □, *Iran* 64 C5
Bakı, *Azerbaijan* 43 K9
Bakırdaği, *Turkey* 66 C6
Bakırköy, *Turkey* 39 H11
Bakkafjörður, *Iceland* 8 C6
Bakony →, *Hungary* 21 H7
Bakony Forest = Bakony Hegyseg, *Hungary* 21 H7
Bakony Hegyseg, *Hungary* 21 H7
Bakori, *Nigeria* 79 C6
Bakouma, *C.A.R.* 73 G9
Baksan, *Russia* 43 J6
Baku = Bakı, *Azerbaijan* 43 K9
Bakutis Coast, *Antarctica* 5 D15
Baky = Bakı, *Azerbaijan* 43 K9
Bala, *Canada* 106 A5
Bâlâ, *Turkey* 66 C5
Bala, L., *U.K.* 12 E4
Balabac I., *Phil.* 55 H2
Balabac Str., *E. Indies* 56 C5
Balabagh, *Afghan.* 62 B4
Ba'labakk, *Lebanon* 69 A5
Balabalangan, Kepulauan, *Indonesia* 56 E5
Bălăciţa, *Romania* 38 E6
Balad, *Iraq* 67 F11
Balad Rūz, *Iraq* 67 F11
Bālādeh, *Fārs, Iran* 65 D6
Bālādeh, *Māzandaran, Iran* 65 B6
Balaghat, *India* 60 J12
Balaghat Ra., *India* 60 K10
Balaguer, *Spain* 28 D5
Balakhna, *Russia* 42 B6
Balaklava, *Australia* 91 E2
Balaklava, *Ukraine* 41 K7
Balakliya, *Ukraine* 41 H9
Balakovo, *Russia* 42 D8
Balancán, *Mexico* 115 D6
Balashov, *Russia* 42 E6
Balasinor, *India* 62 H5
Balasore = Baleshwar, *India* 61 J15
Balassagyarmat, *Hungary* 21 G9
Balât, *Egypt* 76 B2
Balaton, *Hungary* 21 J7
Balayan, *Phil.* 55 E4
Balazote, *Spain* 29 G2
Balbina, Reprêsa da, *Brazil* 121 D6
Balboa, *Panama* 116 E4
Balbriggan, *Ireland* 15 C5
Balcarce, *Argentina* 126 D4
Balcarres, *Canada* 101 C8
Balchik, *Bulgaria* 38 F11
Balclutha, *N.Z.* 87 M2
Bald Hd., *Australia* 89 G2
Bald I., *Australia* 89 F2
Bald Knob, *U.S.A.* 109 H9
Baldock L., *Canada* 101 B9
Baldwin, *Fla., U.S.A.* 105 K4
Baldwin, *Mich., U.S.A.* 104 D3
Baldwinsville, *U.S.A.* 107 C8
Baldy Peak, *U.S.A.* 111 K9
Bale, *Croatia* 33 C10
Bale □, *Ethiopia* 77 F5
Baleares □, *Spain* 28 F7
Baleares, Is., *Spain* 36 B10
Balearic Is. = Baleares, Is., *Spain* 36 B10
Baleia, Pta. da, *Brazil* 123 E4
Balen, *Belgium* 17 F6
Baler, *Phil.* 55 D4
Baler Bay, *Phil.* 55 D4
Balerna, *Switz.* 23 E8
Baleshwar, *India* 61 J15
Balezino, *Russia* 42 B11
Balfate, *Honduras* 116 C2
Balfe's Creek, *Australia* 90 C4
Bali, *Cameroon* 79 D6
Balí, *Greece* 37 D6
Bali, *Indonesia* 56 F5
Bali □, *Indonesia* 56 F5
Bali, Selat, *Indonesia* 57 H16
Baligród, *Poland* 20 F12
Balikeşir, *Turkey* 66 C2
Balikpapan, *Indonesia* 56 E5
Balimbing, *Phil.* 57 C5
Baling, *Malaysia* 59 K3
Balintang Channel, *Phil.* 55 B4
Balipara, *India* 61 F18
Baliza, *Brazil* 125 D7
Balk, *Neths.* 16 C7
Balkan Mts. = Stara Planina, *Bulgaria* 38 F6
Balkhash = Balqash, *Kazakstan* 44 E8
Balkhash, Ozero = Balqash Köl, *Kazakstan* 44 E8
Balla, *Bangla.* 61 G17
Ballachulish, *U.K.* 14 E3
Balladonia, *Australia* 89 F3
Ballarat, *Australia* 91 F3
Ballard, L., *Australia* 89 E3
Ballater, *U.K.* 14 D5
Ballenas, Canal de, *Mexico* 114 B2
Balleny Is., *Antarctica* 5 C11
Ballesteros, *Phil.* 55 B4
Ballia, *India* 63 G11
Ballidu, *Australia* 89 F2
Ballina, *Australia* 91 D5
Ballina, *Mayo, Ireland* 15 B2
Ballina, *Tipp., Ireland* 15 D3
Ballinasloe, *Ireland* 15 C3
Ballinger, *U.S.A.* 109 K5
Ballinrobe, *Ireland* 15 C2
Ballinskelligs B., *Ireland* 15 E1
Ballon, *France* 24 D7
Ballycastle, *U.K.* 15 A5
Ballymena, *U.K.* 15 B5
Ballymena □, *U.K.* 15 B5
Ballymoney, *U.K.* 15 A5
Ballymoney □, *U.K.* 15 A5
Ballyshannon, *Ireland* 15 B3
Balmaceda, *Chile* 128 C2
Balmazújváros, *Hungary* 21 H11
Balmhorn, *Switz.* 22 D5
Balmoral, *Australia* 91 F3
Balmoral, *U.K.* 14 D5
Balmorhea, *U.S.A.* 109 K3
Balonne →, *Australia* 91 D4
Balqash, *Kazakstan* 44 E8
Balqash Köl, *Kazakstan* 44 E8
Balrampur, *India* 63 F10
Balranald, *Australia* 91 E3
Balş, *Romania* 38 E7
Balsapuerto, *Peru* 124 B2
Balsas, *Mexico* 115 D5
Balsas →, *Maranhão, Brazil* 122 C3
Balsas →, *Tocantins, Brazil* 122 C2
Balsas →, *Mexico* 114 D4
Bålsta, *Sweden* 10 E11
Balsthal, *Switz.* 22 B5
Balston Spa, *U.S.A.* 107 D11
Balta, *Romania* 38 E5
Balta, *Ukraine* 41 H5
Balta, *U.S.A.* 108 A4
Baltanás, *Spain* 30 D6
Bălţi, *Moldova* 41 J4
Baltic Sea, *Europe* 9 H18
Baltîm, *Egypt* 76 H7
Baltimore, *Ireland* 15 E2
Baltimore, *U.S.A.* 104 F7
Baltit, *Pakistan* 63 A6
Baltiysk, *Russia* 9 J18
Baltrum, *Germany* 18 B3
Baluchistan □, *Pakistan* 60 F4
Balurghat, *India* 63 G13
Balvi, *Latvia* 9 H22
Balya, *Turkey* 66 C2
Balygychan, *Russia* 45 C16
Balzar, *Ecuador* 120 D2
Bam, *Iran* 65 D8
Bama, *China* 52 E6
Bama, *Nigeria* 79 C7
Bamako, *Mali* 78 C3
Bamba, *Mali* 79 B4
Bambamarca, *Peru* 124 B2
Bambari, *C.A.R.* 73 G9
Bambaroo, *Australia* 90 B4
Bamberg, *Germany* 19 F6
Bamberg, *U.S.A.* 105 J5
Bambesi, *Ethiopia* 77 F3
Bambey, *Senegal* 78 C1
Bambili, *Zaïre* 82 B2
Bambuí, *Brazil* 123 F2
Bamenda, *Cameroon* 79 D7
Bamfield, *Canada* 100 D3
Bāmīān □, *Afghan.* 60 B5
Bamiancheng, *China* 51 C13
Bamkin, *Cameroon* 79 D7
Bampūr, *Iran* 65 E9
Ban Aranyaprathet, *Thailand* 58 F4
Ban Ban, *Laos* 58 C4
Ban Bang Hin, *Thailand* 59 H2
Ban Chiang Klang, *Thailand* 58 C3
Ban Chik, *Laos* 58 D4
Ban Choho, *Thailand* 58 E4
Ban Dan Lan Hoi, *Thailand* 58 D2
Ban Don = Surat Thani, *Thailand* 59 H2
Ban Don, *Vietnam* 58 F6
Ban Don, Ao, *Thailand* 59 H2
Ban Dong, *Thailand* 58 C3
Ban Hong, *Thailand* 58 C2
Ban Kaeng, *Thailand* 58 D3
Ban Keun, *Laos* 58 C4
Ban Khai, *Thailand* 58 F3
Ban Kheun, *Laos* 58 B3
Ban Khlong Kua, *Thailand* 59 J3
Ban Khuan Mao, *Thailand* 59 J2
Ban Khun Yuam, *Thailand* 58 C1
Ban Ko Yai Chim, *Thailand* 59 G2
Ban Kok, *Thailand* 58 D4
Ban Laem, *Thailand* 58 F2
Ban Lao Ngam, *Laos* 58 E6
Ban Le Kathe, *Thailand* 58 E2
Ban Mae Chedi, *Thailand* 58 C2
Ban Mae Laeng, *Thailand* 58 B2

Ban Mae Sariang, *Thailand* 58 C1
Ban Mê Thuôt = Buon Me Thuot, *Vietnam* 58 F7
Ban Mi, *Thailand* 58 E3
Ban Muong Mo, *Laos* 58 C4
Ban Na Mo, *Laos* 58 D5
Ban Na San, *Thailand* 59 H2
Ban Na Tong, *Laos* 58 B3
Ban Nam Bac, *Laos* 58 B4
Ban Nam Ma, *Laos* 58 A3
Ban Ngang, *Laos* 58 E6
Ban Nong Bok, *Laos* 58 D5
Ban Nong Boua, *Laos* 58 E6
Ban Nong Pling, *Thailand* 58 E3
Ban Pak Chan, *Thailand* 59 G2
Ban Phai, *Thailand* 58 D4
Ban Pong, *Thailand* 58 F2
Ban Ron Phibun, *Thailand* 59 H2
Ban Sanam Chai, *Thailand* 59 J3
Ban Sangkha, *Thailand* 58 E4
Ban Tak, *Thailand* 58 D2
Ban Tako, *Thailand* 58 E4
Ban Tha Dua, *Thailand* 58 D2
Ban Tha Li, *Thailand* 58 D3
Ban Tha Nun, *Thailand* 59 H2
Ban Thahine, *Laos* 58 E5
Ban Xien Kok, *Laos* 58 B3
Ban Yen Nhan, *Vietnam* 58 B6
Baña, Punta de la, *Spain* 28 E5
Banaba, *Kiribati* 92 H8
Bañalbufar, *Spain* 36 B9
Banalia, *Zaïre* 82 B2
Banam, *Cambodia* 59 G5
Banamba, *Mali* 78 C3
Banana, *Australia* 90 C5
Bananal, I. do, *Brazil* 123 D1
Banaras = Varanasi, *India* 63 G10
Banas →, *Gujarat, India* 62 H4
Banas →, *Mad. P., India* 63 G9
Bânâs, Ras, *Egypt* 76 C4
Banaz, *Turkey* 66 C3
Banbān, *Si. Arabia* 64 E5
Banbridge, *U.K.* 15 B5
Banbridge □, *U.K.* 15 B5
Banbury, *U.K.* 13 E6
Banchory, *U.K.* 14 D6
Bancroft, *Canada* 98 C4
Band Bonī, *Iran* 65 E8
Band Qīr, *Iran* 65 D6
Banda, *India* 63 G9
Banda, Kepulauan, *Indonesia* 57 E7
Banda Aceh, *Indonesia* 56 C1
Banda Banda, Mt., *Australia* 91 E5
Banda Elat, *Indonesia* 57 F8
Banda Is. = Banda, Kepulauan, *Indonesia* 57 E7
Banda Sea, *Indonesia* 57 F7
Bandai-San, *Japan* 48 F10
Bandama →, *Ivory C.* 78 D3
Bandān, *Iran* 65 D9
Bandanaira, *Indonesia* 57 E7
Bandanwara, *India* 62 F6
Bandar = Machilipatnam, *India* 61 L12
Bandār 'Abbās, *Iran* 65 E8
Bandar-e Anzalī, *Iran* 67 D13
Bandar-e Bushehr = Būshehr, *Iran* 65 D6
Bandar-e Chārak, *Iran* 65 E7
Bandar-e Deylam, *Iran* 65 D6
Bandar-e Khomeynı, *Iran* 65 D6
Bandar-e Lengeh, *Iran* 65 E7
Bandar-e Maqām, *Iran* 65 E7
Bandar-e Ma'shur, *Iran* 65 D6
Bandar-e Nakhīlū, *Iran* 65 E7
Bandar-e Rīg, *Iran* 65 D6
Bandar-e Torkeman, *Iran* 65 B7
Bandar Maharani = Muar, *Malaysia* 59 L4
Bandar Penggaram = Batu Pahat, *Malaysia* 59 M4
Bandar Seri Begawan, *Brunei* 56 C4
Bandawe, *Malawi* 83 E3
Bande, *Belgium* 17 H6
Bande, *Spain* 30 C3
Bandeira, Pico da, *Brazil* 123 F3
Bandeirante, *Brazil* 123 D1
Bandera, *Argentina* 126 B3
Bandera, *U.S.A.* 109 L5
Banderas, B. de, *Mexico* 114 C3
Bandiagara, *Mali* 78 C4
Bandırma, *Turkey* 66 B3
Bandon, *Ireland* 15 E3
Bandon →, *Ireland* 15 E3
Bandula, *Mozam.* 83 F3
Bandundu, *Zaïre* 80 E3
Bandung, *Indonesia* 57 G12
Bandya, *Australia* 89 E3
Bāneh, *Iran* 67 E11
Bañeres, *Spain* 29 G4
Banes, *Cuba* 117 B4
Banff, *Canada* 100 C5
Banff, *U.K.* 14 D6
Banff Nat. Park, *Canada* 100 C5
Banfora, *Burkina Faso* 78 C4
Bang Fai →, *Laos* 58 D5
Bang Hieng →, *Laos* 58 D5
Bang Krathum, *Thailand* 58 D3
Bang Lamung, *Thailand* 58 F3
Bang Mun Nak, *Thailand* 58 D3
Bang Pa In, *Thailand* 58 E3
Bang Rakam, *Thailand* 58 D3
Bang Saphan, *Thailand* 59 G2
Bangala Dam, *Zimbabwe* 83 G3
Bangalore, *India* 60 N10
Bangante, *Cameroon* 79 D7
Bangaon, *India* 63 H13
Bangassou, *C.A.R.* 80 D4
Banggai, Kepulauan, *Indonesia* 57 E6
Banggi, P., *Malaysia* 56 C5
Banghāzī, *Libya* 73 B9
Bangil, *Indonesia* 57 G15
Bangjang, *Sudan* 77 E3
Bangka, P., *Sulawesi, Indonesia* 57 D7
Bangka, P., *Sumatera, Indonesia* 56 E3
Bangka, Selat, *Indonesia* 56 E3
Bangkalan, *Indonesia* 57 G15
Bangkinang, *Indonesia* 56 D2
Bangko, *Indonesia* 56 E2
Bangkok, *Thailand* 58 F3
Bangladesh ■, *Asia* 61 H17
Bangolo, *Ivory C.* 78 D3
Bangong Co, *India* 63 B8
Bangor, *Down, U.K.* 15 B6
Bangor, *Gwynedd, U.K.* 12 D3
Bangor, *Maine, U.S.A.* 99 D6
Bangor, *Pa., U.S.A.* 107 F9
Bangued, *Phil.* 55 C4
Bangui, *C.A.R.* 80 D3
Bangui, *Phil.* 55 B4
Banguru, *Zaïre* 82 B2
Bangweulu, L., *Zambia* 83 E3
Bangweulu Swamp, *Zambia* 83 E3
Bani, *Dom. Rep.* 117 C5
Bani →, *Mali* 78 C4
Bani, Djebel, *Morocco* 74 C3
Bani Bangou, *Niger* 79 B5
Banī Sa'd, *Iraq* 67 F11
Banī Walīd, *Libya* 73 B7
Bania, *Ivory C.* 78 D4
Banihal Pass, *India* 63 C6
Banīnah, *Libya* 73 B9
Bāniyās, *Syria* 66 E6
Banja Luka, *Bos.-H.* 21 L7
Banjar, *Indonesia* 57 G13
Banjarmasin, *Indonesia* 56 E4
Banjarnegara, *Indonesia* 57 G13
Banjul, *Gambia* 78 C1
Banka Banka, *Australia* 90 B1
Banket, *Zimbabwe* 83 F3
Bankilaré, *Niger* 79 C5
Bankipore, *India* 63 G11
Banks I., *B.C., Canada* 100 C3
Banks I., *N.W.T., Canada* 96 A7
Banks Pen., *N.Z.* 87 K4
Banks Str., *Australia* 90 G4
Bankura, *India* 63 H12
Bann →, *Arm., U.K.* 15 B5
Bann →, *L'derry., U.K.* 15 A5
Banna, *Phil.* 55 C4
Bannalec, *France* 24 E3
Bannang Sata, *Thailand* 59 J3
Banning, *U.S.A.* 113 M10
Banningville = Bandundu, *Zaïre* 80 E3
Bannockburn, *Canada* 106 B7
Bannockburn, *U.K.* 14 E5
Bannockburn, *Zimbabwe* 83 G2
Bannu, *Pakistan* 60 C7
Bañolas, *Spain* 28 C7
Banon, *France* 27 D9
Baños de la Encina, *Spain* 31 G7
Baños de Molgas, *Spain* 30 C3
Banská Bystrica, *Slovak Rep.* 20 G9
Banská Štiavnica, *Slovak Rep.* 21 G8
Banswara, *India* 62 H6
Bantayan, *Phil.* 55 F5
Banten, *Indonesia* 57 G12
Bantry, *Ireland* 15 E2
Bantry B., *Ireland* 15 E2
Bantul, *Indonesia* 57 G14
Bantva, *India* 62 J4
Banu, *Afghan.* 60 B6
Banyak, Kepulauan, *Indonesia* 56 D1
Banyo, *Cameroon* 79 D7
Banyuls-sur-Mer, *France* 26 F7
Banyumas, *Indonesia* 57 G13
Banyuwangi, *Indonesia* 57 H16
Banzare Coast, *Antarctica* 5 C9
Banzyville = Mobayi, *Zaïre* 80 D4
Bao Ha, *Vietnam* 58 A5
Bao Lac, *Vietnam* 58 A5
Bao Loc, *Vietnam* 59 G6
Bao'an = Shenzhen, *China* 53 F10
Baocheng, *China* 50 H4
Baode, *China* 50 E6
Baodi, *China* 51 E9
Baoding, *China* 50 E8
Baoji, *China* 50 G4
Baojing, *China* 52 C7
Baokang, *China* 53 B8
Baoshan, *Shanghai, China* 53 B13
Baoshan, *Yunnan, China* 52 E2
Baotou, *China* 50 D6
Baoying, *China* 51 H10
Bap, *India* 62 F5
Bapatla, *India* 61 M12
Bapaume, *France* 25 B9
Bāqerābād, *Iran* 65 C6
Ba'qūbah, *Iraq* 67 F11
Baquedano, *Chile* 126 A2
Bar, *Montenegro, Yug.* 21 N9
Bar, *Ukraine* 41 H4
Bar Bigha, *India* 63 G11
Bar Harbor, *U.S.A.* 99 D6
Bar-le-Duc, *France* 25 D12
Bar-sur-Aube, *France* 25 D11
Bar-sur-Seine, *France* 25 D11
Barabai, *Indonesia* 56 E5
Barabinsk, *Russia* 44 D8
Baraboo, *U.S.A.* 108 D10
Baracaldo, *Spain* 28 B2
Baracoa, *Cuba* 117 B5
Baradero, *Argentina* 126 C4
Baraga, *U.S.A.* 108 B10
Barahona, *Dom. Rep.* 117 C5
Barahona, *Spain* 28 D2
Barail Range, *India* 61 G18
Baraka →, *Sudan* 76 D4
Barakhola, *India* 61 G18
Barakot, *India* 63 J11
Barakpur, *India* 63 H13
Barakula, *Australia* 91 D5
Baralaba, *Australia* 90 C4
Baralzon L., *Canada* 101 B9
Barameiya, *Sudan* 76 D4
Baramula, *India* 63 B6
Baran, *India* 62 G7
Baranavichy, *Belarus* 41 F4
Baranoa, *Colombia* 120 A3
Baranof I., *U.S.A.* 100 B1
Barão de Cocais, *Brazil* 123 E3
Barão de Grajaú, *Brazil* 122 C3
Barão de Melgaço, *Mato Grosso, Brazil* 125 D6
Barão de Melgaço, *Rondônia, Brazil* 125 C5
Baraolt, *Romania* 38 C8
Barapasi, *Indonesia* 57 E9
Barasat, *India* 63 H13
Barat Daya, Kepulauan, *Indonesia* 57 F7
Barataria B., *U.S.A.* 109 L10
Baraut, *India* 62 E7
Baraya, *Colombia* 120 C2
Barbacena, *Brazil* 123 F3
Barbacoas, *Colombia* 120 C2
Barbacoas, *Venezuela* 120 B4
Barbados ■, *W. Indies* 117 D8
Barbalha, *Brazil* 122 C4
Barban, *Croatia* 33 C11
Barbastro, *Spain* 28 C5
Barbate, *Spain* 31 J5
Barberino di Mugello, *Italy* 33 D8
Barberton, *S. Africa* 85 D5
Barberton, *U.S.A.* 106 E3
Barbezieux, *France* 26 C3
Barbosa, *Colombia* 120 B3
Barbourville, *U.S.A.* 105 G4
Barbuda, *W. Indies* 117 C7
Barcaldine, *Australia* 90 C4
Barcarrota, *Spain* 31 G4
Barcellona Pozzo di Gotto, *Italy* 35 D8
Barcelona, *Spain* 28 D7
Barcelona, *Venezuela* 121 A5
Barcelona □, *Spain* 28 D7
Barcelonette, *France* 27 D10
Barcelos, *Brazil* 121 D5
Barcoo →, *Australia* 90 D3
Barcs, *Hungary* 21 K7
Bärdä, *Azerbaijan* 43 K8
Barda del Medio, *Argentina* 128 A3
Bardai, *Chad* 73 D8
Bardas Blancas, *Argentina* 126 D2
Barddhaman, *India* 63 H12
Bardejov, *Slovak Rep.* 20 F11
Bardera, *Somali Rep.* 68 G3
Bardi, *Italy* 32 D6
Bardīyah, *Libya* 73 B9
Bardolino, *Italy* 32 C7
Bardsey I., *U.K.* 12 E3
Bardstown, *U.S.A.* 104 G3
Bareilly, *India* 63 E8
Barentin, *France* 24 C7
Barenton, *France* 24 D6
Barents Sea, *Arctic* 4 B9
Barentu, *Eritrea* 77 D4
Barfleur, *France* 24 C5
Barfleur, Pte. de, *France* 24 C5
Barga, *China* 54 C3
Barga, *Italy* 32 D7
Bargal, *Somali Rep.* 68 E5
Bargara, *Australia* 90 C5
Barge, *Italy* 32 D4
Bargnop, *Sudan* 77 F2
Bargteheide, *Germany* 18 B6
Barguzin, *Russia* 45 D11
Barh, *India* 63 G11
Barhaj, *India* 63 F10
Barhi, *India* 63 G11
Bari, *India* 62 F7
Bari, *Italy* 35 A9
Bari Doab, *Pakistan* 62 D5
Bariadi □, *Tanzania* 82 C3
Barīm, *Yemen* 68 E3
Barima →, *Guyana* 121 B5
Barinas, *Venezuela* 120 B3
Barinas □, *Venezuela* 120 B4
Baring, C., *Canada* 96 B8
Baringo, *Kenya* 82 B4
Baringo □, *Kenya* 82 B4
Baringo, L., *Kenya* 82 B4
Barinitas, *Venezuela* 120 B3
Bariri, *Brazil* 123 F2
Bârîs, *Egypt* 76 C3
Barisal, *Bangla.* 61 H17
Barisan, Bukit, *Indonesia* 56 E2
Barito →, *Indonesia* 56 E4
Barjac, *France* 27 D8
Barjols, *France* 27 E10
Barjūj, Wadi →, *Libya* 75 C7
Bark L., *Canada* 106 A7
Barka = Baraka →, *Sudan* 76 D4
Barkam, *China* 52 B4
Barker, *U.S.A.* 106 C6
Barkley Sound, *Canada* 100 D3
Barkly Downs, *Australia* 90 C2
Barkly East, *S. Africa* 84 E4
Barkly Tableland, *Australia* 90 B2
Barkly West, *S. Africa* 84 D3
Barkol, Wadi →, *Sudan* 76 D3
Barksdale, *U.S.A.* 109 L4
Barlee, L., *Australia* 89 E2
Barlee, Mt., *Australia* 89 D4
Barletta, *Italy* 35 A9
Barlinek, *Poland* 20 C5
Barlovento, *Canary Is.* 36 F2
Barlow L., *Canada* 101 A8
Barmedman, *Australia* 91 E4
Barmer, *India* 62 G4
Barmera, *Australia* 91 E3
Barmouth, *U.K.* 12 E3
Barmstedt, *Germany* 18 B5
Barnagar, *India* 62 H6
Barnard Castle, *U.K.* 12 C6
Barnato, *Australia* 91 E3
Barnaul, *Russia* 44 D9
Barnesville, *U.S.A.* 105 J3
Barnet, *U.K.* 13 F7
Barneveld, *Neths.* 16 D7
Barneveld, *U.S.A.* 107 C9
Barneville-Cartevert, *France* 24 C5
Barngo, *Australia* 90 D4
Barnhart, *U.S.A.* 109 K4
Barnsley, *U.K.* 12 D6
Barnstaple, *U.K.* 13 F3
Barnsville, *U.S.A.* 108 B6
Baro, *Nigeria* 79 D6
Baro →, *Ethiopia* 77 F3
Baroda = Vadodara, *India* 62 H5
Baroda, *India* 62 G7
Baroe, *S. Africa* 84 E3
Baron Ra., *Australia* 88 D4
Barpeta, *India* 61 F17
Barques, Pt. Aux, *U.S.A.* 104 C4
Barquinha, *Portugal* 31 F2
Barquísimeto, *Venezuela* 120 A4
Barr, *France* 25 D14
Barra, *Brazil* 122 D3
Barra, *U.K.* 14 E1
Barra, Sd. of, *U.K.* 14 D1
Barra da Estiva, *Brazil* 123 D3
Barra de Navidad, *Mexico* 114 D4
Barra do Corda, *Brazil* 122 C2
Barra do Mendes, *Brazil* 123 D3
Barra do Piraí, *Brazil* 123 F3
Barra Falsa, Pta. da, *Mozam.* 85 C6
Barra Hd., *U.K.* 14 E1
Barra Mansa, *Brazil* 123 F3
Barraba, *Australia* 91 E5
Barracão do Barreto, *Brazil* 125 B6
Barrackpur = Barakpur, *India* 63 H13
Barrafranca, *Italy* 35 E7
Barraigh = Barra, *U.K.* 14 E1
Barranca, *Lima, Peru* 124 C2
Barranca, *Loreto, Peru* 120 D2
Barrancabermeja, *Colombia* 120 B3
Barrancas, *Colombia* 120 A3
Barrancas, *Venezuela* 121 B5
Barrancos, *Portugal* 31 G4
Barranqueras, *Argentina* 126 B4
Barranquilla, *Colombia* 120 A3
Barras, *Brazil* 122 B3
Barras, *Colombia* 120 D3
Barraute, *Canada* 98 C4
Barre, *Mass., U.S.A.* 107 D12
Barre, *Vt., U.S.A.* 107 B12
Barre do Bugres, *Brazil* 125 C6
Barreal, *Argentina* 126 C2
Barreiras, *Brazil* 123 D3
Barreirinha, *Brazil* 121 D6
Barreirinhas, *Brazil* 122 B3
Barreiro, *Portugal* 31 G1
Barreiros, *Brazil* 122 C4
Barrême, *France* 27 E10
Barren, Nosy, *Madag.* 85 B7
Barretos, *Brazil* 123 F2
Barrhead, *Canada* 100 C6
Barrie, *Canada* 98 D4
Barrier Ra., *Australia* 91 E3
Barrière, *Canada* 100 C4
Barrington, *U.S.A.* 107 E13
Barrington L., *Canada* 101 B8
Barrington Tops, *Australia* 91 E5
Barringun, *Australia* 91 D4
Barro do Garças, *Brazil* 125 D7
Barrow, *U.S.A.* 96 A4
Barrow →, *Ireland* 15 D4
Barrow Creek, *Australia* 90 C1
Barrow I., *Australia* 88 D2
Barrow-in-Furness, *U.K.* 12 C4
Barrow Pt., *Australia* 90 A3
Barrow Pt., *U.S.A.* 94 B4
Barrow Ra., *Australia* 89 E4
Barrow Str., *Canada* 4 B3
Barruecopardo, *Spain* 30 D4
Barruelo, *Spain* 30 C6
Barry, *U.K.* 13 F4
Barry's Bay, *Canada* 98 C4
Barsalogho, *Burkina Faso* 79 C4
Barsat, *Pakistan* 63 A5
Barsham, *Syria* 67 E9
Barsi, *India* 60 K9
Barsø, *Denmark* 11 J3
Barsoi, *India* 61 G15
Barstow, *Calif., U.S.A.* 113 L9
Barstow, *Tex., U.S.A.* 109 K3
Barth, *Germany* 18 A8
Barthélemy, Col, *Vietnam* 58 C5
Bartica, *Guyana* 121 B6
Bartin, *Turkey* 66 B5
Bartlesville, *U.S.A.* 109 G7
Bartlett, *Calif., U.S.A.* 112 J8
Bartlett, *Tex., U.S.A.* 109 K6
Bartlett, L., *Canada* 100 A5
Bartolomeu Dias, *Mozam.* 83 G4
Barton, *Australia* 89 F5
Barton upon Humber, *U.K.* 12 D7
Bartoszyce, *Poland* 20 A10
Bartow, *U.S.A.* 105 M5
Barú, I. de, *Colombia* 120 A2
Barú, Volcan, *Panama* 116 E3
Barumba, *Zaïre* 82 B1
Baruth, *Germany* 18 C9
Barvaux, *Belgium* 17 H6
Barvinkove, *Ukraine* 41 H9
Barwani, *India* 62 H6
Barysaw, *Belarus* 40 E5
Barysh, *Russia* 42 D8
Barzān, *Iraq* 64 B5
Bas-Rhin □, *France* 25 D14
Bašaid, *Serbia, Yug.* 21 K10
Bāsa'idū, *Iran* 65 E7
Basal, *Pakistan* 62 C5
Basankusa, *Zaïre* 80 D3
Basarabeasca, *Moldova* 41 J5
Basawa, *Afghan.* 62 B4
Bascharage, *Lux.* 17 J7
Bascuñán, C., *Chile* 126 B1
Basècles, *Belgium* 17 G3
Basel, *Switz.* 22 A5
Basel-Stadt □, *Switz.* 22 A5
Baselland □, *Switz.* 22 B5
Basento →, *Italy* 35 B9
Bāshī, *Iran* 65 D6
Bashi Channel, *Phil.* 54 D7
Bashkir Republic = Bashkortostan □, *Russia* 44 D6
Bashkortostan □, *Russia* 44 D6
Basilan, *Phil.* 55 H5
Basilan Str., *Phil.* 55 H5
Basildon, *U.K.* 13 F8
Basilicata □, *Italy* 35 B9
Basim = Washim, *India* 60 J10
Basin, *U.S.A.* 110 D9
Basingstoke, *U.K.* 13 F6
Baška, *Croatia* 33 D11
Başkale, *Turkey* 67 C10
Baskatong, Rés., *Canada* 98 C4
Basle = Basel, *Switz.* 22 A5
Basoda, *India* 62 H7
Basodino, *Switz.* 23 D6
Basoka, *Zaïre* 82 B1
Basongo, *Zaïre* 80 E4
Basque, Pays, *France* 26 E2
Basque Provinces = País Vasco □, *Spain* 28 C2
Basra = Al Başrah, *Iraq* 64 D5
Bass Rock, *U.K.* 14 E6
Bass Str., *Australia* 90 F4
Bassano, *Canada* 100 C6
Bassano del Grappa, *Italy* 33 C8
Bassar, *Togo* 79 D5
Bassas da India, *Ind. Oc.* 81 J7
Basse Santa-Su, *Gambia* 78 C2
Basse-Terre, *Guadeloupe* 117 C7
Bassecourt, *Switz.* 22 B4
Bassein, *Burma* 61 L19
Basseterre, *St. Kitts & Nevis* 117 C7
Bassett, *Nebr., U.S.A.* 108 D5
Bassett, *Va., U.S.A.* 105 G6
Bassevelde, *Belgium* 17 F3
Bassi, *India* 62 D7
Bassigny, *France* 25 E12
Bassikounou, *Mauritania* 78 B3
Bassilly, *Belgium* 17 G3
Bassum, *Germany* 18 C4
Båstad, *Sweden* 11 H6
Bastak, *Iran* 65 E7
Baştām, *Iran* 65 B7
Bastar, *India* 61 K12
Bastelica, *France* 27 F13
Basti, *India* 63 F10
Bastia, *France* 27 F13
Bastia Umbra, *Italy* 33 E9
Bastogne, *Belgium* 17 H7
Bastrop, *U.S.A.* 109 K6
Bat Yam, *Israel* 69 C3
Bata, *Eq. Guin.* 80 D1
Bata, *Romania* 38 C5
Bataan, *Phil.* 55 D4
Batabanó, *Cuba* 116 B3
Batabanó, G. de, *Cuba* 116 B3
Batac, *Phil.* 55 B4
Batagoy, *Russia* 45 C14
Batak, *Bulgaria* 39 H7
Batalha, *Portugal* 31 F2
Batama, *Zaïre* 82 B2
Batamay, *Russia* 45 C13
Batan I., *Phil.* 55 A4
Batanes Is., *Phil.* 55 A4
Batang, *China* 52 B2
Batang, *Indonesia* 57 G13
Batangafo, *C.A.R.* 73 G8
Batangas, *Phil.* 55 E4
Batanta, *Indonesia* 57 E8
Batatais, *Brazil* 127 A6
Batavia, *U.S.A.* 106 D6
Bataysk, *Russia* 43 G4
Batchelor, *Australia* 88 B5
Bateman's B., *Australia* 91 F5
Batemans Bay, *Australia* 91 F5
Bates Ra., *Australia* 89 E3
Batesburg, *U.S.A.* 105 J5
Batesville, *Ark., U.S.A.* 109 H9
Batesville, *Miss., U.S.A.* 109 H10

Batesville, *Tex., U.S.A.* 109 L5
Bath, *U.K.* 13 F5
Bath, *Maine, U.S.A.* 99 D6
Bath, *N.Y., U.S.A.* 106 D7
Bath & North East Somerset □, *U.K.* 13 F5
Batheay, *Cambodia* 59 G5
Bathgate, *U.K.* 14 F5
Bathmen, *Neths.* 16 D8
Bathurst = Banjul, *Gambia* 78 C1
Bathurst, *Australia* 91 E4
Bathurst, *Canada* 99 C6
Bathurst, *S. Africa* 84 E4
Bathurst, C., *Canada* 96 A7
Bathurst B., *Australia* 90 A3
Bathurst Harb., *Australia* 90 G4
Bathurst I., *Australia* 88 B5
Bathurst I., *Canada* 4 B2
Bathurst Inlet, *Canada* 96 B9
Batie, *Burkina Faso* 78 D4
Batlow, *Australia* 91 F4
Batman, *Turkey* 67 D9
Batna, *Algeria* 75 A6
Batobato, *Phil.* 55 H7
Batoka, *Zambia* 83 F2
Baton Rouge, *U.S.A.* 109 K9
Batong, Ko, *Thailand* 59 J2
Batopilas, *Mexico* 114 B3
Batouri, *Cameroon* 80 D2
Båtsfjord, *Norway* 8 A23
Battambang, *Cambodia* 58 F4
Batticaloa, *Sri Lanka* 60 R12
Battice, *Belgium* 17 G7
Battipáglia, *Italy* 35 B7
Battle, *U.K.* 13 G8
Battle →, *Canada* 101 C7
Battle Camp, *Australia* 90 B3
Battle Creek, *U.S.A.* 104 D3
Battle Ground, *U.S.A.* 112 E4
Battle Harbour, *Canada* 99 B8
Battle Lake, *U.S.A.* 108 B7
Battle Mountain, *U.S.A.* 110 F5
Battlefields, *Zimbabwe* 83 F2
Battleford, *Canada* 101 C7
Battonya, *Hungary* 21 J11
Batu, *Ethiopia* 68 F2
Batu, Kepulauan, *Indonesia* 56 E1
Batu Caves, *Malaysia* 59 L3
Batu Gajah, *Malaysia* 59 K3
Batu Is. = Batu, Kepulauan, *Indonesia* 56 E1
Batu Pahat, *Malaysia* 59 M4
Batuata, *Indonesia* 57 F6
Batumi, *Georgia* 43 K5
Baturaja, *Indonesia* 56 E2
Baturité, *Brazil* 122 B4
Bau, *Malaysia* 56 D4
Baubau, *Indonesia* 57 F6
Bauchi, *Nigeria* 79 C6
Bauchi □, *Nigeria* 79 C6
Baud, *France* 24 E3
Baudette, *U.S.A.* 108 A7
Baudour, *Belgium* 17 H3
Bauer, C., *Australia* 91 E1
Baugé, *France* 24 E6
Bauhinia Downs, *Australia* 90 C4
Baukau, *Indonesia* 57 F7
Bauma, *Switz.* 23 B7
Baume-les-Dames, *France* 25 E13
Baunatal, *Germany* 18 D5
Baunei, *Italy* 34 B2
Baures, *Bolivia* 125 C5
Bauru, *Brazil* 127 A6
Baús, *Brazil* 125 D7
Bauska, *Latvia* 9 H21
Bautino, *Kazakstan* 43 H10
Bautzen, *Germany* 18 D10
Bavānāt, *Iran* 65 D7
Bavaria = Bayern □, *Germany* 19 F7
Båven, *Sweden* 10 F10
Bavi Sadri, *India* 62 G6
Bavispe →, *Mexico* 114 B3
Bawdwin, *Burma* 61 H20
Bawean, *Indonesia* 56 F4
Bawku, *Ghana* 79 C4
Bawlake, *Burma* 61 K20
Bawolung, *China* 52 C3
Baxley, *U.S.A.* 105 K4
Baxoi, *China* 52 B1
Baxter Springs, *U.S.A.* 109 G7
Bay, L. de, *Phil.* 57 B6
Bay Bulls, *Canada* 99 C9
Bay City, *Mich., U.S.A.* 104 D4
Bay City, *Oreg., U.S.A.* 110 D2
Bay City, *Tex., U.S.A.* 109 L7
Bay de Verde, *Canada* 99 C9
Bay Minette, *U.S.A.* 105 K2
Bay St. Louis, *U.S.A.* 109 K10
Bay Springs, *U.S.A.* 109 K10
Bay View, *N.Z.* 87 H6
Baya, *Zaïre* 83 E2
Bayamo, *Cuba* 116 B4
Bayamón, *Puerto Rico* 117 C6
Bayan Har Shan, *China* 54 C4
Bayan Hot = Alxa Zuoqi, *China* 50 E3
Bayan Obo, *China* 50 D5
Bayan-Ovoo, *Mongolia* 50 C4
Bayana, *India* 62 F7
Bayanaūyl, *Kazakstan* 44 D8
Bayandalay, *Mongolia* 50 C2
Bayanhongor, *Mongolia* 54 B5
Bayard, *U.S.A.* 108 E3
Bayawan, *Phil.* 55 G5
Baybay, *Phil.* 55 F6
Bayburt, *Turkey* 67 B9
Bayerischer Wald, *Germany* 19 F8
Bayern □, *Germany* 19 F7
Bayeux, *France* 24 C6
Bayfield, *Canada* 106 C3
Bayfield, *U.S.A.* 108 B9
Bayındır, *Turkey* 66 C2
Baykal, Oz., *Russia* 45 D11
Baykit, *Russia* 45 C10
Baykonur = Bayqongyr, *Kazakstan* 44 E7
Baynes Mts., *Namibia* 84 B1
Bayombong, *Phil.* 55 C4
Bayon, *France* 25 D13
Bayona, *Spain* 30 C2
Bayonne, *France* 26 E2
Bayonne, *U.S.A.* 107 F10
Bayovar, *Peru* 124 B1
Bayqongyr, *Kazakstan* 44 E7
Bayram-Ali = Bayramaly, *Turkmenistan* 44 F7
Bayramaly, *Turkmenistan* 44 F7
Bayramiç, *Turkey* 66 C2
Bayreuth, *Germany* 19 F7
Bayrischzell, *Germany* 19 H8
Bayrūt, *Lebanon* 69 B4
Bayt Lahm, *West Bank* 69 D4
Baytown, *U.S.A.* 109 L7
Bayzo, *Niger* 79 C5
Baza, *Spain* 29 H2
Bazar Dyuzi, *Russia* 43 K8
Bazardüzü = Bazar Dyuzi, *Russia* 43 K8
Bazarny Karabulak, *Russia* 42 D8
Bazarnyy Syzgan, *Russia* 42 D8
Bazaruto, I. do, *Mozam.* 85 C6
Bazas, *France* 26 D3
Bazhong, *China* 52 B6
Bazmān, Kūh-e, *Iran* 65 D9
Beach, *U.S.A.* 108 B3
Beach City, *U.S.A.* 106 F3
Beachport, *Australia* 91 F2
Beachy Hd., *U.K.* 13 G8
Beacon, *Australia* 89 F2
Beacon, *U.S.A.* 107 E11
Beaconia, *Canada* 101 C9
Beagle, Canal, *S. Amer.* 128 E3
Beagle Bay, *Australia* 88 C3
Bealanana, *Madag.* 85 A8
Beamsville, *Canada* 106 C5
Bear →, *U.S.A.* 112 G5
Béar, C., *France* 26 F7
Bear I., *Ireland* 15 E2
Bear L., *B.C., Canada* 100 B3
Bear L., *Man., Canada* 101 B9
Bear L., *U.S.A.* 110 E8
Bearcreek, *U.S.A.* 110 D9
Beardmore, *Canada* 98 C2
Beardmore Glacier, *Antarctica* 5 E11
Beardstown, *U.S.A.* 108 F9
Béarn, *France* 26 E3
Bearpaw Mts., *U.S.A.* 110 B9
Bearskin Lake, *Canada* 98 B1
Beas de Segura, *Spain* 29 G2
Beasain, *Spain* 28 B2
Beata, C., *Dom. Rep.* 117 C5
Beata, I., *Dom. Rep.* 117 C5
Beatrice, *U.S.A.* 108 E6
Beatrice, *Zimbabwe* 83 F3
Beatrice, C., *Australia* 90 A2
Beatton →, *Canada* 100 B4
Beatton River, *Canada* 100 B4
Beatty, *U.S.A.* 111 H5
Beaucaire, *France* 27 E8
Beauce, Plaine de la, *France* 25 D8
Beauceville, *Canada* 99 C5
Beauchêne, I., *Falk. Is.* 128 D5
Beaudesert, *Australia* 91 D5
Beaufort, *Malaysia* 56 C5
Beaufort, *N.C., U.S.A.* 105 H7
Beaufort, *S.C., U.S.A.* 105 J5
Beaufort Sea, *Arctic* 4 B1
Beaufort West, *S. Africa* 84 E3
Beaugency, *France* 25 E8
Beauharnois, *Canada* 98 C5
Beaujeu, *France* 27 B8
Beaulieu →, *Canada* 100 A6
Beaulieu-sur-Dordogne, *France* 26 D5
Beaulieu-sur-Mer, *France* 27 E11
Beauly, *U.K.* 14 D4
Beauly →, *U.K.* 14 D4
Beaumaris, *U.K.* 12 D3
Beaumetz-lès-Loges, *France* 25 B9
Beaumont, *Belgium* 17 H4
Beaumont, *France* 26 D4
Beaumont, *U.S.A.* 109 K7
Beaumont-de-Lomagne, *France* 26 E4
Beaumont-le-Roger, *France* 24 C7
Beaumont-sur-Oise, *France* 25 C9
Beaumont-sur-Sarthe, *France* 24 D7
Beaune, *France* 25 E11
Beaune-la-Rolande, *France* 25 D9
Beaupréau, *France* 24 E6
Beauraing, *Belgium* 17 H5
Beauséjour, *Canada* 101 C9
Beauvais, *France* 25 C9
Beauval, *Canada* 101 B7
Beauvoir-sur-Mer, *France* 24 F4
Beauvoir-sur-Niort, *France* 26 B3
Beaver, *Alaska, U.S.A.* 96 B5
Beaver, *Okla., U.S.A.* 109 G4
Beaver, *Pa., U.S.A.* 106 F4
Beaver, *Utah, U.S.A.* 111 G7
Beaver →, *B.C., Canada* 100 B4
Beaver →, *Ont., Canada* 98 A2
Beaver →, *Sask., Canada* 101 B7
Beaver City, *U.S.A.* 108 E5
Beaver Dam, *U.S.A.* 108 D10
Beaver Falls, *U.S.A.* 106 F4
Beaver Hill L., *Canada* 101 C10
Beaver I., *U.S.A.* 104 C3
Beaverhill L., *Alta., Canada* 100 C6
Beaverhill L., *N.W.T., Canada* 101 A8
Beaverlodge, *Canada* 100 B5
Beavermouth, *Canada* 100 C5
Beaverstone →, *Canada* 98 B2
Beaverton, *Canada* 106 B5
Beaverton, *U.S.A.* 112 E4
Beawar, *India* 62 F6
Bebedouro, *Brazil* 127 A6
Beboa, *Madag.* 85 B7
Bebra, *Germany* 18 E5
Beccles, *U.K.* 13 E9
Bečej, *Serbia, Yug.* 21 K10
Becerreá, *Spain* 30 C3
Béchar, *Algeria* 75 B4
Beckley, *U.S.A.* 104 G5
Beckum, *Germany* 18 D4
Bečva →, *Czech.* 20 F7
Bédar, *Spain* 29 H3
Bédarieux, *France* 26 E7
Bédarrides, *France* 27 D8
Beddouza, Ras, *Morocco* 74 B3
Bedele, *Ethiopia* 77 F4
Bederkesa, *Germany* 18 B4
Bedeso, *Ethiopia* 77 F5
Bedford, *Canada* 98 C5
Bedford, *S. Africa* 84 E4
Bedford, *U.K.* 13 E7
Bedford, *Ind., U.S.A.* 104 F2
Bedford, *Iowa, U.S.A.* 108 E7
Bedford, *Ohio, U.S.A.* 106 E3
Bedford, *Pa., U.S.A.* 106 F6
Bedford, *Va., U.S.A.* 104 G6
Bedford, C., *Australia* 90 B4
Bedford Downs, *Australia* 88 C4
Bedfordshire □, *U.K.* 13 E7
Będków, *Poland* 20 D9
Bednja →, *Croatia* 33 B13
Bednodemyanovsk, *Russia* 42 D6
Bedónia, *Italy* 32 D6
Bedourie, *Australia* 90 C2
Bedretto, *Switz.* 23 C7
Bedum, *Neths.* 16 B9
Będzin, *Poland* 20 E9
Beech Grove, *U.S.A.* 104 F2
Beechy, *Canada* 101 C7
Beek, *Gelderland, Neths.* 16 E8
Beek, *Limburg, Neths.* 17 G7
Beek, *Noord-Brabant, Neths.* 17 E7
Beekbergen, *Neths.* 16 D7
Beelitz, *Germany* 18 C8
Beenleigh, *Australia* 91 D5
Be'er Menuha, *Israel* 64 D2
Be'er Sheva, *Israel* 69 D3
Beersheba = Be'er Sheva, *Israel* 69 D3
Beerta, *Neths.* 16 B10
Beerze →, *Neths.* 16 E6
Beesd, *Neths.* 16 E6
Beeskow, *Germany* 18 C10
Beeston, *U.K.* 12 E6
Beetaloo, *Australia* 90 B1
Beetsterzwaag, *Neths.* 16 B8
Beetzendorf, *Germany* 18 C7
Beeville, *U.S.A.* 109 L6
Befale, *Zaïre* 80 D4
Befandriana, *Madag.* 85 C7
Befotaka, *Madag.* 85 C8
Bega, *Australia* 91 F4
Bega, Canalul, *Romania* 38 D3
Bégard, *France* 24 D3
Bègles, *France* 26 D3
Begna →, *Norway* 10 D4
Begonte, *Spain* 30 B3
Begusarai, *India* 63 G12
Behābād, *Iran* 65 C8
Behara, *Madag.* 85 C8
Behbehān, *Iran* 65 D6
Behshahr, *Iran* 65 B7
Bei Jiang →, *China* 53 F9
Bei'an, *China* 54 B7
Beibei, *China* 54 D5
Beihai, *China* 52 G7
Beijing, *China* 50 E9
Beijing □, *China* 50 E9
Beilen, *Neths.* 16 C8
Beiliu, *China* 53 F8
Beilngries, *Germany* 19 F7
Beilpajah, *Australia* 91 E3
Beilul, *Eritrea* 77 E5
Beinn na Faoghla = Benbecula, *U.K.* 14 D1
Beipiao, *China* 51 D11
Beira, *Mozam.* 83 F3
Beirut = Bayrūt, *Lebanon* 69 B4
Beitaolaizhao, *China* 51 B13
Beitbridge, *Zimbabwe* 83 G3
Beiuş, *Romania* 38 C5
Beizhen, *Liaoning, China* 51 D11
Beizhen, *Shandong, China* 51 F10
Beizhengzhen, *China* 51 B12
Beja, *Portugal* 31 G3
Béja, *Tunisia* 75 A6
Beja □, *Portugal* 31 H3
Bejaia, *Algeria* 75 A6
Béjar, *Spain* 30 E5
Bejestān, *Iran* 65 C8
Bekaa Valley = Al Biqā □, *Lebanon* 69 A5
Bekasi, *Indonesia* 57 G12
Békés, *Hungary* 21 J11
Békéscsaba, *Hungary* 21 J11
Bekily, *Madag.* 85 C8
Bekkevoort, *Belgium* 17 G5
Bekoji, *Ethiopia* 77 F4
Bekok, *Malaysia* 59 L4
Bekwai, *Ghana* 79 D4
Bela, *India* 63 G9
Bela, *Pakistan* 62 F2
Bela Crkva, *Serbia, Yug.* 21 L11
Bela Palanka, *Serbia, Yug.* 21 M12
Bela Vista, *Brazil* 126 A4
Bela Vista, *Mozam.* 85 D5
Bélâbre, *France* 26 B5
Belalcázar, *Spain* 31 G5
Belarus ■, *Europe* 40 F4
Belau = Palau ■, *Pac. Oc.* 46 J17
Belavenona, *Madag.* 85 C8
Belawan, *Indonesia* 56 D1
Belaya, *Ethiopia* 77 E4
Belaya Glina, *Russia* 43 G5
Belaya Kalitva, *Russia* 43 F5
Belaya Tserkov = Bila Tserkva, *Ukraine* 41 H6
Belcher Is., *Canada* 97 C12
Belchite, *Spain* 28 D4
Belden, *U.S.A.* 112 E5
Belém, *Brazil* 122 B2
Belém de São Francisco, *Brazil* 122 C4
Belén, *Argentina* 126 B2
Belén, *Colombia* 120 C2
Belén, *Paraguay* 126 A4
Belen, *U.S.A.* 111 J10
Beleni, *Turkey* 66 D7
Bélesta, *France* 26 F5
Belet Uen, *Somali Rep.* 68 G4
Belev, *Russia* 42 D3
Belfair, *U.S.A.* 112 C4
Belfast, *S. Africa* 85 D5
Belfast, *U.K.* 15 B6
Belfast, *Maine, U.S.A.* 99 D6
Belfast, *N.Y., U.S.A.* 106 D6
Belfast □, *U.K.* 15 B6
Belfast L., *U.K.* 15 B6
Belfeld, *Neths.* 17 F8
Belfield, *U.S.A.* 108 B3
Belfort, *France* 25 E13
Belfort, Territoire de □, *France* 25 E13
Belfry, *U.S.A.* 110 D9
Belgaum, *India* 60 M9
Belgioioso, *Italy* 32 C6
Belgium ■, *Europe* 17 G5
Belgorod, *Russia* 42 E3
Belgorod-Dnestrovskiy = Bilhorod-Dnistrovskyy, *Ukraine* 41 J6
Belgrade = Beograd, *Serbia, Yug.* 21 L10
Belgrade, *U.S.A.* 110 D8
Belhaven, *U.S.A.* 105 H7
Beli Drim →, *Europe* 21 N10
Beli Manastir, *Croatia* 21 K8
Belice →, *Italy* 34 E5
Belin-Béliet, *France* 26 D3
Belinga, *Gabon* 80 D2
Belinskiy, *Russia* 42 D6
Belinyu, *Indonesia* 56 E3
Beliton Is. = Belitung, *Indonesia* 56 E3
Belitung, *Indonesia* 56 E3
Beliu, *Romania* 38 C5
Belize ■, *Cent. Amer.* 115 D7
Belize City, *Belize* 115 D7
Beljanica, *Serbia, Yug.* 21 L11
Belkovskiy, Ostrov, *Russia* 45 B14
Bell →, *Canada* 98 C4
Bell Bay, *Australia* 90 G4
Bell I., *Canada* 99 B8
Bell-Irving →, *Canada* 100 B3
Bell Peninsula, *Canada* 97 B11
Bell Ville, *Argentina* 126 C3
Bella Bella, *Canada* 100 C3
Bella Coola, *Canada* 100 C3
Bella Flor, *Bolivia* 124 C4
Bella Unión, *Uruguay* 126 C4
Bella Vista, *Corrientes, Argentina* 126 B4
Bella Vista, *Tucuman, Argentina* 126 B2
Bellac, *France* 26 B5
Bellágio, *Italy* 32 C6
Bellaire, *U.S.A.* 106 F4
Bellary, *India* 60 M10
Bellata, *Australia* 91 D4
Belle Fourche, *U.S.A.* 108 C3
Belle Fourche →, *U.S.A.* 108 C3
Belle Glade, *U.S.A.* 105 M5
Belle-Ile, *France* 24 E3
Belle Isle, *Canada* 99 B8
Belle Isle, Str. of, *Canada* 99 B8
Belle-Isle-en-Terre, *France* 24 D3
Belle Plaine, *Iowa, U.S.A.* 108 E8
Belle Plaine, *Minn., U.S.A.* 108 C8
Belle Yella, *Liberia* 78 D3
Belledonne, Chaîne de, *France* 27 C10
Belledune, *Canada* 99 C6
Bellefontaine, *U.S.A.* 104 E4
Bellefonte, *U.S.A.* 106 F7
Bellegarde, *France* 25 E9
Bellegarde-en-Marche, *France* 26 C6
Bellegarde-sur-Valserine, *France* 27 B9
Bellême, *France* 24 D7
Belleoram, *Canada* 99 C8
Belleville, *Canada* 98 D4
Belleville, *France* 27 B8
Belleville, *Ill., U.S.A.* 108 F10
Belleville, *Kans., U.S.A.* 108 F6
Belleville, *N.Y., U.S.A.* 107 C8
Belleville-sur-Vie, *France* 24 F5
Bellevue, *Canada* 100 D6
Bellevue, *Idaho, U.S.A.* 110 E6
Bellevue, *Ohio, U.S.A.* 106 E2
Bellevue, *Wash., U.S.A.* 112 C4
Belley, *France* 27 C9
Bellin = Kangirsuk, *Canada* 97 B13
Bellingen, *Australia* 91 E5
Bellingham, *U.S.A.* 112 B4
Bellingshausen Sea, *Antarctica* 5 C17
Bellinzona, *Switz.* 23 D8
Bello, *Colombia* 120 B2
Bellows Falls, *U.S.A.* 107 C12
Bellpat, *Pakistan* 62 E3
Bellpuig, *Spain* 28 D6
Belluno, *Italy* 33 B9
Bellville, *U.S.A.* 109 L6
Bellwood, *U.S.A.* 106 F6
Bélmez, *Spain* 31 G5
Belmont, *Australia* 91 E5
Belmont, *Canada* 106 D3
Belmont, *S. Africa* 84 D3
Belmont, *U.S.A.* 106 D6
Belmonte, *Brazil* 123 E4
Belmonte, *Portugal* 30 E3
Belmonte, *Spain* 28 F2
Belmopan, *Belize* 115 D7
Belmullet, *Ireland* 15 B2
Belo Horizonte, *Brazil* 123 E3
Belo Jardim, *Brazil* 122 C4
Belo-sur-Mer, *Madag.* 85 C7
Belo-Tsiribihina, *Madag.* 85 B7
Belogorsk = Bilohirsk, *Ukraine* 41 K8
Belogorsk, *Russia* 45 D13
Belogradchik, *Bulgaria* 38 F5
Beloha, *Madag.* 85 D8
Beloit, *Kans., U.S.A.* 108 F5
Beloit, *Wis., U.S.A.* 108 D10
Belokorovichi, *Ukraine* 41 G5
Belomorsk, *Russia* 44 C4
Belonia, *India* 61 H17
Belopolye = Bilopillya, *Ukraine* 41 G8
Belorechensk, *Russia* 43 H4
Belorussia ■ = Belarus ■, *Europe* 40 F4
Belovo, *Russia* 44 D9
Belovodsk, *Ukraine* 41 H10
Beloye, Ozero, *Russia* 40 B9
Beloye More, *Russia* 44 C4
Belozersk, *Russia* 40 B9
Belpasso, *Italy* 35 E7
Belsele, *Belgium* 17 F4
Belsito, *Italy* 34 E6
Beltana, *Australia* 91 E2
Belterra, *Brazil* 121 D7
Beltinci, *Slovenia* 33 B13
Belton, *S.C., U.S.A.* 105 H4
Belton, *Tex., U.S.A.* 109 K6
Belton Res., *U.S.A.* 109 K6
Beltsy = Bălţi, *Moldova* 41 J4
Belturbet, *Ireland* 15 B4
Belukha, *Russia* 44 E9
Beluran, *Malaysia* 56 C5
Belvedere Marittimo, *Italy* 35 C8
Belvès, *France* 26 D5
Belvidere, *Ill., U.S.A.* 108 D10
Belvidere, *N.J., U.S.A.* 107 F9
Belvis de la Jara, *Spain* 31 F6
Belyando →, *Australia* 90 C4
Belyy, *Russia* 40 E7
Belyy, Ostrov, *Russia* 44 B8
Belyy Yar, *Russia* 44 D9
Belzig, *Germany* 18 C8
Belzoni, *U.S.A.* 109 J9
Bemaraha, Lembalemban' i, *Madag.* 85 B7
Bemarivo, *Madag.* 85 C7
Bemarivo →, *Madag.* 85 B8
Bemavo, *Madag.* 85 C8
Bembéréke, *Benin* 79 C5
Bembesi, *Zimbabwe* 83 F2
Bembesi →, *Zimbabwe* 83 F2
Bembézar →, *Spain* 31 H5
Bemidji, *U.S.A.* 108 B7
Bemmel, *Neths.* 16 E7
Ben, *Iran* 65 C6
Ben Cruachan, *U.K.* 14 E3
Ben Dearg, *U.K.* 14 D4
Ben Gardane, *Tunisia* 75 B7
Ben Hope, *U.K.* 14 C4
Ben Lawers, *U.K.* 14 E4
Ben Lomond, *N.S.W., Australia* 91 E5
Ben Lomond, *Tas., Australia* 90 G4
Ben Lomond, *U.K.* 14 E4
Ben Luc, *Vietnam* 59 G6
Ben Macdhui, *U.K.* 14 D5
Ben Mhor, *U.K.* 14 D1
Ben More, *Arg. & Bute, U.K.* 14 E2
Ben More, *Stirl., U.K.* 14 E4
Ben More Assynt, *U.K.* 14 C4
Ben Nevis, *U.K.* 14 E4
Ben Quang, *Vietnam* 58 D6

Ben Slimane, *Morocco* 74 B3
Ben Tre, *Vietnam* 59 G6
Ben Vorlich, *U.K.* 14 E4
Ben Wyvis, *U.K.* 14 D4
Bena, *Nigeria* 79 C6
Bena Dibele, *Zaïre* 80 E4
Benāb, *Iran* 67 D12
Benagalbón, *Spain* 31 J6
Benagerie, *Australia* 91 E3
Benahmed, *Morocco* 74 B3
Benalla, *Australia* 91 F4
Benambra, Mt., *Australia* 91 F4
Benamejí, *Spain* 31 H6
Benares = Varanasi, *India* 63 G10
Bénat, C., *France* 27 E10
Benavente, *Portugal* 31 G2
Benavente, *Spain* 30 C5
Benavides, *Spain* 30 C5
Benavides, *U.S.A.* 109 M5
Benbecula, *U.K.* 14 D1
Benbonyathe, *Australia* 91 E2
Bencubbin, *Australia* 89 F2
Bend, *U.S.A.* 110 D3
Bender Beila, *Somali Rep.* 68 F5
Bendering, *Australia* 89 F2
Bendery = Tighina, *Moldova* 41 J5
Bendigo, *Australia* 91 F3
Bendorf, *Germany* 18 E3
Benē Beraq, *Israel* 69 C3
Beneden Knijpe, *Neths.* 16 C7
Beneditinos, *Brazil* 122 C3
Benedito Leite, *Brazil* 122 C3
Bénéna, *Mali* 78 C4
Benenitra, *Madag.* 85 C8
Benešov, *Czech.* 20 F4
Bénestroff, *France* 25 D13
Benet, *France* 26 B3
Benevento, *Italy* 35 A7
Benfeld, *France* 25 D14
Benga, *Mozam.* 83 F3
Bengal, Bay of, *Ind. Oc.* 61 K16
Bengbu, *China* 51 H9
Benghazi = Banghāzī, *Libya* 73 B9
Bengkalis, *Indonesia* 56 D2
Bengkulu, *Indonesia* 56 E2
Bengkulu □, *Indonesia* 56 E2
Bengough, *Canada* 101 D7
Benguela, *Angola* 81 G2
Benguerir, *Morocco* 74 B3
Benguérua, I., *Mozam.* 85 C6
Benha, *Egypt* 76 H7
Beni, *Zaïre* 82 B2
Beni □, *Bolivia* 125 C4
Beni →, *Bolivia* 125 C4
Beni Abbès, *Algeria* 75 B4
Beni-Haoua, *Algeria* 75 A5
Beni Mazâr, *Egypt* 76 J7
Beni Mellal, *Morocco* 74 B3
Beni Ounif, *Algeria* 75 B4
Beni Saf, *Algeria* 75 A4
Beni Suef, *Egypt* 76 J7
Beniah L., *Canada* 100 A6
Benicarló, *Spain* 28 E5
Benicia, *U.S.A.* 112 G4
Benidorm, *Spain* 29 G4
Benidorm, Islote de, *Spain* 29 G4
Benin ■, *Africa* 79 D5
Benin, Bight of, *W. Afr.* 79 D5
Benin City, *Nigeria* 79 D6
Benisa, *Spain* 29 G5
Benitses, *Greece* 37 A3
Benjamin Aceval, *Paraguay* 126 A4
Benjamin Constant, *Brazil* 120 D3
Benjamin Hill, *Mexico* 114 A2
Benkelman, *U.S.A.* 108 E4
Benkovac, *Croatia* 33 D12
Benlidi, *Australia* 90 C3
Bennebroek, *Neths.* 16 D5
Bennekom, *Neths.* 16 D7
Bennett, *Canada* 100 B2
Bennett, L., *Australia* 88 D5
Bennett, Ostrov, *Russia* 45 B15
Bennettsville, *U.S.A.* 105 H6
Bennington, *U.S.A.* 107 D11
Bénodet, *France* 24 E2
Benoni, *S. Africa* 85 D4
Benoud, *Algeria* 75 B5
Benque Viejo, *Belize* 115 D7
Bensheim, *Germany* 19 F4
Benson, *U.S.A.* 111 L8
Bent, *Iran* 65 E8
Benteng, *Indonesia* 57 F6
Bentinck I., *Australia* 90 B2
Bentiu, *Sudan* 77 F2
Bento Gonçalves, *Brazil* 127 B5
Benton, *Ark., U.S.A.* 109 H8
Benton, *Calif., U.S.A.* 112 H8
Benton, *Ill., U.S.A.* 108 F10
Benton Harbor, *U.S.A.* 104 D2
Bentu Liben, *Ethiopia* 77 F4
Bentung, *Malaysia* 59 L3
Benue □, *Nigeria* 79 D6
Benue →, *Nigeria* 79 D6
Benxi, *China* 51 D12
Benzdorp, *Surinam* 121 C7
Beo, *Indonesia* 57 D7
Beograd, *Serbia, Yug.* 21 L10
Beowawe, *U.S.A.* 110 F5
Bepan Jiang →, *China* 52 E6
Beppu, *Japan* 49 H5
Beqaa Valley = Al Biqā □, *Lebanon* 69 A5
Berati, *Albania* 39 J2
Berau, Teluk, *Indonesia* 57 E8
Berber, *Sudan* 76 D3
Berbera, *Somali Rep.* 68 E4
Berbérati, *C.A.R.* 80 D3
Berberia, C. del, *Spain* 36 C7
Berbice →, *Guyana* 121 B6
Berceto, *Italy* 32 D7
Berchtesgaden, *Germany* 19 H8
Berck-Plage, *France* 25 B8
Berdichev = Berdychiv, *Ukraine* 41 H5
Berdsk, *Russia* 44 D9
Berdyansk, *Ukraine* 41 J9
Berdychiv, *Ukraine* 41 H5
Berea, *U.S.A.* 104 G3
Berebere, *Indonesia* 57 D7
Bereda, *Somali Rep.* 68 E5
Berehove, *Ukraine* 41 H2
Berekum, *Ghana* 78 D4
Berenice, *Egypt* 76 C4
Berens →, *Canada* 101 C9
Berens I., *Canada* 101 C9
Berens River, *Canada* 101 C9
Berestechko, *Ukraine* 41 G3
Bereşti, *Romania* 38 C10
Beretău →, *Romania* 38 B4
Berettyo →, *Hungary* 21 J11
Berettyóújfalu, *Hungary* 21 H11
Berevo, *Mahajanga, Madag.* 85 B7
Berevo, *Toliara, Madag.* 85 B7
Bereza, *Belarus* 41 F3
Berezhany, *Ukraine* 41 H3
Berezina = Byarezina →, *Belarus* 41 F6
Berezivka, *Ukraine* 41 J6
Berezna, *Ukraine* 41 G6
Berezniki, *Russia* 44 D6
Berezovo, *Russia* 44 C7
Berga, *Spain* 28 C6
Bergama, *Turkey* 66 C2
Bergambacht, *Neths.* 16 E5
Bérgamo, *Italy* 32 C6
Bergantiños, *Spain* 30 B2
Bergara, *Spain* 28 B2
Bergedorf, *Germany* 18 B6
Bergeijk, *Neths.* 17 F6
Bergen, *Germany* 18 A9
Bergen, *Neths.* 16 C5
Bergen, *Norway* 9 F11
Bergen, *U.S.A.* 106 C7
Bergen-op-Zoom, *Neths.* 17 F4
Bergerac, *France* 26 D4
Bergheim, *Germany* 18 E2
Berghem, *Neths.* 16 E7
Bergisch Gladbach, *Germany* 18 E3
Bergschenhoek, *Neths.* 16 E5
Bergsjö, *Sweden* 10 C11
Bergues, *France* 25 B9
Bergum, *Neths.* 16 B7
Bergville, *S. Africa* 85 D4
Berhala, Selat, *Indonesia* 56 E2
Berhampore = Baharampur, *India* 63 G13
Berhampur, *India* 61 K14
Berheci →, *Romania* 38 C10
Bering Sea, *Pac. Oc.* 96 C1
Bering Strait, *U.S.A.* 96 B3
Beringen, *Belgium* 17 F6
Beringen, *Switz.* 23 A7
Beringovskiy, *Russia* 45 C18
Berisso, *Argentina* 126 C4
Berja, *Spain* 29 J2
Berkane, *Morocco* 75 B4
Berkel →, *Neths.* 16 D8
Berkeley, *U.K.* 13 F5
Berkeley, *U.S.A.* 112 H4
Berkeley Springs, *U.S.A.* 104 F6
Berkhout, *Neths.* 16 C5
Berkner I., *Antarctica* 5 D18
Berkovitsa, *Bulgaria* 38 F6
Berkshire □, *U.K.* 13 F6
Berlaar, *Belgium* 17 F5
Berland →, *Canada* 100 C5
Berlanga, *Spain* 31 G5
Berlare, *Belgium* 17 F4
Berlenga, I., *Portugal* 31 F1
Berlin, *Germany* 18 C9
Berlin, *Md., U.S.A.* 104 F8
Berlin, *N.H., U.S.A.* 107 B13
Berlin, *Wis., U.S.A.* 104 D1
Bermeja, Sierra, *Spain* 31 J5
Bermejo →, *Formosa, Argentina* 126 B4
Bermejo →, *San Juan, Argentina* 126 C2
Bermeo, *Spain* 28 B2
Bermillo de Sayago, *Spain* 30 D4
Bermuda ■, *Atl. Oc.* 94 F13
Bern, *Switz.* 22 C4
Bern □, *Switz.* 22 C5
Bernado, *U.S.A.* 111 J10
Bernalda, *Italy* 35 B9
Bernalillo, *U.S.A.* 111 J10
Bernardo de Irigoyen, *Argentina* 127 B5
Bernardo O'Higgins □, *Chile* 126 C1
Bernasconi, *Argentina* 126 D3
Bernau, *Bayern, Germany* 19 H8
Bernau, *Brandenburg, Germany* 18 C9
Bernay, *France* 24 C7
Bernburg, *Germany* 18 D7
Berne = Bern, *Switz.* 22 C4
Berne = Bern □, *Switz.* 22 C5
Berner Alpen, *Switz.* 22 D5
Bernese Oberland = Oberland, *Switz.* 22 C5
Bernier I., *Australia* 89 D1
Bernina, Piz, *Switz.* 23 D9
Bernissart, *Belgium* 17 H3
Bernkastel-Kues, *Germany* 19 F3
Beroroha, *Madag.* 85 C8
Béroubouay, *Benin* 79 C5
Beroun, *Czech.* 20 F4
Berounka →, *Czech.* 20 F4
Berovo, *Macedonia* 39 H5
Berrahal, *Algeria* 75 A6
Berre, Étang de, *France* 27 E9
Berrechid, *Morocco* 74 B3
Berri, *Australia* 91 E3
Berriane, *Algeria* 75 B5
Berrouaghia, *Algeria* 75 A5
Berry, *Australia* 91 E5
Berry, *France* 25 F8
Berry Is., *Bahamas* 116 A4
Berryessa L., *U.S.A.* 112 G4
Berryville, *U.S.A.* 109 G8
Bersenbrück, *Germany* 18 C3
Bershad, *Ukraine* 41 H5
Berthold, *U.S.A.* 108 A4
Berthoud, *U.S.A.* 108 E2
Bertincourt, *France* 25 B9
Bertoua, *Cameroon* 80 D2
Bertrand, *U.S.A.* 108 E5
Bertrange, *Lux.* 17 J8
Bertrix, *Belgium* 17 J6
Beruri, *Brazil* 121 D5
Berwick, *U.S.A.* 107 E8
Berwick-upon-Tweed, *U.K.* 12 B5
Berwyn Mts., *U.K.* 12 E4
Beryslav, *Ukraine* 41 J7
Berzasca, *Romania* 38 E4
Besal, *Pakistan* 63 B5
Besalampy, *Madag.* 85 B7
Besançon, *France* 25 E13
Besar, *Indonesia* 56 E5
Beshenkovichi, *Belarus* 40 E5
Beslan, *Russia* 43 J7
Besnard L., *Canada* 101 B7
Besni, *Turkey* 66 D7
Besor, N. →, *Egypt* 69 D3
Bessarabiya, *Moldova* 41 J5
Bessarabka = Basarabeasca, *Moldova* 41 J5
Bessèges, *France* 27 D8
Bessemer, *Ala., U.S.A.* 105 J2
Bessemer, *Mich., U.S.A.* 108 B9
Bessin, *France* 24 C5
Bessines-sur-Gartempe, *France* 26 B5
Best, *Neths.* 17 E6
Bet She'an, *Israel* 69 C4
Bet Shemesh, *Israel* 69 D3
Bet Tadjine, Djebel, *Algeria* 74 C4
Betafo, *Madag.* 85 B8
Betancuria, *Canary Is.* 36 F5
Betanzos, *Bolivia* 125 D4
Betanzos, *Spain* 30 B2
Bétaré Oya, *Cameroon* 80 C2
Bétera, *Spain* 28 F4
Bethal, *S. Africa* 85 D4
Bethanien, *Namibia* 84 D2
Bethany, *U.S.A.* 108 E7
Bethel, *Alaska, U.S.A.* 96 B3
Bethel, *Vt., U.S.A.* 107 C12
Bethel Park, *U.S.A.* 106 F4
Bethlehem = Bayt Lahm, *West Bank* 69 D4
Bethlehem, *S. Africa* 85 D4
Bethlehem, *U.S.A.* 107 F9
Bethulie, *S. Africa* 84 E4
Béthune, *France* 25 B9
Béthune →, *France* 24 C8
Bethungra, *Australia* 91 E4
Betijoque, *Venezuela* 120 B3
Betim, *Brazil* 123 E3
Betioky, *Madag.* 85 C7
Beton-Bazoches, *France* 25 D10
Betong, *Thailand* 59 K3
Betoota, *Australia* 90 D3
Betroka, *Madag.* 85 C8
Betsiamites, *Canada* 99 C6
Betsiamites →, *Canada* 99 C6
Betsiboka →, *Madag.* 85 B8
Bettembourg, *Lux.* 17 J8
Bettiah, *India* 63 F11
Bèttola, *Italy* 32 D6
Betul, *India* 60 J10
Betung, *Malaysia* 56 D4
Betzdorf, *Germany* 18 E3
Beuca, *Romania* 38 E7
Beuil, *France* 27 D10
Beulah, *U.S.A.* 108 B4
Beuvron →, *France* 24 E8
Beveren, *Belgium* 17 F4
Beverley, *Australia* 89 F2
Beverley, *U.K.* 12 D7
Beverlo, *Belgium* 17 F6
Beverly, *Mass., U.S.A.* 107 D14
Beverly, *Wash., U.S.A.* 110 C4
Beverly Hills, *U.S.A.* 113 L8
Beverwijk, *Neths.* 16 D5
Bex, *Switz.* 22 D4
Bey Dağları, *Turkey* 66 D4
Beya, *Russia* 45 D10
Beyānlū, *Iran* 64 C5
Beyin, *Ghana* 78 D4
Beyla, *Guinea* 78 D3
Beynat, *France* 26 C5
Beyneu, *Kazakstan* 44 E6
Beypazarı, *Turkey* 66 B4
Beyşehir, *Turkey* 66 D4
Beyşehir Gölü, *Turkey* 66 D4
Beytüşşebap, *Turkey* 67 D10
Bezhetsk, *Russia* 42 B3
Bezhitsa, *Russia* 44 D4
Béziers, *France* 26 E7
Bezwada = Vijayawada, *India* 61 L12
Bhachau, *India* 60 H7
Bhadarwah, *India* 63 C6
Bhadrakh, *India* 61 J15
Bhadravati, *India* 60 N9
Bhagalpur, *India* 63 G12
Bhakkar, *Pakistan* 62 D4
Bhakra Dam, *India* 62 D7
Bhamo, *Burma* 61 G20
Bhandara, *India* 60 J11
Bhanrer Ra., *India* 62 H8
Bharat = India ■, *Asia* 60 K11
Bharatpur, *India* 62 F7
Bhatinda, *India* 62 D6
Bhatpara, *India* 63 H13
Bhaun, *Pakistan* 62 C5
Bhaunagar = Bhavnagar, *India* 62 J5
Bhavnagar, *India* 62 J5
Bhawanipatna, *India* 61 K12
Bhera, *Pakistan* 62 C5
Bhilsa = Vidisha, *India* 62 H7
Bhilwara, *India* 62 G6
Bhima →, *India* 60 L10
Bhimavaram, *India* 61 L12
Bhimbar, *Pakistan* 63 C6
Bhind, *India* 63 F8
Bhiwandi, *India* 60 K8
Bhiwani, *India* 62 E7
Bhola, *Bangla.* 61 H17
Bhopal, *India* 62 H7
Bhubaneshwar, *India* 61 J14
Bhuj, *India* 62 H3
Bhumiphol Dam = Phumiphon, Khuan, *Thailand* 58 D2
Bhusaval, *India* 60 J9
Bhutan ■, *Asia* 61 F17
Biá →, *Brazil* 120 D4
Biafra, B. of = Bonny, Bight of, *Africa* 79 E6
Biak, *Indonesia* 57 E9
Biała →, *Poland* 20 E10
Biała Podlaska, *Poland* 20 C13
Białogard, *Poland* 20 A5
Białystok, *Poland* 20 B13
Biancavilla, *Italy* 35 E7
Bīārjmand, *Iran* 65 B7
Biaro, *Indonesia* 57 D7
Biarritz, *France* 26 E2
Biasca, *Switz.* 23 D7
Biba, *Egypt* 76 J7
Bibai, *Japan* 48 C10
Bibala, *Angola* 81 G2
Bibane, Bahiret el, *Tunisia* 75 B7
Bibbiena, *Italy* 33 E8
Bibby I., *Canada* 101 A10
Biberach, *Germany* 19 G5
Biberist, *Switz.* 22 B5
Bibey →, *Spain* 30 C3
Bibiani, *Ghana* 78 D4
Biboohra, *Australia* 90 B4
Bibungwa, *Zaïre* 82 C2
Bic, *Canada* 99 C6
Bicaz, *Romania* 38 C9
Biccari, *Italy* 35 A8
Bichena, *Ethiopia* 77 E4
Bichvinta, *Georgia* 43 J5
Bickerton I., *Australia* 90 A2
Bicknell, *Ind., U.S.A.* 104 F2
Bicknell, *Utah, U.S.A.* 111 G8
Bida, *Nigeria* 79 D6
Bidar, *India* 60 L10
Biddeford, *U.S.A.* 99 D5
Biddwara, *Ethiopia* 77 F4
Bideford, *U.K.* 13 F3
Bidon 5 = Poste Maurice Cortier, *Algeria* 75 D5
Bidor, *Malaysia* 59 K3
Bié, Planalto de, *Angola* 81 G3
Bieber, *U.S.A.* 110 F3
Biel, *Switz.* 22 B4
Bielawa, *Poland* 20 E6
Bielé Karpaty, *Europe* 20 F7
Bielefeld, *Germany* 18 C4
Bielersee, *Switz.* 22 B4
Biella, *Italy* 32 C5
Bielsk Podlaski, *Poland* 20 C13
Bielsko-Biała, *Poland* 20 F9
Bien Hoa, *Vietnam* 59 G6
Bienfait, *Canada* 101 D8
Bienne = Biel, *Switz.* 22 B4
Bienvenida, *Spain* 31 G4
Bienvenue, *Fr. Guiana* 121 C7
Bienville, L., *Canada* 98 A5
Biescas, *Spain* 28 C4
Biese →, *Germany* 18 C7
Biesiesfontein, *S. Africa* 84 E2
Bietigheim, *Germany* 19 G5
Bievre, *Belgium* 17 J6
Biferno →, *Italy* 35 A8
Big →, *Canada* 99 B8
Big B., *Canada* 99 A7
Big Bear City, *U.S.A.* 113 L10
Big Bear Lake, *U.S.A.* 113 L10
Big Beaver, *Canada* 101 D7
Big Belt Mts., *U.S.A.* 110 C8
Big Bend, *Swaziland* 85 D5
Big Bend National Park, *U.S.A.* 109 L3
Big Black →, *U.S.A.* 109 J9
Big Blue →, *U.S.A.* 108 F6
Big Cr. →, *Canada* 100 C4
Big Creek, *U.S.A.* 112 H7
Big Cypress Swamp, *U.S.A.* 105 M5
Big Falls, *U.S.A.* 108 A8
Big Fork →, *U.S.A.* 108 A8
Big Horn Mts. = Bighorn Mts., *U.S.A.* 110 D10
Big Lake, *U.S.A.* 109 K4
Big Moose, *U.S.A.* 107 C10
Big Muddy Cr. →, *U.S.A.* 108 A2
Big Pine, *U.S.A.* 111 H4
Big Piney, *U.S.A.* 110 E8
Big Quill L., *Canada* 101 C8
Big Rapids, *U.S.A.* 104 D3
Big River, *Canada* 101 C7
Big Run, *U.S.A.* 106 F6
Big Sable Pt., *U.S.A.* 104 C2
Big Sand L., *Canada* 101 B9
Big Sandy, *U.S.A.* 110 B8
Big Sandy Cr. →, *U.S.A.* 108 F3
Big Sioux →, *U.S.A.* 108 D6
Big Spring, *U.S.A.* 109 J4
Big Springs, *U.S.A.* 108 E3
Big Stone City, *U.S.A.* 108 C6
Big Stone Gap, *U.S.A.* 105 G4
Big Stone L., *U.S.A.* 108 C6
Big Sur, *U.S.A.* 112 J5
Big Timber, *U.S.A.* 110 D9
Big Trout L., *Canada* 98 B1
Biğa, *Turkey* 66 B2
Bigadiç, *Turkey* 66 C3
Biganos, *France* 26 D3
Bigfork, *U.S.A.* 110 B6
Biggar, *Canada* 101 C7
Biggar, *U.K.* 14 F5
Bigge I., *Australia* 88 B4
Biggenden, *Australia* 91 D5
Biggs, *U.S.A.* 112 F5
Bighorn, *U.S.A.* 110 C10
Bighorn →, *U.S.A.* 110 C10
Bighorn Mts., *U.S.A.* 110 D10
Bignona, *Senegal* 78 C1
Bigorre, *France* 26 E4
Bigstone L., *Canada* 101 C9
Biguglia, Étang de, *France* 27 F13
Bigwa, *Tanzania* 82 D4
Bihać, *Bos.-H.* 33 D12
Bihar, *India* 63 G11
Bihar □, *India* 63 G11
Biharamulo, *Tanzania* 82 C3
Biharamulo □, *Tanzania* 82 C3
Bihor, Munţii, *Romania* 38 C5
Bijagós, Arquipélago dos, *Guinea-Biss.* 78 C1
Bijaipur, *India* 62 F7
Bijapur, *Karnataka, India* 60 L9
Bijapur, *Mad. P., India* 61 K12
Bījār, *Iran* 67 E12
Bijeljina, *Bos.-H.* 21 L9
Bijelo Polje, *Montenegro, Yug.* 21 M9
Bijie, *China* 52 D5
Bijnor, *India* 62 E8
Bikaner, *India* 62 E5
Bikapur, *India* 63 F10
Bikeqi, *China* 50 D6
Bikfayyā, *Lebanon* 69 B4
Bikin, *Russia* 45 E14
Bikin →, *Russia* 48 A7
Bikini Atoll, *Pac. Oc.* 92 F8
Bikoué, *Cameroon* 79 E7
Bila Tserkva, *Ukraine* 41 H6
Bilara, *India* 62 F5
Bilaspur, *Mad. P., India* 63 H10
Bilaspur, *Punjab, India* 62 D7
Biläsuvar, *Azerbaijan* 67 C13
Bilauk Taungdan, *Thailand* 58 F2
Bilbao, *Spain* 28 B2
Bilbeis, *Egypt* 76 H7
Bilbo = Bilbao, *Spain* 28 B2
Bilbor, *Romania* 38 B8
Bíldudalur, *Iceland* 8 D2
Bileća, *Bos.-H.* 21 N8
Bilecik, *Turkey* 66 B4
Bilgoraj, *Poland* 20 E12
Bilhorod-Dnistrovskyy, *Ukraine* 41 J6
Bilibino, *Russia* 45 C17
Bilibiza, *Mozam.* 83 E5
Bilir, *Russia* 45 C14
Biliran I., *Phil.* 55 F6
Bill, *U.S.A.* 108 D2
Billabalong, *Australia* 89 E2
Billiluna, *Australia* 88 C4
Billingham, *U.K.* 12 C6
Billings, *U.S.A.* 110 D9
Billiton Is. = Belitung, *Indonesia* 56 E3
Billom, *France* 26 C7
Bilma, *Niger* 73 E7
Bilo Gora, *Croatia* 21 K7
Biloela, *Australia* 90 C5
Bilohirsk, *Ukraine* 41 K8
Biloku, *Guyana* 121 C6
Bilopillya, *Ukraine* 41 G8
Biloxi, *U.S.A.* 109 K10
Bilpa Morea Claypan, *Australia* 90 D2
Bilthoven, *Neths.* 16 D6
Biltine, *Chad* 73 F9
Bilyana, *Australia* 90 B4
Bilyarsk, *Russia* 42 C10
Bilzen, *Belgium* 17 G7
Bima, *Indonesia* 57 F5
Bimban, *Egypt* 76 C3
Bimbila, *Ghana* 79 D5
Bimbo, *C.A.R.* 80 D3
Bimini Is., *Bahamas* 116 A4

Bin Xian, *Heilongjiang, China* 51 B14
Bin Xian, *Shaanxi, China* 50 G5
Bina-Etawah, *India* 62 G8
Binābr, *Iran* 67 D13
Binalbagan, *Phil.* 55 F5
Binalong, *Australia* 91 E4
Bīnālūd, Kūh-e, *Iran* 65 B8
Binatang, *Malaysia* 56 D4
Binbee, *Australia* 90 C4
Binche, *Belgium* 17 H4
Binchuan, *China* 52 E3
Binda, *Australia* 91 D4
Bindle, *Australia* 91 D4
Bindura, *Zimbabwe* 83 F3
Bingara, *N.S.W., Australia* 91 D5
Bingara, *Queens., Australia* 91 D3
Bingen, *Germany* 19 F3
Bingerville, *Ivory C.* 78 D4
Bingham, *U.S.A.* 99 C6
Bingham Canyon, *U.S.A.* 110 F7
Binghamton, *U.S.A.* 107 D9
Bingöl, *Turkey* 67 C9
Bingöl Dağları, *Turkey* 67 C9
Binh Dinh = An Nhon, *Vietnam* 58 F7
Binh Khe, *Vietnam* 58 F7
Binh Son, *Vietnam* 58 E7
Binhai, *China* 51 G10
Binisatua, *Spain* 36 B11
Binjai, *Indonesia* 56 D1
Binnaway, *Australia* 91 E4
Binongko, *Indonesia* 57 F6
Binscarth, *Canada* 101 C8
Bintan, *Indonesia* 56 D2
Bintulu, *Malaysia* 56 D4
Bintuni, *Indonesia* 57 E8
Binyang, *China* 52 F7
Binz, *Germany* 18 A9
Binzert = Bizerte, *Tunisia* 75 A6
Bío Bío □, *Chile* 126 D1
Biograd, *Croatia* 33 E12
Bioko, *Eq. Guin.* 79 E6
Biougra, *Morocco* 74 B3
Bir, *India* 60 K9
Bir, Ras, *Djibouti* 77 E5
Bîr Abu Hashim, *Egypt* 76 C3
Bîr Abu M'nqar, *Egypt* 76 B2
Bîr Abu Muḥammad, *Egypt* 69 F3
Bi'r ad Dabbāghāt, *Jordan* 69 E4
Bîr Adal Deib, *Sudan* 76 C4
Bi'r al Butayyihāt, *Jordan* 69 F4
Bi'r al Mārī, *Jordan* 69 E4
Bi'r al Qattār, *Jordan* 69 F4
Bir Aouine, *Tunisia* 75 B6
Bîr 'Asal, *Egypt* 76 B3
Bîr Autrun, *Sudan* 76 D2
Bîr Beiḍa, *Egypt* 69 E3
Bîr Diqnash, *Egypt* 76 A2
Bir el Abbes, *Algeria* 74 C3
Bîr el 'Abd, *Egypt* 69 D2
Bir el Ater, *Algeria* 75 B6
Bîr el Basur, *Egypt* 76 B2
Bîr el Biarât, *Egypt* 69 F3
Bîr el Duweidar, *Egypt* 69 E1
Bîr el Garârât, *Egypt* 69 D2
Bîr el Gellaz, *Egypt* 76 A2
Bîr el Heisi, *Egypt* 69 F3
Bîr el Jafir, *Egypt* 69 E1
Bîr el Mâlḥi, *Egypt* 69 E2
Bîr el Shaqqa, *Egypt* 76 A2
Bîr el Thamâda, *Egypt* 69 E2
Bîr Fuad, *Egypt* 76 A2
Bîr Gebeil Ḥiṣn, *Egypt* 69 E2
Bi'r Ghadīr, *Syria* 69 A6
Bîr Haimur, *Egypt* 76 C3
Bîr Ḥasana, *Egypt* 69 E2
Bi'r Jadīd, *Iraq* 64 C4
Bir Jdid, *Morocco* 74 B3
Bîr Kanayis, *Egypt* 76 C3
Bîr Kaseiba, *Egypt* 69 E2
Bîr Kerawein, *Egypt* 76 B2
Bîr Lahfân, *Egypt* 69 D2
Bir Lahrache, *Algeria* 75 B6
Bîr Madkûr, *Egypt* 69 E1
Bîr Maql, *Egypt* 76 C3
Bîr Misaha, *Egypt* 76 C2
Bir Mogrein, *Mauritania* 74 C2
Bîr Murr, *Egypt* 76 C3
Bi'r Muṭribah, *Kuwait* 64 D5
Bîr Nakheila, *Egypt* 76 C3
Bîr Qaṭia, *Egypt* 69 E1
Bîr Qatrani, *Egypt* 76 A2
Bîr Ranga, *Egypt* 76 C4
Bîr Sahara, *Egypt* 76 C2
Bîr Seiyâla, *Egypt* 76 B3
Bir Semguine, *Morocco* 74 B3
Bîr Shalatein, *Egypt* 76 C4
Bîr Shebb, *Egypt* 76 C2
Bîr Shût, *Egypt* 76 C4
Bîr Terfawi, *Egypt* 76 C2
Bîr Umm Qubûr, *Egypt* 76 C3
Bîr Ungât, *Egypt* 76 C3
Bîr Za'farâna, *Egypt* 76 J8
Bîr Zeidûn, *Egypt* 76 B3
Bira, *Indonesia* 57 E8
Bîra, *Romania* 38 B10
Biramféro, *Guinea* 78 C3
Birao, *C.A.R.* 73 F9
Birawa, *Zaïre* 82 C2
Bîrca, *Romania* 38 F6
Birch Hills, *Canada* 101 C7
Birch I., *Canada* 101 C9
Birch L., *N.W.T., Canada* 100 A5
Birch L., *Ont., Canada* 98 B1
Birch L., *U.S.A.* 98 C1
Birch Mts., *Canada* 100 B6
Birch River, *Canada* 101 C8
Birchip, *Australia* 91 F3
Bird, *Canada* 101 B10
Bird City, *U.S.A.* 108 F4
Bird I. = Aves, I. de, *W. Indies* 117 C7
Birdaard, *Neths.* 16 B7
Birdlip, *U.K.* 13 F5
Birdsville, *Australia* 90 D2
Birdum, *Australia* 88 C5
Birecik, *Turkey* 67 D8
Birein, *Israel* 69 E3
Bireuen, *Indonesia* 56 C1
Birifo, *Gambia* 78 C2
Birigui, *Brazil* 127 A5
Birkenfeld, *Germany* 19 F3
Birkenhead, *U.K.* 12 D4
Birket Qârûn, *Egypt* 76 J7
Birkhadem, *Algeria* 75 A5
Bîrlad, *Romania* 38 C10
Birmingham, *U.K.* 13 E6
Birmingham, *U.S.A.* 105 J2
Birmitrapur, *India* 61 H14
Birni Ngaouré, *Niger* 79 C5
Birni Nkonni, *Niger* 79 C6
Birnin Gwari, *Nigeria* 79 C6
Birnin Kebbi, *Nigeria* 79 C5
Birnin Kudu, *Nigeria* 79 C6
Birobidzhan, *Russia* 45 E14
Birr, *Ireland* 15 C4
Birrie →, *Australia* 91 D4
Birs →, *Switz.* 22 B5
Birsilpur, *India* 62 E5
Birsk, *Russia* 44 D6
Birtin, *Romania* 38 C5
Birtle, *Canada* 101 C8
Birur, *India* 60 N9
Biryuchiy, *Ukraine* 41 J8
Biržai, *Lithuania* 9 H21
Bîrzava, *Romania* 38 C4
Birzebugga, *Malta* 37 D2
Bisa, *Indonesia* 57 E7
Bisáccia, *Italy* 35 A8
Bisacquino, *Italy* 34 E6
Bisalpur, *India* 63 E8
Bisbee, *U.S.A.* 111 L9
Biscarrosse et de Parentis, Étang de, *France* 26 D2
Biscay, B. of, *Atl. Oc.* 6 F5
Biscayne B., *U.S.A.* 105 N5
Biscéglie, *Italy* 35 A9
Bischofshofen, *Austria* 21 H3
Bischofswerda, *Germany* 18 D10
Bischofszell, *Switz.* 23 B8
Bischwiller, *France* 25 D14
Biscoe Bay, *Antarctica* 5 D13
Biscoe Is., *Antarctica* 5 C17
Biscostasing, *Canada* 98 C3
Biscucuy, *Venezuela* 120 B4
Biševo, *Croatia* 33 F13
Bisha, *Eritrea* 77 D4
Bishah, W. →, *Si. Arabia* 76 C5
Bishan, *China* 52 C6
Bishkek, *Kyrgyzstan* 44 E8
Bishnupur, *India* 63 H12
Bisho, *S. Africa* 85 E4
Bishop, *Calif., U.S.A.* 111 H4
Bishop, *Tex., U.S.A.* 109 M6
Bishop Auckland, *U.K.* 12 C6
Bishop's Falls, *Canada* 99 C8
Bishop's Stortford, *U.K.* 13 F8
Bisignano, *Italy* 35 C9
Bisina, L., *Uganda* 82 B3
Biskra, *Algeria* 75 B6
Bislig, *Phil.* 57 C7
Bismarck, *U.S.A.* 108 B4
Bismarck Arch., *Papua N. G.* 92 H6
Bismark, *Germany* 18 C7
Bismil, *Turkey* 67 D9
Biso, *Uganda* 82 B3
Bison, *U.S.A.* 108 C3
Bīsotūn, *Iran* 67 E12
Bispgården, *Sweden* 10 A10
Bissagos = Bijagós, Arquipélago dos, *Guinea-Biss.* 78 C1
Bissau, *Guinea-Biss.* 78 C1
Bissett, *Canada* 101 C9
Bissikrima, *Guinea* 78 C2
Bistcho L., *Canada* 100 B5
Bistreţu, *Romania* 38 F6
Bistrica = Ilirska-Bistrica, *Slovenia* 33 C11
Bistriţa, *Romania* 38 B7
Bistriţa →, *Romania* 38 C9
Bistriţei, Munţii, *Romania* 38 B8
Biswan, *India* 63 F9
Bitam, *Gabon* 80 D2
Bitburg, *Germany* 19 F2
Bitche, *France* 25 C14
Bithynia, *Turkey* 66 B4
Bitkine, *Chad* 73 F8
Bitlis, *Turkey* 67 C10
Bitola, *Macedonia* 39 H4
Bitolj = Bitola, *Macedonia* 39 H4
Bitonto, *Italy* 35 A9
Bitter Creek, *U.S.A.* 110 F9
Bitter L. = Buheirat-Murrat-el-Kubra, *Egypt* 76 H8
Bitterfeld, *Germany* 18 D8
Bitterfontein, *S. Africa* 84 E2
Bitterroot →, *U.S.A.* 110 C6
Bitterroot Range, *U.S.A.* 110 D6
Bitterwater, *U.S.A.* 112 J6
Bitti, *Italy* 34 B2
Bittou, *Burkina Faso* 79 C4
Biu, *Nigeria* 79 C7
Bivolari, *Romania* 38 B10
Biwa-Ko, *Japan* 49 G8
Biwabik, *U.S.A.* 108 B8
Bixad, *Romania* 38 B6
Biyang, *China* 50 H7
Biysk, *Russia* 44 D9
Bizana, *S. Africa* 85 E4
Bizen, *Japan* 49 G7
Bizerte, *Tunisia* 75 A6
Bjargtangar, *Iceland* 8 D1
Bjelasica, *Montenegro, Yug.* 21 N9
Bjelovar, *Croatia* 21 K6
Bjerringbro, *Denmark* 11 H3
Bjervamoen, *Norway* 10 E3
Bjørnevatn, *Norway* 8 B23
Bjørnøya, *Arctic* 4 B8
Bjuv, *Sweden* 11 H6
Blace, *Serbia, Yug.* 21 M11
Black = Da →, *Vietnam* 58 B5
Black →, *Canada* 106 B5
Black →, *Ark., U.S.A.* 109 H9
Black →, *N.Y., U.S.A.* 107 C8
Black →, *Wis., U.S.A.* 108 D9
Black Diamond, *Canada* 100 C6
Black Forest = Schwarzwald, *Germany* 19 H4
Black Hills, *U.S.A.* 108 C3
Black I., *Canada* 101 C9
Black L., *Canada* 101 B7
Black L., *U.S.A.* 104 C3
Black Mesa, *U.S.A.* 109 G3
Black Mt. = Mynydd Du, *U.K.* 13 F4
Black Mts., *U.K.* 13 F4
Black Range, *U.S.A.* 111 K10
Black River, *Jamaica* 116 C4
Black River Falls, *U.S.A.* 108 C9
Black Sea, *Eurasia* 6 G12
Black Volta →, *Africa* 78 D4
Black Warrior →, *U.S.A.* 105 J2
Blackall, *Australia* 90 C4
Blackball, *N.Z.* 87 K3
Blackbull, *Australia* 90 B3
Blackburn, *U.K.* 12 D5
Blackduck, *U.S.A.* 108 B7
Blackfoot, *U.S.A.* 110 E7
Blackfoot →, *U.S.A.* 110 C7
Blackfoot River Reservoir, *U.S.A.* 110 E8
Blackie, *Canada* 100 C6
Blackpool, *U.K.* 12 D4
Blackriver, *U.S.A.* 106 B1
Blacks Harbour, *Canada* 99 C6
Blacksburg, *U.S.A.* 104 G5
Blacksod B., *Ireland* 15 B2
Blackstone, *U.S.A.* 104 G6
Blackstone →, *Canada* 100 A4
Blackstone Ra., *Australia* 89 E4
Blackville, *Canada* 99 C6
Blackwater, *Australia* 90 C4
Blackwater →, *Ireland* 15 E4
Blackwater →, *U.K.* 15 B5
Blackwater Cr. →, *Australia* 91 D3
Blackwell, *U.S.A.* 109 G6
Blackwells Corner, *U.S.A.* 113 K7
Bladel, *Neths.* 17 F6
Blaenau Ffestiniog, *U.K.* 12 E4
Blaenau Gwent □, *U.K.* 13 F4
Blagodarnoye = Blagodarnyy, *Russia* 43 H6
Blagodarnyy, *Russia* 43 H6
Blagoevgrad, *Bulgaria* 39 G6
Blagoveshchensk, *Russia* 45 D13
Blain, *France* 24 E5
Blaine, *U.S.A.* 112 B4
Blaine Lake, *Canada* 101 C7
Blainville-sur-l'Eau, *France* 25 D13
Blair, *U.S.A.* 108 E6
Blair Athol, *Australia* 90 C4
Blair Atholl, *U.K.* 14 E5
Blairgowrie, *U.K.* 14 E5
Blairmore, *Canada* 100 D6
Blairsden, *U.S.A.* 112 F6
Blairsville, *U.S.A.* 106 F5
Blaj, *Romania* 38 C6
Blake Pt., *U.S.A.* 108 A10
Blakely, *U.S.A.* 105 K3
Blâmont, *France* 25 D13
Blanc, C., *Tunisia* 75 A6
Blanc, Mont, *Alps* 27 C10
Blanca, B., *Argentina* 128 A4
Blanca Peak, *U.S.A.* 111 H11
Blanchard, *U.S.A.* 109 H6
Blanche, C., *Australia* 91 E1
Blanche, L., *S. Austral., Australia* 91 D2
Blanche, L., *W. Austral., Australia* 88 D3
Blanco, *S. Africa* 84 E3
Blanco, *U.S.A.* 109 K5
Blanco →, *Argentina* 126 C2
Blanco, C., *Costa Rica* 116 E2
Blanco, C., *Spain* 36 B9
Blanco, C., *U.S.A.* 110 E1
Blanda →, *Iceland* 8 D3
Blandford Forum, *U.K.* 13 G5
Blanding, *U.S.A.* 111 H9
Blanes, *Spain* 28 D7
Blangy-sur-Bresle, *France* 25 C8
Blanice →, *Czech.* 20 F4
Blankenberge, *Belgium* 17 F2
Blankenburg, *Germany* 18 D6
Blanquefort, *France* 26 D3
Blanquillo, *Uruguay* 127 C4
Blansko, *Czech.* 20 F6
Blantyre, *Malawi* 83 F4
Blaricum, *Neths.* 16 D6
Blarney, *Ireland* 15 E3
Blato, *Croatia* 33 F13
Blatten, *Switz.* 22 D5
Blaubeuren, *Germany* 19 G5
Blåvands Huk, *Denmark* 9 J13
Blaydon, *U.K.* 12 C6
Blaye, *France* 26 C3
Blaye-les-Mines, *France* 26 D6
Blayney, *Australia* 91 E4
Blaze, Pt., *Australia* 88 B5
Bleckede, *Germany* 18 B6
Bled, *Slovenia* 33 B11
Blednaya, Gora, *Russia* 44 B7
Bléharis, *Belgium* 17 G2
Blejeşti, *Romania* 38 E8
Blekinge, *Sweden* 9 H16
Blenheim, *Canada* 106 D2
Blenheim, *N.Z.* 87 J4
Bléone →, *France* 27 D10
Blerick, *Neths.* 17 F8
Bletchley, *U.K.* 13 F7
Blida, *Algeria* 75 A5
Blidet Amor, *Algeria* 75 B6
Blidö, *Sweden* 10 E12
Bligh Sound, *N.Z.* 87 L1
Blind River, *Canada* 98 C3
Blinnenhorn, *Switz.* 23 D6
Blitar, *Indonesia* 57 H15
Blitta, *Togo* 79 D5
Block I., *U.S.A.* 107 E13
Block Island Sd., *U.S.A.* 107 E13
Blodgett Iceberg Tongue, *Antarctica* 5 C9
Bloemendaal, *Neths.* 16 D5
Bloemfontein, *S. Africa* 84 D4
Bloemhof, *S. Africa* 84 D4
Blois, *France* 24 E8
Blokziji, *Neths.* 16 C7
Blönduós, *Iceland* 8 D3
Bloodvein →, *Canada* 101 C9
Bloody Foreland, *Ireland* 15 A3
Bloomer, *U.S.A.* 108 C9
Bloomfield, *Australia* 90 B4
Bloomfield, *Canada* 106 C7
Bloomfield, *Iowa, U.S.A.* 108 E8
Bloomfield, *N. Mex., U.S.A.* 111 H10
Bloomfield, *Nebr., U.S.A.* 108 D6
Bloomington, *Ill., U.S.A.* 108 E10
Bloomington, *Ind., U.S.A.* 104 F2
Bloomington, *Minn., U.S.A.* 108 C8
Bloomsburg, *U.S.A.* 107 F8
Blora, *Indonesia* 57 G14
Blossburg, *U.S.A.* 106 E7
Blouberg, *S. Africa* 85 C4
Blountstown, *U.S.A.* 105 K3
Bludenz, *Austria* 19 H5
Blue Island, *U.S.A.* 104 E2
Blue Lake, *U.S.A.* 110 F2
Blue Mesa Reservoir, *U.S.A.* 111 G10
Blue Mts., *Oreg., U.S.A.* 110 D4
Blue Mts., *Pa., U.S.A.* 107 F8
Blue Mud B., *Australia* 90 A2
Blue Nile = Nîl el Azraq →, *Sudan* 77 D3
Blue Rapids, *U.S.A.* 108 F6
Blue Ridge Mts., *U.S.A.* 105 G5
Blue Stack Mts., *Ireland* 15 B3
Blueberry →, *Canada* 100 B4
Bluefield, *U.S.A.* 104 G5
Bluefields, *Nic.* 116 D3
Bluff, *Australia* 90 C4
Bluff, *N.Z.* 87 M2
Bluff, *U.S.A.* 111 H9
Bluff Knoll, *Australia* 89 F2
Bluff Pt., *Australia* 89 E1
Bluffton, *U.S.A.* 104 E3
Blumenau, *Brazil* 127 B6
Blümisalphorn, *Switz.* 22 D5
Blunt, *U.S.A.* 108 C4
Bly, *U.S.A.* 110 E3
Blyth, *Canada* 106 C3
Blyth, *U.K.* 12 B6
Blythe, *U.S.A.* 113 M12
Blythe Bridge, *U.K.* 12 E5
Bø, *Norway* 10 E3
Bo, *S. Leone* 78 D2
Bo Duc, *Vietnam* 59 G6
Bo Hai, *China* 51 E10
Bo Xian, *China* 50 H8
Boa Esperança, *Brazil* 121 C5
Boa Esperança, Represa, *Brazil* 122 C3
Boa Nova, *Brazil* 123 D3
Boa Viagem, *Brazil* 122 C4
Boa Vista, *Brazil* 121 C5
Boac, *Phil.* 55 E4
Boaco, *Nic.* 116 D2
Bo'ai, *China* 50 G7
Boal, *Spain* 30 B4
Boardman, *U.S.A.* 106 E4
Boatman, *Australia* 91 D4
Bobadah, *Australia* 91 E4
Bobai, *China* 52 F7
Bobbili, *India* 61 K13
Bóbbio, *Italy* 32 D6
Bobcaygeon, *Canada* 98 D4
Böblingen, *Germany* 19 G5
Bobo-Dioulasso, *Burkina Faso* 78 C4
Boboc, *Romania* 38 D9
Bobonaza →, *Ecuador* 120 D2
Bobov Dol, *Bulgaria* 38 G5
Bóbr →, *Poland* 20 C5
Bobraomby, Tanjon' i, *Madag.* 85 A8
Bobrinets, *Ukraine* 41 H7
Bobrov, *Russia* 42 E5
Bobrovitsa, *Ukraine* 41 G6
Bobruysk = Babruysk, *Belarus* 41 F5
Bobures, *Venezuela* 120 B3
Boca de Drago, *Venezuela* 121 A5
Bôca do Acre, *Brazil* 124 B4
Bôca do Jari, *Brazil* 121 D7
Bôca do Moaco, *Brazil* 124 B4
Boca Grande, *Venezuela* 121 B5
Boca Raton, *U.S.A.* 105 M5
Bocaiúva, *Brazil* 123 E3
Bocanda, *Ivory C.* 78 D4
Bocaranga, *C.A.R.* 73 G8
Bocas del Toro, *Panama* 116 E3
Boceguillas, *Spain* 28 D1
Bochnia, *Poland* 20 F10
Bocholt, *Belgium* 17 F7
Bocholt, *Germany* 18 D2
Bochum, *Germany* 18 D3
Bockenem, *Germany* 18 C6
Bocognano, *France* 27 F13
Boconó, *Venezuela* 120 B3
Boconó →, *Venezuela* 120 B4
Bocoyna, *Mexico* 114 B3
Bocq →, *Belgium* 17 H5
Boda, *C.A.R.* 80 D3
Bodaybo, *Russia* 45 D12
Boddington, *Australia* 89 F2
Bodega Bay, *U.S.A.* 112 G3
Bodegraven, *Neths.* 16 D5
Boden, *Sweden* 8 D19
Bodensee, *Europe* 23 A8
Bodenteich, *Germany* 18 C6
Bodhan, *India* 60 K10
Bodinga, *Nigeria* 79 C6
Bodio, *Switz.* 23 D7
Bodmin, *U.K.* 13 G3
Bodmin Moor, *U.K.* 13 G3
Bodø, *Norway* 8 C16
Bodoquena, Serra da, *Brazil* 125 E6
Bodrog →, *Hungary* 21 G11
Bodrum, *Turkey* 66 D2
Boechout, *Belgium* 17 F5
Boekelo, *Neths.* 16 D9
Boelenslaan, *Neths.* 16 B8
Boën, *France* 27 C8
Boende, *Zaïre* 80 E4
Boerne, *U.S.A.* 109 L5
Boertange, *Neths.* 16 B10
Boezinge, *Belgium* 17 G1
Boffa, *Guinea* 78 C2
Bogalusa, *U.S.A.* 109 K10
Bogan Gate, *Australia* 91 E4
Bogantungan, *Australia* 90 C4
Bogata, *U.S.A.* 109 J7
Bogatić, *Serbia, Yug.* 21 L9
Boğazkale, *Turkey* 66 B6
Boğazlıyan, *Turkey* 66 C6
Bogense, *Denmark* 11 J4
Boggabilla, *Australia* 91 D5
Boggabri, *Australia* 91 E5
Boggeragh Mts., *Ireland* 15 D3
Bognor Regis, *U.K.* 13 G7
Bogø, *Denmark* 11 K6
Bogo, *Phil.* 55 F6
Bogodukhov = Bohodukhiv, *Ukraine* 41 G8
Bogong, Mt., *Australia* 91 F4
Bogor, *Indonesia* 57 G12
Bogoroditsk, *Russia* 42 D4
Bogorodsk, *Russia* 42 B6
Bogorodskoye, *Russia* 45 D15
Bogoso, *Ghana* 78 D4
Bogotá, *Colombia* 120 C3
Bogotol, *Russia* 44 D9
Bogra, *Bangla.* 61 G16
Boguchany, *Russia* 45 D10
Boguchar, *Russia* 42 F5
Bogué, *Mauritania* 78 B2
Boguslav, *Ukraine* 41 H6
Bohain-en-Vermandois, *France* 25 C10
Bohemia Downs, *Australia* 88 C4
Bohemian Forest = Böhmerwald, *Germany* 19 F8
Bohena Cr. →, *Australia* 91 E4
Bohinjska Bistrica, *Slovenia* 33 B11
Böhmerwald, *Germany* 19 F8
Bohmte, *Germany* 18 C4
Bohodukhiv, *Ukraine* 41 G8
Bohol, *Phil.* 55 G6
Bohol Sea, *Phil.* 57 C6
Bohotleh, *Somali Rep.* 68 F4
Bohuslän, *Sweden* 9 G14
Boi, *Nigeria* 79 D6
Boi, Pta. de, *Brazil* 127 A6
Boiaçu, *Brazil* 121 D5
Boiano, *Italy* 35 A7
Boileau, C., *Australia* 88 C3
Boipeba, I. de, *Brazil* 123 D4
Bois →, *Brazil* 123 E1
Boischot, *Belgium* 17 F5
Boise, *U.S.A.* 110 E5
Boise City, *U.S.A.* 109 G3
Boissevain, *Canada* 101 D8
Boite →, *Italy* 33 B9
Boitzenburg, *Germany* 18 B9
Boizenburg, *Germany* 18 B6
Bojador C., *W. Sahara* 74 C2
Bojnūrd, *Iran* 65 B8
Bojonegoro, *Indonesia* 57 G14
Boju, *Nigeria* 79 D6

Boka Kotorska, Montenegro, Yug. 21 N8
Bokala, Ivory C. 78 D4
Boké, Guinea 78 C2
Bokhara →, Australia 91 D4
Bokkos, Nigeria 79 D6
Boknafjorden, Norway 9 G11
Bokoro, Chad 73 F8
Bokote, Zaïre 80 E4
Boksitogorsk, Russia 40 C7
Bokungu, Zaïre 80 E4
Bol, Chad 73 F7
Bol, Croatia 33 E13
Bolama, Guinea-Biss. 78 C1
Bolan Pass, Pakistan 60 E5
Bolaños →, Mexico 114 C4
Bolbec, France 24 C7
Boldājī, Iran 65 D6
Boldeşti, Romania 38 D9
Bole, China 54 B3
Bole, Ethiopia 77 F4
Bolekhiv, Ukraine 41 H2
Bolekhov = Bolekhiv, Ukraine 41 H2
Bolesławiec, Poland 20 D5
Bolgatanga, Ghana 79 C4
Bolgrad = Bolhrad, Ukraine 41 K5
Bolhrad, Ukraine 41 K5
Boli, Sudan 77 F2
Bolinao, Phil. 55 C3
Bolinao C., Phil. 57 A5
Bolívar, Argentina 126 D3
Bolívar, Antioquía, Colombia 120 B2
Bolívar, Cauca, Colombia 120 C2
Bolívar, Peru 124 B2
Bolivar, Mo., U.S.A. 109 G8
Bolivar, Tenn., U.S.A. 109 H10
Bolívar □, Colombia 120 B3
Bolívar □, Ecuador 120 D2
Bolívar □, Venezuela 121 B5
Bolivia ■, S. Amer. 125 D5
Bolivian Plateau, S. Amer. 118 E4
Bolkhov, Russia 42 D3
Bollène, France 27 D8
Bollnäs, Sweden 10 C10
Bollon, Australia 91 D4
Bollstabruk, Sweden 10 A11
Bollullos, Spain 31 H4
Bolmen, Sweden 9 H15
Bolobo, Zaïre 80 E3
Bologna, Italy 33 D8
Bologne, France 25 D12
Bologoye, Russia 42 B2
Bolomba, Zaïre 80 D3
Bolonchenticul, Mexico 115 D7
Bolong, Phil. 57 C6
Boloven, Cao Nguyen, Laos 58 E6
Bolpur, India 63 H12
Bolsena, Italy 33 F8
Bolsena, L. di, Italy 33 F8
Bolshaya Chernigovka, Russia 42 D10
Bolshaya Glushitsa, Russia 42 D10
Bolshaya Martynovka, Russia 43 G5
Bolshaya Vradiyevka, Ukraine 41 J6
Bolshereche, Russia 44 D8
Bolshevik, Ostrov, Russia 45 B11
Bolshoi Kavkas = Caucasus Mountains, Eurasia 43 J7
Bolshoy Anyuy →, Russia 45 C17
Bolshoy Atlym, Russia 44 C7
Bolshoy Begichev, Ostrov, Russia 45 B12
Bolshoy Lyakhovskiy, Ostrov, Russia 45 B15
Bolshoy Tokmak = Tokmak, Ukraine 41 J8
Bolshoy Tyuters, Ostrov, Russia 9 G22
Bolsward, Neths. 16 B7
Boltaña, Spain 28 C5
Boltigen, Switz. 22 C4
Bolton, Canada 106 C5
Bolton, U.K. 12 D5
Bolu, Turkey 66 B4
Bolungavík, Iceland 8 C2
Boluo, China 53 F10
Bolvadin, Turkey 66 C4
Bolzano, Italy 33 B8
Bom Comércio, Brazil 125 B4
Bom Conselho, Brazil 122 C4
Bom Despacho, Brazil 123 E2
Bom Jesus, Brazil 122 C3
Bom Jesus da Gurguéia, Serra, Brazil 122 C3
Bom Jesus da Lapa, Brazil 123 D3
Boma, Zaïre 80 F2
Bomaderry, Australia 91 E5
Bombala, Australia 91 F4
Bombarral, Portugal 31 F1
Bombay, India 60 K8
Bomboma, Zaïre 80 D3
Bombombwa, Zaïre 82 B2
Bomi Hills, Liberia 78 D2
Bomili, Zaïre 82 B2
Bømlo, Norway 9 G11
Bommel, Neths. 16 E4
Bomokandi →, Zaïre 82 B2
Bomongo, Zaïre 80 D3
Bomu →, C.A.R. 80 D4
Bon, C., Tunisia 75 A7
Bon Sar Pa, Vietnam 58 F6
Bonaduz, Switz. 23 C8
Bonaire, Neth. Ant. 117 D6
Bonang, Australia 91 F4
Bonanza, Nic. 116 D3
Bonaparte Arch., Australia 88 B3
Boñar, Spain 30 C5
Bonaventure, Canada 99 C6
Bonavista, Canada 99 C9
Bonavista, C., Canada 99 C9
Bonawan, Phil. 55 G5
Bondeno, Italy 33 D8
Bondo, Zaïre 82 B1
Bondoukou, Ivory C. 78 D4
Bondowoso, Indonesia 57 G15
Bone, Teluk, Indonesia 57 E6
Bonefro, Italy 35 A7
Bonerate, Indonesia 57 F6
Bonerate, Kepulauan, Indonesia 57 F6
Bo'ness, U.K. 14 E5
Bonete, Cerro, Argentina 126 B2
Bong Son = Hoai Nhon, Vietnam 58 E7
Bongabong, Phil. 55 E4
Bongandanga, Zaïre 80 D4
Bongor, Chad 73 F8
Bongouanou, Ivory C. 78 D4
Bonham, U.S.A. 109 J6
Bonheiden, Belgium 17 F5
Bonifacio, France 27 G13
Bonifacio, Bouches de, Medit. S. 34 A2
Bonin Is. = Ogasawara Gunto, Pac. Oc. 46 G18
Bonke, Ethiopia 77 F4
Bonn, Germany 18 E3
Bonnat, France 26 B5
Bonne Terre, U.S.A. 109 G9
Bonners Ferry, U.S.A. 110 B5
Bonnétable, France 24 D7
Bonneuil-Matours, France 24 F7
Bonneval, France 24 D8
Bonneville, France 27 B10
Bonney, L., Australia 91 F3
Bonnie Downs, Australia 90 C3
Bonnie Rock, Australia 89 F2
Bonny, Nigeria 79 E6
Bonny →, Nigeria 79 E6
Bonny, Bight of, Africa 79 E6
Bonny-sur-Loire, France 25 E9
Bonnyville, Canada 101 C6
Bonoi, Indonesia 57 E9
Bonorva, Italy 34 B1
Bonsall, U.S.A. 113 M9
Bontang, Indonesia 56 D5
Bonthain, Indonesia 57 F5
Bonthe, S. Leone 78 D2
Bontoc, Phil. 55 C4
Bonyeri, Ghana 78 D4
Bonython Ra., Australia 88 D4
Bookabie, Australia 89 F5
Booker, U.S.A. 109 G4
Boolaboolka L., Australia 91 E3
Booligal, Australia 91 E3
Boom, Belgium 17 F4
Boonah, Australia 91 D5
Boone, Iowa, U.S.A. 108 D8
Boone, N.C., U.S.A. 105 G5
Booneville, Ark., U.S.A. 109 H8
Booneville, Miss., U.S.A. 105 H1
Boonville, Calif., U.S.A. 112 F3
Boonville, Ind., U.S.A. 104 F2
Boonville, Mo., U.S.A. 108 F8
Boonville, N.Y., U.S.A. 107 C9
Boorindal, Australia 91 E4
Boorowa, Australia 91 E4
Boothia, Gulf of, Canada 97 A11
Boothia Pen., Canada 96 A10
Bootle, U.K. 12 D4
Booué, Gabon 80 E2
Boppard, Germany 19 E3
Boquerón □, Paraguay 125 E5
Boquete, Panama 116 E3
Boquilla, Presa de la, Mexico 114 B3
Boquillas del Carmen, Mexico 114 B4
Bor, Czech. 20 F2
Bor, Russia 42 B7
Bor, Serbia, Yug. 21 L12
Bôr, Sudan 77 F3
Bor, Turkey 66 D6
Bor Mashash, Israel 69 D3
Boradā →, Syria 69 B5
Borah Peak, U.S.A. 110 D7
Borama, Somali Rep. 68 F3
Borang, Sudan 77 G3
Borås, Sweden 11 G6
Borāzjān, Iran 65 D6
Borba, Brazil 121 D6
Borba, Portugal 31 G3
Borborema, Planalto da, Brazil 122 C4
Borçka, Turkey 67 B9
Borculo, Neths. 16 D9
Bord Khūn-e Now, Iran 65 D6
Borda, C., Australia 91 F2
Bordeaux, France 26 D3
Borden, Australia 89 F2
Borden, Canada 99 C7
Borden I., Canada 4 B2
Borders □, U.K. 14 F6
Bordertown, Australia 91 F3
Borðeyri, Iceland 8 D3
Bordighera, Italy 32 E4
Bordj bou Arreridj, Algeria 75 A5
Bordj Bourguiba, Tunisia 75 B7
Bordj Fly Ste. Marie, Algeria 74 C4
Bordj-in-Eker, Algeria 75 D6
Bordj Menaiel, Algeria 75 A5
Bordj Messouda, Algeria 75 B6
Bordj Nili, Algeria 75 B5
Bordj Omar Driss, Algeria 75 C6
Bordj Sif Fatima, Algeria 75 B6
Bordj-Tarat, Algeria 75 C6
Bordj Zelfana, Algeria 75 B5
Borensberg, Sweden 11 F9
Borgå = Porvoo, Finland 9 F21
Borgarfjörður, Iceland 8 D7
Borgarnes, Iceland 8 D3
Børgefjellet, Norway 8 D15
Borger, Neths. 16 C9
Borger, U.S.A. 109 H4
Borgerhout, Belgium 17 F4
Borghamn, Sweden 11 F8
Borgholm, Sweden 9 H17
Bórgia, Italy 35 D9
Borgloon, Belgium 17 G6
Borgo San Dalmazzo, Italy 32 D4
Borgo San Lorenzo, Italy 33 E8
Borgo Valsugano, Italy 33 B8
Borgomanero, Italy 32 C5
Borgonovo Val Tidone, Italy 32 C6
Borgorose, Italy 33 F10
Borgosésia, Italy 32 C5
Borgvattnet, Sweden 10 A9
Borikhane, Laos 58 C4
Borisoglebsk, Russia 42 E6
Borisov = Barysaw, Belarus 40 E5
Borisovka, Russia 42 E3
Borja, Peru 120 D2
Borja, Spain 28 D3
Borjas Blancas, Spain 28 D5
Borjomi, Georgia 43 K6
Borken, Germany 18 D2
Borkou, Chad 73 E8
Borkum, Germany 18 B2
Borlänge, Sweden 9 F16
Borley, C., Antarctica 5 C5
Bormida →, Italy 32 D5
Bórmio, Italy 32 B7
Born, Neths. 17 F7
Borna, Germany 18 D8
Borndiep, Neths. 16 B7
Borne, Neths. 16 D9
Bornem, Belgium 17 F4
Borneo, E. Indies 56 D5
Bornholm, Denmark 9 J16
Borno □, Nigeria 79 C7
Bornos, Spain 31 J5
Bornu Yassa, Nigeria 79 C7
Borobudur, Indonesia 57 G14
Borodino, Russia 42 C2
Borogontsy, Russia 45 C14
Boromo, Burkina Faso 78 C4
Boron, U.S.A. 113 L9
Borongan, Phil. 55 F6
Bororen, Australia 90 C5
Borotangba Mts., C.A.R. 77 F1
Borovan, Bulgaria 38 F6
Borovichi, Russia 40 C7
Borovsk, Russia 42 C3
Borrego Springs, U.S.A. 113 M10
Borriol, Spain 28 E4
Borroloola, Australia 90 B2
Borşa, Romania 38 B7
Borssele, Neths. 17 F3
Bort-les-Orgues, France 26 C6
Borth, U.K. 13 E3
Borūjerd, Iran 67 F13
Boryslav, Ukraine 41 H2
Boryspil, Ukraine 41 G6
Borzhomi = Borjomi, Georgia 43 K6
Borzna, Ukraine 41 G7
Borzya, Russia 45 D12
Bosa, Italy 34 B1
Bosanska Dubica, Bos.-H. 33 C13
Bosanska Gradiška, Bos.-H. 21 K7
Bosanska Kostajnica, Bos.-H. 33 C13
Bosanska Krupa, Bos.-H. 33 D13
Bosanski Novi, Bos.-H. 33 C13
Bosanski Šamac, Bos.-H. 21 K8
Bosansko Grahovo, Bos.-H. 33 D13
Bosansko Petrovac, Bos.-H. 33 D13
Bosaso, Somali Rep. 68 E4
Boscastle, U.K. 13 G3
Boscotrecase, Italy 35 B7
Bose, China 52 F6
Boshan, China 51 F9
Boshof, S. Africa 84 D4
Boshrūyeh, Iran 65 C8
Bosilegrad, Serbia, Yug. 21 N12
Boskoop, Neths. 16 D5
Bosna →, Bos.-H. 21 K8
Bosna i Hercegovina = Bosnia-Herzegovina ■, Europe 21 L7
Bosnia-Herzegovina ■, Europe 21 L7
Bosnik, Indonesia 57 E9
Bosobolo, Zaïre 80 D3
Bosporus = Karadeniz Boğazı, Turkey 66 B3
Bossangoa, C.A.R. 73 G8
Bossembélé, C.A.R. 73 G8
Bossier City, U.S.A. 109 J8
Bosso, Niger 79 C7
Bostānābād, Iran 67 D12
Bosten Hu, China 54 B3
Boston, U.K. 12 E7
Boston, U.S.A. 107 D13
Boston Bar, Canada 100 D4
Bosut →, Croatia 21 K8
Boswell, Canada 100 D5
Boswell, Okla., U.S.A. 109 H7
Boswell, Pa., U.S.A. 106 F5
Botad, India 62 H4
Botan →, Turkey 67 D10
Botany B., Australia 91 E5
Botene, Laos 58 D3
Botevgrad, Bulgaria 38 G6
Bothaville, S. Africa 84 D4
Bothnia, G. of, Europe 8 E19
Bothwell, Australia 90 G4
Bothwell, Canada 106 D3
Boticas, Portugal 30 D3
Botletle →, Botswana 84 C3
Botlikh, Russia 43 J8
Botoşani, Romania 38 B9
Botro, Ivory C. 78 D3
Botswana ■, Africa 84 C3
Bottineau, U.S.A. 108 A4
Bottrop, Germany 17 E9
Botucatu, Brazil 127 A6
Botwood, Canada 99 C8
Bou Alam, Algeria 75 B5
Bou Ali, Algeria 75 C4
Bou Djébéha, Mali 78 B4
Bou Guema, Algeria 75 C5
Bou Ismael, Algeria 75 A5
Bou Izakarn, Morocco 74 C3
Boû Lanouâr, Mauritania 74 D1
Bou Saâda, Algeria 75 A5
Bou Salem, Tunisia 75 A6
Bouaké, Ivory C. 78 D3
Bouar, C.A.R. 80 C3
Bouârfa, Morocco 75 B4
Bouca, C.A.R. 73 G8
Boucau, France 26 E2
Boucaut B., Australia 90 A1
Bouches-du-Rhône □, France 27 E9
Bouda, Algeria 75 C4
Boudenib, Morocco 74 B4
Boudry, Switz. 22 C3
Boufarik, Algeria 75 A5
Bougainville, C., Australia 88 B4
Bougainville Reef, Australia 90 B4
Bougaroun, C., Algeria 75 A6
Bougie = Bejaia, Algeria 75 A6
Bougouni, Mali 78 C3
Bouillon, Belgium 17 J6
Bouïra, Algeria 75 A5
Boulder, Colo., U.S.A. 108 E2
Boulder, Mont., U.S.A. 110 C7
Boulder City, U.S.A. 113 K12
Boulder Creek, U.S.A. 112 H4
Boulder Dam = Hoover Dam, U.S.A. 113 K12
Bouli, Mauritania 78 B2
Boulia, Australia 90 C2
Bouligny, France 25 C12
Boulogne →, France 24 E5
Boulogne-sur-Gesse, France 26 E4
Boulogne-sur-Mer, France 25 B8
Bouloire, France 24 E7
Boulsa, Burkina Faso 79 C4
Boultoum, Niger 79 C7
Boumalne, Morocco 74 B3
Boun Neua, Laos 58 B3
Boun Tai, Laos 58 B3
Bouna, Ivory C. 78 D4
Boundary Peak, U.S.A. 112 H8
Boundiali, Ivory C. 78 D3
Bountiful, U.S.A. 110 F8
Bounty Is., Pac. Oc. 92 M9
Bourbon-Lancy, France 26 B7
Bourbon-l'Archambault, France 26 B7
Bourbonnais, France 26 B7
Bourbonne-les-Bains, France 25 E12
Bourem, Mali 79 B4
Bourg, France 26 C3
Bourg-Argental, France 27 C8
Bourg-de-Péage, France 27 C9
Bourg-en-Bresse, France 27 B9
Bourg-St.-Andéol, France 27 D8
Bourg-St.-Maurice, France 27 C10
Bourg-St.-Pierre, Switz. 22 E4
Bourganeuf, France 26 C5
Bourges, France 25 E9
Bourget, Canada 107 A9
Bourget, L. du, France 27 C9
Bourgneuf, B. de, France 24 E4
Bourgneuf-en-Retz, France 24 E5
Bourgogne, France 25 F11
Bourgoin-Jallieu, France 27 C9
Bourgueil, France 24 E7
Bourke, Australia 91 E4
Bournemouth, U.K. 13 G6
Bourriot-Bergonce, France 26 D3
Bouse, U.S.A. 113 M13
Boussac, France 26 B6
Boussens, France 26 E4
Bousso, Chad 73 F8
Boussu, Belgium 17 H3
Boutilimit, Mauritania 78 B2
Boutonne →, France 26 C3
Bouvet I. = Bouvetøya, Antarctica 3 G10
Bouvetøya, Antarctica 3 G10
Bouznika, Morocco 74 B3
Bouzonville, France 25 C13
Bova Marina, Italy 35 E8
Bovalino Marina, Italy 35 D9
Bovec, Slovenia 33 B10
Bovenkarspel, Neths. 16 C6
Bovigny, Belgium 17 H7
Bovill, U.S.A. 110 C5
Bovino, Italy 35 A8
Bow Island, Canada 100 D6
Bowbells, U.S.A. 108 A3
Bowdle, U.S.A. 108 C5
Bowelling, Australia 89 F2
Bowen, Australia 90 C4
Bowen Mts., Australia 91 F4
Bowie, Ariz., U.S.A. 111 K9
Bowie, Tex., U.S.A. 109 J6
Bowkān, Iran 67 D12
Bowland, Forest of, U.K. 12 D5
Bowling Green, Ky., U.S.A. 104 G2
Bowling Green, Ohio, U.S.A. 104 E4
Bowling Green, C., Australia 90 B4
Bowman, U.S.A. 108 B3
Bowman I., Antarctica 5 C8
Bowmans, Australia 91 E2
Bowmanville, Canada 98 D4
Bowmore, U.K. 14 F2
Bowral, Australia 91 E5
Bowraville, Australia 91 E5
Bowron →, Canada 100 C4
Bowser L., Canada 100 B3
Bowsman, Canada 101 C8
Bowwood, Zambia 83 F2
Boxholm, Sweden 11 F9
Boxmeer, Neths. 17 E7
Boxtel, Neths. 17 E6
Boyabat, Turkey 66 B6
Boyaca = Casanare □, Colombia 120 B3
Boyce, U.S.A. 109 K8
Boyer →, Canada 100 B5
Boyle, Ireland 15 C3
Boyne →, Ireland 15 C5
Boyne City, U.S.A. 104 C3
Boynton Beach, U.S.A. 105 M5
Boyoma, Chutes, Zaïre 82 B2
Boyup Brook, Australia 89 F2
Boz Dağ, Turkey 66 D3
Boz Dağları, Turkey 66 C3
Bozburun, Turkey 66 D3
Bozcaada, Turkey 66 C2
Bozdoğan, Turkey 66 D3
Bozeman, U.S.A. 110 D8
Bozen = Bolzano, Italy 33 B8
Bozkır, Turkey 66 D5
Bozouls, France 26 D6
Bozoum, C.A.R. 73 G8
Bozova, Turkey 67 D8
Bozovici, Romania 38 E5
Bozüyük, Turkey 66 C4
Bra, Italy 32 D4
Brabant □, Belgium 17 G5
Brabant L., Canada 101 B8
Brabrand, Denmark 11 H4
Brač, Croatia 33 E13
Bracadale, L., U.K. 14 D2
Bracciano, Italy 33 F9
Bracciano, L. di, Italy 33 F9
Bracebridge, Canada 98 C4
Brach, Libya 73 C7
Bracieux, France 25 E8
Bräcke, Sweden 10 B9
Brackettville, U.S.A. 109 L4
Bracki Kanal, Croatia 33 E13
Brad, Romania 38 C5
Brădano →, Italy 35 B9
Bradenton, U.S.A. 105 M4
Bradford, Canada 106 B5
Bradford, U.K. 12 D6
Bradford, Pa., U.S.A. 106 E6
Bradford, Vt., U.S.A. 107 C12
Brădiceni, Romania 38 D6
Bradley, Ark., U.S.A. 109 J8
Bradley, Calif., U.S.A. 112 K6
Bradley, S. Dak., U.S.A. 108 C6
Bradley Institute, Zimbabwe 83 F3
Bradore Bay, Canada 99 B8
Bradshaw, Australia 88 C5
Brady, U.S.A. 109 K5
Brædstrup, Denmark 11 J3
Braemar, Australia 91 E2
Braeside, Canada 107 A8
Braga, Portugal 30 D2
Braga □, Portugal 30 D2
Bragado, Argentina 126 D3
Bragança, Brazil 122 B2
Bragança, Portugal 30 D4
Bragança □, Portugal 30 D4
Bragança Paulista, Brazil 127 A6
Brahmanbaria, Bangla. 61 H17
Brahmani →, India 61 J15
Brahmaputra →, India 63 G13
Braich-y-pwll, U.K. 12 E3
Braidwood, Australia 91 F4
Brăila, Romania 38 D10
Braine-l'Alleud, Belgium 17 G4
Braine-le-Comte, Belgium 17 G4
Brainerd, U.S.A. 108 B7
Braintree, U.K. 13 F8
Braintree, U.S.A. 107 D14
Brak →, S. Africa 84 D3
Brake, Germany 18 B4
Brakel, Germany 18 D5

Brakel, *Neths.* 16 E6
Brakwater, *Namibia* 84 C2
Brålanda, *Sweden* 11 F6
Bralorne, *Canada* 100 C4
Bramberg, *Germany* 19 E6
Bramming, *Denmark* 11 J2
Brämön, *Sweden* 10 B11
Brampton, *Canada* 98 D4
Bramsche, *Germany* 18 C3
Bramwell, *Australia* 90 A3
Branco →, *Brazil* 121 D5
Branco, C., *Brazil* 122 C5
Brande, *Denmark* 11 J3
Brandenburg = Neubrandenburg, *Germany* 18 B9
Brandenburg, *Germany* 18 C8
Brandenburg □, *Germany* 18 C9
Brandfort, *S. Africa* 84 D4
Brandon, *Canada* 101 D9
Brandon, *U.S.A.* 107 C11
Brandon B., *Ireland* 15 D1
Brandon Mt., *Ireland* 15 D1
Brandsen, *Argentina* 126 D4
Brandval, *Norway* 10 D6
Brandvlei, *S. Africa* 84 E3
Brandýs, *Czech.* 20 E4
Branford, *U.S.A.* 107 E12
Braniewo, *Poland* 20 A9
Bransfield Str., *Antarctica* 5 C18
Branson, *Colo., U.S.A.* 109 G3
Branson, *Mo., U.S.A.* 109 G8
Brantford, *Canada* 98 D3
Brantôme, *France* 26 C4
Branxholme, *Australia* 91 F3
Branzi, *Italy* 32 B6
Bras d'Or, L., *Canada* 99 C7
Brasil, Planalto, *Brazil* 118 E6
Brasiléia, *Brazil* 124 C4
Brasília, *Brazil* 123 E2
Brasília Legal, *Brazil* 121 D6
Braslaw, *Belarus* 9 J22
Braslovce, *Slovenia* 33 B12
Braşov, *Romania* 38 D8
Brass, *Nigeria* 79 E6
Brass →, *Nigeria* 79 E6
Brassac-les-Mines, *France* 26 C7
Brasschaat, *Belgium* 17 F4
Brassey, Banjaran, *Malaysia* 56 D5
Brassey Ra., *Australia* 89 E3
Brasstown Bald, *U.S.A.* 105 H4
Brastad, *Sweden* 9 G14
Bratislava, *Slovak Rep.* 21 G7
Bratsk, *Russia* 45 D11
Brattleboro, *U.S.A.* 107 D12
Braunau, *Austria* 21 G3
Braunschweig, *Germany* 18 C6
Braunton, *U.K.* 13 F3
Brava, *Somali Rep.* 68 G3
Bråviken, *Sweden* 10 F10
Bravo del Norte →, *Mexico* 114 B5
Bravo del Norte, R. → = Grande, Rio →, *U.S.A.* 109 N6
Brawley, *U.S.A.* 113 N11
Bray, *Ireland* 15 C5
Bray, Mt., *Australia* 90 A1
Bray, Pays de, *France* 25 C8
Bray-sur-Seine, *France* 25 D10
Brazeau →, *Canada* 100 C5
Brazil, *U.S.A.* 104 F2
Brazil ■, *S. Amer.* 123 D2
Brazilian Highlands = Brasil, Planalto, *Brazil* 118 E6
Brazo Sur →, *S. Amer.* 126 B4
Brazos →, *U.S.A.* 109 L7
Brazzaville, *Congo* 80 E3
Brčko, *Bos.-H.* 21 L8
Brea, *Peru* 124 A1
Breadalbane, *Australia* 90 C2
Breadalbane, *U.K.* 14 E4
Breaden, L., *Australia* 89 E4
Breaksea Sd., *N.Z.* 87 L1
Bream B., *N.Z.* 87 F5
Bream Hd., *N.Z.* 87 F5
Breas, *Chile* 126 B1
Brebes, *Indonesia* 57 G13
Brechin, *Canada* 106 B5
Brechin, *U.K.* 14 E6
Brecht, *Belgium* 17 F5
Breckenridge, *Colo., U.S.A.* 110 G10
Breckenridge, *Minn., U.S.A.* 108 B6
Breckenridge, *Tex., U.S.A.* 109 J5
Breckland, *U.K.* 13 E8
Brecknock, Pen., *Chile* 128 D2
Břeclav, *Czech.* 20 G6
Brecon, *U.K.* 13 F4
Brecon Beacons, *U.K.* 13 F4
Breda, *Neths.* 17 E5
Bredasdorp, *S. Africa* 84 E3
Bredbo, *Australia* 91 F4
Bredene, *Belgium* 17 F1
Bredstedt, *Germany* 18 A4
Bree, *Belgium* 17 F7
Breezand, *Neths.* 16 C5
Bregalnica →, *Macedonia* 39 H5
Bregenz, *Austria* 19 H5
Bréhal, *France* 24 D5
Bréhat, I. de, *France* 24 D4
Breiðafjörður, *Iceland* 8 D2
Breil-sur-Roya, *France* 27 E11
Breisach, *Germany* 19 G3
Brejinho de Nazaré, *Brazil* 122 D2
Brejo, *Brazil* 122 B3
Bremen, *Germany* 18 B4
Bremen □, *Germany* 18 B4
Bremer I., *Australia* 90 A2
Bremerhaven, *Germany* 18 B4
Bremerton, *U.S.A.* 112 C4
Bremervörde, *Germany* 18 B5
Bremsnes, *Norway* 10 A1
Brenes, *Spain* 31 H5
Brenham, *U.S.A.* 109 K6
Brenner P., *Austria* 19 H7
Breno, *Italy* 32 C7
Brent, *Canada* 98 C4
Brent, *U.K.* 13 F7
Brenta →, *Italy* 33 C9
Brentwood, *U.K.* 13 F8
Brentwood, *U.S.A.* 107 F11
Bréscia, *Italy* 32 C7
Breskens, *Neths.* 17 F3
Breslau = Wrocław, *Poland* 20 D7
Bresle →, *France* 24 B8
Bresles, *France* 25 C9
Bressanone, *Italy* 33 B8
Bressay, *U.K.* 14 A7
Bresse, *France* 25 F12
Bressuire, *France* 24 F6
Brest, *Belarus* 41 F2
Brest, *France* 24 D2
Brest-Litovsk = Brest, *Belarus* 41 F2
Bretagne, *France* 24 D4
Bretçu, *Romania* 38 C9
Breteuil, *Eure, France* 24 D7
Breteuil, *Oise, France* 25 C9
Breton, *Canada* 100 C6
Breton, Pertuis, *France* 26 B2
Breton Sd., *U.S.A.* 109 L10
Brett, C., *N.Z.* 87 F5
Bretten, *Germany* 19 F4
Breukelen, *Neths.* 16 D6
Brevard, *U.S.A.* 105 H4
Breves, *Brazil* 122 B1
Brevik, *Norway* 10 E3
Brewarrina, *Australia* 91 D4
Brewer, *U.S.A.* 99 D6
Brewer, Mt., *U.S.A.* 112 J8
Brewster, *N.Y., U.S.A.* 107 E11
Brewster, *Wash., U.S.A.* 110 B4
Brewster, Kap, *Greenland* 4 B6
Brewton, *U.S.A.* 105 K2
Breyten, *S. Africa* 85 D4
Brezhnev = Naberezhnyye Chelny, *Russia* 42 C11
Brežice, *Slovenia* 33 C12
Brézina, *Algeria* 75 B5
Březnice, *Czech.* 20 F3
Breznik, *Bulgaria* 38 G5
Brezno, *Slovak Rep.* 20 G9
Bria, *C.A.R.* 73 G9
Briançon, *France* 27 D10
Briare, *France* 25 E9
Bribie I., *Australia* 91 D5
Bricquebec, *France* 24 C5
Bridgehampton, *U.S.A.* 107 F12
Bridgend, *U.K.* 13 F4
Bridgend □, *U.K.* 13 F4
Bridgeport, *Calif., U.S.A.* 111 G4
Bridgeport, *Conn., U.S.A.* 107 E11
Bridgeport, *Nebr., U.S.A.* 108 E3
Bridgeport, *Tex., U.S.A.* 109 J6
Bridger, *U.S.A.* 110 D9
Bridgeton, *U.S.A.* 104 F8
Bridgetown, *Australia* 89 F2
Bridgetown, *Barbados* 117 D8
Bridgetown, *Canada* 99 D6
Bridgewater, *Canada* 99 D7
Bridgewater, *Mass., U.S.A.* 107 E14
Bridgewater, *S. Dak., U.S.A.* 108 D6
Bridgewater, C., *Australia* 91 F3
Bridgnorth, *U.K.* 13 E5
Bridgton, *U.S.A.* 107 B14
Bridgwater, *U.K.* 13 F4
Bridlington, *U.K.* 12 C7
Bridport, *Australia* 90 G4
Bridport, *U.K.* 13 G5
Brie, Plaine de la, *France* 25 D9
Brie-Comte-Robert, *France* 25 D9
Briec, *France* 24 D2
Brielle, *Neths.* 16 E4
Brienne-le-Château, *France* 25 D11
Brienon-sur-Armançon, *France* 25 E10
Brienz, *Switz.* 22 C6
Brienzersee, *Switz.* 22 C5
Brig, *Switz.* 22 D5
Brigg, *U.K.* 12 D7
Briggsdale, *U.S.A.* 108 E2
Brigham City, *U.S.A.* 110 F7
Bright, *Australia* 91 F4
Brighton, *Australia* 91 F2
Brighton, *Canada* 98 D4
Brighton, *U.K.* 13 G7
Brighton, *U.S.A.* 108 F2
Brignogan-Plage, *France* 24 D2
Brignoles, *France* 27 E10
Brihuega, *Spain* 28 E2
Brikama, *Gambia* 78 C1
Brilliant, *Canada* 100 D5
Brilliant, *U.S.A.* 106 F4
Brilon, *Germany* 18 D4
Bríndisi, *Italy* 35 B10
Brinje, *Croatia* 33 D12
Brinkley, *U.S.A.* 109 H9
Brinkworth, *Australia* 91 E2
Brinnon, *U.S.A.* 112 C4
Brion, I., *Canada* 99 C7
Brionne, *France* 24 C7
Brionski, *Croatia* 33 D10
Brioude, *France* 26 C7
Briouze, *France* 24 D6
Brisbane, *Australia* 91 D5
Brisbane →, *Australia* 91 D5
Brisighella, *Italy* 33 D8
Bristol, *U.K.* 13 F5
Bristol, *Conn., U.S.A.* 107 E12
Bristol, *Pa., U.S.A.* 107 F10
Bristol, *R.I., U.S.A.* 107 E13
Bristol, *S. Dak., U.S.A.* 108 C6
Bristol, *Tenn., U.S.A.* 105 G4
Bristol □, *U.K.* 13 F5
Bristol B., *U.S.A.* 96 C4
Bristol Channel, *U.K.* 13 F3
Bristol I., *Antarctica* 5 B1
Bristol L., *U.S.A.* 111 J5
Bristow, *U.S.A.* 109 H6
British Columbia □, *Canada* 100 C3
British Isles, *Europe* 6 E5
Brits, *S. Africa* 85 D4
Britstown, *S. Africa* 84 E3
Britt, *Canada* 98 C3
Brittany = Bretagne, *France* 24 D4
Britton, *U.S.A.* 108 C6
Brive-la-Gaillarde, *France* 26 C5
Briviesca, *Spain* 28 C1
Brixen = Bressanone, *Italy* 33 B8
Brixton, *Australia* 90 C3
Brlik, *Kazakstan* 44 E8
Brno, *Czech.* 20 F6
Bro, *Sweden* 10 E11
Broad →, *U.S.A.* 105 J5
Broad Arrow, *Australia* 89 F3
Broad B., *U.K.* 14 C2
Broad Haven, *Ireland* 15 B2
Broad Law, *U.K.* 14 F5
Broad Sd., *Australia* 90 C4
Broadhurst Ra., *Australia* 88 D3
Broads, The, *U.K.* 12 E9
Broadus, *U.S.A.* 108 C2
Broadview, *Canada* 101 C8
Broager, *Denmark* 11 K3
Broaryd, *Sweden* 11 G7
Brochet, *Canada* 101 B8
Brochet, L., *Canada* 101 B8
Brock, *Canada* 101 C7
Brocken, *Germany* 18 D6
Brockport, *U.S.A.* 106 C7
Brockton, *U.S.A.* 107 D13
Brockville, *Canada* 98 D4
Brockway, *Mont., U.S.A.* 108 B2
Brockway, *Pa., U.S.A.* 106 E6
Brocton, *U.S.A.* 106 D5
Brod, *Macedonia* 39 H4
Brodarevo, *Serbia, Yug.* 21 M9
Brodeur Pen., *Canada* 97 A11
Brodick, *U.K.* 14 F3
Brodnica, *Poland* 20 B9
Brody, *Ukraine* 41 G3
Broechem, *Belgium* 17 F5
Broek, *Neths.* 16 D6
Broek op Langedijk, *Neths.* 16 C5
Brogan, *U.S.A.* 110 D5
Broglie, *France* 24 C7
Broken Arrow, *U.S.A.* 109 G7
Broken Bow, *Nebr., U.S.A.* 108 E5
Broken Bow, *Okla., U.S.A.* 109 H7
Broken Hill = Kabwe, *Zambia* 83 E2
Broken Hill, *Australia* 91 E3
Brokind, *Sweden* 11 F9
Brokopondo, *Surinam* 121 B7
Brokopondo □, *Surinam* 121 C6
Bromfield, *U.K.* 13 E5
Bromley, *U.K.* 13 F8
Brønderslev, *Denmark* 11 G3
Brong-Ahafo □, *Ghana* 78 D4
Bronkhorstspruit, *S. Africa* 85 D4
Brønnøysund, *Norway* 8 D15
Bronte, *Italy* 35 E7
Bronte, *U.S.A.* 109 K4
Bronte Park, *Australia* 90 G4
Brook Park, *U.S.A.* 106 E4
Brookfield, *U.S.A.* 108 F8
Brookhaven, *U.S.A.* 109 K9
Brookings, *Oreg., U.S.A.* 110 E1
Brookings, *S. Dak., U.S.A.* 108 C6
Brooklin, *Canada* 106 C6
Brooklyn Park, *U.S.A.* 108 C8
Brookmere, *Canada* 100 D4
Brooks, *Canada* 100 C6
Brooks B., *Canada* 100 C3
Brooks L., *Canada* 101 A7
Brooks Ra., *U.S.A.* 96 B5
Brooksville, *U.S.A.* 105 L4
Brookville, *U.S.A.* 104 F3
Brooloo, *Australia* 91 D5
Broom, L., *U.K.* 14 D3
Broome, *Australia* 88 C3
Broomehill, *Australia* 89 F2
Broons, *France* 24 D4
Brora, *U.K.* 14 C5
Brora →, *U.K.* 14 C5
Brosna →, *Ireland* 15 C4
Broşteni, *Romania* 38 B8
Brotas de Macaúbas, *Brazil* 123 D3
Brothers, *U.S.A.* 110 E3
Brøttum, *Norway* 10 C4
Brou, *France* 24 D8
Brouage, Ramparts de, *France* 26 C2
Brough, *U.K.* 12 C5
Broughton Island, *Canada* 97 B13
Broughty Ferry, *U.K.* 14 E6
Brouwershaven, *Neths.* 16 E3
Brouwershavensche Gat, *Neths.* 16 E3
Brovary, *Ukraine* 41 G6
Brovst, *Denmark* 11 G3
Browerville, *U.S.A.* 108 B7
Brown, Pt., *Australia* 91 E1
Brown Willy, *U.K.* 13 G3
Brownfield, *U.S.A.* 109 J3
Browning, *U.S.A.* 110 B7
Brownlee, *Canada* 101 C7
Brownsville, *Oreg., U.S.A.* 110 D2
Brownsville, *Tenn., U.S.A.* 109 H10
Brownsville, *Tex., U.S.A.* 109 N6
Brownsweg, *Surinam* 121 B6
Brownwood, *U.S.A.* 109 K5
Brownwood, L., *U.S.A.* 109 K5
Browse I., *Australia* 88 B3
Broye →, *Switz.* 22 C3
Brozas, *Spain* 31 F4
Bruas, *Malaysia* 59 K3
Bruay-en-Artois, *France* 25 B9
Bruce, Mt., *Australia* 88 D2
Bruce Pen., *Canada* 106 A3
Bruce Rock, *Australia* 89 F2
Bruche →, *France* 25 D14
Bruchsal, *Germany* 19 F4
Bruck an der Leitha, *Austria* 21 G6
Bruck an der Mur, *Austria* 21 H5
Brue →, *U.K.* 13 F5
Brugelette, *Belgium* 17 G3
Bruges = Brugge, *Belgium* 17 F2
Brugg, *Switz.* 22 B6
Brugge, *Belgium* 17 F2
Brühl, *Germany* 18 E2
Bruinisse, *Neths.* 17 E4
Brûlé, *Canada* 100 C5
Brûlon, *France* 24 E6
Brûly, *Belgium* 17 J5
Brumado, *Brazil* 123 D3
Brumado →, *Brazil* 123 D3
Brumath, *France* 25 D14
Brummen, *Neths.* 16 D8
Brumunddal, *Norway* 10 D4
Brunchilly, *Australia* 90 B1
Brundidge, *U.S.A.* 105 K3
Bruneau, *U.S.A.* 110 E6
Bruneau →, *U.S.A.* 110 E6
Bruneck = Brunico, *Italy* 33 B8
Brunei = Bandar Seri Begawan, *Brunei* 56 C4
Brunei ■, *Asia* 56 D4
Brunette Downs, *Australia* 90 B2
Brunflo, *Sweden* 10 A8
Brunico, *Italy* 33 B8
Brünig, P., *Switz.* 22 C6
Brunkeberg, *Norway* 10 E2
Brunna, *Sweden* 10 E11
Brunnen, *Switz.* 23 C7
Brunner, L., *N.Z.* 87 K3
Bruno, *Canada* 101 C7
Brunsbüttel, *Germany* 18 B5
Brunssum, *Neths.* 17 G7
Brunswick = Braunschweig, *Germany* 18 C6
Brunswick, *Ga., U.S.A.* 105 K5
Brunswick, *Maine, U.S.A.* 99 D6
Brunswick, *Md., U.S.A.* 104 F7
Brunswick, *Mo., U.S.A.* 108 F8
Brunswick, *Ohio, U.S.A.* 106 E3
Brunswick, Pen. de, *Chile* 128 D2
Brunswick B., *Australia* 88 C3
Brunswick Junction, *Australia* 89 F2
Bruntál, *Czech.* 20 F7
Bruny I., *Australia* 90 G4
Brus Laguna, *Honduras* 116 C3
Brusartsi, *Bulgaria* 38 F6
Brush, *U.S.A.* 108 E3
Brushton, *U.S.A.* 107 B10
Brusio, *Switz.* 23 D10
Brusque, *Brazil* 127 B6
Brussel, *Belgium* 17 G4
Brussels = Brussel, *Belgium* 17 G4
Brussels, *Canada* 106 C3
Brustem, *Belgium* 17 G6
Bruthen, *Australia* 91 F4
Bruxelles = Brussel, *Belgium* 17 G4
Bruyères, *France* 25 D13
Bryan, *Ohio, U.S.A.* 104 E3
Bryan, *Tex., U.S.A.* 109 K6
Bryan, Mt., *Australia* 91 E2
Bryanka, *Ukraine* 41 H10
Bryansk, *Russia* 42 D2
Bryansk, *Russia* 43 H8
Bryanskoye = Bryansk, *Russia* 43 H8
Bryant, *U.S.A.* 108 C6
Bryne, *Norway* 9 G11
Bryson City, *U.S.A.* 105 H4
Bryukhovetskaya, *Russia* 43 H4
Brza Palanka, *Serbia, Yug.* 21 L12
Brzava →, *Serbia, Yug.* 21 K10
Brzeg, *Poland* 20 E7
Brzeg Din, *Poland* 20 D6
Bsharri, *Lebanon* 69 A5
Bū Baqarah, *U.A.E.* 65 E8
Bu Craa, *W. Sahara* 74 C2
Bū Ḥasā, *U.A.E.* 65 F7
Bua Yai, *Thailand* 58 E4
Buapinang, *Indonesia* 57 E6
Buayan, *Phil.* 57 C7
Buba, *Guinea-Biss.* 78 C2
Bubanza, *Burundi* 82 C2
Būbiyān, *Kuwait* 65 D6
Bucak, *Turkey* 66 D4
Bucaramanga, *Colombia* 120 B3
Bucas Grande I., *Phil.* 55 G6
Buccaneer Arch., *Australia* 88 C3
Bucchiánico, *Italy* 33 F11
Bucecea, *Romania* 38 B9
Buchach, *Ukraine* 41 H3
Buchan, *U.K.* 14 D6
Buchan Ness, *U.K.* 14 D7
Buchanan, *Canada* 101 C8
Buchanan, *Liberia* 78 D2
Buchanan, L., *Queens., Australia* 90 C4
Buchanan, L., *W. Austral., Australia* 89 E3
Buchanan, L., *U.S.A.* 109 K5
Buchanan Cr. →, *Australia* 90 B2
Buchans, *Canada* 99 C8
Bucharest = Bucureşti, *Romania* 38 E9
Buchholz, *Germany* 18 B5
Buchloe, *Germany* 19 G6
Buchon, Pt., *U.S.A.* 112 K6
Buchs, *Switz.* 23 B8
Bückeburg, *Germany* 18 C5
Buckeye, *U.S.A.* 111 K7
Buckhannon, *U.S.A.* 104 F5
Buckhaven, *U.K.* 14 E5
Buckie, *U.K.* 14 D6
Buckingham, *Canada* 98 C4
Buckingham, *U.K.* 13 F7
Buckingham B., *Australia* 90 A2
Buckinghamshire □, *U.K.* 13 F7
Buckle Hd., *Australia* 88 B4
Buckleboo, *Australia* 91 E2
Buckley, *U.S.A.* 110 C2
Buckley →, *Australia* 90 C2
Bucklin, *U.S.A.* 109 G5
Bucks L., *U.S.A.* 112 F5
Bucquoy, *France* 25 B9
Buctouche, *Canada* 99 C7
Bucureşti, *Romania* 38 E9
Bucyrus, *U.S.A.* 104 E4
Budafok, *Hungary* 21 H9
Budalin, *Burma* 61 H19
Budapest, *Hungary* 21 H9
Budaun, *India* 63 E8
Budd Coast, *Antarctica* 5 C8
Buddusò, *Italy* 34 B2
Bude, *U.K.* 13 G3
Budel, *Neths.* 17 F7
Budennovsk, *Russia* 43 H7
Budeşti, *Romania* 38 E9
Budge Budge = Baj Baj, *India* 63 H13
Budgewoi, *Australia* 91 E5
Budia, *Spain* 28 E2
Budjala, *Zaïre* 80 D3
Búdrio, *Italy* 33 D8
Buea, *Cameroon* 79 E6
Buellton, *U.S.A.* 113 L6
Buena Park, *U.S.A.* 113 M9
Buena Vista, *Bolivia* 125 D5
Buena Vista, *Colo., U.S.A.* 111 G10
Buena Vista, *Va., U.S.A.* 104 G6
Buena Vista L., *U.S.A.* 113 K7
Buenaventura, *Colombia* 120 C2
Buenaventura, *Mexico* 114 B3
Buenaventura, B. de, *Colombia* 120 C2
Buendía, Pantano de, *Spain* 28 E2
Buenópolis, *Brazil* 123 E3
Buenos Aires, *Argentina* 126 C4
Buenos Aires, *Colombia* 120 C3
Buenos Aires, *Costa Rica* 116 E3
Buenos Aires □, *Argentina* 126 D4
Buenos Aires, L., *Chile* 128 C2
Buesaco, *Colombia* 120 C2
Buffalo, *Mo., U.S.A.* 109 G8
Buffalo, *N.Y., U.S.A.* 106 D6
Buffalo, *Okla., U.S.A.* 109 G5
Buffalo, *S. Dak., U.S.A.* 108 C3
Buffalo, *Wyo., U.S.A.* 110 D10
Buffalo →, *Canada* 100 A5
Buffalo Head Hills, *Canada* 100 B5
Buffalo L., *Canada* 100 C6
Buffalo Narrows, *Canada* 101 B7
Buffels →, *S. Africa* 84 D2
Buford, *U.S.A.* 105 H4
Bug → = Buh →, *Ukraine* 41 J6
Bug →, *Poland* 20 C11
Buga, *Colombia* 120 C2
Buganda, *Uganda* 82 C3
Buganga, *Uganda* 82 C3
Bugasong, *Phil.* 55 F5
Bugeat, *France* 26 C5
Bugel, Tanjung, *Indonesia* 56 F4
Buggenhout, *Belgium* 17 F4
Bugibba, *Malta* 37 D1
Bugsuk, *Phil.* 55 G2
Buguma, *Nigeria* 79 E6
Bugun Shara, *Mongolia* 54 B5
Buguruslan, *Russia* 44 D6
Buh →, *Ukraine* 41 J6
Buhăeşti, *Romania* 38 C10
Buheirat-Murrat-el-Kubra, *Egypt* 76 H8
Buhl, *Idaho, U.S.A.* 110 E6
Buhl, *Minn., U.S.A.* 108 B8
Buick, *U.S.A.* 109 G9
Builth Wells, *U.K.* 13 E4
Buinsk, *Russia* 42 C9
Buíque, *Brazil* 122 C4

Buir Nur, *Mongolia* 54 B6
Buis-les-Baronnies, *France* 27 D9
Buitenpost, *Neths.* 16 B8
Buitrago, *Spain* 30 E7
Bujalance, *Spain* 31 H6
Buján, *Spain* 30 C2
Bujaraloz, *Spain* 28 D4
Buje, *Croatia* 33 C10
Bujumbura, *Burundi* 82 C2
Bukachacha, *Russia* 45 D12
Bukama, *Zaïre* 83 D2
Bukavu, *Zaïre* 82 C2
Bukene, *Tanzania* 82 C3
Bukhara = Bukhoro, *Uzbekistan* 44 F7
Bukhoro, *Uzbekistan* 44 F7
Bukima, *Tanzania* 82 C3
Bukit Mertajam, *Malaysia* 59 K3
Bukittinggi, *Indonesia* 56 E2
Bukoba, *Tanzania* 82 C3
Bukoba □, *Tanzania* 82 C3
Bukuru, *Nigeria* 79 D6
Bukuya, *Uganda* 82 B3
Bula, *Guinea-Biss.* 78 C1
Bula, *Indonesia* 57 E8
Bülach, *Switz.* 23 A7
Bulahdelah, *Australia* 91 E5
Bulan, *Phil.* 55 E5
Bulancak, *Turkey* 67 B8
Bulandshahr, *India* 62 E7
Bulanık, *Turkey* 67 C10
Bûlâq, *Egypt* 76 B3
Bulawayo, *Zimbabwe* 83 G2
Buldan, *Turkey* 66 C3
Bulgan, *Mongolia* 54 B5
Bulgar, *Russia* 42 C9
Bulgaria ■, *Europe* 38 G8
Bulgroo, *Australia* 91 D3
Bulgunnia, *Australia* 91 E1
Bulhar, *Somali Rep.* 68 E3
Buli, Teluk, *Indonesia* 57 D7
Buliluyan, C., *Phil.* 55 G2
Bulki, *Ethiopia* 77 F4
Bulkley →, *Canada* 100 B3
Bull Shoals L., *U.S.A.* 109 G8
Bullange, *Belgium* 17 H8
Bullaque →, *Spain* 31 G6
Bullara, *Australia* 88 D1
Bullaring, *Australia* 89 F2
Bullas, *Spain* 29 G3
Bulle, *Switz.* 22 C4
Bulli, *Australia* 91 E5
Bullock Creek, *Australia* 90 B3
Bulloo →, *Australia* 91 D3
Bulloo Downs, *Queens., Australia* 91 D3
Bulloo Downs, *W. Austral., Australia* 88 D2
Bulloo L., *Australia* 91 D3
Bulls, *N.Z.* 87 J5
Bully-les-Mines, *France* 25 B9
Bulnes, *Chile* 126 D1
Bulo Burti, *Somali Rep.* 68 G4
Bulsar = Valsad, *India* 60 J8
Bultfontein, *S. Africa* 84 D4
Bulukumba, *Indonesia* 57 F6
Bulun, *Russia* 45 B13
Bulus, *Russia* 45 C13
Bumba, *Zaïre* 80 D4
Bumbiri I., *Tanzania* 82 C3
Bumhpa Bum, *Burma* 61 F20
Bumi →, *Zimbabwe* 83 F2
Buna, *Kenya* 82 B4
Bunawan, *Agusan del S., Phil.* 55 G6
Bunawan, *Davao del S., Phil.* 55 H6
Bunazi, *Tanzania* 82 C3
Bunbah, Khalīj, *Libya* 73 B9
Bunbury, *Australia* 89 F2
Buncrana, *Ireland* 15 A4
Bundaberg, *Australia* 91 C5
Bünde, *Germany* 18 C4
Bundey →, *Australia* 90 C2
Bundi, *India* 62 G6
Bundooma, *Australia* 90 C1
Bundoran, *Ireland* 15 B3
Bundukia, *Sudan* 77 F3
Bung Kan, *Thailand* 58 C4
Bungatakada, *Japan* 49 H5
Bungil Cr. →, *Australia* 90 D4
Bungo-Suidō, *Japan* 49 H6
Bungoma, *Kenya* 82 B3
Bungu, *Tanzania* 82 D4
Bunia, *Zaïre* 82 B3
Bunji, *Pakistan* 63 B6
Bunkie, *U.S.A.* 109 K8
Bunnell, *U.S.A.* 105 L5
Bunnik, *Neths.* 16 D6
Buñol, *Spain* 29 F4
Bunsbeek, *Belgium* 17 G5
Bunschoten, *Neths.* 16 D6
Buntok, *Indonesia* 56 E4
Bununu, *Nigeria* 79 D6
Bununu Dass, *Nigeria* 79 C6
Bünyan, *Turkey* 66 C6
Bunyu, *Indonesia* 56 D5
Bunza, *Nigeria* 79 C5
Buol, *Indonesia* 57 D6
Buon Brieng, *Vietnam* 58 F7
Buon Me Thuot, *Vietnam* 58 F7
Buong Long, *Cambodia* 58 F6
Buorkhaya, Mys, *Russia* 45 B14
Buqayq, *Si. Arabia* 65 E6
Buqbua, *Egypt* 76 A2
Bur Acaba, *Somali Rep.* 68 G3
Bûr Fuad, *Egypt* 76 H8
Bûr Safâga, *Egypt* 76 B3
Bûr Sa'îd, *Egypt* 76 H8
Bûr Sûdân, *Sudan* 76 D4
Bûr Taufiq, *Egypt* 76 J8
Bura, *Kenya* 82 C4
Burao, *Somali Rep.* 68 F4
Burāq, *Syria* 69 B5
Buras, *U.S.A.* 109 L10
Buraydah, *Si. Arabia* 64 E5
Burbank, *U.S.A.* 113 L8
Burcher, *Australia* 91 E4
Burdekin →, *Australia* 90 B4
Burdett, *Canada* 100 D6
Burdur, *Turkey* 66 D4
Burdur Gölü, *Turkey* 66 D4
Burdwan = Barddhaman, *India* 63 H12
Bure, *Ethiopia* 77 E4
Bure →, *U.K.* 12 E9
Büren, *Germany* 18 D4
Buren, *Neths.* 16 E6
Bureya →, *Russia* 45 E13
Burford, *Canada* 106 C4
Burg, *Germany* 18 C7
Burg auf Fehmarn, *Germany* 18 A7
Burg el Arab, *Egypt* 76 H6
Burg et Tuyur, *Sudan* 76 C2
Burg Stargard, *Germany* 18 B9
Burgas, *Bulgaria* 38 G10
Burgdorf, *Germany* 18 C5
Burgdorf, *Switz.* 22 B5
Burgeo, *Canada* 99 C8
Burgersdorp, *S. Africa* 84 E4
Burges, Mt., *Australia* 89 F3
Burghausen, *Germany* 19 G8
Búrgio, *Italy* 34 E6
Bürglen, *Switz.* 23 C7
Burglengenfeld, *Germany* 19 F8
Burgo de Osma, *Spain* 28 D1
Burgohondo, *Spain* 30 E6
Burgos, *Spain* 28 C1
Burgos □, *Spain* 28 C1
Burgstädt, *Germany* 18 E8
Burgsvik, *Sweden* 9 H18
Burguillos del Cerro, *Spain* 31 G4
Burgundy = Bourgogne, *France* 25 F11
Burhaniye, *Turkey* 66 C2
Burhanpur, *India* 60 J10
Burhou, *U.K.* 24 C4
Buri Pen., *Eritrea* 77 D4
Burias, *Phil.* 55 E5
Burica, Pta., *Costa Rica* 116 E3
Burigi, L., *Tanzania* 82 C3
Burin, *Canada* 99 C8
Buriram, *Thailand* 58 E4
Buriti Alegre, *Brazil* 123 E2
Buriti Bravo, *Brazil* 122 C3
Buriti dos Lopes, *Brazil* 122 B3
Burj Sāfitā, *Syria* 66 E7
Burji, *Ethiopia* 77 F4
Burkburnett, *U.S.A.* 109 H5
Burke, *U.S.A.* 110 C6
Burke →, *Australia* 90 C2
Burketown, *Australia* 90 B2
Burkina Faso ■, *Africa* 78 C4
Burk's Falls, *Canada* 98 C4
Burley, *U.S.A.* 110 E7
Burlingame, *U.S.A.* 112 H4
Burlington, *Canada* 106 C5
Burlington, *Colo., U.S.A.* 108 F3
Burlington, *Iowa, U.S.A.* 108 E9
Burlington, *Kans., U.S.A.* 108 F7
Burlington, *N.C., U.S.A.* 105 G6
Burlington, *N.J., U.S.A.* 107 F10
Burlington, *Vt., U.S.A.* 107 B11
Burlington, *Wash., U.S.A.* 112 B4
Burlington, *Wis., U.S.A.* 104 D1
Burlyu-Tyube, *Kazakstan* 44 E8
Burma ■, *Asia* 61 J20
Burnaby I., *Canada* 100 C2
Burnet, *U.S.A.* 109 K5
Burney, *U.S.A.* 110 F3
Burngup, *Australia* 89 F2
Burnham, *U.S.A.* 106 F7
Burnie, *Australia* 90 G4
Burnley, *U.K.* 12 D5
Burns, *Oreg., U.S.A.* 110 E4
Burns, *Wyo., U.S.A.* 108 E2
Burns Lake, *Canada* 100 C3
Burnside →, *Canada* 96 B9
Burnside, L., *Australia* 89 E3
Burnsville, *U.S.A.* 108 C8
Burnt River, *Canada* 106 B6
Burntwood →, *Canada* 101 B9
Burntwood L., *Canada* 101 B8
Burqān, *Kuwait* 64 D5
Burqin, *China* 54 B3
Burra, *Australia* 91 E2
Burramurra, *Australia* 90 C2
Burreli, *Albania* 39 H3
Burren Junction, *Australia* 91 E4
Burrendong Dam, *Australia* 91 E4
Burriana, *Spain* 28 F4
Burrinjuck Res., *Australia* 91 F4
Burro, Serranías del, *Mexico* 114 B4
Burruyacú, *Argentina* 126 B3
Burry Port, *U.K.* 13 F3
Bursa, *Turkey* 66 B3
Burseryd, *Sweden* 11 G7
Burstall, *Canada* 101 C7
Burton L., *Canada* 98 B4
Burton upon Trent, *U.K.* 12 E6
Burtundy, *Australia* 91 E3
Buru, *Indonesia* 57 E7
Burullus, Bahra el, *Egypt* 76 H7
Burûn, Râs, *Egypt* 69 D2
Burundi ■, *Africa* 82 C3
Bururi, *Burundi* 82 C2
Burutu, *Nigeria* 79 D6
Burwell, *U.S.A.* 108 E5
Bury, *U.K.* 12 D5
Bury St. Edmunds, *U.K.* 13 E8
Buryatia □, *Russia* 45 D11
Buryn, *Ukraine* 41 G7
Busalla, *Italy* 32 D5
Busango Swamp, *Zambia* 83 E2
Buşayrah, *Syria* 67 E9
Buşayyah, *Iraq* 64 D5
Busca, *Italy* 32 D4
Būshehr, *Iran* 65 D6
Būshehr □, *Iran* 65 D6
Bushell, *Canada* 101 B7
Bushenyi, *Uganda* 82 C3
Bushire = Būshehr, *Iran* 65 D6
Bushnell, *Ill., U.S.A.* 108 E9
Bushnell, *Nebr., U.S.A.* 108 E3
Busia □, *Kenya* 82 B3
Busie, *Ghana* 78 C4
Businga, *Zaïre* 80 D4
Buskerud fylke □, *Norway* 10 D3
Busko Zdrój, *Poland* 20 E10
Busovača, *Bos.-H.* 21 L7
Busra ash Shām, *Syria* 69 C5
Bussang, *France* 25 E13
Busselton, *Australia* 89 F2
Busseto, *Italy* 32 D7
Bussigny, *Switz.* 22 C3
Bussum, *Neths.* 16 D6
Bustamante, B., *Argentina* 128 C3
Busto, C., *Spain* 30 B4
Busto Arsízio, *Italy* 32 C5
Busu-Djanoa, *Zaïre* 80 D4
Busuanga, *Phil.* 55 E3
Büsum, *Germany* 18 A4
Buta, *Zaïre* 82 B1
Butare, *Rwanda* 82 C2
Butaritari, *Kiribati* 92 G9
Bute, *U.K.* 14 F3
Bute Inlet, *Canada* 100 C4
Butemba, *Uganda* 82 B3
Butembo, *Zaïre* 82 B2
Butera, *Italy* 35 E7
Bütgenbach, *Belgium* 17 H8
Butha Qi, *China* 54 B7
Butiaba, *Uganda* 82 B3
Butler, *Mo., U.S.A.* 108 F7
Butler, *Pa., U.S.A.* 106 F5
Buton, *Indonesia* 57 E6
Bütschwil, *Switz.* 23 B8
Butte, *Mont., U.S.A.* 110 C7
Butte, *Nebr., U.S.A.* 108 D5
Butte Creek →, *U.S.A.* 112 F5
Butterworth = Gcuwa, *S. Africa* 85 E4
Butterworth, *Malaysia* 59 K3
Buttfield, Mt., *Australia* 89 D4
Button B., *Canada* 101 B10
Buttonwillow, *U.S.A.* 113 K7
Butty Hd., *Australia* 89 F3
Butuan, *Phil.* 55 G6
Butuku-Luba, *Eq. Guin.* 79 E6
Butung = Buton, *Indonesia* 57 E6
Buturlinovka, *Russia* 42 E5
Butzbach, *Germany* 18 E4
Bützow, *Germany* 18 B7
Buxar, *India* 63 G10
Buxton, *Guyana* 121 B6
Buxton, *U.K.* 12 D6
Buxy, *France* 25 F11
Buy, *Russia* 42 A5
Buynaksk, *Russia* 43 J8
Büyük Menderes →, *Turkey* 66 D2
Büyükçekmece, *Turkey* 66 B3
Buzançais, *France* 24 F8
Buzău, *Romania* 38 D9
Buzău →, *Romania* 38 D10
Buzău, Pasul, *Romania* 38 D9
Buzen, *Japan* 49 H5
Buzet, *Croatia* 33 C10
Buzi →, *Mozam.* 83 F3
Buziaş, *Romania* 38 D4
Buzuluk, *Russia* 44 D6
Buzuluk →, *Russia* 42 E6
Buzzards Bay, *U.S.A.* 107 E14
Bwana Mkubwe, *Zaïre* 83 E2
Byala, *Bulgaria* 38 F8
Byala Slatina, *Bulgaria* 38 F6
Byarezina →, *Belarus* 41 F6
Bychawa, *Poland* 20 D12
Bydgoszcz, *Poland* 20 B8
Byelarus = Belarus ■, *Europe* 40 F4
Byelorussia = Belarus ■, *Europe* 40 F4
Byers, *U.S.A.* 108 F2
Byesville, *U.S.A.* 106 G3
Byhalia, *U.S.A.* 109 H10
Bykhaw, *Belarus* 40 F6
Bykhov = Bykhaw, *Belarus* 40 F6
Bykovo, *Russia* 42 F7
Bylas, *U.S.A.* 111 K8
Bylderup-Bov, *Denmark* 11 K3
Bylot I., *Canada* 97 A12
Byrd, C., *Antarctica* 5 C17
Byro, *Australia* 89 E2
Byrock, *Australia* 91 E4
Byron Bay, *Australia* 91 D5
Byrranga, Gory, *Russia* 45 B11
Byrranga Mts. = Byrranga, Gory, *Russia* 45 B11
Byrum, *Denmark* 11 G5
Byske, *Sweden* 8 D19
Byske älv →, *Sweden* 8 D19
Bystrzyca Kłodzka, *Poland* 20 E6
Bytom, *Poland* 20 E8
Bytów, *Poland* 20 A7
Byumba, *Rwanda* 82 C3

C

Ca →, *Vietnam* 58 C5
Ca Mau = Quan Long, *Vietnam* 59 H5
Ca Mau, Mui = Bai Bung, Mui, *Vietnam* 59 H5
Ca Na, *Vietnam* 59 G7
Caacupé, *Paraguay* 126 B4
Caála, *Angola* 81 G3
Caamano Sd., *Canada* 100 C3
Caapiranga, *Brazil* 121 D5
Caazapá, *Paraguay* 126 B4
Caazapá □, *Paraguay* 127 B4
Cabadbaran, *Phil.* 55 G6
Cabalian, *Phil.* 55 F6
Caballeria, C. de, *Spain* 36 A11
Cabana, *Peru* 124 B2
Cabanaconde, *Peru* 124 D3
Cabañaquinta, *Spain* 30 B5
Cabanatuan, *Phil.* 55 D4
Cabanes, *Spain* 28 E5
Cabanillas, *Peru* 124 D3
Cabano, *Canada* 99 C6
Čabar, *Croatia* 33 C11
Cabazon, *U.S.A.* 113 M10
Cabedelo, *Brazil* 122 C5
Cabeza del Buey, *Spain* 31 G5
Cabildo, *Chile* 126 C1
Cabimas, *Venezuela* 120 A3
Cabinda, *Angola* 80 F2
Cabinda □, *Angola* 80 F2
Cabinet Mts., *U.S.A.* 110 C6
Cabo Blanco, *Argentina* 128 C3
Cabo Frio, *Brazil* 123 F3
Cabo Pantoja, *Peru* 120 D2
Cabo Raso, *Argentina* 128 B3
Cabonga, Réservoir, *Canada* 98 C4
Cabool, *U.S.A.* 109 G8
Caboolture, *Australia* 91 D5
Cabora Bassa Dam = Cahora Bassa Dam, *Mozam.* 83 F3
Caborca, *Mexico* 114 A2
Cabot, Mt., *U.S.A.* 107 B13
Cabot Str., *Canada* 99 C8
Cabra, *Spain* 31 H6
Cabra del Santo Cristo, *Spain* 29 H1
Cábras, *Italy* 34 C1
Cabrera, *Spain* 36 B9
Cabrera, Sierra, *Spain* 30 C4
Cabri, *Canada* 101 C7
Cabriel →, *Spain* 29 F3
Cabruta, *Venezuela* 120 B4
Cabugao, *Phil.* 55 C4
Cabuyaro, *Colombia* 120 C3
Cacabelos, *Spain* 30 C4
Čačak, *Serbia, Yug.* 21 M10
Cacao, *Fr. Guiana* 121 C7
Cáceres, *Brazil* 125 D6
Cáceres, *Colombia* 120 B2
Cáceres, *Spain* 31 F4
Cáceres □, *Spain* 31 F4
Cache Bay, *Canada* 98 C4
Cache Cr. →, *U.S.A.* 112 G5
Cachepo, *Portugal* 31 H3
Cachéu, *Guinea-Biss.* 78 C1
Cachi, *Argentina* 126 B2
Cachimbo, *Brazil* 125 B7
Cachimbo, Serra do, *Brazil* 125 B6
Cachoeira, *Brazil* 123 D4
Cachoeira Alta, *Brazil* 123 E1
Cachoeira de Itapemirim, *Brazil* 123 F3
Cachoeira do Sul, *Brazil* 127 C5
Cachoeiro do Arari, *Brazil* 122 B2
Cachopo, *Portugal* 31 H3
Cachuela Esperanza, *Bolivia* 125 C4
Cacólo, *Angola* 80 G3
Caconda, *Angola* 81 G3
Cacongo, *Angola* 80 F2
Caçu, *Brazil* 123 E1
Caculé, *Brazil* 123 D3
Cadarache, *France* 27 E9
Čadca, *Slovak Rep.* 20 F8
Caddo, *U.S.A.* 109 H6
Cadell Cr. →, *Australia* 90 C3
Cadenazzo, *Switz.* 23 D7
Cader Idris, *U.K.* 12 E4
Cadí, Sierra del, *Spain* 28 C6
Cadibarrawirracanna, L., *Australia* 91 D2
Cadillac, *Canada* 98 C4
Cadillac, *France* 26 D3
Cadillac, *U.S.A.* 104 C3
Cadiz, *Phil.* 55 F5
Cádiz, *Spain* 31 J4
Cadiz, *U.S.A.* 106 F4
Cádiz □, *Spain* 31 J5
Cádiz, G. de, *Spain* 31 J4
Cadney Park, *Australia* 91 D1
Cadomin, *Canada* 100 C5
Cadotte →, *Canada* 100 B5
Cadours, *France* 26 E5
Cadoux, *Australia* 89 F2
Caen, *France* 24 C6
Caernarfon, *U.K.* 12 D3
Caernarfon B., *U.K.* 12 D3
Caernarvon = Caernarfon, *U.K.* 12 D3
Caerphilly, *U.K.* 13 F4
Caerphilly □, *U.K.* 13 F4
Caesarea, *Israel* 69 C3
Caeté, *Brazil* 123 E3
Caetité, *Brazil* 123 D3
Cafayate, *Argentina* 126 B2
Cafifi, *Colombia* 120 B3
Cafu, *Angola* 84 B2
Cagayan →, *Phil.* 55 B4
Cagayan de Oro, *Phil.* 55 G6
Cagayan Is., *Phil.* 55 G4
Cagayan Sulu I., *Phil.* 55 H3
Cagli, *Italy* 33 E9
Cágliari, *Italy* 34 C2
Cágliari, G. di, *Italy* 34 C2
Cagnano Varano, *Italy* 35 A8
Cagnes-sur-Mer, *France* 27 E11
Caguán →, *Colombia* 120 D3
Caguas, *Puerto Rico* 117 C6
Caha Mts., *Ireland* 15 E2
Cahama, *Angola* 84 B1
Caher, *Ireland* 15 D4
Caherciveen, *Ireland* 15 E1
Cahora Bassa Dam, *Mozam.* 83 F3
Cahore Pt., *Ireland* 15 D5
Cahors, *France* 26 D5
Cahuapanas, *Peru* 124 B2
Cahuinari →, *Colombia* 120 D3
Cahul, *Moldova* 41 K5
Cai Bau, Dao, *Vietnam* 58 B6
Cai Nuoc, *Vietnam* 59 H5
Caia, *Mozam.* 83 F4
Caiabis, Serra dos, *Brazil* 125 C6
Caianda, *Angola* 83 E1
Caiapó, Serra do, *Brazil* 125 D7
Caiapônia, *Brazil* 125 D7
Caibarién, *Cuba* 116 B4
Caibiran, *Phil.* 55 F6
Caicara, *Bolívar, Venezuela* 120 B4
Caicara, *Monagas, Venezuela* 121 B5
Caicó, *Brazil* 122 C4
Caicos Is., *W. Indies* 117 B5
Caicos Passage, *W. Indies* 117 B5
Cailloma, *Peru* 124 D3
Caine →, *Bolivia* 125 D4
Caird Coast, *Antarctica* 5 D1
Cairn Gorm, *U.K.* 14 D5
Cairn Toul, *U.K.* 14 D5
Cairngorm Mts., *U.K.* 14 D5
Cairns, *Australia* 90 B4
Cairo = El Qâhira, *Egypt* 76 H7
Cairo, *Ga., U.S.A.* 105 K3
Cairo, *Ill., U.S.A.* 109 G10
Cairo Montenotte, *Italy* 32 D5
Caithness, Ord of, *U.K.* 14 C5
Caiundo, *Angola* 81 H3
Caiza, *Bolivia* 125 E4
Cajabamba, *Peru* 124 B2
Cajamarca, *Peru* 124 B2
Cajamarca □, *Peru* 124 B2
Cajapió, *Brazil* 122 B3
Cajarc, *France* 26 D5
Cajatambo, *Peru* 124 C2
Cajàzeiras, *Brazil* 122 C4
Čajetina, *Serbia, Yug.* 21 M9
Çakirgol, *Turkey* 67 B8
Čakovec, *Croatia* 33 B13
Çal, *Turkey* 66 C3
Cala, *Spain* 31 H4
Cala →, *Spain* 31 H4
Cala Cadolar, Punta de, *Spain* 29 G6
Cala d'Or, *Spain* 36 B10
Cala Figuera, C., *Spain* 36 B9
Cala Forcat, *Spain* 36 A10
Cala Mayor, *Spain* 36 B9
Cala Mezquida, *Spain* 36 B11
Cala Millor, *Spain* 36 B10
Cala Ratjada, *Spain* 36 B10
Calabanga, *Phil.* 55 E5
Calabar, *Nigeria* 79 E6
Calabozo, *Venezuela* 120 B4
Calábria □, *Italy* 35 C9
Calaburras, Pta. de, *Spain* 31 J6
Calaceite, *Spain* 28 D5
Calacota, *Bolivia* 124 D4
Calafate, *Argentina* 128 D2
Calahorra, *Spain* 28 C3
Calais, *France* 25 B8
Calais, *U.S.A.* 99 C6
Calais, Pas de, *France* 25 B8
Calalaste, Cord. de, *Argentina* 126 B2
Calama, *Brazil* 125 B5
Calama, *Chile* 126 A2
Calamar, *Bolívar, Colombia* 120 A3
Calamar, *Vaupés, Colombia* 120 C3
Calamarca, *Bolivia* 124 D4
Calamba, *Phil.* 55 F5
Calamian Group, *Phil.* 55 F3
Calamocha, *Spain* 28 E3
Calán Porter, *Spain* 36 B11
Calañas, *Spain* 31 H4
Calanda, *Spain* 28 E4
Calang, *Indonesia* 56 D1
Calangiánus, *Italy* 34 B2
Calapan, *Phil.* 55 E4
Călăraşi, *Romania* 38 E10
Calasparra, *Spain* 29 G3

Calatafimi, *Italy* 34 E5
Calatayud, *Spain* 28 D3
Calato = Kálathos, *Greece* 39 N11
Calauag, *Phil.* 55 E5
Calavà, C., *Italy* 35 D7
Calavite, C., *Phil.* 55 E4
Calayan, *Phil.* 55 B4
Calbayog, *Phil.* 55 E6
Calbe, *Germany* 18 D7
Calca, *Peru* 124 C3
Calcasieu L., *U.S.A.* 109 L8
Calci, *Italy* 32 E7
Calcutta, *India* 63 H13
Caldaro, *Italy* 33 B8
Caldas □, *Colombia* 120 B2
Caldas da Rainha, *Portugal* 31 F1
Caldas de Reyes, *Spain* 30 C2
Caldas Novas, *Brazil* 123 E2
Calder ➝, *U.K.* 12 D6
Caldera, *Chile* 126 B1
Caldwell, *Idaho, U.S.A.* 110 E5
Caldwell, *Kans., U.S.A.* 109 G6
Caldwell, *Tex., U.S.A.* 109 K6
Caledon, *S. Africa* 84 E2
Caledon ➝, *S. Africa* 84 E4
Caledon B., *Australia* 90 A2
Caledonia, *Canada* 106 C5
Caledonia, *U.S.A.* 106 D7
Calella, *Spain* 28 D7
Calemba, *Angola* 84 B2
Calenzana, *France* 27 F12
Caleta Olivia, *Argentina* 128 C3
Calexico, *U.S.A.* 113 N11
Calf of Man, *U.K.* 12 C3
Calgary, *Canada* 100 C6
Calheta, *Madeira* 36 D2
Calhoun, *U.S.A.* 105 H3
Cali, *Colombia* 120 C2
Calicut, *India* 60 P9
Caliente, *U.S.A.* 111 H6
California, *Mo., U.S.A.* 108 F8
California, *Pa., U.S.A.* 106 F5
California □, *U.S.A.* 111 H4
California, Baja, *Mexico* 114 A1
California, Baja, T.N. □ = Baja California □, *Mexico* 114 B2
California, Baja, T.S. □ = Baja California Sur □, *Mexico* 114 B2
California, G. de, *Mexico* 114 B2
California City, *U.S.A.* 113 K9
California Hot Springs, *U.S.A.* 113 K8
Călimănești, *Romania* 38 D7
Călimani, Munţii, *Romania* 38 B8
Călinești, *Romania* 38 D7
Calingasta, *Argentina* 126 C2
Calipatria, *U.S.A.* 113 M11
Calistoga, *U.S.A.* 112 G4
Calitri, *Italy* 35 B8
Calitzdorp, *S. Africa* 84 E3
Callabonna, L., *Australia* 91 D3
Callac, *France* 24 D3
Callan, *Ireland* 15 D4
Callander, *U.K.* 14 E4
Callantsoog, *Neths.* 16 C5
Callao, *Peru* 124 C2
Callaway, *U.S.A.* 108 E5
Calles, *Mexico* 115 C5
Callide, *Australia* 90 C5
Calling Lake, *Canada* 100 B6
Calliope, *Australia* 90 C5
Callosa de Ensarriá, *Spain* 29 G4
Callosa de Segura, *Spain* 29 G4
Calola, *Angola* 84 B2
Calolbon, *Phil.* 55 E6
Caloocan, *Phil.* 55 D4
Calore ➝, *Italy* 35 A7
Caloundra, *Australia* 91 D5
Calpe, *Spain* 29 G5
Calpella, *U.S.A.* 112 F3
Calpine, *U.S.A.* 112 F6
Calstock, *Canada* 98 C3
Caltabellotta, *Italy* 34 E6
Caltagirone, *Italy* 35 E7
Caltanissetta, *Italy* 35 E7
Calulo, *Angola* 80 G2
Calumet, *U.S.A.* 104 B1
Calunda, *Angola* 81 G4
Caluso, *Italy* 32 C4
Calvados □, *France* 24 C6
Calvert, *U.S.A.* 109 K6
Calvert ➝, *Australia* 90 B2
Calvert Hills, *Australia* 90 B2
Calvert I., *Canada* 100 C3
Calvert Ra., *Australia* 88 D3
Calvi, *France* 27 F12
Calvillo, *Mexico* 114 C4
Calvinia, *S. Africa* 84 E2
Calw, *Germany* 19 G4
Calwa, *U.S.A.* 112 J7
Calzada Almuradiel, *Spain* 29 G1
Calzada de Calatrava, *Spain* 31 G7
Cam ➝, *U.K.* 13 E8
Cam Lam, *Vietnam* 59 G7
Cam Pha, *Vietnam* 58 B6
Cam Ranh, *Vietnam* 59 G7
Cam Xuyen, *Vietnam* 58 C6
Camabatela, *Angola* 80 F3
Camacã, *Brazil* 123 E4
Camaçari, *Brazil* 123 D4
Camacha, *Madeira* 36 D3
Camacho, *Mexico* 114 C4
Camacupa, *Angola* 81 G3
Camaguán, *Venezuela* 120 B4
Camagüey, *Cuba* 116 B4
Camaiore, *Italy* 32 E7
Camamu, *Brazil* 123 D4
Camaná, *Peru* 124 D3
Camanche Reservoir, *U.S.A.* 112 G6
Camaquã ➝, *Brazil* 127 C5
Câmara de Lobos, *Madeira* 36 D3
Camararé ➝, *Brazil* 125 C6
Camarat, C., *France* 27 E10
Camaret, *France* 24 D2
Camargo, *Bolivia* 125 E4
Camargue, *France* 27 E8
Camarillo, *U.S.A.* 113 L7
Camariñas, *Spain* 30 B1
Camarón, C., *Honduras* 116 C2
Camarones, *Argentina* 128 B3
Camarones, B., *Argentina* 128 B3
Camas, *U.S.A.* 112 E4
Camas Valley, *U.S.A.* 110 E2
Cambados, *Spain* 30 C2
Cambará, *Brazil* 127 A5
Cambay = Khambhat, *India* 62 H5
Cambay, G. of = Khambat, G. of, *India* 62 J5
Cambil, *Spain* 29 H1
Cambo-les-Bains, *France* 26 E2
Cambodia ■, *Asia* 58 F5
Camborne, *U.K.* 13 G2
Cambrai, *France* 25 B10
Cambria, *U.S.A.* 111 J3
Cambrian Mts., *U.K.* 13 E4
Cambridge, *Canada* 98 D3
Cambridge, *Jamaica* 116 C4
Cambridge, *N.Z.* 87 G5
Cambridge, *U.K.* 13 E8
Cambridge, *Idaho, U.S.A.* 110 D5
Cambridge, *Mass., U.S.A.* 107 D13
Cambridge, *Md., U.S.A.* 104 F7
Cambridge, *Minn., U.S.A.* 108 C8
Cambridge, *N.Y., U.S.A.* 107 C11
Cambridge, *Nebr., U.S.A.* 108 E4
Cambridge, *Ohio, U.S.A.* 106 F3
Cambridge Bay, *Canada* 96 B9
Cambridge G., *Australia* 88 B4
Cambridge Springs, *U.S.A.* 106 E4
Cambridgeshire □, *U.K.* 13 E8
Cambrils, *Spain* 28 D6
Cambuci, *Brazil* 123 F3
Cambundi-Catembo, *Angola* 80 G3
Camden, *Ala., U.S.A.* 105 K2
Camden, *Ark., U.S.A.* 109 J8
Camden, *Maine, U.S.A.* 99 D6
Camden, *N.J., U.S.A.* 107 G9
Camden, *S.C., U.S.A.* 105 H5
Camden Sd., *Australia* 88 C3
Camdenton, *U.S.A.* 109 F8
Çameli, *Turkey* 66 D3
Camembert, *France* 24 D7
Cámeri, *Italy* 32 C5
Camerino, *Italy* 33 E10
Cameron, *Ariz., U.S.A.* 111 J8
Cameron, *La., U.S.A.* 109 L8
Cameron, *Mo., U.S.A.* 108 F7
Cameron, *Tex., U.S.A.* 109 K6
Cameron Falls, *Canada* 98 C2
Cameron Highlands, *Malaysia* 59 K3
Cameron Hills, *Canada* 100 B5
Cameroon ■, *Africa* 73 G7
Camerota, *Italy* 35 B8
Cameroun ➝, *Cameroon* 79 E6
Cameroun, Mt., *Cameroon* 79 E6
Cametá, *Brazil* 122 B2
Camiguin □, *Phil.* 55 G6
Camiguin I., *Phil.* 55 B4
Camiling, *Phil.* 55 D4
Caminha, *Portugal* 30 D2
Camino, *U.S.A.* 112 G6
Camira Creek, *Australia* 91 D5
Camiranga, *Brazil* 122 B2
Camiri, *Bolivia* 125 E5
Camissombo, *Angola* 80 F4
Cammal, *U.S.A.* 106 E7
Camocim, *Brazil* 122 B3
Camogli, *Italy* 32 D6
Camooweal, *Australia* 90 B2
Camopi, *Fr. Guiana* 121 C7
Camopi ➝, *Fr. Guiana* 121 C7
Camotes Is., *Phil.* 55 F6
Camotes Sea, *Phil.* 55 F6
Camp Crook, *U.S.A.* 108 C3
Camp Nelson, *U.S.A.* 113 J8
Camp Wood, *U.S.A.* 109 L4
Campagna, *Italy* 35 B8
Campana, *Argentina* 126 C4
Campana, I., *Chile* 128 C1
Campanário, *Madeira* 36 D2
Campanario, *Spain* 31 G5
Campánia □, *Italy* 35 B7
Campbell, *S. Africa* 84 D3
Campbell, *Calif., U.S.A.* 112 H5
Campbell, *Ohio, U.S.A.* 106 E4
Campbell I., *Pac. Oc.* 92 N8
Campbell L., *Canada* 101 A7
Campbell River, *Canada* 100 C3
Campbell Town, *Australia* 90 G4
Campbellford, *Canada* 106 B7
Campbellpur, *Pakistan* 62 C5
Campbellsville, *U.S.A.* 104 G3
Campbellton, *Canada* 99 C6
Campbelltown, *Australia* 91 E5
Campbeltown, *U.K.* 14 F3
Campeche, *Mexico* 115 D6
Campeche □, *Mexico* 115 D6
Campeche, B. de, *Mexico* 115 D6
Camperdown, *Australia* 91 F3
Camperville, *Canada* 101 C8
Campi Salentina, *Italy* 35 B11
Campidano, *Italy* 34 C1
Campíglia Maríttima, *Italy* 32 E7
Campillo de Altobuey, *Spain* 28 F3
Campillo de Llerena, *Spain* 31 G5
Campillos, *Spain* 31 H6
Campina Grande, *Brazil* 122 C4
Campina Verde, *Brazil* 123 E2
Campinas, *Brazil* 127 A6
Campine, *Belgium* 17 F6
Campli, *Italy* 33 F10
Campo, *Cameroon* 80 D1
Campo, *Spain* 28 C5
Campo Belo, *Brazil* 123 F2
Campo de Criptana, *Spain* 29 F1
Campo de Diauarum, *Brazil* 125 C7
Campo de Gibraltar, *Spain* 31 J5
Campo Flórido, *Brazil* 123 E2
Campo Formoso, *Brazil* 122 D3
Campo Grande, *Brazil* 125 E7
Campo Maíor, *Brazil* 122 B3
Campo Maior, *Portugal* 31 G3
Campo Mourão, *Brazil* 127 A5
Campo Tencia, *Switz.* 23 D7
Campo Túres, *Italy* 33 B8
Campoalegre, *Colombia* 120 C2
Campobasso, *Italy* 35 A7
Campobello di Licata, *Italy* 34 E6
Campobello di Mazara, *Italy* 34 E5
Campofelice di Roccella, *Italy* 34 E6
Camporeale, *Italy* 34 E6
Campos, *Brazil* 123 F3
Campos Altos, *Brazil* 123 E2
Campos Belos, *Brazil* 123 D2
Campos del Puerto, *Spain* 36 B10
Campos Novos, *Brazil* 127 B5
Campos Sales, *Brazil* 122 C3
Camprodón, *Spain* 28 C7
Camptonville, *U.S.A.* 112 F5
Campuya ➝, *Peru* 120 D3
Camrose, *Canada* 100 C6
Camsell Portage, *Canada* 101 B7
Çan, *Turkey* 66 B2
Can Clavo, *Spain* 36 C7
Can Creu, *Spain* 36 C7
Can Gio, *Vietnam* 59 G6
Can Tho, *Vietnam* 59 G5
Canaan, *U.S.A.* 107 D11
Canada ■, *N. Amer.* 96 C10
Cañada de Gómez, *Argentina* 126 C3
Canadian, *U.S.A.* 109 H4
Canadian ➝, *U.S.A.* 109 H7
Canadian Shield, *Canada* 97 C10
Çanakkale, *Turkey* 66 B2
Çanakkale Boğazı, *Turkey* 66 B2
Canal Flats, *Canada* 100 C5
Canalejas, *Argentina* 126 D2
Canals, *Argentina* 126 C3
Canals, *Spain* 29 G4
Canandaigua, *U.S.A.* 106 D7
Cananea, *Mexico* 114 A2
Cañar, *Ecuador* 120 D2
Cañar □, *Ecuador* 120 D2
Canarias, Is., *Atl. Oc.* 36 F4
Canarreos, Arch. de los, *Cuba* 116 B3
Canary Is. = Canarias, Is., *Atl. Oc.* 36 F4
Canastra, Serra da, *Brazil* 123 F2
Canatlán, *Mexico* 114 C4
Canaveral, C., *U.S.A.* 105 L5
Cañaveras, *Spain* 28 E2
Canavieiras, *Brazil* 123 E4
Canbelego, *Australia* 91 E4
Canberra, *Australia* 91 F4
Canby, *Calif., U.S.A.* 110 F3
Canby, *Minn., U.S.A.* 108 C6
Canby, *Oreg., U.S.A.* 112 E4
Cancale, *France* 24 D5
Canche ➝, *France* 25 B8
Canchyuaya, Cordillera de, *Peru* 124 B3
Cancún, *Mexico* 115 C7
Candala, *Somali Rep.* 68 E4
Candarave, *Peru* 124 D3
Candas, *Spain* 30 B5
Candé, *France* 24 E5
Candeias ➝, *Brazil* 125 B5
Candela, *Italy* 35 A8
Candelaria, *Argentina* 127 B4
Candelaria, *Canary Is.* 36 F3
Candelaria, Pta. de la, *Spain* 30 B2
Candeleda, *Spain* 30 E5
Candelo, *Australia* 91 F4
Candia = Iráklion, *Greece* 37 D7
Candia, Sea of = Crete, Sea of, *Greece* 39 N8
Cândido de Abreu, *Brazil* 123 F1
Cândido Mendes, *Brazil* 122 B2
Candle L., *Canada* 101 C7
Candlemas I., *Antarctica* 5 B1
Cando, *U.S.A.* 108 A5
Candon, *Phil.* 55 C4
Canea = Khaniá, *Greece* 37 D6
Canela, *Brazil* 122 D2
Canelli, *Italy* 32 D5
Canelones, *Uruguay* 127 C4
Canet-Plage, *France* 26 F7
Cañete, *Chile* 126 D1
Cañete, *Peru* 124 C2
Cañete, *Spain* 28 E3
Cañete de las Torres, *Spain* 31 H6
Canfranc, *Spain* 28 C4
Cangas, *Spain* 30 C2
Cangas de Narcea, *Spain* 30 B4
Cangas de Onís, *Spain* 30 B5
Canguaretama, *Brazil* 122 C4
Canguçu, *Brazil* 127 C5
Cangxi, *China* 52 B5
Cangyuan, *China* 52 F2
Cangzhou, *China* 50 E9
Canicattì, *Italy* 34 E6
Canicattini Bagni, *Italy* 35 E8
Canim Lake, *Canada* 100 C4
Canindé, *Brazil* 122 B4
Canindé ➝, *Brazil* 122 C3
Canindeyu □, *Paraguay* 127 A4
Canipaan, *Phil.* 56 C5
Canisteo, *U.S.A.* 106 D7
Canisteo ➝, *U.S.A.* 106 D7
Cañitas, *Mexico* 114 C4
Cañizal, *Spain* 30 D5
Canjáyar, *Spain* 29 H2
Çankırı, *Turkey* 66 B5
Cankuzo, *Burundi* 82 C3
Canmore, *Canada* 100 C5
Cann River, *Australia* 91 F4
Canna, *U.K.* 14 D2
Cannanore, *India* 60 P9
Cannes, *France* 27 E11
Canning Town = Port Canning, *India* 63 H13
Cannington, *Canada* 106 B5
Cannock, *U.K.* 12 E5
Cannon Ball ➝, *U.S.A.* 108 B4
Cannondale Mt., *Australia* 90 D4
Caño Colorado, *Colombia* 120 C4
Canoas, *Brazil* 127 B5
Canoe L., *Canada* 101 B7
Canon City, *U.S.A.* 108 F2
Canora, *Canada* 101 C8
Canosa di Púglia, *Italy* 35 A9
Canowindra, *Australia* 91 E4
Canso, *Canada* 99 C7
Canta, *Peru* 124 C2
Cantabria □, *Spain* 30 B6
Cantabria, Sierra de, *Spain* 28 C2
Cantabrian Mts. = Cantábrica, Cordillera, *Spain* 30 C5
Cantábrica, Cordillera, *Spain* 30 C5
Cantal □, *France* 26 C6
Cantal, Plomb du, *France* 26 C6
Cantanhede, *Portugal* 30 E2
Cantaura, *Venezuela* 121 B5
Cantavieja, *Spain* 28 E4
Canterbury, *Australia* 90 D3
Canterbury, *U.K.* 13 F9
Canterbury □, *N.Z.* 87 K3
Canterbury Bight, *N.Z.* 87 L3
Canterbury Plains, *N.Z.* 87 K3
Cantil, *U.S.A.* 113 K9
Cantillana, *Spain* 31 H5
Canto do Buriti, *Brazil* 122 C3
Canton = Guangzhou, *China* 53 F9
Canton, *Ga., U.S.A.* 105 H3
Canton, *Ill., U.S.A.* 108 E9
Canton, *Miss., U.S.A.* 109 J9
Canton, *Mo., U.S.A.* 108 E9
Canton, *N.Y., U.S.A.* 107 B9
Canton, *Ohio, U.S.A.* 106 F3
Canton, *Okla., U.S.A.* 109 G5
Canton, *S. Dak., U.S.A.* 108 D6
Canton L., *U.S.A.* 109 G5
Cantù, *Italy* 32 C6
Canudos, *Brazil* 125 B6
Canumã, *Amazonas, Brazil* 121 D6
Canumã, *Amazonas, Brazil* 125 B5
Canumã ➝, *Brazil* 125 A6
Canutama, *Brazil* 125 B5
Canutillo, *U.S.A.* 111 L10
Canyon, *Tex., U.S.A.* 109 H4
Canyon, *Wyo., U.S.A.* 110 D8
Canyonlands National Park, *U.S.A.* 111 G9
Canyonville, *U.S.A.* 110 E2
Canzo, *Italy* 32 C6
Cao Bang, *Vietnam* 58 A6
Cao He ➝, *China* 51 D13
Cao Lanh, *Vietnam* 59 G5
Cao Xian, *China* 50 G8
Cáorle, *Italy* 33 C9
Cap-aux-Meules, *Canada* 99 C7
Cap-Chat, *Canada* 99 C6
Cap-de-la-Madeleine, *Canada* 98 C5
Cap-Haïtien, *Haiti* 117 C5
Cap St.-Jacques = Vung Tau, *Vietnam* 59 G6
Capa, *Vietnam* 58 A4
Capa Stilo, *Italy* 35 D9
Capáccio, *Italy* 35 B8
Capaia, *Angola* 80 F4
Capanaparo ➝, *Venezuela* 120 B4
Capanema, *Brazil* 122 B2
Caparo ➝, *Barinas, Venezuela* 120 B3
Caparo ➝, *Bolívar, Venezuela* 121 B5
Capatárida, *Venezuela* 120 A3
Capbreton, *France* 26 E2
Capdenac, *France* 26 D6
Cape ➝, *Australia* 90 C4
Cape Barren I., *Australia* 90 G4
Cape Breton Highlands Nat. Park, *Canada* 99 C7
Cape Breton I., *Canada* 99 C7
Cape Charles, *U.S.A.* 104 G8
Cape Coast, *Ghana* 79 D4
Cape Coral, *U.S.A* 105 M5
Cape Dorset, *Canada* 97 B12
Cape Dyer, *Canada* 97 B13
Cape Fear ➝, *U.S.A.* 105 H6
Cape Girardeau, *U.S.A.* 109 G10
Cape Jervis, *Australia* 91 F2
Cape May, *U.S.A.* 104 F8
Cape May Point, *U.S.A.* 103 C12
Cape Palmas, *Liberia* 78 E3
Cape Tormentine, *Canada* 99 C7
Cape Town, *S. Africa* 84 E2
Cape Verde Is. ■, *Atl. Oc.* 70 E1
Cape Vincent, *U.S.A.* 107 B8
Cape York Peninsula, *Australia* 90 A3
Capela, *Brazil* 122 D4
Capela de Campo, *Brazil* 122 B3
Capelinha, *Brazil* 123 E3
Capella, *Australia* 90 C4
Capendu, *France* 26 E6
Capestang, *France* 26 E7
Capim, *Brazil* 122 B2
Capim ➝, *Brazil* 122 B2
Capinópolis, *Brazil* 123 E2
Capinota, *Bolivia* 124 D4
Capitan, *U.S.A.* 111 K11
Capitán Aracena, I., *Chile* 128 D2
Capitán Pastene, *Chile* 128 A2
Capitola, *U.S.A.* 112 J5
Capivara, Serra da, *Brazil* 123 D3
Capizzi, *Italy* 35 E7
Čapljina, *Bos.-H.* 21 M7
Capoche ➝, *Mozam.* 83 F3
Capoeira, *Brazil* 125 B6
Cappadocia, *Turkey* 66 C6
Capraia, *Italy* 32 E6
Caprarola, *Italy* 33 F9
Capreol, *Canada* 98 C3
Caprera, *Italy* 34 A2
Capri, *Italy* 35 B7
Capricorn Group, *Australia* 90 C5
Capricorn Ra., *Australia* 88 D2
Caprino Veronese, *Italy* 32 C7
Caprivi Strip, *Namibia* 84 B3
Captainganj, *India* 63 F10
Captain's Flat, *Australia* 91 F4
Captieux, *France* 26 D3
Cápua, *Italy* 35 A7
Caquetá □, *Colombia* 120 C3
Caquetá ➝, *Colombia* 120 D4
Carabobo, *Venezuela* 120 A4
Carabobo □, *Venezuela* 120 A4
Caracal, *Romania* 38 E7
Caracaraí, *Brazil* 121 C5
Caracas, *Venezuela* 120 A4
Caracol, *Brazil* 122 C3
Caracollo, *Bolivia* 124 D4
Caradoc, *Australia* 91 E3
Caráglio, *Italy* 32 D4
Carahue, *Chile* 128 A2
Caraí, *Brazil* 123 E3
Carajás, Serra dos, *Brazil* 122 C1
Caranapatuba, *Brazil* 125 B5
Carandaiti, *Bolivia* 125 E5
Carangola, *Brazil* 123 F3
Carani, *Australia* 89 F2
Caransebeş, *Romania* 38 D5
Carantec, *France* 24 D3
Caraparaná ➝, *Colombia* 120 D3
Carapelle ➝, *Italy* 35 A8
Caras, *Peru* 124 B2
Caratasca, L., *Honduras* 116 C3
Caratinga, *Brazil* 123 E3
Caraúbas, *Brazil* 122 C4
Caravaca, *Spain* 29 G3
Caravággio, *Italy* 32 C6
Caravelas, *Brazil* 123 E4
Caraveli, *Peru* 124 D3
Caràzinho, *Brazil* 127 B5
Carballino, *Spain* 30 C2
Carballo, *Spain* 30 B2
Carberry, *Canada* 101 D9
Carbia, *Spain* 30 C2
Carbó, *Mexico* 114 B2
Carbon, *Canada* 100 C6
Carbonara, C., *Italy* 34 C2
Carbondale, *Colo., U.S.A.* 110 G10
Carbondale, *Ill., U.S.A.* 109 G10
Carbondale, *Pa., U.S.A.* 107 E9
Carbonear, *Canada* 99 C9
Carboneras, *Spain* 29 J3
Carboneras de Guadazaón, *Spain* 28 F3
Carbonia, *Italy* 34 C1
Carcabuey, *Spain* 31 H6
Carcagente, *Spain* 29 F4
Carcajou, *Canada* 100 B5
Carcar, *Phil.* 55 F5
Carcasse, C., *Haiti* 117 C5
Carcassonne, *France* 26 E6
Carche, *Spain* 29 G3
Carchi □, *Ecuador* 120 C2
Carcross, *Canada* 96 B6
Cardabia, *Australia* 88 D1
Çardak, *Turkey* 66 D3
Cardamon Hills, *India* 60 Q10
Cárdenas, *Cuba* 116 B3
Cárdenas, *San Luis Potosí, Mexico* 115 C5
Cárdenas, *Tabasco, Mexico* 115 D6
Cardenete, *Spain* 28 F3
Cardiel, L., *Argentina* 128 C2
Cardiff, *U.K.* 13 F4
Cardiff □, *U.K.* 13 F4
Cardiff-by-the-Sea, *U.S.A.* 113 M9
Cardigan, *U.K.* 13 E3

Cardigan B., *U.K.* 13 E3
Cardinal, *Canada* 107 B9
Cardón, Punta, *Venezuela* 120 A3
Cardona, *Spain* 28 D6
Cardona, *Uruguay* 126 C4
Cardoner →, *Spain* 28 D6
Cardross, *Canada* 101 D7
Cardston, *Canada* 100 D6
Cardwell, *Australia* 90 B4
Careen L., *Canada* 101 B7
Carei, *Romania* 38 B5
Careiro, *Brazil* 121 D6
Careme, *Indonesia* 57 G13
Carentan, *France* 24 C5
Carey, *Idaho, U.S.A.* 110 E7
Carey, *Ohio, U.S.A.* 104 E4
Carey, L., *Australia* 89 E3
Carey L., *Canada* 101 A8
Careysburg, *Liberia* 78 D2
Cargèse, *France* 27 F12
Carhaix-Plouguer, *France* 24 D3
Carhuamayo, *Peru* 124 C2
Carhuas, *Peru* 124 B2
Carhué, *Argentina* 126 D3
Caria, *Turkey* 66 D3
Cariacica, *Brazil* 123 F3
Caribbean Sea, *W. Indies* 117 C5
Cariboo Mts., *Canada* 100 C4
Caribou, *U.S.A.* 99 C6
Caribou →, *Man., Canada* 101 B10
Caribou →, *N.W.T., Canada* 100 A3
Caribou I., *Canada* 98 C2
Caribou Is., *Canada* 100 A6
Caribou L., *Man., Canada* 101 B9
Caribou L., *Ont., Canada* 98 B2
Caribou Mts., *Canada* 100 B5
Carichic, *Mexico* 114 B3
Carigara, *Phil.* 55 F6
Carignan, *France* 25 C12
Carignano, *Italy* 32 D4
Carillo, *Mexico* 114 B4
Carinda, *Australia* 91 E4
Cariñena, *Spain* 28 D3
Carinhanha, *Brazil* 123 D3
Carinhanha →, *Brazil* 123 D3
Carini, *Italy* 34 D6
Carinola, *Italy* 34 A6
Caripito, *Venezuela* 121 A5
Caritianas, *Brazil* 125 B5
Carlbrod = Dimitrovgrad, *Serbia, Yug.* 21 M12
Carlentini, *Italy* 35 E8
Carleton Place, *Canada* 98 C4
Carletonville, *S. Africa* 84 D4
Carlin, *U.S.A.* 110 F5
Carlingford L., *U.K.* 15 B5
Carlinville, *U.S.A.* 108 F10
Carlisle, *U.K.* 12 C5
Carlisle, *U.S.A.* 106 F7
Carlit, Pic, *France* 26 F5
Carloforte, *Italy* 34 C1
Carlos Casares, *Argentina* 126 D3
Carlos Chagas, *Brazil* 123 E3
Carlos Tejedor, *Argentina* 126 D3
Carlow, *Ireland* 15 D5
Carlow □, *Ireland* 15 D5
Carlsbad, *Calif., U.S.A.* 113 M9
Carlsbad, *N. Mex., U.S.A.* 109 J2
Carlyle, *Canada* 101 D8
Carlyle, *U.S.A.* 108 F10
Carmacks, *Canada* 96 B6
Carmagnola, *Italy* 32 D4
Carman, *Canada* 101 D9
Carmangay, *Canada* 100 C6
Carmanville, *Canada* 99 C9
Carmarthen, *U.K.* 13 F3
Carmarthen B., *U.K.* 13 F3
Carmarthenshire □, *U.K.* 13 F3
Carmaux, *France* 26 D6
Carmel, *U.S.A.* 107 E11
Carmel-by-the-Sea, *U.S.A.* 111 H3
Carmel Valley, *U.S.A.* 112 J5
Carmelo, *Uruguay* 126 C4
Carmen, *Bolivia* 124 C4
Carmen, *Colombia* 120 B2
Carmen, *Paraguay* 127 B4
Carmen →, *Mexico* 114 A3
Carmen, I., *Mexico* 114 B2
Carmen de Patagones, *Argentina* 128 B4
Cármenes, *Spain* 30 C5
Carmensa, *Argentina* 126 D2
Carmi, *U.S.A.* 104 F1
Carmichael, *U.S.A.* 112 G5
Carmila, *Australia* 90 C4
Carmona, *Spain* 31 H5
Carnac, *France* 24 E3
Carnarvon, *Queens., Australia* 90 C4
Carnarvon, *W. Austral., Australia* 89 D1
Carnarvon, *S. Africa* 84 E3
Carnarvon Ra., *Queens., Australia* 90 D4
Carnarvon Ra., *W. Austral., Australia* 89 E3
Carnation, *U.S.A.* 112 C5
Carnaxide, *Portugal* 31 G1
Carndonagh, *Ireland* 15 A4
Carnduff, *Canada* 101 D8
Carnegie, *U.S.A.* 106 F4
Carnegie, L., *Australia* 89 E3
Carnic Alps = Karnische Alpen, *Europe* 21 J3
Carniche Alpi = Karnische Alpen, *Europe* 21 J3
Carnot, *C.A.R.* 80 D3
Carnot, C., *Australia* 91 E2
Carnot B., *Australia* 88 C3
Carnsore Pt., *Ireland* 15 D5
Caro, *U.S.A.* 104 D4
Carol City, *U.S.A.* 105 N5
Carolina, *Brazil* 122 C2
Carolina, *Puerto Rico* 117 C6
Carolina, *S. Africa* 85 D5
Caroline I., *Kiribati* 93 H12
Caroline Is., *Pac. Oc.* 46 J17
Caron, *Canada* 101 C7
Caroni →, *Venezuela* 121 B5
Caroníe = Nébrodi, Monti, *Italy* 35 E7
Caroona, *Australia* 91 E5
Carora, *Venezuela* 120 A3
Carovigno, *Italy* 35 B10
Carpathians, *Europe* 20 F11
Carpaţii Meridionali, *Romania* 38 D8
Carpenédolo, *Italy* 32 C7
Carpentaria, G. of, *Australia* 90 A2
Carpentaria Downs, *Australia* 90 B3
Carpentras, *France* 27 D9
Carpi, *Italy* 32 D7
Carpina, *Brazil* 122 C4
Carpino, *Italy* 35 A8
Carpinteria, *U.S.A.* 113 L7
Carpio, *Spain* 30 D5
Carpolac = Morea, *Australia* 91 F3
Carr Boyd Ra., *Australia* 88 C4
Carrabelle, *U.S.A.* 105 L3
Carranya, *Australia* 88 C4
Carrara, *Italy* 32 D7
Carrascal, *Phil.* 55 G6
Carrascosa del Campo, *Spain* 28 E2
Carrauntoohill, *Ireland* 15 E2
Carretas, Punta, *Peru* 124 C2
Carrick-on-Shannon, *Ireland* 15 C3
Carrick-on-Suir, *Ireland* 15 D4
Carrickfergus, *U.K.* 15 B6
Carrickfergus □, *U.K.* 15 B6
Carrickmacross, *Ireland* 15 C5
Carrieton, *Australia* 91 E2
Carrington, *U.S.A.* 108 B5
Carrión →, *Spain* 30 D6
Carrión de los Condes, *Spain* 30 C6
Carrizal Bajo, *Chile* 126 B1
Carrizalillo, *Chile* 126 B1
Carrizo Cr. →, *U.S.A.* 109 G3
Carrizo Springs, *U.S.A.* 109 L5
Carrizozo, *U.S.A.* 111 K11
Carroll, *U.S.A.* 108 D7
Carrollton, *Ga., U.S.A.* 105 J3
Carrollton, *Ill., U.S.A.* 108 F9
Carrollton, *Ky., U.S.A.* 104 F3
Carrollton, *Mo., U.S.A.* 108 F8
Carrollton, *Ohio, U.S.A.* 106 F3
Carron →, *U.K.* 14 D3
Carron, L., *U.K.* 14 D3
Carrot →, *Canada* 101 C8
Carrot River, *Canada* 101 C8
Carrouges, *France* 24 D6
Carruthers, *Canada* 101 C7
Çarşamba, *Turkey* 66 B7
Carse of Gowrie, *U.K.* 14 E5
Carsóli, *Italy* 33 F10
Carson, *Calif., U.S.A.* 113 M8
Carson, *N. Dak., U.S.A.* 108 B4
Carson →, *U.S.A.* 112 F8
Carson City, *U.S.A.* 112 F7
Carson Sink, *U.S.A.* 110 G4
Carstairs, *U.K.* 14 F5
Cartagena, *Colombia* 120 A2
Cartagena, *Spain* 29 H4
Cartago, *Colombia* 120 C2
Cartago, *Costa Rica* 116 E3
Cartaxo, *Portugal* 31 F2
Cartaya, *Spain* 31 H3
Carteret, *France* 24 C5
Cartersville, *U.S.A.* 105 H3
Carterton, *N.Z.* 87 J5
Carthage, *Ark., U.S.A.* 109 H8
Carthage, *Ill., U.S.A.* 108 E9
Carthage, *Mo., U.S.A.* 109 G7
Carthage, *S. Dak., U.S.A.* 108 C6
Carthage, *Tex., U.S.A.* 109 J7
Cartier I., *Australia* 88 B3
Cartwright, *Canada* 99 B8
Caruaru, *Brazil* 122 C4
Carúpano, *Venezuela* 121 A5
Carutapera, *Brazil* 122 B2
Caruthersville, *U.S.A.* 109 G10
Carvalho, *Brazil* 121 D7
Carvin, *France* 25 B9
Carvoeiro, *Brazil* 121 D5
Carvoeiro, C., *Portugal* 31 F1
Cary, *U.S.A.* 105 H6
Casa Branca, *Brazil* 123 F2
Casa Branca, *Portugal* 31 G2
Casa Grande, *U.S.A.* 111 K8
Casablanca, *Chile* 126 C1
Casablanca, *Morocco* 74 B3
Casacalenda, *Italy* 35 A7
Casal di Principe, *Italy* 35 B7
Casalbordino, *Italy* 33 F11
Casale Monferrato, *Italy* 32 C5
Casalmaggiore, *Italy* 32 D7
Casalpusterlengo, *Italy* 32 C6
Casamance →, *Senegal* 78 C1
Casamássima, *Italy* 35 B9
Casanare □, *Colombia* 120 B3
Casanare →, *Colombia* 120 B4
Casarano, *Italy* 35 B11
Casares, *Spain* 31 J5
Casas Grandes, *Mexico* 114 A3
Casas Ibañez, *Spain* 29 F3
Casasimarro, *Spain* 29 F2
Casatejada, *Spain* 30 F5
Casavieja, *Spain* 30 E6
Cascade, *Idaho, U.S.A.* 110 D5
Cascade, *Mont., U.S.A.* 110 C8
Cascade Locks, *U.S.A.* 112 E5
Cascade Ra., *U.S.A.* 112 D5
Cascade Range, *U.S.A.* 94 E7
Cascais, *Portugal* 31 G1
Cascavel, *Brazil* 127 A5
Cáscina, *Italy* 32 E7
Caselle Torinese, *Italy* 32 C4
Caserta, *Italy* 35 A7
Cashel, *Ireland* 15 D4
Cashmere, *U.S.A.* 110 C3
Cashmere Downs, *Australia* 89 E2
Casibare →, *Colombia* 120 C3
Casiguran, *Phil.* 55 C5
Casilda, *Argentina* 126 C3
Casino, *Australia* 91 D5
Casiquiare →, *Venezuela* 120 C4
Casitas, *Peru* 124 A1
Caslan, *Canada* 100 C6
Čáslav, *Czech.* 20 F5
Casma, *Peru* 124 B2
Casmalia, *U.S.A.* 113 L6
Casola Valsenio, *Italy* 33 D8
Cásoli, *Italy* 33 F11
Caspe, *Spain* 28 D4
Casper, *U.S.A.* 110 E10
Caspian Depression, *Eurasia* 43 G9
Caspian Sea, *Eurasia* 44 E6
Casquets, *U.K.* 24 C4
Cass City, *U.S.A.* 104 D4
Cass Lake, *U.S.A.* 108 B7
Cassá de la Selva, *Spain* 28 D7
Cassano Iónio, *Italy* 35 C9
Cassel, *France* 25 B9
Casselman, *Canada* 107 A9
Casselton, *U.S.A.* 108 B6
Cassiar, *Canada* 100 B3
Cassiar Mts., *Canada* 100 B2
Cassilândia, *Brazil* 125 D7
Cassinga, *Angola* 81 H3
Cassino, *Italy* 34 A6
Cassis, *France* 27 E9
Cassville, *U.S.A.* 109 G8
Cástagneto Carducci, *Italy* 32 E7
Castaic, *U.S.A.* 113 L8
Castanhal, *Brazil* 122 B2
Casteau, *Belgium* 17 G4
Castéggio, *Italy* 32 C6
Castejón de Monegros, *Spain* 28 D4
Castel di Sangro, *Italy* 33 G11
Castel San Giovanni, *Italy* 32 C6
Castel San Pietro Terme, *Italy* 33 D8
Castelbuono, *Italy* 35 E7
Casteldelfino, *Italy* 32 D4
Castelfiorentino, *Italy* 32 E7
Castelfranco Emília, *Italy* 32 D8
Castelfranco Véneto, *Italy* 33 C8
Casteljaloux, *France* 26 D4
Castellabate, *Italy* 35 B7
Castellammare, G. di, *Italy* 34 D5
Castellammare del Golfo, *Italy* 34 D5
Castellammare di Stábia, *Italy* 35 B7
Castellamonte, *Italy* 32 C4
Castellana Grotte, *Italy* 35 B10
Castellane, *France* 27 E10
Castellaneta, *Italy* 35 B9
Castellar de Santisteban, *Spain* 29 G1
Castelleone, *Italy* 32 C6
Castelli, *Argentina* 126 D4
Castelló de Ampurias, *Spain* 28 C8
Castellón □, *Spain* 28 E4
Castellón de la Plana, *Spain* 28 F4
Castellote, *Spain* 28 E4
Castelltersol, *Spain* 28 D7
Castelmáuro, *Italy* 35 A7
Castelnau-de-Médoc, *France* 26 C3
Castelnaudary, *France* 26 E5
Castelnovo ne' Monti, *Italy* 32 D7
Castelnuovo di Val di Cécina, *Italy* 32 E7
Castelo, *Brazil* 123 F3
Castelo Branco, *Portugal* 30 F3
Castelo Branco □, *Portugal* 30 F3
Castelo de Paiva, *Portugal* 30 D2
Castelo de Vide, *Portugal* 31 F3
Castelo do Piauí, *Brazil* 122 C3
Castelsarrasin, *France* 26 D5
Casteltérmini, *Italy* 34 E6
Castelvetrano, *Italy* 34 E5
Casterton, *Australia* 91 F3
Castets, *France* 26 E2
Castiglione del Lago, *Italy* 33 E9
Castiglione della Pescáia, *Italy* 32 F7
Castiglione delle Stiviere, *Italy* 32 C7
Castiglione Fiorentino, *Italy* 33 E8
Castilblanco, *Spain* 31 F5
Castilla, *Peru* 124 B1
Castilla, Playa de, *Spain* 31 H4
Castilla La Mancha □, *Spain* 31 F7
Castilla y Leon □, *Spain* 30 D6
Castillon, Barr. de, *France* 27 E10
Castillon-en-Couserans, *France* 26 F5
Castillon-la-Bataille, *France* 26 D3
Castillonès, *France* 26 D4
Castillos, *Uruguay* 127 C5
Castle Dale, *U.S.A.* 110 G8
Castle Douglas, *U.K.* 14 G5
Castle Rock, *Colo., U.S.A.* 108 F2
Castle Rock, *Wash., U.S.A.* 112 D4
Castlebar, *Ireland* 15 C2
Castleblaney, *Ireland* 15 B5
Castlegar, *Canada* 100 D5
Castlemaine, *Australia* 91 F3
Castlerea, *Ireland* 15 C3
Castlereagh □, *U.K.* 15 B6
Castlereagh →, *Australia* 91 E4
Castlereagh B., *Australia* 90 A2
Castletown, *U.K.* 12 C3
Castletown Bearhaven, *Ireland* 15 E2
Castlevale, *Australia* 90 C4
Castor, *Canada* 100 C6
Castres, *France* 26 E6
Castricum, *Neths.* 16 C5
Castries, *St. Lucia* 117 D7
Castril, *Spain* 29 H2
Castro, *Brazil* 127 A5
Castro, *Chile* 128 B2
Castro Alves, *Brazil* 123 D4
Castro del Río, *Spain* 31 H6
Castro Marim, *Portugal* 31 H3
Castro Urdiales, *Spain* 28 B1
Castro Verde, *Portugal* 31 H2
Castrojeriz, *Spain* 30 C6
Castropol, *Spain* 30 B3
Castroreale, *Italy* 35 D8
Castrovíllari, *Italy* 35 C9
Castroville, *Calif., U.S.A.* 112 J5
Castroville, *Tex., U.S.A.* 109 L5
Castrovirreyna, *Peru* 124 C2
Castuera, *Spain* 31 G5
Casummit Lake, *Canada* 98 B1
Çat, *Turkey* 67 C9
Cat Ba, Dao, *Vietnam* 58 B6
Cat I., *Bahamas* 117 B4
Cat I., *U.S.A.* 109 K10
Cat L., *Canada* 98 B1
Catacamas, *Honduras* 116 D2
Catacáos, *Peru* 124 B1
Cataguases, *Brazil* 123 F3
Catahoula L., *U.S.A.* 109 K8
Çatak, *Turkey* 67 C10
Catalão, *Brazil* 123 E2
Çatalca, *Turkey* 66 B3
Catalina, *Canada* 99 C9
Catalonia = Cataluña □, *Spain* 28 D6
Cataluña □, *Spain* 28 D6
Çatalzeytin, *Turkey* 66 B6
Catamarca, *Argentina* 126 B2
Catamarca □, *Argentina* 126 B2
Catanauan, *Phil.* 55 E5
Catanduanes, *Phil.* 55 E6
Catanduva, *Brazil* 127 A6
Catánia, *Italy* 35 E8
Catánia, G. di, *Italy* 35 E8
Catanzaro, *Italy* 35 D9
Catarman, *Phil.* 55 E6
Catbalogan, *Phil.* 55 F6
Cateel, *Phil.* 55 H7
Catende, *Brazil* 122 C4
Cathcart, *S. Africa* 84 E4
Cathlamet, *U.S.A.* 112 D3
Catio, *Guinea-Biss.* 78 C1
Catismiña, *Venezuela* 121 C5
Catita, *Brazil* 122 C3
Catlettsburg, *U.S.A.* 104 F4
Catoche, C., *Mexico* 115 C7
Catolé do Rocha, *Brazil* 122 C4
Catral, *Spain* 29 G4
Catria, Mt., *Italy* 33 E9
Catrimani, *Brazil* 121 C5
Catrimani →, *Brazil* 121 C5
Catskill, *U.S.A.* 107 D11
Catskill Mts., *U.S.A.* 107 D10
Catt, Mt., *Australia* 90 A1
Cattaraugus, *U.S.A.* 106 D6
Cattólica, *Italy* 33 E9
Cattólica Eraclea, *Italy* 34 E6
Catu, *Brazil* 123 D4
Catuala, *Angola* 84 B2
Catur, *Mozam.* 83 E4
Catwick Is., *Vietnam* 59 G7
Cauca □, *Colombia* 120 C2
Cauca →, *Colombia* 120 B3
Caucaia, *Brazil* 122 B4
Caucasia, *Colombia* 120 B2
Caucasus Mountains, *Eurasia* 43 J7
Caudebec-en-Caux, *France* 24 C7
Caudebec-lès-Elbeuf, *France* 24 C8
Caudete, *Spain* 29 G3
Caudry, *France* 25 B10
Caulnes, *France* 24 D4
Caulónia, *Italy* 35 D9
Caúngula, *Angola* 80 F3
Cauquenes, *Chile* 126 D1
Caura →, *Venezuela* 121 B5
Caurés →, *Brazil* 121 D5
Cauresi →, *Mozam.* 83 F3
Causapscal, *Canada* 99 C6
Caussade, *France* 26 D5
Causse-Méjean, *France* 26 D7
Cauterets, *France* 26 F3
Cautín □, *Chile* 128 A2
Cauvery →, *India* 60 P11
Caux, Pays de, *France* 24 C7
Cava dei Tirreni, *Italy* 35 B7
Cávado →, *Portugal* 30 D2
Cavaillon, *France* 27 E9
Cavalaire-sur-Mer, *France* 27 E10
Cavalcante, *Brazil* 123 D2
Cavalese, *Italy* 33 B8
Cavalier, *U.S.A.* 108 A6
Cavalla = Cavally →, *Africa* 78 E3
Cavallo, I. de, *France* 27 G13
Cavally →, *Africa* 78 E3
Cavan, *Ireland* 15 C4
Cavan □, *Ireland* 15 C4
Cavárzere, *Italy* 33 C9
Cave City, *U.S.A.* 104 G3
Cavenagh Ra., *Australia* 89 E4
Cavendish, *Australia* 91 F3
Caviana, I., *Brazil* 121 C7
Cavite, *Phil.* 55 D4
Cavour, *Italy* 32 D4
Cavtat, *Croatia* 21 N8
Cawndilla L., *Australia* 91 E3
Cawnpore = Kanpur, *India* 63 F9
Caxias, *Brazil* 122 B3
Caxias do Sul, *Brazil* 127 B5
Caxito, *Angola* 80 F2
Çay, *Turkey* 66 C4
Cay Sal Bank, *Bahamas* 116 B3
Cayambe, *Napo, Ecuador* 120 C2
Cayambe, *Quito, Ecuador* 120 C2
Çaycuma, *Turkey* 66 B5
Çayeli, *Turkey* 67 B9
Cayenne, *Fr. Guiana* 121 B7
Cayenne □, *Fr. Guiana* 121 C7
Cayeux-sur-Mer, *France* 25 B8
Cayiralan, *Turkey* 66 C6
Caylus, *France* 26 D5
Cayman Brac, *Cayman Is.* 116 C4
Cayman Is. ■, *W. Indies* 116 C3
Cayo Romano, *Cuba* 117 B4
Cayuga, *Canada* 106 D5
Cayuga, *U.S.A.* 107 D8
Cayuga L., *U.S.A.* 107 D8
Cazalla de la Sierra, *Spain* 31 H5
Căzăneşti, *Romania* 38 E10
Cazaux et de Sanguinet, Étang de, *France* 26 D2
Cazères, *France* 26 E5
Cazin, *Bos.-H.* 33 D12
Čazma, *Croatia* 33 C13
Čazma →, *Croatia* 33 C13
Cazombo, *Angola* 81 G4
Cazorla, *Spain* 29 H1
Cazorla, *Venezuela* 120 B4
Cazorla, Sierra de, *Spain* 29 G2
Cea →, *Spain* 30 C5
Ceadâr-Lunga, *Moldova* 41 J5
Ceanannus Mor, *Ireland* 15 C5
Ceará = Fortaleza, *Brazil* 122 B4
Ceará □, *Brazil* 122 C4
Ceará Mirim, *Brazil* 122 C4
Cebaco, I. de, *Panama* 116 E3
Cebollar, *Argentina* 126 B2
Cebollera, Sierra de, *Spain* 28 D2
Cebreros, *Spain* 30 E6
Cebu, *Phil.* 55 F5
Ceccano, *Italy* 34 A6
Cechi, *Ivory C.* 78 D4
Čechy, *Czech.* 19 F9
Cecil Plains, *Australia* 91 D5
Cécina, *Italy* 32 E7
Cécina →, *Italy* 32 E7
Ceclavin, *Spain* 30 F4
Cedar →, *U.S.A.* 108 E9
Cedar City, *U.S.A.* 111 H7
Cedar Creek Reservoir, *U.S.A.* 109 J6
Cedar Falls, *Iowa, U.S.A.* 108 D8
Cedar Falls, *Wash., U.S.A.* 112 C5
Cedar Key, *U.S.A.* 105 L4
Cedar L., *Canada* 101 C8
Cedar Rapids, *U.S.A.* 108 E9
Cedartown, *U.S.A.* 105 H3
Cedarvale, *Canada* 100 B3
Cedarville, *S. Africa* 85 E4
Cedarville, *U.S.A.* 110 F3
Cedeira, *Spain* 30 B2
Cedral, *Mexico* 114 C4
Cedrino →, *Italy* 34 B2
Cedro, *Brazil* 122 C4
Cedros, I. de, *Mexico* 114 B1
Ceduna, *Australia* 91 E1
Cefalù, *Italy* 35 D7
Cega →, *Spain* 30 D6
Cegléd, *Hungary* 21 H9
Céglie Messápico, *Italy* 35 B10
Cehegín, *Spain* 29 G3
Ceheng, *China* 52 E5
Cehu-Silvaniei, *Romania* 38 B6
Ceira →, *Portugal* 30 E2
Cekhira, *Tunisia* 75 B7
Celano, *Italy* 33 F10
Celanova, *Spain* 30 C3
Celaya, *Mexico* 114 C4
Celbridge, *Ireland* 15 C5
Celebes = Sulawesi □, *Indonesia* 57 E6
Celebes Sea, *Indonesia* 57 D6
Celendín, *Peru* 124 B2
Čelić, *Bos.-H.* 21 L8
Celica, *Ecuador* 120 D2
Celina, *U.S.A.* 104 E3
Celje, *Slovenia* 33 B12

Celle, *Germany* 18 C6
Celles, *Belgium* 17 G2
Celorico da Beira, *Portugal* 30 E3
Cement, *U.S.A.* 109 H5
Çemişgezek, *Turkey* 67 C8
Cenepa →, *Peru* 120 D2
Cengong, *China* 52 D7
Ceno →, *Italy* 32 D7
Cenon, *France* 26 D3
Centallo, *Italy* 32 D4
Centenário do Sul, *Brazil* 123 F1
Center, *N. Dak., U.S.A.* 108 B4
Center, *Tex., U.S.A.* 109 K7
Centerfield, *U.S.A.* 111 G8
Centerville, *Calif., U.S.A.* 112 J7
Centerville, *Iowa, U.S.A.* 108 E8
Centerville, *Pa., U.S.A.* 106 F5
Centerville, *S. Dak., U.S.A.* 108 D6
Centerville, *Tenn., U.S.A.* 105 H2
Centerville, *Tex., U.S.A.* 109 K7
Cento, *Italy* 33 D8
Central, *Brazil* 122 D3
Central, *U.S.A.* 111 K9
Central □, *Kenya* 82 C4
Central □, *Malawi* 83 E3
Central □, *Zambia* 83 E2
Central, Cordillera, *Bolivia* 125 D5
Central, Cordillera, *Colombia* 120 C2
Central, Cordillera, *Costa Rica* 116 D3
Central, Cordillera, *Dom. Rep.* 117 C5
Central, Cordillera, *Peru* 124 B2
Central, Cordillera, *Phil.* 55 C4
Central, Sistema, *Spain* 30 E5
Central African Rep. ■, *Africa* 73 G9
Central City, *Ky., U.S.A.* 104 G2
Central City, *Nebr., U.S.A.* 108 E5
Central I., *Kenya* 82 B4
Central Makran Range, *Pakistan* 60 F4
Central Patricia, *Canada* 98 B1
Central Russian Uplands, *Europe* 6 E13
Central Siberian Plateau, *Russia* 46 C14
Centralia, *Ill., U.S.A.* 108 F10
Centralia, *Mo., U.S.A.* 108 F8
Centralia, *Wash., U.S.A.* 112 D4
Centreville, *Ala., U.S.A.* 105 J2
Centreville, *Miss., U.S.A.* 109 K9
Centúripe, *Italy* 35 E7
Cephalonia = Kefallinía, *Greece* 39 L3
Ceprano, *Italy* 34 A6
Cepu, *Indonesia* 57 G14
Ceram = Seram, *Indonesia* 57 E7
Ceram Sea = Seram Sea, *Indonesia* 57 E7
Cerbère, *France* 26 F7
Cerbicales, Is., *France* 27 G13
Cercal, *Portugal* 31 H2
Cercemaggiore, *Italy* 35 A7
Cerdaña, *Spain* 28 C6
Cerdedo, *Spain* 30 C2
Cère →, *France* 26 D5
Cerea, *Italy* 33 C8
Ceres, *Argentina* 126 B3
Ceres, *Brazil* 123 E2
Ceres, *Italy* 32 C4
Ceres, *S. Africa* 84 E2
Ceres, *U.S.A.* 112 H6
Céret, *France* 26 F6
Cereté, *Colombia* 120 B2
Cerfontaine, *Belgium* 17 H4
Ceridigion □, *U.K.* 13 E3
Cerignola, *Italy* 35 A8
Cerigo = Kíthira, *Greece* 39 N7
Cérilly, *France* 26 B6
Cerisiers, *France* 25 D10
Cerizay, *France* 24 F6
Çerkeş, *Turkey* 66 B5
Çerkeşköy, *Turkey* 66 B2
Cerknica, *Slovenia* 33 C11
Çermik, *Turkey* 67 C8
Cerna →, *Romania* 38 E7
Cernavodă, *Romania* 38 E11
Cernay, *France* 25 E14
Cernik, *Croatia* 21 K7
Cerralvo, I., *Mexico* 114 C3
Cerreto Sannita, *Italy* 35 A7
Cerritos, *Mexico* 114 C4
Cerro Sombrero, *Chile* 128 D3
Certaldo, *Italy* 32 E8
Cervaro →, *Italy* 35 A8
Cervera, *Spain* 28 D6
Cervera de Pisuerga, *Spain* 30 C6
Cervera del Río Alhama, *Spain* 28 C3
Cérvia, *Italy* 33 D9
Cervignano del Friuli, *Italy* 33 C10
Cervinara, *Italy* 35 A7
Cervione, *France* 27 F13
Cervo, *Spain* 30 B3
César □, *Colombia* 120 B3
Cesaro, *Italy* 35 E7
Cesena, *Italy* 33 D9
Cesenático, *Italy* 33 D9
Cēsis, *Latvia* 9 H21
Česká Lípa, *Czech.* 20 E4
Česka Republika = Czech Rep. ■, *Europe* 20 F4
České Budějovice, *Czech.* 20 G4
Ceskomoravská Vrchovina, *Czech.* 20 F5
Český Brod, *Czech.* 20 E4
Český Krumlov, *Czech.* 20 G4
Český Těšin, *Czech.* 20 F8
Çeşme, *Turkey* 66 C2
Cessnock, *Australia* 91 E5
Cestos →, *Liberia* 78 D3
Cétin Grad, *Croatia* 33 C12
Cetina →, *Croatia* 33 E13
Cetraro, *Italy* 35 C8
Ceuta, *N. Afr.* 74 A3
Ceva, *Italy* 32 D5
Cévennes, *France* 26 D7
Ceyhan, *Turkey* 66 D6
Ceyhan →, *Turkey* 66 D6
Ceylânpınar, *Turkey* 67 D9
Ceylon = Sri Lanka ■, *Asia* 60 R12
Cèze →, *France* 27 D8
Cha-am, *Thailand* 58 F2
Chaam, *Neths.* 17 E5
Chabeuil, *France* 27 D9
Chablais, *France* 27 B10
Chablis, *France* 25 E10
Chabounia, *Algeria* 75 A5
Chacabuco, *Argentina* 126 C3
Chachapoyas, *Peru* 124 B2
Chachasp, *Peru* 124 D3
Chachoengsao, *Thailand* 58 F3
Chachran, *Pakistan* 60 E7
Chachro, *Pakistan* 62 G4
Chaco □, *Argentina* 126 B3
Chaco □, *Paraguay* 126 B3
Chad ■, *Africa* 73 E8
Chad, L. = Tchad, L., *Chad* 73 F7
Chadan, *Russia* 45 D10
Chadileuvú →, *Argentina* 126 D2
Chadiza, *Zambia* 83 E3
Chadron, *U.S.A.* 108 D3
Chadyr-Lunga = Ceadâr-Lunga, *Moldova* 41 J5
Chae Hom, *Thailand* 58 C2
Chaem →, *Thailand* 58 C2
Chaeryŏng, *N. Korea* 51 E13
Chagai Hills, *Afghan.* 60 E3
Chagda, *Russia* 45 D14
Chagny, *France* 25 F11
Chagoda, *Russia* 40 C8
Chagos Arch., *Ind. Oc.* 47 K11
Chāh Ākhvor, *Iran* 65 C8
Chāh Bahār, *Iran* 65 E9
Chāh-e-Malek, *Iran* 65 D8
Chāh Kavīr, *Iran* 65 D7
Chahar Burjak, *Afghan.* 60 D3
Chaibasa, *India* 61 H14
Chaillé-les-Marais, *France* 26 B2
Chainat, *Thailand* 58 E3
Chaitén, *Chile* 128 B2
Chaiya, *Thailand* 59 H2
Chaj Doab, *Pakistan* 62 C5
Chajari, *Argentina* 126 C4
Chake Chake, *Tanzania* 82 D4
Chakhānsūr, *Afghan.* 60 D3
Chakonipau, L., *Canada* 99 A6
Chakradharpur, *India* 63 H11
Chakwal, *Pakistan* 62 C5
Chala, *Peru* 124 D3
Chalais, *France* 26 C4
Chalchihuites, *Mexico* 114 C4
Chalcis = Khalkís, *Greece* 39 L6
Chaleur B., *Canada* 99 C6
Chalfant, *U.S.A.* 112 H8
Chalhuanca, *Peru* 124 C3
Chalindrey, *France* 25 E12
Chaling, *China* 53 D9
Chalisgaon, *India* 60 J9
Chalky Inlet, *N.Z.* 87 M1
Challans, *France* 24 F5
Challapata, *Bolivia* 124 D4
Challis, *U.S.A.* 110 D6
Chalna, *India* 63 H13
Chalon-sur-Saône, *France* 25 F11
Chalonnes-sur-Loire, *France* 24 E6
Châlons-en-Champagne, *France* 25 D11
Châlus, *France* 26 C4
Chalyaphum, *Thailand* 58 E4
Cham, *Germany* 19 F8
Cham, *Switz.* 23 B6
Cham, Cu Lao, *Vietnam* 58 E7
Chama, *U.S.A.* 111 H10
Chaman, *Pakistan* 60 D5
Chamba, *India* 62 C7
Chamba, *Tanzania* 83 E4
Chambal →, *India* 63 F8
Chamberlain, *U.S.A.* 108 D5
Chamberlain →, *Australia* 88 C4
Chambers, *U.S.A.* 111 J9
Chambersburg, *U.S.A.* 104 F7
Chambéry, *France* 27 C9
Chambly, *Canada* 107 A11
Chambord, *Canada* 99 C5
Chamchamal, *Iraq* 67 E11
Chamela, *Mexico* 114 D3
Chamical, *Argentina* 126 C2
Chamkar Luong, *Cambodia* 59 G4
Chamonix-Mont Blanc, *France* 27 C10
Champa, *India* 63 H10
Champagne, *Canada* 100 A1
Champagne, *France* 25 D11
Champagne, Plaine de, *France* 25 D11
Champagnole, *France* 25 F12
Champaign, *U.S.A.* 104 E1
Champassak, *Laos* 58 E5
Champaubert, *France* 25 D10
Champdeniers, *France* 26 B3
Champeix, *France* 26 C7
Champlain, *Canada* 104 B9
Champlain, *U.S.A.* 107 B11
Champlain, L., *U.S.A.* 107 B11
Champotón, *Mexico* 115 D6
Chamusca, *Portugal* 31 F2
Chan Chan, *Peru* 124 B2
Chana, *Thailand* 59 J3
Chañaral, *Chile* 126 B1
Chanārān, *Iran* 65 B8
Chanasma, *India* 62 H5
Chancay, *Peru* 124 C2
Chancy, *Switz.* 22 D1
Chandannagar, *India* 63 H13
Chandausi, *India* 63 E8
Chandeleur Is., *U.S.A.* 109 L10
Chandeleur Sd., *U.S.A.* 109 L10
Chandigarh, *India* 62 D7
Chandler, *Australia* 91 D1
Chandler, *Canada* 99 C7
Chandler, *Ariz., U.S.A.* 111 K8
Chandler, *Okla., U.S.A.* 109 H6
Chandless →, *Brazil* 124 B4
Chandmani, *Mongolia* 54 B4
Chandpur, *Bangla.* 61 H17
Chandpur, *India* 62 E8
Chandrapur, *India* 60 K11
Chānf, *Iran* 65 E9
Chang, *Pakistan* 62 F3
Chang, Ko, *Thailand* 59 F4
Ch'ang Chiang = Chang Jiang →, *China* 53 B13
Chang Jiang →, *China* 53 B13
Changa, *India* 63 C7
Changanacheri, *India* 60 Q10
Changane →, *Mozam.* 85 C5
Changbai, *China* 51 D15
Changbai Shan, *China* 51 C15
Changchiak'ou = Zhangjiakou, *China* 50 D8
Ch'angchou = Changzhou, *China* 53 B12
Changchun, *China* 51 C13
Changchunling, *China* 51 B13
Changde, *China* 53 C8
Changdo-ri, *N. Korea* 51 E14
Changfeng, *China* 53 A11
Changhai = Shanghai, *China* 53 B13
Changhua, *China* 53 B12
Changhua, *Taiwan* 53 E13
Changhŭng, *S. Korea* 51 G14
Changhŭngni, *N. Korea* 51 D15
Changjiang, *China* 54 E5
Changjin, *N. Korea* 51 D14
Changjin-chŏsuji, *N. Korea* 51 D14
Changle, *China* 53 E12
Changli, *China* 51 E10
Changling, *China* 51 B12
Changlun, *Malaysia* 59 J3
Changning, *Hunan, China* 53 D9
Changning, *Yunnan, China* 52 E2
Changping, *China* 50 D9
Changsha, *China* 53 C9
Changshan, *China* 53 C12
Changshou, *China* 52 C6
Changshu, *China* 53 B13
Changshun, *China* 52 D6
Changtai, *China* 53 E11
Changting, *China* 53 E11
Changwu, *China* 50 G4
Changxing, *China* 53 B12
Changyang, *China* 53 B8
Changyi, *China* 51 F10
Changyŏn, *N. Korea* 51 E13
Changyuan, *China* 50 G8
Changzhi, *China* 50 F7
Changzhou, *China* 53 B12
Chanhanga, *Angola* 84 B1
Chanlar = Xanlar, *Azerbaijan* 43 K8
Channapatna, *India* 60 N10
Channel Is., *U.K.* 13 H5
Channel Is., *U.S.A.* 113 M7
Channel-Port aux Basques, *Canada* 99 C8
Channing, *Mich., U.S.A.* 104 B1
Channing, *Tex., U.S.A.* 109 H3
Chantada, *Spain* 30 C3
Chanthaburi, *Thailand* 58 F4
Chantilly, *France* 25 C9
Chantonnay, *France* 24 F5
Chantrey Inlet, *Canada* 96 B10
Chanute, *U.S.A.* 109 G7
Chanza →, *Spain* 31 H3
Chao Hu, *China* 53 B11
Chao Phraya →, *Thailand* 58 F3
Chao Phraya Lowlands, *Thailand* 58 E3
Chao Xian, *China* 53 B11
Chao'an, *China* 53 F11
Chaocheng, *China* 50 F8
Chaoyang, *Guangdong, China* 53 F11
Chaoyang, *Liaoning, China* 51 D11
Chapada dos Guimarães, *Brazil* 125 D6
Chapala, *Mozam.* 83 F4
Chapala, L. de, *Mexico* 114 C4
Chaparé →, *Bolivia* 125 D5
Chaparral, *Colombia* 120 C2
Chapayev, *Kazakstan* 42 E10
Chapayevsk, *Russia* 42 D9
Chapecó, *Brazil* 127 B5
Chapel Hill, *U.S.A.* 105 H6
Chapleau, *Canada* 98 C3
Chaplin, *Canada* 101 C7
Chaplino, *Ukraine* 41 H9
Chaplygin, *Russia* 42 D5
Chapra = Chhapra, *India* 63 G11
Châr, *Mauritania* 74 D2
Chara, *Russia* 45 D12
Charadai, *Argentina* 126 B4
Charagua, *Bolivia* 125 D5
Charalá, *Colombia* 120 B3
Charambirá, Punta, *Colombia* 120 C2
Charaña, *Bolivia* 124 D4
Charantsavan, *Armenia* 43 K7
Charapita, *Colombia* 120 D3
Charata, *Argentina* 126 B3
Charcas, *Mexico* 114 C4
Charcoal L., *Canada* 101 B8
Chard, *U.K.* 13 G5
Chardara, *Kazakstan* 44 E7
Chardon, *U.S.A.* 106 E3
Chardzhou = Chärjew, *Turkmenistan* 44 F7
Charente □, *France* 26 C4
Charente →, *France* 26 C2
Charente-Maritime □, *France* 26 C3
Chari →, *Chad* 73 F7
Chārīkār, *Afghan.* 60 B6
Chariton →, *U.S.A.* 108 F8
Charity, *Guyana* 121 B6
Chärjew, *Turkmenistan* 44 F7
Charkhari, *India* 63 G8
Charkhi Dadri, *India* 62 E7
Charleroi, *Belgium* 17 H4
Charleroi, *U.S.A.* 106 F5
Charles, C., *U.S.A.* 104 G8
Charles City, *U.S.A.* 108 D8
Charles L., *Canada* 101 B6
Charles Town, *U.S.A.* 104 F7
Charleston, *Ill., U.S.A.* 104 F1
Charleston, *Miss., U.S.A.* 109 H9
Charleston, *Mo., U.S.A.* 109 G10
Charleston, *S.C., U.S.A.* 105 J6
Charleston, *W. Va., U.S.A.* 104 F5
Charleston Peak, *U.S.A.* 113 J11
Charlestown, *S. Africa* 85 D4
Charlestown, *U.S.A.* 104 F3
Charlesville, *Zaïre* 80 F4
Charleville = Rath Luirc, *Ireland* 15 D3
Charleville, *Australia* 91 D4
Charleville-Mézières, *France* 25 C11
Charlevoix, *U.S.A.* 104 C3
Charlieu, *France* 27 B8
Charlotte, *Mich., U.S.A.* 104 D3
Charlotte, *N.C., U.S.A.* 105 H5
Charlotte Amalie, *Virgin Is.* 117 C7
Charlotte Harbor, *U.S.A.* 105 M4
Charlottesville, *U.S.A.* 104 F6
Charlottetown, *Canada* 99 C7
Charlton, *Australia* 91 F3
Charlton, *U.S.A.* 108 E8
Charlton I., *Canada* 98 B4
Charmes, *France* 25 D13
Charny, *Canada* 99 C5
Charolles, *France* 27 B8
Chârost, *France* 25 F9
Charouine, *Algeria* 75 C4
Charre, *Mozam.* 83 F4
Charroux, *France* 26 B4
Charsadda, *Pakistan* 62 B4
Charters Towers, *Australia* 90 C4
Chartres, *France* 24 D8
Chascomús, *Argentina* 126 D4
Chasefu, *Zambia* 83 E3
Chasovnya-Uchurskaya, *Russia* 45 D14
Chasseneuil-sur-Bonnieure, *France* 26 C4
Chāt, *Iran* 65 B7
Chatal Balkan = Udvoy Balkan, *Bulgaria* 38 G9
Château-Arnoux, *France* 27 D10
Château-Chinon, *France* 25 E10
Château d'Oex, *Switz.* 22 D4
Château-du-Loir, *France* 24 E7
Château-Gontier, *France* 24 E6
Château-la-Vallière, *France* 24 E7
Château-Landon, *France* 25 D9
Château-Porcien, *France* 25 C11
Château-Renault, *France* 24 E7
Château-Salins, *France* 25 D13
Château-Thierry, *France* 25 C10
Châteaubourg, *France* 24 D5
Châteaubriant, *France* 24 E5
Châteaudun, *France* 24 D8
Châteaugiron, *France* 24 D5
Châteaulin, *France* 24 D2
Châteaumeillant, *France* 26 B6
Châteauneuf-du-Faou, *France* 24 D3
Châteauneuf-en-Thymerais, *France* 24 D8
Châteauneuf-sur-Charente, *France* 26 C3
Châteauneuf-sur-Cher, *France* 25 F9
Châteauneuf-sur-Loire, *France* 25 E9
Châteaurenard, *Bouches-du-Rhône, France* 27 E8
Châteaurenard, *Loiret, France* 25 E9
Châteauroux, *France* 25 F8
Châtel-St.-Denis, *Switz.* 22 C3
Châtelaillon-Plage, *France* 26 B2
Châtelaudren, *France* 24 D4
Chatelet, *Belgium* 17 H5
Châtelguyon, *France* 26 C7
Châtellerault, *France* 24 F7
Châtelus-Malvaleix, *France* 26 B6
Chatfield, *U.S.A.* 108 D9
Chatham, *N.B., Canada* 99 C6
Chatham, *Ont., Canada* 98 D3
Chatham, *U.K.* 13 F8
Chatham, *La., U.S.A.* 109 J8
Chatham, *N.Y., U.S.A.* 107 D11
Chatham, I., *Chile* 128 D2
Chatham Is., *Pac. Oc.* 92 M10
Chatham Str., *U.S.A.* 100 B2
Châtillon, *Italy* 32 C4
Châtillon-Coligny, *France* 25 E9
Châtillon-en-Bazois, *France* 25 E10
Châtillon-en-Diois, *France* 27 D9
Châtillon-sur-Indre, *France* 24 F8
Châtillon-sur-Loire, *France* 25 E9
Châtillon-sur-Marne, *France* 25 C10
Châtillon-sur-Seine, *France* 25 E11
Chatmohar, *Bangla.* 63 G13
Chatra, *India* 63 G11
Chatrapur, *India* 61 K14
Chats, L. des, *Canada* 107 A8
Chatsworth, *Canada* 106 B4
Chatsworth, *Zimbabwe* 83 F3
Chattahoochee →, *U.S.A.* 105 K3
Chattanooga, *U.S.A.* 105 H3
Chaturat, *Thailand* 58 E3
Chau Doc, *Vietnam* 59 G5
Chaudanne, Barr. de, *France* 27 E10
Chaudes-Aigues, *France* 26 D7
Chauffailles, *France* 27 B8
Chauk, *Burma* 61 J19
Chaukan La, *Burma* 61 F20
Chaulnes, *France* 25 C9
Chaumont, *France* 25 D12
Chaumont, *U.S.A.* 107 B8
Chaumont-en-Vexin, *France* 25 C8
Chaumont-sur-Loire, *France* 24 E8
Chaunay, *France* 26 B4
Chauny, *France* 25 C10
Chausey, Is., *France* 24 D5
Chaussin, *France* 25 F12
Chautauqua L., *U.S.A.* 106 D5
Chauvigny, *France* 24 F7
Chauvin, *Canada* 101 C6
Chavantina, *Brazil* 125 C7
Chaves, *Brazil* 122 B2
Chaves, *Portugal* 30 D3
Chavuma, *Zambia* 81 G4
Chawang, *Thailand* 59 H2
Chazelles-sur-Lyon, *France* 27 C8
Chazuta, *Peru* 124 B2
Chazy, *U.S.A.* 107 B11
Cheb, *Czech.* 20 E2
Cheboksarskoye Vdkhr., *Russia* 42 B8
Cheboksary, *Russia* 42 B8
Cheboygan, *U.S.A.* 104 C3
Chebsara, *Russia* 40 C10
Chech, Erg, *Africa* 74 D4
Chechaouen, *Morocco* 74 A3
Chechen, Ostrov, *Russia* 43 H8
Chechenia □, *Russia* 43 J7
Checheno-Ingush Republic = Chechenia □, *Russia* 43 J7
Chechnya = Chechenia □, *Russia* 43 J7
Chechon, *S. Korea* 51 F15
Chęciny, *Poland* 20 E10
Checleset B., *Canada* 100 C3
Checotah, *U.S.A.* 109 H7
Chedabucto B., *Canada* 99 C7
Cheduba I., *Burma* 61 K18
Cheepie, *Australia* 91 D4
Chef-Boutonne, *France* 26 B3
Chegdomyn, *Russia* 45 D14
Chegga, *Mauritania* 74 C3
Chegutu, *Zimbabwe* 83 F3
Chehalis, *U.S.A.* 112 D4
Cheiron, Mt., *France* 27 E10
Cheju Do, *S. Korea* 51 H14
Chekalin, *Russia* 42 C3
Chekiang = Zhejiang □, *China* 53 C13
Chel = Kuru, Bahr el →, *Sudan* 77 F2
Chela, Sa. da, *Angola* 84 B1
Chelan, *U.S.A.* 110 C4
Chelan, L., *U.S.A.* 110 C3
Cheleken, *Turkmenistan* 44 F6
Chelforó, *Argentina* 128 A3
Chéliff, O. →, *Algeria* 75 A5
Chelkar = Shalqar, *Kazakstan* 44 E6
Chelkar Tengiz, Solonchak, *Kazakstan* 44 E7
Chellala Dahrania, *Algeria* 75 B5
Chelles, *France* 25 D9
Chełm, *Poland* 20 D13
Chełmek, *Poland* 20 E9
Chełmno, *Poland* 20 B8
Chelmsford, *U.K.* 13 F8
Chełmża, *Poland* 20 B8
Chelsea, *Okla., U.S.A.* 109 G7
Chelsea, *Vt., U.S.A.* 107 C12
Cheltenham, *U.K.* 13 F5
Chelva, *Spain* 28 F4
Chelyabinsk, *Russia* 44 D7
Chelyuskin, C., *Russia* 46 B14

Chemainus, Canada 100 D4
Chembar = Belinskiy, Russia 42 D6
Chemillé, France 24 E6
Chemnitz, Germany 18 E8
Chemult, U.S.A. 110 E3
Chen, Gora, Russia 45 C15
Chen Xian, China 53 E9
Chenab →, Pakistan 62 D4
Chenachane, O. →, Algeria 74 C4
Chenango Forks, U.S.A. 107 D9
Chencha, Ethiopia 77 F4
Chenchiang = Zhenjiang, China 53 A12
Chênée, Belgium 17 G7
Cheney, U.S.A. 110 C5
Cheng Xian, China 50 H3
Chengbu, China 53 D8
Chengcheng, China 50 G5
Chengchou = Zhengzhou, China 50 G7
Chengde, China 51 D9
Chengdong Hu, China 53 A11
Chengdu, China 52 B5
Chenggong, China 52 E4
Chenggu, China 50 H4
Chengjiang, China 52 E4
Chengkou, China 52 B7
Ch'engtu = Chengdu, China 52 B5
Chengwu, China 50 G8
Chengxi Hu, China 53 A11
Chengyang, China 51 F11
Chenjiagang, China 51 G10
Chenkán, Mexico 115 D6
Chenxi, China 53 C8
Cheo Reo, Vietnam 58 F7
Cheom Ksan, Cambodia 58 E5
Chepelare, Bulgaria 39 H7
Chepén, Peru 124 B2
Chepes, Argentina 126 C2
Chepo, Panama 116 E4
Cheptulil, Mt., Kenya 82 B4
Chequamegon B., U.S.A. 108 B9
Cher □, France 25 E9
Cher →, France 24 E7
Cherasco, Italy 32 D4
Cheratte, Belgium 17 G7
Cheraw, U.S.A. 105 H6
Cherbourg, France 24 C5
Cherchell, Algeria 75 A5
Cherdakly, Russia 42 C9
Cherdyn, Russia 44 C6
Cheremkhovo, Russia 45 D11
Cherepanovo, Russia 44 D9
Cherepovets, Russia 40 C9
Chergui, Chott ech, Algeria 75 B5
Cherikov = Cherykaw, Belarus 40 F6
Cherkasy, Ukraine 41 H7
Cherkessk, Russia 43 H6
Cherlak, Russia 44 D8
Chernaya, Russia 45 B9
Cherni, Bulgaria 38 G6
Chernigov = Chernihiv, Ukraine 41 G6
Chernihiv, Ukraine 41 G6
Chernivtsi, Ukraine 41 H3
Chernobyl = Chornobyl, Ukraine 41 G6
Chernogorsk, Russia 45 D10
Chernomorskoye = Chornomorske, Ukraine 41 K7
Chernovtsy = Chernivtsi, Ukraine 41 H3
Chernyakhovsk, Russia 9 J19
Chernyanka, Russia 42 E3
Chernyshovskiy, Russia 45 C12
Chernyye Zemli, Russia 43 H8
Cherokee, Iowa, U.S.A. 108 D7
Cherokee, Okla., U.S.A. 109 G5
Cherokees, Lake O' The, U.S.A. 109 G7
Cherquenco, Chile 128 A2
Cherrapunji, India 61 G17
Cherry Creek, U.S.A. 110 G6
Cherry Valley, U.S.A. 113 M10
Cherryvale, U.S.A. 109 G7
Cherskiy, Russia 45 C17
Cherskogo Khrebet, Russia 45 C15
Chertkovo, Russia 42 F5
Cherven, Belarus 40 F5
Cherven-Bryag, Bulgaria 38 F7
Chervonohrad, Ukraine 41 G3
Cherwell →, U.K. 13 F6
Cherykaw, Belarus 40 F6
Chesapeake, U.S.A. 104 G7
Chesapeake B., U.S.A. 104 F7
Cheshire □, U.K. 12 D5
Cheshskaya Guba, Russia 44 C5
Cheslatta L., Canada 100 C3
Chesley, Canada 106 B3
Cheste, Spain 29 F4
Chester, U.K. 12 D5
Chester, Calif., U.S.A. 110 F3
Chester, Ill., U.S.A. 109 G10
Chester, Mont., U.S.A. 110 B8
Chester, Pa., U.S.A. 104 F8
Chester, S.C., U.S.A. 105 H5
Chesterfield, U.K. 12 D6
Chesterfield, Is., N. Cal. 92 J7
Chesterfield Inlet, Canada 96 B10
Chesterton Ra., Australia 91 D4
Chesterville, Canada 107 A9
Chesuncook L., U.S.A. 99 C6
Chéticamp, Canada 99 C7
Chetumal, B. de, Mexico 115 D7
Chetwynd, Canada 100 B4
Chevanceaux, France 26 C3
Cheviot, The, U.K. 12 B5
Cheviot Hills, U.K. 12 B5
Cheviot Ra., Australia 90 D3
Chew Bahir, Ethiopia 77 G4
Chewelah, U.S.A. 110 B5
Cheyenne, Okla., U.S.A. 109 H5
Cheyenne, Wyo., U.S.A. 108 E2
Cheyenne →, U.S.A. 108 C4
Cheyenne Wells, U.S.A. 108 F3
Cheyne B., Australia 89 F2
Chhabra, India 62 G7
Chhapra, India 63 G11
Chhata, India 62 F7
Chhatarpur, India 63 G8
Chhep, Cambodia 58 F5
Chhindwara, India 63 H8
Chhlong, Cambodia 59 F5
Chhuk, Cambodia 59 G5
Chi →, Thailand 58 E5
Chiai, Taiwan 53 F13
Chiali, Taiwan 53 F13
Chiamis, Indonesia 57 G13
Chiamussu = Jiamusi, China 54 B8
Chiang Dao, Thailand 58 C2
Chiang Kham, Thailand 58 C3
Chiang Khan, Thailand 58 D3
Chiang Khong, Thailand 58 B3
Chiang Mai, Thailand 58 C2
Chiang Saen, Thailand 58 B3
Chiange, Angola 81 H2
Chiapa →, Mexico 115 D6
Chiapa de Corzo, Mexico 115 D6
Chiapas □, Mexico 115 D6
Chiaramonte Gulfi, Italy 35 E7
Chiaravalle, Italy 33 E10
Chiaravalle Centrale, Italy 35 D9
Chiari, Italy 32 C6
Chiasso, Switz. 23 E8
Chiatura, Georgia 43 J6
Chiautla, Mexico 115 D5
Chiávari, Italy 32 D6
Chiavenna, Italy 32 B6
Chiba, Japan 49 G10
Chibabava, Mozam. 85 C5
Chibatu, Indonesia 57 G12
Chibemba, Cunene, Angola 81 H2
Chibemba, Huila, Angola 84 B2
Chibia, Angola 81 H2
Chibougamau, Canada 98 C5
Chibougamau L., Canada 98 C5
Chibuk, Nigeria 79 C7
Chic-Chocs, Mts., Canada 99 C6
Chicacole = Srikakulam, India 61 K13
Chicago, U.S.A. 104 E2
Chicago Heights, U.S.A. 104 E2
Chichagof I., U.S.A. 100 B1
Chichaoua, Morocco 74 B3
Chicheng, China 50 D8
Chichester, U.K. 13 G7
Chichibu, Japan 49 F9
Ch'ich'ihaerh = Qiqihar, China 45 E13
Chickasha, U.S.A. 109 H5
Chiclana de la Frontera, Spain 31 J4
Chiclayo, Peru 124 B2
Chico, U.S.A. 112 F5
Chico →, Chubut, Argentina 128 B3
Chico →, Santa Cruz, Argentina 128 C3
Chicomo, Mozam. 85 C5
Chicontepec, Mexico 115 C5
Chicopee, U.S.A. 107 D12
Chicoutimi, Canada 99 C5
Chicualacuala, Mozam. 85 C5
Chidambaram, India 60 P11
Chidenguele, Mozam. 85 C5
Chidley, C., Canada 97 B13
Chiede, Angola 84 B2
Chiefs Pt., Canada 106 B3
Chiem Hoa, Vietnam 58 A5
Chiemsee, Germany 19 H8
Chiengi, Zambia 83 D2
Chiengmai = Chiang Mai, Thailand 58 C2
Chienti →, Italy 33 E10
Chieri, Italy 32 D4
Chiers →, France 25 C11
Chiese →, Italy 32 C7
Chieti, Italy 33 F11
Chièvres, Belgium 17 G3
Chifeng, China 51 C10
Chigirin, Ukraine 41 H7
Chignecto B., Canada 99 C7
Chigorodó, Colombia 120 B2
Chiguana, Bolivia 126 A2
Chiha-ri, N. Korea 51 E14
Chihli, G. of = Bo Hai, China 51 E10
Chihli, G. of = Po Hai, China 46 F15
Chihuahua, Mexico 114 B3
Chihuahua □, Mexico 114 B3
Chiili, Kazakstan 44 E7
Chik Bollapur, India 60 N10
Chikmagalur, India 60 N9
Chikwawa, Malawi 83 F3
Chilac, Mexico 115 D5
Chilako →, Canada 100 C4
Chilam Chavki, Pakistan 63 B6
Chilanga, Zambia 83 F2
Chilapa, Mexico 115 D5
Chilas, Pakistan 63 B6
Chilaw, Sri Lanka 60 R11
Chilcotin →, Canada 100 C4
Childers, Australia 91 D5
Childress, U.S.A. 109 H4
Chile ■, S. Amer. 128 B2
Chile Chico, Chile 128 C2
Chile Rise, Pac. Oc. 93 L18
Chilecito, Argentina 126 B2
Chilete, Peru 124 B2
Chilia, Braţul →, Romania 38 D12
Chililabombwe, Zambia 83 E2
Chilin = Jilin, China 51 C14
Chilka L., India 61 K14
Chilko →, Canada 100 C4
Chilko, L., Canada 100 C4
Chillagoe, Australia 90 B3
Chillán, Chile 126 D1
Chillicothe, Ill., U.S.A. 108 E10
Chillicothe, Mo., U.S.A. 108 F8
Chillicothe, Ohio, U.S.A. 104 F4
Chilliwack, Canada 100 D4
Chilo, India 62 F5
Chiloane, I., Mozam. 85 C5
Chiloé □, Chile 128 B2
Chiloé, I. de, Chile 128 B2
Chilpancingo, Mexico 115 D5
Chiltern Hills, U.K. 13 F7
Chilton, U.S.A. 104 C1
Chiluage, Angola 80 F4
Chilubi, Zambia 83 E2
Chilubula, Zambia 83 E3
Chilumba, Malawi 83 E3
Chilung, Taiwan 53 E13
Chilwa, L., Malawi 83 F4
Chimaltitán, Mexico 114 C4
Chimán, Panama 116 E4
Chimay, Belgium 17 H4
Chimbay, Uzbekistan 44 E6
Chimborazo, Ecuador 120 D2
Chimborazo □, Ecuador 120 D2
Chimbote, Peru 124 B2
Chimkent = Shymkent, Kazakstan 44 E7
Chimoio, Mozam. 83 F3
Chimpembe, Zambia 83 D2
Chin □, Burma 61 J18
Chin Ling Shan = Qinling Shandi, China 50 H5
China, Mexico 115 B5
China ■, Asia 50 E3
China Lake, U.S.A. 113 K9
Chinacota, Colombia 120 B3
Chinan = Jinan, China 50 F9
Chinandega, Nic. 116 D2
Chinati Peak, U.S.A. 109 K2
Chincha Alta, Peru 124 C2
Chinchilla, Australia 91 D5
Chinchilla de Monte Aragón, Spain 29 G3
Chinchón, Spain 28 E1
Chinchorro, Banco, Mexico 115 D7
Chinchou = Jinzhou, China 51 D11
Chincoteague, U.S.A. 104 G8
Chinde, Mozam. 83 F4
Chindo, S. Korea 51 G14
Chindwin →, Burma 61 J19
Chineni, India 63 C6
Chinga, Mozam. 83 F4
Chingola, Zambia 83 E2
Chingole, Malawi 83 E3
Ch'ingtao = Qingdao, China 51 F11
Chinguetti, Mauritania 74 D2
Chingune, Mozam. 85 C5
Chinhae, S. Korea 51 G15
Chinhanguanine, Mozam. 85 D5
Chinhoyi, Zimbabwe 83 F3
Chiniot, Pakistan 62 D5
Chínipas, Mexico 114 B3
Chinju, S. Korea 51 G15
Chinle, U.S.A. 111 H9
Chinmen, Taiwan 53 E13
Chinmen Tao, Taiwan 53 E13
Chinnampo, N. Korea 51 E13
Chino, Japan 49 G9
Chino, U.S.A. 113 L9
Chino Valley, U.S.A. 111 J7
Chinon, France 24 E7
Chinook, Canada 101 C6
Chinook, U.S.A. 110 B9
Chinsali, Zambia 83 E3
Chióggia, Italy 33 C9
Chíos = Khíos, Greece 39 L9
Chipata, Zambia 83 E3
Chipewyan L., Canada 101 B9
Chipinge, Zimbabwe 83 G3
Chipiona, Spain 31 J4
Chipley, U.S.A. 105 K3
Chipman, Canada 99 C6
Chipoka, Malawi 83 E3
Chippenham, U.K. 13 F5
Chippewa →, U.S.A. 108 C8
Chippewa Falls, U.S.A. 108 C9
Chiquián, Peru 124 C2
Chiquimula, Guatemala 116 D2
Chiquinquira, Colombia 120 B3
Chiquitos, Llanos de, Bolivia 125 D5
Chir →, Russia 43 F6
Chirala, India 60 M12
Chiramba, Mozam. 83 F3
Chirawa, India 62 E6
Chirchiq, Uzbekistan 44 E7
Chirgua →, Venezuela 120 B4
Chiricahua Peak, U.S.A. 111 L9
Chiriquí, G. de, Panama 116 E3
Chiriquí, L. de, Panama 116 E3
Chirivira Falls, Zimbabwe 83 G3
Chirmiri, India 61 H13
Chiromo, Malawi 81 H7
Chirpan, Bulgaria 38 G8
Chirripó Grande, Cerro, Costa Rica 116 E3
Chisamba, Zambia 83 E2
Chisapani Garhi, Nepal 61 F14
Chisasibi, Canada 98 B4
Ch'ishan, Taiwan 53 F13
Chisholm, Canada 100 C6
Chishtian Mandi, Pakistan 62 E5
Chishui, China 52 C5
Chishui He →, China 52 C5
Chisimaio, Somali Rep. 71 G8
Chisimba Falls, Zambia 83 E3
Chişinău, Moldova 41 J5
Chisone →, Italy 32 D4
Chisos Mts., U.S.A. 109 L3
Chistopol, Russia 42 C10
Chita, Colombia 120 B3
Chita, Russia 45 D12
Chitado, Angola 81 H2
Chitembo, Angola 81 G3
Chitipa, Malawi 83 D3
Chitose, Japan 48 C10
Chitral, Pakistan 60 B7
Chitré, Panama 116 E3
Chittagong, Bangla. 61 H17
Chittagong □, Bangla. 61 G17
Chittaurgarh, India 62 G6
Chittoor, India 60 N11
Chitungwiza, Zimbabwe 83 F3
Chiusa, Italy 33 B8
Chiusi, Italy 33 E8
Chiva, Spain 29 F4
Chivacoa, Venezuela 120 A4
Chivasso, Italy 32 C4
Chivay, Peru 124 D3
Chivhu, Zimbabwe 83 F3
Chivilcoy, Argentina 126 C4
Chiwanda, Tanzania 83 E3
Chixi, China 53 G9
Chizera, Zambia 83 E1
Chkalov = Orenburg, Russia 44 D6
Chkolovsk, Russia 42 B6
Chloride, U.S.A. 113 K12
Cho Bo, Vietnam 58 B5
Cho-do, N. Korea 51 E13
Cho Phuoc Hai, Vietnam 59 G6
Choba, Kenya 82 B4
Chobe National Park, Botswana 84 B3
Chochiwŏn, S. Korea 51 F14
Chociwel, Poland 20 B5
Chocó □, Colombia 120 B2
Chocontá, Colombia 120 B3
Choctawhatchee B., U.S.A. 103 D9
Chodecz, Poland 20 C9
Chodziez, Poland 20 C6
Choele Choel, Argentina 128 A3
Choisy-le-Roi, France 25 D9
Choix, Mexico 114 B3
Chojnice, Poland 20 B7
Chojnów, Poland 20 D5
Chōkai-San, Japan 48 E10
Choke, Ethiopia 77 E4
Chokurdakh, Russia 45 B15
Cholame, U.S.A. 112 K6
Cholet, France 24 E6
Choluteca, Honduras 116 D2
Choluteca →, Honduras 116 D2
Chom Bung, Thailand 58 F2
Chom Thong, Thailand 58 C2
Choma, Zambia 83 F2
Chomen Swamp, Ethiopia 77 F4
Chomun, India 62 F6
Chomutov, Czech. 20 E3
Chon Buri, Thailand 58 F3
Chon Thanh, Vietnam 59 G6
Chonan, S. Korea 51 F14
Chone, Ecuador 120 D2
Chong Kai, Cambodia 58 F4
Chong Mek, Thailand 58 E5
Chong'an, China 53 D12
Chongde, China 53 B13
Chŏngdo, S. Korea 51 G15
Chŏngha, S. Korea 51 F15
Chŏngjin, N. Korea 51 D15
Chŏngju, N. Korea 51 E13
Chŏngju, S. Korea 51 F14
Chongli, China 50 D8
Chongming, China 53 B13
Chongming Dao, China 53 B13
Chongoyape, Peru 124 B2
Chongqing, Sichuan, China 52 C6
Chongqing, Sichuan, China 52 B4
Chongren, China 53 D11
Chŏngŭp, S. Korea 51 G14
Chongzuo, China 52 F6
Chŏnju, S. Korea 51 G14
Chonos, Arch. de los, Chile 128 C2
Chop, Ukraine 41 H2
Chopim →, Brazil 127 B5
Chorbat La, India 63 B7
Chorley, U.K. 12 D5
Chornobyl, Ukraine 41 G6
Chornomorske, Ukraine 41 K7
Chorolque, Cerro, Bolivia 126 A2
Chorregon, Australia 90 C3
Chortkiv, Ukraine 41 H3
Chŏrwŏn, S. Korea 51 E14
Chorzów, Poland 20 E8
Chos-Malal, Argentina 126 D1
Chosan, N. Korea 51 D13
Choszczno, Poland 20 B5
Chota, Peru 124 B2
Choteau, U.S.A. 110 C7
Chotila, India 62 H4
Chowchilla, U.S.A. 111 H3
Choybalsan, Mongolia 54 B6
Christchurch, N.Z. 87 K4
Christchurch, U.K. 13 G6
Christian I., Canada 106 B4
Christiana, S. Africa 84 D4
Christiansfeld, Denmark 11 J3
Christiansted, Virgin Is. 117 C7
Christie B., Canada 101 A6
Christina →, Canada 101 B6
Christmas Cr. →, Australia 88 C4
Christmas Creek, Australia 88 C4
Christmas I. = Kiritimati, Kiribati 93 G12
Christmas I., Ind. Oc. 92 J2
Christopher L., Australia 89 D4
Chrudim, Czech. 20 F5
Chrzanów, Poland 20 E9
Chtimba, Malawi 83 E3
Chu = Shu, Kazakstan 44 E8
Chu → = Shu →, Kazakstan 46 E10
Chu →, Vietnam 58 C5
Chu Chua, Canada 100 C4
Chu Lai, Vietnam 58 E7
Chu Xian, China 53 A12
Ch'uanchou = Quanzhou, China 53 E12
Chuankou, China 50 G6
Chūbu □, Japan 49 F8
Chubut □, Argentina 128 B3
Chubut →, Argentina 128 B3
Chuchi L., Canada 100 B4
Chudovo, Russia 40 C6
Chudskoye, Oz., Russia 9 G22
Chūgoku □, Japan 49 G6
Chūgoku-Sanchi, Japan 49 G6
Chuguyev = Chuhuyiv, Ukraine 41 H9
Chugwater, U.S.A. 108 E2
Chuhuyiv, Ukraine 41 H9
Chukchi Sea, Russia 45 C19
Chukotskoye Nagorye, Russia 45 C18
Chula Vista, U.S.A. 113 N9
Chulman, Russia 45 D13
Chulucanas, Peru 124 B1
Chulumani, Bolivia 124 D4
Chulym →, Russia 44 D9
Chum Phae, Thailand 58 D4
Chum Saeng, Thailand 58 E3
Chuma, Bolivia 124 D4
Chumar, India 63 C8
Chumbicha, Argentina 126 B2
Chumerna, Bulgaria 38 G8
Chumikan, Russia 45 D14
Chumphon, Thailand 59 G2
Chumpi, Peru 124 D3
Chumuare, Mozam. 83 E3
Chumunjin, S. Korea 51 F15
Chuna →, Russia 45 D10
Chun'an, China 53 C12
Chunchŏn, S. Korea 51 F14
Chunchura, India 63 H13
Chunga, Zambia 83 F2
Chunggang-ŭp, N. Korea 51 D14
Chunghwa, N. Korea 51 E13
Chungju, S. Korea 51 F14
Chungking = Chongqing, China 52 C6
Chungli, Taiwan 53 E13
Chungmu, S. Korea 51 G15
Chungt'iaoshan = Zhongtiao Shan, China 50 G6
Chungyang Shanmo, Taiwan 53 F13
Chunian, Pakistan 62 D6
Chunya, Tanzania 83 D3
Chunya □, Tanzania 82 D3
Chunyang, China 51 C15
Chuquibamba, Peru 124 D3
Chuquibambilla, Peru 124 C3
Chuquicamata, Chile 126 A2
Chuquisaca □, Bolivia 125 E5
Chur, Switz. 23 C9
Churachandpur, India 61 G18
Churchill, Canada 101 B10
Churchill →, Man., Canada 101 B10
Churchill →, Nfld., Canada 99 B7
Churchill, C., Canada 101 B10
Churchill Falls, Canada 99 B7
Churchill L., Canada 101 B7
Churchill Pk., Canada 100 B3
Churfisten, Switz. 23 B8
Churu, India 62 E6
Churún Merú = Angel Falls, Venezuela 121 B5
Churwalden, Switz. 23 C9
Chushal, India 63 C8
Chusovoy, Russia 44 D6
Chuuronjang, N. Korea 51 D15
Chuvash Republic □ = Chuvashia □, Russia 42 C8
Chuvashia □, Russia 42 C8
Chuwārtah, Iraq 64 C5
Chuxiong, China 52 E3
Ci Xian, China 50 F8
Ciacova, Romania 38 D4
Cianjur, Indonesia 57 G12
Cibadok, Indonesia 57 G12
Cibatu, Indonesia 57 G12
Cibola, U.S.A. 113 M12
Cícero, U.S.A. 104 E2
Cícero Dantas, Brazil 122 D4
Cidacos →, Spain 28 C3

Cide, *Turkey* 66 B5
Ciechanów, *Poland* 20 C10
Ciego de Avila, *Cuba* 116 B4
Ciénaga, *Colombia* 120 A3
Ciénaga de Oro, *Colombia* 120 B2
Cienfuegos, *Cuba* 116 B3
Cieplice Śląskie Zdrój, *Poland* 20 E5
Cierp, *France* 26 F4
Cíes, Is., *Spain* 30 C2
Cieszyn, *Poland* 20 F8
Cieza, *Spain* 29 G3
Çifteler, *Turkey* 66 C4
Cifuentes, *Spain* 28 E2
Cihanbeyli, *Turkey* 66 C5
Cihuatlán, *Mexico* 114 D4
Cijara, Pantano de, *Spain* 31 F6
Cijulang, *Indonesia* 57 G13
Cikajang, *Indonesia* 57 G12
Cikampek, *Indonesia* 57 G12
Cilacap, *Indonesia* 57 G13
Çıldır, *Turkey* 67 B10
Çıldır Gölü, *Turkey* 67 B10
Cili, *China* 53 C8
Cilicia, *Turkey* 66 D5
Cill Chainnigh = Kilkenny, *Ireland* 15 D4
Cilo Dağı, *Turkey* 67 D10
Cima, *U.S.A.* 113 K11
Cimahi, *Indonesia* 57 G12
Cimarron, *Kans., U.S.A.* 109 G4
Cimarron, *N. Mex., U.S.A.* 109 G2
Cimarron →, *U.S.A.* 109 G6
Cimişlia, *Moldova* 41 J5
Cimone, Mte., *Italy* 32 D7
Cîmpina, *Romania* 38 D8
Cîmpulung, *Argeş, Romania* 38 D8
Cîmpulung, *Suceava, Romania* 38 B8
Çinar, *Turkey* 67 D9
Cinca →, *Spain* 28 D5
Cincinnati, *U.S.A.* 104 F3
Cîndeşti, *Romania* 38 D9
Çine, *Turkey* 66 D3
Ciney, *Belgium* 17 H6
Cíngoli, *Italy* 33 E10
Cinigiano, *Italy* 33 F8
Cinto, Mte., *France* 27 F12
Ciorani, *Romania* 38 E9
Čiovo, *Croatia* 33 E13
Cipó, *Brazil* 122 D4
Circeo, Mte., *Italy* 34 A6
Çirçir, *Turkey* 66 C7
Circle, *Alaska, U.S.A.* 96 B5
Circle, *Mont., U.S.A.* 108 B2
Circleville, *Ohio, U.S.A.* 104 F4
Circleville, *Utah, U.S.A.* 111 G7
Cirebon, *Indonesia* 57 G13
Cirencester, *U.K.* 13 F6
Cirey-sur-Vezouze, *France* 25 D13
Ciriè, *Italy* 32 C4
Cirium, *Cyprus* 37 E11
Cirò, *Italy* 35 C10
Ciron →, *France* 26 D3
Cisco, *U.S.A.* 109 J5
Cislău, *Romania* 38 D9
Cisneros, *Colombia* 120 B2
Cisterna di Latina, *Italy* 34 A5
Cisternino, *Italy* 35 B10
Citaré →, *Brazil* 121 C7
Citeli-Ckaro = Tsiteli-Tsqaro, *Georgia* 43 K8
Citlaltépetl, *Mexico* 115 D5
Citrus Heights, *U.S.A.* 112 G5
Citrusdal, *S. Africa* 84 E2
Città della Pieve, *Italy* 33 F9
Città di Castello, *Italy* 33 E9
Città Sant' Angelo, *Italy* 33 F11
Cittadella, *Italy* 33 C8
Cittaducale, *Italy* 33 F9
Cittanova, *Italy* 35 D9
City of Aberdeen □, *U.K.* 14 D6
City of Edinburgh □, *U.K.* 14 F5
City of Glasgow □, *U.K.* 14 F4
Ciucaş, *Romania* 38 D8
Ciudad Altamirano, *Mexico* 114 D4
Ciudad Bolívar, *Venezuela* 121 B5
Ciudad Camargo, *Mexico* 114 B3
Ciudad Chetumal, *Mexico* 115 D7
Ciudad de Valles, *Mexico* 115 C5
Ciudad del Carmen, *Mexico* 115 D6
Ciudad del Este, *Paraguay* 127 B5
Ciudad Delicias = Delicias, *Mexico* 114 B3
Ciudad Guayana, *Venezuela* 121 B5
Ciudad Guerrero, *Mexico* 114 B3
Ciudad Guzmán, *Mexico* 114 D4
Ciudad Juárez, *Mexico* 114 A3
Ciudad Madero, *Mexico* 115 C5
Ciudad Mante, *Mexico* 115 C5
Ciudad Obregón, *Mexico* 114 B3
Ciudad Ojeda, *Venezuela* 120 A3
Ciudad Real, *Spain* 31 G7
Ciudad Real □, *Spain* 31 G7
Ciudad Rodrigo, *Spain* 30 E4
Ciudad Trujillo = Santo Domingo, *Dom. Rep.* 117 C6
Ciudad Victoria, *Mexico* 115 C5
Ciudadela, *Spain* 36 B10
Ciulniţa, *Romania* 38 E10
Civa Burnu, *Turkey* 66 B7
Cividale del Friuli, *Italy* 33 B10
Cívita Castellana, *Italy* 33 F9
Civitanova Marche, *Italy* 33 E10
Civitavécchia, *Italy* 33 F8
Civitella del Tronto, *Italy* 33 F10
Civray, *France* 26 B4
Çivril, *Turkey* 66 C3
Cixerri →, *Italy* 34 C1
Cizre, *Turkey* 67 D10
Clackmannan □, *U.K.* 14 E5
Clacton-on-Sea, *U.K.* 13 F9
Clain →, *France* 24 F7
Claire, L., *Canada* 100 B6
Clairemont, *U.S.A.* 109 J4
Clairton, *U.S.A.* 106 F5
Clairvaux-les-Lacs, *France* 27 B9
Clallam Bay, *U.S.A.* 112 B2
Clamecy, *France* 25 E10
Clanton, *U.S.A.* 105 J2
Clanwilliam, *S. Africa* 84 E2
Clara, *Ireland* 15 C4
Clara →, *Australia* 90 B3
Claraville, *U.S.A.* 113 K8
Clare, *Australia* 91 E2
Clare, *U.S.A.* 104 D3
Clare □, *Ireland* 15 D3
Clare →, *Ireland* 15 C2
Clare I., *Ireland* 15 C2
Claremont, *Calif., U.S.A.* 113 L9
Claremont, *N.H., U.S.A.* 107 C12
Claremont Pt., *Australia* 90 A3
Claremore, *U.S.A.* 109 G7
Claremorris, *Ireland* 15 C3
Clarence →, *Australia* 91 D5
Clarence →, *N.Z.* 87 K4
Clarence, I., *Chile* 128 D2
Clarence I., *Antarctica* 5 C18
Clarence Str., *Australia* 88 B5
Clarence Str., *U.S.A.* 100 B2
Clarence Town, *Bahamas* 117 B5
Clarendon, *Ark., U.S.A.* 109 H9
Clarendon, *Tex., U.S.A.* 109 H4
Clarenville, *Canada* 99 C9
Claresholm, *Canada* 100 C6
Clarie Coast, *Antarctica* 5 C9
Clarinda, *U.S.A.* 108 E7
Clarion, *Iowa, U.S.A.* 108 D8
Clarion, *Pa., U.S.A.* 106 E5
Clarion →, *U.S.A.* 106 E5
Clark, *U.S.A.* 108 C6
Clark, Pt., *Canada* 106 B3
Clark Fork, *U.S.A.* 110 B5
Clark Fork →, *U.S.A.* 110 B5
Clark Hill Res., *U.S.A.* 105 J4
Clarkdale, *U.S.A.* 111 J7
Clarke City, *Canada* 99 B6
Clarke I., *Australia* 90 G4
Clarke L., *Canada* 101 C7
Clarke Ra., *Australia* 90 C4
Clark's Fork →, *U.S.A.* 110 D9
Clark's Harbour, *Canada* 99 D6
Clarks Summit, *U.S.A.* 107 E9
Clarksburg, *U.S.A.* 104 F5
Clarksdale, *U.S.A.* 109 H9
Clarkston, *U.S.A.* 110 C5
Clarksville, *Ark., U.S.A.* 109 H8
Clarksville, *Tenn., U.S.A.* 105 G2
Clarksville, *Tex., U.S.A.* 109 J7
Claro →, *Brazil* 123 E1
Clatskanie, *U.S.A.* 112 D3
Claude, *U.S.A.* 109 H4
Claveria, *Phil.* 55 B4
Clay, *U.S.A.* 112 G5
Clay Center, *U.S.A.* 108 F6
Claypool, *U.S.A.* 111 K8
Claysville, *U.S.A.* 106 F4
Clayton, *Idaho, U.S.A.* 110 D6
Clayton, *N. Mex., U.S.A.* 109 G3
Cle Elum, *U.S.A.* 110 C3
Clear, C., *Ireland* 15 E2
Clear I., *Ireland* 15 E2
Clear L., *U.S.A.* 112 F4
Clear Lake, *S. Dak., U.S.A.* 108 C6
Clear Lake, *Wash., U.S.A.* 110 B2
Clear Lake Reservoir, *U.S.A.* 110 F3
Clearfield, *Pa., U.S.A.* 104 E6
Clearfield, *Utah, U.S.A.* 110 F7
Clearlake Highlands, *U.S.A.* 112 G4
Clearmont, *U.S.A.* 110 D10
Clearwater, *Canada* 100 C4
Clearwater, *U.S.A.* 105 M4
Clearwater →, *Alta., Canada* 100 C6
Clearwater →, *Alta., Canada* 101 B6
Clearwater Cr. →, *Canada* 100 A3
Clearwater Mts., *U.S.A.* 110 C6
Clearwater Prov. Park, *Canada* 101 C8
Cleburne, *U.S.A.* 109 J6
Cleethorpes, *U.K.* 12 D7
Cleeve Hill, *U.K.* 13 F6
Clelles, *France* 27 D9
Clemency, *Lux.* 17 J7
Clerke Reef, *Australia* 88 C2
Clermont, *Australia* 90 C4
Clermont, *France* 25 C9
Clermont-en-Argonne, *France* 25 C12
Clermont-Ferrand, *France* 26 C7
Clermont-l'Hérault, *France* 26 E7
Clerval, *France* 25 E13
Clervaux, *Lux.* 17 H8
Cléry-St.-André, *France* 25 E8
Cles, *Italy* 32 B8
Cleveland, *Australia* 91 D5
Cleveland, *Miss., U.S.A.* 109 J9
Cleveland, *Ohio, U.S.A.* 106 E3
Cleveland, *Okla., U.S.A.* 109 G6
Cleveland, *Tenn., U.S.A.* 105 H3
Cleveland, *Tex., U.S.A.* 109 K7
Cleveland, C., *Australia* 90 B4
Cleveland Heights, *U.S.A.* 106 E3
Clevelândia, *Brazil* 127 B5
Clevelândia do Norte, *Brazil* 121 C7
Clew B., *Ireland* 15 C2
Clewiston, *U.S.A.* 105 M5
Clifden, *Ireland* 15 C1
Clifden, *N.Z.* 87 M1
Cliffdell, *U.S.A.* 112 D5
Clifton, *Australia* 91 D5
Clifton, *Ariz., U.S.A.* 111 K9
Clifton, *Tex., U.S.A.* 109 K6
Clifton Beach, *Australia* 90 B4
Clifton Forge, *U.S.A.* 104 G6
Clifton Hills, *Australia* 91 D2
Climax, *Canada* 101 D7
Clinch →, *U.S.A.* 105 H3
Clingmans Dome, *U.S.A.* 105 H4
Clint, *U.S.A.* 111 L10
Clinton, *B.C., Canada* 100 C4
Clinton, *Ont., Canada* 98 D3
Clinton, *N.Z.* 87 M2
Clinton, *Ark., U.S.A.* 109 H8
Clinton, *Ill., U.S.A.* 108 E10
Clinton, *Ind., U.S.A.* 104 F2
Clinton, *Iowa, U.S.A.* 108 E9
Clinton, *Mass., U.S.A.* 107 D13
Clinton, *Mo., U.S.A.* 108 F8
Clinton, *N.C., U.S.A.* 105 H6
Clinton, *Okla., U.S.A.* 109 H5
Clinton, *S.C., U.S.A.* 105 H5
Clinton, *Tenn., U.S.A.* 105 G3
Clinton, *Wash., U.S.A.* 112 C4
Clinton C., *Australia* 90 C5
Clinton Colden L., *Canada* 96 B9
Clintonville, *U.S.A.* 108 C10
Clipperton, I., *Pac. Oc.* 93 F17
Clisson, *France* 24 E5
Clive L., *Canada* 100 A5
Cliza, *Bolivia* 125 D4
Cloates, Pt., *Australia* 88 D1
Clocolan, *S. Africa* 85 D4
Clodomira, *Argentina* 126 B3
Clonakilty, *Ireland* 15 E3
Clonakilty B., *Ireland* 15 E3
Cloncurry, *Australia* 90 C3
Cloncurry →, *Australia* 90 B3
Clones, *Ireland* 15 B4
Clonmel, *Ireland* 15 D4
Cloppenburg, *Germany* 18 C4
Cloquet, *U.S.A.* 108 B8
Clorinda, *Argentina* 126 B4
Cloud Peak, *U.S.A.* 110 D10
Cloudcroft, *U.S.A.* 111 K11
Cloverdale, *U.S.A.* 112 G4
Clovis, *Calif., U.S.A.* 111 H4
Clovis, *N. Mex., U.S.A.* 109 H3
Cloyes-sur-le-Loir, *France* 24 E8
Cluj-Napoca, *Romania* 38 C6
Clunes, *Australia* 91 F3
Cluny, *France* 27 B8
Cluses, *France* 27 B10
Clusone, *Italy* 32 C6
Clutha →, *N.Z.* 87 M2
Clwyd →, *U.K.* 12 D4
Clyde, *N.Z.* 87 L2
Clyde, *U.S.A.* 106 C8
Clyde →, *U.K.* 14 F4
Clyde, Firth of, *U.K.* 14 F4
Clyde River, *Canada* 97 A13
Clydebank, *U.K.* 14 F4
Clymer, *U.S.A.* 106 D5
Côa →, *Portugal* 30 D3
Coachella, *U.S.A.* 113 M10
Coachella Canal, *U.S.A.* 113 N12
Coahoma, *U.S.A.* 109 J4
Coahuayana →, *Mexico* 114 D4
Coahuayutla, *Mexico* 114 D4
Coahuila □, *Mexico* 114 B4
Coal →, *Canada* 100 B3
Coalane, *Mozam.* 83 F4
Coalcomán, *Mexico* 114 D4
Coaldale, *Canada* 100 D6
Coalgate, *U.S.A.* 109 H6
Coalinga, *U.S.A.* 111 H3
Coalville, *U.K.* 12 E6
Coalville, *U.S.A.* 110 F8
Coaraci, *Brazil* 123 D4
Coari, *Brazil* 121 D5
Coari →, *Brazil* 121 D5
Coari, L. de, *Brazil* 121 D5
Coast □, *Kenya* 82 C4
Coast Mts., *Canada* 100 C3
Coast Ranges, *U.S.A.* 112 G4
Coatbridge, *U.K.* 14 F4
Coatepec, *Mexico* 115 D5
Coatepeque, *Guatemala* 116 D1
Coatesville, *U.S.A.* 104 F8
Coaticook, *Canada* 99 C5
Coats I., *Canada* 97 B11
Coats Land, *Antarctica* 5 D1
Coatzacoalcos, *Mexico* 115 D6
Cobalt, *Canada* 98 C4
Cobán, *Guatemala* 116 C1
Cobar, *Australia* 91 E4
Cóbh, *Ireland* 15 E3
Cobham, *Australia* 91 E3
Cobija, *Bolivia* 124 C4
Cobleskill, *U.S.A.* 107 D10
Coboconk, *Canada* 106 B6
Cobourg, *Canada* 98 D4
Cobourg Pen., *Australia* 88 B5
Cobram, *Australia* 91 F4
Cobre, *U.S.A.* 110 F6
Cóbué, *Mozam.* 83 E3
Coburg, *Germany* 19 E6
Coca, *Spain* 30 D6
Coca →, *Ecuador* 120 D2
Cocachacra, *Peru* 124 D3
Cocal, *Brazil* 122 B3
Cocanada = Kakinada, *India* 61 L13
Cocentaina, *Spain* 29 G4
Cochabamba, *Bolivia* 125 D4
Coche, I., *Venezuela* 121 A5
Cochem, *Germany* 19 E3
Cochemane, *Mozam.* 83 F3
Cochin, *India* 60 Q10
Cochin China = Nam-Phan, *Vietnam* 59 G6
Cochise, *U.S.A.* 111 K9
Cochran, *U.S.A.* 105 J4
Cochrane, *Alta., Canada* 100 C6
Cochrane, *Ont., Canada* 98 C3
Cochrane →, *Canada* 101 B8
Cochrane, L., *Chile* 128 C2
Cockburn, *Australia* 91 E3
Cockburn, Canal, *Chile* 128 D2
Cockburn I., *Canada* 98 C3
Cockburn Ra., *Australia* 88 C4
Cocklebiddy Motel, *Australia* 89 F4
Coco →, *Cent. Amer.* 116 D3
Coco, Pta., *Colombia* 120 C2
Cocoa, *U.S.A.* 105 L5
Cocobeach, *Gabon* 80 D1
Côcos, *Brazil* 123 D3
Côcos →, *Brazil* 123 D3
Cocos, I. del, *Pac. Oc.* 93 G19
Cocos Is., *Ind. Oc.* 92 J1
Cod, C., *U.S.A.* 103 B13
Codajás, *Brazil* 121 D5
Codera, C., *Venezuela* 120 A4
Coderre, *Canada* 101 C7
Codigoro, *Italy* 33 D9
Codó, *Brazil* 122 B3
Codogno, *Italy* 32 C6
Codpa, *Chile* 124 D4
Codroipo, *Italy* 33 C10
Cody, *U.S.A.* 110 D9
Coe Hill, *Canada* 98 D4
Coelemu, *Chile* 126 D1
Coelho Neto, *Brazil* 122 B3
Coen, *Australia* 90 A3
Coeroeni →, *Surinam* 121 C6
Coesfeld, *Germany* 18 D3
Cœur d'Alene, *U.S.A.* 110 C5
Cœur d'Alene L., *U.S.A.* 110 C5
Coevorden, *Neths.* 16 C9
Cofete, *Canary Is.* 36 F5
Coffeyville, *U.S.A.* 109 G7
Coffin B., *Australia* 91 E2
Coffin Bay Peninsula, *Australia* 91 E2
Coffs Harbour, *Australia* 91 E5
Cofrentes, *Spain* 29 F3
Cogealac, *Romania* 38 E11
Coghinas →, *Italy* 34 B1
Coghinas, L. di, *Italy* 34 B2
Cognac, *France* 26 C3
Cogne, *Italy* 32 C4
Cogolludo, *Spain* 28 E1
Cohagen, *U.S.A.* 110 C10
Cohoes, *U.S.A.* 107 D11
Cohuna, *Australia* 91 F3
Coiba, I., *Panama* 116 E3
Coig →, *Argentina* 128 D3
Coihaique, *Chile* 128 C2
Coimbatore, *India* 60 P10
Coimbra, *Brazil* 125 D6
Coimbra, *Portugal* 30 E2
Coimbra □, *Portugal* 30 E2
Coín, *Spain* 31 J6
Coipasa, L. de, *Bolivia* 124 D4
Coipasa, Salar de, *Bolivia* 124 D4
Cojata, *Peru* 124 D4
Cojedes □, *Venezuela* 120 B4
Cojedes →, *Venezuela* 120 B4
Cojimies, *Ecuador* 120 C1
Cojocna, *Romania* 38 C6
Cojutepequé, *El Salv.* 116 D2
Cokeville, *U.S.A.* 110 E8
Colac, *Australia* 91 F3
Colares, *Portugal* 31 G1
Colatina, *Brazil* 123 E3
Colbeck, C., *Antarctica* 5 D13
Colbinabbin, *Australia* 91 F3
Colborne, *Canada* 106 B7
Colby, *U.S.A.* 108 F4
Colchagua □, *Chile* 126 C1
Colchester, *U.K.* 13 F8
Coldstream, *U.K.* 14 F6
Coldwater, *Canada* 106 B5
Coldwater, *U.S.A.* 109 G5
Colebrook, *Australia* 90 G4
Colebrook, *U.S.A.* 107 B13
Coleman, *Canada* 100 D6
Coleman, *U.S.A.* 109 K5
Coleman →, *Australia* 90 B3
Colenso, *S. Africa* 85 D4
Coleraine, *Australia* 91 F3
Coleraine, *U.K.* 15 A5
Coleraine □, *U.K.* 15 A5
Coleridge, L., *N.Z.* 87 K3
Colesberg, *S. Africa* 84 E4
Coleville, *U.S.A.* 112 G7
Colfax, *Calif., U.S.A.* 112 F6
Colfax, *La., U.S.A.* 109 K8
Colfax, *Wash., U.S.A.* 110 C5
Colhué Huapi, L., *Argentina* 128 C3
Cólico, *Italy* 32 B6
Coligny, *France* 27 B9
Coligny, *S. Africa* 85 D4
Colima, *Mexico* 114 D4
Colima □, *Mexico* 114 D4
Colima, Nevado de, *Mexico* 114 D4
Colina, *Chile* 126 C1
Colina do Norte, *Guinea-Biss.* 78 C2
Colinas, *Goiás, Brazil* 123 D2
Colinas, *Maranhão, Brazil* 122 C3
Coll, *U.K.* 14 E2
Collaguasi, *Chile* 126 A2
Collarada, Peña, *Spain* 28 C4
Collarenebri, *Australia* 91 D4
Collbran, *U.S.A.* 111 G10
Colle di Val d'Elsa, *Italy* 33 E8
Colle Salvetti, *Italy* 32 E7
Colle Sannita, *Italy* 35 A7
Collécchio, *Italy* 32 D7
Colleen Bawn, *Zimbabwe* 83 G2
College Park, *U.S.A.* 105 J3
College Station, *U.S.A.* 109 K6
Collette, *Canada* 99 C6
Collie, *Australia* 89 F2
Collier B., *Australia* 88 C3
Collier Ra., *Australia* 88 D2
Colline Metallifere, *Italy* 32 E7
Collingwood, *Canada* 98 D3
Collingwood, *N.Z.* 87 J4
Collins, *Canada* 98 B2
Collinsville, *Australia* 90 C4
Collipulli, *Chile* 126 D1
Collo, *Algeria* 75 A6
Collonges, *France* 27 B9
Collooney, *Ireland* 15 B3
Colmar, *France* 25 D14
Colmars, *France* 27 D10
Colmenar, *Spain* 31 J6
Colmenar de Oreja, *Spain* 28 E1
Colmenar Viejo, *Spain* 30 E7
Colne, *U.K.* 12 D5
Colo →, *Australia* 91 E5
Cologna Véneta, *Italy* 33 C8
Cologne = Köln, *Germany* 18 E2
Colom, I., *Spain* 36 B11
Coloma, *U.S.A.* 112 G6
Colomb-Béchar = Béchar, *Algeria* 75 B4
Colombey-les-Belles, *France* 25 D12
Colombey-les-Deux-Églises, *France* 25 D11
Colômbia, *Brazil* 123 F2
Colombia ■, *S. Amer.* 120 C3
Colombian Basin, *S. Amer.* 94 H12
Colombier, *Switz.* 22 C3
Colombo, *Sri Lanka* 60 R11
Colome, *U.S.A.* 108 D5
Colón, *Argentina* 126 C4
Colón, *Cuba* 116 B3
Colón, *Panama* 116 E4
Colón, *Peru* 124 A1
Colona, *Australia* 89 F5
Colonella, *Italy* 33 F10
Colonia, *Uruguay* 126 C4
Colonia de San Jordi, *Spain* 36 B9
Colonia Dora, *Argentina* 126 B3
Colonial Heights, *U.S.A.* 104 G7
Colonne, C. delle, *Italy* 35 C10
Colonsay, *Canada* 101 C7
Colonsay, *U.K.* 14 E2
Colorado □, *U.S.A.* 111 G10
Colorado →, *Argentina* 128 A4
Colorado →, *N. Amer.* 111 L6
Colorado →, *U.S.A.* 109 L7
Colorado City, *U.S.A.* 109 J4
Colorado Desert, *U.S.A.* 102 D3
Colorado Plateau, *U.S.A.* 111 H8
Colorado River Aqueduct, *U.S.A.* 113 L12
Colorado Springs, *U.S.A.* 108 F2
Colorno, *Italy* 32 D7
Colotlán, *Mexico* 114 C4
Colquechaca, *Bolivia* 125 D4
Colton, *N.Y., U.S.A.* 107 B10
Colton, *Wash., U.S.A.* 110 C5
Columbia, *La., U.S.A.* 109 J8
Columbia, *Miss., U.S.A.* 109 K10
Columbia, *Mo., U.S.A.* 108 F8
Columbia, *Pa., U.S.A.* 107 F8
Columbia, *S.C., U.S.A.* 105 H5
Columbia, *Tenn., U.S.A.* 105 H2
Columbia →, *U.S.A.* 110 C1
Columbia, C., *Canada* 4 A4
Columbia, District of □, *U.S.A.* 104 F7
Columbia, Mt., *Canada* 100 C5
Columbia Basin, *U.S.A.* 110 C4
Columbia Falls, *U.S.A.* 110 B6
Columbia Heights, *U.S.A.* 108 C8
Columbiana, *U.S.A.* 106 F4
Columbretes, Is., *Spain* 28 F5
Columbus, *Ga., U.S.A.* 105 J3
Columbus, *Ind., U.S.A.* 104 F3
Columbus, *Kans., U.S.A.* 109 G7
Columbus, *Miss., U.S.A.* 105 J1
Columbus, *Mont., U.S.A.* 110 D9
Columbus, *N. Dak., U.S.A.* 108 A3
Columbus, *N. Mex., U.S.A.* 111 L10
Columbus, *Nebr., U.S.A.* 108 E6
Columbus, *Ohio, U.S.A.* 104 F4
Columbus, *Tex., U.S.A.* 109 L6
Columbus, *Wis., U.S.A.* 108 D10
Colunga, *Spain* 30 B5
Colusa, *U.S.A.* 112 F4
Colville, *U.S.A.* 110 B5
Colville →, *U.S.A.* 96 A4
Colville, C., *N.Z.* 87 G5

Colwyn Bay, U.K. 12 D4
Coma, Ethiopia 77 F4
Comácchio, Italy 33 D9
Comalcalco, Mexico 115 D6
Comallo, Argentina 128 B2
Comanche, Okla., U.S.A. 109 H6
Comanche, Tex., U.S.A. 109 K5
Comandante Luis Piedrabuena, Argentina 128 C3
Comănești, Romania 38 C9
Comarapa, Bolivia 125 D5
Comayagua, Honduras 116 D2
Combahee →, U.S.A. 105 J5
Combeaufontaine, France 25 E12
Comber, Canada 106 D2
Comblain-au-Pont, Belgium 17 H7
Combles, France 25 B9
Combourg, France 24 D5
Combronde, France 26 C7
Comeragh Mts., Ireland 15 D4
Comet, Australia 90 C4
Comilla, Bangla. 61 H17
Comines, Belgium 17 G1
Comino, Malta 37 C1
Comino, C., Italy 34 B2
Cómiso, Italy 35 F7
Comitán, Mexico 115 D6
Commentry, France 26 B6
Commerce, Ga., U.S.A. 105 H4
Commerce, Tex., U.S.A. 109 J7
Commercy, France 25 D12
Commewijne □, Surinam 121 B7
Committee B., Canada 97 B11
Commonwealth B., Antarctica 5 C10
Commoron Cr. →, Australia 91 D5
Communism Pk. = Kommunizma, Pik, Tajikistan 44 F8
Como, Italy 32 C6
Como, L. di, Italy 32 B6
Comodoro Rivadavia, Argentina 128 C3
Comorin, C., India 60 Q10
Comoro Is. = Comoros ■, Ind. Oc. 70 H8
Comoros ■, Ind. Oc. 70 H8
Comox, Canada 100 D4
Compiègne, France 25 C9
Comporta, Portugal 31 G2
Compostela, Mexico 114 C4
Comprida, I., Brazil 127 A6
Compton, U.S.A. 113 M8
Compton Downs, Australia 91 E4
Comrat, Moldova 41 J5
Con Cuong, Vietnam 58 C5
Con Son, Vietnam 59 H6
Cona Niyeu, Argentina 128 B3
Conakry, Guinea 78 D2
Conara Junction, Australia 90 G4
Concarneau, France 24 E3
Conceição, Brazil 122 C4
Conceição, Mozam. 83 F4
Conceição da Barra, Brazil 123 E4
Conceição do Araguaia, Brazil 122 C2
Conceição do Canindé, Brazil 122 C3
Concepción, Argentina 126 B2
Concepción, Bolivia 125 D5
Concepción, Chile 126 D1
Concepción, Mexico 115 D6
Concepción, Paraguay 126 A4
Concepción, Peru 124 C2
Concepción □, Chile 126 D1
Concepción →, Mexico 114 A2
Concepción, Est. de, Chile 128 D2
Concepción, L., Bolivia 125 D5
Concepción, Punta, Mexico 114 B2
Concepción del Oro, Mexico 114 C4
Concepción del Uruguay, Argentina 126 C4
Conception, Pt., U.S.A. 113 L6
Conception B., Namibia 84 C1
Conception I., Bahamas 117 B4
Concession, Zimbabwe 83 F3
Conchas Dam, U.S.A. 109 H2
Conche, Canada 99 B8
Conches-en-Ouche, France 24 D7
Concho, U.S.A. 111 J9
Concho →, U.S.A. 109 K5
Conchos →, Chihuahua, Mexico 114 B4
Conchos →, Tamaulipas, Mexico 115 B5
Concord, Calif., U.S.A. 112 H4
Concord, N.C., U.S.A. 105 H5
Concord, N.H., U.S.A. 107 C13
Concordia, Argentina 126 C4
Concórdia, Brazil 120 D4
Concordia, Mexico 114 C3
Concordia, U.S.A. 108 F6
Concots, France 26 D5
Concrete, U.S.A. 110 B3
Condamine, Australia 91 D5
Condat, France 26 C6
Conde, Brazil 123 D4
Conde, U.S.A. 108 C5
Condé-sur-l'Escaut, France 25 B10
Condé-sur-Noireau, France 24 D6
Condeúba, Brazil 123 D3
Condobolin, Australia 91 E4
Condom, France 26 E4
Condon, U.S.A. 110 D3
Condove, Italy 32 C4
Conegliano, Italy 33 C9
Conejera, I., Spain 36 B9
Conejos, Mexico 114 B4
Conflans-en-Jarnisy, France 25 C12
Confolens, France 26 B4
Confuso →, Paraguay 126 B4
Congjiang, China 52 E7
Congleton, U.K. 12 D5
Congo = Zaïre →, Africa 80 F2
Congo, Brazil 122 C4
Congo (Kinshasa) = Zaïre ■, Africa 80 E4
Congo ■, Africa 80 E3
Congo Basin, Africa 70 G6
Congonhas, Brazil 123 F3
Congress, U.S.A. 111 J7
Conil, Spain 31 J4
Coniston, Canada 98 C3
Conjeeveram = Kanchipuram, India 60 N11
Conjuboy, Australia 90 B3
Conklin, Canada 101 B6
Conlea, Australia 91 E3
Conn, L., Ireland 15 B2
Connacht □, Ireland 15 C3
Conneaut, U.S.A. 106 E4
Connecticut □, U.S.A. 107 E12
Connecticut →, U.S.A. 107 E12
Connell, U.S.A. 110 C4
Connellsville, U.S.A. 106 F5
Connemara, Ireland 15 C2
Connemaugh →, U.S.A. 106 F5
Connerré, France 24 D7
Connersville, U.S.A. 104 F3
Connors Ra., Australia 90 C4
Conoble, Australia 91 E3
Cononaco →, Ecuador 120 D2
Cononbridge, U.K. 14 D4
Conquest, Canada 101 C7
Conrad, U.S.A. 110 B8
Conran, C., Australia 91 F4
Conroe, U.S.A. 109 K7
Conselheiro Lafaiete, Brazil 123 F3
Conselheiro Pena, Brazil 123 E3
Consort, Canada 101 C6
Constance = Konstanz, Germany 19 H5
Constance, L. = Bodensee, Europe 23 A8
Constanța, Romania 38 E11
Constantina, Spain 31 H5
Constantine, Algeria 75 A6
Constitución, Chile 126 D1
Constitución, Uruguay 126 C4
Consuegra, Spain 31 F7
Consul, Canada 101 D7
Contact, U.S.A. 110 F6
Contai, India 63 J12
Contamana, Peru 124 B3
Contarina, Italy 33 C9
Contas →, Brazil 123 D4
Contes, France 27 E11
Conthey, Switz. 22 D4
Contoocook, U.S.A. 107 C13
Contra Costa, Mozam. 85 D5
Contres, France 24 E8
Contrexéville, France 25 D12
Contumaza, Peru 124 B2
Convención, Colombia 120 B3
Conversano, Italy 35 B10
Conway = Conwy, U.K. 12 D4
Conway = Conwy →, U.K. 12 D4
Conway, Ark., U.S.A. 109 H8
Conway, N.H., U.S.A. 107 C13
Conway, S.C., U.S.A. 105 J6
Conway, L., Australia 91 D2
Conwy, U.K. 12 D4
Conwy →, U.K. 12 D4
Coober Pedy, Australia 91 D1
Cooch Behar = Koch Bihar, India 61 F16
Coodardy, Australia 89 E2
Cook, Australia 89 F5
Cook, U.S.A. 108 B8
Cook, B., Chile 128 E2
Cook, Mt., N.Z. 87 K3
Cook Inlet, U.S.A. 96 C4
Cook Is., Pac. Oc. 93 J11
Cook Strait, N.Z. 87 J5
Cookeville, U.S.A. 105 G3
Cookhouse, S. Africa 84 E4
Cookshire, Canada 107 A13
Cookstown, U.K. 15 B5
Cookstown □, U.K. 15 B5
Cooksville, Canada 106 C5
Cooktown, Australia 90 B4
Coolabah, Australia 91 E4
Cooladdi, Australia 91 D4
Coolah, Australia 91 E4
Coolamon, Australia 91 E4
Coolangatta, Australia 91 D5
Coolgardie, Australia 89 F3
Coolibah, Australia 88 C5
Coolidge, U.S.A. 111 K8
Coolidge Dam, U.S.A. 111 K8
Cooma, Australia 91 F4
Coon Rapids, U.S.A. 108 C8
Coonabarabran, Australia 91 E4
Coonamble, Australia 91 E4
Coonana, Australia 89 F3
Coondapoor, India 60 N9
Coongie, Australia 91 D3
Coongoola, Australia 91 D4
Cooninie, L., Australia 91 D2
Cooper, U.S.A. 109 J7
Cooper →, U.S.A. 105 J6
Cooper Cr. →, Australia 91 D2
Cooperstown, N. Dak., U.S.A. 108 B5
Cooperstown, N.Y., U.S.A. 107 D10
Coorabie, Australia 89 F5
Coorabulka, Australia 90 C3
Coorow, Australia 89 E2
Cooroy, Australia 91 D5
Coos Bay, U.S.A. 110 E1
Cootamundra, Australia 91 E4
Cootehill, Ireland 15 B4
Cooyar, Australia 91 D5
Cooyeana, Australia 90 C2
Copahue Paso, Argentina 126 D1
Copainalá, Mexico 115 D6
Copán, Honduras 116 D2
Copatana, Brazil 120 D4
Cope, U.S.A. 108 F3
Cope, C., Spain 29 H3
Copenhagen = København, Denmark 11 J6
Copertino, Italy 35 B11
Copiapó, Chile 126 B1
Copiapó →, Chile 126 B1
Copley, Australia 91 E2
Copp L., Canada 100 A6
Copparo, Italy 33 D8
Coppename →, Surinam 121 B6
Copper Center, U.S.A. 96 B5
Copper Cliff, Canada 98 C3
Copper Harbor, U.S.A. 104 B2
Copper Queen, Zimbabwe 83 F2
Copperbelt □, Zambia 83 E2
Coppermine = Kuglugtuk, Canada 96 B8
Coppermine →, Canada 96 B8
Copperopolis, U.S.A. 112 H6
Coquet →, U.K. 12 B6
Coquilhatville = Mbandaka, Zaïre 80 D3
Coquille, U.S.A. 110 E1
Coquimbo, Chile 126 B1
Coquimbo □, Chile 126 C1
Corabia, Romania 38 F7
Coração de Jesus, Brazil 123 E3
Coracora, Peru 124 D3
Coradi, Is., Italy 35 B10
Coral Gables, U.S.A. 105 N5
Coral Harbour, Canada 97 B11
Coral Sea, Pac. Oc. 92 J7
Coral Springs, U.S.A. 105 M5
Corantijn →, Surinam 121 B6
Coraopolis, U.S.A. 106 F4
Corato, Italy 35 A9
Corbeil-Essonnes, France 25 D9
Corbie, France 25 C9
Corbières, France 26 F6
Corbigny, France 25 E10
Corbin, U.S.A. 104 G3
Corbion, Belgium 17 J6
Corbones →, Spain 31 H5
Corby, U.K. 13 E7
Corby Glen, U.K. 13 E7
Corcaigh = Cork, Ireland 15 E3
Corcoles →, Spain 29 F1
Corcoran, U.S.A. 111 H4
Corcubión, Spain 30 C1
Cordele, U.S.A. 105 K4
Cordell, U.S.A. 109 H5
Cordenons, Italy 33 C9
Cordes, France 26 D5
Cordisburgo, Brazil 123 E3
Córdoba, Argentina 126 C3
Córdoba, Mexico 115 D5
Córdoba, Spain 31 H6
Córdoba □, Argentina 126 C3
Córdoba □, Colombia 120 B2
Córdoba □, Spain 31 G6
Córdoba, Sierra de, Argentina 126 C3
Cordon, Phil. 55 C4
Cordova, Ala., U.S.A. 105 J2
Cordova, Alaska, U.S.A. 96 B5
Corella, Spain 28 C3
Corella →, Australia 90 B3
Coremas, Brazil 122 C4
Corentyne →, Guyana 121 B6
Corfield, Australia 90 C3
Corfu = Kérkira, Greece 37 A3
Corfu, Str of, Greece 37 A4
Corgo, Spain 30 C3
Corguinho, Brazil 125 D7
Cori, Italy 34 A5
Coria, Spain 30 F4
Corigliano Cálabro, Italy 35 C9
Coringa Is., Australia 90 B4
Corinna, Australia 90 G4
Corinth = Kórinthos, Greece 39 M5
Corinth, Miss., U.S.A. 105 H1
Corinth, N.Y., U.S.A. 107 C11
Corinth, G. of = Korinthiakós Kólpos, Greece 39 L5
Corinth Canal, Greece 39 M6
Corinto, Brazil 123 E3
Corinto, Nic. 116 D2
Cork, Ireland 15 E3
Cork □, Ireland 15 E3
Cork Harbour, Ireland 15 E3
Corlay, France 24 D3
Corleone, Italy 34 E6
Corleto Perticara, Italy 35 B9
Çorlu, Turkey 66 B2
Cormack L., Canada 100 A4
Cormòns, Italy 33 C10
Cormorant, Canada 101 C8
Cormorant L., Canada 101 C8
Corn Is. = Maiz, Is. del, Nic. 116 D3
Cornélio Procópio, Brazil 127 A5
Cornell, U.S.A. 108 C9
Corner Brook, Canada 99 C8
Cornești, Moldova 41 J5
Corníglio, Italy 32 D7
Corning, Ark., U.S.A. 109 G9
Corning, Calif., U.S.A. 110 G2
Corning, Iowa, U.S.A. 108 E7
Corning, N.Y., U.S.A. 106 D7
Corno, Monte, Italy 33 F10
Cornwall, Canada 98 C5
Cornwall □, U.K. 13 G3
Corny Pt., Australia 91 E2
Coro, Venezuela 120 A4
Coroaci, Brazil 123 E3
Coroatá, Brazil 122 B3
Corocoro, Bolivia 124 D4
Corocoro, I., Venezuela 121 B5
Coroico, Bolivia 124 D4
Coromandel, Brazil 123 E2
Coromandel, N.Z. 87 G5
Coromandel Coast, India 60 N12
Corona, Australia 91 E3
Corona, Calif., U.S.A. 113 M9
Corona, N. Mex., U.S.A. 111 J11
Coronado, U.S.A. 113 N9
Coronado, B. de, Costa Rica 116 E3
Coronados, G. de los, Chile 128 B2
Coronados, Is. los, U.S.A. 113 N9
Coronation, Canada 100 C6
Coronation Gulf, Canada 96 B8
Coronation I., Antarctica 5 C18
Coronation I., U.S.A. 100 B2
Coronation Is., Australia 88 B3
Coronda, Argentina 126 C3
Coronel, Chile 126 D1
Coronel Bogado, Paraguay 126 B4
Coronel Dorrego, Argentina 126 D3
Coronel Fabriciano, Brazil 123 E3
Coronel Murta, Brazil 123 E3
Coronel Oviedo, Paraguay 126 B4
Coronel Ponce, Brazil 125 D6
Coronel Pringles, Argentina 126 D3
Coronel Suárez, Argentina 126 D3
Coronel Vidal, Argentina 126 D4
Corongo, Peru 124 B2
Coronie □, Surinam 121 B6
Coropuna, Nevado, Peru 124 D3
Çorovoda, Albania 39 J3
Corowa, Australia 91 F4
Corozal, Belize 115 D7
Corozal, Colombia 120 B2
Corps, France 27 D9
Corpus, Argentina 127 B4
Corpus Christi, U.S.A. 109 M6
Corpus Christi, L., U.S.A. 109 L6
Corque, Bolivia 124 D4
Corral, Chile 128 A2
Corral de Almaguer, Spain 28 F1
Corralejo, Canary Is. 36 F6
Corréggio, Italy 32 D7
Corrente, Brazil 122 D2
Corrente →, Brazil 123 D3
Correntes →, Brazil 125 D6
Correntes, C. das, Mozam. 85 C6
Correntina, Brazil 123 D3
Corrèze □, France 26 C5
Corrèze →, France 26 C5
Corrib, L., Ireland 15 C2
Corrientes, Argentina 126 B4
Corrientes □, Argentina 126 B4
Corrientes →, Argentina 126 C4
Corrientes →, Peru 120 D3
Corrientes, C., Colombia 120 B2
Corrientes, C., Cuba 116 B3
Corrientes, C., Mexico 114 C3
Corrigan, U.S.A. 109 K7
Corrigin, Australia 89 F2
Corry, U.S.A. 106 E5
Corse, France 27 F13
Corse, C., France 27 E13
Corse-du-Sud □, France 27 G13
Corsica = Corse, France 27 F13
Corsicana, U.S.A. 109 J6
Corte, France 27 F13
Corte do Pinto, Portugal 31 H3
Cortegana, Spain 31 H4
Cortez, U.S.A. 111 H9
Cortina d'Ampezzo, Italy 33 B9
Cortland, U.S.A. 107 D8
Cortona, Italy 33 E8
Coruche, Portugal 31 G2
Çoruh →, Turkey 43 K5
Çorum, Turkey 66 B6
Corumbá, Brazil 125 D6
Corumbá →, Brazil 123 E2
Corumbá de Goiás, Brazil 123 E2
Corumbaíba, Brazil 123 E2
Corunna = La Coruña, Spain 30 B2
Corvallis, U.S.A. 110 D2
Corvette, L. de la, Canada 98 B5
Corydon, U.S.A. 108 E8
Cosalá, Mexico 114 C3
Cosamaloapan, Mexico 115 D5
Cosenza, Italy 35 C9
Coshocton, U.S.A. 106 F3
Cosmo Newberry, Australia 89 E3
Cosne-sur-Loire, France 25 E9
Coso Junction, U.S.A. 113 J9
Coso Pk., U.S.A. 113 J9
Cospeito, Spain 30 B3
Cosquín, Argentina 126 C3
Cossato, Italy 32 C5
Cossé-le-Vivien, France 24 E6
Cosson →, France 24 E8
Costa Blanca, Spain 29 G4
Costa Brava, Spain 28 D8
Costa del Sol, Spain 31 J6
Costa Dorada, Spain 28 E6
Costa Mesa, U.S.A. 113 M9
Costa Rica ■, Cent. Amer. 116 D3
Costa Smeralda, Italy 34 A2
Costigliole d'Asti, Italy 32 D5
Costilla, U.S.A. 111 H11
Cosumnes →, U.S.A. 112 G5
Coswig, Germany 18 D8
Cotabato, Phil. 55 H6
Cotacajes →, Bolivia 124 D4
Cotagaita, Bolivia 126 A2
Cotahuasi, Peru 124 D3
Côte d'Azur, France 27 E11
Côte-d'Ivoire ■ = Ivory Coast ■, Africa 78 D3
Côte d'Or, France 25 E11
Côte-d'Or □, France 25 E11
Coteau des Prairies, U.S.A. 108 C6
Coteau du Missouri, U.S.A. 108 B4
Coteau Landing, Canada 107 A10
Cotegipe, Brazil 123 D3
Cotentin, France 24 C5
Côtes-d'Armor □, France 24 D4
Côtes de Meuse, France 25 C12
Côtes-du-Nord = Côtes-d'Armor □, France 24 D4
Cotiella, Spain 28 C5
Cotillo, Canary Is. 36 F5
Cotina →, Bos.-H. 21 M8
Cotoca, Bolivia 125 D5
Cotonou, Benin 79 D5
Cotopaxi, Ecuador 120 D2
Cotopaxi □, Ecuador 120 D2
Cotronei, Italy 35 C9
Cotswold Hills, U.K. 13 F5
Cottage Grove, U.S.A. 110 E2
Cottbus, Germany 18 D10
Cottingham, U.K. 12 C5
Cottonwood, U.S.A. 111 J7
Cotulla, U.S.A. 109 L5
Coubre, Pte. de la, France 26 C2
Couches, France 25 F11
Couço, Portugal 31 G2
Coudersport, U.S.A. 106 E6
Couedic, C. du, Australia 91 F2
Couëron, France 24 E5
Couesnon →, France 24 D5
Couhé, France 26 B4
Coulanges-sur-Yonne, France 25 E10
Coulee City, U.S.A. 110 C4
Coulman I., Antarctica 5 D11
Coulommiers, France 25 D10
Coulon →, France 27 E9
Coulonge →, Canada 98 C4
Coulonges-sur-l'Autize, France 26 B3
Coulterville, U.S.A. 112 H6
Council, Alaska, U.S.A. 96 B3
Council, Idaho, U.S.A. 110 D5
Council Bluffs, U.S.A. 108 E7
Council Grove, U.S.A. 108 F6
Coupeville, U.S.A. 112 B4
Courantyne →, S. Amer. 121 B6
Courcelles, Belgium 17 H4
Courçon, France 26 B3
Couronne, C., France 27 E9
Cours-la-Ville, France 27 B8
Coursan, France 26 E7
Courseulles-sur-Mer, France 24 C6
Court-St.-Etienne, Belgium 17 G5
Courtenay, Canada 100 D3
Courtland, U.S.A. 112 G5
Courtrai = Kortrijk, Belgium 17 G2
Courtright, Canada 106 D2
Courville-sur-Eure, France 24 D8
Coushatta, U.S.A. 109 J8
Coutances, France 24 C5
Couterne, France 24 D6
Coutras, France 26 C3
Coutts, Canada 100 D6
Couvet, Switz. 22 C3
Couvin, Belgium 17 H4
Covarrubias, Spain 28 C1
Coveñas, Colombia 120 B2
Coventry, U.K. 13 E6
Coventry L., Canada 101 A7
Covilhã, Portugal 30 E3
Covington, Ga., U.S.A. 105 J4
Covington, Ky., U.S.A. 104 F3
Covington, Okla., U.S.A. 109 G6
Covington, Tenn., U.S.A. 109 H10
Cowal, L., Australia 91 E4
Cowan, Canada 101 C8
Cowan, L., Australia 89 F3
Cowan L., Canada 101 C7
Cowangie, Australia 91 F3
Cowansville, Canada 107 A12
Cowarie, Australia 91 D2
Cowcowing Lakes, Australia 89 F2
Cowdenbeath, U.K. 14 E5
Cowell, Australia 91 E2
Cowes, U.K. 13 G6
Cowlitz →, U.S.A. 112 D4
Cowra, Australia 91 E4
Coxilha Grande, Brazil 127 B5
Coxim, Brazil 125 D7
Coxim →, Brazil 125 D7
Cox's Bazar, Bangla. 61 J17
Cox's Cove, Canada 99 C8

Coyame, *Mexico* 114 B3
Coyote Wells, *U.S.A.* 113 N11
Coyuca de Benítez, *Mexico* 115 D4
Coyuca de Catalan, *Mexico* 114 D4
Cozad, *U.S.A.* 108 E5
Cozumel, *Mexico* 115 C7
Cozumel, I. de, *Mexico* 115 C7
Craboon, *Australia* 91 E4
Cracow = Kraków, *Poland* 20 E9
Cracow, *Australia* 91 D5
Cradock, *S. Africa* 84 E4
Craig, *Alaska, U.S.A.* 100 B2
Craig, *Colo., U.S.A.* 110 F10
Craigavon, *U.K.* 15 B5
Craigmore, *Zimbabwe* 83 G3
Crailsheim, *Germany* 19 F6
Craiova, *Romania* 38 E6
Cramsie, *Australia* 90 C3
Cranberry Portage, *Canada* 101 C8
Cranbrook, *Tas., Australia* 90 G4
Cranbrook, *W. Austral., Australia* 89 F2
Cranbrook, *Canada* 100 D5
Crandon, *U.S.A.* 108 C10
Crane, *Oreg., U.S.A.* 110 E4
Crane, *Tex., U.S.A.* 109 K3
Cranston, *U.S.A.* 107 E13
Craon, *France* 24 E6
Craonne, *France* 25 C10
Craponne-sur-Arzon, *France* 26 C7
Crasna, *Romania* 38 C10
Crater L., *U.S.A.* 110 E2
Crateús, *Brazil* 122 C3
Crati →, *Italy* 35 C9
Crato, *Brazil* 122 C4
Crato, *Portugal* 31 F3
Cravo Norte, *Colombia* 120 B3
Cravo Norte →, *Colombia* 120 B3
Crawford, *U.S.A.* 108 D3
Crawfordsville, *U.S.A.* 104 E2
Crawley, *U.K.* 13 F7
Crazy Mts., *U.S.A.* 110 C8
Crean L., *Canada* 101 C7
Crécy-en-Brie, *France* 25 D9
Crécy-en-Ponthieu, *France* 25 B8
Crediton, *Canada* 106 C3
Credo, *Australia* 89 F3
Cree →, *Canada* 101 B7
Cree →, *U.K.* 14 G4
Cree L., *Canada* 101 B7
Creede, *U.S.A.* 111 H10
Creel, *Mexico* 114 B3
Creighton, *U.S.A.* 108 D6
Creil, *France* 25 C9
Crema, *Italy* 32 C6
Cremona, *Italy* 32 C7
Crepori →, *Brazil* 125 B6
Crépy, *France* 25 C10
Crépy-en-Valois, *France* 25 C9
Cres, *Croatia* 33 D11
Cresbard, *U.S.A.* 108 C5
Crescent, *Okla., U.S.A.* 109 H6
Crescent, *Oreg., U.S.A.* 110 E3
Crescent City, *U.S.A.* 110 F1
Crescentino, *Italy* 32 C5
Crespino, *Italy* 33 D8
Crespo, *Argentina* 126 C3
Cressy, *Australia* 91 F3
Crest, *France* 27 D9
Cresta, Mt., *Phil.* 55 C5
Crested Butte, *U.S.A.* 111 G10
Crestline, *Calif., U.S.A.* 113 L9
Crestline, *Ohio, U.S.A.* 106 F2
Creston, *Canada* 100 D5
Creston, *Calif., U.S.A.* 112 K6
Creston, *Iowa, U.S.A.* 108 E7
Creston, *Wash., U.S.A.* 110 C4
Crestview, *Calif., U.S.A.* 112 H8
Crestview, *Fla., U.S.A.* 105 K2
Crete = Kríti, *Greece* 37 D7
Crete, *U.S.A.* 108 E6
Crete, Sea of, *Greece* 39 N8
Creus, C. de, *Spain* 28 C8
Creuse □, *France* 26 B6
Creuse →, *France* 26 B4
Creuzburg, *Germany* 18 D6
Crevalcore, *Italy* 33 D8
Crèvecœur-le-Grand, *France* 25 C9
Crevillente, *Spain* 29 G4
Crewe, *U.K.* 12 D5
Criciúma, *Brazil* 127 B6
Crieff, *U.K.* 14 E5
Crikvenica, *Croatia* 33 C11
Crimea □, *Ukraine* 41 K8
Crimean Pen. = Krymskyy Pivostriv, *Ukraine* 41 K8
Crimmitschau, *Germany* 18 E8
Cristalândia, *Brazil* 122 D2
Cristino Castro, *Brazil* 122 C3
Crişul Alb →, *Romania* 38 C4
Crişul Negru →, *Romania* 38 C4
Crişul Repede →, *Romania* 38 C3
Crivitz, *Germany* 18 B7
Crixás, *Brazil* 123 D2
Crna Gora = Montenegro □, *Yugoslavia* 21 N9
Crni Drim →, *Macedonia* 39 H3
Črnomelj, *Slovenia* 33 C12
Croagh Patrick, *Ireland* 15 C2
Croatia ■, *Europe* 33 C13
Crocker, Banjaran, *Malaysia* 56 C5
Crockett, *U.S.A.* 109 K7
Crocodile = Krokodil →, *Mozam.* 85 D5
Crocodile Is., *Australia* 90 A1
Crocq, *France* 26 C6
Croisette, C., *France* 27 E9
Croisic, Pte. du, *France* 24 E4
Croix, L. La, *Canada* 98 C1
Croker, C., *Australia* 88 B5
Croker I., *Australia* 88 B5
Cromarty, *Canada* 101 B10
Cromarty, *U.K.* 14 D4
Cromer, *U.K.* 12 E9
Cromwell, *N.Z.* 87 L2
Cronat, *France* 25 F10
Cronulla, *Australia* 91 E5
Crooked →, *Canada* 100 C4
Crooked →, *U.S.A.* 110 D3
Crooked I., *Bahamas* 117 B5
Crooked Island Passage, *Bahamas* 117 B5
Crookston, *Minn., U.S.A.* 108 B6
Crookston, *Nebr., U.S.A.* 108 D4
Crooksville, *U.S.A.* 104 F4
Crookwell, *Australia* 91 E4
Crosby, *Minn., U.S.A.* 108 B8
Crosby, *N. Dak., U.S.A.* 101 D8
Crosby, *Pa., U.S.A.* 106 E6
Crosbyton, *U.S.A.* 109 J4
Cross →, *Nigeria* 79 E6
Cross City, *U.S.A.* 105 L4
Cross Fell, *U.K.* 12 C5
Cross L., *Canada* 101 C9
Cross Plains, *U.S.A.* 109 J5
Cross River □, *Nigeria* 79 D6
Cross Sound, *U.S.A.* 96 C6
Crossett, *U.S.A.* 109 J9
Crossfield, *Canada* 100 C6
Crosshaven, *Ireland* 15 E3
Croton-on-Hudson, *U.S.A.* 107 E11
Crotone, *Italy* 35 C10
Crow →, *Canada* 100 B4
Crow Agency, *U.S.A.* 110 D10
Crow Hd., *Ireland* 15 E1
Crowell, *U.S.A.* 109 J5
Crowley, *U.S.A.* 109 K8
Crowley, L., *U.S.A.* 112 H8
Crown Point, *U.S.A.* 104 E2
Crows Landing, *U.S.A.* 112 H5
Crows Nest, *Australia* 91 D5
Crowsnest Pass, *Canada* 100 D6
Croydon, *Australia* 90 B3
Croydon, *U.K.* 13 F7
Crozet Is., *Ind. Oc.* 3 G12
Crozon, *France* 24 D2
Cruz, C., *Cuba* 116 C4
Cruz Alta, *Brazil* 127 B5
Cruz das Almas, *Brazil* 123 D4
Cruz de Malta, *Brazil* 122 C3
Cruz del Eje, *Argentina* 126 C3
Cruzeiro, *Brazil* 123 F2
Cruzeiro do Oeste, *Brazil* 127 A5
Cruzeiro do Sul, *Brazil* 124 B3
Cry L., *Canada* 100 B3
Crystal Bay, *U.S.A.* 112 F7
Crystal Brook, *Australia* 91 E2
Crystal City, *Mo., U.S.A.* 108 F9
Crystal City, *Tex., U.S.A.* 109 L5
Crystal Falls, *U.S.A.* 104 B1
Crystal River, *U.S.A.* 105 L4
Crystal Springs, *U.S.A.* 109 K9
Csongrád, *Hungary* 21 J10
Csorna, *Hungary* 21 H7
Csurgo, *Hungary* 21 J7
Cu Lao Hon, *Vietnam* 59 G7
Cua Rao, *Vietnam* 58 C5
Cuácua →, *Mozam.* 83 F4
Cuamato, *Angola* 84 B2
Cuamba, *Mozam.* 83 E4
Cuando →, *Angola* 81 H4
Cuando Cubango □, *Angola* 84 B3
Cuangar, *Angola* 84 B2
Cuanza →, *Angola* 70 G5
Cuarto →, *Argentina* 126 C3
Cuatrociénegas, *Mexico* 114 B4
Cuauhtémoc, *Mexico* 114 B3
Cuba, *Portugal* 31 G3
Cuba, *N. Mex., U.S.A.* 111 J10
Cuba, *N.Y., U.S.A.* 106 D6
Cuba ■, *W. Indies* 116 B4
Cuballing, *Australia* 89 F2
Cubango →, *Africa* 84 B3
Çubuk, *Turkey* 66 B5
Cuchi, *Angola* 81 G3
Cuchillo-Có, *Argentina* 128 A4
Cuchivero →, *Venezuela* 120 B4
Cuchumatanes, Sierra de los, *Guatemala* 116 C1
Cucuí, *Brazil* 120 C4
Cucurpe, *Mexico* 114 A2
Cucurrupí, *Colombia* 120 C2
Cúcuta, *Colombia* 120 B3
Cudalbi, *Romania* 38 D10
Cuddalore, *India* 60 P11
Cuddapah, *India* 60 M11
Cuddapan, L., *Australia* 90 D3
Cudgewa, *Australia* 91 F4
Cudillero, *Spain* 30 B4
Cue, *Australia* 89 E2
Cuéllar, *Spain* 30 D6
Cuenca, *Ecuador* 120 D2
Cuenca, *Spain* 28 E2
Cuenca □, *Spain* 28 F2
Cuenca, Serranía de, *Spain* 28 F3
Cuerdo del Pozo, Pantano de la, *Spain* 28 D2
Cuernavaca, *Mexico* 115 D5
Cuero, *U.S.A.* 109 L6
Cuers, *France* 27 E10
Cuervo, *U.S.A.* 109 H2
Cuesmes, *Belgium* 17 H3
Cuevas, Cerro, *Bolivia* 125 E4
Cuevas del Almanzora, *Spain* 29 H3
Cuevo, *Bolivia* 125 E5
Cuiabá, *Brazil* 125 D6
Cuiabá →, *Brazil* 125 D6
Cuilco, *Guatemala* 116 C1
Cuillin Hills, *U.K.* 14 D2
Cuillin Sd., *U.K.* 14 D2
Cuima, *Angola* 81 G3
Cuiseaux, *France* 27 B9
Cuité, *Brazil* 122 C4
Cuito →, *Angola* 84 B3
Cuitzeo, L. de, *Mexico* 114 D4
Cuiuni →, *Brazil* 121 D5
Cukai, *Malaysia* 59 K4
Culan, *France* 26 B6
Culbertson, *U.S.A.* 108 A2
Culcairn, *Australia* 91 F4
Culebra, Sierra de la, *Spain* 30 D4
Culemborg, *Neths.* 16 E6
Culfa, *Azerbaijan* 67 C11
Culgoa →, *Australia* 91 D4
Culiacán, *Mexico* 114 C3
Culiacán →, *Mexico* 114 C3
Culion, *Phil.* 55 F4
Culiseu →, *Brazil* 125 C7
Cúllar de Baza, *Spain* 29 H2
Cullarin Ra., *Australia* 91 E4
Cullen, *U.K.* 14 D6
Cullen Pt., *Australia* 90 A3
Cullera, *Spain* 29 F4
Cullman, *U.S.A.* 105 H2
Culloden, *U.K.* 14 D4
Culoz, *France* 27 C9
Culpeper, *U.S.A.* 104 F7
Culuene →, *Brazil* 125 C7
Culver, Pt., *Australia* 89 F3
Culverden, *N.Z.* 87 K4
Cumaná, *Venezuela* 121 A5
Cumare, *Colombia* 120 C3
Cumari, *Brazil* 123 E2
Cumberland, *Canada* 100 D3
Cumberland, *Md., U.S.A.* 104 F6
Cumberland, *Wis., U.S.A.* 108 C8
Cumberland →, *U.S.A.* 105 G2
Cumberland I., *U.S.A.* 105 K5
Cumberland Is., *Australia* 90 C4
Cumberland L., *Canada* 101 C8
Cumberland Pen., *Canada* 97 B13
Cumberland Plateau, *U.S.A.* 105 H3
Cumberland Sd., *Canada* 97 B13
Cumborah, *Australia* 91 D4
Cumbres Mayores, *Spain* 31 G4
Cumbria □, *U.K.* 12 C5
Cumbrian Mts., *U.K.* 12 C4
Cumbum, *India* 60 M11
Cuminá →, *Brazil* 121 D6
Cuminapanema →, *Brazil* 121 D7
Cummings Mt., *U.S.A.* 113 K8
Cummins, *Australia* 91 E2
Cumnock, *Australia* 91 E4
Cumnock, *U.K.* 14 F4
Cumpas, *Mexico* 114 A3
Cumplida, Pta., *Canary Is.* 36 F2
Çumra, *Turkey* 66 D5
Cuncumén, *Chile* 126 C1
Cundeelee, *Australia* 89 F3
Cunderdin, *Australia* 89 F2
Cundinamarca □, *Colombia* 120 C3
Cunene →, *Angola* 84 B1
Cúneo, *Italy* 32 D4
Cunillera, I., *Spain* 36 C7
Cunlhat, *France* 26 C7
Cunnamulla, *Australia* 91 D4
Cuorgnè, *Italy* 32 C4
Cupar, *Canada* 101 C8
Cupar, *U.K.* 14 E5
Cupica, G. de, *Colombia* 120 B2
Ćuprija, *Serbia, Yug.* 21 M11
Curaçá, *Brazil* 122 C4
Curaçao, *Neth. Ant.* 117 D6
Curacautín, *Chile* 128 A2
Curahuara de Carangas, *Bolivia* 124 D4
Curanilahue, *Chile* 126 D1
Curaray →, *Peru* 120 D3
Curatabaca, *Venezuela* 121 B5
Cure →, *France* 25 E10
Curepto, *Chile* 126 D1
Curiapo, *Venezuela* 121 B5
Curicó, *Chile* 126 C1
Curicó □, *Chile* 126 C1
Curicuriari →, *Brazil* 120 D4
Curimatá, *Brazil* 122 D3
Curiplaya, *Colombia* 120 C3
Curitiba, *Brazil* 127 B6
Currabubula, *Australia* 91 E5
Currais Novos, *Brazil* 122 C4
Curralinho, *Brazil* 122 B2
Currant, *U.S.A.* 110 G6
Curraweena, *Australia* 91 E4
Currawilla, *Australia* 90 D3
Current →, *U.S.A.* 109 G9
Currie, *Australia* 90 F3
Currie, *U.S.A.* 110 F6
Currituck Sd., *U.S.A.* 105 G8
Curtea de Argeş, *Romania* 38 D7
Curtis, *Spain* 30 B2
Curtis, *U.S.A.* 108 E4
Curtis Group, *Australia* 90 F4
Curtis I., *Australia* 90 C5
Curuá →, *Pará, Brazil* 121 D7
Curuá →, *Pará, Brazil* 125 B7
Curuá, I., *Brazil* 122 A1
Curuaés →, *Brazil* 125 B7
Curuápanema →, *Brazil* 121 D6
Curuçá, *Brazil* 122 B2
Curuguaty, *Paraguay* 127 A4
Curup, *Indonesia* 56 E2
Curupira, Serra, *S. Amer.* 121 C5
Cururu →, *Brazil* 125 B6
Cururupu, *Brazil* 122 B3
Curuzú Cuatiá, *Argentina* 126 B4
Curvelo, *Brazil* 123 E3
Cushing, *U.S.A.* 109 H6
Cushing, Mt., *Canada* 100 B3
Cusihuiriáchic, *Mexico* 114 B3
Cusna, Mte., *Italy* 32 D7
Cusset, *France* 26 B7
Custer, *U.S.A.* 108 D3
Cut Bank, *U.S.A.* 110 B7
Cutervo, *Peru* 124 B2
Cuthbert, *U.S.A.* 105 K3
Cutler, *U.S.A.* 112 J7
Cutral-Có, *Argentina* 128 A3
Cutro, *Italy* 35 C9
Cuttaburra →, *Australia* 91 D3
Cuttack, *India* 61 J14
Cuvier, C., *Australia* 89 D1
Cuvier I., *N.Z.* 87 G5
Cuxhaven, *Germany* 18 B4
Cuyabeno, *Ecuador* 120 D2
Cuyahoga Falls, *U.S.A.* 106 E3
Cuyapo, *Phil.* 55 D4
Cuyo, *Phil.* 55 F4
Cuyo East Pass, *Phil.* 55 F4
Cuyo West Pass, *Phil.* 55 F4
Cuyuni →, *Guyana* 121 B6
Cuzco, *Bolivia* 124 E4
Cuzco, *Peru* 124 C3
Cuzco □, *Peru* 124 C3
Cwmbran, *U.K.* 13 F4
Cyangugu, *Rwanda* 82 C2
Cyclades = Kikládhes, *Greece* 39 M7
Cygnet, *Australia* 90 G4
Cynthiana, *U.S.A.* 104 F3
Cypress Hills, *Canada* 101 D7
Cyprus ■, *Asia* 66 E5
Cyrenaica, *Libya* 73 C9
Cyrene = Shaḩḩāt, *Libya* 73 B9
Czar, *Canada* 101 C6
Czarne, *Poland* 20 B6
Czech Rep. ■, *Europe* 20 F4
Czersk, *Poland* 20 B7
Częstochowa, *Poland* 20 E9

D

Da →, *Vietnam* 58 B5
Da Hinggan Ling, *China* 54 B7
Da Lat, *Vietnam* 59 G7
Da Nang, *Vietnam* 58 D7
Da Qaidam, *China* 54 C4
Da Yunhe →, *China* 51 G11
Da'an, *China* 51 B13
Daarlerveen, *Neths.* 16 D9
Dab'a, Râs el, *Egypt* 76 H6
Daba Shan, *China* 52 B7
Dabai, *Nigeria* 79 C6
Dabajuro, *Venezuela* 120 A3
Dabakala, *Ivory C.* 78 D4
Dabeiba, *Colombia* 120 B2
Dabhoi, *India* 62 H5
Dąbie, *Poland* 20 B4
Dabie Shan, *China* 53 B10
Dabo, *Indonesia* 56 E2
Dabola, *Guinea* 78 C2
Dabou, *Ivory C.* 78 D4
Daboya, *Ghana* 79 D4
Dabrowa Tarnówska, *Poland* 20 E10
Dabu, *China* 53 E11
Dabung, *Malaysia* 59 K4
Dabus →, *Ethiopia* 77 E4
Dacato →, *Ethiopia* 77 F5
Dacca = Dhaka, *Bangla.* 63 H14
Dacca = Dhaka □, *Bangla.* 63 G14
Dachau, *Germany* 19 G7
Dadanawa, *Guyana* 121 C6
Daday, *Turkey* 66 B5
Dade City, *U.S.A.* 105 L4
Dades, Oued →, *Morocco* 74 B3
Dadiya, *Nigeria* 79 D7
Dadra and Nagar Haveli □, *India* 60 J8
Dadri = Charkhi Dadri, *India* 62 E7
Dadu, *Pakistan* 62 F2
Dadu He →, *China* 52 C4
Dăeni, *Romania* 38 E11
Daet, *Phil.* 55 D5
Dafang, *China* 52 D5
Dagana, *Senegal* 78 B1
Dagash, *Sudan* 76 D3
Dagestan □, *Russia* 43 J8
Dagestanskiye Ogni, *Russia* 43 J9
Daggett, *U.S.A.* 113 L10
Daghestan Republic = Dagestan □, *Russia* 43 J8
Daghfeli, *Sudan* 76 D3
Dağlıq Qarabağ = Nagorno-Karabakh, *Azerbaijan* 67 C12
Dagö = Hiiumaa, *Estonia* 9 G20
Dagu, *China* 51 E9
Daguan, *China* 52 D4
Dagupan, *Phil.* 55 C4
Dahab, *Egypt* 76 B3
Dahlak Kebir, *Eritrea* 68 D3
Dahlenburg, *Germany* 18 B6
Dahlonega, *U.S.A.* 105 H4
Dahme, *Germany* 18 D9
Dahod, *India* 62 H6
Dahomey = Benin ■, *Africa* 79 D5
Dahong Shan, *China* 53 B9
Dahra, *Senegal* 78 B1
Dahra, Massif de, *Algeria* 75 A5
Dai Hao, *Vietnam* 58 C6
Dai-Sen, *Japan* 49 G6
Dai Shan, *China* 53 B14
Dai Xian, *China* 50 E7
Daicheng, *China* 50 E9
Daimiel, *Spain* 29 F1
Daingean, *Ireland* 15 C4
Dainkog, *China* 52 A1
Daintree, *Australia* 90 B4
Daiō-Misaki, *Japan* 49 G8
Dairût, *Egypt* 76 B3
Daisetsu-Zan, *Japan* 48 C11
Dajarra, *Australia* 90 C2
Dajin Chuan →, *China* 52 B3
Dak Dam, *Cambodia* 58 F6
Dak Nhe, *Vietnam* 58 E6
Dak Pek, *Vietnam* 58 E6
Dak Song, *Vietnam* 59 F6
Dak Sui, *Vietnam* 58 E6
Dakar, *Senegal* 78 C1
Dakhla, *W. Sahara* 74 D1
Dakhla, El Wâhât el-, *Egypt* 76 B2
Dakingari, *Nigeria* 79 C5
Dakor, *India* 62 H5
Dakoro, *Niger* 79 C6
Dakota City, *U.S.A.* 108 D6
Đakovica, *Serbia, Yug.* 21 N10
Đakovo, *Croatia* 21 K8
Dalaba, *Guinea* 78 C2
Dalachi, *China* 50 F3
Dalai Nur, *China* 50 C9
Dālakī, *Iran* 65 D6
Dalälven, *Sweden* 9 F17
Dalaman, *Turkey* 66 D3
Dalaman →, *Turkey* 66 D3
Dalandzadgad, *Mongolia* 50 C3
Dalarna, *Sweden* 9 F16
Dālbandīn, *Pakistan* 60 E4
Dalbeattie, *U.K.* 14 G5
Dalbosjön, *Sweden* 11 F6
Dalby, *Australia* 91 D5
Dalby, *Sweden* 11 J7
Dalen, *Neths.* 16 C9
Dalen, *Norway* 10 E2
Dalfsen, *Neths.* 16 C8
Dalga, *Egypt* 76 B3
Dalgān, *Iran* 65 E8
Dalhart, *U.S.A.* 109 G3
Dalhousie, *Canada* 99 C6
Dalhousie, *India* 62 C6
Dali, *Shaanxi, China* 50 G5
Dali, *Yunnan, China* 52 E3
Dalian, *China* 51 E11
Daliang Shan, *China* 52 D4
Dalias, *Spain* 29 J2
Daling He →, *China* 51 D11
Dāliyat el Karmel, *Israel* 69 C4
Dalkeith, *U.K.* 14 F5
Dall I., *U.S.A.* 100 C2
Dallarnil, *Australia* 91 D5
Dallas, *Oreg., U.S.A.* 110 D2
Dallas, *Tex., U.S.A.* 109 J6
Dallol, *Ethiopia* 77 E5
Dalmacija, *Croatia* 21 M7
Dalmatia = Dalmacija, *Croatia* 21 M7
Dalmellington, *U.K.* 14 F4
Dalnegorsk, *Russia* 45 E14
Dalnerechensk, *Russia* 45 E14
Daloa, *Ivory C.* 78 D3
Dalou Shan, *China* 52 C6
Dalsjöfors, *Sweden* 11 G7
Dalskog, *Sweden* 11 F6
Dalsland, *Sweden* 9 G14
Daltenganj, *India* 63 G11
Dalton, *Canada* 98 C3
Dalton, *Ga., U.S.A.* 105 H3
Dalton, *Mass., U.S.A.* 107 D11
Dalton, *Nebr., U.S.A.* 108 E3
Dalton Iceberg Tongue, *Antarctica* 5 C9
Dalupiri I., *Phil.* 55 B4
Dalvík, *Iceland* 8 D4
Daly →, *Australia* 88 B5
Daly City, *U.S.A.* 112 H4
Daly L., *Canada* 101 B7
Daly Waters, *Australia* 90 B1
Dam Doi, *Vietnam* 59 H5
Dam Ha, *Vietnam* 58 B6
Daman, *India* 60 J8
Dāmaneh, *Iran* 65 C6
Damanhûr, *Egypt* 76 H7
Damanzhuang, *China* 50 E9
Damar, *Indonesia* 57 F7
Damaraland, *Namibia* 84 C2
Damascus = Dimashq, *Syria* 69 B5
Damaturu, *Nigeria* 79 C7
Damāvand, *Iran* 65 C7
Damāvand, Qolleh-ye, *Iran* 65 C7
Damba, *Angola* 80 F3
Dame Marie, *Haiti* 117 C5
Dāmghān, *Iran* 65 B7
Dămienesti, *Romania* 38 C10
Damietta = Dumyât, *Egypt* 76 H7
Daming, *China* 50 F8

Damīr Qābū, *Syria* 64 B4
Dammam = Ad Dammām, *Si. Arabia* 65 E6
Dammarie, *France* 24 D8
Dammartin-en-Goële, *France* 25 C9
Dammastock, *Switz.* 23 C6
Damme, *Germany* 18 C4
Damodar →, *India* 63 H12
Damoh, *India* 63 H8
Damous, *Algeria* 75 A5
Dampier, *Australia* 88 D2
Dampier, Selat, *Indonesia* 57 E8
Dampier Arch., *Australia* 88 D2
Damrei, Chuor Phnum, *Cambodia* 59 G4
Damville, *France* 24 D8
Damvillers, *France* 25 C12
Dan-Gulbi, *Nigeria* 79 C6
Dana, *Indonesia* 57 F6
Dana, L., *Canada* 98 B4
Dana, Mt., *U.S.A.* 112 H7
Danakil Depression, *Ethiopia* 77 E5
Danao, *Phil.* 55 F6
Danbury, *U.S.A.* 107 E11
Danby L., *U.S.A.* 111 J6
Dand, *Afghan.* 62 D1
Dandaragan, *Australia* 89 F2
Dandeldhura, *Nepal* 63 E9
Dandeli, *India* 60 M9
Dandenong, *Australia* 91 F4
Dandong, *China* 51 D13
Danfeng, *China* 50 H6
Danforth, *U.S.A.* 99 C6
Dangan Liedao, *China* 53 F10
Danger Is. = Pukapuka, *Cook Is.* 93 J11
Danger Pt., *S. Africa* 84 E2
Dangla, *Ethiopia* 77 E4
Dangora, *Nigeria* 79 C6
Dangrek, Phnom, *Thailand* 58 E5
Dangriga, *Belize* 115 D7
Dangshan, *China* 50 G9
Dangtu, *China* 53 B12
Dangyang, *China* 53 B8
Daniel, *U.S.A.* 110 E8
Daniel's Harbour, *Canada* 99 B8
Danielskuil, *S. Africa* 84 D3
Danielson, *U.S.A.* 107 E13
Danilov, *Russia* 42 A5
Danilovka, *Russia* 42 E7
Daning, *China* 50 F6
Danissa, *Kenya* 82 B5
Danja, *Nigeria* 79 C6
Dankalwa, *Nigeria* 79 C7
Dankama, *Nigeria* 79 C6
Dankhar Gompa, *India* 60 C11
Dankov, *Russia* 42 D4
Danleng, *China* 52 B4
Danlí, *Honduras* 116 D2
Dannemora, *U.S.A.* 107 B11
Dannenberg, *Germany* 18 B7
Dannevirke, *N.Z.* 87 J6
Dannhauser, *S. Africa* 85 D5
Dansville, *U.S.A.* 106 D7
Dantan, *India* 63 J12
Dante, *Somali Rep.* 68 E5
Danube = Dunărea →, *Europe* 41 K5
Danube →, *Europe* 6 F11
Danvers, *U.S.A.* 107 D14
Danville, *Ill., U.S.A.* 104 E2
Danville, *Ky., U.S.A.* 104 G3
Danville, *Va., U.S.A.* 105 G6
Danyang, *China* 53 B12
Danzhai, *China* 52 D6
Danzig = Gdańsk, *Poland* 20 A8
Dao, *Phil.* 57 B6
Dão →, *Portugal* 30 E2
Dao Xian, *China* 53 E8
Daocheng, *China* 52 C3
Daora, *W. Sahara* 74 C2
Daoud = Aïn Beïda, *Algeria* 75 A6
Daoulas, *France* 24 D2
Dapaong, *Togo* 79 C5
Dapitan, *Phil.* 55 G5
Daqing Shan, *China* 50 D6
Daqu Shan, *China* 53 B14
Dar Banda, *Africa* 70 F6
Dar el Beida = Casablanca, *Morocco* 74 B3
Dar es Salaam, *Tanzania* 82 D4
Dar Mazār, *Iran* 65 D8
Dar'ā, *Syria* 69 C5
Dar'ā □, *Syria* 69 C5
Dārāb, *Iran* 65 D7
Daraj, *Libya* 75 B7
Dārān, *Iran* 65 C6
Daravica, *Serbia, Yug.* 21 N10
Daraw, *Egypt* 76 C3
Dārayyā, *Syria* 69 B5
Darazo, *Nigeria* 79 C7
Darband, *Pakistan* 62 B5
Darband, Kūh-e, *Iran* 65 D8
Darbhanga, *India* 63 F11
Darby, *U.S.A.* 110 C6
Dardanelle, *Ark., U.S.A.* 109 H8
Dardanelle, *Calif., U.S.A.* 112 G7
Dardanelles = Çanakkale Boğazı, *Turkey* 66 B2
Darende, *Turkey* 66 C7
Dārestān, *Iran* 65 D8
Darfo, *Italy* 32 C7
Dârfûr, *Sudan* 73 F9
Dargai, *Pakistan* 62 B4
Dargan Ata, *Uzbekistan* 44 E7
Dargaville, *N.Z.* 87 F4
Darhan Muminggan Lianheqi, *China* 50 D6
Dari, *Sudan* 77 F3
Darıca, *Turkey* 66 B3
Darién, G. del, *Colombia* 120 B2
Darién, Serranía del, *Colombia* 120 B2
Dariganga, *Mongolia* 50 B7
Darinskoye, *Kazakstan* 42 E10
Darjeeling = Darjiling, *India* 63 F13
Darjiling, *India* 63 F13
Dark Cove, *Canada* 99 C9
Darkan, *Australia* 89 F2
Darkhazīneh, *Iran* 65 D6
Darkot Pass, *Pakistan* 63 A5
Darling →, *Australia* 91 E3
Darling Downs, *Australia* 91 D5
Darling Ra., *Australia* 89 F2
Darlington, *U.K.* 12 C6
Darlington, *S.C., U.S.A.* 105 H6
Darlington, *Wis., U.S.A.* 108 D9
Darlington, L., *S. Africa* 84 E4
Darlot, L., *Australia* 89 E3
Darłowo, *Poland* 20 A6
Darmstadt, *Germany* 19 F4
Darnah, *Libya* 73 B9
Darnall, *S. Africa* 85 D5
Darnétal, *France* 24 C8
Darney, *France* 25 D13
Darnley, C., *Antarctica* 5 C6
Darnley B., *Canada* 96 B7
Daroca, *Spain* 28 D3
Darr, *Australia* 90 C3
Darr →, *Australia* 90 C3
Darrington, *U.S.A.* 110 B3
Darsser Ort, *Germany* 18 A8
Dart →, *U.K.* 13 G4
Dart, C., *Antarctica* 5 D14
Dartmoor, *U.K.* 13 G4
Dartmouth, *Australia* 90 C3
Dartmouth, *Canada* 99 D7
Dartmouth, *U.K.* 13 G4
Dartmouth, L., *Australia* 91 D4
Dartuch, C., *Spain* 36 B10
Darvaza, *Turkmenistan* 44 E6
Darvel, Teluk, *Malaysia* 57 D5
Darwha, *India* 60 J10
Darwin, *Australia* 88 B5
Darwin, *U.S.A.* 113 J9
Darwin, Mt., *Chile* 128 D3
Darwin River, *Australia* 88 B5
Daryoi Amu = Amudarya →, *Uzbekistan* 44 E6
Dās, *U.A.E.* 65 E7
Dashetai, *China* 50 D5
Dashhowuz, *Turkmenistan* 44 E6
Dashkesan = Daşkäsän, *Azerbaijan* 43 K7
Dasht, *Iran* 65 B8
Dasht →, *Pakistan* 60 G2
Dasht-e Mārgow, *Afghan.* 60 D3
Dasht-i-Nawar, *Afghan.* 62 C3
Daska, *Pakistan* 62 C6
Daşkäsän, *Azerbaijan* 43 K7
Dassa-Zoume, *Benin* 79 D5
Datça, *Turkey* 66 D2
Datia, *India* 63 G8
Datian, *China* 53 E11
Datong, *Anhui, China* 53 B11
Datong, *Shanxi, China* 50 D7
Datu, Tanjung, *Indonesia* 56 D3
Datu Piang, *Phil.* 55 H6
Daugava →, *Latvia* 9 H21
Daugavpils, *Latvia* 9 J22
Daule, *Ecuador* 120 D2
Daule →, *Ecuador* 120 D2
Daulpur, *India* 62 F7
Daun, *Germany* 19 E2
Dauphin, *Canada* 101 C8
Dauphin I., *U.S.A.* 105 K1
Dauphin L., *Canada* 101 C9
Dauphiné, *France* 27 C9
Daura, *Borno, Nigeria* 79 C7
Daura, *Kaduna, Nigeria* 79 C6
Dausa, *India* 62 F7
Däväçi, *Azerbaijan* 43 K9
Davangere, *India* 60 M9
Davao, *Phil.* 55 H6
Davao, G. of, *Phil.* 55 H6
Dāvar Panāh, *Iran* 65 E9
Davenport, *Calif., U.S.A.* 112 H4
Davenport, *Iowa, U.S.A.* 108 E9
Davenport, *Wash., U.S.A.* 110 C4
Davenport Downs, *Australia* 90 C3
Davenport Ra., *Australia* 90 C1
David, *Panama* 116 E3
David City, *U.S.A.* 108 E6
David Gorodok = Davyd Haradok, *Belarus* 41 F4
Davidson, *Canada* 101 C7
Davis, *U.S.A.* 112 G5
Davis Dam, *U.S.A.* 113 K12
Davis Inlet, *Canada* 99 A7
Davis Mts., *U.S.A.* 109 K2
Davis Sea, *Antarctica* 5 C7
Davis Str., *N. Amer.* 97 B14
Davos, *Switz.* 23 C9
Davy L., *Canada* 101 B7
Davyd Haradok, *Belarus* 41 F4
Dawa →, *Ethiopia* 77 G5
Dawaki, *Bauchi, Nigeria* 79 D6
Dawaki, *Kano, Nigeria* 79 C6
Dawes Ra., *Australia* 90 C5
Dawson, *Canada* 96 B6
Dawson, *Ga., U.S.A.* 105 K3
Dawson, *N. Dak., U.S.A.* 108 B5
Dawson, I., *Chile* 128 D2
Dawson Creek, *Canada* 100 B4
Dawson Inlet, *Canada* 101 A10
Dawson Ra., *Australia* 90 C4
Dawu, *China* 52 B3
Dax, *France* 26 E2
Daxian, *China* 52 B6
Daxin, *China* 52 F6
Daxindian, *China* 51 F11
Daxinggou, *China* 51 C15
Daxue Shan, *Sichuan, China* 52 B3
Daxue Shan, *Yunnan, China* 52 F2
Dayao, *China* 52 E3
Daye, *China* 53 B10
Dayi, *China* 52 B4
Daylesford, *Australia* 91 F3
Dayong, *China* 53 C8
Dayr az Zawr, *Syria* 67 E9
Daysland, *Canada* 100 C6
Dayton, *Nev., U.S.A.* 112 F7
Dayton, *Ohio, U.S.A.* 104 F3
Dayton, *Pa., U.S.A.* 106 F5
Dayton, *Tenn., U.S.A.* 105 H3
Dayton, *Wash., U.S.A.* 110 C4
Daytona Beach, *U.S.A.* 105 L5
Dayu, *China* 53 E10
Dayville, *U.S.A.* 110 D4
Dazhu, *China* 52 B6
Dazu, *China* 52 C5
De Aar, *S. Africa* 84 E3
De Bilt, *Neths.* 16 D6
De Funiak Springs, *U.S.A.* 105 K2
De Grey, *Australia* 88 D2
De Grey →, *Australia* 88 D2
De Kalb, *U.S.A.* 108 E10
De Koog, *Neths.* 16 B5
De Land, *U.S.A.* 105 L5
De Leon, *U.S.A.* 109 J5
De Panne, *Belgium* 17 F1
De Pere, *U.S.A.* 104 C1
De Queen, *U.S.A.* 109 H7
De Quincy, *U.S.A.* 109 K8
De Ridder, *U.S.A.* 109 K8
De Rijp, *Neths.* 16 C5
De Smet, *U.S.A.* 108 C6
De Soto, *U.S.A.* 108 F9
De Tour Village, *U.S.A.* 104 C4
De Witt, *U.S.A.* 109 H9
Dead Sea, *Asia* 69 D4
Deadwood, *U.S.A.* 108 C3
Deadwood L., *Canada* 100 B3
Deakin, *Australia* 89 F4
Deal, *U.K.* 13 F9
Deal I., *Australia* 90 F4
Dealesville, *S. Africa* 84 D4
De'an, *China* 53 C10
Dean, Forest of, *U.K.* 13 F5
Deán Funes, *Argentina* 126 C3
Dearborn, *U.S.A.* 98 D3
Dease →, *Canada* 100 B3
Dease L., *Canada* 100 B2
Dease Lake, *Canada* 100 B2
Death Valley, *U.S.A.* 113 J10
Death Valley Junction, *U.S.A.* 113 J10
Death Valley National Monument, *U.S.A.* 113 J10
Deauville, *France* 24 C7
Deba Habe, *Nigeria* 79 C7
Debaltsevo, *Ukraine* 41 H10
Debao, *China* 52 F6
Debar, *Macedonia* 39 H3
Debden, *Canada* 101 C7
Debdou, *Morocco* 75 B4
Dębica, *Poland* 20 E11
Dęblin, *Poland* 20 D11
Débo, L., *Mali* 78 B4
Debolt, *Canada* 100 B5
Deborah East, L., *Australia* 89 F2
Deborah West, L., *Australia* 89 F2
Debre Birhan, *Ethiopia* 77 F4
Debre Markos, *Ethiopia* 77 E4
Debre May, *Ethiopia* 77 E4
Debre Sina, *Ethiopia* 77 F4
Debre Tabor, *Ethiopia* 77 E4
Debre Zebit, *Ethiopia* 77 E4
Debrecen, *Hungary* 21 H11
Dečani, *Serbia, Yug.* 21 N10
Decatur, *Ala., U.S.A.* 105 H2
Decatur, *Ga., U.S.A.* 105 J3
Decatur, *Ill., U.S.A.* 108 F10
Decatur, *Ind., U.S.A.* 104 E3
Decatur, *Tex., U.S.A.* 109 J6
Decazeville, *France* 26 D6
Deccan, *India* 60 M10
Deception L., *Canada* 101 B8
Dechang, *China* 52 D4
Děčín, *Czech.* 20 E4
Decize, *France* 25 F10
Deckerville, *U.S.A.* 106 C2
Decollatura, *Italy* 35 C9
Decorah, *U.S.A.* 108 D9
Dedéagach = Alexandroúpolis, *Greece* 39 J8
Dedemsvaart, *Neths.* 16 C8
Dedham, *U.S.A.* 107 D13
Dédougou, *Burkina Faso* 78 C4
Dedovichi, *Russia* 40 D5
Dedza, *Malawi* 83 E3
Dee →, *C. of Aberd., U.K.* 14 D6
Dee →, *Wales, U.K.* 12 D4
Deep B., *Canada* 100 A5
Deep Well, *Australia* 90 C1
Deepwater, *Australia* 91 D5
Deer →, *Canada* 101 B10
Deer Lake, *Nfld., Canada* 99 C8
Deer Lake, *Ont., Canada* 101 C10
Deer Lodge, *U.S.A.* 110 C7
Deer Park, *U.S.A.* 110 C5
Deer River, *U.S.A.* 108 B8
Deeral, *Australia* 90 B4
Deerdepoort, *S. Africa* 84 C4
Deerlijk, *Belgium* 17 G2
Deferiet, *U.S.A.* 107 B9
Defiance, *U.S.A.* 104 E3
Dêgê, *China* 52 B2
Degebe →, *Portugal* 31 G3
Degeh Bur, *Ethiopia* 68 F3
Degema, *Nigeria* 79 E6
Degersheim, *Switz.* 23 B8
Deggendorf, *Germany* 19 G8
Deh Bīd, *Iran* 65 D7
Deh-e Shīr, *Iran* 65 D7
Dehaj, *Iran* 65 D7
Dehdez, *Iran* 65 D6
Dehestān, *Iran* 65 D7
Dehgolān, *Iran* 67 E12
Dehi Titan, *Afghan.* 60 C3
Dehibat, *Tunisia* 75 B7
Dehlorān, *Iran* 67 F12
Dehnow-e Kūhestān, *Iran* 65 E8
Dehra Dun, *India* 62 D8
Dehri, *India* 63 G11
Dehua, *China* 53 E12
Dehui, *China* 51 B13
Deinze, *Belgium* 17 G3
Dej, *Romania* 38 B6
Dejiang, *China* 52 C7
Dekemhare, *Eritrea* 77 D4
Dekese, *Zaïre* 80 E4
Del Mar, *U.S.A.* 113 N9
Del Norte, *U.S.A.* 111 H10
Del Rio, *U.S.A.* 109 L4
Delai, *Sudan* 76 D4
Delano, *U.S.A.* 113 K7
Delareyville, *S. Africa* 84 D4
Delavan, *U.S.A.* 108 D10
Delaware, *U.S.A.* 104 E4
Delaware □, *U.S.A.* 104 F8
Delaware →, *U.S.A.* 104 F8
Delaware B., *U.S.A.* 103 C12
Delegate, *Australia* 91 F4
Delémont, *Switz.* 22 B4
Delft, *Neths.* 16 D4
Delfzijl, *Neths.* 16 B9
Delgado, C., *Mozam.* 83 E5
Delgerhet, *Mongolia* 50 B6
Delgo, *Sudan* 76 C3
Delhi, *Canada* 106 D4
Delhi, *India* 62 E7
Delhi, *U.S.A.* 107 D10
Delia, *Canada* 100 C6
Delice, *Turkey* 66 C6
Delicias, *Mexico* 114 B3
Delījān, *Iran* 65 C6
Déline, *Canada* 96 B7
Delitzsch, *Germany* 18 D8
Dell City, *U.S.A.* 111 L11
Dell Rapids, *U.S.A.* 108 D6
Delle, *France* 25 E14
Dellys, *Algeria* 75 A5
Delmar, *U.S.A.* 107 D11
Delmenhorst, *Germany* 18 B4
Delmiro Gouveia, *Brazil* 122 C4
Delnice, *Croatia* 33 C11
Delong, Ostrova, *Russia* 45 B15
Deloraine, *Australia* 90 G4
Deloraine, *Canada* 101 D8
Delphi, *U.S.A.* 104 E2
Delphos, *U.S.A.* 104 E3
Delportshoop, *S. Africa* 84 D3
Delray Beach, *U.S.A.* 105 M5
Delsbo, *Sweden* 10 C10
Delta, *Colo., U.S.A.* 111 G9
Delta, *Utah, U.S.A.* 110 G7
Delta □, *Nigeria* 79 D6
Delta Amacuro □, *Venezuela* 121 B5
Delungra, *Australia* 91 D5
Delvinákion, *Greece* 39 K3
Delvinë, *Albania* 39 K3
Demanda, Sierra de la, *Spain* 28 C1
Demavand = Damāvand, *Iran* 65 C7
Demba, *Zaïre* 80 F4
Dembecha, *Ethiopia* 77 E4
Dembi, *Ethiopia* 77 F4
Dembia, *Zaïre* 82 B2
Dembidolo, *Ethiopia* 77 F3
Demer →, *Belgium* 17 G5
Demidov, *Russia* 40 E6
Deming, *N. Mex., U.S.A.* 111 K10
Deming, *Wash., U.S.A.* 112 B4
Demini →, *Brazil* 121 D5
Demirci, *Turkey* 66 C3
Demirköy, *Turkey* 66 B2
Demmin, *Germany* 18 B9
Demnate, *Morocco* 74 B3
Demonte, *Italy* 32 D4
Demopolis, *U.S.A.* 105 J2
Dempo, *Indonesia* 56 E2
Demyansk, *Russia* 40 D7
Den Burg, *Neths.* 16 B5
Den Chai, *Thailand* 58 D3
Den Dungen, *Neths.* 17 E6
Den Haag = 's-Gravenhage, *Neths.* 16 D4
Den Ham, *Neths.* 16 D8
Den Helder, *Neths.* 16 C5
Den Hulst, *Neths.* 16 C8
Den Oever, *Neths.* 16 C6
Denain, *France* 25 B10
Denair, *U.S.A.* 112 H6
Denau, *Uzbekistan* 44 F7
Denbigh, *U.K.* 12 D4
Denbighshire □, *U.K.* 12 D4
Dendang, *Indonesia* 56 E3
Dender →, *Belgium* 17 F4
Denderhoutem, *Belgium* 17 G4
Denderleeuw, *Belgium* 17 G4
Dendermonde, *Belgium* 17 F4
Deneba, *Ethiopia* 77 F4
Denekamp, *Neths.* 16 D10
Deng Xian, *China* 53 A9
Dengchuan, *China* 52 E3
Denge, *Nigeria* 79 C6
Dengfeng, *China* 50 G7
Dengi, *Nigeria* 79 D6
Dengkou, *China* 50 D4
Denham, *Australia* 89 E1
Denham Ra., *Australia* 90 C4
Denham Sd., *Australia* 89 E1
Denia, *Spain* 29 G5
Denial B., *Australia* 91 E1
Deniliquin, *Australia* 91 F3
Denison, *Iowa, U.S.A.* 108 D7
Denison, *Tex., U.S.A.* 109 J6
Denison Plains, *Australia* 88 C4
Denizli, *Turkey* 66 D3
Denman Glacier, *Antarctica* 5 C7
Denmark, *Australia* 89 F2
Denmark ■, *Europe* 11 J3
Denmark Str., *Atl. Oc.* 4 C6
Dennison, *U.S.A.* 106 F3
Denpasar, *Indonesia* 56 F5
Denton, *Mont., U.S.A.* 110 C9
Denton, *Tex., U.S.A.* 109 J6
D'Entrecasteaux, Pt., *Australia* 89 F2
Dents du Midi, *Switz.* 22 D3
Denu, *Ghana* 79 D5
Denver, *U.S.A.* 108 F2
Denver City, *U.S.A.* 109 J3
Deoband, *India* 62 E7
Deoghar, *India* 63 G12
Deolali, *India* 60 K8
Deoli = Devli, *India* 62 G6
Deoria, *India* 63 F10
Deosai Mts., *Pakistan* 63 B6
Deping, *China* 51 F9
Deposit, *U.S.A.* 107 D9
Depot Springs, *Australia* 89 E3
Deputatskiy, *Russia* 45 C14
Dêqên, *China* 52 C2
Deqing, *China* 53 F8
Dera Ghazi Khan, *Pakistan* 62 D4
Dera Ismail Khan, *Pakistan* 62 D4
Derbent, *Russia* 43 J9
Derby, *Australia* 88 C3
Derby, *U.K.* 12 E6
Derby, *Conn., U.S.A.* 107 E11
Derby, *N.Y., U.S.A.* 106 D6
Derbyshire □, *U.K.* 12 E6
Dereli, *Turkey* 67 B8
Derg →, *U.K.* 15 B4
Derg, L., *Ireland* 15 D3
Dergachi = Derhaci, *Ukraine* 41 G9
Dergaon, *India* 61 F19
Derhaci, *Ukraine* 41 G9
Derik, *Turkey* 67 D9
Derinkuyu, *Turkey* 66 C6
Dernieres, Isles, *U.S.A.* 109 L9
Dêrong, *China* 52 C2
Derry = Londonderry, *U.K.* 15 B4
Derryveagh Mts., *Ireland* 15 B3
Derudub, *Sudan* 76 D4
Derval, *France* 24 E5
Dervéni, *Greece* 39 L5
Derwent, *Canada* 101 C6
Derwent →, *Derby, U.K.* 12 E6
Derwent →, *N. Yorks., U.K.* 12 D7
Derwent Water, *U.K.* 12 C4
Des Moines, *Iowa, U.S.A.* 108 E8
Des Moines, *N. Mex., U.S.A.* 109 G3
Des Moines →, *U.S.A.* 108 E9
Desaguadero →, *Argentina* 126 C2
Desaguadero →, *Bolivia* 124 D4
Descanso, Pta., *Mexico* 113 N9
Descartes, *France* 26 B4
Deschaillons, *Canada* 99 C5
Descharme →, *Canada* 101 B7
Deschutes →, *U.S.A.* 110 D3
Dese, *Ethiopia* 68 E2
Deseado, C., *Chile* 128 D2
Desenzano del Garda, *Italy* 32 C7
Desert Center, *U.S.A.* 113 M11
Desert Hot Springs, *U.S.A.* 113 M10
Désirade, I., *Guadeloupe* 117 C7
Deskenatlata L., *Canada* 100 A6
Desna →, *Ukraine* 41 G6
Desnătui →, *Romania* 38 E6
Desolación, I., *Chile* 128 D2
Despeñaperros, Paso, *Spain* 29 G1
Despotovac, *Serbia, Yug.* 21 L11
Dessau, *Germany* 18 D8
Dessel, *Belgium* 17 F6
Dessye = Dese, *Ethiopia* 68 E2
D'Estrees B., *Australia* 91 F2
Desuri, *India* 62 G5
Desvres, *France* 25 B8
Det Udom, *Thailand* 58 E5
Dete, *Zimbabwe* 83 F2
Detinja →, *Serbia, Yug.* 21 M9

Detmold, *Germany* 18 D4
Detour, Pt., *U.S.A.* 104 C2
Detroit, *Mich., U.S.A.* 98 D3
Detroit, *Tex., U.S.A.* 109 J7
Detroit Lakes, *U.S.A.* 108 B7
Deurne, *Belgium* 17 F4
Deurne, *Neths.* 17 F7
Deutsche Bucht, *Germany* 18 A4
Deutschlandsberg, *Austria* 21 J5
Deux-Sèvres □, *France* 24 F6
Deva, *Romania* 38 D5
Devakottai, *India* 60 Q11
Devaprayag, *India* 63 D8
Dévaványa, *Hungary* 21 H10
Deveci Dağları, *Turkey* 66 B7
Develi, *Turkey* 66 C6
Deventer, *Neths.* 16 D8
Deveron →, *U.K.* 14 D6
Devgadh Bariya, *India* 62 H5
Devils Den, *U.S.A.* 112 K7
Devils Lake, *U.S.A.* 108 A5
Devils Paw, *Canada* 100 B2
Devizes, *U.K.* 13 F6
Devli, *India* 62 G6
Devnya, *Bulgaria* 38 F10
Devolii →, *Albania* 39 J3
Devon, *Canada* 100 C6
Devon □, *U.K.* 13 G4
Devon I., *Canada* 4 B3
Devonport, *Australia* 90 G4
Devonport, *N.Z.* 87 G5
Devonport, *U.K.* 13 G3
Devrek, *Turkey* 66 B4
Devrekâni, *Turkey* 66 B5
Devrez →, *Turkey* 66 B6
Dewas, *India* 62 H7
Dewetsdorp, *S. Africa* 84 D4
Dewsbury, *U.K.* 12 D6
Dexing, *China* 53 C11
Dexter, *Mo., U.S.A.* 109 G9
Dexter, *N. Mex., U.S.A.* 109 J2
Dey-Dey, L., *Australia* 89 E5
Deyang, *China* 52 B5
Deyhūk, *Iran* 65 C8
Deyyer, *Iran* 65 E6
Dezadeash L., *Canada* 100 A1
Dezfūl, *Iran* 67 F13
Dezhneva, Mys, *Russia* 45 C19
Dezhou, *China* 50 F9
Dháfni, *Greece* 37 D7
Dhahaban, *Si. Arabia* 76 C4
Dhahiriya = Aẓ Ẓāhirīyah, *West Bank* 69 D3
Dhahran = Aẓ Ẓahrān, *Si. Arabia* 65 E6
Dhaka, *Bangla.* 63 H14
Dhaka □, *Bangla.* 63 G14
Dhali, *Cyprus* 37 D12
Dhamar, *Yemen* 68 E3
Dhamási, *Greece* 39 K5
Dhampur, *India* 63 E8
Dhamtari, *India* 61 J12
Dhanbad, *India* 63 H12
Dhangarhi, *Nepal* 61 E12
Dhankuta, *Nepal* 63 F12
Dhar, *India* 62 H6
Dharampur, *India* 62 H6
Dharamsala = Dharmsala, *India* 62 C7
Dharmapuri, *India* 60 N11
Dharmsala, *India* 62 C7
Dharwad, *India* 60 M9
Dhaulagiri, *Nepal* 63 E10
Dhebar, L., *India* 62 G6
Dheftera, *Cyprus* 37 D12
Dhenkanal, *India* 61 J14
Dhenoúsa, *Greece* 39 M8
Dherinia, *Cyprus* 37 D12
Dheskáti, *Greece* 39 K4
Dhespotikó, *Greece* 39 N7
Dhestina, *Greece* 39 L5
Dhiarrizos →, *Cyprus* 37 E11
Dhībān, *Jordan* 69 D4
Dhíkti Óros, *Greece* 37 D7
Dhimitsána, *Greece* 39 M5
Dhírfis, *Greece* 39 L6
Dhodhekánisos, *Greece* 39 N10
Dholiana, *Greece* 39 K3
Dholka, *India* 62 H5
Dhoraji, *India* 62 J4
Dhoxáton, *Greece* 39 H7
Dhráhstis, Ákra, *Greece* 37 A3
Dhrangadhra, *India* 62 H4
Dhrápanon, Ákra, *Greece* 37 D6
Dhrol, *India* 62 H4
Dhuburi, *India* 61 F16
Dhule, *India* 60 J9
Dhut →, *Somali Rep.* 68 E5
Di Linh, *Vietnam* 59 G7
Di Linh, Cao Nguyen, *Vietnam* 59 G7
Día, *Greece* 37 D7
Diablo, Mt., *U.S.A.* 112 H5
Diablo Range, *U.S.A.* 112 J5
Diafarabé, *Mali* 78 C4
Diala, *Mali* 78 C3
Dialakoro, *Mali* 78 C3
Diallassagou, *Mali* 78 C4
Diamante, *Argentina* 126 C3
Diamante →, *Argentina* 126 C2
Diamantina, *Brazil* 123 E3
Diamantina →, *Australia* 91 D2
Diamantino, *Brazil* 125 C6
Diamond Bar, *U.S.A.* 113 L9
Diamond Harbour, *India* 63 H13
Diamond Is., *Australia* 90 B5
Diamond Mts., *U.S.A.* 110 G6
Diamond Springs, *U.S.A.* 112 G6
Diamondville, *U.S.A.* 110 F8
Dianbai, *China* 53 G8
Diancheng, *China* 53 G8
Diano Marina, *Italy* 32 E5
Dianópolis, *Brazil* 123 D2
Dianra, *Ivory C.* 78 D3
Diapaga, *Burkina Faso* 79 C5
Diapangou, *Burkina Faso* 79 C5
Diariguila, *Guinea* 78 C2
Dībā, *Oman* 65 E8
Dibaya, *Zaïre* 80 F4
Dibaya-Lubue, *Zaïre* 80 E3
Dibbi, *Ethiopia* 68 G3
Dibete, *Botswana* 84 C4
Dibrugarh, *India* 61 F19
Dickinson, *U.S.A.* 108 B3
Dickson, *Russia* 44 B9
Dickson, *U.S.A.* 105 G2
Dickson City, *U.S.A.* 107 E9
Dicle Nehri →, *Turkey* 67 D9
Dicomano, *Italy* 33 E8
Didam, *Neths.* 16 E8
Didesa, W. →, *Ethiopia* 77 E4
Didiéni, *Mali* 78 C3
Didsbury, *Canada* 100 C6
Didwana, *India* 62 F6
Die, *France* 27 D9
Diébougou, *Burkina Faso* 78 C4
Diefenbaker L., *Canada* 101 C7
Diego Garcia, *Ind. Oc.* 3 E13
Diekirch, *Lux.* 17 J8
Diélette, *France* 24 C5
Diéma, *Mali* 78 C3
Diémbéring, *Senegal* 78 C1
Diemen, *Neths.* 16 D5
Dien Ban, *Vietnam* 58 E7
Dien Bien, *Vietnam* 58 B4
Dien Khanh, *Vietnam* 59 F7
Diepenbeek, *Belgium* 17 G6
Diepenheim, *Neths.* 16 D9
Diepenveen, *Neths.* 16 D8
Diepholz, *Germany* 18 C4
Diepoldsau, *Switz.* 23 B9
Dieppe, *France* 24 C8
Dieren, *Neths.* 16 D8
Dierks, *U.S.A.* 109 H7
Diessen, *Neths.* 17 F6
Diessenhofen, *Switz.* 23 A7
Diest, *Belgium* 17 G6
Dietikon, *Switz.* 23 B6
Dieulefit, *France* 27 D9
Dieuze, *France* 25 D13
Diever, *Neths.* 16 C8
Differdange, *Lux.* 17 J7
Dig, *India* 62 F7
Digba, *Zaïre* 82 B2
Digby, *Canada* 99 D6
Digges, *Canada* 101 B10
Digges Is., *Canada* 97 B12
Dighinala, *Bangla.* 61 H18
Dighton, *U.S.A.* 108 F4
Digne-les-Bains, *France* 27 D10
Digoin, *France* 26 B7
Digor, *Turkey* 67 B10
Digos, *Phil.* 55 H6
Digranes, *Iceland* 8 C6
Digul →, *Indonesia* 57 F9
Dihang →, *India* 61 F19
Dīhōk, *Iraq* 67 D10
Dijlah, Nahr →, *Asia* 64 D5
Dijle →, *Belgium* 17 G5
Dijon, *France* 25 E12
Dikala, *Sudan* 77 G3
Dikimdya, *Russia* 45 D13
Dikkil, *Djibouti* 77 E5
Dikomu di Kai, *Botswana* 84 C3
Diksmuide, *Belgium* 17 F1
Dikson = Dickson, *Russia* 44 B9
Dikwa, *Nigeria* 79 C7
Dila, *Ethiopia* 77 F4
Dilbeek, *Belgium* 17 G4
Dili, *Indonesia* 57 F7
Dilijan, *Armenia* 43 K7
Dilizhan = Dilijan, *Armenia* 43 K7
Dillenburg, *Germany* 18 E4
Dilley, *U.S.A.* 109 L5
Dilling, *Sudan* 77 E2
Dillingen, *Germany* 19 G6
Dillingham, *U.S.A.* 96 C4
Dillon, *Canada* 101 B7
Dillon, *Mont., U.S.A.* 110 D7
Dillon, *S.C., U.S.A.* 105 H6
Dillon →, *Canada* 101 B7
Dilolo, *Zaïre* 80 G4
Dilsen, *Belgium* 17 F7
Dilston, *Australia* 90 G4
Dimas, *Mexico* 114 C3
Dimashq, *Syria* 69 B5
Dimashq □, *Syria* 69 B5
Dimbaza, *S. Africa* 85 E4
Dimbokro, *Ivory C.* 78 D4
Dimboola, *Australia* 91 F3
Dîmboviţa →, *Romania* 38 E9
Dîmbovnic →, *Romania* 38 E8
Dimbulah, *Australia* 90 B4
Dimitrovgrad, *Bulgaria* 39 G8
Dimitrovgrad, *Russia* 42 C9
Dimitrovgrad, *Serbia, Yug.* 21 M12
Dimitrovo = Pernik, *Bulgaria* 38 G6
Dimmitt, *U.S.A.* 109 H3
Dimo, *Sudan* 77 F2
Dimona, *Israel* 69 D4
Dimovo, *Bulgaria* 38 F5
Dinagat, *Phil.* 55 F6
Dinajpur, *Bangla.* 61 G16
Dinan, *France* 24 D4
Dīnān Āb, *Iran* 65 C8
Dinant, *Belgium* 17 H5
Dinapur, *India* 63 G11
Dinar, *Turkey* 66 C4
Dīnār, Kūh-e, *Iran* 65 D6
Dinara Planina, *Croatia* 33 E13
Dinard, *France* 24 D4
Dinaric Alps = Dinara Planina, *Croatia* 33 E13
Dinder, Nahr ed →, *Sudan* 77 E3
Dindigul, *India* 60 P11
Ding Xian, *China* 50 E8
Dingalan, *Phil.* 55 D4
Dingbian, *China* 50 F4
Dingelstädt, *Germany* 18 D6
Dinghai, *China* 53 B14
Dingle, *Ireland* 15 D1
Dingle B., *Ireland* 15 D1
Dingmans Ferry, *U.S.A.* 107 E10
Dingnan, *China* 53 E10
Dingo, *Australia* 90 C4
Dingolfing, *Germany* 19 G8
Dingtao, *China* 50 G8
Dinguiraye, *Guinea* 78 C2
Dingwall, *U.K.* 14 D4
Dingxi, *China* 50 G3
Dingxiang, *China* 50 E7
Dingyuan, *China* 53 A11
Dinh, Mui, *Vietnam* 59 G7
Dinh Lap, *Vietnam* 58 B6
Dinkel →, *Neths.* 16 D9
Dinokwe, *Botswana* 84 C4
Dinosaur National Monument, *U.S.A.* 110 F9
Dinslaken, *Germany* 17 E9
Dintel →, *Neths.* 17 E4
Dinteloord, *Neths.* 17 E4
Dinuba, *U.S.A.* 111 H4
Dinxperlo, *Neths.* 16 E9
Diósgyör, *Hungary* 21 G10
Diourbel, *Senegal* 78 C1
Diplo, *Pakistan* 62 G3
Dipolog, *Phil.* 55 G5
Dipşa, *Romania* 38 C7
Dir, *Pakistan* 60 B7
Diré, *Mali* 78 B4
Dire Dawa, *Ethiopia* 68 F3
Diriamba, *Nic.* 116 D2
Dirico, *Angola* 81 H4
Dirk Hartog I., *Australia* 89 E1
Dirranbandi, *Australia* 91 D4
Disa, *India* 62 G5
Disa, *Sudan* 77 E3
Disappointment, C., *U.S.A.* 110 C1
Disappointment, L., *Australia* 88 D3
Disaster B., *Australia* 91 F4
Discovery B., *Australia* 91 F3
Disentis, *Switz.* 23 C7
Dishna, *Egypt* 76 B3
Disina, *Nigeria* 79 C6
Disko, *Greenland* 4 C5
Disko Bugt, *Greenland* 4 C5
Disna = Dzisna →, *Belarus* 40 E5
Dison, *Belgium* 17 G7
Disteghil Sar, *Pakistan* 63 A6
Distrito Federal □, *Brazil* 123 E2
Distrito Federal □, *Venezuela* 120 A4
Disûq, *Egypt* 76 H7
Diu, *India* 62 J4
Dīvāndarreh, *Iran* 67 E12
Dives →, *France* 24 C6
Dives-sur-Mer, *France* 24 C6
Divichi = Däväçi, *Azerbaijan* 43 K9
Divide, *U.S.A.* 110 D7
Dividing Ra., *Australia* 89 E2
Divinópolis, *Brazil* 123 F3
Divisões, Serra dos, *Brazil* 123 E1
Divnoye, *Russia* 43 H6
Divo, *Ivory C.* 78 D3
Divriği, *Turkey* 67 C8
Dīwāl Kol, *Afghan.* 62 B2
Dixie Mt., *U.S.A.* 112 F6
Dixon, *Calif., U.S.A.* 112 G5
Dixon, *Ill., U.S.A.* 108 E10
Dixon, *Mont., U.S.A.* 110 C6
Dixon, *N. Mex., U.S.A.* 111 H11
Dixon Entrance, *U.S.A.* 100 C2
Dixonville, *Canada* 100 B5
Diyadin, *Turkey* 67 C10
Diyālā →, *Iraq* 67 F11
Diyarbakır, *Turkey* 67 D9
Djado, *Niger* 73 D7
Djakarta = Jakarta, *Indonesia* 57 G12
Djamâa, *Algeria* 75 B6
Djamba, *Angola* 84 B1
Djambala, *Congo* 80 E2
Djanet, *Algeria* 75 D6
Djawa = Jawa, *Indonesia* 57 G14
Djebiniana, *Tunisia* 75 A7
Djelfa, *Algeria* 75 B5
Djema, *C.A.R.* 82 A2
Djendel, *Algeria* 75 A5
Djeneïene, *Tunisia* 75 B7
Djenné, *Mali* 78 C4
Djenoun, Garet el, *Algeria* 75 C6
Djerba, *Tunisia* 75 B7
Djerba, I. de, *Tunisia* 73 B7
Djerid, Chott, *Tunisia* 75 B6
Djibo, *Burkina Faso* 79 C4
Djibouti, *Djibouti* 68 E3
Djibouti ■, *Africa* 68 E3
Djolu, *Zaïre* 80 D4
Djougou, *Benin* 79 D5
Djoum, *Cameroon* 80 D2
Djourab, *Chad* 73 E8
Djugu, *Zaïre* 82 B3
Djúpivogur, *Iceland* 8 D6
Djursholm, *Sweden* 10 E12
Djursland, *Denmark* 11 H4
Dmitriya Lapteva, Proliv, *Russia* 45 B15
Dmitriyev Lgovskiy, *Russia* 42 D2
Dmitrov, *Russia* 42 B3
Dmitrovsk-Orlovskiy, *Russia* 42 D2
Dnepr → = Dnipro →, *Ukraine* 41 J7
Dneprodzerzhinsk = Dniprodzerzhynsk, *Ukraine* 41 H8
Dneprodzerzhinskoye Vdkhr. = Dniprodzerzhynske Vdskh., *Ukraine* 41 H8
Dnepropetrovsk = Dnipropetrovsk, *Ukraine* 41 H8
Dneprorudnoye = Dniprorudne, *Ukraine* 41 J8
Dnestr → = Dnister →, *Europe* 41 J6
Dnestrovski = Belgorod, *Russia* 42 E3
Dnieper → = Dnipro →, *Ukraine* 41 J7
Dniester → = Dnister →, *Europe* 41 J6
Dnipro →, *Ukraine* 41 J7
Dniprodzerzhynsk, *Ukraine* 41 H8
Dniprodzerzhynske Vdskh., *Ukraine* 41 H8
Dnipropetrovsk, *Ukraine* 41 H8
Dniprorudne, *Ukraine* 41 J8
Dnister →, *Europe* 41 J6
Dnistrovskyy Lyman, *Ukraine* 41 J6
Dno, *Russia* 40 D5
Dnyapro = Dnipro →, *Ukraine* 41 J7
Doan Hung, *Vietnam* 58 B5
Doba, *Chad* 73 G8
Dobbiaco, *Italy* 33 B9
Dobbyn, *Australia* 90 B3
Dobele, *Latvia* 9 H20
Döbeln, *Germany* 18 D9
Doberai, Jazirah, *Indonesia* 57 E8
Dobiegniew, *Poland* 20 C5
Doblas, *Argentina* 126 D3
Dobo, *Indonesia* 57 F8
Doboj, *Bos.-H.* 21 L8
Dobra, *Dîmbovita, Romania* 38 E8
Dobra, *Hunedoara, Romania* 38 D5
Dobreta-Turnu-Severin, *Romania* 38 E5
Dobrich, *Bulgaria* 38 F10
Dobrinishta, *Bulgaria* 39 H6
Dobrodzień, *Poland* 20 E8
Dobropole, *Ukraine* 41 H9
Dobruja, *Romania* 38 E11
Dobrush, *Belarus* 41 F6
Dobtong, *Sudan* 77 F3
Doc, Mui, *Vietnam* 58 D6
Doce →, *Brazil* 123 E4
Doda, *India* 63 C6
Dodecanese = Dhodhekánisos, *Greece* 39 N10
Dodewaard, *Neths.* 16 E7
Dodge Center, *U.S.A.* 108 C8
Dodge City, *U.S.A.* 109 G5
Dodge L., *Canada* 101 B7
Dodgeville, *U.S.A.* 108 D9
Dodo, *Sudan* 77 F2
Dodola, *Ethiopia* 77 F4
Dodoma, *Tanzania* 82 D4
Dodoma □, *Tanzania* 82 D4
Dodsland, *Canada* 101 C7
Dodson, *U.S.A.* 110 B9
Doesburg, *Neths.* 16 D8
Doetinchem, *Neths.* 16 E8
Dog Creek, *Canada* 100 C4
Dog L., *Man., Canada* 101 C9
Dog L., *Ont., Canada* 98 C2
Doğanşehir, *Turkey* 66 C7
Dogi, *Afghan.* 60 C3
Dogliani, *Italy* 32 D4
Dogondoutchi, *Niger* 79 C5
Dogran, *Pakistan* 62 D5
Doğubayazıt, *Turkey* 67 C11
Doguéraoua, *Niger* 79 C6
Doha = Ad Dawhah, *Qatar* 65 E6
Dohazari, *Bangla.* 61 H18
Doi, *Indonesia* 57 D7
Doi Luang, *Thailand* 58 C3
Doi Saket, *Thailand* 58 C2
Doig →, *Canada* 100 B4
Dois Irmãos, Sa., *Brazil* 122 C3
Dokka →, *Norway* 10 D4
Dokkum, *Neths.* 16 B7
Dokkumer Ee →, *Neths.* 16 B7
Dokri, *Pakistan* 62 F3
Dokuchayevsk, *Ukraine* 41 J9
Dol-de-Bretagne, *France* 24 D5
Doland, *U.S.A.* 108 C5
Dolbeau, *Canada* 99 C5
Dole, *France* 25 E12
Doleib, Wadi →, *Sudan* 77 E3
Dolgellau, *U.K.* 12 E4
Dolgelley = Dolgellau, *U.K.* 12 E4
Dolianova, *Italy* 34 C2
Dolinskaya = Dolynska, *Ukraine* 41 H7
Dollart, *Neths.* 16 B10
Dolna Banya, *Bulgaria* 38 G6
Dolni Dŭbnik, *Bulgaria* 38 F7
Dolo, *Ethiopia* 77 G5
Dolo, *Italy* 33 C9
Dolomites = Dolomiti, *Italy* 33 B8
Dolomiti, *Italy* 33 B8
Dolores, *Argentina* 126 D4
Dolores, *Uruguay* 126 C4
Dolores, *U.S.A.* 111 H9
Dolores →, *U.S.A.* 111 G9
Dolphin, C., *Falk. Is.* 128 D5
Dolphin and Union Str., *Canada* 96 B8
Dolynska, *Ukraine* 41 H7
Dolzhanskaya, *Russia* 43 G3
Dom, *Switz.* 22 D5
Dom Joaquim, *Brazil* 123 E3
Dom Pedrito, *Brazil* 127 C5
Dom Pedro, *Brazil* 122 B3
Doma, *Nigeria* 79 D6
Domaniç, *Turkey* 66 C3
Domasi, *Malawi* 83 F4
Domat Ems, *Switz.* 23 C8
Domazlice, *Czech.* 20 F2
Dombarovskiy, *Russia* 44 D6
Dombås, *Norway* 9 E13
Dombasle-sur-Meurthe, *France* 25 D13
Dombes, *France* 27 B8
Dombóvár, *Hungary* 21 J8
Domburg, *Neths.* 17 E3
Domérat, *France* 26 B6
Domeyko, *Chile* 126 B1
Domeyko, Cordillera, *Chile* 126 A2
Domfront, *France* 24 D6
Dominador, *Chile* 126 A2
Dominica ■, *W. Indies* 117 C7
Dominica Passage, *W. Indies* 117 C7
Dominican Rep. ■, *W. Indies* 117 C5
Dömitz, *Germany* 18 B7
Domme, *France* 26 D5
Dommel →, *Neths.* 17 E6
Domo, *Ethiopia* 68 F4
Domodóssola, *Italy* 32 B5
Dompaire, *France* 25 D13
Dompierre-sur-Besbre, *France* 26 B7
Dompim, *Ghana* 78 D4
Domrémy-la-Pucelle, *France* 25 D12
Domsjö, *Sweden* 10 A12
Domville, Mt., *Australia* 91 D5
Domvraína, *Greece* 39 L5
Domžale, *Slovenia* 33 B11
Don →, *Russia* 43 G4
Don →, *C. of Aberd., U.K.* 14 D6
Don →, *S. Yorks. U.K.* 12 D7
Don, C., *Australia* 88 B5
Don Benito, *Spain* 31 G5
Don Duong, *Vietnam* 59 G7
Don Martín, Presa de, *Mexico* 114 B4
Dona Ana = Nhamaabué, *Mozam.* 83 F4
Donaghadee, *U.K.* 15 B6
Donald, *Australia* 91 F3
Donalda, *Canada* 100 C6
Donaldsonville, *U.S.A.* 109 K9
Donalsonville, *U.S.A.* 105 K3
Donau = Dunărea →, *Europe* 41 K5
Donau →, *Austria* 21 G7
Donaueschingen, *Germany* 19 H4
Donauwörth, *Germany* 19 G6
Doncaster, *U.K.* 12 D6
Dondo, *Angola* 80 F2
Dondo, *Mozam.* 83 F3
Dondo, Teluk, *Indonesia* 57 D6
Dondra Head, *Sri Lanka* 60 S12
Donegal, *Ireland* 15 B3
Donegal □, *Ireland* 15 B4
Donegal B., *Ireland* 15 B3
Donets →, *Russia* 43 G5
Donetsk, *Ukraine* 41 J9
Dong Ba Thin, *Vietnam* 59 F7
Dong Dang, *Vietnam* 58 B6
Dong Giam, *Vietnam* 58 C5
Dong Ha, *Vietnam* 58 D6
Dong Hene, *Laos* 58 D5
Dong Hoi, *Vietnam* 58 D6
Dong Jiang →, *China* 53 F10
Dong Khe, *Vietnam* 58 A6
Dong Ujimqin Qi, *China* 50 B9
Dong Van, *Vietnam* 58 A5
Dong Xoai, *Vietnam* 59 G6
Donga, *Nigeria* 79 D7
Dong'an, *China* 53 D8
Dongara, *Australia* 89 E1
Dongbei, *China* 51 D13
Dongchuan, *China* 52 D4
Dongen, *Neths.* 17 E5
Donges, *France* 24 E4
Dongfang, *China* 58 C7
Dongfeng, *China* 51 C13
Donggala, *Indonesia* 57 E5
Donggan, *China* 52 F5
Donggou, *China* 51 E13
Dongguan, *China* 53 F9
Dongguang, *China* 50 F9
Donghai Dao, *China* 53 G8

Dongjingcheng, *China* 51 B15
Donglan, *China* 52 E6
Dongliu, *China* 53 B11
Dongmen, *China* 52 F6
Dongning, *China* 51 B16
Dongnyi, *China* 52 C3
Dongola, *Sudan* 76 D3
Dongou, *Congo* 80 D3
Dongping, *China* 50 G9
Dongshan, *China* 53 F11
Dongsheng, *China* 50 E6
Dongtai, *China* 51 H11
Dongting Hu, *China* 53 C9
Dongxiang, *China* 53 C11
Dongxing, *China* 52 G7
Dongyang, *China* 53 C13
Dongzhi, *China* 53 B11
Donington, C., *Australia* 91 E2
Doniphan, *U.S.A.* 109 G9
Donja Stubica, *Croatia* 33 C13
Donji Dušnik, *Serbia, Yug.* 21 M12
Donji Miholjac, *Croatia* 21 K8
Donji Milanovac, *Serbia, Yug.* 21 L12
Donji Vakuf, *Bos.-H.* 21 L7
Dønna, *Norway* 8 C15
Donna, *U.S.A.* 109 M5
Donnaconna, *Canada* 99 C5
Donnelly's Crossing, *N.Z.* 87 F4
Donnybrook, *Australia* 89 F2
Donnybrook, *S. Africa* 85 D4
Donora, *U.S.A.* 106 F5
Donor's Hill, *Australia* 90 B3
Donostia = San Sebastián, *Spain* 28 B3
Donskoy, *Russia* 42 D4
Donsol, *Phil.* 55 E5
Donya Lendava, *Slovenia* 33 B13
Donzère, *France* 27 D8
Donzère-Mondragon, Barr. de, *France* 27 D8
Donzy, *France* 25 E10
Doon →, *U.K.* 14 F4
Doorn, *Neths.* 16 D6
Dora, L., *Australia* 88 D3
Dora Báltea →, *Italy* 32 C5
Dora Ripária →, *Italy* 32 C4
Doran L., *Canada* 101 A7
Dorchester, *U.K.* 13 G5
Dorchester, C., *Canada* 97 B12
Dordogne □, *France* 26 C4
Dordogne →, *France* 26 C3
Dordrecht, *Neths.* 16 E5
Dordrecht, *S. Africa* 84 E4
Dore →, *France* 26 C7
Dore, Mts., *France* 26 C6
Doré L., *Canada* 101 C7
Doré Lake, *Canada* 101 C7
Dores do Indaiá, *Brazil* 123 E2
Dorfen, *Germany* 19 G8
Dorgali, *Italy* 34 B2
Dori, *Burkina Faso* 79 C4
Doring →, *S. Africa* 84 E2
Doringbos, *S. Africa* 84 E2
Dorion, *Canada* 98 C5
Dormaa-Ahenkro, *Ghana* 78 D4
Dormo, Ras, *Eritrea* 77 E5
Dornach, *Switz.* 22 B5
Dornberg, *Slovenia* 33 C10
Dornbirn, *Austria* 19 H5
Dornes, *France* 25 F10
Dornoch, *U.K.* 14 D4
Dornoch Firth, *U.K.* 14 D4
Dornogovĭ □, *Mongolia* 50 B6
Doro, *Mali* 79 B4
Dorogobuzh, *Russia* 40 E7
Dorohoi, *Romania* 38 B9
Döröö Nuur, *Mongolia* 54 B4
Dorr, *Iran* 65 C6
Dorre I., *Australia* 89 E1
Dorrigo, *Australia* 91 E5
Dorris, *U.S.A.* 110 F3
Dorset, *Canada* 106 A6
Dorset, *U.S.A.* 106 E4
Dorset □, *U.K.* 13 G5
Dorsten, *Germany* 18 D2
Dortmund, *Germany* 18 D3
Dörtyol, *Turkey* 66 D7
Dorum, *Germany* 18 B4
Doruma, *Zaïre* 82 B2
Dorūneh, *Iran* 65 C8
Dos Bahías, C., *Argentina* 128 B3
Dos Hermanas, *Spain* 31 H5
Dos Palos, *U.S.A.* 112 J6
Dosso, *Niger* 79 C5
Dothan, *U.S.A.* 105 K3
Dottignies, *Belgium* 17 G2
Doty, *U.S.A.* 112 D3
Douai, *France* 25 B10
Douala, *Cameroon* 79 E6
Douarnenez, *France* 24 D2
Double Island Pt., *Australia* 91 D5
Doubrava →, *Czech.* 20 F5
Doubs □, *France* 25 E13
Doubs →, *France* 25 F12
Doubtful Sd., *N.Z.* 87 L1
Doubtless B., *N.Z.* 87 F4
Doudeville, *France* 24 C7
Doué-la-Fontaine, *France* 24 E6
Douentza, *Mali* 78 C4
Douglas, *S. Africa* 84 D3
Douglas, *U.K.* 12 C3
Douglas, *Alaska, U.S.A.* 100 B2
Douglas, *Ariz., U.S.A.* 111 L9
Douglas, *Ga., U.S.A.* 105 K4
Douglas, *Wyo., U.S.A.* 108 D2
Douglastown, *Canada* 99 C7
Douglasville, *U.S.A.* 105 J3
Douirat, *Morocco* 74 B4
Doukáton, Ákra, *Greece* 39 L3
Doulevant-le-Château, *France* 25 D11
Doullens, *France* 25 B9
Doumé, *Cameroon* 80 D2
Douna, *Mali* 78 C3
Dounreay, *U.K.* 14 C5
Dour, *Belgium* 17 H3
Dourada, Serra, *Brazil* 123 D2
Dourados, *Brazil* 127 A5
Dourados →, *Brazil* 127 A5
Dourdan, *France* 25 D9
Douro →, *Europe* 30 D2
Douvaine, *France* 27 B10
Douz, *Tunisia* 75 B6
Douze →, *France* 26 E3
Dove →, *U.K.* 12 E6
Dove Creek, *U.S.A.* 111 H9
Dover, *Australia* 90 G4
Dover, *U.K.* 13 F9
Dover, *Del., U.S.A.* 104 F8
Dover, *N.H., U.S.A.* 107 C14
Dover, *N.J., U.S.A.* 107 F10
Dover, *Ohio, U.S.A.* 106 F3
Dover, Pt., *Australia* 89 F4
Dover, Str. of, *Europe* 24 B8
Dover-Foxcroft, *U.S.A.* 99 C6
Dover Plains, *U.S.A.* 107 E11
Dovey = Dyfi →, *U.K.* 13 E4
Dovrefjell, *Norway* 10 B3
Dow Rūd, *Iran* 65 C6
Dowa, *Malawi* 83 E3
Dowagiac, *U.S.A.* 104 E2
Dowgha'i, *Iran* 65 B8
Dowlatābād, *Iran* 65 D8
Down □, *U.K.* 15 B6
Downey, *Calif., U.S.A.* 113 M8
Downey, *Idaho, U.S.A.* 110 E7
Downham Market, *U.K.* 13 E8
Downieville, *U.S.A.* 112 F6
Downpatrick, *U.K.* 15 B6
Downpatrick Hd., *Ireland* 15 B2
Dowsārī, *Iran* 65 D8
Doyle, *U.S.A.* 112 E6
Doylestown, *U.S.A.* 107 F9
Draa, C., *Morocco* 74 C2
Draa, Oued →, *Morocco* 74 C2
Drac →, *France* 27 C9
Drachten, *Neths.* 16 B8
Drăgănești, *Romania* 38 E7
Drăgănești-Viașca, *Romania* 38 E8
Dragaš, *Serbia, Yug.* 21 N10
Drăgășani, *Romania* 38 E7
Dragichyn, *Belarus* 41 F3
Dragonera, I., *Spain* 36 B9
Draguignan, *France* 27 E10
Drain, *U.S.A.* 110 E2
Drake, *Australia* 91 D5
Drake, *U.S.A.* 108 B4
Drake Passage, *S. Ocean* 5 B17
Drakensberg, *S. Africa* 85 E4
Dráma, *Greece* 39 H7
Drammen, *Norway* 10 E4
Drangajökull, *Iceland* 8 C2
Drangedal, *Norway* 10 E3
Dranov, Ostrov, *Romania* 38 E12
Dras, *India* 63 B6
Drau = Drava →, *Croatia* 21 K8
Drava →, *Croatia* 21 K8
Draveil, *France* 25 D9
Dravograd, *Slovenia* 33 B12
Drawa →, *Poland* 20 C5
Drawno, *Poland* 20 B5
Drayton Valley, *Canada* 100 C6
Dreibergen, *Neths.* 16 D6
Drenthe □, *Neths.* 16 C9
Drentsche Hoofdvaart, *Neths.* 16 C8
Drepanum, C., *Cyprus* 37 E11
Dresden, *Canada* 106 D2
Dresden, *Germany* 18 D9
Dreux, *France* 24 D8
Driel, *Neths.* 16 E7
Driffield, *U.K.* 12 C7
Driftwood, *U.S.A.* 106 E6
Driggs, *U.S.A.* 110 E8
Drin i zi →, *Albania* 39 H3
Drina →, *Bos.-H.* 21 L9
Drincea →, *Romania* 38 E5
Drini →, *Albania* 38 G3
Drinjača →, *Bos.-H.* 21 L9
Drissa = Vyerkhnyadzvinsk, *Belarus* 40 E4
Drivstua, *Norway* 10 B3
Drniš, *Croatia* 33 E13
Drøbak, *Norway* 10 E4
Drochia, *Moldova* 41 H4
Drogheda, *Ireland* 15 C5
Drogichin = Dragichyn, *Belarus* 41 F3
Drogobych = Drohobych, *Ukraine* 41 H2
Drohobych, *Ukraine* 41 H2
Droichead Atha = Drogheda, *Ireland* 15 C5
Droichead Nua, *Ireland* 15 C5
Droitwich, *U.K.* 13 E5
Drôme □, *France* 27 D9
Drôme →, *France* 27 D8
Dromedary, C., *Australia* 91 F5
Dronero, *Italy* 32 D4
Dronfield, *Australia* 90 C3
Dronne →, *France* 26 C3
Dronninglund, *Denmark* 11 G4
Dronrijp, *Neths.* 16 B7
Dropt →, *France* 26 D3
Drumbo, *Canada* 106 C4
Drumheller, *Canada* 100 C6
Drummond, *U.S.A.* 110 C7
Drummond I., *U.S.A.* 98 C3
Drummond Pt., *Australia* 91 E2
Drummond Ra., *Australia* 90 C4
Drummondville, *Canada* 98 C5
Drumright, *U.S.A.* 109 H6
Drunen, *Neths.* 17 E6
Druskininkai, *Lithuania* 9 J20
Drut →, *Belarus* 41 F6
Druten, *Neths.* 16 E7
Druya, *Belarus* 40 E4
Druzhina, *Russia* 45 C15
Drvar, *Bos.-H.* 33 D13
Drvenik, *Croatia* 33 E13
Dry Tortugas, *U.S.A.* 116 B3
Dryanovo, *Bulgaria* 38 G8
Dryden, *Canada* 101 D10
Dryden, *U.S.A.* 109 K3
Drygalski I., *Antarctica* 5 C7
Drysdale →, *Australia* 88 B4
Drysdale I., *Australia* 90 A2
Dschang, *Cameroon* 79 D7
Du Bois, *U.S.A.* 106 E6
Du Quoin, *U.S.A.* 108 G10
Duanesburg, *U.S.A.* 107 D10
Duaringa, *Australia* 90 C4
Ḍubā, *Si. Arabia* 64 E2
Dubai = Dubayy, *U.A.E.* 65 E7
Dubăsari, *Moldova* 41 J5
Dubăsari Vdkhr., *Moldova* 41 J5
Dubawnt →, *Canada* 101 A8
Dubawnt, L., *Canada* 101 A8
Dubayy, *U.A.E.* 65 E7
Dubbeldam, *Neths.* 16 E5
Dubbo, *Australia* 91 E4
Dubele, *Zaïre* 82 B2
Dübendorf, *Switz.* 23 B7
Dubica, *Croatia* 33 C13
Dublin, *Ireland* 15 C5
Dublin, *Ga., U.S.A.* 105 J4
Dublin, *Tex., U.S.A.* 109 J5
Dublin □, *Ireland* 15 C5
Dublin B., *Ireland* 15 C5
Dubna, *Russia* 42 B3
Dubno, *Ukraine* 41 G3
Dubois, *U.S.A.* 110 D7
Dubossary = Dubăsari, *Moldova* 41 J5
Dubossary Vdkhr. = Dubăsari Vdkhr., *Moldova* 41 J5
Dubovka, *Russia* 43 F7
Dubovskoye, *Russia* 43 G6
Dubrajpur, *India* 63 H12
Dubréka, *Guinea* 78 D2
Dubrovitsa = Dubrovytsya, *Ukraine* 41 G4
Dubrovnik, *Croatia* 21 N8
Dubrovskoye, *Russia* 45 D12
Dubrovytsya, *Ukraine* 41 G4
Dubuque, *U.S.A.* 108 D9
Duchang, *China* 53 C11
Duchesne, *U.S.A.* 110 F8
Duchess, *Australia* 90 C2
Ducie I., *Pac. Oc.* 93 K15
Duck Cr. →, *Australia* 88 D2
Duck Lake, *Canada* 101 C7
Duck Mountain Prov. Park, *Canada* 101 C8
Duckwall, Mt., *U.S.A.* 112 H6
Düdelange, *Lux.* 17 K8
Duderstadt, *Germany* 18 D6
Dudhi, *India* 61 G13
Düdingen, *Switz.* 22 C4
Dudinka, *Russia* 45 C9
Dudley, *U.K.* 13 E5
Dueñas, *Spain* 30 D6
Dueré, *Brazil* 123 D2
Duero = Douro →, *Europe* 30 D2
Duffel, *Belgium* 17 F5
Dufftown, *U.K.* 14 D5
Dufourspitz, *Switz.* 22 E5
Dugi Otok, *Croatia* 33 E12
Dugo Selo, *Croatia* 33 C13
Duifken Pt., *Australia* 90 A3
Duisburg, *Germany* 18 D2
Duitama, *Colombia* 120 B3
Duiveland, *Neths.* 17 E4
Duiwelskloof, *S. Africa* 85 C5
Dūkdamīn, *Iran* 65 C8
Duke I., *U.S.A.* 100 C2
Dukhān, *Qatar* 65 E6
Dukhovshchina, *Russia* 40 E7
Duki, *Pakistan* 60 D6
Duku, *Bauchi, Nigeria* 79 C7
Duku, *Sokoto, Nigeria* 79 C5
Dulag, *Phil.* 55 F6
Dulce →, *Argentina* 126 C3
Dulce, G., *Costa Rica* 116 E3
Dulf, *Iraq* 64 C5
Dŭlgopol, *Bulgaria* 38 F10
Dulit, Banjaran, *Malaysia* 56 D4
Duliu, *China* 50 E9
Dullewala, *Pakistan* 62 D4
Dülmen, *Germany* 18 D3
Dulovo, *Bulgaria* 38 F10
Dulq Maghār, *Syria* 67 D8
Dululu, *Australia* 90 C5
Duluth, *U.S.A.* 108 B8
Dum Dum, *India* 63 H13
Dum Duma, *India* 61 F19
Dum Hadjer, *Chad* 73 F8
Dūmā, *Lebanon* 69 A4
Dūmā, *Syria* 69 B5
Dumaguete, *Phil.* 55 G5
Dumai, *Indonesia* 56 D2
Dumaran, *Phil.* 55 F3
Dumas, *Ark., U.S.A.* 109 J9
Dumas, *Tex., U.S.A.* 109 H4
Dumbarton, *U.K.* 14 F4
Dumbleyung, *Australia* 89 F2
Dumfries, *U.K.* 14 F5
Dumfries & Galloway □, *U.K.* 14 F5
Dumka, *India* 63 G12
Dümmer See, *Germany* 18 C4
Dumoine →, *Canada* 98 C4
Dumoine L., *Canada* 98 C4
Dumraon, *India* 63 G11
Dumyât, *Egypt* 76 H7
Dumyât, Masabb, *Egypt* 76 H7
Dún Dealgan = Dundalk, *Ireland* 15 B5
Dun Laoghaire, *Ireland* 15 C5
Dun-le-Palestel, *France* 26 B5
Dun-sur-Auron, *France* 25 F9
Duna = Dunărea →, *Europe* 41 K5
Duna →, *Hungary* 21 K8
Dunaföldvár, *Hungary* 21 J8
Dunaj = Dunărea →, *Europe* 41 K5
Dunaj →, *Slovak Rep.* 21 H8
Dunajec →, *Poland* 20 E10
Dunajska Streda, *Slovak Rep.* 21 H7
Dunapatai, *Hungary* 21 J9
Dunărea →, *Europe* 41 K5
Dunaújváros, *Hungary* 21 J8
Dunav = Dunărea →, *Europe* 41 K5
Dunav →, *Serbia, Yug.* 21 L11
Dunay, *Russia* 48 C6
Dunback, *N.Z.* 87 L3
Dunbar, *Australia* 90 B3
Dunbar, *U.K.* 14 E6
Dunblane, *U.K.* 14 E5
Duncan, *Canada* 100 D4
Duncan, *Ariz., U.S.A.* 111 K9
Duncan, *Okla., U.S.A.* 109 H6
Duncan, L., *Canada* 98 B4
Duncan L., *Canada* 100 A6
Duncan Town, *Bahamas* 116 B4
Duncannon, *U.S.A.* 106 F7
Dundalk, *Canada* 106 B4
Dundalk, *Ireland* 15 B5
Dundalk Bay, *Ireland* 15 C5
Dundas, *Canada* 98 D4
Dundas, L., *Australia* 89 F3
Dundas I., *Canada* 100 C2
Dundas Str., *Australia* 88 B5
Dundee, *S. Africa* 85 D5
Dundee, *U.K.* 14 E6
Dundee City □, *U.K.* 14 E6
Dundgovĭ □, *Mongolia* 50 B4
Dundoo, *Australia* 91 D3
Dundrum, *U.K.* 15 B6
Dundrum B., *U.K.* 15 B6
Dundwara, *India* 63 F8
Dunedin, *N.Z.* 87 L3
Dunedin, *U.S.A.* 105 L4
Dunedin →, *Canada* 100 B4
Dunfermline, *U.K.* 14 E5
Dungannon, *Canada* 106 C3
Dungannon, *U.K.* 15 B5
Dungannon □, *U.K.* 15 B5
Dungarpur, *India* 62 H5
Dungarvan, *Ireland* 15 D4
Dungarvan Harbour, *Ireland* 15 D4
Dungeness, *U.K.* 13 G8
Dungo, L. do, *Angola* 84 B2
Dungog, *Australia* 91 E5
Dungu, *Zaïre* 82 B2
Dungunâb, *Sudan* 76 C4
Dungunâb, Khalij, *Sudan* 76 C4
Dunhua, *China* 51 C15
Dunhuang, *China* 54 B4
Dunières, *France* 27 C8
Dunk I., *Australia* 90 B4
Dunkeld, *U.K.* 14 E5
Dunkerque, *France* 25 A9
Dunkery Beacon, *U.K.* 13 F4
Dunkirk = Dunkerque, *France* 25 A9
Dunkirk, *U.S.A.* 106 D5
Dunkuj, *Sudan* 77 E3
Dunkwa, *Central, Ghana* 78 D4
Dunkwa, *Central, Ghana* 79 D4
Dunlap, *U.S.A.* 108 E7
Dúnleary = Dun Laoghaire, *Ireland* 15 C5
Dunmanus B., *Ireland* 15 E2
Dunmara, *Australia* 90 B1
Dunmore, *U.S.A.* 107 E9
Dunmore Hd., *Ireland* 15 D1
Dunmore Town, *Bahamas* 116 A4
Dunn, *U.S.A.* 105 H6
Dunnellon, *U.S.A.* 105 L4
Dunnet Hd., *U.K.* 14 C5
Dunning, *U.S.A.* 108 E4
Dunnville, *Canada* 106 D5
Dunolly, *Australia* 91 F3
Dunoon, *U.K.* 14 F4
Dunqul, *Egypt* 76 C3
Duns, *U.K.* 14 F6
Dunseith, *U.S.A.* 108 A4
Dunsmuir, *U.S.A.* 110 F2
Dunstable, *U.K.* 13 F7
Dunstan Mts., *N.Z.* 87 L2
Dunster, *Canada* 100 C5
Dunvegan L., *Canada* 101 A7
Duolun, *China* 50 C9
Duong Dong, *Vietnam* 59 G4
Dupree, *U.S.A.* 108 C4
Dupuyer, *U.S.A.* 110 B7
Duque de Caxias, *Brazil* 123 F3
Duque de York, I., *Chile* 128 D1
Durack →, *Australia* 88 C4
Durack Ra., *Australia* 88 C4
Durağan, *Turkey* 66 B6
Durance →, *France* 27 E8
Durand, *U.S.A.* 104 D4
Durango = Victoria de Durango, *Mexico* 114 C4
Durango, *Spain* 28 B2
Durango, *U.S.A.* 111 H10
Durango □, *Mexico* 114 C4
Duranillin, *Australia* 89 F2
Durant, *U.S.A.* 109 J6
Duratón →, *Spain* 30 D6
Durazno, *Uruguay* 126 C4
Durazzo = Durrësi, *Albania* 39 H2
Durban, *France* 26 F6
Durban, *S. Africa* 85 D5
Dúrcal, *Spain* 31 J7
Düren, *Germany* 18 E2
Durg, *India* 61 J12
Durgapur, *India* 63 H12
Durham, *Canada* 98 D3
Durham, *U.K.* 12 C6
Durham, *Calif., U.S.A.* 112 F5
Durham, *N.C., U.S.A.* 105 G6
Durham □, *U.K.* 12 C6
Durham Downs, *Australia* 91 D4
Durmitor, *Montenegro, Yug.* 21 M9
Durness, *U.K.* 14 C4
Durrësi, *Albania* 39 H2
Durrie, *Australia* 90 D3
Dursunbey, *Turkey* 66 C3
Durtal, *France* 24 E6
Duru, *Zaïre* 82 B2
D'Urville, Tanjung, *Indonesia* 57 E9
D'Urville I., *N.Z.* 87 J4
Duryea, *U.S.A.* 107 E9
Dusa Mareb, *Somali Rep.* 68 F4
Dûsh, *Egypt* 76 C3
Dushak, *Turkmenistan* 44 F7
Dushan, *China* 52 E6
Dushanbe, *Tajikistan* 44 F7
Dusheti, *Georgia* 43 J7
Dusky Sd., *N.Z.* 87 L1
Dussejour, C., *Australia* 88 B4
Düsseldorf, *Germany* 18 D2
Dussen, *Neths.* 16 E5
Dutch Harbor, *U.S.A.* 96 C3
Dutlwe, *Botswana* 84 C3
Dutsan Wai, *Nigeria* 79 C6
Dutton, *Canada* 106 D3
Dutton →, *Australia* 90 C3
Duved, *Sweden* 10 A6
Duvno, *Bos.-H.* 21 M7
Duyun, *China* 52 D6
Düzce, *Turkey* 66 B4
Duzdab = Zāhedān, *Iran* 65 D9
Dvina, Severnaya →, *Russia* 44 C5
Dvinsk = Daugavpils, *Latvia* 9 J22
Dvor, *Croatia* 33 C13
Dwarka, *India* 62 H3
Dwellingup, *Australia* 89 F2
Dwight, *Canada* 106 A5
Dwight, *U.S.A.* 104 E1
Dyatkovo, *Russia* 42 D2
Dyatlovo = Dzyatlava, *Belarus* 40 F3
Dyer, C., *Canada* 97 B13
Dyer Plateau, *Antarctica* 5 D17
Dyersburg, *U.S.A.* 109 G10
Dyfi →, *U.K.* 13 E4
Dyje →, *Czech.* 20 G6
Dyle →, *Belgium* 17 G5
Dymer, *Ukraine* 41 G6
Dynevor Downs, *Australia* 91 D3
Dynów, *Poland* 20 F12
Dysart, *Canada* 101 C8
Dzamin Üüd, *Mongolia* 50 C6
Dzerzhinsk, *Russia* 42 B6
Dzhalinda, *Russia* 45 D13
Dzhambul = Zhambyl, *Kazakstan* 44 E8
Dzhankoy, *Ukraine* 41 K8
Dzhanybek, *Kazakstan* 42 F8
Dzhardzhan, *Russia* 45 C13
Dzharylhach, Ostriv, *Ukraine* 41 J7
Dzhetygara = Zhetiqara, *Kazakstan* 44 D7
Dzhezkazgan = Zhezqazghan, *Kazakstan* 44 E7
Dzhizak = Jizzakh, *Uzbekistan* 44 E7
Dzhugdzur, Khrebet, *Russia* 45 D14
Dzhvari = Jvari, *Georgia* 43 J6
Działdowa, *Poland* 20 B10
Działoszyn, *Poland* 20 D8
Dzierzgoń, *Poland* 20 B9
Dzierzoniów, *Poland* 20 E6
Dzilam de Bravo, *Mexico* 115 C7
Dzioua, *Algeria* 75 B6
Dzisna, *Belarus* 40 E5
Dzisna →, *Belarus* 40 E5

Dzungaria = Junggar Pendi, China 54 B3
Dzungarian Gate = Alataw Shankou, China 54 B3
Dzuumod, Mongolia 54 B5
Dzyarzhynsk, Belarus 40 F4
Dzyatlava, Belarus 40 F3

E

Eabamet, L., Canada 98 B2
Eads, U.S.A. 108 F3
Eagle, U.S.A. 110 G10
Eagle →, Canada 99 B8
Eagle Butte, U.S.A. 108 C4
Eagle Grove, U.S.A. 108 D8
Eagle L., Calif., U.S.A. 110 F3
Eagle L., Maine, U.S.A. 99 C6
Eagle Lake, U.S.A. 109 L6
Eagle Mountain, U.S.A. 113 M11
Eagle Nest, U.S.A. 111 H11
Eagle Pass, U.S.A. 109 L4
Eagle Pk., U.S.A. 112 G7
Eagle Pt., Australia 88 C3
Eagle River, U.S.A. 108 C10
Ealing, U.K. 13 F7
Earaheedy, Australia 89 E3
Earl Grey, Canada 101 C8
Earle, U.S.A. 109 H9
Earlimart, U.S.A. 113 K7
Earn →, U.K. 14 E5
Earn, L., U.K. 14 E4
Earnslaw, Mt., N.Z. 87 L2
Earth, U.S.A. 109 H3
Easley, U.S.A. 105 H4
East Angus, Canada 99 C5
East Aurora, U.S.A. 106 D6
East Ayrshire □, U.K. 14 F4
East B., U.S.A. 109 L10
East Bengal, Bangla. 61 G17
East Beskids = Vychodné Beskydy, Europe 41 H2
East Brady, U.S.A. 106 F5
East C., N.Z. 87 G7
East Chicago, U.S.A. 104 E2
East China Sea, Asia 54 C7
East Coulee, Canada 100 C6
East Dunbartonshire □, U.K. 14 F4
East Falkland, Falk. Is. 128 D5
East Grand Forks, U.S.A. 108 B6
East Greenwich, U.S.A. 107 E13
East Hartford, U.S.A. 107 E12
East Helena, U.S.A. 110 C8
East Indies, Asia 57 E6
East Jordan, U.S.A. 104 C3
East Lansing, U.S.A. 104 D3
East Liverpool, U.S.A. 106 F4
East London, S. Africa 85 E4
East Lothian □, U.K. 14 F6
East Main = Eastmain, Canada 98 B4
East Orange, U.S.A. 107 F10
East Pacific Ridge, Pac. Oc. 93 J17
East Palestine, U.S.A. 106 F4
East Pine, Canada 100 B4
East Point, U.S.A. 105 J3
East Providence, U.S.A. 107 E13
East Pt., Canada 99 C7
East Renfrewshire □, U.K. 14 F4
East Retford = Retford, U.K. 12 D7
East Riding □, U.K. 12 D7
East St. Louis, U.S.A. 108 F9
East Schelde → = Oosterschelde, Neths. 17 E4
East Siberian Sea, Russia 45 B17
East Stroudsburg, U.S.A. 107 E9
East Sussex □, U.K. 13 G8
East Tawas, U.S.A. 104 C4
East Toorale, Australia 91 E4
East Walker →, U.S.A. 112 G7
Eastbourne, N.Z. 87 J5
Eastbourne, U.K. 13 G8
Eastend, Canada 101 D7
Easter Islands = Pascua, I. de, Pac. Oc. 93 K17
Eastern □, Kenya 82 B4
Eastern □, Uganda 82 B3
Eastern Cape □, S. Africa 84 E4
Eastern Cr. →, Australia 90 C3
Eastern Ghats, India 60 N11
Eastern Group = Lau Group, Fiji 87 C9
Eastern Group, Australia 89 F3
Eastern Province □, S. Leone 78 D2
Eastern Transvaal = Mpumalanga □, S. Africa 85 B5
Easterville, Canada 101 C9
Easthampton, U.S.A. 107 D12
Eastland, U.S.A. 109 J5
Eastleigh, U.K. 13 G6
Eastmain, Canada 98 B4
Eastmain →, Canada 98 B4
Eastman, Canada 107 A12
Eastman, U.S.A. 105 J4
Easton, Md., U.S.A. 104 F7
Easton, Pa., U.S.A. 107 F9
Easton, Wash., U.S.A. 112 C5
Eastport, U.S.A. 99 D6
Eastsound, U.S.A. 112 B4
Eaton, U.S.A. 108 E2
Eatonia, Canada 101 C7
Eatonton, U.S.A. 105 J4
Eatontown, U.S.A. 107 F10
Eatonville, U.S.A. 112 D4
Eau Claire, Fr. Guiana 121 C7
Eau Claire, U.S.A. 108 C9
Eauze, France 26 E4
Ebagoola, Australia 90 A3
Eban, Nigeria 79 D5
Ebbw Vale, U.K. 13 F4
Ebeggui, Algeria 75 C6
Ebeltoft, Denmark 9 H14
Ebensburg, U.S.A. 106 F6
Ebensee, Austria 21 H3
Eber Gölü, Turkey 66 C4
Eberbach, Germany 19 F4
Eberswalde-Finow, Germany 18 C9
Ebetsu, Japan 48 C10
Ebian, China 52 C4
Ebikon, Switz. 23 B6
Ebingen, Germany 19 G5
Ebnat-Kappel, Switz. 23 B8
Eboli, Italy 35 B8
Ebolowa, Cameroon 79 E7
Ebrach, Germany 19 F6
Ébrié, Lagune, Ivory C. 78 D4
Ebro →, Spain 28 E5
Ebro, Pantano del, Spain 30 B7
Ebstorf, Germany 18 B6
Ecaussines-d' Enghien, Belgium 17 G4
Eceabat, Turkey 66 B2
Ech Cheliff, Algeria 75 A5
Echallens, Switz. 22 C3
Echeng, China 53 B10
Echigo-Sammyaku, Japan 49 F9
Echizen-Misaki, Japan 49 G7
Echmiadzin = Yejmiadzin, Armenia 43 K7
Echo Bay, N.W.T., Canada 96 B8
Echo Bay, Ont., Canada 98 C3
Echoing →, Canada 101 B10
Echt, Neths. 17 F7
Echternach, Lux. 17 J8
Echuca, Australia 91 F3
Ecija, Spain 31 H5
Eckernförde, Germany 18 A5
Eclipse Is., Australia 88 B4
Écommoy, France 24 E7
Ecoporanga, Brazil 123 E3
Écos, France 25 C8
Écouché, France 24 D6
Ecuador ■, S. Amer. 120 D2
Écueillé, France 24 E8
Ed, Sweden 11 F5
Ed Dabbura, Sudan 76 D3
Ed Dâmer, Sudan 76 D3
Ed Debba, Sudan 76 D3
Ed-Déffa, Egypt 76 A2
Ed Deim, Sudan 77 E2
Ed Dueim, Sudan 77 E3
Edah, Australia 89 E2
Edam, Canada 101 C7
Edam, Neths. 16 C6
Eday, U.K. 14 B6
Edd, Eritrea 68 E3
Eddrachillis B., U.K. 14 C3
Eddystone, U.K. 13 G3
Eddystone Pt., Australia 90 G4
Ede, Neths. 16 D7
Ede, Nigeria 79 D5
Édea, Cameroon 79 E7
Edegem, Belgium 17 F4
Edehon L., Canada 101 A9
Edekel, Adrar, Algeria 75 D6
Eden, Australia 91 F4
Eden, N.C., U.S.A. 105 G6
Eden, N.Y., U.S.A. 106 D6
Eden, Tex., U.S.A. 109 K5
Eden, Wyo., U.S.A. 110 E9
Eden →, U.K. 12 C4
Eden L., Canada 101 B8
Edenburg, S. Africa 84 D4
Edendale, S. Africa 85 D5
Edenderry, Ireland 15 C4
Edenton, U.S.A. 105 G7
Edenville, S. Africa 85 D4
Eder →, Germany 18 D5
Eder-Stausee, Germany 18 D4
Edgar, U.S.A. 108 E5
Edgartown, U.S.A. 107 E14
Edge Hill, U.K. 13 E6
Edgefield, U.S.A. 105 J5
Edgeley, U.S.A. 108 B5
Edgemont, U.S.A. 108 D3
Edgeøya, Svalbard 4 B9
Édhessa, Greece 39 J5
Edievale, N.Z. 87 L2
Edina, Liberia 78 D2
Edina, U.S.A. 108 E8
Edinburg, U.S.A. 109 M5
Edinburgh, U.K. 14 F5
Edinița, Moldova 41 H4
Edirne, Turkey 66 B2
Edison, U.S.A. 112 B4
Edithburgh, Australia 91 F2
Edjeleh, Algeria 75 C6
Edjudina, Australia 89 E3
Edmeston, U.S.A. 107 D9
Edmond, U.S.A. 109 H6
Edmonds, U.S.A. 112 C4
Edmonton, Australia 90 B4
Edmonton, Canada 100 C6
Edmund L., Canada 101 C10
Edmundston, Canada 99 C6
Edna, U.S.A. 109 L6
Edna Bay, U.S.A. 100 B2
Edo □, Nigeria 79 D6
Edolo, Italy 32 B7
Edremit, Turkey 66 C2
Edremit Körfezi, Turkey 66 C2
Edsbyn, Sweden 10 C9
Edsele, Sweden 10 A10
Edson, Canada 100 C5
Eduardo Castex, Argentina 126 D3
Edward →, Australia 91 F3
Edward, L., Africa 82 C2
Edward I., Canada 98 C2
Edward River, Australia 90 A3
Edward VII Land, Antarctica 5 E13
Edwards, U.S.A. 113 L9
Edwards Plateau, U.S.A. 109 K4
Edwardsville, U.S.A. 107 E9
Edzo, Canada 100 A5
Eefde, Neths. 16 D8
Eekloo, Belgium 17 F3
Eelde, Neths. 16 B9
Eem →, Neths. 16 D6
Eems →, Neths. 16 B9
Eems Kanaal, Neths. 16 B9
Eenrum, Neths. 16 B8
Eernegem, Belgium 17 F2
Eerste Valthermond, Neths. 16 C9
Eferi, Algeria 75 D6
Effingham, U.S.A. 104 F1
Effretikon, Switz. 23 B7
Eforie Sud, Romania 38 E11
Ega →, Spain 28 C3
Égadi, Ísole, Italy 34 E5
Eganville, Canada 98 C4
Egeland, U.S.A. 108 A5
Egenolf L., Canada 101 B9
Eger = Cheb, Czech. 20 E2
Eger, Hungary 21 H10
Eger →, Hungary 21 H10
Egersund, Norway 9 G12
Egg L., Canada 101 B7
Eggenburg, Austria 20 G5
Eggenfelden, Germany 19 G8
Eggiwil, Switz. 22 C5
Éghezée, Belgium 17 G5
Eginbah, Australia 88 D2
Égletons, France 26 C6
Eglisau, Switz. 23 A7
Egmond-aan-Zee, Neths. 16 C5
Egmont, C., N.Z. 87 H4
Egmont, Mt., N.Z. 87 H5
Eğridir, Turkey 66 D4
Eğridir Gölü, Turkey 66 D4
Egtved, Denmark 11 J3
Éguas →, Brazil 123 D3
Egume, Nigeria 79 D6
Éguzon, France 26 B5
Egvekinot, Russia 45 C19
Egypt ■, Africa 76 J7
Eha Amufu, Nigeria 79 D6
Ehime □, Japan 49 H6
Ehingen, Germany 19 G5
Ehrenberg, U.S.A. 113 M12
Ehrwald, Austria 19 H6
Eibar, Spain 28 B2
Eibergen, Neths. 16 D9
Eichstätt, Germany 19 G7
Eider →, Germany 18 A4
Eidsvold, Australia 91 D5
Eidsvoll, Norway 9 F14
Eifel, Germany 19 E2
Eiffel Flats, Zimbabwe 83 F3
Eigg, U.K. 14 E2
Eighty Mile Beach, Australia 88 C3
Eil, Somali Rep. 68 F4
Eil, L., U.K. 14 E3
Eildon, L., Australia 91 F4
Eileen L., Canada 101 A7
Eilenburg, Germany 18 D8
Ein el Luweiqa, Sudan 77 E3
Einasleigh, Australia 90 B3
Einasleigh →, Australia 90 B3
Einbeck, Germany 18 D5
Eindhoven, Neths. 17 F6
Einsiedeln, Switz. 23 B7
Eire = Ireland ■, Europe 15 D4
Eiríksjökull, Iceland 8 D3
Eirlandsche Gat, Neths. 16 B5
Eirunepé, Brazil 124 B4
Eisden, Belgium 17 G7
Eisenach, Germany 18 E6
Eisenberg, Germany 18 E7
Eisenerz, Austria 21 H4
Eisenhüttenstadt, Germany 18 C10
Eisenstadt, Austria 21 H6
Eiserfeld, Germany 18 E3
Eisfeld, Germany 18 E6
Eisleben, Germany 18 D7
Eivissa = Ibiza, Spain 36 C7
Ejby, Denmark 11 J3
Eje, Sierra del, Spain 30 C4
Ejea de los Caballeros, Spain 28 C3
Ejutla, Mexico 115 D5
Ekalaka, U.S.A. 108 C2
Ekeren, Belgium 17 F4
Eket, Nigeria 79 E6
Eketahuna, N.Z. 87 J5
Ekhínos, Greece 39 H8
Ekibastuz, Kazakstan 44 D8
Ekimchan, Russia 45 D14
Ekoli, Zaïre 82 C1
Eksel, Belgium 17 F6
Eksjö, Sweden 9 H16
Ekwan →, Canada 98 B3
Ekwan Pt., Canada 98 B3
El Aaiún, W. Sahara 74 C2
El Aargub, Mauritania 74 D1
El Abiodh-Sidi-Cheikh, Algeria 75 B5
El 'Agrûd, Egypt 69 E3
El Aïoun, Morocco 75 B4
El 'Aiyat, Egypt 76 J7
El Alamein, Egypt 76 H6
El Alto, Peru 124 A1
El 'Aqaba, W. →, Egypt 69 E2
El 'Arag, Egypt 76 B2
El Arahal, Spain 31 H5
El Arenal, Spain 36 B9
El Aricha, Algeria 75 B4
El Arīhā, West Bank 69 D4
El Arish, Australia 90 B4
El 'Arîsh, Egypt 69 D2
El 'Arîsh, W. →, Egypt 69 D2
El Arrouch, Algeria 75 A6
El Asnam = Ech Cheliff, Algeria 75 A5
El Astillero, Spain 30 B7
El Badâri, Egypt 76 B3
El Bahrein, Egypt 76 B2
El Ballâs, Egypt 76 B3
El Balyana, Egypt 76 B3
El Banco, Colombia 120 B3
El Baqeir, Sudan 76 D3
El Barco de Ávila, Spain 30 E5
El Barco de Valdeorras, Spain 30 C4
El Bauga, Sudan 76 D3
El Baúl, Venezuela 120 B4
El Bawiti, Egypt 76 J6
El Bayadh, Algeria 75 B5
El Bierzo, Spain 30 C4
El Bluff, Nic. 116 D3
El Bolsón, Argentina 128 B2
El Bonillo, Spain 29 G2
El Brûk, W. →, Egypt 69 E2
El Buheirat □, Sudan 77 F2
El Caín, Argentina 128 B3
El Cajon, U.S.A. 113 N10
El Callao, Venezuela 121 B5
El Camp, Spain 28 D6
El Campo, U.S.A. 109 L6
El Carmen, Bolivia 125 C5
El Carmen, Venezuela 120 C4
El Castillo, Spain 31 H4
El Centro, U.S.A. 113 N11
El Cerro, Bolivia 125 D5
El Cerro, Spain 31 H4
El Cocuy, Colombia 120 B3
El Compadre, Mexico 113 N10
El Corcovado, Argentina 128 B2
El Coronil, Spain 31 H5
El Cuy, Argentina 128 A3
El Cuyo, Mexico 115 C7
El Dab'a, Egypt 76 H6
El Daheir, Egypt 69 D3
El Deir, Egypt 76 B3
El Dere, Somali Rep. 68 G4
El Descanso, Mexico 113 N10
El Desemboque, Mexico 114 A2
El Dilingat, Egypt 76 H7
El Diviso, Colombia 120 C2
El Djem, Tunisia 75 A7
El Djouf, Mauritania 72 E3
El Dorado, Ark., U.S.A. 109 J8
El Dorado, Kans., U.S.A. 109 G6
El Dorado, Venezuela 121 B5
El Eglab, Algeria 74 C4
El Escorial, Spain 30 E6
El Eulma, Algeria 75 A6
El Faiyûm, Egypt 76 J7
El Fâsher, Sudan 77 E2
El Fashn, Egypt 76 J7
El Ferrol, Spain 30 B2
El Fifi, Sudan 77 E1
El Fuerte, Mexico 114 B3
El Gal, Somali Rep. 68 E5
El Gebir, Sudan 77 E2
El Gedida, Egypt 76 B2
El Geneina = Al Junaynah, Sudan 73 F9
El Geteina, Sudan 77 E3
El Gezira □, Sudan 77 E3
El Gîza, Egypt 76 H7
El Goléa, Algeria 75 B5
El Hadeb, W. Sahara 74 C2
El Hadjira, Algeria 75 B6
El Hagiz, Sudan 77 D4
El Hajeb, Morocco 74 B3
El Hammam, Egypt 76 H6
El Hammâmi, Mauritania 74 D2
El Hank, Mauritania 74 D3
El Hasian, W. Sahara 74 C2
El Hawata, Sudan 77 E3
El Heiz, Egypt 76 B2
El 'Idisât, Egypt 76 B3
El Iskandarîya, Egypt 76 H6
El Jadida, Morocco 74 B3
El Jebelein, Sudan 77 E3
El Kab, Sudan 76 D3
El Kabrît, G., Egypt 69 F2
El Kala, Algeria 75 A6
El Kalâa, Morocco 74 B3
El Kamlin, Sudan 77 D3
El Kantara, Algeria 75 A6
El Kantara, Tunisia 75 B7
El Karaba, Sudan 76 D3
El Kef, Tunisia 75 A6
El Khandaq, Sudan 76 D3
El Khârga, Egypt 76 B3
El Khartûm, Sudan 77 D3
El Khartûm □, Sudan 77 D3
El Khartûm Bahrî, Sudan 77 D3
El Khroub, Algeria 75 A6
El Kseur, Algeria 75 A5
El Ksiba, Morocco 74 B3
El Kuntilla, Egypt 69 E3
El Laqâwa, Sudan 77 E2
El Laqeita, Egypt 76 B3
El Leiya, Sudan 77 D4
El Mafâza, Sudan 77 E3
El Mahalla el Kubra, Egypt 76 H7
El Mahârîq, Egypt 76 B3
El Mahmûdîya, Egypt 76 H7
El Maitén, Argentina 128 B2
El Maiz, Algeria 75 C4
El-Maks el-Bahari, Egypt 76 C3
El Manshâh, Egypt 76 B3
El Mansour, Algeria 75 C4
El Mansûra, Egypt 76 H7
El Mantico, Venezuela 121 B5
El Manzala, Egypt 76 H7
El Marâgha, Egypt 76 B3
El Masid, Sudan 77 D3
El Matariya, Egypt 76 H8
El Medano, Canary Is. 36 F3
El Meghaier, Algeria 75 B6
El Meraguen, Algeria 75 C4
El Metemma, Sudan 77 D3
El Miamo, Venezuela 121 B5
El Milagro, Argentina 126 C2
El Milia, Algeria 75 A6
El Minyâ, Egypt 76 J7
El Molar, Spain 28 E1
El Monte, U.S.A. 113 L8
El Mreyye, Mauritania 78 B3
El Obeid, Sudan 77 E3
El Odaiya, Sudan 77 E2
El Oro, Mexico 115 D4
El Oro □, Ecuador 120 D2
El Oued, Algeria 75 B6
El Palmar, Bolivia 125 D5
El Palmar, Venezuela 121 B5
El Palmito, Presa, Mexico 114 B3
El Panadés, Spain 28 D6
El Pardo, Spain 30 E7
El Paso, U.S.A. 111 L10
El Paso Robles, U.S.A. 112 K6
El Pedernoso, Spain 29 F2
El Pedroso, Spain 31 H5
El Pobo de Dueñas, Spain 28 E3
El Portal, U.S.A. 111 H4
El Porvenir, Mexico 114 A3
El Prat de Llobregat, Spain 28 D7
El Progreso, Honduras 116 C2
El Provencío, Spain 29 F2
El Pueblito, Mexico 114 B3
El Pueblo, Canary Is. 36 F2
El Puerto de Santa María, Spain 31 J4
El Qâhira, Egypt 76 H7
El Qantara, Egypt 69 E1
El Qasr, Egypt 76 B2
El Quseima, Egypt 69 E3
El Qusîya, Egypt 76 B3
El Râshda, Egypt 76 B2
El Reno, U.S.A. 109 H6
El Ribero, Spain 30 C2
El Ridisiya, Egypt 76 C3
El Rio, U.S.A. 113 L7
El Ronquillo, Spain 31 H4
El Roque, Pta., Canary Is. 36 F4
El Rosarito, Mexico 114 B2
El Rubio, Spain 31 H5
El Saff, Egypt 76 J7
El Saheira, W. →, Egypt 69 E2
El Salto, Mexico 114 C3
El Salvador ■, Cent. Amer. 116 D2
El Sancejo, Spain 31 H5
El Sauce, Nic. 116 D2
El Shallal, Egypt 76 C3
El Simbillawein, Egypt 76 H7
El Sombrero, Venezuela 120 B4
El Suweis, Egypt 76 J8
El Tamarâni, W. →, Egypt 69 E3
El Thamad, Egypt 69 F3
El Tigre, Venezuela 121 B5
El Tîh, G., Egypt 69 F2
El Tîna, Khalîg, Egypt 69 D1
El Tocuyo, Venezuela 120 B4
El Tofo, Chile 126 B1
El Tránsito, Chile 126 B1
El Tûr, Egypt 76 J8
El Turbio, Argentina 128 D2
El Uqsur, Egypt 76 B3
El Vado, Spain 28 D1
El Vallés, Spain 28 D7
El Venado, Mexico 114 C4
El Vigía, Venezuela 120 B3
El Wabeira, Egypt 69 F2
El Wak, Kenya 82 B5
El Waqf, Egypt 76 B3
El Wâsta, Egypt 76 J7
El Weguet, Ethiopia 77 F5
El Wuz, Sudan 77 D3
Elafónisos, Greece 39 N5
Élassa, Greece 39 P9
Elassón, Greece 39 K5
Elat, Israel 69 F3
Elâzığ, Turkey 67 C8
Elba, Italy 32 F7
Elba, U.S.A. 105 K2
Elbasani, Albania 39 H3
Elbe, U.S.A. 112 D4
Elbe →, Europe 18 B4
Elbe-Seiten Kanal, Germany 18 C6
Elbert, Mt., U.S.A. 111 G10
Elberta, U.S.A. 104 C2
Elberton, U.S.A. 105 H4
Elbeuf, France 24 C8
Elbing = Elbląg, Poland 20 A9
Elbistan, Turkey 66 C7
Elbląg, Poland 20 A9

Elbow, *Canada* 101 C7
Elbrus, *Asia* 43 J6
Elburg, *Neths.* 16 D7
Elburz Mts. = Alborz, Reshteh-ye Kūhhā-ye, *Iran* 65 C7
Elche, *Spain* 29 G4
Elche de la Sierra, *Spain* 29 G2
Elcho I., *Australia* 90 A2
Elda, *Spain* 29 G4
Eldon, *Mo., U.S.A.* 108 F8
Eldon, *Wash., U.S.A.* 112 C3
Eldora, *U.S.A.* 108 D8
Eldorado, *Argentina* 127 B5
Eldorado, *Canada* 101 B7
Eldorado, *Mexico* 114 C3
Eldorado, *Ill., U.S.A.* 104 G1
Eldorado, *Tex., U.S.A.* 109 K4
Eldorado Springs, *U.S.A.* 109 G8
Eldoret, *Kenya* 82 B4
Eldred, *U.S.A.* 106 E6
Elea, C., *Cyprus* 37 D13
Electra, *U.S.A.* 109 H5
Elefantes →, *Mozam.* 85 C5
Elefantes, G., *Chile* 128 C2
Elektrogorsk, *Russia* 42 C4
Elektrostal, *Russia* 42 C4
Elele, *Nigeria* 79 D6
Elephant Butte Reservoir, *U.S.A.* 111 K10
Elephant I., *Antarctica* 5 C18
Elesbão Veloso, *Brazil* 122 C3
Eleşkirt, *Turkey* 67 C10
Eleuthera, *Bahamas* 116 A4
Elgepiggen, *Norway* 10 B5
Elgeyo-Marakwet □, *Kenya* 82 B4
Elgg, *Switz.* 23 B7
Elgin, *N.B., Canada* 99 C6
Elgin, *Ont., Canada* 107 B8
Elgin, *U.K.* 14 D5
Elgin, *Ill., U.S.A.* 104 D1
Elgin, *N. Dak., U.S.A.* 108 B4
Elgin, *Nebr., U.S.A.* 108 E5
Elgin, *Nev., U.S.A.* 111 H6
Elgin, *Oreg., U.S.A.* 110 D5
Elgin, *Tex., U.S.A.* 109 K6
Elgon, Mt., *Africa* 82 B3
Eliase, *Indonesia* 57 F8
Elida, *U.S.A.* 109 J3
Elikón, *Greece* 39 L5
Elim, *S. Africa* 84 E2
Elisabethville = Lubumbashi, *Zaïre* 83 E2
Eliseu Martins, *Brazil* 122 C3
Elista, *Russia* 43 G7
Elizabeth, *Australia* 91 E2
Elizabeth, *U.S.A.* 107 F10
Elizabeth City, *U.S.A.* 105 G7
Elizabethton, *U.S.A.* 105 G4
Elizabethtown, *Ky., U.S.A.* 104 G3
Elizabethtown, *N.Y., U.S.A.* 107 B11
Elizabethtown, *Pa., U.S.A.* 107 F8
Elizondo, *Spain* 28 B3
Ełk, *Poland* 20 B12
Elk City, *U.S.A.* 109 H5
Elk Creek, *U.S.A.* 112 F4
Elk Grove, *U.S.A.* 112 G5
Elk Island Nat. Park, *Canada* 100 C6
Elk Lake, *Canada* 98 C3
Elk Point, *Canada* 101 C6
Elk River, *Idaho, U.S.A.* 110 C5
Elk River, *Minn., U.S.A.* 108 C8
Elkedra, *Australia* 90 C2
Elkedra →, *Australia* 90 C2
Elkhart, *Ind., U.S.A.* 104 E3
Elkhart, *Kans., U.S.A.* 109 G4
Elkhorn, *Canada* 101 D8
Elkhorn →, *U.S.A.* 108 E6
Elkhovo, *Bulgaria* 38 G9
Elkin, *U.S.A.* 105 G5
Elkins, *U.S.A.* 104 F6
Elko, *Canada* 100 D5
Elko, *U.S.A.* 110 F6
Ell, L., *Australia* 89 E4
Ellecom, *Neths.* 16 D8
Ellef Ringnes I., *Canada* 4 B2
Ellendale, *Australia* 88 C3
Ellendale, *U.S.A.* 108 B5
Ellensburg, *U.S.A.* 110 C3
Ellenville, *U.S.A.* 107 E10
Ellery, Mt., *Australia* 91 F4
Ellesmere, L., *N.Z.* 87 M4
Ellesmere I., *Canada* 4 B4
Ellesmere Port, *U.K.* 12 D5
Ellezelles, *Belgium* 17 G3
Ellice Is. = Tuvalu ■, *Pac. Oc.* 92 H9
Ellinwood, *U.S.A.* 108 F5
Elliot, *Australia* 90 B1
Elliot, *S. Africa* 85 E4
Elliot Lake, *Canada* 98 C3
Elliotdale = Xhora, *S. Africa* 85 E4
Ellis, *U.S.A.* 108 F5
Elliston, *Australia* 91 E1
Ellisville, *U.S.A.* 109 K10
Ellon, *U.K.* 14 D6
Ellore = Eluru, *India* 61 L12
Ells →, *Canada* 100 B6
Ellsworth, *U.S.A.* 108 F5
Ellsworth Land, *Antarctica* 5 D16
Ellsworth Mts., *Antarctica* 5 D16
Ellwangen, *Germany* 19 G6
Ellwood City, *U.S.A.* 106 F4
Elm, *Switz.* 23 C8
Elma, *Canada* 101 D9
Elma, *U.S.A.* 112 D3
Elmadağ, *Turkey* 66 C5
Elmalı, *Turkey* 66 D3
Elmhurst, *U.S.A.* 104 E2
Elmina, *Ghana* 79 D4
Elmira, *Canada* 106 C4
Elmira, *U.S.A.* 106 D8
Elmore, *Australia* 91 F3
Elmore, *U.S.A.* 113 M11
Elmshorn, *Germany* 18 B5
Elmvale, *Canada* 106 B5
Elne, *France* 26 F6
Elora, *Canada* 106 C4
Elorza, *Venezuela* 120 B4
Eloúnda, *Greece* 37 D7
Eloy, *U.S.A.* 111 K8
Éloyes, *France* 25 D13
Elrose, *Canada* 101 C7
Elsas, *Canada* 98 C3
Elsie, *U.S.A.* 112 E3
Elsinore = Helsingør, *Denmark* 11 H6
Elsinore, *U.S.A.* 111 G7
Elspe, *Germany* 18 D4
Elspeet, *Neths.* 16 D7
Elst, *Neths.* 16 E7
Elster →, *Germany* 18 D7
Elsterwerda, *Germany* 18 D9
Elten, *Neths.* 16 E8
Eltham, *N.Z.* 87 H5
Elton, *Russia* 43 F8
Elton, Ozero, *Russia* 43 F8
Eluru, *India* 61 L12
Elvas, *Portugal* 31 G3
Elven, *France* 24 E4
Elverum, *Norway* 10 D5
Elvire →, *Australia* 88 C4
Elvo →, *Italy* 32 C5
Elvran, *Norway* 10 A5
Elwood, *Ind., U.S.A.* 104 E3
Elwood, *Nebr., U.S.A.* 108 E5
Elx = Elche, *Spain* 29 G4
Ely, *U.K.* 13 E8
Ely, *Minn., U.S.A.* 108 B9
Ely, *Nev., U.S.A.* 110 G6
Elyria, *U.S.A.* 106 E2
Elz →, *Germany* 19 G3
Emāmrūd, *Iran* 65 B7
Emba = Embi, *Kazakstan* 44 E6
Emba → = Embi →, *Kazakstan* 44 E6
Embarcación, *Argentina* 126 A3
Embarras Portage, *Canada* 101 B6
Embetsu, *Japan* 48 B10
Embi, *Kazakstan* 44 E6
Embi →, *Kazakstan* 44 E6
Embira →, *Brazil* 124 B3
Embóna, *Greece* 37 C9
Embrach, *Switz.* 23 A7
Embrun, *France* 27 D10
Embu, *Kenya* 82 C4
Embu □, *Kenya* 82 C4
Emden, *Germany* 18 B3
Emerald, *Australia* 90 C4
Emerson, *Canada* 101 D9
Emery, *U.S.A.* 111 G8
Emet, *Turkey* 66 C3
Emi Koussi, *Chad* 73 E8
Emília-Romagna □, *Italy* 32 D7
Emílius, Mte., *Italy* 32 C4
Eminabad, *Pakistan* 62 C6
Emirdağ, *Turkey* 66 C4
Emlenton, *U.S.A.* 106 E5
Emlichheim, *Germany* 18 C2
Emme →, *Switz.* 22 B5
Emmeloord, *Neths.* 16 C7
Emmen, *Neths.* 16 C9
Emmendingen, *Germany* 19 G3
Emmental, *Switz.* 22 C4
Emmer-Compascuum, *Neths.* 16 C10
Emmerich, *Germany* 18 D2
Emmet, *Australia* 90 C3
Emmetsburg, *U.S.A.* 108 D7
Emmett, *U.S.A.* 110 E5
Empalme, *Mexico* 114 B2
Empangeni, *S. Africa* 85 D5
Empedrado, *Argentina* 126 B4
Emperor Seamount Chain, *Pac. Oc.* 92 D9
Empoli, *Italy* 32 E7
Emporia, *Kans., U.S.A.* 108 F6
Emporia, *Va., U.S.A.* 105 G7
Emporium, *U.S.A.* 106 E6
Empress, *Canada* 101 C6
Emptinne, *Belgium* 17 H6
Empty Quarter = Rub' al Khali, *Si. Arabia* 68 D4
Ems →, *Germany* 18 B3
Emsdale, *Canada* 106 A5
Emsdetten, *Germany* 18 C3
Emu, *China* 51 C15
Emu Park, *Australia* 90 C5
'En 'Avrona, *Israel* 69 F3
En Nahud, *Sudan* 77 E2
Ena, *Japan* 49 G8
Enafors, *Sweden* 10 A6
Enambú, *Colombia* 120 C3
Enana, *Namibia* 84 B2
Enånger, *Sweden* 10 C11
Enaratoli, *Indonesia* 57 E9
Enard B., *U.K.* 14 C3
Enare = Inarijärvi, *Finland* 8 B22
Encantadas, Serra, *Brazil* 127 C5
Encanto, C., *Phil.* 57 A6
Encarnación, *Paraguay* 127 B4
Encarnación de Diaz, *Mexico* 114 C4
Enchi, *Ghana* 78 D4
Encinal, *U.S.A.* 109 L5
Encinitas, *U.S.A.* 113 M9
Encino, *U.S.A.* 111 J11
Encontrados, *Venezuela* 120 B3
Encounter B., *Australia* 91 F2
Encruzilhada, *Brazil* 123 E3
Ende, *Indonesia* 57 F6
Endeavour, *Canada* 101 C8
Endeavour Str., *Australia* 90 A3
Endelave, *Denmark* 11 J4
Enderbury I., *Kiribati* 92 H10
Enderby, *Canada* 100 C5
Enderby I., *Australia* 88 D2
Enderby Land, *Antarctica* 5 C5
Enderlin, *U.S.A.* 108 B6
Endicott, *N.Y., U.S.A.* 107 D8
Endicott, *Wash., U.S.A.* 110 C5
Endimari →, *Brazil* 124 B4
Endyalgout I., *Australia* 88 B5
Ene →, *Peru* 124 C3
Enewetak Atoll, *Pac. Oc.* 92 F8
Enez, *Turkey* 66 B2
Enfield, *U.K.* 13 F7
Engadin, *Switz.* 19 J6
Engaño, C., *Dom. Rep.* 117 C6
Engaño, C., *Phil.* 57 A6
Engcobo, *S. Africa* 85 E4
Engelberg, *Switz.* 23 C6
Engels, *Russia* 42 E8
Engemann L., *Canada* 101 B7
Enger, *Norway* 10 D4
Enggano, *Indonesia* 56 F2
Enghien, *Belgium* 17 G4
Engil, *Morocco* 74 B4
Engkilili, *Malaysia* 56 D4
England, *U.S.A.* 109 H9
England □, *U.K.* 7 E5
Englee, *Canada* 99 B8
Englehart, *Canada* 98 C4
Engler L., *Canada* 101 B7
Englewood, *Colo., U.S.A.* 108 F2
Englewood, *Kans., U.S.A.* 109 G5
English →, *Canada* 101 C10
English Bazar = Ingraj Bazar, *India* 63 G13
English Channel, *Europe* 13 G6
English River, *Canada* 98 C1
Enguri →, *Georgia* 43 J5
Enid, *U.S.A.* 109 G6
Enipévs →, *Greece* 39 K5
Enkhuizen, *Neths.* 16 C6
Enköping, *Sweden* 10 E11
Enle, *China* 52 E3
Enna, *Italy* 35 E7
Ennadai, *Canada* 101 A8
Ennadai L., *Canada* 101 A8
Ennedi, *Chad* 73 E9
Enngonia, *Australia* 91 D4
Ennis, *Ireland* 15 D3
Ennis, *Mont., U.S.A.* 110 D8
Ennis, *Tex., U.S.A.* 109 J6
Enniscorthy, *Ireland* 15 D5
Enniskillen, *U.K.* 15 B4
Ennistimon, *Ireland* 15 D2
Enns →, *Austria* 21 G4
Enontekiö, *Finland* 8 B20
Enping, *China* 53 F9
Enriquillo, L., *Dom. Rep.* 117 C5
Ens, *Neths.* 16 C7
Enschede, *Neths.* 16 D9
Ensenada, *Argentina* 126 C4
Ensenada, *Mexico* 114 A1
Enshi, *China* 52 B7
Ensiola, Pta., *Spain* 36 B9
Ensisheim, *France* 25 E14
Entebbe, *Uganda* 82 B3
Enter, *Neths.* 16 D9
Enterprise, *Canada* 100 A5
Enterprise, *Oreg., U.S.A.* 110 D5
Enterprise, *Utah, U.S.A.* 111 H7
Entlebuch, *Switz.* 22 C6
Entre Ríos, *Bolivia* 126 A3
Entre Rios, *Bahia, Brazil* 123 D4
Entre Rios, *Pará, Brazil* 125 B7
Entre Ríos □, *Argentina* 126 C4
Entrepeñas, Pantano de, *Spain* 28 E2
Enugu, *Nigeria* 79 D6
Enugu □, *Nigeria* 79 D6
Enugu Ezike, *Nigeria* 79 D6
Enumclaw, *U.S.A.* 112 C5
Envermeu, *France* 24 C8
Envigado, *Colombia* 120 B2
Envira, *Brazil* 124 B3
Enz →, *Germany* 19 F5
Enza →, *Italy* 32 D7
Eólie, Ís., *Italy* 35 D7
Epanomí, *Greece* 39 J5
Epe, *Neths.* 16 D7
Epe, *Nigeria* 79 D5
Épernay, *France* 25 C10
Épernon, *France* 25 D8
Ephesus, *Turkey* 66 D2
Ephraim, *U.S.A.* 110 G8
Ephrata, *U.S.A.* 110 C4
Epila, *Spain* 28 D3
Épinac-les-Mines, *France* 25 F11
Épinal, *France* 25 D13
Epira, *Guyana* 121 B6
Episkopi, *Cyprus* 37 E11
Episkopí, *Greece* 37 D6
Episkopi Bay, *Cyprus* 37 E11
Eppan = Appiano, *Italy* 33 B8
Epping, *U.K.* 13 F8
Epukiro, *Namibia* 84 C2
Equatorial Guinea ■, *Africa* 80 D1
Equeipa, *Venezuela* 121 B5
Er Rahad, *Sudan* 77 E3
Er Rif, *Morocco* 75 A4
Er Roseires, *Sudan* 77 E3
Erāwadī Myit = Irrawaddy →, *Burma* 61 M19
Erba, *Italy* 32 C6
Erba, *Sudan* 76 D4
Erbaa, *Turkey* 66 B7
Erbil = Arbīl, *Iraq* 67 D11
Erçis, *Turkey* 67 C10
Erdao Jiang →, *China* 51 C14
Erdek, *Turkey* 66 B2
Erdemli, *Turkey* 66 D6
Erdene, *Mongolia* 50 B6
Erding, *Germany* 19 G7
Erdre →, *France* 24 E5
Erebato →, *Venezuela* 121 B5
Erebus, Mt., *Antarctica* 5 D11
Erechim, *Brazil* 127 B5
Ereğli, *Konya, Turkey* 66 D6
Ereğli, *Zonguldak, Turkey* 66 B4
Erei, Monti, *Italy* 35 E7
Erembodegem, *Belgium* 17 G4
Erenhot, *China* 50 C7
Eresma →, *Spain* 30 D6
Erewadi Myitwanya, *Burma* 61 M19
Erfenisdam, *S. Africa* 84 D4
Erfoud, *Morocco* 74 B4
Erft →, *Germany* 18 D2
Erfurt, *Germany* 18 E7
Ergani, *Turkey* 67 C8
Ergeni Vozvyshennost, *Russia* 43 G7
Ērgli, *Latvia* 9 H21
Erhlin, *Taiwan* 53 F13
Eria →, *Spain* 30 C5
Eriba, *Sudan* 77 D4
Eriboll, L., *U.K.* 14 C4
Érica, *Neths.* 16 C9
Érice, *Italy* 34 D5
Erie, *U.S.A.* 106 D4
Erie, L., *N. Amer.* 106 D3
Erie Canal, *U.S.A.* 106 C6
Erieau, *Canada* 106 D3
Erigavo, *Somali Rep.* 68 E4
Erikoúsa, *Greece* 37 A3
Eriksdale, *Canada* 101 C9
Erikslund, *Sweden* 10 B9
Erímanthos, *Greece* 39 M4
Erimo-misaki, *Japan* 48 D11
Eriswil, *Switz.* 22 B5
Erithraí, *Greece* 39 L6
Eritrea ■, *Africa* 77 E4
Erjas →, *Portugal* 31 F3
Erlangen, *Germany* 19 F7
Erldunda, *Australia* 90 D1
Ermelo, *Neths.* 16 D7
Ermelo, *S. Africa* 85 D4
Ermenak, *Turkey* 66 D5
Ermióni, *Greece* 39 M6
Ermones, *Greece* 37 A3
Ermoúpolis = Síros, *Greece* 39 M7
Ernakulam = Cochin, *India* 60 Q10
Erne →, *Ireland* 15 B3
Erne, Lower L., *U.K.* 15 B4
Erne, Upper L., *U.K.* 15 B4
Ernée, *France* 24 D6
Ernest Giles Ra., *Australia* 89 E3
Ernstberg, *Germany* 19 E2
Erode, *India* 60 P10
Eromanga, *Australia* 91 D3
Erongo, *Namibia* 84 C2
Erp, *Neths.* 17 E7
Erquelinnes, *Belgium* 17 H4
Erquy, *France* 24 D4
Erquy, C. d', *France* 24 D4
Err, Piz d', *Switz.* 23 C9
Errabiddy, *Australia* 89 E2
Erramala Hills, *India* 60 M11
Errer →, *Ethiopia* 77 F5
Errigal, *Ireland* 15 A3
Erris Hd., *Ireland* 15 B1
Erseka, *Albania* 39 J3
Erskine, *U.S.A.* 108 B7
Erstein, *France* 25 D14
Erstfeld, *Switz.* 23 C7
Ertil, *Russia* 42 E5
Ertis → = Irtysh →, *Russia* 44 C7
Ertvelde, *Belgium* 17 F3
Eruh, *Turkey* 67 D10
Eruwa, *Nigeria* 79 D5
Ervy-le-Châtel, *France* 25 D10
Erwin, *U.S.A.* 105 G4
Eryuan, *China* 52 D2
Erzgebirge, *Germany* 18 E9
Erzin, *Russia* 45 D10
Erzincan, *Turkey* 67 C8
Erzurum, *Turkey* 67 C9
Es Caló, *Spain* 36 C8
Es Caná, *Spain* 36 B8
Es Sahrâ' Esh Sharqîya, *Egypt* 76 B3
Es Sînâ', *Egypt* 76 J8
Es Sûkî, *Sudan* 77 E3
Esambo, *Zaïre* 82 C1
Esan-Misaki, *Japan* 48 D10
Esashi, *Hokkaidō, Japan* 48 B11
Esashi, *Hokkaidō, Japan* 48 D10
Esbjerg, *Denmark* 11 J2
Escada, *Brazil* 122 C4
Escalante, *U.S.A.* 111 H8
Escalante →, *U.S.A.* 111 H8
Escalón, *Mexico* 114 B4
Escalona, *Spain* 30 E6
Escambia →, *U.S.A.* 105 K2
Escanaba, *U.S.A.* 104 C2
Escaut →, *Belgium* 17 F3
Esch-sur-Alzette, *Lux.* 17 J7
Eschede, *Germany* 18 C6
Escholzmatt, *Switz.* 22 C5
Eschwege, *Germany* 18 D6
Eschweiler, *Germany* 18 E2
Escoma, *Bolivia* 124 D4
Escondido, *U.S.A.* 113 M9
Escuinapa, *Mexico* 114 C3
Escuintla, *Guatemala* 116 D1
Eséka, *Cameroon* 79 E7
Esenguly, *Turkmenistan* 44 F6
Esens, *Germany* 18 B3
Esera →, *Spain* 28 C5
Eşfahān, *Iran* 65 C6
Esfīdeh, *Iran* 65 C8
Esgueva →, *Spain* 30 D6
Esh Sham = Dimashq, *Syria* 69 B5
Esh Shamâlîya □, *Sudan* 76 D2
Eshan, *China* 52 E4
Eshowe, *S. Africa* 85 D5
Esiama, *Ghana* 78 E4
Esil → = Ishim →, *Russia* 44 D8
Esino →, *Italy* 33 E10
Esk →, *Cumb., U.K.* 14 G5
Esk →, *N. Yorks., U.K.* 12 C7
Eskifjörður, *Iceland* 8 D7
Eskilstuna, *Sweden* 10 E10
Eskimalatya, *Turkey* 67 C8
Eskimo Pt., *Canada* 101 A10
Eskişehir, *Turkey* 66 C4
Esla →, *Spain* 30 D4
Esla, Pantano del, *Spain* 30 D4
Eslāmābād-e Gharb, *Iran* 67 E12
Eslöv, *Sweden* 11 J7
Eşme, *Turkey* 66 C3
Esmeralda, I., *Chile* 128 C1
Esmeraldas, *Ecuador* 120 C2
Esmeraldas □, *Ecuador* 120 C2
Esmeraldas →, *Ecuador* 120 C2
Esneux, *Belgium* 17 G7
Espada, Pta., *Colombia* 120 A3
Espalion, *France* 26 D6
Espalmador, I., *Spain* 36 C7
Espanola, *Canada* 98 C3
Espardell, I. del, *Spain* 36 C7
Esparraguera, *Spain* 28 D6
Esparta, *Costa Rica* 116 E3
Espejo, *Spain* 31 H6
Esperança, *Brazil* 122 C4
Esperance, *Australia* 89 F3
Esperance B., *Australia* 89 F3
Esperantinópolis, *Brazil* 122 B3
Esperanza, *Santa Cruz, Argentina* 128 D2
Esperanza, *Santa Fe, Argentina* 126 C3
Esperanza, *Phil.* 55 G6
Espéraza, *France* 26 F6
Espichel, C., *Portugal* 31 G1
Espiel, *Spain* 31 G5
Espigão, Serra do, *Brazil* 127 B5
Espinal, *Colombia* 120 C3
Espinar, *Peru* 124 C3
Espinazo, Sierra del = Espinhaço, Serra do, *Brazil* 123 E3
Espinhaço, Serra do, *Brazil* 123 E3
Espinho, *Portugal* 30 D2
Espinilho, Serra do, *Brazil* 127 B5
Espino, *Venezuela* 120 B4
Espinosa de los Monteros, *Spain* 30 B7
Espírito Santo □, *Brazil* 123 F3
Espíritu Santo, B. del, *Mexico* 115 D7
Espíritu Santo, I., *Mexico* 114 C2
Espita, *Mexico* 115 C7
Espiye, *Turkey* 67 B8
Esplanada, *Brazil* 123 D4
Espluga de Francolí, *Spain* 28 D6
Espoo, *Finland* 9 F21
Espuña, Sierra, *Spain* 29 H3
Espungabera, *Mozam.* 85 C5
Esquel, *Argentina* 128 B2
Esquina, *Argentina* 126 B4
Essaouira, *Morocco* 74 B3
Essebie, *Zaïre* 82 B3
Essen, *Belgium* 17 F4
Essen, *Germany* 18 D2
Essendon, Mt., *Australia* 89 E3
Essequibo →, *Guyana* 121 B6
Essex, *Canada* 106 D2
Essex, *Calif., U.S.A.* 113 L11
Essex, *N.Y., U.S.A.* 107 B11
Essex □, *U.K.* 13 F8
Esslingen, *Germany* 19 G5
Essonne □, *France* 25 D9
Essvik, *Sweden* 10 B11
Estaca, Pta. del, *Spain* 30 B3
Estadilla, *Spain* 28 C5
Estados, I. de Los, *Argentina* 128 D4
Estagel, *France* 26 F6
Eştahbānāt, *Iran* 65 D7
Estallenchs, *Spain* 36 B9
Estância, *Brazil* 122 D4
Estancia, *U.S.A.* 111 J10
Estārm, *Iran* 65 D8
Estarreja, *Portugal* 30 E2
Estats, Pic d', *Spain* 28 C6
Estavayer-le-Lac, *Switz.* 22 C3
Estcourt, *S. Africa* 85 D4
Este, *Italy* 33 C8
Esteban, *Spain* 30 B4
Estelí, *Nic.* 116 D2
Estella, *Spain* 28 C2

Estelline, *S. Dak., U.S.A.* 108 C6
Estelline, *Tex., U.S.A.* 109 H4
Estena →, *Spain* 31 F6
Estepa, *Spain* 31 H6
Estepona, *Spain* 31 J5
Esterhazy, *Canada* 101 C8
Esternay, *France* 25 D10
Esterri de Aneu, *Spain* 28 C6
Estevan, *Canada* 101 D8
Estevan Group, *Canada* 100 C3
Estherville, *U.S.A.* 108 D7
Estissac, *France* 25 D10
Eston, *Canada* 101 C7
Estonia ■, *Europe* 9 G21
Estoril, *Portugal* 31 G1
Estouk, *Mali* 79 B5
Estrêla, Serra da, *Portugal* 30 E3
Estrella, *Spain* 29 G1
Estremoz, *Portugal* 31 G3
Estrondo, Serra do, *Brazil* 122 C2
Esztergom, *Hungary* 21 H8
Et Tîdra, *Mauritania* 78 B1
Étables-sur-Mer, *France* 24 D4
Etadunna, *Australia* 91 D2
Etah, *India* 63 F8
Étain, *France* 25 C12
Etalle, *Belgium* 17 J7
Etamamu, *Canada* 99 B8
Étampes, *France* 25 D9
Étang-sur-Arroux, *France* 27 B8
Etanga, *Namibia* 84 B1
Étaples, *France* 25 B8
Etawah, *India* 63 F8
Etawah →, *U.S.A.* 105 H3
Etawney L., *Canada* 101 B9
Ete, *Nigeria* 79 D6
Éthe, *Belgium* 17 J7
Ethel, *U.S.A.* 112 D4
Ethel, Oued el →, *Algeria* 74 C4
Ethel Creek, *Australia* 88 D3
Ethelbert, *Canada* 101 C8
Ethiopia ■, *Africa* 68 F3
Ethiopian Highlands, *Ethiopia* 46 J7
Etive, L., *U.K.* 14 E3
Etna, *Italy* 35 E8
Etoile, *Zaïre* 83 E2
Etolin I., *U.S.A.* 100 B2
Etosha Pan, *Namibia* 84 B2
Etowah, *U.S.A.* 105 H3
Étrépagny, *France* 25 C8
Étretat, *France* 24 C7
Ettelbruck, *Lux.* 17 J8
Etten, *Neths.* 17 E5
Ettlingen, *Germany* 19 G4
Ettrick Water →, *U.K.* 14 F6
Etuku, *Zaïre* 82 C2
Etzatlán, *Mexico* 114 C4
Eu, *France* 24 B8
Euboea = Évvoia, *Greece* 39 L7
Eucla Motel, *Australia* 89 F4
Euclid, *U.S.A.* 106 E3
Euclides da Cunha, *Brazil* 122 D4
Eucumbene, L., *Australia* 91 F4
Eudora, *U.S.A.* 109 J9
Eufaula, *Ala., U.S.A.* 105 K3
Eufaula, *Okla., U.S.A.* 109 H7
Eufaula L., *U.S.A.* 109 H7
Eugene, *U.S.A.* 110 E2
Eugowra, *Australia* 91 E4
Eulo, *Australia* 91 D4
Eunice, *La., U.S.A.* 109 K8
Eunice, *N. Mex., U.S.A.* 109 J3
Eupen, *Belgium* 17 G8
Euphrates = Furāt, Nahr al →, *Asia* 64 D5
Eure □, *France* 24 C8
Eure →, *France* 24 C8
Eure-et-Loir □, *France* 24 D8
Eureka, *Canada* 4 B3
Eureka, *Calif., U.S.A.* 110 F1
Eureka, *Kans., U.S.A.* 109 G6
Eureka, *Mont., U.S.A.* 110 B6
Eureka, *Nev., U.S.A.* 110 G5
Eureka, *S. Dak., U.S.A.* 108 C5
Eureka, *Utah, U.S.A.* 110 G7
Eureka, Mt., *Australia* 89 E3
Euroa, *Australia* 91 F4
Europa, I., *Ind. Oc.* 81 J8
Europa, Picos de, *Spain* 30 B6
Europa, Pta. de, *Gib.* 31 J5
Europa Pt. = Europa, Pta. de, *Gib.* 31 J5
Europoort, *Neths.* 16 E4
Euskirchen, *Germany* 18 E2
Eustis, *U.S.A.* 105 L5
Eutin, *Germany* 18 A6
Eutsuk L., *Canada* 100 C3
Eva, *Brazil* 121 D6
Eva Downs, *Australia* 90 B1
Evale, *Angola* 84 B2
Evans, *U.S.A.* 108 E2
Evans Head, *Australia* 91 D5
Evans L., *Canada* 98 B4
Evans Mills, *U.S.A.* 107 B9
Evanston, *Ill., U.S.A.* 104 D2
Evanston, *Wyo., U.S.A.* 110 F8
Evansville, *Ind., U.S.A.* 104 F2
Evansville, *Wis., U.S.A.* 108 D10
Évaux-les-Bains, *France* 26 B6
Evaz, *Iran* 65 E7
Eveleth, *U.S.A.* 108 B8
Evensk, *Russia* 45 C16
Evenstad, *Norway* 10 C5
Everard, L., *Australia* 91 E1
Everard Park, *Australia* 89 E5
Everard Ras., *Australia* 89 E5
Evere, *Belgium* 17 G4
Everest, Mt., *Nepal* 63 E12
Everett, *Pa., U.S.A.* 106 F6
Everett, *Wash., U.S.A.* 112 C4
Evergem, *Belgium* 17 F3
Everglades, The, *U.S.A.* 105 N5
Everglades City, *U.S.A.* 105 N5
Everglades National Park, *U.S.A.* 105 N5
Evergreen, *U.S.A.* 105 K2
Everson, *U.S.A.* 110 B2
Evesham, *U.K.* 13 E6
Évian-les-Bains, *France* 27 B10
Evinayong, *Eq. Guin.* 80 D2
Évinos →, *Greece* 39 L4
Évisa, *France* 27 F12
Evje, *Norway* 9 G12
Évora, *Portugal* 31 G3
Évora □, *Portugal* 31 G3
Evowghlī, *Iran* 67 C11
Évreux, *France* 24 C8
Évron, *France* 24 D6
Évros →, *Bulgaria* 66 B2
Evrótas →, *Greece* 39 N5
Évvoia, *Greece* 39 L7
Évvoia □, *Greece* 39 L6
Ewe, L., *U.K.* 14 D3
Ewing, *U.S.A.* 108 D5
Ewo, *Congo* 80 E2
Exaltación, *Bolivia* 125 C4
Excelsior Springs, *U.S.A.* 108 F7
Excideuil, *France* 26 C5
Exe →, *U.K.* 13 G4
Exeter, *Canada* 106 C3
Exeter, *U.K.* 13 G4
Exeter, *Calif., U.S.A.* 111 H4
Exeter, *N.H., U.S.A.* 107 D14
Exeter, *Nebr., U.S.A.* 108 E6
Exloo, *Neths.* 16 C9
Exmes, *France* 24 D7
Exmoor, *U.K.* 13 F4
Exmouth, *Australia* 88 D1
Exmouth, *U.K.* 13 G4
Exmouth G., *Australia* 88 D1
Expedition Ra., *Australia* 90 C4
Extremadura □, *Spain* 31 F4
Exuma Sound, *Bahamas* 116 B4
Eyasi, L., *Tanzania* 82 C4
Eyeberry L., *Canada* 101 A8
Eyemouth, *U.K.* 14 F6
Eygurande, *France* 26 C6
Eyjafjörður, *Iceland* 8 C4
Eymet, *France* 26 D4
Eymoutiers, *France* 26 C5
Eynesil, *Turkey* 67 B8
Eyre, *Australia* 89 F4
Eyre (North), L., *Australia* 91 D2
Eyre (South), L., *Australia* 91 D2
Eyre Cr. →, *Australia* 91 D2
Eyre Mts., *N.Z.* 87 L2
Eyre Pen., *Australia* 91 E2
Eysturoy, *Færoe Is.* 8 E9
Eyvānkī, *Iran* 65 C6
Ez Zeidab, *Sudan* 76 D3
Ezcaray, *Spain* 28 C2
Ezine, *Turkey* 66 C2
Ezmul, *Mauritania* 74 D1
Ezouza →, *Cyprus* 37 E11

F

F.Y.R.O.M. = Macedonia ■, *Europe* 39 H4
Fabens, *U.S.A.* 111 L10
Fåborg, *Denmark* 11 J4
Fabriano, *Italy* 33 E9
Făcăeni, *Romania* 38 E10
Facatativá, *Colombia* 120 C3
Fachi, *Niger* 72 E7
Facture, *France* 26 D3
Fada, *Chad* 73 E9
Fada-n-Gourma, *Burkina Faso* 79 C5
Faddeyevskiy, Ostrov, *Russia* 45 B15
Fadghāmī, *Syria* 67 E9
Fadlab, *Sudan* 76 D3
Faenza, *Italy* 33 D8
Færoe Is. = Føroyar, *Atl. Oc.* 8 F9
Fafa, *Mali* 79 B5
Fafe, *Portugal* 30 D2
Fagam, *Nigeria* 79 C7
Făgăras, *Romania* 38 D7
Făgăras, Munţii, *Romania* 38 D7
Fågelsjö, *Sweden* 10 C8
Fagersta, *Sweden* 9 F16
Făget, *Romania* 38 D5
Fagnano, L., *Argentina* 128 D3
Fagnano Castello, *Italy* 35 C9
Fagnières, *France* 25 D11
Fahlīān, *Iran* 65 D6
Fahraj, *Kermān, Iran* 65 D8
Fahraj, *Yazd, Iran* 65 D7
Faial, *Madeira* 36 D3
Faido, *Switz.* 23 D7
Fair Hd., *U.K.* 15 A5
Fair Oaks, *U.S.A.* 112 G5
Fairbank, *U.S.A.* 111 L8
Fairbanks, *U.S.A.* 96 B5
Fairbury, *U.S.A.* 108 E6
Fairfax, *U.S.A.* 109 G6
Fairfield, *Ala., U.S.A.* 105 J2
Fairfield, *Calif., U.S.A.* 112 G4
Fairfield, *Conn., U.S.A.* 107 E11
Fairfield, *Idaho, U.S.A.* 110 E6
Fairfield, *Ill., U.S.A.* 104 F1
Fairfield, *Iowa, U.S.A.* 108 E9
Fairfield, *Mont., U.S.A.* 110 C8
Fairfield, *Tex., U.S.A.* 109 K7
Fairford, *Canada* 101 C9
Fairhope, *U.S.A.* 105 K2
Fairlie, *N.Z.* 87 L3
Fairmead, *U.S.A.* 112 H6
Fairmont, *Minn., U.S.A.* 108 D7
Fairmont, *W. Va., U.S.A.* 104 F5
Fairmount, *U.S.A.* 113 L8
Fairplay, *U.S.A.* 111 G11
Fairport, *U.S.A.* 106 C7
Fairport Harbor, *U.S.A.* 106 E3
Fairview, *Australia* 90 B3
Fairview, *Canada* 100 B5
Fairview, *Mont., U.S.A.* 108 B2
Fairview, *Okla., U.S.A.* 109 G5
Fairview, *Utah, U.S.A.* 110 G8
Fairweather, Mt., *U.S.A.* 96 C6
Faisalabad, *Pakistan* 62 D5
Faith, *U.S.A.* 108 C3
Faizabad, *India* 63 F10
Fajardo, *Puerto Rico* 117 C6
Fakfak, *Indonesia* 57 E8
Fakobli, *Ivory C.* 78 D3
Fakse, *Denmark* 11 J6
Fakse Bugt, *Denmark* 11 J6
Fakse Ladeplads, *Denmark* 11 J6
Faku, *China* 51 C12
Falaise, *France* 24 D6
Falaise, Mui, *Vietnam* 58 C5
Falam, *Burma* 61 H18
Falces, *Spain* 28 C3
Fălciu, *Romania* 38 C11
Falcón □, *Venezuela* 120 A4
Falcon, C., *Algeria* 75 A4
Falcón, C., *Spain* 36 C7
Falcon Dam, *U.S.A.* 109 M5
Falconara Marittima, *Italy* 33 E10
Falconer, *U.S.A.* 106 D5
Faléa, *Mali* 78 C2
Faleshty = Fălești, *Moldova* 41 J4
Fălești, *Moldova* 41 J4
Falfurrias, *U.S.A.* 109 M5
Falher, *Canada* 100 B5
Falirakí, *Greece* 37 C10
Falkenberg, *Germany* 18 D9
Falkenberg, *Sweden* 11 H6
Falkensee, *Germany* 18 C9
Falkenstein, *Germany* 18 E8
Falkirk, *U.K.* 14 F5
Falkirk □, *U.K.* 14 F5
Falkland, East, I., *Falk. Is.* 128 D5
Falkland, West, I., *Falk. Is.* 128 D4
Falkland Is. □, *Atl. Oc.* 128 D5
Falkland Sd., *Falk. Is.* 128 D5
Falköping, *Sweden* 11 F7
Fall River, *U.S.A.* 107 E13
Fall River Mills, *U.S.A.* 110 F3
Fallbrook, *U.S.A.* 111 K5
Fallbrook, *Calif., U.S.A.* 113 M9
Fallon, *Mont., U.S.A.* 108 B2
Fallon, *Nev., U.S.A.* 110 G4
Falls City, *Nebr., U.S.A.* 108 E7
Falls City, *Oreg., U.S.A.* 110 D2
Falls Creek, *U.S.A.* 106 E6
Falmouth, *Jamaica* 116 C4
Falmouth, *U.K.* 13 G2
Falmouth, *U.S.A.* 104 F3
False B., *S. Africa* 84 E2
Falset, *Spain* 28 D5
Falso, C., *Honduras* 116 C3
Falster, *Denmark* 11 K5
Falsterbo, *Sweden* 11 J6
Fălticeni, *Romania* 38 B9
Falun, *Sweden* 9 F16
Famagusta, *Cyprus* 66 E5
Famagusta Bay, *Cyprus* 37 D13
Famatina, Sierra de, *Argentina* 126 B2
Family L., *Canada* 101 C9
Famoso, *U.S.A.* 113 K7
Fan Xian, *China* 50 G8
Fana, *Mali* 78 C3
Fandriana, *Madag.* 85 C8
Fang, *Thailand* 58 C2
Fang Xian, *China* 53 A8
Fangchang, *China* 53 B12
Fangcheng, *Guangxi Zhuangzu, China* 52 G7
Fangcheng, *Henan, China* 50 H7
Fangliao, *Taiwan* 53 F13
Fangshan, *China* 50 E6
Fangzi, *China* 51 F10
Fani i Madh →, *Albania* 39 H3
Fanjiatun, *China* 51 C13
Fannich, L., *U.K.* 14 D4
Fannūj, *Iran* 65 E8
Fanny Bay, *Canada* 100 D4
Fanø, *Denmark* 11 J2
Fano, *Italy* 33 E10
Fanshaw, *U.S.A.* 100 B2
Fanshi, *China* 50 E7
Fao = Al Fāw, *Iraq* 65 D6
Faqirwali, *Pakistan* 62 E5
Fara in Sabina, *Italy* 33 F9
Faradje, *Zaïre* 82 B2
Farafangana, *Madag.* 85 C8
Farâfra, El Wâhât el-, *Egypt* 76 B2
Farāh, *Afghan.* 60 C3
Farāh □, *Afghan.* 60 C3
Farahalana, *Madag.* 85 A9
Faraid, Gebel, *Egypt* 76 C4
Faramana, *Burkina Faso* 78 C4
Faranah, *Guinea* 78 C2
Farasān, Jazā'ir, *Si. Arabia* 68 D3
Farasan Is. = Farasān, Jazā'ir, *Si. Arabia* 68 D3
Faratsiho, *Madag.* 85 B8
Fardes →, *Spain* 29 H1
Fareham, *U.K.* 13 G6
Farewell, C., *N.Z.* 87 J4
Farewell C. = Farvel, Kap, *Greenland* 4 D5
Farghona, *Uzbekistan* 44 E8
Fargo, *U.S.A.* 108 B6
Fār'iah, W. al →, *West Bank* 69 C4
Faribault, *U.S.A.* 108 C8
Faridkot, *India* 62 D6
Faridpur, *Bangla.* 63 H13
Färila, *Sweden* 10 C9
Farim, *Guinea-Biss.* 78 C1
Farīmān, *Iran* 65 C8
Farina, *Australia* 91 E2
Farinha →, *Brazil* 122 C2
Fariones, Pta., *Canary Is.* 36 E6
Fâriskûr, *Egypt* 76 H7
Farmerville, *U.S.A.* 109 J8
Farmington, *Calif., U.S.A.* 112 H6
Farmington, *N.H., U.S.A.* 107 C13
Farmington, *N. Mex., U.S.A.* 111 H9
Farmington, *Utah, U.S.A.* 110 F8
Farmington →, *U.S.A.* 107 E12
Farmville, *U.S.A.* 104 G6
Farnborough, *U.K.* 13 F7
Farne Is., *U.K.* 12 B6
Farnham, *Canada* 107 A12
Faro, *Brazil* 121 D6
Faro, *Portugal* 31 H3
Fårö, *Sweden* 9 H18
Faro □, *Portugal* 31 H2
Farquhar, C., *Australia* 89 D1
Farrars Cr. →, *Australia* 90 D3
Farrāshband, *Iran* 65 D7
Farrell, *U.S.A.* 106 E4
Farrell Flat, *Australia* 91 E2
Farrokhī, *Iran* 65 C8
Farruch, C., *Spain* 36 B10
Farrukhabad-cum-Fatehgarh, *India* 63 F8
Fārs □, *Iran* 65 D7
Fársala, *Greece* 39 K5
Farsø, *Denmark* 11 H3
Farsund, *Norway* 9 G12
Fartak, Râs, *Si. Arabia* 64 D2
Fartura, Serra da, *Brazil* 127 B5
Faru, *Nigeria* 79 C6
Fārūj, *Iran* 65 B8
Farum, *Denmark* 11 J6
Farvel, Kap, *Greenland* 4 D5
Farwell, *U.S.A.* 109 H3
Fasā, *Iran* 65 D7
Fasano, *Italy* 35 B10
Fashoda, *Sudan* 77 F3
Fastiv, *Ukraine* 41 G5
Fastnet Rock, *Ireland* 15 E2
Fastov = Fastiv, *Ukraine* 41 G5
Fatagar, Tanjung, *Indonesia* 57 E8
Fatehgarh, *India* 63 F8
Fatehpur, *Raj., India* 62 F6
Fatehpur, *Ut. P., India* 63 G9
Fatesh, *Russia* 42 D2
Fatick, *Senegal* 78 C1
Fatima, *Canada* 99 C7
Fátima, *Portugal* 31 F2
Fatoya, *Guinea* 78 C3
Fatsa, *Turkey* 66 B7
Faucille, Col de la, *France* 27 B10
Faulkton, *U.S.A.* 108 C5
Faulquemont, *France* 25 C13
Fauquembergues, *France* 25 B9
Faure I., *Australia* 89 E1
Făurei, *Romania* 38 D10
Fauresmith, *S. Africa* 84 D4
Fauske, *Norway* 8 C16
Fauvillers, *Belgium* 17 J7
Favara, *Italy* 34 E6
Favaritx, C., *Spain* 36 A11
Favignana, *Italy* 34 E5
Favignana, I., *Italy* 34 E5
Favourable Lake, *Canada* 98 B1
Fawn →, *Canada* 98 A2
Fawnskin, *U.S.A.* 113 L10
Faxaflói, *Iceland* 8 D2
Faya-Largeau, *Chad* 73 E8
Fayd, *Si. Arabia* 64 E4
Fayence, *France* 27 E10
Fayette, *Ala., U.S.A.* 105 J2
Fayette, *Mo., U.S.A.* 108 F8
Fayetteville, *Ark., U.S.A.* 109 G7
Fayetteville, *N.C., U.S.A.* 105 H6
Fayetteville, *Tenn., U.S.A.* 105 H2
Fayón, *Spain* 28 D5
Fazenda Nova, *Brazil* 123 E1
Fazilka, *India* 62 D6
Fazilpur, *Pakistan* 62 E4
Fdérik, *Mauritania* 74 D2
Feale →, *Ireland* 15 D2
Fear, C., *U.S.A.* 105 J7
Feather →, *U.S.A.* 110 G3
Feather Falls, *U.S.A.* 112 F5
Featherston, *N.Z.* 87 J5
Featherstone, *Zimbabwe* 83 F3
Fécamp, *France* 24 C7
Fedala = Mohammedia, *Morocco* 74 B3
Federación, *Argentina* 126 C4
Fedeshkūh, *Iran* 65 D7
Fedjadj, Chott el, *Tunisia* 75 B6
Fehmarn, *Germany* 18 A7
Fehmarn Bælt, *Europe* 9 J14
Fei Xian, *China* 51 G9
Feijó, *Brazil* 124 B3
Feilding, *N.Z.* 87 J5
Feira de Santana, *Brazil* 123 D4
Feixiang, *China* 50 F8
Fejø, *Denmark* 11 K5
Feke, *Turkey* 66 D6
Felanitx, *Spain* 36 B10
Feldberg, *Baden-W., Germany* 19 H3
Feldberg, *Mecklenburg-Vorpommern, Germany* 18 B9
Feldkirch, *Austria* 19 H5
Felipe Carrillo Puerto, *Mexico* 115 D7
Felixlândia, *Brazil* 123 E3
Felixstowe, *U.K.* 13 F9
Felletin, *France* 26 C6
Felton, *U.K.* 12 B6
Felton, *U.S.A.* 112 H4
Feltre, *Italy* 33 B8
Femø, *Denmark* 11 K5
Femunden, *Norway* 10 B5
Fen He →, *China* 50 G6
Fenelon Falls, *Canada* 106 B6
Feneroa, *Ethiopia* 77 E4
Feng Xian, *Jiangsu, China* 50 G9
Feng Xian, *Shaanxi, China* 50 H4
Fengári, *Greece* 39 J8
Fengcheng, *Jiangxi, China* 53 C10
Fengcheng, *Liaoning, China* 51 D13
Fengdu, *China* 52 C6
Fengfeng, *China* 50 F8
Fenggang, *China* 52 D6
Fenghua, *China* 53 C13
Fenghuang, *China* 52 D7
Fenghuangzui, *China* 52 A7
Fengjie, *China* 52 B7
Fengkai, *China* 53 F8
Fengle, *China* 53 B9
Fengning, *China* 50 D9
Fengqing, *China* 52 E2
Fengqiu, *China* 50 G8
Fengrun, *China* 51 E10
Fengshan, *Guangxi Zhuangzu, China* 52 E7
Fengshan, *Guangxi Zhuangzu, China* 52 E6
Fengtai, *Anhui, China* 53 A11
Fengtai, *Beijing, China* 50 E9
Fengxian, *China* 53 B13
Fengxiang, *China* 50 G4
Fengxin, *China* 53 C10
Fengyang, *China* 51 H9
Fengyi, *China* 52 E3
Fengzhen, *China* 50 D7
Fenit, *Ireland* 15 D2
Fennimore, *U.S.A.* 108 D9
Feno, C. de, *France* 27 G12
Fenoarivo Afovoany, *Madag.* 85 B8
Fenoarivo Atsinanana, *Madag.* 85 B8
Fens, The, *U.K.* 12 E8
Fenton, *U.S.A.* 104 D4
Fenxi, *China* 50 F6
Fenyang, *China* 50 F6
Fenyi, *China* 53 D10
Feodosiya, *Ukraine* 41 K8
Fer, C. de, *Algeria* 75 A6
Ferdows, *Iran* 65 C8
Fère-Champenoise, *France* 25 D10
Fère-en-Tardenois, *France* 25 C10
Ferentino, *Italy* 34 A6
Ferfer, *Somali Rep.* 68 F4
Fergana = Farghona, *Uzbekistan* 44 E8
Fergus, *Canada* 98 D3
Fergus Falls, *U.S.A.* 108 B6
Fériana, *Tunisia* 75 B6
Feričanci, *Croatia* 21 K8
Ferkane, *Algeria* 75 B6
Ferkéssédougou, *Ivory C.* 78 D3
Ferlach, *Austria* 21 J4
Ferland, *Canada* 98 B2
Ferlo, Vallée du, *Senegal* 78 B2
Fermanagh □, *U.K.* 15 B4
Fermo, *Italy* 33 E10
Fermoselle, *Spain* 30 D4
Fermoy, *Ireland* 15 D3
Fernán Nuñéz, *Spain* 31 H6
Fernández, *Argentina* 126 B3
Fernandina Beach, *U.S.A.* 105 K5
Fernando de Noronha, *Brazil* 122 B5
Fernando Póo = Bioko, *Eq. Guin.* 79 E6
Fernandópolis, *Brazil* 123 F1
Ferndale, *Calif., U.S.A.* 110 F1
Ferndale, *Wash., U.S.A.* 112 B4
Fernie, *Canada* 100 D5
Fernlees, *Australia* 90 C4
Fernley, *U.S.A.* 110 G4
Ferozepore = Firozpur, *India* 62 D6
Férrai, *Greece* 39 J9
Ferrandina, *Italy* 35 B9
Ferrara, *Italy* 33 D8
Ferrato, C., *Italy* 34 C2
Ferreira do Alentejo, *Portugal* 31 G2
Ferreñafe, *Peru* 124 B2
Ferrerías, *Spain* 36 B11

Ferret, C., France 26 D2
Ferrette, France 25 E14
Ferriday, U.S.A. 109 K9
Ferrières, France 25 D9
Ferriete, Italy 32 D6
Ferrol = El Ferrol, Spain 30 B2
Ferrol, Pen. de, Peru 124 B2
Ferron, U.S.A. 111 G8
Ferros, Brazil 123 E3
Ferryland, Canada 99 C9
Fertile, U.S.A. 108 B6
Fertília, Italy 34 B1
Fès, Morocco 74 B4
Feschaux, Belgium 17 H5
Feshi, Zaïre 80 F3
Fessenden, U.S.A. 108 B5
Fetești, Romania 38 E10
Fethiye, Turkey 66 D3
Fetlar, U.K. 14 A8
Feuerthalen, Switz. 23 A7
Feuilles →, Canada 97 C12
Feurs, France 27 C8
Fezzan, Libya 73 C8
Ffestiniog, U.K. 12 E4
Fiambalá, Argentina 126 B2
Fianarantsoa, Madag. 85 C8
Fianarantsoa □, Madag. 85 B8
Fianga, Cameroon 73 G8
Fichtelgebirge, Germany 19 E7
Ficksburg, S. Africa 85 D4
Fidenza, Italy 32 D7
Fiditi, Nigeria 79 D5
Field, Canada 98 C3
Field →, Australia 90 C2
Field I., Australia 88 B5
Fieri, Albania 39 J2
Fiesch, Switz. 22 D6
Fife □, U.K. 14 E5
Fife Ness, U.K. 14 E6
Fifth Cataract, Sudan 76 D3
Figeac, France 26 D6
Figline Valdarno, Italy 33 E8
Figtree, Zimbabwe 83 G2
Figueira Castelo Rodrigo, Portugal 30 E4
Figueira da Foz, Portugal 30 E2
Figueiró dos Vinhos, Portugal 30 F2
Figueras, Spain 28 C7
Figuig, Morocco 75 B4
Fihaonana, Madag. 85 B8
Fiherenana, Madag. 85 B8
Fiherenana →, Madag. 85 C7
Fiji ■, Pac. Oc. 87 C8
Fika, Nigeria 79 C7
Filabres, Sierra de los, Spain 29 H2
Filadélfia, Bolivia 124 C4
Filadélfia, Brazil 122 C2
Filadélfia, Italy 35 D9
Filer, U.S.A. 110 E6
Filey, U.K. 12 C7
Filfla, Malta 37 D1
Filiași, Romania 38 E6
Filiátes, Greece 39 K3
Filiatrá, Greece 39 M4
Filicudi, Italy 35 D7
Filiourí →, Greece 39 H8
Filipstad, Sweden 9 G16
Filisur, Switz. 23 C9
Fillmore, Canada 101 D8
Fillmore, Calif., U.S.A. 113 L8
Fillmore, Utah, U.S.A. 111 G7
Filottrano, Italy 33 E10
Finale Lígure, Italy 32 D5
Finale nell' Emília, Italy 33 D8
Fiñana, Spain 29 H2
Finch, Canada 107 A9
Findhorn →, U.K. 14 D5
Findlay, U.S.A. 104 E4
Finger L., Canada 101 C10
Fíngõe, Mozam. 83 E3
Finike, Turkey 66 D4
Finistère □, France 24 D2
Finisterre, Spain 30 C1
Finisterre, C., Spain 30 C1
Finke, Australia 90 D1
Finke →, Australia 91 D2
Finland ■, Europe 8 E22
Finland, G. of, Europe 9 G21
Finlay →, Canada 100 B3
Finley, Australia 91 F4
Finley, U.S.A. 108 B6
Finn →, Ireland 15 B4
Finnigan, Mt., Australia 90 B4
Finniss, C., Australia 91 E1
Finnmark, Norway 8 B20
Finnsnes, Norway 8 B18
Finspång, Sweden 9 G16
Finsteraarhorn, Switz. 22 C6
Finsterwalde, Germany 18 D9
Finsterwolde, Neths. 16 B10
Fiora →, Italy 33 F8
Fiorenzuola d'Arda, Italy 32 D6
Fīq, Syria 69 C4
Firat = Furāt, Nahr al →, Asia 64 D5
Fire River, Canada 98 C3
Firebag →, Canada 101 B6
Firebaugh, U.S.A. 112 J6
Firedrake L., Canada 101 A8
Firenze, Italy 33 E8
Firk →, Iraq 64 D5
Firmi, France 26 D6
Firminy, France 27 C8
Firozabad, India 63 F8
Firozpur, India 62 D6
Fīrūzābād, Iran 65 D7
Fīrūzkūh, Iran 65 C7
Firvale, Canada 100 C3
Fish →, Namibia 84 D2
Fish →, S. Africa 84 E3
Fisher, Australia 89 F5
Fisher B., Canada 101 C9
Fishguard, U.K. 13 F3
Fishing L., Canada 101 C9
Fismes, France 25 C10
Fitchburg, U.S.A. 107 D13
Fitero, Spain 28 C3
Fitri, L., Chad 73 F8
Fitz Roy, Argentina 128 C3
Fitzgerald, Canada 100 B6
Fitzgerald, U.S.A. 105 K4
Fitzmaurice →, Australia 88 B5
Fitzroy →, Queens., Australia 90 C5
Fitzroy →, W. Austral., Australia 88 C3
Fitzroy Crossing, Australia 88 C4
Fitzwilliam I., Canada 106 A3
Fiume = Rijeka, Croatia 33 C11
Fiumefreddo Brúzio, Italy 35 C9
Five Points, U.S.A. 112 J6
Fivizzano, Italy 32 D7
Fizi, Zaïre 82 C2
Fjellerup, Denmark 11 H4
Fjerritslev, Denmark 11 G3
Fkih ben Salah, Morocco 74 B3
Flå, Norway 10 A4
Flagler, U.S.A. 108 F3
Flagstaff, U.S.A. 111 J8
Flaherty I., Canada 98 A4
Flåm, Norway 9 F12
Flambeau →, U.S.A. 108 C9
Flamborough Hd., U.K. 12 C7
Flaming Gorge Dam, U.S.A. 110 F9
Flaming Gorge Reservoir, U.S.A. 110 F9
Flamingo, Teluk, Indonesia 57 F9
Flanders = West-Vlaanderen □, Belgium 17 G2
Flandre Occidentale = West-Vlaanderen □, Belgium 17 G2
Flandre Orientale = Oost-Vlaanderen □, Belgium 17 F3
Flandreau, U.S.A. 108 C6
Flanigan, U.S.A. 112 E7
Flannan Is., U.K. 14 C1
Flåsjön, Sweden 8 D16
Flat →, Canada 100 A3
Flat River, U.S.A. 109 G9
Flathead L., U.S.A. 110 C6
Flattery, C., Australia 90 A4
Flattery, C., U.S.A. 112 B2
Flavy-le-Martel, France 25 C10
Flawil, Switz. 23 B8
Flaxton, U.S.A. 108 A3
Fleetwood, U.K. 12 D4
Flekkefjord, Norway 9 G12
Flémalle, Belgium 17 G6
Flemington, U.S.A. 106 E7
Flensburg, Germany 18 A5
Flensburger Förde, Germany 18 A5
Flers, France 24 D6
Flesherton, Canada 106 B4
Flesko, Tanjung, Indonesia 57 D6
Fleurance, France 26 E4
Fleurier, Switz. 22 C3
Fleurus, Belgium 17 H5
Flevoland □, Neths. 16 C7
Flims, Switz. 23 C8
Flin Flon, Canada 101 C8
Flinders →, Australia 90 B3
Flinders B., Australia 89 F2
Flinders Group, Australia 90 A3
Flinders I., Australia 90 F4
Flinders Ranges, Australia 91 E2
Flinders Reefs, Australia 90 B4
Flint, U.K. 12 D4
Flint, U.S.A. 104 D4
Flint →, U.S.A. 105 K3
Flint I., Kiribati 93 J12
Flinton, Australia 91 D4
Flintshire □, U.K. 12 D4
Flix, Spain 28 D5
Flixecourt, France 25 B9
Flobecq, Belgium 17 G3
Flodden, U.K. 12 B5
Floodwood, U.S.A. 108 B8
Flora, Norway 10 A5
Flora, U.S.A. 104 F1
Florac, France 26 D7
Florala, U.S.A. 105 K2
Florânia, Brazil 122 C4
Floreffe, Belgium 17 H5
Florence = Firenze, Italy 33 E8
Florence, Ala., U.S.A. 105 H2
Florence, Ariz., U.S.A. 111 K8
Florence, Colo., U.S.A. 108 F2
Florence, Oreg., U.S.A. 110 E1
Florence, S.C., U.S.A. 105 H6
Florence, L., Australia 91 D2
Florennes, Belgium 17 H5
Florensac, France 26 E7
Florenville, Belgium 17 J6
Flores, Brazil 122 C4
Flores, Guatemala 116 C2
Flores, Indonesia 57 F6
Flores I., Canada 100 D3
Flores Sea, Indonesia 57 F6
Floresta, Brazil 122 C4
Florești, Moldova 41 J5
Floresville, U.S.A. 109 L5
Floriano, Brazil 122 C3
Florianópolis, Brazil 127 B6
Florida, Cuba 116 B4
Florida, Uruguay 127 C4
Florida □, U.S.A. 105 L5
Florida, Straits of, U.S.A. 116 B3
Florida B., U.S.A. 116 A3
Florida Keys, U.S.A. 103 F10
Florídia, Italy 35 E8
Floridsdorf, Austria 21 G6
Flórina, Greece 39 J4
Florø, Norway 9 F11
Flower Station, Canada 107 A8
Flower's Cove, Canada 99 B8
Floydada, U.S.A. 109 J4
Fluk, Indonesia 57 E7
Flumen →, Spain 28 D4
Flumendosa →, Italy 34 C2
Fluminimaggiore, Italy 34 C1
Flushing = Vlissingen, Neths. 17 F3
Fluviá →, Spain 28 C8
Flying Fish, C., Antarctica 5 D15
Foam Lake, Canada 101 C8
Foča, Bos.-H. 21 M8
Foça, Turkey 66 C2
Focșani, Romania 38 D10
Fogang, China 53 F9
Foggaret el Arab, Algeria 75 C5
Foggaret ez Zoua, Algeria 75 C5
Fóggia, Italy 35 A8
Foggo, Nigeria 79 C6
Foglia →, Italy 33 E9
Fogo, Canada 99 C9
Fogo I., Canada 99 C9
Fohnsdorf, Austria 21 H4
Föhr, Germany 18 A4
Foia, Portugal 31 H2
Foix, France 26 F5
Fokino, Russia 42 D2
Folda, Nord-Trøndelag, Norway 8 D14
Folda, Nordland, Norway 8 C16
Foleyet, Canada 98 C3
Folgefonni, Norway 9 F12
Foligno, Italy 33 F9
Folkestone, U.K. 13 F9
Folkston, U.S.A. 105 K5
Follett, U.S.A. 109 G4
Follónica, Italy 32 F7
Follónica, G. di, Italy 32 F7
Folsom Res., U.S.A. 112 G5
Fond-du-Lac, Canada 101 B7
Fond du Lac, U.S.A. 108 D10
Fond-du-Lac →, Canada 101 B7
Fonda, U.S.A. 107 D10
Fondi, Italy 34 A6
Fonfría, Spain 30 D4
Fongen, Norway 10 A5
Fonni, Italy 34 B2
Fonsagrada, Spain 30 B3
Fonseca, G. de, Cent. Amer. 116 D2
Fontaine-Française, France 25 E12
Fontainebleau, France 25 D9
Fontana, U.S.A. 113 L9
Fontana, L., Argentina 128 B2
Fontas →, Canada 100 B4
Fonte Boa, Brazil 120 D4
Fontem, Cameroon 79 D6
Fontenay-le-Comte, France 26 B3
Fontur, Iceland 8 C6
Fonyód, Hungary 21 J7
Foochow = Fuzhou, China 53 D12
Foping, China 50 H4
Foppiano, Italy 32 B5
Forbach, France 25 C13
Forbes, Australia 91 E4
Forbesganj, India 63 F12
Forcados, Nigeria 79 D6
Forcados →, Nigeria 79 D6
Forcall →, Spain 28 E4
Forcalquier, France 27 E9
Forchheim, Germany 19 F7
Forclaz, Col de la, Switz. 22 D4
Ford City, Calif., U.S.A. 113 K7
Ford City, Pa., U.S.A. 106 F5
Førde, Norway 9 F11
Ford's Bridge, Australia 91 D4
Fordyce, U.S.A. 109 J8
Forécariah, Guinea 78 D2
Forel, Mt., Greenland 4 C6
Foremost, Canada 100 D6
Forenza, Italy 35 B8
Forest, Belgium 17 G4
Forest, Canada 106 C3
Forest, U.S.A. 109 J10
Forest City, Iowa, U.S.A. 108 D8
Forest City, N.C., U.S.A. 105 H5
Forest City, Pa., U.S.A. 107 E9
Forest Grove, U.S.A. 112 E3
Forestburg, Canada 100 C6
Foresthill, U.S.A. 112 F6
Forestier Pen., Australia 90 G4
Forestville, Canada 99 C6
Forestville, Calif., U.S.A. 112 G4
Forestville, Wis., U.S.A. 104 C2
Forez, Mts. du, France 26 C7
Forfar, U.K. 14 E6
Forges-les-Eaux, France 25 C8
Forks, U.S.A. 112 C2
Forlì, Italy 33 D9
Forman, U.S.A. 108 B6
Formazza, Italy 32 B5
Formby Pt., U.K. 12 D4
Formentera, Spain 36 C7
Formentor, C. de, Spain 36 B10
Former Yugoslav Republic of Macedonia = Macedonia ■, Europe 39 H4
Fórmia, Italy 34 A6
Formiga, Brazil 123 F2
Formigine, Italy 32 D7
Formiguères, France 26 F6
Formosa = Taiwan ■, Asia 53 F13
Formosa, Argentina 126 B4
Formosa, Brazil 123 E2
Formosa □, Argentina 126 B3
Formosa, Serra, Brazil 125 C6
Formosa Bay, Kenya 82 C5
Formosa Strait, Asia 53 E12
Formoso →, Brazil 123 D2
Fornells, Spain 36 A11
Fornos de Algodres, Portugal 30 E3
Fornovo di Taro, Italy 32 D7
Føroyar, Atl. Oc. 8 F9
Forres, U.K. 14 D5
Forrest, Vic., Australia 91 F3
Forrest, W. Austral., Australia 89 F4
Forrest, Mt., Australia 89 D4
Forrest City, U.S.A. 109 H9
Forrières, Belgium 17 H6
Forsa, Sweden 10 C10
Forsayth, Australia 90 B3
Forsmo, Sweden 10 A11
Forssa, Finland 9 F20
Forst, Germany 18 D10
Forster, Australia 91 E5
Forsyth, Ga., U.S.A. 105 J4
Forsyth, Mont., U.S.A. 110 C10
Fort Albany, Canada 98 B3
Fort Apache, U.S.A. 111 K9
Fort Assiniboine, Canada 100 C6
Fort Augustus, U.K. 14 D4
Fort Beaufort, S. Africa 84 E4
Fort Benton, U.S.A. 110 C8
Fort Bragg, U.S.A. 110 G2
Fort Bridger, U.S.A. 110 F8
Fort Chipewyan, Canada 101 B6
Fort Collins, U.S.A. 108 E2
Fort-Coulonge, Canada 98 C4
Fort Davis, U.S.A. 109 K3
Fort-de-France, Martinique 117 D7
Fort de Possel = Possel, C.A.R. 80 C3
Fort Defiance, U.S.A. 111 J9
Fort Dodge, U.S.A. 108 D7
Fort Edward, U.S.A. 107 C11
Fort Frances, Canada 101 D10
Fort Garland, U.S.A. 111 H11
Fort George = Chisasibi, Canada 98 B4
Fort Good-Hope, Canada 96 B7
Fort Hancock, U.S.A. 111 L11
Fort Hertz = Putao, Burma 61 F20
Fort Hope, Canada 98 B2
Fort Irwin, U.S.A. 113 K10
Fort Jameson = Chipata, Zambia 83 E3
Fort Kent, U.S.A. 99 C6
Fort Klamath, U.S.A. 110 E3
Fort-Lamy = Ndjamena, Chad 73 F7
Fort Laramie, U.S.A. 108 D2
Fort Lauderdale, U.S.A. 105 M5
Fort Liard, Canada 100 A4
Fort Liberté, Haiti 117 C5
Fort Lupton, U.S.A. 108 E2
Fort Mackay, Canada 100 B6
Fort McKenzie, Canada 99 A6
Fort Macleod, Canada 100 D6
Fort MacMahon, Algeria 75 C5
Fort McMurray, Canada 100 B6
Fort McPherson, Canada 96 B6
Fort Madison, U.S.A. 108 E9
Fort Meade, U.S.A. 105 M5
Fort Miribel, Algeria 75 C5
Fort Morgan, U.S.A. 108 E3
Fort Myers, U.S.A. 105 M5
Fort Nelson, Canada 100 B4
Fort Nelson →, Canada 100 B4
Fort Norman = Tulita, Canada 96 B7
Fort Payne, U.S.A. 105 H3
Fort Peck, U.S.A. 110 B10
Fort Peck Dam, U.S.A. 110 C10
Fort Peck L., U.S.A. 110 C10
Fort Pierce, U.S.A. 105 M5
Fort Pierre, U.S.A. 108 C4
Fort Pierre Bordes = Ti-n-Zaouaténe, Algeria 75 E5
Fort Plain, U.S.A. 107 D10
Fort Portal, Uganda 82 B3
Fort Providence, Canada 100 A5
Fort Qu'Appelle, Canada 101 C8
Fort Resolution, Canada 100 A6
Fort Rixon, Zimbabwe 83 G2
Fort Rosebery = Mansa, Zambia 83 E2
Fort Ross, U.S.A. 112 G3
Fort Rupert = Waskaganish, Canada 98 B4
Fort St. James, Canada 100 C4
Fort St. John, Canada 100 B4
Fort Sandeman, Pakistan 62 D3
Fort Saskatchewan, Canada 100 C6
Fort Scott, U.S.A. 109 G7
Fort Severn, Canada 98 A2
Fort Shevchenko, Kazakstan 43 H10
Fort Simpson, Canada 100 A4
Fort Smith, Canada 100 B6
Fort Smith, U.S.A. 109 H7
Fort Stanton, U.S.A. 111 K11
Fort Stockton, U.S.A. 109 K3
Fort Sumner, U.S.A. 109 H2
Fort Trinquet = Bir Mogrein, Mauritania 74 C2
Fort Valley, U.S.A. 105 J4
Fort Vermilion, Canada 100 B5
Fort Walton Beach, U.S.A. 105 K2
Fort Wayne, U.S.A. 104 E3
Fort William, U.K. 14 E3
Fort Worth, U.S.A. 109 J6
Fort Yates, U.S.A. 108 B4
Fort Yukon, U.S.A. 96 B5
Fortaleza, Bolivia 124 C4
Fortaleza, Brazil 122 B4
Forteau, Canada 99 B8
Forth →, U.K. 14 E5
Forth, Firth of, U.K. 14 E6
Forthassa Rharbia, Algeria 75 B4
Fortín Coronel Eugenio Garay, Paraguay 125 E5
Fortín Garrapatal, Paraguay 125 E5
Fortín General Pando, Paraguay 125 D6
Fortín Madrejón, Paraguay 125 E6
Fortín Uno, Argentina 128 A3
Fortore →, Italy 33 G12
Fortrose, U.K. 14 D4
Fortuna, Spain 29 G3
Fortuna, Calif., U.S.A. 110 F1
Fortuna, N. Dak., U.S.A. 108 A3
Fortune B., Canada 99 C8
Fos-sur-Mer, France 27 E8
Foshan, China 53 F9
Fosna, Norway 8 E14
Fosnavåg, Norway 9 E11
Fossacésia, Italy 33 F11
Fossano, Italy 32 D4
Fosses-la-Ville, Belgium 17 H5
Fossil, U.S.A. 110 D3
Fossilbrook, Australia 90 B3
Fossombrone, Italy 33 E9
Fosston, U.S.A. 108 B7
Foster, Canada 107 A12
Foster →, Canada 101 B7
Fosters Ra., Australia 90 C1
Fostoria, U.S.A. 104 E4
Fougamou, Gabon 80 E2
Fougères, France 24 D5
Foul Pt., Sri Lanka 60 Q12
Foula, U.K. 14 A6
Foulness I., U.K. 13 F8
Foulpointe, Madag. 85 B8
Foum Assaka, Morocco 74 C2
Foum Zguid, Morocco 74 B3
Foumban, Cameroon 79 D7
Foundiougne, Senegal 78 C1
Fountain, Colo., U.S.A. 108 F2
Fountain, Utah, U.S.A. 110 G8
Fountain Springs, U.S.A. 113 K8
Fourchambault, France 25 E10
Fourchu, Canada 99 C7
Fouriesburg, S. Africa 84 D4
Fourmies, France 25 B11
Foúrnoi, Greece 39 M9
Fours, France 25 F10
Fouta Djalon, Guinea 78 C2
Foux, Cap-à-, Haiti 117 C5
Foveaux Str., N.Z. 87 M2
Fowey, U.K. 13 G3
Fowler, Calif., U.S.A. 111 H4
Fowler, Colo., U.S.A. 108 F2
Fowler, Kans., U.S.A. 109 G4
Fowlers B., Australia 89 F5
Fowlerton, U.S.A. 109 L5
Fowman, Iran 67 D13
Fox →, Canada 101 B10
Fox Valley, Canada 101 C7
Foxe Basin, Canada 97 B12
Foxe Chan., Canada 97 B11
Foxe Pen., Canada 97 B12
Foxhol, Neths. 16 B9
Foxpark, U.S.A. 110 F10
Foxton, N.Z. 87 J5
Foyle, Lough, U.K. 15 A4
Foynes, Ireland 15 D2
Foz, Spain 30 B3
Fóz do Cunene, Angola 84 B1
Foz do Gregório, Brazil 124 B3
Foz do Iguaçu, Brazil 127 B5
Foz do Riosinho, Brazil 124 B3
Frackville, U.S.A. 107 F8
Fraga, Spain 28 D5
Fraire, Belgium 17 H5
Frameries, Belgium 17 H3
Framingham, U.S.A. 107 D13
Franca, Brazil 123 F2
Francavilla al Mare, Italy 33 F11
Francavilla Fontana, Italy 35 B10
France ■, Europe 7 F6
Frances, Australia 91 F3
Frances →, Canada 100 A3
Frances L., Canada 100 A3
Francés Viejo, C., Dom. Rep. 117 C6
Franceville, Gabon 80 E2
Franche-Comté, France 25 F12
Franches Montagnes, Switz. 22 B4
Francisco de Orellana, Ecuador 120 D2
Francisco I. Madero, Coahuila, Mexico 114 B4
Francisco I. Madero, Durango, Mexico 114 C4
Francisco Sá, Brazil 123 E3
Francistown, Botswana 85 C4
Francofonte, Italy 35 E7

François, Canada 99 C8
François L., Canada 100 C3
Francorchamps, Belgium 17 H7
Franeker, Neths. 16 B7
Frankado, Djibouti 77 E5
Frankenberg, Germany 18 D4
Frankenthal, Germany 19 F4
Frankenwald, Germany 19 E7
Frankfort, S. Africa 85 D4
Frankfort, Ind., U.S.A. 104 E2
Frankfort, Kans., U.S.A. 108 F6
Frankfort, Ky., U.S.A. 104 F3
Frankfort, Mich., U.S.A. 104 C2
Frankfurt, Brandenburg, Germany 18 C10
Frankfurt, Hessen, Germany 19 E4
Fränkische Alb, Germany 19 F7
Fränkische Rezal →, Germany 19 F7
Fränkische Saale →, Germany 19 E5
Fränkische Schweiz, Germany 19 F7
Frankland →, Australia 89 G2
Franklin, Ky., U.S.A. 105 G2
Franklin, La., U.S.A. 109 L9
Franklin, Mass., U.S.A. 107 D13
Franklin, N.H., U.S.A. 107 C13
Franklin, Nebr., U.S.A. 108 E5
Franklin, Pa., U.S.A. 106 E5
Franklin, Tenn., U.S.A. 105 H2
Franklin, Va., U.S.A. 105 G7
Franklin, W. Va., U.S.A. 104 F6
Franklin B., Canada 96 B7
Franklin D. Roosevelt L., U.S.A. 110 B4
Franklin I., Antarctica 5 D11
Franklin L., U.S.A. 110 F6
Franklin Mts., Canada 96 B7
Franklin Str., Canada 96 A10
Franklinton, U.S.A. 109 K9
Franklinville, U.S.A. 106 D6
Franks Pk., U.S.A. 110 E9
Frankston, Australia 91 F4
Fränsta, Sweden 10 B10
Frantsa Iosifa, Zemlya, Russia 44 A6
Franz, Canada 98 C3
Franz Josef Land = Frantsa Iosifa, Zemlya, Russia 44 A6
Franzburg, Germany 18 A8
Frascati, Italy 34 A5
Fraser →, B.C., Canada 100 D4
Fraser →, Nfld., Canada 99 A7
Fraser, Mt., Australia 89 E2
Fraser I., Australia 91 D5
Fraser Lake, Canada 100 C4
Fraserburg, S. Africa 84 E3
Fraserburgh, U.K. 14 D6
Fraserdale, Canada 98 C3
Frasne, France 25 F13
Frauenfeld, Switz. 23 A7
Fray Bentos, Uruguay 126 C4
Frazier Downs, Australia 88 C3
Frechilla, Spain 30 C6
Fredericia, Denmark 11 J3
Frederick, Md., U.S.A. 104 F7
Frederick, Okla., U.S.A. 109 H5
Frederick, S. Dak., U.S.A. 108 C5
Frederick Sd., U.S.A. 100 B2
Fredericksburg, Tex., U.S.A. 109 K5
Fredericksburg, Va., U.S.A. 104 F7
Fredericktown, U.S.A. 109 G9
Frederico I. Madero, Presa, Mexico 114 B3
Fredericton, Canada 99 C6
Fredericton Junc., Canada 99 C6
Frederikshåb, Greenland 4 C5
Frederikshavn, Denmark 11 G4
Frederikssund, Denmark 11 J6
Frederiksted, Virgin Is. 117 C7
Fredonia, Ariz., U.S.A. 111 H7
Fredonia, Kans., U.S.A. 109 G7
Fredonia, N.Y., U.S.A. 106 D5
Fredrikstad, Norway 10 E4
Free State □, S. Africa 84 D4
Freehold, U.S.A. 107 F10
Freel Peak, U.S.A. 112 G7
Freeland, U.S.A. 107 E9
Freels, C., Canada 99 C9
Freeman, Calif., U.S.A. 113 K9
Freeman, S. Dak., U.S.A. 108 D6
Freeport, Bahamas 116 A4
Freeport, Canada 99 D6
Freeport, Ill., U.S.A. 108 D10
Freeport, N.Y., U.S.A. 107 F11
Freeport, Tex., U.S.A. 109 L7
Freetown, S. Leone 78 D2
Frégate, L., Canada 98 B5
Fregenal de la Sierra, Spain 31 G4
Fregene, Italy 34 A5
Fréhel, C., France 24 D4
Freiberg, Germany 18 E9
Freibourg = Fribourg, Switz. 22 C4
Freiburg, Baden-W., Germany 19 H3
Freiburg, Niedersachsen, Germany 18 B5
Freiburger Alpen, Switz. 22 C4
Freire, Chile 128 A2
Freirina, Chile 126 B1
Freising, Germany 19 G7
Freistadt, Austria 20 G4
Freital, Germany 18 E9
Fréjus, France 27 E10
Fremantle, Australia 89 F2
Fremont, Calif., U.S.A. 111 H2
Fremont, Mich., U.S.A. 104 D3
Fremont, Nebr., U.S.A. 108 E6
Fremont, Ohio, U.S.A. 104 E4
Fremont →, U.S.A. 111 G8
Fremont L., U.S.A. 110 E9
French Camp, U.S.A. 112 H5
French Creek →, U.S.A. 106 E5
French Guiana ■, S. Amer. 121 C7
French Pass, N.Z. 87 J4
French Polynesia ■, Pac. Oc. 93 J13
Frenchglen, U.S.A. 110 E4
Frenchman Butte, Canada 101 C7
Frenchman Cr. →, Mont., U.S.A. 110 B10
Frenchman Cr. →, Nebr., U.S.A. 108 E4
Frenda, Algeria 75 A5
Fresco →, Brazil 125 B7
Freshfield, C., Antarctica 5 C10
Fresnay-sur-Sarthe, France 24 D7
Fresnillo, Mexico 114 C4
Fresno, U.S.A. 111 H4
Fresno Alhandiga, Spain 30 E5
Fresno Reservoir, U.S.A. 110 B9
Freudenstadt, Germany 19 G4
Freux, Belgium 17 J6
Frévent, France 25 B9
Frew →, Australia 90 C2
Frewena, Australia 90 B2
Freycinet Pen., Australia 90 G4
Freyming-Merlebach, France 25 C13
Freyung, Germany 19 G9
Fria, Guinea 78 C2
Fria, C., Namibia 84 B1
Friant, U.S.A. 112 J7
Frías, Argentina 126 B2
Fribourg, Switz. 22 C4
Fribourg □, Switz. 22 C4
Frick, Switz. 22 A6
Friday Harbor, U.S.A. 112 B3
Friedberg, Bayern, Germany 19 G6
Friedberg, Hessen, Germany 19 E4
Friedland, Germany 18 B9
Friedrichshafen, Germany 19 H5
Friedrichskoog, Germany 18 A4
Friedrichstadt, Germany 18 A5
Friendly Is. = Tonga ■, Pac. Oc. 87 D11
Friesack, Germany 18 C8
Friesche Wad, Neths. 16 B7
Friesland □, Neths. 16 B7
Friesoythe, Germany 18 B3
Frillesås, Sweden 11 G6
Frio →, U.S.A. 109 L5
Frio, C., Brazil 118 F6
Friona, U.S.A. 109 H3
Frisian Is., Europe 18 B2
Fristad, Sweden 11 G7
Fritch, U.S.A. 109 H4
Fritsla, Sweden 11 G6
Fritzlar, Germany 18 D5
Friuli-Venézia Giulia □, Italy 33 B10
Frobisher B., Canada 97 B13
Frobisher Bay = Iqaluit, Canada 97 B13
Frobisher L., Canada 101 B7
Frohavet, Norway 8 E13
Froid, U.S.A. 108 A2
Froid-Chapelle, Belgium 17 H4
Frolovo, Russia 42 F6
Fromberg, U.S.A. 110 D9
Frome, U.K. 13 F5
Frome, L., Australia 91 E2
Frome Downs, Australia 91 E2
Frómista, Spain 30 C6
Front Range, U.S.A. 110 G11
Front Royal, U.S.A. 104 F6
Fronteira, Portugal 31 F3
Fronteiras, Brazil 122 C3
Frontera, Canary Is. 36 G2
Frontera, Mexico 115 D6
Frontignan, France 26 E7
Frosinone, Italy 34 A6
Frosolone, Italy 35 A7
Frostburg, U.S.A. 104 F6
Frostisen, Norway 8 B17
Frouard, France 25 D13
Frøya, Norway 8 E13
Fruges, France 25 B9
Frumoasa, Romania 38 C8
Frunze = Bishkek, Kyrgyzstan 44 E8
Frutal, Brazil 123 F2
Frutigen, Switz. 22 C5
Frýdek-Místek, Czech. 20 F8
Frýdlant, Czech. 20 E5
Fu Jiang →, China 52 C6
Fu Xian, Liaoning, China 51 E11
Fu Xian, Shaanxi, China 50 F5
Fu'an, China 53 D12
Fubian, China 52 B4
Fucécchio, Italy 32 E7
Fucheng, China 50 F9
Fuchou = Fuzhou, China 53 D12
Fuchū, Japan 49 G6
Fuchuan, China 53 E8
Fuchun Jiang →, China 53 B13
Fúcino, Conca del, Italy 33 F10
Fuding, China 53 D13
Fuencaliente, Canary Is. 36 F2
Fuencaliente, Spain 31 G6
Fuencaliente, Pta., Canary Is. 36 F2
Fuengirola, Spain 31 J6
Fuente Alamo, Albacete, Spain 29 G3
Fuente Álamo, Murcia, Spain 29 H3
Fuente de Cantos, Spain 31 G4
Fuente del Maestre, Spain 31 G4
Fuente el Fresno, Spain 31 F7
Fuente Ovejuna, Spain 31 G5
Fuentes de Andalucía, Spain 31 H5
Fuentes de Ebro, Spain 28 D4
Fuentes de León, Spain 31 G4
Fuentes de Oñoro, Spain 30 E4
Fuentesaúco, Spain 30 D5
Fuerte →, Mexico 114 B3
Fuerte Olimpo, Paraguay 126 A4
Fuerteventura, Canary Is. 36 F6
Fufeng, China 50 G4
Fuga I., Phil. 55 B4
Fugong, China 52 D2
Fugou, China 50 G8
Fugu, China 50 E6
Fuhai, China 54 B3
Fuḥaymī, Iraq 67 E10
Fuji, Japan 49 G9
Fuji-San, Japan 49 G9
Fuji-yoshida, Japan 49 G9
Fujian □, China 53 E12
Fujinomiya, Japan 49 G9
Fujisawa, Japan 49 G9
Fukien = Fujian □, China 53 E12
Fukuchiyama, Japan 49 G7
Fukue-Shima, Japan 49 H4
Fukui, Japan 49 F8
Fukui □, Japan 49 G8
Fukuoka, Japan 49 H5
Fukuoka □, Japan 49 H5
Fukushima, Japan 48 F10
Fukushima □, Japan 48 F10
Fukuyama, Japan 49 G6
Fulda, Germany 18 E5
Fulda →, Germany 18 D5
Fuling, China 52 C6
Fullerton, Calif., U.S.A. 113 M9
Fullerton, Nebr., U.S.A. 108 E5
Fulongquan, China 51 B13
Fulton, Mo., U.S.A. 108 F9
Fulton, N.Y., U.S.A. 107 C8
Fulton, Tenn., U.S.A. 105 G1
Fuluälven →, Sweden 10 C7
Fulufjället, Sweden 10 C6
Fumay, France 25 C11
Fumel, France 26 D4
Fumin, China 52 E4
Funabashi, Japan 49 G10
Funchal, Madeira 36 D3
Fundación, Colombia 120 A3
Fundão, Brazil 123 E3
Fundão, Portugal 30 E3
Fundy, B. of, Canada 99 D6
Funing, Hebei, China 51 E10
Funing, Jiangsu, China 51 H10
Funing, Yunnan, China 52 F5
Funiu Shan, China 50 H7
Funsi, Ghana 78 C4
Funtua, Nigeria 79 C6
Fuping, Hebei, China 50 E8
Fuping, Shaanxi, China 50 G5
Fuqing, China 53 E12
Fuquan, China 52 D6
Fur, Denmark 11 H3
Furano, Japan 48 C11
Furāt, Nahr al →, Asia 64 D5
Fürg, Iran 65 D7
Furkapass, Switz. 23 C7
Furmanov, Russia 42 B5
Furmanovo, Kazakstan 42 F9
Furnás, Spain 36 B8
Furnas, Reprêsa de, Brazil 123 F2
Furneaux Group, Australia 90 G4
Furness, U.K. 12 C4
Furqlus, Syria 69 A6
Fürstenau, Germany 18 C3
Fürstenberg, Germany 18 B9
Fürstenfeld, Austria 21 H6
Fürstenfeldbruck, Germany 19 G7
Fürstenwalde, Germany 18 C10
Fürth, Germany 19 F6
Furth im Wald, Germany 19 F8
Furtwangen, Germany 19 G4
Furukawa, Japan 48 E10
Furusund, Sweden 10 E12
Fury and Hecla Str., Canada 97 B11
Fusagasuga, Colombia 120 C3
Fuscaldo, Italy 35 C9
Fushan, Shandong, China 51 F11
Fushan, Shanxi, China 50 G6
Fushun, Liaoning, China 51 D12
Fushun, Sichuan, China 52 C5
Fusio, Switz. 23 D7
Fusong, China 51 C14
Füssen, Germany 19 H6
Fusui, China 52 F6
Futrono, Chile 128 B2
Futuna, Wall. & F. Is. 87 B8
Fuwa, Egypt 76 H7
Fuxin, China 51 C11
Fuyang, Anhui, China 50 H8
Fuyang, Zhejiang, China 53 B12
Fuyang He →, China 50 E9
Fuying Dao, China 53 D13
Fuyu, China 51 B13
Fuyuan, Heilongjiang, China 54 B8
Fuyuan, Yunnan, China 52 E5
Fuzhou, China 53 D12
Fylde, U.K. 12 D5
Fyn, Denmark 11 J4
Fyne, L., U.K. 14 F3
Fyns Amtskommune □, Denmark 11 J4
Fyresvatn, Norway 10 E2

G

Gaanda, Nigeria 79 C7
Gabarin, Nigeria 79 C7
Gabas →, France 26 E3
Gabela, Angola 80 G2
Gabès, Tunisia 75 B7
Gabès, G. de, Tunisia 75 B7
Gabgaba, W. →, Egypt 76 C3
Gabon ■, Africa 80 E2
Gaborone, Botswana 84 C4
Gabriels, U.S.A. 107 B10
Gābrīk, Iran 65 E8
Gabrovo, Bulgaria 38 G8
Gacé, France 24 D7
Gāch Sār, Iran 65 B6
Gachsārān, Iran 65 D6
Gacko, Bos.-H. 21 M8
Gadag, India 60 M9
Gadamai, Sudan 77 D4
Gadap, Pakistan 62 G2
Gadarwara, India 63 H8
Gadebusch, Germany 18 B7
Gadein, Sudan 77 F2
Gadhada, India 62 J4
Gadmen, Switz. 23 C6
Gádor, Sierra de, Spain 29 J2
Gadsden, Ala., U.S.A. 105 H2
Gadsden, Ariz., U.S.A. 111 K6
Gadwal, India 60 L10
Gadyach = Hadyach, Ukraine 41 G8
Găeşti, Romania 38 E8
Gaeta, Italy 34 A6
Gaeta, G. di, Italy 34 A6
Gaffney, U.S.A. 105 H5
Gafsa, Tunisia 75 B6
Gagarin, Russia 42 C2
Gagetown, Canada 99 C6
Gagino, Russia 42 C7
Gagliano del Capo, Italy 35 C11
Gagnoa, Ivory C. 78 D3
Gagnon, Canada 99 B6
Gagnon, L., Canada 101 A6
Gagra, Georgia 43 J5
Gahini, Rwanda 82 C3
Gahmar, India 63 G10
Gai Xian, China 51 D12
Gaïdhouronísi, Greece 37 E7
Gail, U.S.A. 109 J4
Gail →, Austria 21 J3
Gaillac, France 26 E5
Gaillimh = Galway, Ireland 15 C2
Gaillon, France 24 C8
Gaimán, Argentina 128 B3
Gaines, U.S.A. 106 E7
Gainesville, Fla., U.S.A. 105 L4
Gainesville, Ga., U.S.A. 105 H4
Gainesville, Mo., U.S.A. 109 G8
Gainesville, Tex., U.S.A. 109 J6
Gainsborough, U.K. 12 D7
Gairdner, L., Australia 91 E2
Gairloch, L., U.K. 14 D3
Gais, Switz. 23 B8
Gakuch, Pakistan 63 A5
Galán, Cerro, Argentina 126 B2
Galana →, Kenya 82 C5
Galangue, Angola 81 G3
Galápagos, Pac. Oc. 118 D1
Galashiels, U.K. 14 F6
Galaţi, Romania 38 D11
Galatia, Turkey 66 C5
Galatina, Italy 35 B11
Galátone, Italy 35 B11
Galax, U.S.A. 105 G5
Galaxídhion, Greece 39 L5
Galbraith, Australia 90 B3
Galcaio, Somali Rep. 68 F4
Galdhøpiggen, Norway 10 C2
Galeana, Mexico 114 C4
Galela, Indonesia 57 D7
Galera, Spain 29 H2
Galera, Pta., Chile 128 A2
Galera Point, Trin. & Tob. 117 D7
Galesburg, U.S.A. 108 E9
Galeton, U.S.A. 106 E7
Galheirão →, Brazil 123 D2
Galheiros, Brazil 123 D2
Gali, Georgia 43 J5
Galich, Russia 42 A6
Galiche, Bulgaria 38 F6
Galicia □, Spain 30 C3
Galilee = Hagalil, Israel 69 C4
Galilee, L., Australia 90 C4
Galilee, Sea of = Yam Kinneret, Israel 69 C4
Galinoporni, Cyprus 37 D13
Galion, U.S.A. 106 F2
Galite, Is. de la, Tunisia 75 A6
Galiuro Mts., U.S.A. 111 K8
Gallabat, Sudan 77 E4
Gallarate, Italy 32 C5
Gallardon, France 25 D8
Gallatin, U.S.A. 105 G2
Galle, Sri Lanka 60 R12
Gállego →, Spain 28 D4
Gallegos →, Argentina 128 D3
Galley Hd., Ireland 15 E3
Galliate, Italy 32 C5
Gallinas, Pta., Colombia 120 A3
Gallipoli = Gelibolu, Turkey 66 B2
Gallípoli, Italy 35 B11
Gallipolis, U.S.A. 104 F4
Gällivare, Sweden 8 C19
Gallo, C., Italy 34 D6
Gallocanta, L. de, Spain 28 E3
Galloway, U.K. 14 G4
Galloway, Mull of, U.K. 14 G4
Gallup, U.S.A. 111 J9
Gallur, Spain 28 D3
Galong, Australia 91 E4
Galoya, Sri Lanka 60 Q12
Galt, U.S.A. 112 G5
Galtström, Sweden 10 B11
Galtür, Austria 19 J6
Galty Mts., Ireland 15 D3
Galtymore, Ireland 15 D3
Galva, U.S.A. 108 E9
Galvarino, Chile 128 A2
Galve de Sorbe, Spain 28 D1
Galveston, U.S.A. 109 L7
Galveston B., U.S.A. 109 L7
Gálvez, Argentina 126 C3
Gálvez, Spain 31 F6
Galway, Ireland 15 C2
Galway □, Ireland 15 C2
Galway B., Ireland 15 C2
Gam →, Vietnam 58 B5
Gamagori, Japan 49 G8
Gamari, L., Ethiopia 77 E5
Gamawa, Nigeria 79 C7
Gamay, Phil. 55 E6
Gambaga, Ghana 79 C4
Gambat, Pakistan 62 F3
Gambela, Ethiopia 77 F3
Gambia ■, W. Afr. 78 C1
Gambia →, W. Afr. 78 C1
Gambier, C., Australia 88 B5
Gambier Is., Australia 91 F2
Gamboli, Pakistan 62 E3
Gamboma, Congo 80 E3
Gamerco, U.S.A. 111 J9
Gamlakarleby = Kokkola, Finland 8 E20
Gammon →, Canada 101 C9
Gammouda, Tunisia 75 A6
Gamu-Gofa □, Ethiopia 77 F4
Gan, France 26 E3
Gan Gan, Argentina 128 B3
Gan Goriama, Mts., Cameroon 79 D7
Gan Jiang →, China 53 C10
Ganado, Ariz., U.S.A. 111 J9
Ganado, Tex., U.S.A. 109 L6
Gananoque, Canada 98 D4
Ganāveh, Iran 65 D6
Gäncä, Azerbaijan 43 K8
Gand = Gent, Belgium 17 F3
Ganda, Angola 81 G2
Gandak →, India 63 G11
Gandava, Pakistan 62 E2
Gander, Canada 99 C9
Gander L., Canada 99 C9
Ganderowe Falls, Zimbabwe 83 F2
Gandesa, Spain 28 D5
Gandhi Sagar, India 62 G6
Gandi, Nigeria 79 C6
Gandía, Spain 29 G4
Gandino, Italy 32 C6
Gando, Pta., Canary Is. 36 G4
Gandole, Nigeria 79 D7
Gandu, Brazil 123 D4
Ganedidalem = Gani, Indonesia 57 E7
Ganetti, Sudan 76 D3
Ganga →, India 63 H14
Ganga, Mouths of the, India 63 J13
Ganganagar, India 62 E5
Gangapur, India 62 F7
Gangara, Niger 79 C6
Gangaw, Burma 61 H19
Gangdisê Shan, China 61 D12
Ganges = Ganga →, India 63 H14
Ganges, France 26 E7
Gangoh, India 62 E7
Gangtok, India 61 F16
Gangu, China 50 G3
Gangyao, China 51 B14
Gani, Indonesia 57 E7
Ganj, India 63 F8
Gannat, France 26 B7
Gannett Peak, U.S.A. 110 E9
Gannvalley, U.S.A. 108 C5
Ganquan, China 50 F5
Gänserdorf, Austria 21 G6
Ganshui, China 52 C6
Gansu □, China 50 G3
Ganta, Liberia 78 D3
Gantheaume, C. Australia 91 F2
Gantheaume B., Australia 89 E1
Gantsevichi = Hantsavichy, Belarus 41 F4
Ganyem, Indonesia 57 E10
Ganyu, China 51 G10
Ganyushkino, Kazakstan 43 G9
Ganzhou, China 53 E10
Gao, Mali 79 B5
Gao Xian, China 52 C5
Gao'an, China 53 C10

Gaohe, *China* 53 F9
Gaohebu, *China* 53 B11
Gaokeng, *China* 53 D9
Gaolan Dao, *China* 53 G9
Gaoligong Shan, *China* 52 E2
Gaomi, *China* 51 F10
Gaoping, *China* 50 G7
Gaotang, *China* 50 F9
Gaoua, *Burkina Faso* 78 C4
Gaoual, *Guinea* 78 C2
Gaoxiong = Kaohsiung, *Taiwan* 53 F13
Gaoyang, *China* 50 E8
Gaoyou, *China* 53 A12
Gaoyou Hu, *China* 51 H10
Gaoyuan, *China* 51 F9
Gaozhou, *China* 53 G8
Gap, *France* 27 D10
Gapan, *Phil.* 55 D4
Gar, *China* 54 C2
Garabogazköl Aylagy, *Turkmenistan* 44 E6
Garachico, *Canary Is.* 36 F3
Garachiné, *Panama* 116 E4
Garafia, *Canary Is.* 36 F2
Garajonay, *Canary Is.* 36 F2
Garanhuns, *Brazil* 122 C4
Garawe, *Liberia* 78 E3
Garba Tula, *Kenya* 82 B4
Garber, *U.S.A.* 109 G6
Garberville, *U.S.A.* 110 F2
Garça, *Brazil* 123 F2
Garças →, *Mato Grosso, Brazil* 125 D7
Garças →, *Pernambuco, Brazil* 122 C4
Garcias, *Brazil* 125 E7
Gard, *Somali Rep.* 68 F4
Gard □, *France* 27 D8
Gard →, *France* 27 E8
Garda, L. di, *Italy* 32 C7
Gardanne, *France* 27 E9
Garde L., *Canada* 101 A7
Gardelegen, *Germany* 18 C7
Garden City, *Kans., U.S.A.* 109 G4
Garden City, *Tex., U.S.A.* 109 K4
Garden Grove, *U.S.A.* 113 M9
Gardēz, *Afghan.* 62 C3
Gardiner, *U.S.A.* 110 D8
Gardiners I., *U.S.A.* 107 E12
Gardner, *U.S.A.* 107 D13
Gardner Canal, *Canada* 100 C3
Gardnerville, *U.S.A.* 112 G7
Gare Tigre, *Fr. Guiana* 121 C7
Garéssio, *Italy* 32 D5
Garey, *U.S.A.* 113 L6
Garfield, *U.S.A.* 110 C5
Gargan, Mt., *France* 26 C5
Gargano, Mte., *Italy* 35 A8
Gargouna, *Mali* 79 B5
Garhshankar, *India* 62 D7
Garibaldi Prov. Park, *Canada* 100 D4
Garies, *S. Africa* 84 E2
Garigliano →, *Italy* 34 A6
Garissa, *Kenya* 82 C4
Garissa □, *Kenya* 82 C5
Garkida, *Nigeria* 79 C7
Garko, *Nigeria* 79 C6
Garland, *Tex., U.S.A.* 109 J6
Garland, *Utah, U.S.A.* 110 F7
Garlasco, *Italy* 32 C5
Garm, *Tajikistan* 44 F8
Garmāb, *Iran* 65 C8
Garmisch-Partenkirchen, *Germany* 19 H7
Garmsār, *Iran* 65 C7
Garner, *U.S.A.* 108 D8
Garnett, *U.S.A.* 108 F7
Garo Hills, *India* 63 G14
Garoe, *Somali Rep.* 68 F4
Garonne →, *France* 26 C3
Garonne, Canal Latéral à la →, *France* 26 D4
Garoua, *Cameroon* 79 D7
Garrel, *Germany* 18 C3
Garrigue, *France* 26 E7
Garrison, *Mont., U.S.A.* 110 C7
Garrison, *N. Dak., U.S.A.* 108 B4
Garrison, *Tex., U.S.A.* 109 K7
Garrison Res. = Sakakawea, L., *U.S.A.* 108 B3
Garrovillas, *Spain* 31 F4
Garrucha, *Spain* 29 H3
Garry →, *U.K.* 14 E5
Garry, L., *Canada* 96 B9
Garsen, *Kenya* 82 C5
Garson L., *Canada* 101 B6
Gartempe →, *France* 26 B4
Gartz, *Germany* 18 B10
Garu, *Ghana* 79 C4
Garub, *Namibia* 84 D2
Garut, *Indonesia* 57 G12
Garvão, *Portugal* 31 H2
Garvie Mts., *N.Z.* 87 L2
Garwa = Garoua, *Cameroon* 79 D7
Garwa, *India* 63 G10
Garwolin, *Poland* 20 D11
Gary, *U.S.A.* 104 E2
Garz, *Germany* 18 A9
Garzê, *China* 52 B3
Garzón, *Colombia* 120 C2
Gas-San, *Japan* 48 E10
Gasan Kuli = Esenguly, *Turkmenistan* 44 F6
Gascogne, *France* 26 E4
Gascogne, G. de, *Europe* 28 B2
Gascony = Gascogne, *France* 26 E4
Gascoyne →, *Australia* 89 D1
Gascoyne Junc. T.O., *Australia* 89 E2
Gascueña, *Spain* 28 E2
Gash, Wadi →, *Ethiopia* 77 D4
Gashaka, *Nigeria* 79 D7
Gasherbrum, *Pakistan* 63 B7
Gashua, *Nigeria* 79 C7
Gaspé, *Canada* 99 C7
Gaspé, C. de, *Canada* 99 C7
Gaspé, Pén. de, *Canada* 99 C6
Gaspésie, Parc Prov. de la, *Canada* 99 C6
Gassaway, *U.S.A.* 104 F5
Gasselte, *Neths.* 16 C9
Gasselternijveen, *Neths.* 16 C9
Gàssino Torinese, *Italy* 32 C4
Gassol, *Nigeria* 79 D7
Gasteiz = Vitoria, *Spain* 28 C2
Gastonia, *U.S.A.* 105 H5
Gastoúni, *Greece* 39 M4
Gastoúri, *Greece* 39 K2
Gastre, *Argentina* 128 B3
Gata, C., *Cyprus* 37 E12
Gata, C. de, *Spain* 29 J2
Gata, Sierra de, *Spain* 30 E4
Gataga →, *Canada* 100 B3
Gătaia, *Romania* 38 D4
Gatchina, *Russia* 40 C6
Gates, *U.S.A.* 106 C7
Gateshead, *U.K.* 12 C6
Gatesville, *U.S.A.* 109 K6
Gaths, *Zimbabwe* 83 G3
Gatico, *Chile* 126 A1
Gâtinais, *France* 25 D9
Gâtine, Hauteurs de, *France* 26 B3
Gatineau →, *Canada* 98 C4
Gatineau, Parc de la, *Canada* 98 C4
Gattaran, *Phil.* 55 B4
Gattinara, *Italy* 32 C5
Gatun, L., *Panama* 116 E4
Gatyana, *S. Africa* 85 E4
Gau, *Fiji* 87 D8
Gaucín, *Spain* 31 J5
Gauer L., *Canada* 101 B9
Gauhati, *India* 63 F14
Gauja →, *Latvia* 9 H21
Gaula →, *Norway* 8 E14
Gaurain-Ramecroix, *Belgium* 17 G3
Gausta, *Norway* 10 E2
Gauteng □, *S. Africa* 85 D4
Gāv Koshī, *Iran* 65 D8
Gavá, *Spain* 28 D6
Gāvakān, *Iran* 65 D7
Gavarnie, *France* 26 F3
Gavāter, *Iran* 65 E9
Gāvbandī, *Iran* 65 E7
Gavdhopoúla, *Greece* 37 E6
Gávdhos, *Greece* 37 E6
Gavere, *Belgium* 17 G3
Gavião, *Portugal* 31 F3
Gaviota, *U.S.A.* 113 L6
Gävle, *Sweden* 9 F17
Gävleborgs län □, *Sweden* 10 C10
Gavorrano, *Italy* 32 F7
Gavray, *France* 24 D5
Gavrilov Yam, *Russia* 42 B4
Gawachab, *Namibia* 84 D2
Gawilgarh Hills, *India* 60 J10
Gawler, *Australia* 91 E2
Gaxun Nur, *China* 54 B5
Gaya, *India* 63 G11
Gaya, *Niger* 79 C5
Gaya, *Nigeria* 79 C6
Gaylord, *U.S.A.* 104 C3
Gayndah, *Australia* 91 D5
Gaysin = Haysyn, *Ukraine* 41 H5
Gayvoron = Hayvoron, *Ukraine* 41 H5
Gaza, *Gaza Strip* 69 D3
Gaza □, *Mozam.* 85 C5
Gaza Strip □, *Asia* 69 D3
Gazaoua, *Niger* 79 C6
Gāzbor, *Iran* 65 D8
Gazi, *Zaïre* 82 B1
Gaziantep, *Turkey* 66 D7
Gazipaşa, *Turkey* 66 D5
Gazli, *Uzbekistan* 44 E7
Gbarnga, *Liberia* 78 D3
Gbekebo, *Nigeria* 79 D5
Gboko, *Nigeria* 79 D6
Gbongan, *Nigeria* 79 D5
Gcuwa, *S. Africa* 85 E4
Gdańsk, *Poland* 20 A8
Gdańska, Zatoka, *Poland* 20 A9
Gdov, *Russia* 9 G22
Gdynia, *Poland* 20 A8
Gebe, *Indonesia* 57 D7
Gebeit Mine, *Sudan* 76 C4
Gebze, *Turkey* 66 B3
Gecha, *Ethiopia* 77 F4
Gedaref, *Sudan* 77 E4
Gede, Tanjung, *Indonesia* 56 F3
Gedinne, *Belgium* 17 J5
Gediz, *Turkey* 66 C3
Gediz →, *Turkey* 66 C2
Gedo, *Ethiopia* 77 F4
Gèdre, *France* 26 F4
Gedser, *Denmark* 11 K5
Gedser Odde, *Denmark* 11 K5
Geegully Cr. →, *Australia* 88 C3
Geel, *Belgium* 17 F5
Geelong, *Australia* 91 F3
Geelvink Chan., *Australia* 89 E1
Geer →, *Belgium* 17 G7
Geesthacht, *Germany* 18 B6
Geffen, *Neths.* 16 E6
Geidam, *Nigeria* 79 C7
Geikie →, *Canada* 101 B8
Geili, *Sudan* 77 D3
Geilo, *Norway* 10 D2
Geisingen, *Germany* 19 H4
Geislingen, *Germany* 19 G5
Geita, *Tanzania* 82 C3
Geita □, *Tanzania* 82 C3
Gejiu, *China* 52 F4
Gel →, *Sudan* 77 F2
Gel River, *Sudan* 77 F2
Gela, *Italy* 35 E7
Gela, G. di, *Italy* 35 F7
Geladi, *Ethiopia* 68 F4
Gelderland □, *Neths.* 16 D8
Geldermalsen, *Neths.* 16 E6
Geldern, *Germany* 18 D2
Geldrop, *Neths.* 17 F7
Geleen, *Neths.* 17 G7
Gelehun, *S. Leone* 78 D2
Gelendost, *Turkey* 66 C4
Gelendzhik, *Russia* 43 H4
Gelibolu, *Turkey* 66 B2
Gelidonya Burnu, *Turkey* 66 D4
Gelnhausen, *Germany* 19 E5
Gelsenkirchen, *Germany* 18 D3
Gelting, *Germany* 18 A5
Gemas, *Malaysia* 59 L4
Gembloux, *Belgium* 17 G5
Gemena, *Zaïre* 80 D3
Gemerek, *Turkey* 66 C7
Gemert, *Neths.* 17 E7
Gemlik, *Turkey* 66 B3
Gemona del Friuli, *Italy* 33 B10
Gemsa, *Egypt* 76 B3
Gemünden, *Germany* 19 E5
Genale, *Ethiopia* 77 F4
Genappe, *Belgium* 17 G4
Genç, *Turkey* 67 C9
Gençay, *France* 26 B4
Gendringen, *Neths.* 16 E8
Gendt, *Neths.* 16 E7
Geneina, Gebel, *Egypt* 76 J8
Genemuiden, *Neths.* 16 C8
General Acha, *Argentina* 126 D3
General Alvear, *Buenos Aires, Argentina* 126 D3
General Alvear, *Mendoza, Argentina* 126 D2
General Artigas, *Paraguay* 126 B4
General Belgrano, *Argentina* 126 D4
General Cabrera, *Argentina* 126 C3
General Carrera, L., *Chile* 128 C2
General Cepeda, *Mexico* 114 B4
General Conesa, *Argentina* 128 B4
General Guido, *Argentina* 126 D4
General Juan Madariaga, *Argentina* 126 D4
General La Madrid, *Argentina* 126 D3
General Lorenzo Vintter, *Argentina* 128 B4
General MacArthur, *Phil.* 55 F6
General Martin Miguel de Güemes, *Argentina* 126 A3
General Paz, *Argentina* 126 B4
General Pico, *Argentina* 126 D3
General Pinedo, *Argentina* 126 B3
General Pinto, *Argentina* 126 C3
General Sampaio, *Brazil* 122 B4
General Santos, *Phil.* 55 H6
General Toshevo, *Bulgaria* 38 F11
General Trevino, *Mexico* 115 B5
General Trías, *Mexico* 114 B3
General Viamonte, *Argentina* 126 D3
General Villegas, *Argentina* 126 D3
General Vintter, L., *Argentina* 128 B2
Generoso, Mte., *Switz.* 23 E8
Genesee, *Idaho, U.S.A.* 110 C5
Genesee, *Pa., U.S.A.* 106 E7
Genesee →, *U.S.A.* 106 C7
Geneseo, *Ill., U.S.A.* 108 E9
Geneseo, *Kans., U.S.A.* 108 F5
Geneseo, *N.Y., U.S.A.* 106 D7
Geneva = Genève, *Switz.* 22 D2
Geneva, *Ala., U.S.A.* 105 K3
Geneva, *N.Y., U.S.A.* 106 D7
Geneva, *Nebr., U.S.A.* 108 E6
Geneva, *Ohio, U.S.A.* 106 E4
Geneva, L. = Léman, L., *Europe* 22 D3
Geneva, L., *U.S.A.* 104 D1
Genève, *Switz.* 22 D2
Genève □, *Switz.* 22 D2
Gengenbach, *Germany* 19 G4
Gengma, *China* 52 F2
Genichesk = Henichesk, *Ukraine* 41 J8
Genil →, *Spain* 31 H5
Génissiat, Barr. de, *France* 27 B9
Genk, *Belgium* 17 G7
Genlis, *France* 25 E12
Gennargentu, Mti. del, *Italy* 34 C2
Gennep, *Neths.* 17 E7
Gennes, *France* 24 E6
Genoa = Génova, *Italy* 32 D5
Genoa, *Australia* 91 F4
Genoa, *N.Y., U.S.A.* 107 D8
Genoa, *Nebr., U.S.A.* 108 E6
Genoa, *Nev., U.S.A.* 112 F7
Genoa →, *Argentina* 128 B2
Génova, *Italy* 32 D5
Génova, G. di, *Italy* 32 E6
Gent, *Belgium* 17 F3
Gentbrugge, *Belgium* 17 F3
Genthin, *Germany* 18 C8
Gentio do Ouro, *Brazil* 122 D3
Geographe B., *Australia* 89 F2
Geographe Chan., *Australia* 89 D1
Geokchay = Göyçay, *Azerbaijan* 43 K8
Georga, Zemlya, *Russia* 44 A5
George, *S. Africa* 84 E3
George →, *Canada* 99 A6
George, L., *N.S.W., Australia* 91 F4
George, L., *S. Austral., Australia* 91 F3
George, L., *W. Austral., Australia* 88 D3
George, L., *Uganda* 82 B3
George, L., *Fla., U.S.A.* 105 L5
George, L., *N.Y., U.S.A.* 107 C11
George Gill Ra., *Australia* 88 D5
George River = Kangiqsualujjuaq, *Canada* 97 C13
George Sound, *N.Z.* 87 L1
George Town, *Bahamas* 116 B4
George Town, *Malaysia* 59 K3
George V Land, *Antarctica* 5 C10
George VI Sound, *Antarctica* 5 D17
George West, *U.S.A.* 109 L5
Georgetown, *Australia* 90 B3
Georgetown, *Ont., Canada* 98 D4
Georgetown, *P.E.I., Canada* 99 C7
Georgetown, *Cayman Is.* 116 C3
Georgetown, *Gambia* 78 C2
Georgetown, *Guyana* 121 B6
Georgetown, *Calif., U.S.A.* 112 G6
Georgetown, *Colo., U.S.A.* 110 G11
Georgetown, *Ky., U.S.A.* 104 F3
Georgetown, *S.C., U.S.A.* 105 J6
Georgetown, *Tex., U.S.A.* 109 K6
Georgia □, *U.S.A.* 105 J4
Georgia ■, *Asia* 43 J6
Georgia, Str. of, *Canada* 100 D4
Georgian B., *Canada* 98 C3
Georgina →, *Australia* 90 C2
Georgina Downs, *Australia* 90 C2
Georgiu-Dezh = Liski, *Russia* 42 E4
Georgiyevsk, *Russia* 43 H6
Gera, *Germany* 18 E8
Geraardsbergen, *Belgium* 17 G3
Geral, Serra, *Bahia, Brazil* 123 D3
Geral, Serra, *Goiás, Brazil* 122 D2
Geral, Serra, *Sta. Catarina, Brazil* 127 B6
Geral de Goiás, Serra, *Brazil* 123 D2
Geral do Paranã Serra, *Brazil* 123 E2
Geraldine, *U.S.A.* 110 C8
Geraldton, *Australia* 89 E1
Geraldton, *Canada* 98 C2
Gérardmer, *France* 25 D13
Gercüş, *Turkey* 67 D9
Gerede, *Turkey* 66 B5
Gereshk, *Afghan.* 60 D4
Gérgal, *Spain* 29 H2
Gerik, *Malaysia* 59 K3
Gering, *U.S.A.* 108 E3
Gerlach, *U.S.A.* 110 F4
Gerlachovka, *Slovak Rep.* 20 F10
Gerlogubi, *Ethiopia* 68 F4
Germansen Landing, *Canada* 100 B4
Germany ■, *Europe* 18 E6
Germersheim, *Germany* 19 F4
Germī, *Iran* 67 C13
Germiston, *S. Africa* 85 D4
Gernsheim, *Germany* 19 F4
Gero, *Japan* 49 G8
Gerolstein, *Germany* 19 E2
Gerolzhofen, *Germany* 19 F6
Gerona, *Spain* 28 D7
Gerona □, *Spain* 28 C7
Gérouville, *Belgium* 17 J6
Gerrard, *Canada* 100 C5
Gers □, *France* 26 E4
Gers →, *France* 26 D4
Gersfeld, *Germany* 18 E5
Gerze, *Turkey* 66 B6
Geseke, *Germany* 18 D4
Geser, *Indonesia* 57 E8
Gesso →, *Italy* 32 D4
Gestro, Wabi →, *Ethiopia* 77 G5
Gesves, *Belgium* 17 H6
Getafe, *Spain* 30 E7
Gethsémani, *Canada* 99 B7
Gettysburg, *Pa., U.S.A.* 104 F7
Gettysburg, *S. Dak., U.S.A.* 108 C5
Getz Ice Shelf, *Antarctica* 5 D14
Geul →, *Neths.* 17 G7
Gevaş, *Turkey* 67 C10
Gévaudan, *France* 26 D7
Gevgelija, *Macedonia* 39 H5
Gévora →, *Spain* 31 G4
Gex, *France* 27 B10
Geyser, *U.S.A.* 110 C8
Geyserville, *U.S.A.* 112 G4
Geyve, *Turkey* 66 B4
Ghâbat el Arab = Wang Kai, *Sudan* 77 F2
Ghaghara →, *India* 63 G11
Ghalla, Wadi el →, *Sudan* 77 E2
Ghallamane, *Mauritania* 74 D3
Ghana ■, *W. Afr.* 79 D4
Ghansor, *India* 63 H9
Ghanzi, *Botswana* 84 C3
Ghanzi □, *Botswana* 84 C3
Gharb el Istiwa'iya □, *Sudan* 77 F2
Gharbîya, Es Sahrâ el, *Egypt* 76 B2
Ghard Abû Muharik, *Egypt* 76 B2
Ghardaïa, *Algeria* 75 B5
Ghârib, G., *Egypt* 76 J8
Gharyān, *Libya* 75 B7
Gharyān □, *Libya* 75 B7
Ghat, *Libya* 75 D7
Ghatal, *India* 63 H12
Ghatampur, *India* 63 F9
Ghaţţī, *Si. Arabia* 64 D3
Ghawdex = Gozo, *Malta* 37 C1
Ghazal, Bahr el →, *Chad* 73 F8
Ghazâl, Bahr el →, *Sudan* 77 F3
Ghazaouet, *Algeria* 75 A4
Ghaziabad, *India* 62 E7
Ghazipur, *India* 63 G10
Ghaznī, *Afghan.* 62 C3
Ghaznī □, *Afghan.* 60 C6
Ghedi, *Italy* 32 C7
Ghèlinsor, *Somali Rep.* 68 F4
Ghent = Gent, *Belgium* 17 F3
Gheorghe Gheorghiu-Dej = Oneşti, *Romania* 38 C9
Gheorgheni, *Romania* 38 C8
Ghergani, *Romania* 38 E8
Gherla, *Romania* 38 B6
Ghilarza, *Italy* 34 B1
Ghisonaccia, *France* 27 F13
Ghisoni, *France* 27 F13
Ghizao, *Afghan.* 62 C1
Ghizar →, *Pakistan* 63 A5
Ghogha, *India* 62 J5
Ghot Ogrein, *Egypt* 76 A2
Ghotaru, *India* 62 F4
Ghotki, *Pakistan* 62 E3
Ghowr □, *Afghan.* 60 C4
Ghudaf, W. al →, *Iraq* 67 F10
Ghudāmis, *Libya* 75 B6
Ghughri, *India* 63 H9
Ghugus, *India* 60 K11
Ghulam Mohammad Barrage, *Pakistan* 62 G3
Ghūrīān, *Afghan.* 60 B2
Gia Dinh, *Vietnam* 59 G6
Gia Lai = Pleiku, *Vietnam* 58 F7
Gia Nghia, *Vietnam* 59 G6
Gia Ngoc, *Vietnam* 58 E7
Gia Vuc, *Vietnam* 58 E7
Gian, *Phil.* 57 C7
Giannutri, *Italy* 32 F8
Giant Forest, *U.S.A.* 112 J8
Giant Mts. = Krkonoše, *Czech.* 20 E5
Giants Causeway, *U.K.* 15 A5
Giarabub = Al Jaghbūb, *Libya* 73 C9
Giarre, *Italy* 35 E8
Giaveno, *Italy* 32 C4
Gibara, *Cuba* 116 B4
Gibb River, *Australia* 88 C4
Gibbon, *U.S.A.* 108 E5
Gibe →, *Ethiopia* 77 F4
Gibellina, *Italy* 34 E6
Gibraléon, *Spain* 31 H4
Gibraltar ■, *Europe* 31 J5
Gibraltar, Str. of, *Medit. S.* 31 K5
Gibson Desert, *Australia* 88 D4
Gibsons, *Canada* 100 D4
Gibsonville, *U.S.A.* 112 F6
Giddings, *U.S.A.* 109 K6
Gidole, *Ethiopia* 77 F4
Gien, *France* 25 E9
Giessen, *Germany* 18 E4
Gieten, *Neths.* 16 B9
Gīfān, *Iran* 65 B8
Gifatin, Geziret, *Egypt* 76 B3
Gifford Creek, *Australia* 88 D2
Gifhorn, *Germany* 18 C6
Gifu, *Japan* 49 G8
Gifu □, *Japan* 49 G8
Gigant, *Russia* 43 G5
Giganta, Sa. de la, *Mexico* 114 B2
Gigen, *Bulgaria* 38 F7
Gigha, *U.K.* 14 F3
Giglio, *Italy* 32 F7
Gignac, *France* 26 E7
Gigüela →, *Spain* 29 F1
Gijón, *Spain* 30 B5
Gil I., *Canada* 100 C3
Gila →, *U.S.A.* 111 K6
Gila Bend, *U.S.A.* 111 K7
Gila Bend Mts., *U.S.A.* 111 K7
Gīlān □, *Iran* 65 B6
Gilbert →, *Australia* 90 B3
Gilbert Is., *Kiribati* 92 G9
Gilbert Plains, *Canada* 101 C8
Gilbert River, *Australia* 90 B3
Gilberton, *Australia* 90 B3
Gilbués, *Brazil* 122 C2
Gilf el Kebîr, Hadabat el, *Egypt* 76 C2
Gilford I., *Canada* 100 C3
Gilgandra, *Australia* 91 E4
Gilgil, *Kenya* 82 C4
Gilgit, *India* 63 B6
Gilgit →, *Pakistan* 63 B6
Giljeva Planina, *Serbia, Yug.* 21 M10

Gillam, *Canada* 101 B10
Gilleleje, *Denmark* 11 H6
Gillen, L., *Australia* 89 E3
Gilles, L., *Australia* 91 E2
Gillette, *U.S.A.* 108 C2
Gilliat, *Australia* 90 C3
Gillingham, *U.K.* 13 F8
Gilly, *Belgium* 17 H4
Gilmer, *U.S.A.* 109 J7
Gilmore, *Australia* 91 F4
Gilmore, L., *Australia* 89 F3
Gilmour, *Canada* 98 D4
Gilo →, *Ethiopia* 77 F3
Gilort →, *Romania* 38 E6
Gilroy, *U.S.A.* 111 H3
Gilze, *Neths.* 17 E5
Gimbi, *Ethiopia* 77 F4
Gimigliano, *Italy* 35 D9
Gimli, *Canada* 101 C9
Gimone →, *France* 26 E5
Gimont, *France* 26 E4
Gin Gin, *Australia* 91 D5
Ginâh, *Egypt* 76 B3
Gindie, *Australia* 90 C4
Gingin, *Australia* 89 F2
Gîngiova, *Romania* 38 F6
Ginir, *Ethiopia* 68 F3
Ginosa, *Italy* 35 B9
Ginzo de Limia, *Spain* 30 C3
Giohar, *Somali Rep.* 68 G4
Gióia, G. di, *Italy* 35 D8
Gióia del Colle, *Italy* 35 B9
Gióia Táuro, *Italy* 35 D8
Gioiosa Iónica, *Italy* 35 D9
Gióna, Óros, *Greece* 39 L5
Giovi, Passo dei, *Italy* 32 D5
Giovinazzo, *Italy* 35 A9
Gir Hills, *India* 62 J4
Girab, *India* 62 F4
Girâfi, W. →, *Egypt* 69 F3
Giraltovce, *Slovak Rep.* 20 F11
Girard, *Kans., U.S.A.* 109 G7
Girard, *Ohio, U.S.A.* 106 E4
Girard, *Pa., U.S.A.* 106 D4
Girardot, *Colombia* 120 C3
Girdle Ness, *U.K.* 14 D6
Giresun, *Turkey* 67 B8
Girga, *Egypt* 76 B3
Giridih, *India* 63 G12
Girifalco, *Italy* 35 D9
Girilambone, *Australia* 91 E4
Girne = Kyrenia, *Cyprus* 66 E5
Giro, *Nigeria* 79 C5
Giromagny, *France* 25 E13
Girona = Gerona, *Spain* 28 D7
Gironde □, *France* 26 D3
Gironde →, *France* 26 C2
Gironella, *Spain* 28 C6
Giru, *Australia* 90 B4
Girvan, *U.K.* 14 F4
Gisborne, *N.Z.* 87 H7
Gisenyi, *Rwanda* 82 C2
Gislaved, *Sweden* 9 H15
Gisors, *France* 25 C8
Gistel, *Belgium* 17 F1
Giswil, *Switz.* 22 C6
Gitega, *Burundi* 82 C2
Gits, *Belgium* 17 F2
Giuba →, *Somali Rep.* 68 G3
Giubiasco, *Switz.* 23 D8
Giugliano in Campania, *Italy* 35 B7
Giulianova, *Italy* 33 F10
Giurgeni, *Romania* 38 E10
Giurgiu, *Romania* 38 F8
Give, *Denmark* 11 J3
Givet, *France* 25 B11
Givors, *France* 27 C8
Givry, *Belgium* 17 H4
Givry, *France* 25 F11
Giyon, *Ethiopia* 77 F4
Giza = El Giza, *Egypt* 76 H7
Gizhiga, *Russia* 45 C17
Gizhiginskaya Guba, *Russia* 45 C16
Giżycko, *Poland* 20 A11
Gizzeria, *Italy* 35 D9
Gjegjani, *Albania* 39 H3
Gjerstad, *Norway* 10 F3
Gjirokastra, *Albania* 39 J3
Gjoa Haven, *Canada* 96 B10
Gjøl, *Denmark* 11 G3
Gjøvik, *Norway* 10 D4
Glace Bay, *Canada* 99 C8
Glacier Bay, *U.S.A.* 100 B1
Glacier Nat. Park, *Canada* 100 C5
Glacier Park, *U.S.A.* 110 B7
Glacier Peak, *U.S.A.* 110 B3
Gladewater, *U.S.A.* 109 J7
Gladstone, *Queens., Australia* 90 C5
Gladstone, *S. Austral., Australia* 91 E2
Gladstone, *W. Austral., Australia* 89 E1
Gladstone, *Canada* 101 C9
Gladstone, *U.S.A.* 104 C2
Gladwin, *U.S.A.* 104 D3
Gladys L., *Canada* 100 B2
Glåma = Glomma →, *Norway* 10 E4
Gláma, *Iceland* 8 D2
Glamis, *U.S.A.* 113 N11
Glamoč, *Bos.-H.* 33 D13
Glan, *Sweden* 11 F10
Glanerbrug, *Neths.* 16 D9
Glarner Alpen, *Switz.* 23 C8
Glärnisch, *Switz.* 23 C7
Glarus, *Switz.* 23 B8
Glarus □, *Switz.* 23 C8
Glasco, *Kans., U.S.A.* 108 F6
Glasco, *N.Y., U.S.A.* 107 D11
Glasgow, *U.K.* 14 F4
Glasgow, *Ky., U.S.A.* 104 G3
Glasgow, *Mont., U.S.A.* 110 B10
Glastonbury, *U.K.* 13 F5
Glastonbury, *U.S.A.* 107 E12
Glatt →, *Switz.* 23 B7
Glattfelden, *Switz.* 23 A7
Glauchau, *Germany* 18 E8
Glazov, *Russia* 42 A11
Gleiwitz = Gliwice, *Poland* 20 E8
Glen, *U.S.A.* 107 B13
Glen Affric, *U.K.* 14 D4
Glen Canyon Dam, *U.S.A.* 111 H8
Glen Canyon National Recreation Area, *U.S.A.* 111 H8
Glen Coe, *U.K.* 14 E4
Glen Cove, *U.S.A.* 107 F11
Glen Garry, *U.K.* 14 D3
Glen Innes, *Australia* 91 D5
Glen Lyon, *U.S.A.* 107 E8
Glen Mor, *U.K.* 14 D4
Glen Moriston, *U.K.* 14 D4
Glen Orchy, *U.K.* 14 E4
Glen Spean, *U.K.* 14 E4
Glen Ullin, *U.S.A.* 108 B4
Glénan, Is. de, *France* 24 E2
Glenburgh, *Australia* 89 E2
Glencoe, *Canada* 106 D3
Glencoe, *S. Africa* 85 D5
Glencoe, *U.S.A.* 108 C7
Glendale, *Ariz., U.S.A.* 111 K7
Glendale, *Calif., U.S.A.* 113 L8
Glendale, *Oreg., U.S.A.* 110 E2
Glendale, *Zimbabwe* 83 F3
Glendive, *U.S.A.* 108 B2
Glendo, *U.S.A.* 108 D2
Glenelg, *Australia* 91 E2
Glenelg →, *Australia* 91 F3
Glenflorrie, *Australia* 88 D2
Glengarriff, *Ireland* 15 E2
Glengyle, *Australia* 90 C2
Glenmora, *U.S.A.* 109 K8
Glenmorgan, *Australia* 91 D4
Glenn, *U.S.A.* 112 F4
Glenns Ferry, *U.S.A.* 110 E6
Glenorchy, *Australia* 90 G4
Glenore, *Australia* 90 B3
Glenormiston, *Australia* 90 C2
Glenreagh, *Australia* 91 E5
Glenrock, *U.S.A.* 110 E11
Glenrothes, *U.K.* 14 E5
Glens Falls, *U.S.A.* 107 C11
Glenties, *Ireland* 15 B3
Glenville, *U.S.A.* 104 F5
Glenwood, *Alta., Canada* 100 D6
Glenwood, *Nfld., Canada* 99 C9
Glenwood, *Ark., U.S.A.* 109 H8
Glenwood, *Hawaii, U.S.A.* 102 J17
Glenwood, *Iowa, U.S.A.* 108 E7
Glenwood, *Minn., U.S.A.* 108 C7
Glenwood, *Wash., U.S.A.* 112 D5
Glenwood Springs, *U.S.A.* 110 G10
Gletsch, *Switz.* 23 C6
Glettinganes, *Iceland* 8 D7
Glina, *Croatia* 33 C13
Glittertind, *Norway* 10 C2
Gliwice, *Poland* 20 E8
Globe, *U.S.A.* 111 K8
Glödnitz, *Austria* 21 J4
Głogów, *Poland* 20 D6
Glomma →, *Norway* 10 E4
Glorieuses, Is., *Ind. Oc.* 85 A8
Glossop, *U.K.* 12 D6
Gloucester, *Australia* 91 E5
Gloucester, *U.K.* 13 F5
Gloucester, *U.S.A.* 107 D14
Gloucester I., *Australia* 90 B4
Gloucestershire □, *U.K.* 13 F5
Gloversville, *U.S.A.* 107 C10
Glovertown, *Canada* 99 C9
Główno, *Poland* 20 D9
Głubczyce, *Poland* 20 E7
Glubokiy, *Russia* 43 F5
Glubokoye = Hlybokaye, *Belarus* 40 E4
Głuchołazy, *Poland* 20 E7
Glücksburg, *Germany* 18 A5
Glückstadt, *Germany* 18 B5
Glukhov = Hlukhiv, *Ukraine* 41 G7
Glusk, *Belarus* 41 F5
Glyngøre, *Denmark* 11 H2
Gmünd, *Kärnten, Austria* 21 J3
Gmünd, *Niederösterreich, Austria* 20 G5
Gnarp, *Sweden* 10 B11
Gnesta, *Sweden* 10 E11
Gniew, *Poland* 20 B8
Gniezno, *Poland* 20 C7
Gnoien, *Germany* 18 B8
Gnowangerup, *Australia* 89 F2
Go Cong, *Vietnam* 59 G6
Gō-no-ura, *Japan* 49 H4
Go Quao, *Vietnam* 59 H5
Goa, *India* 60 M8
Goa □, *India* 60 M8
Goalen Hd., *Australia* 91 F5
Goalpara, *India* 61 F17
Goalundo Ghat, *Bangla.* 63 H13
Goaso, *Ghana* 78 D4
Goat Fell, *U.K.* 14 F3
Goba, *Ethiopia* 68 F2
Goba, *Mozam.* 85 D5
Gobabis, *Namibia* 84 C2
Gobernador Gregores, *Argentina* 128 C2
Gobi, *Asia* 50 C5
Gobō, *Japan* 49 H7
Gobo, *Sudan* 77 F3
Goch, *Germany* 18 D2
Gochas, *Namibia* 84 C2
Godavari →, *India* 61 L13
Godavari Point, *India* 61 L13
Godbout, *Canada* 99 C6
Godda, *India* 63 G12
Godegård, *Sweden* 11 F9
Goderich, *Canada* 98 D3
Goderville, *France* 24 C7
Godhavn, *Greenland* 4 C5
Godhra, *India* 62 H5
Gödöllö, *Hungary* 21 H9
Godoy Cruz, *Argentina* 126 C2
Gods →, *Canada* 101 B10
Gods L., *Canada* 101 C10
Godthåb, *Greenland* 97 B14
Godwin Austen = K2, *Pakistan* 63 B7
Goeie Hoop, Kaap die = Good Hope, C. of, *S. Africa* 84 E2
Goéland, L. au, *Canada* 98 C4
Goeree, *Neths.* 16 E4
Goes, *Neths.* 17 F3
Gogama, *Canada* 98 C3
Gogango, *Australia* 90 C5
Gogebic, L., *U.S.A.* 108 B10
Gogra = Ghaghara →, *India* 63 G11
Gogriâl, *Sudan* 77 F2
Goiana, *Brazil* 122 C5
Goianésia, *Brazil* 123 E2
Goiânia, *Brazil* 123 E2
Goiás, *Brazil* 123 E1
Goiás □, *Brazil* 122 D2
Goiatuba, *Brazil* 123 E2
Goio-Ere, *Brazil* 127 A5
Goirle, *Neths.* 17 E6
Góis, *Portugal* 30 E2
Gojam □, *Ethiopia* 77 E4
Gojeb, Wabi →, *Ethiopia* 77 F4
Gojō, *Japan* 49 G7
Gojra, *Pakistan* 62 D5
Gokarannath, *India* 63 F9
Gökçeada, *Turkey* 66 B1
Gökırmak →, *Turkey* 66 B6
Göksu →, *Turkey* 66 D6
Göksun, *Turkey* 66 C7
Gokteik, *Burma* 61 H20
Gokurt, *Pakistan* 62 E2
Gola, *India* 63 E9
Golakganj, *India* 63 F13
Golan Heights = Hagolan, *Syria* 69 B4
Golāshkerd, *Iran* 65 E8
Golaya Pristen = Hola Pristan, *Ukraine* 41 J7
Gölbaşı, *Adiyaman, Turkey* 66 D7
Gölbaşı, *Ankara, Turkey* 66 C5
Golchikha, *Russia* 4 B12
Golconda, *U.S.A.* 110 F5
Gölcük, *Kocaeli, Turkey* 66 B3
Gölcük, *Niğde, Turkey* 66 C6
Gold Beach, *U.S.A.* 110 E1
Gold Coast, *Australia* 91 D5
Gold Coast, *W. Afr.* 79 E4
Gold Hill, *U.S.A.* 110 E2
Goldach, *Switz.* 23 B8
Goldau, *Switz.* 23 B7
Goldberg, *Germany* 18 B8
Golden, *Canada* 100 C5
Golden, *U.S.A.* 108 F2
Golden B., *N.Z.* 87 J4
Golden Gate, *U.S.A.* 110 H2
Golden Hinde, *Canada* 100 D3
Golden Lake, *Canada* 106 A7
Golden Prairie, *Canada* 101 C7
Golden Vale, *Ireland* 15 D3
Goldendale, *U.S.A.* 110 D3
Goldfield, *U.S.A.* 111 H5
Goldfields, *Canada* 101 B7
Goldsand L., *Canada* 101 B8
Goldsboro, *U.S.A.* 105 H7
Goldsmith, *U.S.A.* 109 K3
Goldsworthy, *Australia* 88 D2
Goldthwaite, *U.S.A.* 109 K5
Golegã, *Portugal* 31 F2
Goleniów, *Poland* 20 B4
Golestānak, *Iran* 65 D7
Goleta, *U.S.A.* 113 L7
Golfito, *Costa Rica* 116 E3
Golfo Aranci, *Italy* 34 B2
Gölgeli Dağları, *Turkey* 66 D3
Goliad, *U.S.A.* 109 L6
Golija, *Serbia, Yug.* 21 M10
Gölköy, *Turkey* 66 B7
Golo →, *France* 27 F13
Golpāyegān, *Iran* 65 C6
Gölpazarı, *Turkey* 66 B4
Golra, *Pakistan* 62 C5
Golspie, *U.K.* 14 D5
Golyama Kamchiya →, *Bulgaria* 38 F10
Goma, *Rwanda* 82 C2
Goma, *Zaïre* 82 C2
Gomati →, *India* 63 G10
Gombari, *Zaïre* 82 B2
Gombe, *Nigeria* 79 C7
Gombe →, *Tanzania* 82 C3
Gombi, *Nigeria* 79 C7
Gomel = Homyel, *Belarus* 41 F6
Gomera, *Canary Is.* 36 F2
Gómez Palacio, *Mexico* 114 B4
Gomīshān, *Iran* 65 B7
Gommern, *Germany* 18 C7
Gomogomo, *Indonesia* 57 F8
Gomoh, *India* 61 H15
Gompa = Ganta, *Liberia* 78 D3
Goms, *Switz.* 22 D6
Gonābād, *Iran* 65 C8
Gonaïves, *Haiti* 117 C5
Gonâve, G. de la, *Haiti* 117 C5
Gonâve, I. de la, *Haiti* 117 C5
Gonbab-e Kāvūs, *Iran* 65 B7
Gonda, *India* 63 F9
Gondal, *India* 62 J4
Gonder, *Ethiopia* 77 E4
Gonder □, *Ethiopia* 77 E4
Gondia, *India* 60 J12
Gondola, *Mozam.* 83 F3
Gondomar, *Portugal* 30 D2
Gondomar, *Spain* 30 C2
Gondrecourt-le-Château, *France* 25 D12
Gönen, *Turkey* 66 B2
Gong Xian, *China* 52 C5
Gong'an, *China* 53 B9
Gongcheng, *China* 53 E8
Gongga Shan, *China* 52 C3
Gongguan, *China* 52 G7
Gonghe, *China* 54 C5
Gongola →, *Nigeria* 79 D7
Gongolgon, *Australia* 91 E4
Gongshan, *China* 52 D2
Gongtan, *China* 52 C7
Goniadz, *Poland* 20 B12
Goniri, *Nigeria* 79 C7
Gonjo, *China* 52 B2
Gonnesa, *Italy* 34 C1
Gónnos, *Greece* 39 K5
Gonnosfanádiga, *Italy* 34 C1
Gonzaga, *Phil.* 55 B5
Gonzales, *Calif., U.S.A.* 111 H3
Gonzales, *Tex., U.S.A.* 109 L6
González Chaves, *Argentina* 126 D3
Good Hope, C. of, *S. Africa* 84 E2
Gooderham, *Canada* 98 D4
Goodeve, *Canada* 101 C8
Gooding, *U.S.A.* 110 E6
Goodland, *U.S.A.* 108 F4
Goodnight, *U.S.A.* 109 H4
Goodooga, *Australia* 91 D4
Goodsoil, *Canada* 101 C7
Goodsprings, *U.S.A.* 111 J6
Goole, *U.K.* 12 D7
Goolgowi, *Australia* 91 E4
Goomalling, *Australia* 89 F2
Goombalie, *Australia* 91 D4
Goonda, *Mozam.* 83 F3
Goondiwindi, *Australia* 91 D5
Goongarrie, L., *Australia* 89 F3
Goonyella, *Australia* 90 C4
Goor, *Neths.* 16 D9
Gooray, *Australia* 91 D5
Goose →, *Canada* 99 B7
Goose L., *U.S.A.* 110 F3
Gop, *India* 60 H6
Gopalganj, *India* 63 F11
Goppenstein, *Switz.* 22 D5
Göppingen, *Germany* 19 G5
Gor, *Spain* 29 H2
Góra, *Poland* 20 D6
Gorakhpur, *India* 63 F10
Gorbatov, *Russia* 42 B6
Gorbea, Peña, *Spain* 28 B2
Gorda, *U.S.A.* 112 K5
Gorda, Pta., *Canary Is.* 36 F2
Gorda, Pta., *Nic.* 116 D3
Gordan B., *Australia* 88 B5
Gordon, *U.S.A.* 108 D3
Gordon →, *Australia* 90 G4
Gordon, I., *Chile* 128 D3
Gordon Downs, *Australia* 88 C4
Gordon L., *Alta., Canada* 101 B6
Gordon L., *N.W.T., Canada* 100 A6
Gordonvale, *Australia* 90 B4
Gore, *Australia* 91 D5
Goré, *Chad* 73 G8
Gore, *Ethiopia* 77 F4
Gore, *N.Z.* 87 M2
Gore Bay, *Canada* 98 C3
Görele, *Turkey* 67 B8
Goreme, *Turkey* 66 C6
Gorey, *Ireland* 15 D5
Gorg, *Iran* 65 D8
Gorgān, *Iran* 65 B7
Gorgona, isola, *Italy* 32 E6
Gorgora, *Ethiopia* 77 E4
Gorham, *U.S.A.* 107 B13
Gori, *Georgia* 43 J7
Gorinchem, *Neths.* 16 E5
Gorinhatã, *Brazil* 123 E2
Goris, *Armenia* 67 C12
Goritsy, *Russia* 42 B3
Gorízia, *Italy* 33 C10
Gorki = Horki, *Belarus* 40 E6
Gorki = Nizhniy Novgorod, *Russia* 42 B7
Gorkiy = Nizhniy Novgorod, *Russia* 42 B7
Gorkovskoye Vdkhr., *Russia* 42 B6
Gørlev, *Denmark* 11 J5
Gorlice, *Poland* 20 F11
Görlitz, *Germany* 18 D10
Gorlovka = Horlivka, *Ukraine* 41 H10
Gorman, *Calif., U.S.A.* 113 L8
Gorman, *Tex., U.S.A.* 109 J5
Gorna Dzhumayo = Blagoevgrad, *Bulgaria* 39 G6
Gorna Oryakhovitsa, *Bulgaria* 38 F8
Gornja Radgona, *Slovenia* 33 B13
Gornja Tuzla, *Bos.-H.* 21 L8
Gornji Grad, *Slovenia* 33 B11
Gornji Milanovac, *Serbia, Yug.* 21 M10
Gornji Vakuf, *Bos.-H.* 21 M7
Gorno-Altay □, *Russia* 44 D9
Gorno-Altaysk, *Russia* 44 D9
Gorno Slinkino = Gornopravdinsk, *Russia* 44 C8
Gornopravdinsk, *Russia* 44 C8
Gornyatskiy, *Russia* 43 F5
Gornyi, *Russia* 48 B6
Gornyy, *Russia* 42 E9
Gorodenka = Horodenka, *Ukraine* 41 H3
Gorodets, *Russia* 42 B6
Gorodishche = Horodyshche, *Ukraine* 41 H6
Gorodishche, *Russia* 42 D7
Gorodnya = Horodnya, *Ukraine* 41 G6
Gorodok = Haradok, *Belarus* 40 E6
Gorodok = Horodok, *Ukraine* 41 H2
Gorodovikovsk, *Russia* 43 G5
Gorokhov = Horokhiv, *Ukraine* 41 G3
Gorokhovets, *Russia* 42 B6
Gorom Gorom, *Burkina Faso* 79 C4
Goromonzi, *Zimbabwe* 83 F3
Gorongose →, *Mozam.* 85 C5
Gorongoza, *Mozam.* 83 F3
Gorongoza, Sa. da, *Mozam.* 83 F3
Gorontalo, *Indonesia* 57 D6
Goronyo, *Nigeria* 79 C6
Gorredijk, *Neths.* 16 C8
Gorron, *France* 24 D6
Gorshechnoye, *Russia* 42 E4
Gorssel, *Neths.* 16 D8
Gort, *Ireland* 15 C3
Gortis, *Greece* 37 D6
Goryachiy Klyuch, *Russia* 43 H4
Gorzkowice, *Poland* 20 D9
Gorzów Śląski, *Poland* 20 D8
Gorzów Wielkopolski, *Poland* 20 C5
Göschenen, *Switz.* 23 C7
Gosford, *Australia* 91 E5
Goshen, *Calif., U.S.A.* 112 J7
Goshen, *Ind., U.S.A.* 104 E3
Goshen, *N.Y., U.S.A.* 107 E10
Goshogawara, *Japan* 48 D10
Goslar, *Germany* 18 D6
Gospič, *Croatia* 33 D12
Gosport, *U.K.* 13 G6
Gossau, *Switz.* 23 B8
Gosse →, *Australia* 90 B1
Gostivar, *Macedonia* 39 H3
Gostyń, *Poland* 20 D7
Gostynin, *Poland* 20 C9
Göta älv →, *Sweden* 11 G5
Göta kanal, *Sweden* 9 G16
Götaland, *Sweden* 9 G15
Göteborg, *Sweden* 11 G5
Götene, *Sweden* 11 F7
Gotha, *Germany* 18 E6
Gothenburg = Göteborg, *Sweden* 11 G5
Gothenburg, *U.S.A.* 108 E4
Gotland, *Sweden* 9 H18
Gotse Delchev, *Bulgaria* 39 H6
Gotska Sandön, *Sweden* 9 G18
Gōtsu, *Japan* 49 G6
Göttingen, *Germany* 18 D5
Gottwald = Zmiyev, *Ukraine* 41 H9
Gottwaldov = Zlin, *Czech.* 20 F7
Goubangzi, *China* 51 D11
Gouda, *Neths.* 16 D5
Goúdhoura, Ákra, *Greece* 37 E8
Goudiry, *Senegal* 78 C2
Gough I., *Atl. Oc.* 2 G9
Gouin, Rés., *Canada* 98 C5
Gouitafla, *Ivory C.* 78 D3
Goulburn, *Australia* 91 E4
Goulburn Is., *Australia* 90 A1
Goulia, *Ivory C.* 78 C3
Goulimine, *Morocco* 74 C3
Goulmina, *Morocco* 74 B4
Gounou-Gaya, *Chad* 73 G8
Goúra, *Greece* 39 M5
Gouraya, *Algeria* 75 A5
Gourdon, *France* 26 D5
Gouré, *Niger* 79 C7
Gouri, *Chad* 73 E8
Gourits →, *S. Africa* 84 E3
Gourma Rharous, *Mali* 79 B4
Goúrnais, *Greece* 37 D7
Gournay-en-Bray, *France* 25 C8
Gourock Ra., *Australia* 91 F4
Goursi, *Burkina Faso* 78 C4
Gouvêa, *Brazil* 123 E3
Gouverneur, *U.S.A.* 107 B9
Gouviá, *Greece* 37 A3
Gouzon, *France* 26 B6

Govan, *Canada* 101 C8
Governador Valadares, *Brazil* 123 E3
Governor's Harbour, *Bahamas* 116 A4
Gowan Ra., *Australia* 90 C4
Gowanda, *U.S.A.* 106 D6
Gowd-e Zirreh, *Afghan.* 60 E3
Gower, *U.K.* 13 F3
Gowna, L., *Ireland* 15 C4
Goya, *Argentina* 126 B4
Göyçay, *Azerbaijan* 43 K8
Goyder Lagoon, *Australia* 91 D2
Goyllarisquisga, *Peru* 124 C2
Göynük, *Turkey* 66 B4
Goz Beïda, *Chad* 73 F9
Goz Regeb, *Sudan* 77 D4
Gozo, *Malta* 37 C1
Graaff-Reinet, *S. Africa* 84 E3
Grabow, *Germany* 18 B7
Grabs, *Switz.* 23 B8
Gračac, *Croatia* 33 D12
Gračanica, *Bos.-H.* 21 L8
Graçay, *France* 25 E8
Grace, *U.S.A.* 110 E8
Graceville, *U.S.A.* 108 C6
Gracias a Dios, C., *Honduras* 116 C3
Graciosa, I., *Canary Is.* 36 E6
Gradaús, *Brazil* 122 C1
Gradaús, Serra dos, *Brazil* 122 C1
Gradets, *Bulgaria* 38 G9
Grado, *Italy* 33 C10
Grado, *Spain* 30 B4
Gradule, *Australia* 91 D4
Grady, *U.S.A.* 109 H3
Graeca, Lacul, *Romania* 38 E9
Grafenau, *Germany* 19 G9
Gräfenberg, *Germany* 19 F7
Grafton, *Australia* 91 D5
Grafton, *U.S.A.* 108 A6
Gragnano, *Italy* 35 B7
Graham, *Canada* 98 C1
Graham, *N.C., U.S.A.* 105 G6
Graham, *Tex., U.S.A.* 109 J5
Graham →, *Canada* 100 B4
Graham, Mt., *U.S.A.* 111 K9
Graham Bell, Os., *Russia* 44 A7
Graham I., *Canada* 100 C2
Graham Land, *Antarctica* 5 C17
Grahamdale, *Canada* 101 C9
Grahamstown, *S. Africa* 84 E4
Graïba, *Tunisia* 75 B7
Graide, *Belgium* 17 J6
Graie, Alpi, *Europe* 32 C4
Grain Coast, *W. Afr.* 78 E3
Grajaú, *Brazil* 122 C2
Grajaú →, *Brazil* 122 B3
Grajewo, *Poland* 20 B12
Gramada, *Bulgaria* 38 F5
Gramat, *France* 26 D5
Grammichele, *Italy* 35 E7
Grampian Highlands = Grampian Mts., *U.K.* 14 E5
Grampian Mts., *U.K.* 14 E5
Gran →, *Surinam* 121 C6
Gran Altiplanicie Central, *Argentina* 128 C3
Gran Canaria, *Canary Is.* 36 F4
Gran Chaco, *S. Amer.* 126 B3
Gran Paradiso, *Italy* 32 C4
Gran Sasso d'Italia, *Italy* 33 F10
Granada, *Nic.* 116 D2
Granada, *Spain* 29 H1
Granada, *U.S.A.* 109 F3
Granada □, *Spain* 31 H7
Granadilla de Abona, *Canary Is.* 36 F3
Granard, *Ireland* 15 C4
Granbury, *U.S.A.* 109 J6
Granby, *Canada* 98 C5
Grand →, *Mo., U.S.A.* 108 F8
Grand →, *S. Dak., U.S.A.* 108 C4
Grand Bahama, *Bahamas* 116 A4
Grand Bank, *Canada* 99 C8
Grand Bassam, *Ivory C.* 78 D4
Grand Béréby, *Ivory C.* 78 E3
Grand-Bourg, *Guadeloupe* 117 C7
Grand Canal = Yun Ho →, *China* 51 E9
Grand Canyon, *U.S.A.* 111 H7
Grand Canyon National Park, *U.S.A.* 111 H7
Grand Cayman, *Cayman Is.* 116 C3
Grand Cess, *Liberia* 78 E3
Grand Coulee, *U.S.A.* 110 C4
Grand Coulee Dam, *U.S.A.* 110 C4
Grand Erg Occidental, *Algeria* 75 B5
Grand Erg Oriental, *Algeria* 75 C6
Grand Falls, *Canada* 99 C8
Grand Forks, *Canada* 100 D5
Grand Forks, *U.S.A.* 108 B6
Grand-Fougeray, *France* 24 E5
Grand Haven, *U.S.A.* 104 D2
Grand I., *U.S.A.* 104 B2
Grand Island, *U.S.A.* 108 E5
Grand Isle, *U.S.A.* 109 L10
Grand Junction, *U.S.A.* 111 G9
Grand L., *N.B., Canada* 99 C6
Grand L., *Nfld., Canada* 99 C8
Grand L., *Nfld., Canada* 99 B7
Grand L., *U.S.A.* 109 L8
Grand Lac Victoria, *Canada* 98 C4
Grand Lahou, *Ivory C.* 78 D3
Grand Lake, *U.S.A.* 110 F11
Grand-Leez, *Belgium* 17 G5
Grand-Lieu, L. de, *France* 24 E5
Grand Manan I., *Canada* 99 D6
Grand Marais, *Canada* 108 B9
Grand Marais, *U.S.A.* 104 B3
Grand-Mère, *Canada* 98 C5
Grand Popo, *Benin* 79 D5
Grand Portage, *U.S.A.* 98 C2
Grand Prairie, *U.S.A.* 109 J6
Grand Rapids, *Canada* 101 C9
Grand Rapids, *Mich., U.S.A.* 104 D2
Grand Rapids, *Minn., U.S.A.* 108 B8
Grand St.-Bernard, Col du, *Europe* 22 E4
Grand Santi, *Fr. Guiana* 121 C7
Grand Teton, *U.S.A.* 110 E8
Grand Valley, *U.S.A.* 110 G9
Grand View, *Canada* 101 C8
Grandas de Salime, *Spain* 30 B4
Grande →, *Jujuy, Argentina* 126 A2
Grande →, *Mendoza, Argentina* 126 D2
Grande →, *Bolivia* 125 D5
Grande →, *Bahia, Brazil* 122 D3
Grande →, *Minas Gerais, Brazil* 123 F1
Grande →, *Spain* 29 F4
Grande →, *Venezuela* 121 B5
Grande, B., *Argentina* 128 D3
Grande, I., *Brazil* 123 F3
Grande, Rio →, *U.S.A.* 109 N6
Grande, Serra, *Piauí, Brazil* 122 C2
Grande, Serra, *Tocantins, Brazil* 122 D2
Grande Baie, *Canada* 99 C5
Grande Baleine, R. de la →, *Canada* 98 A4
Grande Cache, *Canada* 100 C5
Grande de Santiago →, *Mexico* 114 C3
Grande Dixence, Barr. de la, *Switz.* 22 D4
Grande-Entrée, *Canada* 99 C7
Grande Prairie, *Canada* 100 B5
Grande-Rivière, *Canada* 99 C7
Grande Sauldre →, *France* 25 E9
Grande-Vallée, *Canada* 99 C6
Grandes-Bergeronnes, *Canada* 99 C6
Grandfalls, *U.S.A.* 109 K3
Grandoe Mines, *Canada* 100 B3
Grândola, *Portugal* 31 G2
Grandpré, *France* 25 C11
Grandson, *Switz.* 22 C3
Grandview, *U.S.A.* 110 C4
Grandvilliers, *France* 25 C8
Graneros, *Chile* 126 C1
Grangemouth, *U.K.* 14 E5
Granger, *Wash., U.S.A.* 110 C3
Granger, *Wyo., U.S.A.* 110 F9
Grangeville, *U.S.A.* 110 D5
Granite City, *U.S.A.* 108 F9
Granite Falls, *U.S.A.* 108 C7
Granite Mt., *U.S.A.* 113 M10
Granite Peak, *Australia* 89 E3
Granite Peak, *U.S.A.* 110 D9
Granity, *N.Z.* 87 J3
Granja, *Brazil* 122 B3
Granja de Moreruela, *Spain* 30 D5
Granja de Torrehermosa, *Spain* 31 G5
Granollers, *Spain* 28 D7
Gransee, *Germany* 18 B9
Grant, *U.S.A.* 108 E4
Grant, Mt., *U.S.A.* 110 G4
Grant City, *U.S.A.* 108 E7
Grant I., *Australia* 88 B5
Grant Range, *U.S.A.* 111 G6
Grantham, *U.K.* 12 E7
Grantown-on-Spey, *U.K.* 14 D5
Grants, *U.S.A.* 111 J10
Grants Pass, *U.S.A.* 110 E2
Grantsburg, *U.S.A.* 108 C8
Grantsville, *U.S.A.* 110 F7
Granville, *France* 24 D5
Granville, *N. Dak., U.S.A.* 108 A4
Granville, *N.Y., U.S.A.* 104 D9
Granville L., *Canada* 101 B8
Grao de Gandía, *Spain* 29 F4
Grapeland, *U.S.A.* 109 K7
Gras, L. de, *Canada* 96 B8
Graskop, *S. Africa* 85 C5
Grass →, *Canada* 101 B9
Grass Range, *U.S.A.* 110 C9
Grass River Prov. Park, *Canada* 101 C8
Grass Valley, *Calif., U.S.A.* 112 F6
Grass Valley, *Oreg., U.S.A.* 110 D3
Grassano, *Italy* 35 B9
Grasse, *France* 27 E10
Grassmere, *Australia* 91 E3
Graubünden □, *Switz.* 23 C9
Graulhet, *France* 26 E5
Graus, *Spain* 28 C5
Gravatá, *Brazil* 122 C4
Grave, *Neths.* 16 E7
Grave, Pte. de, *France* 26 C2
's-Graveland, *Neths.* 16 D6
Gravelbourg, *Canada* 101 D7
Gravelines, *France* 25 B9
's-Gravendeel, *Neths.* 16 E5
's-Gravenhage, *Neths.* 16 D4
Gravenhurst, *Canada* 106 B5
's-Gravenpolder, *Neths.* 17 F3
's-Gravensande, *Neths.* 16 D4
Gravesend, *Australia* 91 D5
Gravesend, *U.K.* 13 F8
Gravina di Púglia, *Italy* 35 B9
Gravois, Pointe-à-, *Haiti* 117 C5
Gravone →, *France* 27 G12
Gray, *France* 25 E12
Grayling, *U.S.A.* 104 C3
Grayling →, *Canada* 100 B3
Grays Harbor, *U.S.A.* 110 C1
Grays L., *U.S.A.* 110 E8
Grays River, *U.S.A.* 112 D3
Grayson, *Canada* 101 C8
Grayvoron, *Russia* 42 E2
Graz, *Austria* 21 H5
Grazalema, *Spain* 31 J5
Greasy L., *Canada* 100 A4
Great Abaco I., *Bahamas* 116 A4
Great Artesian Basin, *Australia* 90 C3
Great Australian Bight, *Australia* 89 F5
Great Bahama Bank, *Bahamas* 116 B4
Great Barrier I., *N.Z.* 87 G5
Great Barrier Reef, *Australia* 90 B4
Great Barrington, *U.S.A.* 107 D11
Great Basin, *U.S.A.* 110 G5
Great Bear →, *Canada* 96 B7
Great Bear L., *Canada* 96 B7
Great Belt = Store Bælt, *Denmark* 11 J5
Great Bend, *Kans., U.S.A.* 108 F5
Great Bend, *Pa., U.S.A.* 107 E9
Great Blasket I., *Ireland* 15 D1
Great Britain, *Europe* 6 E5
Great Central, *Canada* 100 D3
Great Dividing Ra., *Australia* 90 C4
Great Driffield = Driffield, *U.K.* 12 C7
Great Exuma I., *Bahamas* 116 B4
Great Falls, *Canada* 101 C9
Great Falls, *U.S.A.* 110 C8
Great Fish = Groot Vis →, *S. Africa* 84 E4
Great Guana Cay, *Bahamas* 116 B4
Great Harbour Deep, *Canada* 99 B8
Great I., *Canada* 101 B9
Great Inagua I., *Bahamas* 117 B5
Great Indian Desert = Thar Desert, *India* 62 F4
Great Karoo, *S. Africa* 84 E3
Great Lake, *Australia* 90 G4
Great Malvern, *U.K.* 13 E5
Great Ormes Head, *U.K.* 12 D4
Great Ouse →, *U.K.* 12 E8
Great Palm I., *Australia* 90 B4
Great Plains, *N. Amer.* 102 A6
Great Ruaha →, *Tanzania* 82 D4
Great Saint Bernard P. = Grand St.-Bernard, Col du, *Europe* 22 E4
Great Salt L., *U.S.A.* 110 F7
Great Salt Lake Desert, *U.S.A.* 110 F7
Great Salt Plains L., *U.S.A.* 109 G5
Great Sandy Desert, *Australia* 88 D3
Great Sangi = Sangihe, P., *Indonesia* 57 D7
Great Scarcies →, *S. Leone* 78 D2
Great Slave L., *Canada* 100 A5
Great Smoky Mts. Nat. Pk., *U.S.A.* 105 H4
Great Stour = Stour →, *U.K.* 13 F9
Great Victoria Desert, *Australia* 89 E4
Great Wall, *China* 50 E5
Great Whernside, *U.K.* 12 C6
Great Yarmouth, *U.K.* 12 E9
Greater Antilles, *W. Indies* 117 C5
Greater London □, *U.K.* 13 F7
Greater Manchester □, *U.K.* 12 D5
Greater Sunda Is., *Indonesia* 56 F4
Grebbestad, *Sweden* 11 F5
Grebenka = Hrebenka, *Ukraine* 41 G7
Greco, C., *Cyprus* 37 E13
Greco, Mte., *Italy* 34 A6
Gredos, Sierra de, *Spain* 30 E5
Greece, *U.S.A.* 106 C7
Greece ■, *Europe* 39 K6
Greeley, *Colo., U.S.A.* 108 E2
Greeley, *Nebr., U.S.A.* 108 E5
Green →, *Ky., U.S.A.* 104 G2
Green →, *Utah, U.S.A.* 111 G9
Green B., *U.S.A.* 104 C2
Green Bay, *U.S.A.* 104 C2
Green C., *Australia* 91 F5
Green Cove Springs, *U.S.A.* 105 L5
Green River, *U.S.A.* 111 G8
Greenbank, *U.S.A.* 112 B4
Greenbush, *Mich., U.S.A.* 106 B1
Greenbush, *Minn., U.S.A.* 108 A6
Greencastle, *U.S.A.* 104 F2
Greene, *U.S.A.* 107 D9
Greenfield, *Calif., U.S.A.* 112 J5
Greenfield, *Calif., U.S.A.* 113 K8
Greenfield, *Ind., U.S.A.* 104 F3
Greenfield, *Iowa, U.S.A.* 108 E7
Greenfield, *Mass., U.S.A.* 107 D12
Greenfield, *Mo., U.S.A.* 109 G8
Greenfield Park, *Canada* 107 A11
Greenland ■, *N. Amer.* 4 C5
Greenland Sea, *Arctic* 4 B7
Greenock, *U.K.* 14 F4
Greenore, *Ireland* 15 B5
Greenore Pt., *Ireland* 15 D5
Greenough →, *Australia* 89 E1
Greenport, *U.S.A.* 107 E12
Greensboro, *Ga., U.S.A.* 105 J4
Greensboro, *N.C., U.S.A.* 105 G6
Greensburg, *Ind., U.S.A.* 104 F3
Greensburg, *Kans., U.S.A.* 109 G5
Greensburg, *Pa., U.S.A.* 106 F5
Greenville, *Liberia* 78 D3
Greenville, *Ala., U.S.A.* 105 K2
Greenville, *Calif., U.S.A.* 112 E6
Greenville, *Ill., U.S.A.* 108 F10
Greenville, *Maine, U.S.A.* 99 C6
Greenville, *Mich., U.S.A.* 104 D3
Greenville, *Miss., U.S.A.* 109 J9
Greenville, *N.C., U.S.A.* 105 H7
Greenville, *Ohio, U.S.A.* 104 E3
Greenville, *Pa., U.S.A.* 106 E4
Greenville, *S.C., U.S.A.* 105 H4
Greenville, *Tenn., U.S.A.* 105 G4
Greenville, *Tex., U.S.A.* 109 J6
Greenwater Lake Prov. Park, *Canada* 101 C8
Greenwich, *U.K.* 13 F8
Greenwich, *Conn., U.S.A.* 107 E11
Greenwich, *N.Y., U.S.A.* 107 C11
Greenwich, *Ohio, U.S.A.* 106 E2
Greenwood, *Canada* 100 D5
Greenwood, *Miss., U.S.A.* 109 J9
Greenwood, *S.C., U.S.A.* 105 H4
Greenwood, Mt., *Australia* 88 B5
Gregório →, *Brazil* 124 B3
Gregory, *U.S.A.* 108 D5
Gregory →, *Australia* 90 B2
Gregory, L., *S. Austral., Australia* 91 D2
Gregory, L., *W. Austral., Australia* 89 E2
Gregory Downs, *Australia* 90 B2
Gregory L., *Australia* 88 D4
Gregory Ra., *Queens., Australia* 90 B3
Gregory Ra., *W. Austral., Australia* 88 D3
Greiffenberg, *Germany* 18 B9
Greifswald, *Germany* 18 A9
Greifswalder Bodden, *Germany* 18 A9
Grein, *Austria* 21 G4
Greiz, *Germany* 18 E8
Gremikha, *Russia* 44 C4
Grenå, *Denmark* 11 H4
Grenada, *U.S.A.* 109 J10
Grenada ■, *W. Indies* 117 D7
Grenade, *France* 26 E5
Grenadines, *W. Indies* 117 D7
Grenchen, *Switz.* 22 B4
Grenen, *Denmark* 11 G4
Grenfell, *Australia* 91 E4
Grenfell, *Canada* 101 C8
Grenoble, *France* 27 C9
Grenora, *U.S.A.* 108 A3
Grenville, C., *Australia* 90 A3
Grenville Chan., *Canada* 100 C3
Gréoux-les-Bains, *France* 27 E9
Gresham, *U.S.A.* 112 E4
Gresik, *Indonesia* 57 G15
Grëssoney St. Jean, *Italy* 32 C4
Gretna Green, *U.K.* 14 F5
Grevelingen Krammer, *Neths.* 16 E4
Greven, *Germany* 18 C3
Grevená, *Greece* 39 J4
Grevenbroich, *Germany* 18 D2
Grevenmacher, *Lux.* 17 J8
Grevesmühlen, *Germany* 18 B7
Grevie, *Sweden* 11 H6
Grey →, *N.Z.* 87 K3
Grey, C., *Australia* 90 A2
Grey Ra., *Australia* 91 D3
Grey Res., *Canada* 99 C8
Greybull, *U.S.A.* 110 D9
Greymouth, *N.Z.* 87 K3
Greytown, *N.Z.* 87 J5
Greytown, *S. Africa* 85 D5
Gribanovskiy, *Russia* 42 E5
Gribbell I., *Canada* 100 C3
Gridley, *U.S.A.* 112 F5
Griekwastad, *S. Africa* 84 D3
Griffin, *U.S.A.* 105 J3
Griffith, *Australia* 91 E4
Grijpskerk, *Neths.* 16 B8
Grillby, *Sweden* 10 E11
Grimari, *C.A.R.* 73 G9
Grimaylov = Hrymayliv, *Ukraine* 41 H4
Grimbergen, *Belgium* 17 G4
Grimes, *U.S.A.* 112 F5
Grimma, *Germany* 18 D8
Grimmen, *Germany* 18 A9
Grimsby, *Canada* 106 C5
Grimsby, *U.K.* 12 D7
Grimselpass, *Switz.* 23 C6
Grímsey, *Iceland* 8 C5
Grimshaw, *Canada* 100 B5
Grimstad, *Norway* 11 F2
Grindelwald, *Switz.* 22 C6
Grindsted, *Denmark* 11 J2
Grindu, *Romania* 38 E9
Grinnell, *U.S.A.* 108 E8
Griñón, *Spain* 30 E7
Grintavec, *Slovenia* 33 B11
Grip, *Norway* 10 A1
Gris-Nez, C., *France* 25 B8
Grisolles, *France* 26 E5
Grisons = Graubünden □, *Switz.* 23 C9
Grivegnée, *Belgium* 17 G7
Grmeč Planina, *Bos.-H.* 33 D13
Groais I., *Canada* 99 B8
Groblersdal, *S. Africa* 85 D4
Grobming, *Austria* 21 H3
Grodno = Hrodna, *Belarus* 40 F2
Grodzisk Mázowiecki, *Poland* 20 C10
Grodzisk Wielkopolski, *Poland* 20 C6
Grodzyanka = Hrodzyanka, *Belarus* 40 F5
Groenlo, *Neths.* 16 D9
Groesbeck, *U.S.A.* 109 K6
Groesbeek, *Neths.* 16 E7
Groix, *France* 24 E3
Groix, I. de, *France* 24 E3
Grójec, *Poland* 20 D10
Grolloo, *Neths.* 16 C9
Gronau, *Niedersachsen, Germany* 18 C5
Gronau, *Nordrhein-Westfalen, Germany* 18 C3
Grong, *Norway* 8 D15
Groningen, *Neths.* 16 B9
Groningen, *Surinam* 121 B6
Groningen □, *Neths.* 16 B9
Groninger Wad, *Neths.* 16 B9
Gronsveld, *Neths.* 17 G7
Groom, *U.S.A.* 109 H4
Groot →, *S. Africa* 84 E3
Groot Berg →, *S. Africa* 84 E2
Groot-Brakrivier, *S. Africa* 84 E3
Groot-Kei →, *S. Africa* 85 E4
Groot Vis →, *S. Africa* 84 E4
Groote Eylandt, *Australia* 90 A2
Grootebroek, *Neths.* 16 C6
Grootfontein, *Namibia* 84 B2
Grootlaagte →, *Africa* 84 C3
Grootvloer, *S. Africa* 84 E3
Gros C., *Canada* 100 A6
Grosa, Pta., *Spain* 36 B8
Grósio, *Italy* 32 B7
Grosne →, *France* 27 B8
Gross Glockner, *Austria* 21 H2
Grossenbrode, *Germany* 18 A7
Grossenhain, *Germany* 18 D9
Grosseto, *Italy* 32 F8
Groswater B., *Canada* 99 B8
Grote Gette →, *Neths.* 17 G6
Grote Nete →, *Belgium* 17 F5
Groton, *Conn., U.S.A.* 107 E12
Groton, *S. Dak., U.S.A.* 108 C5
Grottáglie, *Italy* 35 B10
Grottaminarda, *Italy* 35 A8
Grottammare, *Italy* 33 F10
Grouard Mission, *Canada* 100 B5
Grouin, Pte. du, *France* 24 D5
Groundhog →, *Canada* 98 C3
Grouse Creek, *U.S.A.* 110 F7
Grouw, *Neths.* 16 B7
Grove City, *U.S.A.* 106 E4
Groveland, *U.S.A.* 112 H6
Grover City, *U.S.A.* 113 K6
Groveton, *N.H., U.S.A.* 107 B13
Groveton, *Tex., U.S.A.* 109 K7
Grožnjan, *Croatia* 33 C10
Groznyy, *Russia* 43 J7
Grubbenvorst, *Neths.* 17 F8
Grudziądz, *Poland* 20 B8
Gruissan, *France* 26 E7
Grumo Áppula, *Italy* 35 A9
Grünberg, *Germany* 18 E4
Grundy Center, *U.S.A.* 108 D8
Gruver, *U.S.A.* 109 G4
Gruyères, *Switz.* 22 C4
Gryazi, *Russia* 42 D4
Gryazovets, *Russia* 40 C11
Gstaad, *Switz.* 22 D4
Gua, *India* 61 H14
Gua Musang, *Malaysia* 59 K3
Guacanayabo, G. de, *Cuba* 116 B4
Guacara, *Venezuela* 120 A4
Guachípas →, *Argentina* 126 B2
Guachiría →, *Colombia* 120 B3
Guadajoz →, *Spain* 31 H6
Guadalajara, *Mexico* 114 C4
Guadalajara, *Spain* 28 E1
Guadalajara □, *Spain* 28 E2
Guadalcanal, *Solomon Is.* 92 H8
Guadalcanal, *Spain* 31 G5
Guadalén →, *Spain* 31 G7
Guadales, *Argentina* 126 C2
Guadalete →, *Spain* 31 J4
Guadalhorce →, *Spain* 31 J6
Guadalimar →, *Spain* 29 G1
Guadalmena →, *Spain* 29 G2
Guadalmez →, *Spain* 31 G5
Guadalope →, *Spain* 28 D4
Guadalquivir →, *Spain* 31 J4

Guadalupe = Guadeloupe ■, W. Indies 117 C7
Guadalupe, Brazil 122 C3
Guadalupe, Mexico 113 N10
Guadalupe, Spain 31 F5
Guadalupe, U.S.A. 113 L6
Guadalupe →, Mexico 113 N10
Guadalupe →, U.S.A. 109 L6
Guadalupe, Sierra de, Spain 31 F5
Guadalupe Bravos, Mexico 114 A3
Guadalupe I., Pac. Oc. 94 G8
Guadalupe Peak, U.S.A. 111 L11
Guadalupe y Calvo, Mexico 114 B3
Guadarrama, Sierra de, Spain 30 E6
Guadauta, Georgia 43 J5
Guadeloupe ■, W. Indies 117 C7
Guadeloupe Passage, W. Indies 117 C7
Guadiamar →, Spain 31 J4
Guadiana →, Portugal 31 H3
Guadiana Menor →, Spain 29 H1
Guadiaro →, Spain 31 J5
Guadiato →, Spain 31 H5
Guadiela →, Spain 28 E2
Guadix, Spain 29 H1
Guafo, Boca del, Chile 128 B2
Guafo, I., Chile 128 B2
Guainía □, Colombia 120 C4
Guainía →, Colombia 120 C4
Guaíra, Brazil 127 A5
Guaitecas, Is., Chile 128 B2
Guajará-Mirim, Brazil 125 C4
Guajira □, Colombia 120 A3
Guajira, Pen. de la, Colombia 120 A3
Gualaceo, Ecuador 120 D2
Gualán, Guatemala 116 C2
Gualdo Tadino, Italy 33 E9
Gualeguay, Argentina 126 C4
Gualeguaychú, Argentina 126 C4
Gualicho, Salina, Argentina 128 B3
Gualjaina, Argentina 128 B2
Guam ■, Pac. Oc. 92 F6
Guamá, Brazil 122 B2
Guamá →, Brazil 122 B2
Guamblin, I., Chile 128 B1
Guaminí, Argentina 126 D3
Guamote, Ecuador 120 D2
Guampí, Sierra de, Venezuela 121 B4
Guamúchil, Mexico 114 B3
Guan Xian, China 52 B4
Guanabacoa, Cuba 116 B3
Guanacaste, Cordillera del, Costa Rica 116 D2
Guanaceví, Mexico 114 B3
Guanahani = San Salvador, Bahamas 117 B5
Guanajay, Cuba 116 B3
Guanajuato, Mexico 114 C4
Guanajuato □, Mexico 114 C4
Guanambi, Brazil 123 D3
Guanare, Venezuela 120 B4
Guanare →, Venezuela 120 B4
Guandacol, Argentina 126 B2
Guane, Cuba 116 B3
Guang'an, China 52 B6
Guangchang, China 53 D11
Guangde, China 53 B12
Guangdong □, China 53 F9
Guangfeng, China 53 C12
Guanghan, China 52 B5
Guanghua, China 53 A8
Guangji, China 53 C10
Guangling, China 50 E8
Guangning, China 53 F9
Guangrao, China 51 F10
Guangshun, China 52 D6
Guangwu, China 50 F3
Guangxi Zhuangzu Zizhiqu □, China 52 E7
Guangyuan, China 52 A5
Guangze, China 53 D11
Guangzhou, China 53 F9
Guanhães, Brazil 123 E3
Guanipa →, Venezuela 121 B5
Guanling, China 52 E5
Guannan, China 51 G10
Guanta, Venezuela 121 A5
Guantánamo, Cuba 117 B4
Guantao, China 50 F8
Guanyang, China 53 E8
Guanyun, China 51 G10
Guapí, Colombia 120 C2
Guápiles, Costa Rica 116 D3
Guaporé →, Brazil 125 C4
Guaqui, Bolivia 124 D4
Guara, Sierra de, Spain 28 C4
Guarabira, Brazil 122 C4
Guaranda, Ecuador 120 D2
Guarapari, Brazil 123 F3
Guarapuava, Brazil 123 G1
Guaratinguetá, Brazil 127 A6
Guaratuba, Brazil 127 B6
Guarda, Portugal 30 E3
Guarda □, Portugal 30 E3
Guardafui, C. = Asir, Ras, Somali Rep. 68 E5
Guardamar del Segura, Spain 29 G4
Guardavalle, Italy 35 D9
Guardiagrele, Italy 33 F11
Guardo, Spain 30 C6
Guareña, Spain 31 G4
Guareña →, Spain 30 D5
Guaria □, Paraguay 126 B4
Guárico □, Venezuela 120 B4
Guarrojo →, Colombia 120 C3
Guarujá, Brazil 127 A6
Guarus, Brazil 123 F3
Guasave, Mexico 114 B3
Guascama, Pta., Colombia 120 C2
Guasdualito, Venezuela 120 B3
Guasipati, Venezuela 121 B5
Guastalla, Italy 32 D7
Guatemala, Guatemala 116 D1
Guatemala ■, Cent. Amer. 116 C1
Guatire, Venezuela 120 A4
Guaviare □, Colombia 120 C3
Guaviare →, Colombia 120 C4
Guaxupé, Brazil 127 A6
Guayabero →, Colombia 120 C3
Guayama, Puerto Rico 117 C6
Guayaneco, Arch., Chile 128 C1
Guayaquil, Ecuador 120 D2
Guayaquil, G. de, Ecuador 120 D1
Guayaramerín, Bolivia 125 C4
Guayas →, Ecuador 120 D2
Guaymas, Mexico 114 B2
Guazhou, China 53 A12
Guba, Zaïre 83 E2
Gûbâl, Madîq, Egypt 76 B3
Gubat, Phil. 55 E6
Gúbbio, Italy 33 E9
Gubio, Nigeria 79 C7
Gubkin, Russia 42 E3
Gudata = Guadauta, Georgia 43 J5
Gudbrandsdalen, Norway 9 F14
Guddu Barrage, Pakistan 60 E6
Gudenå →, Denmark 11 H3
Gudermes, Russia 43 J8
Gudivada, India 61 L12
Gudur, India 60 M11
Guebwiller, France 25 E14
Guecho, Spain 28 B2
Guékédou, Guinea 78 D2
Guelma, Algeria 75 A6
Guelph, Canada 98 D3
Guemar, Algeria 75 B6
Guéméné-Penfao, France 24 E5
Guéméné-sur-Scorff, France 24 D3
Guéné, Benin 79 C5
Güepi, Peru 120 D2
Guer, France 24 E4
Güer Aike, Argentina 128 D3
Guérande, France 24 E4
Guercif, Morocco 75 B4
Guéréda, Chad 73 F9
Guéret, France 26 B5
Guérigny, France 25 E10
Guerneville, U.S.A. 112 G4
Guernica, Spain 28 B2
Guernsey, U.K. 13 H5
Guernsey, U.S.A. 108 D2
Guerrara, Oasis, Algeria 75 B5
Guerrara, Saoura, Algeria 75 C4
Guerrero □, Mexico 115 D5
Guerzim, Algeria 75 C4
Gueugnon, France 27 B8
Gueydan, U.S.A. 109 K8
Gügher, Iran 65 D8
Guglionesi, Italy 35 A7
Gui Jiang →, China 53 F8
Gui Xian, China 52 F7
Guia, Canary Is. 36 F4
Guia de Isora, Canary Is. 36 F3
Guia Lopes da Laguna, Brazil 127 A4
Guiana, S. Amer. 118 C4
Guichi, China 53 B11
Guider, Cameroon 79 D7
Guidimouni, Niger 79 C6
Guiding, China 52 D6
Guidong, China 53 D9
Guiglo, Ivory C. 78 D3
Guijá, Mozam. 85 C5
Guijo de Coria, Spain 30 E4
Guildford, U.K. 13 F7
Guilford, U.S.A. 99 C6
Guilin, China 53 E8
Guillaumes, France 27 D10
Guillestre, France 27 D10
Guilvinec, France 24 E2
Güímar, Canary Is. 36 F3
Guimarães, Brazil 122 B3
Guimarães, Portugal 30 D2
Guimaras, Phil. 55 F5
Guinda, U.S.A. 112 G4
Guinea, Africa 70 F4
Guinea ■, W. Afr. 78 C2
Guinea, Gulf of, Atl. Oc. 79 E5
Guinea-Bissau ■, Africa 78 C2
Güines, Cuba 116 B3
Guingamp, France 24 D3
Guipavas, France 24 D2
Guiping, China 53 F8
Guipúzcoa □, Spain 28 B2
Guir, O. →, Algeria 75 B4
Guiratinga, Brazil 125 D7
Güiria, Venezuela 121 A5
Guiscard, France 25 C10
Guise, France 25 C10
Guitiriz, Spain 30 B3
Guiuan, Phil. 55 F6
Guixi, China 53 C11
Guiyang, Guizhou, China 52 D6
Guiyang, Hunan, China 53 E9
Guizhou □, China 52 D6
Gujan-Mestras, France 26 D2
Gujarat □, India 62 H4
Gujiang, China 53 D10
Gujranwala, Pakistan 62 C6
Gujrat, Pakistan 62 C6
Gukovo, Russia 43 F5
Gulbarga, India 60 L10
Gulbene, Latvia 9 H22
Gulf, The, Asia 65 E6
Gulfport, U.S.A. 109 K10
Gulgong, Australia 91 E4
Gulin, China 52 C5
Gulistan, Pakistan 62 D2
Gull Lake, Canada 101 C7
Gullegem, Belgium 17 G2
Güllük, Turkey 66 D2
Gulma, Nigeria 79 C5
Gulmarg, India 63 B6
Gülnar, Turkey 66 D5
Gulpen, Neths. 17 G7
Gülşehir, Turkey 66 C6
Gulshad, Kazakstan 44 E8
Gulsvik, Norway 10 D3
Gulu, Uganda 82 B3
Gulwe, Tanzania 82 D4
Gulyaypole = Hulyaypole, Ukraine 41 J9
Gum Lake, Australia 91 E3
Gumal →, Pakistan 62 D4
Gumbaz, Pakistan 62 D3
Gumel, Nigeria 79 C6
Gumiel de Hizán, Spain 28 D1
Gumlu, Australia 90 B4
Gumma □, Japan 49 F9
Gummersbach, Germany 18 D3
Gummi, Nigeria 79 C6
Gümüşhaciköy, Turkey 66 B6
Gümüşhane, Turkey 67 B8
Gumzai, Indonesia 57 F8
Guna, Ethiopia 77 E4
Guna, India 62 G7
Gundagai, Australia 91 F4
Gundelfingen, Germany 19 G6
Gundih, Indonesia 57 G14
Güneydoğu Toroslar, Turkey 67 C9
Gungu, Zaïre 80 F3
Gunisao →, Canada 101 C9
Gunisao L., Canada 101 C9
Gunnbjørn Fjeld, Greenland 4 C6
Gunnedah, Australia 91 E5
Gunningbar Cr. →, Australia 91 E4
Gunnison, Colo., U.S.A. 111 G10
Gunnison, Utah, U.S.A. 110 G8
Gunnison →, U.S.A. 111 G9
Gunpowder, Australia 90 B2
Guntakal, India 60 M10
Guntersville, U.S.A. 105 H2
Guntong, Malaysia 59 K3
Guntur, India 61 L12
Gunungapi, Indonesia 57 F7
Gunungsitoli, Indonesia 56 D1
Günz →, Germany 19 G6
Gunza, Angola 80 G2
Günzburg, Germany 19 G6
Gunzenhausen, Germany 19 F6
Guo He →, China 51 H9
Guoyang, China 50 H9
Gupis, Pakistan 63 A5
Gura Humorului, Romania 38 B8
Gurag, Ethiopia 77 F4
Gurdaspur, India 62 C6
Gurdon, U.S.A. 109 J8
Gurgaon, India 62 E7
Gürgentepe, Turkey 66 B7
Gurgueia →, Brazil 122 C3
Gurha, India 62 G4
Guri, Embalse de, Venezuela 121 B5
Gurjaani, Georgia 43 K7
Gurk →, Austria 21 J4
Gurkha, Nepal 63 E11
Gurley, Australia 91 D4
Gürpınar, Turkey 67 C10
Gurué, Mozam. 83 F4
Gurun, Malaysia 59 K3
Gürün, Turkey 66 C7
Gurupá, Brazil 121 D7
Gurupá, I. Grande de, Brazil 121 D7
Gurupi, Brazil 123 D2
Gurupi →, Brazil 122 B2
Gurupi, Serra do, Brazil 122 C2
Guryev = Atyraū, Kazakstan 44 E6
Gus-Khrustalnyy, Russia 42 C5
Gusau, Nigeria 79 C6
Gusev, Russia 9 J20
Gushan, China 51 E12
Gushgy, Turkmenistan 44 F7
Gushi, China 53 A10
Gushiago, Ghana 79 D4
Gusinje, Montenegro, Yug. 21 N9
Gusinoozersk, Russia 45 D11
Gúspini, Italy 34 C1
Gustanj, Slovenia 33 B11
Gustine, U.S.A. 111 H3
Güstrow, Germany 18 B8
Gusum, Sweden 11 F10
Guta = Kalárovo, Slovak Rep. 21 H7
Gütersloh, Germany 18 D4
Gutha, Australia 89 E2
Guthalongra, Australia 90 B4
Guthrie, U.S.A. 109 H6
Gutian, China 53 D12
Gutiérrez, Bolivia 125 D5
Guttannen, Switz. 23 C6
Guttenberg, U.S.A. 108 D9
Guyana ■, S. Amer. 121 B6
Guyane française ■ = French Guiana ■, S. Amer. 121 C7
Guyang, China 50 D6
Guyenne, France 26 D4
Guymon, U.S.A. 109 G4
Guyra, Australia 91 E5
Guyuan, Hebei, China 50 D8
Guyuan, Ningxia Huizu, China 50 F4
Guzhang, China 52 C7
Guzhen, China 51 H9
Guzmán, L. de, Mexico 114 A3
Gvardeysk, Russia 9 J19
Gvardeyskoye, Ukraine 41 K8
Gwa, Burma 61 L19
Gwaai, Zimbabwe 83 F2
Gwabegar, Australia 91 E4
Gwadabawa, Nigeria 79 C6
Gwādar, Pakistan 60 G3
Gwagwada, Nigeria 79 C6
Gwalia, Australia 89 E3
Gwalior, India 62 F8
Gwanda, Zimbabwe 83 G2
Gwandu, Nigeria 79 C5
Gwane, Zaïre 82 B2
Gwaram, Nigeria 79 C7
Gwarzo, Nigeria 79 C6
Gweebarra B., Ireland 15 B3
Gweedore, Ireland 15 A3
Gweru, Zimbabwe 83 F2
Gwi, Nigeria 79 D6
Gwinn, U.S.A. 104 B2
Gwio Kura, Nigeria 79 C7
Gwol, Ghana 78 C4
Gwoza, Nigeria 79 C7
Gwydir →, Australia 91 D4
Gwynedd □, U.K. 12 E3
Gyandzha = Gäncä, Azerbaijan 43 K8
Gyaring Hu, China 54 C4
Gydanskiy P-ov., Russia 44 C8
Gympie, Australia 91 D5
Gyoma, Hungary 21 J10
Gyöngyös, Hungary 21 H9
Györ, Hungary 21 H7
Gypsum Pt., Canada 100 A6
Gypsumville, Canada 101 C9
Gyula, Hungary 21 J11
Gyumri, Armenia 43 K6
Gyzylarbat, Turkmenistan 44 F6
Gzhatsk = Gagarin, Russia 42 C2

H

Ha 'Arava →, Israel 69 E4
Ha Coi, Vietnam 58 B6
Ha Dong, Vietnam 58 B5
Ha Giang, Vietnam 58 A5
Ha Tien, Vietnam 59 G5
Ha Tinh, Vietnam 58 C5
Ha Trung, Vietnam 58 C5
Haacht, Belgium 17 G5
Haag, Germany 19 G8
Haaksbergen, Neths. 16 D9
Haaltert, Belgium 17 G4
Haamstede, Neths. 17 E3
Haapsalu, Estonia 9 G20
Haarlem, Neths. 16 D5
Haast →, N.Z. 87 K2
Haast Bluff, Australia 88 D5
Haastrecht, Neths. 16 E5
Hab Nadi Chauki, Pakistan 62 G2
Habaswein, Kenya 82 B4
Habay, Canada 100 B5
Habay-la-Neuve, Belgium 17 J7
Ḩabbānīyah, Iraq 67 F10
Ḩabbānīyah, Hawr al, Iraq 67 F10
Haboro, Japan 48 B10
Haccourt, Belgium 17 G7
Hachenburg, Germany 18 E3
Hachijō-Jima, Japan 49 H9
Hachinohe, Japan 48 D10
Hachiōji, Japan 49 G9
Hachŏn, N. Korea 51 D15
Hachy, Belgium 17 J7
Hacıbektaş, Turkey 66 C6
Hacılar, Turkey 66 C6
Hackensack, U.S.A. 107 F10
Hadali, Pakistan 62 C5
Hadarba, Ras, Sudan 76 C4
Hadarom □, Israel 69 E3
Haddington, U.K. 14 F6
Hadejia, Nigeria 79 C7
Hadejia →, Nigeria 79 C7
Haden, Australia 91 D5
Hadera, Israel 69 C3
Hadera, N. →, Israel 69 C3
Haderslev, Denmark 11 J3
Hadhramaut = Haḑramawt, Yemen 68 D4
Hadım, Turkey 66 D5
Hadjeb El Aïoun, Tunisia 75 A6
Hadong, S. Korea 51 G14
Haḑramawt, Yemen 68 D4
Ḩadrānīyah, Iraq 64 C4
Hadrian's Wall, U.K. 12 C5
Hadsten, Denmark 11 H4
Hadsund, Denmark 11 H4
Hadyach, Ukraine 41 G8
Haeju, N. Korea 51 E13
Haenam, S. Korea 51 G14
Haerhpin = Harbin, China 51 B14
Hafar al Bāţin, Si. Arabia 64 D5
Hafik, Turkey 66 C7
Ḩafīrat al 'Aydā, Si. Arabia 64 E3
Hafizabad, Pakistan 62 C5
Haflong, India 61 G18
Hafnarfjörður, Iceland 8 D3
Hafun, Ras, Somali Rep. 68 E5
Hagalil, Israel 69 C4
Hagen, Germany 18 D3
Hagenow, Germany 18 B7
Hagerman, U.S.A. 109 J2
Hagerstown, U.S.A. 104 F7
Hagetmau, France 26 E3
Hagfors, Sweden 9 F15
Häggenås, Sweden 10 A8
Hagi, Japan 49 G5
Hagolan, Syria 69 B4
Hagondange-Briey, France 25 C13
Hags Hd., Ireland 15 D2
Hague, C. de la, France 24 C5
Hague, The = 's-Gravenhage, Neths. 16 D4
Haguenau, France 25 D14
Hai □, Tanzania 82 C4
Hai Duong, Vietnam 58 B6
Hai'an, Guangdong, China 53 G8
Hai'an, Jiangsu, China 53 A13
Haicheng, Fujian, China 53 E11
Haicheng, Liaoning, China 51 D12
Haidar Khel, Afghan. 62 C3
Haifa = Hefa, Israel 69 C3
Haifeng, China 53 F10
Haig, Australia 89 F4
Haiger, Germany 18 E4
Haikang, China 53 G8
Haikou, China 54 D6
Ḩā'il, Si. Arabia 64 E4
Hailar, China 54 B6
Hailey, U.S.A. 110 E6
Haileybury, Canada 98 C4
Hailin, China 51 B15
Hailing Dao, China 53 G8
Hailong, China 51 C13
Hailun, China 54 B7
Hailuoto, Finland 8 D21
Haimen, Guangdong, China 53 F11
Haimen, Jiangsu, China 53 B13
Haimen, Zhejiang, China 53 C13
Hainan □, China 54 E5
Hainaut □, Belgium 17 H4
Haines, U.S.A. 110 D5
Haines City, U.S.A. 105 L5
Haines Junction, Canada 100 A1
Haining, China 53 B13
Haiphong, Vietnam 54 D5
Haiti ■, W. Indies 117 C5
Haiya Junction, Sudan 76 D4
Haiyan, China 53 B13
Haiyang, China 51 F11
Haiyuan, Guangxi Zhuangzu, China 52 F6
Haiyuan, Ningxia Huizu, China 50 F3
Haizhou, China 51 G10
Haizhou Wan, China 51 G10
Hajar Bangar, Sudan 73 F9
Hajdúböszörmény, Hungary 21 H11
Hajdúszoboszló, Hungary 21 H11
Hajipur, India 63 G11
Ḩājjī Muḩsin, Iraq 64 C5
Ḩājjīābād, Eşfahan, Iran 65 C7
Ḩājjīābād, Hormozgān, Iran 65 D7
Hakansson, Mts., Zaïre 83 D2
Håkantorp, Sweden 11 F6
Hakkâri, Turkey 67 D10
Hakkâri Dağları, Turkey 67 C10
Hakken-Zan, Japan 49 G7
Hakodate, Japan 48 D10
Haku-San, Japan 49 F8
Hakui, Japan 49 F8
Hala, Pakistan 60 G6
Ḩalab, Syria 66 D7
Ḩalabjah, Iraq 67 E11
Halaib, Sudan 76 C4
Halanzy, Belgium 17 J7
Ḩālat 'Ammār, Si. Arabia 64 D3
Halbā, Lebanon 69 A5
Halberstadt, Germany 18 D7
Halcombe, N.Z. 87 J5
Halcon, Mt., Phil. 57 B6
Halden, Norway 10 E5
Haldensleben, Germany 18 C7
Haldia, India 61 H16
Haldwani, India 63 E8
Hale →, Australia 90 C2
Haleakala Crater, U.S.A. 102 H16
Halen, Belgium 17 G6
Haleyville, U.S.A. 105 H2
Half Assini, Ghana 78 D4
Halfway →, Canada 100 B4
Haliburton, Canada 98 C4
Halifax, Australia 90 B4
Halifax, Canada 99 D7
Halifax, U.K. 12 D6
Halifax B., Australia 90 B4
Halifax I., Namibia 84 D2
Ḩalīl →, Iran 65 E8
Hall, Austria 19 H7
Hall Beach, Canada 97 B11
Hall Pt., Australia 88 C3
Halland, Sweden 9 H15
Hallands län □, Sweden 11 H6
Hallands Väderö, Sweden 11 H6

Hallandsås, Sweden 11 H7
Halle, Belgium 17 G4
Halle, Nordrhein-Westfalen, Germany 18 C4
Halle, Sachsen-Anhalt, Germany 18 D7
Hällefors, Sweden 9 G16
Hallein, Austria 21 H3
Hällekis, Sweden 11 F7
Hallett, Australia 91 E2
Hallettsville, U.S.A. 109 L6
Hällevadsholm, Sweden 11 F5
Halliday, U.S.A. 108 B3
Halliday L., Canada 101 A7
Hallim, S. Korea 51 H14
Hallingdalselva →, Norway 9 F13
Hallock, U.S.A. 101 D9
Halls Creek, Australia 88 C4
Hallsberg, Sweden 9 G16
Hallstahammar, Sweden 10 E10
Hallstead, U.S.A. 107 E9
Halmahera, Indonesia 57 D7
Halmeu, Romania 38 B6
Halmstad, Sweden 11 H6
Halq el Oued, Tunisia 75 A7
Hals, Denmark 11 H4
Halsafjorden, Norway 10 A2
Hälsingborg = Helsingborg, Sweden 11 H6
Hälsingland, Sweden 9 F16
Halstad, U.S.A. 108 B6
Haltdalen, Norway 10 B5
Haltern, Germany 18 D3
Halti, Finland 8 B19
Halul, Qatar 65 E7
Ḩalvān, Iran 65 C8
Ham, France 25 C10
Ham Tan, Vietnam 59 G6
Ham Yen, Vietnam 58 A5
Hamab, Namibia 84 D2
Hamad, Sudan 77 D3
Hamada, Japan 49 G6
Hamadān, Iran 67 E13
Hamadān □, Iran 65 C6
Hamadia, Algeria 75 A5
Hamāh, Syria 66 E7
Hamamatsu, Japan 49 G8
Hamar, Norway 10 D5
Hamâta, Gebel, Egypt 76 C3
Hambantota, Sri Lanka 60 R12
Hamber Prov. Park, Canada 100 C5
Hamburg, Germany 18 B5
Hamburg, Ark., U.S.A. 109 J9
Hamburg, Iowa, U.S.A. 108 E7
Hamburg, N.Y., U.S.A. 106 D6
Hamburg, Pa., U.S.A. 107 F9
Hamburg □, Germany 18 B6
Ḩamḑ, W. al →, Si. Arabia 64 E3
Hamden, U.S.A. 107 E12
Häme, Finland 9 F20
Hämeenlinna, Finland 9 F21
Hamélé, Ghana 78 C4
Hamelin Pool, Australia 89 E1
Hameln, Germany 18 C5
Hamer Koke, Ethiopia 77 F4
Hamerkaz □, Israel 69 C3
Hamersley Ra., Australia 88 D2
Hamhung, N. Korea 51 E14
Hami, China 54 B4
Hamilton, Australia 91 F3
Hamilton, Canada 98 D4
Hamilton, N.Z. 87 G5
Hamilton, U.K. 14 F4
Hamilton, Mo., U.S.A. 108 F8
Hamilton, Mont., U.S.A. 110 C6
Hamilton, N.Y., U.S.A. 107 D9
Hamilton, Ohio, U.S.A. 104 F3
Hamilton, Tex., U.S.A. 109 K5
Hamilton →, Australia 90 C2
Hamilton City, U.S.A. 112 F4
Hamilton Hotel, Australia 90 C3
Hamilton Inlet, Canada 99 B8
Hamina, Finland 9 F22
Hamiota, Canada 101 C8
Hamlet, U.S.A. 105 H6
Hamley Bridge, Australia 91 E2
Hamlin = Hameln, Germany 18 C5
Hamlin, N.Y., U.S.A. 106 C7
Hamlin, Tex., U.S.A. 109 J4
Hamm, Germany 18 D3
Hammam Bouhadjar, Algeria 75 A4
Hammamet, Tunisia 75 A7
Hammamet, G. de, Tunisia 75 A7
Hammarstrand, Sweden 10 A10
Hamme, Belgium 17 F4
Hamme-Mille, Belgium 17 G5
Hammel, Denmark 11 H3
Hammelburg, Germany 19 E5
Hammerfest, Norway 8 A20
Hammond, Ind., U.S.A. 104 E2
Hammond, La., U.S.A. 109 K9
Hammonton, U.S.A. 104 F8
Hamoir, Belgium 17 H7
Hamont, Belgium 17 F7
Hamoyet, Jebel, Sudan 76 D4
Hampden, N.Z. 87 L3
Hampshire □, U.K. 13 F6
Hampshire Downs, U.K. 13 F6
Hampton, Ark., U.S.A. 109 J8
Hampton, Iowa, U.S.A. 108 D8
Hampton, N.H., U.S.A. 107 D14
Hampton, S.C., U.S.A. 105 J5
Hampton, Va., U.S.A. 104 G7
Hampton Tableland, Australia 89 F4
Hamrat esh Sheykh, Sudan 77 E2
Hamur, Turkey 67 C10
Hamyang, S. Korea 51 G14
Han Jiang →, China 53 F11
Han Shui →, China 53 B10
Hana, U.S.A. 102 H17
Hanak, Si. Arabia 64 E3
Hanamaki, Japan 48 E10
Hanang, Tanzania 82 C4
Hanau, Germany 19 E4
Hanbogd, Mongolia 50 C4
Hancheng, China 50 G6
Hanchuan, China 53 B9
Hancock, Mich., U.S.A. 108 B10
Hancock, Minn., U.S.A. 108 C7
Hancock, N.Y., U.S.A. 107 E9
Handa, Japan 49 G8
Handa, Somali Rep. 68 E5
Handan, China 50 F8
Handen, Sweden 10 E12
Handeni, Tanzania 82 D4
Handeni □, Tanzania 82 D4
Handub, Sudan 76 D4
Handwara, India 63 B6
Handzame, Belgium 17 F2
Hanegev, Israel 69 E3
Haney, Canada 100 D4
Hanford, U.S.A. 111 H4
Hang Chat, Thailand 58 C2
Hang Dong, Thailand 58 C2
Hangang →, S. Korea 51 F14
Hangayn Nuruu, Mongolia 54 B4
Hangchou = Hangzhou, China 53 B13
Hanggin Houqi, China 50 D4
Hanggin Qi, China 50 E5
Hangu, China 51 E9
Hangzhou, China 53 B13
Hangzhou Wan, China 53 B13
Hanhongor, Mongolia 50 C3
Ḩanīdh, Si. Arabia 65 E6
Ḩanīsh, Yemen 68 E3
Hanjiang, China 53 E12
Hankinson, U.S.A. 108 B6
Hanko, Finland 9 G20
Hankou, China 53 B10
Hanksville, U.S.A. 111 G8
Hanle, India 63 C8
Hanmer Springs, N.Z. 87 K4
Hann →, Australia 88 C4
Hann, Mt., Australia 88 C4
Hanna, Canada 100 C6
Hannaford, U.S.A. 108 B5
Hannah, U.S.A. 108 A5
Hannah B., Canada 98 B4
Hannibal, U.S.A. 108 F9
Hannik, Sudan 76 D3
Hannover, Germany 18 C5
Hannut, Belgium 17 G6
Hanoi, Vietnam 54 D5
Hanover = Hannover, Germany 18 C5
Hanover, Canada 106 B3
Hanover, S. Africa 84 E3
Hanover, N.H., U.S.A. 107 C12
Hanover, Ohio, U.S.A. 106 F2
Hanover, Pa., U.S.A. 104 F7
Hanover, I., Chile 128 D2
Hanshou, China 53 C8
Hansi, India 62 E6
Hanson, L., Australia 91 E2
Hantsavichy, Belarus 41 F4
Hanyang, China 53 B10
Hanyin, China 52 A7
Hanyuan, China 52 C4
Hanzhong, China 50 H4
Hanzhuang, China 51 G9
Haora, India 63 H13
Haoxue, China 53 B9
Haparanda, Sweden 8 D21
Hapert, Neths. 17 F6
Happy, U.S.A. 109 H4
Happy Camp, U.S.A. 110 F2
Happy Valley-Goose Bay, Canada 99 B7
Hapsu, N. Korea 51 D15
Hapur, India 62 E7
Ḩaql, Si. Arabia 69 F3
Haquira, Peru 124 C3
Har, Indonesia 57 F8
Har-Ayrag, Mongolia 50 B5
Har Hu, China 54 C4
Har Us Nuur, Mongolia 54 B4
Har Yehuda, Israel 69 D3
Ḩaraḑ, Si. Arabia 68 C4
Haradok, Belarus 40 E6
Haranomachi, Japan 48 F10
Harardera, Somali Rep. 68 G4
Harare, Zimbabwe 83 F3
Harat, Eritrea 77 D4
Harazé, Chad 73 F8
Harbin, China 51 B14
Harbiye, Turkey 66 D7
Harboør, Denmark 11 H2
Harbor Beach, U.S.A. 104 D4
Harbor Springs, U.S.A. 104 C3
Harbour Breton, Canada 99 C8
Harbour Grace, Canada 99 C9
Harburg, Germany 18 B5
Hårby, Denmark 11 J4
Harda, India 62 H7
Hardangerfjorden, Norway 9 F12
Hardangervidda, Norway 9 F12
Hardap Dam, Namibia 84 C2
Hardegarijp, Neths. 16 B7
Hardenberg, Neths. 16 C9
Harderwijk, Neths. 16 D7
Hardey →, Australia 88 D2
Hardin, U.S.A. 110 D10
Harding, S. Africa 85 E4
Harding Ra., Australia 88 C3
Hardisty, Canada 100 C6
Hardman, U.S.A. 110 D4
Hardoi, India 63 F9
Hardwar = Haridwar, India 62 E8
Hardwick, U.S.A. 107 B12
Hardy, U.S.A. 109 G9
Hardy, Pen., Chile 128 E3
Hare B., Canada 99 B8
Hareid, Norway 9 E12
Harelbeke, Belgium 17 G2
Haren, Germany 18 C3
Haren, Neths. 16 B9
Harer, Ethiopia 68 F3
Harerge □, Ethiopia 77 F5
Hareto, Ethiopia 77 F4
Harfleur, France 24 C7
Hargeisa, Somali Rep. 68 F3
Hari →, Indonesia 56 E2
Haria, Canary Is. 36 E6
Haricha, Hamada el, Mali 74 D4
Haridwar, India 62 E8
Haringhata →, Bangla. 61 J16
Haringvliet, Neths. 16 E4
Harīrūd →, Asia 60 A2
Härjedalen, Sweden 9 E15
Harlan, Iowa, U.S.A. 108 E7
Harlan, Ky., U.S.A. 105 G4
Harlech, U.K. 12 E3
Harlem, U.S.A. 110 B9
Harlingen, Neths. 16 B6
Harlingen, U.S.A. 109 M6
Harlowton, U.S.A. 110 C9
Harmånger, Sweden 10 C11
Harmil, Eritrea 77 D5
Harney Basin, U.S.A. 110 E4
Harney L., U.S.A. 110 E4
Harney Peak, U.S.A. 108 D3
Härnön, Sweden 10 B12
Härnösand, Sweden 10 B11
Haro, Spain 28 C2
Harp L., Canada 99 A7
Harper, Liberia 78 E3
Harplinge, Sweden 11 H6
Harrand, Pakistan 62 E4
Harriman, U.S.A. 105 H3
Harrington Harbour, Canada 99 B8
Harris, U.K. 14 D2
Harris, Sd. of, U.K. 14 D1
Harris L., Australia 91 E2
Harrisburg, Ill., U.S.A. 109 G10
Harrisburg, Nebr., U.S.A. 108 E3
Harrisburg, Oreg., U.S.A. 110 D2
Harrisburg, Pa., U.S.A. 106 F8
Harrismith, S. Africa 85 D4
Harrison, Ark., U.S.A. 109 G8
Harrison, Idaho, U.S.A. 110 C5
Harrison, Nebr., U.S.A. 108 D3
Harrison, C., Canada 99 B8
Harrison Bay, U.S.A. 96 A4
Harrison L., Canada 100 D4
Harrisonburg, U.S.A. 104 F6
Harrisonville, U.S.A. 108 F7
Harriston, Canada 98 D3
Harrisville, U.S.A. 106 B1
Harrogate, U.K. 12 D6
Harrow, U.K. 13 F7
Harsefeld, Germany 18 B5
Harsīn, Iran 67 E12
Harskamp, Neths. 16 D7
Harstad, Norway 8 B17
Hart, U.S.A. 104 D2
Hart, L., Australia 91 E2
Hartbees →, S. Africa 84 D3
Hartberg, Austria 21 H5
Hartford, Conn., U.S.A. 107 E12
Hartford, Ky., U.S.A. 104 G2
Hartford, S. Dak., U.S.A. 108 D6
Hartford, Wis., U.S.A. 108 D10
Hartford City, U.S.A. 104 E3
Hartland, Canada 99 C6
Hartland Pt., U.K. 13 F3
Hartlepool, U.K. 12 C6
Hartlepool □, U.K. 12 C6
Hartley Bay, Canada 100 C3
Hartmannberge, Namibia 84 B1
Hartney, Canada 101 D8
Harts →, S. Africa 84 D3
Hartselle, U.S.A. 105 H2
Hartshorne, U.S.A. 109 H7
Hartsville, U.S.A. 105 H5
Hartwell, U.S.A. 105 H4
Harunabad, Pakistan 62 E5
Harvand, Iran 65 D7
Harvey, Australia 89 F2
Harvey, Ill., U.S.A. 104 E2
Harvey, N. Dak., U.S.A. 108 B5
Harwich, U.K. 13 F9
Haryana □, India 62 E7
Haryn →, Belarus 41 F4
Harz, Germany 18 D6
Harzé, Belgium 17 H7
Harzgerode, Germany 18 D7
Hasaheisa, Sudan 77 E3
Hasan Kīādeh, Iran 65 B6
Ḩasanābād, Iran 65 C7
Hasanpur, India 62 E8
Haselünne, Germany 18 C3
Hashimoto, Japan 49 G7
Hashtjerd, Iran 65 C6
Håsjö, Sweden 10 A10
Haskell, Okla., U.S.A. 109 H7
Haskell, Tex., U.S.A. 109 J5
Haslach, Germany 19 G4
Haslev, Denmark 11 J5
Hasparren, France 26 E2
Hassa, Turkey 66 D7
Hasselt, Belgium 17 G6
Hasselt, Neths. 16 C8
Hassene, Adrar, Algeria 75 D5
Hassfurt, Germany 19 E6
Hassi bou Khelala, Algeria 75 B4
Hassi Djafou, Algeria 75 B5
Hassi el Abiod, Algeria 75 B5
Hassi el Biod, Algeria 75 C6
Hassi el Hadjar, Algeria 75 B5
Hassi Imoulaye, Algeria 75 C6
Hassi Inifel, Algeria 75 C5
Hassi Messaoud, Algeria 75 B6
Hassi Tartrat, Algeria 75 B6
Hassi Zerzour, Morocco 74 B4
Hässleholm, Sweden 9 H15
Hastière-Lavaux, Belgium 17 H5
Hastings, N.Z. 87 H6
Hastings, U.K. 13 G8
Hastings, Mich., U.S.A. 104 D3
Hastings, Minn., U.S.A. 108 C8
Hastings, Nebr., U.S.A. 108 E5
Hastings Ra., Australia 91 E5
Hat Yai, Thailand 59 J3
Hatanbulag, Mongolia 50 C5
Hatay = Antalya, Turkey 66 D4
Hatch, U.S.A. 111 K10
Hatches Creek, Australia 90 C2
Hatchet L., Canada 101 B8
Haţeg, Romania 38 D5
Haţeg, Mţii., Romania 38 D6
Hatert, Neths. 16 E7
Hateruma-Shima, Japan 49 M1
Hatfield P.O., Australia 91 E3
Hatgal, Mongolia 54 A5
Hathras, India 62 F8
Hatia, Bangla. 61 H17
Hato de Corozal, Colombia 120 B3
Hato Mayor, Dom. Rep. 117 C6
Hattah, Australia 91 E3
Hattem, Neths. 16 D8
Hatteras, C., U.S.A. 105 H8
Hattiesburg, U.S.A. 109 K10
Hatvan, Hungary 21 H9
Hau Bon = Cheo Reo, Vietnam 58 F7
Hau Duc, Vietnam 58 E7
Haug, Norway 10 D4
Haugastøl, Norway 10 D1
Haugesund, Norway 9 G11
Haukipudas, Finland 8 D21
Haulerwijk, Neths. 16 B8
Haultain →, Canada 101 B7
Hauraki G., N.Z. 87 G5
Haut Atlas, Morocco 74 B3
Haut-Rhin □, France 25 E14
Haut Zaïre □, Zaïre 82 B2
Haute-Corse □, France 27 F13
Haute-Garonne □, France 26 E5
Haute-Loire □, France 26 C7
Haute-Marne □, France 25 D12
Haute-Saône □, France 25 E13
Haute-Savoie □, France 27 C10
Haute-Vienne □, France 26 C5
Hauterive, Canada 99 C6
Hautes-Alpes □, France 27 D10
Hautes Fagnes = Hohe Venn, Belgium 17 H8
Hautes-Pyrénées □, France 26 F4
Hauteville-Lompnès, France 27 C9
Hautmont, France 25 B10
Hautrage, Belgium 17 H3
Hauts-de-Seine □, France 25 D9
Hauts Plateaux, Algeria 75 B4
Hauzenberg, Germany 19 G9
Havana = La Habana, Cuba 116 B3
Havana, U.S.A. 108 E9
Havant, U.K. 13 G7
Havasu, L., U.S.A. 113 L12
Havel →, Germany 18 C8
Havelange, Belgium 17 H6
Havelian, Pakistan 62 B5
Havelock, N.B., Canada 99 C6
Havelock, Ont., Canada 98 D4
Havelock, N.Z. 87 J4
Havelte, Neths. 16 C8
Haverfordwest, U.K. 13 F3
Haverhill, U.S.A. 107 D13
Havering, U.K. 13 F8
Haverstraw, U.S.A. 107 E11
Håverud, Sweden 11 F6
Havlíčkův Brod, Czech. 20 F5
Havneby, Denmark 11 J2
Havre, U.S.A. 110 B9
Havre-Aubert, Canada 99 C7
Havre-St.-Pierre, Canada 99 B7
Havza, Turkey 66 B6
Haw →, U.S.A. 105 H6
Hawaii □, U.S.A. 102 H16
Hawaii I., Pac. Oc. 102 J17
Hawaiian Is., Pac. Oc. 102 H17
Hawaiian Ridge, Pac. Oc. 93 E11
Hawarden, Canada 101 C7
Hawarden, U.S.A. 108 D6
Hawea, L., N.Z. 87 L2
Hawera, N.Z. 87 H5
Hawick, U.K. 14 F6
Hawk Junction, Canada 98 C3
Hawke B., N.Z. 87 H6
Hawker, Australia 91 E2
Hawkesbury, Canada 98 C5
Hawkesbury I., Canada 100 C3
Hawkesbury Pt., Australia 90 A1
Hawkinsville, U.S.A. 105 J4
Hawkwood, Australia 91 D5
Hawley, U.S.A. 108 B6
Hawrān, Syria 69 C5
Ḩawrān, W. →, Iraq 67 F10
Hawsh Mūssá, Lebanon 69 B4
Hawthorne, U.S.A. 110 G4
Hawzen, Ethiopia 77 E4
Haxtun, U.S.A. 108 E3
Hay, Australia 91 E3
Hay →, Australia 90 C2
Hay →, Canada 100 A5
Hay, C., Australia 88 B4
Hay L., Canada 100 B5
Hay Lakes, Canada 100 C6
Hay-on-Wye, U.K. 13 E4
Hay River, Canada 100 A5
Hay Springs, U.S.A. 108 D3
Haya, Indonesia 57 E7
Hayachine-San, Japan 48 E10
Hayange, France 25 C13
Hayden, Ariz., U.S.A. 111 K8
Hayden, Colo., U.S.A. 110 F10
Haydon, Australia 90 B3
Hayes, U.S.A. 108 C4
Hayes →, Canada 101 B10
Haymana, Turkey 66 C5
Haynesville, U.S.A. 109 J8
Hayrabolu, Turkey 66 B2
Hays, Canada 100 C6
Hays, U.S.A. 108 F5
Haysyn, Ukraine 41 H5
Hayvoron, Ukraine 41 H5
Hayward, Calif., U.S.A. 112 H4
Hayward, Wis., U.S.A. 108 B9
Haywards Heath, U.K. 13 F7
Hazafon □, Israel 69 C4
Hazarām, Kūh-e, Iran 65 D8
Hazard, U.S.A. 104 G4
Hazaribag, India 63 H11
Hazaribag Road, India 63 G11
Hazebrouck, France 25 B9
Hazelton, Canada 100 B3
Hazelton, U.S.A. 108 B4
Hazen, N. Dak., U.S.A. 108 B4
Hazen, Nev., U.S.A. 110 G4
Hazerswoude, Neths. 16 D5
Hazlehurst, Ga., U.S.A. 105 K4
Hazlehurst, Miss., U.S.A. 109 K9
Hazleton, U.S.A. 107 F9
Hazlett, L., Australia 88 D4
Ḩazor, Israel 69 B4
He Xian, Anhui, China 53 B12
He Xian, Guangxi Zhuangzu, China 53 E8
Head of Bight, Australia 89 F5
Headlands, Zimbabwe 83 F3
Healdsburg, U.S.A. 112 G4
Healdton, U.S.A. 109 H6
Healesville, Australia 91 F4
Heanor, U.K. 12 D6
Heard I., Ind. Oc. 3 G13
Hearne, U.S.A. 109 K6
Hearne B., Canada 101 A9
Hearne L., Canada 100 A6
Hearst, Canada 98 C3
Heart →, U.S.A. 108 B4
Heart's Content, Canada 99 C9
Heath →, Bolivia 124 C4
Heath Pt., Canada 99 C7
Heath Steele, Canada 99 C6
Heavener, U.S.A. 109 H7
Hebbronville, U.S.A. 109 M5
Hebei □, China 50 E9
Hebel, Australia 91 D4
Heber, U.S.A. 113 N11
Heber Springs, U.S.A. 109 H9
Hebert, Canada 101 C7
Hebgen L., U.S.A. 110 D8
Hebi, China 50 G8
Hebrides, U.K. 14 D1
Hebron = Al Khalīl, West Bank 69 D4
Hebron, Canada 97 C13
Hebron, N. Dak., U.S.A. 108 B3
Hebron, Nebr., U.S.A. 108 E6
Hecate Str., Canada 100 C2
Hechi, China 52 E7
Hechingen, Germany 19 G4
Hechtel, Belgium 17 F6
Hechuan, China 52 B6
Hecla, U.S.A. 108 C5
Hecla I., Canada 101 C9
Heddal, Norway 10 E3
Hédé, France 24 D5
Hede, Sweden 10 B7
Hedemora, Sweden 9 F16
Hedley, U.S.A. 109 H4
Hedmark fylke □, Norway 10 C5
Hedrum, Norway 10 E4
Heeg, Neths. 16 C7
Heegermeer, Neths. 16 C7
Heemskerk, Neths. 16 C5
Heemstede, Neths. 16 D5
Heer, Neths. 17 G7
Heerde, Neths. 16 D8
's Heerenburg, Neths. 16 E8
Heerenveen, Neths. 16 C7
Heerhugowaard, Neths. 16 C5
Heerlen, Neths. 17 G7
Heers, Belgium 17 G6
Heesch, Neths. 16 E7
Heestert, Belgium 17 G2

Heeze, *Neths.* 17 F7
Ḥefa, *Israel* 69 C3
Ḥefa □, *Israel* 69 C4
Hefei, *China* 53 B11
Hegang, *China* 54 B8
Hegyalja, *Hungary* 21 G11
Heichengzhen, *China* 50 F4
Heide, *Germany* 18 A5
Heidelberg, *Germany* 19 F4
Heidelberg, *S. Africa* 84 E3
Heidenheim, *Germany* 19 G6
Heijing, *China* 52 E3
Heilbron, *S. Africa* 85 D4
Heilbronn, *Germany* 19 F5
Heiligenblut, *Austria* 21 H2
Heiligenhafen, *Germany* 18 A6
Heiligenstadt, *Germany* 18 D6
Heilongjiang □, *China* 51 B14
Heilunkiang = Heilongjiang □, *China* 51 B14
Heimaey, *Iceland* 8 E3
Heino, *Neths.* 16 D8
Heinola, *Finland* 9 F22
Heinsch, *Belgium* 17 J7
Heinze Is., *Burma* 61 M20
Heishan, *China* 51 D12
Heishui, *Liaoning, China* 51 C10
Heishui, *Sichuan, China* 52 A4
Heist, *Belgium* 17 F2
Heist-op-den-Berg, *Belgium* 17 F5
Hejaz = Al Ḥijāz, *Si. Arabia* 68 B2
Hejian, *China* 50 E9
Hejiang, *China* 52 C5
Hejin, *China* 50 G6
Hekelgem, *Belgium* 17 G4
Hekımhan, *Turkey* 66 C7
Hekla, *Iceland* 8 E4
Hekou, *Gansu, China* 50 F2
Hekou, *Guangdong, China* 53 F9
Hekou, *Yunnan, China* 54 D5
Helagsfjället, *Sweden* 10 B6
Helan Shan, *China* 50 E3
Helchteren, *Belgium* 17 F6
Helden, *Neths.* 17 F7
Helechosa, *Spain* 31 F6
Helena, *Ark., U.S.A.* 109 H9
Helena, *Mont., U.S.A.* 110 C7
Helendale, *U.S.A.* 113 L9
Helensburgh, *U.K.* 14 E4
Helensville, *N.Z.* 87 G5
Helgeland, *Norway* 8 C15
Helgeroa, *Norway* 10 F3
Helgoland, *Germany* 18 A3
Heligoland = Helgoland, *Germany* 18 A3
Heligoland B. = Deutsche Bucht, *Germany* 18 A4
Heliopolis, *Egypt* 76 H7
Hella, *Iceland* 8 E3
Hellebæk, *Denmark* 11 H6
Hellendoorn, *Neths.* 16 D8
Hellevoetsluis, *Neths.* 16 E4
Hellín, *Spain* 29 G3
Helmand □, *Afghan.* 60 D4
Helmand →, *Afghan.* 60 D2
Helme →, *Germany* 18 D7
Helmond, *Neths.* 17 F7
Helmsdale, *U.K.* 14 C5
Helmstedt, *Germany* 18 C7
Helnæs, *Denmark* 11 J4
Helong, *China* 51 C15
Helper, *U.S.A.* 110 G8
Helsingborg, *Sweden* 11 H6
Helsinge, *Denmark* 11 H6
Helsingfors = Helsinki, *Finland* 9 F21
Helsingør, *Denmark* 11 H6
Helsinki, *Finland* 9 F21
Helston, *U.K.* 13 G2
Helvellyn, *U.K.* 12 C4
Helvoirt, *Neths.* 17 E6
Helwân, *Egypt* 76 J7
Hemet, *U.S.A.* 113 M10
Hemingford, *U.S.A.* 108 D3
Hemphill, *U.S.A.* 109 K8
Hempstead, *U.S.A.* 109 K6
Hemse, *Sweden* 9 H18
Hemsö, *Sweden* 10 B12
Henan □, *China* 50 G8
Henares →, *Spain* 28 E1
Henashi-Misaki, *Japan* 48 D9
Hendaye, *France* 26 E2
Hendek, *Turkey* 66 B4
Henderson, *Argentina* 126 D3
Henderson, *Ky., U.S.A.* 104 G2
Henderson, *N.C., U.S.A.* 105 G6
Henderson, *Nev., U.S.A.* 113 J12
Henderson, *Tenn., U.S.A.* 105 H1
Henderson, *Tex., U.S.A.* 109 J7
Hendersonville, *U.S.A.* 105 H4
Hendījān, *Iran* 65 D6
Hendon, *Australia* 91 D5
Heng Xian, *China* 52 F7
Hengcheng, *China* 50 E4
Hengdaohezi, *China* 51 B15
Hengelo, *Gelderland, Neths.* 16 D8
Hengelo, *Overijssel, Neths.* 16 D9
Hengfeng, *China* 53 C10
Hengshan, *Hunan, China* 53 D9
Hengshan, *Shaanxi, China* 50 F5
Hengshui, *China* 50 F8
Hengyang, *Hunan, China* 53 D9
Hengyang, *Hunan, China* 53 D9
Henichesk, *Ukraine* 41 J8
Hénin-Beaumont, *France* 25 B9
Henlopen, C., *U.S.A.* 104 F8
Hennan, *Sweden* 10 B9
Hennebont, *France* 24 E3
Hennenman, *S. Africa* 84 D4
Hennessey, *U.S.A.* 109 G6
Hennigsdorf, *Germany* 18 C9
Henrichemont, *France* 25 E9
Henrietta, *U.S.A.* 109 J5
Henrietta, Ostrov, *Russia* 45 B16
Henrietta Maria, C., *Canada* 98 A3
Henry, *U.S.A.* 108 E10
Henryetta, *U.S.A.* 109 H6
Hensall, *Canada* 106 C3
Hentiyn Nuruu, *Mongolia* 54 B5
Henty, *Australia* 91 F4
Henzada, *Burma* 61 L19
Heping, *China* 53 E10
Heppner, *U.S.A.* 110 D4
Hepu, *China* 52 G7
Hepworth, *Canada* 106 B3
Heqing, *China* 52 D3
Hequ, *China* 50 E6
Héraðsflói, *Iceland* 8 D6
Héraðsvötn →, *Iceland* 8 D4
Herald Cays, *Australia* 90 B4
Herāt, *Afghan.* 60 B3
Herāt □, *Afghan.* 60 B3
Hérault □, *France* 26 E7
Hérault →, *France* 26 E7
Herbault, *France* 24 E8
Herbert →, *Australia* 90 B4
Herbert Downs, *Australia* 90 C2
Herberton, *Australia* 90 B4
Herbignac, *France* 24 E4
Herborn, *Germany* 18 E4
Herby, *Poland* 20 E8
Hercegnovi, *Montenegro, Yug.* 21 N8
Herðubreið, *Iceland* 8 D5
Hereford, *U.K.* 13 E5
Hereford, *U.S.A.* 109 H3
Hereford and Worcester □, *U.K.* 13 E5
Herefoss, *Norway* 11 F2
Herent, *Belgium* 17 G5
Herentals, *Belgium* 17 F5
Herenthout, *Belgium* 17 F5
Herfølge, *Denmark* 11 J6
Herford, *Germany* 18 C4
Héricourt, *France* 25 E13
Herington, *U.S.A.* 108 F6
Herisau, *Switz.* 23 B8
Hérisson, *France* 26 B6
Herk →, *Belgium* 17 G6
Herkenbosch, *Neths.* 17 F8
Herkimer, *U.S.A.* 107 D10
Herlong, *U.S.A.* 112 E6
Herm, *U.K.* 24 C4
Hermagor-Pressegger See, *Austria* 21 J3
Herman, *U.S.A.* 108 C6
Hermann, *U.S.A.* 108 F9
Hermannsburg, *Germany* 18 C6
Hermannsburg Mission, *Australia* 88 D5
Hermanus, *S. Africa* 84 E2
Herment, *France* 26 C6
Hermidale, *Australia* 91 E4
Hermiston, *U.S.A.* 110 D4
Hermitage, *N.Z.* 87 K3
Hermite, I., *Chile* 128 E3
Hermon, Mt. = Ash Shaykh, J., *Lebanon* 69 B4
Hermosillo, *Mexico* 114 B2
Hernád →, *Hungary* 21 H11
Hernandarias, *Paraguay* 127 B5
Hernandez, *U.S.A.* 112 J6
Hernando, *Argentina* 126 C3
Hernando, *U.S.A.* 109 H10
Herne, *Belgium* 17 G4
Herne, *Germany* 17 E10
Herne Bay, *U.K.* 13 F9
Herning, *Denmark* 11 H2
Heroica = Caborca, *Mexico* 114 A2
Heroica Nogales = Nogales, *Mexico* 114 A2
Heron Bay, *Canada* 98 C2
Herradura, Pta. de la, *Canary Is.* 36 F5
Herreid, *U.S.A.* 108 C4
Herrera, *Spain* 31 H6
Herrera de Alcántar, *Spain* 31 F3
Herrera de Pisuerga, *Spain* 30 C6
Herrera del Duque, *Spain* 31 F5
Herrick, *Australia* 90 G4
Herrin, *U.S.A.* 109 G10
Herrljunga, *Sweden* 11 F7
Hersbruck, *Germany* 19 F7
Herseaux, *Belgium* 17 G2
Herselt, *Belgium* 17 F5
Hersonissos, *Greece* 37 D7
Herstal, *Belgium* 17 G7
Hertford, *U.K.* 13 F7
Hertfordshire □, *U.K.* 13 F7
's-Hertogenbosch, *Neths.* 17 E6
Hertzogville, *S. Africa* 84 D4
Hervás, *Spain* 30 E5
Herve, *Belgium* 17 G7
Herwijnen, *Neths.* 16 E6
Herzberg, *Brandenburg, Germany* 18 D9
Herzberg, *Niedersachsen, Germany* 18 D6
Herzele, *Belgium* 17 G3
Herzliyya, *Israel* 69 C3
Herzogenbuchsee, *Switz.* 22 B5
Ḥeşār, *Fārs, Iran* 65 D6
Ḥeşār, *Markazī, Iran* 65 C6
Hesdin, *France* 25 B9
Hesel, *Germany* 18 B3
Heshui, *China* 50 G5
Heshun, *China* 50 F7
Hesperange, *Lux.* 17 J8
Hesperia, *U.S.A.* 113 L9
Hesse = Hessen □, *Germany* 18 E5
Hessen □, *Germany* 18 E5
Hetch Hetchy Aqueduct, *U.S.A.* 112 H5
Hettinger, *U.S.A.* 108 C3
Hettstedt, *Germany* 18 D7
Heugem, *Neths.* 17 G7
Heule, *Belgium* 17 G2
Heusden, *Belgium* 17 F6
Heusden, *Neths.* 16 E6
Hève, C. de la, *France* 24 C7
Heverlee, *Belgium* 17 G5
Hewett, C., *Canada* 97 A13
Hexham, *U.K.* 12 C5
Hexi, *Yunnan, China* 52 E4
Hexi, *Zhejiang, China* 53 D12
Hexigten Qi, *China* 51 C9
Ḥeydarābād, *Iran* 65 D7
Heyfield, *Australia* 91 F4
Heysham, *U.K.* 12 C5
Heythuysen, *Neths.* 17 F7
Heyuan, *China* 53 F10
Heywood, *Australia* 91 F3
Heze, *China* 50 G8
Hezhang, *China* 52 D5
Hi Vista, *U.S.A.* 113 L9
Hialeah, *U.S.A.* 105 N5
Hiawatha, *Kans., U.S.A.* 108 F7
Hiawatha, *Utah, U.S.A.* 110 G8
Hibbing, *U.S.A.* 108 B8
Hibbs B., *Australia* 90 G4
Hibernia Reef, *Australia* 88 B3
Hickory, *U.S.A.* 105 H5
Hicks, Pt., *Australia* 91 F4
Hicksville, *U.S.A.* 107 F11
Hida, *Romania* 38 B6
Hida-Gawa →, *Japan* 49 G8
Hida-Sammyaku, *Japan* 49 F8
Hidaka-Sammyaku, *Japan* 48 C11
Hidalgo, *Mexico* 115 C5
Hidalgo □, *Mexico* 115 C5
Hidalgo, Presa M., *Mexico* 114 B3
Hidalgo, Pta. del, *Canary Is.* 36 F3
Hidalgo del Parral, *Mexico* 114 B3
Hiddensee, *Germany* 18 A9
Hidrolândia, *Brazil* 123 E2
Hieflau, *Austria* 21 H4
Hiendelaencina, *Spain* 28 D1
Hierro, *Canary Is.* 36 G1
Higashiajima-San, *Japan* 48 F10
Higashiōsaka, *Japan* 49 G7
Higgins, *U.S.A.* 109 G4
Higgins Corner, *U.S.A.* 112 F5
Higginsville, *Australia* 89 F3
High Atlas = Haut Atlas, *Morocco* 74 B3
High I., *Canada* 99 A7
High Island, *U.S.A.* 109 L7
High Level, *Canada* 100 B5
High Point, *U.S.A.* 105 H6
High Prairie, *Canada* 100 B5
High River, *Canada* 100 C6
High Springs, *U.S.A.* 105 L4
High Tatra = Tatry, *Slovak Rep.* 20 F9
High Veld, *Africa* 70 J6
High Wycombe, *U.K.* 13 F7
Highbury, *Australia* 90 B3
Highland □, *U.K.* 14 D4
Highland Park, *U.S.A.* 104 D2
Highmore, *U.S.A.* 108 C5
Highrock L., *Canada* 101 B7
Higüay, *Dom. Rep.* 117 C6
Hihya, *Egypt* 76 H7
Hiiumaa, *Estonia* 9 G20
Híjar, *Spain* 28 D4
Ḥijāz □, *Si. Arabia* 68 C2
Hijken, *Neths.* 16 C8
Hijo = Tagum, *Phil.* 55 H6
Hikari, *Japan* 49 H5
Hiko, *U.S.A.* 111 H6
Hikone, *Japan* 49 G8
Hikurangi, *N.Z.* 87 F5
Hikurangi, Mt., *N.Z.* 87 H6
Hildburghausen, *Germany* 19 E6
Hildesheim, *Germany* 18 C5
Hill →, *Australia* 89 F2
Hill City, *Idaho, U.S.A.* 110 E6
Hill City, *Kans., U.S.A.* 108 F5
Hill City, *Minn., U.S.A.* 108 B8
Hill City, *S. Dak., U.S.A.* 108 D3
Hill Island L., *Canada* 101 A7
Hillared, *Sweden* 11 G7
Hillcrest Center, *U.S.A.* 113 K8
Hillegom, *Neths.* 16 D5
Hillerød, *Denmark* 11 J6
Hillingdon, *U.K.* 13 F7
Hillman, *U.S.A.* 104 C4
Hillmond, *Canada* 101 C7
Hillsboro, *Kans., U.S.A.* 108 F6
Hillsboro, *N. Dak., U.S.A.* 108 B6
Hillsboro, *N.H., U.S.A.* 107 C13
Hillsboro, *N. Mex., U.S.A.* 111 K10
Hillsboro, *Oreg., U.S.A.* 112 E4
Hillsboro, *Tex., U.S.A.* 109 J6
Hillsborough, *Grenada* 117 D7
Hillsdale, *Mich., U.S.A.* 104 E3
Hillsdale, *N.Y., U.S.A.* 107 D11
Hillside, *Australia* 88 D2
Hillsport, *Canada* 98 C2
Hillston, *Australia* 91 E4
Hilo, *U.S.A.* 102 J17
Hilton, *U.S.A.* 106 C7
Hilvan, *Turkey* 67 D8
Hilvarenbeek, *Neths.* 17 F6
Hilversum, *Neths.* 16 D6
Himachal Pradesh □, *India* 62 D7
Himalaya, *Asia* 63 E11
Himamaylan, *Phil.* 55 F5
Himara, *Albania* 39 J2
Himatnagar, *India* 60 H8
Himeji, *Japan* 49 G7
Himi, *Japan* 49 F8
Himmerland, *Denmark* 11 H3
Ḥimş, *Syria* 69 A5
Ḥimş □, *Syria* 69 A5
Hinche, *Haiti* 117 C5
Hinchinbrook I., *Australia* 90 B4
Hinckley, *U.K.* 13 E6
Hinckley, *U.S.A.* 110 G7
Hindås, *Sweden* 11 G6
Hindaun, *India* 62 F7
Hindmarsh, L., *Australia* 91 F3
Hindsholm, *Denmark* 11 J4
Hindu Bagh, *Pakistan* 62 D2
Hindu Kush, *Asia* 60 B7
Hindubagh, *Pakistan* 60 D5
Hindupur, *India* 60 N10
Hines Creek, *Canada* 100 B5
Hinganghat, *India* 60 J11
Hingeon, *Belgium* 17 G5
Hingham, *U.S.A.* 110 B8
Hingoli, *India* 60 K10
Hinigaran, *Phil.* 55 F5
Hinis, *Turkey* 67 C9
Hinna = Imi, *Ethiopia* 68 F3
Hinna, *Nigeria* 79 C7
Hinnøya, *Norway* 8 B16
Hinojosa del Duque, *Spain* 31 G5
Hinsdale, *U.S.A.* 110 B10
Hinterrhein →, *Switz.* 23 C8
Hinton, *Canada* 100 C5
Hinton, *U.S.A.* 104 G5
Hinwil, *Switz.* 23 B7
Hınzır Burnu, *Turkey* 66 D6
Hippolytushoef, *Neths.* 16 C5
Hirado, *Japan* 49 H4
Hirakud Dam, *India* 61 J13
Hiratsuka, *Japan* 49 G9
Hirfanlı Baraji, *Turkey* 66 C5
Hirhafok, *Algeria* 75 D6
Hîrlău, *Romania* 38 B9
Hiroo, *Japan* 48 C11
Hirosaki, *Japan* 48 D10
Hiroshima, *Japan* 49 G6
Hiroshima □, *Japan* 49 G6
Hirsholmene, *Denmark* 11 G4
Hirson, *France* 25 C11
Hîrşova, *Romania* 38 E10
Hirtshals, *Denmark* 11 G3
Hisar, *India* 62 E6
Hisb →, *Iraq* 64 D5
Ḥismá, *Si. Arabia* 64 D3
Hispaniola, *W. Indies* 117 C5
Hīt, *Iraq* 67 F10
Hita, *Japan* 49 H5
Hitachi, *Japan* 49 F10
Hitchin, *U.K.* 13 F7
Hitoyoshi, *Japan* 49 H5
Hitra, *Norway* 8 E13
Hitzacker, *Germany* 18 B7
Ḥiyyon, N. →, *Israel* 69 E4
Hjalmar L., *Canada* 101 A7
Hjälmare kanal, *Sweden* 10 E9
Hjälmaren, *Sweden* 10 E9
Hjartdal, *Norway* 10 E2
Hjerkinn, *Norway* 10 B3
Hjørring, *Denmark* 11 G3
Hjortkvarn, *Sweden* 11 F9
Hlinsko, *Czech.* 20 F5
Hluhluwe, *S. Africa* 85 D5
Hlukhiv, *Ukraine* 41 G7
Hlyboka, *Ukraine* 41 H3
Hlybokaye, *Belarus* 40 E4
Ho, *Ghana* 79 D5
Ho Chi Minh City = Phanh Bho Ho Chi Minh, *Vietnam* 59 G6
Ho Thuong, *Vietnam* 58 C5
Hoa Binh, *Vietnam* 58 B5
Hoa Da, *Vietnam* 59 G7
Hoa Hiep, *Vietnam* 59 G5
Hoai Nhon, *Vietnam* 58 E7
Hoang Lien Son, *Vietnam* 58 A4
Hoare B., *Canada* 97 B13
Hobart, *Australia* 90 G4
Hobart, *U.S.A.* 109 H5
Hobbs, *U.S.A.* 109 J3
Hobbs Coast, *Antarctica* 5 D14
Hobo, *Colombia* 120 C2
Hoboken, *Belgium* 17 F4
Hoboken, *U.S.A.* 107 F10
Hobro, *Denmark* 11 H3
Hobscheid, *Lux.* 17 J7
Hoburgen, *Sweden* 9 H18
Hochdorf, *Switz.* 23 B6
Hochschwab, *Austria* 21 H5
Höchstadt, *Germany* 19 F6
Hockenheim, *Germany* 19 F4
Hodaka-Dake, *Japan* 49 F8
Hodgson, *Canada* 101 C9
Hódmezövásárhely, *Hungary* 21 J10
Hodna, Chott el, *Algeria* 75 A5
Hodna, Monts du, *Algeria* 75 A5
Hodonín, *Czech.* 20 G7
Hoeamdong, *N. Korea* 51 C16
Hœdic, I. de, *France* 24 E4
Hoegaarden, *Belgium* 17 G5
Hoek van Holland, *Neths.* 16 E4
Hoeksche Waard, *Neths.* 16 E4
Hoenderloo, *Neths.* 16 D7
Hoengsŏng, *S. Korea* 51 F14
Hoensbroek, *Neths* 17 G7
Hoeryong, *N. Korea* 51 C15
Hoeselt, *Belgium* 17 G6
Hoeven, *Neths.* 17 E5
Hoeyang, *N. Korea* 51 E14
Hof, *Germany* 19 E7
Hofgeismar, *Germany* 18 D5
Hofmeyr, *S. Africa* 84 E4
Höfn, *Iceland* 8 D6
Hofors, *Sweden* 9 F17
Hofsjökull, *Iceland* 8 D4
Hōfu, *Japan* 49 G5
Hogan Group, *Australia* 90 F4
Hogansville, *U.S.A.* 105 J3
Hogeland, *U.S.A.* 110 B9
Hoggar = Ahaggar, *Algeria* 75 D6
Högsäter, *Sweden* 11 F6
Hogsty Reef, *Bahamas* 117 B5
Hoh →, *U.S.A.* 112 C2
Hoh Xil Shan, *China* 54 C3
Hohe Rhön, *Germany* 19 E5
Hohe Tauern, *Austria* 21 H2
Hohe Venn, *Belgium* 17 H8
Hohenau, *Austria* 20 G6
Hohenems, *Austria* 19 H5
Hohenstein-Ernstthal, *Germany* 18 E8
Hohenwald, *U.S.A.* 105 H2
Hohenwestedt, *Germany* 18 A5
Hohhot, *China* 50 D6
Hóhlakas, *Greece* 37 D9
Hohoe, *Ghana* 79 D5
Hoi An, *Vietnam* 58 E7
Hoi Xuan, *Vietnam* 58 B5
Hoisington, *U.S.A.* 108 F5
Højer, *Denmark* 11 K2
Hōjō, *Japan* 49 H6
Hökerum, *Sweden* 11 G7
Hokianga Harbour, *N.Z.* 87 F4
Hokitika, *N.Z.* 87 K3
Hokkaidō □, *Japan* 48 C11
Hokksund, *Norway* 10 E3
Hol-Hol, *Djibouti* 77 E5
Hola Pristan, *Ukraine* 41 J7
Holbæk, *Denmark* 11 J5
Holbrook, *Australia* 91 F4
Holbrook, *U.S.A.* 111 J8
Holden, *Canada* 100 C6
Holden, *U.S.A.* 110 G7
Holdenville, *U.S.A.* 109 H6
Holderness, *U.K.* 12 D7
Holdfast, *Canada* 101 C7
Holdich, *Argentina* 128 C3
Holdrege, *U.S.A.* 108 E5
Holguín, *Cuba* 116 B4
Hollabrunn, *Austria* 20 G6
Hollams Bird I., *Namibia* 84 C1
Holland, *U.S.A.* 104 D2
Hollandia = Jayapura, *Indonesia* 57 E10
Hollandsch Diep, *Neths.* 17 E5
Hollandsch IJssel →, *Neths.* 16 E5
Hollfeld, *Germany* 19 F7
Hollidaysburg, *U.S.A.* 106 F6
Hollis, *U.S.A.* 109 H5
Hollister, *Calif., U.S.A.* 111 H3
Hollister, *Idaho, U.S.A.* 110 E6
Hollum, *Neths.* 16 B7
Holly, *U.S.A.* 108 F3
Holly Hill, *U.S.A.* 105 L5
Holly Springs, *U.S.A.* 109 H10
Hollywood, *Calif., U.S.A.* 111 J4
Hollywood, *Fla., U.S.A.* 105 N5
Holm, *Sweden* 10 B10
Holman Island, *Canada* 96 A8
Hólmavík, *Iceland* 8 D3
Holmes Reefs, *Australia* 90 B4
Holmestrand, *Norway* 10 E4
Holmsbu, *Norway* 10 E4
Holmsjön, *Sweden* 10 B9
Holmsland Klit, *Denmark* 11 J2
Holmsund, *Sweden* 8 E19
Holroyd →, *Australia* 90 A3
Holstebro, *Denmark* 11 H2
Holsworthy, *U.K.* 13 G3
Holte, *Denmark* 11 J6
Holten, *Neths.* 16 D8
Holton, *Canada* 99 B8
Holton, *U.S.A.* 108 F7
Holtville, *U.S.A.* 113 N11
Holwerd, *Neths.* 16 B7
Holy Cross, *U.S.A.* 96 B4
Holy I., *Angl., U.K.* 12 D3
Holy I., *Northumb., U.K.* 12 B6
Holyhead, *U.K.* 12 D3
Holyoke, *Colo., U.S.A.* 108 E3
Holyoke, *Mass., U.S.A.* 107 D12
Holyrood, *Canada* 99 C9
Holzkirchen, *Germany* 19 H7
Holzminden, *Germany* 18 D5
Homa Bay, *Kenya* 82 C3
Homa Bay □, *Kenya* 82 C3
Homalin, *Burma* 61 G19
Homand, *Iran* 65 C8
Homberg, *Germany* 18 D5
Hombori, *Mali* 79 B4
Homburg, *Germany* 19 F3

Home B., *Canada* 97 B13
Home Hill, *Australia* 90 B4
Homedale, *U.S.A.* 110 E5
Homer, *Alaska, U.S.A.* 96 C4
Homer, *La., U.S.A.* 109 J8
Homestead, *Australia* 90 C4
Homestead, *Fla., U.S.A.* 105 N5
Homestead, *Oreg., U.S.A.* 110 D5
Homewood, *U.S.A.* 112 F6
Hominy, *U.S.A.* 109 G6
Homoine, *Mozam.* 85 C6
Homoljske Planina, *Serbia, Yug.* 21 L11
Homorod, *Romania* 38 C8
Homs = Ḥimṣ, *Syria* 69 A5
Homyel, *Belarus* 41 F6
Hon Chong, *Vietnam* 59 G5
Hon Me, *Vietnam* 58 C5
Hon Quan, *Vietnam* 59 G6
Honan = Henan □, *China* 50 G8
Honbetsu, *Japan* 48 C11
Honcut, *U.S.A.* 112 F5
Honda, *Colombia* 120 B3
Honda Bay, *Phil.* 55 G3
Hondeklipbaai, *S. Africa* 84 E2
Hondo, *Japan* 49 H5
Hondo, *U.S.A.* 109 L5
Hondo →, *Belize* 115 D7
Honduras ■, *Cent. Amer.* 116 D2
Honduras, G. de, *Caribbean* 116 C2
Hønefoss, *Norway* 9 F14
Honesdale, *U.S.A.* 107 E9
Honey L., *U.S.A.* 112 E6
Honfleur, *France* 24 C7
Hong Gai, *Vietnam* 58 B6
Hong He →, *China* 50 H8
Hong Kong ■, *Asia* 53 F10
Hong'an, *China* 53 B10
Hongchŏn, *S. Korea* 51 F14
Honghai Wan, *China* 53 F10
Honghu, *China* 53 C9
Hongjiang, *China* 52 D7
Hongliu He →, *China* 50 F5
Hongor, *Mongolia* 50 B7
Hongsa, *Laos* 58 C3
Hongshui He →, *China* 52 F7
Hongsŏng, *S. Korea* 51 F14
Hongtong, *China* 50 F6
Honguedo, Détroit d', *Canada* 99 C7
Hongwon, *N. Korea* 51 E14
Hongya, *China* 52 C4
Hongyuan, *China* 52 A4
Hongze Hu, *China* 51 H10
Honiara, *Solomon Is.* 92 H7
Honiton, *U.K.* 13 G4
Honjō, *Japan* 48 E10
Honkorâb, Ras, *Egypt* 76 C4
Honningsvåg, *Norway* 8 A21
Honolulu, *U.S.A.* 102 H16
Honshū, *Japan* 49 G9
Hontoria del Pinar, *Spain* 28 D1
Hood, Mt., *U.S.A.* 110 D3
Hood, Pt., *Australia* 89 F2
Hood River, *U.S.A.* 110 D3
Hoodsport, *U.S.A.* 112 C3
Hooge, *Germany* 18 A4
Hoogerheide, *Neths.* 17 F4
Hoogeveen, *Neths.* 16 C8
Hoogeveensche Vaart, *Neths.* 16 C8
Hoogezand, *Neths.* 16 B9
Hooghly → = Hugli →, *India* 63 J13
Hooghly-Chinsura = Chunchura, *India* 63 H13
Hoogkerk, *Neths.* 16 B9
Hooglede, *Belgium* 17 G2
Hoogstraten, *Belgium* 17 F5
Hoogvliet, *Neths.* 16 E4
Hook Hd., *Ireland* 15 D5
Hook I., *Australia* 90 C4
Hook of Holland = Hoek van Holland, *Neths.* 16 E4
Hooker, *U.S.A.* 109 G4
Hooker Creek, *Australia* 88 C5
Hoopeston, *U.S.A.* 104 E2
Hoopstad, *S. Africa* 84 D4
Hoorn, *Neths.* 16 C6
Hoover Dam, *U.S.A.* 113 K12
Hooversville, *U.S.A.* 106 F6
Hop Bottom, *U.S.A.* 107 E9
Hopa, *Turkey* 67 B9
Hope, *Canada* 100 D4
Hope, *Ariz., U.S.A.* 113 M13
Hope, *Ark., U.S.A.* 109 J8
Hope, *N. Dak., U.S.A.* 108 B6
Hope, L., *Australia* 91 D2
Hope, Pt., *U.S.A.* 96 B3
Hope Town, *Bahamas* 116 A4
Hopedale, *Canada* 99 A7
Hopefield, *S. Africa* 84 E2
Hopei = Hebei □, *China* 50 E9
Hopelchén, *Mexico* 115 D7
Hopetoun, *Vic., Australia* 91 F3
Hopetoun, *W. Austral., Australia* 89 F3
Hopetown, *S. Africa* 84 D3
Hopkins, *U.S.A.* 108 E7
Hopkins, L., *Australia* 88 D4
Hopkinsville, *U.S.A.* 105 G2
Hopland, *U.S.A.* 112 G3
Hoptrup, *Denmark* 11 J3
Hoquiam, *U.S.A.* 112 D3
Horasan, *Turkey* 67 B10
Horcajo de Santiago, *Spain* 28 F1
Horden Hills, *Australia* 88 D5
Horezu, *Romania* 38 D6
Horgen, *Switz.* 23 B7
Horinger, *China* 50 D6
Horki, *Belarus* 40 E6
Horlick Mts., *Antarctica* 5 E15
Horlivka, *Ukraine* 41 H10
Hormoz, *Iran* 65 E7
Hormoz, Jaz. ye, *Iran* 65 E8
Hormuz, Str. of, *The Gulf* 65 E8
Horn, *Iceland* 8 C2
Horn, *Neths.* 17 F7
Horn →, *Canada* 100 A5
Horn, Cape = Hornos, C. de, *Chile* 128 E3
Horn Head, *Ireland* 15 A3
Horn I., *Australia* 90 A3
Horn I., *U.S.A.* 105 K1
Horn Mts., *Canada* 100 A5
Hornachuelos, *Spain* 31 H5
Hornavan, *Sweden* 8 C17
Hornbæk, *Denmark* 11 H6
Hornbeck, *U.S.A.* 109 K8
Hornbrook, *U.S.A.* 110 F2
Hornburg, *Germany* 18 C6
Horncastle, *U.K.* 12 D7
Hornell, *U.S.A.* 106 D7
Hornell L., *Canada* 100 A5
Hornepayne, *Canada* 98 C3
Hornitos, *U.S.A.* 112 H6
Hornos, C. de, *Chile* 128 E3
Hornoy, *France* 25 C8
Hornsby, *Australia* 91 E5
Hornsea, *U.K.* 12 D7
Hornslandet, *Sweden* 10 C11
Hornslet, *Denmark* 11 H4
Hornu, *Belgium* 17 H3
Hörnum, *Germany* 18 A4
Horobetsu, *Japan* 48 C10
Horodenka, *Ukraine* 41 H3
Horodnya, *Ukraine* 41 G6
Horodok, *Khmelnytskyy, Ukraine* 41 H4
Horodok, *Lviv, Ukraine* 41 H2
Horodyshche, *Ukraine* 41 H6
Horokhiv, *Ukraine* 41 G3
Horqin Youyi Qianqi, *China* 51 A12
Horqueta, *Paraguay* 126 A4
Horred, *Sweden* 11 G6
Horse Creek, *U.S.A.* 108 E3
Horse Is., *Canada* 99 B8
Horsefly L., *Canada* 100 C4
Horsens, *Denmark* 11 J3
Horsens Fjord, *Denmark* 11 J4
Horsham, *Australia* 91 F3
Horsham, *U.K.* 13 F7
Horst, *Neths.* 17 F8
Horten, *Norway* 10 E4
Hortobágy →, *Hungary* 21 H11
Horton, *U.S.A.* 108 F7
Horton →, *Canada* 96 B7
Horw, *Switz.* 23 B6
Horwood, L., *Canada* 98 C3
Hosaina, *Ethiopia* 77 F4
Hose, Gunung-Gunung, *Malaysia* 56 D4
Ḥoseynābād, *Khuzestān, Iran* 65 C6
Ḥoseynābād, *Kordestān, Iran* 67 E12
Hoshangabad, *India* 62 H7
Hoshiarpur, *India* 62 D6
Hosingen, *Lux.* 17 H8
Hosmer, *U.S.A.* 108 C5
Hospental, *Switz.* 23 C7
Hospet, *India* 60 M10
Hospitalet de Llobregat, *Spain* 28 D7
Hoste, I., *Chile* 128 E3
Hostens, *France* 26 D3
Hot, *Thailand* 58 C2
Hot Creek Range, *U.S.A.* 110 G5
Hot Springs, *Ark., U.S.A.* 109 H8
Hot Springs, *S. Dak., U.S.A.* 108 D3
Hotagen, *Sweden* 8 E16
Hotan, *China* 54 C2
Hotazel, *S. Africa* 84 D3
Hotchkiss, *U.S.A.* 111 G10
Hotham, C., *Australia* 88 B5
Hoting, *Sweden* 8 D17
Hotte, Massif de la, *Haiti* 117 C5
Hottentotsbaai, *Namibia* 84 D1
Hotton, *Belgium* 17 H6
Houat, I. de, *France* 24 E4
Houck, *U.S.A.* 111 J9
Houdan, *France* 25 D8
Houdeng-Goegnies, *Belgium* 17 H4
Houei Sai, *Laos* 58 B3
Houffalize, *Belgium* 17 H7
Houghton, *U.S.A.* 108 B10
Houghton L., *U.S.A.* 104 C3
Houghton-le-Spring, *U.K.* 12 C6
Houhora Heads, *N.Z.* 87 F4
Houille →, *Belgium* 17 H5
Houlton, *U.S.A.* 99 C6
Houma, *U.S.A.* 109 L9
Houndé, *Burkina Faso* 78 C4
Hourtin, *France* 26 C2
Hourtin-Carcans, Étang d', *France* 26 C2
Houston, *Canada* 100 C3
Houston, *Mo., U.S.A.* 109 G9
Houston, *Tex., U.S.A.* 109 L7
Houten, *Neths.* 16 D6
Houthalen, *Belgium* 17 F6
Houthem, *Belgium* 17 G1
Houthulst, *Belgium* 17 G2
Houtman Abrolhos, *Australia* 89 E1
Houyet, *Belgium* 17 H6
Hov, *Denmark* 11 J4
Hova, *Sweden* 11 F8
Høvåg, *Norway* 11 F2
Hovd, *Mongolia* 54 B4
Hove, *U.K.* 13 G7
Hoveyzeh, *Iran* 65 D6
Hövsgöl, *Mongolia* 50 C5
Hövsgöl Nuur, *Mongolia* 54 A5
Howakil, *Eritrea* 77 D5
Howar, Wadi →, *Sudan* 77 D2
Howard, *Australia* 91 D5
Howard, *Kans., U.S.A.* 109 G6
Howard, *Pa., U.S.A.* 106 E7
Howard, *S. Dak., U.S.A.* 108 C6
Howard I., *Australia* 90 A2
Howard L., *Canada* 101 A7
Howe, *U.S.A.* 110 E7
Howe, C., *Australia* 91 F5
Howell, *U.S.A.* 104 D4
Howick, *Canada* 107 A11
Howick, *S. Africa* 85 D5
Howick Group, *Australia* 90 A4
Howitt, L., *Australia* 91 D2
Howland I., *Pac. Oc.* 92 G10
Howley, *Canada* 99 C8
Howrah = Haora, *India* 63 H13
Howth Hd., *Ireland* 15 C5
Höxter, *Germany* 18 D5
Hoy, *U.K.* 14 C5
Hoya, *Germany* 18 C5
Høyanger, *Norway* 9 F12
Hoyerswerda, *Germany* 18 D10
Hoyos, *Spain* 30 E4
Hpungan Pass, *Burma* 61 F20
Hradec Králové, *Czech.* 20 E5
Hranice, *Czech.* 20 F7
Hrazdan, *Armenia* 43 K7
Hrebenka, *Ukraine* 41 G7
Hrodna, *Belarus* 40 F2
Hrodzyanka, *Belarus* 40 F5
Hron →, *Slovak Rep.* 21 H8
Hrubieszów, *Poland* 20 E13
Hrvatska = Croatia ■, *Europe* 33 C13
Hrymayliv, *Ukraine* 41 H4
Hsenwi, *Burma* 61 H20
Hsiamen = Xiamen, *China* 53 E12
Hsian = Xi'an, *China* 50 G5
Hsinchu, *Taiwan* 53 E13
Hsinhailien = Lianyungang, *China* 51 G10
Hsüchou = Xuzhou, *China* 51 G9
Hu Xian, *China* 50 G5
Hua Hin, *Thailand* 58 F2
Hua Xian, *Henan, China* 50 G8
Hua Xian, *Shaanxi, China* 50 G5
Hua'an, *China* 53 E11
Huacaya, *Bolivia* 125 E5
Huacheng, *China* 53 E10
Huachinera, *Mexico* 114 A3
Huacho, *Peru* 124 C2
Huachón, *Peru* 124 C2
Huade, *China* 50 D7
Huadian, *China* 51 C14
Huai He →, *China* 53 A12
Huai Yot, *Thailand* 59 J2
Huai'an, *Hebei, China* 50 D8
Huai'an, *Jiangsu, China* 51 H10
Huaibei, *China* 50 G9
Huaide, *China* 51 C13
Huaidezhen, *China* 51 C13
Huaihua, *China* 52 D7
Huaiji, *China* 53 F9
Huainan, *China* 53 A11
Huaining, *China* 53 B11
Huairen, *China* 50 E7
Huairou, *China* 50 D9
Huaiyang, *China* 50 H8
Huaiyuan, *Anhui, China* 51 H9
Huaiyuan, *Guangxi Zhuangzu, China* 52 E7
Huajianzi, *China* 51 D13
Huajuapan de Leon, *Mexico* 115 D5
Hualapai Peak, *U.S.A.* 111 J7
Hualien, *Taiwan* 53 E13
Huallaga →, *Peru* 124 B2
Huallanca, *Peru* 124 B2
Huamachuco, *Peru* 124 B2
Huambo, *Angola* 81 G3
Huan Jiang →, *China* 50 G5
Huan Xian, *China* 50 F4
Huancabamba, *Peru* 124 B2
Huancane, *Peru* 124 D4
Huancapi, *Peru* 124 C3
Huancavelica, *Peru* 124 C2
Huancavelica □, *Peru* 124 C3
Huancayo, *Peru* 124 C2
Huanchaca, *Bolivia* 124 E4
Huanchaca, Serranía de, *Bolivia* 125 C5
Huang Hai = Yellow Sea, *China* 51 G12
Huang He →, *China* 51 F10
Huang Xian, *China* 51 F11
Huangchuan, *China* 53 A10
Huanggang, *China* 53 B10
Huangling, *China* 50 G5
Huangliu, *China* 54 E5
Huanglong, *China* 50 G5
Huanglongtan, *China* 53 A8
Huangmei, *China* 53 B10
Huangpi, *China* 53 B10
Huangping, *China* 52 D6
Huangshi, *China* 53 B10
Huangsongdian, *China* 51 C14
Huangyan, *China* 53 C13
Huangyangsi, *China* 53 D8
Huaning, *China* 52 E4
Huanjiang, *China* 52 E7
Huanta, *Peru* 124 C3
Huantai, *China* 51 F9
Huánuco, *Peru* 124 B2
Huánuco □, *Peru* 124 B2
Huanuni, *Bolivia* 124 D4
Huanzo, Cordillera de, *Peru* 124 C3
Huaping, *China* 52 D3
Huaral, *Peru* 124 C2
Huaraz, *Peru* 124 B2
Huari, *Peru* 124 B2
Huarmey, *Peru* 124 C2
Huarochiri, *Peru* 124 C2
Huarocondo, *Peru* 124 C3
Huarong, *China* 53 C9
Huascarán, *Peru* 124 B2
Huascarán, Nevado, *Peru* 124 B2
Huasco, *Chile* 126 B1
Huasco →, *Chile* 126 B1
Huasna, *U.S.A.* 113 K6
Huatabampo, *Mexico* 114 B3
Huauchinango, *Mexico* 115 C5
Huautla de Jiménez, *Mexico* 115 D5
Huaxi, *China* 52 D6
Huay Namota, *Mexico* 114 C4
Huayin, *China* 50 G6
Huayllay, *Peru* 124 C2
Huayuan, *China* 52 C7
Huazhou, *China* 53 G8
Hubbard, *U.S.A.* 109 K6
Hubbart Pt., *Canada* 101 B10
Hubei □, *China* 53 B9
Hubli-Dharwad = Dharwad, *India* 60 M9
Huchang, *N. Korea* 51 D14
Hückelhoven, *Germany* 18 D2
Huddersfield, *U.K.* 12 D6
Hudi, *Sudan* 76 D3
Hudiksvall, *Sweden* 10 C11
Hudson, *Canada* 101 C10
Hudson, *Mass., U.S.A.* 107 D13
Hudson, *Mich., U.S.A.* 104 E3
Hudson, *N.Y., U.S.A.* 107 D11
Hudson, *Wis., U.S.A.* 108 C8
Hudson, *Wyo., U.S.A.* 110 E9
Hudson →, *U.S.A.* 107 F10
Hudson Bay, *N.W.T., Canada* 97 C11
Hudson Bay, *Sask., Canada* 101 C8
Hudson Falls, *U.S.A.* 107 C11
Hudson Mts., *Antarctica* 5 D16
Hudson Str., *Canada* 97 B13
Hudson's Hope, *Canada* 100 B4
Hue, *Vietnam* 58 D6
Huebra →, *Spain* 30 D4
Huechucuicui, Pta., *Chile* 128 B2
Huedin, *Romania* 38 C6
Huehuetenango, *Guatemala* 116 C1
Huejúcar, *Mexico* 114 C4
Huelgoat, *France* 24 D3
Huelma, *Spain* 29 H1
Huelva, *Spain* 31 H4
Huelva □, *Spain* 31 H4
Huelva →, *Spain* 31 H5
Huentelauquén, *Chile* 126 C1
Huércal Overa, *Spain* 29 H3
Huerta, Sa. de la, *Argentina* 126 C2
Huertas, C. de las, *Spain* 29 G4
Huerva →, *Spain* 28 D4
Huesca, *Spain* 28 C4
Huesca □, *Spain* 28 C5
Huéscar, *Spain* 29 H2
Huetamo, *Mexico* 114 D4
Huete, *Spain* 28 E2
Hugh →, *Australia* 90 D1
Hughenden, *Australia* 90 C3
Hughes, *Australia* 89 F4
Hugli →, *India* 63 J13
Hugo, *U.S.A.* 108 F3
Hugoton, *U.S.A.* 109 G4
Hui Xian, *Gansu, China* 50 H4
Hui Xian, *Henan, China* 50 G7
Hui'an, *China* 53 E12
Hui'anbu, *China* 50 F4
Huichang, *China* 53 E10
Huichapán, *Mexico* 115 C5
Huidong, *China* 52 D4
Huifa He →, *China* 51 C14
Huila □, *Colombia* 120 C2
Huila, Nevado del, *Colombia* 120 C2
Huilai, *China* 53 F11
Huili, *China* 52 D4
Huimin, *China* 51 F9
Huinan, *China* 51 C14
Huinca Renancó, *Argentina* 126 C3
Huining, *China* 50 G3
Huinong, *China* 50 E4
Huise, *Belgium* 17 G3
Huishui, *China* 52 D6
Huisne →, *France* 24 E7
Huissen, *Neths.* 16 E7
Huiting, *China* 50 G9
Huitong, *China* 52 D7
Huixtla, *Mexico* 115 D6
Huize, *China* 52 D4
Huizen, *Neths.* 16 D6
Huizhou, *China* 53 F10
Hukawng Valley, *Burma* 61 F20
Hukou, *China* 53 C11
Hukuntsi, *Botswana* 84 C3
Hula, *Ethiopia* 77 F4
Hulan, *China* 54 B7
Ḥulayfā', *Si. Arabia* 64 E4
Huld, *Mongolia* 50 B3
Hulin He →, *China* 51 B12
Hull = Kingston upon Hull, *U.K.* 12 D7
Hull, *Canada* 98 C4
Hull →, *U.K.* 12 D7
Hulst, *Neths.* 17 F4
Hulun Nur, *China* 54 B6
Hulyaypole, *Ukraine* 41 J9
Humahuaca, *Argentina* 126 A2
Humaitá, *Brazil* 125 B5
Humaitá, *Paraguay* 126 B4
Humansdorp, *S. Africa* 84 E3
Humbe, *Angola* 84 B1
Humber →, *U.K.* 12 D7
Humbert River, *Australia* 88 C5
Humble, *U.S.A.* 109 L8
Humboldt, *Canada* 101 C7
Humboldt, *Iowa, U.S.A.* 108 D7
Humboldt, *Tenn., U.S.A.* 109 H10
Humboldt →, *U.S.A.* 110 F4
Humboldt Gletscher, *Greenland* 4 B4
Hume, *U.S.A.* 112 J8
Hume, L., *Australia* 91 F4
Humenné, *Slovak Rep.* 20 G11
Humphreys, Mt., *U.S.A.* 112 H8
Humphreys Peak, *U.S.A.* 111 J8
Humpolec, *Czech.* 20 F5
Humptulips, *U.S.A.* 112 C3
Hūn, *Libya* 73 C8
Hun Jiang →, *China* 51 D13
Húnaflói, *Iceland* 8 D3
Hunan □, *China* 53 D9
Hunchun, *China* 51 C16
Hundested, *Denmark* 11 J5
Hundred Mile House, *Canada* 100 C4
Hunedoara, *Romania* 38 D5
Hünfeld, *Germany* 18 E5
Hung Yen, *Vietnam* 58 B6
Hungary ■, *Europe* 21 H9
Hungary, Plain of, *Europe* 6 F10
Hungerford, *Australia* 91 D3
Hŭngnam, *N. Korea* 51 E14
Huni Valley, *Ghana* 78 D4
Hunsberge, *Namibia* 84 D2
Hunsrück, *Germany* 19 F3
Hunstanton, *U.K.* 12 E8
Hunte →, *Germany* 18 C4
Hunter, *N. Dak., U.S.A.* 108 B6
Hunter, *N.Y., U.S.A.* 107 D10
Hunter I., *Australia* 90 G3
Hunter I., *Canada* 100 C3
Hunter Ra., *Australia* 91 E5
Hunters Road, *Zimbabwe* 83 F2
Hunterville, *N.Z.* 87 H5
Huntingburg, *U.S.A.* 104 F2
Huntingdon, *Canada* 98 C5
Huntingdon, *U.K.* 13 E7
Huntingdon, *U.S.A.* 106 F6
Huntington, *Ind., U.S.A.* 104 E3
Huntington, *N.Y., U.S.A.* 107 F11
Huntington, *Oreg., U.S.A.* 110 D5
Huntington, *Utah, U.S.A.* 110 G8
Huntington, *W. Va., U.S.A.* 104 F4
Huntington Beach, *U.S.A.* 113 M8
Huntington Park, *U.S.A.* 111 K4
Huntly, *N.Z.* 87 G5
Huntly, *U.K.* 14 D6
Huntsville, *Canada* 98 C4
Huntsville, *Ala., U.S.A.* 105 H2
Huntsville, *Tex., U.S.A.* 109 K7
Hunyani →, *Zimbabwe* 83 F3
Hunyuan, *China* 50 E7
Hunza →, *India* 63 B6
Huo Xian, *China* 50 F6
Huong Hoa, *Vietnam* 58 D6
Huong Khe, *Vietnam* 58 C5
Huonville, *Australia* 90 G4
Huoqiu, *China* 53 A11
Huoshan, *Anhui, China* 53 A12
Huoshan, *Anhui, China* 53 B11
Hupeh = Hubei □, *China* 53 B9
Ḥūr, *Iran* 65 D8
Hure Qi, *China* 51 C11
Hurezani, *Romania* 38 E6
Hurghada, *Egypt* 76 B3
Hurley, *N. Mex., U.S.A.* 111 K9
Hurley, *Wis., U.S.A.* 108 B9
Huron, *Calif., U.S.A.* 112 J6
Huron, *Ohio, U.S.A.* 106 E2
Huron, *S. Dak., U.S.A.* 108 C5
Huron, L., *U.S.A.* 106 B2
Hurricane, *U.S.A.* 111 H7
Hurso, *Ethiopia* 77 F5
Hurum, *Norway* 10 C2
Hurunui →, *N.Z.* 87 K4
Hurup, *Denmark* 11 H2
Húsavík, *Iceland* 8 C5
Huşi, *Romania* 38 C11
Huskvarna, *Sweden* 9 H16
Hussar, *Canada* 100 C6
Hustadvika, *Norway* 8 E12
Husum, *Germany* 18 A5
Husum, *Sweden* 10 A13
Hutchinson, *Kans., U.S.A.* 109 F6

Hutchinson, *Minn., U.S.A.* 108 C7
Huttig, *U.S.A.* 109 J8
Hutton, Mt., *Australia* 91 D4
Huttwil, *Switz.* 22 B5
Huwun, *Ethiopia* 77 G5
Huy, *Belgium* 17 G6
Hvammstangi, *Iceland* 8 D3
Hvar, *Croatia* 33 E13
Hvarski Kanal, *Croatia* 33 E13
Hvítá →, *Iceland* 8 D3
Hwachon-chosuji, *S. Korea* 51 E14
Hwang Ho = Huang He →, *China* 51 F10
Hwange, *Zimbabwe* 83 F2
Hwange Nat. Park, *Zimbabwe* 84 B4
Hyannis, *U.S.A.* 108 E4
Hyargas Nuur, *Mongolia* 54 B4
Hybo, *Sweden* 10 C10
Hyde Park, *Guyana* 121 B6
Hyden, *Australia* 89 F2
Hyderabad, *India* 60 L11
Hyderabad, *Pakistan* 62 G3
Hyères, *France* 27 E10
Hyères, Is. d', *France* 27 F10
Hyesan, *N. Korea* 51 D15
Hyland →, *Canada* 100 B3
Hyltebruk, *Sweden* 11 H7
Hymia, *India* 63 C8
Hyndman Peak, *U.S.A.* 110 E6
Hyōgo □, *Japan* 49 G7
Hyrum, *U.S.A.* 110 F8
Hysham, *U.S.A.* 110 C10
Hythe, *U.K.* 13 F9
Hyūga, *Japan* 49 H5
Hyvinge = Hyvinkää, *Finland* 9 F21
Hyvinkää, *Finland* 9 F21

I

I-n-Échaï, *Mali* 74 D4
I-n-Gall, *Niger* 79 B6
Iabès, Erg, *Algeria* 75 C4
Iaco →, *Brazil* 124 B4
Iaçu, *Brazil* 123 D3
Iakora, *Madag.* 85 C8
Iaşi, *Romania* 38 B10
Iauaretê, *Colombia* 120 C4
Iba, *Phil.* 55 D3
Ibadan, *Nigeria* 79 D5
Ibagué, *Colombia* 120 C2
Ibaiti, *Brazil* 123 F1
Iballja, *Albania* 38 G3
Ibăneşti, *Romania* 38 C7
Ibar →, *Serbia, Yug.* 21 M10
Ibaraki □, *Japan* 49 F10
Ibarra, *Ecuador* 120 C2
Ibba, *Sudan* 77 G2
Ibba, Bahr el →, *Sudan* 77 F2
Ibbenbüren, *Germany* 18 C3
Ibembo, *Zaïre* 82 B1
Ibera, L., *Argentina* 126 B4
Iberian Peninsula, *Europe* 6 H5
Iberico, Sistema, *Spain* 28 E2
Iberville, *Canada* 98 C5
Iberville, Lac d', *Canada* 98 A5
Ibi, *Nigeria* 79 D6
Ibiá, *Brazil* 123 E2
Ibicaraí, *Brazil* 123 D4
Ibicuí, *Brazil* 123 D4
Ibicuy, *Argentina* 126 C4
Ibioapaba, Sa. da, *Brazil* 122 B3
Ibipetuba, *Brazil* 122 D3
Ibitiara, *Brazil* 123 D3
Ibiza, *Spain* 36 C7
Íblei, Monti, *Italy* 35 E7
Ibo, *Mozam.* 83 E5
Ibonma, *Indonesia* 57 E8
Ibotirama, *Brazil* 123 D3
Ibrāhīm →, *Lebanon* 69 A4
Ibshawâi, *Egypt* 76 J7
Ibu, *Indonesia* 57 D7
Iburg, *Germany* 18 C4
Ibusuki, *Japan* 49 J5
Icá, *Peru* 124 C2
Ica □, *Peru* 124 C2
Iça →, *Brazil* 124 A4
Icabarú, *Venezuela* 121 C5
Icabarú →, *Venezuela* 121 C5
Içana, *Brazil* 120 C4
Içana →, *Brazil* 120 C4
Icatu, *Brazil* 122 B3
Içel = Mersin, *Turkey* 66 D6
Iceland ■, *Europe* 8 D4
Icha, *Russia* 45 D16
Ich'ang = Yichang, *China* 53 B8
Ichchapuram, *India* 61 K14
Ichihara, *Japan* 49 G10
Ichikawa, *Japan* 49 G9
Ichilo →, *Bolivia* 125 D5
Ichinohe, *Japan* 48 D10
Ichinomiya, *Japan* 49 G8
Ichinoseki, *Japan* 48 E10
Ichnya, *Ukraine* 41 G7
Ichŏn, *S. Korea* 51 F14
Icht, *Morocco* 74 C3
Ichtegem, *Belgium* 17 F2
Icó, *Brazil* 122 C4
Icod, *Canary Is.* 36 F3
Icoraci, *Brazil* 122 B2
Icy Str., *U.S.A.* 100 B1
Ida Grove, *U.S.A.* 108 D7
Ida Valley, *Australia* 89 E3
Idabel, *U.S.A.* 109 J7
Idaga Hamus, *Ethiopia* 77 E4
Idah, *Nigeria* 79 D6
Idaho □, *U.S.A.* 110 D6
Idaho City, *U.S.A.* 110 E6
Idaho Falls, *U.S.A.* 110 E7
Idaho Springs, *U.S.A.* 110 G11
Idanha-a-Nova, *Portugal* 30 F3
Idar-Oberstein, *Germany* 19 F3
Idd el Ghanam, *Sudan* 73 F9
Iddan, *Somali Rep.* 68 F4
Idehan, *Libya* 75 C7
Idehan Marzūq, *Libya* 73 D7
Idelès, *Algeria* 75 D6
Idfû, *Egypt* 76 C3
Ídhi Óros, *Greece* 37 D6
Ídhra, *Greece* 39 M6
Idi, *Indonesia* 56 C1
Idiofa, *Zaïre* 80 E3
Idku, Bahra el, *Egypt* 76 H7
Idlib, *Syria* 66 E7
Idria, *U.S.A.* 112 J6
Idrija, *Slovenia* 33 B11
Idritsa, *Russia* 40 D5
Idstein, *Germany* 19 E4
Idutywa, *S. Africa* 85 E4
Ieper, *Belgium* 17 G1
Ierápetra, *Greece* 37 E7
Ierissós, *Greece* 39 J6
Ierzu, *Italy* 34 C2
Iesi, *Italy* 33 E10
Ifach, Punta, *Spain* 29 G5
'Ifāl, W. al →, *Si. Arabia* 64 D2
Ifanadiana, *Madag.* 85 C8
Ife, *Nigeria* 79 D5
Iférouâne, *Niger* 79 B6
Iffley, *Australia* 90 B3
Ifni, *Morocco* 74 C2
Ifon, *Nigeria* 79 D6
Iforas, Adrar des, *Mali* 79 B5
Ifould, L., *Australia* 89 F5
Ifrane, *Morocco* 74 B3
Iganga, *Uganda* 82 B3
Igara Paraná →, *Colombia* 120 D3
Igarapava, *Brazil* 123 F2
Igarapé Açu, *Brazil* 122 B2
Igarapé-Mirim, *Brazil* 122 B2
Igarka, *Russia* 44 C9
Igatimi, *Paraguay* 127 A4
Igbetti, *Nigeria* 79 D5
Igbo-Ora, *Nigeria* 79 D5
Igboho, *Nigeria* 79 D5
Iğdır, *Turkey* 67 C11
Iggesund, *Sweden* 10 C11
Ighil Izane, *Algeria* 75 A5
Iglésias, *Italy* 34 C1
Igli, *Algeria* 75 B4
Igloolik, *Canada* 97 B11
Igma, Gebel el, *Egypt* 76 J8
Ignace, *Canada* 98 C1
İğneada Burnu, *Turkey* 66 B3
Igra, *Russia* 42 B11
Iguaçu →, *Brazil* 127 B5
Iguaçu, Cat. del, *Brazil* 127 B5
Iguaçu Falls = Iguaçu, Cat. del, *Brazil* 127 B5
Iguala, *Mexico* 115 D5
Igualada, *Spain* 28 D6
Iguape, *Brazil* 123 F2
Iguassu = Iguaçu →, *Brazil* 127 B5
Iguatu, *Brazil* 122 C4
Iguéla, *Gabon* 80 E1
Igunga □, *Tanzania* 82 C3
Iheya-Shima, *Japan* 49 L3
Ihiala, *Nigeria* 79 D6
Ihosy, *Madag.* 85 C8
Ihotry, L., *Madag.* 85 C7
Ii, *Finland* 8 D21
Ii-Shima, *Japan* 49 L3
Iida, *Japan* 49 G8
Iijoki →, *Finland* 8 D21
Iisalmi, *Finland* 8 E22
Iiyama, *Japan* 49 F9
Iizuka, *Japan* 49 H5
Ijâfene, *Mauritania* 74 D3
Ijebu-Igbo, *Nigeria* 79 D5
Ijebu-Ode, *Nigeria* 79 D5
IJmuiden, *Neths.* 16 D5
IJssel →, *Neths.* 16 C7
IJsselmeer, *Neths.* 16 C6
IJsselmuiden, *Neths.* 16 C7
IJsselstein, *Neths.* 16 D6
Ijuí →, *Brazil* 127 B4
IJzendijke, *Neths.* 17 F3
IJzer →, *Belgium* 17 F1
Ikale, *Nigeria* 79 D6
Ikare, *Nigeria* 79 D6
Ikaría, *Greece* 39 M9
Ikast, *Denmark* 11 H3
Ikeda, *Japan* 49 G6
Ikeja, *Nigeria* 79 D5
Ikela, *Zaïre* 80 E4
Ikerre-Ekiti, *Nigeria* 79 D6
Ikhtiman, *Bulgaria* 38 G6
Iki, *Japan* 49 H4
Ikimba L., *Tanzania* 82 C3
Ikire, *Nigeria* 79 D5
İkizdere, *Turkey* 67 B9
Ikom, *Nigeria* 79 D6
Ikopa →, *Madag.* 85 B8
Ikot Ekpene, *Nigeria* 79 D6
Ikungu, *Tanzania* 82 C3
Ikurun, *Nigeria* 79 D5
Ila, *Nigeria* 79 D5
Ilagan, *Phil.* 55 C4
Īlām, *Iran* 67 F12
Ilam, *Nepal* 63 F12
Ilan, *Taiwan* 53 E13
Ilanskiy, *Russia* 45 D10
Ilanz, *Switz.* 23 C8
Ilaro, *Nigeria* 79 D5
Iława, *Poland* 20 B9
Ilbilbie, *Australia* 90 C4
Ile-à-la-Crosse, *Canada* 101 B7
Ile-à-la-Crosse, Lac, *Canada* 101 B7
Île-de-France, *France* 25 D9
Ilebo, *Zaïre* 80 E4
Ileje □, *Tanzania* 83 D3
Ilek, *Russia* 44 D6
Ilek →, *Russia* 44 D6
Ilero, *Nigeria* 79 D5
Ilesha, *Kwara, Nigeria* 79 D5
Ilesha, *Oyo, Nigeria* 79 D5
Ilford, *Canada* 101 B9
Ilfracombe, *Australia* 90 C3
Ilfracombe, *U.K.* 13 F3
Ilgaz, *Turkey* 66 B5
Ilgaz Dağları, *Turkey* 66 B5
Ilgın, *Turkey* 66 C4
Ilha Grande, *Brazil* 121 D4
Ilha Grande, B. da, *Brazil* 123 F3
Ílhavo, *Portugal* 30 E2
Ilhéus, *Brazil* 123 D4
Ili →, *Kazakstan* 44 E8
Iliç, *Turkey* 67 C8
Ilich, *Kazakstan* 44 E7
Ilichevsk, *Azerbaijan* 67 C11
Iliff, *U.S.A.* 108 E3
Iligan, *Phil.* 55 G6
Iligan Bay, *Phil.* 55 G6
Ilikí, L., *Greece* 39 L6
Ilin I., *Phil.* 55 E4
Iliodhrómia, *Greece* 39 K6
Ilion, *U.S.A.* 107 D9
Ilirska-Bistrica, *Slovenia* 33 C11
Ilkeston, *U.K.* 12 E6
Illampu = Ancohuma, Nevada, *Bolivia* 124 D4
Illana B., *Phil.* 55 H5
Illapel, *Chile* 126 C1
Ille-et-Vilaine □, *France* 24 D5
Ille-sur-Têt, *France* 26 F6
Iller →, *Germany* 19 G5
Illescas, *Spain* 30 E7
Illetas, *Spain* 36 B9
Illichivsk, *Ukraine* 41 J6
Illiers-Combray, *France* 24 D8
Illimani, *Bolivia* 124 D4
Illinois □, *U.S.A.* 103 C9
Illinois →, *U.S.A.* 103 C8
Illium = Troy, *Turkey* 66 C2
Illizi, *Algeria* 75 C6
Illora, *Spain* 31 H7
Ilm →, *Germany* 18 D7
Ilmajoki, *Finland* 9 E20
Ilmen, Ozero, *Russia* 40 C6
Ilmenau, *Germany* 18 E6
Ilo, *Peru* 124 D3
Ilobu, *Nigeria* 79 D5
Iloilo, *Phil.* 55 F5
Ilora, *Nigeria* 79 D5
Ilorin, *Nigeria* 79 D5
Ilovatka, *Russia* 42 E7
Ilovlya, *Russia* 43 F7
Ilovlya →, *Russia* 43 F7
Ilubabor □, *Ethiopia* 77 F3
Ilva Mică, *Romania* 38 B7
Ilwaco, *U.S.A.* 112 D2
Ilwaki, *Indonesia* 57 F7
Ilyichevsk = Illichivsk, *Ukraine* 41 J6
Imabari, *Japan* 49 G6
Imaloto →, *Madag.* 85 C8
İmamoğlu, *Turkey* 66 D6
Imandra, Ozero, *Russia* 44 C4
Imari, *Japan* 49 H4
Imasa, *Sudan* 76 D4
Imatra, *Finland* 40 B5
Imbâbah, *Egypt* 76 H7
Imbabura □, *Ecuador* 120 C2
Imbaimadai, *Guyana* 121 B5
Imbler, *U.S.A.* 110 D5
Imdahane, *Morocco* 74 B3
imeni 26 Bakinskikh Komissarov = Neftçala, *Azerbaijan* 67 C13
Imeni Poliny Osipenko, *Russia* 45 D14
Imeri, Serra, *Brazil* 120 C4
Imerimandroso, *Madag.* 85 B8
Imesan, *Mauritania* 74 D1
Imi, *Ethiopia* 68 F3
Imishly = Imişli, *Azerbaijan* 43 L9
Imişli, *Azerbaijan* 43 L9
Imitek, *Morocco* 74 C3
Imlay, *U.S.A.* 110 F4
Imlay City, *U.S.A.* 106 C1
Immenstadt, *Germany* 19 H6
Immingham, *U.K.* 12 D7
Immokalee, *U.S.A.* 105 M5
Imo □, *Nigeria* 79 D6
Imola, *Italy* 33 D8
Imotski, *Croatia* 21 M7
Imperatriz, *Amazonas, Brazil* 124 B4
Imperatriz, *Maranhão, Brazil* 122 C2
Impéria, *Italy* 32 E5
Imperial, *Canada* 101 C7
Imperial, *Peru* 124 C2
Imperial, *Calif., U.S.A.* 113 N11
Imperial, *Nebr., U.S.A.* 108 E4
Imperial Beach, *U.S.A.* 113 N9
Imperial Dam, *U.S.A.* 113 N12
Imperial Reservoir, *U.S.A.* 113 N12
Imperial Valley, *U.S.A.* 113 N11
Imperieuse Reef, *Australia* 88 C2
Impfondo, *Congo* 80 D3
Imphal, *India* 61 G18
Imphy, *France* 26 B7
İmranlı, *Turkey* 67 C8
Imroz = Gökçeada, *Turkey* 66 B1
Imst, *Austria* 19 H6
Imuruan B., *Phil.* 57 B5
In Belbel, *Algeria* 75 C5
In Delimane, *Mali* 79 B5
In Rhar, *Algeria* 75 C5
In Salah, *Algeria* 75 C5
In Tallak, *Mali* 79 B5
Ina, *Japan* 49 G8
Inajá, *Brazil* 122 C4
Inangahua Junction, *N.Z.* 87 J3
Inanwatan, *Indonesia* 57 E8
Iñapari, *Peru* 124 C4
Inari, *Finland* 8 B22
Inarijärvi, *Finland* 8 B22
Inawashiro-Ko, *Japan* 48 F10
Inca, *Spain* 36 B9
Incaguasi, *Chile* 126 B1
İnce Burun, *Turkey* 66 A6
İncekum Burnu, *Turkey* 66 D5
Inchon, *S. Korea* 51 F14
Incio, *Spain* 30 C3
Incirliova, *Turkey* 66 D2
Incomáti →, *Mozam.* 85 D5
Inda Silase, *Ethiopia* 77 E4
Indalsälven →, *Sweden* 10 B11
Indaw, *Burma* 61 G20
Indbir, *Ethiopia* 77 F4
Independence, *Calif., U.S.A.* 111 H4
Independence, *Iowa, U.S.A.* 108 D9
Independence, *Kans., U.S.A.* 109 G7
Independence, *Mo., U.S.A.* 108 F7
Independence, *Oreg., U.S.A.* 110 D2
Independence Fjord, *Greenland* 4 A6
Independence Mts., *U.S.A.* 110 F5
Independência, *Brazil* 122 C3
Independenţa, *Romania* 38 D10
Index, *U.S.A.* 112 C5
India ■, *Asia* 60 K11
Indian →, *U.S.A.* 105 M5
Indian Cabins, *Canada* 100 B5
Indian Harbour, *Canada* 99 B8
Indian Head, *Canada* 101 C8
Indian Ocean 46 K11
Indian Springs, *U.S.A.* 113 J11
Indiana, *U.S.A.* 106 F5
Indiana □, *U.S.A.* 104 E3
Indianapolis, *U.S.A.* 104 F2
Indianola, *Iowa, U.S.A.* 108 E8
Indianola, *Miss., U.S.A.* 109 J9
Indiapora, *Brazil* 123 E1
Indiga, *Russia* 44 C5
Indigirka →, *Russia* 45 B15
Inđija, *Serbia, Yug.* 21 K10
Indio, *U.S.A.* 113 M10
Indonesia ■, *Asia* 56 F5
Indore, *India* 62 H6
Indramayu, *Indonesia* 57 G13
Indravati →, *India* 61 K12
Indre □, *France* 25 F8
Indre →, *France* 24 E7
Indre-et-Loire □, *France* 24 E7
Indus →, *Pakistan* 62 G2
Indus, Mouth of the, *Pakistan* 62 H2
İnebolu, *Turkey* 66 B5
Inegöl, *Turkey* 66 B3
Inés, Mt., *Argentina* 128 C3
Ineu, *Romania* 38 C4
Inezgane, *Morocco* 74 B3
Infantes, *Spain* 29 G1
Infiernillo, Presa del, *Mexico* 114 D4
Infiesto, *Spain* 30 B5
Ingapirca, *Ecuador* 120 D2
Ingelmunster, *Belgium* 17 G2
Ingende, *Zaïre* 80 E3
Ingeniero Jacobacci, *Argentina* 128 B3
Ingenio, *Canary Is.* 36 G4
Ingenio Santa Ana, *Argentina* 126 B2
Ingersoll, *Canada* 106 C4
Ingham, *Australia* 90 B4
Ingleborough, *U.K.* 12 C5
Inglewood, *Queens., Australia* 91 D5
Inglewood, *Vic., Australia* 91 F3
Inglewood, *N.Z.* 87 H5
Inglewood, *U.S.A.* 113 M8
Ingólfshöfði, *Iceland* 8 E5
Ingolstadt, *Germany* 19 G7
Ingomar, *U.S.A.* 110 C10
Ingonish, *Canada* 99 C7
Ingore, *Guinea-Biss.* 78 C1
Ingraj Bazar, *India* 63 G13
Ingrid Christensen Coast, *Antarctica* 5 C6
Ingul → = Inhul →, *Ukraine* 41 J7
Ingulec = Inhulec, *Ukraine* 41 J7
Ingulets → = Inhulets →, *Ukraine* 41 J7
Inguri → = Enguri →, *Georgia* 43 J5
Ingushetia □, *Russia* 43 J7
Ingwavuma, *S. Africa* 85 D5
Inhaca, I., *Mozam.* 85 D5
Inhafenga, *Mozam.* 85 C5
Inhambane, *Mozam.* 85 C6
Inhambane □, *Mozam.* 85 C5
Inhambupe, *Brazil* 123 D4
Inhaminga, *Mozam.* 83 F4
Inharrime, *Mozam.* 85 C6
Inharrime →, *Mozam.* 85 C6
Inhul →, *Ukraine* 41 J7
Inhulec, *Ukraine* 41 J7
Inhulets →, *Ukraine* 41 J7
Inhuma, *Brazil* 122 C3
Inhumas, *Brazil* 123 E2
Iniesta, *Spain* 29 F3
Ining = Yining, *China* 44 E9
Inini □, *Fr. Guiana* 121 C7
Inírida →, *Colombia* 120 C4
Inishbofin, *Ireland* 15 C1
Inishmore, *Ireland* 15 C2
Inishowen Pen., *Ireland* 15 A4
Injune, *Australia* 91 D4
Inklin, *Canada* 100 B2
Inklin →, *Canada* 100 B2
Inkom, *U.S.A.* 110 E7
Inle L., *Burma* 61 J20
Inn →, *Austria* 19 G9
Innamincka, *Australia* 91 D3
Inner Hebrides, *U.K.* 14 D2
Inner Mongolia = Nei Monggol Zizhiqu □, *China* 50 C6
Inner Sound, *U.K.* 14 D3
Innerkip, *Canada* 106 C4
Innerkirchen, *Switz.* 22 C6
Innerste →, *Germany* 18 C5
Innetalling I., *Canada* 98 A4
Innisfail, *Australia* 90 B4
Innisfail, *Canada* 100 C6
In'no-shima, *Japan* 49 G6
Innsbruck, *Austria* 19 H7
Inny →, *Ireland* 15 C4
Inocência, *Brazil* 123 E1
Inongo, *Zaïre* 80 E3
Inoucdjouac = Inukjuak, *Canada* 97 C12
Inowrocław, *Poland* 20 C8
Inpundong, *N. Korea* 51 D14
Inquisivi, *Bolivia* 124 D4
Ins, *Switz.* 22 B4
Inscription, C., *Australia* 89 E1
Insein, *Burma* 61 L20
Însurăţei, *Romania* 38 E10
Intendente Alvear, *Argentina* 126 D3
Interior, *U.S.A.* 108 D4
Interlaken, *Switz.* 25 F14
International Falls, *U.S.A.* 108 A8
Intiyaco, *Argentina* 126 B3
Intragna, *Switz.* 23 D7
Intutu, *Peru* 120 D3
Inukjuak, *Canada* 97 C12
Inútil, B., *Chile* 128 D2
Inuvik, *Canada* 96 B6
Inveraray, *U.K.* 14 E3
Inverbervie, *U.K.* 14 E6
Invercargill, *N.Z.* 87 M2
Inverclyde □, *U.K.* 14 F4
Inverell, *Australia* 91 D5
Invergordon, *U.K.* 14 D4
Invermere, *Canada* 100 C5
Inverness, *Canada* 99 C7
Inverness, *U.K.* 14 D4
Inverness, *U.S.A.* 105 L4
Inverurie, *U.K.* 14 D6
Inverway, *Australia* 88 C4
Investigator Group, *Australia* 91 E1
Investigator Str., *Australia* 91 F2
Inya, *Russia* 44 D9
Inyanga, *Zimbabwe* 83 F3
Inyangani, *Zimbabwe* 83 F3
Inyantue, *Zimbabwe* 83 F2
Inyo Mts., *U.S.A.* 111 H5
Inyokern, *U.S.A.* 113 K9
Inza, *Russia* 42 D8
Inzhavino, *Russia* 42 D6
Iō-Jima, *Japan* 49 J5
Ioánnina, *Greece* 39 K3
Iola, *U.S.A.* 109 G7
Ion Corvin, *Romania* 38 E10
Iona, *U.K.* 14 E2
Ione, *Calif., U.S.A.* 112 G6
Ione, *Wash., U.S.A.* 110 B5
Ionia, *U.S.A.* 104 D3
Ionian Is. = Iónioi Nísoi, *Greece* 39 L3
Ionian Sea, *Medit. S.* 6 H9
Iónioi Nísoi, *Greece* 39 L3
Íos, *Greece* 39 N8
Iowa □, *U.S.A.* 108 D8
Iowa City, *U.S.A.* 108 E9
Iowa Falls, *U.S.A.* 108 D8
Ipala, *Tanzania* 82 C3
Ipameri, *Brazil* 123 E2
Iparía, *Peru* 124 B3
Ipáti, *Greece* 39 L5
Ipatinga, *Brazil* 123 E3
Ipatovo, *Russia* 43 H6
Ipel →, *Europe* 21 G9
Ipiales, *Colombia* 120 C2
Ipiaú, *Brazil* 123 D4

Ipin = Yibin, *China* 52 C5
Ipirá, *Brazil* 123 D4
Ipiranga, *Brazil* 120 D4
Ipixuna, *Brazil* 124 B3
Ipixuna →, *Amazonas, Brazil* 124 B3
Ipixuna →, *Amazonas, Brazil* 125 B5
Ipoh, *Malaysia* 59 K3
Iporá, *Brazil* 123 D1
Ippy, *C.A.R.* 73 G9
Ipsala, *Turkey* 66 B2
Ipsárion Óros, *Greece* 39 J7
Ipswich, *Australia* 91 D5
Ipswich, *U.K.* 13 E9
Ipswich, *Mass., U.S.A.* 107 D14
Ipswich, *S. Dak., U.S.A.* 108 C5
Ipu, *Brazil* 122 B3
Ipueiras, *Brazil* 122 B3
Ipupiara, *Brazil* 123 D3
Iqaluit, *Canada* 97 B13
Iquique, *Chile* 124 E3
Iquitos, *Peru* 120 D3
Irabu-Jima, *Japan* 49 M2
Iracoubo, *Fr. Guiana* 121 B7
Īrafshān, *Iran* 65 E9
Irahuan, *Phil.* 55 G3
Iráklia, *Greece* 39 N8
Iráklion, *Greece* 37 D7
Iráklion □, *Greece* 37 D7
Irala, *Paraguay* 127 B5
Iramba □, *Tanzania* 82 C3
Iran ■, *Asia* 65 C7
Iran, Gunung-Gunung, *Malaysia* 56 D4
Iran, Plateau of, *Asia* 46 F9
Iran Ra. = Iran, Gunung-Gunung, *Malaysia* 56 D4
Īrānshahr, *Iran* 65 E9
Irapa, *Venezuela* 121 A5
Irapuato, *Mexico* 114 C4
Iraq ■, *Asia* 67 F10
Irarrar, O. →, *Mali* 75 D5
Irati, *Brazil* 127 B5
Irbid, *Jordan* 69 C4
Irbid □, *Jordan* 69 C5
Irebu, *Zaïre* 80 E3
Irecê, *Brazil* 122 D3
Iregua →, *Spain* 28 C7
Ireland ■, *Europe* 15 D4
Ireland's Eye, *Ireland* 15 C5
Irele, *Nigeria* 79 D6
Ireng →, *Brazil* 121 C6
Iret, *Russia* 45 C16
Irgiz, Bolshaya →, *Russia* 42 D9
Irhârharene, *Algeria* 75 C6
Irharrhar, O. →, *Algeria* 75 C6
Irherm, *Morocco* 74 B3
Irhil Mgoun, *Morocco* 74 B3
Irhyangdong, *N. Korea* 51 D15
Iri, *S. Korea* 51 G14
Irian Jaya □, *Indonesia* 57 E9
Irié, *Guinea* 78 D3
Iriga, *Phil.* 55 E5
Iringa, *Tanzania* 82 D4
Iringa □, *Tanzania* 82 D4
Iriomote-Jima, *Japan* 49 M1
Iriona, *Honduras* 116 C2
Iriri →, *Brazil* 121 D7
Iriri Novo →, *Brazil* 125 B7
Irish Republic ■, *Europe* 15 D4
Irish Sea, *U.K.* 12 D3
Irkineyeva, *Russia* 45 D10
Irkutsk, *Russia* 45 D11
Irma, *Canada* 101 C6
Irō-Zaki, *Japan* 49 G9
Iroise, Mer d', *France* 24 D2
Iron Baron, *Australia* 91 E2
Iron Gate = Portile de Fier, *Europe* 38 E5
Iron Knob, *Australia* 91 E2
Iron Mountain, *U.S.A.* 104 C1
Iron Ra., *Australia* 90 A3
Iron River, *U.S.A.* 108 B10
Ironbridge, *U.K.* 13 E5
Irondequoit, *U.S.A.* 106 C7
Ironstone Kopje, *Botswana* 84 D3
Ironton, *Mo., U.S.A.* 109 G9
Ironton, *Ohio, U.S.A.* 104 F4
Ironwood, *U.S.A.* 108 B9
Iroquois Falls, *Canada* 98 C3
Irosin, *Phil.* 55 E6
Irpin, *Ukraine* 41 G6
Irrara Cr. →, *Australia* 91 D4
Irrawaddy □, *Burma* 61 L19
Irrawaddy →, *Burma* 61 M19
Irsina, *Italy* 35 B9
Irtysh →, *Russia* 44 C7
Irumu, *Zaïre* 82 B2
Irún, *Spain* 28 B3
Irunea = Pamplona, *Spain* 28 C3
Irurzun, *Spain* 28 C3
Irvine, *Canada* 101 D6
Irvine, *U.K.* 14 F4
Irvine, *Calif., U.S.A.* 113 M9
Irvine, *Ky., U.S.A.* 104 G4
Irvinestown, *U.K.* 15 B4
Irving, *U.S.A.* 109 J6
Irvona, *U.S.A.* 106 F6
Irwin →, *Australia* 89 E1
Irymple, *Australia* 91 E3
Is-sur-Tille, *France* 25 E12
Isa, *Nigeria* 79 C6
Isaac →, *Australia* 90 C4
Isabel, *U.S.A.* 108 C4
Isabela, I., *Mexico* 114 C3
Isabella, *Phil.* 55 H5
Isabella, Cord., *Nic.* 116 D2
Isabella Ra., *Australia* 88 D3
Ísafjarðardjúp, *Iceland* 8 C2
Ísafjörður, *Iceland* 8 C2
Isagarh, *India* 62 G7
Isahaya, *Japan* 49 H5
Isaka, *Tanzania* 82 C3
Isakly, *Russia* 42 C10
Isana = Içana →, *Brazil* 120 C4
Isangi, *Zaïre* 80 D4
Isar →, *Germany* 19 G8
Isarco →, *Italy* 33 B8
Ísari, *Greece* 39 M5
Isbergues, *France* 25 B9
Iscayachi, *Bolivia* 125 E4
Íschia, *Italy* 34 B6
Iscuandé, *Colombia* 120 C2
Isdell →, *Australia* 88 C3
Ise, *Japan* 49 G8
Ise-Wan, *Japan* 49 G8
Isefjord, *Denmark* 11 J5
Iseltwald, *Switz.* 22 C5
Isenthal, *Switz.* 23 C7
Iseo, *Italy* 32 C7
Iseo, L. d', *Italy* 32 C7
Iseramagazi, *Tanzania* 82 C3
Isère □, *France* 27 C9
Isère →, *France* 27 D8
Iserlohn, *Germany* 18 D3
Isérnia, *Italy* 35 A7
Iseyin, *Nigeria* 79 D5
Isherton, *Guyana* 121 C6
Ishigaki-Shima, *Japan* 49 M2
Ishikari-Gawa →, *Japan* 48 C10
Ishikari-Sammyaku, *Japan* 48 C11
Ishikari-Wan, *Japan* 48 C10
Ishikawa □, *Japan* 49 F8
Ishim, *Russia* 44 D7
Ishim →, *Russia* 44 D8
Ishinomaki, *Japan* 48 E10
Ishioka, *Japan* 49 F10
Ishkuman, *Pakistan* 63 A5
Ishpeming, *U.S.A.* 104 B2
Isigny-sur-Mer, *France* 24 C5
Isil Kul, *Russia* 44 D8
Isiolo, *Kenya* 82 B4
Isiolo □, *Kenya* 82 B4
Isiro, *Zaïre* 82 B2
Isisford, *Australia* 90 C3
Iskenderun, *Turkey* 66 D7
Iskenderun Körfezi, *Turkey* 66 D6
Iskilip, *Turkey* 66 B6
Iskŭr →, *Bulgaria* 38 F7
Iskut →, *Canada* 100 B2
Isla →, *U.K.* 14 E5
Isla Cristina, *Spain* 31 H3
Isla Vista, *U.S.A.* 113 L7
Islâhiye, *Turkey* 66 D7
Islamabad, *Pakistan* 62 C5
Islamkot, *Pakistan* 62 G4
Island →, *Canada* 100 A4
Island Falls, *Canada* 98 C3
Island Falls, *U.S.A.* 99 C6
Island L., *Canada* 101 C10
Island Lagoon, *Australia* 91 E2
Island Pond, *U.S.A.* 107 B13
Islands, B. of, *Canada* 99 C8
Islay, *U.K.* 14 F2
Isle →, *France* 26 D3
Isle aux Morts, *Canada* 99 C8
Isle of Wight □, *U.K.* 13 G6
Isle Royale, *U.S.A.* 108 A10
Isleta, *U.S.A.* 111 J10
Isleton, *U.S.A.* 112 G5
Ismail = Izmayil, *Ukraine* 41 K5
Ismâ'ilîya, *Egypt* 76 H8
Ismaning, *Germany* 19 G7
Ismay, *U.S.A.* 108 B2
Isna, *Egypt* 76 B3
Isogstalo, *India* 63 B8
Isola del Gran Sasso d'Italia, *Italy* 33 F10
Ísola del Liri, *Italy* 34 A6
Ísola della Scala, *Italy* 32 C8
Ísola di Capo Rizzuto, *Italy* 35 D10
Isparta, *Turkey* 66 D4
Isperikh, *Bulgaria* 38 F9
Íspica, *Italy* 35 F7
Israel ■, *Asia* 69 D3
Issano, *Guyana* 121 B6
Issia, *Ivory C.* 78 D3
Issoire, *France* 26 C7
Issoudun, *France* 25 F8
Issyk-Kul = Ysyk-Köl, *Kyrgyzstan* 46 E11
Issyk-Kul, Ozero = Ysyk-Köl, Ozero, *Kyrgyzstan* 44 E8
Ist, *Croatia* 33 D11
Istaihah, *U.A.E.* 65 F7
Istanbul, *Turkey* 66 B3
Istmina, *Colombia* 120 B2
Istok, *Serbia, Yug.* 21 N10
Istokpoga, L., *U.S.A.* 105 M5
Istra, *Croatia* 33 C11
Istranca Dağları, *Turkey* 66 B2
Istres, *France* 27 E8
Istria = Istra, *Croatia* 33 C11
Itá, *Paraguay* 126 B4
Itabaiana, *Paraíba, Brazil* 122 C4
Itabaiana, *Sergipe, Brazil* 122 D4
Itabaianinha, *Brazil* 122 D4
Itaberaba, *Brazil* 123 D3
Itaberaí, *Brazil* 123 E2
Itabira, *Brazil* 123 E3
Itabirito, *Brazil* 123 F3
Itaboca, *Brazil* 121 D5
Itabuna, *Brazil* 123 D4
Itacajá, *Brazil* 122 C2
Itacaunas →, *Brazil* 122 C2
Itacoatiara, *Brazil* 121 D6
Itacuaí →, *Brazil* 124 A3
Itaguaçu, *Brazil* 123 E3
Itaguari →, *Brazil* 123 D3
Itaguatins, *Brazil* 122 C2
Itaim →, *Brazil* 122 C3
Itainópolis, *Brazil* 122 C3
Itaipú, Represa de, *Brazil* 127 B5
Itaituba, *Brazil* 121 D6
Itajaí, *Brazil* 127 B6
Itajubá, *Brazil* 123 F2
Itajuípe, *Brazil* 123 D4
Itaka, *Tanzania* 83 D3
Italy ■, *Europe* 7 G8
Itamataré, *Brazil* 122 B2
Itambacuri, *Brazil* 123 E3
Itambé, *Brazil* 123 E3
Itampolo, *Madag.* 85 C7
Itanhauã →, *Brazil* 121 D5
Itanhém, *Brazil* 123 E3
Itapaci, *Brazil* 123 D2
Itapagé, *Brazil* 122 B4
Itaparica, I. de, *Brazil* 123 D4
Itapebi, *Brazil* 123 E4
Itapecuru-Mirim, *Brazil* 122 B3
Itaperuna, *Brazil* 123 F3
Itapetinga, *Brazil* 123 E3
Itapetininga, *Brazil* 127 A6
Itapeva, *Brazil* 127 A6
Itapicuru →, *Bahia, Brazil* 122 D4
Itapicuru →, *Maranhão, Brazil* 122 B3
Itapinima, *Brazil* 125 B5
Itapipoca, *Brazil* 122 B4
Itapiranga, *Brazil* 121 D6
Itapiúna, *Brazil* 122 B4
Itaporanga, *Brazil* 122 C4
Itapuá □, *Paraguay* 127 B4
Itapuranga, *Brazil* 123 E2
Itaquari, *Brazil* 123 F3
Itaquatiara, *Brazil* 121 D6
Itaquí, *Brazil* 126 B4
Itararé, *Brazil* 127 A6
Itarsi, *India* 62 H7
Itarumã, *Brazil* 123 E1
Itatí, *Argentina* 126 B4
Itatira, *Brazil* 122 B4
Itatuba, *Brazil* 125 B5
Itatupa, *Brazil* 121 D7
Itaueira, *Brazil* 122 C3
Itaueira →, *Brazil* 122 C3
Itaúna, *Brazil* 123 F3
Itbayat, *Phil.* 55 A4
Itchen →, *U.K.* 13 G6
Ite, *Peru* 124 D3
Itezhi Tezhi, L., *Zambia* 83 F2
Ithaca = Itháki, *Greece* 39 L3
Ithaca, *U.S.A.* 107 D8
Itháki, *Greece* 39 L3
Itinga, *Brazil* 123 E3
Itiquira, *Brazil* 125 D7
Itiquira →, *Brazil* 125 D6
Itiruçu, *Brazil* 123 D3
Itiúba, *Brazil* 122 D4
Ito, *Japan* 49 G9
Itoigawa, *Japan* 49 F8
Iton →, *France* 24 C8
Itonamas →, *Bolivia* 125 C5
Itsa, *Egypt* 76 J7
Íttiri, *Italy* 34 B1
Ittoqqortoormiit = Scoresbysund, *Greenland* 4 B6
Itu, *Brazil* 127 A6
Itu, *Nigeria* 79 D6
Ituaçu, *Brazil* 123 D3
Ituango, *Colombia* 120 B2
Ituiutaba, *Brazil* 123 E2
Itumbiara, *Brazil* 123 E2
Ituna, *Canada* 101 C8
Itunge Port, *Tanzania* 83 D3
Ituni, *Guyana* 121 B6
Itupiranga, *Brazil* 122 C2
Iturama, *Brazil* 123 E1
Iturbe, *Argentina* 126 A2
Ituri →, *Zaïre* 82 B2
Iturup, Ostrov, *Russia* 45 E15
Ituverava, *Brazil* 123 F2
Ituxi →, *Brazil* 125 B5
Ituyuro →, *Argentina* 126 A3
Itzehoe, *Germany* 18 B5
Ivaí →, *Brazil* 127 A5
Ivalo, *Finland* 8 B22
Ivalojoki →, *Finland* 8 B22
Ivanava, *Belarus* 41 F3
Ivangorod, *Russia* 40 C5
Ivanhoe, *N.S.W., Australia* 91 E3
Ivanhoe, *W. Austral., Australia* 88 C4
Ivanhoe, *U.S.A.* 112 J7
Ivanhoe L., *Canada* 101 A7
Ivanić Grad, *Croatia* 33 C13
Ivanjica, *Serbia, Yug.* 21 M10
Ivanjšcice, *Croatia* 33 B13
Ivankoyskoye Vdkhr., *Russia* 42 B3
Ivano-Frankivsk, *Ukraine* 41 H3
Ivano-Frankovsk = Ivano-Frankivsk, *Ukraine* 41 H3
Ivanovo = Ivanava, *Belarus* 41 F3
Ivanovo, *Russia* 42 B5
Ivato, *Madag.* 85 C8
Ivatsevichy, *Belarus* 41 F3
Ivaylovgrad, *Bulgaria* 39 H9
Ivinheima →, *Brazil* 127 A5
Ivohibe, *Madag.* 85 C8
Ivolândia, *Brazil* 123 E1
Ivory Coast ■, *Africa* 78 D3
Ivrea, *Italy* 32 C4
Ivujivik, *Canada* 97 B12
Iwahig, *Phil.* 56 C5
Iwaizumi, *Japan* 48 E10
Iwaki, *Japan* 49 F10
Iwakuni, *Japan* 49 G6
Iwamizawa, *Japan* 48 C10
Iwanai, *Japan* 48 C10
Iwata, *Japan* 49 G8
Iwate □, *Japan* 48 E10
Iwate-San, *Japan* 48 E10
Iwo, *Nigeria* 79 D5
Ixiamas, *Bolivia* 124 C4
Ixopo, *S. Africa* 85 E5
Ixtepec, *Mexico* 115 D5
Ixtlán del Río, *Mexico* 114 C4
Iyo, *Japan* 49 H6
Izabal, L. de, *Guatemala* 116 C2
Izamal, *Mexico* 115 C7
Izberbash, *Russia* 43 J8
Izegem, *Belgium* 17 G2
Izena-Shima, *Japan* 49 L3
Izhevsk, *Russia* 44 D6
Izmayil, *Ukraine* 41 K5
Izmir, *Turkey* 66 C2
Izmit, *Turkey* 66 B3
Iznajar, *Spain* 31 H6
Iznalloz, *Spain* 29 H1
Iznik, *Turkey* 66 B3
Iznik Gölü, *Turkey* 66 B3
Izobil'nyy, *Russia* 43 H5
Izola, *Slovenia* 33 C10
Izozog, Bañados de, *Bolivia* 125 D5
Izra, *Syria* 69 C5
Iztochni Rodopi, *Bulgaria* 39 H8
Izu-Shotō, *Japan* 49 G10
Izumi-sano, *Japan* 49 G7
Izumo, *Japan* 49 G6
Izyaslav, *Ukraine* 41 G4
Izyum, *Ukraine* 41 H9

J

J.F. Rodrigues, *Brazil* 122 B1
Jaba, *Ethiopia* 77 F4
Jabal el Awliya, *Sudan* 77 D3
Jabal Lubnān, *Lebanon* 69 B4
Jabalón →, *Spain* 31 G6
Jabalpur, *India* 63 H8
Jabbūl, *Syria* 64 B3
Jablah, *Syria* 66 E6
Jablanac, *Croatia* 33 D11
Jablonec, *Czech.* 20 E5
Jabłonowo, *Poland* 20 B9
Jaboatão, *Brazil* 122 C4
Jaboticabal, *Brazil* 127 A6
Jaburu, *Brazil* 125 B5
Jaca, *Spain* 28 C4
Jacaré →, *Brazil* 122 D3
Jacareí, *Brazil* 127 A6
Jacarèzinho, *Brazil* 127 A6
Jaciara, *Brazil* 125 D7
Jacinto, *Brazil* 123 E3
Jaciparaná, *Brazil* 125 B5
Jackman, *U.S.A.* 99 C5
Jacksboro, *U.S.A.* 109 J5
Jackson, *Australia* 91 D4
Jackson, *Ala., U.S.A.* 105 K2
Jackson, *Calif., U.S.A.* 112 G6
Jackson, *Ky., U.S.A.* 104 G4
Jackson, *Mich., U.S.A.* 104 D3
Jackson, *Minn., U.S.A.* 108 D7
Jackson, *Miss., U.S.A.* 109 J9
Jackson, *Mo., U.S.A.* 109 G10
Jackson, *Ohio, U.S.A.* 104 F4
Jackson, *Tenn., U.S.A.* 105 H1
Jackson, *Wyo., U.S.A.* 110 E8
Jackson B., *N.Z.* 87 K2
Jackson L., *U.S.A.* 110 E8
Jacksons, *N.Z.* 87 K3
Jacksonville, *Ala., U.S.A.* 105 J3
Jacksonville, *Calif., U.S.A.* 112 H6
Jacksonville, *Fla., U.S.A.* 105 K5
Jacksonville, *Ill., U.S.A.* 108 F9
Jacksonville, *N.C., U.S.A.* 105 H7
Jacksonville, *Oreg., U.S.A.* 110 E2
Jacksonville, *Tex., U.S.A.* 109 K7
Jacksonville Beach, *U.S.A.* 105 K5
Jacmel, *Haiti* 117 C5
Jacob Lake, *U.S.A.* 111 H7
Jacobabad, *Pakistan* 62 E3
Jacobina, *Brazil* 122 D3
Jacques-Cartier, Mt., *Canada* 99 C6
Jacqueville, *Ivory C.* 78 D4
Jacuí →, *Brazil* 127 C5
Jacumba, *U.S.A.* 113 N10
Jacundá →, *Brazil* 122 B1
Jade, *Germany* 18 B4
Jadebusen, *Germany* 18 B4
Jadoigne, *Belgium* 17 G5
Jadotville = Likasi, *Zaïre* 83 E2
Jadraque, *Spain* 28 E2
Jādū, *Libya* 75 B7
Jaén, *Peru* 124 B2
Jaén, *Spain* 31 H7
Jaén □, *Spain* 31 H7
Jafène, *Africa* 74 D3
Jaffa = Tel Aviv-Yafo, *Israel* 69 C3
Jaffa, C., *Australia* 91 F2
Jaffna, *Sri Lanka* 60 Q12
Jagadhri, *India* 62 D7
Jagadishpur, *India* 63 G11
Jagdalpur, *India* 61 K12
Jagersfontein, *S. Africa* 84 D4
Jagraon, *India* 60 D9
Jagst →, *Germany* 19 F5
Jagtial, *India* 60 K11
Jaguaquara, *Brazil* 123 D4
Jaguariaíva, *Brazil* 127 A6
Jaguaribe, *Brazil* 122 C4
Jaguaribe →, *Brazil* 122 B4
Jaguaruana, *Brazil* 122 B4
Jagüey Grande, *Cuba* 116 B3
Jahangirabad, *India* 62 E8
Jahrom, *Iran* 65 D7
Jaicós, *Brazil* 122 C3
Jailolo, *Indonesia* 57 D7
Jailolo, Selat, *Indonesia* 57 D7
Jaipur, *India* 62 F6
Jājarm, *Iran* 65 B8
Jajce, *Bos.-H.* 21 L7
Jakarta, *Indonesia* 57 G12
Jakobstad = Pietarsaari, *Finland* 8 E20
Jakupica, *Macedonia* 39 H4
Jal, *U.S.A.* 109 J3
Jalalabad, *Afghan.* 62 B4
Jalalabad, *India* 63 F8
Jalalpur Jattan, *Pakistan* 62 C6
Jalama, *U.S.A.* 113 L6
Jalapa, *Guatemala* 116 D2
Jalapa Enríquez, *Mexico* 115 D5
Jalasjärvi, *Finland* 9 E20
Jalaun, *India* 63 F8
Jales, *Brazil* 123 F1
Jaleswar, *Nepal* 63 F11
Jalgaon, *Maharashtra, India* 60 J10
Jalgaon, *Maharashtra, India* 60 J9
Jalhay, *Belgium* 17 G7
Jalībah, *Iraq* 64 D5
Jalingo, *Nigeria* 79 D7
Jalisco □, *Mexico* 114 C4
Jalkot, *Pakistan* 63 B5
Jallas →, *Spain* 30 C1
Jalna, *India* 60 K9
Jalón →, *Spain* 28 D3
Jalpa, *Mexico* 114 C4
Jalpaiguri, *India* 61 F16
Jaluit I., *Pac. Oc.* 92 G8
Jalūlā, *Iraq* 67 E11
Jamaari, *Nigeria* 79 C6
Jamaica ■, *W. Indies* 116 C4
Jamalpur, *Bangla.* 61 G16
Jamalpur, *India* 63 G12
Jamalpurganj, *India* 63 H13
Jamanxim →, *Brazil* 125 A6
Jamari, *Brazil* 125 B5
Jamari →, *Brazil* 125 B5
Jambe, *Indonesia* 57 E8
Jambes, *Belgium* 17 H5
Jambi, *Indonesia* 56 E2
Jambi □, *Indonesia* 56 E2
Jambusar, *India* 62 H5
James →, *U.S.A.* 108 D6
James B., *Canada* 97 C11
James Ras., *Australia* 88 D5
James Ross I., *Antarctica* 5 C18
Jamestown, *Australia* 91 E2
Jamestown, *S. Africa* 84 E4
Jamestown, *Ky., U.S.A.* 104 G3
Jamestown, *N. Dak., U.S.A.* 108 B5
Jamestown, *N.Y., U.S.A.* 106 D5
Jamestown, *Pa., U.S.A.* 106 E4
Jamestown, *Tenn., U.S.A.* 105 G3
Jamīlābād, *Iran* 65 C6
Jamiltepec, *Mexico* 115 D5
Jamkhandi, *India* 60 L9
Jammerbugt, *Denmark* 11 G3
Jammu, *India* 62 C6
Jammu & Kashmir □, *India* 63 B7
Jamnagar, *India* 62 H4
Jamoigne, *Belgium* 17 J6
Jampur, *Pakistan* 62 E4
Jamrud, *Pakistan* 62 C4
Jämsä, *Finland* 9 F21
Jamshedpur, *India* 63 H12
Jamtara, *India* 63 H12
Jämtland, *Sweden* 8 E15
Jämtlands län □, *Sweden* 10 B7
Jan L., *Canada* 101 C8
Jan Mayen, *Arctic* 4 B7
Janakkala, *Finland* 9 F21
Janaúba, *Brazil* 123 E3
Janaucu, I., *Brazil* 122 A1
Jand, *Pakistan* 62 C5
Janda, L. de la, *Spain* 31 J5
Jandaia, *Brazil* 123 E1
Jandaq, *Iran* 65 C7
Jandia, *Canary Is.* 36 F5
Jandia, Pta. de, *Canary Is.* 36 F5
Jandiatuba →, *Brazil* 120 D4
Jandola, *Pakistan* 62 C4
Jandowae, *Australia* 91 D5
Jandrain-Jandrenouilles, *Belgium* 17 G5
Jándula →, *Spain* 31 G6
Janesville, *U.S.A.* 108 D10
Janga, *Ghana* 79 C4
Jango, *Brazil* 125 E6
Janīn, *West Bank* 69 C4
Janjina, *Croatia* 21 N7
Janos, *Mexico* 114 A3
Jánosháza, *Hungary* 21 H7
Janów Podlaski, *Poland* 20 C13
Januária, *Brazil* 123 E3
Janub Dârfûr □, *Sudan* 77 E2

Janub Kordofân □, *Sudan* 77 E3
Janubio, *Canary Is.* 36 F6
Janville, *France* 25 D8
Janzé, *France* 24 E5
Jaora, *India* 62 H6
Japan ■, *Asia* 49 G8
Japan, Sea of, *Asia* 48 E7
Japan Trench, *Pac. Oc.* 46 F18
Japen = Yapen, *Indonesia* 57 E9
Japurá →, *Brazil* 120 D4
Jaque, *Panama* 120 B2
Jarābulus, *Syria* 67 D8
Jaraguá, *Brazil* 123 E2
Jaraguari, *Brazil* 125 E7
Jaraicejo, *Spain* 31 F5
Jaraiz, *Spain* 30 E5
Jarama →, *Spain* 28 E1
Jaramānah, *Syria* 66 F7
Jaramillo, *Argentina* 128 C3
Jarandilla, *Spain* 30 E5
Jaranwala, *Pakistan* 62 D5
Jarash, *Jordan* 69 C4
Jarauçu →, *Brazil* 121 D7
Jardim, *Brazil* 126 A4
Jardín →, *Spain* 29 G2
Jardines de la Reina, Is., *Cuba* 116 B4
Jargalang, *China* 51 C12
Jargalant = Hovd, *Mongolia* 54 B4
Jargeau, *France* 25 E9
Jari →, *Brazil* 121 D7
Jarīr, W. al →, *Si. Arabia* 64 E4
Jarmen, *Germany* 18 B9
Jarnac, *France* 26 C3
Jarny, *France* 25 C12
Jarocin, *Poland* 20 D7
Jarosław, *Poland* 20 E12
Järpås, *Sweden* 11 F6
Järpen, *Sweden* 10 A7
Jarrahdale, *Australia* 89 F2
Jarres, Plaine des, *Laos* 58 C4
Jarso, *Ethiopia* 77 F4
Jartai, *China* 50 E3
Jaru, *Brazil* 125 C5
Jaru →, *Brazil* 125 C5
Jarud Qi, *China* 51 B11
Järvenpää, *Finland* 9 F21
Jarvis, *Canada* 106 D4
Jarvis I., *Pac. Oc.* 93 H12
Jarwa, *India* 63 F10
Jaša Tomić, *Serbia, Yug.* 21 K10
Jāsimīyah, *Iraq* 67 F11
Jasin, *Malaysia* 59 L4
Jāsk, *Iran* 65 E8
Jasło, *Poland* 20 F11
Jason, Is., *Falk. Is.* 128 D4
Jasper, *Alta., Canada* 100 C5
Jasper, *Ont., Canada* 107 B9
Jasper, *Ala., U.S.A.* 105 J2
Jasper, *Fla., U.S.A.* 105 K4
Jasper, *Minn., U.S.A.* 108 D6
Jasper, *Tex., U.S.A.* 109 K8
Jasper Nat. Park, *Canada* 100 C5
Jastrebarsko, *Croatia* 33 C12
Jastrzębie Zdrój, *Poland* 20 F8
Jászárokszállás, *Hungary* 21 H10
Jászberény, *Hungary* 21 H9
Jászladány, *Hungary* 21 H10
Jataí, *Brazil* 123 E1
Jatapu →, *Brazil* 121 D6
Jati, *Pakistan* 62 G3
Jatibarang, *Indonesia* 57 G13
Jatinegara, *Indonesia* 57 G12
Játiva, *Spain* 29 G4
Jatobal, *Brazil* 122 B2
Jaú, *Brazil* 127 A6
Jaú →, *Brazil* 121 D5
Jauaperí →, *Brazil* 121 D5
Jauche, *Belgium* 17 G5
Jauja, *Peru* 124 C2
Jaunpur, *India* 63 G10
Jauru →, *Brazil* 125 D6
Java = Jawa, *Indonesia* 57 G14
Java Sea, *Indonesia* 56 E3
Java Trench, *Ind. Oc.* 92 H2
Jávea, *Spain* 29 G5
Javhlant = Ulyasutay, *Mongolia* 54 B4
Javier, I., *Chile* 128 C2
Javron, *France* 24 D6
Jawa, *Indonesia* 57 G14
Jawor, *Poland* 20 D6
Jaworzno, *Poland* 20 E9
Jay, *U.S.A.* 109 G7
Jaya, Puncak, *Indonesia* 57 E9
Jayanca, *Peru* 124 B2
Jayanti, *India* 61 F16
Jayapura, *Indonesia* 57 E10
Jayawijaya, Pegunungan, *Indonesia* 57 E9
Jaynagar, *India* 61 F15
Jayrūd, *Syria* 66 F7
Jayton, *U.S.A.* 109 J4
Jazīreh-ye Shīf, *Iran* 65 D6
Jazminal, *Mexico* 114 C4
Jazzīn, *Lebanon* 69 B4
Jean, *U.S.A.* 113 K11
Jean Marie River, *Canada* 100 A4
Jean Rabel, *Haiti* 117 C5
Jeanerette, *U.S.A.* 109 L9
Jeanette, Ostrov, *Russia* 45 B16
Jeannette, *U.S.A.* 106 F5
Jebba, *Morocco* 74 A4
Jebba, *Nigeria* 79 D5
Jebel, Bahr el →, *Sudan* 77 F3
Jebel Qerri, *Sudan* 77 D3
Jeberos, *Peru* 124 B2
Jedburgh, *U.K.* 14 F6
Jedda = Jiddah, *Si. Arabia* 68 C2
Jędrzejów, *Poland* 20 E10
Jedway, *Canada* 100 C2
Jeetzel →, *Germany* 18 B7
Jefferson, *Iowa, U.S.A.* 108 D7
Jefferson, *Ohio, U.S.A.* 106 E4
Jefferson, *Tex., U.S.A.* 109 J7
Jefferson, *Wis., U.S.A.* 108 D10
Jefferson, Mt., *Nev., U.S.A.* 110 G5
Jefferson, Mt., *Oreg., U.S.A.* 110 D3
Jefferson City, *Mo., U.S.A.* 108 F8
Jefferson City, *Tenn., U.S.A.* 105 G4
Jeffersonville, *U.S.A.* 104 F3
Jega, *Nigeria* 79 C5
Jēkabpils, *Latvia* 9 H21
Jelenia Góra, *Poland* 20 E5
Jelgava, *Latvia* 9 H20
Jelli, *Sudan* 77 F3
Jellicoe, *Canada* 98 C2
Jemaja, *Indonesia* 56 D3
Jemaluang, *Malaysia* 59 L4
Jemappes, *Belgium* 17 H3
Jember, *Indonesia* 57 H15
Jembongan, *Malaysia* 56 C5
Jemeppe, *Belgium* 17 G7
Jemnice, *Czech.* 20 F5
Jena, *Germany* 18 E7
Jena, *U.S.A.* 109 K8
Jendouba, *Tunisia* 75 A6
Jenkins, *U.S.A.* 104 G4
Jenner, *U.S.A.* 112 G3
Jennings, *U.S.A.* 109 K8
Jennings →, *Canada* 100 B2
Jeparit, *Australia* 91 F3
Jequié, *Brazil* 123 D3
Jequitaí →, *Brazil* 123 E3
Jequitinhonha, *Brazil* 123 E3
Jequitinhonha →, *Brazil* 123 E4
Jerada, *Morocco* 75 B4
Jerantut, *Malaysia* 59 L4
Jérémie, *Haiti* 117 C5
Jeremoabo, *Brazil* 122 D4
Jerez, Punta, *Mexico* 115 C5
Jerez de García Salinas, *Mexico* 114 C4
Jerez de la Frontera, *Spain* 31 J4
Jerez de los Caballeros, *Spain* 31 G4
Jericho = Arīḩā, *Syria* 64 C3
Jericho = El Arīḩā, *West Bank* 69 D4
Jericho, *Australia* 90 C4
Jerichow, *Germany* 18 C8
Jerilderie, *Australia* 91 F4
Jermyn, *U.S.A.* 107 E9
Jerome, *U.S.A.* 111 J8
Jersey, *U.K.* 13 H5
Jersey City, *U.S.A.* 107 F10
Jersey Shore, *U.S.A.* 106 E7
Jerseyville, *U.S.A.* 108 F9
Jerusalem, *Israel* 69 D4
Jervis B., *Australia* 91 F5
Jesenice, *Slovenia* 33 B11
Jesenké, *Slovak Rep.* 21 G10
Jesselton = Kota Kinabalu, *Malaysia* 56 C5
Jessnitz, *Germany* 18 D8
Jessore, *Bangla.* 61 H16
Jesup, *U.S.A.* 105 K5
Jesús, *Peru* 124 B2
Jesús Carranza, *Mexico* 115 D5
Jesús María, *Argentina* 126 C3
Jetmore, *U.S.A.* 109 F5
Jetpur, *India* 62 J4
Jette, *Belgium* 17 G4
Jevnaker, *Norway* 10 D4
Jewett, *Ohio, U.S.A.* 106 F3
Jewett, *Tex., U.S.A.* 109 K6
Jewett City, *U.S.A.* 107 E13
Jeyḩūnābād, *Iran* 65 C6
Jeypore, *India* 61 K13
Jeziorany, *Poland* 20 B10
Jhajjar, *India* 62 E7
Jhal Jhao, *Pakistan* 60 F4
Jhalawar, *India* 62 G7
Jhang Maghiana, *Pakistan* 62 D5
Jhansi, *India* 63 G8
Jharia, *India* 63 H12
Jharsuguda, *India* 61 J14
Jhelum, *Pakistan* 62 C5
Jhelum →, *Pakistan* 62 D5
Jhunjhunu, *India* 62 E6
Ji Xian, *Hebei, China* 50 F8
Ji Xian, *Henan, China* 50 G8
Ji Xian, *Shanxi, China* 50 F6
Jia Xian, *Henan, China* 50 H7
Jia Xian, *Shaanxi, China* 50 E6
Jiading, *China* 53 B13
Jiahe, *China* 53 E9
Jialing Jiang →, *China* 52 C6
Jiamusi, *China* 54 B8
Ji'an, *Jiangxi, China* 53 D10
Ji'an, *Jilin, China* 51 D14
Jianchang, *China* 51 D11
Jianchangying, *China* 51 D10
Jianchuan, *China* 52 D2
Jiande, *China* 53 C12
Jiangbei, *China* 52 C6
Jiangcheng, *China* 52 F3
Jiangdi, *China* 52 D4
Jiange, *China* 52 A5
Jiangjin, *China* 52 C6
Jiangkou, *China* 52 D7
Jiangle, *China* 53 D11
Jiangling, *China* 53 B9
Jiangmen, *China* 53 F9
Jiangshan, *China* 53 C12
Jiangsu □, *China* 51 H10
Jiangxi □, *China* 53 D10
Jiangyin, *China* 53 B13
Jiangyong, *China* 53 E8
Jiangyou, *China* 52 B5
Jianhe, *China* 52 D7
Jianli, *China* 53 C9
Jianning, *China* 53 D11
Jian'ou, *China* 53 D12
Jianshi, *China* 52 B7
Jianshui, *China* 52 F4
Jianyang, *Fujian, China* 53 D12
Jianyang, *Sichuan, China* 52 B5
Jiao Xian, *China* 51 F11
Jiaohe, *Hebei, China* 50 E9
Jiaohe, *Jilin, China* 51 C14
Jiaoling, *China* 53 E11
Jiaozhou Wan, *China* 51 F11
Jiaozuo, *China* 50 G7
Jiashan, *China* 53 A11
Jiawang, *China* 51 G9
Jiaxiang, *China* 50 G9
Jiaxing, *China* 53 B13
Jiayi = Chiai, *Taiwan* 53 F13
Jiayu, *China* 53 C9
Jibão, Serra do, *Brazil* 123 D3
Jibiya, *Nigeria* 79 C6
Jibou, *Romania* 38 B6
Jibuti = Djibouti ■, *Africa* 68 E3
Jicarón, I., *Panama* 116 E3
Jičín, *Czech.* 20 E5
Jiddah, *Si. Arabia* 68 C2
Jido, *India* 61 E19
Jieshou, *China* 50 H8
Jiexiu, *China* 50 F6
Jieyang, *China* 53 F11
Jigawa □, *Nigeria* 79 C6
Jiggalong, *Australia* 88 D3
Jihlava, *Czech.* 20 F5
Jijel, *Algeria* 75 A6
Jijiga, *Ethiopia* 68 F3
Jijona, *Spain* 29 G4
Jikamshi, *Nigeria* 79 C6
Jilin, *China* 51 C14
Jilin □, *China* 51 C13
Jiloca →, *Spain* 28 D3
Jilong = Chilung, *Taiwan* 53 E13
Jima, *Ethiopia* 77 F4
Jimbolia, *Romania* 38 D3
Jimena de la Frontera, *Spain* 31 J5
Jiménez, *Mexico* 114 B4
Jimo, *China* 51 F11
Jin Jiang →, *China* 53 C10
Jin Xian, *Hebei, China* 50 E8
Jin Xian, *Liaoning, China* 51 E11
Jinan, *China* 50 F9
Jincheng, *China* 50 G7
Jinchuan, *China* 52 B4
Jind, *India* 62 E7
Jindabyne, *Australia* 91 F4
Jindrichuv Hradeç, *Czech.* 20 F5
Jing He →, *China* 50 G5
Jing Shan, *China* 53 B8
Jing Xian, *Anhui, China* 53 B12
Jing Xian, *Hunan, China* 52 D7
Jing'an, *China* 53 C10
Jingbian, *China* 50 F5
Jingchuan, *China* 50 G4
Jingde, *China* 53 B12
Jingdezhen, *China* 53 C11
Jingdong, *China* 52 E3
Jinggu, *China* 52 F3
Jinghai, *China* 50 E9
Jinghong, *China* 52 F3
Jingjiang, *China* 53 A13
Jingle, *China* 50 E6
Jingmen, *China* 53 B9
Jingning, *China* 50 G3
Jingpo Hu, *China* 51 C15
Jingshan, *China* 53 B9
Jingtai, *China* 50 F3
Jingxi, *China* 52 F6
Jingxing, *China* 50 E8
Jingyang, *China* 50 G5
Jingyu, *China* 51 C14
Jingyuan, *China* 50 F3
Jingziguan, *China* 50 H6
Jinhua, *China* 53 C12
Jining, *Nei Mongol Zizhiqu, China* 50 D7
Jining, *Shandong, China* 50 G9
Jinja, *Uganda* 82 B3
Jinjang, *Malaysia* 59 L3
Jinji, *China* 50 F4
Jinjiang, *Fujian, China* 53 E12
Jinjiang, *Yunnan, China* 52 D3
Jinjie, *China* 52 F6
Jinjini, *Ghana* 78 D4
Jinkou, *China* 53 B10
Jinmen Dao, *China* 53 E12
Jinnah Barrage, *Pakistan* 60 C7
Jinning, *China* 52 E4
Jinotega, *Nic.* 116 D2
Jinotepe, *Nic.* 116 D2
Jinping, *Guizhou, China* 52 D7
Jinping, *Yunnan, China* 52 F4
Jinsha, *China* 52 D6
Jinsha Jiang →, *China* 52 C5
Jinshan, *China* 53 B13
Jinshi, *China* 53 C8
Jintan, *China* 53 B12
Jinxi, *Jiangxi, China* 53 D11
Jinxi, *Liaoning, China* 51 D11
Jinxian, *China* 53 C11
Jinxiang, *China* 50 G9
Jinyun, *China* 53 C13
Jinzhai, *China* 53 B10
Jinzhou, *China* 51 D11
Jiparaná →, *Brazil* 125 B5
Jipijapa, *Ecuador* 120 D1
Jiquilpan, *Mexico* 114 D4
Jishan, *China* 50 G6
Jishou, *China* 52 C7
Jishui, *China* 53 D10
Jisr ash Shughūr, *Syria* 66 E7
Jitarning, *Australia* 89 F2
Jitra, *Malaysia* 59 J3
Jiu →, *Romania* 38 F6
Jiudengkou, *China* 50 E4
Jiujiang, *Guangdong, China* 53 F9
Jiujiang, *Jiangxi, China* 53 C10
Jiuling Shan, *China* 53 C10
Jiulong, *China* 52 C3
Jiuquan, *China* 54 C4
Jiutai, *China* 51 B13
Jiuxiangcheng, *China* 50 H8
Jiuxincheng, *China* 50 E8
Jiuyuhang, *China* 53 B12
Jixi, *Anhui, China* 53 B12
Jixi, *Heilongjiang, China* 51 B16
Jiyang, *China* 51 F9
Jīzān, *Si. Arabia* 68 D3
Jize, *China* 50 F8
Jizera →, *Czech.* 20 E4
Jizō-Zaki, *Japan* 49 G6
Jizzakh, *Uzbekistan* 44 E7
Joaçaba, *Brazil* 127 B5
Joaíma, *Brazil* 123 E3
João, *Brazil* 122 B1
João Amaro, *Brazil* 123 D3
João Câmara, *Brazil* 122 C4
João Pessoa, *Brazil* 122 C5
João Pinheiro, *Brazil* 123 E2
Joaquim Távora, *Brazil* 123 F2
Joaquín V. González, *Argentina* 126 B3
Jobourg, Nez de, *France* 24 C5
Jódar, *Spain* 29 H1
Jodhpur, *India* 62 F5
Jœuf, *France* 25 C13
Jofane, *Mozam.* 85 C5
Jõgeva, *Estonia* 9 G22
Joggins, *Canada* 99 C7
Jogjakarta = Yogyakarta, *Indonesia* 57 G14
Johannesburg, *S. Africa* 85 D4
Johannesburg, *U.S.A.* 113 K9
John Day, *U.S.A.* 110 D4
John Day →, *U.S.A.* 110 D3
John H. Kerr Reservoir, *U.S.A.* 105 G6
John o' Groats, *U.K.* 14 C5
Johnnie, *U.S.A.* 113 J10
John's Ra., *Australia* 90 C1
Johnson, *U.S.A.* 109 G4
Johnson City, *N.Y., U.S.A.* 107 D9
Johnson City, *Tenn., U.S.A.* 105 G4
Johnson City, *Tex., U.S.A.* 109 K5
Johnsonburg, *U.S.A.* 106 E6
Johnsondale, *U.S.A.* 113 K8
Johnson's Crossing, *Canada* 100 A2
Johnston, L., *Australia* 89 F3
Johnston Falls = Mambilima Falls, *Zambia* 83 E2
Johnston I., *Pac. Oc.* 93 F11
Johnstone Str., *Canada* 100 C3
Johnstown, *N.Y., U.S.A.* 107 C10
Johnstown, *Pa., U.S.A.* 106 F6
Johor Baharu, *Malaysia* 59 M4
Jõhvi, *Estonia* 9 G22
Joigny, *France* 25 E10
Joinvile, *Brazil* 127 B6
Joinville, *France* 25 D12
Joinville I., *Antarctica* 5 C18
Jojutla, *Mexico* 115 D5
Jokkmokk, *Sweden* 8 C18
Jökulsá á Bru →, *Iceland* 8 D6
Jökulsá á Fjöllum →, *Iceland* 8 C5
Jolfā, *Āzarbājān-e Sharqī, Iran* 67 C11
Jolfā, *Eşfahan, Iran* 65 C6
Joliet, *U.S.A.* 104 E1
Joliette, *Canada* 98 C5
Jolo, *Phil.* 55 J4
Jolon, *U.S.A.* 112 K5
Jomalig, *Phil.* 55 D5
Jombang, *Indonesia* 57 G15
Jomda, *China* 52 B2
Jome, *Indonesia* 57 E7
Jomfruland, *Norway* 11 F3
Jönåker, *Sweden* 11 F10
Jonava, *Lithuania* 9 J21
Jones Sound, *Canada* 4 B3
Jonesboro, *Ark., U.S.A.* 109 H9
Jonesboro, *Ill., U.S.A.* 109 G10
Jonesboro, *La., U.S.A.* 109 J8
Jonesport, *U.S.A.* 99 D6
Jonglei, *Sudan* 77 F3
Jonglei □, *Sudan* 77 F3
Joniškis, *Lithuania* 9 H20
Jönköping, *Sweden* 9 H16
Jonquière, *Canada* 99 C5
Jonsberg, *Sweden* 11 F10
Jonsered, *Sweden* 11 G6
Jonzac, *France* 26 C3
Joplin, *U.S.A.* 109 G7
Jordan, *U.S.A.* 110 C10
Jordan ■, *Asia* 69 E5
Jordan →, *Asia* 69 D4
Jordan Valley, *U.S.A.* 110 E5
Jordânia, *Brazil* 123 E3
Jorge, C., *Chile* 128 D1
Jorhat, *India* 61 F19
Jörn, *Sweden* 8 D19
Jorong, *Indonesia* 56 E4
Jørpeland, *Norway* 9 G11
Jorquera →, *Chile* 126 B2
Jos, *Nigeria* 79 D6
José Batlle y Ordóñez, *Uruguay* 127 C4
José de San Martín, *Argentina* 128 B2
Joseph, *U.S.A.* 110 D5
Joseph, L., *Nfld., Canada* 99 B6
Joseph, L., *Ont., Canada* 106 A5
Joseph Bonaparte G., *Australia* 88 B4
Joseph City, *U.S.A.* 111 J8
Joshua Tree, *U.S.A.* 113 L10
Joshua Tree National Monument, *U.S.A.* 113 M10
Josselin, *France* 24 E4
Jostedalsbreen, *Norway* 9 F12
Jotunheimen, *Norway* 10 C2
Jourdanton, *U.S.A.* 109 L5
Joure, *Neths.* 16 C7
Joussard, *Canada* 100 B5
Joutseno, *Finland* 40 B5
Jovellanos, *Cuba* 116 B3
Joyeuse, *France* 27 D8
Józefów, *Poland* 20 C11
Ju Xian, *China* 51 F10
Juan Aldama, *Mexico* 114 C4
Juan Bautista Alberdi, *Argentina* 126 C3
Juan de Fuca Str., *Canada* 112 B2
Juan de Nova, *Ind. Oc.* 85 B7
Juan Fernández, Arch. de, *Pac. Oc.* 118 G2
Juan José Castelli, *Argentina* 126 B3
Juan L. Lacaze, *Uruguay* 126 C4
Juanjuí, *Peru* 124 B2
Juankoski, *Finland* 8 E23
Juárez, *Argentina* 126 D4
Juárez, *Mexico* 113 N11
Juárez, Sierra de, *Mexico* 114 A1
Juatinga, Ponta de, *Brazil* 123 F3
Juàzeiro, *Brazil* 122 C3
Juàzeiro do Norte, *Brazil* 122 C4
Jubayl, *Lebanon* 69 A4
Jubbah, *Si. Arabia* 64 D4
Jubbulpore = Jabalpur, *India* 63 H8
Jübek, *Germany* 18 A5
Jubga, *Russia* 43 H4
Jubilee L., *Australia* 89 E4
Juby, C., *Morocco* 74 C2
Júcar →, *Spain* 29 F4
Júcaro, *Cuba* 116 B4
Juchitán, *Mexico* 115 D5
Judaea = Har Yehuda, *Israel* 69 D3
Judenburg, *Austria* 21 H4
Judith →, *U.S.A.* 110 C9
Judith, Pt., *U.S.A.* 107 E13
Judith Gap, *U.S.A.* 110 C9
Jufari →, *Brazil* 121 D5
Jugoslavia = Yugoslavia ■, *Europe* 21 M10
Juigalpa, *Nic.* 116 D2
Juillac, *France* 26 C5
Juist, *Germany* 18 B2
Juiz de Fora, *Brazil* 123 F3
Jujuy □, *Argentina* 126 A2
Julesburg, *U.S.A.* 108 E3
Juli, *Peru* 124 D4
Julia Cr. →, *Australia* 90 C3
Julia Creek, *Australia* 90 C3
Juliaca, *Peru* 124 D3
Julian, *U.S.A.* 113 M10
Julian Alps = Julijske Alpe, *Slovenia* 33 B11
Julianakanaal, *Neths.* 17 F7
Julianatop, *Surinam* 121 C6
Julianehåb, *Greenland* 4 C5
Jülich, *Germany* 18 E2
Julierpass, *Switz.* 23 D9
Julijske Alpe, *Slovenia* 33 B11
Julimes, *Mexico* 114 B3
Jullundur, *India* 62 D6
Julu, *China* 50 F8
Jumbo, *Zimbabwe* 83 F3
Jumbo Pk., *U.S.A.* 113 J12
Jumentos Cays, *Bahamas* 117 B4
Jumet, *Belgium* 17 H4
Jumilla, *Spain* 29 G3
Jumla, *Nepal* 63 E10
Jumna = Yamuna →, *India* 63 G9
Junagadh, *India* 62 J4
Junction, *Tex., U.S.A.* 109 K5
Junction, *Utah, U.S.A.* 111 G7
Junction B., *Australia* 90 A1
Junction City, *Kans., U.S.A.* 108 F6
Junction City, *Oreg., U.S.A.* 110 D2
Junction Pt., *Australia* 90 A1
Jundah, *Australia* 90 C3
Jundiaí, *Brazil* 127 A6
Juneau, *U.S.A.* 96 C6

Junee, *Australia* 91 E4
Jungfrau, *Switz.* 22 C5
Junggar Pendi, *China* 54 B3
Junglinster, *Lux.* 17 J8
Jungshahi, *Pakistan* 62 G2
Juniata →, *U.S.A.* 106 F7
Junín, *Argentina* 126 C3
Junín, *Peru* 124 C2
Junín □, *Peru* 124 C3
Junín de los Andes, *Argentina* 128 A2
Jūniyah, *Lebanon* 69 B4
Juntura, *U.S.A.* 110 E4
Juparanã, L., *Brazil* 123 E3
Jupiter →, *Canada* 99 C7
Juquiá, *Brazil* 123 F2
Jur, Nahr el →, *Sudan* 77 F2
Jura = Jura, Mts. du, *Europe* 25 F13
Jura = Schwäbische Alb, *Germany* 19 G5
Jura, *U.K.* 14 F3
Jura □, *France* 25 F12
Jura, Mts. du, *Europe* 25 F13
Jura, Sd. of, *U.K.* 14 F3
Jura Suisse, *Switz.* 22 B3
Jurado, *Colombia* 120 B2
Jurbarkas, *Lithuania* 9 J20
Jurilovca, *Romania* 38 E11
Jūrmala, *Latvia* 9 H20
Jurong, *China* 53 B12
Juruá →, *Brazil* 120 D4
Juruena, *Brazil* 125 C6
Juruena →, *Brazil* 125 B6
Juruti, *Brazil* 121 D6
Jussey, *France* 25 E12
Justo Daract, *Argentina* 126 C2
Jutaí, *Brazil* 124 B4
Jutaí →, *Brazil* 120 D4
Jüterbog, *Germany* 18 D9
Juticalpa, *Honduras* 116 D2
Jutland = Jylland, *Denmark* 11 H3
Jutphaas, *Neths.* 16 D6
Juventud, I. de la, *Cuba* 116 B3
Juvigny-sous-Andaine, *France* 24 D6
Juvisy-sur-Orge, *France* 25 D9
Juwain, *Afghan.* 60 D2
Jūy Zar, *Iran* 67 F12
Juye, *China* 50 G9
Juzennecourt, *France* 25 D11
Jvari, *Georgia* 43 J6
Jylland, *Denmark* 11 H3
Jyväskylä, *Finland* 9 E21

K

K2, *Pakistan* 63 B7
Kaap Plateau, *S. Africa* 84 D3
Kaapkruis, *Namibia* 84 C1
Kaapstad = Cape Town, *S. Africa* 84 E2
Kaatsheuvel, *Neths.* 17 E6
Kabaena, *Indonesia* 57 F6
Kabala, *S. Leone* 78 D2
Kabale, *Uganda* 82 C3
Kabalo, *Zaïre* 82 D2
Kabambare, *Zaïre* 82 C2
Kabango, *Zaïre* 83 D2
Kabanjahe, *Indonesia* 56 D1
Kabankalan, *Phil.* 55 G5
Kabara, *Mali* 78 B4
Kabardinka, *Russia* 43 H4
Kabardino-Balkar Republic = Kabardino Balkaria □, *Russia* 43 J6
Kabardino Balkaria □, *Russia* 43 J6
Kabare, *Indonesia* 57 E8
Kabarega Falls, *Uganda* 82 B3
Kabasalan, *Phil.* 55 H5
Kabba, *Nigeria* 79 D6
Kabin Buri, *Thailand* 58 F3
Kabinakagami L., *Canada* 98 C3
Kabīr, Zab al →, *Iraq* 67 D10
Kabkabīyah, *Sudan* 73 F9
Kabna, *Sudan* 76 D3
Kabompo, *Zambia* 83 E1
Kabompo →, *Zambia* 81 G4
Kabondo, *Zaïre* 83 D2
Kabongo, *Zaïre* 82 D2
Kabou, *Togo* 79 D5
Kaboudia, Rass, *Tunisia* 75 A7
Kabra, *Australia* 90 C5
Kabūd Gonbad, *Iran* 65 B8
Kabugao, *Phil.* 55 B4
Kābul, *Afghan.* 62 B3
Kābul □, *Afghan.* 60 B6
Kabul →, *Pakistan* 62 C5
Kabunga, *Zaïre* 82 C2
Kaburuang, *Indonesia* 57 D7
Kabushiya, *Sudan* 77 D3
Kabwe, *Zambia* 83 E2
Kačanik, *Serbia, Yug.* 21 N11
Kachchh, Gulf of, *India* 62 H3
Kachchh, Rann of, *India* 62 G4
Kachebera, *Zambia* 83 E3
Kachin □, *Burma* 61 F20
Kachira, L., *Uganda* 82 C3
Kachiry, *Kazakstan* 44 D8
Kachisi, *Ethiopia* 77 F4
Kachot, *Cambodia* 59 G4
Kaçkar, *Turkey* 67 B9
Kadan Kyun, *Burma* 56 B1
Kadanai →, *Afghan.* 62 D1
Kadarkút, *Hungary* 21 J7
Kade, *Ghana* 79 D4
Kadi, *India* 62 H5
Kadina, *Australia* 91 E2
Kadınhanı, *Turkey* 66 C5
Kadirli, *Turkey* 66 D7
Kadiyevka = Stakhanov, *Ukraine* 41 H10
Kadoka, *U.S.A.* 108 D4
Kadom, *Russia* 42 C6
Kadoma, *Zimbabwe* 83 F2
Kâdugli, *Sudan* 77 E2
Kaduna, *Nigeria* 79 C6
Kaduna □, *Nigeria* 79 C6
Kaduy, *Russia* 40 C9
Kaédi, *Mauritania* 78 B2
Kaelé, *Cameroon* 79 C7
Kaeng Khoï, *Thailand* 58 E3
Kaesŏng, *N. Korea* 51 F14
Kāf, *Si. Arabia* 64 D3
Kafakumba, *Zaïre* 80 F4
Kafan = Kapan, *Armenia* 67 C12
Kafanchan, *Nigeria* 79 D6
Kafareti, *Nigeria* 79 C7
Kaffrine, *Senegal* 78 C1
Kafia Kingi, *Sudan* 73 G9
Kafinda, *Zambia* 83 E3
Kafirévs, Ákra, *Greece* 39 L7
Kafr el Dauwâr, *Egypt* 76 H7
Kafr el Sheikh, *Egypt* 76 H7
Kafue, *Zambia* 83 F2
Kafue →, *Zambia* 81 H5
Kafue Flats, *Zambia* 83 F2
Kafue Nat. Park, *Zambia* 83 F2
Kafulwe, *Zambia* 83 D2
Kaga, *Afghan.* 62 B4
Kaga Bandoro, *C.A.R.* 73 G8
Kagan, *Uzbekistan* 44 F7
Kagawa □, *Japan* 49 G6
Kagera □, *Tanzania* 82 C3
Kagera →, *Uganda* 82 C3
Kağizman, *Turkey* 67 B10
Kagoshima, *Japan* 49 J5
Kagoshima □, *Japan* 49 J5
Kagul = Cahul, *Moldova* 41 K5
Kahak, *Iran* 65 B6
Kahama, *Tanzania* 82 C3
Kahama □, *Tanzania* 82 C3
Kahang, *Malaysia* 59 L4
Kahayan →, *Indonesia* 56 E4
Kahe, *Tanzania* 82 C4
Kahemba, *Zaïre* 80 F3
Kahil, Djebel bou, *Algeria* 75 B5
Kahniah →, *Canada* 100 B4
Kahnūj, *Iran* 65 E8
Kahoka, *U.S.A.* 108 E9
Kahoolawe, *U.S.A.* 102 H16
Kahramanmaraş, *Turkey* 66 D7
Kâhta, *Turkey* 67 D8
Kahuta, *Pakistan* 62 C5
Kai, Kepulauan, *Indonesia* 57 F8
Kai Besar, *Indonesia* 57 F8
Kai Is. = Kai, Kepulauan, *Indonesia* 57 F8
Kai Kecil, *Indonesia* 57 F8
Kai Xian, *China* 52 B7
Kaiama, *Nigeria* 79 D5
Kaiapoi, *N.Z.* 87 K4
Kaieteur Falls, *Guyana* 121 B6
Kaifeng, *China* 50 G8
Kaihua, *China* 53 C12
Kaikohe, *N.Z.* 87 F4
Kaikoura, *N.Z.* 87 K4
Kaikoura Ra., *N.Z.* 87 J4
Kailahun, *S. Leone* 78 D2
Kaili, *China* 52 D6
Kailu, *China* 51 C11
Kailua Kona, *U.S.A.* 102 J17
Kaimana, *Indonesia* 57 E8
Kaimanawa Mts., *N.Z.* 87 H5
Kaimganj, *India* 63 F8
Kaimur Hills, *India* 63 G9
Kaingaroa Forest, *N.Z.* 87 H6
Kainji Res., *Nigeria* 79 C5
Kainuu, *Finland* 8 D23
Kaipara Harbour, *N.Z.* 87 G5
Kaiping, *China* 53 F9
Kaipokok B., *Canada* 99 B8
Kairana, *India* 62 E7
Kaironi, *Indonesia* 57 E8
Kairouan, *Tunisia* 75 A7
Kaiserslautern, *Germany* 19 F3
Kaitaia, *N.Z.* 87 F4
Kaitangata, *N.Z.* 87 M2
Kaithal, *India* 62 E7
Kaitu →, *Pakistan* 62 C4
Kaiwi Channel, *U.S.A.* 102 H16
Kaiyang, *China* 52 D6
Kaiyuan, *Liaoning, China* 51 C13
Kaiyuan, *Yunnan, China* 52 F4
Kajaani, *Finland* 8 D22
Kajabbi, *Australia* 90 B3
Kajana = Kajaani, *Finland* 8 D22
Kajang, *Malaysia* 59 L3
Kajaran, *Armenia* 67 C12
Kajiado, *Kenya* 82 C4
Kajiado □, *Kenya* 82 C4
Kajo Kaji, *Sudan* 77 G3
Kaka, *Sudan* 77 E3
Kakabeka Falls, *Canada* 98 C2
Kakamas, *S. Africa* 84 D3
Kakamega, *Kenya* 82 B3
Kakamega □, *Kenya* 82 B3
Kakanj, *Bos.-H.* 21 L8
Kakanui Mts., *N.Z.* 87 L3
Kake, *Japan* 49 G6
Kakegawa, *Japan* 49 G9
Kakeroma-Jima, *Japan* 49 K4
Kakhib, *Russia* 43 J8
Kakhovka, *Ukraine* 41 J7
Kakhovske Vdskh., *Ukraine* 41 J7
Kakinada, *India* 61 L13
Kakisa →, *Canada* 100 A5
Kakisa L., *Canada* 100 A5
Kakogawa, *Japan* 49 G7
Kakwa →, *Canada* 100 C5
Kāl Gūsheh, *Iran* 65 D8
Kal Safīd, *Iran* 67 E12
Kala, *Nigeria* 79 C7
Kalaa-Kebira, *Tunisia* 75 A7
Kalabagh, *Pakistan* 62 C4
Kalabahi, *Indonesia* 57 F6
Kalabáka, *Greece* 39 K4
Kalabo, *Zambia* 81 G4
Kalach, *Russia* 42 E5
Kalach na Donu, *Russia* 43 F6
Kaladan →, *Burma* 61 J18
Kaladar, *Canada* 106 B7
Kalahari, *Africa* 84 C3
Kalahari Gemsbok Nat. Park, *S. Africa* 84 D3
Kalajoki, *Finland* 8 D20
Kālak, *Iran* 65 E8
Kalakamati, *Botswana* 85 C4
Kalakan, *Russia* 45 D12
Kalakh, *Syria* 64 C3
K'alak'unlun Shank'ou, *Pakistan* 63 B7
Kalam, *Pakistan* 63 B5
Kalama, *U.S.A.* 112 E4
Kalama, *Zaïre* 82 C2
Kalámai, *Greece* 39 M5
Kalamariá, *Greece* 39 J5
Kalamata = Kalámai, *Greece* 39 M5
Kalamazoo, *U.S.A.* 104 D3
Kalamazoo →, *U.S.A.* 104 D2
Kalambo Falls, *Tanzania* 83 D3
Kálamos, *Greece* 39 L3
Kalannie, *Australia* 89 F2
Kalāntarī, *Iran* 65 C7
Kalao, *Indonesia* 57 F6
Kalaotoa, *Indonesia* 57 F6
Kälarne, *Sweden* 10 B10
Kalárovo, *Slovak Rep.* 21 H7
Kalasin, *Thailand* 58 D4
Kalat, *Pakistan* 60 E5
Kalāteh, *Iran* 65 B7
Kalāteh-ye-Ganj, *Iran* 65 E8
Kálathos, *Greece* 39 N11
Kalaus →, *Russia* 43 H7
Kalávrita, *Greece* 39 L5
Kalbarri, *Australia* 89 E1
Kale, *Turkey* 66 D3
Kalecik, *Turkey* 66 B5
Kalegauk Kyun, *Burma* 61 M20
Kalehe, *Zaïre* 82 C2
Kalema, *Tanzania* 82 C3
Kalemie, *Zaïre* 82 D2
Kalety, *Poland* 20 E8
Kalewa, *Burma* 61 H19
Kalgan = Zhangjiakou, *China* 50 D8
Kalgoorlie-Boulder, *Australia* 89 F3
Kaliakra, Nos, *Bulgaria* 38 F11
Kalianda, *Indonesia* 56 F3
Kalibo, *Phil.* 55 F5
Kaliganj, *Bangla.* 63 H13
Kalima, *Zaïre* 82 C2
Kalimantan, *Indonesia* 56 E4
Kalimantan Barat □, *Indonesia* 56 E4
Kalimantan Selatan □, *Indonesia* 56 E5
Kalimantan Tengah □, *Indonesia* 56 E4
Kalimantan Timur □, *Indonesia* 56 D5
Kálimnos, *Greece* 39 N10
Kalimpong, *India* 63 F13
Kalinin = Tver, *Russia* 42 B2
Kaliningrad, *Russia* 9 J19
Kalininsk, *Russia* 42 E7
Kalinkavichy, *Belarus* 41 F5
Kalinkovichi = Kalinkavichy, *Belarus* 41 F5
Kalinovik, *Bos.-H.* 21 M8
Kalipetrovo, *Bulgaria* 38 E10
Kaliro, *Uganda* 82 B3
Kalispell, *U.S.A.* 110 B6
Kalisz, *Poland* 20 D8
Kaliua, *Tanzania* 82 D3
Kalix, *Sweden* 8 D20
Kalix →, *Sweden* 8 D20
Kalka, *India* 62 D7
Kalkan, *Turkey* 66 D3
Kalkaska, *U.S.A.* 104 C3
Kalkfeld, *Namibia* 84 C2
Kalkfontein, *Botswana* 84 C3
Kalkrand, *Namibia* 84 C2
Kållandsö, *Sweden* 11 F7
Kallavesi, *Finland* 8 E22
Kallithéa, *Greece* 39 M6
Kallonís, Kólpos, *Greece* 39 K9
Kallsjön, *Sweden* 8 E15
Kalmalo, *Nigeria* 79 C6
Kalmar, *Sweden* 9 H17
Kalmthout, *Belgium* 17 F4
Kalmyk Republic = Kalmykia □, *Russia* 43 G8
Kalmykia □, *Russia* 43 G8
Kalmykovo, *Kazakstan* 44 E6
Kalna, *India* 63 H13
Kalocsa, *Hungary* 21 J9
Kalokhorio, *Cyprus* 37 E12
Kaloko, *Zaïre* 82 D2
Kalol, *Gujarat, India* 62 H5
Kalol, *Gujarat, India* 62 H5
Kalolímnos, *Greece* 39 M10
Kalomo, *Zambia* 83 F2
Kalpi, *India* 63 F8
Kaltbrunn, *Switz.* 23 B8
Kaltern = Caldaro, *Italy* 33 B8
Kaltungo, *Nigeria* 79 D7
Kalu, *Pakistan* 62 G2
Kaluga, *Russia* 42 C3
Kalulushi, *Zambia* 83 E2
Kalundborg, *Denmark* 11 J5
Kalush, *Ukraine* 41 H3
Kałuszyn, *Poland* 20 C11
Kalutara, *Sri Lanka* 60 R11
Kalyazin, *Russia* 42 B3
Kama, *Zaïre* 82 C2
Kama →, *Russia* 44 D6
Kamachumu, *Tanzania* 82 C3
Kamaishi, *Japan* 48 E10
Kamalia, *Pakistan* 62 D5
Kaman, *Turkey* 66 C5
Kamapanda, *Zambia* 83 E1
Kamaran, *Yemen* 68 D3
Kamativi, *Zimbabwe* 83 F2
Kamba, *Nigeria* 79 C5
Kambalda, *Australia* 89 F3
Kambar, *Pakistan* 62 F3
Kambia, *S. Leone* 78 D2
Kambolé, *Zambia* 83 D3
Kambos, *Cyprus* 37 D11
Kambove, *Zaïre* 83 E2
Kamchatka, P-ov., *Russia* 45 D16
Kamchatka Pen. = Kamchatka, P-ov., *Russia* 45 D16
Kamen, *Russia* 44 D9
Kamen-Rybolov, *Russia* 48 B6
Kamenjak, Rt., *Croatia* 33 D10
Kamenka = Kaminka, *Ukraine* 41 H7
Kamenka, *Kazakstan* 42 E10
Kamenka, *Russia* 42 D6
Kamenka, *Russia* 42 E4
Kamenka Bugskaya = Kamyanka-Buzka, *Ukraine* 41 G3
Kamenka Dneprovskaya = Kamyanka-Dniprovska, *Ukraine* 41 J8
Kamennomostskiy, *Russia* 43 H5
Kamenolomini, *Russia* 43 G5
Kamensk-Shakhtinskiy, *Russia* 43 F5
Kamensk Uralskiy, *Russia* 44 D7
Kamenskiy, *Russia* 42 E7
Kamenskoye, *Russia* 45 C17
Kamenyak, *Bulgaria* 38 F9
Kamenz, *Germany* 18 D10
Kameoka, *Japan* 49 G7
Kamiah, *U.S.A.* 110 C5
Kamień Pomorski, *Poland* 20 B4
Kamieskroon, *S. Africa* 84 E2
Kamilukuak, L., *Canada* 101 A8
Kamin-Kashyrskyy, *Ukraine* 41 G3
Kamina, *Zaïre* 83 D1
Kaminak L., *Canada* 101 A9
Kaminka, *Ukraine* 41 H7
Kaminoyama, *Japan* 48 E10
Kamiros, *Greece* 37 C9
Kamituga, *Zaïre* 82 C2
Kamloops, *Canada* 100 C4
Kamnik, *Slovenia* 33 B11
Kamo, *Armenia* 43 K7
Kamo, *Japan* 48 F9
Kamoa Mts., *Guyana* 121 C6
Kamoke, *Pakistan* 62 C6
Kamp →, *Austria* 21 G5
Kampala, *Uganda* 82 B3
Kampar, *Malaysia* 59 K3
Kampar →, *Indonesia* 56 D2
Kampen, *Neths.* 16 C7
Kamperland, *Neths.* 17 E3
Kamphaeng Phet, *Thailand* 58 D2
Kampolombo, L., *Zambia* 83 E2
Kampong To, *Thailand* 59 J3
Kampot, *Cambodia* 59 G5
Kampti, *Burkina Faso* 78 C4
Kampuchea = Cambodia ■, *Asia* 58 F5
Kampung →, *Indonesia* 57 F9
Kampung Air Putih, *Malaysia* 59 K4
Kampung Jerangau, *Malaysia* 59 K4
Kampung Raja, *Malaysia* 59 K4
Kampungbaru = Tolitoli, *Indonesia* 57 D6
Kamrau, Teluk, *Indonesia* 57 E8
Kamsack, *Canada* 101 C8
Kamskoye Ustye, *Russia* 42 C9
Kamuchawie L., *Canada* 101 B8
Kamui-Misaki, *Japan* 48 C10
Kamyanets-Podilskyy, *Ukraine* 41 H4
Kamyanka-Buzka, *Ukraine* 41 G3
Kamyanka-Dniprovska, *Ukraine* 41 J8
Kāmyārān, *Iran* 67 E12
Kamyshin, *Russia* 42 E7
Kamyzyak, *Russia* 43 G9
Kanaaupscow, *Canada* 98 B4
Kanab, *U.S.A.* 111 H7
Kanab →, *U.S.A.* 111 H7
Kanagi, *Japan* 48 D10
Kanairiktok →, *Canada* 99 A7
Kanália, *Greece* 39 K5
Kananga, *Zaïre* 80 F4
Kanarraville, *U.S.A.* 111 H7
Kanash, *Russia* 42 C8
Kanaskat, *U.S.A.* 112 C5
Kanawha →, *U.S.A.* 104 F4
Kanazawa, *Japan* 49 F8
Kanchanaburi, *Thailand* 58 E2
Kanchenjunga, *Nepal* 63 F13
Kanchipuram, *India* 60 N11
Kanda Kanda, *Zaïre* 80 F4
Kandahar = Qandahār, *Afghan.* 60 D4
Kandalaksha, *Russia* 44 C4
Kandalu, *Afghan.* 60 E3
Kandangan, *Indonesia* 56 E5
Kandanos, *Greece* 37 D5
Kander →, *Switz.* 22 C5
Kandersteg, *Switz.* 22 D5
Kandhíla, *Greece* 39 M5
Kandhkot, *Pakistan* 62 E3
Kandhla, *India* 62 E7
Kandi, *Benin* 79 C5
Kandi, *India* 63 H13
Kandıra, *Turkey* 66 B4
Kandla, *India* 62 H4
Kandos, *Australia* 91 E4
Kandy, *Sri Lanka* 60 R12
Kane, *U.S.A.* 106 E6
Kane Basin, *Greenland* 4 B4
Kanevskaya, *Russia* 43 G4
Kanfanar, *Croatia* 33 C10
Kangaba, *Mali* 78 C3
Kangal, *Turkey* 66 C7
Kangān, *Fārs, Iran* 65 E7
Kangān, *Hormozgān, Iran* 65 E8
Kangar, *Malaysia* 59 J3
Kangaroo I., *Australia* 91 F2
Kangasala, *Finland* 9 F21
Kangāvar, *Iran* 67 E12
Kangding, *China* 52 B3
Kăngdong, *N. Korea* 51 E14
Kangean, Kepulauan, *Indonesia* 56 F5
Kangean Is. = Kangean, Kepulauan, *Indonesia* 56 F5
Kanggye, *N. Korea* 51 D14
Kanggyŏng, *S. Korea* 51 F14
Kanghwa, *S. Korea* 51 F14
Kangiqsualujjuaq, *Canada* 97 C13
Kangiqsujuaq, *Canada* 97 B12
Kangirsuk, *Canada* 97 B13
Kangnŭng, *S. Korea* 51 F15
Kango, *Gabon* 80 D2
Kangping, *China* 51 C12
Kangto, *India* 61 F18
Kani, *Ivory C.* 78 D3
Kaniama, *Zaïre* 82 D1
Kaniapiskau →, *Canada* 99 A6
Kaniapiskau L., *Canada* 99 B6
Kanin, Poluostrov, *Russia* 44 C5
Kanin Nos, Mys, *Russia* 44 C5
Kanin Pen. = Kanin, Poluostrov, *Russia* 44 C5
Kaniva, *Australia* 91 F3
Kanjiža, *Serbia, Yug.* 21 J10
Kanjut Sar, *Pakistan* 63 A6
Kankaanpää, *Finland* 9 F20
Kankakee, *U.S.A.* 104 E2
Kankakee →, *U.S.A.* 104 E1
Kankan, *Guinea* 78 C3
Kankendy = Xankändi, *Azerbaijan* 67 C12
Kanker, *India* 61 J12
Kankunskiy, *Russia* 45 D13
Kannapolis, *U.S.A.* 105 H5
Kannauj, *India* 63 F8
Kannod, *India* 60 H10
Kano, *Nigeria* 79 C6
Kano □, *Nigeria* 79 C6
Kan'onji, *Japan* 49 G6
Kanoroba, *Ivory C.* 78 D3
Kanowit, *Malaysia* 56 D4
Kanowna, *Australia* 89 F3
Kanoya, *Japan* 49 J5
Kanpetlet, *Burma* 61 J18
Kanpur, *India* 63 F9
Kansas □, *U.S.A.* 108 F6
Kansas →, *U.S.A.* 108 F7
Kansas City, *Kans., U.S.A.* 108 F7
Kansas City, *Mo., U.S.A.* 108 F7
Kansenia, *Zaïre* 83 E2
Kansk, *Russia* 45 D10
Kansŏng, *S. Korea* 51 E15
Kansu = Gansu □, *China* 50 G3
Kantang, *Thailand* 59 J2
Kantché, *Niger* 79 C6
Kanté, *Togo* 79 D5
Kantemirovka, *Russia* 42 F4
Kantharalak, *Thailand* 58 E5
Kantō □, *Japan* 49 F9
Kantô-Sanchi, *Japan* 49 G9
Kanturk, *Ireland* 15 D3
Kanuma, *Japan* 49 F9
Kanus, *Namibia* 84 D2
Kanye, *Botswana* 84 C4
Kanzenze, *Zaïre* 83 E2
Kanzi, Ras, *Tanzania* 82 D4
Kaohsiung, *Taiwan* 53 F13
Kaokoveld, *Namibia* 84 B1
Kaolack, *Senegal* 78 C1
Kaoshan, *China* 51 B13
Kapadvanj, *India* 62 H5

Kapan, *Armenia* 67 C12
Kapanga, *Zaïre* 80 F4
Kapchagai = Qapshaghay, *Kazakstan* 44 E8
Kapellen, *Belgium* 17 F4
Kapéllo, Ákra, *Greece* 39 N6
Kapema, *Zaïre* 83 E2
Kapfenberg, *Austria* 21 H5
Kapiri Mposhi, *Zambia* 83 E2
Kapiskau →, *Canada* 98 B3
Kapit, *Malaysia* 56 D4
Kapiti I., *N.Z.* 87 J5
Kaplice, *Czech.* 20 G4
Kapoe, *Thailand* 59 H2
Kapoeta, *Sudan* 77 G3
Kapos →, *Hungary* 21 J8
Kaposvár, *Hungary* 21 J7
Kapowsin, *U.S.A.* 112 D4
Kappeln, *Germany* 18 A5
Kapps, *Namibia* 84 C2
Kaprije, *Croatia* 33 E12
Kaprijke, *Belgium* 17 F3
Kapsan, *N. Korea* 51 D15
Kapsukas = Marijampolė, *Lithuania* 9 J20
Kapuas →, *Indonesia* 56 E3
Kapuas Hulu, Pegunungan, *Malaysia* 56 D4
Kapuas Hulu Ra. = Kapuas Hulu, Pegunungan, *Malaysia* 56 D4
Kapulo, *Zaïre* 83 D2
Kapunda, *Australia* 91 E2
Kapuni, *N.Z.* 87 H5
Kapurthala, *India* 62 D6
Kapuskasing, *Canada* 98 C3
Kapuskasing →, *Canada* 98 C3
Kapustin Yar, *Russia* 43 F7
Kaputar, *Australia* 91 E5
Kaputir, *Kenya* 82 B4
Kapuvár, *Hungary* 21 H7
Kara, *Russia* 44 C7
Kara Bogaz Gol, Zaliv = Garabogazköl Aylagy, *Turkmenistan* 44 E6
Kara Kalpak Republic □ = Karakalpakstan □, *Uzbekistan* 44 E6
Kara Kum, *Turkmenistan* 44 F6
Kara Sea, *Russia* 44 B7
Karabiğa, *Turkey* 66 B2
Karabük, *Turkey* 66 B5
Karaburun, *Turkey* 66 C2
Karaburuni, *Albania* 39 J2
Karabutak = Qarabutaq, *Kazakstan* 44 E7
Karacabey, *Turkey* 66 B3
Karacasu, *Turkey* 66 D3
Karachala = Qaraçala, *Azerbaijan* 43 L9
Karachayevsk, *Russia* 43 J5
Karachev, *Russia* 42 D2
Karachey-Cherkessia □, *Russia* 43 J5
Karachi, *Pakistan* 62 G2
Karad, *India* 60 L9
Karadeniz Boğazı, *Turkey* 66 B3
Karaga, *Ghana* 79 D4
Karaganda = Qaraghandy, *Kazakstan* 44 E8
Karagayly, *Kazakstan* 44 E8
Karaginskiy, Ostrov, *Russia* 45 D17
Karagüney Dağları, *Turkey* 66 B6
Karagwe □, *Tanzania* 82 C3
Karaikal, *India* 60 P11
Karaikkudi, *India* 60 P11
Karaisali, *Turkey* 66 D6
Karaj, *Iran* 65 C6
Karak, *Malaysia* 59 L4
Karakalpakstan □, *Uzbekistan* 44 E6
Karakas, *Kazakstan* 44 E9
Karakelong, *Indonesia* 57 D7
Karakitang, *Indonesia* 57 D7
Karaklis = Vanadzor, *Armenia* 43 K7
Karakoçan, *Turkey* 67 C9
Karakoram Pass, *Pakistan* 63 B7
Karakoram Ra., *Pakistan* 63 B7
Karakurt, *Turkey* 67 B10
Karalon, *Russia* 45 D12
Karaman, *Turkey* 66 D5
Karamay, *China* 54 B3
Karambu, *Indonesia* 56 E5
Karamea Bight, *N.Z.* 87 J3
Karamsad, *India* 62 H5
Karand, *Iran* 67 E12
Karanganyar, *Indonesia* 57 G13
Karapınar, *Turkey* 66 D5
Karasburg, *Namibia* 84 D2
Karasino, *Russia* 44 C9
Karasjok, *Norway* 8 B21
Karasu, *Turkey* 66 B4
Karasuk, *Russia* 44 D8
Karasuyama, *Japan* 49 F10
Karataş, *Turkey* 66 D6
Karataş Burnu, *Turkey* 66 D6
Karatau = Qarataū, *Kazakstan* 44 E8
Karatau, Khrebet, *Kazakstan* 44 E7
Karauli, *India* 62 F7
Karavostasi, *Cyprus* 37 D11
Karawang, *Indonesia* 57 G12
Karawanken, *Europe* 21 J4
Karayazı, *Turkey* 67 C10
Karazhal, *Kazakstan* 44 E8
Karbalā, *Iraq* 67 F11
Kårböle, *Sweden* 10 C9
Karcag, *Hungary* 21 H10
Karcha →, *Pakistan* 63 B7
Karda, *Russia* 45 D11
Kardhámila, *Greece* 39 L9
Kardhítsa, *Greece* 39 K4
Kärdla, *Estonia* 9 G20
Kareeberge, *S. Africa* 84 E3
Kareima, *Sudan* 76 D3
Karelia □, *Russia* 44 C4
Karelian Republic □ = Karelia □, *Russia* 44 C4
Kārevāndar, *Iran* 65 E9
Kargasok, *Russia* 44 D9
Kargat, *Russia* 44 D9
Kargı, *Turkey* 66 B6
Kargil, *India* 63 B7
Kargopol, *Russia* 40 B10
Karguéri, *Niger* 79 C7
Karia ba Mohammed, *Morocco* 74 B3
Karīān, *Iran* 65 E8
Kariba, *Zimbabwe* 83 F2
Kariba, L., *Zimbabwe* 83 F2
Kariba Dam, *Zimbabwe* 83 F2
Kariba Gorge, *Zambia* 83 F2
Karibib, *Namibia* 84 C2
Karimata, Kepulauan, *Indonesia* 56 E3
Karimata, Selat, *Indonesia* 56 E3
Karimata Is. = Karimata, Kepulauan, *Indonesia* 56 E3
Karimnagar, *India* 60 K11
Karimunjawa, Kepulauan, *Indonesia* 56 F4
Karin, *Somali Rep.* 68 E4
Karīt, *Iran* 65 C8
Kariya, *Japan* 49 G8
Karjala, *Finland* 40 A5
Karkaralinsk = Qarqaraly, *Kazakstan* 44 E8
Karkinitska Zatoka, *Ukraine* 41 K7
Karkinitskiy Zaliv = Karkinitska Zatoka, *Ukraine* 41 K7
Karkur Tohl, *Egypt* 76 C2
Karl Liebknecht, *Russia* 42 E2
Karl-Marx-Stadt = Chemnitz, *Germany* 18 E8
Karla, L. = Voiviïs Límni, *Greece* 39 K5
Karlivka, *Ukraine* 41 H8
Karlobag, *Croatia* 33 D12
Karlovac, *Croatia* 33 C12
Karlovka = Karlivka, *Ukraine* 41 H8
Karlovo, *Bulgaria* 38 G7
Karlovy Vary, *Czech.* 20 E2
Karlsbad = Karlovy Vary, *Czech.* 20 E2
Karlsborg, *Sweden* 11 F8
Karlshamn, *Sweden* 9 H16
Karlskoga, *Sweden* 9 G16
Karlskrona, *Sweden* 9 H16
Karlsruhe, *Germany* 19 F4
Karlstad, *Sweden* 9 G15
Karlstad, *U.S.A.* 108 A6
Karlstadt, *Germany* 19 F5
Karnal, *India* 62 E7
Karnali →, *Nepal* 63 E9
Karnaphuli Res., *Bangla.* 61 H18
Karnataka □, *India* 60 N10
Karnes City, *U.S.A.* 109 L6
Karnische Alpen, *Europe* 21 J3
Karo, *Mali* 78 C4
Karoi, *Zimbabwe* 83 F2
Karonga, *Malawi* 83 D3
Karoonda, *Australia* 91 F2
Karora, *Sudan* 76 D4
Káros, *Greece* 39 N8
Karousádhes, *Greece* 39 K2
Karpasia □, *Cyprus* 37 D13
Kárpathos, *Greece* 39 P10
Kárpathos, Stenón, *Greece* 39 P10
Karpuz Burnu = Apostolos Andreas, C., *Cyprus* 66 E6
Karrebæk, *Denmark* 11 J5
Kars, *Turkey* 67 B10
Karsakpay, *Kazakstan* 44 E7
Karsha, *Kazakstan* 42 F10
Karshi = Qarshi, *Uzbekistan* 44 F7
Karsiyang, *India* 63 F13
Karst, *Croatia* 33 C11
Kartaly, *Russia* 44 D7
Kartapur, *India* 62 D6
Karthaus, *U.S.A.* 106 E6
Kartuzy, *Poland* 20 A8
Karufa, *Indonesia* 57 E8
Karumba, *Australia* 90 B3
Karumo, *Tanzania* 82 C3
Karumwa, *Tanzania* 82 C3
Karungu, *Kenya* 82 C3
Karup, *Denmark* 11 H3
Karviná, *Czech.* 20 F8
Karwar, *India* 60 M9
Karwi, *India* 63 G9
Kaş, *Turkey* 66 D3
Kasache, *Malawi* 83 E3
Kasai →, *Zaïre* 80 E3
Kasai Oriental □, *Zaïre* 82 C1
Kasaji, *Zaïre* 83 E1
Kasama, *Zambia* 83 E3
Kasan-dong, *N. Korea* 51 D14
Kasane, *Namibia* 84 B3
Kasanga, *Tanzania* 83 D3
Kasangulu, *Zaïre* 80 E3
Kasaragod, *India* 60 N9
Kasba L., *Canada* 101 A8
Kasba Tadla, *Morocco* 74 B3
Kāseh Garān, *Iran* 64 C5
Kasempa, *Zambia* 83 E2
Kasenga, *Zaïre* 83 E2
Kasese, *Uganda* 82 B3
Kasewa, *Zambia* 83 E2
Kasganj, *India* 63 F8
Kashabowie, *Canada* 98 C1
Kāshān, *Iran* 65 C6
Kashi, *China* 54 C2
Kashimbo, *Zaïre* 83 E2
Kashin, *Russia* 42 B3
Kashipur, *India* 63 E8
Kashira, *Russia* 42 C4
Kashiwazaki, *Japan* 49 F9
Kashk-e Kohneh, *Afghan.* 60 B3
Kāshmar, *Iran* 65 C8
Kashmir, *Asia* 63 C7
Kashmor, *Pakistan* 62 E3
Kashpirovka, *Russia* 42 D9
Kashun Noerh = Gaxun Nur, *China* 54 B5
Kasimov, *Russia* 42 C5
Kasinge, *Zaïre* 82 D2
Kasiruta, *Indonesia* 57 E7
Kaskaskia →, *U.S.A.* 108 G10
Kaskattama →, *Canada* 101 B10
Kaskinen, *Finland* 9 E19
Kaslo, *Canada* 100 D5
Kasmere L., *Canada* 101 B8
Kasongo, *Zaïre* 82 C2
Kasongo Lunda, *Zaïre* 80 F3
Kásos, *Greece* 39 P9
Kásos, Stenón, *Greece* 39 P9
Kaspi, *Georgia* 43 K7
Kaspiysk, *Russia* 43 J8
Kaspiyskiy, *Russia* 43 H8
Kassab ed Doleib, *Sudan* 77 E3
Kassaba, *Egypt* 76 C2
Kassalâ, *Sudan* 77 D4
Kassalâ □, *Sudan* 77 D4
Kassel, *Germany* 18 D5
Kassinger, *Sudan* 76 D3
Kassiópi, *Greece* 37 A3
Kassue, *Indonesia* 57 F9
Kastamonu, *Turkey* 66 B5
Kastav, *Croatia* 33 C11
Kastélli, *Greece* 37 D5
Kastéllion, *Greece* 37 D7
Kastellou, Ákra, *Greece* 39 P10
Kasterlee, *Belgium* 17 F5
Kastóri, *Greece* 39 M5
Kastoría, *Greece* 39 J4
Kastornoye, *Russia* 42 E4
Kástron, *Greece* 39 K8
Kastsyukovichy, *Belarus* 40 F7
Kasulu, *Tanzania* 82 C3
Kasulu □, *Tanzania* 82 C3
Kasumi, *Japan* 49 G7
Kasumkent, *Russia* 43 K9
Kasungu, *Malawi* 83 E3
Kasur, *Pakistan* 62 D6
Kata, *Russia* 45 D11
Kataba, *Zambia* 83 F2
Katako Kombe, *Zaïre* 82 C1
Katákolon, *Greece* 39 M4
Katale, *Tanzania* 82 C3
Katamatite, *Australia* 91 F4
Katanda, *Kivu, Zaïre* 82 C2
Katanda, *Shaba, Zaïre* 82 D1
Katanga = Shaba □, *Zaïre* 82 D2
Katangi, *India* 60 J11
Katangli, *Russia* 45 D15
Katavi Swamp, *Tanzania* 82 D3
Kateríni, *Greece* 39 J5
Katha, *Burma* 61 G20
Katherîna, Gebel, *Egypt* 76 J8
Katherine, *Australia* 88 B5
Kathiawar, *India* 62 H4
Kathikas, *Cyprus* 37 E11
Kati, *Mali* 78 C3
Katihar, *India* 63 G12
Katima Mulilo, *Zambia* 84 B3
Katimbira, *Malawi* 83 E3
Katingan = Mendawai →, *Indonesia* 56 E4
Katiola, *Ivory C.* 78 D3
Katmandu, *Nepal* 63 F11
Kato Akhaïa, *Greece* 39 L4
Káto Arkhánai, *Greece* 37 D7
Káto Khorió, *Greece* 37 D7
Kato Pyrgos, *Cyprus* 37 D11
Káto Stavros, *Greece* 39 J6
Katompe, *Zaïre* 82 D2
Katonga →, *Uganda* 82 B3
Katoomba, *Australia* 91 E5
Katowice, *Poland* 20 E9
Katrine, L., *U.K.* 14 E4
Katrineholm, *Sweden* 10 E10
Katsepe, *Madag.* 85 B8
Katsina, *Nigeria* 79 C6
Katsina □, *Nigeria* 79 C6
Katsina Ala →, *Nigeria* 79 D6
Katsumoto, *Japan* 49 H4
Katsuura, *Japan* 49 G10
Katsuyama, *Japan* 49 F8
Kattaviá, *Greece* 37 D9
Kattegat, *Denmark* 11 H5
Katumba, *Zaïre* 82 D2
Katungu, *Kenya* 82 C5
Katwa, *India* 63 H13
Katwijk-aan-Zee, *Neths.* 16 D4
Kauai, *U.S.A.* 102 H15
Kauai Channel, *U.S.A.* 102 H15
Kaub, *Germany* 19 E3
Kaufbeuren, *Germany* 19 H6
Kaufman, *U.S.A.* 109 J6
Kauhajoki, *Finland* 9 E20
Kaukauna, *U.S.A.* 104 C1
Kaukauveld, *Namibia* 84 C3
Kaunas, *Lithuania* 9 J20
Kaura Namoda, *Nigeria* 79 C6
Kautokeino, *Norway* 8 B20
Kavacha, *Russia* 45 C17
Kavadarci, *Macedonia* 39 H5
Kavaja, *Albania* 39 H2
Kavak, *Turkey* 66 B7
Kavalerovo, *Russia* 48 B7
Kavali, *India* 60 M12
Kavála, *Greece* 39 J7
Kavār, *Iran* 65 D7
Kavarna, *Bulgaria* 38 F11
Kavkaz, *Russia* 43 H3
Kavos, *Greece* 37 B4
Kaw, *Fr. Guiana* 121 C7
Kawa, *Sudan* 77 E3
Kawagama L., *Canada* 106 A6
Kawagoe, *Japan* 49 G9
Kawaguchi, *Japan* 49 G9
Kawaihae, *U.S.A.* 102 H17
Kawambwa, *Zambia* 83 D2
Kawanoe, *Japan* 49 G6
Kawardha, *India* 63 J9
Kawasaki, *Japan* 49 G9
Kawene, *Canada* 98 C1
Kawerau, *N.Z.* 87 H6
Kawhia Harbour, *N.Z.* 87 H5
Kawio, Kepulauan, *Indonesia* 57 D7
Kawnro, *Burma* 61 H21
Kawthoolei = Kawthule □, *Burma* 61 L20
Kawthule □, *Burma* 61 L20
Kaya, *Burkina Faso* 79 C4
Kayah □, *Burma* 61 K20
Kayan →, *Indonesia* 56 D5
Kaycee, *U.S.A.* 110 E10
Kayeli, *Indonesia* 57 E7
Kayenta, *U.S.A.* 111 H8
Kayes, *Mali* 78 C2
Kayima, *S. Leone* 78 D2
Kayl, *Lux.* 17 K8
Kayoa, *Indonesia* 57 D7
Kayomba, *Zambia* 83 E1
Kayoro, *Ghana* 79 C4
Kayrunnera, *Australia* 91 E3
Kaysatskoye, *Russia* 42 F8
Kayseri, *Turkey* 66 C6
Kaysville, *U.S.A.* 110 F8
Kayuagung, *Indonesia* 56 E2
Kazachye, *Russia* 45 B14
Kazakstan ■, *Asia* 44 E7
Kazan, *Russia* 42 C9
Kazan-Rettō, *Pac. Oc.* 92 E6
Kazanlŭk, *Bulgaria* 38 G8
Kazanskaya, *Russia* 42 F5
Kazatin = Kozyatyn, *Ukraine* 41 H5
Kazbek, *Russia* 43 J7
Kāzerūn, *Iran* 65 D6
Kazi Magomed = Qazimämmäd, *Azerbaijan* 43 K9
Kazincbarcika, *Hungary* 21 G10
Kaztalovka, *Kazakstan* 42 F9
Kazumba, *Zaïre* 80 F4
Kazuno, *Japan* 48 D10
Kazym →, *Russia* 44 C7
Kcynia, *Poland* 20 C7
Ké-Macina, *Mali* 78 C3
Kéa, *Greece* 39 M7
Keams Canyon, *U.S.A.* 111 J8
Kearney, *U.S.A.* 108 E5
Keban, *Turkey* 67 C8
Keban Baraji, *Turkey* 67 C8
Kebbi □, *Nigeria* 79 C6
Kébi, *Ivory C.* 78 D3
Kebili, *Tunisia* 75 B6
Kebnekaise, *Sweden* 8 C18
Kebri Dehar, *Ethiopia* 68 F3
Kebumen, *Indonesia* 57 G13
Kecel, *Hungary* 21 J9
Kechika →, *Canada* 100 B3
Kecskemét, *Hungary* 21 J9
Kedada, *Ethiopia* 77 F4
Kedgwick, *Canada* 99 C6
Kédhros Óros, *Greece* 37 D6
Kedia Hill, *Botswana* 84 C3
Kediniai, *Lithuania* 9 J21
Kediri, *Indonesia* 57 G15
Kédougou, *Senegal* 78 C2
Kedzierzyn, *Poland* 20 E8
Keeler, *U.S.A.* 112 J9
Keeley L., *Canada* 101 C7
Keeling Is. = Cocos Is., *Ind. Oc.* 92 J1
Keene, *Calif., U.S.A.* 113 K8
Keene, *N.H., U.S.A.* 107 D12
Keeper Hill, *Ireland* 15 D3
Keer-Weer, C., *Australia* 90 A3
Keerbergen, *Belgium* 17 F5
Keeseville, *U.S.A.* 107 B11
Keeten Mastgat, *Neths.* 17 E4
Keetmanshoop, *Namibia* 84 D2
Keewatin, *U.S.A.* 108 B8
Keewatin □, *Canada* 101 A9
Keewatin →, *Canada* 101 B8
Kefa □, *Ethiopia* 77 F4
Kefallinía, *Greece* 39 L3
Kefamenanu, *Indonesia* 57 F6
Keffi, *Nigeria* 79 D6
Keflavík, *Iceland* 8 D2
Keg River, *Canada* 100 B5
Kegaska, *Canada* 99 B7
Kehl, *Germany* 19 G3
Keighley, *U.K.* 12 D6
Keila, *Estonia* 9 G21
Keimoes, *S. Africa* 84 D3
Keita, *Niger* 79 C6
Keitele, *Finland* 8 E22
Keith, *Australia* 91 F3
Keith, *U.K.* 14 D6
Keith Arm, *Canada* 96 B7
Kejser Franz Joseph Fjord = Kong Franz Joseph Fd., *Greenland* 4 B6
Kekri, *India* 62 G6
Kël, *Russia* 45 C13
Kelamet, *Eritrea* 77 D4
Kelan, *China* 50 E6
Kelang, *Malaysia* 59 L3
Kelantan →, *Malaysia* 59 J4
Kelheim, *Germany* 19 G7
Kelibia, *Tunisia* 75 A7
Kelkit, *Turkey* 67 B8
Kelkit →, *Turkey* 66 B7
Kellé, *Congo* 80 E2
Keller, *U.S.A.* 110 B4
Kellerberrin, *Australia* 89 F2
Kellett, C., *Canada* 4 B1
Kelleys I., *U.S.A.* 106 E2
Kellogg, *U.S.A.* 110 C5
Kells = Ceanannus Mor, *Ireland* 15 C5
Kélo, *Chad* 73 G8
Kelokedhara, *Cyprus* 37 E11
Kelowna, *Canada* 100 D5
Kelsey Bay, *Canada* 100 C3
Kelseyville, *U.S.A.* 112 G4
Kelso, *N.Z.* 87 L2
Kelso, *U.K.* 14 F6
Kelso, *U.S.A.* 112 D4
Keluang, *Malaysia* 59 L4
Kelvington, *Canada* 101 C8
Kem, *Russia* 44 C4
Kem-Kem, *Morocco* 74 B4
Kema, *Indonesia* 57 D7
Kemah, *Turkey* 67 C8
Kemaliye, *Turkey* 67 C8
Kemano, *Canada* 100 C3
Kemasik, *Malaysia* 59 K4
Kembolcha, *Ethiopia* 77 E4
Kemer, *Turkey* 66 D4
Kemerovo, *Russia* 44 D9
Kemi, *Finland* 8 D21
Kemi älv = Kemijoki →, *Finland* 8 D21
Kemijärvi, *Finland* 8 C22
Kemijoki →, *Finland* 8 D21
Kemmel, *Belgium* 17 G1
Kemmerer, *U.S.A.* 110 F8
Kemmuna = Comino, *Malta* 37 C1
Kemp, L., *U.S.A.* 109 J5
Kemp Land, *Antarctica* 5 C5
Kempsey, *Australia* 91 E5
Kempt, L., *Canada* 98 C5
Kempten, *Germany* 19 H6
Kemptville, *Canada* 98 C4
Kenadsa, *Algeria* 75 B4
Kendal, *Indonesia* 56 F4
Kendal, *U.K.* 12 C5
Kendall, *Australia* 91 E5
Kendall →, *Australia* 90 A3
Kendallville, *U.S.A.* 104 E3
Kendari, *Indonesia* 57 E6
Kendawangan, *Indonesia* 56 E4
Kende, *Nigeria* 79 C5
Kendenup, *Australia* 89 F2
Kendrapara, *India* 61 J15
Kendrew, *S. Africa* 84 E3
Kendrick, *U.S.A.* 110 C5
Kene Thao, *Laos* 58 D3
Kenedy, *U.S.A.* 109 L6
Kenema, *S. Leone* 78 D2
Keng Kok, *Laos* 58 D5
Keng Tawng, *Burma* 61 J21
Keng Tung, *Burma* 61 J21
Kenge, *Zaïre* 80 E3
Kengeja, *Tanzania* 82 D4
Kenhardt, *S. Africa* 84 D3
Kenitra, *Morocco* 74 B3
Kenli, *China* 51 F10
Kenmare, *Ireland* 15 E2
Kenmare, *U.S.A.* 108 A3
Kenmare →, *Ireland* 15 E2
Kennebec, *U.S.A.* 108 D5
Kennedy, *Zimbabwe* 83 F2
Kennedy Ra., *Australia* 89 D2
Kennedy Taungdeik, *Burma* 61 H18
Kenner, *U.S.A.* 109 L9
Kennet →, *U.K.* 13 F7
Kenneth Ra., *Australia* 88 D2
Kennett, *U.S.A.* 109 G9
Kennewick, *U.S.A.* 110 C4
Kénogami, *Canada* 99 C5
Kenogami →, *Canada* 98 B3
Kenora, *Canada* 101 D10
Kenosha, *U.S.A.* 104 D2
Kensington, *Canada* 99 C7
Kensington, *U.S.A* 108 F5
Kensington Downs, *Australia* 90 C3
Kent, *Ohio, U.S.A* 106 E3
Kent, *Oreg., U.S.A.* 110 D3
Kent, *Tex., U.S.A.* 109 K2

Kent, Wash., U.S.A. 112 C4
Kent □, U.K. 13 F8
Kent Group, Australia 90 F4
Kent Pen., Canada 96 B9
Kentau, Kazakstan 44 E7
Kentland, U.S.A. 104 E2
Kenton, U.S.A. 104 E4
Kentucky □, U.S.A. 104 G3
Kentucky →, U.S.A. 104 F3
Kentucky L., U.S.A. 105 G2
Kentville, Canada 99 C7
Kentwood, U.S.A. 109 K9
Kenya ■, Africa 82 B4
Kenya, Mt., Kenya 82 C4
Keo Neua, Deo, Vietnam 58 C5
Keokuk, U.S.A. 108 E9
Kep, Cambodia 59 G5
Kep, Vietnam 58 B6
Kepi, Indonesia 57 F9
Kępno, Poland 20 D7
Kerala □, India 60 P10
Kerama-Rettō, Japan 49 L3
Keran, Pakistan 63 B5
Kerang, Australia 91 F3
Keraudren, C., Australia 88 C2
Kerava, Finland 9 F21
Kerch, Ukraine 41 K9
Kerchenskiy Proliv, Black Sea 41 K9
Kerchoual, Mali 79 B5
Kerempe Burnu, Turkey 66 A5
Keren, Eritrea 77 D4
Kerewan, Gambia 78 C1
Kerguelen, Ind. Oc. 3 G13
Keri Kera, Sudan 77 E3
Kericho, Kenya 82 C4
Kericho □, Kenya 82 C4
Kerinci, Indonesia 56 E2
Kerkdriel, Neths. 16 E6
Kerkenna, Is., Tunisia 75 B7
Kerki, Turkmenistan 44 F7
Kérkira, Greece 37 A3
Kerkrade, Neths. 17 G8
Kerma, Sudan 76 D3
Kermadec Is., Pac. Oc. 92 K10
Kermadec Trench, Pac. Oc. 92 L10
Kermān, Iran 65 D8
Kerman, U.S.A. 112 J6
Kermān □, Iran 65 D8
Kermānshāh = Bākhtarān, Iran 67 E12
Kerme Körfezi, Turkey 66 D2
Kermit, U.S.A. 109 K3
Kern →, U.S.A. 113 K7
Kerns, Switz. 23 C6
Kernville, U.S.A. 113 K8
Keroh, Malaysia 59 K3
Kerrobert, Canada 101 C7
Kerrville, U.S.A. 109 K5
Kerry □, Ireland 15 D2
Kerry Hd., Ireland 15 D2
Kersa, Ethiopia 77 F5
Kerteminde, Denmark 11 J4
Kertosono, Indonesia 57 G15
Kerulen →, Asia 54 B6
Kerzaz, Algeria 75 C4
Kerzers, Switz. 22 C4
Kesagami →, Canada 98 B4
Kesagami L., Canada 98 B3
Keşan, Turkey 66 B2
Kesch, Piz, Switz. 23 C9
Kesennuma, Japan 48 E10
Keshit, Iran 65 D8
Keşiş Dağ, Turkey 67 C8
Keskin, Turkey 66 C5
Kessel, Belgium 17 F5
Kessel, Neths. 17 F8
Kessel-Lo, Belgium 17 G5
Kestell, S. Africa 85 D4
Kestenga, Russia 44 C4
Kesteren, Neths. 16 E7
Keswick, U.K. 12 C4
Keszthely, Hungary 21 J7
Ket →, Russia 44 D9
Keta, Ghana 79 D5
Ketapang, Indonesia 56 E4
Ketchikan, U.S.A. 96 C6
Ketchum, U.S.A. 110 E6
Kete Krachi, Ghana 79 D4
Ketef, Khalîg Umm el, Egypt 76 C4
Ketelmeer, Neths. 16 C7
Keti Bandar, Pakistan 62 G2
Ketri, India 62 E6
Kętrzyn, Poland 20 A11
Kettering, U.K. 13 E7
Kettering, U.S.A. 104 F3
Kettle →, Canada 101 B11
Kettle Falls, U.S.A. 110 B4
Kettleman City, U.S.A. 112 J7
Keuruu, Finland 9 E21
Kevin, U.S.A. 110 B8
Kewanee, U.S.A. 108 E10
Kewaunee, U.S.A. 104 C2
Keweenaw B., U.S.A. 104 B1
Keweenaw Pen., U.S.A. 104 B2
Keweenaw Pt., U.S.A. 104 B2
Key Harbour, Canada 98 C3
Key West, U.S.A. 103 F10
Keyser, U.S.A. 104 F6
Keystone, U.S.A. 108 D3
Kezhma, Russia 45 D11
Kežmarok, Slovak Rep. 20 F10
Khabarovo, Russia 44 C7
Khabarovsk, Russia 45 E14
Khabr, Iran 65 D8
Khābūr →, Syria 67 E9
Khachmas = Xaçmaz, Azerbaijan 43 K9
Khachrod, India 62 H6
Khadari, W. el →, Sudan 77 E2
Khadro, Pakistan 62 F3
Khadyzhensk, Russia 43 H4
Khadzhilyangar, India 63 B8
Khagaria, India 63 G12
Khaipur, Bahawalpur, Pakistan 62 E5
Khaipur, Hyderabad, Pakistan 62 F3
Khair, India 62 F7
Khairabad, India 63 F9
Khairagarh, India 63 J9
Khairpur, Pakistan 60 F6
Khakassia □, Russia 44 D9
Khakhea, Botswana 84 C3
Khalafābād, Iran 65 D6
Khalfallah, Algeria 75 B5
Khalilabad, India 63 F10
Khalīlī, Iran 65 E7
Khalkhāl, Iran 67 D13
Khálki, Greece 39 K5
Khalkís, Greece 39 L6
Khalmer-Sede = Tazovskiy, Russia 44 C8
Khalmer Yu, Russia 44 C7
Khalturin, Russia 44 D5
Khalūf, Oman 68 C6
Kham Keut, Laos 58 C5
Khamas Country, Botswana 84 C4
Khambat, G. of, India 62 J5
Khambhaliya, India 62 H3
Khambhat, India 62 H5
Khamilonísion, Greece 39 P9
Khamīr, Iran 65 E7
Khamir, Yemen 68 D3
Khamsa, Egypt 69 E1
Khān Abū Shāmat, Syria 69 B5
Khān Azād, Iraq 64 C5
Khān Mujiddah, Iraq 64 C4
Khān Shaykhūn, Syria 66 E7
Khān Yūnis, Gaza Strip 69 D3
Khānaqīn, Iraq 67 E11
Khānbāghī, Iran 65 B7
Khandrá, Greece 39 P9
Khandwa, India 60 J10
Khandyga, Russia 45 C14
Khāneh, Iran 64 B5
Khanewal, Pakistan 62 D4
Khanh Duong, Vietnam 58 F7
Khaniá, Greece 37 D6
Khaniá □, Greece 37 D6
Khaníon, Kólpos, Greece 37 D5
Khanka, Ozero, Asia 45 E14
Khankendy = Xankändi, Azerbaijan 67 C12
Khanna, India 62 D7
Khanpur, Pakistan 62 E4
Khanty-Mansiysk, Russia 44 C7
Khapalu, Pakistan 63 B7
Khapcheranga, Russia 45 E12
Kharabali, Russia 43 G8
Kharagpur, India 63 H12
Khárakas, Greece 37 D7
Kharan Kalat, Pakistan 60 E4
Kharānaq, Iran 65 C7
Kharda, India 60 K9
Khardung La, India 63 B7
Khârga, El Wâhât el, Egypt 76 B3
Khargon, India 60 J9
Kharit, Wadi el →, Egypt 76 C3
Khārk, Jazireh, Iran 65 D6
Kharkiv, Ukraine 41 H9
Kharkov = Kharkiv, Ukraine 41 H9
Kharmanli, Bulgaria 39 H8
Kharovsk, Russia 40 C11
Kharta, Turkey 66 B3
Khartoum = El Khartûm, Sudan 77 D3
Khasan, Russia 48 C5
Khasavyurt, Russia 43 J8
Khāsh, Iran 60 E2
Khashm el Girba, Sudan 77 E4
Khashuri, Georgia 43 J6
Khaskovo, Bulgaria 39 H8
Khatanga, Russia 45 B11
Khatanga →, Russia 45 B11
Khatauli, India 62 E7
Khātūnābād, Iran 65 C6
Khatyrka, Russia 45 C18
Khaybar, Harrat, Si. Arabia 64 E4
Khāzimiyah, Iraq 64 C4
Khazzân Jabal el Awliyâ, Sudan 77 D3
Khe Bo, Vietnam 58 C5
Khe Long, Vietnam 58 B5
Khed Brahma, India 60 G8
Khekra, India 62 E7
Khemarak Phouminville, Cambodia 59 G4
Khemis Miliana, Algeria 75 A5
Khemissèt, Morocco 74 B3
Khemmarat, Thailand 58 D5
Khenāmān, Iran 65 D8
Khenchela, Algeria 75 A6
Khenifra, Morocco 74 B3
Kherrata, Algeria 75 A6
Kherson, Ukraine 41 J7
Khersónisos Akrotíri, Greece 37 D6
Kheta →, Russia 45 B11
Khilok, Russia 45 D12
Khimki, Russia 42 C3
Khíos, Greece 39 L9
Khirbat Qanāfār, Lebanon 69 B4
Khiuma = Hiiumaa, Estonia 9 G20
Khiva, Uzbekistan 44 E7
Khīyāv, Iran 64 B5
Khlong Khlung, Thailand 58 D2
Khmelnik, Ukraine 41 H4
Khmelnitskiy = Khmelnytskyy, Ukraine 41 H4
Khmelnytskyy, Ukraine 41 H4
Khmer Rep. = Cambodia ■, Asia 58 F5
Khoai, Hon, Vietnam 59 H5
Khodoriv, Ukraine 41 H3
Khodzent = Khudzhand, Tajikistan 44 E7
Khojak P., Afghan. 60 D5
Khok Kloi, Thailand 59 H2
Khok Pho, Thailand 59 J3
Kholm, Russia 40 D6
Kholmsk, Russia 45 E15
Khomas Hochland, Namibia 84 C2
Khomeyn, Iran 65 C6
Khon Kaen, Thailand 58 D4
Khong, Laos 58 E5
Khong Sedone, Laos 58 E5
Khonuu, Russia 45 C15
Khoper →, Russia 42 F6
Khor el 'Atash, Sudan 77 E3
Khóra, Greece 39 M4
Khóra Sfakíon, Greece 37 D6
Khorāsān □, Iran 65 C8
Khorat = Nakhon Ratchasima, Thailand 58 E4
Khorat, Cao Nguyen, Thailand 58 E4
Khorb el Ethel, Algeria 74 C3
Khorixas, Namibia 84 C1
Khorol, Ukraine 41 H7
Khorramābād, Khorāsān, Iran 65 C8
Khorramābād, Lorestān, Iran 67 F13
Khorrāmshahr, Iran 65 D6
Khorugh, Tajikistan 44 F8
Khosravī, Iran 65 D6
Khosrowābād, Khuzestān, Iran 65 D6
Khosrowābād, Kordestān, Iran 67 E12
Khosūyeh, Iran 65 D7
Khotyn, Ukraine 41 H4
Khouribga, Morocco 74 B3
Khowai, Bangla. 61 G17
Khoyniki, Belarus 41 G5
Khrami →, Georgia 43 K7
Khrenovoye, Russia 42 E5
Khristianá, Greece 39 N8
Khrysokhou B., Cyprus 37 D11
Khu Khan, Thailand 58 E5
Khudzhand, Tajikistan 44 E7
Khuff, Si. Arabia 64 E5
Khūgīānī, Afghan. 62 D1
Khulna, Bangla. 61 H16
Khulna □, Bangla. 61 H16
Khulo, Georgia 43 K6
Khumago, Botswana 84 C3
Khūnsorkh, Iran 65 E8
Khūr, Iran 65 C8
Khurai, India 62 G8
Khurayş, Si. Arabia 65 E6
Khūrīyā Mūrīyā, Jazā 'ir, Oman 68 D6
Khurja, India 62 E7
Khūsf, Iran 65 C8
Khush, Afghan. 60 C3
Khushab, Pakistan 62 C5
Khust, Ukraine 41 H2
Khuzdar, Pakistan 62 F2
Khūzestān □, Iran 65 D6
Khvājeh, Iran 64 B5
Khvalynsk, Russia 42 D9
Khvānsār, Iran 65 D7
Khvatovka, Russia 42 D8
Khvor, Iran 65 C7
Khvorgū, Iran 65 E8
Khvormūj, Iran 65 D6
Khvoy, Iran 67 C11
Khvoynaya, Russia 40 C8
Khyber Pass, Afghan. 62 B4
Kiabukwa, Zaïre 83 D1
Kiama, Australia 91 E5
Kiamba, Phil. 55 H6
Kiambi, Zaïre 82 D2
Kiambu, Kenya 82 C4
Kiangsi = Jiangxi □, China 53 D10
Kiangsu = Jiangsu □, China 51 H10
Kibæk, Denmark 11 H2
Kibanga Port, Uganda 82 B3
Kibangou, Congo 80 E2
Kibara, Tanzania 82 C3
Kibare, Mts., Zaïre 82 D2
Kibombo, Zaïre 82 C2
Kibondo, Tanzania 82 C3
Kibondo □, Tanzania 82 C3
Kibumbu, Burundi 82 C2
Kibungu, Rwanda 82 C3
Kibuye, Burundi 82 C2
Kibuye, Rwanda 82 C2
Kibwesa, Tanzania 82 D2
Kibwezi, Kenya 82 C4
Kichiga, Russia 45 D17
Kicking Horse Pass, Canada 100 C5
Kidal, Mali 79 B5
Kidderminster, U.K. 13 E5
Kidete, Tanzania 82 D4
Kidira, Senegal 78 C2
Kidnappers, C., N.Z. 87 H6
Kidston, Australia 90 B3
Kidugallo, Tanzania 82 D4
Kiel, Germany 18 A6
Kiel Canal = Nord-Ostsee-Kanal →, Germany 18 A5
Kielce, Poland 20 E10
Kieldrecht, Belgium 17 F4
Kieler Bucht, Germany 18 A6
Kien Binh, Vietnam 59 H5
Kien Tan, Vietnam 59 G5
Kienge, Zaïre 83 E2
Kiessé, Niger 79 C5
Kiev = Kyyiv, Ukraine 41 G6
Kiffa, Mauritania 78 B2
Kifisiá, Greece 39 L6
Kifissós →, Greece 39 L6
Kifrī, Iraq 67 E11
Kigali, Rwanda 82 C3
Kigarama, Tanzania 82 C3
Kigoma □, Tanzania 82 D2
Kigoma-Ujiji, Tanzania 82 C2
Kigomasha, Ras, Tanzania 82 C4
Kihee, Australia 91 D3
Kihnu, Estonia 9 G21
Kii-Sanchi, Japan 49 G7
Kii-Suidō, Japan 49 H7
Kikaiga-Shima, Japan 49 K4
Kikinda, Serbia, Yug. 21 K10
Kikládhes, Greece 39 M7
Kikwit, Zaïre 80 E3
Kílalki, Greece 39 N10
Kilauea Crater, U.S.A. 102 J17
Kilchberg, Switz. 23 B7
Kilcoy, Australia 91 D5
Kildare, Ireland 15 C5
Kildare □, Ireland 15 C5
Kilgore, U.S.A. 109 J7
Kilifi, Kenya 82 C4
Kilifi □, Kenya 82 C4
Kilimanjaro, Tanzania 82 C4
Kilimanjaro □, Tanzania 82 C4
Kilimli, Turkey 66 B4
Kilindini, Kenya 82 C4
Kilis, Turkey 66 D7
Kiliya, Ukraine 41 K5
Kilju, N. Korea 51 D15
Kilkee, Ireland 15 D2
Kilkenny, Ireland 15 D4
Kilkenny □, Ireland 15 D4
Kilkieran B., Ireland 15 C2
Kilkís, Greece 39 J5
Killala, Ireland 15 B2
Killala B., Ireland 15 B2
Killaloe, Ireland 15 D3
Killaloe Sta., Canada 106 A7
Killam, Canada 100 C6
Killarney, Australia 91 D5
Killarney, Canada 98 C3
Killarney, Ireland 15 D2
Killarney, Lakes of, Ireland 15 E2
Killary Harbour, Ireland 15 C2
Killdeer, Canada 101 D7
Killdeer, U.S.A. 108 B3
Killeen, U.S.A. 109 K6
Killiecrankie, Pass of, U.K. 14 E5
Killin, U.K. 14 E4
Killíni, Ilía, Greece 39 M4
Killíni, Korinthía, Greece 39 M5
Killybegs, Ireland 15 B3
Kilmarnock, U.K. 14 F4
Kilmez, Russia 42 B10
Kilmez →, Russia 42 B10
Kilmore, Australia 91 F3
Kilondo, Tanzania 83 D3
Kilosa, Tanzania 82 D4
Kilosa □, Tanzania 82 D4
Kilrush, Ireland 15 D2
Kilwa □, Tanzania 83 D4
Kilwa Kisiwani, Tanzania 83 D4
Kilwa Kivinje, Tanzania 83 D4
Kilwa Masoko, Tanzania 83 D4
Kim, U.S.A. 109 G3
Kimaam, Indonesia 57 F9
Kimamba, Tanzania 82 D4
Kimba, Australia 91 E2
Kimball, Nebr., U.S.A. 108 E3
Kimball, S. Dak., U.S.A. 108 D5
Kimberley, Canada 100 D5
Kimberley, S. Africa 84 D3
Kimberley Downs, Australia 88 C3
Kimberly, U.S.A. 110 E6
Kimchaek, N. Korea 51 D15
Kimchŏn, S. Korea 51 F15
Kími, Greece 39 L7
Kimje, S. Korea 51 G14
Kimmirut, Canada 97 B13
Kímolos, Greece 39 N7
Kimovsk, Russia 42 C3
Kimparana, Mali 78 C4
Kimry, Russia 42 B3
Kimsquit, Canada 100 C3
Kimstad, Sweden 11 F9
Kinabalu, Gunong, Malaysia 56 C5
Kínaros, Greece 39 N9
Kinaskan L., Canada 100 B2
Kinbasket L., Canada 100 C5
Kincaid, Canada 101 D7
Kincardine, Canada 98 D3
Kinda, Zaïre 83 D2
Kinder Scout, U.K. 12 D6
Kindersley, Canada 101 C7
Kindia, Guinea 78 C2
Kindu, Zaïre 82 C2
Kinel, Russia 42 D10
Kineshma, Russia 42 B6
Kinesi, Tanzania 82 C3
King, L., Australia 89 F2
King, Mt., Australia 90 D4
King City, U.S.A. 111 H3
King Cr. →, Australia 90 C2
King Edward →, Australia 88 B4
King Frederick VI Land = Kong Frederik VI.s Kyst, Greenland 4 C5
King George B., Falk. Is. 128 D4
King George I., Antarctica 5 C18
King George Is., Canada 97 C11
King I. = Kadan Kyun, Burma 56 B1
King I., Australia 90 F3
King I., Canada 100 C3
King Leopold Ras., Australia 88 C4
King Sd., Australia 88 C3
King William I., Canada 96 B10
King William's Town, S. Africa 84 E4
Kingaroy, Australia 91 D5
Kingfisher, U.S.A. 109 H6
Kingirbān, Iraq 64 C5
Kingisepp = Kuressaare, Estonia 9 G20
Kingisepp, Russia 40 C5
Kingman, Ariz., U.S.A. 113 K12
Kingman, Kans., U.S.A. 109 G5
Kingoonya, Australia 91 E2
Kings →, U.S.A. 111 H4
Kings Canyon National Park, U.S.A. 111 H4
King's Lynn, U.K. 12 E8
Kings Mountain, U.S.A. 105 H5
King's Peak, U.S.A. 110 F8
Kingsbridge, U.K. 13 G4
Kingsburg, U.S.A. 111 H4
Kingscote, Australia 91 F2
Kingscourt, Ireland 15 C5
Kingsley, U.S.A. 108 D7
Kingsport, U.S.A. 105 G4
Kingston, Canada 98 D4
Kingston, Jamaica 116 C4
Kingston, N.Z. 87 L2
Kingston, N.Y., U.S.A. 107 E10
Kingston, Pa., U.S.A. 107 E9
Kingston, R.I., U.S.A. 107 E13
Kingston Pk., U.S.A. 113 K11
Kingston South East, Australia 91 F2
Kingston upon Hull, U.K. 12 D7
Kingston upon Hull □, U.K. 12 D7
Kingston-upon-Thames, U.K. 13 F7
Kingstown, St. Vincent 117 D7
Kingstree, U.S.A. 105 J6
Kingsville, Canada 98 D3
Kingsville, U.S.A. 109 M6
Kingussie, U.K. 14 D4
Kınık, Turkey 66 C2
Kinistino, Canada 101 C7
Kinkala, Congo 80 E2
Kinki □, Japan 49 H8
Kinleith, N.Z. 87 H5
Kinmount, Canada 106 B6
Kinna, Sweden 11 G6
Kinnaird, Canada 100 D5
Kinnairds Hd., U.K. 14 D7
Kinnared, Sweden 11 G7
Kinnarodden, Norway 6 A11
Kino, Mexico 114 B2
Kinoje →, Canada 98 B3
Kinomoto, Japan 49 G8
Kinoni, Uganda 82 C3
Kinrooi, Belgium 17 F7
Kinross, U.K. 14 E5
Kinsale, Ireland 15 E3
Kinsale, Old Hd. of, Ireland 15 E3
Kinsha = Chang Jiang →, China 53 B13
Kinshasa, Zaïre 80 E3
Kinsley, U.S.A. 109 G5
Kinston, U.S.A. 105 H7
Kintampo, Ghana 79 D4
Kintap, Indonesia 56 E5
Kintore Ra., Australia 88 D4
Kintyre, U.K. 14 F3
Kintyre, Mull of, U.K. 14 F3
Kinushseo →, Canada 98 A3
Kinuso, Canada 100 B5
Kinyangiri, Tanzania 82 C3
Kinzig →, Germany 19 G3
Kinzua, U.S.A. 106 E6
Kinzua Dam, U.S.A. 106 E5
Kiosk, Canada 98 C4
Kiowa, Kans., U.S.A. 109 G5
Kiowa, Okla., U.S.A. 109 H7
Kipahigan L., Canada 101 B8
Kipanga, Tanzania 82 D4
Kiparissía, Greece 39 M4
Kiparissiakós Kólpos, Greece 39 M4
Kipembawe, Tanzania 82 D3
Kipengere Ra., Tanzania 83 D3
Kipili, Tanzania 82 D3
Kipini, Kenya 82 C5
Kipling, Canada 101 C8
Kippure, Ireland 15 C5

Kipushi, *Zaïre* 83 E2
Kiratpur, *India* 62 E8
Kirchberg, *Switz.* 22 B5
Kirchhain, *Germany* 18 E4
Kirchheim, *Germany* 19 G5
Kirchheim-Bolanden, *Germany* 19 F4
Kirensk, *Russia* 45 D11
Kirgella Rocks, *Australia* 89 F3
Kirghizia ■ = Kyrgyzstan ■, *Asia* 44 E8
Kirghizstan = Kyrgyzstan ■, *Asia* 44 E8
Kiri, *Zaïre* 80 E3
Kiribati ■, *Pac. Oc.* 92 H10
Kırıkhan, *Turkey* 66 D7
Kırıkkale, *Turkey* 66 C5
Kirillov, *Russia* 40 C10
Kirin = Jilin, *China* 51 C14
Kirin = Jilin □, *China* 51 C13
Kirishi, *Russia* 40 C7
Kiritimati, *Kiribati* 93 G12
Kırka, *Turkey* 66 C4
Kirkcaldy, *U.K.* 14 E5
Kirkcudbright, *U.K.* 14 G4
Kirkee, *India* 60 K8
Kirkenær, *Norway* 10 D6
Kirkenes, *Norway* 8 B23
Kirkintilloch, *U.K.* 14 F4
Kirkjubæjarklaustur, *Iceland* 8 E4
Kirkkonummi, *Finland* 9 F21
Kirkland, *U.S.A.* 111 J7
Kirkland Lake, *Canada* 98 C3
Kırklareli, *Turkey* 66 B2
Kirksville, *U.S.A.* 108 E8
Kirkūk, *Iraq* 67 E11
Kirkwall, *U.K.* 14 C6
Kirkwood, *S. Africa* 84 E4
Kirn, *Germany* 19 F3
Kirov, *Russia* 42 C2
Kirov, *Russia* 44 D5
Kirovabad = Gäncä, *Azerbaijan* 43 K8
Kirovakan = Vanadzor, *Armenia* 43 K7
Kirovograd = Kirovohrad, *Ukraine* 41 H7
Kirovohrad, *Ukraine* 41 H7
Kirovsk = Babadayhan, *Turkmenistan* 44 F7
Kirovsk, *Russia* 44 C4
Kirovskiy, *Russia* 43 H9
Kirovskiy, *Kamchatka, Russia* 45 D16
Kirovskiy, *Primorsk, Russia* 48 B6
Kirriemuir, *U.K.* 14 E6
Kirsanov, *Russia* 42 D6
Kırşehir, *Turkey* 66 C6
Kirtachi, *Niger* 79 C5
Kirthar Range, *Pakistan* 62 F2
Kiruna, *Sweden* 8 C19
Kirundu, *Zaïre* 82 C2
Kirup, *Australia* 89 F2
Kirya, *Russia* 42 C8
Kiryū, *Japan* 49 F9
Kisaga, *Tanzania* 82 C3
Kisalaya, *Nic.* 116 D3
Kisámou, Kólpos, *Greece* 37 D5
Kisanga, *Zaïre* 82 B2
Kisangani, *Zaïre* 82 B2
Kisar, *Indonesia* 57 F7
Kisaran, *Indonesia* 56 D1
Kisarawe, *Tanzania* 82 D4
Kisarawe □, *Tanzania* 82 D4
Kisarazu, *Japan* 49 G9
Kisbér, *Hungary* 21 H8
Kiselevsk, *Russia* 44 D9
Kishanganga →, *Pakistan* 63 B5
Kishanganj, *India* 63 F13
Kishangarh, *India* 62 F4
Kishi, *Nigeria* 79 D5
Kishinev = Chişinău, *Moldova* 41 J5
Kishiwada, *Japan* 49 G7
Kishtwar, *India* 63 C6
Kisii, *Kenya* 82 C3
Kisii □, *Kenya* 82 C3
Kisiju, *Tanzania* 82 D4
Kisir, *Turkey* 67 B10
Kisizi, *Uganda* 82 C2
Kiska I., *U.S.A.* 96 C1
Kiskatinaw →, *Canada* 100 B4
Kiskittogisu L., *Canada* 101 C9
Kiskőrös, *Hungary* 21 J9
Kiskundorozsma, *Hungary* 21 J10
Kiskunfélegyháza, *Hungary* 21 J9
Kiskunhalas, *Hungary* 21 J9
Kiskunmajsa, *Hungary* 21 J9
Kislovodsk, *Russia* 43 J6
Kismayu = Chisimaio, *Somali Rep.* 71 G8
Kiso-Gawa →, *Japan* 49 G8
Kiso-Sammyaku, *Japan* 49 G8
Kisofukushima, *Japan* 49 G8
Kisoro, *Uganda* 82 C2
Kispest, *Hungary* 21 H9
Kissidougou, *Guinea* 78 D2
Kissimmee, *U.S.A.* 105 L5
Kissimmee →, *U.S.A.* 105 M5
Kississing L., *Canada* 101 B8
Kissónerga, *Cyprus* 37 E11
Kistanje, *Croatia* 33 E12
Kisújszállás, *Hungary* 21 H10
Kisumu, *Kenya* 82 C3
Kisvárda, *Hungary* 21 G12
Kiswani, *Tanzania* 82 C4
Kiswere, *Tanzania* 83 D4
Kit Carson, *U.S.A.* 108 F3
Kita, *Mali* 78 C3
Kitab, *Uzbekistan* 44 F7
Kitaibaraki, *Japan* 49 F10
Kitakami, *Japan* 48 E10
Kitakami-Gawa →, *Japan* 48 E10
Kitakami-Sammyaku, *Japan* 48 E10
Kitakata, *Japan* 48 F9
Kitakyūshū, *Japan* 49 H5
Kitale, *Kenya* 82 B4
Kitami, *Japan* 48 C11
Kitami-Sammyaku, *Japan* 48 B11
Kitangiri, L., *Tanzania* 82 C3
Kitaya, *Tanzania* 83 E5
Kitchener, *Australia* 89 F3
Kitchener, *Canada* 98 D3
Kitee, *Finland* 40 A6
Kitega = Gitega, *Burundi* 82 C2
Kitengo, *Zaïre* 82 D1
Kiteto □, *Tanzania* 82 C4
Kitgum, *Uganda* 82 B3
Kíthira, *Greece* 39 N7
Kíthnos, *Greece* 39 M7
Kiti, *Cyprus* 37 E12
Kiti, C., *Cyprus* 37 E12
Kitikmeot □, *Canada* 96 A9
Kitimat, *Canada* 100 C3
Kitinen →, *Finland* 8 C22
Kitiyab, *Sudan* 77 D3
Kítros, *Greece* 39 J5
Kitsuki, *Japan* 49 H5
Kittakittaooloo, L., *Australia* 91 D2
Kittanning, *U.S.A.* 106 F5
Kittatinny Mts., *U.S.A.* 107 E10
Kittery, *U.S.A.* 105 D10
Kittilä, *Finland* 8 C21
Kitui, *Kenya* 82 C4
Kitui □, *Kenya* 82 C4
Kitwe, *Zambia* 83 E2
Kitzbühel, *Austria* 19 H8
Kitzingen, *Germany* 19 F6
Kivarli, *India* 62 G5
Kivertsi, *Ukraine* 41 G3
Kividhes, *Cyprus* 37 E11
Kivu □, *Zaïre* 82 C2
Kivu, L., *Zaïre* 82 C2
Kiyev = Kyyiv, *Ukraine* 41 G6
Kiyevskoye Vdkhr. = Kyyivske Vdskh., *Ukraine* 41 G6
Kiziguru, *Rwanda* 82 C3
Kızıl Irmak →, *Turkey* 66 B6
Kizil Jilga, *India* 63 B8
Kizil Yurt, *Russia* 43 J8
Kızılcahamam, *Turkey* 66 B5
Kızılhisar, *Turkey* 66 D3
Kızılırmak, *Turkey* 66 B5
Kızıltepe, *Turkey* 67 D9
Kizimkazi, *Tanzania* 82 D4
Kizlyar, *Russia* 43 J8
Kizyl-Arvat = Gyzylarbat, *Turkmenistan* 44 F6
Kjellerup, *Denmark* 11 H3
Kjölur, *Iceland* 8 D4
Kladanj, *Bos.-H.* 21 L8
Kladno, *Czech.* 20 E4
Kladovo, *Serbia, Yug.* 21 L12
Klaeng, *Thailand* 58 F3
Klagenfurt, *Austria* 21 J4
Klagshamn, *Sweden* 11 J6
Klagstorp, *Sweden* 11 J7
Klaipėda, *Lithuania* 9 J19
Klaksvík, *Færoe Is.* 8 E9
Klamath →, *U.S.A.* 110 F1
Klamath Falls, *U.S.A.* 110 E3
Klamath Mts., *U.S.A.* 110 F2
Klanjec, *Croatia* 33 B12
Klappan →, *Canada* 100 B3
Klarälven →, *Sweden* 9 G15
Klaten, *Indonesia* 57 G14
Klatovy, *Czech.* 20 F3
Klausen = Chiusa, *Italy* 33 B8
Klawer, *S. Africa* 84 E2
Klawock, *U.S.A.* 100 B2
Klazienaveen, *Neths.* 16 C10
Kleczew, *Poland* 20 C8
Kleena Kleene, *Canada* 100 C4
Klein, *U.S.A.* 110 C9
Klein-Karas, *Namibia* 84 D2
Kleine Gette →, *Belgium* 17 G6
Kleine Nete →, *Belgium* 17 F5
Klekovača, *Bos.-H.* 33 D13
Klenovec, *Macedonia* 39 H3
Klenovec, *Slovak Rep.* 20 G9
Klerksdorp, *S. Africa* 84 D4
Kletnya, *Russia* 40 F7
Kletsk = Klyetsk, *Belarus* 41 F4
Kletskiy, *Russia* 43 F6
Kleve, *Germany* 18 D2
Klickitat, *U.S.A.* 110 D3
Klickitat →, *U.S.A.* 112 E5
Klidhes, *Cyprus* 37 D13
Klimovichi, *Belarus* 40 F6
Klin, *Russia* 42 B3
Klinaklini →, *Canada* 100 C3
Klintsy, *Russia* 41 F7
Klipdale, *S. Africa* 84 E2
Klipplaat, *S. Africa* 84 E3
Klitmøller, *Denmark* 11 G2
Kljajićevo, *Serbia, Yug.* 21 K9
Ključ, *Bos.-H.* 33 D13
Kłobuck, *Poland* 20 E8
Kłodzko, *Poland* 20 E6
Kloetinge, *Neths.* 17 F3
Klondike, *Canada* 96 B6
Kloosterzande, *Neths.* 17 F4
Klosterneuburg, *Austria* 21 G6
Klosters, *Switz.* 23 C9
Kloten, *Switz.* 23 B7
Klötze, *Germany* 18 C7
Klouto, *Togo* 79 D5
Kluane L., *Canada* 96 B6
Kluczbork, *Poland* 20 E8
Klundert, *Neths.* 17 E5
Klyetsk, *Belarus* 41 F4
Klyuchevskaya, Gora, *Russia* 45 D17
Knaresborough, *U.K.* 12 C6
Knee L., *Man., Canada* 101 B10
Knee L., *Sask., Canada* 101 B7
Kneïss, Is., *Tunisia* 75 B7
Knesselare, *Belgium* 17 F2
Knezha, *Bulgaria* 38 F7
Knić, *Serbia, Yug.* 21 M10
Knight Inlet, *Canada* 100 C3
Knighton, *U.K.* 13 E4
Knights Ferry, *U.S.A.* 112 H6
Knights Landing, *U.S.A.* 112 G5
Knin, *Croatia* 33 D13
Knittelfeld, *Austria* 21 H4
Knjaževac, *Serbia, Yug.* 21 M12
Knob, C., *Australia* 89 F2
Knockmealdown Mts., *Ireland* 15 D4
Knokke, *Belgium* 17 F2
Knossós, *Greece* 37 D7
Knox, *U.S.A.* 104 E2
Knox, C., *Canada* 100 C2
Knox City, *U.S.A.* 109 J5
Knox Coast, *Antarctica* 5 C8
Knoxville, *Iowa, U.S.A.* 108 E8
Knoxville, *Tenn., U.S.A.* 105 H4
Knutshø, *Norway* 10 B3
Knysna, *S. Africa* 84 E3
Knyszyn, *Poland* 20 B12
Ko Kha, *Thailand* 58 C2
Ko Tao, *Thailand* 59 G2
Koartac = Quaqtaq, *Canada* 97 B13
Koba, *Aru, Indonesia* 57 F8
Koba, *Bangka, Indonesia* 56 E3
Kobarid, *Slovenia* 33 B10
Kobayashi, *Japan* 49 J5
Kobdo = Hovd, *Mongolia* 54 B4
Kōbe, *Japan* 49 G7
Kobelyaky, *Ukraine* 41 H8
København, *Denmark* 11 J6
Kōbi-Sho, *Japan* 49 M1
Koblenz, *Germany* 19 E3
Koblenz, *Switz.* 22 A6
Kobo, *Ethiopia* 77 E4
Kobroor, Kepulauan, *Indonesia* 57 F8
Kobryn, *Belarus* 41 F3
Kobuleti, *Georgia* 43 K5
Kobyłka, *Poland* 20 C11
Kobylkino, *Russia* 42 C6
Kocaeli = İzmit, *Turkey* 66 B3
Kočani, *Macedonia* 39 H5
Koceljevo, *Serbia, Yug.* 21 L9
Kočevje, *Slovenia* 33 C11
Koch Bihar, *India* 61 F16
Kochang, *S. Korea* 51 G14
Kochas, *India* 63 G10
Kocher →, *Germany* 19 F5
Kocheya, *Russia* 45 D13
Kōchi, *Japan* 49 H6
Kōchi □, *Japan* 49 H6
Kochiu = Gejiu, *China* 52 F4
Kodiak, *U.S.A.* 96 C4
Kodiak I., *U.S.A.* 96 C4
Kodinar, *India* 62 J4
Kodori →, *Georgia* 43 J5
Koekelare, *Belgium* 17 F1
Koersel, *Belgium* 17 F6
Koes, *Namibia* 84 D2
Koffiefontein, *S. Africa* 84 D4
Kofiau, *Indonesia* 57 E7
Koforidua, *Ghana* 79 D4
Kōfu, *Japan* 49 G9
Koga, *Japan* 49 F9
Kogaluk →, *Canada* 99 A7
Kogan, *Australia* 91 D5
Køge, *Denmark* 9 J15
Kogi □, *Nigeria* 79 D6
Kogin Baba, *Nigeria* 79 D7
Koh-i-Bābā, *Afghan.* 60 B5
Koh-i-Khurd, *Afghan.* 62 C1
Kohat, *Pakistan* 62 C4
Kohima, *India* 61 G19
Kohkīlūyeh va Būyer Aḥmadi □, *Iran* 65 D6
Kohler Ra., *Antarctica* 5 D15
Kohtla-Järve, *Estonia* 9 G22
Koillismaa, *Finland* 8 D23
Koin-dong, *N. Korea* 51 D14
Kojō, *N. Korea* 51 E14
Kojonup, *Australia* 89 F2
Kojūr, *Iran* 65 B6
Koka, *Sudan* 76 C3
Kokand = Qŭqon, *Uzbekistan* 44 E8
Kokanee Glacier Prov. Park, *Canada* 100 D5
Kokas, *Indonesia* 57 E8
Kokchetav = Kökshetaū, *Kazakstan* 44 D7
Kokemäenjoki →, *Finland* 9 F19
Kokerite, *Guyana* 121 B6
Kokhma, *Russia* 42 B5
Kokkola, *Finland* 8 E20
Koko, *Nigeria* 79 C5
Koko Kyunzu, *Burma* 61 M18
Kokolopozo, *Ivory C.* 78 D3
Kokomo, *U.S.A.* 104 E2
Kokonau, *Indonesia* 57 E9
Kokoro, *Niger* 79 C5
Koksan, *N. Korea* 51 E14
Kökshetaū, *Kazakstan* 44 D7
Koksoak →, *Canada* 97 C13
Kokstad, *S. Africa* 85 E4
Kokubu, *Japan* 49 J5
Kokuora, *Russia* 45 B15
Kola, *Indonesia* 57 F8
Kola, *Russia* 44 C4
Kola Pen. = Kolskiy Poluostrov, *Russia* 44 C4
Kolahoi, *India* 63 B6
Kolahun, *Liberia* 78 D2
Kolaka, *Indonesia* 57 E6
Kolar, *India* 60 N11
Kolar Gold Fields, *India* 60 N11
Kolari, *Finland* 8 C20
Kolayat, *India* 60 F8
Kolby Kås, *Denmark* 11 J4
Kolchugino = Leninsk-Kuznetskiy, *Russia* 44 D9
Kolchugino, *Russia* 42 B4
Kolda, *Senegal* 78 C2
Kolding, *Denmark* 11 J3
Kole, *Zaïre* 80 E4
Koléa, *Algeria* 75 A5
Kolepom = Yos Sudarso, Pulau, *Indonesia* 57 F9
Kolguyev, Ostrov, *Russia* 44 C5
Kolham, *Neths.* 16 B9
Kolhapur, *India* 60 L9
Kolia, *Ivory C.* 78 D3
Kolín, *Czech.* 20 E5
Kolind, *Denmark* 11 H4
Kolkas Rags, *Latvia* 9 H20
Kölleda, *Germany* 18 D7
Kollum, *Neths.* 16 B8
Kolmanskop, *Namibia* 84 D2
Köln, *Germany* 18 E2
Koło, *Poland* 20 C8
Kołobrzeg, *Poland* 20 A5
Kolokani, *Mali* 78 C3
Kolomna, *Russia* 42 C4
Kolomyya, *Ukraine* 41 H3
Kolondiéba, *Mali* 78 C3
Kolonodale, *Indonesia* 57 E6
Kolosib, *India* 61 G18
Kolpashevo, *Russia* 44 D9
Kolpino, *Russia* 40 C6
Kolpny, *Russia* 42 D3
Kolskiy Poluostrov, *Russia* 44 C4
Kolubara →, *Serbia, Yug.* 21 L10
Koluszki, *Poland* 20 D9
Kolwezi, *Zaïre* 83 E2
Kolyma →, *Russia* 45 C17
Kolymskoye Nagorye, *Russia* 45 C16
Kôm Ombo, *Egypt* 76 C3
Komandorskiye Is. = Komandorskiye Ostrova, *Russia* 45 D17
Komandorskiye Ostrova, *Russia* 45 D17
Komárno, *Slovak Rep.* 21 H8
Komárom, *Hungary* 21 H8
Komatipoort, *S. Africa* 85 D5
Komatou Yialou, *Cyprus* 37 D13
Komatsu, *Japan* 49 F8
Komatsujima, *Japan* 49 H7
Kombissiri, *Burkina Faso* 79 C4
Kombori, *Burkina Faso* 78 C4
Komen, *Slovenia* 33 C10
Komenda, *Ghana* 79 D4
Komi □, *Russia* 44 C6
Komiža, *Croatia* 33 E13
Komló, *Hungary* 21 J8
Kommunarsk = Alchevsk, *Ukraine* 41 H10
Kommunizma, Pik, *Tajikistan* 44 F8
Komodo, *Indonesia* 57 F5
Komoé, *Ivory C.* 78 D4
Komono, *Congo* 80 E2
Komoran, Pulau, *Indonesia* 57 F9
Komoro, *Japan* 49 F9
Komotini, *Greece* 39 H8
Kompasberg, *S. Africa* 84 E3
Kompong Bang, *Cambodia* 59 F5
Kompong Cham, *Cambodia* 59 F5
Kompong Chhnang, *Cambodia* 59 F5
Kompong Chikreng, *Cambodia* 58 F5
Kompong Kleang, *Cambodia* 58 F5
Kompong Luong, *Cambodia* 59 G5
Kompong Pranak, *Cambodia* 58 F5
Kompong Som, *Cambodia* 59 G4
Kompong Som, Chhung, *Cambodia* 59 G4
Kompong Speu, *Cambodia* 59 G5
Kompong Sralao, *Cambodia* 58 E5
Kompong Thom, *Cambodia* 58 F5
Kompong Trabeck, *Cambodia* 58 F5
Kompong Trabeck, *Cambodia* 59 G5
Kompong Trach, *Cambodia* 59 G5
Kompong Tralach, *Cambodia* 59 G5
Komrat = Comrat, *Moldova* 41 J5
Komsberg, *S. Africa* 84 E3
Komsomolets, Ostrov, *Russia* 45 A10
Komsomolsk, *Russia* 42 B5
Komsomolsk, *Russia* 45 D14
Komsomolskiy, *Russia* 42 C7
Konakovo, *Russia* 42 B3
Konarhá □, *Afghan.* 60 B7
Konārī, *Iran* 65 D6
Konawa, *U.S.A.* 109 H6
Konch, *India* 63 G8
Kondakovo, *Russia* 45 C16
Konde, *Tanzania* 82 C4
Kondinin, *Australia* 89 F2
Kondoa, *Tanzania* 82 C4
Kondoa □, *Tanzania* 82 D4
Kondókali, *Greece* 37 A3
Kondopaga, *Russia* 40 A8
Kondratyevo, *Russia* 45 D10
Kondrovo, *Russia* 42 C2
Konduga, *Nigeria* 79 C7
Köneürgench, *Turkmenistan* 44 E6
Konevo, *Russia* 40 A10
Kong, *Ivory C.* 78 D4
Kong →, *Cambodia* 58 F5
Kong, Koh, *Cambodia* 59 G4
Kong Christian IX.s Land, *Greenland* 4 C6
Kong Christian X.s Land, *Greenland* 4 B6
Kong Franz Joseph Fd., *Greenland* 4 B6
Kong Frederik IX.s Land, *Greenland* 4 C5
Kong Frederik VI.s Kyst, *Greenland* 4 C5
Kong Frederik VIII.s Land, *Greenland* 4 B6
Kong Oscar Fjord, *Greenland* 4 B6
Kongeå →, *Denmark* 11 J3
Kongju, *S. Korea* 51 F14
Konglu, *Burma* 61 F20
Kongolo, *Kasai Or., Zaïre* 82 D1
Kongolo, *Shaba, Zaïre* 82 D2
Kongor, *Sudan* 77 F3
Kongoussi, *Burkina Faso* 79 C4
Kongsberg, *Norway* 10 E3
Kongsvinger, *Norway* 10 D6
Kongwa, *Tanzania* 82 D4
Koni, *Zaïre* 83 E2
Koni, Mts., *Zaïre* 83 E2
Königsberg = Kaliningrad, *Russia* 9 J19
Königslutter, *Germany* 18 C6
Königswusterhausen, *Germany* 18 C9
Konin, *Poland* 20 C8
Kónitsa, *Greece* 39 J3
Köniz, *Switz.* 22 C4
Konjice, *Slovenia* 33 B12
Konkiep, *Namibia* 84 D2
Konkouré →, *Guinea* 78 D2
Könnern, *Germany* 18 D7
Kono, *S. Leone* 78 D2
Konolfingen, *Switz.* 22 C5
Konongo, *Ghana* 79 D4
Konosha, *Russia* 40 B11
Kōnosu, *Japan* 49 F9
Konotop, *Ukraine* 41 G7
Konqi He →, *China* 54 B4
Końskie, *Poland* 20 D10
Konstantinovka = Kostyantynivka, *Ukraine* 41 H9
Konstantinovsk, *Russia* 43 G5
Konstanz, *Germany* 19 H5
Kont, *Iran* 65 E9
Kontagora, *Nigeria* 79 C6
Kontich, *Belgium* 17 F4
Kontum, *Vietnam* 58 E7
Kontum, Plateau du, *Vietnam* 58 E7
Konya, *Turkey* 66 D5
Konya Ovası, *Turkey* 66 C5
Konz, *Germany* 19 F2
Konza, *Kenya* 82 C4
Kookynie, *Australia* 89 E3
Kooline, *Australia* 88 D2
Kooloonong, *Australia* 91 E3
Koolyanobbing, *Australia* 89 F2
Koondrook, *Australia* 91 F3
Koonibba, *Australia* 91 E1
Koorawatha, *Australia* 91 E4
Koorda, *Australia* 89 F2
Kooskia, *U.S.A.* 110 C6
Kootenai →, *Canada* 110 B5
Kootenay L., *Canada* 100 D5
Kootenay Nat. Park, *Canada* 100 C5
Kootjieskolk, *S. Africa* 84 E3
Kopanovka, *Russia* 43 G8
Kopaonik, *Serbia, Yug.* 21 M11
Kópavogur, *Iceland* 8 D3
Koper, *Slovenia* 33 C10
Kopervik, *Norway* 9 G11
Kopeysk, *Russia* 44 D7
Kopi, *Australia* 91 E2
Köping, *Sweden* 10 E10
Kopiste, *Croatia* 33 F13
Köpmanholmen, *Sweden* 10 A12
Koppang, *Norway* 10 C5
Kopperå, *Norway* 10 A5
Koppies, *S. Africa* 85 D4
Koprivnica, *Croatia* 33 B13

Kopychyntsi, *Ukraine* 41 H3
Korab, *Macedonia* 39 H3
Korakiána, *Greece* 37 A3
Korba, *India* 63 H10
Korbach, *Germany* 18 D4
Korbu, G., *Malaysia* 59 K3
Korça, *Albania* 39 J3
Korce = Korça, *Albania* 39 J3
Korčula, *Croatia* 33 F14
Korčulanski Kanal, *Croatia* 33 E13
Kord Küy, *Iran* 65 B7
Kord Sheykh, *Iran* 65 D7
Kordestān □, *Iran* 64 C5
Kordofân, *Sudan* 73 F10
Korea, North ■, *Asia* 51 E14
Korea, South ■, *Asia* 51 F15
Korea Bay, *Korea* 51 E13
Korea Strait, *Asia* 51 G15
Korenevo, *Russia* 42 E2
Korenovsk, *Russia* 43 H4
Korets, *Ukraine* 41 G4
Korgan, *Turkey* 66 B7
Korgus, *Sudan* 76 D3
Korhogo, *Ivory C.* 78 D3
Koribundu, *S. Leone* 78 D2
Korim, *Indonesia* 57 E9
Korinthiakós Kólpos, *Greece* 39 L5
Kórinthos, *Greece* 39 M5
Korioumé, *Mali* 78 B4
Koríssa, Límni, *Greece* 37 B3
Kōriyama, *Japan* 48 F10
Korkuteli, *Turkey* 66 D4
Kormakiti, C., *Cyprus* 37 D11
Körmend, *Hungary* 21 H6
Kornat, *Croatia* 33 E12
Korneshty = Corneşti, *Moldova* 41 J5
Kornsjø, *Norway* 10 F5
Kornstad, *Norway* 10 B1
Koro, *Fiji* 87 C8
Koro, *Ivory C.* 78 D3
Koro, *Mali* 78 C4
Koro Sea, *Fiji* 87 C9
Korocha, *Russia* 42 E3
Köroğlu Dağları, *Turkey* 66 B5
Korogwe, *Tanzania* 82 D4
Korogwe □, *Tanzania* 82 D4
Koroit, *Australia* 91 F3
Koronadal, *Phil.* 55 H6
Koronowo, *Poland* 20 B7
Koror, *Pac. Oc.* 57 C8
Körös →, *Hungary* 21 J10
Korosten, *Ukraine* 41 G5
Korostyshev, *Ukraine* 41 G5
Korotoyak, *Russia* 42 E4
Korraraika, Helodranon' i, *Madag.* 85 B7
Korsakov, *Russia* 45 E15
Korshunovo, *Russia* 45 D12
Korsør, *Denmark* 9 J14
Korsun Shevchenkovskiy, *Ukraine* 41 H6
Korsze, *Poland* 20 A11
Kortemark, *Belgium* 17 F2
Kortessem, *Belgium* 17 G6
Korti, *Sudan* 76 D3
Kortrijk, *Belgium* 17 G2
Korwai, *India* 62 G8
Koryakskoye Nagorye, *Russia* 45 C18
Koryŏng, *S. Korea* 51 G15
Koryukovka, *Ukraine* 41 G7
Kos, *Greece* 39 N10
Kosa, *Ethiopia* 77 F4
Kosaya Gora, *Russia* 42 C3
Kościan, *Poland* 20 C6
Kościerzyna, *Poland* 20 A7
Kosciusko, *U.S.A.* 109 J10
Kosciusko, Mt., *Australia* 91 F4
Kosciusko I., *U.S.A.* 100 B2
Kösély →, *Hungary* 21 H11
Kosha, *Sudan* 76 C3
K'oshih = Kashi, *China* 54 C2
Koshiki-Rettō, *Japan* 49 J4
Kosi, *India* 62 F7
Košice, *Slovak Rep.* 20 G11
Kosjerić, *Serbia, Yug.* 21 M9
Koskhinoú, *Greece* 37 C10
Kosŏng, *N. Korea* 51 E15
Kosovska-Mitrovica = Titova-Mitrovica, *Serbia, Yug.* 21 N10
Kostajnica, *Croatia* 33 C13
Kostanjevica, *Slovenia* 33 C12
Kostelec, *Czech.* 20 E6
Koster, *S. Africa* 84 D4
Kôstî, *Sudan* 77 E3
Kostopil, *Ukraine* 41 G4
Kostroma, *Russia* 42 B5
Kostromskoye Vdkhr., *Russia* 42 B5
Kostyantynivka, *Ukraine* 41 H9
Kostyukovichi = Kastsyukovichy, *Belarus* 40 F7
Koszalin, *Poland* 20 A6
Köszeg, *Hungary* 21 H6
Kot Addu, *Pakistan* 62 D4
Kot Moman, *Pakistan* 62 C5
Kota, *India* 62 G6
Kota Baharu, *Malaysia* 59 J4
Kota Belud, *Malaysia* 56 C5
Kota Kinabalu, *Malaysia* 56 C5
Kota Tinggi, *Malaysia* 59 M4
Kotaagung, *Indonesia* 56 F2
Kotabaru, *Indonesia* 56 E5
Kotabumi, *Indonesia* 56 E2
Kotagede, *Indonesia* 57 G14
Kotamobagu, *Indonesia* 57 D6
Kotaneelee →, *Canada* 100 A4
Kotawaringin, *Indonesia* 56 E4
Kotcho L., *Canada* 100 B4
Kotelnich, *Russia* 42 A9
Kotelnikovo, *Russia* 43 G6
Kotelnyy, Ostrov, *Russia* 45 B14
Köthen, *Germany* 18 D7
Kothi, *India* 63 G9
Kotiro, *Pakistan* 62 F2
Kotka, *Finland* 9 F22
Kotlas, *Russia* 44 C5
Kotli, *Pakistan* 62 C5
Kotmul, *Pakistan* 63 B6
Kotonkoro, *Nigeria* 79 C6
Kotor, *Montenegro, Yug.* 21 N8
Kotoriba, *Croatia* 33 B13
Kotovo, *Russia* 42 E7
Kotovsk, *Russia* 42 D5
Kotovsk, *Ukraine* 41 J5
Kotputli, *India* 62 F7
Kotri, *Pakistan* 62 G3
Kótronas, *Greece* 39 N5
Kottayam, *India* 60 Q10
Kotturu, *India* 60 M10
Kotuy →, *Russia* 45 B11
Kotzebue, *U.S.A.* 96 B3
Kouango, *C.A.R.* 80 C4
Koudekerke, *Neths.* 17 F3
Koudougou, *Burkina Faso* 78 C4
Koufonísi, *Greece* 37 E8
Kougaberge, *S. Africa* 84 E3
Kouibli, *Ivory C.* 78 D3
Kouilou →, *Congo* 80 E2
Kouki, *C.A.R.* 80 C3
Koula Moutou, *Gabon* 80 E2
Koulen, *Cambodia* 58 F5
Koulikoro, *Mali* 78 C3
Kouloúra, *Greece* 37 A3
Koúm-bournoú, Ákra, *Greece* 37 C10
Koumala, *Australia* 90 C4
Koumankou, *Mali* 78 C3
Koumbia, *Burkina Faso* 78 C4
Koumbia, *Guinea* 78 C2
Koumboum, *Guinea* 78 C2
Koumpenntoum, *Senegal* 78 C2
Koumra, *Chad* 73 G8
Koundara, *Guinea* 78 C2
Kounradskiy, *Kazakstan* 44 E8
Kountze, *U.S.A.* 109 K7
Koupéla, *Burkina Faso* 79 C4
Kouris →, *Cyprus* 37 E11
Kourou, *Fr. Guiana* 121 B7
Kouroussa, *Guinea* 78 C3
Koussané, *Mali* 78 C2
Kousseri, *Cameroon* 73 F7
Koutiala, *Mali* 78 C3
Kouto, *Ivory C.* 78 D3
Kouvé, *Togo* 79 D5
Kouvola, *Finland* 9 F22
Kovačica, *Serbia, Yug.* 21 K10
Kovel, *Ukraine* 41 G3
Kovin, *Serbia, Yug.* 21 L10
Kovrov, *Russia* 42 B5
Kowanyama, *Australia* 90 B3
Kowkash, *Canada* 98 B2
Kowloon, *H.K.* 53 F10
Kowŏn, *N. Korea* 51 E14
Köyceğiz, *Turkey* 66 D3
Koyuk, *U.S.A.* 96 B3
Koyukuk →, *U.S.A.* 96 B4
Koyulhisar, *Turkey* 66 B7
Koza, *Japan* 49 L3
Kozan, *Turkey* 66 D6
Kozáni, *Greece* 39 J4
Kozara, *Bos.-H.* 33 D14
Kozarac, *Bos.-H.* 33 D13
Kozelets, *Ukraine* 41 G6
Kozelsk, *Russia* 42 C2
Kozhikode = Calicut, *India* 60 P9
Kozje, *Slovenia* 33 B12
Kozlovets, *Bulgaria* 38 F8
Kozlovka, *Russia* 42 C9
Kozlu, *Turkey* 66 B4
Kozluk, *Turkey* 67 C9
Koźmin, *Poland* 20 D7
Kozmodemyansk, *Russia* 42 B8
Kozyatyn, *Ukraine* 41 H5
Kpabia, *Ghana* 79 D4
Kpalimé, *Togo* 79 D5
Kpandae, *Ghana* 79 D4
Kpessi, *Togo* 79 D5
Kra, Isthmus of = Kra, Kho Khot, *Thailand* 59 G2
Kra, Kho Khot, *Thailand* 59 G2
Kra Buri, *Thailand* 59 G2
Krabbendijke, *Neths.* 17 F4
Krabi, *Thailand* 59 H2
Kragan, *Indonesia* 57 G14
Kragerø, *Norway* 10 F3
Kragujevac, *Serbia, Yug.* 21 L10
Krajina, *Bos.-H.* 33 D13
Krakatau = Rakata, Pulau, *Indonesia* 56 F3
Krakor, *Cambodia* 58 F5
Kraków, *Poland* 20 E9
Kraksaan, *Indonesia* 57 G15
Kråkstad, *Norway* 10 E4
Kralanh, *Cambodia* 58 F4
Králiky, *Czech.* 20 E6
Kraljevo, *Serbia, Yug.* 21 M10
Kralovice, *Czech.* 20 F3
Kralupy, *Czech.* 20 E4
Kramatorsk, *Ukraine* 41 H9
Kramfors, *Sweden* 10 B11
Kramis, C., *Algeria* 75 A5
Krångede, *Sweden* 10 A10
Kranj, *Slovenia* 33 B11
Kranjska Gora, *Slovenia* 33 B10
Krankskop, *S. Africa* 85 D5
Krapina, *Croatia* 33 B12
Krapina →, *Croatia* 33 C12
Krapkowice, *Poland* 20 E7
Kraskino, *Russia* 45 E14
Krāslava, *Latvia* 40 E4
Kraslice, *Czech.* 20 E2
Krasnaya Gorbatka, *Russia* 42 C5
Krasnaya Polyana, *Russia* 43 J5
Kraśnik, *Poland* 20 E12
Kraśnik Fabryczny, *Poland* 20 E12
Krasnoarmeisk, *Ukraine* 41 H9
Krasnoarmeysk, *Russia* 42 E7
Krasnoarmeyskiy, *Russia* 43 G6
Krasnodar, *Russia* 43 H4
Krasnodon, *Ukraine* 41 H10
Krasnogorskiy, *Russia* 42 B9
Krasnograd = Krasnohrad, *Ukraine* 41 H8
Krasnogvardeyskoye, *Russia* 43 H5
Krasnogvardyesk, *Ukraine* 41 K8
Krasnohrad, *Ukraine* 41 H8
Krasnokutsk, *Ukraine* 41 G8
Krasnolesnyy, *Russia* 42 E4
Krasnoperekopsk, *Ukraine* 41 J7
Krasnorechenskiy, *Russia* 48 B7
Krasnoselkupsk, *Russia* 44 C9
Krasnoslobodsk, *Russia* 42 C6
Krasnoslobodsk, *Russia* 43 F7
Krasnoturinsk, *Russia* 44 D7
Krasnoufimsk, *Russia* 44 D6
Krasnouralsk, *Russia* 44 D7
Krasnovodsk = Türkmenbashi, *Turkmenistan* 44 E6
Krasnoyarsk, *Russia* 45 D10
Krasnoye = Krasnyy, *Russia* 40 E6
Krasnozavodsk, *Russia* 42 B4
Krasny Sulin, *Russia* 43 G5
Krasnystaw, *Poland* 20 E13
Krasnyy, *Russia* 40 E6
Krasnyy Kholm, *Russia* 42 A3
Krasnyy Kut, *Russia* 42 E8
Krasnyy Liman, *Ukraine* 41 H9
Krasnyy Luch, *Ukraine* 41 H10
Krasnyy Profintern, *Russia* 42 B5
Krasnyy Yar, *Russia* 42 D10
Krasnyy Yar, *Russia* 42 E7
Krasnyy Yar, *Russia* 43 G9
Krasnyye Baki, *Russia* 42 B7
Krasnyyoskolske Vdskh., *Ukraine* 41 H9
Kraszna →, *Hungary* 21 G12
Kratie, *Cambodia* 58 F6
Krau, *Indonesia* 57 E10
Kravanh, Chuor Phnum, *Cambodia* 59 G4
Krefeld, *Germany* 18 D2
Krémaston, Límni, *Greece* 39 L4
Kremenchug = Kremenchuk, *Ukraine* 41 H7
Kremenchuk, *Ukraine* 41 H7
Kremenchuksk Vdskh., *Ukraine* 41 H7
Kremenets, *Ukraine* 41 G3
Kremennaya, *Ukraine* 41 H10
Kremges = Svitlovodsk, *Ukraine* 41 H7
Kremikovtsi, *Bulgaria* 38 G6
Kremmen, *Germany* 18 C9
Kremmling, *U.S.A.* 110 F10
Krems, *Austria* 21 G5
Kremsmünster, *Austria* 21 G4
Kretinga, *Lithuania* 9 J19
Krettamia, *Algeria* 74 C4
Krettsy, *Russia* 40 C7
Kreuzberg, *Germany* 19 E5
Kreuzlingen, *Switz.* 23 A8
Kribi, *Cameroon* 79 E6
Krichem, *Bulgaria* 38 G7
Krichev = Krychaw, *Belarus* 40 F6
Krim, *Slovenia* 33 C11
Krimpen, *Neths.* 16 E5
Kriós, Ákra, *Greece* 37 D5
Krishna →, *India* 61 M12
Krishnanagar, *India* 63 H13
Kristiansand, *Norway* 9 G13
Kristianstad, *Sweden* 9 H16
Kristiansund, *Norway* 10 A1
Kristiinankaupunki, *Finland* 9 E19
Kristinehamn, *Sweden* 9 G16
Kristinestad = Kristiinankaupunki, *Finland* 9 E19
Kríti, *Greece* 37 D7
Kritsá, *Greece* 37 D7
Kriva →, *Macedonia* 38 G4
Kriva Palanka, *Macedonia* 38 G5
Krivaja →, *Bos.-H.* 21 L8
Krivoy Rog = Kryvyy Rih, *Ukraine* 41 J7
Križevci, *Croatia* 33 B13
Krk, *Croatia* 33 C11
Krka →, *Slovenia* 33 C12
Krkonoše, *Czech.* 20 E5
Krnov, *Czech.* 20 E7
Krobia, *Poland* 20 D6
Krokeaí, *Greece* 39 N5
Krokodil →, *Mozam.* 85 D5
Krokom, *Sweden* 10 A8
Krolevets, *Ukraine* 41 G7
Kroměříz, *Czech.* 20 F7
Krommenie, *Neths.* 16 D5
Kromy, *Russia* 42 D2
Kronach, *Germany* 19 E7
Kronprins Olav Kyst, *Antarctica* 5 C5
Kronshtadt, *Russia* 40 C5
Kroonstad, *S. Africa* 84 D4
Kröpelin, *Germany* 18 A7
Kropotkin, *Irkutsk, Russia* 45 D12
Kropotkin, *Krasnodar, Russia* 43 H5
Kropp, *Germany* 18 A5
Krościenko, *Poland* 20 F10
Krosno, *Poland* 20 F11
Krosno Odrzańskie, *Poland* 20 C5
Krotoszyn, *Poland* 20 D7
Krotovka, *Russia* 42 D10
Kroussón, *Greece* 37 D6
Krško, *Slovenia* 33 C12
Kruger Nat. Park, *S. Africa* 85 C5
Krugersdorp, *S. Africa* 85 D4
Kruiningen, *Neths.* 17 F4
Kruisfontein, *S. Africa* 84 E3
Kruishoutem, *Belgium* 17 G3
Kruisland, *Neths.* 17 E4
Kruja, *Albania* 39 H2
Krulevshchina = Krulyewshchyna, *Belarus* 40 E4
Krulyewshchyna, *Belarus* 40 E4
Kruma, *Albania* 38 G3
Krumbach, *Germany* 19 G6
Krung Thep = Bangkok, *Thailand* 58 F3
Krupanj, *Serbia, Yug.* 21 L9
Krupinica →, *Slovak Rep.* 21 G8
Krupki, *Belarus* 40 E5
Kruševac, *Serbia, Yug.* 21 M11
Kruzof I., *U.S.A.* 100 B1
Krychaw, *Belarus* 40 F6
Krymsk, *Russia* 43 H4
Krymskiy Poluostrov = Krymskyy Pivostriv, *Ukraine* 41 K8
Krymskyy Pivostriv, *Ukraine* 41 K8
Krynica Morska, *Poland* 20 A9
Krynki, *Poland* 20 B13
Kryvyy Rih, *Ukraine* 41 J7
Krzywiń, *Poland* 20 D6
Krzyz, *Poland* 20 C6
Ksabi, *Morocco* 74 B4
Ksar Chellala, *Algeria* 75 A5
Ksar el Boukhari, *Algeria* 75 A5
Ksar el Kebir, *Morocco* 74 B3
Ksar es Souk = Ar Rachidiya, *Morocco* 74 B4
Ksar Rhilane, *Tunisia* 75 B6
Ksour, Mts. des, *Algeria* 75 B4
Kstovo, *Russia* 42 B7
Kuala, *Indonesia* 56 D3
Kuala Berang, *Malaysia* 59 K4
Kuala Dungun, *Malaysia* 59 K4
Kuala Kangsar, *Malaysia* 59 K3
Kuala Kelawang, *Malaysia* 59 L4
Kuala Kerai, *Malaysia* 59 K4
Kuala Kubu Baharu, *Malaysia* 59 L3
Kuala Lipis, *Malaysia* 59 K4
Kuala Lumpur, *Malaysia* 59 L3
Kuala Nerang, *Malaysia* 59 J3
Kuala Pilah, *Malaysia* 59 L4
Kuala Rompin, *Malaysia* 59 L4
Kuala Selangor, *Malaysia* 59 L3
Kuala Terengganu, *Malaysia* 59 K4
Kualajelai, *Indonesia* 56 E4
Kualakapuas, *Indonesia* 56 E4
Kualakurun, *Indonesia* 56 E4
Kualapembuang, *Indonesia* 56 E4
Kualasimpang, *Indonesia* 56 D1
Kuancheng, *China* 51 D10
Kuandang, *Indonesia* 57 D6
Kuandian, *China* 51 D13
Kuangchou = Guangzhou, *China* 53 F9
Kuantan, *Malaysia* 59 L4
Kuba = Quba, *Azerbaijan* 43 K9
Kuban →, *Russia* 43 H3
Kubenskoye, Ozero, *Russia* 40 C10
Kubokawa, *Japan* 49 H6
Kubrat, *Bulgaria* 38 F9
Kučevo, *Serbia, Yug.* 21 L11
Kucha Gompa, *India* 63 B7
Kuchaman, *India* 62 F6
Kuchino-eruba-Jima, *Japan* 49 J5
Kuchino-Shima, *Japan* 49 K4
Kuchinotsu, *Japan* 49 H5
Kucing, *Malaysia* 56 D4
Kuçova, *Albania* 39 J2
Kud →, *Pakistan* 62 F2
Kuda, *India* 60 H7
Kudat, *Malaysia* 56 C5
Kudus, *Indonesia* 57 G14
Kudymkar, *Russia* 44 D6
Kueiyang = Guiyang, *China* 52 D6
Kufra Oasis = Al Kufrah, *Libya* 73 D9
Kufstein, *Austria* 19 H8
Kugluktuk, *Canada* 96 B8
Kugong I., *Canada* 98 A4
Kūh-e-Hazārām, *Iran* 65 D8
Kūhak, *Iran* 60 F3
Kūhbonān, *Iran* 65 D8
Kūhestak, *Iran* 65 E8
Kūhīn, *Iran* 65 C6
Kūhīrī, *Iran* 65 E9
Kuhnsdorf, *Austria* 21 J4
Kūhpāyeh, *Eşfahan, Iran* 65 C7
Kūhpāyeh, *Kermān, Iran* 65 D8
Kui Buri, *Thailand* 59 F2
Kuinre, *Neths.* 16 C7
Kuito, *Angola* 81 G3
Kujang, *N. Korea* 51 E14
Kuji, *Japan* 48 D10
Kujū-San, *Japan* 49 H5
Kukawa, *Nigeria* 79 C7
Kukerin, *Australia* 89 F2
Kukmor, *Russia* 42 B10
Kukup, *Malaysia* 59 M4
Kukvidze, *Russia* 42 E6
Kula, *Serbia, Yug.* 21 K9
Kula, *Turkey* 66 C3
Kulai, *Malaysia* 59 M4
Kulal, Mt., *Kenya* 82 B4
Kulaly, Ostrov, *Kazakstan* 43 H10
Kulasekarappattinam, *India* 60 Q11
Kuldiga, *Latvia* 9 H19
Kuldja = Yining, *China* 44 E9
Kuldu, *Sudan* 77 E2
Kulebaki, *Russia* 42 C6
Kulen Vakuf, *Bos.-H.* 33 D13
Kulgam, *India* 63 C6
Kulim, *Malaysia* 59 K3
Kulin, *Australia* 89 F2
Kulja, *Australia* 89 F2
Kulm, *U.S.A.* 108 B5
Kulmbach, *Germany* 19 E7
Kŭlob, *Tajikistan* 44 F7
Kulp, *Turkey* 67 C9
Kulsary, *Kazakstan* 44 E6
Kulti, *India* 63 H12
Kulu, *Turkey* 66 C5
Kulumbura, *Australia* 88 B4
Kulunda, *Russia* 44 D8
Kulungar, *Afghan.* 62 C3
Kūlvand, *Iran* 65 D7
Kulwin, *Australia* 91 F3
Kulyab = Kŭlob, *Tajikistan* 44 F7
Kum Tekei, *Kazakstan* 44 E8
Kuma →, *Russia* 43 H8
Kumaganum, *Nigeria* 79 C7
Kumagaya, *Japan* 49 F9
Kumai, *Indonesia* 56 E4
Kumamba, Kepulauan, *Indonesia* 57 E9
Kumamoto, *Japan* 49 H5
Kumamoto □, *Japan* 49 H5
Kumanovo, *Macedonia* 38 G4
Kumara, *N.Z.* 87 K3
Kumarl, *Australia* 89 F3
Kumasi, *Ghana* 78 D4
Kumayri = Gyumri, *Armenia* 43 K6
Kumba, *Cameroon* 79 E6
Kumbakonam, *India* 60 P11
Kumbarilla, *Australia* 91 D5
Kumbo, *Cameroon* 79 D7
Kümchŏn, *N. Korea* 51 E14
Kumdok, *India* 63 C8
Kume-Shima, *Japan* 49 L3
Kumeny, *Russia* 42 A9
Kŭmhwa, *S. Korea* 51 E14
Kumi, *Uganda* 82 B3
Kumla, *Sweden* 9 G16
Kumluca, *Turkey* 66 D4
Kummerower See, *Germany* 18 B8
Kumo, *Nigeria* 79 C7
Kumon Bum, *Burma* 61 F20
Kumylzhenskaya, *Russia* 42 F6
Kunama, *Australia* 91 F4
Kunashir, Ostrov, *Russia* 45 E15
Kunda, *Estonia* 9 G22
Kundla, *India* 62 J4
Kungala, *Australia* 91 D5
Kungälv, *Sweden* 11 G5
Kunghit I., *Canada* 100 C2
Kungrad = Qŭnghirot, *Uzbekistan* 44 E6
Kungsbacka, *Sweden* 11 G6
Kungur, *Russia* 44 D6
Kungurri, *Australia* 90 C4
Kunhar →, *Pakistan* 63 B5
Kunhegyes, *Hungary* 21 H10
Kuningan, *Indonesia* 57 G13
Kunlong, *Burma* 61 H21
Kunlun Shan, *Asia* 54 C3
Kunming, *China* 52 E4
Kunrade, *Neths.* 17 G7
Kunsan, *S. Korea* 51 G14
Kunshan, *China* 53 B13
Kununurra, *Australia* 88 C4
Kunwarara, *Australia* 90 C5
Kunya-Urgench = Köneürgench, *Turkmenistan* 44 E6
Künzelsau, *Germany* 19 F5
Kuopio, *Finland* 8 E22
Kupa →, *Croatia* 33 C13
Kupang, *Indonesia* 57 F6
Kupres, *Bos.-H.* 21 L7
Kupyansk, *Ukraine* 41 H9
Kupyansk-Uzlovoi, *Ukraine* 41 H9
Kuqa, *China* 54 B3
Kür →, *Azerbaijan* 67 C13
Kura = Kür →, *Azerbaijan* 67 C13
Kuranda, *Australia* 90 B4
Kurashiki, *Japan* 49 G6
Kurayoshi, *Japan* 49 G6
Kürdämir, *Azerbaijan* 43 K9

Kurdistan, *Asia* 67 D10
Kŭrdzhali, *Bulgaria* 39 H8
Kure, *Japan* 49 G6
Küre, *Turkey* 66 B5
Küre Dağları, *Turkey* 66 B6
Kuressaare, *Estonia* 9 G20
Kurgaldzhinskiy, *Kazakstan* 44 D8
Kurgan, *Russia* 44 D7
Kurganinsk, *Russia* 43 H5
Kurgannaya = Kurganinsk, *Russia* 43 H5
Kuria Maria Is. = Khūrīyā Mūrīyā, Jazā 'ir, *Oman* 68 D6
Kuridala, *Australia* 90 C3
Kurigram, *Bangla.* 61 G16
Kurikka, *Finland* 9 E20
Kuril Is. = Kurilskiye Ostrova, *Russia* 45 E15
Kuril Trench, *Pac. Oc.* 46 E19
Kurilsk, *Russia* 45 E15
Kurilskiye Ostrova, *Russia* 45 E15
Kuringen, *Belgium* 17 G6
Kurino, *Japan* 49 J5
Kurinskaya Kosa, *Azerbaijan* 67 C13
Kurkur, *Egypt* 76 C3
Kurlovskiy, *Russia* 42 C5
Kurmuk, *Sudan* 77 E3
Kurnool, *India* 60 M10
Kuro-Shima, *Kagoshima, Japan* 49 J4
Kuro-Shima, *Okinawa, Japan* 49 M2
Kurow, *N.Z.* 87 L3
Kurrajong, *Australia* 91 E5
Kurram →, *Pakistan* 62 C4
Kurri Kurri, *Australia* 91 E5
Kursavka, *Russia* 43 H6
Kurshskiy Zaliv, *Russia* 9 J19
Kursk, *Russia* 42 E3
Kuršumlija, *Serbia, Yug.* 21 M11
Kurşunlu, *Turkey* 66 B5
Kurtalan, *Turkey* 67 D9
Kuru, Bahr el →, *Sudan* 77 F2
Kurucaşile, *Turkey* 66 B5
Kuruktag, *China* 54 B3
Kuruman, *S. Africa* 84 D3
Kuruman →, *S. Africa* 84 D3
Kurume, *Japan* 49 H5
Kurunegala, *Sri Lanka* 60 R12
Kurupukari, *Guyana* 121 C6
Kurya, *Russia* 45 C11
Kus Gölü, *Turkey* 66 B2
Kuşadası, *Turkey* 66 D2
Kusatsu, *Japan* 49 F9
Kusawa L., *Canada* 100 A1
Kusel, *Germany* 19 F3
Kushchevskaya, *Russia* 43 G4
Kushikino, *Japan* 49 J5
Kushima, *Japan* 49 J5
Kushimoto, *Japan* 49 H7
Kushiro, *Japan* 48 C12
Kushiro →, *Japan* 48 C12
Kūshk, *Iran* 65 D8
Kushka = Gushgy, *Turkmenistan* 44 F7
Kūshkī, *Īlām, Iran* 64 C5
Kūshkī, *Khorāsān, Iran* 65 B8
Kūshkū, *Iran* 65 E7
Kushol, *India* 63 C7
Kushtia, *Bangla.* 61 H16
Kushum →, *Kazakstan* 42 F10
Kuskokwim →, *U.S.A.* 96 B3
Kuskokwim B., *U.S.A.* 96 C3
Küsnacht, *Switz.* 23 B7
Kussharo-Ko, *Japan* 48 C12
Küssnacht, *Switz.* 23 B6
Kustanay = Qostanay, *Kazakstan* 44 D7
Kut, Ko, *Thailand* 59 G4
Kütahya, *Turkey* 66 C4
Kutaisi, *Georgia* 43 J6
Kutaraja = Banda Aceh, *Indonesia* 56 C1
Kutch, Gulf of = Kachchh, Gulf of, *India* 62 H3
Kutch, Rann of = Kachchh, Rann of, *India* 62 G4
Kutina, *Croatia* 33 C13
Kutiyana, *India* 62 J4
Kutkashen, *Azerbaijan* 43 K8
Kutná Hora, *Czech.* 20 F5
Kutno, *Poland* 20 C9
Kuttabul, *Australia* 90 C4
Kutu, *Zaïre* 80 E3
Kutum, *Sudan* 77 E1
Kuujjuaq, *Canada* 97 C13
Kuŭp-tong, *N. Korea* 51 D14
Kuurne, *Belgium* 17 G2
Kuusamo, *Finland* 8 D23
Kuusankoski, *Finland* 9 F22
Kuvshinovo, *Russia* 42 B2
Kuwait = Al Kuwayt, *Kuwait* 64 D5
Kuwait ■, *Asia* 64 D5
Kuwana, *Japan* 49 G8
Kuybyshev = Samara, *Russia* 42 D10
Kuybyshev, *Russia* 44 D8
Kuybyshevo, *Ukraine* 41 J9
Kuybyshevskoye Vdkhr., *Russia* 42 C9
Kuye He →, *China* 50 E6
Kūyeh, *Iran* 64 B5
Kūysanjaq, *Iraq* 67 D11
Kuyumba, *Russia* 45 C10
Kuzey Anadolu Dağları, *Turkey* 66 B7
Kuznetsk, *Russia* 42 D8
Kvænangen, *Norway* 8 A19
Kvaløy, *Norway* 8 B18
Kvam, *Norway* 10 C3
Kvareli = Qvareli, *Georgia* 43 K7
Kvarner, *Croatia* 33 D11
Kvarnerič, *Croatia* 33 D11
Kviteseid, *Norway* 10 E2
Kwabhaca, *S. Africa* 85 E4
Kwadacha →, *Canada* 100 B3
Kwakhanai, *Botswana* 84 C3
Kwakoegron, *Surinam* 121 B6
Kwale, *Kenya* 82 C4
Kwale, *Nigeria* 79 D6
Kwale □, *Kenya* 82 C4
KwaMashu, *S. Africa* 85 D5
Kwamouth, *Zaïre* 80 E3
Kwando →, *Africa* 84 B3
Kwangdaeri, *N. Korea* 51 D14
Kwangju, *S. Korea* 51 G14
Kwango →, *Zaïre* 71 G5
Kwangsi-Chuang = Guangxi Zhuangzu Zizhiqu □, *China* 52 E7
Kwangtung = Guangdong □, *China* 53 F9
Kwara □, *Nigeria* 79 D5
Kwataboahegan →, *Canada* 98 B3
Kwatisore, *Indonesia* 57 E8
KwaZulu Natal □, *S. Africa* 85 D5
Kweichow = Guizhou □, *China* 52 D6
Kwekwe, *Zimbabwe* 83 F2
Kwimba □, *Tanzania* 82 C3
Kwinana New Town, *Australia* 89 F2
Kwoka, *Indonesia* 57 E8
Kyabé, *Chad* 73 G8
Kyabra Cr. →, *Australia* 91 D3
Kyabram, *Australia* 91 F4
Kyaikto, *Burma* 58 D1
Kyakhta, *Russia* 45 D11
Kyancutta, *Australia* 91 E2
Kyangin, *Burma* 61 K19
Kyaukpadaung, *Burma* 61 J19
Kyaukpyu, *Burma* 61 K18
Kyaukse, *Burma* 61 J20
Kyburz, *U.S.A.* 112 G6
Kyenjojo, *Uganda* 82 B3
Kyle Dam, *Zimbabwe* 83 G3
Kyle of Lochalsh, *U.K.* 14 D3
Kyll →, *Germany* 19 F2
Kyllburg, *Germany* 19 E2
Kymijoki →, *Finland* 9 F22
Kyneton, *Australia* 91 F3
Kynuna, *Australia* 90 C3
Kyō-ga-Saki, *Japan* 49 G7
Kyoga, L., *Uganda* 82 B3
Kyogle, *Australia* 91 D5
Kyongju, *S. Korea* 51 G15
Kyongpyaw, *Burma* 61 L19
Kyŏngsŏng, *N. Korea* 51 D15
Kyōto, *Japan* 49 G7
Kyōto □, *Japan* 49 G7
Kyparissovouno, *Cyprus* 37 D12
Kyperounda, *Cyprus* 37 E11
Kyren, *Russia* 45 D11
Kyrenia, *Cyprus* 66 E5
Kyrgyzstan ■, *Asia* 44 E8
Kyritz, *Germany* 18 C8
Kyrönjoki →, *Finland* 8 E19
Kyrtylakh, *Russia* 45 C13
Kystatyam, *Russia* 45 C13
Kythréa, *Cyprus* 37 D12
Kyulyunken, *Russia* 45 C14
Kyunhla, *Burma* 61 H19
Kyuquot, *Canada* 100 C3
Kyurdamir = Kürdämir, *Azerbaijan* 43 K9
Kyūshū, *Japan* 49 H5
Kyūshū □, *Japan* 49 H5
Kyūshū-Sanchi, *Japan* 49 H5
Kyustendil, *Bulgaria* 38 G5
Kyusyur, *Russia* 45 B13
Kywong, *Australia* 91 E4
Kyyiv, *Ukraine* 41 G6
Kyyivske Vdskh., *Ukraine* 41 G6
Kyzyl, *Russia* 45 D10
Kyzyl Kum, *Uzbekistan* 44 E7
Kyzyl-Kyya, *Kyrgyzstan* 44 E8
Kzyl-Orda = Qyzylorda, *Kazakstan* 44 E7

L

La Albuera, *Spain* 31 G4
La Albufera, *Spain* 29 F4
La Alcarria, *Spain* 28 E2
La Algaba, *Spain* 31 H4
La Almarcha, *Spain* 28 F2
La Almunia de Doña Godina, *Spain* 28 D3
La Asunción, *Venezuela* 121 A5
La Banda, *Argentina* 126 B3
La Bañeza, *Spain* 30 C5
La Barca, *Mexico* 114 C4
La Barge, *U.S.A.* 110 E8
La Bassée, *France* 25 B9
La Bastide-Puylaurent, *France* 26 D7
La Baule, *France* 24 E4
La Belle, *U.S.A.* 105 M5
La Biche →, *Canada* 100 B4
La Bisbal, *Spain* 28 D8
La Blanquilla, *Venezuela* 121 A5
La Bomba, *Mexico* 114 A1
La Bresse, *France* 25 D13
La Bureba, *Spain* 28 C1
La Cal →, *Bolivia* 125 D6
La Calera, *Chile* 126 C1
La Campiña, *Spain* 31 H6
La Canal, *Spain* 36 C7
La Cañiza, *Spain* 30 C2
La Capelle, *France* 25 C10
La Carlota, *Argentina* 126 C3
La Carlota, *Phil.* 55 F5
La Carolina, *Spain* 31 G7
La Cavalerie, *France* 26 D7
La Ceiba, *Honduras* 116 C2
La Chaise-Dieu, *France* 26 C7
La Chaize-le-Vicomte, *France* 24 F5
La Chapelle d'Angillon, *France* 25 E9
La Chapelle-Glain, *France* 24 E5
La Charité-sur-Loire, *France* 25 E10
La Chartre-sur-le-Loir, *France* 24 E7
La Châtaigneraie, *France* 26 B3
La Châtre, *France* 26 B5
La Chaux de Fonds, *Switz.* 22 B3
La Chorrera, *Colombia* 120 D3
La Ciotat, *France* 27 E9
La Clayette, *France* 27 B8
La Cocha, *Argentina* 126 B2
La Concepción = Ri-Aba, *Eq. Guin.* 79 E6
La Concepción, *Venezuela* 120 A3
La Concordia, *Mexico* 115 D6
La Conner, *U.S.A.* 110 B2
La Coruña, *Spain* 30 B2
La Coruña □, *Spain* 30 B2
La Côte, *Switz.* 22 D2
La Côte-St.-André, *France* 27 C9
La Courtine-le-Trucq, *France* 26 C6
La Crau, *France* 27 E8
La Crete, *Canada* 100 B5
La Crosse, *Kans., U.S.A.* 108 F5
La Crosse, *Wis., U.S.A.* 108 D9
La Cruz, *Costa Rica* 116 D2
La Cruz, *Mexico* 114 C3
La Dorada, *Colombia* 120 B3
La Ensenada, *Chile* 128 B2
La Escondida, *Mexico* 114 C5
La Esmeralda, *Paraguay* 126 A3
La Esperanza, *Argentina* 128 B3
La Esperanza, *Cuba* 116 B3
La Esperanza, *Honduras* 116 D2
La Estrada, *Spain* 30 C2
La Fayette, *U.S.A.* 105 H3
La Fé, *Cuba* 116 B3
La Fère, *France* 25 C10
La Ferté-Bernard, *France* 24 D7
La Ferté-Macé, *France* 24 D6
La Ferté-St.-Aubin, *France* 25 E8
La Ferté-sous-Jouarre, *France* 25 D10
La Ferté-Vidame, *France* 24 D7
La Flèche, *France* 24 E6
La Follette, *U.S.A.* 105 G3
La Fregeneda, *Spain* 30 E4
La Fría, *Venezuela* 120 B3
La Fuente de San Esteban, *Spain* 30 E4
La Gineta, *Spain* 29 F2
La Gloria, *Colombia* 120 B3
La Gran Sabana, *Venezuela* 121 B5
La Grand-Combe, *France* 27 D8
La Grande, *U.S.A.* 110 D4
La Grande-Motte, *France* 27 E8
La Grange, *Calif., U.S.A.* 112 H6
La Grange, *Ga., U.S.A.* 105 J3
La Grange, *Ky., U.S.A.* 104 F3
La Grange, *Tex., U.S.A.* 109 L6
La Grita, *Venezuela* 120 B3
La Guaira, *Venezuela* 120 A4
La Guardia, *Spain* 30 D2
La Gudiña, *Spain* 30 C3
La Güera, *Mauritania* 74 D1
La Guerche-de-Bretagne, *France* 24 E5
La Guerche-sur-l'Aubois, *France* 25 F9
La Habana, *Cuba* 116 B3
La Harpe, *U.S.A.* 108 E9
La Haye-du-Puits, *France* 24 C5
La Horqueta, *Venezuela* 121 B5
La Horra, *Spain* 30 D7
La Independencia, *Mexico* 115 D6
La Isabela, *Dom. Rep.* 117 C5
La Jara, *U.S.A.* 111 H11
La Joya, *Peru* 124 D3
La Junquera, *Spain* 28 C7
La Junta, *U.S.A.* 109 F3
La Laguna, *Canary Is.* 36 F3
La Libertad, *Guatemala* 116 C1
La Libertad, *Mexico* 114 B2
La Libertad □, *Peru* 124 B2
La Ligua, *Chile* 126 C1
La Línea de la Concepción, *Spain* 31 J5
La Loche, *Canada* 101 B7
La Londe-les-Maures, *France* 27 E10
La Lora, *Spain* 30 C7
La Loupe, *France* 24 D8
La Louvière, *Belgium* 17 H4
La Machine, *France* 25 F10
La Maddalena, *Italy* 34 A2
La Malbaie, *Canada* 99 C5
La Mancha, *Spain* 29 F2
La Mariña, *Spain* 30 B3
La Mesa, *Calif., U.S.A.* 113 N9
La Mesa, *N. Mex., U.S.A.* 111 K10
La Misión, *Mexico* 114 A1
La Mothe-Achard, *France* 24 F5
La Motte, *France* 27 D10
La Motte-Chalançon, *France* 27 D9
La Moure, *U.S.A.* 108 B5
La Muela, *Spain* 28 D3
La Mure, *France* 27 D9
La Negra, *Chile* 126 A1
La Neuveville, *Switz.* 22 B4
La Oliva, *Canary Is.* 36 F6
La Oraya, *Peru* 124 C2
La Orotava, *Canary Is.* 36 F3
La Pacaudière, *France* 26 B7
La Palma, *Canary Is.* 36 F2
La Palma, *Panama* 116 E4
La Palma del Condado, *Spain* 31 H4
La Paloma, *Chile* 126 C1
La Pampa □, *Argentina* 126 D2
La Paragua, *Venezuela* 121 B5
La Paz, *Entre Ríos, Argentina* 126 C4
La Paz, *San Luis, Argentina* 126 C2
La Paz, *Bolivia* 124 D4
La Paz, *Honduras* 116 D2
La Paz, *Mexico* 114 C2
La Paz, *Phil.* 55 D4
La Paz □, *Bolivia* 124 D4
La Paz Centro, *Nic.* 116 D2
La Pedrera, *Colombia* 120 D4
La Perouse Str., *Asia* 48 B11
La Pesca, *Mexico* 115 C5
La Piedad, *Mexico* 114 C4
La Pine, *U.S.A.* 110 E3
La Plant, *U.S.A.* 108 C4
La Plata, *Argentina* 126 D4
La Plata, *Colombia* 120 C2
La Plata, L., *Argentina* 128 B2
La Pobla de Lillet, *Spain* 28 C6
La Pola de Gordón, *Spain* 30 C5
La Porte, *U.S.A.* 104 E2
La Puebla, *Spain* 28 F8
La Puebla de Cazalla, *Spain* 31 H5
La Puebla de los Infantes, *Spain* 31 H5
La Puebla de Montalbán, *Spain* 30 F6
La Puerta, *Spain* 29 G2
La Punt, *Switz.* 23 C9
La Purísima, *Mexico* 114 B2
La Push, *U.S.A.* 112 C2
La Quiaca, *Argentina* 126 A2
La Rambla, *Spain* 31 H6
La Reine, *Canada* 98 C4
La Réole, *France* 26 D3
La Restinga, *Canary Is.* 36 G2
La Rioja, *Argentina* 126 B2
La Rioja □, *Argentina* 126 B2
La Rioja □, *Spain* 28 C2
La Robla, *Spain* 30 C5
La Roche, *Switz.* 22 C4
La Roche-Bernard, *France* 24 E4
La Roche-Canillac, *France* 26 C5
La Roche-en-Ardenne, *Belgium* 17 H7
La Roche-sur-Yon, *France* 24 F5
La Rochefoucauld, *France* 26 C4
La Rochelle, *France* 26 B2
La Roda, *Albacete, Spain* 29 F2
La Roda, *Sevilla, Spain* 31 H6
La Romana, *Dom. Rep.* 117 C6
La Ronge, *Canada* 101 B7
La Rumorosa, *Mexico* 113 N10
La Sabina, *Spain* 36 C7
La Sagra, *Spain* 29 H2
La Salle, *U.S.A.* 108 E10
La Sanabria, *Spain* 30 C4
La Santa, *Canary Is.* 36 E6
La Sarraz, *Switz.* 22 C3
La Sarre, *Canada* 98 C4
La Scie, *Canada* 99 C8
La Selva, *Spain* 28 D7
La Selva Beach, *U.S.A.* 112 J5
La Serena, *Chile* 126 B1
La Serena, *Spain* 31 G5
La Seyne-sur-Mer, *France* 27 E9
La Sila, *Italy* 35 C9
La Solana, *Spain* 29 G1
La Souterraine, *France* 26 B5
La Spézia, *Italy* 32 D6
La Suze-sur-Sarthe, *France* 24 E7
La Tagua, *Colombia* 120 C3
La Teste, *France* 26 D2
La Tortuga, *Venezuela* 117 D6
La Tour-du-Pin, *France* 27 C9
La Tranche-sur-Mer, *France* 24 F5
La Tremblade, *France* 26 C2
La Tuque, *Canada* 98 C5
La Unión, *Chile* 128 B2
La Unión, *Colombia* 120 C2
La Unión, *El Salv.* 116 D2
La Unión, *Mexico* 114 D4
La Unión, *Peru* 124 B2
La Unión, *Spain* 29 H4
La Urbana, *Venezuela* 120 B4
La Vecilla, *Spain* 30 C5
La Vega, *Dom. Rep.* 117 C5
La Vega, *Peru* 124 C2
La Vela, *Venezuela* 120 A4
La Veleta, *Spain* 31 H7
La Venta, *Mexico* 115 D6
La Ventura, *Mexico* 114 C4
La Venturosa, *Colombia* 120 B4
La Victoria, *Venezuela* 120 A4
La Voulte-sur-Rhône, *France* 27 D8
La Zarza, *Spain* 31 H4
Laaber →, *Germany* 19 G8
Laage, *Germany* 18 B8
Laba →, *Russia* 43 H4
Labason, *Phil.* 55 G5
Labastide-Murat, *France* 26 D5
Labastide-Rouairoux, *France* 26 E6
Labbézenga, *Mali* 79 B5
Labe = Elbe →, *Europe* 18 B4
Labé, *Guinea* 78 C2
Laberec →, *Slovak Rep.* 20 G11
Laberge, L., *Canada* 100 A1
Labin, *Croatia* 33 C11
Labinsk, *Russia* 43 H5
Labis, *Malaysia* 59 L4
Labo, *Phil.* 55 D5
Laboe, *Germany* 18 A6
Labouheyre, *France* 26 D3
Laboulaye, *Argentina* 126 C3
Labra, Peña, *Spain* 30 B6
Labrador, Coast of □, *Canada* 99 B7
Labrador City, *Canada* 99 B6
Lábrea, *Brazil* 125 B5
Labrède, *France* 26 D3
Labuan, Pulau, *Malaysia* 56 C5
Labuha, *Indonesia* 57 E7
Labuhan, *Indonesia* 57 G11
Labuhanbajo, *Indonesia* 57 F6
Labuissière, *Belgium* 17 H4
Labuk, Telok, *Malaysia* 56 C5
Labyrinth, L., *Australia* 91 E2
Labytnangi, *Russia* 44 C7
Lac Allard, *Canada* 99 B7
Lac Bouchette, *Canada* 99 C5
Lac du Flambeau, *U.S.A.* 108 B10
Lac Édouard, *Canada* 98 C5
Lac La Biche, *Canada* 100 C6
Lac la Martre = Wha Ti, *Canada* 96 B8
Lac-Mégantic, *Canada* 99 C5
Lac Seul, Res., *Canada* 98 B1
Lac Thien, *Vietnam* 58 F7
Lacanau, *France* 26 D2
Lacanau, Étang de, *France* 26 D2
Lacantúm →, *Mexico* 115 D6
Lacara →, *Spain* 31 G4
Lacaune, *France* 26 E6
Lacaune, Mts. de, *France* 26 E6
Laccadive Is. = Lakshadweep Is, *Ind. Oc.* 46 H11
Lacepede B., *Australia* 91 F2
Lacepede Is., *Australia* 88 C3
Lacerdónia, *Mozam.* 83 F4
Lacey, *U.S.A.* 112 C4
Lachay, Pta., *Peru* 124 C2
Lachen, *Switz.* 23 B7
Lachhmangarh, *India* 62 F6
Lachi, *Pakistan* 62 C4
Lachine, *Canada* 98 C5
Lachlan →, *Australia* 91 E3
Lachute, *Canada* 98 C5
Lackawanna, *U.S.A.* 106 D6
Lacolle, *Canada* 107 A11
Lacombe, *Canada* 100 C6
Lacona, *U.S.A.* 107 C8
Láconi, *Italy* 34 C2
Laconia, *U.S.A.* 107 C13
Lacq, *France* 26 E3
Lacrosse, *U.S.A.* 110 C5
Ladakh Ra., *India* 63 B8
Ladário, *Brazil* 125 D6
Ládhon →, *Greece* 39 M4
Ladik, *Turkey* 66 B6
Ladismith, *S. Africa* 84 E3
Lādīz, *Iran* 65 D9
Ladnun, *India* 62 F6
Ladoga, L. = Ladozhskoye Ozero, *Russia* 40 B6
Ladon, *France* 25 D9
Ladozhskoye Ozero, *Russia* 40 B6
Ladrillero, G., *Chile* 128 C1
Lady Grey, *S. Africa* 84 E4
Ladybrand, *S. Africa* 84 D4
Ladysmith, *Canada* 100 D4
Ladysmith, *S. Africa* 85 D4
Ladysmith, *U.S.A.* 108 C9
Lae, *Papua N. G.* 92 H6
Laem Ngop, *Thailand* 59 F4
Laem Pho, *Thailand* 59 J3
Læsø, *Denmark* 11 G4
Læsø Rende, *Denmark* 11 G4
Lafayette, *Colo., U.S.A.* 108 F2
Lafayette, *Ind., U.S.A.* 104 E2
Lafayette, *La., U.S.A.* 109 K9
Lafayette, *Tenn., U.S.A.* 105 G3
Laferte →, *Canada* 100 A5
Lafia, *Nigeria* 79 D6
Lafiagi, *Nigeria* 79 D6
Lafleche, *Canada* 101 D7
Lafon, *Sudan* 77 F3
Laforsen, *Sweden* 10 C9
Lagan →, *Sweden* 11 H7

Lagan →, *U.K.* 15 B6
Lagarfljót →, *Iceland* 8 D6
Lagarto, *Brazil* 122 D4
Lage, *Germany* 18 D4
Lage, *Spain* 30 B2
Lage-Mierde, *Neths.* 17 F6
Lågen →, *Oppland, Norway* 9 F14
Lågen →, *Vestfold, Norway* 9 G14
Lägerdorf, *Germany* 18 B5
Laghouat, *Algeria* 75 B5
Lagnieu, *France* 27 C9
Lagny, *France* 25 D9
Lago, *Italy* 35 C9
Lago Posadas, *Argentina* 128 C2
Lago Ranco, *Chile* 128 B2
Lagôa, *Portugal* 31 H2
Lagoaça, *Portugal* 30 D4
Lagodekhi, *Georgia* 43 K8
Lagónegro, *Italy* 35 B8
Lagonoy Gulf, *Phil.* 55 E5
Lagos, *Nigeria* 79 D5
Lagos, *Portugal* 31 H2
Lagos de Moreno, *Mexico* 114 C4
Lagrange, *Australia* 88 C3
Lagrange B., *Australia* 88 C3
Laguardia, *Spain* 28 C2
Laguépie, *France* 26 D5
Laguna, *Brazil* 127 B6
Laguna, *U.S.A.* 111 J10
Laguna Beach, *U.S.A.* 113 M9
Laguna de la Janda, *Spain* 31 J5
Laguna Limpia, *Argentina* 126 B4
Laguna Madre, *U.S.A.* 115 B5
Lagunas, *Chile* 126 A2
Lagunas, *Peru* 124 B2
Lagunillas, *Bolivia* 125 D5
Lahad Datu, *Malaysia* 57 C5
Lahan Sai, *Thailand* 58 E4
Lahanam, *Laos* 58 D5
Laharpur, *India* 63 F9
Lahat, *Indonesia* 56 E2
Lahewa, *Indonesia* 56 D1
Lahiang Lahiang, *Phil.* 55 H4
Lāhījān, *Iran* 65 B6
Lahn →, *Germany* 19 E3
Laholm, *Sweden* 11 H7
Laholmsbukten, *Sweden* 11 H6
Lahontan Reservoir, *U.S.A.* 110 G4
Lahore, *Pakistan* 62 D6
Lahr, *Germany* 19 G3
Lahti, *Finland* 9 F21
Lahtis = Lahti, *Finland* 9 F21
Laï, *Chad* 73 G8
Lai Chau, *Vietnam* 58 A4
Lai'an, *China* 53 A12
Laibin, *China* 52 F7
Laidley, *Australia* 91 D5
Laifeng, *China* 52 C7
L'Aigle, *France* 24 D7
Laignes, *France* 25 E11
L'Aiguillon-sur-Mer, *France* 26 B2
Laikipia □, *Kenya* 82 B4
Laingsburg, *S. Africa* 84 E3
Lainio älv →, *Sweden* 8 C20
Lairg, *U.K.* 14 C4
Laishui, *China* 50 E8
Laiwu, *China* 51 F9
Laixi, *China* 51 F11
Laiyang, *China* 51 F11
Laiyuan, *China* 50 E8
Laizhou Wan, *China* 51 F10
Laja →, *Mexico* 114 C4
Lajere, *Nigeria* 79 C7
Lajes, *Rio Grande do N., Brazil* 122 C4
Lajes, *Sta. Catarina, Brazil* 127 B5
Lajinha, *Brazil* 123 F3
Lajkovac, *Serbia, Yug.* 21 L10
Lajosmizse, *Hungary* 21 H9
Lak Sao, *Laos* 58 C5
Lakaband, *Pakistan* 62 D3
Lake Alpine, *U.S.A.* 112 G7
Lake Andes, *U.S.A.* 108 D5
Lake Anse, *U.S.A.* 104 B1
Lake Arthur, *U.S.A.* 109 K8
Lake Cargelligo, *Australia* 91 E4
Lake Charles, *U.S.A.* 109 K8
Lake City, *Colo., U.S.A.* 111 G10
Lake City, *Fla., U.S.A.* 105 K4
Lake City, *Iowa, U.S.A.* 108 D7
Lake City, *Mich., U.S.A.* 104 C3
Lake City, *Minn., U.S.A.* 108 C8
Lake City, *Pa., U.S.A.* 106 D4
Lake City, *S.C., U.S.A.* 105 J6
Lake George, *U.S.A.* 107 C11
Lake Grace, *Australia* 89 F2
Lake Harbour = Kimmirut, *Canada* 97 B13
Lake Havasu City, *U.S.A.* 113 L12
Lake Hughes, *U.S.A.* 113 L8
Lake Isabella, *U.S.A.* 113 K8
Lake King, *Australia* 89 F2
Lake Lenore, *Canada* 101 C8
Lake Louise, *Canada* 100 C5
Lake Mead National Recreation Area, *U.S.A.* 113 K12
Lake Mills, *U.S.A.* 108 D8
Lake Nash, *Australia* 90 C2
Lake Providence, *U.S.A.* 109 J9
Lake River, *Canada* 98 B3
Lake Superior Prov. Park, *Canada* 98 C3
Lake Village, *U.S.A.* 109 J9
Lake Wales, *U.S.A.* 105 M5
Lake Worth, *U.S.A.* 105 M5
Lakefield, *Canada* 98 D4
Lakeland, *Australia* 90 B3
Lakeland, *U.S.A.* 105 L5
Lakemba, *Fiji* 87 D9
Lakeport, *U.S.A.* 112 F4
Lakes Entrance, *Australia* 91 F4
Lakeside, *Ariz., U.S.A.* 111 J9
Lakeside, *Calif., U.S.A.* 113 N10
Lakeside, *Nebr., U.S.A.* 108 D3
Lakeview, *U.S.A.* 110 E3
Lakewood, *Colo., U.S.A.* 108 F2
Lakewood, *N.J., U.S.A.* 107 F10
Lakewood, *Ohio, U.S.A.* 106 E3
Lakewood Center, *U.S.A.* 112 C4
Lakhaniá, *Greece* 37 D9
Lakhonpheng, *Laos* 58 E5
Lakhpat, *India* 62 H3
Läki, *Azerbaijan* 43 K8
Lakin, *U.S.A.* 109 G4
Lakitusaki →, *Canada* 98 B3
Lákkoi, *Greece* 37 D5
Lakonikós Kólpos, *Greece* 39 N5
Lakor, *Indonesia* 57 F7
Lakota, *Ivory C.* 78 D3
Lakota, *U.S.A.* 108 A5
Laksefjorden, *Norway* 8 A22
Lakselv, *Norway* 8 A21
Lakshadweep Is., *Ind. Oc.* 46 H11
Lakshmikantapur, *India* 63 H13
Lala Ghat, *India* 61 G18
Lala Musa, *Pakistan* 62 C5
Lalago, *Tanzania* 82 C3
Lalapanzi, *Zimbabwe* 83 F3
Lalganj, *India* 63 G11
Lalibela, *Ethiopia* 77 E4
Lalin, *China* 51 B14
Lalín, *Spain* 30 C2
Lalin He →, *China* 51 B13
Lalinde, *France* 26 D4
Lalitapur = Patan, *Nepal* 61 F14
Lalitpur, *India* 63 G8
Lam, *Vietnam* 58 B6
Lam Pao Res., *Thailand* 58 D4
Lama Kara, *Togo* 79 D5
Lamaing, *Burma* 61 M20
Lamar, *Colo., U.S.A.* 108 F3
Lamar, *Mo., U.S.A.* 109 G7
Lamarque, *Argentina* 128 A3
Lamas, *Peru* 124 B2
Lamastre, *France* 27 D8
Lamballe, *France* 24 D4
Lambaréné, *Gabon* 80 E2
Lambasa, *Fiji* 87 C8
Lambay I., *Ireland* 15 C5
Lambayeque □, *Peru* 124 B2
Lambert, *U.S.A.* 108 B2
Lambert Glacier, *Antarctica* 5 D6
Lamberts Bay, *S. Africa* 84 E2
Lambesc, *France* 27 E9
Lámbia, *Greece* 39 M4
Lambro →, *Italy* 32 C6
Lame, *Nigeria* 79 C6
Lame Deer, *U.S.A.* 110 D10
Lamego, *Portugal* 30 D3
Lamèque, *Canada* 99 C7
Lameroo, *Australia* 91 F3
Lamesa, *U.S.A.* 109 J4
Lamía, *Greece* 39 L5
Lamitan, *Phil.* 55 H5
Lammermuir Hills, *U.K.* 14 F6
Lamon Bay, *Phil.* 55 D5
Lamont, *Canada* 100 C6
Lamont, *U.S.A.* 113 K8
Lampa, *Peru* 124 D3
Lampang, *Thailand* 58 C2
Lampasas, *U.S.A.* 109 K5
Lampaul, *France* 24 D1
Lampazos de Naranjo, *Mexico* 114 B4
Lampeter, *U.K.* 13 E3
Lampione, *Medit. S.* 75 A7
Lampman, *Canada* 101 D8
Lamprey, *Canada* 101 B10
Lampung □, *Indonesia* 56 F2
Lamu, *Kenya* 82 C5
Lamu □, *Kenya* 82 C5
Lamud, *Peru* 124 B2
Lamy, *U.S.A.* 111 J11
Lan Xian, *China* 50 E6
Lanai I., *U.S.A.* 102 H16
Lanak La, *India* 63 B8
Lanaken, *Belgium* 17 G7
Lanak'o Shank'ou = Lanak La, *India* 63 B8
Lanao, L., *Phil.* 55 H6
Lanark, *Canada* 107 A8
Lanark, *U.K.* 14 F5
Lancang, *China* 52 F2
Lancang Jiang →, *China* 52 G3
Lancashire □, *U.K.* 12 D5
Lancaster, *Canada* 107 A10
Lancaster, *U.K.* 12 C5
Lancaster, *Calif., U.S.A.* 113 L8
Lancaster, *Ky., U.S.A.* 104 G3
Lancaster, *N.H., U.S.A.* 107 B13
Lancaster, *N.Y., U.S.A.* 106 D6
Lancaster, *Pa., U.S.A.* 107 F8
Lancaster, *S.C., U.S.A.* 105 H5
Lancaster, *Wis., U.S.A.* 108 D9
Lancaster Sd., *Canada* 97 A11
Lancer, *Canada* 101 C7
Lanchow = Lanzhou, *China* 50 F2
Lanciano, *Italy* 33 F11
Lanco, *Chile* 128 A2
Lancones, *Peru* 124 A1
Lancun, *China* 51 F11
Łancut, *Poland* 20 E12
Lancy, *Switz.* 22 D2
Landau, *Bayern, Germany* 19 G8
Landau, *Rhld-Pfz., Germany* 19 F4
Landeck, *Austria* 19 H6
Landen, *Belgium* 17 G6
Lander, *U.S.A.* 110 E9
Lander →, *Australia* 88 D5
Landerneau, *France* 24 D2
Landeryd, *Sweden* 11 G7
Landes, *France* 26 D3
Landes □, *France* 26 E3
Landete, *Spain* 28 F3
Landi Kotal, *Pakistan* 62 B4
Landivisiau, *France* 24 D2
Landor, *Australia* 89 E2
Landquart, *Switz.* 23 C9
Landquart →, *Switz.* 23 C9
Landrecies, *France* 25 B10
Land's End, *U.K.* 13 G2
Landsberg, *Germany* 19 G6
Landsborough Cr. →, *Australia* 90 C3
Landshut, *Germany* 19 G8
Landskrona, *Sweden* 11 J6
Landstuhl, *Germany* 19 F3
Landvetter, *Sweden* 11 G6
Laneffe, *Belgium* 17 H5
Lanesboro, *U.S.A.* 107 E9
Lanett, *U.S.A.* 105 J3
Lang Bay, *Canada* 100 D4
Lang Qua, *Vietnam* 58 A5
Lang Shan, *China* 50 D4
Lang Son, *Vietnam* 58 B6
Lang Suan, *Thailand* 59 H2
La'nga Co, *China* 61 D12
Lángadhás, *Greece* 39 J6
Langádhia, *Greece* 39 M5
Långan →, *Sweden* 10 A8
Langar, *Iran* 65 C9
Langara I., *Canada* 100 C2
Langatabbetje, *Surinam* 121 C7
Langdai, *China* 52 D5
Langdon, *U.S.A.* 108 A5
Langdorp, *Belgium* 17 G5
Langeac, *France* 26 C7
Langeais, *France* 24 E7
Langeb Baraka →, *Sudan* 76 D4
Langeberg, *S. Africa* 84 E3
Langeberge, *S. Africa* 84 D3
Langeland, *Denmark* 11 K4
Langemark, *Belgium* 17 G1
Langen, *Germany* 19 F4
Langenburg, *Canada* 101 C8
Langeneß, *Germany* 18 A4
Langenthal, *Switz.* 22 B5
Langeoog, *Germany* 18 B3
Langeskov, *Denmark* 11 J4
Langesund, *Norway* 10 F3
Länghem, *Sweden* 11 G7
Langhirano, *Italy* 32 D7
Langholm, *U.K.* 14 F6
Langhus, *Norway* 10 E4
Langjökull, *Iceland* 8 D3
Langkawi, P., *Malaysia* 59 J2
Langklip, *S. Africa* 84 D3
Langkon, *Malaysia* 56 C5
Langlade, *St- P. & M.* 99 C8
Langlois, *U.S.A.* 110 E1
Langnau, *Switz.* 22 C5
Langogne, *France* 26 D7
Langon, *France* 26 D3
Langøya, *Norway* 8 B16
Langres, *France* 25 E12
Langres, Plateau de, *France* 25 E12
Langsa, *Indonesia* 56 D1
Långsele, *Sweden* 10 A11
Langtry, *U.S.A.* 109 L4
Langu, *Thailand* 59 J2
Languedoc, *France* 26 E7
Langwies, *Switz.* 23 C9
Langxi, *China* 53 B12
Langxiangzhen, *China* 50 E9
Langzhong, *China* 52 B5
Lanigan, *Canada* 101 C7
Lankao, *China* 50 G8
Länkäran, *Azerbaijan* 67 C13
Lannemezan, *France* 26 E4
Lannilis, *France* 24 D2
Lannion, *France* 24 D3
L'Annonciation, *Canada* 98 C5
Lanouaille, *France* 26 C5
Lanping, *China* 52 D2
Lansdale, *U.S.A.* 107 F9
Lansdowne, *Australia* 91 E5
Lansdowne, *Canada* 107 B8
Lansdowne House, *Canada* 98 B2
L'Anse, *U.S.A.* 98 C2
L'Anse au Loup, *Canada* 99 B8
Lansford, *U.S.A.* 107 F9
Lanshan, *China* 53 E9
Lansing, *U.S.A.* 104 D3
Lanslebourg-Mont-Cenis, *France* 27 C10
Lanta Yai, Ko, *Thailand* 59 J2
Lantian, *China* 50 G5
Lanus, *Argentina* 126 C4
Lanusei, *Italy* 34 C2
Lanuza, *Phil.* 55 G7
Lanxi, *China* 53 C12
Lanzarote, *Canary Is.* 36 E6
Lanzhou, *China* 50 F2
Lanzo Torinese, *Italy* 32 C4
Lao →, *Italy* 35 C8
Lao Bao, *Laos* 58 D6
Lao Cai, *Vietnam* 58 A4
Laoag, *Phil.* 55 B4
Laoang, *Phil.* 55 E6
Laoha He →, *China* 51 C11
Laois □, *Ireland* 15 D4
Laon, *France* 25 C10
Laona, *U.S.A.* 104 C1
Laos ■, *Asia* 58 D5
Lapa, *Brazil* 127 B6
Lapalisse, *France* 26 B7
Laparan, *Phil.* 57 C6
Lapeer, *U.S.A.* 104 D4
Lapithos, *Cyprus* 37 D12
Lapland = Lappland, *Europe* 8 B21
Laporte, *U.S.A.* 107 E8
Lapovo, *Serbia, Yug.* 21 L11
Lappeenranta, *Finland* 9 F23
Lappland, *Europe* 8 B21
Laprida, *Argentina* 126 D3
Lapseki, *Turkey* 66 B2
Laptev Sea, *Russia* 45 B13
Lapua, *Finland* 8 E20
Lăpuşul →, *Romania* 38 B6
L'Áquila, *Italy* 33 F10
Lār, *Āzarbājān-e Sharqī, Iran* 64 B5
Lār, *Fārs, Iran* 65 E7
Lara □, *Venezuela* 120 A4
Larabanga, *Ghana* 78 D4
Laracha, *Spain* 30 B2
Larache, *Morocco* 74 A3
Laragne-Montéglin, *France* 27 D9
Laramie, *U.S.A.* 108 E2
Laramie Mts., *U.S.A.* 108 E2
Laranjeiras, *Brazil* 122 D4
Laranjeiras do Sul, *Brazil* 127 B5
Larantuka, *Indonesia* 57 F6
Larap, *Phil.* 55 D5
Larat, *Indonesia* 57 F8
L'Arbresle, *France* 27 C8
Larde, *Mozam.* 83 F4
Larder Lake, *Canada* 98 C4
Lardhos, Ákra, *Greece* 37 C10
Lardhos, Órmos, *Greece* 37 C10
Laredo, *Spain* 28 B1
Laredo, *U.S.A.* 109 M5
Laredo Sd., *Canada* 100 C3
Laren, *Neths.* 16 D6
Largentière, *France* 27 D8
L'Argentière-la-Bessée, *France* 27 D10
Largo, *U.S.A.* 105 M4
Largs, *U.K.* 14 F4
Lari, *Italy* 32 E7
Lariang, *Indonesia* 57 E5
Larimore, *U.S.A.* 108 B6
Lārīn, *Iran* 65 C7
Larino, *Italy* 35 A7
Lárisa, *Greece* 39 K5
Larkana, *Pakistan* 62 F3
Larnaca, *Cyprus* 66 E5
Larnaca Bay, *Cyprus* 37 E12
Larne, *U.K.* 15 B6
Larned, *U.S.A.* 108 F5
Larochette, *Belgium* 17 J8
Laroquebrou, *France* 26 D6
Larrimah, *Australia* 88 C5
Larsen Ice Shelf, *Antarctica* 5 C17
Larvik, *Norway* 10 E4
Laryak, *Russia* 44 C8
Larzac, Causse du, *France* 26 E7
Las Alpujarras, *Spain* 29 J1
Las Animas, *U.S.A.* 108 F3
Las Anod, *Somali Rep.* 68 F4
Las Blancos, *Spain* 29 H4
Las Brenãs, *Argentina* 126 B3
Las Cabezas de San Juan, *Spain* 31 J5
Las Chimeneas, *Mexico* 113 N10
Las Coloradas, *Argentina* 128 A2
Las Cruces, *U.S.A.* 111 K10
Las Flores, *Argentina* 126 D4
Las Heras, *Argentina* 126 C2
Las Horquetas, *Argentina* 128 C2
Las Khoreh, *Somali Rep.* 68 E4
Las Lajas, *Argentina* 128 A2
Las Lomas, *Peru* 124 A1
Las Lomitas, *Argentina* 126 A3
Las Marismas, *Spain* 31 H4
Las Mercedes, *Venezuela* 120 B4
Las Navas de la Concepción, *Spain* 31 H5
Las Navas de Tolosa, *Spain* 31 G7
Las Navas del Marqués, *Spain* 30 E6
Las Palmas, *Argentina* 126 B4
Las Palmas, *Canary Is.* 36 F4
Las Palmas →, *Mexico* 113 N10
Las Piedras, *Uruguay* 127 C4
Las Pipinas, *Argentina* 126 D4
Las Plumas, *Argentina* 128 B3
Las Rosas, *Argentina* 126 C3
Las Tablas, *Panama* 116 E3
Las Termas, *Argentina* 126 B3
Las Truchas, *Mexico* 114 D4
Las Varillas, *Argentina* 126 C3
Las Vegas, *N. Mex., U.S.A.* 111 J11
Las Vegas, *Nev., U.S.A.* 113 J11
Lascano, *Uruguay* 127 C5
Lashburn, *Canada* 101 C7
Lashio, *Burma* 61 H20
Lashkar, *India* 62 F8
Łasin, *Poland* 20 B9
Lasíthi, *Greece* 37 D7
Lasíthi □, *Greece* 37 D7
Laško, *Slovenia* 33 B12
Lassance, *Brazil* 123 E3
Lassay, *France* 24 D6
Lassen Pk., *U.S.A.* 110 F3
Last Mountain L., *Canada* 101 C7
Lastchance Cr. →, *U.S.A.* 112 E5
Lastoursville, *Gabon* 80 E2
Lastovo, *Croatia* 33 F13
Lastovski Kanal, *Croatia* 33 F13
Lat Yao, *Thailand* 58 E2
Latacunga, *Ecuador* 120 D2
Latakia = Al Lādhiqīyah, *Syria* 66 E6
Latchford, *Canada* 98 C4
Laterza, *Italy* 35 B9
Latham, *Australia* 89 E2
Lathen, *Germany* 18 C3
Lathrop Wells, *U.S.A.* 113 J10
Latiano, *Italy* 35 B10
Latina, *Italy* 34 A5
Latisana, *Italy* 33 C10
Latium = Lazio □, *Italy* 33 F9
Laton, *U.S.A.* 112 J7
Latorica →, *Slovak Rep.* 21 G11
Latouche Treville, C., *Australia* 88 C3
Latrobe, *Australia* 90 G4
Latrobe, *U.S.A.* 106 F5
Latrónico, *Italy* 35 B9
Latvia ■, *Europe* 9 H20
Lau Group, *Fiji* 87 C9
Lauca →, *Bolivia* 124 D4
Lauchhammer, *Germany* 18 D9
Lauenburg, *Germany* 18 B6
Läufelfingen, *Switz.* 22 B5
Laufen, *Switz.* 22 B5
Lauffen, *Germany* 19 F5
Laujar, *Spain* 29 J2
Laukaa, *Finland* 9 E21
Launceston, *Australia* 90 G4
Launceston, *U.K.* 13 G3
Laune →, *Ireland* 15 D2
Laupheim, *Germany* 19 G5
Laura, *Australia* 90 B3
Laureana di Borrello, *Italy* 35 D9
Laurel, *Miss., U.S.A.* 109 K10
Laurel, *Mont., U.S.A.* 110 D9
Laurencekirk, *U.K.* 14 E6
Laurens, *U.S.A.* 105 H4
Laurentian Plateau, *Canada* 99 B6
Laurentides, Parc Prov. des, *Canada* 99 C5
Lauria, *Italy* 35 B8
Laurie L., *Canada* 101 B8
Laurinburg, *U.S.A.* 105 H6
Laurium, *U.S.A.* 104 B1
Lausanne, *Switz.* 22 C3
Laut, *Indonesia* 56 D3
Laut Kecil, Kepulauan, *Indonesia* 56 E5
Lautaro, *Chile* 128 A2
Lauterbach, *Germany* 18 E5
Lauterbrunnen, *Switz.* 22 C5
Lauterecken, *Germany* 19 F3
Lautoka, *Fiji* 87 C7
Lauwe, *Belgium* 17 G2
Lauwers, *Neths.* 16 A8
Lauwers Zee, *Neths.* 16 B8
Lauzon, *Canada* 99 C5
Lava Hot Springs, *U.S.A.* 110 E7
Lavadores, *Spain* 30 C2
Lavagna, *Italy* 32 D6
Laval, *France* 24 D6
Lavalle, *Argentina* 126 B2
Lávara, *Greece* 39 H9
Lavardac, *France* 26 D4
Lavaur, *France* 26 E5
Lavaux, *Switz.* 22 D3
Lavelanet, *France* 26 F5
Lavello, *Italy* 35 A8
Laverne, *U.S.A.* 109 G5
Laverton, *Australia* 89 E3
Lavos, *Portugal* 30 E2
Lavras, *Brazil* 123 F3
Lavre, *Portugal* 31 G2
Lavrentiya, *Russia* 45 C19
Lávrion, *Greece* 39 M7
Lávris, *Greece* 37 D6
Lavumisa, *Swaziland* 85 D5
Lawas, *Malaysia* 56 D5
Lawele, *Indonesia* 57 F6
Lawn Hill, *Australia* 90 B2
Lawng Pit, *Burma* 61 G20
Lawqah, *Si. Arabia* 64 D4
Lawra, *Ghana* 78 C4
Lawrence, *N.Z.* 87 L2
Lawrence, *Kans., U.S.A.* 108 F7
Lawrence, *Mass., U.S.A.* 107 D13
Lawrenceburg, *Ind., U.S.A.* 104 F3
Lawrenceburg, *Tenn., U.S.A.* 105 H2
Lawrenceville, *U.S.A.* 105 J4
Laws, *U.S.A.* 112 H8
Lawton, *U.S.A.* 109 H5
Lawu, *Indonesia* 57 G14
Laxford, L., *U.K.* 14 C3
Lay →, *France* 26 B2
Laylān, *Iraq* 64 C5
Layon →, *France* 24 E6
Laysan I., *Pac. Oc.* 93 E11
Laytonville, *U.S.A.* 110 G2
Lazarevskoye, *Russia* 43 J4
Lazio □, *Italy* 33 F9
Lazo, *Russia* 48 C6
Le Barcarès, *France* 26 F7
Le Beausset, *France* 27 E9

Le Blanc, *France* 26 B5
Le Bleymard, *France* 26 D7
Le Bourgneuf-la-Fôret, *France* 24 D6
Le Bouscat, *France* 26 D3
Le Brassus, *Switz.* 22 C2
Le Bugue, *France* 26 D4
Le Canourgue, *France* 26 D7
Le Cateau, *France* 25 B10
Le Chambon-Feugerolles, *France* 27 C8
Le Château-d'Oléron, *France* 26 C2
Le Châtelard, *Switz.* 22 D3
Le Châtelet, *France* 26 B6
Le Châtelet-en-Brie, *France* 25 D9
Le Chesne, *France* 25 C11
Le Cheylard, *France* 27 D8
Le Conquet, *France* 24 D2
Le Creusot, *France* 25 F11
Le Croisic, *France* 24 E4
Le Donjon, *France* 26 B7
Le Dorat, *France* 26 B5
Le François, *Martinique* 117 D7
Le Grand-Lucé, *France* 24 E7
Le Grand-Pressigny, *France* 24 F7
Le Havre, *France* 24 C7
Le Lavandou, *France* 27 E10
Le Lion-d'Angers, *France* 24 E6
Le Locle, *Switz.* 22 B3
Le Louroux-Béconnais, *France* 24 E6
Le Luc, *France* 27 E10
Le Madonie, *Italy* 34 E6
Le Maire, Estr. de, *Argentina* 128 D4
Le Mans, *France* 24 E7
Le Mars, *U.S.A.* 108 D6
Le Mêle-sur-Sarthe, *France* 24 D7
Le Merlerault, *France* 24 D7
Le Monastier-sur-Gazeille, *France* 26 D7
Le Monêtier-les-Bains, *France* 27 D10
Le Mont d'Or, *France* 25 F13
Le Mont-Dore, *France* 26 C6
Le Mont-St.-Michel, *France* 24 D5
Le Moule, *Guadeloupe* 117 C7
Le Muy, *France* 27 E10
Le Palais, *France* 24 E3
Le Perthus, *France* 26 F6
Le Pont, *Switz.* 22 C2
Le Pouldu, *France* 24 E3
Le Puy-en-Velay, *France* 26 C7
Le Quesnoy, *France* 25 B10
Le Roy, *U.S.A.* 109 F7
Le Sentier, *Switz.* 22 C2
Le Sueur, *U.S.A.* 108 C8
Le Teil, *France* 27 D8
Le Teilleul, *France* 24 D6
Le Theil, *France* 24 D7
Le Thillot, *France* 25 E13
Le Thuy, *Vietnam* 58 D6
Le Touquet-Paris-Plage, *France* 25 B8
Le Tréport, *France* 24 B8
Le Val-d'Ajol, *France* 25 E13
Le Verdon-sur-Mer, *France* 26 C2
Le Vigan, *France* 26 E7
Lea →, *U.K.* 13 F7
Leach, *Cambodia* 59 F4
Lead, *U.S.A.* 108 C3
Leader, *Canada* 101 C7
Leadhills, *U.K.* 14 F5
Leadville, *U.S.A.* 111 G10
Leaf →, *U.S.A.* 109 K10
Leakey, *U.S.A.* 109 L5
Leamington, *Canada* 98 D3
Leamington, *U.S.A.* 110 G7
Leamington Spa = Royal Leamington Spa, *U.K.* 13 E6
Le'an, *China* 53 D10
Leandro Norte Alem, *Argentina* 127 B4
Learmonth, *Australia* 88 D1
Leask, *Canada* 101 C7
Leavenworth, *Kans., U.S.A.* 108 F7
Leavenworth, *Wash., U.S.A.* 110 C3
Łeba, *Poland* 20 A7
Lebak, *Phil.* 55 H6
Lebam, *U.S.A.* 112 D3
Lebanon, *Ind., U.S.A.* 104 E2
Lebanon, *Kans., U.S.A.* 108 F5
Lebanon, *Ky., U.S.A.* 104 G3
Lebanon, *Mo., U.S.A.* 109 G8
Lebanon, *Oreg., U.S.A.* 110 D2
Lebanon, *Pa., U.S.A.* 107 F8
Lebanon, *Tenn., U.S.A.* 105 G2
Lebanon ■, *Asia* 69 B4
Lebbeke, *Belgium* 17 G4
Lebec, *U.S.A.* 113 L8
Lebedyan, *Russia* 42 D4
Lebedyn, *Ukraine* 41 G8
Lebomboberge, *S. Africa* 85 C5
Lębork, *Poland* 20 A7
Lebrija, *Spain* 31 J4
Lebu, *Chile* 126 D1
Lecce, *Italy* 35 B11
Lecco, *Italy* 32 C6
Lecco, L. di, *Italy* 32 C6
Lécera, *Spain* 28 D4
Lech, *Austria* 19 H6
Lech →, *Germany* 19 G6
Lechang, *China* 53 E9
Lechtaler Alpen, *Austria* 19 H6
Lectoure, *France* 26 E4
Łęczyca, *Poland* 20 C9
Ledbury, *U.K.* 13 E5
Lede, *Belgium* 17 G3
Ledeberg, *Belgium* 17 F3
Ledesma, *Spain* 30 D5
Ledong, *China* 58 C7
Leduc, *Canada* 100 C6
Ledyczek, *Poland* 20 B6
Lee, *U.S.A.* 107 D11
Lee →, *Ireland* 15 E3
Lee Vining, *U.S.A.* 112 H7
Leech L., *U.S.A.* 108 B7
Leedey, *U.S.A.* 109 H5
Leeds, *U.K.* 12 D6
Leeds, *U.S.A.* 105 J2
Leek, *Neths.* 16 B8
Leek, *U.K.* 12 D5
Leende, *Neths.* 17 F7
Leer, *Germany* 18 B3
Leerdam, *Neths.* 16 E6
Leersum, *Neths.* 16 E6
Leesburg, *U.S.A.* 105 L5
Leesville, *U.S.A.* 109 K8
Leeton, *Australia* 91 E4
Leetonia, *U.S.A.* 106 F4
Leeu Gamka, *S. Africa* 84 E3
Leeuwarden, *Neths.* 16 B7
Leeuwin, C., *Australia* 89 F2
Leeward Is., *Atl. Oc.* 117 C7
Lefka, *Cyprus* 37 D11
Lefkoniko, *Cyprus* 37 D12
Lefors, *U.S.A.* 109 H4
Lefroy, L., *Australia* 89 F3
Legal, *Canada* 100 C6
Leganés, *Spain* 30 E7
Legazpi, *Phil.* 55 E5
Legendre I., *Australia* 88 D2
Leghorn = Livorno, *Italy* 32 E7
Legionowo, *Poland* 20 C10
Léglise, *Belgium* 17 J7
Legnago, *Italy* 33 C8
Legnano, *Italy* 32 C5
Legnica, *Poland* 20 D6
Legrad, *Croatia* 33 B13
Legume, *Australia* 91 D5
Leh, *India* 63 B7
Lehi, *U.S.A.* 110 F8
Lehighton, *U.S.A.* 107 F9
Lehrte, *Germany* 18 C5
Lehututu, *Botswana* 84 C3
Lei Shui →, *China* 53 D9
Leiah, *Pakistan* 62 D4
Leibnitz, *Austria* 21 J5
Leibo, *China* 52 C4
Leicester, *U.K.* 13 E6
Leicestershire □, *U.K.* 13 E6
Leichhardt →, *Australia* 90 B2
Leichhardt Ra., *Australia* 90 C4
Leiden, *Neths.* 16 D5
Leiderdorp, *Neths.* 16 D5
Leidschendam, *Neths.* 16 D4
Leie →, *Belgium* 25 A10
Leignon, *Belgium* 17 H6
Leine →, *Germany* 18 C5
Leinster, *Australia* 89 E3
Leinster □, *Ireland* 15 C4
Leinster, Mt., *Ireland* 15 D5
Leipzig, *Germany* 18 D8
Leiria, *Portugal* 31 F2
Leiria □, *Portugal* 31 F2
Leirvik, *Norway* 9 G11
Leisler, Mt., *Australia* 88 D4
Leith, *U.K.* 14 F5
Leith Hill, *U.K.* 13 F7
Leitha →, *Europe* 21 H7
Leitrim, *Ireland* 15 B3
Leitrim □, *Ireland* 15 B3
Leiyang, *China* 53 D9
Leiza, *Spain* 28 B3
Leizhou Bandao, *China* 54 D6
Leizhou Wan, *China* 53 G8
Lek →, *Neths.* 16 E5
Leka, *Norway* 8 D14
Leke, *Belgium* 17 F1
Lekkerkerk, *Neths.* 16 E5
Leksula, *Indonesia* 57 E7
Lékva Ori, *Greece* 37 D6
Leland, *U.S.A.* 109 J9
Leland Lakes, *Canada* 101 A6
Leleque, *Argentina* 128 B2
Lelystad, *Neths.* 16 D7
Lema, *Nigeria* 79 C5
Léman, L., *Europe* 22 D3
Lemelerveld, *Neths.* 16 D8
Lemera, *Zaïre* 82 C2
Lemery, *Phil.* 55 E4
Lemgo, *Germany* 18 C4
Lemhi Ra., *U.S.A.* 110 D7
Lemmer, *Neths.* 16 C7
Lemmon, *U.S.A.* 108 C3
Lemon Grove, *U.S.A.* 113 N9
Lemoore, *U.S.A.* 111 H4
Lempdes, *France* 26 C7
Lemsid, *W. Sahara* 74 C2
Lemvig, *Denmark* 11 H2
Lena →, *Russia* 45 B13
Lencloître, *France* 24 F7
Lençóis, *Brazil* 123 D3
Léndas, *Greece* 37 E6
Lendeh, *Iran* 65 D6
Lendelede, *Belgium* 17 G2
Lendinara, *Italy* 33 C8
Lengerich, *Germany* 18 C3
Lenggong, *Malaysia* 59 K3
Lenggries, *Germany* 19 H7
Lengua de Vaca, Pta., *Chile* 126 C1
Lenina, Kanal →, *Russia* 43 J7
Leninabad = Khudzhand, *Tajikistan* 44 E7
Leninakan = Gyumri, *Armenia* 43 K6
Leningrad = Sankt-Peterburg, *Russia* 40 C6
Lenino, *Ukraine* 41 K8
Leninogorsk, *Kazakstan* 44 D9
Leninsk, *Russia* 43 F7
Leninsk-Kuznetskiy, *Russia* 44 D9
Leninskoye, *Russia* 42 A8
Leninskoye, *Russia* 45 E14
Lenk, *Switz.* 22 D4
Lenkoran = Länkäran, *Azerbaijan* 67 C13
Lenmalu, *Indonesia* 57 E8
Lenne →, *Germany* 18 D3
Lennox, I., *Chile* 128 E3
Lennoxville, *Canada* 107 A13
Leno, *Italy* 32 C7
Lenoir, *U.S.A.* 105 H5
Lenoir City, *U.S.A.* 105 H3
Lenora, *U.S.A.* 108 F4
Lenore L., *Canada* 101 C8
Lenox, *U.S.A.* 107 D11
Lens, *Belgium* 17 G3
Lens, *France* 25 B9
Lens St. Remy, *Belgium* 17 G6
Lensk, *Russia* 45 C12
Lent, *Neths.* 16 E7
Lentekhi, *Georgia* 43 J6
Lentini, *Italy* 35 E8
Lenwood, *U.S.A.* 113 L9
Lenzburg, *Switz.* 22 B6
Lenzen, *Germany* 18 B7
Lenzerheide, *Switz.* 23 C9
Léo, *Burkina Faso* 78 C4
Leoben, *Austria* 21 H5
Leodhas = Lewis, *U.K.* 14 C2
Leola, *U.S.A.* 108 C5
Leominster, *U.K.* 13 E5
Leominster, *U.S.A.* 107 D13
Léon, *France* 26 E2
León, *Mexico* 114 C4
León, *Nic.* 116 D2
León, *Spain* 30 C5
Leon, *U.S.A.* 108 E8
León □, *Spain* 30 C5
León, Montañas de, *Spain* 30 C4
Leonardtown, *U.S.A.* 104 F7
Leone, Mte., *Switz.* 22 D6
Leonforte, *Italy* 35 E7
Leongatha, *Australia* 91 F4
Leonídhion, *Greece* 39 M5
Leonora, *Australia* 89 E3
Léopold II, Lac = Mai-Ndombe, L., *Zaïre* 80 E3
Leopoldina, *Brazil* 123 F3
Leopoldo Bulhões, *Brazil* 123 E2
Leopoldsburg, *Belgium* 17 F6
Léopoldville = Kinshasa, *Zaïre* 80 E3
Leoti, *U.S.A.* 108 F4
Leova, *Moldova* 41 J5
Leoville, *Canada* 101 C7
Lépa, L. do, *Angola* 84 B2
Lepe, *Spain* 31 H3
Lepel = Lyepyel, *Belarus* 40 E5
Lepikha, *Russia* 45 C13
Leping, *China* 53 C11
Lepontine, Alpi, *Italy* 23 D6
Leppävirta, *Finland* 9 E22
Lequeitio, *Spain* 28 B2
Lercara Friddi, *Italy* 34 E6
Lerdo, *Mexico* 114 B4
Léré, *Chad* 73 G7
Lere, *Nigeria* 79 D6
Leribe, *Lesotho* 85 D4
Lérici, *Italy* 32 D6
Lérida, *Spain* 28 D5
Lérida □, *Spain* 28 C6
Lérins, Is. de, *France* 27 E11
Lerma, *Spain* 30 C7
Léros, *Greece* 39 M9
Lérouville, *France* 25 D12
Lerwick, *U.K.* 14 A7
Les Abrets, *France* 27 C9
Les Andelys, *France* 24 C8
Les Arcs, *France* 27 E10
Les Baux-de-Provence, *France* 27 E8
Les Bois, *Switz.* 22 B3
Les Cayes, *Haiti* 117 C5
Les Diablerets, *Switz.* 22 D4
Les Échelles, *France* 27 C9
Les Essarts, *France* 24 F5
Les Étroits, *Canada* 99 C6
Les Eyzies-de-Tayac-Sireuil, *France* 26 D5
Les Herbiers, *France* 24 F5
Les Minquiers, *Chan. Is.* 24 D4
Les Ponts-de-Cé, *France* 24 E6
Les Riceys, *France* 25 E11
Les Sables-d'Olonne, *France* 26 B2
Les Vans, *France* 27 D8
Les Verrières, *Switz.* 22 C2
Lesbos = Lésvos, *Greece* 39 K9
Leshan, *China* 52 C4
Lésina, L. di, *Italy* 33 G12
Lesja, *Norway* 10 B2
Lesjaverk, *Norway* 10 B2
Leskov I., *Antarctica* 5 B1
Leskovac, *Serbia, Yug.* 21 M11
Leslie, *U.S.A.* 109 H8
Lesneven, *France* 24 D2
Lešnica, *Serbia, Yug.* 21 L9
Lesnoye, *Russia* 42 A2
Lesopilnoye, *Russia* 48 A7
Lesotho ■, *Africa* 85 D4
Lesozavodsk, *Russia* 45 E14
Lesparre-Médoc, *France* 26 C3
Lessay, *France* 24 C5
Lesse →, *Belgium* 17 H5
Lesser Antilles, *W. Indies* 117 C7
Lesser Slave L., *Canada* 100 B5
Lesser Sunda Is., *Indonesia* 57 F6
Lessines, *Belgium* 17 G3
Lester, *U.S.A.* 112 C5
Lestock, *Canada* 101 C8
Lesuer I., *Australia* 88 B4
Lésvos, *Greece* 39 K9
Leszno, *Poland* 20 D6
Letchworth, *U.K.* 13 F7
Letea, Ostrov, *Romania* 38 D12
Lethbridge, *Canada* 100 D6
Lethem, *Guyana* 121 C6
Leti, Kepulauan, *Indonesia* 57 F7
Leti Is. = Leti, Kepulauan, *Indonesia* 57 F7
Letiahau →, *Botswana* 84 C3
Leticia, *Colombia* 120 D4
Leting, *China* 51 E10
Letjiesbos, *S. Africa* 84 E3
Letlhakeng, *Botswana* 84 C3
Letpadan, *Burma* 61 L19
Letpan, *Burma* 61 K19
Letterkenny, *Ireland* 15 B4
Leu, *Romania* 38 E7
Leucadia, *U.S.A.* 113 M9
Leucate, *France* 26 F7
Leucate, Étang de, *France* 26 F7
Leuk, *Switz.* 22 D5
Leukerbad, *Switz.* 22 D5
Leupegem, *Belgium* 17 G3
Leuser, G., *Indonesia* 56 D1
Leutkirch, *Germany* 19 H6
Leuven, *Belgium* 17 G5
Leuze, *Hainaut, Belgium* 17 G3
Leuze, *Namur, Belgium* 17 G5
Lev Tolstoy, *Russia* 42 D4
Levádhia, *Greece* 39 L5
Levan, *U.S.A.* 110 G8
Levanger, *Norway* 8 E14
Levant, I. du, *France* 27 E10
Lévanto, *Italy* 32 D6
Levanzo, *Italy* 34 E5
Levelland, *U.S.A.* 109 J3
Leven, *U.K.* 14 E6
Leven, L., *U.K.* 14 E5
Leven, Toraka, *Madag.* 85 A8
Levens, *France* 27 E11
Leveque C., *Australia* 88 C3
Leverano, *Italy* 35 B10
Leverkusen, *Germany* 18 D2
Levet, *France* 25 F9
Levice, *Slovak Rep.* 21 G8
Levico, *Italy* 33 C8
Levie, *France* 27 G13
Levier, *France* 25 F13
Levin, *N.Z.* 87 J5
Lévis, *Canada* 99 C5
Levis, L., *Canada* 100 A5
Levítha, *Greece* 39 M9
Levittown, *N.Y., U.S.A.* 107 F11
Levittown, *Pa., U.S.A.* 107 F10
Levkás, *Greece* 39 L3
Levkímmi, *Greece* 37 B4
Levkímmi, Ákra, *Greece* 37 B4
Levkôsia = Nicosia, *Cyprus* 66 E5
Levoča, *Slovak Rep.* 20 F10
Levroux, *France* 25 F8
Levski, *Bulgaria* 38 F8
Levskigrad = Karlovo, *Bulgaria* 38 G7
Lewellen, *U.S.A.* 108 E3
Lewes, *U.K.* 13 G8
Lewes, *U.S.A.* 104 F8
Lewis, *U.K.* 14 C2
Lewis →, *U.S.A.* 112 E4
Lewis, Butt of, *U.K.* 14 C2
Lewis Ra., *Australia* 88 D4
Lewis Range, *U.S.A.* 110 C7
Lewisburg, *Pa., U.S.A.* 106 F8
Lewisburg, *Tenn., U.S.A.* 105 H2
Lewisporte, *Canada* 99 C8
Lewiston, *Idaho, U.S.A.* 110 C5
Lewiston, *Maine, U.S.A.* 105 C11
Lewistown, *Mont., U.S.A.* 110 C9
Lewistown, *Pa., U.S.A.* 106 F7
Lexington, *Ill., U.S.A.* 108 E10
Lexington, *Ky., U.S.A.* 104 F3
Lexington, *Miss., U.S.A.* 109 J9
Lexington, *Mo., U.S.A.* 108 F8
Lexington, *N.C., U.S.A.* 105 H5
Lexington, *Nebr., U.S.A.* 108 E5
Lexington, *Ohio, U.S.A.* 106 F2
Lexington, *Oreg., U.S.A.* 110 D4
Lexington, *Tenn., U.S.A.* 105 H1
Lexington Park, *U.S.A.* 104 F7
Leye, *China* 52 E6
Leyre →, *France* 26 D2
Leysin, *Switz.* 22 D4
Leyte, *Phil.* 55 F6
Leyte Gulf, *Phil.* 55 F6
Lezay, *France* 26 B4
Lezha, *Albania* 39 H2
Lezhi, *China* 52 B5
Lézignan-Corbières, *France* 26 E6
Lezoux, *France* 26 C7
Lgov, *Russia* 42 E2
Lhasa, *China* 54 D4
Lhazê, *China* 54 D3
Lhokkruet, *Indonesia* 56 D1
Lhokseumawe, *Indonesia* 56 C1
Lhuntsi Dzong, *India* 61 F17
Li, *Thailand* 58 D2
Li Shui →, *China* 53 C9
Li Xian, *Gansu, China* 50 G3
Li Xian, *Hebei, China* 50 E8
Li Xian, *Hunan, China* 53 C8
Li Xian, *Sichuan, China* 52 B4
Liádhoi, *Greece* 39 N9
Lian Xian, *China* 53 E9
Liancheng, *China* 53 E11
Lianga, *Phil.* 55 G7
Liangcheng, *Nei Mongol Zizhiqu, China* 50 D7
Liangcheng, *Shandong, China* 51 G10
Liangdang, *China* 50 H4
Lianghekou, *China* 52 C7
Liangping, *China* 52 B6
Lianhua, *China* 53 D9
Lianjiang, *Fujian, China* 53 D12
Lianjiang, *Guangdong, China* 53 G8
Lianping, *China* 53 E10
Lianshan, *China* 53 E9
Lianshanguan, *China* 51 D12
Lianshui, *China* 51 H10
Lianyuan, *China* 53 D8
Lianyungang, *China* 51 G10
Liao He →, *China* 51 D11
Liaocheng, *China* 50 F8
Liaodong Bandao, *China* 51 E12
Liaodong Wan, *China* 51 D11
Liaoning □, *China* 51 D12
Liaoyang, *China* 51 D12
Liaoyuan, *China* 51 C13
Liaozhong, *China* 51 D12
Liapádhes, *Greece* 39 K2
Liard →, *Canada* 100 A4
Liari, *Pakistan* 62 G2
Líbano, *Colombia* 120 C2
Libau = Liepāja, *Latvia* 9 H19
Libby, *U.S.A.* 110 B6
Libenge, *Zaïre* 80 D3
Liberal, *Kans., U.S.A.* 109 G4
Liberal, *Mo., U.S.A.* 109 G7
Liberdade, *Brazil* 124 C3
Liberdade →, *Brazil* 125 B7
Liberec, *Czech.* 20 E5
Liberia, *Costa Rica* 116 D2
Liberia ■, *W. Afr.* 78 D3
Libertad, *Venezuela* 120 B4
Liberty, *Mo., U.S.A.* 108 F7
Liberty, *Tex., U.S.A.* 109 K7
Libin, *Belgium* 17 J6
Lîbîya, Sahrâ', *Africa* 73 C9
Libo, *China* 52 E6
Libobo, Tanjung, *Indonesia* 57 E7
Libode, *S. Africa* 85 E4
Libonda, *Zambia* 81 G4
Libourne, *France* 26 D3
Libramont, *Belgium* 17 J6
Libreville, *Gabon* 80 D1
Libya ■, *N. Afr.* 73 C8
Libyan Desert = Lîbîya, Sahrâ', *Africa* 73 C9
Libyan Plateau = Ed-Déffa, *Egypt* 76 A2
Licantén, *Chile* 126 D1
Licata, *Italy* 34 E6
Lice, *Turkey* 67 C9
Licheng, *China* 50 F7
Lichfield, *U.K.* 12 E6
Lichinga, *Mozam.* 83 E4
Lichtaart, *Belgium* 17 F5
Lichtenburg, *S. Africa* 84 D4
Lichtenfels, *Germany* 19 E7
Lichtenvoorde, *Neths.* 16 E9
Lichtervelde, *Belgium* 17 F2
Lichuan, *Hubei, China* 52 B7
Lichuan, *Jiangxi, China* 53 D11
Licosa, Punta, *Italy* 35 B7
Lida, *Belarus* 9 K21
Lida, *U.S.A.* 111 H5
Lidingö, *Sweden* 10 E12
Lidköping, *Sweden* 11 F7
Lido, *Italy* 33 C9
Lido, *Niger* 79 C5
Lido di Roma = Ostia, Lido di, *Italy* 34 A5
Lidzbark Warminski, *Poland* 20 A10
Liebenwalde, *Germany* 18 C9
Lieberose, *Germany* 18 D10
Liebig, Mt., *Australia* 88 D5
Liechtenstein ■, *Europe* 23 B9
Liederkerke, *Belgium* 17 G4
Liège, *Belgium* 17 G7
Liège □, *Belgium* 17 G7
Liegnitz = Legnica, *Poland* 20 D6
Liempde, *Neths.* 17 E6
Lienart, *Zaïre* 82 B2
Lienyünchiangshih = Lianyungang, *China* 51 G10
Lienz, *Austria* 21 J2
Liepāja, *Latvia* 9 H19
Lier, *Belgium* 17 F5
Lierneux, *Belgium* 17 H7
Lieshout, *Neths.* 17 E7
Liestal, *Switz.* 22 B5
Liévin, *France* 25 B9
Lièvre →, *Canada* 98 C4
Liezen, *Austria* 21 H4

Liffey →, Ireland 15 C5
Lifford, Ireland 15 B4
Liffré, France 24 D5
Lifjell, Norway 10 E2
Lifudzin, Russia 48 B7
Ligao, Phil. 55 E5
Lightning Ridge, Australia 91 D4
Lignano Sabbiadoro, Italy 33 C10
Ligny-en-Barrois, France 25 D12
Ligny-le-Châtel, France 25 E10
Ligoúrion, Greece 39 M6
Ligueil, France 24 E7
Liguria □, Italy 32 D6
Ligurian Sea, Medit. S. 32 E5
Lihou Reefs and Cays, Australia 90 B5
Lihue, U.S.A. 102 H15
Lijiang, China 52 D3
Likasi, Zaïre 83 E2
Likati, Zaïre 80 D4
Likhoslavl, Russia 42 B2
Likhovskoy, Russia 43 F5
Likoma I., Malawi 83 E3
Likumburu, Tanzania 83 D4
L'Île-Bouchard, France 24 E7
L'Ile-Rousse, France 27 F12
Liling, China 53 D9
Lille, Belgium 17 F5
Lille, France 25 B10
Lille Bælt, Denmark 11 J3
Lillebonne, France 24 C7
Lillehammer, Norway 10 C4
Lillers, France 25 B9
Lillesand, Norway 11 F2
Lilleshall, U.K. 13 E5
Lillestrøm, Norway 10 E5
Lillian Point, Mt., Australia 89 E4
Lillo, Spain 28 F1
Lillooet →, Canada 100 D4
Lilongwe, Malawi 83 E3
Liloy, Phil. 57 C6
Lim →, Bos.-H. 21 M9
Lima, Indonesia 57 E7
Lima, Peru 124 C2
Lima, Mont., U.S.A. 110 D7
Lima, Ohio, U.S.A. 104 E3
Lima □, Peru 124 C2
Lima →, Portugal 30 D2
Limages, Canada 107 A9
Liman, Russia 43 H8
Limassol, Cyprus 66 E5
Limavady, U.K. 15 A5
Limavady □, U.K. 15 B5
Limay →, Argentina 128 A3
Limay Mahuida, Argentina 126 D2
Limbang, Brunei 56 D5
Limbara, Mte., Italy 34 B2
Limbaži, Latvia 9 H21
Limbdi, India 62 H4
Limbe, Cameroon 79 E6
Limbourg, Belgium 17 G7
Limbri, Australia 91 E5
Limbunya, Australia 88 C4
Limburg, Germany 19 E4
Limburg □, Belgium 17 F6
Limburg □, Neths. 17 F7
Limeira, Brazil 127 A6
Limerick, Ireland 15 D3
Limerick □, Ireland 15 D3
Limestone, U.S.A. 106 D6
Limestone →, Canada 101 B10
Limfjorden, Denmark 11 H3
Limia = Lima →, Portugal 30 D2
Limingen, Norway 8 D15
Limmared, Sweden 11 G7
Limmat →, Switz. 23 B6
Limmen, Neths. 16 C5
Limmen Bight, Australia 90 A2
Limmen Bight →, Australia 90 B2
Límni, Greece 39 L6
Límnos, Greece 39 K8
Limoeiro, Brazil 122 C4
Limoeiro do Norte, Brazil 122 C4
Limoges, France 26 C5
Limón, Costa Rica 116 D3
Limon, U.S.A. 108 F3
Limone Piemonte, Italy 32 D4
Limousin, France 26 C5
Limousin, Plateaux du, France 26 C5
Limoux, France 26 E6
Limpopo →, Africa 85 D5
Limuru, Kenya 82 C4
Lin Xian, China 50 F6
Lin'an, China 53 B12
Linapacan I., Phil. 55 F3
Linapacan Str., Phil. 55 F3
Linares, Chile 126 D1
Linares, Colombia 120 C2
Linares, Mexico 115 C5
Linares, Spain 29 G1
Linares □, Chile 126 D1
Línas Mte., Italy 34 C1
Lincang, China 52 F3
Lincheng, China 50 F8
Linchuan, China 53 D11
Lincoln, Argentina 126 C3
Lincoln, N.Z. 87 K4
Lincoln, U.K. 12 D7
Lincoln, Calif., U.S.A. 112 G5
Lincoln, Ill., U.S.A. 108 E10
Lincoln, Kans., U.S.A. 108 F5
Lincoln, Maine, U.S.A. 99 C6
Lincoln, N.H., U.S.A. 107 B13
Lincoln, N. Mex., U.S.A. 111 K11
Lincoln, Nebr., U.S.A. 108 E6
Lincoln Hav = Lincoln Sea, Arctic 4 A5
Lincoln Sea, Arctic 4 A5
Lincolnshire □, U.K. 12 D7
Lincolnshire Wolds, U.K. 12 D7
Lincolnton, U.S.A. 105 H5
L'Incudine, France 27 G13
Lind, U.S.A. 110 C4
Linda, U.S.A. 112 F5
Lindau, Germany 19 H5
Linde →, Neths. 16 C7
Linden, Guyana 121 B6
Linden, Calif., U.S.A. 112 G5
Linden, Tex., U.S.A. 109 J7
Lindenheuvel, Neths. 17 G7
Lindenhurst, U.S.A. 107 F11
Linderöd, Sweden 11 J7
Linderödsåsen, Sweden 11 J7
Lindesnes, Norway 9 H12
Líndhos, Greece 66 D3
Lindi, Tanzania 83 D4
Lindi □, Tanzania 83 D4
Lindi →, Zaïre 82 B2
Lindoso, Portugal 30 D2
Lindow, Germany 18 C8
Lindsay, Canada 98 D4
Lindsay, Calif., U.S.A. 111 H4
Lindsay, Okla., U.S.A. 109 H6
Lindsborg, U.S.A. 108 F6
Linfen, China 50 F6
Ling Xian, Hunan, China 53 D9
Ling Xian, Shandong, China 50 F9
Lingao, China 58 C7
Lingayen, Phil. 57 A6
Lingayen G., Phil. 55 C4
Lingbi, China 51 H9
Lingchuan, Guangxi Zhuangzu, China 53 E8
Lingchuan, Shanxi, China 50 G7
Lingen, Germany 18 C3
Lingga, Indonesia 56 E2
Lingga, Kepulauan, Indonesia 56 E2
Lingga Arch. = Lingga, Kepulauan, Indonesia 56 E2
Lingle, U.S.A. 108 D2
Lingling, China 53 D8
Lingqiu, China 50 E8
Lingshan, China 52 F7
Lingshi, China 50 F6
Lingshou, China 50 E8
Lingshui, China 58 C8
Lingtai, China 50 G4
Linguéré, Senegal 78 B1
Lingwu, China 50 E4
Lingyuan, China 51 D10
Lingyun, China 52 E6
Linh Cam, Vietnam 58 C5
Linhai, China 53 C13
Linhares, Brazil 123 E3
Linhe, China 50 D4
Linjiang, China 51 D14
Linköping, Sweden 11 F9
Linkou, China 51 B16
Linli, China 53 C8
Linlithgow, U.K. 14 F5
Linnhe, L., U.K. 14 E3
Linosa, I., Medit. S. 75 A7
Linqi, China 50 G7
Linqing, China 50 F8
Linqu, China 51 F10
Linru, China 50 G7
Lins, Brazil 127 A6
Linshui, China 52 B6
Lintao, China 50 G2
Linth →, Switz. 19 H5
Linthal, Switz. 23 C8
Lintlaw, Canada 101 C8
Linton, Canada 99 C5
Linton, Ind., U.S.A. 104 F2
Linton, N. Dak., U.S.A. 108 B4
Lintong, China 50 G5
Linville, Australia 91 D5
Linwood, Canada 106 C4
Linwu, China 53 E9
Linxi, China 51 C10
Linxia, China 54 C5
Linxiang, China 53 C9
Linyanti →, Africa 84 B4
Linyi, China 51 G10
Linz, Austria 21 G4
Linz, Germany 18 E3
Linzhenzhen, China 50 F5
Linzi, China 51 F10
Lion, G. du, France 27 E8
Lionárisso, Cyprus 37 D13
Lioni, Italy 35 B8
Lions, G. of = Lion, G. du, France 27 E8
Lion's Den, Zimbabwe 83 F3
Lion's Head, Canada 98 D3
Liozno = Lyozna, Belarus 40 E6
Lipa, Phil. 55 E4
Lipali, Mozam. 83 F4
Lípari, Italy 35 D7
Lípari, Is. = Eólie, Ís., Italy 35 D7
Lipcani, Moldova 41 H4
Lipetsk, Russia 42 D4
Liping, China 52 D7
Lipkany = Lipcani, Moldova 41 H4
Lipljan, Serbia, Yug. 21 N11
Lipno, Poland 20 C9
Lipova, Romania 38 C4
Lipovcy Manzovka, Russia 48 B6
Lipovets, Ukraine 41 H5
Lippe →, Germany 18 D2
Lippstadt, Germany 18 D4
Lipscomb, U.S.A. 109 G4
Lipsko, Poland 20 D11
Lipsói, Greece 39 M9
Liptovsky Svaty Milkulaš, Slovak Rep. 20 F9
Liptrap C., Australia 91 F4
Lipu, China 53 E8
Lira, Uganda 82 B3
Liri →, Italy 34 A6
Liria, Spain 28 F4
Lisala, Zaïre 80 D4
Lisboa, Portugal 31 G1
Lisboa □, Portugal 31 G1
Lisbon = Lisboa, Portugal 31 G1
Lisbon, N. Dak., U.S.A. 108 B6
Lisbon, N.H., U.S.A. 107 B13
Lisbon, Ohio, U.S.A. 106 F4
Lisburn, U.K. 15 B5
Lisburne, C., U.S.A. 96 B3
Liscannor, B., Ireland 15 D2
Liscia →, Italy 34 A2
Lishe Jiang →, China 52 E3
Lishi, China 50 F6
Lishu, China 51 C13
Lishui, Jiangsu, China 53 B12
Lishui, Zhejiang, China 53 C12
Lisianski I., Pac. Oc. 92 E10
Lisichansk = Lysychansk, Ukraine 41 H10
Lisieux, France 24 C7
Liski, Russia 42 E4
L'Isle-Adam, France 25 C9
L'Isle-Jourdain, Gers, France 26 E5
L'Isle-Jourdain, Vienne, France 26 B4
L'Isle-sur-le-Doubs, France 25 E13
Lisle-sur-Tarn, France 26 E5
Lismore, Australia 91 D5
Lismore, Ireland 15 D4
Lisse, Neths. 16 D5
List, Germany 18 A4
Lista, Norway 9 G12
Lister, Mt., Antarctica 5 D11
Liston, Australia 91 D5
Listowel, Canada 98 D3
Listowel, Ireland 15 D2
Lit-et-Mixe, France 26 D2
Litang, Guangxi Zhuangzu, China 52 F7
Litang, Sichuan, China 52 B3
Litang, Malaysia 57 C5
Litang Qu →, China 52 C3
Litani →, Lebanon 69 B4
Litchfield, Calif., U.S.A. 112 E6
Litchfield, Conn., U.S.A. 107 E11
Litchfield, Ill., U.S.A. 108 F10
Litchfield, Minn., U.S.A. 108 C7
Lithgow, Australia 91 E5
Líthinon, Ákra, Greece 37 E6
Lithuania ■, Europe 9 J20
Litija, Slovenia 33 B11
Litókhoron, Greece 39 J5
Litoměřice, Czech. 20 E4
Little Abaco I., Bahamas 116 A4
Little Barrier I., N.Z. 87 G5
Little Belt Mts., U.S.A. 110 C8
Little Blue →, U.S.A. 108 F6
Little Cadotte →, Canada 100 B5
Little Cayman, I., Cayman Is. 116 C3
Little Churchill →, Canada 101 B9
Little Colorado →, U.S.A. 111 H8
Little Current, Canada 98 C3
Little Current →, Canada 98 B3
Little Falls, Minn., U.S.A. 108 C7
Little Falls, N.Y., U.S.A. 107 C10
Little Fork →, U.S.A. 108 A8
Little Grand Rapids, Canada 101 C9
Little Humboldt →, U.S.A. 110 F5
Little Inagua I., Bahamas 117 B5
Little Karoo, S. Africa 84 E3
Little Lake, U.S.A. 113 K9
Little Laut Is. = Laut Kecil, Kepulauan, Indonesia 56 E5
Little Minch, U.K. 14 D2
Little Missouri →, U.S.A. 108 B3
Little Ouse →, U.K. 13 E8
Little Rann, India 62 H4
Little Red →, U.S.A. 109 H9
Little River, N.Z. 87 K4
Little Rock, U.S.A. 109 H8
Little Ruaha →, Tanzania 82 D4
Little Sable Pt., U.S.A. 104 D2
Little Sioux →, U.S.A. 108 E6
Little Smoky →, Canada 100 C5
Little Snake →, U.S.A. 110 F9
Little Valley, U.S.A. 106 D6
Little Wabash →, U.S.A. 104 G1
Littlefield, U.S.A. 109 J3
Littlefork, U.S.A. 108 A8
Littlehampton, U.K. 13 G7
Littleton, U.S.A. 107 B13
Liu He →, China 51 D11
Liu Jiang →, China 52 F7
Liuba, China 50 H4
Liucheng, China 52 E7
Liugou, China 51 D10
Liuhe, China 51 C13
Liuheng Dao, China 53 C14
Liukang Tenggaja, Indonesia 57 F5
Liuli, Tanzania 83 E3
Liuwa Plain, Zambia 81 G4
Liuyang, China 53 C9
Liuzhou, China 52 E7
Liuzhuang, China 51 H11
Livadherón, Greece 39 J4
Livadhia, Cyprus 37 E12
Livarot, France 24 D7
Live Oak, Calif., U.S.A. 112 F5
Live Oak, Fla., U.S.A. 105 K4
Liveras, Cyprus 37 D11
Liveringa, Australia 88 C3
Livermore, U.S.A. 112 H5
Livermore, Mt., U.S.A. 109 K2
Liverpool, Australia 91 E5
Liverpool, Canada 99 D7
Liverpool, U.K. 12 D5
Liverpool Plains, Australia 91 E5
Liverpool Ra., Australia 91 E5
Livingston, Guatemala 116 C2
Livingston, Calif., U.S.A. 112 H6
Livingston, Mont., U.S.A. 110 D8
Livingston, Tex., U.S.A. 109 K7
Livingstone, Zambia 83 F2
Livingstone Mts., Tanzania 83 D3
Livingstonia, Malawi 83 E3
Livny, Russia 42 D3
Livonia, U.S.A. 104 D4
Livorno, Italy 32 E7
Livramento, Brazil 127 C4
Livramento do Brumado, Brazil 123 D3
Livron-sur-Drôme, France 27 D8
Liwale, Tanzania 83 D4
Liwale □, Tanzania 83 D4
Lixi, China 52 D3
Liyang, China 53 B12
Lizard I., Australia 90 A4
Lizard Pt., U.K. 13 H2
Lizarda, Brazil 122 C2
Lizzano, Italy 35 B10
Ljubija, Bos.-H. 33 D13
Ljubljana, Slovenia 33 B11
Ljubno, Slovenia 33 B11
Ljubuški, Bos.-H. 21 M7
Ljung, Sweden 11 F7
Ljungan →, Sweden 10 B11
Ljungaverk, Sweden 10 B10
Ljungby, Sweden 9 H15
Ljusdal, Sweden 10 C10
Ljusnan →, Sweden 9 F17
Ljusne, Sweden 9 F17
Ljutomer, Slovenia 33 B13
Llagostera, Spain 28 D7
Llamellín, Peru 124 B2
Llancanelo, Salina, Argentina 126 D2
Llandeilo, U.K. 13 F3
Llandovery, U.K. 13 F4
Llandrindod Wells, U.K. 13 E4
Llandudno, U.K. 12 D4
Llanelli, U.K. 13 F3
Llanes, Spain 30 B6
Llangollen, U.K. 12 E4
Llanidloes, U.K. 13 E4
Llano, U.S.A. 109 K5
Llano →, U.S.A. 109 K5
Llano Estacado, U.S.A. 109 J3
Llanos, S. Amer. 118 C3
Llanquihue □, Chile 128 B2
Llanquihue, L., Chile 128 B1
Llebetx, C., Spain 36 B9
Lleida = Lérida, Spain 28 D5
Llentrisca, C., Spain 36 C7
Llera, Mexico 115 C5
Llerena, Spain 31 G4
Llica, Bolivia 124 D4
Llico, Chile 126 C1
Llobregat →, Spain 28 D7
Lloret de Mar, Spain 28 D7
Lloyd B., Australia 90 A3
Lloyd L., Canada 101 B7
Lloydminster, Canada 101 C6
Lluchmayor, Spain 36 B9
Llullaillaco, Volcán, S. Amer. 126 A2
Lo, Belgium 17 G1
Lo →, Vietnam 58 B5
Loa, U.S.A. 111 G8
Loa →, Chile 126 A1
Loano, Italy 32 D5
Lobatse, Botswana 84 D4
Löbau, Germany 18 D10
Lobbes, Belgium 17 H4
Lobenstein, Germany 18 E7
Lobería, Argentina 126 D4
Lobito, Angola 81 G2
Lobón, Canal de, Spain 31 G4
Lobos, Argentina 126 D4
Lobos, I., Mexico 114 B2
Lobos, I. de, Canary Is. 36 F6
Lobos de Tierra, I., Peru 124 B1
Loc Binh, Vietnam 58 B6
Loc Ninh, Vietnam 59 G6
Locarno, Switz. 23 D7
Loch Garman = Wexford, Ireland 15 D5
Lochaber, U.K. 14 E4
Lochcarron, U.K. 14 D3
Lochem, Neths. 16 D8
Loches, France 24 E8
Lochgelly, U.K. 14 E5
Lochgilphead, U.K. 14 E3
Lochinver, U.K. 14 C3
Lochnagar, Australia 90 C4
Lochnagar, U.K. 14 E5
Łochów, Poland 20 C11
Lochy →, U.K. 14 E3
Lock, Australia 91 E2
Lock Haven, U.S.A. 106 E7
Lockeford, U.S.A. 112 G5
Lockeport, Canada 99 D6
Lockerbie, U.K. 14 F5
Lockhart, U.S.A. 109 L6
Lockhart, L., Australia 89 F2
Lockney, U.S.A. 109 H4
Lockport, U.S.A. 106 C6
Locminé, France 24 E4
Locri, Italy 35 D9
Locronan, France 24 D2
Loctudy, France 24 E2
Lod, Israel 69 D3
Lodeinoye Pole, Russia 40 B7
Lodève, France 26 E7
Lodge Grass, U.S.A. 110 D10
Lodgepole, U.S.A. 108 E3
Lodgepole Cr. →, U.S.A. 108 E2
Lodhran, Pakistan 62 E4
Lodi, Italy 32 C6
Lodi, U.S.A. 112 G5
Lodja, Zaïre 82 C1
Lodosa, Spain 28 C2
Lödöse, Sweden 11 F6
Lodwar, Kenya 82 B4
Łódź, Poland 20 D9
Loei, Thailand 58 D3
Loenen, Neths. 16 D8
Loengo, Zaïre 82 C2
Loeriesfontein, S. Africa 84 E2
Lofoten, Norway 8 B15
Lofsdalen, Sweden 10 B7
Lofsen →, Sweden 10 B7
Logan, Kans., U.S.A. 108 F5
Logan, Ohio, U.S.A. 104 F4
Logan, Utah, U.S.A. 110 F8
Logan, W. Va., U.S.A. 104 G5
Logan, Mt., Canada 96 B5
Logan Pass, U.S.A. 100 D6
Logandale, U.S.A. 113 J12
Logansport, Ind., U.S.A. 104 E2
Logansport, La., U.S.A. 109 K8
Logo, Sudan 77 F3
Logone →, Chad 73 F8
Logroño, Spain 28 C2
Logrosán, Spain 31 F5
Løgstør, Denmark 11 H3
Lohardaga, India 63 H11
Lohja, Finland 9 F21
Lohr, Germany 19 F5
Loi-kaw, Burma 61 K20
Loimaa, Finland 9 F20
Loir →, France 24 E6
Loir-et-Cher □, France 24 E8
Loire □, France 27 C8
Loire →, France 24 E4
Loire-Atlantique □, France 24 E5
Loiret □, France 25 E9
Loitz, Germany 18 B9
Loja, Ecuador 124 A2
Loja, Spain 31 H6
Loja □, Ecuador 120 D2
Loji, Indonesia 57 E7
Loka, Sudan 77 G3
Lokandu, Zaïre 82 C2
Løken, Norway 10 E5
Lokeren, Belgium 17 F3
Lokhvitsa, Ukraine 41 G7
Lokichokio, Kenya 82 B3
Lokitaung, Kenya 82 B4
Lokkan tekojärvi, Finland 8 C22
Løkken, Denmark 11 G3
Løkken, Norway 10 A3
Loknya, Russia 40 D6
Lokoja, Nigeria 79 D6
Lokolama, Zaïre 80 E3
Lokot, Russia 42 D2
Lol →, Sudan 77 F2
Lola, Guinea 78 D3
Lola, Mt., U.S.A. 112 F6
Lolibai, Gebel, Sudan 77 G3
Lolimi, Sudan 77 G3
Loliondo, Tanzania 82 C4
Lolland, Denmark 11 K5
Lollar, Germany 18 E4
Lolo, U.S.A. 110 C6
Lolodorf, Cameroon 79 E7
Lom, Bulgaria 38 F6
Lom →, Bulgaria 38 F6
Lom Kao, Thailand 58 D3
Lom Sak, Thailand 58 D3
Loma, U.S.A. 110 C8
Loma Linda, U.S.A. 113 L9
Lomami →, Zaïre 82 B1
Lomas de Zamóra, Argentina 126 C4
Lombadina, Australia 88 C3
Lombárdia □, Italy 32 C6
Lombardy = Lombárdia □, Italy 32 C6
Lombez, France 26 E4
Lomblen, Indonesia 57 F6
Lombok, Indonesia 56 F5
Lomé, Togo 79 D5
Lomela, Zaïre 80 E4
Lomela →, Zaïre 80 E4
Lomello, Italy 32 C5
Lometa, U.S.A. 109 K5
Lomié, Cameroon 80 D2
Lomma, Sweden 11 J7
Lomme →, Belgium 17 H6
Lommel, Belgium 17 F6
Lomond, Canada 100 C6

Lomond, L., U.K. 14 E4
Lomphat, Cambodia 58 F6
Lompobatang, Indonesia 57 F5
Lompoc, U.S.A. 113 L6
Lomsegga, Norway 10 C2
Łomza, Poland 20 B12
Loncoche, Chile 128 A2
Loncopuè, Argentina 128 A2
Londa, India 60 M9
Londerzeel, Belgium 17 G4
Londiani, Kenya 82 C4
Londinières, France 24 C8
London, Canada 98 D3
London, U.K. 13 F7
London, Ky., U.S.A. 104 G3
London, Ohio, U.S.A. 104 F4
London, Greater □, U.K. 13 F7
Londonderry, U.K. 15 B4
Londonderry □, U.K. 15 B4
Londonderry, C., Australia 88 B4
Londonderry, I., Chile 128 E2
Londrina, Brazil 127 A5
Lone Pine, U.S.A. 111 H4
Long Beach, Calif., U.S.A. 113 M8
Long Beach, N.Y., U.S.A. 107 F11
Long Beach, Wash., U.S.A. 112 D2
Long Branch, U.S.A. 107 F11
Long Creek, U.S.A. 110 D4
Long Eaton, U.K. 12 E6
Long I., Australia 90 C4
Long I., Bahamas 117 B4
Long I., U.S.A. 107 F11
Long Island Sd., U.S.A. 107 E12
Long L., Canada 98 C2
Long Lake, U.S.A. 107 C10
Long Pine, U.S.A. 108 D5
Long Point B., Canada 106 D4
Long Pt., Nfld., Canada 99 C8
Long Pt., Ont., Canada 106 D4
Long Range Mts., Canada 99 C8
Long Reef, Australia 88 B4
Long Str. = Longa, Proliv, Russia 4 C16
Long Thanh, Vietnam 59 G6
Long Xian, China 50 G4
Long Xuyen, Vietnam 59 G5
Longá, Greece 39 N4
Longa, Proliv, Russia 4 C16
Long'an, China 52 F6
Longarone, Italy 33 B9
Longchang, China 52 C5
Longchi, China 52 C4
Longchuan, Guangdong, China 53 E10
Longchuan, Yunnan, China 52 E1
Longde, China 50 G4
Longeau, France 25 E12
Longford, Australia 90 G4
Longford, Ireland 15 C4
Longford □, Ireland 15 C4
Longguan, China 50 D8
Longhua, China 51 D9
Longhui, China 53 D8
Longido, Tanzania 82 C4
Longiram, Indonesia 56 E5
Longkou, Jiangxi, China 53 D10
Longkou, Shandong, China 51 F11
Longlac, Canada 98 C2
Longli, China 52 D6
Longlier, Belgium 17 J6
Longlin, China 52 E5
Longling, China 52 E2
Longmen, China 53 F10
Longming, China 52 F6
Longmont, U.S.A. 108 E2
Longnan, China 53 E10
Longnawan, Indonesia 56 D4
Longobucco, Italy 35 C9
Longquan, China 53 C12
Longreach, Australia 90 C3
Longshan, China 52 C7
Longsheng, China 53 E8
Longton, Australia 90 C4
Longtown, U.K. 13 F5
Longué-Jumelles, France 24 E6
Longueau, France 25 C9
Longueuil, Canada 107 A11
Longuyon, France 25 C12
Longview, Canada 100 C6
Longview, Tex., U.S.A. 109 J7
Longview, Wash., U.S.A. 112 D4
Longvilly, Belgium 17 H7
Longwy, France 25 C12
Longxi, China 50 G3
Longyou, China 53 C12
Longzhou, China 52 F6
Lonigo, Italy 33 C8
Löningen, Germany 18 C3
Lonja →, Croatia 33 C13
Lonoke, U.S.A. 109 H9
Lonquimay, Chile 128 A2
Lons-le-Saunier, France 25 F12
Lønstrup, Denmark 11 G3
Lookout, C., Canada 98 A3
Lookout, C., U.S.A. 105 H7
Loolmalasin, Tanzania 82 C4
Loon →, Alta., Canada 100 B5
Loon →, Man., Canada 101 B8
Loon Lake, Canada 101 C7
Loon-op-Zand, Neths. 17 E6
Loongana, Australia 89 F4
Loop Hd., Ireland 15 D2
Loosduinen, Neths. 16 D4
Lop Buri, Thailand 58 E3
Lop Nor = Lop Nur, China 54 B4
Lop Nur, China 54 B4
Lopare, Bos.-H. 21 L8
Lopatin, Russia 43 J8
Lopatina, G., Russia 45 D15
Lopaye, Sudan 77 F3
Lopera, Spain 31 H6
Lopez, Phil. 55 E5
Lopez, C., Gabon 80 E1
Loppersum, Neths. 16 B9
Lopphavet, Norway 8 A19
Lora →, Afghan. 60 D4
Lora, Hamun-i-, Pakistan 60 E4
Lora Cr. →, Australia 91 D2
Lora del Río, Spain 31 H5
Lorain, U.S.A. 106 E2
Loralai, Pakistan 62 D3
Lorca, Spain 29 H3
Lord Howe I., Pac. Oc. 92 L7
Lord Howe Ridge, Pac. Oc. 92 L8
Lordsburg, U.S.A. 111 K9
Loreto, Bolivia 125 D5
Loreto, Brazil 122 C2
Loreto, Italy 33 E10
Loreto, Mexico 114 B2
Loreto □, Peru 120 D3
Loreto Aprutino, Italy 33 F10
Lorgues, France 27 E10
Lorica, Colombia 120 B2
Lorient, France 24 E3
Lorn, U.K. 14 E3
Lorn, Firth of, U.K. 14 E3
Lorne, Australia 91 F3
Lorovouno, Cyprus 37 D11
Lörrach, Germany 19 H3
Lorraine, France 25 D12
Lorrainville, Canada 98 C4
Los, Îles de, Guinea 78 D2
Los Alamos, Calif., U.S.A. 113 L6
Los Alamos, N. Mex., U.S.A. 111 J10
Los Altos, U.S.A. 112 H4
Los Andes, Chile 126 C1
Los Angeles, Chile 126 D1
Los Angeles, U.S.A. 113 L8
Los Angeles Aqueduct, U.S.A. 113 K9
Los Antiguos, Argentina 128 C2
Los Banos, U.S.A. 111 H3
Los Barrios, Spain 31 J5
Los Blancos, Argentina 126 A3
Los Cristianos, Canary Is. 36 F3
Los Gatos, U.S.A. 112 H5
Los Hermanos, Venezuela 117 D7
Los Islotes, Canary Is. 36 E6
Los Lagos, Chile 128 A2
Los Llanos de Aridane, Canary Is. 36 F2
Los Lomas, Peru 124 A1
Los Lunas, U.S.A. 111 J10
Los Menucos, Argentina 128 B3
Los Mochis, Mexico 114 B3
Los Monegros, Spain 28 D4
Los Monos, Argentina 128 C3
Los Olivos, U.S.A. 113 L6
Los Palacios, Cuba 116 B3
Los Palacios y Villafranca, Spain 31 H5
Los Reyes, Mexico 114 D4
Los Ríos □, Ecuador 120 D2
Los Roques, Venezuela 120 A4
Los Santos de Maimona, Spain 31 G4
Los Teques, Venezuela 120 A4
Los Testigos, Venezuela 121 A5
Los Vilos, Chile 126 C1
Los Yébenes, Spain 31 F7
Losada →, Colombia 120 C3
Loshkalakh, Russia 45 C15
Lošinj, Croatia 33 D11
Losser, Neths. 16 D10
Lossiemouth, U.K. 14 D5
Lot □, France 26 D5
Lot →, France 26 D4
Lot-et-Garonne □, France 26 D4
Lota, Chile 126 D1
Løten, Norway 10 D5
Lotfābād, Iran 65 B8
Lothair, S. Africa 85 D5
Lothiers, France 25 F8
Lötschbergtunnel, Switz. 22 D5
Lottefors, Sweden 10 C10
Lotung, Taiwan 53 E13
Lotzwil, Switz. 22 B5
Loubomo, Congo 80 E2
Loudéac, France 24 D4
Loudi, China 53 D8
Loudon, U.S.A. 105 H3
Loudonville, U.S.A. 106 F2
Loudun, France 24 E7
Loué, France 24 E6
Loue →, France 25 E12
Louga, Senegal 78 B1
Loughborough, U.K. 12 E6
Loughrea, Ireland 15 C3
Loughros More B., Ireland 15 B3
Louhans, France 27 B9
Louis Trichardt, S. Africa 85 C4
Louis XIV, Pte., Canada 98 B4
Louisa, U.S.A. 104 F4
Louisbourg, Canada 99 C8
Louise I., Canada 100 C2
Louiseville, Canada 98 C5
Louisiade Arch., Papua N. G. 92 J7
Louisiana, U.S.A. 108 F9
Louisiana □, U.S.A. 109 K9
Louisville, Ky., U.S.A. 104 F3
Louisville, Miss., U.S.A. 109 J10
Loulay, France 26 B3
Loulé, Portugal 31 H2
Louny, Czech. 20 E3
Loup City, U.S.A. 108 E5
Lourdes, France 26 E3
Lourdes-du-Blanc-Sablon, Canada 99 B8
Lourenço, Brazil 121 C7
Lourenço-Marques = Maputo, Mozam. 85 D5
Loures, Portugal 31 G1
Lourinhã, Portugal 31 F1
Lousã, Portugal 30 E2
Louth, Australia 91 E4
Louth, Ireland 15 C5
Louth, U.K. 12 D7
Louth □, Ireland 15 C5
Louvain = Leuven, Belgium 17 G5
Louveigné, Belgium 17 G7
Louviers, France 24 C8
Louwsburg, S. Africa 85 D5
Lovat →, Russia 40 C6
Love, Canada 101 C8
Lovech, Bulgaria 38 F7
Loveland, U.S.A. 108 E2
Lovell, U.S.A. 110 D9
Lovelock, U.S.A. 110 F4
Lóvere, Italy 32 C7
Loviisa, Finland 9 F22
Loving, U.S.A. 109 J2
Lovington, U.S.A. 109 J3
Lovios, Spain 30 D2
Lovisa = Loviisa, Finland 9 F22
Lovran, Croatia 33 C11
Low Pt., Australia 89 F4
Low Tatra = Nízké Tatry, Slovak Rep. 20 G9
Lowa, Zaïre 82 C2
Lowa →, Zaïre 82 C2
Lowell, U.S.A. 107 D13
Lower Arrow L., Canada 100 D5
Lower California = Baja California, Mexico 114 A1
Lower Hutt, N.Z. 87 J5
Lower L., U.S.A. 110 F3
Lower Lake, U.S.A. 112 G4
Lower Post, Canada 100 B3
Lower Red L., U.S.A. 108 B7
Lower Saxony = Niedersachsen □, Germany 18 C5
Lower Tunguska = Tunguska, Nizhnyaya →, Russia 45 C9
Lowestoft, U.K. 13 E9
Łowicz, Poland 20 C9
Lowville, U.S.A. 107 C9
Loxton, Australia 91 E3
Loxton, S. Africa 84 E3
Loyalton, U.S.A. 112 F6
Loyalty Is. = Loyauté, Is., N. Cal. 92 K8
Loyang = Luoyang, China 50 G7
Loyauté, Is., N. Cal. 92 K8
Loyev = Loyew, Belarus 41 G6
Loyew, Belarus 41 G6
Loyoro, Uganda 82 B3
Lož, Slovenia 33 C11
Lozère □, France 26 D7
Loznica, Serbia, Yug. 21 L9
Lozova, Ukraine 41 H9
Luachimo, Angola 80 F4
Luacono, Angola 80 G4
Lualaba →, Zaïre 82 B5
Luampa, Zambia 83 F1
Lu'an, China 53 B11
Luan Chau, Vietnam 58 B4
Luan He →, China 51 E10
Luan Xian, China 51 E10
Luancheng, Guangxi Zhuangzu, China 52 F7
Luancheng, Hebei, China 50 F8
Luanda, Angola 80 F2
Luang Prabang, Laos 58 C4
Luang Thale, Thailand 59 J3
Luangwa, Zambia 83 F3
Luangwa →, Zambia 83 E3
Luangwa Valley, Zambia 83 E3
Luanne, China 51 D9
Luanping, China 51 D9
Luanshya, Zambia 83 E2
Luapula □, Zambia 83 E2
Luapula →, Africa 83 D2
Luarca, Spain 30 B4
Luashi, Zaïre 83 E1
Luau, Angola 80 G4
Lubalo, Angola 80 F3
Lubań, Poland 20 D5
Lubana, Ozero = Lubānas Ezers, Latvia 9 H22
Lubānas Ezers, Latvia 9 H22
Lubang, Phil. 55 E4
Lubang Is., Phil. 57 B6
Lubartów, Poland 20 D12
Lubawa, Poland 20 B9
Lubbeek, Belgium 17 G5
Lübben, Germany 18 D9
Lübbenau, Germany 18 D9
Lubbock, U.S.A. 109 J4
Lübeck, Germany 18 B6
Lübecker Bucht, Germany 18 A7
Lubefu, Zaïre 82 C1
Lubefu →, Zaïre 82 C1
Lubero = Luofu, Zaïre 82 C2
Lubicon L., Canada 100 B5
Lublin, Poland 20 D12
Lubliniec, Poland 20 E8
Lubnān, J., Lebanon 69 B4
Lubny, Ukraine 41 G7
Lubon, Poland 20 C6
Lubongola, Zaïre 82 C2
Lubsko, Poland 20 D4
Lübtheen, Germany 18 B7
Lubuagan, Phil. 55 C4
Lubudi →, Zaïre 83 D2
Lubuk Antu, Malaysia 56 D4
Lubuklinggau, Indonesia 56 E2
Lubuksikaping, Indonesia 56 D2
Lubumbashi, Zaïre 83 E2
Lubunda, Zaïre 82 D2
Lubungu, Zambia 83 E2
Lubutu, Zaïre 82 C2
Luc An Chau, Vietnam 58 A5
Luc-en-Diois, France 27 D9
Lucan, Canada 106 C3
Lucban, Phil. 55 D4
Lucca, Italy 32 E7
Luce Bay, U.K. 14 G4
Lucea, Jamaica 116 C4
Lucedale, U.S.A. 105 K1
Lucena, Phil. 55 E4
Lucena, Spain 31 H6
Lucena del Cid, Spain 28 E4
Lučenec, Slovak Rep. 21 G9
Lucens, Switz. 22 C3
Lucera, Italy 35 A8
Lucerne = Luzern, Switz. 23 B6
Lucerne, U.S.A. 112 F4
Lucerne Valley, U.S.A. 113 L10
Lucero, Mexico 114 A3
Luchena →, Spain 29 H3
Lucheng, China 50 F7
Lucheringo →, Mozam. 83 E4
Luchiang, Taiwan 53 E13
Lüchow, Germany 18 C7
Luchuan, China 53 F8
Lucie →, Surinam 121 C6
Lucira, Angola 81 G2
Luckau, Germany 18 D9
Luckenwalde, Germany 18 C9
Lucknow, India 63 F9
Luçon, France 26 B2
Lüda = Dalian, China 51 E11
Luda Kamchiya →, Bulgaria 38 F10
Ludbreg, Croatia 33 B13
Lüdenscheid, Germany 18 D3
Lüderitz, Namibia 84 D2
Ludewe □, Tanzania 83 D3
Ludhiana, India 62 D6
Ludian, China 52 D4
Luding Qiao, China 52 C4
Lüdinghausen, Germany 18 D3
Ludington, U.S.A. 104 D2
Ludlow, U.K. 13 E5
Ludlow, Calif., U.S.A. 113 L10
Ludlow, Vt., U.S.A. 107 C12
Ludus, Romania 38 C7
Ludvika, Sweden 9 F16
Ludwigsburg, Germany 19 G5
Ludwigshafen, Germany 19 F4
Ludwigslust, Germany 18 B7
Ludza, Latvia 40 D4
Luebo, Zaïre 80 F4
Lueki, Zaïre 82 C2
Luena, Zaïre 83 D2
Luena, Zambia 83 E3
Luepa, Venezuela 121 B5
Lüeyang, China 50 H4
Lufeng, Guangdong, China 53 F10
Lufeng, Yunnan, China 52 E4
Lufira →, Zaïre 83 D2
Lufkin, U.S.A. 109 K7
Lufupa, Zaïre 83 E1
Luga, Russia 40 C5
Luga →, Russia 40 C5
Lugano, Switz. 23 D7
Lugano, L. di, Switz. 23 E8
Lugansk = Luhansk, Ukraine 41 H10
Lugard's Falls, Kenya 82 C4
Lugela, Mozam. 83 F4
Lugenda →, Mozam. 83 E4
Lugh Ganana, Somali Rep. 68 G3
Lugnaquilla, Ireland 15 D5
Lugnvik, Sweden 10 B11
Lugo, Italy 33 D8
Lugo, Spain 30 B3
Lugo □, Spain 30 C3
Lugoj, Romania 38 D4
Lugones, Spain 30 B5
Lugovoy, Kazakstan 44 E8
Luhansk, Ukraine 41 H10
Luhe, China 53 A12
Luhe →, Germany 18 B6
Luhuo, China 52 B3
Luiana, Angola 84 B3
Luimneach = Limerick, Ireland 15 D3
Luino, Italy 32 C5
Luís Correia, Brazil 122 B3
Luís Gonçalves, Brazil 122 C1
Luitpold Coast, Antarctica 5 D1
Luiza, Zaïre 80 F4
Luizi, Zaïre 82 D2
Luján, Argentina 126 C4
Lujiang, China 53 B11
Lukanga Swamp, Zambia 83 E2
Lukenie →, Zaïre 80 E3
Lukhisaral, India 63 G12
Lŭki, Bulgaria 39 H7
Lukolela, Equateur, Zaïre 80 E3
Lukolela, Kasai Or., Zaïre 82 D1
Lukosi, Zimbabwe 83 F2
Lukovit, Bulgaria 38 F7
Łuków, Poland 20 D12
Lukoyanov, Russia 42 C7
Lule älv →, Sweden 8 D19
Luleå, Sweden 8 D20
Lüleburgaz, Turkey 66 B2
Luliang, China 52 E4
Luling, U.S.A. 109 L6
Lulong, China 51 E10
Lulonga →, Zaïre 80 D3
Lulua →, Zaïre 80 E4
Luluabourg = Kananga, Zaïre 80 F4
Lumai, Angola 81 G4
Lumajang, Indonesia 57 H15
Lumbala N'guimbo, Angola 81 G4
Lumberton, Miss., U.S.A. 109 K10
Lumberton, N.C., U.S.A. 105 H6
Lumberton, N. Mex., U.S.A. 111 H10
Lumbres, France 25 B9
Lumbwa, Kenya 82 C4
Lummen, Belgium 17 G6
Lumsden, N.Z. 87 L2
Lumut, Malaysia 59 K3
Lumut, Tg., Indonesia 56 E3
Luna, Phil. 55 C4
Lunan, China 52 E4
Lunavada, India 62 H5
Lunca, Romania 38 B8
Lund, Sweden 11 J7
Lund, U.S.A. 110 G6
Lundazi, Zambia 83 E3
Lunderskov, Denmark 11 J3
Lundi →, Zimbabwe 83 G3
Lundu, Malaysia 56 D3
Lundy, U.K. 13 F3
Lune →, U.K. 12 C5
Lüneburg, Germany 18 B6
Lüneburg Heath = Lüneburger Heide, Germany 18 C6
Lüneburger Heide, Germany 18 C6
Lunel, France 27 E8
Lünen, Germany 18 D3
Lunenburg, Canada 99 D7
Lunéville, France 25 D13
Lunga →, Zambia 83 E2
Lungern, Switz. 22 C6
Lungi Airport, S. Leone 78 D2
Lunglei, India 61 H18
Luni, India 62 F5
Luni →, India 62 G4
Luninets = Luninyets, Belarus 41 F4
Luning, U.S.A. 110 G4
Lunino, Russia 42 D7
Luninyets, Belarus 41 F4
Lunner, Norway 10 D4
Lunsemfwa →, Zambia 83 E3
Lunsemfwa Falls, Zambia 83 E2
Lunteren, Neths. 16 D7
Luo He →, China 50 G6
Luocheng, China 52 E7
Luochuan, China 50 G5
Luoci, China 52 E4
Luodian, China 52 E6
Luoding, China 53 F8
Luofu, Zaïre 82 C2
Luohe, China 50 H8
Luojiang, China 52 B5
Luonan, China 50 G6
Luoning, China 50 G6
Luoshan, China 53 A10
Luotian, China 53 B10
Luoyang, China 50 G7
Luoyuan, China 53 D12
Luozi, Zaïre 80 E2
Luozigou, China 51 C16
Lupanshui, China 52 D5
Lupeni, Romania 38 D6
Lupilichi, Mozam. 83 E4
Lupoing, China 52 E5
Luquan, China 52 E4
Luque, Paraguay 126 B4
Luque, Spain 31 H6
Luray, U.S.A. 104 F6
Lure, France 25 E13
Luremo, Angola 80 F3
Lurgan, U.K. 15 B5
Luri, France 27 F13
Luribay, Bolivia 124 D4
Lurin, Peru 124 C2
Lusaka, Zambia 83 F2
Lusambo, Zaïre 82 C1
Lusangaye, Zaïre 82 C2
Luseland, Canada 101 C7
Lushan, Henan, China 50 H7
Lushan, Sichuan, China 52 B4
Lushi, China 50 G6
Lushnja, Albania 39 J2
Lushoto, Tanzania 82 C4
Lushoto □, Tanzania 82 C4
Lushui, China 52 E2
Lüshun, China 51 E11
Lusignan, France 26 B4
Lusigny-sur-Barse, France 25 D11
Lusk, U.S.A. 108 D2
Lussac-les-Châteaux, France 26 B4
Lussanvira, Brazil 123 F1
Luta = Dalian, China 51 E11
Luton, U.K. 13 F7
Lutong, Malaysia 56 D4

Lutry, *Switz.* 22 C3
Lutselke, *Canada* 101 A6
Lutsk, *Ukraine* 41 G3
Lützow Holmbukta, *Antarctica* 5 C4
Lutzputs, *S. Africa* 84 D3
Luverne, *U.S.A.* 108 D6
Luvua, *Zaïre* 83 D2
Luvua →, *Zaïre* 82 D2
Luwegu →, *Tanzania* 83 D4
Luwuk, *Indonesia* 57 E6
Luxembourg, *Lux.* 17 J8
Luxembourg □, *Belgium* 17 J7
Luxembourg ■, *Europe* 17 J8
Luxeuil-les-Bains, *France* 25 E13
Luxi, *Hunan, China* 53 C8
Luxi, *Yunnan, China* 52 E4
Luxi, *Yunnan, China* 52 E2
Luxor = El Uqsur, *Egypt* 76 B3
Luy →, *France* 26 E2
Luy-de-Béarn →, *France* 26 E3
Luy-de-France →, *France* 26 E3
Luyi, *China* 50 H8
Luyksgestel, *Neths.* 17 F6
Luz-St.-Sauveur, *France* 26 F4
Luzern, *Switz.* 23 B6
Luzern □, *Switz.* 22 B5
Luzhai, *China* 52 E7
Luzhou, *China* 52 C5
Luziânia, *Brazil* 123 E2
Luzilândia, *Brazil* 122 B3
Luzon, *Phil.* 55 D4
Luzy, *France* 25 F10
Luzzi, *Italy* 35 C9
Lviv, *Ukraine* 41 H3
Lvov = Lviv, *Ukraine* 41 H3
Lyakhavichy, *Belarus* 41 F4
Lyakhovskiye, Ostrova, *Russia* 45 B15
Lyaki = Läki, *Azerbaijan* 43 K8
Lyallpur = Faisalabad, *Pakistan* 62 D5
Lycaonia, *Turkey* 66 D5
Lychen, *Germany* 18 B9
Lychkova, *Russia* 40 D7
Lycia, *Turkey* 66 D3
Lycksele, *Sweden* 8 D18
Lydda = Lod, *Israel* 69 D3
Lydenburg, *S. Africa* 85 D5
Lydia, *Turkey* 66 C3
Lyell, *N.Z.* 87 J4
Lyell I., *Canada* 100 C2
Lyepyel, *Belarus* 40 E5
Lygnern, *Sweden* 11 G6
Lyman, *U.S.A.* 110 F8
Lyme Regis, *U.K.* 13 G5
Lymington, *U.K.* 13 G6
Łyna →, *Poland* 9 J19
Lynchburg, *U.S.A.* 104 G6
Lynd →, *Australia* 90 B3
Lynd Ra., *Australia* 91 D4
Lynden, *Canada* 106 C4
Lynden, *U.S.A.* 112 B4
Lyndhurst, *Queens., Australia* 90 B3
Lyndhurst, *S. Austral., Australia* 91 E2
Lyndon →, *Australia* 89 D1
Lyndonville, *N.Y., U.S.A.* 106 C6
Lyndonville, *Vt., U.S.A.* 107 B12
Lyngdal, *Norway* 10 E3
Lyngen, *Norway* 8 B19
Lynher Reef, *Australia* 88 C3
Lynn, *U.S.A.* 107 D14
Lynn Canal, *U.S.A.* 100 B1
Lynn Lake, *Canada* 101 B8
Lynnwood, *U.S.A.* 112 C4
Lynton, *U.K.* 13 F4
Lyntupy, *Belarus* 9 J22
Lynx L., *Canada* 101 A7
Lyø, *Denmark* 11 J4
Lyon, *France* 27 C8
Lyonnais, *France* 27 C8
Lyons = Lyon, *France* 27 C8
Lyons, *Colo., U.S.A.* 108 E2
Lyons, *Ga., U.S.A.* 105 J4
Lyons, *Kans., U.S.A.* 108 F5
Lyons, *N.Y., U.S.A.* 106 C8
Lyozna, *Belarus* 40 E6
Lyrestad, *Sweden* 11 F8
Lys = Leie →, *Belgium* 25 A10
Lysekil, *Sweden* 11 F5
Lyskovo, *Russia* 42 B7
Lyss, *Switz.* 22 B4
Lysychansk, *Ukraine* 41 H10
Lytle, *U.S.A.* 109 L5
Lyttelton, *N.Z.* 87 K4
Lytton, *Canada* 100 C4
Lyuban, *Russia* 40 C6
Lyubertsy, *Russia* 42 C3
Lyubim, *Russia* 42 A5
Lyuboml, *Ukraine* 41 G3
Lyubotyn, *Ukraine* 41 H8
Lyubytino, *Russia* 40 C7
Lyudinovo, *Russia* 42 D2

M

Ma →, *Vietnam* 58 C5
Ma'adaba, *Jordan* 69 E4
Maamba, *Zambia* 84 B4
Ma'ān, *Jordan* 69 E4
Ma'ān □, *Jordan* 69 F5
Maanselkä, *Finland* 8 C23
Ma'anshan, *China* 53 B12
Maarheeze, *Neths.* 17 F7
Maarianhamina, *Finland* 9 F18
Maarn, *Neths.* 16 D6
Ma'arrat an Nu'mān, *Syria* 66 E7
Maarssen, *Neths.* 16 D6
Maartensdijk, *Neths.* 16 D6
Maas →, *Neths.* 16 E5
Maasbracht, *Belgium* 17 F7
Maasbree, *Neths.* 17 F8
Maasdam, *Neths.* 16 E5
Maasdijk, *Neths.* 16 E4
Maaseik, *Belgium* 17 F7
Maasland, *Neths.* 16 E4
Maasniel, *Neths.* 17 F8
Maassluis, *Neths.* 16 E4
Maastricht, *Neths.* 17 G7
Maave, *Mozam.* 85 C5
Mabaruma, *Guyana* 121 B6
Mabel L., *Canada* 100 C5
Mabenge, *Zaïre* 82 B1
Mabian, *China* 52 C4
Mablethorpe, *U.K.* 12 D8
Maboma, *Zaïre* 82 B2
Mabrouk, *Mali* 79 B4
Mabton, *U.S.A.* 110 C3
Mac Bac, *Vietnam* 59 H6
Macachín, *Argentina* 126 D3
Macaé, *Brazil* 123 F3
Macaíba, *Brazil* 122 C4
Macajuba, *Brazil* 123 D3
McAlester, *U.S.A.* 109 H7
McAllen, *U.S.A.* 109 M5
Macamic, *Canada* 98 C4
Macao = Macau ■, *China* 53 F9
Macão, *Portugal* 31 F3
Macapá, *Brazil* 121 C7
Macará, *Ecuador* 120 D2
Macarani, *Brazil* 123 E3
Macarena, Serranía de la, *Colombia* 120 C3
McArthur →, *Australia* 90 B2
McArthur, Port, *Australia* 90 B2
McArthur River, *Australia* 90 B2
Macas, *Ecuador* 120 D2
Macate, *Peru* 124 B2
Macau, *Brazil* 122 C4
Macau ■, *China* 53 F9
Macaúbas, *Brazil* 123 D3
Macaya →, *Colombia* 120 C3
McBride, *Canada* 100 C4
McCall, *U.S.A.* 110 D5
McCamey, *U.S.A.* 109 K3
McCammon, *U.S.A.* 110 E7
McCauley I., *Canada* 100 C2
McCleary, *U.S.A.* 112 C3
Macclesfield, *U.K.* 12 D5
McClintock, *Canada* 101 B10
M'Clintock Chan., *Canada* 96 A9
McClintock Ra., *Australia* 88 C4
McCloud, *U.S.A.* 110 F2
McCluer I., *Australia* 88 B5
McClure, *U.S.A.* 106 F7
McClure, L., *U.S.A.* 112 H6
M'Clure Str., *Canada* 4 B2
McClusky, *U.S.A.* 108 B4
McComb, *U.S.A.* 109 K9
McConaughy, L., *U.S.A.* 108 E4
McCook, *U.S.A.* 108 E4
McCullough Mt., *U.S.A.* 113 K11
McCusker →, *Canada* 101 B7
McDame, *Canada* 100 B3
McDermitt, *U.S.A.* 110 F5
Macdonald, L., *Australia* 88 D4
McDonald Is., *Ind. Oc.* 3 G13
Macdonnell Ranges, *Australia* 88 D5
McDouall Peak, *Australia* 91 D1
Macdougall L., *Canada* 96 B10
MacDowell L., *Canada* 98 B1
Macduff, *U.K.* 14 D6
Maceda, *Spain* 30 C3
Macedonia ■, *Europe* 39 H4
Maceió, *Brazil* 122 C4
Maceira, *Portugal* 31 F2
Macenta, *Guinea* 78 D3
Macerata, *Italy* 33 E10
McFarland, *U.S.A.* 113 K7
McFarlane →, *Canada* 101 B7
Macfarlane, L., *Australia* 91 E2
McGehee, *U.S.A.* 109 J9
McGill, *U.S.A.* 110 G6
Macgillycuddy's Reeks, *Ireland* 15 D2
MacGregor, *Canada* 101 D9
McGregor, *U.S.A.* 108 D9
McGregor →, *Canada* 100 B4
McGregor Ra., *Australia* 91 D3
Mach, *Pakistan* 60 E5
Māch Kowr, *Iran* 65 E9
Machacalis, *Brazil* 123 E3
Machado = Jiparaná →, *Brazil* 125 B5
Machagai, *Argentina* 126 B3
Machakos, *Kenya* 82 C4
Machakos □, *Kenya* 82 C4
Machala, *Ecuador* 120 D2
Machanga, *Mozam.* 85 C6
Machattie, L., *Australia* 90 C2
Machava, *Mozam.* 85 D5
Machece, *Mozam.* 83 F4
Machecoul, *France* 24 F5
Machelen, *Belgium* 17 G4
Macheng, *China* 53 B10
Machevna, *Russia* 45 C18
Machezo, *Spain* 31 F6
Machias, *U.S.A.* 99 D6
Machichaco, C., *Spain* 28 B2
Machichi →, *Canada* 101 B10
Machico, *Madeira* 36 D3
Machilipatnam, *India* 61 L12
Machiques, *Venezuela* 120 A3
Machupicchu, *Peru* 124 C3
Machynlleth, *U.K.* 13 E4
McIlwraith Ra., *Australia* 90 A3
Măcin, *Romania* 38 D11
Macina, *Mali* 78 C4
McIntosh, *U.S.A.* 108 C4
McIntosh L., *Canada* 101 B8
Macintosh Ra., *Australia* 89 E4
Macintyre →, *Australia* 91 D5
Macizo Galaico, *Spain* 30 C3
Mackay, *Australia* 90 C4
Mackay, *U.S.A.* 110 E7
MacKay →, *Canada* 100 B6
Mackay, L., *Australia* 88 D4
McKay Ra., *Australia* 88 D3
McKeesport, *U.S.A.* 106 F5
McKenna, *U.S.A.* 112 D4
Mackenzie, *Canada* 100 B4
Mackenzie, *Guyana* 121 B6
McKenzie, *U.S.A.* 105 G1
Mackenzie →, *Australia* 90 C4
Mackenzie →, *Canada* 96 B6
McKenzie →, *U.S.A.* 110 D2
Mackenzie Bay, *Canada* 4 B1
Mackenzie City = Linden, *Guyana* 121 B6
Mackenzie Highway, *Canada* 100 B5
Mackenzie Mts., *Canada* 96 B6
Mackinaw City, *U.S.A.* 104 C3
McKinlay, *Australia* 90 C3
McKinlay →, *Australia* 90 C3
McKinley, Mt., *U.S.A.* 96 B4
McKinley Sea, *Arctic* 4 A7
McKinney, *U.S.A.* 109 J6
Mackinnon Road, *Kenya* 82 C4
Macksville, *Australia* 91 E5
McLaughlin, *U.S.A.* 108 C4
Maclean, *Australia* 91 D5
McLean, *U.S.A.* 109 H4
McLeansboro, *U.S.A.* 108 F10
Maclear, *S. Africa* 85 E4
Macleay →, *Australia* 91 E5
McLennan, *Canada* 100 B5
MacLeod, B., *Canada* 101 A7
McLeod, L., *Australia* 89 D1
MacLeod Lake, *Canada* 100 C4
McLoughlin, Mt., *U.S.A.* 110 E2
McLure, *Canada* 100 C4
McMechen, *U.S.A.* 106 G4
McMillan, L., *U.S.A.* 109 J2
McMinnville, *Oreg., U.S.A.* 110 D2
McMinnville, *Tenn., U.S.A.* 105 H3
McMorran, *Canada* 101 C7
McMurdo Sd., *Antarctica* 5 D11
McMurray = Fort McMurray, *Canada* 100 B6
McMurray, *U.S.A.* 112 B4
McNary, *U.S.A.* 111 J9
MacNutt, *Canada* 101 C8
Macodoene, *Mozam.* 85 C6
Macomb, *U.S.A.* 108 E9
Macomer, *Italy* 34 B1
Mâcon, *France* 27 B8
Macon, *Ga., U.S.A.* 105 J4
Macon, *Miss., U.S.A.* 105 J1
Macon, *Mo., U.S.A.* 108 F8
Macondo, *Angola* 81 G4
Macossa, *Mozam.* 83 F3
Macoun L., *Canada* 101 B8
Macovane, *Mozam.* 85 C6
McPherson, *U.S.A.* 108 F6
McPherson Pk., *U.S.A.* 113 L7
McPherson Ra., *Australia* 91 D5
Macquarie Harbour, *Australia* 90 G4
Macquarie Is., *Pac. Oc.* 92 N7
MacRobertson Land, *Antarctica* 5 D6
Macroom, *Ireland* 15 E3
Macroy, *Australia* 88 D2
MacTier, *Canada* 106 A5
Macubela, *Mozam.* 83 F4
Macugnaga, *Italy* 32 C4
Macuiza, *Mozam.* 83 F3
Macujer, *Colombia* 120 C3
Macusani, *Peru* 124 C3
Macuse, *Mozam.* 83 F4
Macuspana, *Mexico* 115 D6
Macusse, *Angola* 84 B3
McVille, *U.S.A.* 108 B5
Madadeni, *S. Africa* 85 D5
Madagali, *Nigeria* 79 C7
Madagascar ■, *Africa* 85 C8
Madā'in Sālih, *Si. Arabia* 64 E3
Madama, *Niger* 73 D7
Madame I., *Canada* 99 C7
Madaoua, *Niger* 79 C6
Madara, *Nigeria* 79 C7
Madaripur, *Bangla.* 61 H17
Madauk, *Burma* 61 L20
Madawaska, *Canada* 106 A7
Madawaska →, *Canada* 98 C4
Madaya, *Burma* 61 H20
Madbar, *Sudan* 77 F3
Maddaloni, *Italy* 35 A7
Made, *Neths.* 17 E5
Madeira, *Atl. Oc.* 36 D3
Madeira →, *Brazil* 121 D6
Madeleine, Is. de la, *Canada* 99 C7
Maden, *Turkey* 67 C8
Madera, *U.S.A.* 111 H3
Madha, *India* 60 L9
Madhubani, *India* 63 F12
Madhya Pradesh □, *India* 62 J7
Madian, *China* 53 A11
Madidi →, *Bolivia* 124 C4
Madikeri, *India* 60 N9
Madill, *U.S.A.* 109 H6
Madimba, *Zaïre* 80 E3
Ma'din, *Syria* 67 E8
Madīnat ash Sha'b, *Yemen* 68 E3
Madingou, *Congo* 80 E2
Madirovalo, *Madag.* 85 B8
Madison, *Calif., U.S.A.* 112 G5
Madison, *Fla., U.S.A.* 105 K4
Madison, *Ind., U.S.A.* 104 F3
Madison, *Nebr., U.S.A.* 108 E6
Madison, *Ohio, U.S.A.* 106 E3
Madison, *S. Dak., U.S.A.* 108 D6
Madison, *Wis., U.S.A.* 108 D10
Madison →, *U.S.A.* 110 D8
Madisonville, *Ky., U.S.A.* 104 G2
Madisonville, *Tex., U.S.A.* 109 K7
Madista, *Botswana* 84 C4
Madiun, *Indonesia* 57 G14
Madley, *U.K.* 13 E5
Madol, *Sudan* 77 F2
Madon →, *France* 25 D13
Madona, *Latvia* 9 H22
Madras = Tamil Nadu □, *India* 60 P10
Madras, *India* 60 N12
Madras, *U.S.A.* 110 D3
Madre, L., *Mexico* 115 B5
Madre, Laguna, *U.S.A.* 109 M6
Madre, Sierra, *Phil.* 55 C5
Madre de Dios □, *Peru* 124 C3
Madre de Dios →, *Bolivia* 124 C4
Madre de Dios, I., *Chile* 128 D1
Madre del Sur, Sierra, *Mexico* 115 D5
Madre Occidental, Sierra, *Mexico* 114 B3
Madre Oriental, Sierra, *Mexico* 114 C4
Madri, *India* 62 G5
Madrid, *Spain* 30 E7
Madrid □, *Spain* 30 E7
Madridejos, *Spain* 31 F7
Madrigal de las Altas Torres, *Spain* 30 D6
Madrona, Sierra, *Spain* 31 G6
Madroñera, *Spain* 31 F5
Madu, *Sudan* 77 E2
Madura, Selat, *Indonesia* 57 G15
Madura Motel, *Australia* 89 F4
Madurai, *India* 60 Q11
Madurantakam, *India* 60 N11
Madzhalis, *Russia* 43 J8
Mae Chan, *Thailand* 58 B2
Mae Hong Son, *Thailand* 58 C2
Mae Khlong →, *Thailand* 58 F3
Mae Phrik, *Thailand* 58 D2
Mae Ramat, *Thailand* 58 D2
Mae Rim, *Thailand* 58 C2
Mae Sot, *Thailand* 58 D2
Mae Suai, *Thailand* 58 C2
Mae Tha, *Thailand* 58 C2
Maebashi, *Japan* 49 F9
Maella, *Spain* 28 D5
Măeruş, *Romania* 38 D8
Maesteg, *U.K.* 13 F4
Maestra, Sierra, *Cuba* 116 B4
Maestrazgo, Mts. del, *Spain* 28 E4
Maevatanana, *Madag.* 85 B8
Mafeking = Mafikeng, *S. Africa* 84 D4
Mafeking, *Canada* 101 C8
Maféré, *Ivory C.* 78 D4
Mafeteng, *Lesotho* 84 D4
Maffe, *Belgium* 17 H6
Maffra, *Australia* 91 F4
Mafia I., *Tanzania* 82 D4
Mafikeng, *S. Africa* 84 D4
Mafra, *Brazil* 127 B6
Mafra, *Portugal* 31 G1
Mafungabusi Plateau, *Zimbabwe* 83 F2
Magadan, *Russia* 45 D16
Magadi, *Kenya* 82 C4
Magadi, L., *Kenya* 82 C4
Magaliesburg, *S. Africa* 85 D4
Magallanes □, *Chile* 128 D2
Magallanes, Estrecho de, *Chile* 128 D2
Magangué, *Colombia* 120 B3
Magaria, *Niger* 79 C6
Magburaka, *S. Leone* 78 D2
Magdalen Is. = Madeleine, Is. de la, *Canada* 99 C7
Magdalena, *Argentina* 126 D4
Magdalena, *Bolivia* 125 C5
Magdalena, *Malaysia* 56 D5
Magdalena, *Mexico* 114 A2
Magdalena, *U.S.A.* 111 J10
Magdalena □, *Colombia* 120 A3
Magdalena →, *Colombia* 120 A3
Magdalena →, *Mexico* 114 A2
Magdalena, B., *Mexico* 114 C2
Magdalena, I., *Chile* 128 B2
Magdalena, Llano de la, *Mexico* 114 C2
Magdeburg, *Germany* 18 C7
Magdelaine Cays, *Australia* 90 B5
Magdub, *Sudan* 77 E2
Magee, *U.S.A.* 109 K10
Magee, I., *U.K.* 15 B6
Magelang, *Indonesia* 57 G14
Magellan's Str. = Magallanes, Estrecho de, *Chile* 128 D2
Magenta, *Italy* 32 C5
Magenta, L., *Australia* 89 F2
Magerøya, *Norway* 8 A21
Maggia, *Switz.* 23 D7
Maggia →, *Switz.* 23 D7
Maggiorasca, Mte., *Italy* 32 D6
Maggiore, L., *Italy* 32 C5
Maghama, *Mauritania* 78 B2
Magherafelt, *U.K.* 15 B5
Maghnia, *Algeria* 75 B4
Magione, *Italy* 33 E9
Magistralnyy, *Russia* 45 D11
Magliano in Toscana, *Italy* 33 F8
Máglie, *Italy* 35 B11
Magnac-Laval, *France* 26 B5
Magnetic Pole (North) = North Magnetic Pole, *Canada* 4 B2
Magnetic Pole (South) = South Magnetic Pole, *Antarctica* 5 C9
Magnitogorsk, *Russia* 44 D6
Magnolia, *Ark., U.S.A.* 109 J8
Magnolia, *Miss., U.S.A.* 109 K9
Magnor, *Norway* 10 E6
Magny-en-Vexin, *France* 25 C8
Magog, *Canada* 99 C5
Magoro, *Uganda* 82 B3
Magosa = Famagusta, *Cyprus* 66 E5
Magouládhes, *Greece* 37 A3
Magoye, *Zambia* 83 F2
Magpie L., *Canada* 99 B7
Magrath, *Canada* 100 D6
Magro →, *Spain* 29 F4
Magrur, Wadi →, *Sudan* 77 D2
Magu □, *Tanzania* 82 C3
Maguan, *China* 52 F5
Maguarinho, C., *Brazil* 122 B2
Mağusa = Famagusta, *Cyprus* 66 E5
Maguse L., *Canada* 101 A9
Maguse Pt., *Canada* 101 A10
Magwe, *Burma* 61 J19
Maha Sarakham, *Thailand* 58 D4
Mahābād, *Iran* 67 D11
Mahabharat Lekh, *Nepal* 63 E9
Mahabo, *Madag.* 85 C7
Mahadeo Hills, *India* 62 H8
Mahagi, *Zaïre* 82 B3
Mahaicony, *Guyana* 121 B6
Mahajamba →, *Madag.* 85 B8
Mahajamba, Helodranon' i, *Madag.* 85 B8
Mahajan, *India* 62 E5
Mahajanga, *Madag.* 85 B8
Mahajanga □, *Madag.* 85 B8
Mahajilo →, *Madag.* 85 B8
Mahakam →, *Indonesia* 56 E5
Mahalapye, *Botswana* 84 C4
Maḩallāt, *Iran* 65 C6
Māhān, *Iran* 65 D8
Mahanadi →, *India* 61 J15
Mahanoro, *Madag.* 85 B8
Mahanoy City, *U.S.A.* 107 F8
Maharashtra □, *India* 60 J9
Maharès, *Tunisia* 75 B7
Mahari Mts., *Tanzania* 82 D2
Mahasham, W. →, *Egypt* 69 E3
Mahasolo, *Madag.* 85 B8
Mahattat ash Shīdīyah, *Jordan* 69 F4
Mahattat 'Unayzah, *Jordan* 69 E4
Mahaxay, *Laos* 58 D5
Mahbes, *W. Sahara* 74 C3
Mahbubnagar, *India* 60 L10
Maḩḑah, *Oman* 65 E7
Mahdia, *Guyana* 121 B6
Mahdia, *Tunisia* 75 A7
Mahe, *India* 63 C8
Mahenge, *Tanzania* 83 D4
Maheno, *N.Z.* 87 L3
Mahesana, *India* 62 H5
Mahia Pen., *N.Z.* 87 H6
Mahilyow, *Belarus* 40 F6
Mahirija, *Morocco* 75 B4
Mahmiya, *Sudan* 77 D3
Mahmud Kot, *Pakistan* 62 D4
Mahmudia, *Romania* 38 D12
Mahnomen, *U.S.A.* 108 B7
Mahoba, *India* 63 G8
Mahón, *Spain* 36 B11
Mahone Bay, *Canada* 99 D7
Mahuta, *Nigeria* 79 C5
Mai-Ndombe, L., *Zaïre* 80 E3
Mai-Sai, *Thailand* 58 B2
Maicao, *Colombia* 120 A3
Maîche, *France* 25 E13
Maici →, *Brazil* 125 B5
Maicurú →, *Brazil* 121 D7
Máida, *Italy* 35 D9
Maidan Khula, *Afghan.* 62 C3
Maidenhead, *U.K.* 13 F7
Maidi, *Yemen* 77 D5
Maidstone, *Canada* 101 C7
Maidstone, *U.K.* 13 F8
Maiduguri, *Nigeria* 79 C7
Maignelay, *France* 25 C9
Maigo, *Phil.* 55 G5
Maigualida, Sierra, *Venezuela* 121 B6
Maigudo, *Ethiopia* 77 F4

Maijdi, Bangla. 61 H17
Maikala Ra., India 61 J12
Mailly-le-Camp, France 25 D11
Mailsi, Pakistan 62 E5
Main →, Germany 19 F4
Main →, U.K. 15 B5
Main Centre, Canada 101 C7
Mainburg, Germany 19 G7
Maine, France 24 E6
Maine □, U.S.A. 99 C6
Maine →, Ireland 15 D2
Maine-et-Loire □, France 24 E6
Maïne-Soroa, Niger 79 C7
Maingkwan, Burma 61 F20
Mainit, L., Phil. 55 G6
Mainland, Orkney, U.K. 14 C5
Mainland, Shet., U.K. 14 A7
Mainpuri, India 63 F8
Maintenon, France 25 D8
Maintirano, Madag. 85 B7
Mainvault, Belgium 17 G3
Mainz, Germany 19 F4
Maipú, Argentina 126 D4
Maiquetía, Venezuela 120 A4
Maira →, Italy 32 D4
Mairabari, India 61 F18
Mairipotaba, Brazil 123 E2
Maisí, Cuba 117 B5
Maisi, Pta. de, Cuba 117 B5
Maisse, France 25 D9
Maissin, Belgium 17 J6
Maitland, N.S.W., Australia 91 E5
Maitland, S. Austral., Australia 91 E2
Maitland →, Canada 106 C3
Maiyema, Nigeria 79 C5
Maiyuan, China 53 E11
Maiz, Is. del, Nic. 116 D3
Maizuru, Japan 49 G7
Majagual, Colombia 120 B3
Majalengka, Indonesia 57 G13
Majari →, Brazil 121 C5
Majene, Indonesia 57 E5
Majes →, Peru 124 D3
Maji, Ethiopia 77 F4
Majiang, China 52 D6
Major, Canada 101 C7
Majorca = Mallorca, Spain 36 B10
Majuriã, Brazil 125 B5
Maka, Senegal 78 C2
Makak, Cameroon 79 E7
Makale, Indonesia 57 E5
Makamba, Burundi 82 C2
Makari, Cameroon 80 B2
Makarikari = Makgadikgadi Salt Pans, Botswana 84 C4
Makarovo, Russia 45 D11
Makarska, Croatia 21 M7
Makaryev, Russia 42 B6
Makasar = Ujung Pandang, Indonesia 57 F5
Makasar, Selat, Indonesia 57 E5
Makasar, Str. of = Makasar, Selat, Indonesia 57 E5
Makat, Kazakstan 44 E6
Makedonija = Macedonia ■, Europe 39 H4
Makena, U.S.A. 102 H16
Makeni, S. Leone 78 D2
Makeyevka = Makiyivka, Ukraine 41 H9
Makgadikgadi Salt Pans, Botswana 84 C4
Makhachkala, Russia 43 J8
Makharadze = Ozurgeti, Georgia 43 K5
Makhmūr, Iraq 67 E10
Makian, Indonesia 57 D7
Makindu, Kenya 82 C4
Makinsk, Kazakstan 44 D8
Makiyivka, Ukraine 41 H9
Makkah, Si. Arabia 68 C2
Makkovik, Canada 99 A8
Makkum, Neths. 16 B6
Makó, Hungary 21 J10
Makokou, Gabon 80 D2
Makongo, Zaïre 82 B2
Makoro, Zaïre 82 B2
Makoua, Congo 80 E3
Makrá, Greece 39 N8
Makrai, India 60 H10
Makran Coast Range, Pakistan 60 G4
Makrana, India 62 F6
Makriyialos, Greece 37 D7
Maksimkin Yar, Russia 44 D9
Maktar, Tunisia 75 A6
Mākū, Iran 67 C11
Makumbi, Zaïre 80 F4
Makunda, Botswana 84 C3
Makurazaki, Japan 49 J5
Makurdi, Nigeria 79 D6
Makūyeh, Iran 65 D7
Makwassie, S. Africa 84 D4
Mal B., Ireland 15 D2
Mal i Nemërçkës, Albania 39 J3
Mala, Peru 124 C2
Mala, Pta., Panama 116 E3
Mala Belozërka, Ukraine 41 J8
Mala Kapela, Croatia 33 D12
Mala Vyska, Ukraine 41 H6
Malabang, Phil. 55 H6
Malabar Coast, India 60 P9
Malabo = Rey Malabo, Eq. Guin. 79 E6
Malabon, Phil. 55 D4
Malacca, Str. of, Indonesia 59 L3
Malacky, Slovak Rep. 21 G7
Malad City, U.S.A. 110 E7
Maladzyechna, Belarus 40 E4
Málaga, Colombia 120 B3
Málaga, Spain 31 J6
Malaga, U.S.A. 109 J2
Málaga □, Spain 31 J6
Malagarasi, Tanzania 82 D3
Malagarasi →, Tanzania 82 D2
Malagón, Spain 31 F7
Malagón →, Spain 31 H3
Malaimbandy, Madag. 85 C8
Malakâl, Sudan 77 F3
Malakand, Pakistan 62 B4
Malakoff, U.S.A. 109 J7
Malamyzh, Russia 45 E14
Malang, Indonesia 57 G15
Malangen, Norway 8 B18
Malanje, Angola 80 F3
Mälaren, Sweden 10 E11
Malargüe, Argentina 126 D2
Malartic, Canada 98 C4
Malaryta, Belarus 41 G3
Malatya, Turkey 67 C8
Malawi ■, Africa 83 E3
Malawi, L., Africa 83 E3
Malay Pen., Asia 59 J3
Malaya Belozërka = Mala Belozërka, Ukraine 41 J8
Malaya Vishera, Russia 40 C7
Malaya Viska = Mala Vyska, Ukraine 41 H6
Malaybalay, Phil. 55 G6
Malāyer, Iran 67 E13
Malaysia ■, Asia 56 D4
Malazgirt, Turkey 67 C10
Malbon, Australia 90 C3
Malbooma, Australia 91 E1
Malbork, Poland 20 A9
Malcésine, Italy 32 C7
Malchin, Germany 18 B8
Malchow, Germany 18 B8
Malcolm, Australia 89 E3
Malcolm, Pt., Australia 89 F3
Maldegem, Belgium 17 F2
Malden, Mass., U.S.A. 107 D13
Malden, Mo., U.S.A. 109 G10
Malden I., Kiribati 93 H12
Maldives ■, Ind. Oc. 46 J11
Maldonado, Uruguay 127 C5
Maldonado, Punta, Mexico 115 D5
Malè, Italy 32 B7
Maléa, Ákra, Greece 39 N6
Malegaon, India 60 J9
Malei, Mozam. 83 F4
Malek Kandī, Iran 67 D12
Malela, Zaïre 82 C2
Malema, Mozam. 83 E4
Máleme, Greece 37 D5
Malerkotla, India 62 D6
Máles, Greece 37 D7
Malesherbes, France 25 D9
Malestroit, France 24 E4
Malfa, Italy 35 D7
Malgobek, Russia 43 J7
Malgomaj, Sweden 8 D17
Malgrat, Spain 28 D7
Malha, Sudan 77 D2
Malheur →, U.S.A. 110 D5
Malheur L., U.S.A. 110 E4
Mali, Guinea 78 C2
Mali ■, Africa 78 B4
Mali →, Burma 61 G20
Mali Kanal, Serbia, Yug. 21 K9
Malibu, U.S.A. 113 L8
Malik, Indonesia 57 E6
Malili, Indonesia 57 E6
Malimba, Mts., Zaïre 82 D2
Malin Hd., Ireland 15 A4
Malindi, Kenya 82 C5
Malines = Mechelen, Belgium 17 F4
Malino, Indonesia 57 D6
Malinyi, Tanzania 83 D4
Malipo, China 52 F5
Maliqi, Albania 39 J3
Malita, Phil. 57 C7
Malkara, Turkey 66 B2
Małkinia Górna, Poland 20 C12
Malko Tŭrnovo, Bulgaria 39 H10
Mallacoota, Australia 91 F4
Mallacoota Inlet, Australia 91 F4
Mallaig, U.K. 14 E3
Mallawan, India 63 F9
Mallawi, Egypt 76 B3
Malleco □, Chile 128 A2
Mallemort, France 27 E9
Málles Venosta, Italy 32 B7
Mállia, Greece 37 D7
Mallión, Kólpos, Greece 37 D7
Mallorca, Spain 36 B10
Mallorytown, Canada 107 B9
Mallow, Ireland 15 D3
Malmberget, Sweden 8 C19
Malmédy, Belgium 17 H8
Malmesbury, S. Africa 84 E2
Malmö, Sweden 11 J6
Malmöhus län □, Sweden 11 J7
Malmslätt, Sweden 11 F9
Malmyzh, Russia 42 B10
Maloarkhangelsk, Russia 42 D3
Maloca, Brazil 121 C6
Maloja, Switz. 23 D9
Maloja, P., Switz. 23 D9
Malolos, Phil. 57 B6
Malombe L., Malawi 83 E4
Malone, U.S.A. 107 B10
Malong, China 52 E4
Måløy, Norway 9 F11
Maloyaroslovets, Russia 42 C3
Malpartida, Spain 31 F4
Malpaso, Canary Is. 36 G1
Malpica, Spain 30 B2
Mals = Málles Venosta, Italy 32 B7
Malta, Brazil 122 C4
Malta, Idaho, U.S.A. 110 E7
Malta, Mont., U.S.A. 110 B10
Malta ■, Europe 37 D1
Malta Channel, Medit. S. 34 F6
Maltahöhe, Namibia 84 C2
Malters, Switz. 22 B6
Malton, Canada 106 C5
Malton, U.K. 12 C7
Maluku, Indonesia 57 E7
Maluku □, Indonesia 57 E7
Maluku Sea = Molucca Sea, Indonesia 57 E6
Malumfashi, Nigeria 79 C6
Malvan, India 60 L8
Malvern, U.S.A. 109 H8
Malvern Hills, U.K. 13 E5
Malvik, Norway 10 A4
Malvinas, Is. = Falkland Is. □, Atl. Oc. 128 D5
Malya, Tanzania 82 C3
Malyn, Ukraine 41 G5
Malyy Lyakhovskiy, Ostrov, Russia 45 B15
Malyy Nimnyr, Russia 45 D13
Mama, Russia 45 D12
Mamadysh, Russia 42 C10
Mamanguape, Brazil 122 C4
Mamasa, Indonesia 57 E5
Mambasa, Zaïre 82 B2
Mamberamo →, Indonesia 57 E9
Mambilima Falls, Zambia 83 E2
Mambirima, Zaïre 83 E2
Mambo, Tanzania 82 C4
Mambrui, Kenya 82 C5
Mamburao, Phil. 55 E4
Mameigwess L., Canada 98 B2
Mamer, Lux. 17 J8
Mamers, France 24 D7
Mamfe, Cameroon 79 D6
Mamiña, Chile 124 E4
Mámmola, Italy 35 D9
Mammoth, U.S.A. 111 K8
Mamoré →, Bolivia 125 C4
Mamou, Guinea 78 C2
Mampatá, Guinea-Biss. 78 C2
Mampong, Ghana 79 D4
Mamuil Malal, Paso, S. Amer. 128 A2
Mamuju, Indonesia 57 E5
Man, Ivory C. 78 D3
Man, I. of, U.K. 12 C3
Man Na, Burma 61 H20
Mana, Fr. Guiana 121 B7
Mana →, Fr. Guiana 121 B7
Måna →, Norway 10 E2
Manaar, G. of = Mannar, G. of, Asia 60 Q11
Manabí □, Ecuador 120 D1
Manacacías →, Colombia 120 C3
Manacapuru, Brazil 121 D5
Manacapuru →, Brazil 121 D5
Manacor, Spain 36 B10
Manado, Indonesia 57 D6
Manage, Belgium 17 G4
Managua, Nic. 116 D2
Managua, L., Nic. 116 D2
Manakara, Madag. 85 C8
Manama = Al Manāmah, Bahrain 65 E6
Manambao →, Madag. 85 B7
Manambato, Madag. 85 A8
Manambolo →, Madag. 85 B7
Manambolosy, Madag. 85 B8
Mananara, Madag. 85 B8
Mananara →, Madag. 85 C8
Mananjary, Madag. 85 C8
Manantenina, Madag. 85 C8
Manaos = Manaus, Brazil 121 D6
Manapire →, Venezuela 120 B4
Manapouri, N.Z. 87 L1
Manapouri, L., N.Z. 87 L1
Manas, China 54 B3
Manas →, India 61 F17
Manaslu, Nepal 63 E11
Manasquan, U.S.A. 107 F10
Manassa, U.S.A. 111 H11
Manaung, Burma 61 K18
Manaus, Brazil 121 D6
Manavgat, Turkey 66 D4
Manawan L., Canada 101 B8
Manay, Phil. 55 H7
Manbij, Syria 66 D7
Mancelona, U.S.A. 104 C3
Mancha Real, Spain 31 H7
Manche □, France 24 C5
Manchester, U.K. 12 D5
Manchester, Calif., U.S.A. 112 G3
Manchester, Conn., U.S.A. 107 E12
Manchester, Ga., U.S.A. 105 J3
Manchester, Iowa, U.S.A. 108 D9
Manchester, Ky., U.S.A. 104 G4
Manchester, N.H., U.S.A. 107 D13
Manchester, N.Y., U.S.A. 106 D7
Manchester, Vt., U.S.A. 107 C11
Manchester L., Canada 101 A7
Manchuria = Dongbei, China 51 D13
Manchurian Plain, China 46 E16
Manciano, Italy 33 F8
Mancifa, Ethiopia 77 F5
Mancora, Pta., Peru 124 A1
Mand →, Iran 65 D7
Manda, Chunya, Tanzania 82 D3
Manda, Ludewe, Tanzania 83 E3
Mandabé, Madag. 85 C7
Mandaguari, Brazil 127 A5
Mandah, Mongolia 50 B5
Mandal, Norway 9 G12
Mandalay, Burma 61 J20
Mandale = Mandalay, Burma 61 J20
Mandalgovi, Mongolia 50 B4
Mandalī, Iraq 67 F11
Mandan, U.S.A. 108 B4
Mandaon, Phil. 55 E5
Mandar, Teluk, Indonesia 57 E5
Mandas, Italy 34 C2
Mandaue, Phil. 55 F5
Mandelieu-la-Napoule, France 27 E10
Mandera, Kenya 82 B5
Mandera □, Kenya 82 B5
Manderfeld, Belgium 17 H8
Mandi, India 62 D7
Mandimba, Mozam. 83 E4
Mandioli, Indonesia 57 E7
Mandioré, L., S. Amer. 125 D6
Mandla, India 63 H9
Mandø, Denmark 11 J2
Mandoto, Madag. 85 B8
Mandoúdhion, Greece 39 L6
Mandra, Pakistan 62 C5
Mandrare →, Madag. 85 D8
Mandritsara, Madag. 85 B8
Mandsaur, India 62 G6
Mandurah, Australia 89 F2
Mandúria, Italy 35 B10
Mandvi, India 62 H3
Mandya, India 60 N10
Mandzai, Pakistan 62 D2
Mané, Burkina Faso 79 C4
Maneh, Iran 65 B8
Manengouba, Mts., Cameroon 79 D6
Maneroo, Australia 90 C3
Maneroo Cr. →, Australia 90 C3
Manfalût, Egypt 76 B3
Manfred, Australia 91 E3
Manfredónia, Italy 35 A8
Manfredónia, G. di, Italy 35 A9
Manga, Brazil 123 D3
Manga, Burkina Faso 79 C4
Manga, Niger 79 C7
Mangabeiras, Chapada das, Brazil 122 D2
Mangalia, Romania 38 F11
Mangalore, India 60 N9
Manganeses, Spain 30 D5
Mangaweka, N.Z. 87 H5
Manggar, Indonesia 56 E3
Manggawitu, Indonesia 57 E8
Mangkalihat, Tanjung, Indonesia 57 D5
Mangla Dam, Pakistan 63 C5
Manglares, C., Colombia 120 C2
Manglaur, India 62 E7
Mangnai, China 54 C4
Mango, Togo 79 C5
Mangoche, Malawi 83 E4
Mangoky →, Madag. 85 C7
Mangole, Indonesia 57 E7
Mangombe, Zaïre 82 C2
Mangonui, N.Z. 87 F4
Mangualde, Portugal 30 E3
Mangueigne, Chad 73 F9
Mangueira, L. da, Brazil 127 C5
Manguéni, Hamada, Niger 75 D7
Mangum, U.S.A. 109 H5
Mangyshlak Poluostrov, Kazakstan 44 E6
Manhattan, U.S.A. 108 F6
Manhiça, Mozam. 85 D5
Manhuaçu, Brazil 123 F3
Manhumirim, Brazil 123 F3
Maní, Colombia 120 C3
Mania →, Madag. 85 B8
Maniago, Italy 33 B9
Manica, Mozam. 85 B5
Manica e Sofala □, Mozam. 85 B5
Manicaland □, Zimbabwe 83 F3
Manicoré, Brazil 125 B5
Manicoré →, Brazil 125 B5
Manicouagan →, Canada 99 C6
Manīfah, Si. Arabia 65 E6
Manifold, Australia 90 C5
Manifold, C., Australia 90 C5
Maniganggo, China 52 B2
Manigotagan, Canada 101 C9
Manihiki, Cook Is. 93 J11
Manika, Plateau de la, Zaïre 83 E2
Manila, Phil. 55 D4
Manila, U.S.A. 110 F9
Manila B., Phil. 55 D4
Manilla, Australia 91 E5
Manimpé, Mali 78 C3
Maningrida, Australia 90 A1
Manipur □, India 61 G18
Manipur →, Burma 61 H19
Manisa, Turkey 66 C2
Manistee, U.S.A. 104 C2
Manistee →, U.S.A. 104 C2
Manistique, U.S.A. 104 C2
Manito L., Canada 101 C7
Manitoba □, Canada 101 B9
Manitoba, L., Canada 101 C9
Manitou, Canada 101 D9
Manitou I., U.S.A. 98 C2
Manitou Is., U.S.A. 104 C2
Manitou L., Canada 99 B6
Manitou Springs, U.S.A. 108 F2
Manitoulin I., Canada 98 C3
Manitowaning, Canada 98 C3
Manitowoc, U.S.A. 104 C2
Manitsauá-Missu →, Brazil 125 C7
Manizales, Colombia 120 B2
Manja, Madag. 85 C7
Manjacaze, Mozam. 85 C5
Manjakandriana, Madag. 85 B8
Manjhand, Pakistan 62 G3
Manjil, Iran 65 B6
Manjimup, Australia 89 F2
Manjra →, India 60 K10
Mankato, Kans., U.S.A. 108 F5
Mankato, Minn., U.S.A. 108 C8
Mankayane, Swaziland 85 D5
Mankono, Ivory C. 78 D3
Mankota, Canada 101 D7
Manlay, Mongolia 50 B4
Manlleu, Spain 28 C7
Manly, Australia 91 E5
Manmad, India 60 J9
Mann Ras., Australia 89 E5
Manna, Indonesia 56 E2
Mannahill, Australia 91 E3
Mannar, Sri Lanka 60 Q11
Mannar, G. of, Asia 60 Q11
Mannar I., Sri Lanka 60 Q11
Männedorf, Switz. 23 B7
Mannheim, Germany 19 F4
Manning, Canada 100 B5
Manning, Oreg., U.S.A. 112 E3
Manning, S.C., U.S.A. 105 J5
Manning Prov. Park, Canada 100 D4
Mannington, U.S.A. 104 F5
Mannu →, Italy 34 C2
Mannu, C., Italy 34 B1
Mannum, Australia 91 E2
Mano, S. Leone 78 D2
Manoa, Bolivia 125 B4
Manokwari, Indonesia 57 E8
Manombo, Madag. 85 C7
Manono, Zaïre 82 D2
Manosque, France 27 E9
Manouane, L., Canada 99 B5
Manpojin, N. Korea 51 D14
Manresa, Spain 28 D6
Mansa, Gujarat, India 62 H5
Mansa, Punjab, India 62 E6
Mansa, Zambia 83 E2
Mansehra, Pakistan 62 B5
Mansel I., Canada 97 B11
Mansfield, Australia 91 F4
Mansfield, U.K. 12 D6
Mansfield, La., U.S.A. 109 J8
Mansfield, Mass., U.S.A. 107 D13
Mansfield, Ohio, U.S.A. 106 F2
Mansfield, Pa., U.S.A. 106 E7
Mansfield, Wash., U.S.A. 110 C4
Mansidão, Brazil 122 D3
Mansilla de las Mulas, Spain 30 C5
Mansle, France 26 C4
Manso →, Brazil 123 D2
Mansoa, Guinea-Biss. 78 C1
Manson Creek, Canada 100 B4
Mansoura, Algeria 75 A5
Manta, Ecuador 120 D1
Manta, B. de, Ecuador 120 D1
Mantalingajan, Mt., Phil. 55 G2
Mantare, Tanzania 82 C3
Manteca, U.S.A. 111 H3
Mantecal, Venezuela 120 B4
Mantena, Brazil 123 E3
Manteo, U.S.A. 105 H8
Mantes-la-Jolie, France 25 D8
Manthani, India 60 K11
Manthelan, France 24 E7
Manti, U.S.A. 110 G8
Mantiqueira, Serra da, Brazil 123 F3
Manton, U.S.A. 104 C3
Mantorp, Sweden 11 F9
Mántova, Italy 32 C7
Mänttä, Finland 9 E21
Mantua = Mántova, Italy 32 C7
Manturovo, Russia 42 A7
Manu, Peru 124 C3
Manu →, Peru 124 C3
Manua Is., Amer. Samoa 87 B14
Manuae, Cook Is. 93 J12
Manuel Alves →, Brazil 123 D2
Manuel Alves Grande →, Brazil 122 C2
Manuel Urbano, Brazil 124 B4
Manui, Indonesia 57 E6
Manuripi →, Bolivia 124 C4
Manville, U.S.A. 108 D2
Many, U.S.A. 109 K8
Manyara, L., Tanzania 82 C4
Manych →, Russia 43 G5
Manych-Gudilo, Ozero, Russia 43 G6
Manyonga →, Tanzania 82 C3
Manyoni, Tanzania 82 D3
Manyoni □, Tanzania 82 D3
Manzai, Pakistan 62 C4
Manzala, Bahra el, Egypt 76 H7
Manzanares, Spain 29 F1

Manzaneda, Cabeza de, *Spain* 30 C3
Manzanillo, *Cuba* 116 B4
Manzanillo, *Mexico* 114 D4
Manzanillo, Pta., *Panama* 116 E4
Manzano Mts., *U.S.A.* 111 J10
Manzarīyeh, *Iran* 65 C6
Manzhouli, *China* 54 B6
Manzini, *Swaziland* 85 D5
Mao, *Chad* 73 F8
Maoke, Pegunungan, *Indonesia* 57 E9
Maolin, *China* 51 C12
Maoming, *China* 53 G8
Maowen, *China* 52 B4
Maoxing, *China* 51 B13
Mapam Yumco, *China* 54 C3
Mapastepec, *Mexico* 115 D6
Mapia, Kepulauan, *Indonesia* 57 D8
Mapimí, *Mexico* 114 B4
Mapimí, Bolsón de, *Mexico* 114 B4
Maping, *China* 53 B9
Mapinga, *Tanzania* 82 D4
Mapinhane, *Mozam.* 85 C6
Mapire, *Venezuela* 121 B5
Maple Creek, *Canada* 101 D7
Maple Valley, *U.S.A.* 112 C4
Mapleton, *U.S.A.* 110 D2
Mapuera →, *Brazil* 121 D6
Maputo, *Mozam.* 85 D5
Maputo, B. de, *Mozam.* 85 D5
Maqiaohe, *China* 51 B16
Maqnā, *Si. Arabia* 64 D2
Maqteïr, *Mauritania* 74 D2
Maquela do Zombo, *Angola* 80 F3
Maquinchao, *Argentina* 128 B3
Maquoketa, *U.S.A.* 108 D9
Mar, Serra do, *Brazil* 127 B6
Mar Chiquita, L., *Argentina* 126 C3
Mar del Plata, *Argentina* 126 D4
Mar Menor, *Spain* 29 H4
Mara, *Guyana* 121 B6
Mara, *Tanzania* 82 C3
Mara □, *Tanzania* 82 C3
Maraã, *Brazil* 120 D4
Marabá, *Brazil* 122 C2
Maracá, I. de, *Brazil* 121 C7
Maracaibo, *Venezuela* 120 A3
Maracaibo, L. de, *Venezuela* 120 B3
Maracaju, *Brazil* 127 A4
Maracajú, Serra de, *Brazil* 125 E6
Maracanã, *Brazil* 122 B2
Maracás, *Brazil* 123 D3
Maracay, *Venezuela* 120 A4
Marādah, *Libya* 73 C8
Maradi, *Niger* 79 C6
Maradun, *Nigeria* 79 C6
Marāgheh, *Iran* 67 D12
Maragogipe, *Brazil* 123 D4
Marāh, *Si. Arabia* 64 E5
Marajó, B. de, *Brazil* 122 B2
Marajó, I. de, *Brazil* 122 B2
Marākand, *Iran* 64 B5
Maralal, *Kenya* 82 B4
Maralinga, *Australia* 89 F5
Marama, *Australia* 91 F3
Marampa, *S. Leone* 78 D2
Maran, *Malaysia* 59 L4
Marana, *U.S.A.* 111 K8
Maranboy, *Australia* 88 B5
Maranchón, *Spain* 28 D2
Marand, *Iran* 67 C11
Marang, *Malaysia* 59 K4
Maranguape, *Brazil* 122 B4
Maranhão = São Luís, *Brazil* 122 B3
Maranhão □, *Brazil* 122 B2
Marano, L. di, *Italy* 33 C10
Maranoa →, *Australia* 91 D4
Marañón →, *Peru* 124 A3
Marão, *Mozam.* 85 C5
Marapi →, *Brazil* 121 C6
Marari, *Brazil* 124 B4
Maraş = Kahramanmaraş, *Turkey* 66 D7
Mărăşeşti, *Romania* 38 D10
Maratea, *Italy* 35 C8
Marateca, *Portugal* 31 G2
Marathasa □, *Cyprus* 37 E11
Marathókambos, *Greece* 39 M9
Marathon, *Australia* 90 C3
Marathon, *Canada* 98 C2
Marathón, *Greece* 39 L6
Marathon, *N.Y., U.S.A.* 107 D8
Marathon, *Tex., U.S.A.* 109 K3
Marathóvouno, *Cyprus* 37 D12
Maratua, *Indonesia* 57 D5
Maraú, *Brazil* 123 D4
Maravatío, *Mexico* 114 D4
Marawi City, *Phil.* 55 G6
Marāwih, *U.A.E.* 65 E7
Marbella, *Spain* 31 J6
Marble Bar, *Australia* 88 D2
Marble Falls, *U.S.A.* 109 K5
Marblehead, *U.S.A.* 107 D14
Marburg, *Germany* 18 E4
Marby, *Sweden* 10 A8
Marcal →, *Hungary* 21 H7
Marcapata, *Peru* 124 C3
Marcaria, *Italy* 32 C7
March, *U.K.* 13 E8
Marchand = Rommani, *Morocco* 74 B3
Marche, *France* 26 B5
Marche □, *Italy* 33 E10
Marche-en-Famenne, *Belgium* 17 H6
Marchena, *Spain* 31 H5
Marches = Marche □, *Italy* 33 E10
Marciana Marina, *Italy* 32 F7
Marcianise, *Italy* 35 A7
Marcigny, *France* 27 B8
Marcillat-en-Combraille, *France* 26 B6
Marcinelle, *Belgium* 17 H4
Marck, *France* 25 B8
Marckolsheim, *France* 25 D14
Marcona, *Peru* 124 D2
Marcos Juárez, *Argentina* 126 C3
Marcus I. = Minami-Tori-Shima, *Pac. Oc.* 92 E7
Marcus Necker Ridge, *Pac. Oc.* 92 F9
Marcy, Mt., *U.S.A.* 107 B11
Mardan, *Pakistan* 62 B5
Mardie, *Australia* 88 D2
Mardin, *Turkey* 67 D9
Marechal Deodoro, *Brazil* 122 C4
Maree, L., *U.K.* 14 D3
Mareeba, *Australia* 90 B4
Marek = Stanke Dimitrov, *Bulgaria* 38 G6
Marek, *Indonesia* 57 E6
Maremma, *Italy* 32 F8
Maréna, *Mali* 78 C3
Marenberg, *Slovenia* 33 B12
Marengo, *U.S.A.* 108 E8
Marennes, *France* 26 C2
Marenyi, *Kenya* 82 C4
Marerano, *Madag.* 85 C7
Maréttimo, *Italy* 34 E5
Mareuil-sur-Lay, *France* 26 B2
Marfa, *U.S.A.* 109 K2
Marfa Pt., *Malta* 37 D1
Marganets = Marhanets, *Ukraine* 41 J8
Margaret →, *Australia* 88 C4
Margaret Bay, *Canada* 100 C3
Margaret L., *Canada* 100 B5
Margaret River, *Australia* 88 C4
Margarita, I. de, *Venezuela* 121 A5
Margarítion, *Greece* 39 K3
Margaritovo, *Russia* 48 C7
Margate, *S. Africa* 85 E5
Margate, *U.K.* 13 F9
Margelan = Marghilon, *Uzbekistan* 44 E8
Margeride, Mts. de la, *France* 26 D7
Margherita di Savoia, *Italy* 35 A9
Marghilon, *Uzbekistan* 44 E8
Margosatubig, *Phil.* 55 H5
Marguerite, *Canada* 100 C4
Marhanets, *Ukraine* 41 J8
Marhoum, *Algeria* 75 B4
Mari El □, *Russia* 42 B8
Mari Republic □ = Mari El □, *Russia* 42 B8
María Elena, *Chile* 126 A2
María Grande, *Argentina* 126 C4
Maria I., *N. Terr., Australia* 90 A2
Maria I., *Tas., Australia* 90 G4
Maria van Diemen, C., *N.Z.* 87 F4
Mariager, *Denmark* 11 H4
Mariager Fjord, *Denmark* 11 H4
Mariakani, *Kenya* 82 C4
Marian L., *Canada* 100 A5
Mariana Trench, *Pac. Oc.* 46 H18
Marianao, *Cuba* 116 B3
Marianna, *Ark., U.S.A.* 109 H9
Marianna, *Fla., U.S.A.* 105 K3
Mariánské Lázně, *Czech.* 20 F2
Marias →, *U.S.A.* 110 C8
Mariato, Punta, *Panama* 116 E3
Mariazell, *Austria* 21 H5
Ma'rib, *Yemen* 68 D4
Maribo, *Denmark* 11 K5
Maribor, *Slovenia* 33 B12
Marico →, *Africa* 84 C4
Maricopa, *Ariz., U.S.A.* 111 K7
Maricopa, *Calif., U.S.A.* 113 K7
Maricourt, *Canada* 97 C12
Marîdî, *Sudan* 77 G2
Maridi, Wadi →, *Sudan* 77 F2
Marié →, *Brazil* 120 D4
Marie Byrd Land, *Antarctica* 5 D14
Marie-Galante, *Guadeloupe* 117 C7
Mariecourt = Kangiqsujuaq, *Canada* 97 B12
Mariefred, *Sweden* 10 E11
Marienbad = Mariánské Lázně, *Czech.* 20 F2
Marienberg, *Germany* 18 E9
Marienberg, *Neths.* 16 D9
Marienbourg, *Belgium* 17 H5
Mariental, *Namibia* 84 C2
Marienville, *U.S.A.* 106 E5
Mariestad, *Sweden* 11 F7
Marietta, *Ga., U.S.A.* 105 J3
Marietta, *Ohio, U.S.A.* 104 F5
Marieville, *Canada* 107 A11
Marignane, *France* 27 E9
Marihatag, *Phil.* 55 G7
Mariinsk, *Russia* 44 D9
Mariinskiy Posad, *Russia* 42 B8
Marijampolė, *Lithuania* 9 J20
Marília, *Brazil* 127 A5
Marillana, *Australia* 88 D2
Marín, *Spain* 30 C2
Marina, *U.S.A.* 112 J5
Marina di Cirò, *Italy* 35 C10
Marina Plains, *Australia* 90 A3
Marinduque, *Phil.* 55 E5
Marine City, *U.S.A.* 104 D4
Marineo, *Italy* 34 E6
Marinette, *U.S.A.* 104 C2
Maringá, *Brazil* 127 A5
Marinha Grande, *Portugal* 31 F2
Marion, *Ala., U.S.A.* 105 J2
Marion, *Ill., U.S.A.* 109 G10
Marion, *Ind., U.S.A.* 104 E3
Marion, *Iowa, U.S.A.* 108 D9
Marion, *Kans., U.S.A.* 108 F6
Marion, *Mich., U.S.A.* 104 C3
Marion, *N.C., U.S.A.* 105 H4
Marion, *Ohio, U.S.A.* 104 E4
Marion, *S.C., U.S.A.* 105 H6
Marion, *Va., U.S.A.* 105 G5
Marion, L., *U.S.A.* 105 J5
Maripa, *Venezuela* 121 B4
Maripasoula, *Fr. Guiana* 121 C7
Mariposa, *U.S.A.* 111 H4
Mariscal Estigarribia, *Paraguay* 126 A3
Maritime Alps = Maritimes, Alpes, *Europe* 27 D11
Maritimes, Alpes, *Europe* 27 D11
Maritsa = Évros →, *Bulgaria* 66 B2
Maritsa, *Greece* 37 C10
Mariupol, *Ukraine* 41 J9
Marīvān, *Iran* 67 E12
Markam, *China* 52 C2
Markazī □, *Iran* 65 C6
Markdale, *Canada* 106 B4
Marke, *Belgium* 17 G2
Marked Tree, *U.S.A.* 109 H9
Markelsdorfer Huk, *Germany* 18 A6
Marken, *Neths.* 16 D6
Markermeer, *Neths.* 16 C6
Market Drayton, *U.K.* 12 E5
Market Harborough, *U.K.* 13 E7
Markham, *Canada* 106 C5
Markham, Mt., *Antarctica* 5 E11
Markham L., *Canada* 101 A8
Marki, *Poland* 20 C11
Markleeville, *U.S.A.* 112 G7
Markoupoulon, *Greece* 39 M6
Markovo, *Russia* 45 C17
Markoye, *Burkina Faso* 79 C5
Marks, *Russia* 42 E8
Marksville, *U.S.A.* 109 K8
Markt Schwaben, *Germany* 19 G7
Marktredwitz, *Germany* 19 E8
Marla, *Australia* 91 D1
Marlboro, *U.S.A.* 107 D13
Marlborough, *Australia* 90 C4
Marlborough Downs, *U.K.* 13 F6
Marle, *France* 25 C10
Marlin, *U.S.A.* 109 K6
Marlow, *Germany* 18 A8
Marlow, *U.S.A.* 109 H6
Marly-le-Grand, *Switz.* 22 C4
Marmagao, *India* 60 M8
Marmande, *France* 26 D4
Marmara, *Turkey* 66 B2
Marmara, Sea of = Marmara Denizi, *Turkey* 66 B3
Marmara Denizi, *Turkey* 66 B3
Marmaris, *Turkey* 66 D3
Marmarth, *U.S.A.* 108 B3
Marmelos →, *Brazil* 125 B5
Marmion, Mt., *Australia* 89 E2
Marmion L., *Canada* 98 C1
Marmolada, Mte., *Italy* 33 B8
Marmolejo, *Spain* 31 G6
Marmora, *Canada* 98 D4
Marnay, *France* 25 E12
Marne, *Germany* 18 B5
Marne □, *France* 25 D11
Marne →, *France* 25 D9
Marneuli, *Georgia* 43 K7
Maroa, *Venezuela* 120 C4
Maroala, *Madag.* 85 B8
Maroantsetra, *Madag.* 85 B8
Maromandia, *Madag.* 85 A8
Marondera, *Zimbabwe* 83 F3
Maroni →, *Fr. Guiana* 121 B7
Maronne →, *France* 26 C5
Maroochydore, *Australia* 91 D5
Maroona, *Australia* 91 F3
Maros →, *Hungary* 21 J10
Marosakoa, *Madag.* 85 B8
Marostica, *Italy* 33 C8
Maroua, *Cameroon* 79 C7
Marovoay, *Madag.* 85 B8
Marowijne □, *Surinam* 121 C7
Marowijne →, *Surinam* 121 B7
Marquard, *S. Africa* 84 D4
Marqueira, *Portugal* 31 G1
Marquesas Is. = Marquises, Is., *Pac. Oc.* 93 H14
Marquette, *U.S.A.* 104 B2
Marquise, *France* 25 B8
Marquises, Is., *Pac. Oc.* 93 H14
Marra, Gebel, *Sudan* 77 F2
Marracuene, *Mozam.* 85 D5
Marradi, *Italy* 33 D8
Marrakech, *Morocco* 74 B3
Marrawah, *Australia* 90 G3
Marrecas, Serra das, *Brazil* 122 C3
Marree, *Australia* 91 D2
Marrilla, *Australia* 88 D1
Marrimane, *Mozam.* 85 C5
Marromeu, *Mozam.* 85 B6
Marroquí, Punta, *Spain* 31 K5
Marrowie Cr. →, *Australia* 91 E4
Marrubane, *Mozam.* 83 F4
Marrum, *Neths.* 16 B7
Marrupa, *Mozam.* 83 E4
Marsá Matrûh, *Egypt* 76 A2
Marsá Susah, *Libya* 73 B9
Marsabit, *Kenya* 82 B4
Marsabit □, *Kenya* 82 B4
Marsala, *Italy* 34 E5
Marsalforn, *Malta* 37 C1
Marsberg, *Germany* 18 D4
Marsciano, *Italy* 33 F9
Marsden, *Australia* 91 E4
Marsdiep, *Neths.* 16 C5
Marseillan, *France* 26 E7
Marseille, *France* 27 E9
Marseilles = Marseille, *France* 27 E9
Marsh I., *U.S.A.* 109 L9
Marsh L., *U.S.A.* 108 C6
Marshall, *Liberia* 78 D2
Marshall, *Ark., U.S.A.* 109 H8
Marshall, *Mich., U.S.A.* 104 D3
Marshall, *Minn., U.S.A.* 108 C7
Marshall, *Mo., U.S.A.* 108 F8
Marshall, *Tex., U.S.A.* 109 J7
Marshall →, *Australia* 90 C2
Marshall Is. ■, *Pac. Oc.* 92 G9
Marshalltown, *U.S.A.* 108 D8
Marshfield, *Mo., U.S.A.* 109 G8
Marshfield, *Wis., U.S.A.* 108 C9
Marshūn, *Iran* 65 B6
Mársico Nuovo, *Italy* 35 B8
Märsta, *Sweden* 10 E11
Marstal, *Denmark* 11 K4
Marstrand, *Sweden* 11 G5
Mart, *U.S.A.* 109 K6
Marta →, *Italy* 33 F8
Martaban, *Burma* 61 L20
Martaban, G. of, *Burma* 61 L20
Martano, *Italy* 35 B11
Martapura, *Kalimantan, Indonesia* 56 E4
Martapura, *Sumatera, Indonesia* 56 E2
Marte, *Nigeria* 79 C7
Martel, *France* 26 D5
Martelange, *Belgium* 17 J7
Martés, Sierra, *Spain* 29 F4
Martha's Vineyard, *U.S.A.* 107 E14
Martigné-Ferchaud, *France* 24 E5
Martigny, *Switz.* 22 D4
Martigues, *France* 27 E9
Martil, *Morocco* 74 A3
Martin, *Slovak Rep.* 20 F8
Martin, *S. Dak., U.S.A.* 108 D4
Martin, *Tenn., U.S.A.* 109 G10
Martín →, *Spain* 28 D4
Martin L., *U.S.A.* 105 J3
Martina, *Switz.* 23 C10
Martina Franca, *Italy* 35 B10
Martinborough, *N.Z.* 87 J5
Martinez, *U.S.A.* 112 G4
Martinho Campos, *Brazil* 123 E2
Martinique ■, *W. Indies* 117 D7
Martinique Passage, *W. Indies* 117 C7
Martínon, *Greece* 39 L6
Martinópolis, *Brazil* 127 A5
Martins Ferry, *U.S.A.* 106 F4
Martinsburg, *Pa., U.S.A.* 106 F6
Martinsburg, *W. Va., U.S.A.* 104 F7
Martinsville, *Ind., U.S.A.* 104 F2
Martinsville, *Va., U.S.A.* 105 G6
Marton, *N.Z.* 87 J5
Martorell, *Spain* 28 D6
Martos, *Spain* 31 H7
Martuni, *Armenia* 43 K7
Maru, *Nigeria* 79 C6
Marudi, *Malaysia* 56 D4
Ma'ruf, *Afghan.* 60 D5
Marugame, *Japan* 49 G6
Marúggio, *Italy* 35 B10
Maruim, *Brazil* 122 D4
Marulan, *Australia* 91 E5
Marum, *Neths.* 16 B8
Marunga, *Angola* 84 B3
Marungu, Mts., *Zaïre* 82 D2
Marvast, *Iran* 65 D7
Marvejols, *France* 26 D7
Marwar, *India* 62 G5
Mary, *Turkmenistan* 44 F7
Mary Frances L., *Canada* 101 A7
Mary Kathleen, *Australia* 90 C2
Maryborough = Port Laoise, *Ireland* 15 C4
Maryborough, *Queens., Australia* 91 D5
Maryborough, *Vic., Australia* 91 F3
Maryfield, *Canada* 101 D8
Maryland □, *U.S.A.* 104 F7
Maryland Junction, *Zimbabwe* 83 F3
Maryport, *U.K.* 12 C4
Mary's Harbour, *Canada* 99 B8
Marystown, *Canada* 99 C8
Marysvale, *U.S.A.* 111 G7
Marysville, *Canada* 100 D5
Marysville, *Calif., U.S.A.* 112 F5
Marysville, *Kans., U.S.A.* 108 F6
Marysville, *Mich., U.S.A.* 106 D2
Marysville, *Ohio, U.S.A.* 104 E4
Marysville, *Wash., U.S.A.* 112 B4
Maryvale, *Australia* 91 D5
Maryville, *U.S.A.* 105 H4
Marzo, Punta, *Colombia* 120 B2
Marzūq, *Libya* 73 C7
Masahunga, *Tanzania* 82 C3
Masai, *Malaysia* 59 M4
Masai Steppe, *Tanzania* 82 C4
Masaka, *Uganda* 82 C3
Masalembo, Kepulauan, *Indonesia* 56 F4
Masalima, Kepulauan, *Indonesia* 56 F5
Masallı, *Azerbaijan* 67 C13
Masamba, *Indonesia* 57 E6
Masan, *S. Korea* 51 G15
Masanasa, *Spain* 29 F4
Masasi, *Tanzania* 83 E4
Masasi □, *Tanzania* 83 E4
Masaya, *Nic.* 116 D2
Masba, *Nigeria* 79 C7
Masbate, *Phil.* 55 E5
Mascara, *Algeria* 75 A5
Mascota, *Mexico* 114 C4
Masela, *Indonesia* 57 F7
Maseru, *Lesotho* 84 D4
Mashaba, *Zimbabwe* 83 G3
Mashābih, *Si. Arabia* 64 E3
Mashan, *China* 52 F7
Masherbrum, *Pakistan* 63 B7
Mashhad, *Iran* 65 B8
Mashi, *Nigeria* 79 C6
Mashīz, *Iran* 65 D8
Mashkel, Hamun-i-, *Pakistan* 60 E3
Mashki Chāh, *Pakistan* 60 E3
Mashonaland Central □, *Zimbabwe* 85 B5
Mashonaland East □, *Zimbabwe* 85 B5
Mashonaland West □, *Zimbabwe* 85 B4
Mashtaga = Maştağa, *Azerbaijan* 43 K10
Masi Manimba, *Zaïre* 80 E3
Masindi, *Uganda* 82 B3
Masindi Port, *Uganda* 82 B3
Masisea, *Peru* 124 B3
Masisi, *Zaïre* 82 C2
Masjed Soleyman, *Iran* 65 D6
Mask, L., *Ireland* 15 C2
Maslinica, *Croatia* 33 E13
Masnou, *Spain* 28 D7
Masoala, Tanjon' i, *Madag.* 85 B9
Masoarivo, *Madag.* 85 B7
Masohi, *Indonesia* 57 E7
Masomeloka, *Madag.* 85 C8
Mason, *Nev., U.S.A.* 112 G7
Mason, *Tex., U.S.A.* 109 K5
Mason City, *U.S.A.* 108 D8
Maspalomas, *Canary Is.* 36 G4
Maspalomas, Pta., *Canary Is.* 36 G4
Masqat, *Oman* 68 C6
Massa, *Italy* 32 D7
Massa, O. →, *Morocco* 74 B3
Massa Maríttima, *Italy* 32 E7
Massachusetts □, *U.S.A.* 107 D12
Massachusetts B., *U.S.A.* 107 D14
Massafra, *Italy* 35 B10
Massaguet, *Chad* 73 F8
Massakory, *Chad* 73 F8
Massanella, *Spain* 36 B9
Massangena, *Mozam.* 85 C5
Massapê, *Brazil* 122 B3
Massarosa, *Italy* 32 E7
Massat, *France* 26 F5
Massawa = Mitsiwa, *Eritrea* 77 D4
Massena, *U.S.A.* 107 B10
Massénya, *Chad* 73 F8
Masset, *Canada* 100 C2
Massiac, *France* 26 C7
Massif Central, *France* 26 D7
Massillon, *U.S.A.* 106 F3
Massinga, *Mozam.* 85 C6
Masson, *Canada* 107 A9
Masson I., *Antarctica* 5 C7
Maştağa, *Azerbaijan* 43 K10
Mastanli = Momchilgrad, *Bulgaria* 39 H8
Masterton, *N.Z.* 87 J5
Mástikho, Ákra, *Greece* 39 L9
Mastuj, *Pakistan* 63 A5
Mastung, *Pakistan* 60 E5
Mastūrah, *Si. Arabia* 76 C4
Masty, *Belarus* 40 F3
Masuda, *Japan* 49 G5
Masvingo, *Zimbabwe* 83 G3
Masvingo □, *Zimbabwe* 83 G3
Maswa □, *Tanzania* 82 C3
Maşyāf, *Syria* 66 E7
Mata de São João, *Brazil* 123 D4
Matabeleland North □, *Zimbabwe* 83 F2
Matabeleland South □, *Zimbabwe* 83 G2
Mataboor, *Indonesia* 57 E9
Matachel →, *Spain* 31 G4
Matachewan, *Canada* 98 C3
Matacuni →, *Venezuela* 121 C4
Matad, *Mongolia* 54 B6
Matadi, *Zaïre* 80 F2
Matagalpa, *Nic.* 116 D2
Matagami, *Canada* 98 C4
Matagami, L., *Canada* 98 C4

Matagorda, *U.S.A.* 109 L7
Matagorda B., *U.S.A.* 109 L6
Matagorda I., *U.S.A.* 109 L6
Matak, P., *Indonesia* 59 L6
Matakana, *Australia* 91 E4
Mátala, *Greece* 37 E6
Matalaque, *Peru* 124 D3
Matam, *Senegal* 78 B2
Matameye, *Niger* 79 C6
Matamoros, *Campeche, Mexico* 115 D6
Matamoros, *Coahuila, Mexico* 114 B4
Matamoros, *Puebla, Mexico* 115 D5
Matamoros, *Tamaulipas, Mexico* 115 B5
Ma'ṭan as Sarra, *Libya* 73 D9
Matandu →, *Tanzania* 83 D3
Matane, *Canada* 99 C6
Matang, *China* 52 F5
Matankari, *Niger* 79 C5
Matanzas, *Cuba* 116 B3
Matapan, C. = Taínaron, Ákra, *Greece* 39 N5
Matapédia, *Canada* 99 C6
Matara, *Sri Lanka* 60 S12
Mataram, *Indonesia* 56 F5
Matarani, *Peru* 124 D3
Mataranka, *Australia* 88 B5
Matarma, Râs, *Egypt* 69 E1
Mataró, *Spain* 28 D7
Matarraña →, *Spain* 28 D5
Matatiele, *S. Africa* 85 E4
Mataura, *N.Z.* 87 M2
Mategua, *Bolivia* 125 C5
Matehuala, *Mexico* 114 C4
Mateira, *Brazil* 123 E1
Mateke Hills, *Zimbabwe* 83 G3
Matélica, *Italy* 33 E10
Matera, *Italy* 35 B9
Mátészalka, *Hungary* 21 H12
Matetsi, *Zimbabwe* 83 F2
Mateur, *Tunisia* 75 A6
Matfors, *Sweden* 10 B11
Matha, *France* 26 C3
Matheson Island, *Canada* 101 C9
Mathis, *U.S.A.* 109 L6
Mathura, *India* 62 F7
Mati, *Phil.* 55 H7
Mati →, *Albania* 39 H2
Matías Romero, *Mexico* 115 D5
Matibane, *Mozam.* 83 E5
Matima, *Botswana* 84 C3
Matiri Ra., *N.Z.* 87 J4
Matlock, *U.K.* 12 D6
Matmata, *Tunisia* 75 B6
Matna, *Sudan* 77 E4
Mato →, *Venezuela* 121 B4
Mato, Serrania de, *Venezuela* 120 B4
Mato Grosso □, *Brazil* 125 C6
Mato Grosso, Planalto do, *Brazil* 125 C7
Mato Grosso, Plateau of, *Brazil* 118 E5
Mato Grosso do Sul □, *Brazil* 125 D7
Matochkin Shar, *Russia* 44 B6
Matopo Hills, *Zimbabwe* 83 G2
Matopos, *Zimbabwe* 83 G2
Matosinhos, *Portugal* 30 D2
Matour, *France* 27 B8
Matsena, *Nigeria* 79 C7
Matsesta, *Russia* 43 J4
Matsu Tao, *Taiwan* 53 E13
Matsue, *Japan* 49 G6
Matsumae, *Japan* 48 D10
Matsumoto, *Japan* 49 F9
Matsusaka, *Japan* 49 G8
Matsuura, *Japan* 49 H4
Matsuyama, *Japan* 49 H6
Mattagami →, *Canada* 98 B3
Mattancheri, *India* 60 Q10
Mattawa, *Canada* 98 C4
Mattawamkeag, *U.S.A.* 99 C6
Matterhorn, *Switz.* 22 E5
Matthew Town, *Bahamas* 117 B5
Matthew's Ridge, *Guyana* 121 B5
Mattice, *Canada* 98 C3
Mattituck, *U.S.A.* 107 F12
Mattmar, *Sweden* 10 A7
Matuba, *Mozam.* 85 C5
Matucana, *Peru* 124 C2
Matun, *Afghan.* 62 C3
Maturín, *Venezuela* 121 B5
Matveyev Kurgan, *Russia* 43 G4
Mau, *India* 63 G10
Mau Escarpment, *Kenya* 82 C4
Mau Ranipur, *India* 63 G8
Maubeuge, *France* 25 B10
Maubourguet, *France* 26 E4
Maud, Pt., *Australia* 88 D1
Maude, *Australia* 91 E3
Maudin Sun, *Burma* 61 M19
Maués, *Brazil* 121 D6
Mauganj, *India* 61 G12
Maui, *U.S.A.* 102 H16
Maulamyaing = Moulmein, *Burma* 61 L20
Maule □, *Chile* 126 D1
Mauléon-Licharre, *France* 26 E3
Maullín, *Chile* 128 B2
Maumee, *U.S.A.* 104 E4
Maumee →, *U.S.A.* 104 E4
Maumere, *Indonesia* 57 F6
Maun, *Botswana* 84 B3
Mauna Kea, *U.S.A.* 102 J17
Mauna Loa, *U.S.A.* 102 J17
Maungmagan Kyunzu, *Burma* 61 M20
Maupin, *U.S.A.* 110 D3
Maure-de-Bretagne, *France* 24 E5
Maurepas, L., *U.S.A.* 109 K9
Maures, *France* 27 E10
Mauriac, *France* 26 C6
Maurice, L., *Australia* 89 E5
Maurienne, *France* 27 C10
Mauritania ■, *Africa* 74 D3
Mauritius ■, *Ind. Oc.* 70 J9
Mauron, *France* 24 D4
Maurs, *France* 26 D6
Mauston, *U.S.A.* 108 D9
Mauterndorf, *Austria* 21 H3
Mauvezin, *France* 26 E4
Mauzé-sur-le-Mignon, *France* 26 B3
Mavaca →, *Venezuela* 121 C4
Mavinga, *Angola* 81 H4
Mavli, *India* 62 G5
Mavrova, *Albania* 39 J2
Mavuradonha Mts., *Zimbabwe* 83 F3
Mawa, *Zaïre* 82 B2
Mawana, *India* 62 E7
Mawand, *Pakistan* 62 E3
Mawk Mai, *Burma* 61 J20
Mawlaik, *Burma* 61 H19
Mawquq, *Si. Arabia* 64 E4
Mawson Coast, *Antarctica* 5 C6
Max, *U.S.A.* 108 B4
Maxcanú, *Mexico* 115 C6
Maxesibeni, *S. Africa* 85 E4
Maxhamish L., *Canada* 100 B4
Maxixe, *Mozam.* 85 C6
Maxville, *Canada* 107 A10
Maxwell, *U.S.A.* 112 F4
Maxwelton, *Australia* 90 C3
May Downs, *Australia* 90 C4
May Pen, *Jamaica* 116 C4
Maya, *Spain* 28 B3
Maya →, *Russia* 45 D14
Maya Mts., *Belize* 115 D7
Mayaguana, *Bahamas* 117 B5
Mayagüez, *Puerto Rico* 117 C6
Mayahi, *Niger* 79 C6
Mayals, *Spain* 28 D5
Mayāmey, *Iran* 65 B7
Mayang, *China* 52 D7
Mayarí, *Cuba* 117 B4
Maybell, *U.S.A.* 110 F9
Maychew, *Ethiopia* 77 E4
Maydān, *Iraq* 67 E11
Maydena, *Australia* 90 G4
Mayen, *Germany* 19 E3
Mayenne, *France* 24 D6
Mayenne □, *France* 24 D6
Mayenne →, *France* 24 E6
Mayer, *U.S.A.* 111 J7
Mayerthorpe, *Canada* 100 C5
Mayfield, *U.S.A.* 105 G1
Mayhill, *U.S.A.* 111 K11
Maykop, *Russia* 43 H5
Maymyo, *Burma* 58 A1
Maynard, *U.S.A.* 112 C4
Maynard Hills, *Australia* 89 E2
Mayne →, *Australia* 90 C3
Maynooth, *Ireland* 15 C5
Mayo, *Canada* 96 B6
Mayo □, *Ireland* 15 C2
Mayo →, *Argentina* 128 C3
Mayo →, *Peru* 124 B2
Mayo L., *Canada* 96 B6
Mayon Volcano, *Phil.* 55 E5
Mayor I., *N.Z.* 87 G6
Mayorga, *Spain* 30 C5
Mayotte, I., *Mayotte* 71 H8
Mayraira Pt., *Phil.* 55 B4
Mayskiy, *Russia* 43 J7
Mayson L., *Canada* 101 B7
Maysville, *U.S.A.* 104 F4
Mayu, *Indonesia* 57 D7
Mayville, *N. Dak., U.S.A.* 108 B6
Mayville, *N.Y., U.S.A.* 106 D5
Mayya, *Russia* 45 C14
Mazabuka, *Zambia* 83 F2
Mazagán = El Jadida, *Morocco* 74 B3
Mazagão, *Brazil* 121 D7
Mazamet, *France* 26 E6
Mazán, *Peru* 120 D3
Māzandarān □, *Iran* 65 B7
Mazapil, *Mexico* 114 C4
Mazar, O. →, *Algeria* 75 B5
Mazara del Vallo, *Italy* 34 E5
Mazarredo, *Argentina* 128 C3
Mazarrón, *Spain* 29 H3
Mazarrón, G. de, *Spain* 29 H3
Mazaruni →, *Guyana* 121 B6
Mazatán, *Mexico* 114 B2
Mazatenango, *Guatemala* 116 D1
Mazatlán, *Mexico* 114 C3
Mažeikiai, *Lithuania* 9 H20
Māzhān, *Iran* 65 C8
Mazīnān, *Iran* 65 B8
Mazoe, *Mozam.* 83 F3
Mazoe →, *Mozam.* 83 F3
Mazowe, *Zimbabwe* 83 F3
Mazrûb, *Sudan* 77 E2
Mazu Dao, *China* 53 D12
Mazurian Lakes = Mazurski, Pojezierze, *Poland* 20 B10
Mazurski, Pojezierze, *Poland* 20 B10
Mazyr, *Belarus* 41 F5
Mazzarino, *Italy* 35 E7
Mbaba, *Senegal* 78 C1
Mbabane, *Swaziland* 85 D5
Mbagne, *Mauritania* 78 B2
M'bahiakro, *Ivory C.* 78 D4
Mbaïki, *C.A.R.* 80 D3
Mbala, *Zambia* 83 D3
Mbale, *Uganda* 82 B3
Mbalmayo, *Cameroon* 79 E7
Mbamba Bay, *Tanzania* 83 E3
Mbandaka, *Zaïre* 80 D3
Mbanga, *Cameroon* 79 E6
Mbanza Congo, *Angola* 80 F2
Mbanza Ngungu, *Zaïre* 80 F2
Mbarara, *Uganda* 82 C3
Mbashe →, *S. Africa* 85 E4
Mbatto, *Ivory C.* 78 D4
Mbenkuru →, *Tanzania* 83 D4
Mberengwa, *Zimbabwe* 83 G2
Mberengwa, Mt., *Zimbabwe* 83 G2
Mberubu, *Nigeria* 79 D6
Mbesuma, *Zambia* 83 D3
Mbeya, *Tanzania* 83 D3
Mbeya □, *Tanzania* 82 D3
Mbinga, *Tanzania* 83 E4
Mbinga □, *Tanzania* 83 E3
Mbini □, *Eq. Guin.* 80 D2
Mboki, *C.A.R.* 77 F2
Mboro, *Senegal* 78 B1
Mboune, *Senegal* 78 C2
Mbour, *Senegal* 78 C1
Mbout, *Mauritania* 78 B2
Mbozi □, *Tanzania* 83 D3
Mbuji-Mayi, *Zaïre* 82 D1
Mbulu, *Tanzania* 82 C4
Mbulu □, *Tanzania* 82 C4
Mburucuyá, *Argentina* 126 B4
Mcherrah, *Algeria* 74 C4
Mchinja, *Tanzania* 83 D4
Mchinji, *Malawi* 83 E3
Mdennah, *Mauritania* 74 D3
Mead, L., *U.S.A.* 113 J12
Meade, *U.S.A.* 109 G4
Meadow, *Australia* 89 E1
Meadow Lake, *Canada* 101 C7
Meadow Lake Prov. Park, *Canada* 101 C7
Meadow Valley Wash →, *U.S.A.* 113 J12
Meadville, *U.S.A.* 106 E4
Meaford, *Canada* 98 D3
Mealhada, *Portugal* 30 E2
Mealy Mts., *Canada* 99 B8
Meander River, *Canada* 100 B5
Meares, C., *U.S.A.* 110 D2
Mearim →, *Brazil* 122 B3
Meath □, *Ireland* 15 C5
Meath Park, *Canada* 101 C7
Meaulne, *France* 26 B6
Meaux, *France* 25 D9
Mebechi-Gawa →, *Japan* 48 D10
Mecanhelas, *Mozam.* 83 F4
Mecaya →, *Colombia* 120 C2
Mecca = Makkah, *Si. Arabia* 68 C2
Mecca, *U.S.A.* 113 M10
Mechanicsburg, *U.S.A.* 106 F8
Mechanicville, *U.S.A.* 107 D11
Mechara, *Ethiopia* 77 F5
Mechelen, *Antwerpen, Belgium* 17 F4
Mechelen, *Limburg, Belgium* 17 G7
Mecheria, *Algeria* 75 B4
Mechernich, *Germany* 18 E2
Mechetinskaya, *Russia* 43 G5
Mechra Benâbbou, *Morocco* 74 B3
Mecitözü, *Turkey* 66 B6
Mecklenburg-Vorpommern □, *Germany* 18 B8
Mecklenburger Bucht, *Germany* 18 A7
Meconta, *Mozam.* 83 E4
Meda, *Australia* 88 C3
Meda, *Portugal* 30 E3
Medan, *Indonesia* 56 D1
Médanos, *Argentina* 128 A4
Medanosa, Pta., *Argentina* 128 C3
Medéa, *Algeria* 75 A5
Medeiros Neto, *Brazil* 123 E3
Medel, Pic, *Switz.* 23 C7
Medellín, *Colombia* 120 B2
Medelpad, *Sweden* 9 E17
Medemblik, *Neths.* 16 C6
Médenine, *Tunisia* 75 B7
Mederdra, *Mauritania* 78 B1
Medford, *Mass., U.S.A.* 107 D13
Medford, *Oreg., U.S.A.* 110 E2
Medford, *Wis., U.S.A.* 108 C9
Medgidia, *Romania* 38 E11
Medi, *Sudan* 77 F3
Media Agua, *Argentina* 126 C2
Media Luna, *Argentina* 126 C2
Mediaş, *Romania* 38 C7
Medical Lake, *U.S.A.* 110 C5
Medicina, *Italy* 33 D8
Medicine Bow, *U.S.A.* 110 F10
Medicine Bow Pk., *U.S.A.* 110 F10
Medicine Bow Ra., *U.S.A.* 110 F10
Medicine Hat, *Canada* 101 D6
Medicine Lake, *U.S.A.* 108 A2
Medicine Lodge, *U.S.A.* 109 G5
Medina = Al Madīnah, *Si. Arabia* 64 E3
Medina, *Brazil* 123 E3
Medina, *Colombia* 120 C3
Medina, *N. Dak., U.S.A.* 108 B5
Medina, *N.Y., U.S.A.* 106 C6
Medina, *Ohio, U.S.A.* 106 E3
Medina →, *U.S.A.* 109 L5
Medina de Ríoseco, *Spain* 30 D5
Medina del Campo, *Spain* 30 D6
Medina L., *U.S.A.* 109 L5
Medina-Sidonia, *Spain* 31 J5
Medinaceli, *Spain* 28 D2
Medinipur, *India* 63 H12
Mediterranean Sea, *Europe* 6 H7
Medjerda, O. →, *Tunisia* 75 A7
Medley, *Canada* 101 C6
Médoc, *France* 26 C3
Medstead, *Canada* 101 C7
Medulin, *Croatia* 33 D10
Medveda, *Serbia, Yug.* 21 N11
Medvedevo, *Russia* 42 B8
Medveditsa →, *Russia* 42 F6
Medveditsa →, *Russia* 42 B3
Medvedok, *Russia* 42 B10
Medvezhi, Ostrava, *Russia* 45 B17
Medvezhyegorsk, *Russia* 44 C4
Medway →, *U.K.* 13 F8
Medzilaborce, *Slovak Rep.* 20 F11
Meeberrie, *Australia* 89 E2
Meekatharra, *Australia* 89 E2
Meeker, *U.S.A.* 110 F10
Meer, *Belgium* 17 F5
Meerane, *Germany* 18 E8
Meerbeke, *Belgium* 17 G4
Meerhout, *Belgium* 17 F6
Meerle, *Belgium* 17 F5
Meersburg, *Germany* 19 H5
Meerssen, *Neths.* 17 G7
Meerut, *India* 62 E7
Meeteetse, *U.S.A.* 110 D9
Meeuwen, *Belgium* 17 F7
Mega, *Ethiopia* 77 G4
Megálo Petalí, *Greece* 39 M7
Megalópolis, *Greece* 39 M5
Meganísi, *Greece* 39 L3
Mégara, *Greece* 39 M6
Megève, *France* 27 C10
Meghalaya □, *India* 61 G17
Meghezez, *Ethiopia* 77 F4
Mégiscane, L., *Canada* 98 C4
Megra, *Russia* 40 B9
Mehadia, *Romania* 38 E5
Mehaigne →, *Belgium* 17 G6
Mehaïguene, O. →, *Algeria* 75 B5
Meheisa, *Sudan* 76 D3
Mehndawal, *India* 63 F10
Mehr Jān, *Iran* 65 C7
Mehrābād, *Iran* 67 D12
Mehrān, *Iran* 67 F12
Mehrīz, *Iran* 65 D7
Mehun-sur-Yèvre, *France* 25 E9
Mei Jiang →, *China* 53 E11
Mei Xian, *Guangdong, China* 53 E11
Mei Xian, *Shaanxi, China* 50 G4
Meia Ponte →, *Brazil* 123 E2
Meicheng, *China* 53 C12
Meichengzhen, *China* 53 C8
Meichuan, *China* 53 B10
Meiganga, *Cameroon* 80 C2
Meijel, *Neths.* 17 F7
Meiktila, *Burma* 61 J19
Meilen, *Switz.* 23 B7
Meiningen, *Germany* 18 E6
Meio →, *Brazil* 123 D3
Meira, Sierra de, *Spain* 30 B3
Meiringen, *Switz.* 22 C6
Meishan, *China* 52 B4
Meissen, *Germany* 18 D9
Meissner, *Germany* 18 D5
Meitan, *China* 52 D6
Mejillones, *Chile* 126 A1
Meka, *Australia* 89 E2
Mékambo, *Gabon* 80 D2
Mekdela, *Ethiopia* 77 E4
Mekele, *Ethiopia* 77 E4
Mekhtar, *Pakistan* 60 D6
Meknès, *Morocco* 74 B3
Meko, *Nigeria* 79 D5
Mekong →, *Asia* 59 H6
Mekongga, *Indonesia* 57 E6
Mekvari = Kür →, *Azerbaijan* 67 C13
Melagiri Hills, *India* 60 N10
Melah, Sebkhet el, *Algeria* 75 C4
Melaka, *Malaysia* 59 L4
Melalap, *Malaysia* 56 C5
Mélambes, *Greece* 37 D6
Melanesia, *Pac. Oc.* 92 H7
Melbourne, *Australia* 91 F3
Melbourne, *U.S.A.* 105 L5
Melchor Múzquiz, *Mexico* 114 B4
Melchor Ocampo, *Mexico* 114 C4
Méldola, *Italy* 33 D9
Meldorf, *Germany* 18 A5
Melegnano, *Italy* 32 C6
Melenci, *Serbia, Yug.* 21 K10
Melenki, *Russia* 42 C5
Mélèzes →, *Canada* 97 C12
Melfi, *Chad* 73 F8
Melfi, *Italy* 35 B8
Melfort, *Canada* 101 C8
Melfort, *Zimbabwe* 83 F3
Melgaço, *Madeira* 30 C2
Melgar de Fernamental, *Spain* 30 C6
Melhus, *Norway* 10 A4
Melick, *Neths.* 17 F8
Melide, *Switz.* 23 E7
Meligalá, *Greece* 39 M4
Melilla, *N. Afr.* 75 A4
Melipilla, *Chile* 126 C1
Mélissa, Ákra, *Greece* 37 D6
Melita, *Canada* 101 D8
Mélito di Porto Salvo, *Italy* 35 E8
Melitopol, *Ukraine* 41 J8
Melk, *Austria* 21 G5
Mellansel, *Sweden* 8 E18
Melle, *Belgium* 17 G3
Melle, *France* 26 B3
Melle, *Germany* 18 C4
Mellégue, O. →, *Tunisia* 75 A6
Mellen, *U.S.A.* 108 B9
Mellerud, *Sweden* 11 F6
Mellette, *U.S.A.* 108 C5
Mellid, *Spain* 30 C2
Mellieha, *Malta* 37 D1
Mellit, *Sudan* 77 E2
Mellizo Sur, Cerro *Chile* 128 C2
Mellrichstadt, *Germany* 19 E6
Melnik, *Bulgaria* 39 H6
Mělník, *Czech.* 20 E4
Melo, *Uruguay* 127 C5
Melolo, *Indonesia* 57 F6
Melouprey, *Cambodia* 58 F5
Melrhir, Chott, *Algeria* 75 B6
Melrose, *N.S.W., Australia* 91 E4
Melrose, *W. Austral., Australia* 89 E3
Melrose, *U.K.* 14 F6
Melrose, *U.S.A.* 109 H3
Mels, *Switz.* 23 B8
Melsele, *Belgium* 17 F4
Melstone, *U.S.A.* 110 C10
Melsungen, *Germany* 18 D5
Melton Mowbray, *U.K.* 12 E7
Melun, *France* 25 D9
Melut, *Sudan* 77 E3
Melville, *Canada* 101 C8
Melville, C., *Australia* 90 A3
Melville, L., *Canada* 99 B8
Melville B., *Australia* 90 A2
Melville I., *Australia* 88 B5
Melville I., *Canada* 4 B2
Melville Pen., *Canada* 97 B11
Melvin →, *Canada* 100 B5
Memaliaj, *Albania* 39 J2
Memba, *Mozam.* 83 E5
Memboro, *Indonesia* 57 F5
Membrilla, *Spain* 29 G1
Memel = Klaipėda, *Lithuania* 9 J19
Memel, *S. Africa* 85 D4
Memmingen, *Germany* 19 H6
Mempawah, *Indonesia* 56 D3
Memphis, *Tenn., U.S.A.* 109 H10
Memphis, *Tex., U.S.A.* 109 H4
Mena, *Ukraine* 41 G7
Mena, *U.S.A.* 109 H7
Mena →, *Ethiopia* 77 F5
Menai Strait, *U.K.* 12 D3
Ménaka, *Mali* 79 B5
Menaldum, *Neths.* 16 B7
Menan = Chao Phraya →, *Thailand* 58 F3
Menarandra →, *Madag.* 85 D7
Menard, *U.S.A.* 109 K5
Menasha, *U.S.A.* 104 C1
Menate, *Indonesia* 56 E4
Mendawai →, *Indonesia* 56 E4
Mende, *France* 26 D7
Mendebo, *Ethiopia* 77 F4
Mendez, *Mexico* 115 B5
Mendhar, *India* 63 C6
Mendi, *Ethiopia* 77 F4
Mendip Hills, *U.K.* 13 F5
Mendocino, *U.S.A.* 110 G2
Mendocino, C., *U.S.A.* 110 F1
Mendota, *Calif., U.S.A.* 111 H3
Mendota, *Ill., U.S.A.* 108 E10
Mendoza, *Argentina* 126 C2
Mendoza □, *Argentina* 126 C2
Mendrisio, *Switz.* 23 E7
Mene Grande, *Venezuela* 120 B3
Menemen, *Turkey* 66 C2
Menen, *Belgium* 17 G2
Menéndez, L., *Argentina* 128 B2
Menfi, *Italy* 34 E5
Mengcheng, *China* 53 A11
Mengdingjie, *China* 52 F2
Mengeš, *Slovenia* 33 B11
Menggala, *Indonesia* 56 E3
Menghai, *China* 52 G3
Mengíbar, *Spain* 31 H7
Mengjin, *China* 50 G7
Mengla, *China* 52 G3
Menglian, *China* 52 F2
Mengoub, *Algeria* 74 C3
Mengshan, *China* 53 E8
Mengyin, *China* 51 G9
Mengzhe, *China* 52 F3
Mengzi, *China* 52 F4
Menihek L., *Canada* 99 B6
Menin = Menen, *Belgium* 17 G2
Menindee, *Australia* 91 E3
Menindee L., *Australia* 91 E3
Meningie, *Australia* 91 F2
Menlo Park, *U.S.A.* 112 H4
Menominee, *U.S.A.* 104 C2
Menominee →, *U.S.A.* 104 C2
Menomonie, *U.S.A.* 108 C9

Menongue, *Angola* 81 G3
Menorca, *Spain* 36 B11
Mentakab, *Malaysia* 59 L4
Mentawai, Kepulauan, *Indonesia* 56 E1
Menton, *France* 27 E11
Mentor, *U.S.A.* 106 E3
Menzel-Bourguiba, *Tunisia* 75 A6
Menzel Chaker, *Tunisia* 75 B7
Menzel-Temime, *Tunisia* 75 A7
Menzies, *Australia* 89 E3
Me'ona, *Israel* 69 B4
Meoqui, *Mexico* 114 B3
Mepaco, *Mozam.* 83 F3
Meppel, *Neths.* 16 C8
Meppen, *Germany* 18 C3
Mequinenza, *Spain* 28 D5
Mer, *France* 24 E8
Mer Rouge, *U.S.A.* 109 J9
Merabéllou, Kólpos, *Greece* 37 D7
Meramangye, L., *Australia* 89 E5
Meran = Merano, *Italy* 33 B8
Merano, *Italy* 33 B8
Merate, *Italy* 32 C6
Merauke, *Indonesia* 57 F10
Merbabu, *Indonesia* 57 G14
Merbein, *Australia* 91 E3
Merca, *Somali Rep.* 68 G3
Mercadal, *Spain* 36 B11
Mercato Saraceno, *Italy* 33 E9
Merced, *U.S.A.* 111 H3
Merced Pk., *U.S.A.* 112 H7
Mercedes, *Buenos Aires, Argentina* 126 C4
Mercedes, *Corrientes, Argentina* 126 B4
Mercedes, *San Luis, Argentina* 126 C2
Mercedes, *Uruguay* 126 C4
Merceditas, *Chile* 126 B1
Mercer, *N.Z.* 87 G5
Mercer, *U.S.A.* 106 E4
Merchtem, *Belgium* 17 G4
Mercier, *Bolivia* 124 C4
Mercury, *U.S.A.* 113 J11
Mercy C., *Canada* 97 B13
Merdrignac, *France* 24 D4
Mere, *Belgium* 17 G3
Meredith, C., *Falk. Is.* 128 D4
Meredith, L., *U.S.A.* 109 H4
Merefa, *Ukraine* 41 H9
Merelbeke, *Belgium* 17 G3
Méréville, *France* 25 D9
Merga = Nukheila, *Sudan* 76 D2
Mergui Arch. = Myeik Kyunzu, *Burma* 59 G1
Mérida, *Mexico* 115 C7
Mérida, *Spain* 31 G4
Mérida, *Venezuela* 120 B3
Mérida □, *Venezuela* 120 B3
Mérida, Cord. de, *Venezuela* 120 B3
Meriden, *U.S.A.* 107 E12
Meridian, *Calif., U.S.A.* 112 F5
Meridian, *Idaho, U.S.A.* 110 E5
Meridian, *Miss., U.S.A.* 105 J1
Meridian, *Tex., U.S.A.* 109 K6
Mering, *Germany* 19 G7
Meriruma, *Brazil* 121 C7
Merkel, *U.S.A.* 109 J4
Merksem, *Belgium* 17 F4
Merksplas, *Belgium* 17 F5
Mermaid Reef, *Australia* 88 C2
Mern, *Denmark* 11 J6
Merowe, *Sudan* 76 D3
Merredin, *Australia* 89 F2
Merrick, *U.K.* 14 F4
Merrickville, *Canada* 107 B9
Merrill, *Oreg., U.S.A.* 110 E3
Merrill, *Wis., U.S.A.* 108 C10
Merriman, *U.S.A.* 108 D4
Merritt, *Canada* 100 C4
Merriwa, *Australia* 91 E5
Merriwagga, *Australia* 91 E4
Merry I., *Canada* 98 A4
Merrygoen, *Australia* 91 E4
Merryville, *U.S.A.* 109 K8
Mersa Fatma, *Eritrea* 68 E3
Mersch, *Lux.* 17 J8
Merseburg, *Germany* 18 D7
Mersey →, *U.K.* 12 D5
Merseyside □, *U.K.* 12 D5
Mersin, *Turkey* 66 D6
Mersing, *Malaysia* 59 L4
Merta, *India* 62 F6
Mertert, *Lux.* 17 J8
Merthyr Tydfil, *U.K.* 13 F4
Merthyr Tydfil □, *U.K.* 13 F4
Mértola, *Portugal* 31 H3
Mertzig, *Lux.* 17 J8
Mertzon, *U.S.A.* 109 K4
Méru, *France* 25 C9
Meru, *Kenya* 82 B4
Meru, *Tanzania* 82 C4
Meru □, *Kenya* 82 B4
Merville, *France* 25 B9
Méry-sur-Seine, *France* 25 D10
Merzifon, *Turkey* 66 B6
Merzig, *Germany* 19 F2
Merzouga, Erg Tin, *Algeria* 75 D7
Mesa, *U.S.A.* 111 K8
Mesach Mellet, *Libya* 75 D7
Mesagne, *Italy* 35 B10
Mesanagrós, *Greece* 37 C9
Mesaoría □, *Cyprus* 37 D12
Mesarás, Kólpos, *Greece* 37 D6
Meschede, *Germany* 18 D4
Mescit, *Turkey* 67 B9
Mesfinto, *Ethiopia* 77 E4
Mesgouez, L., *Canada* 98 B4
Meshchovsk, *Russia* 42 C2
Meshed = Mashhad, *Iran* 65 B8
Meshoppen, *U.S.A.* 107 E8
Meshra er Req, *Sudan* 77 F2
Mesick, *U.S.A.* 104 C3
Mesilinka →, *Canada* 100 B4
Mesilla, *U.S.A.* 111 K10
Meslay-du-Maine, *France* 24 E6
Mesocco, *Switz.* 23 D8
Mesolóngion, *Greece* 39 L4
Mesopotamia = Al Jazirah, *Iraq* 67 E10
Mesoraca, *Italy* 35 C9
Mesquite, *U.S.A.* 111 H6
Mess Cr. →, *Canada* 100 B2
Messac, *France* 24 E5
Messad, *Algeria* 75 B5
Messalo →, *Mozam.* 83 E4
Méssaména, *Cameroon* 79 E7
Messancy, *Belgium* 17 J7
Messier, Canal, *Chile* 128 C2
Messina, *Italy* 35 D8
Messina, *S. Africa* 85 C5
Messina, Str. di, *Italy* 35 D8
Messíni, *Greece* 39 M5
Messiniakós Kólpos, *Greece* 39 N5
Messkirch, *Germany* 19 H5
Messonghi, *Greece* 37 B3
Mesta →, *Bulgaria* 39 H7
Mestanza, *Spain* 31 G6
Mestre, *Italy* 33 C9
Mestre, Espigão, *Brazil* 123 D2
Městys Zelezná Ruda, *Czech.* 20 F3
Mesudiye, *Turkey* 66 B7
Meta □, *Colombia* 120 C3
Meta →, *S. Amer.* 120 B4
Metairie, *U.S.A.* 109 L9
Metaline Falls, *U.S.A.* 110 B5
Metán, *Argentina* 126 B3
Metangula, *Mozam.* 83 E3
Metáuro →, *Italy* 33 E10
Metema, *Ethiopia* 77 E4
Metengobalame, *Mozam.* 83 E3
Méthana, *Greece* 39 M6
Methven, *N.Z.* 87 K3
Methy L., *Canada* 101 B7
Metil, *Mozam.* 83 F4
Metlakatla, *U.S.A.* 100 B2
Metlaoui, *Tunisia* 75 B6
Metlika, *Slovenia* 33 C12
Metropolis, *U.S.A.* 109 G10
Mettet, *Belgium* 17 H5
Mettur Dam, *India* 60 P10
Metz, *France* 25 C13
Meulaboh, *Indonesia* 56 D1
Meulan, *France* 25 C8
Meung-sur-Loire, *France* 25 E8
Meureudu, *Indonesia* 56 C1
Meurthe →, *France* 25 D13
Meurthe-et-Moselle □, *France* 25 D13
Meuse □, *France* 25 C12
Meuse →, *Europe* 17 G7
Meuselwitz, *Germany* 18 D8
Mexborough, *U.K.* 12 D6
Mexia, *U.S.A.* 109 K6
Mexiana, I., *Brazil* 122 A2
Mexicali, *Mexico* 114 A1
Mexican Plateau, *Mexico* 94 G9
México, *Mexico* 115 D5
Mexico, *Maine, U.S.A.* 107 B14
Mexico, *Mo., U.S.A.* 108 F9
México □, *Mexico* 114 D5
Mexico ■, *Cent. Amer.* 114 C4
Mexico, G. of, *Cent. Amer.* 115 C7
Meyenburg, *Germany* 18 B8
Meymac, *France* 26 C6
Meymaneh, *Afghan.* 60 B4
Meyrargues, *France* 27 E9
Meyrueis, *France* 26 D7
Meyssac, *France* 26 C5
Mezdra, *Bulgaria* 38 F6
Mèze, *France* 26 E7
Mezen, *Russia* 44 C5
Mezen →, *Russia* 44 C5
Mézene, *France* 27 D8
Mezha →, *Russia* 40 E6
Mézidon, *France* 24 C6
Mézilhac, *France* 27 D8
Mézin, *France* 26 D4
Mezöberény, *Hungary* 21 J11
Mezőkövácsháza, *Hungary* 21 J10
Mezőkövesd, *Hungary* 21 H10
Mézos, *France* 26 D2
Mezötúr, *Hungary* 21 J10
Mezquital, *Mexico* 114 C4
Mezzolombardo, *Italy* 32 B8
Mgeta, *Tanzania* 83 D4
Mglin, *Russia* 41 F7
Mhlaba Hills, *Zimbabwe* 83 F3
Mhow, *India* 62 H6
Miahuatlán, *Mexico* 115 D5
Miajadas, *Spain* 31 F5
Miallo, *Australia* 90 B4
Miami, *Ariz., U.S.A.* 111 K8
Miami, *Fla., U.S.A.* 105 N5
Miami, *Tex., U.S.A.* 109 H4
Miami →, *U.S.A.* 104 F3
Miami Beach, *U.S.A.* 105 N5
Mian Xian, *China* 50 H4
Mianchi, *China* 50 G6
Mīāndowāb, *Iran* 67 D12
Miandrivazo, *Madag.* 85 B8
Mīāneh, *Iran* 67 D12
Mianning, *China* 52 C4
Mianwali, *Pakistan* 62 C4
Mianyang, *Hubei, China* 53 B9
Mianyang, *Sichuan, China* 52 B5
Mianzhu, *China* 52 B5
Miaoli, *Taiwan* 53 E13
Miarinarivo, *Madag.* 85 B8
Miass, *Russia* 44 D7
Miastko, *Poland* 20 A6
Michelstadt, *Germany* 19 F5
Michigan □, *U.S.A.* 104 C3
Michigan, L., *U.S.A.* 104 C2
Michigan City, *U.S.A.* 104 E2
Michikamau L., *Canada* 99 B7
Michipicoten, *Canada* 98 C3
Michipicoten I., *Canada* 98 C2
Michoacan □, *Mexico* 114 D4
Michurin, *Bulgaria* 38 G10
Michurinsk, *Russia* 42 D5
Miclere, *Australia* 90 C4
Mico, Pta., *Nic.* 116 D3
Micronesia, Federated States of ■, *Pac. Oc.* 92 G7
Midai, P., *Indonesia* 59 L6
Midale, *Canada* 101 D8
Middagsfjället, *Sweden* 10 A6
Middelbeers, *Neths.* 17 F6
Middelburg, *Neths.* 17 F3
Middelburg, *Eastern Cape, S. Africa* 84 E3
Middelburg, *Mpumalanga, S. Africa* 85 D4
Middelfart, *Denmark* 11 J3
Middelharnis, *Neths.* 16 E4
Middelkerke, *Belgium* 17 F1
Middelrode, *Neths.* 17 E6
Middelwit, *S. Africa* 84 C4
Middle Alkali L., *U.S.A.* 110 F3
Middle Fork Feather →, *U.S.A.* 112 F5
Middle I., *Australia* 89 F3
Middle Loup →, *U.S.A.* 108 E5
Middleboro, *U.S.A.* 107 E14
Middleburg, *N.Y., U.S.A.* 107 D10
Middleburg, *Pa., U.S.A.* 106 F7
Middlebury, *U.S.A.* 107 B11
Middleport, *U.S.A.* 104 F4
Middlesboro, *U.S.A.* 105 G4
Middlesbrough, *U.K.* 12 C6
Middlesbrough □, *U.K.* 12 C6
Middlesex, *Belize* 116 C2
Middlesex, *U.S.A.* 107 F10
Middleton, *Australia* 90 C3
Middleton, *Canada* 99 D6
Middletown, *Calif., U.S.A.* 112 G4
Middletown, *Conn., U.S.A.* 107 E12
Middletown, *N.Y., U.S.A.* 107 E10
Middletown, *Ohio, U.S.A.* 104 F3
Middletown, *Pa., U.S.A.* 107 F8
Midelt, *Morocco* 74 B4
Midi, Canal du →, *France* 26 E5
Midi d'Ossau, Pic du, *France* 26 F3
Midland, *Canada* 98 D4
Midland, *Calif., U.S.A.* 113 M12
Midland, *Mich., U.S.A.* 104 D3
Midland, *Pa., U.S.A.* 106 F4
Midland, *Tex., U.S.A.* 109 K3
Midlands □, *Zimbabwe* 83 F2
Midleton, *Ireland* 15 E3
Midlothian, *U.S.A.* 109 J6
Midlothian □, *U.K.* 14 F5
Midongy, Tangorombohitr' i, *Madag.* 85 C8
Midongy Atsimo, *Madag.* 85 C8
Midou →, *France* 26 E3
Midouze →, *France* 26 E3
Midsayap, *Phil.* 55 H6
Midu, *China* 52 E3
Midway Is., *Pac. Oc.* 92 E10
Midway Wells, *U.S.A.* 113 N11
Midwest, *U.S.A.* 103 B9
Midwest, *Wyo., U.S.A.* 110 E10
Midwest City, *U.S.A.* 109 H6
Midwolda, *Neths.* 16 B9
Midyat, *Turkey* 67 D9
Midzŏr, *Bulgaria* 38 F5
Mie □, *Japan* 49 G8
Miechów, *Poland* 20 E10
Międzychód, *Poland* 20 C5
Międzyrzec Podlaski, *Poland* 20 D12
Międzyrzecz, *Poland* 20 C5
Miélan, *France* 26 E4
Mielec, *Poland* 20 E11
Mienga, *Angola* 84 B2
Miercurea Ciuc, *Romania* 38 C8
Mieres, *Spain* 30 B5
Mierlo, *Neths.* 17 F7
Mieso, *Ethiopia* 77 F5
Mifflintown, *U.S.A.* 106 F7
Mifraz Hefa, *Israel* 69 C4
Migdāl, *Israel* 69 C4
Migennes, *France* 25 E10
Migliarino, *Italy* 33 D8
Miguel Alemán, Presa, *Mexico* 115 D5
Miguel Alves, *Brazil* 122 B3
Miguel Calmon, *Brazil* 122 D3
Mihaliççık, *Turkey* 66 C4
Mihara, *Japan* 49 G6
Mijares →, *Spain* 28 F4
Mijas, *Spain* 31 J6
Mikese, *Tanzania* 82 D4
Mikha-Tskhakaya = Senaki, *Georgia* 43 J6
Mikhailovka = Mykhaylivka, *Ukraine* 41 J8
Mikhaylov, *Russia* 42 C4
Mikhaylovgrad, *Bulgaria* 38 F6
Mikhaylovka, *Russia* 42 E6
Mikhnevo, *Russia* 42 C3
Mikínai, *Greece* 39 M5
Mikkeli, *Finland* 9 F22
Mikkwa →, *Canada* 100 B6
Mikniya, *Sudan* 77 D3
Mikołajki, *Poland* 20 B11
Míkonos, *Greece* 39 M8
Mikrón Dhérion, *Greece* 39 H9
Mikulov, *Czech.* 20 G6
Mikumi, *Tanzania* 82 D4
Milaca, *U.S.A.* 108 C8
Milagro, *Ecuador* 120 D2
Milagros, *Phil.* 55 E5
Milan = Milano, *Italy* 32 C6
Milan, *Mo., U.S.A.* 108 E8
Milan, *Tenn., U.S.A.* 105 H1
Milang, *Australia* 91 E2
Milange, *Mozam.* 83 F4
Milano, *Italy* 32 C6
Milâs, *Turkey* 66 D2
Milatos, *Greece* 37 D7
Milazzo, *Italy* 35 D8
Milbank, *U.S.A.* 108 C6
Milden, *Canada* 101 C7
Mildmay, *Canada* 106 B3
Mildura, *Australia* 91 E3
Mile, *China* 52 E4
Miléai, *Greece* 39 K6
Miles, *Australia* 91 D5
Miles, *U.S.A.* 109 K4
Miles City, *U.S.A.* 108 B2
Milestone, *Canada* 101 D8
Mileto, *Italy* 35 D9
Miletto, Mte., *Italy* 35 A7
Miletus, *Turkey* 66 D2
Mileura, *Australia* 89 E2
Milford, *Calif., U.S.A.* 112 E6
Milford, *Conn., U.S.A.* 107 E11
Milford, *Del., U.S.A.* 104 F8
Milford, *Mass., U.S.A.* 107 D13
Milford, *Pa., U.S.A.* 107 E10
Milford, *Utah, U.S.A.* 111 G7
Milford Haven, *U.K.* 13 F2
Milford Sd., *N.Z.* 87 L1
Milgun, *Australia* 89 D2
Milh, Bahr al, *Iraq* 67 F10
Miliana, *Aïn Salah, Algeria* 75 C5
Miliana, *Médéa, Algeria* 75 A5
Miling, *Australia* 89 F2
Militello in Val di Catánia, *Italy* 35 E7
Milk →, *U.S.A.* 110 B10
Milk, Wadi el →, *Sudan* 76 D3
Milk River, *Canada* 100 D6
Mill, *Neths.* 17 E7
Mill City, *U.S.A.* 110 D2
Mill I., *Antarctica* 5 C8
Mill Valley, *U.S.A.* 112 H4
Millau, *France* 26 D7
Millbridge, *Canada* 106 B7
Millbrook, *Canada* 106 B6
Mille Lacs, L. des, *Canada* 98 C1
Mille Lacs L., *U.S.A.* 108 B8
Milledgeville, *U.S.A.* 105 J4
Millen, *U.S.A.* 105 J5
Miller, *U.S.A.* 108 C5
Millerovo, *Russia* 43 F5
Millersburg, *Ohio, U.S.A.* 106 F3
Millersburg, *Pa., U.S.A.* 106 F8
Millerton, *U.S.A.* 107 E11
Millerton L., *U.S.A.* 112 J7
Millevaches, Plateau de, *France* 26 C6
Millicent, *Australia* 91 F3
Millingen, *Neths.* 16 E8
Millinocket, *U.S.A.* 99 C6
Millmerran, *Australia* 91 D5
Mills L., *Canada* 100 A5
Millsboro, *U.S.A.* 106 G4
Milltown Malbay, *Ireland* 15 D2
Millville, *U.S.A.* 104 F8
Millwood L., *U.S.A.* 109 J8
Milly-la-Forêt, *France* 25 D9
Milna, *Croatia* 33 E13
Milne →, *Australia* 90 C2
Milne Inlet, *Canada* 97 A11
Milnor, *U.S.A.* 108 B6
Milo, *Canada* 100 C6
Mílos, *Greece* 39 N7
Miloševo, *Serbia, Yug.* 21 K10
Milparinka P.O., *Australia* 91 D3
Miltenberg, *Germany* 19 F5
Milton, *Canada* 106 C5
Milton, *N.Z.* 87 M2
Milton, *U.K.* 14 D4
Milton, *Calif., U.S.A.* 112 G6
Milton, *Fla., U.S.A.* 105 K2
Milton, *Pa., U.S.A.* 106 F8
Milton-Freewater, *U.S.A.* 110 D4
Milton Keynes, *U.K.* 13 E7
Miltou, *Chad* 73 F8
Milverton, *Canada* 106 C4
Milwaukee, *U.S.A.* 104 D2
Milwaukee Deep, *Atl. Oc.* 117 C6
Milwaukie, *U.S.A.* 112 E4
Mim, *Ghana* 78 D4
Mimizan, *France* 26 D2
Mimoso, *Brazil* 123 E2
Min Chiang →, *China* 53 E12
Min Jiang →, *China* 52 C5
Min Xian, *China* 50 G3
Mina, *U.S.A.* 111 G4
Mina Pirquitas, *Argentina* 126 A2
Mīnā Su'ud, *Si. Arabia* 65 D6
Mīnā'al Aḥmadī, *Kuwait* 65 D6
Mīnāb, *Iran* 65 E8
Minago →, *Canada* 101 C9
Minaki, *Canada* 101 D10
Minamata, *Japan* 49 H5
Minami-Tori-Shima, *Pac. Oc.* 92 E7
Minas, *Uruguay* 127 C4
Minas, Sierra de las, *Guatemala* 116 C2
Minas Basin, *Canada* 99 C7
Minas de Rio Tinto, *Spain* 31 H4
Minas de San Quintín, *Spain* 31 G6
Minas Gerais □, *Brazil* 123 E2
Minas Novas, *Brazil* 123 E3
Minatitlán, *Mexico* 115 D6
Minbu, *Burma* 61 J19
Mincio →, *Italy* 32 C7
Mindanao, *Phil.* 55 H6
Mindanao Sea = Bohol Sea, *Phil.* 57 C6
Mindanao Trench, *Pac. Oc.* 55 F7
Mindel →, *Germany* 19 G6
Mindelheim, *Germany* 19 G6
Minden, *Canada* 106 B6
Minden, *Germany* 18 C4
Minden, *La., U.S.A.* 109 J8
Minden, *Nev., U.S.A.* 112 G7
Mindiptana, *Indonesia* 57 F10
Mindoro, *Phil.* 55 E4
Mindoro Str., *Phil.* 55 E4
Mindouli, *Congo* 80 E2
Mine, *Japan* 49 G5
Minehead, *U.K.* 13 F4
Mineiros, *Brazil* 125 D7
Mineola, *U.S.A.* 109 J7
Mineral King, *U.S.A.* 112 J8
Mineral Wells, *U.S.A.* 109 J5
Mineralnyye Vody, *Russia* 43 H6
Minersville, *Pa., U.S.A.* 107 F8
Minersville, *Utah, U.S.A.* 111 G7
Minerva, *U.S.A.* 106 F3
Minervino Murge, *Italy* 35 A9
Minetto, *U.S.A.* 107 C8
Mingäçevir, *Azerbaijan* 43 K8
Mingäçevir Su Anbarı, *Azerbaijan* 43 K8
Mingan, *Canada* 99 B7
Mingechaur = Mingäçevir, *Azerbaijan* 43 K8
Mingechaurskoye Vdkhr. = Mingäçevir Su Anbarı, *Azerbaijan* 43 K8
Mingela, *Australia* 90 B4
Mingenew, *Australia* 89 E2
Mingera Cr. →, *Australia* 90 C2
Minggang, *China* 53 A10
Mingin, *Burma* 61 H19
Minglanilla, *Spain* 28 F3
Minglun, *China* 52 E7
Mingorria, *Spain* 30 E6
Mingt'iehkaitafan = Mintaka Pass, *Pakistan* 63 A6
Mingxi, *China* 53 D11
Mingyuegue, *China* 51 C15
Minho = Miño →, *Spain* 30 D2
Minhou, *China* 53 E12
Minićevo, *Serbia, Yug.* 21 M12
Minidoka, *U.S.A.* 110 E7
Minigwal, L., *Australia* 89 E3
Minilya, *Australia* 89 D1
Minilya →, *Australia* 89 D1
Minipi, L., *Canada* 99 B7
Mink L., *Canada* 100 A5
Minna, *Nigeria* 79 D6
Minneapolis, *Kans., U.S.A.* 108 F6
Minneapolis, *Minn., U.S.A.* 108 C8
Minnedosa, *Canada* 101 C9
Minnesota □, *U.S.A.* 108 B7
Minnesund, *Norway* 10 D5
Minnie Creek, *Australia* 89 D2
Minnipa, *Australia* 91 E2
Minnitaki L., *Canada* 98 C1
Mino, *Japan* 49 G8
Miño →, *Spain* 30 D2
Minorca = Menorca, *Spain* 36 B11
Minore, *Australia* 91 E4
Minot, *U.S.A.* 108 A4
Minqin, *China* 50 E2
Minqing, *China* 53 D12
Minsen, *Germany* 18 B3
Minsk, *Belarus* 40 F4
Mińsk Mazowiecki, *Poland* 20 C11
Mintaka Pass, *Pakistan* 63 A6
Minto, *U.S.A.* 96 B5
Minton, *Canada* 101 D8
Minturn, *U.S.A.* 110 G10
Minturno, *Italy* 34 A6
Minûf, *Egypt* 76 H7
Minusinsk, *Russia* 45 D10
Minutang, *India* 61 E20
Minvoul, *Gabon* 80 D2
Minya el Qamh, *Egypt* 76 H7
Mionica, *Serbia, Yug.* 21 L10
Mir, *Niger* 79 C7
Mīr Kūh, *Iran* 65 E8
Mīr Shahdād, *Iran* 65 E8
Mira, *Italy* 33 C9
Mira, *Portugal* 30 E2
Mira →, *Colombia* 120 C2
Mira →, *Portugal* 31 H2
Mira por vos Cay, *Bahamas* 117 B5
Mirabella Eclano, *Italy* 35 A7
Miracema do Norte, *Brazil* 122 C2

Mirador, Brazil 122 C3
Miraflores, Colombia 120 C3
Miraj, India 60 L9
Miram Shah, Pakistan 62 C4
Miramar, Argentina 126 D4
Miramar, Mozam. 85 C6
Miramas, France 27 E8
Mirambeau, France 26 C3
Miramichi B., Canada 99 C7
Miramont-de-Guyenne, France 26 D4
Miranda, Brazil 125 E6
Miranda □, Venezuela 120 A4
Miranda →, Brazil 125 D6
Miranda de Ebro, Spain 28 C2
Miranda do Corvo, Spain 30 E2
Miranda do Douro, Portugal 30 D4
Mirande, France 26 E4
Mirandela, Portugal 30 D3
Mirando City, U.S.A. 109 M5
Mirándola, Italy 32 D8
Mirandópolis, Brazil 127 A5
Mirango, Malawi 83 E3
Mirani, Australia 90 C4
Mirano, Italy 33 C9
Mirassol, Brazil 127 A6
Mirbāţ, Oman 68 D5
Mirear, Egypt 76 C4
Mirebeau, Côte-d'Or, France 25 E12
Mirebeau, Vienne, France 24 F7
Mirecourt, France 25 D13
Mirgorod = Myrhorod, Ukraine 41 H7
Miri, Malaysia 56 D4
Miriam Vale, Australia 90 C5
Mirim, L., S. Amer. 127 C5
Mirimire, Venezuela 120 A4
Miriti, Brazil 125 B6
Mirnyy, Russia 45 C12
Mirond L., Canada 101 B8
Mirpur, Pakistan 63 C5
Mirpur Bibiwari, Pakistan 62 E2
Mirpur Khas, Pakistan 62 G3
Mirpur Sakro, Pakistan 62 G2
Mirria, Niger 79 C6
Mirror, Canada 100 C6
Mîrşani, Romania 38 E6
Miryang, S. Korea 51 G15
Mirzaani, Georgia 43 K8
Mirzapur, India 63 G10
Mirzapur-cum-Vindhyachal = Mirzapur, India 63 G10
Misantla, Mexico 115 D5
Misawa, Japan 48 D10
Miscou I., Canada 99 C7
Mish'āb, Ra'as al, Si. Arabia 65 D6
Mishagua →, Peru 124 C3
Mishan, China 54 B8
Mishawaka, U.S.A. 104 E2
Mishbih, Gebel, Egypt 76 C3
Mishima, Japan 49 G9
Misilmeri, Italy 34 D6
Misión, Mexico 113 N10
Misión Fagnano, Argentina 128 D3
Misiones □, Argentina 127 B5
Misiones □, Paraguay 126 B4
Miskah, Si. Arabia 64 E4
Miskitos, Cayos, Nic. 116 D3
Miskolc, Hungary 21 G10
Misoke, Zaïre 82 C2
Misool, Indonesia 57 E8
Misrātah, Libya 73 B8
Missanabie, Canada 98 C3
Missão Velha, Brazil 122 C4
Missinaibi →, Canada 98 B3
Missinaibi L., Canada 98 C3
Mission, S. Dak., U.S.A. 108 D4
Mission, Tex., U.S.A. 109 M5
Mission City, Canada 100 D4
Mission Viejo, U.S.A. 113 M9
Missisa L., Canada 98 B2
Missisagi →, Canada 98 C3
Mississippi □, U.S.A. 109 J10
Mississippi →, U.S.A. 109 L10
Mississippi L., Canada 107 A8
Mississippi River Delta, U.S.A. 109 L9
Mississippi Sd., U.S.A. 109 K10
Missoula, U.S.A. 110 C6
Missour, Morocco 74 B4
Missouri □, U.S.A. 108 F8
Missouri →, U.S.A. 108 F9
Missouri Valley, U.S.A. 108 E7
Mist, U.S.A. 112 E3
Mistake B., Canada 101 A10
Mistassini →, Canada 99 C5
Mistassini L., Canada 98 B5
Mistastin L., Canada 99 A7
Mistatim, Canada 101 C8
Mistelbach, Austria 20 G6
Misterbianco, Italy 35 E8
Mistretta, Italy 35 E7
Misty L., Canada 101 B8
Misurata = Misrātah, Libya 73 B8
Mit Ghamr, Egypt 76 H7
Mitatib, Sudan 77 D4
Mitchell, Australia 91 D4
Mitchell, Canada 106 C3
Mitchell, Ind., U.S.A. 104 F2
Mitchell, Nebr., U.S.A. 108 E3
Mitchell, Oreg., U.S.A. 110 D3
Mitchell, S. Dak., U.S.A. 108 D5
Mitchell →, Australia 90 B3
Mitchell, Mt., U.S.A. 105 H4
Mitchell Ras., Australia 90 A2
Mitchelstown, Ireland 15 D3
Mitha Tiwana, Pakistan 62 C5
Mitilíni, Greece 39 K9
Mito, Japan 49 F10
Mitrofanovka, Russia 42 F4
Mitrovica = Titova-Mitrovica, Serbia, Yug. 21 N10
Mitsinjo, Madag. 85 B8
Mitsiwa, Eritrea 77 D4
Mitsiwa Channel, Eritrea 77 D5
Mitsukaidō, Japan 49 F9
Mittagong, Australia 91 E5
Mittelland, Switz. 22 C4
Mittellandkanal →, Germany 18 C3
Mittenwalde, Germany 18 C9
Mitterteich, Germany 19 F8
Mittweida, Germany 18 E8
Mitú, Colombia 120 C3
Mituas, Colombia 120 C4
Mitumba, Tanzania 82 D3
Mitumba, Chaîne des, Zaïre 82 D2
Mitumba Mts. = Mitumba, Chaîne des, Zaïre 82 D2
Mitwaba, Zaïre 83 D2
Mityana, Uganda 82 B3
Mitzic, Gabon 80 D2
Mixteco →, Mexico 115 D5
Miyagi □, Japan 48 E10
Miyâh, W. el →, Egypt 76 B3
Miyah, W. el →, Syria 64 C3
Miyake-Jima, Japan 49 G9
Miyako, Japan 48 E10
Miyako-Jima, Japan 49 M2
Miyako-Rettō, Japan 49 M2
Miyakonojō, Japan 49 J5
Miyanoura-Dake, Japan 49 J5
Miyazaki, Japan 49 J5
Miyazaki □, Japan 49 H5
Miyazu, Japan 49 G7
Miyet, Bahr el = Dead Sea, Asia 69 D4
Miyi, China 52 D4
Miyoshi, Japan 49 G6
Miyun, China 50 D9
Miyun Shuiku, China 51 D9
Mizdah, Libya 75 B7
Mizen Hd., Cork, Ireland 15 E2
Mizen Hd., Wick., Ireland 15 D5
Mizhi, China 50 F6
Mizil, Romania 38 E9
Mizoram □, India 61 H18
Mizpe Ramon, Israel 69 E3
Mizusawa, Japan 48 E10
Mjöbäck, Sweden 11 G6
Mjölby, Sweden 11 F9
Mjörn, Sweden 11 G6
Mjøsa, Norway 10 D5
Mkata, Tanzania 82 D4
Mkokotoni, Tanzania 82 D4
Mkomazi, Tanzania 82 C4
Mkomazi →, S. Africa 85 E5
Mkulwe, Tanzania 83 D3
Mkumbi, Ras, Tanzania 82 D4
Mkushi, Zambia 83 E2
Mkushi River, Zambia 83 E2
Mkuze, S. Africa 85 D5
Mladá Boleslav, Czech. 20 E4
Mladenovac, Serbia, Yug. 21 L10
Mlala Hills, Tanzania 82 D3
Mlange, Malawi 83 F4
Mlava →, Serbia, Yug. 21 L11
Mława, Poland 20 B10
Mlinište, Bos.-H. 33 D13
Mljet, Croatia 21 N7
Młynary, Poland 20 A9
Mmabatho, S. Africa 84 D4
Mme, Cameroon 79 D7
Mo i Rana, Norway 8 C16
Moa, Indonesia 57 F7
Moa →, S. Leone 78 D2
Moab, U.S.A. 111 G9
Moabi, Gabon 80 E2
Moaco →, Brazil 124 B4
Moala, Fiji 87 D8
Moalie Park, Australia 91 D3
Moaña, Spain 30 C2
Moba, Zaïre 82 D2
Mobārakābād, Iran 65 D7
Mobārakīyeh, Iran 65 C6
Mobaye, C.A.R. 80 D4
Mobayi, Zaïre 80 D4
Moberly, U.S.A. 108 F8
Moberly →, Canada 100 B4
Mobile, U.S.A. 105 K1
Mobile B., U.S.A. 105 K2
Mobridge, U.S.A. 108 C4
Mobutu Sese Seko, L. = Albert L., Africa 82 B3
Moc Chau, Vietnam 58 B5
Moc Hoa, Vietnam 59 G5
Mocabe Kasari, Zaïre 83 D2
Mocajuba, Brazil 122 B2
Moçambique, Mozam. 83 F5
Moçâmedes = Namibe, Angola 81 H2
Mocapra →, Venezuela 120 B4
Mocha, I., Chile 128 A2
Mochudi, Botswana 84 C4
Mocimboa da Praia, Mozam. 83 E5
Moclips, U.S.A. 112 C2
Mocoa, Colombia 120 C2
Mococa, Brazil 127 A6
Mocorito, Mexico 114 B3
Moctezuma, Mexico 114 B3
Moctezuma →, Mexico 115 C5
Mocuba, Mozam. 83 F4
Mocúzari, Presa, Mexico 114 B3
Modane, France 27 C10
Modasa, India 62 H5
Modave, Belgium 17 H6
Modder →, S. Africa 84 D3
Modderrivier, S. Africa 84 D3
Módena, Italy 32 D7
Modena, U.S.A. 111 H7
Modesto, U.S.A. 111 H3
Módica, Italy 35 F7
Modigliana, Italy 33 D8
Modo, Sudan 77 F3
Modra, Slovak Rep. 21 G7
Moe, Australia 91 F4
Moebase, Mozam. 83 F4
Moëlan-sur-Mer, France 24 E3
Moengo, Surinam 121 B7
Moergestel, Neths. 17 E6
Moers, Germany 17 F9
Moësa →, Switz. 23 D8
Moffat, U.K. 14 F5
Moga, India 62 D6
Mogadishu = Muqdisho, Somali Rep. 68 G4
Mogador = Essaouira, Morocco 74 B3
Mogadouro, Portugal 30 D4
Mogalakwena →, S. Africa 85 C4
Mogami →, Japan 48 E10
Mogán, Canary Is. 36 G4
Mogaung, Burma 61 G20
Møgeltønder, Denmark 11 K2
Mogente, Spain 29 G4
Mogho, Ethiopia 77 G5
Mogi das Cruzes, Brazil 127 A6
Mogi-Guaçu →, Brazil 127 A6
Mogi-Mirim, Brazil 127 A6
Mogielnica, Poland 20 D10
Mogilev = Mahilyow, Belarus 40 F6
Mogilev-Podolskiy = Mohyliv-Podilskyy, Ukraine 41 H4
Mogilno, Poland 20 C7
Mogincual, Mozam. 83 F5
Mogliano Véneto, Italy 33 C9
Mogocha, Russia 45 D12
Mogoi, Indonesia 57 E8
Mogok, Burma 61 H20
Moguer, Spain 31 H4
Mogumber, Australia 89 F2
Mohács, Hungary 21 K8
Mohales Hoek, Lesotho 84 E4
Mohall, U.S.A. 108 A4
Moḩammadābād, Iran 65 B8
Mohammadia, Algeria 75 A5
Mohammedia, Morocco 74 B3
Mohave, L., U.S.A. 113 K12
Mohawk →, U.S.A. 107 D11
Möhne →, Germany 18 D3
Moholm, Sweden 11 F8
Mohoro, Tanzania 82 D4
Mohyliv-Podilskyy, Ukraine 41 H4
Moia, Sudan 77 F2
Moidart, L., U.K. 14 E3
Moineşti, Romania 38 C9
Moirans, France 27 C9
Moirans-en-Montagne, France 27 B9
Moíres, Greece 37 D6
Moisaküla, Estonia 9 G21
Moisie, Canada 99 B6
Moisie →, Canada 99 B6
Moissac, France 26 D5
Moïssala, Chad 73 G8
Moita, Portugal 31 G2
Mojácar, Spain 29 H3
Mojados, Spain 30 D6
Mojave, U.S.A. 113 K8
Mojave Desert, U.S.A. 113 L10
Mojiang, China 52 F3
Mojo, Bolivia 126 A2
Mojo, Ethiopia 77 F4
Mojokerto, Indonesia 57 G15
Mojos, Llanos de, Bolivia 125 D5
Moju →, Brazil 122 B2
Mokai, N.Z. 87 H5
Mokambo, Zaïre 83 E2
Mokameh, India 63 G11
Mokelumne →, U.S.A. 112 G5
Mokelumne Hill, U.S.A. 112 G6
Mokhós, Greece 37 D7
Mokhotlong, Lesotho 85 D4
Moknine, Tunisia 75 A7
Mokokchung, India 61 F19
Mokra Gora, Serbia, Yug. 21 N10
Mokronog, Slovenia 33 C12
Moksha →, Russia 42 C6
Mokshan, Russia 42 D7
Mol, Belgium 17 F6
Mola, C. de la, Spain 28 F9
Mola di Bari, Italy 35 A10
Moláoi, Greece 39 N5
Molat, Croatia 33 D11
Molchanovo, Russia 44 D9
Mold, U.K. 12 D4
Moldavia, Romania 38 C10
Moldavia ■ = Moldova ■, Europe 41 J5
Molde, Norway 8 E12
Moldova ■, Europe 41 J5
Moldova Nouă, Romania 38 E4
Moldoveana, Romania 38 D7
Molepolole, Botswana 84 C4
Moléson, Switz. 22 C4
Molfetta, Italy 35 A9
Molina de Aragón, Spain 28 E3
Moline, U.S.A. 108 E9
Molinella, Italy 33 D8
Molinos, Argentina 126 B2
Moliro, Zaïre 82 D3
Molise □, Italy 33 G11
Moliterno, Italy 35 B8
Mollahat, Bangla. 63 H13
Mölle, Sweden 11 H6
Molledo, Spain 30 B6
Mollendo, Peru 124 D3
Mollerin, L., Australia 89 F2
Mollerusa, Spain 28 D5
Mollina, Spain 31 H6
Mölln, Germany 18 B6
Mölltorp, Sweden 11 F8
Mölndal, Sweden 11 G6
Molochansk, Ukraine 41 J8
Molochnoye, Ozero, Ukraine 41 J8
Molodechno = Maladzyechna, Belarus 40 E4
Molokai, U.S.A. 102 H16
Molong, Australia 91 E4
Molopo →, Africa 84 D3
Mólos, Greece 39 L5
Molotov = Perm, Russia 44 D6
Moloundou, Cameroon 80 D3
Molsheim, France 25 D14
Molson L., Canada 101 C9
Molteno, S. Africa 84 E4
Molu, Indonesia 57 F8
Molucca Sea, Indonesia 57 E6
Moluccas = Maluku, Indonesia 57 E7
Moma, Mozam. 83 F4
Moma, Zaïre 82 C1
Mombaça, Brazil 122 C4
Mombasa, Kenya 82 C4
Mombetsu, Japan 48 B11
Mombuey, Spain 30 C4
Momchilgrad, Bulgaria 39 H8
Momi, Zaïre 82 C2
Momignies, Belgium 17 H4
Mompós, Colombia 120 B3
Møn, Denmark 11 K6
Mon →, Burma 61 J19
Mona, Canal de la, W. Indies 117 C6
Mona, Isla, Puerto Rico 117 C6
Mona, Pta., Costa Rica 116 E3
Mona, Pta., Spain 31 J7
Monach Is., U.K. 14 D1
Monaco ■, Europe 27 E11
Monadhliath Mts., U.K. 14 D4
Monagas □, Venezuela 121 B5
Monaghan, Ireland 15 B5
Monaghan □, Ireland 15 B5
Monahans, U.S.A. 109 K3
Monapo, Mozam. 83 E5
Monarch Mt., Canada 100 C3
Monastir = Bitola, Macedonia 39 H4
Monastir, Tunisia 75 A7
Moncada, Phil. 55 D4
Moncada, Spain 28 F4
Moncalieri, Italy 32 D4
Moncalvo, Italy 32 C5
Moncão, Portugal 30 C2
Moncarapacho, Portugal 31 H3
Moncayo, Sierra del, Spain 28 D3
Mönchengladbach, Germany 18 D2
Monchique, Portugal 31 H2
Monclova, Mexico 114 B4
Moncontour, France 24 D4
Moncoutant, France 26 B3
Moncton, Canada 99 C7
Mondego →, Portugal 30 E2
Mondego, C., Portugal 30 E2
Mondeodo, Indonesia 57 E6
Mondolfo, Italy 33 E10
Mondoñedo, Spain 30 B3
Mondovì, Italy 32 D4
Mondovi, U.S.A. 108 C9
Mondragon, France 27 D8
Mondragon, Phil. 55 E6
Mondragone, Italy 34 A6
Mondrain I., Australia 89 F3
Monduli □, Tanzania 82 C4
Monemvasía, Greece 39 N6
Monessen, U.S.A. 106 F5
Monesterio, Spain 31 G4
Monestier-de-Clermont, France 27 D9
Monett, U.S.A. 109 G8
Monfalcone, Italy 33 C10
Monflanquin, France 26 D4
Monforte, Portugal 31 F3
Monforte de Lemos, Spain 30 C3
Mong Hsu, Burma 61 J21
Mong Kung, Burma 61 J20
Mong Nai, Burma 61 J20
Mong Pawk, Burma 61 H21
Mong Ton, Burma 61 J21
Mong Wa, Burma 61 J22
Mong Yai, Burma 61 H21
Mongalla, Sudan 77 F3
Mongers, L., Australia 89 E2
Monghyr = Munger, India 63 G12
Mongibello = Etna, Italy 35 E8
Mongo, Chad 73 F8
Mongolia ■, Asia 45 E10
Mongonu, Nigeria 79 C7
Mongororo, Chad 73 F9
Mongu, Zambia 81 H4
Môngua, Angola 84 B2
Monistrol-d'Allier, France 26 D7
Monistrol-sur-Loire, France 27 C8
Monkey Bay, Malawi 83 E4
Monkey River, Belize 115 D7
Monkira, Australia 90 C3
Monkoto, Zaïre 80 E4
Monmouth, U.K. 13 F5
Monmouth, U.S.A. 108 E9
Monmouthshire □, U.K. 13 F5
Mono L., U.S.A. 111 H4
Monolith, U.S.A. 113 K8
Monólithos, Greece 37 C9
Monongahela, U.S.A. 106 F5
Monópoli, Italy 35 B10
Monor, Hungary 21 H9
Monóvar, Spain 29 G4
Monqoumba, C.A.R. 80 D3
Monreal del Campo, Spain 28 E3
Monreale, Italy 34 D6
Monroe, Ga., U.S.A. 105 J4
Monroe, La., U.S.A. 109 J8
Monroe, Mich., U.S.A. 104 E4
Monroe, N.C., U.S.A. 105 H5
Monroe, N.Y., U.S.A. 107 E10
Monroe, Utah, U.S.A. 111 G7
Monroe, Wash., U.S.A. 112 C5
Monroe, Wis., U.S.A. 108 D10
Monroe City, U.S.A. 108 F9
Monroeville, Ala., U.S.A. 105 K2
Monroeville, Pa., U.S.A. 106 F5
Monrovia, Liberia 78 D2
Mons, Belgium 17 H3
Monsaraz, Portugal 31 G3
Monse, Indonesia 57 E6
Monsefú, Peru 124 B2
Monségur, France 26 D4
Monsélice, Italy 33 C8
Monster, Neths. 16 D4
Mont Cenis, Col du, France 27 C10
Mont-de-Marsan, France 26 E3
Mont-Joli, Canada 99 C6
Mont-Laurier, Canada 98 C4
Mont-St.-Michel, Le = Le Mont-St.-Michel, France 24 D5
Mont-sous-Vaudrey, France 25 F12
Mont-sur-Marchienne, Belgium 17 H4
Mont Tremblant Prov. Park, Canada 98 C5
Montabaur, Germany 18 E3
Montagnac, France 26 E7
Montagnana, Italy 33 C8
Montagu, S. Africa 84 E3
Montagu I., Antarctica 5 B1
Montague, Canada 99 C7
Montague, U.S.A. 110 F2
Montague, I., Mexico 114 A2
Montague Ra., Australia 89 E2
Montague Sd., Australia 88 B4
Montaigu, France 24 F5
Montalbán, Spain 28 E4
Montalbano di Elicona, Italy 35 D8
Montalbano Iónico, Italy 35 B9
Montalbo, Spain 28 F2
Montalcino, Italy 33 E8
Montalegre, Portugal 30 D3
Montalto di Castro, Italy 33 F8
Montalto Uffugo, Italy 35 C9
Montalvo, U.S.A. 113 L7
Montamarta, Spain 30 D5
Montaña, Peru 124 B3
Montana, Switz. 22 D4
Montana □, U.S.A. 110 C9
Montaña Clara, I., Canary Is. 36 E6
Montánchez, Spain 31 F4
Montañita, Colombia 120 C2
Montargis, France 25 E9
Montauban, France 26 D5
Montauk, U.S.A. 107 E13
Montauk Pt., U.S.A. 107 E13
Montbard, France 25 E11
Montbéliard, France 25 E13
Montblanch, Spain 28 D6
Montbrison, France 27 C8
Montcalm, Pic de, France 26 F5
Montceau-les-Mines, France 25 F11
Montchanin, France 27 B8
Montclair, U.S.A. 107 F10
Montcornet, France 25 C11
Montcuq, France 26 D5
Montdidier, France 25 C9
Monte Albán, Mexico 115 D5
Monte Alegre, Brazil 121 D7
Monte Alegre de Goiás, Brazil 123 D2
Monte Alegre de Minas, Brazil 123 E2
Monte Azul, Brazil 123 E3
Monte Bello Is., Australia 88 D2
Monte-Carlo, Monaco 27 E11
Monte Carmelo, Brazil 123 E2
Monte Caseros, Argentina 126 C4
Monte Comán, Argentina 126 C2
Monte Cristi, Dom. Rep. 117 C5
Monte Dinero, Argentina 128 D3
Monte Lindo →, Paraguay 126 A4
Monte Quemado, Argentina 126 B3
Monte Redondo, Portugal 30 F2
Monte Rio, U.S.A. 112 G4
Monte San Giovanni Campano, Italy 34 A6
Monte San Savino, Italy 33 E8

Monte Sant' Ángelo, *Italy* 35 A8
Monte Santu, C. di, *Italy* 34 B2
Monte Vista, *U.S.A.* 111 H10
Monteagudo, *Argentina* 127 B5
Monteagudo, *Bolivia* 125 D5
Montealegre, *Spain* 29 G3
Montebello, *Canada* 98 C5
Montebelluna, *Italy* 33 C9
Montebourg, *France* 24 C5
Montecastrilli, *Italy* 33 F9
Montecatini Terme, *Italy* 32 E7
Montecito, *U.S.A.* 113 L7
Montecristi, *Ecuador* 120 D1
Montecristo, *Italy* 32 F7
Montefalco, *Italy* 33 F9
Montefiascone, *Italy* 33 F9
Montefrío, *Spain* 31 H6
Montegnée, *Belgium* 17 G7
Montego Bay, *Jamaica* 116 C4
Montegranaro, *Italy* 33 E10
Monteiro, *Brazil* 122 C4
Montejicar, *Spain* 29 H1
Montejinnie, *Australia* 88 C5
Montelíbano, *Colombia* 120 B2
Montélimar, *France* 27 D8
Montella, *Italy* 35 B8
Montellano, *Spain* 31 J5
Montello, *U.S.A.* 108 D10
Montelupo Fiorentino, *Italy* 32 E8
Montemor-o-Novo, *Portugal* 31 G2
Montemor-o-Velho, *Portugal* 30 E2
Montemorelos, *Mexico* 115 B5
Montendre, *France* 26 C3
Montenegro, *Brazil* 127 B5
Montenegro □, *Yugoslavia* 21 N9
Montenero di Bisáccia, *Italy* 33 G11
Montepuez, *Mozam.* 83 E4
Montepuez →, *Mozam.* 83 E5
Montepulciano, *Italy* 33 E8
Montereale, *Italy* 33 F10
Montereau-Fault-Yonne, *France* 25 D9
Monterey, *U.S.A.* 111 H3
Monterey B., *U.S.A.* 112 J5
Montería, *Colombia* 120 B2
Montero, *Bolivia* 125 D5
Monteros, *Argentina* 126 B2
Monterotondo, *Italy* 33 F9
Monterrey, *Mexico* 114 B4
Montes Altos, *Brazil* 122 C2
Montes Claros, *Brazil* 123 E3
Montesano, *U.S.A.* 112 D3
Montesárchio, *Italy* 35 A7
Montescaglioso, *Italy* 35 B9
Montesilvano Marina, *Italy* 33 F11
Montevarchi, *Italy* 33 E8
Montevideo, *Uruguay* 127 C4
Montevideo, *U.S.A.* 108 C7
Montezuma, *U.S.A.* 108 E8
Montfaucon, *France* 25 C12
Montfaucon-en-Velay, *France* 27 C8
Montfort, *France* 24 D5
Montfort, *Neths.* 17 F7
Montfort-l'Amaury, *France* 25 D8
Montgenèvre, *France* 27 D10
Montgomery = Sahiwal, *Pakistan* 62 D5
Montgomery, *U.K.* 13 E4
Montgomery, *Ala., U.S.A.* 105 J2
Montgomery, *W. Va., U.S.A.* 104 F5
Montguyon, *France* 26 C3
Monthey, *Switz.* 22 D3
Monticelli d'Ongina, *Italy* 32 C6
Monticello, *Ark., U.S.A.* 109 J9
Monticello, *Fla., U.S.A.* 105 K4
Monticello, *Ind., U.S.A.* 104 E2
Monticello, *Iowa, U.S.A.* 108 D9
Monticello, *Ky., U.S.A.* 105 G3
Monticello, *Minn., U.S.A.* 108 C8
Monticello, *Miss., U.S.A.* 109 K9
Monticello, *N.Y., U.S.A.* 107 E10
Monticello, *Utah, U.S.A.* 111 H9
Montichiari, *Italy* 32 C7
Montier-en-Der, *France* 25 D11
Montignac, *France* 26 C5
Montignies-sur-Sambre, *Belgium* 17 H4
Montigny, *France* 25 C13
Montigny-sur-Aube, *France* 25 E11
Montijo, *Spain* 31 G4
Montijo, Presa de, *Spain* 31 G4
Montilla, *Spain* 31 H6
Montlhéry, *France* 25 D9
Montluçon, *France* 26 B6
Montmagny, *Canada* 99 C5
Montmarault, *France* 26 B6
Montmartre, *Canada* 101 C8
Montmédy, *France* 25 C12
Montmélian, *France* 27 C10
Montmirail, *France* 25 D10
Montmoreau-St.-Cybard, *France* 26 C4
Montmorency, *Canada* 99 C5
Montmorillon, *France* 26 B4
Montmort, *France* 25 D10
Monto, *Australia* 90 C5
Montoir-sur-le-Loir, *France* 24 E7
Montório al Vomano, *Italy* 33 F10
Montoro, *Spain* 31 G6
Montour Falls, *U.S.A.* 106 D8
Montpelier, *Idaho, U.S.A.* 110 E8
Montpelier, *Ohio, U.S.A.* 104 E3
Montpelier, *Vt., U.S.A.* 107 B12
Montpellier, *France* 26 E7
Montpezat-de-Quercy, *France* 26 D5
Montpon-Ménestérol, *France* 26 D4
Montréal, *Canada* 98 C5
Montréal, *France* 26 E6
Montreal L., *Canada* 101 C7
Montreal Lake, *Canada* 101 C7
Montredon-Labessonnié, *France* 26 E6
Montréjeau, *France* 26 E4
Montrésor, *France* 24 E8
Montreuil, *France* 25 B8
Montreuil-Bellay, *France* 24 E6
Montreux, *Switz.* 22 D3
Montrevault, *France* 24 E5
Montrevel-en-Bresse, *France* 27 B9
Montrichard, *France* 24 E8
Montrose, *U.K.* 14 E6
Montrose, *Colo., U.S.A.* 111 G10
Montrose, *Pa., U.S.A.* 107 E9
Monts, Pte. des, *Canada* 99 C6
Monts-sur-Guesnes, *France* 24 F7
Montsalvy, *France* 26 D6
Montsant, Sierra de, *Spain* 28 D5
Montsauche, *France* 25 E11
Montsech, Sierra del, *Spain* 28 C5
Montseny, *Spain* 28 D2
Montserrat, *Spain* 28 D6
Montserrat ■, *W. Indies* 117 C7
Montuenga, *Spain* 30 D6
Montuiri, *Spain* 36 B9
Monveda, *Zaïre* 80 D4
Monywa, *Burma* 61 H19
Monza, *Italy* 32 C6
Monze, *Zambia* 83 F2
Monze, C., *Pakistan* 62 G2
Monzón, *Spain* 28 D5
Mooi River, *S. Africa* 85 D4
Mook, *Neths.* 16 E7
Moolawatana, *Australia* 91 D2
Mooliabeenee, *Australia* 89 F2
Mooloogool, *Australia* 89 E2
Moomin Cr. →, *Australia* 91 D4
Moonah →, *Australia* 90 C2
Moonbeam, *Canada* 98 C3
Moonda, L., *Australia* 90 D3
Moonie, *Australia* 91 D5
Moonie →, *Australia* 91 D4
Moonta, *Australia* 91 E2
Moora, *Australia* 89 F2
Mooraberree, *Australia* 90 D3
Moorarie, *Australia* 89 E2
Moorcroft, *U.S.A.* 108 C2
Moore →, *Australia* 89 F2
Moore, L., *Australia* 89 E2
Moore Reefs, *Australia* 90 B4
Moorefield, *U.S.A.* 104 F6
Moores Res., *U.S.A.* 107 B13
Mooresville, *U.S.A.* 105 H5
Moorfoot Hills, *U.K.* 14 F5
Moorhead, *U.S.A.* 108 B6
Mooroopna, *Australia* 91 F4
Moorpark, *U.S.A.* 113 L8
Moorreesburg, *S. Africa* 84 E2
Moorslede, *Belgium* 17 G2
Moosburg, *Germany* 19 G7
Moose →, *Canada* 98 B3
Moose Factory, *Canada* 98 B3
Moose I., *Canada* 101 C9
Moose Jaw, *Canada* 101 C7
Moose Jaw →, *Canada* 101 C7
Moose Lake, *Canada* 101 C8
Moose Lake, *U.S.A.* 108 B8
Moose Mountain Cr. →, *Canada* 101 D8
Moose Mountain Prov. Park, *Canada* 101 D8
Moose River, *Canada* 98 B3
Moosehead L., *U.S.A.* 99 C6
Moosomin, *Canada* 101 C8
Moosonee, *Canada* 98 B3
Moosup, *U.S.A.* 107 E13
Mopeia Velha, *Mozam.* 83 F4
Mopipi, *Botswana* 84 C3
Mopoi, *C.A.R.* 82 A2
Mopti, *Mali* 78 C4
Moqatta, *Sudan* 77 E4
Moquegua, *Peru* 124 D3
Moquegua □, *Peru* 124 D3
Mór, *Hungary* 21 H8
Móra, *Portugal* 31 G2
Mora, *Sweden* 9 F16
Mora, *Minn., U.S.A.* 108 C8
Mora, *N. Mex., U.S.A.* 111 J11
Mora de Ebro, *Spain* 28 D5
Mora de Rubielos, *Spain* 28 E4
Mora la Nueva, *Spain* 28 D5
Morača →, *Montenegro, Yug.* 21 N9
Morada Nova, *Brazil* 122 C4
Morada Nova de Minas, *Brazil* 123 E2
Moradabad, *India* 63 E8
Morafenobe, *Madag.* 85 B7
Morąg, *Poland* 20 B9
Moral de Calatrava, *Spain* 29 G1
Moraleja, *Spain* 30 E4
Morales, *Colombia* 120 C2
Moramanga, *Madag.* 85 B8
Moran, *Kans., U.S.A.* 109 G7
Moran, *Wyo., U.S.A.* 110 E8
Moranbah, *Australia* 90 C4
Morano Cálabro, *Italy* 35 C9
Morant Cays, *Jamaica* 116 C4
Morant Pt., *Jamaica* 116 C4
Morar, L., *U.K.* 14 E3
Moratalla, *Spain* 29 G3
Moratuwa, *Sri Lanka* 60 R11
Morava →, *Slovak Rep.* 20 G6
Moravia, *U.S.A.* 108 E8
Moravian Hts. = Ceskomoravská Vrchovina, *Czech.* 20 F5
Moravica →, *Serbia, Yug.* 21 M10
Moravice →, *Czech.* 20 F7
Moraviţa, *Romania* 21 K11
Moravská Třebová, *Czech.* 20 F6
Morawa, *Australia* 89 E2
Morawhanna, *Guyana* 121 B6
Moray □, *U.K.* 14 D5
Moray Firth, *U.K.* 14 D5
Morbach, *Germany* 19 F3
Morbegno, *Italy* 32 B6
Morbi, *India* 62 H4
Morbihan □, *France* 24 E4
Morcenx, *France* 26 D3
Mordelles, *France* 24 D5
Morden, *Canada* 101 D9
Mordovian Republic □ = Mordvinia □, *Russia* 42 C7
Mordovo, *Russia* 42 D5
Mordvinia □, *Russia* 42 C7
Møre og Romsdal fylke □, *Norway* 10 B2
Morea, *Australia* 91 F3
Morea, *Greece* 6 H10
Moreau →, *U.S.A.* 108 C4
Morecambe, *U.K.* 12 C5
Morecambe B., *U.K.* 12 C5
Moree, *Australia* 91 D4
Morehead, *U.S.A.* 104 F4
Morehead City, *U.S.A.* 105 H7
Morelia, *Mexico* 114 D4
Morella, *Australia* 90 C3
Morella, *Spain* 28 E4
Morelos, *Mexico* 114 B3
Morelos □, *Mexico* 115 D5
Morena, Sierra, *Spain* 31 G7
Morenci, *U.S.A.* 111 K9
Moreni, *Romania* 38 E8
Moreno Valley, *U.S.A.* 113 M10
Morero, *Bolivia* 125 C4
Moreru →, *Brazil* 125 C6
Moresby I., *Canada* 100 C2
Morestel, *France* 27 C9
Moret-sur-Loing, *France* 25 D9
Moreton, *Australia* 90 A3
Moreton I., *Australia* 91 D5
Moreuil, *France* 25 C9
Morey, *Spain* 36 B10
Morez, *France* 27 B10
Morgan, *Australia* 91 E2
Morgan, *U.S.A.* 110 F8
Morgan City, *U.S.A.* 109 L9
Morgan Hill, *U.S.A.* 112 H5
Morganfield, *U.S.A.* 104 G2
Morganton, *U.S.A.* 105 H5
Morgantown, *U.S.A.* 104 F6
Morgat, *France* 24 D2
Morgenzon, *S. Africa* 85 D4
Morges, *Switz.* 22 C2
Morghak, *Iran* 65 D8
Morhange, *France* 25 D13
Mori, *Italy* 32 C7
Morialmée, *Belgium* 17 H5
Morice L., *Canada* 100 C3
Morichal, *Colombia* 120 C3
Morichal Largo →, *Venezuela* 121 B5
Moriki, *Nigeria* 79 C6
Morinville, *Canada* 100 C6
Morioka, *Japan* 48 E10
Moris, *Mexico* 114 B3
Morlaàs, *France* 26 E3
Morlaix, *France* 24 D3
Morlanwelz, *Belgium* 17 H4
Mormanno, *Italy* 35 C8
Mormant, *France* 25 D9
Mornington, *Vic., Australia* 91 F4
Mornington, *W. Austral., Australia* 88 C4
Mornington, I., *Chile* 128 C1
Mornington I., *Australia* 90 B2
Mórnos →, *Greece* 39 L4
Moro, *Sudan* 77 E3
Moro G., *Phil.* 55 H5
Morocco ■, *N. Afr.* 74 B3
Morococha, *Peru* 124 C2
Morogoro, *Tanzania* 82 D4
Morogoro □, *Tanzania* 82 D4
Moroleón, *Mexico* 114 C4
Morombe, *Madag.* 85 C7
Moron, *Argentina* 126 C4
Morón, *Cuba* 116 B4
Mörön →, *Mongolia* 54 B6
Morón de Almazán, *Spain* 28 D2
Morón de la Frontera, *Spain* 31 H5
Morona →, *Peru* 120 D2
Morona-Santiago □, *Ecuador* 120 D2
Morondava, *Madag.* 85 C7
Morondo, *Ivory C.* 78 D3
Morongo Valley, *U.S.A.* 113 L10
Moronou, *Ivory C.* 78 D4
Morotai, *Indonesia* 57 D7
Moroto, *Uganda* 82 B3
Moroto Summit, *Kenya* 82 B3
Morozovsk, *Russia* 43 F5
Morpeth, *U.K.* 12 B6
Morphou, *Cyprus* 66 E5
Morphou Bay, *Cyprus* 37 D11
Morrilton, *U.S.A.* 109 H8
Morrinhos, *Ceara, Brazil* 122 B3
Morrinhos, *Minas Gerais, Brazil* 123 E2
Morrinsville, *N.Z.* 87 G5
Morris, *Canada* 101 D9
Morris, *Ill., U.S.A.* 104 E1
Morris, *Minn., U.S.A.* 108 C7
Morris, Mt., *Australia* 89 E5
Morrisburg, *Canada* 98 D4
Morrison, *U.S.A.* 108 E10
Morristown, *Ariz., U.S.A.* 111 K7
Morristown, *N.J., U.S.A.* 107 F10
Morristown, *S. Dak., U.S.A.* 108 C4
Morristown, *Tenn., U.S.A.* 105 G4
Morro, Pta., *Chile* 126 B1
Morro Bay, *U.S.A.* 111 J3
Morro del Jable, *Canary Is.* 36 F5
Morro do Chapéu, *Brazil* 123 D3
Morro Jable, Pta. de, *Canary Is.* 36 F5
Morros, *Brazil* 122 B3
Morrosquillo, G. de, *Colombia* 116 E4
Morrumbene, *Mozam.* 85 C6
Mors, *Denmark* 11 H2
Morshansk, *Russia* 42 D5
Mörsil, *Sweden* 10 A7
Mortagne →, *France* 25 D13
Mortagne-au-Perche, *France* 24 D7
Mortagne-sur-Gironde, *France* 26 C3
Mortagne-sur-Sèvre, *France* 24 F6
Mortain, *France* 24 D6
Mortara, *Italy* 32 C5
Morteau, *France* 25 E13
Morteros, *Argentina* 126 C3
Mortes, R. das →, *Brazil* 123 D1
Mortlake, *Australia* 91 F3
Morton, *Tex., U.S.A.* 109 J3
Morton, *Wash., U.S.A.* 112 D4
Mortsel, *Belgium* 17 F4
Morundah, *Australia* 91 E4
Moruya, *Australia* 91 F5
Morvan, *France* 25 E11
Morven, *Australia* 91 D4
Morvern, *U.K.* 14 E3
Morwell, *Australia* 91 F4
Mosalsk, *Russia* 42 C2
Mosbach, *Germany* 19 F5
Mošćenice, *Croatia* 33 C11
Mosciano Sant' Ángelo, *Italy* 33 F10
Moscos Is., *Burma* 58 E1
Moscow = Moskva, *Russia* 42 C3
Moscow, *U.S.A.* 110 C5
Mosel →, *Europe* 19 E3
Moselle = Mosel →, *Europe* 19 E3
Moselle □, *France* 25 D13
Moses Lake, *U.S.A.* 110 C4
Mosgiel, *N.Z.* 87 L3
Moshi, *Tanzania* 82 C4
Moshi □, *Tanzania* 82 C4
Moshupa, *Botswana* 84 C4
Mosjøen, *Norway* 8 D15
Moskenesøya, *Norway* 8 C15
Moskenstraumen, *Norway* 8 C15
Moskva, *Russia* 42 C3
Moskva →, *Russia* 42 C4
Moslavačka Gora, *Croatia* 33 C13
Mosomane, *Botswana* 84 C4
Moson-magyaróvar, *Hungary* 21 H7
Mospino, *Ukraine* 41 J9
Mosquera, *Colombia* 120 C2
Mosquero, *U.S.A.* 109 H3
Mosqueruela, *Spain* 28 E4
Mosquitia, *Honduras* 116 C3
Mosquitos, G. de los, *Panama* 116 E3
Moss, *Norway* 10 E4
Moss Vale, *Australia* 91 E5
Mossaka, *Congo* 80 E3
Mossâmedes, *Brazil* 123 E1
Mossbank, *Canada* 101 D7
Mossburn, *N.Z.* 87 L2
Mosselbaai, *S. Africa* 84 E3
Mossendjo, *Congo* 80 E2
Mosses, Col des, *Switz.* 22 D4
Mossgiel, *Australia* 91 E3
Mossman, *Australia* 90 B4
Mossoró, *Brazil* 122 C4
Mossuril, *Mozam.* 83 E5
Mossy →, *Canada* 101 C8
Most, *Czech.* 20 E3
Mosta, *Malta* 37 D1
Moşţafáābād, *Iran* 65 C7
Mostaganem, *Algeria* 75 A5
Mostar, *Bos.-H.* 21 M7
Mostardas, *Brazil* 127 C5
Mostefa, Rass, *Tunisia* 75 A7
Mostiska = Mostyska, *Ukraine* 41 H2
Móstoles, *Spain* 30 E7
Mosty = Masty, *Belarus* 40 F3
Mostyska, *Ukraine* 41 H2
Mosul = Al Mawşil, *Iraq* 67 D10
Mosulpo, *S. Korea* 51 H14
Mota del Cuervo, *Spain* 28 F2
Mota del Marqués, *Spain* 30 D5
Motagua →, *Guatemala* 116 C2
Motala, *Sweden* 11 F9
Motherwell, *U.K.* 14 F5
Motihari, *India* 63 F11
Motilla del Palancar, *Spain* 28 F3
Motnik, *Slovenia* 33 B11
Motocurunya, *Venezuela* 121 C5
Motovun, *Croatia* 33 C10
Motozintla de Mendoza, *Mexico* 115 D6
Motril, *Spain* 29 J1
Motru →, *Romania* 38 E6
Mott, *U.S.A.* 108 B3
Móttola, *Italy* 35 B10
Motueka, *N.Z.* 87 J4
Motueka →, *N.Z.* 87 J4
Motul, *Mexico* 115 C7
Mouanda, *Gabon* 80 E2
Mouchalagane →, *Canada* 99 B6
Mouding, *China* 52 E3
Moudjeria, *Mauritania* 78 B2
Moudon, *Switz.* 22 C3
Mouila, *Gabon* 80 E2
Moulamein, *Australia* 91 F3
Moulianá, *Greece* 37 D7
Moulins, *France* 26 B7
Moulmein, *Burma* 61 L20
Moulouya, O. →, *Morocco* 75 A4
Moulton, *U.S.A.* 109 L6
Moultrie, *U.S.A.* 105 K4
Moultrie, L., *U.S.A.* 105 J5
Mound City, *Mo., U.S.A.* 108 E7
Mound City, *S. Dak., U.S.A.* 108 C4
Moúnda, Ákra, *Greece* 39 L3
Moundou, *Chad* 73 G8
Moundsville, *U.S.A.* 106 G4
Moung, *Cambodia* 58 F4
Mount Airy, *U.S.A.* 105 G5
Mount Albert, *Canada* 106 B5
Mount Amherst, *Australia* 88 C4
Mount Angel, *U.S.A.* 110 D2
Mount Augustus, *Australia* 88 D2
Mount Barker, *S. Austral., Australia* 91 F2
Mount Barker, *W. Austral., Australia* 89 F2
Mount Carmel, *U.S.A.* 104 F2
Mount Clemens, *U.S.A.* 98 D3
Mount Coolon, *Australia* 90 C4
Mount Darwin, *Zimbabwe* 83 F3
Mount Desert I., *U.S.A.* 99 D6
Mount Dora, *U.S.A.* 105 L5
Mount Douglas, *Australia* 90 C4
Mount Eba, *Australia* 91 E2
Mount Edgecumbe, *U.S.A.* 100 B1
Mount Elizabeth, *Australia* 88 C4
Mount Fletcher, *S. Africa* 85 E4
Mount Forest, *Canada* 98 D3
Mount Gambier, *Australia* 91 F3
Mount Garnet, *Australia* 90 B4
Mount Hope, *N.S.W., Australia* 91 E4
Mount Hope, *S. Austral., Australia* 91 E2
Mount Hope, *U.S.A.* 104 G5
Mount Horeb, *U.S.A.* 108 D10
Mount Howitt, *Australia* 91 D3
Mount Isa, *Australia* 90 C2
Mount Keith, *Australia* 89 E3
Mount Laguna, *U.S.A.* 113 N10
Mount Larcom, *Australia* 90 C5
Mount Lofty Ra., *Australia* 91 E2
Mount McKinley National Park, *U.S.A.* 96 B5
Mount Magnet, *Australia* 89 E2
Mount Margaret, *Australia* 91 D3
Mount Maunganui, *N.Z.* 87 G6
Mount Molloy, *Australia* 90 B4
Mount Monger, *Australia* 89 F3
Mount Morgan, *Australia* 90 C5
Mount Morris, *U.S.A.* 106 D7
Mount Mulligan, *Australia* 90 B3
Mount Narryer, *Australia* 89 E2
Mount Olympus = Uludağ, *Turkey* 66 B3
Mount Oxide Mine, *Australia* 90 B2
Mount Pearl, *Canada* 99 C9
Mount Perry, *Australia* 91 D5
Mount Phillips, *Australia* 88 D2
Mount Pleasant, *Iowa, U.S.A.* 108 E9
Mount Pleasant, *Mich., U.S.A.* 104 D3
Mount Pleasant, *Pa., U.S.A.* 106 F5
Mount Pleasant, *S.C., U.S.A.* 105 J6
Mount Pleasant, *Tenn., U.S.A.* 105 H2
Mount Pleasant, *Tex., U.S.A.* 109 J7
Mount Pleasant, *Utah, U.S.A.* 110 G8
Mount Pocono, *U.S.A.* 107 E9
Mount Rainier National Park, *U.S.A.* 112 D5
Mount Revelstoke Nat. Park, *Canada* 100 C5
Mount Robson Prov. Park, *Canada* 100 C5
Mount Sandiman, *Australia* 89 D2
Mount Shasta, *U.S.A.* 110 F2
Mount Signal, *U.S.A.* 113 N11
Mount Sterling, *Ill., U.S.A.* 108 F9
Mount Sterling, *Ky., U.S.A.* 104 F4
Mount Surprise, *Australia* 90 B3

Mount Union, *U.S.A.* 106 F7
Mount Vernon, *Australia* 88 D2
Mount Vernon, *Ind., U.S.A.* 108 F10
Mount Vernon, *N.Y., U.S.A.* 107 F11
Mount Vernon, *Ohio, U.S.A.* 106 F2
Mount Vernon, *Wash., U.S.A.* 112 B4
Mountain Center, *U.S.A.* 113 M10
Mountain City, *Nev., U.S.A.* 110 F6
Mountain City, *Tenn., U.S.A.* 105 G5
Mountain Grove, *U.S.A.* 109 G8
Mountain Home, *Ark., U.S.A.* 109 G8
Mountain Home, *Idaho, U.S.A.* 110 E6
Mountain Iron, *U.S.A.* 108 B8
Mountain Park, *Canada* 100 C5
Mountain Pass, *U.S.A.* 113 K11
Mountain View, *Ark., U.S.A.* 109 H8
Mountain View, *Calif., U.S.A.* 111 H2
Mountainair, *U.S.A.* 111 J10
Mountmellick, *Ireland* 15 C4
Moura, *Australia* 90 C4
Moura, *Brazil* 121 D5
Moura, *Portugal* 31 G3
Mourão, *Portugal* 31 G3
Mourdi, Dépression du, *Chad* 73 E9
Mourdiah, *Mali* 78 C3
Mourenx-Ville-Nouvelle, *France* 26 E3
Mouri, *Ghana* 79 D4
Mourilyan, *Australia* 90 B4
Mourmelon-le-Grand, *France* 25 C11
Mourne →, *U.K.* 15 B4
Mourne Mts., *U.K.* 15 B5
Mournies, *Greece* 37 D6
Mouscron, *Belgium* 17 G2
Moussoro, *Chad* 73 F8
Mouthe, *France* 25 F13
Moutier, *Switz.* 22 B4
Moûtiers, *France* 27 C10
Moutohara, *N.Z.* 87 H6
Moutong, *Indonesia* 57 D6
Mouy, *France* 25 C9
Mouzáki, *Greece* 39 K4
Movas, *Mexico* 114 B3
Moville, *Ireland* 15 A4
Moxhe, *Belgium* 17 G6
Moxotó →, *Brazil* 122 C4
Moy →, *Ireland* 15 B3
Moyale, *Kenya* 68 G2
Moyamba, *S. Leone* 78 D2
Moyen Atlas, *Morocco* 74 B3
Moyle □, *U.K.* 15 A5
Moyo, *Indonesia* 56 F5
Moyobamba, *Peru* 124 B2
Moyyero →, *Russia* 45 C11
Moyynty, *Kazakstan* 44 E8
Mozambique = Moçambique, *Mozam.* 83 F5
Mozambique ■, *Africa* 83 F4
Mozambique Chan., *Africa* 85 B7
Mozdok, *Russia* 43 J7
Mozdūrān, *Iran* 65 B9
Mozhaysk, *Russia* 42 C3
Mozhga, *Russia* 42 B11
Mozhnābād, *Iran* 65 C9
Mozirje, *Slovenia* 33 B11
Mozyr = Mazyr, *Belarus* 41 F5
Mpanda, *Tanzania* 82 D3
Mpanda □, *Tanzania* 82 D3
Mpésoba, *Mali* 78 C3
Mpika, *Zambia* 83 E3
Mpulungu, *Zambia* 83 D3
Mpumalanga, *S. Africa* 85 D5
Mpumalanga □, *S. Africa* 85 B5
Mpwapwa, *Tanzania* 82 D4
Mpwapwa □, *Tanzania* 82 D4
Mqinvartsveri = Kazbek, *Russia* 43 J7
Mrągowo, *Poland* 20 B11
Mramor, *Serbia, Yug.* 21 M11
Mrimina, *Morocco* 74 C3
Mrkonjić Grad, *Bos.-H.* 21 L7
Mrkopalj, *Croatia* 33 C11
Msab, Oued en →, *Algeria* 75 B6
Msaken, *Tunisia* 75 A7
Msambansovu, *Zimbabwe* 83 F3
M'sila, *Algeria* 75 A5
Msoro, *Zambia* 83 E3
Msta →, *Russia* 40 C6
Mstislavl = Mstsislaw, *Belarus* 40 E6
Mstsislaw, *Belarus* 40 E6
Mtama, *Tanzania* 83 E4
Mtilikwe →, *Zimbabwe* 83 G3
Mtsensk, *Russia* 42 D3
Mtskheta, *Georgia* 43 K7
Mtubatuba, *S. Africa* 85 D5
Mtwara-Mikindani, *Tanzania* 83 E5
Mu Gia, Deo, *Vietnam* 58 D5
Mu Us Shamo, *China* 50 E5
Muaná, *Brazil* 122 B2
Muang Chiang Rai, *Thailand* 58 C2
Muang Lamphun, *Thailand* 58 C2
Muang Pak Beng, *Laos* 58 C3
Muar, *Malaysia* 59 L4
Muarabungo, *Indonesia* 56 E2
Muaraenim, *Indonesia* 56 E2
Muarajuloi, *Indonesia* 56 E4
Muarakaman, *Indonesia* 56 E5
Muaratebo, *Indonesia* 56 E2
Muaratembesi, *Indonesia* 56 E2
Muaratewe, *Indonesia* 56 E4
Mubarakpur, *India* 63 F10
Mubarraz = Al Mubarraz, *Si. Arabia* 65 E6
Mubende, *Uganda* 82 B3
Mubi, *Nigeria* 79 C7
Mubur, P., *Indonesia* 59 L6
Mucajaí →, *Brazil* 121 C5
Mucajaí, Serra do, *Brazil* 121 C5
Muchachos, Roque de los, *Canary Is.* 36 F2
Mücheln, *Germany* 18 D7
Muchinga Mts., *Zambia* 83 E3
Muchkapskiy, *Russia* 42 E6
Muck, *U.K.* 14 E2
Muckadilla, *Australia* 91 D4
Muco →, *Colombia* 120 C3
Muconda, *Angola* 80 G4
Mucuim →, *Brazil* 125 B5
Mucur, *Turkey* 66 C6
Mucura, *Brazil* 121 D5
Mucuri, *Brazil* 123 E4
Mucurici, *Brazil* 123 E3
Mucusso, *Angola* 84 B3
Muda, *Canary Is.* 36 F6
Mudan Jiang →, *China* 51 A15
Mudanjiang, *China* 51 B15
Mudanya, *Turkey* 66 B3
Muddy Cr. →, *U.S.A.* 111 H8
Mudgee, *Australia* 91 E4
Mudjatik →, *Canada* 101 B7
Mudurnu, *Turkey* 66 B4
Muecate, *Mozam.* 83 E4
Muêda, *Mozam.* 83 E4
Mueller Ra., *Australia* 88 C4
Muende, *Mozam.* 83 E3
Muerto, Mar, *Mexico* 115 D6
Muertos, Punta de los, *Spain* 29 J3
Mufindi □, *Tanzania* 83 D4
Mufu Shan, *China* 53 C10
Mufulira, *Zambia* 83 E2
Mufumbiro Range, *Africa* 82 C2
Mugardos, *Spain* 30 B2
Muge, *Portugal* 31 F2
Muge →, *Portugal* 31 F2
Múggia, *Italy* 33 C10
Mughayrā', *Si. Arabia* 64 D3
Mugi, *Japan* 49 H7
Mugia, *Spain* 30 B1
Mugila, Mts., *Zaïre* 82 D2
Muğla, *Turkey* 66 D3
Müglizh, *Bulgaria* 38 G8
Mugu, *Nepal* 63 E10
Muhammad, Râs, *Egypt* 76 B3
Muhammad Qol, *Sudan* 76 C4
Muhammadabad, *India* 63 F10
Muhesi →, *Tanzania* 82 D4
Muheza □, *Tanzania* 82 C4
Mühldorf, *Germany* 19 G8
Mühlhausen, *Germany* 18 D6
Mühlig Hofmann fjell, *Antarctica* 5 D3
Muhos, *Finland* 8 D22
Muhu, *Estonia* 9 G20
Muhutwe, *Tanzania* 82 C3
Muiden, *Neths.* 16 D6
Muikamachi, *Japan* 49 F9
Muine Bheag, *Ireland* 15 D5
Muiños, *Spain* 30 D3
Muir, L., *Australia* 89 F2
Mukacheve, *Ukraine* 41 H2
Mukachevo = Mukacheve, *Ukraine* 41 H2
Mukah, *Malaysia* 56 D4
Mukawwa, Geziret, *Egypt* 76 C4
Mukdahan, *Thailand* 58 D5
Mukden = Shenyang, *China* 51 D12
Mukhtolovo, *Russia* 42 C6
Mukhtuya = Lensk, *Russia* 45 C12
Mukinbudin, *Australia* 89 F2
Mukishi, *Zaïre* 83 D1
Mukomuko, *Indonesia* 56 E2
Mukomwenze, *Zaïre* 82 D2
Muktsar, *India* 62 D6
Mukur, *Afghan.* 62 C2
Mukutawa →, *Canada* 101 C9
Mukwela, *Zambia* 83 F2
Mula, *Spain* 29 G3
Mulange, *Zaïre* 82 C2
Mulchén, *Chile* 126 D1
Mulde →, *Germany* 18 D8
Mule Creek, *U.S.A.* 108 D2
Muleba, *Tanzania* 82 C3
Muleba □, *Tanzania* 82 C3
Mulegns, *Switz.* 23 C9
Muleshoe, *U.S.A.* 109 H3
Mulgathing, *Australia* 91 E1
Mulgrave, *Canada* 99 C7
Mulhacén, *Spain* 29 H1
Mülheim, *Germany* 18 D2
Mulhouse, *France* 25 E14
Muli, *China* 52 D3
Muling, *China* 51 B16
Mull, *U.K.* 14 E3
Mullaittvu, *Sri Lanka* 60 Q12
Mullen, *U.S.A.* 108 D4
Mullengudgery, *Australia* 91 E4
Mullens, *U.S.A.* 104 G5
Muller, Pegunungan, *Indonesia* 56 D4
Mullet Pen., *Ireland* 15 B1
Mullewa, *Australia* 89 E2
Müllheim, *Germany* 19 H3
Mulligan →, *Australia* 90 C2
Mullin, *U.S.A.* 109 K5
Mullingar, *Ireland* 15 C4
Mullins, *U.S.A.* 105 H6
Mullumbimby, *Australia* 91 D5
Mulobezi, *Zambia* 83 F2
Multan, *Pakistan* 62 D4
Multrå, *Sweden* 10 A11
Mulumbe, Mts., *Zaïre* 83 D2
Mulungushi Dam, *Zambia* 83 E2
Mulvane, *U.S.A.* 109 G6
Mulwad, *Sudan* 76 D3
Mulwala, *Australia* 91 F4
Mumbaī = Bombay, *India* 60 K8
Mumbwa, *Zambia* 83 E2
Mumra, *Russia* 43 H8
Mun →, *Thailand* 58 E5
Muna, *Indonesia* 57 F6
Munamagi, *Estonia* 9 H22
Münchberg, *Germany* 19 E7
Müncheberg, *Germany* 18 C10
München, *Germany* 19 G7
Munchen-Gladbach = Mönchengladbach, *Germany* 18 D2
Muncho Lake, *Canada* 100 B3
Munchŏn, *N. Korea* 51 E14
Münchwilen, *Switz.* 23 B7
Muncie, *U.S.A.* 104 E3
Muncoonie, L., *Australia* 90 D2
Mundala, *Indonesia* 57 E10
Mundare, *Canada* 100 C6
Munday, *U.S.A.* 109 J5
Münden, *Germany* 18 D5
Mundiwindi, *Australia* 88 D3
Mundo →, *Spain* 29 G2
Mundo Novo, *Brazil* 123 D3
Mundra, *India* 62 H3
Mundrabilla, *Australia* 89 F4
Munducurus, *Brazil* 121 D6
Munera, *Spain* 29 F2
Mungallala, *Australia* 91 D4
Mungallala Cr. →, *Australia* 91 D4
Mungana, *Australia* 90 B3
Mungaoli, *India* 62 G8
Mungari, *Mozam.* 83 F3
Mungbere, *Zaïre* 82 B2
Munger, *India* 63 G12
Mungindi, *Australia* 91 D4
Munhango, *Angola* 81 G3
Munich = München, *Germany* 19 G7
Munising, *U.S.A.* 104 B2
Munka-Ljungby, *Sweden* 11 H6
Munkedal, *Sweden* 11 F5
Munku-Sardyk, *Russia* 45 D11
Münnerstadt, *Germany* 19 E6
Muñoz Gamero, Pen., *Chile* 128 D2
Munroe L., *Canada* 101 B9
Munsan, *S. Korea* 51 F14
Münsingen, *Switz.* 22 C5
Munster, *France* 25 D14
Munster, *Niedersachsen, Germany* 18 C6
Münster, *Nordrhein-Westfalen, Germany* 18 D3
Münster, *Switz.* 23 D6
Munster □, *Ireland* 15 D3
Muntadgin, *Australia* 89 F2
Muntele Mare, *Romania* 38 C6
Muntok, *Indonesia* 56 E3
Munyama, *Zambia* 83 F2
Munzur Dağları, *Turkey* 67 C8
Muong Beng, *Laos* 58 B3
Muong Boum, *Vietnam* 58 A4
Muong Et, *Laos* 58 B5
Muong Hai, *Laos* 58 B3
Muong Hiem, *Laos* 58 B4
Muong Houn, *Laos* 58 B3
Muong Hung, *Vietnam* 58 B4
Muong Kau, *Laos* 58 E5
Muong Khao, *Laos* 58 C4
Muong Khoua, *Laos* 58 B4
Muong Liep, *Laos* 58 C3
Muong May, *Laos* 58 E6
Muong Ngeun, *Laos* 58 B3
Muong Ngoi, *Laos* 58 B4
Muong Nhie, *Vietnam* 58 A4
Muong Nong, *Laos* 58 D6
Muong Ou Tay, *Laos* 58 A3
Muong Oua, *Laos* 58 C3
Muong Peun, *Laos* 58 B4
Muong Phalane, *Laos* 58 D5
Muong Phieng, *Laos* 58 C3
Muong Phine, *Laos* 58 D6
Muong Sai, *Laos* 58 B3
Muong Saiapoun, *Laos* 58 C3
Muong Sen, *Vietnam* 58 C5
Muong Sing, *Laos* 58 B3
Muong Son, *Laos* 58 B4
Muong Soui, *Laos* 58 C4
Muong Va, *Laos* 58 B4
Muong Xia, *Vietnam* 58 B5
Muonio, *Finland* 8 C20
Muonionjoki →, *Finland* 8 C20
Muotathal, *Switz.* 23 C7
Mupa, *Angola* 81 H3
Muping, *China* 51 F11
Muqaddam, Wadi →, *Sudan* 76 D3
Muqdisho, *Somali Rep.* 68 G4
Mur-de-Bretagne, *France* 24 D4
Mura →, *Slovenia* 33 B13
Muradiye, *Turkey* 67 C10
Murakami, *Japan* 48 E9
Murallón, Cuerro, *Chile* 128 C2
Muralto, *Switz.* 23 D7
Muranda, *Rwanda* 82 C2
Murang'a, *Kenya* 82 C4
Murashi, *Russia* 44 D5
Murat, *France* 26 C6
Murat →, *Turkey* 67 C9
Muratlı, *Turkey* 66 B2
Muravera, *Italy* 34 C2
Murayama, *Japan* 48 E10
Murban, *U.A.E.* 65 F7
Murça, *Portugal* 30 D3
Murchison →, *Australia* 89 E1
Murchison, Mt., *Antarctica* 5 D11
Murchison Falls = Kabarega Falls, *Uganda* 82 B3
Murchison House, *Australia* 89 E1
Murchison Ra., *Australia* 90 C1
Murchison Rapids, *Malawi* 83 F3
Murcia, *Spain* 29 G3
Murcia □, *Spain* 29 H3
Murdo, *U.S.A.* 108 D4
Murdoch Pt., *Australia* 90 A3
Mureş →, *Romania* 38 C3
Mureşul = Mureş →, *Romania* 38 C3
Muret, *France* 26 E5
Murfatlar, *Romania* 38 E11
Murfreesboro, *U.S.A.* 105 H2
Murg, *Switz.* 23 B8
Murg →, *Germany* 19 G4
Murgab = Murghob, *Tajikistan* 44 F8
Murgenthal, *Switz.* 22 B5
Murghob, *Tajikistan* 44 F8
Murgon, *Australia* 91 D5
Murgoo, *Australia* 89 E2
Muri, *Switz.* 23 B6
Muria, *Indonesia* 57 G14
Muriaé, *Brazil* 123 F3
Murias de Paredes, *Spain* 30 C4
Murici, *Brazil* 122 C4
Muriel Mine, *Zimbabwe* 83 F3
Müritz-see, *Germany* 18 B8
Murka, *Kenya* 82 C4
Murmansk, *Russia* 44 C4
Murmerwoude, *Neths.* 16 B8
Murnau, *Germany* 19 H7
Muro, *France* 27 F12
Muro, *Spain* 36 B10
Muro, C. de, *France* 27 G12
Muro Lucano, *Italy* 35 B8
Murom, *Russia* 42 C6
Muroran, *Japan* 48 C10
Muros, *Spain* 30 C1
Muros y de Noya, Ría de, *Spain* 30 C2
Muroto, *Japan* 49 H7
Muroto-Misaki, *Japan* 49 H7
Murphy, *U.S.A.* 110 E5
Murphys, *U.S.A.* 112 G6
Murphysboro, *U.S.A.* 109 G10
Murrat, *Sudan* 76 D2
Murray, *Ky., U.S.A.* 105 G1
Murray, *Utah, U.S.A.* 110 F8
Murray →, *Australia* 91 F2
Murray →, *Canada* 100 B4
Murray, L., *U.S.A.* 105 H5
Murray Bridge, *Australia* 91 F2
Murray Downs, *Australia* 90 C1
Murray Harbour, *Canada* 99 C7
Murraysburg, *S. Africa* 84 E3
Murree, *Pakistan* 62 C5
Murrieta, *U.S.A.* 113 M9
Murrin Murrin, *Australia* 89 E3
Murrumbidgee →, *Australia* 91 E3
Murrumburrah, *Australia* 91 E4
Murrurundi, *Australia* 91 E5
Murshid, *Sudan* 76 C3
Murshidabad, *India* 63 G13
Murska Sobota, *Slovenia* 33 B13
Murten, *Switz.* 22 C4
Murtensee, *Switz.* 22 C4
Murtle L., *Canada* 100 C5
Murtoa, *Australia* 91 F3
Murtosa, *Portugal* 30 E2
Muru →, *Brazil* 124 B3
Murungu, *Tanzania* 82 C3
Murwara, *India* 63 H9
Murwillumbah, *Australia* 91 D5
Mürz →, *Austria* 21 H5
Mürzzuschlag, *Austria* 21 H5
Muş, *Turkey* 67 C9
Mûsa, G., *Egypt* 76 J8
Musa Khel, *Pakistan* 62 D3
Mūsá Qal'eh, *Afghan.* 60 C4
Musaffargarh, *Pakistan* 60 D7
Musala, *Bulgaria* 38 G6
Musala, *Indonesia* 56 D1
Musan, *N. Korea* 51 C15
Musangu, *Zaïre* 83 E1
Musasa, *Tanzania* 82 C3
Musay'īd, *Qatar* 65 E6
Muscat = Masqat, *Oman* 68 C6
Muscat & Oman = Oman ■, *Asia* 68 C6
Muscatine, *U.S.A.* 108 E9
Musel, *Spain* 30 B5
Musgrave, *Australia* 90 A3
Musgrave Ras., *Australia* 89 E5
Mushie, *Zaïre* 80 E3
Mushin, *Nigeria* 79 D5
Musi →, *Indonesia* 56 E2
Muskeg →, *Canada* 100 A4
Muskegon, *U.S.A.* 104 D2
Muskegon →, *U.S.A.* 104 D2
Muskegon Heights, *U.S.A.* 104 D2
Muskogee, *U.S.A.* 109 H7
Muskwa →, *Canada* 100 B4
Muslīmiyah, *Syria* 64 B3
Musmar, *Sudan* 76 D4
Musofu, *Zambia* 83 E2
Musoma, *Tanzania* 82 C3
Musoma □, *Tanzania* 82 C3
Musquaro, L., *Canada* 99 B7
Musquodoboit Harbour, *Canada* 99 D7
Musselburgh, *U.K.* 14 F5
Musselkanaal, *Neths.* 16 C10
Musselshell →, *U.S.A.* 110 C10
Mussidan, *France* 26 C4
Mussomeli, *Italy* 34 E6
Musson, *Belgium* 17 J7
Mussoorie, *India* 62 D8
Mussuco, *Angola* 84 B2
Mustafakemalpaşa, *Turkey* 66 B3
Mustang, *Nepal* 63 E10
Musters, L., *Argentina* 128 C3
Musudan, *N. Korea* 51 D15
Muswellbrook, *Australia* 91 E5
Mût, *Egypt* 76 B2
Mut, *Turkey* 66 D5
Mutanda, *Mozam.* 85 C5
Mutanda, *Zambia* 83 E2
Mutare, *Zimbabwe* 83 F3
Muting, *Indonesia* 57 F10
Mutoray, *Russia* 45 C11
Mutshatsha, *Zaïre* 83 E1
Mutsu, *Japan* 48 D10
Mutsu-Wan, *Japan* 48 D10
Muttaburra, *Australia* 90 C3
Mutuáli, *Mozam.* 83 E4
Mutunópolis, *Brazil* 123 D2
Muweilih, *Egypt* 69 E3
Muxima, *Angola* 80 F2
Muy Muy, *Nic.* 116 D2
Muyinga, *Burundi* 82 C3
Muynak, *Uzbekistan* 44 E6
Muzaffarabad, *Pakistan* 63 B5
Muzaffargarh, *Pakistan* 62 D4
Muzaffarnagar, *India* 62 E7
Muzaffarpur, *India* 63 F11
Muzhi, *Russia* 44 C7
Muzillac, *France* 24 E4
Muzon, C., *U.S.A.* 100 C2
Muztag, *China* 54 C3
Mvôlô, *Sudan* 77 F2
Mvuma, *Zimbabwe* 83 F3
Mvurwi, *Zimbabwe* 83 F3
Mwadui, *Tanzania* 82 C3
Mwambo, *Tanzania* 83 E5
Mwandi, *Zambia* 83 F1
Mwanza, *Tanzania* 82 C3
Mwanza, *Zaïre* 82 D2
Mwanza, *Zambia* 83 F1
Mwanza □, *Tanzania* 82 C3
Mwaya, *Tanzania* 83 D3
Mweelrea, *Ireland* 15 C2
Mweka, *Zaïre* 80 E4
Mwenezi, *Zimbabwe* 83 G3
Mwenezi →, *Mozam.* 83 G3
Mwenga, *Zaïre* 82 C2
Mweru, L., *Zambia* 83 D2
Mweza Range, *Zimbabwe* 83 G3
Mwilambwe, *Zaïre* 82 D5
Mwimbi, *Tanzania* 83 D3
Mwinilunga, *Zambia* 83 E1
My Tho, *Vietnam* 59 G6
Mya, O. →, *Algeria* 75 B5
Myajlar, *India* 62 F4
Myanaung, *Burma* 61 K19
Myanmar = Burma ■, *Asia* 61 J20
Myaungmya, *Burma* 61 L19
Myeik Kyunzu, *Burma* 59 G1
Myerstown, *U.S.A.* 107 F8
Myingyan, *Burma* 61 J19
Myitkyina, *Burma* 61 G20
Myjava, *Slovak Rep.* 20 G7
Mykhaylivka, *Ukraine* 41 J8
Mykines, *Færoe Is.* 8 E9
Mykolayiv, *Ukraine* 41 J7
Mymensingh, *Bangla.* 61 G17
Mynydd Du, *U.K.* 13 F4
Mýrdalsjökull, *Iceland* 8 E4
Myrhorod, *Ukraine* 41 H7
Myroodah, *Australia* 88 C3
Myrtle Beach, *U.S.A.* 105 J6
Myrtle Creek, *U.S.A.* 110 E2
Myrtle Point, *U.S.A.* 110 E1
Myrtou, *Cyprus* 37 D12
Mysen, *Norway* 10 E5
Mysia, *Turkey* 66 C2
Myslenice, *Poland* 20 F9
Myślibórz, *Poland* 20 C4
Mysłowice, *Poland* 20 E9
Mysore = Karnataka □, *India* 60 N10
Mysore, *India* 60 N10
Mystic, *U.S.A.* 107 E13
Myszków, *Poland* 20 E9
Mythen, *Switz.* 23 B7
Mytishchi, *Russia* 42 C3
Myton, *U.S.A.* 110 F8
Mývatn, *Iceland* 8 D5
Mzimba, *Malawi* 83 E3
Mzimkulu →, *S. Africa* 85 E5
Mzimvubu →, *S. Africa* 85 E4
Mzuzu, *Malawi* 83 E3

N

N' Dioum, *Senegal* 78 B2
Na Hearadh = Harris, *U.K.* 14 D2
Na Noi, *Thailand* 58 C3
Na Phao, *Laos* 58 D5
Na Sam, *Vietnam* 58 A6
Na San, *Vietnam* 58 B5
Naab →, *Germany* 19 F8
Naaldwijk, *Neths.* 16 E4
Na'am, *Sudan* 77 F2
Naantali, *Finland* 9 F19
Naarden, *Neths.* 16 D6
Naas, *Ireland* 15 C5
Nababiep, *S. Africa* 84 D2
Nabadwip = Navadwip, *India* 63 H13
Nabari, *Japan* 49 G8
Nabawa, *Australia* 89 E1
Nabberu, L., *Australia* 89 E3
Nabburg, *Germany* 19 F8
Naberezhnyye Chelny, *Russia* 42 C11
Nabeul, *Tunisia* 75 A7
Nabha, *India* 62 D7
Nabīd, *Iran* 65 D8
Nabire, *Indonesia* 57 E9
Nabisar, *Pakistan* 62 G3
Nabisipi →, *Canada* 99 B7
Nabiswera, *Uganda* 82 B3
Nablus = Nābulus, *West Bank* 69 C4
Naboomspruit, *S. Africa* 85 C4
Nabua, *Phil.* 55 E5
Nābulus, *West Bank* 69 C4
Nacala, *Mozam.* 83 E5
Nacala-Velha, *Mozam.* 83 E5
Nacaome, *Honduras* 116 D2
Nacaroa, *Mozam.* 83 E4
Naches, *U.S.A.* 110 C3
Naches →, *U.S.A.* 112 D6
Nachingwea, *Tanzania* 83 E4
Nachingwea □, *Tanzania* 83 E4
Nachna, *India* 62 F4
Náchod, *Czech.* 20 E6
Nacimiento Reservoir, *U.S.A.* 112 K6
Nacka, *Sweden* 10 E12
Nackara, *Australia* 91 E2
Naco, *Mexico* 114 A3
Naco, *U.S.A.* 111 L9
Nacogdoches, *U.S.A.* 109 K7
Nácori Chico, *Mexico* 114 B3
Nacozari, *Mexico* 114 A3
Nadi, *Sudan* 76 D3
Nadiad, *India* 62 H5
Nădlac, *Romania* 38 C3
Nador, *Morocco* 75 A4
Nadur, *Malta* 37 C1
Nadūshan, *Iran* 65 C7
Nadvirna, *Ukraine* 41 H3
Nadvornaya = Nadvirna, *Ukraine* 41 H3
Nadym, *Russia* 44 C8
Nadym →, *Russia* 44 C8
Nærbø, *Norway* 9 G11
Næstved, *Denmark* 11 J5
Nafada, *Nigeria* 79 C7
Näfels, *Switz.* 23 B8
Naftshahr, *Iran* 67 E11
Nafud Desert = An Nafūd, *Si. Arabia* 64 D4
Nafūsah, Jabal, *Libya* 75 B7
Nag Hammâdi, *Egypt* 76 B3
Naga, *Phil.* 55 E5
Naga, Kreb en, *Africa* 74 D3
Nagagami →, *Canada* 98 C3
Nagahama, *Japan* 49 G8
Nagai, *Japan* 48 E10
Nagaland □, *India* 61 F19
Nagano, *Japan* 49 F9
Nagano □, *Japan* 49 F9
Nagaoka, *Japan* 49 F9
Nagappattinam, *India* 60 P11
Nagar Parkar, *Pakistan* 62 G4
Nagasaki, *Japan* 49 H4
Nagasaki □, *Japan* 49 H4
Nagato, *Japan* 49 G5
Nagaur, *India* 62 F5
Nagercoil, *India* 60 Q10
Nagina, *India* 63 E8
Nagīneh, *Iran* 65 C8
Nagir, *Pakistan* 63 A6
Nagold, *Germany* 19 G4
Nagold →, *Germany* 19 G4
Nagoorin, *Australia* 90 C5
Nagorno-Karabakh, *Azerbaijan* 67 C12
Nagornyy, *Russia* 45 D13
Nagoya, *Japan* 49 G8
Nagpur, *India* 60 J11
Nagua, *Dom. Rep.* 117 C6
Nagykanizsa, *Hungary* 21 J7
Nagykőrös, *Hungary* 21 H9
Nagyléta, *Hungary* 21 H11
Naha, *Japan* 49 L3
Nahanni Butte, *Canada* 100 A4
Nahanni Nat. Park, *Canada* 100 A3
Nahariyya, *Israel* 66 F6
Nahāvand, *Iran* 67 E13
Nahe →, *Germany* 19 F3
Nahîya, W. →, *Egypt* 76 J7
Nahlin, *Canada* 100 B2
Nahuel Huapi, L., *Argentina* 128 B2
Naicá, *Mexico* 114 B3
Naicam, *Canada* 101 C8
Nā'ifah, *Si. Arabia* 68 D5
Naila, *Germany* 19 E7
Nain, *Canada* 99 A7
Nā'īn, *Iran* 65 C7
Naini Tal, *India* 63 E8
Nainpur, *India* 60 H12
Naintré, *France* 24 F7
Naipu, *Romania* 38 E8
Naira, *Indonesia* 57 E7
Nairn, *U.K.* 14 D5
Nairobi, *Kenya* 82 C4
Naissaar, *Estonia* 9 G21
Naivasha, *Kenya* 82 C4
Naivasha, L., *Kenya* 82 C4
Najac, *France* 26 D5
Najafābād, *Iran* 65 C6
Nájera, *Spain* 28 C2
Najerilla →, *Spain* 28 C2
Najibabad, *India* 62 E8
Najin, *N. Korea* 51 C16
Najmah, *Si. Arabia* 65 E6
Naju, *S. Korea* 51 G14
Nakadōri-Shima, *Japan* 49 H4
Nakalagba, *Zaïre* 82 B2
Nakaminato, *Japan* 49 F10
Nakamura, *Japan* 49 H6
Nakano, *Japan* 49 F9
Nakano-Shima, *Japan* 49 K4
Nakashibetsu, *Japan* 48 C12
Nakfa, *Eritrea* 77 D4
Nakhichevan = Naxçıvan, *Azerbaijan* 67 C11
Nakhichevan Republic □ = Naxçıvan □, *Azerbaijan* 67 C11
Nakhl, *Egypt* 69 F2
Nakhl-e Taqī, *Iran* 65 E7
Nakhodka, *Russia* 45 E14
Nakhon Nayok, *Thailand* 58 E3
Nakhon Pathom, *Thailand* 58 F3
Nakhon Phanom, *Thailand* 58 D5
Nakhon Ratchasima, *Thailand* 58 E4
Nakhon Sawan, *Thailand* 58 E3
Nakhon Si Thammarat, *Thailand* 59 H3
Nakhon Thai, *Thailand* 58 D3
Nakina, *B.C., Canada* 100 B2
Nakina, *Ont., Canada* 98 B2
Nakło nad Noteią, *Poland* 20 B7
Nakodar, *India* 62 D6
Nakskov, *Denmark* 11 K5
Näkten, *Sweden* 10 B8
Naktong →, *S. Korea* 51 G15
Nakuru, *Kenya* 82 C4
Nakuru □, *Kenya* 82 C4
Nakuru, L., *Kenya* 82 C4
Nakusp, *Canada* 100 C5
Nal →, *Pakistan* 62 G1
Nalchik, *Russia* 43 J6
Nälden, *Sweden* 10 A8
Näldsjön, *Sweden* 10 A8
Nalerigu, *Ghana* 79 C4
Nalgonda, *India* 60 L11
Nalhati, *India* 63 G12
Nalinnes, *Belgium* 17 H4
Nallamalai Hills, *India* 60 M11
Nallıhan, *Turkey* 66 B4
Nalón →, *Spain* 30 B4
Nālūt, *Libya* 75 B7
Nam Can, *Vietnam* 59 H5
Nam Co, *China* 54 C4
Nam Dinh, *Vietnam* 58 B6
Nam Du, Hon, *Vietnam* 59 H5
Nam Ngum Dam, *Laos* 58 C4
Nam-Phan, *Vietnam* 59 G6
Nam Phong, *Thailand* 58 D4
Nam Tha, *Laos* 58 B3
Nam Tok, *Thailand* 58 E2
Namacunde, *Angola* 84 B2
Namacurra, *Mozam.* 85 B6
Namak, Daryācheh-ye, *Iran* 65 C7
Namak, Kavir-e, *Iran* 65 C8
Namaland, *Namibia* 84 C2
Namangan, *Uzbekistan* 44 E8
Namapa, *Mozam.* 83 E4
Namaqualand, *S. Africa* 84 D2
Namasagali, *Uganda* 82 B3
Namber, *Indonesia* 57 E8
Nambour, *Australia* 91 D5
Nambucca Heads, *Australia* 91 E5
Namche Bazar, *Nepal* 63 F12
Namchonjŏm, *N. Korea* 51 E14
Namêche, *Belgium* 17 H6
Namecunda, *Mozam.* 83 E4
Nameh, *Indonesia* 56 D5
Nameponda, *Mozam.* 83 F4
Nametil, *Mozam.* 83 F4
Namew L., *Canada* 101 C8
Namib Desert = Namibwoestyn, *Namibia* 84 C2
Namibe, *Angola* 81 H2
Namibe □, *Angola* 84 B1
Namibia ■, *Africa* 84 C2
Namibwoestyn, *Namibia* 84 C2
Namīn, *Iran* 67 C13
Namlea, *Indonesia* 57 E7
Namoi →, *Australia* 91 E4
Namous, O. en →, *Algeria* 75 B4
Nampa, *U.S.A.* 110 E5
Nampō-Shotō, *Japan* 49 J10
Nampula, *Mozam.* 83 F4
Namrole, *Indonesia* 57 E7
Namse Shankou, *China* 61 E13
Namsen →, *Norway* 8 D14
Namsos, *Norway* 8 D14
Namtsy, *Russia* 45 C13
Namtu, *Burma* 61 H20
Namtumbo, *Tanzania* 83 E4
Namu, *Canada* 100 C3
Namur, *Belgium* 17 H5
Namur □, *Belgium* 17 H6
Namutoni, *Namibia* 84 B2
Namwala, *Zambia* 83 F2
Namwŏn, *S. Korea* 51 G14
Namysłów, *Poland* 20 D7
Nan, *Thailand* 58 C3
Nan →, *Thailand* 58 E3
Nan Xian, *China* 53 C9
Nanaimo, *Canada* 100 D4
Nanam, *N. Korea* 51 D15
Nanan, *China* 53 E12
Nanango, *Australia* 91 D5
Nan'ao, *China* 53 F11
Nanao, *Japan* 49 F8
Nanbu, *China* 52 B6
Nanchang, *China* 53 C10
Nancheng, *China* 53 D11
Nanching = Nanjing, *China* 53 A12
Nanchong, *China* 52 B6
Nanchuan, *China* 52 C6
Nancy, *France* 25 D13
Nanda Devi, *India* 63 D8
Nandan, *China* 52 E6
Nandan, *Japan* 49 G7
Nanded, *India* 60 K10
Nandewar Ra., *Australia* 91 E5
Nandi, *Fiji* 87 C7
Nandi □, *Kenya* 82 B4
Nandurbar, *India* 60 J9
Nandyal, *India* 60 M11
Nanfeng, *Guangdong, China* 53 F8
Nanfeng, *Jiangxi, China* 53 D11
Nanga, *Australia* 89 E1
Nanga-Eboko, *Cameroon* 79 E7
Nanga Parbat, *Pakistan* 63 B6
Nangade, *Mozam.* 83 E4
Nangapinoh, *Indonesia* 56 E4
Nangarhár □, *Afghan.* 60 B7
Nangatayap, *Indonesia* 56 E4
Nangeya Mts., *Uganda* 82 B3
Nangis, *France* 25 D10
Nangong, *China* 50 F8
Nanhua, *China* 52 E3
Nanhuang, *China* 51 F11
Nanhui, *China* 53 B13
Nanjeko, *Zambia* 83 F1
Nanji Shan, *China* 53 D13
Nanjian, *China* 52 E3
Nanjiang, *China* 52 A6
Nanjing, *Fujian, China* 53 E11
Nanjing, *Jiangsu, China* 53 A12
Nanjirinji, *Tanzania* 83 D4
Nankana Sahib, *Pakistan* 62 D5
Nankang, *China* 53 E10
Nanking = Nanjing, *China* 53 A12
Nankoku, *Japan* 49 H6
Nanling, *China* 53 B12
Nanning, *China* 52 F7
Nannup, *Australia* 89 F2
Nanpan Jiang →, *China* 52 E6
Nanpara, *India* 63 F9
Nanpi, *China* 50 E9
Nanping, *Fujian, China* 53 D12
Nanping, *Henan, China* 53 C9
Nanri Dao, *China* 53 E12
Nanripe, *Mozam.* 83 E4
Nansei-Shotō = Ryūkyū-rettō, *Japan* 49 M2
Nansen Sd., *Canada* 4 A3
Nansio, *Tanzania* 82 C3
Nant, *France* 26 D7
Nantes, *France* 24 E5
Nanteuil-le-Haudouin, *France* 25 C9
Nantiat, *France* 26 B5
Nanticoke, *U.S.A.* 107 E8
Nanton, *Canada* 100 C6
Nantong, *China* 53 A13
Nantua, *France* 27 B9
Nantucket I., *U.S.A.* 94 E12
Nanuque, *Brazil* 123 E3
Nanusa, Kepulauan, *Indonesia* 57 D7
Nanutarra, *Australia* 88 D2
Nanxiong, *China* 53 E10
Nanyang, *China* 50 H7
Nanyi Hu, *China* 53 B12
Nanyuan, *China* 50 E9
Nanyuki, *Kenya* 82 B4
Nanzhang, *China* 53 B8
Nao, C. de la, *Spain* 29 G5
Naococane L., *Canada* 99 B5
Naoetsu, *Japan* 49 F9
Náousa, *Greece* 39 J5
Naozhou Dao, *China* 53 G8
Napa, *U.S.A.* 112 G4
Napa →, *U.S.A.* 112 G4
Napanee, *Canada* 98 D4
Napanoch, *U.S.A.* 107 E10
Nape, *Laos* 58 C5
Nape Pass = Keo Neua, Deo, *Vietnam* 58 C5
Napf, *Switz.* 22 B5
Napier, *N.Z.* 87 H6
Napier Broome B., *Australia* 88 B4
Napier Downs, *Australia* 88 C3
Napier Pen., *Australia* 90 A2
Naples = Nápoli, *Italy* 35 B7
Naples, *U.S.A.* 105 M5
Napo, *China* 52 F5
Napo □, *Ecuador* 120 D2
Napo →, *Peru* 120 D3
Napoleon, *N. Dak., U.S.A.* 108 B5
Napoleon, *Ohio, U.S.A.* 104 E3
Nápoli, *Italy* 35 B7
Nápoli, G. di, *Italy* 35 B7
Napopo, *Zaïre* 82 B2
Nappa Merrie, *Australia* 91 D3
Naqâda, *Egypt* 76 B3
Naqadeh, *Iran* 67 D11
Naqqāsh, *Iran* 65 C6
Nara, *Japan* 49 G7
Nara, *Mali* 78 B3
Nara □, *Japan* 49 G8
Nara Canal, *Pakistan* 62 G3
Nara Visa, *U.S.A.* 109 H3
Naracoorte, *Australia* 91 F3
Naradhan, *Australia* 91 E4
Narasapur, *India* 61 L12
Narathiwat, *Thailand* 59 J3
Narayanganj, *Bangla.* 61 H17
Narayanpet, *India* 60 L10
Narbonne, *France* 26 E7
Narcea →, *Spain* 30 B4
Nardīn, *Iran* 65 B7
Nardò, *Italy* 35 B11
Narembeen, *Australia* 89 F2
Nares Str., *Arctic* 94 A13
Naretha, *Australia* 89 F3
Narew →, *Poland* 20 C10
Nari →, *Pakistan* 62 E2
Narin, *Afghan.* 60 A6
Narindra, Helodranon' i, *Madag.* 85 A8
Narino □, *Colombia* 120 C2
Narita, *Japan* 49 G10
Narmada →, *India* 62 J5
Narman, *Turkey* 67 B9
Narmland, *Sweden* 9 F15
Narnaul, *India* 62 E7
Narni, *Italy* 33 F9
Naro, *Ghana* 78 C4
Naro, *Italy* 34 E6
Naro Fominsk, *Russia* 42 C3
Narodnaya, *Russia* 46 C9
Narok, *Kenya* 82 C4
Narok □, *Kenya* 82 C4
Narón, *Spain* 30 B2
Narooma, *Australia* 91 F5
Narowal, *Pakistan* 62 C6
Narrabri, *Australia* 91 E4
Narran →, *Australia* 91 D4
Narrandera, *Australia* 91 E4
Narraway →, *Canada* 100 B5
Narrogin, *Australia* 89 F2
Narromine, *Australia* 91 E4
Narsimhapur, *India* 63 H8
Nartkala, *Russia* 43 J6
Naruto, *Japan* 49 G7
Narva, *Estonia* 40 C5
Narva →, *Russia* 9 G22
Narvik, *Norway* 8 B17
Narvskoye Vdkhr., *Russia* 40 C5
Narwana, *India* 62 E7
Naryan-Mar, *Russia* 44 C6
Naryilco, *Australia* 91 D3
Narym, *Russia* 44 D9
Narymskoye, *Kazakstan* 44 E9
Naryn, *Kyrgyzstan* 44 E8
Nasa, *Norway* 8 C16
Nasarawa, *Nigeria* 79 D6
Năsăud, *Romania* 38 B7
Naseby, *N.Z.* 87 L3
Naselle, *U.S.A.* 112 D3
Naser, Buheirat en, *Egypt* 76 C3
Nashua, *Iowa, U.S.A.* 108 D8
Nashua, *Mont., U.S.A.* 110 B10
Nashua, *N.H., U.S.A.* 107 D13
Nashville, *Ark., U.S.A.* 109 J8
Nashville, *Ga., U.S.A.* 105 K4
Nashville, *Tenn., U.S.A.* 105 G2
Našice, *Croatia* 21 K8
Nasielsk, *Poland* 20 C10
Nasik, *India* 60 K8
Nasipit, *Phil.* 55 G6
Nasirabad, *India* 62 F6
Naskaupi →, *Canada* 99 B7
Naso, *Italy* 35 D7
Naşriān-e Pā'īn, *Iran* 64 C5
Nass →, *Canada* 100 B3
Nassau, *Bahamas* 116 A4
Nassau, *U.S.A.* 107 D11
Nassau, B., *Chile* 128 E3
Nasser, L. = Naser, Buheirat en, *Egypt* 76 C3
Nasser City = Kôm Ombo, *Egypt* 76 C3
Nassian, *Ivory C.* 78 D4
Nässjö, *Sweden* 9 H16
Nasugbu, *Phil.* 55 D4
Näsviken, *Sweden* 10 C10
Nat Kyizin, *Burma* 61 M20
Nata, *Botswana* 84 C4
Natagaima, *Colombia* 120 C2
Natal, *Brazil* 122 C4
Natal, *Canada* 100 D6
Natal, *Indonesia* 56 D1
Natalinci, *Serbia, Yug.* 21 L10
Naţanz, *Iran* 65 C6
Natashquan, *Canada* 99 B7
Natashquan →, *Canada* 99 B7
Natchez, *U.S.A.* 109 K9
Natchitoches, *U.S.A.* 109 K8
Naters, *Switz.* 22 D5
Nathalia, *Australia* 91 F4
Nathdwara, *India* 62 G5
Nati, Pta., *Spain* 36 A10
Natimuk, *Australia* 91 F3
Nation →, *Canada* 100 B4
National City, *U.S.A.* 113 N9
Natitingou, *Benin* 79 C5
Natividad, I., *Mexico* 114 B1
Natoma, *U.S.A.* 108 F5
Natron, L., *Tanzania* 82 C4
Natrona Heights, *U.S.A.* 106 F5
Natrûn, W. el →, *Egypt* 76 H7
Natuna Besar, Kepulauan, *Indonesia* 59 L7
Natuna Is. = Natuna Besar, Kepulauan, *Indonesia* 59 L7
Natuna Selatan, Kepulauan, *Indonesia* 59 L7
Natural Bridge, *U.S.A.* 107 B9
Naturaliste, C., *Australia* 90 G4
Nau Qala, *Afghan.* 62 B3
Naubinway, *U.S.A.* 98 C2
Naucelle, *France* 26 D6
Nauders, *Austria* 19 J6
Nauen, *Germany* 18 C8
Naugatuck, *U.S.A.* 107 E11
Naumburg, *Germany* 18 D7
Nā'ūr at Tunayb, *Jordan* 69 D4
Nauru ■, *Pac. Oc.* 92 H8
Naushahra = Nowshera, *Pakistan* 60 B8
Nauta, *Peru* 120 D3
Nautanwa, *India* 61 F13
Nautla, *Mexico* 115 C5
Nava, *Mexico* 114 B4
Nava del Rey, *Spain* 30 D5
Navacerrada, Puerto de, *Spain* 30 E7
Navadwip, *India* 63 H13
Navahermosa, *Spain* 31 F6
Navahrudak, *Belarus* 40 F3
Navajo Reservoir, *U.S.A.* 111 H10
Navalcarnero, *Spain* 30 E6
Navalmoral de la Mata, *Spain* 30 F5
Navalvillar de Pela, *Spain* 31 F5
Navan = An Uaimh, *Ireland* 15 C5
Navapolatsk, *Belarus* 40 E5
Navarino, I., *Chile* 128 E3
Navarra □, *Spain* 28 C3
Navarre, *U.S.A.* 106 F3
Navarrenx, *France* 26 E3
Navarro →, *U.S.A.* 112 F3
Navasota, *U.S.A.* 109 K6
Navassa, *W. Indies* 117 C4
Nave, *Italy* 32 C7
Naver →, *U.K.* 14 C4
Navia, *Spain* 30 B4
Navia →, *Spain* 30 B4
Navia de Suarna, *Spain* 30 C4
Navidad, *Chile* 126 C1
Navlya, *Russia* 42 D2
Navoi = Nawoiy, *Uzbekistan* 44 E7
Navojoa, *Mexico* 114 B3
Navolato, *Mexico* 114 C3
Návpaktos, *Greece* 39 L4
Návplion, *Greece* 39 M5
Navrongo, *Ghana* 79 C4
Navsari, *India* 60 J8
Nawa Kot, *Pakistan* 62 E4
Nawabganj, *Ut. P., India* 63 F9
Nawabganj, *Ut. P., India* 63 E8
Nawabshah, *Pakistan* 62 F3
Nawada, *India* 63 G11
Nawakot, *Nepal* 63 F11
Nawalgarh, *India* 62 F6
Nawanshahr, *India* 63 C6
Nawi, *Sudan* 76 D3
Nawoiy, *Uzbekistan* 44 E7
Naxçıvan, *Azerbaijan* 67 C11
Naxçıvan □, *Azerbaijan* 67 C11
Náxos, *Greece* 39 M8
Nay, *France* 26 E3
Nāy Band, *Iran* 65 E7
Naya →, *Colombia* 120 C2
Nayakhan, *Russia* 45 C16
Nayarit □, *Mexico* 114 C4
Nayé, *Senegal* 78 C2
Nayong, *China* 52 D5
Nayoro, *Japan* 48 B11
Nayyāl, W. →, *Si. Arabia* 64 D3
Nazaré, *Bahia, Brazil* 123 D4
Nazaré, *Pará, Brazil* 125 B7
Nazaré, *Tocantins, Brazil* 122 C2
Nazaré, *Portugal* 31 F1
Nazareth = Nazerat, *Israel* 69 C4
Nazas, *Mexico* 114 B4
Nazas →, *Mexico* 114 B4
Naze, The, *U.K.* 13 F9
Nazerat, *Israel* 69 C4
Nāzīk, *Iran* 67 C11
Nazilli, *Turkey* 66 D3
Nazir Hat, *Bangla.* 61 H17
Nazko, *Canada* 100 C4
Nazko →, *Canada* 100 C4
Nazret, *Ethiopia* 77 F4
Nchanga, *Zambia* 83 E2
Ncheu, *Malawi* 83 E3
Ndala, *Tanzania* 82 C3
Ndalatando, *Angola* 80 F2
Ndali, *Benin* 79 D5
Ndareda, *Tanzania* 82 C4
Ndélé, *C.A.R.* 73 G9
Ndendé, *Gabon* 80 E2
Ndjamena, *Chad* 73 F7
Ndjolé, *Gabon* 80 E2
Ndola, *Zambia* 83 E2

Ndoto Mts., *Kenya* 82 B4
Nduguti, *Tanzania* 82 C3
Nea →, *Norway* 10 A5
Néa Flippiás, *Greece* 39 K3
Neagh, Lough, *U.K.* 15 B5
Neah Bay, *U.S.A.* 112 B2
Neale, L., *Australia* 88 D5
Neápolis, *Kozan, Greece* 39 J4
Neápolis, *Kríti, Greece* 37 D7
Neápolis, *Lakonia, Greece* 39 N6
Near Is., *U.S.A.* 96 C1
Neath, *U.K.* 13 F4
Neath Port Talbot □, *U.K.* 13 F4
Nebbou, *Burkina Faso* 79 C4
Nebine Cr. →, *Australia* 91 D4
Nebitdag, *Turkmenistan* 44 F6
Nebolchy, *Russia* 40 C7
Nebraska □, *U.S.A.* 108 E5
Nebraska City, *U.S.A.* 108 E7
Nébrodi, Monti, *Italy* 35 E7
Necedah, *U.S.A.* 108 C9
Nechako →, *Canada* 100 C4
Neches →, *U.S.A.* 109 L8
Neckar →, *Germany* 19 F4
Necochea, *Argentina* 126 D4
Nedelišće, *Croatia* 33 B13
Neder Rijn →, *Neths.* 16 E8
Nederbrakel, *Belgium* 17 G3
Nederweert, *Neths.* 17 F7
Nédha →, *Greece* 39 M4
Nedroma, *Algeria* 75 A4
Neede, *Neths.* 16 D9
Needles, *U.S.A.* 113 L12
Needles, The, *U.K.* 13 G6
Ñeembucú □, *Paraguay* 126 B4
Neemuch = Nimach, *India* 62 G6
Neenah, *U.S.A.* 104 C1
Neepawa, *Canada* 101 C9
Neer, *Neths.* 17 F7
Neerpelt, *Belgium* 17 F6
Nefta, *Tunisia* 75 B6
Neftah Sidi Boubekeur, *Algeria* 75 A5
Neftçala, *Azerbaijan* 67 C13
Neftegorsk, *Russia* 43 H4
Neftekumsk, *Russia* 43 H7
Neftenbach, *Switz.* 23 A7
Negapatam = Nagappattinam, *India* 60 P11
Negaunee, *U.S.A.* 104 B2
Negele, *Ethiopia* 68 F2
Negev Desert = Hanegev, *Israel* 69 E3
Negombo, *Sri Lanka* 60 R11
Negotin, *Serbia, Yug.* 21 L12
Negra, Peña, *Spain* 30 C4
Negra, Pta., *Mauritania* 74 D1
Negra, Pta., *Peru* 124 B1
Negra Pt., *Phil.* 57 A6
Negrais, C. = Maudin Sun, *Burma* 61 M19
Negreira, *Spain* 30 C2
Négrine, *Algeria* 75 B6
Negro →, *Argentina* 128 B4
Negro →, *Bolivia* 125 C5
Negro →, *Brazil* 121 D6
Negro →, *Uruguay* 127 C4
Negros, *Phil.* 55 G5
Nehalem →, *U.S.A.* 112 E3
Nehāvand, *Iran* 65 C6
Nehbandān, *Iran* 65 D9
Neheim, *Germany* 18 D3
Nehoiaşu, *Romania* 38 D9
Nei Monggol Zizhiqu □, *China* 50 C6
Neidpath, *Canada* 101 C7
Neihart, *U.S.A.* 110 C8
Neijiang, *China* 52 C5
Neilton, *U.S.A.* 110 C2
Neiqiu, *China* 50 F8
Neira de Jusá, *Spain* 30 C3
Neiva, *Colombia* 120 C2
Neixiang, *China* 50 H6
Nejanilini L., *Canada* 101 B9
Nejo, *Ethiopia* 77 F4
Nekā, *Iran* 65 B7
Nekemte, *Ethiopia* 77 F4
Nêkheb, *Egypt* 76 B3
Neksø, *Denmark* 9 J16
Nelas, *Portugal* 30 E3
Nelia, *Australia* 90 C3
Nelidovo, *Russia* 40 D7
Neligh, *U.S.A.* 108 D5
Nelkan, *Russia* 45 D14
Nellore, *India* 60 M11
Nelma, *Russia* 45 E14
Nelson, *Canada* 100 D5
Nelson, *N.Z.* 87 J4
Nelson, *U.K.* 12 D5
Nelson, *U.S.A.* 111 J7
Nelson →, *Canada* 101 C9
Nelson, C., *Australia* 91 F3
Nelson, Estrecho, *Chile* 128 D2
Nelson Forks, *Canada* 100 B4
Nelson House, *Canada* 101 B9
Nelson L., *Canada* 101 B8
Nelspoort, *S. Africa* 84 E3
Nelspruit, *S. Africa* 85 D5
Néma, *Mauritania* 78 B3
Neman, *Russia* 9 J20
Neman →, *Lithuania* 9 J19
Nemeiben L., *Canada* 101 B7
Nemira, *Romania* 38 C9
Nemours, *France* 25 D9
Nemunas = Neman →, *Lithuania* 9 J19
Nemuro, *Japan* 48 C12
Nemuro-Kaikyō, *Japan* 48 C12
Nemuy, *Russia* 45 D14
Nen Jiang →, *China* 51 B13
Nenagh, *Ireland* 15 D3
Nenana, *U.S.A.* 96 B5
Nenasi, *Malaysia* 59 L4
Nene →, *U.K.* 12 E8
Nenjiang, *China* 54 B7
Neno, *Malawi* 83 F3
Neodesha, *U.S.A.* 109 G7
Neópolis, *Brazil* 122 D4
Neosho, *U.S.A.* 109 G7
Neosho →, *U.S.A.* 109 H7
Nepal ■, *Asia* 63 F11
Nepalganj, *Nepal* 63 E9
Nephi, *U.S.A.* 110 G8
Nephin, *Ireland* 15 B2
Neptune, *U.S.A.* 107 F10
Néra →, *Romania* 38 E4
Nérac, *France* 26 D4
Nerchinsk, *Russia* 45 D12
Nerchinskiy Zavod, *Russia* 45 D12
Nereju, *Romania* 38 D9
Nerekhta, *Russia* 42 B5
Néret L., *Canada* 99 B5
Neringa, *Lithuania* 9 J19
Nerja, *Spain* 31 J7
Nerl →, *Russia* 42 B5
Nerpio, *Spain* 29 G2
Nerva, *Spain* 31 H4
Nes, *Neths.* 16 B7
Nesbyen, *Norway* 10 D3
Nesebūr, *Bulgaria* 38 G10
Nesland, *Norway* 10 E1
Neslandsvatn, *Norway* 10 F3
Nesle, *France* 25 C9
Nesodden, *Norway* 10 E4
Nesque →, *France* 27 E8
Ness, L., *U.K.* 14 D4
Nesslau, *Switz.* 23 B8
Nesterov, *Ukraine* 41 G2
Néstos →, *Greece* 39 H7
Nesvizh = Nyasvizh, *Belarus* 41 F4
Netanya, *Israel* 69 C3
Nète →, *Belgium* 17 F4
Netherdale, *Australia* 90 C4
Netherlands ■, *Europe* 16 E6
Netherlands Antilles ■, *W. Indies* 120 A4
Neto →, *Italy* 35 C10
Nettancourt, *France* 25 D11
Nettilling L., *Canada* 97 B12
Nettuno, *Italy* 34 A5
Netzahualcoyotl, Presa, *Mexico* 115 D6
Neu-Isenburg, *Germany* 19 E4
Neu-Ulm, *Germany* 19 G6
Neubrandenburg, *Germany* 18 B9
Neubukow, *Germany* 18 A7
Neuburg, *Germany* 19 G7
Neuchâtel, *Switz.* 22 C3
Neuchâtel □, *Switz.* 22 C3
Neuchâtel, Lac de, *Switz.* 22 C3
Neudau, *Austria* 21 H6
Neuenegg, *Switz.* 22 C4
Neuenhaus, *Germany* 18 C2
Neuf-Brisach, *France* 25 D14
Neufahrn, *Germany* 19 G8
Neufchâteau, *Belgium* 17 J6
Neufchâteau, *France* 25 D12
Neufchâtel-en-Bray, *France* 24 C8
Neufchâtel-sur-Aisne, *France* 25 C11
Neuhaus, *Germany* 18 B6
Neuhausen, *Switz.* 23 A7
Neuillé-Pont-Pierre, *France* 24 E7
Neuilly-St.-Front, *France* 25 C10
Neukalen, *Germany* 18 B8
Neumarkt, *Germany* 19 F7
Neumarkt-Sankt Veit, *Germany* 19 G8
Neumünster, *Germany* 18 A5
Neung-sur-Beuvron, *France* 25 E8
Neunkirchen, *Austria* 21 H6
Neunkirchen, *Germany* 19 F3
Neuquén, *Argentina* 128 A3
Neuquén □, *Argentina* 126 D2
Neuquén →, *Argentina* 128 A3
Neuruppin, *Germany* 18 C8
Neuse →, *U.S.A.* 105 H7
Neusiedler See, *Austria* 21 H6
Neuss, *Germany* 17 F9
Neussargues-Moissac, *France* 26 C7
Neustadt, *Baden-W., Germany* 19 H4
Neustadt, *Bayern, Germany* 19 F8
Neustadt, *Bayern, Germany* 19 G7
Neustadt, *Bayern, Germany* 19 F6
Neustadt, *Bayern, Germany* 19 E7
Neustadt, *Brandenburg, Germany* 18 C8
Neustadt, *Hessen, Germany* 18 E5
Neustadt, *Niedersachsen, Germany* 18 C5
Neustadt, *Rhld-Pfz., Germany* 19 F4
Neustadt, *Schleswig-Holstein, Germany* 18 A6
Neustadt, *Thüringen, Germany* 18 E7
Neustrelitz, *Germany* 18 B9
Neuvic, *France* 26 C6
Neuville, *Belgium* 17 H5
Neuville-aux-Bois, *France* 25 D9
Neuville-de-Poitou, *France* 26 B4
Neuville-sur-Saône, *France* 27 C8
Neuvy-le-Roi, *France* 24 E7
Neuvy-St.-Sépulchre, *France* 26 B5
Neuvy-sur-Barangeon, *France* 25 E9
Neuwerk, *Germany* 18 B4
Neuwied, *Germany* 18 E3
Neva →, *Russia* 40 C6
Nevada, *U.S.A.* 109 G7
Nevada □, *U.S.A.* 110 G5
Nevada, Sierra, *Spain* 29 H1
Nevada, Sierra, *U.S.A.* 110 G3
Nevada City, *U.S.A.* 112 F6
Nevado, Cerro, *Argentina* 126 D2
Nevanka, *Russia* 45 D10
Nevel, *Russia* 40 D5
Nevele, *Belgium* 17 F3
Nevers, *France* 25 F10
Nevertire, *Australia* 91 E4
Neville, *Canada* 101 D7
Nevinnomyssk, *Russia* 43 H6
Nevis, *W. Indies* 117 C7
Nevrokop = Gotse Delchev, *Bulgaria* 39 H6
Nevşehir, *Turkey* 66 C6
New →, *Guyana* 121 C6
New Albany, *Ind., U.S.A.* 104 F3
New Albany, *Miss., U.S.A.* 109 H10
New Albany, *Pa., U.S.A.* 107 E8
New Amsterdam, *Guyana* 121 B6
New Angledool, *Australia* 91 D4
New Bedford, *U.S.A.* 107 E14
New Bern, *U.S.A.* 105 H7
New Bethlehem, *U.S.A.* 106 E5
New Bloomfield, *U.S.A.* 106 F7
New Boston, *U.S.A.* 109 J7
New Braunfels, *U.S.A.* 109 L5
New Brighton, *N.Z.* 87 K4
New Brighton, *U.S.A.* 106 F4
New Britain, *Papua N. G.* 92 H7
New Britain, *U.S.A.* 107 E12
New Brunswick, *U.S.A.* 107 F10
New Brunswick □, *Canada* 99 C6
New Bussa, *Nigeria* 79 D5
New Caledonia ■, *Pac. Oc.* 92 K8
New Castle, *Ind., U.S.A.* 104 F3
New Castle, *Pa., U.S.A.* 106 E4
New City, *U.S.A.* 107 E11
New Cumberland, *U.S.A.* 106 F4
New Cuyama, *U.S.A.* 113 L7
New Delhi, *India* 62 E7
New Denver, *Canada* 100 D5
New Don Pedro Reservoir, *U.S.A.* 112 H6
New England, *U.S.A.* 108 B3
New England Ra., *Australia* 91 E5
New Forest, *U.K.* 13 G6
New Glasgow, *Canada* 99 C7
New Guinea, *Oceania* 46 K17
New Hamburg, *Canada* 106 C4
New Hampshire □, *U.S.A.* 107 C13
New Hampton, *U.S.A.* 108 D8
New Hanover, *S. Africa* 85 D5
New Haven, *Conn., U.S.A.* 107 E12
New Haven, *Mich., U.S.A.* 106 D2
New Hazelton, *Canada* 100 B3
New Hebrides = Vanuatu ■, *Pac. Oc.* 92 J8
New Iberia, *U.S.A.* 109 K9
New Ireland, *Papua N. G.* 92 H7
New Jersey □, *U.S.A.* 107 F10
New Kensington, *U.S.A.* 106 F5
New Lexington, *U.S.A.* 104 F4
New Liskeard, *Canada* 98 C4
New London, *Conn., U.S.A.* 107 E12
New London, *Minn., U.S.A.* 108 C7
New London, *Ohio, U.S.A.* 106 E2
New London, *Wis., U.S.A.* 108 C10
New Madrid, *U.S.A.* 109 G10
New Meadows, *U.S.A.* 110 D5
New Melones L., *U.S.A.* 112 H6
New Mexico □, *U.S.A.* 111 J10
New Milford, *Conn., U.S.A.* 107 E11
New Milford, *Pa., U.S.A.* 107 E9
New Norcia, *Australia* 89 F2
New Norfolk, *Australia* 90 G4
New Orleans, *U.S.A.* 109 K9
New Philadelphia, *U.S.A.* 106 F3
New Plymouth, *N.Z.* 87 H5
New Plymouth, *U.S.A.* 110 E5
New Providence, *Bahamas* 116 A4
New Radnor, *U.K.* 13 E4
New Richmond, *U.S.A.* 108 C8
New Roads, *U.S.A.* 109 K9
New Rochelle, *U.S.A.* 107 F11
New Rockford, *U.S.A.* 108 B5
New Ross, *Ireland* 15 D5
New Salem, *U.S.A.* 108 B4
New Scone, *U.K.* 14 E5
New Siberian Is. = Novaya Sibir, Ostrov, *Russia* 45 B16
New Siberian Is. = Novosibirskiye Ostrova, *Russia* 45 B15
New Smyrna Beach, *U.S.A.* 105 L5
New South Wales □, *Australia* 91 E4
New Springs, *Australia* 89 E3
New Town, *U.S.A.* 108 A3
New Ulm, *U.S.A.* 108 C7
New Waterford, *Canada* 99 C7
New Westminster, *Canada* 100 D4
New York □, *U.S.A.* 107 D9
New York City, *U.S.A.* 107 F11
New Zealand ■, *Oceania* 87 J5
Newala, *Tanzania* 83 E4
Newala □, *Tanzania* 83 E4
Newark, *Del., U.S.A.* 104 F8
Newark, *N.J., U.S.A.* 107 F10
Newark, *N.Y., U.S.A.* 106 C7
Newark, *Ohio, U.S.A.* 106 F2
Newark-on-Trent, *U.K.* 12 D7
Newaygo, *U.S.A.* 104 D3
Newberg, *U.S.A.* 110 D2
Newberry, *Mich., U.S.A.* 104 B3
Newberry, *S.C., U.S.A.* 105 H5
Newberry Springs, *U.S.A.* 113 L10
Newbridge = Droichead Nua, *Ireland* 15 C5
Newbrook, *Canada* 100 C6
Newburgh, *U.S.A.* 107 E10
Newbury, *U.K.* 13 F6
Newbury, *U.S.A.* 107 B12
Newburyport, *U.S.A.* 107 D14
Newcastle, *Australia* 91 E5
Newcastle, *Canada* 99 C6
Newcastle, *S. Africa* 85 D4
Newcastle, *U.K.* 15 B6
Newcastle, *Calif., U.S.A.* 112 G5
Newcastle, *Wyo., U.S.A.* 108 D2
Newcastle Emlyn, *U.K.* 13 E3
Newcastle Ra., *Australia* 88 C5
Newcastle-under-Lyme, *U.K.* 12 D5
Newcastle-upon-Tyne, *U.K.* 12 C6
Newcastle Waters, *Australia* 90 B1
Newdegate, *Australia* 89 F2
Newell, *U.S.A.* 108 C3
Newfoundland □, *Canada* 99 B8
Newfoundland I., *N. Amer.* 94 E14
Newhalem, *U.S.A.* 100 D4
Newhall, *U.S.A.* 113 L8
Newham, *U.K.* 13 F8
Newhaven, *U.K.* 13 G8
Newkirk, *U.S.A.* 109 G6
Newman, *Australia* 88 D2
Newman, *U.S.A.* 112 H5
Newmarket, *Canada* 106 B5
Newmarket, *Ireland* 15 D3
Newmarket, *U.K.* 13 E8
Newmarket, *U.S.A.* 107 C14
Newnan, *U.S.A.* 105 J3
Newport, *I. of W., U.K.* 13 G6
Newport, *Newp., U.K.* 13 F5
Newport, *Ark., U.S.A.* 109 H9
Newport, *Ky., U.S.A.* 104 F3
Newport, *N.H., U.S.A.* 107 C12
Newport, *Oreg., U.S.A.* 110 D1
Newport, *Pa., U.S.A.* 106 F7
Newport, *R.I., U.S.A.* 107 E13
Newport, *Tenn., U.S.A.* 105 H4
Newport, *Vt., U.S.A.* 107 B12
Newport, *Wash., U.S.A.* 110 B5
Newport □, *U.K.* 13 F4
Newport Beach, *U.S.A.* 113 M9
Newport News, *U.S.A.* 104 G7
Newquay, *U.K.* 13 G2
Newry, *U.K.* 15 B5
Newry & Mourne □, *U.K.* 15 B5
Newton, *Iowa, U.S.A.* 108 E8
Newton, *Mass., U.S.A.* 107 D13
Newton, *Miss., U.S.A.* 109 J10
Newton, *N.C., U.S.A.* 105 H5
Newton, *N.J., U.S.A.* 107 E10
Newton, *Tex., U.S.A.* 109 K8
Newton Abbot, *U.K.* 13 G4
Newton Boyd, *Australia* 91 D5
Newton Stewart, *U.K.* 14 G4
Newtonmore, *U.K.* 14 D4
Newtown, *U.K.* 13 E4
Newtownabbey □, *U.K.* 15 B6
Newtownards, *U.K.* 15 B6
Newville, *U.S.A.* 106 F7
Nexon, *France* 26 C5
Neya, *Russia* 42 A6
Neyrīz, *Iran* 65 D7
Neyshābūr, *Iran* 65 B8
Nezhin = Nizhyn, *Ukraine* 41 G6
Nezperce, *U.S.A.* 110 C5
Ngabang, *Indonesia* 56 D3
Ngabordamlu, Tanjung, *Indonesia* 57 F8
Ngambé, *Cameroon* 79 D7
Ngami Depression, *Botswana* 84 C3
Ngamo, *Zimbabwe* 83 F2
Nganglong Kangri, *China* 61 C12
Nganjuk, *Indonesia* 57 G14
Ngao, *Thailand* 58 C2
Ngaoundéré, *Cameroon* 80 C2
Ngapara, *N.Z.* 87 L3
Ngara, *Tanzania* 82 C3
Ngara □, *Tanzania* 82 C3
Ngawi, *Indonesia* 57 G14
Nghia Lo, *Vietnam* 58 B5
Ngoma, *Malawi* 83 E3
Ngomahura, *Zimbabwe* 83 G3
Ngomba, *Tanzania* 83 D3
Ngop, *Sudan* 77 F3
Ngoring Hu, *China* 54 C4
Ngorkou, *Mali* 78 B4
Ngorongoro, *Tanzania* 82 C4
Ngozi, *Burundi* 82 C2
Ngudu, *Tanzania* 82 C3
Nguigmi, *Niger* 73 F7
Ngukurr, *Australia* 90 A1
Ngunga, *Tanzania* 82 C3
Nguru, *Nigeria* 79 C7
Nguru Mts., *Tanzania* 82 D4
Nguyen Binh, *Vietnam* 58 A5
Nha Trang, *Vietnam* 59 F7
Nhacoongo, *Mozam.* 85 C6
Nhamaabué, *Mozam.* 83 F4
Nhambiquara, *Brazil* 125 C6
Nhamundá, *Brazil* 121 D6
Nhamundá →, *Brazil* 121 D6
Nhangutazi, L., *Mozam.* 85 C5
Nhecolândia, *Brazil* 125 D6
Nhill, *Australia* 91 F3
Nho Quan, *Vietnam* 58 B5
Nhulunbuy, *Australia* 90 A2
Nia-nia, *Zaïre* 82 B2
Niafounké, *Mali* 78 B4
Niagara, *U.S.A.* 104 C1
Niagara Falls, *Canada* 98 D4
Niagara Falls, *U.S.A.* 106 C6
Niagara-on-the-Lake, *Canada* 106 C5
Niah, *Malaysia* 56 D4
Niamey, *Niger* 79 C5
Nianforando, *Guinea* 78 D2
Nianfors, *Sweden* 10 C10
Niangara, *Zaïre* 82 B2
Nias, *Indonesia* 56 D1
Niassa □, *Mozam.* 83 E4
Nibbiano, *Italy* 32 D6
Nibe, *Denmark* 11 H3
Nicaragua ■, *Cent. Amer.* 116 D2
Nicaragua, L. de, *Nic.* 116 D2
Nicastro, *Italy* 35 D9
Nice, *France* 27 E11
Niceville, *U.S.A.* 105 K2
Nichinan, *Japan* 49 J5
Nicholás, Canal, *W. Indies* 116 B3
Nicholasville, *U.S.A.* 104 G3
Nichols, *U.S.A.* 107 D8
Nicholson, *Australia* 88 C4
Nicholson, *U.S.A.* 107 E9
Nicholson →, *Australia* 90 B2
Nicholson Ra., *Australia* 89 E2
Nickerie □, *Surinam* 121 C6
Nickerie →, *Surinam* 121 B6
Nicobar Is., *Ind. Oc.* 46 J13
Nicoclí, *Colombia* 120 B2
Nicola, *Canada* 100 C4
Nicolet, *Canada* 98 C5
Nicolls Town, *Bahamas* 116 A4
Nicosia, *Cyprus* 66 E5
Nicosia, *Italy* 35 E7
Nicótera, *Italy* 35 D8
Nicoya, *Costa Rica* 116 D2
Nicoya, G. de, *Costa Rica* 116 E3
Nicoya, Pen. de, *Costa Rica* 116 E2
Nidau, *Switz.* 22 B4
Nidd →, *U.K.* 12 C6
Nidda, *Germany* 18 E5
Nidda →, *Germany* 19 E4
Nidwalden □, *Switz.* 23 C6
Nidzica, *Poland* 20 B10
Niebüll, *Germany* 18 A4
Nied →, *Germany* 25 C13
Niederaula, *Germany* 18 E5
Niederbipp, *Switz.* 22 B5
Niederbronn-les-Bains, *France* 25 D14
Niedere Tauern, *Austria* 21 H4
Niedersachsen □, *Germany* 18 C5
Niekerkshoop, *S. Africa* 84 D3
Niel, *Belgium* 17 F4
Niellé, *Ivory C.* 78 C3
Niemba, *Zaïre* 82 D2
Niemen = Neman →, *Lithuania* 9 J19
Nienburg, *Germany* 18 C5
Niers →, *Germany* 18 D2
Niesen, *Switz.* 22 C5
Niesky, *Germany* 18 D10
Nieu Bethesda, *S. Africa* 84 E3
Nieuw-Amsterdam, *Neths.* 16 C9
Nieuw Amsterdam, *Surinam* 121 B6
Nieuw Beijerland, *Neths.* 16 E4
Nieuw-Dordrecht, *Neths.* 16 C9
Nieuw Loosdrecht, *Neths.* 16 D6
Nieuw Nickerie, *Surinam* 121 B6
Nieuw-Schoonebeek, *Neths.* 16 C10
Nieuw-Vennep, *Neths.* 16 D5
Nieuw-Vossemeer, *Neths.* 17 E4
Nieuwe-Niedorp, *Neths.* 16 C5
Nieuwe-Pekela, *Neths.* 16 B9
Nieuwe-Schans, *Neths.* 16 B10
Nieuwendijk, *Neths.* 16 E5
Nieuwerkerken, *Belgium* 17 G6
Nieuwkoop, *Neths.* 16 D5
Nieuwleusen, *Neths.* 16 C8
Nieuwnamen, *Neths.* 17 F4
Nieuwolda, *Neths.* 16 B9
Nieuwoudtville, *S. Africa* 84 E2
Nieuwpoort, *Belgium* 17 F1
Nieuwveen, *Neths.* 16 D5
Nieves, *Spain* 30 C2
Nieves, Pico de las, *Canary Is.* 36 G4
Nièvre □, *France* 25 E10
Niğde, *Turkey* 66 D6
Nigel, *S. Africa* 85 D4
Niger □, *Nigeria* 79 C6
Niger ■, *W. Afr.* 79 B6
Niger →, *W. Afr.* 79 D6
Nigeria ■, *W. Afr.* 79 D6
Nightcaps, *N.Z.* 87 L2
Nigríta, *Greece* 39 J6
Nihtaur, *India* 63 E8
Nii-Jima, *Japan* 49 G9
Niigata, *Japan* 48 F9

Niigata □, *Japan* 49 F9
Niihama, *Japan* 49 H6
Niihau, *U.S.A.* 102 H14
Niimi, *Japan* 49 G6
Niitsu, *Japan* 48 F9
Níjar, *Spain* 29 J2
Nijil, *Jordan* 69 E4
Nijkerk, *Neths.* 16 D7
Nijlen, *Belgium* 17 F5
Nijmegen, *Neths.* 16 E7
Nijverdal, *Neths.* 16 D8
Nīk Pey, *Iran* 67 D13
Nike, *Nigeria* 79 D6
Nikiniki, *Indonesia* 57 F6
Nikki, *Benin* 79 D5
Nikkō, *Japan* 49 F9
Nikolayev = Mykolayiv, *Ukraine* 41 J7
Nikolayevsk, *Russia* 42 E7
Nikolayevsk-na-Amur, *Russia* 45 D15
Nikolsk, *Russia* 42 D8
Nikolskoye, *Russia* 45 D17
Nikopol, *Bulgaria* 38 F7
Nikopol, *Ukraine* 41 J8
Niksar, *Turkey* 66 B7
Nīkshahr, *Iran* 65 E9
Nikšić, *Montenegro, Yug.* 21 N8
Nîl, Nahr en →, *Africa* 76 H7
Nîl el Abyad →, *Sudan* 77 D3
Nîl el Azraq →, *Sudan* 77 D3
Niland, *U.S.A.* 113 M11
Nile = Nîl, Nahr en →, *Africa* 76 H7
Nile Delta, *Egypt* 76 H7
Niles, *U.S.A.* 106 E4
Nilo Peçanha, *Brazil* 123 D4
Nimach, *India* 62 G6
Nimbahera, *India* 62 G6
Nîmes, *France* 27 E8
Nimfaíon, Ákra = Pínnes, Ákra, *Greece* 39 J7
Nimmitabel, *Australia* 91 F4
Nimule, *Sudan* 77 G3
Nin, *Croatia* 33 D12
Nīnawá, *Iraq* 67 D10
Nindigully, *Australia* 91 D4
Ninemile, *U.S.A.* 100 B2
Nineveh = Nīnawá, *Iraq* 67 D10
Ning Xian, *China* 50 G4
Ningaloo, *Australia* 88 D1
Ning'an, *China* 51 B15
Ningbo, *China* 53 C13
Ningcheng, *China* 51 D10
Ningde, *China* 53 D12
Ningdu, *China* 53 D10
Ninggang, *China* 53 D9
Ningguo, *China* 53 B12
Ninghai, *China* 53 C13
Ninghua, *China* 53 D11
Ningjin, *China* 50 F8
Ningjing Shan, *China* 52 B2
Ninglang, *China* 52 D3
Ningling, *China* 50 G8
Ningming, *China* 52 F6
Ningnan, *China* 52 D4
Ningpo = Ningbo, *China* 53 C13
Ningqiang, *China* 50 H4
Ningshan, *China* 50 H5
Ningsia Hui A.R. = Ningxia Huizu Zizhiqu □, *China* 50 E3
Ningwu, *China* 50 E7
Ningxia Huizu Zizhiqu □, *China* 50 E3
Ningxiang, *China* 53 C9
Ningyang, *China* 50 G9
Ningyuan, *China* 53 E8
Ninh Binh, *Vietnam* 58 B5
Ninh Giang, *Vietnam* 58 B6
Ninh Hoa, *Vietnam* 58 F7
Ninh Ma, *Vietnam* 58 F7
Ninove, *Belgium* 17 G4
Nioaque, *Brazil* 127 A4
Niobrara, *U.S.A.* 108 D6
Niobrara →, *U.S.A.* 108 D6
Niono, *Mali* 78 C3
Nioro du Rip, *Senegal* 78 C1
Nioro du Sahel, *Mali* 78 B3
Niort, *France* 26 B3
Nipawin, *Canada* 101 C8
Nipawin Prov. Park, *Canada* 101 C8
Nipigon, *Canada* 98 C2
Nipigon, L., *Canada* 98 C2
Nipin →, *Canada* 101 B7
Nipishish L., *Canada* 99 B7
Nipissing L., *Canada* 98 C4
Nipomo, *U.S.A.* 113 K6
Nipton, *U.S.A.* 113 K11
Niquelândia, *Brazil* 123 D2
Nīr, *Iran* 67 C12
Nirasaki, *Japan* 49 G9
Nirmal, *India* 60 K11
Nirmali, *India* 63 F12
Niš, *Serbia, Yug.* 21 M11
Nisa, *Portugal* 31 F3
Nişāb, *Si. Arabia* 64 D5
Nişāb, *Yemen* 68 E4
Nišava →, *Serbia, Yug.* 21 M11
Niscemi, *Italy* 35 E7
Nishinomiya, *Japan* 49 G7
Nishin'omote, *Japan* 49 J5
Nishiwaki, *Japan* 49 G7
Nísíros, *Greece* 39 N10
Niskibi →, *Canada* 98 A2
Nispen, *Neths.* 17 F4
Nisqually →, *U.S.A.* 112 C4
Nissáki, *Greece* 37 A3
Nissan →, *Sweden* 11 H6
Nissedal, *Norway* 10 E2
Nisser, *Norway* 10 E2
Nissum Bredning, *Denmark* 9 H13
Nissum Fjord, *Denmark* 11 H2
Nistelrode, *Neths.* 17 E7
Nistru = Dnister →, *Europe* 41 J6
Nisutlin →, *Canada* 100 A2
Nitchequon, *Canada* 99 B5
Niterói, *Brazil* 123 F3
Nith →, *U.K.* 14 F5
Nitra, *Slovak Rep.* 21 G8
Nittedal, *Norway* 10 D4
Nittenau, *Germany* 19 F8
Niuafo'ou, *Tonga* 87 B11
Niue, *Cook Is.* 93 J11
Niulan Jiang →, *China* 52 D4
Niut, *Indonesia* 56 D4
Niutou Shan, *China* 53 C13
Niuzhuang, *China* 51 D12
Nivala, *Finland* 8 E21
Nivelles, *Belgium* 17 G4
Nivernais, *France* 25 E10
Nixon, *U.S.A.* 109 L6
Nizamabad, *India* 60 K11
Nizamghat, *India* 61 E19
Nizhne Kolymsk, *Russia* 45 C17
Nizhne-Vartovsk, *Russia* 44 C8
Nizhneangarsk, *Russia* 45 D11
Nizhnegorskiy = Nyzhnohirskyy, *Ukraine* 41 K8
Nizhnekamsk, *Russia* 42 C10
Nizhneudinsk, *Russia* 45 D10
Nizhneyansk, *Russia* 45 B14
Nizhniy Chir, *Russia* 43 F6
Nizhniy Lomov, *Russia* 42 D6
Nizhniy Novgorod, *Russia* 42 B7
Nizhniy Tagil, *Russia* 44 D6
Nizhyn, *Ukraine* 41 G6
Nizip, *Turkey* 66 D7
Nízké Tatry, *Slovak Rep.* 20 G9
Nizza Monferrato, *Italy* 32 D5
Njakwa, *Malawi* 83 E3
Njanji, *Zambia* 83 E3
Njinjo, *Tanzania* 83 D4
Njombe, *Tanzania* 83 D3
Njombe □, *Tanzania* 83 D3
Njombe →, *Tanzania* 82 D4
Nkambe, *Cameroon* 79 D7
Nkana, *Zambia* 83 E2
Nkawkaw, *Ghana* 79 D4
Nkayi, *Zimbabwe* 83 F2
Nkhata Bay, *Malawi* 80 G6
Nkhota Kota, *Malawi* 83 E3
Nkongsamba, *Cameroon* 79 E6
Nkurenkuru, *Namibia* 84 B2
Nkwanta, *Ghana* 78 D4
Nmai →, *Burma* 61 G20
Noakhali = Maijdi, *Bangla.* 61 H17
Noatak, *U.S.A.* 96 B3
Nobel, *Canada* 106 A4
Nobeoka, *Japan* 49 H5
Noblejas, *Spain* 28 F1
Noblesville, *U.S.A.* 104 E3
Noce →, *Italy* 32 B8
Nocera Inferiore, *Italy* 35 B7
Nocera Terinese, *Italy* 35 C9
Nocera Umbra, *Italy* 33 E9
Noci, *Italy* 35 B10
Nockatunga, *Australia* 91 D3
Nocona, *U.S.A.* 109 J6
Noda, *Japan* 49 G9
Noel, *U.S.A.* 109 G7
Nogales, *Mexico* 114 A2
Nogales, *U.S.A.* 111 L8
Nōgata, *Japan* 49 H5
Nogent-en-Bassigny, *France* 25 D12
Nogent-le-Rotrou, *France* 24 D7
Nogent-sur-Seine, *France* 25 D10
Noggerup, *Australia* 89 F2
Noginsk, *Moskva, Russia* 42 C4
Noginsk, *Sib., Russia* 45 C10
Nogoa →, *Australia* 90 C4
Nogoyá, *Argentina* 126 C4
Nogueira de Ramuin, *Spain* 30 C3
Noguera Pallaresa →, *Spain* 28 D5
Noguera Ribagorzana →, *Spain* 28 D5
Nohar, *India* 62 E6
Noire, Montagne, *France* 26 E6
Noire, Mts., *France* 24 D3
Noirétable, *France* 26 C7
Noirmoutier, I. de, *France* 24 F4
Noirmoutier-en-l'Ile, *France* 24 F4
Nojane, *Botswana* 84 C3
Nojima-Zaki, *Japan* 49 G9
Nok Kundi, *Pakistan* 60 E3
Nokaneng, *Botswana* 84 B3
Nokhtuysk, *Russia* 45 C12
Nokia, *Finland* 9 F20
Nokomis, *Canada* 101 C8
Nokomis L., *Canada* 101 B8
Nol, *Sweden* 11 G6
Nola, *C.A.R.* 80 D3
Nola, *Italy* 35 B7
Nolay, *France* 25 F11
Noli, C. di, *Italy* 32 D5
Nolinsk, *Russia* 42 B9
Noma Omuramba →, *Namibia* 84 B3
Noman L., *Canada* 101 A7
Nombre de Dios, *Panama* 116 E4
Nome, *U.S.A.* 96 B3
Nomo-Zaki, *Japan* 49 H4
Nonacho L., *Canada* 101 A7
Nonancourt, *France* 24 D8
Nonant-le-Pin, *France* 24 D7
Nonda, *Australia* 90 C3
Nong Chang, *Thailand* 58 E2
Nong Het, *Laos* 58 C4
Nong Khai, *Thailand* 58 D4
Nong'an, *China* 51 B13
Nongoma, *S. Africa* 85 D5
Nonoava, *Mexico* 114 B3
Nonthaburi, *Thailand* 58 F3
Nontron, *France* 26 C4
Nonza, *France* 27 F13
Noonamah, *Australia* 88 B5
Noonan, *U.S.A.* 108 A3
Noondoo, *Australia* 91 D4
Noonkanbah, *Australia* 88 C3
Noord-Bergum, *Neths.* 16 B8
Noord Brabant □, *Neths.* 17 E6
Noord Holland □, *Neths.* 16 D5
Noordbeveland, *Neths.* 17 E3
Noordeloos, *Neths.* 16 E5
Noordhollandsch Kanaal, *Neths.* 16 C5
Noordhorn, *Neths.* 16 B8
Noordoostpolder, *Neths.* 16 C7
Noordwijk aan Zee, *Neths.* 16 D4
Noordwijk-Binnen, *Neths.* 16 D4
Noordwijkerhout, *Neths.* 16 D5
Noordzee Kanaal, *Neths.* 16 D5
Noorwolde, *Neths.* 16 C8
Nootka, *Canada* 100 D3
Nootka I., *Canada* 100 D3
Nóqui, *Angola* 80 F2
Nora, *Eritrea* 77 D5
Noranda, *Canada* 98 C4
Nórcia, *Italy* 33 F10
Norco, *U.S.A.* 113 M9
Nord □, *France* 25 B10
Nord-Ostsee-Kanal →, *Germany* 18 A5
Nordagutu, *Norway* 10 E3
Nordaustlandet, *Svalbard* 4 B9
Nordborg, *Denmark* 11 J3
Nordby, *Århus, Denmark* 11 J4
Nordby, *Ribe, Denmark* 11 J2
Norddeich, *Germany* 18 B3
Nordegg, *Canada* 100 C5
Norden, *Germany* 18 B3
Nordenham, *Germany* 18 B4
Norderhov, *Norway* 10 D4
Norderney, *Germany* 18 B3
Nordfjord, *Norway* 9 F11
Nordfriesische Inseln, *Germany* 18 A4
Nordhausen, *Germany* 18 D6
Nordhorn, *Germany* 18 C3
Norðoyar, *Færoe Is.* 8 E9
Nordjyllands Amtskommune □, *Denmark* 11 H4
Nordkapp, *Norway* 8 A21
Nordkapp, *Svalbard* 4 A9
Nordkinn = Kinnarodden, *Norway* 6 A11
Nordkinn-halvøya, *Norway* 8 A22
Nördlingen, *Germany* 19 G6
Nordrhein-Westfalen □, *Germany* 18 D3
Nordstrand, *Germany* 18 A4
Nordvik, *Russia* 45 B12
Nore, *Norway* 10 D3
Norefjell, *Norway* 10 D3
Norembega, *Canada* 98 C3
Noresund, *Norway* 10 D3
Norfolk, *Nebr., U.S.A.* 108 D6
Norfolk, *Va., U.S.A.* 104 G7
Norfolk □, *U.K.* 12 E9
Norfolk Broads, *U.K.* 12 E9
Norfolk I., *Pac. Oc.* 92 K8
Norfork Res., *U.S.A.* 109 G8
Norg, *Neths.* 16 B8
Norilsk, *Russia* 45 C9
Norley, *Australia* 91 D3
Norma, Mt., *Australia* 90 C3
Normal, *U.S.A.* 108 E10
Norman, *U.S.A.* 109 H6
Norman →, *Australia* 90 B3
Norman Wells, *Canada* 96 B7
Normanby →, *Australia* 90 A3
Normandie, *France* 24 D7
Normandie, Collines de, *France* 24 D6
Normandin, *Canada* 98 C5
Normandy = Normandie, *France* 24 D7
Normanhurst, Mt., *Australia* 89 E3
Normanton, *Australia* 90 B3
Norquay, *Canada* 101 C8
Norquinco, *Argentina* 128 B2
Norrbotten □, *Sweden* 8 C19
Nørre Åby, *Denmark* 11 J3
Nørre Nebel, *Denmark* 11 J2
Norre Vorupør, *Denmark* 11 H2
Nørresundby, *Denmark* 11 G3
Norris, *U.S.A.* 110 D8
Norristown, *U.S.A.* 107 F9
Norrköping, *Sweden* 11 F10
Norrland, *Sweden* 9 E16
Norrtälje, *Sweden* 10 E12
Norseman, *Australia* 89 F3
Norsholm, *Sweden* 11 F9
Norsk, *Russia* 45 D14
Norte, Pta., *Argentina* 128 B4
Norte, Pta. del, *Canary Is.* 36 G2
Norte de Santander □, *Colombia* 120 B3
Nortelândia, *Brazil* 125 C6
North Adams, *U.S.A.* 107 D11
North Ayrshire □, *U.K.* 14 F4
North Battleford, *Canada* 101 C7
North Bay, *Canada* 98 C4
North Belcher Is., *Canada* 98 A4
North Bend, *Canada* 100 D4
North Bend, *Oreg., U.S.A.* 110 E1
North Bend, *Pa., U.S.A.* 106 E7
North Bend, *Wash., U.S.A.* 112 C5
North Berwick, *U.K.* 14 E6
North Berwick, *U.S.A.* 107 C14
North C., *Canada* 99 C7
North C., *N.Z.* 87 F4
North Canadian →, *U.S.A.* 109 H7
North Cape = Nordkapp, *Norway* 8 A21
North Cape = Nordkapp, *Svalbard* 4 A9
North Caribou L., *Canada* 98 B1
North Carolina □, *U.S.A.* 105 H5
North Channel, *Canada* 98 C3
North Channel, *U.K.* 14 G3
North Charleston, *U.S.A.* 105 J6
North Chicago, *U.S.A.* 104 D2
North Dakota □, *U.S.A.* 108 B5
North Dandalup, *Australia* 89 F2
North Down □, *U.K.* 15 B6
North Downs, *U.K.* 13 F8
North East, *U.S.A.* 106 D5
North East Frontier Agency = Arunachal Pradesh □, *India* 61 E19
North East Lincolnshire □, *U.K.* 12 D7
North East Providence Chan., *W. Indies* 116 A4
North Eastern □, *Kenya* 82 B5
North Esk →, *U.K.* 14 E6
North European Plain, *Europe* 6 E10
North Foreland, *U.K.* 13 F9
North Fork, *U.S.A.* 112 H7
North Fork American →, *U.S.A.* 112 G5
North Fork Feather →, *U.S.A.* 112 F5
North Frisian Is. = Nordfriesische Inseln, *Germany* 18 A4
North Henik L., *Canada* 101 A9
North Highlands, *U.S.A.* 112 G5
North Horr, *Kenya* 82 B4
North I., *Kenya* 82 B4
North I., *N.Z.* 87 H5
North Kingsville, *U.S.A.* 106 E4
North Knife →, *Canada* 101 B10
North Koel →, *India* 63 G10
North Korea ■, *Asia* 51 E14
North Lakhimpur, *India* 61 F19
North Lanarkshire □, *U.K.* 14 F5
North Las Vegas, *U.S.A.* 113 J11
North Lincolnshire □, *U.K.* 12 D7
North Little Rock, *U.S.A.* 109 H8
North Loup →, *U.S.A.* 108 E5
North Magnetic Pole, *Canada* 4 B2
North Minch, *U.K.* 14 C3
North Nahanni →, *Canada* 100 A4
North Olmsted, *U.S.A.* 106 E3
North Ossetia □, *Russia* 43 J7
North Pagai, I. = Pagai Utara, *Indonesia* 56 E2
North Palisade, *U.S.A.* 111 H4
North Platte, *U.S.A.* 108 E4
North Platte →, *U.S.A.* 108 E4
North Pole, *Arctic* 4 A
North Portal, *Canada* 101 D8
North Powder, *U.S.A.* 110 D5
North Pt., *Canada* 99 C7
North Rhine Westphalia □ = Nordrhein-Westfalen □, *Germany* 18 D3
North Ronaldsay, *U.K.* 14 B6
North Saskatchewan →, *Canada* 101 C7
North Sea, *Europe* 6 D6
North Somerset □, *U.K.* 13 F5
North Sporades = Voríai Sporádhes, *Greece* 39 K6
North Sydney, *Canada* 99 C7
North Taranaki Bight, *N.Z.* 87 H5
North Thompson →, *Canada* 100 C4
North Tonawanda, *U.S.A.* 106 C6
North Troy, *U.S.A.* 107 B12
North Truchas Pk., *U.S.A.* 111 J11
North Twin I., *Canada* 98 B3
North Tyne →, *U.K.* 12 C5
North Uist, *U.K.* 14 D1
North Vancouver, *Canada* 100 D4
North Vernon, *U.S.A.* 104 F3
North Wabasca L., *Canada* 100 B6
North Walsham, *U.K.* 12 E9
North-West □, *S. Africa* 84 D4
North West C., *Australia* 88 D1
North West Christmas I. Ridge, *Pac. Oc.* 93 G11
North West Frontier □, *Pakistan* 62 C4
North West Highlands, *U.K.* 14 D3
North West Providence Channel, *W. Indies* 116 A4
North West River, *Canada* 99 B7
North West Territories □, *Canada* 96 B9
North Western □, *Zambia* 83 E2
North York Moors, *U.K.* 12 C7
North Yorkshire □, *U.K.* 12 C6
Northallerton, *U.K.* 12 C6
Northam, *S. Africa* 84 C4
Northampton, *Australia* 89 E1
Northampton, *U.K.* 13 E7
Northampton, *Mass., U.S.A.* 107 D12
Northampton, *Pa., U.S.A.* 107 F9
Northampton Downs, *Australia* 90 C4
Northamptonshire □, *U.K.* 13 E7
Northbridge, *U.S.A.* 107 D13
Northcliffe, *Australia* 89 F2
Northeim, *Germany* 18 D6
Northern □, *Malawi* 83 E3
Northern □, *Uganda* 82 B3
Northern □, *Zambia* 83 E3
Northern Cape □, *S. Africa* 84 D3
Northern Circars, *India* 61 L13
Northern Indian L., *Canada* 101 B9
Northern Ireland □, *U.K.* 15 B5
Northern Light, L., *Canada* 98 C1
Northern Marianas ■, *Pac. Oc.* 92 F6
Northern Province □, *S. Leone* 78 D2
Northern Territory □, *Australia* 88 D5
Northern Transvaal □, *S. Africa* 85 C4
Northfield, *U.S.A.* 108 C8
Northland □, *N.Z.* 87 F4
Northome, *U.S.A.* 108 B7
Northport, *Ala., U.S.A.* 105 J2
Northport, *Mich., U.S.A.* 104 C3
Northport, *Wash., U.S.A.* 110 B5
Northumberland □, *U.K.* 12 B5
Northumberland, C., *Australia* 91 F3
Northumberland Is., *Australia* 90 C4
Northumberland Str., *Canada* 99 C7
Northwich, *U.K.* 12 D5
Northwood, *Iowa, U.S.A.* 108 D8
Northwood, *N. Dak., U.S.A.* 108 B6
Norton, *U.S.A.* 108 F5
Norton, *Zimbabwe* 83 F3
Norton Sd., *U.S.A.* 96 B3
Nortorf, *Germany* 18 A5
Norwalk, *Calif., U.S.A.* 113 M8
Norwalk, *Conn., U.S.A.* 107 E11
Norwalk, *Ohio, U.S.A.* 106 E2
Norway, *U.S.A.* 104 C2
Norway ■, *Europe* 8 E14
Norway House, *Canada* 101 C9
Norwegian Sea, *Atl. Oc.* 4 C8
Norwich, *Canada* 106 D4
Norwich, *U.K.* 12 E9
Norwich, *Conn., U.S.A.* 107 E12
Norwich, *N.Y., U.S.A.* 107 D9
Norwood, *Canada* 106 B7
Noshiro, *Japan* 48 D10
Nosivka, *Ukraine* 41 G6
Nosok, *Russia* 44 B9
Nosovka = Nosivka, *Ukraine* 41 G6
Noss Hd., *U.K.* 14 C5
Nossa Senhora da Glória, *Brazil* 122 D4
Nossa Senhora das Dores, *Brazil* 122 D4
Nossa Senhora do Livramento, *Brazil* 125 D6
Nossebro, *Sweden* 11 F6
Nossob →, *S. Africa* 84 D3
Nosy Bé, *Madag.* 81 G9
Nosy Boraha, *Madag.* 85 B8
Nosy Mitsio, *Madag.* 81 G9
Nosy Varika, *Madag.* 85 C8
Noteć →, *Poland* 20 C5
Notigi Dam, *Canada* 101 B9
Notikewin →, *Canada* 100 B5
Notios Evvoïkos Kólpos, *Greece* 39 L7
Noto, *Italy* 35 F8
Noto, G. di, *Italy* 35 F8
Notodden, *Norway* 10 E3
Notre-Dame, *Canada* 99 C7
Notre Dame B., *Canada* 99 C8
Notre Dame de Koartac = Quaqtaq, *Canada* 97 B13
Notre Dame d'Ivugivic = Ivujivik, *Canada* 97 B12
Notsé, *Togo* 79 D5
Nottaway →, *Canada* 98 B4
Nøtterøy, *Norway* 10 E4
Nottingham, *U.K.* 12 E6
Nottinghamshire □, *U.K.* 12 D7
Nottoway →, *U.S.A.* 104 G7
Notwane →, *Botswana* 84 C4
Nouâdhibou, *Mauritania* 74 D1
Nouâdhibou, Ras, *Mauritania* 74 D1
Nouakchott, *Mauritania* 78 B1
Nouméa, *N. Cal.* 92 K8
Noupoort, *S. Africa* 84 E3

Nouveau Comptoir = Wemindji, *Canada* 98 B4
Nouvelle-Calédonie = New Caledonia ■, *Pac. Oc.* 92 K8
Nouzonville, *France* 25 C11
Nová Baňa, *Slovak Rep.* 21 G8
Nová Bystřice, *Czech.* 20 F5
Nova Casa Nova, *Brazil* 122 C3
Nova Cruz, *Brazil* 122 C4
Nova Era, *Brazil* 123 E3
Nova Esperança, *Brazil* 127 A5
Nova Friburgo, *Brazil* 123 F3
Nova Gaia = Cambundi-Catembo, *Angola* 80 G3
Nova Gradiška, *Croatia* 21 K7
Nova Granada, *Brazil* 123 F2
Nova Iguaçu, *Brazil* 123 F3
Nova Iorque, *Brazil* 122 C3
Nova Kakhovka, *Ukraine* 41 J7
Nova Lamego, *Guinea-Biss.* 78 C2
Nova Lima, *Brazil* 127 A7
Nova Lisboa = Huambo, *Angola* 81 G3
Nova Lusitânia, *Mozam.* 83 F3
Nova Mambone, *Mozam.* 85 C6
Nova Odesa, *Ukraine* 41 J6
Nova Ponte, *Brazil* 123 E2
Nova Scotia □, *Canada* 99 C7
Nova Sofala, *Mozam.* 85 C5
Nova Venécia, *Brazil* 123 E3
Nova Vida, *Brazil* 125 C5
Nova Zagora, *Bulgaria* 38 G8
Novaleksandrovskaya = Novoaleksandrovsk, *Russia* 43 H5
Novannenskiy = Novoannenskiy, *Russia* 42 E6
Novara, *Italy* 32 C5
Novato, *U.S.A.* 112 G4
Novaya Kakhovka = Nova Kakhovka, *Ukraine* 41 J7
Novaya Kazanka, *Kazakstan* 43 F9
Novaya Ladoga, *Russia* 40 B7
Novaya Lyalya, *Russia* 44 D7
Novaya Sibir, Ostrov, *Russia* 45 B16
Novaya Zemlya, *Russia* 44 B6
Novelda, *Spain* 29 G4
Novellara, *Italy* 32 D7
Noventa Vicentina, *Italy* 33 C8
Novgorod, *Russia* 40 C6
Novgorod-Severskiy = Novhorod-Siverskyy, *Ukraine* 41 G7
Novhorod-Siverskyy, *Ukraine* 41 G7
Novi Bečej, *Serbia, Yug.* 21 K10
Novi Grad, *Croatia* 33 C10
Novi Krichim, *Bulgaria* 38 G7
Novi Lígure, *Italy* 32 D5
Novi Pazar, *Bulgaria* 38 F10
Novi Pazar, *Serbia, Yug.* 21 M10
Novi Sad, *Serbia, Yug.* 21 K9
Novi Vinodolski, *Croatia* 33 C11
Novigrad, *Croatia* 33 D12
Noville, *Belgium* 17 H7
Novo Acôrdo, *Brazil* 122 D2
Novo Aripuanã, *Brazil* 121 E5
Nôvo Cruzeiro, *Brazil* 123 E3
Nôvo Hamburgo, *Brazil* 127 B5
Novo Horizonte, *Brazil* 123 F2
Novo Mesto, *Slovenia* 33 C12
Novo Remanso, *Brazil* 122 C3
Novoaleksandrovsk, *Russia* 43 H5
Novoannenskiy, *Russia* 42 E6
Novoataysk, *Russia* 44 D9
Novoazovsk, *Ukraine* 41 J10
Novocheboksarsk, *Russia* 42 B8
Novocherkassk, *Russia* 43 G5
Novodevichye, *Russia* 42 D9
Novogrudok = Navahrudak, *Belarus* 40 F3
Novohrad-Volynskyy, *Ukraine* 41 G4
Novokachalinsk, *Russia* 48 B6
Novokazalinsk = Zhangaqazaly, *Kazakstan* 44 E7
Novokhopersk, *Russia* 42 E5
Novokuybyshevsk, *Russia* 42 D9
Novokuznetsk, *Russia* 44 D9
Novomirgorod, *Ukraine* 41 H6
Novomoskovsk, *Russia* 42 C4
Novomoskovsk, *Ukraine* 41 H8
Novopolotsk = Navapolatsk, *Belarus* 40 E5
Novorossiysk, *Russia* 43 H3
Novorybnoye, *Russia* 45 B11
Novorzhev, *Russia* 40 D5
Novoselytsya, *Ukraine* 41 H4
Novoshakhtinsk, *Russia* 43 G4
Novosibirsk, *Russia* 44 D9
Novosibirskiye Ostrova, *Russia* 45 B15
Novosil, *Russia* 42 D3
Novosokolniki, *Russia* 40 D6
Novotitarovskaya, *Russia* 43 H4
Novotroitsk, *Russia* 44 D6
Novoukrayinka, *Ukraine* 41 H6
Novouljanovsk, *Russia* 42 C9
Novouzensk, *Russia* 42 E9
Novovolynsk, *Ukraine* 41 G3
Novovoronezhskiy, *Russia* 42 E4
Novozybkov, *Russia* 41 F6
Novska, *Croatia* 21 K6
Novy Bug = Novyy Buh, *Ukraine* 41 J7
Nový Bydzov, *Czech.* 20 E5
Nowy Dwór Mazowiecki, *Poland* 20 C10
Novyy Afon, *Georgia* 43 J5
Novyy Buh, *Ukraine* 41 J7
Novyy Oskol, *Russia* 42 E3
Novyy Port, *Russia* 44 C8
Now Shahr, *Iran* 65 B6
Nowa Deba, *Poland* 20 E11
Nowa Ruda, *Poland* 20 E6
Nowa Sól, *Poland* 20 D5
Nowbarān, *Iran* 65 C6
Nowe, *Poland* 20 B8
Nowghāb, *Iran* 65 C8
Nowgong, *India* 61 F18
Nowogard, *Poland* 20 B5
Nowogród, *Poland* 20 B11
Nowra, *Australia* 91 E5
Nowshera, *Pakistan* 60 B8
Nowy Korczyn, *Poland* 20 E10
Nowy Sącz, *Poland* 20 F10
Noxen, *U.S.A.* 107 E8
Noxon, *U.S.A.* 110 C6
Noya, *Spain* 30 C2
Noyant, *France* 24 E7
Noyers, *France* 25 E10
Noyes I., *U.S.A.* 100 B2
Noyon, *France* 25 C9
Noyon, *Mongolia* 50 C2
Nozay, *France* 24 E5
Nsa, O. en →, *Algeria* 75 B6
Nsanje, *Malawi* 83 F4
Nsawam, *Ghana* 79 D4
Nsomba, *Zambia* 83 E2
Nsukka, *Nigeria* 79 D6
Nu Jiang →, *China* 52 C1
Nu Shan, *China* 52 D2
Nuba Mts. = Nubah, Jibalan, *Sudan* 77 E3
Nubah, Jibalan, *Sudan* 77 E3
Nubia, *Africa* 70 D7
Nubian Desert = Nûbîya, Es Sahrâ En, *Sudan* 76 C3
Nûbîya, Es Sahrâ En, *Sudan* 76 C3
Ñuble □, *Chile* 126 D1
Nuboai, *Indonesia* 57 E9
Nubra →, *India* 63 B7
Nueces →, *U.S.A.* 109 M6
Nueltin L., *Canada* 101 A9
Nuenen, *Neths.* 17 F7
Nueva, I., *Chile* 128 E3
Nueva Antioquia, *Colombia* 120 B4
Nueva Asunción □, *Paraguay* 126 A3
Nueva Esparta □, *Venezuela* 121 A5
Nueva Gerona, *Cuba* 116 B3
Nueva Imperial, *Chile* 128 A2
Nueva Palmira, *Uruguay* 126 C4
Nueva Rosita, *Mexico* 114 B4
Nueva San Salvador, *El Salv.* 116 D2
Nuéve de Julio, *Argentina* 126 D3
Nuevitas, *Cuba* 116 B4
Nuevo, G., *Argentina* 128 B4
Nuevo Guerrero, *Mexico* 115 B5
Nuevo Laredo, *Mexico* 115 B5
Nuevo León □, *Mexico* 114 C4
Nuevo Mundo, Cerro, *Bolivia* 124 E4
Nuevo Rocafuerte, *Ecuador* 120 D2
Nugget Pt., *N.Z.* 87 M2
Nugrus, Gebel, *Egypt* 76 C3
Nuhaka, *N.Z.* 87 H6
Nuits-St.-Georges, *France* 25 E11
Nukey Bluff, *Australia* 91 E2
Nukheila, *Sudan* 76 D2
Nukhuyb, *Iraq* 67 F10
Nuku'alofa, *Tonga* 87 E11
Nukus, *Uzbekistan* 44 E6
Nuland, *Neths.* 16 E6
Nulato, *U.S.A.* 96 B4
Nules, *Spain* 28 F4
Nullagine →, *Australia* 88 D3
Nullarbor, *Australia* 89 F5
Nullarbor Plain, *Australia* 89 F4
Numalla, L., *Australia* 91 D3
Numan, *Nigeria* 79 D7
Numansdorp, *Neths.* 16 E4
Numata, *Japan* 49 F9
Numatinna →, *Sudan* 77 F2
Numazu, *Japan* 49 G9
Numbulwar, *Australia* 90 A2
Numfoor, *Indonesia* 57 E8
Numurkah, *Australia* 91 F4
Nunaksaluk I., *Canada* 99 A7
Nuneaton, *U.K.* 13 E6
Nungo, *Mozam.* 83 E4
Nungwe, *Tanzania* 82 C3
Nunivak I., *U.S.A.* 96 B3
Nunkun, *India* 63 C7
Nunspeet, *Neths.* 16 D7
Nùoro, *Italy* 34 B2
Nuquí, *Colombia* 120 B2
Nūrābād, *Iran* 65 E8
Nure →, *Italy* 32 C6
Nuremberg = Nürnberg, *Germany* 19 F7
Nuri, *Mexico* 114 B3
Nurina, *Australia* 89 F4
Nuriootpa, *Australia* 91 E2
Nurlat, *Russia* 42 C10
Nurmes, *Finland* 8 E23
Nürnberg, *Germany* 19 F7
Nurran, L. = Terewah, L., *Australia* 91 D4
Nurrari Lakes, *Australia* 89 E5
Nurri, *Italy* 34 C2
Nusa Barung, *Indonesia* 57 H15
Nusa Kambangan, *Indonesia* 57 G13
Nusa Tenggara Barat □, *Indonesia* 56 F5
Nusa Tenggara Timur □, *Indonesia* 57 F6
Nusaybin, *Turkey* 67 D9
Nushki, *Pakistan* 62 E2
Nutak, *Canada* 97 C13
Nuth, *Neths.* 17 G7
Nutwood Downs, *Australia* 90 B1
Nuuk = Godthåb, *Greenland* 97 B14
Nuwakot, *Nepal* 63 E10
Nuweiba', *Egypt* 76 B3
Nuweveldberge, *S. Africa* 84 E3
Nuyts, C., *Australia* 89 F5
Nuyts Arch., *Australia* 91 E1
Nxau-Nxau, *Botswana* 84 B3
Nyaake, *Liberia* 78 E3
Nyack, *U.S.A.* 107 E11
Nyadal, *Sweden* 10 B11
Nyah West, *Australia* 91 F3
Nyahanga, *Tanzania* 82 C3
Nyahua, *Tanzania* 82 D3
Nyahururu, *Kenya* 82 B4
Nyainqentanglha Shan, *China* 54 C4
Nyakanazi, *Tanzania* 82 C3
Nyakrom, *Ghana* 79 D4
Nyâlâ, *Sudan* 77 E1
Nyamandhlovu, *Zimbabwe* 83 F2
Nyambiti, *Tanzania* 82 C3
Nyamwaga, *Tanzania* 82 C3
Nyandekwa, *Tanzania* 82 C3
Nyanding →, *Sudan* 77 F3
Nyandoma, *Russia* 40 B11
Nyangana, *Namibia* 84 B3
Nyanguge, *Tanzania* 82 C3
Nyankpala, *Ghana* 79 D4
Nyanza, *Burundi* 82 C2
Nyanza, *Rwanda* 82 C2
Nyanza □, *Kenya* 82 C3
Nyarling →, *Canada* 100 A6
Nyasa, L. = Malawi, L., *Africa* 83 E3
Nyasvizh, *Belarus* 41 F4
Nyazura, *Zimbabwe* 83 F3
Nyazwidzi →, *Zimbabwe* 83 F3
Nyborg, *Denmark* 11 J4
Nybro, *Sweden* 9 H16
Nyda, *Russia* 44 C8
Nyeri, *Kenya* 82 C4
Nyerol, *Sudan* 77 F3
Nyhem, *Sweden* 10 B9
Nyiel, *Sudan* 77 F3
Nyinahin, *Ghana* 78 D4
Nyirbátor, *Hungary* 21 H12
Nyíregyháza, *Hungary* 21 H11
Nykøbing, *Storstrøm, Denmark* 11 K5
Nykøbing, *Vestsjælland, Denmark* 11 J5
Nykøbing, *Viborg, Denmark* 11 H2
Nyköping, *Sweden* 11 F11
Nykvarn, *Sweden* 10 E11
Nyland, *Sweden* 10 A11
Nylstroom, *S. Africa* 85 C4
Nymagee, *Australia* 91 E4
Nymburk, *Czech.* 20 E5
Nynäshamn, *Sweden* 10 F11
Nyngan, *Australia* 91 E4
Nyoman = Neman →, *Lithuania* 9 J19
Nyon, *Switz.* 22 D2
Nyong →, *Cameroon* 79 E6
Nyons, *France* 27 D9
Nyord, *Denmark* 11 J6
Nyou, *Burkina Faso* 79 C4
Nysa, *Poland* 20 E7
Nysa →, *Europe* 18 C10
Nyssa, *U.S.A.* 110 E5
Nysted, *Denmark* 11 K5
Nyunzu, *Zaïre* 82 D2
Nyurbe, *Russia* 45 C12
Nyzhnohirskyy, *Ukraine* 41 K8
Nzega, *Tanzania* 82 C3
Nzega □, *Tanzania* 82 C3
N'Zérékoré, *Guinea* 78 D3
Nzeto, *Angola* 80 F2
Nzilo, Chutes de, *Zaïre* 83 E2
Nzubuka, *Tanzania* 82 C3

O

Ō-Shima, *Nagasaki, Japan* 49 G4
Ō-Shima, *Shizuoka, Japan* 49 G9
Oacoma, *U.S.A.* 108 D5
Oahe, L., *U.S.A.* 108 C4
Oahe Dam, *U.S.A.* 108 C4
Oahu, *U.S.A.* 102 H16
Oak Creek, *U.S.A.* 110 F10
Oak Harbor, *U.S.A.* 112 B4
Oak Hill, *U.S.A.* 104 G5
Oak Park, *U.S.A.* 104 E2
Oak Ridge, *U.S.A.* 105 G3
Oak View, *U.S.A.* 113 L7
Oakan-Dake, *Japan* 48 C12
Oakbank, *Australia* 91 E3
Oakdale, *Calif., U.S.A.* 111 H3
Oakdale, *La., U.S.A.* 109 K8
Oakengates, *U.K.* 12 E5
Oakes, *U.S.A.* 108 B5
Oakesdale, *U.S.A.* 110 C5
Oakey, *Australia* 91 D5
Oakham, *U.K.* 12 E7
Oakhurst, *U.S.A.* 112 H7
Oakland, *Calif., U.S.A.* 111 H2
Oakland, *Oreg., U.S.A.* 110 E2
Oakland City, *U.S.A.* 104 F2
Oakley, *Idaho, U.S.A.* 110 E7
Oakley, *Kans., U.S.A.* 108 F4
Oakover →, *Australia* 88 D3
Oakridge, *U.S.A.* 110 E2
Oakville, *U.S.A.* 112 D3
Oamaru, *N.Z.* 87 L3
Oasis, *Calif., U.S.A.* 113 M10
Oasis, *Nev., U.S.A.* 112 H9
Oates Land, *Antarctica* 5 C11
Oatman, *U.S.A.* 113 K12
Oaxaca, *Mexico* 115 D5
Oaxaca □, *Mexico* 115 D5
Ob →, *Russia* 44 C7
Oba, *Canada* 98 C3
Obala, *Cameroon* 79 E7
Obama, *Japan* 49 G7
Oban, *U.K.* 14 E3
Obbia, *Somali Rep.* 68 F4
Obdam, *Neths.* 16 C5
Obed, *Canada* 100 C5
Ober-Aagau, *Switz.* 22 B5
Obera, *Argentina* 127 B4
Oberalppass, *Switz.* 23 C7
Oberalpstock, *Switz.* 23 C7
Oberammergau, *Germany* 19 H7
Oberdrauburg, *Austria* 21 J2
Oberengadin, *Switz.* 23 C9
Oberentfelden, *Switz.* 22 B6
Oberhausen, *Germany* 18 D2
Oberkirch, *Germany* 19 G4
Oberland, *Switz.* 22 C5
Oberlin, *Kans., U.S.A.* 108 F4
Oberlin, *La., U.S.A.* 109 K8
Oberlin, *Ohio, U.S.A.* 106 E2
Obernai, *France* 25 D14
Oberndorf, *Germany* 19 G4
Oberon, *Australia* 91 E4
Oberpfälzer Wald, *Germany* 19 F8
Obersiggenthal, *Switz.* 23 B6
Oberstdorf, *Germany* 19 H6
Oberwil, *Switz.* 22 A5
Obi, Kepulauan, *Indonesia* 57 E7
Obi Is. = Obi, Kepulauan, *Indonesia* 57 E7
Obiaruku, *Nigeria* 79 D6
Óbidos, *Brazil* 121 D6
Óbidos, *Portugal* 31 F1
Obihiro, *Japan* 48 C11
Obilatu, *Indonesia* 57 E7
Obilnoye, *Russia* 43 G7
Obing, *Germany* 19 H8
Obisfelde, *Germany* 18 C6
Objat, *France* 26 C5
Obluchye, *Russia* 45 E14
Obninsk, *Russia* 42 C3
Obo, *C.A.R.* 82 A2
Obo, *Ethiopia* 77 G4
Oboa, Mt., *Uganda* 82 B3
Obock, *Djibouti* 77 E5
Oborniki, *Poland* 20 C6
Oboyan, *Russia* 42 E3
Obozerskaya = Obozerskiy, *Russia* 44 C5
Obozerskiy, *Russia* 44 C5
Obrovac, *Croatia* 33 D12
Obruk, *Turkey* 66 C5
Observatory Inlet, *Canada* 100 B3
Obshchi Syrt, *Russia* 6 E16
Obskaya Guba, *Russia* 44 C8
Obuasi, *Ghana* 79 D4
Obubra, *Nigeria* 79 D6
Obwalden □, *Switz.* 22 C6
Obzor, *Bulgaria* 38 G10
Ocala, *U.S.A.* 105 L4
Ocamo →, *Venezuela* 121 C4
Ocampo, *Mexico* 114 B3
Ocaña, *Colombia* 120 B3
Ocaña, *Spain* 28 F1
Ocanomowoc, *U.S.A.* 108 D10
Ocate, *U.S.A.* 109 G2
Occidental, Cordillera, *Colombia* 120 C3
Occidental, Cordillera, *Peru* 124 C3
Ocean City, *N.J., U.S.A.* 104 F8
Ocean City, *Wash., U.S.A.* 112 C2
Ocean I. = Banaba, *Kiribati* 92 H8
Ocean Park, *U.S.A.* 112 D2
Oceano, *U.S.A.* 113 K6
Oceanport, *U.S.A.* 107 F10
Oceanside, *U.S.A.* 113 M9
Ochagavia, *Spain* 28 C3
Ochakiv, *Ukraine* 41 J6
Ochamchira, *Georgia* 43 J5
Ochamps, *Belgium* 17 J6
Ochil Hills, *U.K.* 14 E5
Ochre River, *Canada* 101 C9
Ochsenfurt, *Germany* 19 F6
Ochsenhausen, *Germany* 19 G5
Ocilla, *U.S.A.* 105 K4
Ocmulgee →, *U.S.A.* 105 K4
Ocna Sibiului, *Romania* 38 D7
Ocnița, *Moldova* 41 H4
Ocoña, *Peru* 124 D3
Ocoña →, *Peru* 124 D3
Oconee →, *U.S.A.* 105 K4
Oconto, *U.S.A.* 104 C2
Oconto Falls, *U.S.A.* 104 C1
Ocosingo, *Mexico* 115 D6
Ocotal, *Nic.* 116 D2
Ocotlán, *Mexico* 114 C4
Ocquier, *Belgium* 17 H6
Ocreza →, *Portugal* 31 F3
Octave, *U.S.A.* 111 J7
Octeville, *France* 24 C5
Ocumare del Tuy, *Venezuela* 120 A4
Ocuri, *Bolivia* 125 D4
Oda, *Ghana* 79 D4
Ōda, *Japan* 49 G6
Oda, J., *Sudan* 76 C4
Ódáðahraun, *Iceland* 8 D5
Ödåkra, *Sweden* 11 H6
Odate, *Japan* 48 D10
Odawara, *Japan* 49 G9
Odda, *Norway* 9 F12
Odder, *Denmark* 11 J4
Oddur, *Somali Rep.* 68 G3
Ödeborg, *Sweden* 11 F5
Odei →, *Canada* 101 B9
Odemira, *Portugal* 31 H2
Ödemiş, *Turkey* 66 C3
Odendaalsrus, *S. Africa* 84 D4
Odense, *Denmark* 11 J4
Odenwald, *Germany* 19 F5
Oder →, *Germany* 18 B10
Oderzo, *Italy* 33 C9
Odesa, *Ukraine* 41 J6
Odessa = Odesa, *Ukraine* 41 J6
Odessa, *Canada* 107 B8
Odessa, *Tex., U.S.A.* 109 K3
Odessa, *Wash., U.S.A.* 110 C4
Odiakwe, *Botswana* 84 C4
Odiel →, *Spain* 31 H4
Odienné, *Ivory C.* 78 D3
Odintsovo, *Russia* 42 C3
Odiongan, *Phil.* 55 E4
Odobeşti, *Romania* 38 D10
O'Donnell, *U.S.A.* 109 J4
Odoorn, *Neths.* 16 C9
Odorheiu Secuiesc, *Romania* 38 C8
Odoyevo, *Russia* 42 D3
Odra = Oder →, *Germany* 18 B10
Odra →, *Poland* 20 B4
Odra →, *Spain* 30 C6
Odžaci, *Serbia, Yug.* 21 K9
Odzi, *Zimbabwe* 85 B5
Oedelem, *Belgium* 17 F2
Oegstgeest, *Neths.* 16 D4
Oeiras, *Brazil* 122 C3
Oeiras, *Portugal* 31 G1
Oelrichs, *U.S.A.* 108 D3
Oelsnitz, *Germany* 18 E8
Oelwein, *U.S.A.* 108 D9
Oenpelli, *Australia* 88 B5
Of, *Turkey* 67 B9
Ofanto →, *Italy* 35 A9
Offa, *Nigeria* 79 D5
Offaly □, *Ireland* 15 C4
Offenbach, *Germany* 19 E4
Offenburg, *Germany* 19 G3
Offerdal, *Sweden* 10 A8
Offida, *Italy* 33 F10
Offranville, *France* 24 C8
Ofidhousa, *Greece* 39 N9
Ofotfjorden, *Norway* 8 B17
Ōfunato, *Japan* 48 E10
Oga, *Japan* 48 E9
Oga-Hantō, *Japan* 48 E9
Ogahalla, *Canada* 98 B2
Ōgaki, *Japan* 49 G8
Ogallala, *U.S.A.* 108 E4
Ogasawara Gunto, *Pac. Oc.* 46 G18
Ogbomosho, *Nigeria* 79 D5
Ogden, *Iowa, U.S.A.* 108 D8
Ogden, *Utah, U.S.A.* 110 F7
Ogdensburg, *U.S.A.* 107 B9
Ogeechee →, *U.S.A.* 105 K5
Ogilby, *U.S.A.* 113 N12
Oglio →, *Italy* 32 C7
Ogmore, *Australia* 90 C4
Ognon →, *France* 25 E12
Ogoja, *Nigeria* 79 D6
Ogoki →, *Canada* 98 B2
Ogoki L., *Canada* 98 B2
Ogoki Res., *Canada* 98 B2
Ogooué →, *Gabon* 80 E1
Ogosta →, *Bulgaria* 38 F6
Ogowe = Ogooué →, *Gabon* 80 E1
Ogr = Sharafa, *Sudan* 77 E2
Ogre, *Latvia* 9 H21
Ogrein, *Sudan* 76 D3
Ogulin, *Croatia* 33 C12
Ogun □, *Nigeria* 79 D5
Oguta, *Nigeria* 79 D6
Ogwashi-Uku, *Nigeria* 79 D6
Ogwe, *Nigeria* 79 E6
Ohai, *N.Z.* 87 L2
Ohakune, *N.Z.* 87 H5
Ohanet, *Algeria* 75 C6
Ohata, *Japan* 48 D10
Ohau, L., *N.Z.* 87 L2
Ohey, *Belgium* 17 H6
Ohio □, *U.S.A.* 104 E3
Ohio →, *U.S.A.* 104 G1
Ohre →, *Czech.* 20 E4
Ohre →, *Germany* 18 C7

Ohrid, *Macedonia* 39 H3
Ohridsko Jezero, *Macedonia* 39 H3
Ohrigstad, *S. Africa* 85 C5
Öhringen, *Germany* 19 F5
Oiapoque →, *Brazil* 121 C7
Oikou, *China* 51 E9
Oil City, *U.S.A.* 106 E5
Oildale, *U.S.A.* 113 K7
Oirschot, *Neths.* 17 E6
Oise □, *France* 25 C9
Oise →, *France* 25 D9
Oisterwijk, *Neths.* 17 E6
Ōita, *Japan* 49 H5
Ōita □, *Japan* 49 H5
Oiticica, *Brazil* 122 C3
Ojai, *U.S.A.* 113 L7
Ojinaga, *Mexico* 114 B4
Ojiya, *Japan* 49 F9
Ojos del Salado, Cerro, *Argentina* 126 B2
Oka →, *Russia* 42 B7
Okaba, *Indonesia* 57 F9
Okahandja, *Namibia* 84 C2
Okahukura, *N.Z.* 87 H5
Okanagan L., *Canada* 100 C5
Okandja, *Gabon* 80 E2
Okanogan, *U.S.A.* 110 B4
Okanogan →, *U.S.A.* 110 B4
Okaputa, *Namibia* 84 C2
Okara, *Pakistan* 62 D5
Okarito, *N.Z.* 87 K3
Okaukuejo, *Namibia* 84 B2
Okavango Swamps, *Botswana* 84 B3
Okaya, *Japan* 49 F9
Okayama, *Japan* 49 G6
Okayama □, *Japan* 49 G6
Okazaki, *Japan* 49 G8
Oke-Iho, *Nigeria* 79 D5
Okeechobee, *U.S.A.* 105 M5
Okeechobee, L., *U.S.A.* 105 M5
Okefenokee Swamp, *U.S.A.* 105 K4
Okehampton, *U.K.* 13 G3
Okene, *Nigeria* 79 D6
Oker →, *Germany* 18 C6
Okha, *Russia* 45 D15
Ókhi Óros, *Greece* 39 L7
Okhotsk, *Russia* 45 D15
Okhotsk, Sea of, *Asia* 45 D15
Okhotskiy Perevoz, *Russia* 45 C14
Okhtyrka, *Ukraine* 41 G8
Oki-Shotō, *Japan* 49 F6
Okiep, *S. Africa* 84 D2
Okigwi, *Nigeria* 79 D6
Okija, *Nigeria* 79 D6
Okinawa □, *Japan* 49 L3
Okinawa-Guntō, *Japan* 49 L3
Okinawa-Jima, *Japan* 49 L4
Okino-erabu-Shima, *Japan* 49 L4
Okitipupa, *Nigeria* 79 D5
Oklahoma □, *U.S.A.* 109 H6
Oklahoma City, *U.S.A.* 109 H6
Okmulgee, *U.S.A.* 109 H7
Oknitsa = Ocnița, *Moldova* 41 H4
Okolo, *Uganda* 82 B3
Okolona, *U.S.A.* 109 H10
Okrika, *Nigeria* 79 E6
Oktabrsk = Oktyabrsk, *Kazakstan* 44 E6
Oktyabrsk, *Kazakstan* 44 E6
Oktyabrsk, *Russia* 42 D9
Oktyabrskiy = Aktsyabrski, *Belarus* 41 F5
Oktyabrskiy, *Russia* 43 G5
Oktyabrskoy Revolyutsii, Os., *Russia* 45 B10
Oktyabrskoye = Zhovtneve, *Ukraine* 41 J7
Oktyabrskoye, *Russia* 44 C7
Okulovka, *Russia* 40 C7
Okuru, *N.Z.* 87 K2
Okushiri-Tō, *Japan* 48 C9
Okuta, *Nigeria* 79 D5
Okwa →, *Botswana* 84 C3
Ola, *U.S.A.* 109 H8
Ólafsfjörður, *Iceland* 8 C4
Ólafsvík, *Iceland* 8 D2
Olancha, *U.S.A.* 113 J8
Olancha Pk., *U.S.A.* 113 J8
Olanchito, *Honduras* 116 C2
Öland, *Sweden* 9 H17
Olargues, *France* 26 E6
Olary, *Australia* 91 E3
Olascoaga, *Argentina* 126 D3
Olathe, *U.S.A.* 108 F7
Olavarría, *Argentina* 126 D3
Oława, *Poland* 20 E7
Ólbia, *Italy* 34 B2
Ólbia, G. di, *Italy* 34 B2
Old Bahama Chan. = Bahama, Canal Viejo de, *W. Indies* 116 B4
Old Baldy Pk. = San Antonio, Mt., *U.S.A.* 113 L9
Old Cork, *Australia* 90 C3
Old Crow, *Canada* 96 B6
Old Dale, *U.S.A.* 113 L11
Old Dongola, *Sudan* 76 D3
Old Fletton, *U.K.* 13 E7
Old Forge, *N.Y., U.S.A.* 107 C10
Old Forge, *Pa., U.S.A.* 107 E9
Old Fort →, *Canada* 101 B6
Old Shinyanga, *Tanzania* 82 C3
Old Speck Mt., *U.S.A.* 107 B14
Old Town, *U.S.A.* 99 D6
Old Wives L., *Canada* 101 C7
Oldbury, *U.K.* 13 F5
Oldcastle, *Ireland* 15 C4
Oldeani, *Tanzania* 82 C4
Oldenburg, *Niedersachsen, Germany* 18 B4
Oldenburg, *Schleswig-Holstein, Germany* 18 A6
Oldenzaal, *Neths.* 16 D9
Oldham, *U.K.* 12 D5
Oldman →, *Canada* 100 D6
Olds, *Canada* 100 C6
Olean, *U.S.A.* 106 D6
Oléggio, *Italy* 32 C5
Oleiros, *Portugal* 30 F3
Olekma →, *Russia* 45 C13
Olekminsk, *Russia* 45 C13
Oleksandriya, *Ukraine* 41 H7
Oleksandriya, *Ukraine* 41 G4
Oleksandrovka, *Ukraine* 41 H7
Olema, *U.S.A.* 112 G4
Olen, *Belgium* 17 F5
Olenek, *Russia* 45 C12
Olenek →, *Russia* 45 B13
Olenino, *Russia* 42 B1
Oléron, I. d', *France* 26 C2
Oleśnica, *Poland* 20 D7
Olesno, *Poland* 20 E8
Olevsk, *Ukraine* 41 G4
Olga, *Russia* 45 E14
Olga, L., *Canada* 98 C4
Olga, Mt., *Australia* 89 E5
Ølgod, *Denmark* 11 J2
Olhão, *Portugal* 31 H3
Olib, *Croatia* 33 D11
Oliena, *Italy* 34 B2
Oliete, *Spain* 28 D4
Olifants →, *Africa* 85 C5
Olifantshoek, *S. Africa* 84 D3
Ólimbos, *Greece* 39 P10
Ólimbos, Óros, *Greece* 39 J5
Olímpia, *Brazil* 127 A6
Olinda, *Brazil* 122 C5
Olindiná, *Brazil* 122 D4
Olite, *Spain* 28 C3
Oliva, *Argentina* 126 C3
Oliva, *Spain* 29 G4
Oliva, Punta del, *Spain* 30 B5
Oliva de la Frontera, *Spain* 31 G4
Olivares, *Spain* 28 F2
Olivehurst, *U.S.A.* 112 F5
Oliveira, *Brazil* 123 F3
Oliveira de Azemeis, *Portugal* 30 E2
Oliveira dos Brejinhos, *Brazil* 123 D3
Olivenza, *Spain* 31 G3
Oliver, *Canada* 100 D5
Oliver L., *Canada* 101 B8
Olivone, *Switz.* 23 C7
Olkhovka, *Russia* 42 F7
Olkusz, *Poland* 20 E9
Ollagüe, *Chile* 126 A2
Olloy, *Belgium* 17 H5
Olmedo, *Spain* 30 D6
Olmos, *Peru* 124 B2
Olney, *Ill., U.S.A.* 104 F1
Olney, *Tex., U.S.A.* 109 J5
Oloma, *Cameroon* 79 E7
Olomane →, *Canada* 99 B7
Olomouc, *Czech.* 20 F7
Olonets, *Russia* 40 B7
Olongapo, *Phil.* 55 D4
Oloron, Gave d' →, *France* 26 E2
Oloron-Ste.-Marie, *France* 26 E3
Olot, *Spain* 28 C7
Olovo, *Bos.-H.* 21 L8
Olovyannaya, *Russia* 45 D12
Oloy →, *Russia* 45 C16
Olpe, *Germany* 18 D3
Olshanka, *Ukraine* 41 H6
Olshany, *Ukraine* 41 G8
Olst, *Neths.* 16 D8
Olsztyn, *Poland* 20 B10
Olt →, *Romania* 38 F7
Olten, *Switz.* 22 B5
Oltenița, *Romania* 38 E9
Olton, *U.S.A.* 109 H3
Oltu, *Turkey* 67 B9
Olur, *Turkey* 67 B10
Olutanga, *Phil.* 55 H5
Olvega, *Spain* 28 D3
Olvera, *Spain* 31 J5
Olymbos, *Cyprus* 37 D12
Olympia, *Greece* 39 M4
Olympia, *U.S.A.* 112 D4
Olympic Mts., *U.S.A.* 112 C3
Olympic Nat. Park, *U.S.A.* 112 C3
Olympus, *Cyprus* 66 E5
Olympus, Mt. = Ólimbos, Óros, *Greece* 39 J5
Olympus, Mt., *U.S.A.* 112 C3
Olyphant, *U.S.A.* 107 E9
Om →, *Russia* 44 D8
Om Hajer, *Eritrea* 77 E4
Om Koi, *Thailand* 58 D2
Ōma, *Japan* 48 D10
Ōmachi, *Japan* 49 F8
Omae-Zaki, *Japan* 49 G9
Ōmagari, *Japan* 48 E10
Omagh, *U.K.* 15 B4
Omagh □, *U.K.* 15 B4
Omaha, *U.S.A.* 108 E7
Omak, *U.S.A.* 110 B4
Omalos, *Greece* 37 D5
Oman ■, *Asia* 68 C6
Oman, G. of, *Asia* 65 E8
Omaruru, *Namibia* 84 C2
Omaruru →, *Namibia* 84 C1
Omate, *Peru* 124 D3
Ombai, Selat, *Indonesia* 57 F6
Omboué, *Gabon* 80 E1
Ombrone →, *Italy* 32 F8
Omdurmân, *Sudan* 77 D3
Omegna, *Italy* 32 C5
Omeonga, *Zaïre* 82 C1
Ometepe, I. de, *Nic.* 116 D2
Ometepec, *Mexico* 115 D5
Ominato, *Japan* 48 D10
Omineca →, *Canada* 100 B4
Omiš, *Croatia* 33 E13
Omišalj, *Croatia* 33 C11
Omitara, *Namibia* 84 C2
Ōmiya, *Japan* 49 G9
Omme Å →, *Denmark* 11 J2
Ommen, *Neths.* 16 C8
Ömnögovĭ □, *Mongolia* 50 C3
Omo →, *Ethiopia* 77 F4
Omodhos, *Cyprus* 37 E11
Omolon →, *Russia* 45 C16
Omono-Gawa →, *Japan* 48 E10
Omsk, *Russia* 44 D8
Omsukchan, *Russia* 45 C16
Ōmu, *Japan* 48 B11
Omul, Vf., *Romania* 38 D8
Ōmura, *Japan* 49 H4
Omuramba Omatako →, *Namibia* 81 H4
Omurtag, *Bulgaria* 38 F9
Ōmuta, *Japan* 49 H5
On, *Belgium* 17 H6
Oña, *Spain* 28 C1
Onaga, *U.S.A.* 108 F6
Onalaska, *U.S.A.* 108 D9
Onamia, *U.S.A.* 108 B8
Onancock, *U.S.A.* 104 G8
Onang, *Indonesia* 57 E5
Onaping L., *Canada* 98 C3
Oñate, *Spain* 28 B2
Onavas, *Mexico* 114 B3
Onawa, *U.S.A.* 108 D6
Onaway, *U.S.A.* 104 C3
Oncócua, *Angola* 84 B1
Onda, *Spain* 28 F4
Ondaejin, *N. Korea* 51 D15
Ondangua, *Namibia* 84 B2
Ondárroa, *Spain* 28 B2
Ondas →, *Brazil* 123 D3
Ondava →, *Slovak Rep.* 20 G11
Onderdijk, *Neths.* 16 C6
Ondjiva, *Angola* 84 B2
Ondo, *Nigeria* 79 D5
Ondo □, *Nigeria* 79 D6
Öndörhaan, *Mongolia* 54 B6
Öndörshil, *Mongolia* 50 B5
Öndverðarnes, *Iceland* 8 D1
Onega, *Russia* 44 C4
Onega →, *Russia* 6 C13
Onega, G. of = Onezhskaya Guba, *Russia* 44 C4
Onega, L. = Onezhskoye Ozero, *Russia* 40 B8
Onehunga, *N.Z.* 87 G5
Oneida, *U.S.A.* 107 C9
Oneida L., *U.S.A.* 107 C9
O'Neill, *U.S.A.* 108 D5
Onekotan, Ostrov, *Russia* 45 E16
Onema, *Zaïre* 82 C1
Oneonta, *Ala., U.S.A.* 105 J2
Oneonta, *N.Y., U.S.A.* 107 D9
Onești, *Romania* 38 C9
Onezhskaya Guba, *Russia* 44 C4
Onezhskoye Ozero, *Russia* 40 B8
Ongarue, *N.Z.* 87 H5
Ongerup, *Australia* 89 F2
Ongjin, *N. Korea* 51 F13
Ongkharak, *Thailand* 58 E3
Ongniud Qi, *China* 51 C10
Ongoka, *Zaïre* 82 C2
Ongole, *India* 60 M12
Ongon, *Mongolia* 50 B7
Onguren, *Russia* 45 D11
Onhaye, *Belgium* 17 H5
Oni, *Georgia* 43 J6
Onida, *U.S.A.* 108 C4
Onilahy →, *Madag.* 85 C7
Onitsha, *Nigeria* 79 D6
Onoda, *Japan* 49 G5
Onpyŏng-ni, *S. Korea* 51 H14
Ons, Is. d', *Spain* 30 C2
Onsala, *Sweden* 11 G6
Onslow, *Australia* 88 D2
Onslow B., *U.S.A.* 105 H7
Onstwedde, *Neths.* 16 B10
Ontake-San, *Japan* 49 G8
Ontaneda, *Spain* 30 B7
Ontario, *Calif., U.S.A.* 113 L9
Ontario, *Oreg., U.S.A.* 110 D5
Ontario □, *Canada* 98 B2
Ontario, L., *U.S.A.* 98 D4
Onteniente, *Spain* 29 G4
Ontonagon, *U.S.A.* 108 B10
Ontur, *Spain* 29 G3
Onyx, *U.S.A.* 113 K8
Oodnadatta, *Australia* 91 D2
Ooldea, *Australia* 89 F5
Ooltgensplaat, *Neths.* 17 E4
Oombulgurri, *Australia* 88 C4
Oona River, *Canada* 100 C2
Oordegem, *Belgium* 17 G3
Oorindi, *Australia* 90 C3
Oost-Vlaanderen □, *Belgium* 17 F3
Oost-Vlieland, *Neths.* 16 B6
Oostakker, *Belgium* 17 F3
Oostburg, *Neths.* 17 F3
Oostduinkerke, *Belgium* 17 F1
Oostelijk-Flevoland, *Neths.* 16 C7
Oostende, *Belgium* 17 F1
Oosterbeek, *Neths.* 16 E7
Oosterdijk, *Neths.* 16 C6
Oosterend, *Friesland, Neths.* 16 B6
Oosterend, *Noord-Holland, Neths.* 16 B5
Oosterhout, *Neths.* 17 E5
Oosterschelde, *Neths.* 17 E4
Oosterwolde, *Neths.* 16 B8
Oosterzele, *Belgium* 17 G3
Oostkamp, *Belgium* 17 F2
Oostmalle, *Belgium* 17 F5
Oostrozebekke, *Belgium* 17 G2
Oostvleteven, *Belgium* 17 G1
Oostvoorne, *Neths.* 16 E4
Oostzaan, *Neths.* 16 D5
Ootacamund, *India* 60 P10
Ootmarsum, *Neths.* 16 D9
Ootsa L., *Canada* 100 C3
Opala, *Russia* 45 D16
Opala, *Zaïre* 82 C1
Opanake, *Sri Lanka* 60 R12
Opasatika, *Canada* 98 C3
Opasquia, *Canada* 101 C10
Opatija, *Croatia* 33 C11
Opava, *Czech.* 20 F7
Opeinde, *Neths.* 16 B8
Opelousas, *U.S.A.* 109 K8
Opémisca, L., *Canada* 98 C5
Opglabbeek, *Belgium* 17 F7
Opheim, *U.S.A.* 110 B10
Ophthalmia Ra., *Australia* 88 D2
Opi, *Nigeria* 79 D6
Opinaca →, *Canada* 98 B4
Opinaca L., *Canada* 98 B4
Opiskotish, L., *Canada* 99 B6
Oploo, *Neths.* 17 E7
Opmeer, *Neths.* 16 C5
Opobo, *Nigeria* 79 E6
Opochka, *Russia* 40 D5
Opoczno, *Poland* 20 D10
Opol, *Phil.* 55 G6
Opole, *Poland* 20 E7
Oporto = Porto, *Portugal* 30 D2
Opotiki, *N.Z.* 87 H6
Opp, *U.S.A.* 105 K2
Oppdal, *Norway* 9 E13
Oppenheim, *Germany* 19 F4
Opperdoes, *Neths.* 16 C6
Óppido Mamertina, *Italy* 35 D8
Oppland fylke □, *Norway* 10 C3
Oppstad, *Norway* 10 D5
Oprtalj, *Croatia* 33 C10
Opua, *N.Z.* 87 F5
Opunake, *N.Z.* 87 H4
Opuzen, *Croatia* 21 M7
Ora, *Cyprus* 37 E12
Ora, *Italy* 33 B8
Ora Banda, *Australia* 89 F3
Oracle, *U.S.A.* 111 K8
Oradea, *Romania* 38 B4
Öræfajökull, *Iceland* 8 D5
Orahovac, *Serbia, Yug.* 21 N10
Orai, *India* 63 G8
Oraison, *France* 27 E9
Oral = Zhayyq →, *Kazakstan* 44 E6
Oral, *Kazakstan* 44 E10
Oran, *Algeria* 75 A4
Oran, *Argentina* 126 A3
Orange = Oranje →, *S. Africa* 84 D2
Orange, *Australia* 91 E4
Orange, *France* 27 D8
Orange, *Calif., U.S.A.* 113 M9
Orange, *Mass., U.S.A.* 107 D12
Orange, *Tex., U.S.A.* 109 K8
Orange, *Va., U.S.A.* 104 F6
Orange, C., *Brazil* 121 C7
Orange Cove, *U.S.A.* 112 J7
Orange Free State □ = Free State □, *S. Africa* 84 D4
Orange Grove, *U.S.A.* 109 M6
Orange Walk, *Belize* 115 D7
Orangeburg, *U.S.A.* 105 J5
Orangeville, *Canada* 98 D3
Orani, *Phil.* 55 D4
Oranienburg, *Germany* 18 C9
Oranje →, *S. Africa* 84 D2
Oranje Vrystaat □ = Free State □, *S. Africa* 84 D4
Oranjemund, *Namibia* 84 D2
Oranjerivier, *S. Africa* 84 D3
Oras, *Phil.* 55 E6
Orăștie, *Romania* 38 D6
Orașul Stalin = Brașov, *Romania* 38 D8
Orava →, *Slovak Rep.* 20 F9
Oravita, *Romania* 38 D4
Orb →, *France* 26 E7
Orba →, *Italy* 32 D5
Ørbæk, *Denmark* 11 J4
Orbe, *Switz.* 22 C3
Orbec, *France* 24 C7
Orbetello, *Italy* 33 F8
Órbigo →, *Spain* 30 C5
Orbost, *Australia* 91 F4
Orce, *Spain* 29 H2
Orce →, *Spain* 29 H2
Orchies, *France* 25 B10
Orchila, I., *Venezuela* 120 A4
Orco →, *Italy* 32 C4
Orcopampa, *Peru* 124 D3
Orcutt, *U.S.A.* 113 L6
Ord →, *Australia* 88 C4
Ord, Mt., *Australia* 88 C4
Ordenes, *Spain* 30 B2
Orderville, *U.S.A.* 111 H7
Ording = St-Peter-Ording, *Germany* 18 A4
Ordos = Mu Us Shamo, *China* 50 E5
Ordu, *Turkey* 66 B7
Ordubad, *Azerbaijan* 67 C12
Orduña, *Álava, Spain* 28 C7
Orduña, *Granada, Spain* 29 H1
Ordway, *U.S.A.* 108 F3
Ordzhonikidze = Vladikavkaz, *Russia* 43 J7
Ordzhonikidze, *Ukraine* 41 J8
Ore, *Zaïre* 82 B2
Ore Mts. = Erzgebirge, *Germany* 18 E9
Orealla, *Guyana* 121 B6
Orebić, *Croatia* 21 M7
Örebro, *Sweden* 9 G16
Oregon, *U.S.A.* 108 D10
Oregon □, *U.S.A.* 110 E3
Oregon City, *U.S.A.* 112 E4
Orekhov = Orikhiv, *Ukraine* 41 J8
Orekhovo-Zuyevo, *Russia* 42 C4
Orel, *Russia* 42 D3
Orel →, *Ukraine* 41 H8
Orellana, Canal de, *Spain* 31 F5
Orellana, Pantano de, *Spain* 31 F5
Orellana la Vieja, *Spain* 31 F5
Orem, *U.S.A.* 110 F8
Ören, *Turkey* 66 D2
Orenburg, *Russia* 44 D6
Orense, *Spain* 30 C3
Orense □, *Spain* 30 C3
Orepuki, *N.Z.* 87 M1
Orestiás, *Greece* 39 H9
Øresund, *Europe* 11 J6
Orford Ness, *U.K.* 13 E9
Organà, *Spain* 28 C6
Organos, Pta. de los, *Canary Is.* 36 F2
Orgaz, *Spain* 31 F7
Orgeyev = Orhei, *Moldova* 41 J5
Orgon, *France* 27 E9
Orhaneli, *Turkey* 66 C3
Orhangazi, *Turkey* 66 B3
Orhei, *Moldova* 41 J5
Orhon Gol →, *Mongolia* 54 A5
Ória, *Italy* 35 B10
Orient, *Australia* 91 D3
Oriental, Cordillera, *Bolivia* 125 D4
Oriental, Cordillera, *Colombia* 120 B3
Oriente, *Argentina* 126 D3
Origny-Ste.-Benoîte, *France* 25 C10
Orihuela, *Spain* 29 G4
Orihuela del Tremedal, *Spain* 28 E3
Orikhiv, *Ukraine* 41 J8
Oriku, *Albania* 39 J2
Orinduik, *Guyana* 121 C5
Orinoco →, *Venezuela* 121 B5
Orissa □, *India* 61 K14
Orissaare, *Estonia* 9 G20
Oristano, *Italy* 34 C1
Oristano, G. di, *Italy* 34 C1
Orituco →, *Venezuela* 120 B4
Orizaba, *Mexico* 115 D5
Orizona, *Brazil* 123 E2
Orjen, *Bos.-H.* 21 N8
Orjiva, *Spain* 29 J1
Orkanger, *Norway* 10 A3
Örkelljunga, *Sweden* 11 H7
Örkény, *Hungary* 21 H9
Orkla →, *Norway* 10 A3
Orkney, *S. Africa* 84 D4
Orkney □, *U.K.* 14 C6
Orkney Is., *U.K.* 14 C6
Orland, *U.S.A.* 112 F4
Orlando, *U.S.A.* 105 L5
Orlando, C. d', *Italy* 35 D7
Orléanais, *France* 25 E9
Orléans, *France* 25 E8
Orleans, *U.S.A.* 107 B12
Orléans, I. d', *Canada* 99 C5
Orlice →, *Czech.* 20 E6
Orlov, *Slovak Rep.* 20 F10
Orlov Gay, *Russia* 42 E9
Ormara, *Pakistan* 60 G4
Ormea, *Italy* 32 D4
Ormília, *Greece* 39 J6
Ormoc, *Phil.* 55 F6
Ormond, *N.Z.* 87 H6
Ormond Beach, *U.S.A.* 105 L5
Ormož, *Slovenia* 33 B13
Ormstown, *Canada* 107 A11
Ornans, *France* 25 E13
Orne □, *France* 24 D7
Orne →, *France* 24 C6
Ørnhøj, *Denmark* 11 H2
Ornö, *Sweden* 10 E12
Örnsköldsvik, *Sweden* 10 A12
Oro, *N. Korea* 51 D14
Oro →, *Mexico* 114 B3
Oro Grande, *U.S.A.* 113 L9
Orobie, Alpi, *Italy* 32 B6

Orocué, *Colombia* 120 C3
Orodo, *Nigeria* 79 D6
Orogrande, *U.S.A.* 111 K10
Orol, *Spain* 30 B3
Orol Dengizi = Aral Sea, *Asia* 44 E7
Oromocto, *Canada* 99 C6
Oron, *Nigeria* 79 E6
Oron, *Switz.* 22 C3
Orono, *Canada* 106 C6
Oropesa, *Spain* 30 F5
Oroquieta, *Phil.* 55 G5
Orós, *Brazil* 122 C4
Orosei, G. di, *Italy* 34 B2
Orosháza, *Hungary* 21 J10
Orotukan, *Russia* 45 C16
Oroville, *Calif., U.S.A.* 112 F5
Oroville, *Wash., U.S.A.* 110 B4
Oroville, L., *U.S.A.* 112 F5
Orroroo, *Australia* 91 E2
Orrville, *U.S.A.* 106 F3
Orsara di Púglia, *Italy* 35 A8
Orsha, *Belarus* 40 E6
Orsières, *Switz.* 22 D4
Orsk, *Russia* 44 D6
Ørslev, *Denmark* 11 J5
Orsogna, *Italy* 33 F11
Orşova, *Romania* 38 E5
Ørsted, *Denmark* 11 H4
Orta, L. d', *Italy* 32 C5
Orta Nova, *Italy* 35 A8
Ortaca, *Turkey* 66 D3
Ortaköy, *Çorum, Turkey* 66 B6
Ortaköy, *Niğde, Turkey* 66 C6
Orte, *Italy* 33 F9
Ortegal, C., *Spain* 30 B3
Orteguaza →, *Colombia* 120 C2
Orthez, *France* 26 E3
Ortho, *Belgium* 17 H7
Ortigueira, *Spain* 30 B3
Orting, *U.S.A.* 112 C4
Ortles, *Italy* 32 B7
Ortón →, *Bolivia* 124 C4
Ortona, *Italy* 33 F11
Orūmīyeh, *Iran* 67 D11
Orūmīyeh, Daryācheh-ye, *Iran* 67 D11
Orune, *Italy* 34 B2
Oruro, *Bolivia* 124 D4
Oruro □, *Bolivia* 124 D4
Orust, *Sweden* 11 F5
Oruzgān □, *Afghan.* 60 C5
Orvault, *France* 24 E5
Orvieto, *Italy* 33 F9
Orwell, *U.S.A.* 106 E4
Orwell →, *U.K.* 13 E9
Oryakhovo, *Bulgaria* 38 F6
Orzinuovi, *Italy* 32 C6
Orzysz, *Poland* 20 B11
Osa, Pen. de, *Costa Rica* 116 E3
Osage, *Iowa, U.S.A.* 108 D8
Osage, *Wyo., U.S.A.* 108 D2
Osage →, *U.S.A.* 108 F9
Osage City, *U.S.A.* 108 F7
Ōsaka, *Japan* 49 G7
Osan, *S. Korea* 51 F14
Osawatomie, *U.S.A.* 108 F7
Osborne, *U.S.A.* 108 F5
Osceola, *Ark., U.S.A.* 109 H10
Osceola, *Iowa, U.S.A.* 108 E8
Oschatz, *Germany* 18 D9
Oschersleben, *Germany* 18 C7
Óschiri, *Italy* 34 B2
Oscoda, *U.S.A.* 106 B1
Ösel = Saaremaa, *Estonia* 9 G20
Osery, *Russia* 42 C4
Osh, *Kyrgyzstan* 44 E8
Oshawa, *Canada* 98 D4
Oshkosh, *Nebr., U.S.A.* 108 E3
Oshkosh, *Wis., U.S.A.* 108 C10
Oshmyany = Ashmyany, *Belarus* 9 J21
Oshnovīyeh, *Iran* 64 B5
Oshogbo, *Nigeria* 79 D5
Oshtorīnān, *Iran* 67 E13
Oshwe, *Zaïre* 80 E3
Osijek, *Croatia* 21 K8
Ósilo, *Italy* 34 B1
Osimo, *Italy* 33 E10
Osintorf, *Belarus* 40 E6
Osipenko = Berdyansk, *Ukraine* 41 J9
Osipovichi = Asipovichy, *Belarus* 40 F5
Osizweni, *S. Africa* 85 D5
Oskaloosa, *U.S.A.* 108 E8
Oskarshamn, *Sweden* 9 H17
Oskélanéo, *Canada* 98 C4
Öskemen, *Kazakstan* 44 E9
Oskol →, *Ukraine* 41 H9
Oslo, *Norway* 10 E4
Oslob, *Phil.* 55 G5
Oslofjorden, *Norway* 10 E4
Osmanabad, *India* 60 K10
Osmancık, *Turkey* 66 B6
Osmaniye, *Turkey* 66 D7
Ösmo, *Sweden* 10 F11
Osnabrück, *Germany* 18 C4
Osor, *Italy* 33 D11
Osorio, *Brazil* 127 B5
Osorno, *Chile* 128 B2
Osorno, *Spain* 30 C6
Osorno □, *Chile* 128 B2
Osorno, Vol., *Chile* 128 B2
Osoyoos, *Canada* 100 D5
Osøyri, *Norway* 9 F11
Ospika →, *Canada* 100 B4
Osprey Reef, *Australia* 90 A4
Oss, *Neths.* 16 E7
Ossa, Mt., *Australia* 90 G4
Óssa, Oros, *Greece* 39 K5
Ossa de Montiel, *Spain* 29 G2
Ossabaw I., *U.S.A.* 105 K5
Osse →, *France* 26 D4
Ossendrecht, *Neths.* 17 F4
Ossining, *U.S.A.* 107 E11
Ossipee, *U.S.A.* 107 C13
Ossokmanuan L., *Canada* 99 B7
Ossora, *Russia* 45 D17
Ostashkov, *Russia* 42 B1
Oste →, *Germany* 18 B5
Ostend = Oostende, *Belgium* 17 F1
Oster, *Ukraine* 41 G6
Osterburg, *Germany* 18 C7
Osterburken, *Germany* 19 F5
Österdalälven, *Sweden* 9 F16
Østerdalen, *Norway* 9 F14
Östergötlands län □, *Sweden* 11 F9
Osterholz-Scharmbeck, *Germany* 18 B4
Østerild, *Denmark* 11 G2
Ostermundigen, *Switz.* 22 C4
Östersund, *Sweden* 10 A8
Østfold fylke □, *Norway* 10 E5
Ostfriesische Inseln, *Germany* 18 B3
Ostfriesland, *Germany* 18 B3
Óstia, Lido di, *Italy* 34 A5
Ostíglia, *Italy* 33 C8
Ostra, *Italy* 33 E10
Ostrava, *Czech.* 20 F8
Ostróda, *Poland* 20 B9
Ostrogozhsk, *Russia* 42 E4
Ostrogróg Szamotuły, *Poland* 20 C6
Ostroh, *Ukraine* 41 G4
Ostrołęka, *Poland* 20 B11
Ostrov, *Bulgaria* 38 F7
Ostrov, *Romania* 38 E10
Ostrov, *Russia* 40 D5
Ostrów Mazowiecka, *Poland* 20 C11
Ostrów Wielkopolski, *Poland* 20 D7
Ostrowiec-Świętokrzyski, *Poland* 20 E11
Ostrzeszów, *Poland* 20 D7
Ostseebad Kühlungsborn, *Germany* 18 A7
Osttirol □, *Austria* 19 J8
Ostuni, *Italy* 35 B10
Osum →, *Bulgaria* 38 F7
Osumi →, *Albania* 39 J3
Ōsumi-Kaikyō, *Japan* 49 J5
Ōsumi-Shotō, *Japan* 49 J5
Osun □, *Nigeria* 79 D5
Osuna, *Spain* 31 H5
Oswego, *U.S.A.* 107 C8
Oswestry, *U.K.* 12 E4
Oświęcim, *Poland* 20 E9
Otago □, *N.Z.* 87 L2
Otago Harbour, *N.Z.* 87 L3
Ōtake, *Japan* 49 G6
Otaki, *N.Z.* 87 J5
Otaru, *Japan* 48 C10
Otaru-Wan = Ishikari-Wan, *Japan* 48 C10
Otava →, *Czech.* 20 F4
Otavalo, *Ecuador* 120 C2
Otavi, *Namibia* 84 B2
Otchinjau, *Angola* 84 B1
Otelec, *Romania* 38 D3
Otero de Rey, *Spain* 30 B3
Othello, *U.S.A.* 110 C4
Othonoí, *Greece* 39 K2
Óthris, Óros, *Greece* 39 K5
Otira Gorge, *N.Z.* 87 K3
Otis, *U.S.A.* 108 E3
Otjiwarongo, *Namibia* 84 C2
Otočac, *Croatia* 33 D12
Otoineppu, *Japan* 48 B11
Otorohanga, *N.Z.* 87 H5
Otoskwin →, *Canada* 98 B2
Otosquen, *Canada* 101 C8
Otra →, *Norway* 9 G13
Otradnyy, *Russia* 42 D10
Otranto, *Italy* 35 B11
Otranto, C. d', *Italy* 35 B11
Otranto, Str. of, *Italy* 35 B11
Otse, *S. Africa* 84 D4
Ōtsu, *Japan* 49 G7
Ōtsuki, *Japan* 49 G9
Otta, *Norway* 10 C3
Ottawa = Outaouais →, *Canada* 98 C5
Ottawa, *Canada* 98 C4
Ottawa, *Ill., U.S.A.* 108 E10
Ottawa, *Kans., U.S.A.* 108 F7
Ottawa Is., *Canada* 97 C11
Ottélé, *Cameroon* 79 E7
Otter L., *Canada* 101 B8
Otter Rapids, *Ont., Canada* 98 B3
Otter Rapids, *Sask., Canada* 101 B8
Otterndorf, *Germany* 18 B4
Otterup, *Denmark* 11 J4
Otterville, *Canada* 106 D4
Ottignies, *Belgium* 17 G5
Otto Beit Bridge, *Zimbabwe* 83 F2
Ottosdal, *S. Africa* 84 D4
Ottsjön, *Sweden* 10 A7
Ottumwa, *U.S.A.* 108 E8
Otu, *Nigeria* 79 D5
Otukpa, *Nigeria* 79 D6
Oturkpo, *Nigeria* 79 D6
Otway, B., *Chile* 128 D2
Otway, C., *Australia* 91 F3
Otwock, *Poland* 20 C11
Ötz, *Austria* 19 H6
Ötz →, *Austria* 19 H6
Ötztaler Alpen, *Austria* 19 J7
Ou →, *Laos* 58 B4
Ou Neua, *Laos* 58 A3
Ou-Sammyaku, *Japan* 48 E10
Ouachita →, *U.S.A.* 109 K9
Ouachita, L., *U.S.A.* 109 H8
Ouachita Mts., *U.S.A.* 109 H7
Ouadâne, *Mauritania* 74 D2
Ouadda, *C.A.R.* 73 G9
Ouagadougou, *Burkina Faso* 79 C4
Ouahigouya, *Burkina Faso* 78 C4
Ouahila, *Algeria* 74 C3
Ouahran = Oran, *Algeria* 75 A4
Oualâta, *Mauritania* 78 B3
Ouallene, *Algeria* 75 D5
Ouanda Djallé, *C.A.R.* 73 G9
Ouango, *C.A.R.* 80 D4
Ouarâne, *Mauritania* 74 D2
Ouargla, *Algeria* 75 B6
Ouarkziz, Djebel, *Algeria* 74 C3
Ouarzazate, *Morocco* 74 B3
Ouatagouna, *Mali* 79 B5
Oubangi →, *Zaïre* 80 E3
Oubarakai, O. →, *Algeria* 75 C6
Ouche →, *France* 25 E12
Oud-Beijerland, *Neths.* 16 E4
Oud-Gastel, *Neths.* 17 E4
Oud Turnhout, *Belgium* 17 F6
Ouddorp, *Neths.* 16 E3
Oude-Pekela, *Neths.* 16 B10
Oude Rijn →, *Neths.* 16 D4
Oudega, *Neths.* 16 B8
Oudenaarde, *Belgium* 17 G3
Oudenbosch, *Neths.* 17 E5
Oudenburg, *Belgium* 17 F2
Ouderkerk, *Utrecht, Neths.* 16 D5
Ouderkerk, *Zuid-Holland, Neths.* 16 E5
Oudeschild, *Neths.* 16 B5
Oudewater, *Neths.* 16 D5
Oudkarspel, *Neths.* 16 C5
Oudon, *France* 24 E5
Oudon →, *France* 24 E6
Oudtshoorn, *S. Africa* 84 E3
Oued Zem, *Morocco* 74 B3
Ouellé, *Ivory C.* 78 D4
Ouenza, *Algeria* 75 A6
Ouessa, *Burkina Faso* 78 C4
Ouessant, I. d', *France* 24 D1
Ouesso, *Congo* 80 D3
Ouest, Pte., *Canada* 99 C7
Ouezzane, *Morocco* 74 B3
Ouffet, *Belgium* 17 H6
Ouidah, *Benin* 79 D5
Ouistreham, *France* 24 C6
Oujda, *Morocco* 75 B4
Oujeft, *Mauritania* 74 D2
Oulainen, *Finland* 8 D21
Ould Yenjé, *Mauritania* 78 B2
Ouled Djellal, *Algeria* 75 B6
Ouled Naïl, Mts. des, *Algeria* 75 B5
Oulmès, *Morocco* 74 B3
Oulu, *Finland* 8 D21
Oulujärvi, *Finland* 8 D22
Oulujoki →, *Finland* 8 D21
Oulx, *Italy* 32 C3
Oum Chalouba, *Chad* 73 E9
Oum-el-Bouaghi, *Algeria* 75 A6
Oum el Ksi, *Algeria* 74 C3
Oum-er-Rbia, O. →, *Morocco* 74 B3
Oumè, *Ivory C.* 78 D3
Ounane, Dj., *Algeria* 75 C6
Ounasjoki →, *Finland* 8 C21
Ounguati, *Namibia* 84 C2
Ounianga-Kébir, *Chad* 73 E9
Ounianga Sérir, *Chad* 73 E9
Our →, *Lux.* 17 J8
Ouray, *U.S.A.* 111 G10
Ourcq →, *France* 25 C10
Ourém, *Brazil* 122 B2
Ourense = Orense, *Spain* 30 C3
Ouricuri, *Brazil* 122 C3
Ourinhos, *Brazil* 127 A6
Ourique, *Portugal* 31 H2
Ouro Fino, *Brazil* 127 A6
Ouro Prêto, *Brazil* 123 F3
Ouro Sogui, *Senegal* 78 B2
Oursi, *Burkina Faso* 79 C4
Ourthe →, *Belgium* 17 H7
Ouse, *Australia* 90 G4
Ouse →, *E. Susx., U.K.* 13 G8
Ouse →, *N. Yorks., U.K.* 12 C8
Oust, *France* 26 F5
Oust →, *France* 24 E4
Outaouais →, *Canada* 98 C5
Outardes →, *Canada* 99 C6
Outat Oulad el Haj, *Morocco* 75 B4
Outer Hebrides, *U.K.* 14 D1
Outer I., *Canada* 99 B8
Outes, *Spain* 30 C2
Outjo, *Namibia* 84 C2
Outlook, *Canada* 101 C7
Outlook, *U.S.A.* 108 A2
Outokumpu, *Finland* 8 E23
Outreau, *France* 25 B8
Ouvèze →, *France* 27 E8
Ouyen, *Australia* 91 F3
Ouzouer-le-Marché, *France* 25 E8
Ovada, *Italy* 32 D5
Ovalau, *Fiji* 87 C8
Ovalle, *Chile* 126 C1
Ovamboland, *Namibia* 84 B2
Ovar, *Portugal* 30 E2
Ovejas, *Colombia* 120 B2
Overdinkel, *Neths.* 16 D10
Overflakkee, *Neths.* 16 E4
Overijse, *Belgium* 17 G5
Overijssel □, *Neths.* 16 D9
Overijsselsch Kanaal →, *Neths.* 16 C8
Overland Park, *U.S.A.* 108 F7
Overpelt, *Belgium* 17 F6
Overton, *U.S.A.* 113 J12
Övertorneå, *Sweden* 8 C20
Ovid, *U.S.A.* 108 E3
Ovidiopol, *Ukraine* 41 J6
Oviedo, *Spain* 30 B5
Oviedo □, *Spain* 30 B5
Oviken, *Sweden* 10 A8
Oviksfjällen, *Sweden* 10 B7
Oviši, *Latvia* 9 H19
Övör Hangay □, *Mongolia* 50 B2
Ovoro, *Nigeria* 79 D6
Øvre Årdal, *Norway* 9 F12
Ovruch, *Ukraine* 41 G5
Owaka, *N.Z.* 87 M2
Owambo = Ovamboland, *Namibia* 84 B2
Owase, *Japan* 49 G8
Owatonna, *U.S.A.* 108 C8
Owbeh, *Afghan.* 60 B3
Owego, *U.S.A.* 107 D8
Owen Falls Dam, *Uganda* 82 B3
Owen Sound, *Canada* 98 D3
Owendo, *Gabon* 80 D1
Owens →, *U.S.A.* 112 J9
Owens L., *U.S.A.* 113 J9
Owensboro, *U.S.A.* 104 G2
Owensville, *U.S.A.* 108 F9
Owerri, *Nigeria* 79 D6
Owl →, *Canada* 101 B10
Owo, *Nigeria* 79 D6
Owosso, *U.S.A.* 104 D3
Owyhee, *U.S.A.* 110 F5
Owyhee →, *U.S.A.* 110 E5
Owyhee, L., *U.S.A.* 110 E5
Oxapampa, *Peru* 124 C2
Öxarfjörður, *Iceland* 8 C5
Oxelösund, *Sweden* 11 F11
Oxford, *N.Z.* 87 K4
Oxford, *U.K.* 13 F6
Oxford, *Miss., U.S.A.* 109 H10
Oxford, *N.C., U.S.A.* 105 G6
Oxford, *Ohio, U.S.A.* 104 F3
Oxford L., *Canada* 101 C9
Oxfordshire □, *U.K.* 13 F6
Oxley, *Australia* 91 E3
Oxnard, *U.S.A.* 113 L7
Oxus = Amudarya →, *Uzbekistan* 44 E6
Oya, *Malaysia* 56 D4
Oyama, *Japan* 49 F9
Oyapock →, *Fr. Guiana* 121 C7
Oyem, *Gabon* 80 D2
Oyen, *Canada* 101 C6
Øyeren, *Norway* 10 E5
Oykel →, *U.K.* 14 D4
Oymyakon, *Russia* 45 C15
Oyo, *Nigeria* 79 D5
Oyo □, *Nigeria* 79 D5
Oyón, *Peru* 124 C2
Oyonnax, *France* 27 B9
Oyster Bay, *U.S.A.* 107 F11
Ōyübari, *Japan* 48 C11
Özalp, *Turkey* 67 C10
Ozamiz, *Phil.* 55 G5
Ozark, *Ala., U.S.A.* 105 K3
Ozark, *Ark., U.S.A.* 109 H8
Ozark, *Mo., U.S.A.* 109 G8
Ozark Plateau, *U.S.A.* 109 G9
Ozarks, L. of the, *U.S.A.* 108 F8
Ózd, *Hungary* 21 G10
Ozernoye, *Russia* 42 E10
Ozette L., *U.S.A.* 112 B2
Ozieri, *Italy* 34 B2
Ozinki, *Russia* 42 E9
Ozona, *U.S.A.* 109 K4
Ozorków, *Poland* 20 D9
Ozuluama, *Mexico* 115 C5
Ozurgeti, *Georgia* 43 K5

P

Pa, *Burkina Faso* 78 C4
Pa-an, *Burma* 61 L20
Pa Mong Dam, *Thailand* 58 D4
Paal, *Belgium* 17 F6
Paamiut = Frederikshåb, *Greenland* 4 C5
Paar →, *Germany* 19 G6
Paarl, *S. Africa* 84 E2
Paauilo, *U.S.A.* 102 H17
Pab Hills, *Pakistan* 62 F2
Pabianice, *Poland* 20 D9
Pabna, *Bangla.* 61 G16
Pabo, *Uganda* 82 B3
Pacaás Novos, Serra dos, *Brazil* 125 C5
Pacaipampa, *Peru* 124 B2
Pacaja →, *Brazil* 122 B1
Pacajus, *Brazil* 122 B4
Pacaraima, Sierra, *Venezuela* 121 C5
Pacarán, *Peru* 124 C2
Pacaraos, *Peru* 124 C2
Pacasmayo, *Peru* 124 B2
Paceco, *Italy* 34 E5
Pachacamac, *Peru* 124 C2
Pachhar, *India* 62 G7
Pachino, *Italy* 35 F8
Pachitea →, *Peru* 124 B3
Pachiza, *Peru* 124 B2
Pacho, *Colombia* 120 B3
Pachpadra, *India* 60 G8
Pachuca, *Mexico* 115 C5
Pacific, *Canada* 100 C3
Pacific-Antarctic Ridge, *Pac. Oc.* 93 M16
Pacific Grove, *U.S.A.* 111 H3
Pacific Ocean, *Pac. Oc.* 93 G14
Pacifica, *U.S.A.* 112 H4
Pacitan, *Indonesia* 57 H14
Packwood, *U.S.A* 112 D5
Pacuí →, *Brazil* 123 E2
Pacy-sur-Eure, *France* 24 C8
Padaido, Kepulauan, *Indonesia* 57 E9
Padang, *Indonesia* 56 E2
Padangpanjang, *Indonesia* 56 E2
Padangsidempuan, *Indonesia* 56 D1
Padauari →, *Brazil* 121 D5
Padborg, *Denmark* 11 K3
Padcaya, *Bolivia* 125 E5
Paddockwood, *Canada* 101 C7
Paderborn, *Germany* 18 D4
Padilla, *Bolivia* 125 D5
Padloping Island, *Canada* 97 B13
Pádova, *Italy* 33 C8
Padra, *India* 62 H5
Padrauna, *India* 63 F10
Padre I., *U.S.A.* 109 M6
Padro, Mte., *France* 27 F12
Padrón, *Spain* 30 C2
Padstow, *U.K.* 13 G3
Padua = Pádova, *Italy* 33 C8
Paducah, *Ky., U.S.A.* 104 G1
Paducah, *Tex., U.S.A.* 109 H4
Padul, *Spain* 31 H7
Padula, *Italy* 35 B8
Paengnyong-do, *S. Korea* 51 F13
Paeroa, *N.Z.* 87 G5
Paesana, *Italy* 32 D4
Pafúri, *Mozam.* 85 C5
Pag, *Croatia* 33 D11
Paga, *Ghana* 79 C4
Pagadian, *Phil.* 55 H5
Pagai Selatan, P., *Indonesia* 56 E2
Pagai Utara, *Indonesia* 56 E2
Pagalu = Annobón, *Atl. Oc.* 70 G4
Pagastikós Kólpos, *Greece* 39 K6
Pagatan, *Indonesia* 56 E5
Page, *Ariz., U.S.A.* 111 H8
Page, *N. Dak., U.S.A.* 108 B6
Paglieta, *Italy* 33 F11
Pagny-sur-Moselle, *France* 25 D13
Pago Pago, *Amer. Samoa* 87 B13
Pagosa Springs, *U.S.A.* 111 H10
Pagwa River, *Canada* 98 B2
Pahala, *U.S.A.* 102 J17
Pahang →, *Malaysia* 59 L4
Pahiatua, *N.Z.* 87 J5
Pahokee, *U.S.A.* 105 M5
Pahrump, *U.S.A.* 113 J11
Pahute Mesa, *U.S.A.* 112 H10
Pai, *Thailand* 58 C2
Paia, *U.S.A.* 102 H16
Paicines, *U.S.A.* 112 J5
Paide, *Estonia* 9 G21
Paignton, *U.K.* 13 G4
Paiho, *Taiwan* 53 F13
Paiján, *Peru* 124 B2
Päijänne, *Finland* 9 F21
Paimbœuf, *France* 24 E4
Paimpol, *France* 24 D3
Painan, *Indonesia* 56 E2
Painesville, *U.S.A.* 106 E3
Paint Hills = Wemindji, *Canada* 98 B4
Paint L., *Canada* 101 B9
Paint Rock, *U.S.A.* 109 K5
Painted Desert, *U.S.A.* 111 J8
Paintsville, *U.S.A.* 104 G4
País Vasco □, *Spain* 28 C2
Paisley, *Canada* 106 B3
Paisley, *U.K.* 14 F4
Paisley, *U.S.A.* 110 E3
Paita, *Peru* 124 B1
Paiva →, *Portugal* 30 D2
Paizhou, *China* 53 B9
Pajares, *Spain* 30 B5
Pajares, Puerto de, *Spain* 30 C5
Pak Lay, *Laos* 58 C3
Pak Phanang, *Thailand* 59 H3
Pak Sane, *Laos* 58 C4
Pak Song, *Laos* 58 E6
Pak Suong, *Laos* 58 C4
Pakaraima Mts., *Guyana* 121 B5
Pákhnes, *Greece* 37 D6
Pakistan ■, *Asia* 62 E3
Pakkading, *Laos* 58 C4
Pakokku, *Burma* 61 J19
Pakpattan, *Pakistan* 62 D5
Pakrac, *Croatia* 21 K7

Paks, *Hungary* 21 J8
Pakse, *Laos* 58 E5
Paktīā □, *Afghan.* 60 C6
Pakwach, *Uganda* 82 B3
Pala, *Chad* 73 G8
Pala, *U.S.A.* 113 M9
Pala, *Zaïre* 82 D2
Palabek, *Uganda* 82 B3
Palacios, *U.S.A.* 109 L6
Palafrugell, *Spain* 28 D8
Palagiano, *Italy* 35 B10
Palagonía, *Italy* 35 E7
Palagruža, *Croatia* 33 F13
Palaiókastron, *Greece* 37 D8
Palaiokhóra, *Greece* 37 D5
Palam, *India* 60 K10
Palamás, *Greece* 39 K5
Palamós, *Spain* 28 D8
Palampur, *India* 62 C7
Palana, *Australia* 90 F4
Palana, *Russia* 45 D16
Palanan, *Phil.* 55 C5
Palanan Pt., *Phil.* 55 C5
Palandri, *Pakistan* 63 C5
Palanga, *Lithuania* 9 J19
Palangkaraya, *Indonesia* 56 E4
Palani Hills, *India* 60 P10
Palanpur, *India* 62 G5
Palanro, *Indonesia* 57 E5
Palapye, *Botswana* 84 C4
Palas, *Pakistan* 63 B5
Palatka, *Russia* 45 C16
Palatka, *U.S.A.* 105 L5
Palau ■, *Pac. Oc.* 46 J17
Palawan, *Phil.* 55 G3
Palayankottai, *India* 60 Q10
Palazzo, Pte., *France* 27 F12
Palazzo San Gervásio, *Italy* 35 B8
Palazzolo Acréide, *Italy* 35 E7
Palca, *Chile* 124 D4
Paldiski, *Estonia* 9 G21
Paleleh, *Indonesia* 57 D6
Palembang, *Indonesia* 56 E2
Palena →, *Chile* 128 B2
Palena, L., *Chile* 128 B2
Palencia, *Spain* 30 C6
Palencia □, *Spain* 30 C6
Paleokastrítsa, *Greece* 37 A3
Paleometokho, *Cyprus* 37 D12
Palermo, *Colombia* 120 C2
Palermo, *Italy* 34 D6
Palermo, *U.S.A.* 110 G3
Palestine, *Asia* 69 D4
Palestine, *U.S.A.* 109 K7
Palestrina, *Italy* 34 A5
Paletwa, *Burma* 61 J18
Palghat, *India* 60 P10
Palgrave, Mt., *Australia* 88 D2
Pali, *India* 62 G5
Palinuro, C., *Italy* 35 B8
Palisade, *U.S.A.* 108 E4
Paliseul, *Belgium* 17 J6
Palitana, *India* 62 J4
Palizada, *Mexico* 115 D6
Palizzi Marina, *Italy* 35 E8
Palk Bay, *Asia* 60 Q11
Palk Strait, *Asia* 60 Q11
Palkānah, *Iraq* 64 C5
Palla Road = Dinokwe, *Botswana* 84 C4
Pallanza = Verbánia, *Italy* 32 C5
Pallasovka, *Russia* 42 E8
Pallisa, *Uganda* 82 B3
Pallu, *India* 62 E6
Palm Bay, *U.S.A.* 105 L5
Palm Beach, *U.S.A.* 105 M6
Palm Desert, *U.S.A.* 113 M10
Palm Is., *Australia* 90 B4
Palm Springs, *U.S.A.* 113 M10
Palma, *Mozam.* 83 E5
Palma →, *Brazil* 123 D2
Palma, B. de, *Spain* 36 B9
Palma de Mallorca, *Spain* 36 B9
Palma del Río, *Spain* 31 H5
Palma di Montechiaro, *Italy* 34 E6
Palma Soriano, *Cuba* 116 B4
Palmanova, *Italy* 33 C10
Palmares, *Brazil* 122 C4
Palmarito, *Venezuela* 120 B3
Palmarola, *Italy* 34 B5
Palmas, *Brazil* 127 B5
Palmas, C., *Liberia* 78 E3
Pálmas, G. di, *Italy* 34 C1
Palmas de Monte Alto, *Brazil* 123 D3
Palmdale, *U.S.A.* 113 L8
Palmeira, *Brazil* 123 G2
Palmeira dos Índios, *Brazil* 122 C4
Palmeirais, *Brazil* 122 C3
Palmeiras →, *Brazil* 123 D2
Palmeirinhas, Pta. das, *Angola* 80 F2
Palmela, *Portugal* 31 G2
Palmelo, *Brazil* 123 E2
Palmer, *U.S.A.* 96 B5
Palmer →, *Australia* 90 B3
Palmer Arch., *Antarctica* 5 C17
Palmer Lake, *U.S.A.* 108 F2
Palmer Land, *Antarctica* 5 D18
Palmerston, *Canada* 106 C4
Palmerston, *N.Z.* 87 L3
Palmerston North, *N.Z.* 87 J5
Palmerton, *U.S.A.* 107 F9
Palmetto, *U.S.A.* 105 M4
Palmi, *Italy* 35 D8
Palmira, *Argentina* 126 C2
Palmira, *Colombia* 120 C2
Palmyra = Tudmur, *Syria* 67 E8
Palmyra, *Mo., U.S.A.* 108 F9
Palmyra, *N.Y., U.S.A.* 106 C7
Palmyra Is., *Pac. Oc.* 93 G11
Palo Alto, *U.S.A.* 111 H2
Palo del Colle, *Italy* 35 A9
Palo Verde, *U.S.A.* 113 M12
Palombara Sabina, *Italy* 33 F9
Palompon, *Phil.* 55 F6
Palopo, *Indonesia* 57 E6
Palos, C. de, *Spain* 29 H4
Palos Verdes, *U.S.A.* 113 M8
Palos Verdes, Pt., *U.S.A.* 113 M8
Palouse, *U.S.A.* 110 C5
Palpa, *Peru* 124 C2
Palparara, *Australia* 90 C3
Pålsboda, *Sweden* 10 E9
Palu, *Indonesia* 57 E5
Palu, *Turkey* 67 C9
Paluan, *Phil.* 57 B6
Palwal, *India* 62 E7
Pama, *Burkina Faso* 79 C5
Pamanukan, *Indonesia* 57 G12
Pamekasan, *Indonesia* 57 G15
Pamiers, *France* 26 E5
Pamirs, *Tajikistan* 44 F8
Pamlico →, *U.S.A.* 105 H7
Pamlico Sd., *U.S.A.* 105 H8
Pampa, *U.S.A.* 109 H4
Pampa de Agma, *Argentina* 128 B3
Pampa de las Salinas, *Argentina* 126 C2
Pampa Grande, *Bolivia* 125 D5
Pampa Hermosa, *Peru* 124 B2
Pampanua, *Indonesia* 57 E6
Pamparato, *Italy* 32 D4
Pampas, *Argentina* 126 D3
Pampas, *Peru* 124 C3
Pampas →, *Peru* 124 C3
Pamphylia, *Turkey* 66 D4
Pamplona, *Colombia* 120 B3
Pamplona, *Spain* 28 C3
Pampoenpoort, *S. Africa* 84 E3
Pan Xian, *China* 52 E5
Pana, *U.S.A.* 108 F10
Panabo, *Phil.* 55 H6
Panaca, *U.S.A.* 111 H6
Panagyurishte, *Bulgaria* 38 G7
Panaitan, *Indonesia* 57 G11
Panaji, *India* 60 M8
Panamá, *Panama* 116 E4
Panama ■, *Cent. Amer.* 116 E4
Panamá, G. de, *Panama* 116 E4
Panama Canal, *Panama* 116 E4
Panama City, *U.S.A.* 105 K3
Panamint Range, *U.S.A.* 113 J9
Panamint Springs, *U.S.A.* 113 J9
Panão, *Peru* 124 B2
Panaon I., *Phil.* 55 F6
Panare, *Thailand* 59 J3
Panarea, *Italy* 35 D8
Panaro →, *Italy* 32 D8
Panarukan, *Indonesia* 57 G15
Panay, *Phil.* 55 F5
Panay, G., *Phil.* 57 B6
Pancake Range, *U.S.A.* 111 G6
Pančevo, *Serbia, Yug.* 21 L10
Pancorbo, Paso, *Spain* 28 C1
Pandan, *Antique, Phil.* 55 F5
Pandan, *Catanduanes, Phil.* 55 D6
Pandegelang, *Indonesia* 57 G12
Pandharpur, *India* 60 L9
Pandilla, *Spain* 28 D1
Pando, *Uruguay* 127 C4
Pando □, *Bolivia* 124 C4
Pando, L. = Hope, L., *Australia* 91 D2
Pandokrátor, *Greece* 37 A3
Pandora, *Costa Rica* 116 E3
Panevėžys, *Lithuania* 9 J21
Panfilov, *Kazakstan* 44 E8
Panfilovo, *Russia* 42 E6
Pang-Long, *Burma* 61 H21
Pang-Yang, *Burma* 61 H21
Panga, *Zaïre* 82 B2
Pangalanes, Canal des, *Madag.* 85 C8
Pangani, *Tanzania* 82 D4
Pangani □, *Tanzania* 82 D4
Pangani →, *Tanzania* 82 D4
Pangfou = Bengbu, *China* 51 H9
Pangil, *Zaïre* 82 C2
Pangkah, Tanjung, *Indonesia* 57 G15
Pangkajene, *Indonesia* 57 E5
Pangkalanbrandan, *Indonesia* 56 D1
Pangkalanbuun, *Indonesia* 56 E4
Pangkalansusu, *Indonesia* 56 D1
Pangkalpinang, *Indonesia* 56 E3
Pangkoh, *Indonesia* 56 E4
Pangnirtung, *Canada* 97 B13
Pangrango, *Indonesia* 57 G12
Panguipulli, *Chile* 128 A2
Panguitch, *U.S.A.* 111 H7
Pangutaran Group, *Phil.* 55 H4
Panhandle, *U.S.A.* 109 H4
Pani Mines, *India* 62 H5
Pania-Mutombo, *Zaïre* 82 D1
Panipat, *India* 62 E7
Panjal Range, *India* 62 C7
Panjgur, *Pakistan* 60 F4
Panjim = Panaji, *India* 60 M8
Panjinad Barrage, *Pakistan* 60 E7
Panjwai, *Afghan.* 62 D1
Pankshin, *Nigeria* 79 D6
Panmunjŏm, *N. Korea* 51 F14
Panna, *India* 63 G9
Panna Hills, *India* 63 G9
Pano Lefkara, *Cyprus* 37 E12
Pano Panayia, *Cyprus* 37 E11
Panorama, *Brazil* 127 A5
Pánormon, *Greece* 37 D6
Panshan, *China* 51 D12
Panshi, *China* 51 C14
Pantar, *Indonesia* 57 F6
Pante Macassar, *Indonesia* 57 F6
Pantelleria, *Italy* 34 F5
Pantón, *Spain* 30 C3
Pánuco, *Mexico* 115 C5
Panyam, *Nigeria* 79 D6
Panyu, *China* 53 F9
Pao →, *Anzoátegui, Venezuela* 121 B5
Pao →, *Apure, Venezuela* 120 B4
Páola, *Italy* 35 C9
Paola, *Malta* 37 D2
Paola, *U.S.A.* 108 F7
Paonia, *U.S.A.* 111 G10
Paoting = Baoding, *China* 50 E8
Paot'ou = Baotou, *China* 50 D6
Paoua, *C.A.R.* 73 G8
Pápa, *Hungary* 21 H7
Papagayo →, *Mexico* 115 D5
Papagayo, G. de, *Costa Rica* 116 D2
Papakura, *N.Z.* 87 G5
Papantla, *Mexico* 115 C5
Papar, *Malaysia* 56 C5
Pápas, Ákra, *Greece* 39 L4
Papenburg, *Germany* 18 B3
Paphlagonia, *Turkey* 66 B5
Paphos, *Cyprus* 66 E5
Papien Chiang = Da →, *Vietnam* 58 B5
Papigochic →, *Mexico* 114 B3
Paposo, *Chile* 126 B1
Papoutsa, *Cyprus* 37 E12
Papua New Guinea ■, *Oceania* 92 H6
Papuča, *Croatia* 33 D12
Papudo, *Chile* 126 C1
Papuk, *Croatia* 21 K7
Papun, *Burma* 61 K20
Papunya, *Australia* 88 D5
Pará = Belém, *Brazil* 122 B2
Pará □, *Brazil* 125 A7
Pará □, *Surinam* 121 B6
Parábita, *Italy* 35 B11
Paraburdoo, *Australia* 88 D2
Paracale, *Phil.* 55 D5
Paracas, Pen., *Peru* 124 C2
Paracatu, *Brazil* 123 E2
Paracatu →, *Brazil* 123 E2
Paracel Is., *S. China Sea* 56 A4
Parachilna, *Australia* 91 E2
Parachinar, *Pakistan* 62 C4
Paraćin, *Serbia, Yug.* 21 M11
Paracuru, *Brazil* 122 B4
Parada, Punta, *Peru* 124 D2
Paradas, *Spain* 31 H5
Paradela, *Spain* 30 C3
Paradhísi, *Greece* 37 C10
Paradip, *India* 61 J15
Paradise, *Calif., U.S.A.* 112 F5
Paradise, *Mont., U.S.A.* 110 C6
Paradise, *Nev., U.S.A.* 113 J11
Paradise →, *Canada* 99 B8
Paradise Valley, *U.S.A.* 110 F5
Parado, *Indonesia* 57 F5
Paragould, *U.S.A.* 109 G9
Paraguá →, *Bolivia* 125 C5
Paragua →, *Venezuela* 121 B5
Paraguaçu →, *Brazil* 123 D4
Paraguaçu Paulista, *Brazil* 127 A5
Paraguaipoa, *Venezuela* 120 A3
Paraguaná, Pen. de, *Venezuela* 120 A3
Paraguarí, *Paraguay* 126 B4
Paraguarí □, *Paraguay* 126 B4
Paraguay ■, *S. Amer.* 126 A4
Paraguay →, *Paraguay* 126 B4
Paraíba = João Pessoa, *Brazil* 122 C5
Paraíba □, *Brazil* 122 C4
Paraíba do Sul →, *Brazil* 123 F3
Parainen, *Finland* 9 F20
Paraiso, *Mexico* 115 D6
Parak, *Iran* 65 E7
Parakhino Paddubye, *Russia* 40 C7
Parakou, *Benin* 79 D5
Paralimni, *Cyprus* 37 D12
Paramaribo, *Surinam* 121 B6
Parambu, *Brazil* 122 C3
Paramillo, Nudo del, *Colombia* 120 B2
Paramirim, *Brazil* 123 D3
Paramirim →, *Brazil* 123 D3
Paramithiá, *Greece* 39 K3
Paramushir, Ostrov, *Russia* 45 D16
Paran →, *Israel* 69 E4
Paraná, *Argentina* 126 C3
Paranã, *Brazil* 123 D2
Paraná □, *Brazil* 127 A5
Paraná →, *Argentina* 126 C4
Paranaguá, *Brazil* 127 B6
Paranaíba →, *Brazil* 123 F1
Paranapanema →, *Brazil* 127 A5
Paranapiacaba, Serra do, *Brazil* 127 A6
Paranavaí, *Brazil* 127 A5
Parang, *Jolo, Phil.* 55 J4
Parang, *Mindanao, Phil.* 57 C6
Parangaba, *Brazil* 122 B4
Parapóla, *Greece* 39 N6
Paraspóri, Ákra, *Greece* 39 P10
Paratinga, *Brazil* 123 D3
Paratoo, *Australia* 91 E2
Parattah, *Australia* 90 G4
Paraúna, *Brazil* 123 E1
Paray-le-Monial, *France* 27 B8
Parbati →, *India* 62 G7
Parbhani, *India* 60 K10
Parchim, *Germany* 18 B7
Parczew, *Poland* 20 D12
Pardes Hanna, *Israel* 69 C3
Pardilla, *Spain* 30 D7
Pardo →, *Bahia, Brazil* 123 E4
Pardo →, *Mato Grosso, Brazil* 127 A5
Pardo →, *Minas Gerais, Brazil* 123 E3
Pardo →, *São Paulo, Brazil* 123 F2
Pardubice, *Czech.* 20 E5
Pare, *Indonesia* 57 G15
Pare □, *Tanzania* 82 C4
Pare Mts., *Tanzania* 82 C4
Parecis, Serra dos, *Brazil* 125 C6
Paredes de Nava, *Spain* 30 C6
Pareh, *Iran* 64 B5
Parelhas, *Brazil* 122 C4
Paren, *Russia* 45 C17
Parent, *Canada* 98 C5
Parent, L., *Canada* 98 C4
Parentis-en-Born, *France* 26 D2
Parepare, *Indonesia* 57 E5
Parfino, *Russia* 40 D6
Pargo, Pta. do, *Madeira* 36 D2
Paria, G. de, *Venezuela* 121 A5
Paria, Pen. de, *Venezuela* 121 A5
Pariaguán, *Venezuela* 121 B5
Pariaman, *Indonesia* 56 E2
Paricatuba, *Brazil* 121 D5
Paricutín, Cerro, *Mexico* 114 D4
Parigi, *Java, Indonesia* 57 G13
Parigi, *Sulawesi, Indonesia* 57 E6
Parika, *Guyana* 121 B6
Parikkala, *Finland* 40 B5
Parima, Serra, *Brazil* 121 C5
Parinari, *Peru* 124 A3
Pariñas, Pta., *S. Amer.* 118 D2
Parîngul Mare, *Romania* 38 D6
Parintins, *Brazil* 121 D6
Pariparit Kyun, *Burma* 61 M18
Paris, *Canada* 98 D3
Paris, *France* 25 D9
Paris, *Idaho, U.S.A.* 110 E8
Paris, *Ky., U.S.A.* 104 F3
Paris, *Tenn., U.S.A.* 105 G1
Paris, *Tex., U.S.A.* 109 J7
Paris, Ville de □, *France* 25 D9
Parish, *U.S.A.* 107 C8
Pariti, *Indonesia* 57 F6
Park, *U.S.A.* 112 B4
Park City, *U.S.A.* 110 F8
Park Falls, *U.S.A.* 108 C9
Park Range, *U.S.A.* 110 G10
Park Rapids, *U.S.A.* 108 B7
Park River, *U.S.A.* 108 A6
Park Rynie, *S. Africa* 85 E5
Parkā Bandar, *Iran* 65 E8
Parkano, *Finland* 9 E20
Parker, *Ariz., U.S.A.* 113 L12
Parker, *S. Dak., U.S.A.* 108 D6
Parker Dam, *U.S.A.* 113 L12
Parkersburg, *U.S.A.* 104 F5
Parkerview, *Canada* 101 C8
Parkes, *Australia* 91 E4
Parkfield, *U.S.A.* 112 K6
Parkland, *U.S.A.* 112 C4
Parkside, *Canada* 101 C7
Parkston, *U.S.A.* 108 D5
Parksville, *Canada* 100 D4
Parma, *Italy* 32 D7
Parma, *Idaho, U.S.A.* 110 E5
Parma, *Ohio, U.S.A.* 106 E3
Parma →, *Italy* 32 D7
Parnaguá, *Brazil* 122 D3
Parnaíba, *Piauí, Brazil* 122 B3
Parnaíba, *São Paulo, Brazil* 125 D7
Parnaíba →, *Brazil* 122 B3
Parnamirim, *Brazil* 122 C4
Parnarama, *Brazil* 122 C3
Parnassós, *Greece* 39 L5
Párnis, *Greece* 39 L6
Párnon Óros, *Greece* 39 M5
Parnu, *Estonia* 9 G21
Paroo →, *Australia* 91 E3
Páros, *Greece* 39 M8
Parowan, *U.S.A.* 111 H7
Parpaillon, *France* 27 D10
Parral, *Chile* 126 D1
Parramatta, *Australia* 91 E5
Parras, *Mexico* 114 B4
Parrett →, *U.K.* 13 F5
Parris I., *U.S.A.* 105 J5
Parrsboro, *Canada* 99 C7
Parry Is., *Canada* 4 B2
Parry Sound, *Canada* 98 C3
Parsberg, *Germany* 19 F7
Parshall, *U.S.A.* 108 B3
Parsnip →, *Canada* 100 B4
Parsons, *U.S.A.* 109 G7
Parsons Ra., *Australia* 90 A2
Partanna, *Italy* 34 E5
Parthenay, *France* 24 F6
Partinico, *Italy* 34 D6
Paru →, *Brazil* 121 D7
Parú →, *Venezuela* 120 C4
Paru de Oeste →, *Brazil* 121 C6
Parucito →, *Venezuela* 120 B4
Paruro, *Peru* 124 C3
Parvān □, *Afghan.* 60 B6
Parvatipuram, *India* 61 K13
Parys, *S. Africa* 84 D4
Pas-de-Calais □, *France* 25 B9
Pasadena, *Calif., U.S.A.* 113 L8
Pasadena, *Tex., U.S.A.* 109 L7
Pasaje, *Ecuador* 120 D2
Pasaje →, *Argentina* 126 B3
Pasay, *Phil.* 55 D4
Pascagoula, *U.S.A.* 109 K10
Pascagoula →, *U.S.A.* 109 K10
Paşcani, *Romania* 38 B9
Pasco, *U.S.A.* 110 C4
Pasco □, *Peru* 124 C2
Pasco, Cerro de, *Peru* 124 C2
Pascua, I. de, *Pac. Oc.* 93 K17
Pasewalk, *Germany* 18 B10
Pasfield L., *Canada* 101 B7
Pasha →, *Russia* 40 B7
Pashiwari, *Pakistan* 63 B6
Pashmakli = Smolyan, *Bulgaria* 39 H7
Pasinler, *Turkey* 67 C9
Pasirian, *Indonesia* 57 H15
Paskūh, *Iran* 65 E9
Pasley, C., *Australia* 89 F3
Pašman, *Croatia* 33 E12
Pasni, *Pakistan* 60 G3
Paso Cantinela, *Mexico* 113 N11
Paso de Indios, *Argentina* 128 B3
Paso de los Libres, *Argentina* 126 B4
Paso de los Toros, *Uruguay* 126 C4
Paso Flores, *Argentina* 128 B2
Paso Robles, *U.S.A.* 111 J3
Pasorapa, *Bolivia* 125 D5
Paspébiac, *Canada* 99 C6
Pasrur, *Pakistan* 62 C6
Passage West, *Ireland* 15 E3
Passaic, *U.S.A.* 107 F10
Passau, *Germany* 19 G9
Passendale, *Belgium* 17 G2
Passero, C., *Italy* 35 F8
Passo Fundo, *Brazil* 127 B5
Passos, *Brazil* 123 F2
Passow, *Germany* 18 B10
Passwang, *Switz.* 22 B5
Passy, *France* 27 C10
Pastavy, *Belarus* 9 J22
Pastaza □, *Ecuador* 120 D2
Pastaza →, *Peru* 120 D2
Pastęk, *Poland* 20 A9
Pasto, *Colombia* 120 C2
Pastos Bons, *Brazil* 122 C3
Pastrana, *Spain* 28 E2
Pasuruan, *Indonesia* 57 G15
Patagonia, *Argentina* 128 C2
Patagonia, *U.S.A.* 111 L8
Patambar, *Iran* 65 D9
Patan, *India* 60 H8
Patan, *Maharashtra, India* 62 H5
Patan, *Nepal* 61 F14
Patani, *Indonesia* 57 D7
Pataudi, *India* 62 E7
Patay, *France* 25 D8
Patchewollock, *Australia* 91 F3
Patchogue, *U.S.A.* 107 F11
Patea, *N.Z.* 87 H5
Pategi, *Nigeria* 79 D6
Patensie, *S. Africa* 84 E3
Paternò, *Italy* 35 E7
Pateros, *U.S.A.* 110 B4
Paterson, *U.S.A.* 107 F10
Paterson Ra., *Australia* 88 D3
Paterswolde, *Neths.* 16 B9
Pathankot, *India* 62 C6
Pathfinder Reservoir, *U.S.A.* 110 E10
Pathiu, *Thailand* 59 G2
Pathum Thani, *Thailand* 58 E3
Pati, *Indonesia* 57 G14
Patía, *Colombia* 120 C2
Patía →, *Colombia* 120 C2
Patiala, *India* 62 D7
Patine Kouka, *Senegal* 78 C2
Pativilca, *Peru* 124 C2
Patkai Bum, *India* 61 F19
Pátmos, *Greece* 39 M9
Patna, *India* 63 G11
Patnos, *Turkey* 67 C10
Patonga, *Uganda* 82 B3
Patos, *Brazil* 122 C4
Patos, L. dos, *Brazil* 127 C5
Patos de Minas, *Brazil* 123 E2
Patquía, *Argentina* 126 C2
Pátrai, *Greece* 39 L4
Pátraikós Kólpos, *Greece* 39 L4
Patras = Pátrai, *Greece* 39 L4
Patricio Lynch, I., *Chile* 128 C1
Patrocínio, *Brazil* 123 E2
Patta, *Kenya* 82 C5
Pattada, *Italy* 34 B2
Pattani, *Thailand* 59 J3
Patten, *U.S.A.* 99 C6
Patterson, *Calif., U.S.A.* 111 H3
Patterson, *La., U.S.A.* 109 L9
Patterson, Mt., *U.S.A.* 112 G7
Patti, *India* 62 D6
Patti, *Italy* 35 D7
Pattoki, *Pakistan* 62 D5
Patton, *U.S.A.* 106 F6
Patu, *Brazil* 122 C4
Patuakhali, *Bangla.* 61 H17
Patuca →, *Honduras* 116 C3

Patuca, Punta, *Honduras* 116 C3
Pâturages, *Belgium* 17 H3
Pátzcuaro, *Mexico* 114 D4
Pau, *France* 26 E3
Pau, Gave de →, *France* 26 E2
Pau d' Arco, *Brazil* 122 C2
Pau dos Ferros, *Brazil* 122 C4
Paucartambo, *Peru* 124 C3
Pauillac, *France* 26 C3
Pauini, *Brazil* 124 B4
Pauini →, *Brazil* 121 D5
Pauk, *Burma* 61 J19
Paul I., *Canada* 99 A7
Paul Isnard, *Fr. Guiana* 121 C7
Paulhan, *France* 26 E7
Paulis = Isiro, *Zaïre* 82 B2
Paulista, *Brazil* 122 C5
Paulistana, *Brazil* 122 C3
Paullina, *U.S.A.* 108 D7
Paulo Afonso, *Brazil* 122 C4
Paulo de Faria, *Brazil* 123 F2
Paulpietersburg, *S. Africa* 85 D5
Pauls Valley, *U.S.A.* 109 H6
Pauma Valley, *U.S.A.* 113 M10
Pausa, *Peru* 124 D3
Pauto →, *Colombia* 120 B3
Pāveh, *Iran* 67 E12
Pavelets, *Russia* 42 D4
Pavia, *Italy* 32 C6
Pāvilosta, *Latvia* 9 H19
Pavlikeni, *Bulgaria* 38 F8
Pavlodar, *Kazakstan* 44 D8
Pavlograd = Pavlohrad, *Ukraine* 41 H8
Pavlohrad, *Ukraine* 41 H8
Pavlovo, *Oka, Russia* 42 C6
Pavlovo, *Sakha, Russia* 45 C12
Pavlovsk, *Russia* 42 E5
Pavlovskaya, *Russia* 43 G4
Pavlovskiy-Posad, *Russia* 42 C4
Pavullo nel Frignano, *Italy* 32 D7
Pawhuska, *U.S.A.* 109 G6
Pawling, *U.S.A.* 107 E11
Pawnee, *U.S.A.* 109 G6
Pawnee City, *U.S.A.* 108 E6
Pawtucket, *U.S.A.* 107 E13
Paximádhia, *Greece* 37 D6
Paxoí, *Greece* 39 K3
Paxton, *Ill., U.S.A.* 104 E1
Paxton, *Nebr., U.S.A.* 108 E4
Payakumbuh, *Indonesia* 56 E2
Payerne, *Switz.* 22 C3
Payette, *U.S.A.* 110 D5
Paymogo, *Spain* 31 H3
Payne Bay = Kangirsuk, *Canada* 97 B13
Paynes Find, *Australia* 89 E2
Paynesville, *Liberia* 78 D2
Paynesville, *U.S.A.* 108 C7
Paysandú, *Uruguay* 126 C4
Payson, *Ariz., U.S.A.* 111 J8
Payson, *Utah, U.S.A.* 110 F8
Paz →, *Guatemala* 116 D1
Paz, B. la, *Mexico* 114 C2
Pāzanān, *Iran* 65 D6
Pazar, *Turkey* 67 B9
Pazarcık, *Turkey* 66 D7
Pazardzhik, *Bulgaria* 38 G7
Pazaryolu, *Turkey* 67 B9
Pazin, *Croatia* 33 C10
Pazña, *Bolivia* 124 D4
Pčinja →, *Macedonia* 39 H4
Pe Ell, *U.S.A.* 112 D3
Peabody, *U.S.A.* 107 D14
Peace →, *Canada* 100 B6
Peace Point, *Canada* 100 B6
Peace River, *Canada* 100 B5
Peach Springs, *U.S.A.* 111 J7
Peak, The = Kinder Scout, *U.K.* 12 D6
Peak Downs, *Australia* 90 C4
Peak Downs Mine, *Australia* 90 C4
Peak Hill, *N.S.W., Australia* 91 E4
Peak Hill, *W. Austral., Australia* 89 E2
Peak Ra., *Australia* 90 C4
Peake, *Australia* 91 F2
Peake Cr. →, *Australia* 91 D2
Peale, Mt., *U.S.A.* 111 G9
Pearblossom, *U.S.A.* 113 L9
Pearl →, *U.S.A.* 109 K10
Pearl City, *U.S.A.* 102 H16
Pearsall, *U.S.A.* 109 L5
Pearse I., *Canada* 100 C2
Peary Land, *Greenland* 4 A6
Pease →, *U.S.A.* 109 H5
Pebane, *Mozam.* 83 F4
Pebas, *Peru* 120 D3
Pebble, I., *Falk. Is.* 128 D5
Pebble Beach, *U.S.A.* 112 J5
Peć, *Serbia, Yug.* 21 N10
Peçanha, *Brazil* 123 E3
Péccioli, *Italy* 32 E7
Pechea, *Romania* 38 D10
Pechenga, *Russia* 44 C4
Pechenizhyn, *Ukraine* 41 H3
Pechiguera, Pta., *Canary Is.* 36 F6
Pechnezhskoye Vdkhr., *Ukraine* 41 G9
Pechora →, *Russia* 44 C6
Pechorskaya Guba, *Russia* 44 C6
Pecica, *Romania* 38 C4
Pečka, *Serbia, Yug.* 21 L9
Pécora, C., *Italy* 34 C1
Pečory, *Russia* 9 H22
Pecos, *U.S.A.* 109 K3
Pecos →, *U.S.A.* 109 L3
Pécs, *Hungary* 21 J8
Pedder, L., *Australia* 90 G4
Peddie, *S. Africa* 85 E4
Pédernales, *Dom. Rep.* 117 C5
Pedieos →, *Cyprus* 37 D12
Pedirka, *Australia* 91 D2
Pedra Azul, *Brazil* 123 E3
Pedra Grande, Recifes de, *Brazil* 123 E4
Pedras Negras, *Brazil* 125 C5
Pedreiras, *Brazil* 122 B3
Pedro Afonso, *Brazil* 122 C2
Pedro Cays, *Jamaica* 116 C4
Pedro Chico, *Colombia* 120 C3
Pedro de Valdivia, *Chile* 126 A2
Pedro Juan Caballero, *Paraguay* 127 A4
Pedro Muñoz, *Spain* 29 F2
Pedrógão Grande, *Portugal* 30 F2
Peebinga, *Australia* 91 E3
Peebles, *U.K.* 14 F5
Peekskill, *U.S.A.* 107 E11
Peel, *U.K.* 12 C3
Peel →, *Australia* 91 E5
Peel →, *Canada* 96 B6
Peene →, *Germany* 18 A9
Peera Peera Poolanna L., *Australia* 91 D2
Peers, *Canada* 100 C5
Pegasus Bay, *N.Z.* 87 K4
Pegnitz, *Germany* 19 F7
Pegnitz →, *Germany* 19 F6
Pego, *Spain* 29 G4
Pegu, *Burma* 61 L20
Pegu Yoma, *Burma* 61 K19
Pehuajó, *Argentina* 126 D3
Pei Xian, *China* 50 G9
Peichiang, *Taiwan* 53 F13
Peine, *Chile* 126 A2
Peine, *Germany* 18 C6
Peip'ing = Beijing, *China* 50 E9
Peipus, L. = Chudskoye, Oz., *Russia* 9 G22
Peissenberg, *Germany* 19 H7
Peitz, *Germany* 18 D10
Peixe, *Brazil* 123 D2
Peixe →, *Brazil* 123 F1
Peixoto de Azeredo →, *Brazil* 125 C6
Peize, *Neths.* 16 B8
Pek →, *Serbia, Yug.* 21 L11
Pekalongan, *Indonesia* 57 G13
Pekan, *Malaysia* 59 L4
Pekanbaru, *Indonesia* 56 D2
Pekin, *U.S.A.* 108 E10
Peking = Beijing, *China* 50 E9
Pelabuhan Kelang, *Malaysia* 59 L3
Pelabuhan Ratu, Teluk, *Indonesia* 57 G12
Pelabuhanratu, *Indonesia* 57 G12
Pélagos, *Greece* 39 K7
Pelaihari, *Indonesia* 56 E4
Pelat, Mt., *France* 27 D10
Peleaga, Vf., *Romania* 38 D5
Pelechuco, *Bolivia* 124 C4
Pelée, Mt., *Martinique* 117 D7
Pelee, Pt., *Canada* 98 D3
Pelee I., *Canada* 98 D3
Pelejo, *Peru* 124 B2
Pelekech, *Kenya* 82 B4
Peleng, *Indonesia* 57 E6
Pelham, *U.S.A.* 105 K3
Pelhřimov, *Czech.* 20 F5
Pelican L., *Canada* 101 C8
Pelican Narrows, *Canada* 101 B8
Pelican Rapids, *Canada* 101 C8
Pelkosenniemi, *Finland* 8 C22
Pella, *S. Africa* 84 D2
Pella, *U.S.A.* 108 E8
Péllaro, *Italy* 35 D8
Pello, *Finland* 8 C21
Pellworm, *Germany* 18 A4
Pelly →, *Canada* 96 B6
Pelly Bay, *Canada* 97 B11
Pelly L., *Canada* 96 B9
Peloponnese = Pelopónnisos □, *Greece* 39 M5
Pelopónnisos □, *Greece* 39 M5
Peloritani, Monti, *Italy* 35 D8
Peloro, C., *Italy* 35 D8
Pelorus Sd., *N.Z.* 87 J4
Pelotas, *Brazil* 127 C5
Pelvoux, Massif du, *France* 27 D10
Pemalang, *Indonesia* 57 G13
Pematangsiantar, *Indonesia* 56 D1
Pemba, *Mozam.* 83 E5
Pemba, *Zambia* 83 F2
Pemba Channel, *Tanzania* 82 D4
Pemba I., *Tanzania* 82 D4
Pemberton, *Australia* 89 F2
Pemberton, *Canada* 100 C4
Pembina, *U.S.A.* 108 A6
Pembina →, *U.S.A.* 101 D9
Pembine, *U.S.A.* 104 C2
Pembroke, *Canada* 98 C4
Pembroke, *U.K.* 13 F3
Pembroke, *U.S.A.* 105 J5
Pembrokeshire □, *U.K.* 13 F3
Pen-y-Ghent, *U.K.* 12 C5
Peña, Sierra de la, *Spain* 28 C4
Peña de Francia, Sierra de, *Spain* 30 E4
Penafiel, *Portugal* 30 D2
Peñafiel, *Spain* 30 D6
Peñaflor, *Spain* 31 H5
Peñalara, Pico, *Spain* 30 E7
Penalva, *Brazil* 122 B2
Penamacôr, *Portugal* 30 E3
Penang = Pinang, *Malaysia* 59 K3
Penápolis, *Brazil* 127 A6
Peñaranda de Bracamonte, *Spain* 30 E5
Peñarroya-Pueblonuevo, *Spain* 31 G5
Peñas, C. de, *Spain* 30 B5
Penas, G. de, *Chile* 128 C2
Peñas, Pta., *Venezuela* 121 A5
Peñas de San Pedro, *Spain* 29 G2
Peñas del Chache, *Canary Is.* 36 E6
Peñausende, *Spain* 30 D5
Pench'i = Benxi, *China* 51 D12
Pend Oreille →, *U.S.A.* 110 B5
Pend Oreille L., *U.S.A.* 110 C5
Pendembu, *S. Leone* 78 D2
Pendências, *Brazil* 122 C4
Pender B., *Australia* 88 C3
Pendleton, *Calif., U.S.A.* 113 M9
Pendleton, *Oreg., U.S.A.* 110 D4
Penedo, *Brazil* 122 D4
Penetanguishene, *Canada* 98 D4
Peng Xian, *China* 52 B4
Pengalengan, *Indonesia* 57 G12
Penge, *Kasai Or., Zaïre* 82 D1
Penge, *Kivu, Zaïre* 82 C2
Penglai, *China* 51 F11
Pengshui, *China* 52 C7
Penguin, *Australia* 90 G4
Pengxi, *China* 52 B5
Pengze, *China* 53 C11
Penhalonga, *Zimbabwe* 83 F3
Peniche, *Portugal* 31 F1
Penicuik, *U.K.* 14 F5
Penida, *Indonesia* 56 F5
Peninsular Malaysia □, *Malaysia* 59 L4
Peñíscola, *Spain* 28 E5
Penitente, Serra dos, *Brazil* 122 C2
Penmarch, *France* 24 E2
Penmarch, Pte. de, *France* 24 E2
Penn Hills, *U.S.A.* 106 F5
Penn Yan, *U.S.A.* 106 D7
Pennabilli, *Italy* 33 E9
Pennant, *Canada* 101 C7
Penne, *Italy* 33 F10
Penner →, *India* 60 M12
Pennine, Alpi, *Alps* 32 B4
Pennines, *U.K.* 12 C5
Pennington, *U.S.A.* 112 F5
Pennino, Mte., *Italy* 33 E9
Pennsylvania □, *U.S.A.* 104 E6
Penny, *Canada* 100 C4
Peno, *Russia* 42 B1
Penola, *Australia* 91 F3
Penong, *Australia* 89 F5
Penonomé, *Panama* 116 E3
Penrith, *Australia* 91 E5
Penrith, *U.K.* 12 C5
Pensacola, *U.S.A.* 105 K2
Pensacola Mts., *Antarctica* 5 E1
Pense, *Canada* 101 C8
Penshurst, *Australia* 91 F3
Pentecoste, *Brazil* 122 B4
Penticton, *Canada* 100 D5
Pentland, *Australia* 90 C4
Pentland Firth, *U.K.* 14 C5
Pentland Hills, *U.K.* 14 F5
Penylan L., *Canada* 101 A7
Penza, *Russia* 42 D7
Penzance, *U.K.* 13 G2
Penzberg, *Germany* 19 H7
Penzhino, *Russia* 45 C17
Penzhinskaya Guba, *Russia* 45 C17
Penzlin, *Germany* 18 B9
Peoria, *Ariz., U.S.A.* 111 K7
Peoria, *Ill., U.S.A.* 108 E10
Pepingen, *Belgium* 17 G4
Pepinster, *Belgium* 17 G7
Pera Hd., *Australia* 90 A3
Perabumulih, *Indonesia* 56 E2
Perakhóra, *Greece* 39 L5
Perales de Alfambra, *Spain* 28 E3
Perales del Puerto, *Spain* 30 E4
Peralta, *Spain* 28 C3
Pérama, *Kérkira, Greece* 37 A3
Pérama, *Kríti, Greece* 37 D6
Peräpohjola, *Finland* 8 C22
Percé, *Canada* 99 C7
Perche, *France* 24 D8
Perche, Collines du, *France* 24 D7
Percival Lakes, *Australia* 88 D4
Percy, *France* 24 D5
Percy Is., *Australia* 90 C5
Perdido →, *Argentina* 128 B3
Perdido, Mte., *Spain* 26 F4
Perdu, Mt. = Perdido, Mte., *Spain* 26 F4
Pereira, *Colombia* 120 C2
Pereira Barreto, *Brazil* 123 F1
Perekerten, *Australia* 91 E3
Perelazovskiy, *Russia* 43 F6
Perené →, *Peru* 124 C3
Perenjori, *Australia* 89 E2
Pereslavl-Zalesskiy, *Russia* 42 B4
Pereyaslav-Khmelnytskyy, *Ukraine* 41 G6
Pérez, I., *Mexico* 115 C7
Pergamino, *Argentina* 126 C3
Pergau →, *Malaysia* 59 K3
Pérgine Valsugana, *Italy* 33 B8
Pérgola, *Italy* 33 E9
Perham, *U.S.A.* 108 B7
Perhentian, Kepulauan, *Malaysia* 59 K4
Periam, *Romania* 38 C3
Péribonca →, *Canada* 99 C5
Péribonca, L., *Canada* 99 B5
Perico, *Argentina* 126 A2
Pericos, *Mexico* 114 B3
Périers, *France* 24 C5
Périgord, *France* 26 D4
Périgueux, *France* 26 C4
Perijá, Sierra de, *Colombia* 120 B3
Peristéra, *Greece* 39 K6
Peristerona →, *Cyprus* 37 D12
Perito Moreno, *Argentina* 128 C2
Peritoró, *Brazil* 122 B3
Perković, *Croatia* 33 E13
Perlas, Arch. de las, *Panama* 116 E4
Perlas, Punta de, *Nic.* 116 D3
Perleberg, *Germany* 18 B7
Perm, *Russia* 44 D6
Pernambuco = Recife, *Brazil* 122 C5
Pernambuco □, *Brazil* 122 C4
Pernatty Lagoon, *Australia* 91 E2
Pernik, *Bulgaria* 38 G6
Peron, C., *Australia* 89 E1
Peron Is., *Australia* 88 B5
Peron Pen., *Australia* 89 E1
Péronne, *France* 25 C9
Péronnes, *Belgium* 17 H4
Perosa Argentina, *Italy* 32 D4
Perow, *Canada* 100 C3
Perpendicular Pt., *Australia* 91 E5
Perpignan, *France* 26 F6
Perris, *U.S.A.* 113 M9
Perros-Guirec, *France* 24 D3
Perry, *Fla., U.S.A.* 105 K4
Perry, *Ga., U.S.A.* 105 J4
Perry, *Iowa, U.S.A.* 108 E7
Perry, *Maine, U.S.A.* 105 C12
Perry, *Okla., U.S.A.* 109 G6
Perryton, *U.S.A.* 109 G4
Perryville, *U.S.A.* 109 G10
Perşembe, *Turkey* 66 B7
Perseverancia, *Bolivia* 125 C5
Pershotravensk, *Ukraine* 41 G4
Persia = Iran ■, *Asia* 65 C7
Persian Gulf = Gulf, The, *Asia* 65 E6
Perstorp, *Sweden* 11 H7
Pertek, *Turkey* 67 C8
Perth, *Australia* 89 F2
Perth, *Canada* 98 D4
Perth, *U.K.* 14 E5
Perth & Kinross □, *U.K.* 14 E5
Perth Amboy, *U.S.A.* 107 F10
Pertuis, *France* 27 E9
Peru, *Ill., U.S.A.* 108 E10
Peru, *Ind., U.S.A.* 104 E2
Peru ■, *S. Amer.* 120 D2
Peru-Chile Trench, *Pac. Oc.* 93 K20
Perúgia, *Italy* 33 E9
Perušić, *Croatia* 33 D12
Péruwelz, *Belgium* 17 G3
Pervomaysk, *Russia* 42 C6
Pervomaysk, *Ukraine* 41 H6
Pervouralsk, *Russia* 44 D6
Perwez, *Belgium* 17 G5
Pes, Pta. del, *Spain* 36 C7
Pésaro, *Italy* 33 E9
Pescara, *Italy* 33 F11
Pescara →, *Italy* 33 F11
Peschanokopskoye, *Russia* 43 G5
Péscia, *Italy* 32 E7
Pescina, *Italy* 33 G10
Peseux, *Switz.* 22 C3
Peshawar, *Pakistan* 62 B4
Peshtigo, *U.S.A.* 104 C2
Peski, *Russia* 42 E6
Pêso da Régua, *Portugal* 30 D3
Pesqueira, *Brazil* 122 C4
Pessac, *France* 26 D3
Pessoux, *Belgium* 17 H6
Pestovo, *Russia* 40 C8
Pestravka, *Russia* 42 D9
Petah Tiqwa, *Israel* 69 C3
Petaling Jaya, *Malaysia* 59 L3
Petaloudhes, *Greece* 37 C10
Petaluma, *U.S.A.* 112 G4
Petange, *Lux.* 17 J7
Petatlán, *Mexico* 114 D4
Petauke, *Zambia* 83 E3
Petawawa, *Canada* 98 C4
Petegem, *Belgium* 17 G3
Petén Itzá, L., *Guatemala* 116 C2
Peter I.s Øy, *Antarctica* 5 C16
Peter Pond L., *Canada* 101 B7
Peterbell, *Canada* 98 C3
Peterborough, *Australia* 91 E2
Peterborough, *Canada* 97 D12
Peterborough, *U.K.* 13 E7
Peterborough, *U.S.A.* 107 D13
Peterhead, *U.K.* 14 D7
Petermann Bjerg, *Greenland* 94 B17
Peter's Mine, *Guyana* 121 B6
Petersburg, *Alaska, U.S.A.* 100 B2
Petersburg, *Ind., U.S.A.* 104 F2
Petersburg, *Va., U.S.A.* 104 G7
Petersburg, *W. Va., U.S.A.* 104 F6
Petford, *Australia* 90 B3
Petília Policastro, *Italy* 35 C9
Petit Bois I., *U.S.A.* 105 K1
Petit-Cap, *Canada* 99 C7
Petit Goâve, *Haiti* 117 C5
Petit Lac Manicouagan, *Canada* 99 B6
Petit Saint Bernard, Col du, *Italy* 32 C3
Petitcodiac, *Canada* 99 C6
Petite Baleine →, *Canada* 98 A4
Petite Saguenay, *Canada* 99 C5
Petitsikapau, L., *Canada* 99 B6
Petlad, *India* 62 H5
Peto, *Mexico* 115 C7
Petone, *N.Z.* 87 J5
Petoskey, *U.S.A.* 104 C3
Petra, *Jordan* 69 E4
Petra, *Spain* 36 B10
Petra, Ostrova, *Russia* 4 B13
Petra Velikogo, Zaliv, *Russia* 48 C5
Petralia Sottana, *Italy* 35 E7
Petrel, *Spain* 29 G4
Petreto-Bicchisano, *France* 27 G12
Petrich, *Bulgaria* 39 H6
Petrijanec, *Croatia* 33 B13
Petrikov = Pyetrikaw, *Belarus* 41 F5
Petrinja, *Croatia* 33 C13
Petrodvorets, *Russia* 40 C5
Petrograd = Sankt-Peterburg, *Russia* 40 C6
Petrolândia, *Brazil* 122 C4
Petrolia, *Canada* 98 D3
Petrolina, *Brazil* 122 C3
Petropavl, *Kazakstan* 44 D7
Petropavlovsk = Petropavl, *Kazakstan* 44 D7
Petropavlovsk-Kamchatskiy, *Russia* 45 D16
Petropavlovskiy = Akhtubinsk, *Russia* 43 F8
Petrópolis, *Brazil* 123 F3
Petroşani, *Romania* 38 D6
Petrova Gora, *Croatia* 33 C12
Petrovac, *Montenegro, Yug.* 21 N8
Petrovsk, *Russia* 42 D7
Petrovsk-Zabaykalskiy, *Russia* 45 D11
Petrovskaya, *Russia* 43 H3
Petrovskoye = Svetlograd, *Russia* 43 H6
Petrozavodsk, *Russia* 40 B8
Petrus Steyn, *S. Africa* 85 D4
Petrusburg, *S. Africa* 84 D4
Peumo, *Chile* 126 C1
Peureulak, *Indonesia* 56 D1
Pevek, *Russia* 45 C18
Peveragno, *Italy* 32 D4
Peyrehorade, *France* 26 E2
Peyruis, *France* 27 D9
Pézenas, *France* 26 E7
Pfaffenhofen, *Germany* 19 G7
Pfäffikon, *Switz.* 23 B7
Pfarrkirchen, *Germany* 19 G8
Pfeffenhausen, *Germany* 19 G7
Pforzheim, *Germany* 19 G4
Pfullendorf, *Germany* 19 H5
Pfungstadt, *Germany* 19 F4
Phagwara, *India* 60 D9
Phaistós, *Greece* 37 D6
Phala, *Botswana* 84 C4
Phalera = Phulera, *India* 62 F6
Phalodi, *India* 62 F5
Phalsbourg, *France* 25 D14
Phan, *Thailand* 58 C2
Phan Rang, *Vietnam* 59 G7
Phan Ri = Hoa Da, *Vietnam* 59 G7
Phan Thiet, *Vietnam* 59 G7
Phanat Nikhom, *Thailand* 58 F3
Phangan, Ko, *Thailand* 59 H3
Phangnga, *Thailand* 59 H2
Phanh Bho Ho Chi Minh, *Vietnam* 59 G6
Phanom Sarakham, *Thailand* 58 F3
Pharenda, *India* 63 F10
Phatthalung, *Thailand* 59 J3
Phayao, *Thailand* 58 C2
Phelps, *N.Y., U.S.A.* 106 D7
Phelps, *Wis., U.S.A.* 108 B10
Phelps L., *Canada* 101 B8
Phenix City, *U.S.A.* 105 J3
Phet Buri, *Thailand* 58 F2
Phetchabun, *Thailand* 58 D3
Phetchabun, Thiu Khao, *Thailand* 58 E3
Phetchaburi = Phet Buri, *Thailand* 58 F2
Phi Phi, Ko, *Thailand* 59 J2
Phiafay, *Laos* 58 E6
Phibun Mangsahan, *Thailand* 58 E5
Phichai, *Thailand* 58 D3
Phichit, *Thailand* 58 D3
Philadelphia, *Miss., U.S.A.* 109 J10
Philadelphia, *N.Y., U.S.A.* 107 B9
Philadelphia, *Pa., U.S.A.* 107 F9
Philip, *U.S.A.* 108 C4
Philippeville, *Belgium* 17 H5
Philippi L., *Australia* 90 C2
Philippines ■, *Asia* 55 F5
Philippolis, *S. Africa* 84 E4
Philippopolis = Plovdiv, *Bulgaria* 38 G7
Philipsburg, *Mont., U.S.A.* 110 C7
Philipsburg, *Pa., U.S.A.* 106 F6

Philipstown = Daingean, Ireland 15 C4
Philipstown, S. Africa 84 E3
Phillip I., Australia 91 F4
Phillips, Tex., U.S.A. 109 H4
Phillips, Wis., U.S.A. 108 C9
Phillipsburg, Kans., U.S.A. 108 F5
Phillipsburg, N.J., U.S.A. 107 F9
Phillott, Australia 91 D4
Philmont, U.S.A. 107 D11
Philomath, U.S.A. 110 D2
Phimai, Thailand 58 E4
Phitsanulok, Thailand 58 D3
Phnom Dangrek, Thailand 58 E5
Phnom Penh, Cambodia 59 G5
Phoenix, Ariz., U.S.A. 111 K7
Phoenix, N.Y., U.S.A. 107 C8
Phoenix Is., Kiribati 92 H10
Phoenixville, U.S.A. 107 F9
Phon, Thailand 58 E4
Phon Tiou, Laos 58 D5
Phong →, Thailand 58 D4
Phong Saly, Laos 58 B4
Phong Tho, Vietnam 58 A4
Phonhong, Laos 58 C4
Phonum, Thailand 59 H2
Phosphate Hill, Australia 90 C2
Photharam, Thailand 58 F2
Phra Chedi Sam Ong, Thailand 58 E2
Phra Nakhon Si Ayutthaya, Thailand 58 E3
Phra Thong, Ko, Thailand 59 H2
Phrae, Thailand 58 C3
Phrom Phiram, Thailand 58 D3
Phrygia, Turkey 66 C4
Phu Dien, Vietnam 58 C5
Phu Loi, Laos 58 B4
Phu Ly, Vietnam 58 B5
Phu Tho, Vietnam 58 B5
Phuc Yen, Vietnam 58 B5
Phuket, Thailand 59 J2
Phuket, Ko, Thailand 59 J2
Phulera, India 62 F6
Phumiphon, Khuan, Thailand 58 D2
Phun Phin, Thailand 59 H2
Piacá, Brazil 122 C2
Piacenza, Italy 32 C6
Piaçubaçu, Brazil 122 D4
Piádena, Italy 32 C7
Pialba, Australia 91 D5
Pian Cr. →, Australia 91 E4
Piana, France 27 F12
Pianella, Italy 33 F11
Pianoro, Italy 33 D8
Pianosa, Puglia, Italy 33 F12
Pianosa, Toscana, Italy 32 F7
Piapot, Canada 101 D7
Piare →, Italy 33 C9
Pias, Portugal 31 G3
Piaseczno, Poland 20 C11
Piatã, Brazil 123 D3
Piatra, Romania 38 F8
Piatra Neamţ, Romania 38 C9
Piauí □, Brazil 122 C3
Piaui →, Brazil 122 C3
Piave →, Italy 33 C9
Piazza Ármerina, Italy 35 E7
Pibor →, Sudan 77 F3
Pibor Post, Sudan 77 F3
Pica, Chile 124 E4
Picardie, France 25 C9
Picardie, Plaine de, France 25 C9
Picardy = Picardie, France 25 C9
Picayune, U.S.A. 109 K10
Picerno, Italy 35 B8
Pichilemu, Chile 126 C1
Pichincha, □, Ecuador 120 D2
Pickerel L., Canada 98 C1
Pickle Lake, Canada 98 B1
Pico Truncado, Argentina 128 C3
Picos, Brazil 122 C3
Picos Ancares, Sierra de, Spain 30 C4
Picota, Peru 124 B2
Picquigny, France 25 C9
Picton, Australia 91 E5
Picton, Canada 98 D4
Picton, N.Z. 87 J5
Picton, I., Chile 128 E3
Pictou, Canada 99 C7
Picture Butte, Canada 100 D6
Picuí, Brazil 122 C4
Picún Leufú, Argentina 128 A3
Pidurutalagala, Sri Lanka 60 R12
Piedecuesta, Colombia 120 B3
Piedicavallo, Italy 32 C4
Piedmont = Piemonte □, Italy 32 D4
Piedmont, U.S.A. 105 J3
Piedmont Plateau, U.S.A. 105 J5
Piedmonte d'Alife, Italy 35 A7
Piedra →, Spain 28 D3
Piedra del Anguila, Argentina 128 B2
Piedra Lais, Venezuela 120 C4
Piedrabuena, Spain 31 F6
Piedrahita, Spain 30 E5
Piedras, R. de las →, Peru 124 C4
Piedras Negras, Mexico 114 B4
Pieksämäki, Finland 9 E22
Piemonte □, Italy 32 D4
Pierce, U.S.A. 110 C6
Piercefield, U.S.A. 107 B10
Pierre, U.S.A. 108 C4
Pierre Bénite, Barrage de la, France 27 C8
Pierre-de-Bresse, France 27 B9
Pierrefeu-du-Var, France 27 E10
Pierrefonds, France 25 C9
Pierrefontaine-les-Varans, France 25 E13
Pierrefort, France 26 D6
Pierrelatte, France 27 D8
Piešťany, Slovak Rep. 20 G7
Piesting →, Austria 21 G6
Piet Retief, S. Africa 85 D5
Pietarsaari, Finland 8 E20
Pietermaritzburg, S. Africa 85 D5
Pietersburg, S. Africa 85 C4
Pietraperzia, Italy 35 E7
Pietrasanta, Italy 32 E7
Pietrosul, Romania 38 B8
Pietrosul, Romania 38 B7
Pieve di Cadore, Italy 33 B9
Pieve di Teco, Italy 32 D4
Pievepélago, Italy 32 D7
Pigádhia, Greece 39 P10
Pigeon, U.S.A. 104 D4
Piggott, U.S.A. 109 G9
Pigna, Italy 32 E4
Pigüe, Argentina 126 D3
Pihani, India 63 F9
Pihlajavesi, Finland 9 F23
Pijnacker, Neths. 16 D4
Pikalevo, Russia 40 C8
Pikes Peak, U.S.A. 108 F2
Piketberg, S. Africa 84 E2
Pikeville, U.S.A. 104 G4
Pikou, China 51 E12
Pikwitonei, Canada 101 B9
Piła, Poland 20 B6
Pila, Spain 29 G3
Pilani, India 62 E6
Pilar, Brazil 122 C4
Pilar, Paraguay 126 B4
Pilas Group, Phil. 57 C6
Pilaya →, Bolivia 125 E5
Pilcomayo →, Paraguay 126 B4
Pilibhit, India 63 E8
Pilica →, Poland 20 D11
Pilkhawa, India 62 E7
Pillaro, Ecuador 120 D2
Pílos, Greece 39 N4
Pilot Mound, Canada 101 D9
Pilot Point, U.S.A. 109 J6
Pilot Rock, U.S.A. 110 D4
Pilsen = Plzeň, Czech. 20 F3
Pilštanj, Slovenia 33 B12
Pima, U.S.A. 111 K9
Pimba, Australia 91 E2
Pimenta Bueno, Brazil 125 C5
Pimentel, Peru 124 B2
Pina, Spain 28 D4
Pinamalayan, Phil. 55 E4
Pinang, Malaysia 59 K3
Pinar, C. del, Spain 36 B10
Pinar del Río, Cuba 116 B3
Pınarbaşı, Turkey 66 C7
Pınarhisar, Turkey 66 B2
Pinchang, China 52 B6
Pincher Creek, Canada 100 D6
Pinchi L., Canada 100 C4
Pinckneyville, U.S.A. 108 F10
Pîncota, Romania 38 C4
Pind Dadan Khan, Pakistan 62 C5
Pindar, Australia 89 E2
Pindaré →, Brazil 122 B3
Pindaré Mirim, Brazil 122 B2
Pindi Gheb, Pakistan 62 C5
Pindiga, Nigeria 79 D7
Pindobal, Brazil 122 B2
Pindos Óros, Greece 39 K4
Pindus Mts. = Pindos Óros, Greece 39 K4
Pine, U.S.A. 111 J8
Pine →, Canada 101 B7
Pine, C., Canada 99 C9
Pine Bluff, U.S.A. 109 H8
Pine City, U.S.A. 108 C8
Pine Falls, Canada 101 C9
Pine Flat L., U.S.A. 112 J7
Pine Pass, Canada 100 B4
Pine Point, Canada 100 A6
Pine Ridge, U.S.A. 108 D3
Pine River, Canada 101 C8
Pine River, U.S.A. 108 B7
Pine Valley, U.S.A. 113 N10
Pinecrest, U.S.A. 112 G6
Pinedale, U.S.A. 112 J7
Pinega →, Russia 44 C5
Pinehill, Australia 90 C4
Pinerolo, Italy 32 D4
Pineto, Italy 33 F11
Pinetop, U.S.A. 111 J9
Pinetown, S. Africa 85 D5
Pinetree, U.S.A. 110 E11
Pineville, Ky., U.S.A. 105 G4
Pineville, La., U.S.A. 109 K8
Piney, France 25 D11
Ping →, Thailand 58 E3
Pingaring, Australia 89 F2
Pingba, China 52 D6
Pingchuan, China 52 D3
Pingding, China 50 F7
Pingdingshan, China 50 H7
Pingdong, Taiwan 53 F13
Pingdu, China 51 F10
Pingelly, Australia 89 F2
Pingguo, China 52 F6
Pinghe, China 53 E11
Pinghu, China 53 B13
Pingjiang, China 53 C9
Pingle, China 53 E8
Pingli, China 52 A7
Pingliang, China 50 G4
Pinglu, China 50 E7
Pingluo, China 50 E4
Pingnan, Fujian, China 53 D12
Pingnan, Guangxi Zhuangzu, China 53 F8
Pingquan, China 51 D10
Pingrup, Australia 89 F2
Pingtan, China 53 E12
Pingtang, China 52 E6
P'ingtung, Taiwan 53 F13
Pingwu, China 50 H3
Pingxiang, Guangxi Zhuangzu, China 52 F6
Pingxiang, Jiangxi, China 53 D9
Pingyao, China 50 F7
Pingyi, China 51 G9
Pingyin, China 50 F9
Pingyuan, Guangdong, China 53 E10
Pingyuan, Shandong, China 50 F9
Pingyuanjie, China 52 F4
Pinhal, Brazil 127 A6
Pinheiro, Brazil 122 B2
Pinhel, Portugal 30 E3
Pinhuá →, Brazil 125 B4
Pini, Indonesia 56 D1
Piniós →, Ilía, Greece 39 M4
Piniós →, Trikkala, Greece 39 K5
Pinjarra, Australia 89 F2
Pink →, Canada 101 B8
Pinnacles, Australia 89 E3
Pinnacles, U.S.A. 112 J5
Pinnaroo, Australia 91 F3
Pinneberg, Germany 18 B5
Pínnes, Ákra, Greece 39 J7
Pino Hachado, Paso, S. Amer. 128 A2
Pinon Hills, U.S.A. 113 L9
Pinos, Mexico 114 C4
Pinos, Mt., U.S.A. 113 L7
Pinos Pt., U.S.A. 111 H3
Pinos Puente, Spain 31 H7
Pinotepa Nacional, Mexico 115 D5
Pinrang, Indonesia 57 E5
Pinsk, Belarus 41 F4
Pintados, Chile 124 E4
Pintumba, Australia 89 F5
Pinyang, China 53 D13
Pinyug, Russia 44 C5
Pinzolo, Italy 32 B7
Pio XII, Brazil 122 B2
Pioche, U.S.A. 111 H6
Piombino, Italy 32 F7
Piombino, Canale di, Italy 32 F7
Pioner, Os., Russia 45 B10
Pionki, Poland 20 D11
Piorini →, Brazil 121 D5
Piorini, L., Brazil 121 D5
Piotrków Trybunalski, Poland 20 D9
Piove di Sacco, Italy 33 C9
Pīp, Iran 65 E9
Pipar, India 62 F5
Piparia, India 62 H8
Pipestone, U.S.A. 108 D6
Pipestone →, Canada 98 B2
Pipestone Cr. →, Canada 101 D8
Pipmuacan, Rés., Canada 99 C5
Pippingarra, Australia 88 D2
Pipriac, France 24 E5
Piqua, U.S.A. 104 E3
Piquet Carneiro, Brazil 122 C4
Piquiri →, Brazil 127 A5
Pīr Sohrāb, Iran 65 E9
Piracanjuba, Brazil 123 E2
Piracicaba, Brazil 127 A6
Piracuruca, Brazil 122 B3
Piræus = Piraiévs, Greece 39 M6
Piraiévs, Greece 39 M6
Piráino, Italy 35 D7
Pirajuí, Brazil 127 A6
Piran, Slovenia 33 C10
Pirané, Argentina 126 B4
Piranhas, Brazil 122 C4
Pirano = Piran, Slovenia 33 C10
Pirapemas, Brazil 122 B3
Pirapora, Brazil 123 E3
Piray →, Bolivia 125 D5
Pires do Rio, Brazil 123 E2
Pírgos, Ilía, Greece 39 M4
Pírgos, Messinia, Greece 39 N5
Pirgovo, Bulgaria 38 F8
Piriac-sur-Mer, France 24 E4
Piribebuy, Paraguay 126 B4
Pirin Planina, Bulgaria 39 H6
Pirineos, Spain 28 C6
Piripiri, Brazil 122 B3
Piritu, Venezuela 120 B4
Pirmasens, Germany 19 F3
Pirna, Germany 18 E9
Pirot, Serbia, Yug. 21 M12
Piru, Indonesia 57 E7
Piru, U.S.A. 113 L8
Piryatin = Pyryatyn, Ukraine 41 G7
Pisa, Italy 32 E7
Pisac, Peru 124 C3
Pisagua, Chile 124 D3
Pisarovina, Croatia 33 C12
Pisciotta, Italy 35 B8
Pisco, Peru 124 C2
Písek, Czech. 20 F4
Pishan, China 54 C2
Pishin Lora →, Pakistan 62 E1
Pisidia, Turkey 66 D4
Pising, Indonesia 57 F6
Pismo Beach, U.S.A. 113 K6
Pissis, Cerro, Argentina 126 B2
Pissos, France 26 D3
Pissouri, Cyprus 37 E11
Pisticci, Italy 35 B9
Pistóia, Italy 32 E7
Pistol B., Canada 101 A10
Pisuerga →, Spain 30 D6
Pisz, Poland 20 B11
Pitalito, Colombia 120 C2
Pitanga, Brazil 123 F1
Pitangui, Brazil 123 E3
Pitarpunga, L., Australia 91 E3
Pitcairn I., Pac. Oc. 93 K14
Pite älv →, Sweden 8 D19
Piteå, Sweden 8 D19
Piterka, Russia 42 E8
Piteşti, Romania 38 E7
Pithapuram, India 61 L13
Pithara, Australia 89 F2
Píthion, Greece 39 H9
Pithiviers, France 25 D9
Pitigliano, Italy 33 F8
Pitkyaranta, Russia 40 B6
Pitlochry, U.K. 14 E5
Pitrufquén, Chile 128 A2
Pitsilia □, Cyprus 37 E12
Pitt I., Canada 100 C3
Pittem, Belgium 17 F2
Pittsburg, Kans., U.S.A. 109 G7
Pittsburg, Tex., U.S.A. 109 J7
Pittsburgh, U.S.A. 106 F5
Pittsfield, Ill., U.S.A. 108 F9
Pittsfield, Mass., U.S.A. 107 D11
Pittsfield, N.H., U.S.A. 107 C13
Pittston, U.S.A. 107 E9
Pittsworth, Australia 91 D5
Pituri →, Australia 90 C2
Piuí, Brazil 123 F2
Pium, Brazil 122 D2
Piura, Peru 124 B1
Piura □, Peru 124 A2
Pivijay, Colombia 120 A3
Pixley, U.S.A. 112 K7
Piyai, Greece 39 K4
Pizarro, Colombia 120 C2
Pizol, Switz. 23 C8
Pizzo, Italy 35 D9
Placentia, Canada 99 C9
Placentia B., Canada 99 C9
Placer, Phil. 55 F5
Placerville, U.S.A. 112 G6
Placetas, Cuba 116 B4
Plaffeien, Switz. 22 C4
Plain Dealing, U.S.A. 109 J8
Plainfield, U.S.A. 107 F10
Plains, Kans., U.S.A. 109 G4
Plains, Mont., U.S.A. 110 C6
Plains, Tex., U.S.A. 109 J3
Plainview, Nebr., U.S.A. 108 D6
Plainview, Tex., U.S.A. 109 H4
Plainville, U.S.A. 108 F5
Plainwell, U.S.A. 104 D3
Plaisance, France 26 E4
Pláka, Greece 39 J8
Pláka, Ákra, Greece 37 D8
Plakhino, Russia 44 C9
Plana Cays, Bahamas 117 B5
Planada, U.S.A. 112 H6
Plancoët, France 24 D4
Plandište, Serbia, Yug. 21 K11
Planeta Rica, Colombia 120 B2
Planina, Slovenia 33 B12
Planina, Slovenia 33 C11
Plankinton, U.S.A. 108 D5
Plano, U.S.A. 109 J6
Plant City, U.S.A. 105 L4
Plaquemine, U.S.A. 109 K9
Plasencia, Spain 30 E4
Plaški, Croatia 33 C12
Plaster City, U.S.A. 113 N11
Plaster Rock, Canada 99 C6
Plastun, Russia 48 B8
Plata, Río de la, S. Amer. 126 C4
Platani →, Italy 34 E6
Plátanos, Greece 37 D5
Plateau □, Nigeria 79 D6
Plateau du Coteau du Missouri, U.S.A. 108 B4
Plato, Colombia 120 B3
Platta, Piz, Switz. 23 D9
Platte, U.S.A. 108 D5
Platte →, Mo., U.S.A. 108 F7
Platte →, Nebr., U.S.A. 94 E10
Platteville, U.S.A. 108 E2
Plattling, Germany 19 G8
Plattsburgh, U.S.A. 107 B11
Plattsmouth, U.S.A. 108 E7
Plau, Germany 18 B8
Plauen, Germany 18 E8
Plavinas, Latvia 9 H21
Plavnica, Montenegro, Yug. 21 N9
Plavsk, Russia 42 D3
Playa Blanca, Canary Is. 36 F6
Playa Blanca Sur, Canary Is. 36 F6
Playa de las Americas, Canary Is. 36 F3
Playa de Mogán, Canary Is. 36 G4
Playa del Inglés, Canary Is. 36 G4
Playa Esmerelda, Canary Is. 36 F5
Playgreen L., Canada 101 C9
Pleasant Bay, Canada 99 C7
Pleasant Hill, Calif., U.S.A. 112 H4
Pleasant Hill, Mo., U.S.A. 108 F7
Pleasanton, U.S.A. 109 L5
Pleasantville, U.S.A. 104 F8
Pléaux, France 26 C6
Pleiku, Vietnam 58 F7
Plélan-le-Grand, France 24 D4
Plémet-la-Pierre, France 24 D4
Pléneuf-Val-André, France 24 D4
Pleniţa, Romania 38 E6
Plenty →, Australia 90 C2
Plenty, B. of, N.Z. 87 G6
Plentywood, U.S.A. 108 A2
Plessisville, Canada 99 C5
Plestin-les-Grèves, France 24 D3
Pleszew, Poland 20 D7
Pleternica, Croatia 21 K7
Pletipi L., Canada 99 B5
Pleven, Bulgaria 38 F7
Plevlja, Montenegro, Yug. 21 M9
Płock, Poland 20 C9
Plöcken Passo, Italy 33 B9
Ploegsteert, Belgium 17 G1
Ploemeur, France 24 E3
Ploërmel, France 24 E4
Ploieşti, Romania 38 E9
Plombières-les-Bains, France 25 E13
Plomin, Croatia 33 C11
Plön, Germany 18 A6
Plöner See, Germany 18 A6
Plonge, Lac la, Canada 101 B7
Płońsk, Poland 20 C10
Płoty, Poland 20 B5
Plouaret, France 24 D3
Plouay, France 24 E3
Ploudalmézeau, France 24 D2
Plougasnou, France 24 D3
Plouha, France 24 D4
Plouhinec, France 24 E2
Plovdiv, Bulgaria 38 G7
Plum, U.S.A. 106 F5
Plum I., U.S.A. 107 E12
Plumas, U.S.A. 112 F7
Plummer, U.S.A. 110 C5
Plumtree, Zimbabwe 83 G2
Plunge, Lithuania 9 J19
Pluvigner, France 24 E3
Plymouth, U.K. 13 G3
Plymouth, Calif., U.S.A. 112 G6
Plymouth, Ind., U.S.A. 104 E2
Plymouth, Mass., U.S.A. 107 E14
Plymouth, N.C., U.S.A. 105 H7
Plymouth, N.H., U.S.A. 107 C13
Plymouth, Pa., U.S.A. 107 E9
Plymouth, Wis., U.S.A. 104 D2
Plynlimon = Pumlumon Fawr, U.K. 13 E4
Plyusa, Russia 40 C5
Plyusa →, Russia 40 C5
Plyussa = Plyusa, Russia 40 C5
Plyussa → = Plyusa →, Russia 40 C5
Plzeň, Czech. 20 F3
Pniewy, Poland 20 C6
Pô, Burkina Faso 79 C4
Po →, Italy 33 D9
Po, Foci del, Italy 33 D9
Po Hai = Bo Hai, China 51 E10
Po Hai, China 46 F15
Pobé, Benin 79 D5
Pobeda, Russia 45 C15
Pobedino, Russia 45 E15
Pobedy Pik, Kyrgyzstan 44 E8
Pobiedziska, Poland 20 C7
Pobla de Segur, Spain 28 C5
Pobladura de Valle, Spain 30 C5
Pocahontas, Ark., U.S.A. 109 G9
Pocahontas, Iowa, U.S.A. 108 D7
Pocatello, U.S.A. 110 E7
Pochep, Russia 41 F7
Pochinki, Russia 42 C7
Pochinok, Russia 40 E7
Pochutla, Mexico 115 D5
Poci, Venezuela 121 B5
Pocinhos, Brazil 122 C4
Pocito Casas, Mexico 114 B2
Poções, Brazil 123 D3
Pocomoke City, U.S.A. 104 F8
Poconé, Brazil 125 D6
Poços de Caldas, Brazil 127 A6
Poddebice, Poland 20 D8
Poděbrady, Czech. 20 E5
Podensac, France 26 D3
Podgorica, Montenegro, Yug. 21 N9
Podilska Vysochyna, Ukraine 41 H4
Podkamennaya Tunguska →, Russia 45 C10
Podlapac, Croatia 33 D12
Podolsk, Russia 42 C3
Podor, Senegal 78 B1
Podporozhy, Russia 40 B8
Podravska Slatina, Croatia 21 K7
Podujevo, Serbia, Yug. 21 N11
Poel, Germany 18 B7
Pofadder, S. Africa 84 D2
Pogamasing, Canada 98 C3
Poggiardo, Italy 35 B11
Poggibonsi, Italy 33 E8
Pogoanele, Romania 38 E9
Pogradeci, Albania 39 J3
Pogranitšnyi, Russia 48 B5

Poh, *Indonesia* 57 E6
Pohang, *S. Korea* 51 F15
Pohjanmaa, *Finland* 8 E20
Pohnpei, *Pac. Oc.* 92 G7
Pohorelá, *Slovak Rep.* 20 G10
Pohorje, *Slovenia* 33 B12
Poiana Mare, *Romania* 38 F6
Poinsett, C., *Antarctica* 5 C8
Point Edward, *Canada* 98 D3
Point Pedro, *Sri Lanka* 60 Q12
Point Pleasant, *N.J., U.S.A.* 107 F10
Point Pleasant, *W. Va., U.S.A.* 104 F4
Pointe-à-la Hache, *U.S.A.* 109 L10
Pointe-à-Pitre, *Guadeloupe* 117 C7
Pointe Noire, *Congo* 80 E2
Poirino, *Italy* 32 D4
Poisonbush Ra., *Australia* 88 D3
Poissy, *France* 25 D9
Poitiers, *France* 24 F7
Poitou, *France* 26 B3
Poitou, Seuil du, *France* 26 B4
Poix de Picardie, *France* 25 C8
Poix-Terron, *France* 25 C11
Pojoaque Valley, *U.S.A.* 111 J11
Pokaran, *India* 60 F7
Pokataroo, *Australia* 91 D4
Pokhvistnevo, *Russia* 42 D11
Poko, *Sudan* 77 F3
Poko, *Zaïre* 82 B2
Pokrov, *Russia* 42 C4
Pokrovsk = Engels, *Russia* 42 E8
Pokrovsk, *Russia* 45 C13
Pokrovskoye, *Russia* 43 G4
Pol, *Spain* 30 B3
Pola = Pula, *Croatia* 33 D10
Pola, *Russia* 40 D7
Pola de Allande, *Spain* 30 B4
Pola de Lena, *Spain* 30 B5
Pola de Siero, *Spain* 30 B5
Pola de Somiedo, *Spain* 30 B4
Polacca, *U.S.A.* 111 J8
Polan, *Iran* 65 E9
Poland ■, *Europe* 20 C9
Polanów, *Poland* 20 A6
Polatlı, *Turkey* 66 C5
Polatsk, *Belarus* 40 E5
Polcura, *Chile* 126 D1
Polden Hills, *U.K.* 13 F5
Polessk, *Russia* 9 J19
Polesye = Pripet Marshes, *Europe* 41 F5
Polgar, *Hungary* 21 H11
Pŏlgyo-ri, *S. Korea* 51 G14
Poli, *Cameroon* 80 C2
Políaigos, *Greece* 39 N7
Policastro, G. di, *Italy* 35 C8
Police, *Poland* 20 B4
Polignano a Mare, *Italy* 35 B10
Poligny, *France* 25 F12
Políkhnitas, *Greece* 39 K9
Polillo Is., *Phil.* 55 D4
Polillo Strait, *Phil.* 55 D4
Polis, *Cyprus* 37 D11
Polístena, *Italy* 35 D9
Políyiros, *Greece* 39 J6
Polk, *U.S.A.* 106 E5
Polla, *Italy* 35 B8
Pollachi, *India* 60 P10
Pollensa, *Spain* 36 B10
Pollensa, B. de, *Spain* 36 B10
Póllica, *Italy* 35 B8
Pollino, Mte., *Italy* 35 C9
Pollock, *U.S.A.* 108 C4
Polna, *Russia* 40 C5
Polnovat, *Russia* 44 C7
Polo, *U.S.A.* 108 E10
Pology, *Ukraine* 41 J9
Polonne, *Ukraine* 41 G4
Polonnoye = Polonne, *Ukraine* 41 G4
Polson, *U.S.A.* 110 C6
Poltava, *Ukraine* 41 H8
Põltsamaa, *Estonia* 9 G21
Polunochnoye, *Russia* 44 C7
Põlva, *Estonia* 9 G22
Polynesia, *Pac. Oc.* 93 H11
Polynésie française = French Polynesia ■, *Pac. Oc.* 93 J13
Pomarance, *Italy* 32 E7
Pomárico, *Italy* 35 B9
Pomaro, *Mexico* 114 D4
Pombal, *Brazil* 122 C4
Pombal, *Portugal* 30 F2
Pómbia, *Greece* 37 D6
Pomeroy, *Ohio, U.S.A.* 104 F4
Pomeroy, *Wash., U.S.A.* 110 C5
Pomichna, *Ukraine* 41 H6
Pomona, *U.S.A.* 113 L9
Pomorie, *Bulgaria* 38 G10
Pomos, *Cyprus* 37 D11
Pomos, C., *Cyprus* 37 D11
Pompano Beach, *U.S.A.* 105 M5
Pompei, *Italy* 35 B7
Pompey, *France* 25 D13
Pompeys Pillar, *U.S.A.* 110 D10
Ponape = Pohnpei, *Pac. Oc.* 92 G7
Ponask, L., *Canada* 98 B1
Ponass L., *Canada* 101 C8
Ponca, *U.S.A.* 108 D6
Ponca City, *U.S.A.* 109 G6
Ponce, *Puerto Rico* 117 C6
Ponchatoula, *U.S.A.* 109 K9
Poncheville, L., *Canada* 98 B4
Poncin, *France* 27 B9
Pond, *U.S.A.* 113 K7
Pond Inlet, *Canada* 97 A12
Pondicherry, *India* 60 P11
Pondrôme, *Belgium* 17 H6
Ponds, I. of, *Canada* 99 B8
Ponferrada, *Spain* 30 C4
Pongo, Wadi →, *Sudan* 77 F2
Poniatowa, *Poland* 20 D12
Ponikva, *Slovenia* 33 B12
Ponnani, *India* 60 P9
Ponnyadaung, *Burma* 61 J19
Ponoka, *Canada* 100 C6
Ponorogo, *Indonesia* 57 G14
Ponoy →, *Russia* 44 C5
Pons, *France* 26 C3
Pons, *Spain* 28 D6
Ponsul →, *Portugal* 31 F3
Pont-à-Celles, *Belgium* 17 G4
Pont-à-Mousson, *France* 25 D13
Pont-Audemer, *France* 24 C7
Pont-Aven, *France* 24 E3
Pont Canavese, *Italy* 32 C4
Pont-de-Roide, *France* 25 E13
Pont-de-Salars, *France* 26 D6
Pont-de-Vaux, *France* 25 F11
Pont-de-Veyle, *France* 27 B8
Pont-l'Abbé, *France* 24 E2
Pont-l'Évêque, *France* 24 C7
Pont-St.-Esprit, *France* 27 D8
Pont-Saint-Martin, *Italy* 32 C4
Pont-sur-Yonne, *France* 25 D10
Ponta de Pedras, *Brazil* 122 B2
Ponta do Sol, *Madeira* 36 D2
Ponta Grossa, *Brazil* 127 B5
Ponta Pora, *Brazil* 127 A4
Pontacq, *France* 26 E3
Pontailler-sur-Saône, *France* 25 E12
Pontal →, *Brazil* 122 C3
Pontalina, *Brazil* 123 E2
Pontarlier, *France* 25 F13
Pontassieve, *Italy* 33 E8
Pontaubault, *France* 24 D5
Pontaumur, *France* 26 C6
Pontcharra, *France* 27 C10
Pontchartrain L., *U.S.A.* 109 K9
Pontchâteau, *France* 24 E4
Ponte Alta, Serra do, *Brazil* 123 E2
Ponte Alta do Norte, *Brazil* 122 D2
Ponte Branca, *Brazil* 125 D7
Ponte da Barca, *Portugal* 30 D2
Ponte de Sor, *Portugal* 31 F3
Ponte dell'Ólio, *Italy* 32 D6
Ponte di Legno, *Italy* 32 B7
Ponte do Lima, *Portugal* 30 D2
Ponte do Pungué, *Mozam.* 83 F3
Ponte-Leccia, *France* 27 F13
Ponte nelle Alpi, *Italy* 33 B9
Ponte Nova, *Brazil* 123 F3
Ponte San Pietro, *Italy* 32 C6
Pontebba, *Italy* 33 B10
Pontecorvo, *Italy* 34 A6
Pontedera, *Italy* 32 E7
Pontefract, *U.K.* 12 D6
Ponteix, *Canada* 101 D7
Pontelandolfo, *Italy* 35 A7
Pontevedra, *Spain* 30 C2
Pontevedra □, *Spain* 30 C2
Pontevedra, R. de →, *Spain* 30 C2
Pontevico, *Italy* 32 C7
Pontiac, *Ill., U.S.A.* 108 E10
Pontiac, *Mich., U.S.A.* 104 D4
Pontian Kecil, *Malaysia* 59 M4
Pontianak, *Indonesia* 56 E3
Pontine Is. = Ponziane, Ísole, *Italy* 34 B5
Pontine Mts. = Kuzey Anadolu Dağları, *Turkey* 66 B7
Pontínia, *Italy* 34 A6
Pontivy, *France* 24 D4
Pontoise, *France* 25 C9
Ponton →, *Canada* 100 B5
Pontorson, *France* 24 D5
Pontrémoli, *Italy* 32 D6
Pontresina, *Switz.* 23 D9
Pontrieux, *France* 24 D3
Pontypool, *Canada* 106 B6
Pontypool, *U.K.* 13 F4
Pontypridd, *U.K.* 13 F4
Ponza, *Italy* 34 B5
Ponziane, Ísole, *Italy* 34 B5
Poochera, *Australia* 91 E1
Poole, *U.K.* 13 G6
Pooley I., *Canada* 100 C3
Poona = Pune, *India* 60 K8
Pooncarie, *Australia* 91 E3
Poopelloe L., *Australia* 91 E3
Poopó, *Bolivia* 124 D4
Poopó, L. de, *Bolivia* 124 D4
Popanyinning, *Australia* 89 F2
Popayán, *Colombia* 120 C2
Poperinge, *Belgium* 17 G1
Popigay, *Russia* 45 B12
Popilta, L., *Australia* 91 E3
Popio L., *Australia* 91 E3
Poplar, *U.S.A.* 108 A2
Poplar →, *Man., Canada* 101 C9
Poplar →, *N.W.T., Canada* 100 A4
Poplar Bluff, *U.S.A.* 109 G9
Poplarville, *U.S.A.* 109 K10
Popocatépetl, Volcán, *Mexico* 115 D5
Popokabaka, *Zaïre* 80 F3
Pópoli, *Italy* 33 F10
Popovača, *Croatia* 33 C13
Popovo, *Bulgaria* 38 F9
Poppel, *Belgium* 17 F6
Poprád, *Slovak Rep.* 20 F10
Poprád →, *Slovak Rep.* 20 F10
Porali →, *Pakistan* 62 G2
Porangaba, *Brazil* 124 B3
Porangatu, *Brazil* 123 D2
Porbandar, *India* 62 J3
Porce →, *Colombia* 120 B3
Porcher I., *Canada* 100 C2
Porco, *Bolivia* 125 D4
Porcos →, *Brazil* 123 D2
Porcuna, *Spain* 31 H6
Porcupine →, *Canada* 101 B8
Porcupine →, *U.S.A.* 96 B5
Pordenone, *Italy* 33 C9
Poreč, *Croatia* 33 C10
Porecatu, *Brazil* 123 F1
Poretskoye, *Russia* 42 C8
Pori, *Finland* 9 F19
Porkhov, *Russia* 40 D5
Porlamar, *Venezuela* 121 A5
Porlezza, *Italy* 32 B6
Porma →, *Spain* 30 C5
Pornic, *France* 24 E4
Poronaysk, *Russia* 45 E15
Póros, *Greece* 39 M6
Poroshiri-Dake, *Japan* 48 C11
Poroto Mts., *Tanzania* 83 D3
Porpoise B., *Antarctica* 5 C9
Porquerolles, I. de, *France* 27 F10
Porrentruy, *Switz.* 22 B4
Porreras, *Spain* 36 B10
Porretta, Passo di, *Italy* 32 D7
Porsangen, *Norway* 8 A21
Porsgrunn, *Norway* 10 E3
Port Adelaide, *Australia* 91 E2
Port Alberni, *Canada* 100 D4
Port Alfred, *Canada* 99 C5
Port Alfred, *S. Africa* 84 E4
Port Alice, *Canada* 100 C3
Port Allegany, *U.S.A.* 106 E6
Port Allen, *U.S.A.* 109 K9
Port Alma, *Australia* 90 C5
Port Angeles, *U.S.A.* 112 B3
Port Antonio, *Jamaica* 116 C4
Port Aransas, *U.S.A.* 109 M6
Port Arthur = Lüshun, *China* 51 E11
Port Arthur, *Australia* 90 G4
Port Arthur, *U.S.A.* 109 L8
Port au Port B., *Canada* 99 C8
Port-au-Prince, *Haiti* 117 C5
Port Augusta, *Australia* 91 E2
Port Augusta West, *Australia* 91 E2
Port Austin, *U.S.A.* 98 D3
Port Bell, *Uganda* 82 B3
Port Bergé Vaovao, *Madag.* 85 B8
Port Blandford, *Canada* 99 C9
Port Bou, *Spain* 28 C8
Port Bouët, *Ivory C.* 78 D4
Port Bradshaw, *Australia* 90 A2
Port Broughton, *Australia* 91 E2
Port Burwell, *Canada* 98 D3
Port Canning, *India* 63 H13
Port-Cartier, *Canada* 99 B6
Port Chalmers, *N.Z.* 87 L3
Port Chester, *U.S.A.* 107 F11
Port Clements, *Canada* 100 C2
Port Clinton, *U.S.A.* 104 E4
Port Colborne, *Canada* 98 D4
Port Coquitlam, *Canada* 100 D4
Port Credit, *Canada* 106 C5
Port Curtis, *Australia* 90 C5
Port Dalhousie, *Canada* 106 C5
Port Darwin, *Australia* 88 B5
Port Darwin, *Falk. Is.* 128 D5
Port Davey, *Australia* 90 G4
Port-de-Bouc, *France* 27 E8
Port-de-Paix, *Haiti* 117 C5
Port Dickson, *Malaysia* 59 L3
Port Douglas, *Australia* 90 B4
Port Dover, *Canada* 106 D4
Port Edward, *Canada* 100 C2
Port Elgin, *Canada* 98 D3
Port Elizabeth, *S. Africa* 84 E4
Port Ellen, *U.K.* 14 F2
Port-en-Bessin, *France* 24 C6
Port Erin, *U.K.* 12 C3
Port Essington, *Australia* 88 B5
Port Etienne = Nouâdhibou, *Mauritania* 74 D1
Port Fairy, *Australia* 91 F3
Port Fouâd = Bûr Fuad, *Egypt* 76 H8
Port Gamble, *U.S.A.* 112 C4
Port-Gentil, *Gabon* 80 E1
Port Gibson, *U.S.A.* 109 K9
Port Glasgow, *U.K.* 14 F4
Port Harcourt, *Nigeria* 79 E6
Port Hardy, *Canada* 100 C3
Port Harrison = Inukjuak, *Canada* 97 C12
Port Hawkesbury, *Canada* 99 C7
Port Hedland, *Australia* 88 D2
Port Henry, *U.S.A.* 107 B11
Port Hood, *Canada* 99 C7
Port Hope, *Canada* 98 D4
Port Hueneme, *U.S.A.* 113 L7
Port Huron, *U.S.A.* 104 D4
Port Iliç, *Azerbaijan* 67 C13
Port Isabel, *U.S.A.* 109 M6
Port Jefferson, *U.S.A.* 107 F11
Port Jervis, *U.S.A.* 107 E10
Port-Joinville, *France* 24 F4
Port Katon, *Russia* 43 G4
Port Kelang = Pelabuhan Kelang, *Malaysia* 59 L3
Port Kembla, *Australia* 91 E5
Port Kenny, *Australia* 91 E1
Port-la-Nouvelle, *France* 26 E7
Port Lairge = Waterford, *Ireland* 15 D4
Port Laoise, *Ireland* 15 C4
Port Lavaca, *U.S.A.* 109 L6
Port-Leucate, *France* 26 F7
Port Lincoln, *Australia* 91 E2
Port Loko, *S. Leone* 78 D2
Port Louis, *France* 24 E3
Port Lyautey = Kenitra, *Morocco* 74 B3
Port MacDonnell, *Australia* 91 F3
Port Macquarie, *Australia* 91 E5
Port Maria, *Jamaica* 116 C4
Port Mellon, *Canada* 100 D4
Port-Menier, *Canada* 99 C7
Port Morant, *Jamaica* 116 C4
Port Moresby, *Papua N. G.* 92 H6
Port Mourant, *Guyana* 121 B6
Port Mouton, *Canada* 99 D7
Port Musgrave, *Australia* 90 A3
Port-Navalo, *France* 24 E4
Port Nelson, *Canada* 101 B10
Port Nolloth, *S. Africa* 84 D2
Port Nouveau-Québec = Kangiqsualujjuaq, *Canada* 97 C13
Port O'Connor, *U.S.A.* 109 L6
Port of Spain, *Trin. & Tob.* 117 D7
Port Orchard, *U.S.A.* 112 C4
Port Orford, *U.S.A.* 110 E1
Port Pegasus, *N.Z.* 87 M1
Port Perry, *Canada* 98 D4
Port Phillip B., *Australia* 91 F3
Port Pirie, *Australia* 91 E2
Port Radium = Echo Bay, *Canada* 96 B8
Port Renfrew, *Canada* 100 D4
Port Roper, *Australia* 90 A2
Port Rowan, *Canada* 98 D3
Port Safaga = Bûr Safâga, *Egypt* 76 B3
Port Said = Bûr Sa'îd, *Egypt* 76 H8
Port St. Joe, *U.S.A.* 105 L3
Port St. Johns, *S. Africa* 85 E4
Port-St.-Louis-du-Rhône, *France* 27 E8
Port San Vicente, *Phil.* 55 B5
Port Sanilac, *U.S.A.* 98 D3
Port Saunders, *Canada* 99 B8
Port Severn, *Canada* 106 B5
Port Shepstone, *S. Africa* 85 E5
Port Simpson, *Canada* 100 C2
Port Stanley = Stanley, *Falk. Is.* 128 D5
Port Stanley, *Canada* 98 D3
Port Sudan = Bûr Sûdân, *Sudan* 76 D4
Port-sur-Saône, *France* 25 E13
Port Talbot, *U.K.* 13 F4
Port Taufiq = Bûr Taufiq, *Egypt* 76 J8
Port Townsend, *U.S.A.* 112 B4
Port-Vendres, *France* 26 F7
Port Wakefield, *Australia* 91 E2
Port Washington, *U.S.A.* 104 D2
Port Weld, *Malaysia* 59 K3
Portachuelo, *Bolivia* 125 D5
Portadown, *U.K.* 15 B5
Portage, *U.S.A.* 108 D10
Portage La Prairie, *Canada* 101 D9
Portageville, *U.S.A.* 109 G10
Portalegre, *Portugal* 31 F3
Portalegre □, *Portugal* 31 F3
Portales, *U.S.A.* 109 H3
Portarlington, *Ireland* 15 C4
Porteirinha, *Brazil* 123 E3
Portel, *Brazil* 122 B1
Portel, *Portugal* 31 G3
Porter L., *N.W.T., Canada* 101 A7
Porter L., *Sask., Canada* 101 B7
Porterville, *S. Africa* 84 E2
Porterville, *U.S.A.* 111 H4
Porthcawl, *U.K.* 13 F4
Porthill, *U.S.A.* 110 B5
Portile de Fier, *Europe* 38 E5
Portimão, *Portugal* 31 H2
Portland, *N.S.W., Australia* 91 E4
Portland, *Vic., Australia* 91 F3
Portland, *Canada* 107 B8
Portland, *Conn., U.S.A.* 107 E12
Portland, *Maine, U.S.A.* 99 D5
Portland, *Mich., U.S.A.* 104 D3
Portland, *Oreg., U.S.A.* 112 E4
Portland, I. of, *U.K.* 13 G5
Portland B., *Australia* 91 F3
Portland Bill, *U.K.* 13 G5
Portland Prom., *Canada* 97 C12
Portlands Roads, *Australia* 90 A3
Portneuf, *Canada* 99 C5
Pôrto, *Brazil* 122 B3
Porto, *France* 27 F12
Porto, *Portugal* 30 D2
Porto □, *Portugal* 30 D2
Porto, G. de, *France* 27 F12
Pôrto Acre, *Brazil* 124 B4
Pôrto Alegre, *Pará, Brazil* 121 D7
Pôrto Alegre, *Rio Grande do S., Brazil* 127 C5
Porto Amboim = Gunza, *Angola* 80 G2
Porto Argentera, *Italy* 32 D4
Porto Azzurro, *Italy* 32 F7
Porto Botte, *Italy* 34 C1
Pôrto Cajueiro, *Brazil* 125 C6
Porto Civitanova, *Italy* 33 E10
Porto Cristo, *Spain* 36 B10
Pôrto da Fôlha, *Brazil* 122 C4
Pôrto de Móz, *Brazil* 121 D7
Pôrto de Pedras, *Brazil* 122 C4
Pôrto des Meinacos, *Brazil* 125 C7
Porto Empédocle, *Italy* 34 E6
Pôrto Esperança, *Brazil* 125 D6
Pôrto Esperidão, *Brazil* 125 D6
Pôrto Franco, *Brazil* 122 C2
Porto Garibaldi, *Italy* 33 D9
Pôrto Grande, *Brazil* 121 C7
Pôrto Jofre, *Brazil* 125 D6
Pórto Lágo, *Greece* 39 J8
Pôrto Mendes, *Brazil* 127 A5
Porto Moniz, *Madeira* 36 D2
Pôrto Murtinho, *Brazil* 125 E6
Pôrto Nacional, *Brazil* 122 D2
Porto Novo, *Benin* 79 D5
Porto Petro, *Spain* 36 B10
Porto Recanati, *Italy* 33 E10
Porto San Giórgio, *Italy* 33 E10
Pôrto Santana, *Brazil* 121 D7
Porto Santo, *Madeira* 72 B1
Porto Santo Stéfano, *Italy* 32 F8
Pôrto São José, *Brazil* 127 A5
Pôrto Seguro, *Brazil* 123 E4
Porto Tolle, *Italy* 33 D9
Porto Tórres, *Italy* 34 B1
Pôrto União, *Brazil* 127 B5
Pôrto Válter, *Brazil* 124 B3
Porto-Vecchio, *France* 27 G13
Pôrto Velho, *Brazil* 125 B5
Portobelo, *Panama* 116 E4
Portoferráio, *Italy* 32 F7
Portogruaro, *Italy* 33 C9
Portola, *U.S.A.* 112 F6
Portomaggiore, *Italy* 33 D8
Portoscuso, *Italy* 34 C1
Portovénere, *Italy* 32 D6
Portovíejo, *Ecuador* 120 D1
Portpatrick, *U.K.* 14 G3
Portree, *U.K.* 14 D2
Portrush, *U.K.* 15 A5
Portsall, *France* 24 D2
Portsmouth, *Domin.* 117 C7
Portsmouth, *U.K.* 13 G6
Portsmouth, *N.H., U.S.A.* 107 C14
Portsmouth, *Ohio, U.S.A.* 104 F4
Portsmouth, *R.I., U.S.A.* 107 E13
Portsmouth, *Va., U.S.A.* 104 G7
Portsoy, *U.K.* 14 D6
Porttipahtan tekojärvi, *Finland* 8 B22
Portugal ■, *Europe* 30 F3
Portugalete, *Spain* 28 B1
Portuguesa □, *Venezuela* 120 B4
Portumna, *Ireland* 15 C3
Portville, *U.S.A.* 106 D6
Porvenir, *Bolivia* 124 C4
Porvenir, *Chile* 128 D2
Porvoo, *Finland* 9 F21
Porzuna, *Spain* 31 F6
Posada →, *Italy* 34 B2
Posadas, *Argentina* 127 B4
Posadas, *Spain* 31 H5
Poschiavo, *Switz.* 23 D10
Posets, *Spain* 28 C5
Poshan = Boshan, *China* 51 F9
Posht-e-Badam, *Iran* 65 C7
Posídhion, Ákra, *Greece* 39 K6
Poso, *Indonesia* 57 E6
Posoegroenoe, *Surinam* 121 C6
Posong, *S. Korea* 51 G14
Posse, *Brazil* 123 D2
Possel, *C.A.R.* 80 C3
Possession I., *Antarctica* 5 D11
Pössneck, *Germany* 18 E7
Post, *U.S.A.* 109 J4
Post Falls, *U.S.A.* 110 C5
Postavy = Pastavy, *Belarus* 9 J22
Poste Maurice Cortier, *Algeria* 75 D5
Postmasburg, *S. Africa* 84 D3
Postojna, *Slovenia* 33 C11
Poston, *U.S.A.* 113 M12
Potchefstroom, *S. Africa* 84 D4
Poté, *Brazil* 123 E3
Poteau, *U.S.A.* 109 H7
Poteet, *U.S.A.* 109 L5
Potelu, Lacul, *Romania* 38 F7
Potenza, *Italy* 35 B8
Potenza →, *Italy* 33 E10
Potenza Picena, *Italy* 33 E10
Poteriteri, L., *N.Z.* 87 M1
Potes, *Spain* 30 B6
Potgietersrus, *S. Africa* 85 C4
Poti, *Georgia* 43 J5
Potiraguá, *Brazil* 123 E4
Potiskum, *Nigeria* 79 C7
Potomac →, *U.S.A.* 104 F7
Potosí, *Bolivia* 125 D4
Potosí □, *Bolivia* 124 E4
Potosi Mt., *U.S.A.* 113 K11
Pototan, *Phil.* 55 F5
Potrerillos, *Chile* 126 B2
Potsdam, *Germany* 18 C9
Potsdam, *U.S.A.* 107 B10
Pottenstein, *Germany* 19 F7
Potter, *U.S.A.* 108 E3

Pottery Hill = Abû Ballas, Egypt 76 C2
Pottstown, U.S.A. 107 F9
Pottsville, U.S.A. 107 F8
Pottuvil, Sri Lanka 60 R12
P'otzu, Taiwan 53 F13
Pouancé, France 24 E5
Pouce Coupé, Canada 100 B4
Poughkeepsie, U.S.A. 107 E11
Pouilly-sur-Loire, France 25 E9
Poulaphouca Res., Ireland 15 C5
Poulsbo, U.S.A. 112 C4
Pourri, Mt., France 27 C10
Pouso Alegre, Mato Grosso, Brazil 125 C6
Pouso Alegre, Minas Gerais, Brazil 127 A6
Pouzauges, France 24 F6
Povenets, Russia 44 C4
Poverty B., N.Z. 87 H7
Póvoa de Lanhosa, Portugal 30 D2
Póvoa de Varzim, Portugal 30 D2
Povorino, Russia 42 E6
Powassan, Canada 98 C4
Poway, U.S.A. 113 N9
Powder →, U.S.A. 108 B2
Powder River, U.S.A. 110 E10
Powell, U.S.A. 110 D9
Powell L., U.S.A. 111 H8
Powell River, Canada 100 D4
Powers, Mich., U.S.A. 104 C2
Powers, Oreg., U.S.A. 110 E1
Powers Lake, U.S.A. 108 A3
Powys □, U.K. 13 E4
Poxoreu, Brazil 125 D7
Poyang Hu, China 53 C11
Poyarkovo, Russia 45 E13
Poza de la Sal, Spain 28 C1
Poza Rica, Mexico 115 C5
Pozanti, Turkey 66 D6
Požarevac, Serbia, Yug. 21 L11
Poznań, Poland 20 C6
Pozo, U.S.A. 113 K6
Pozo Alcón, Spain 29 H2
Pozo Almonte, Chile 124 E4
Pozo Colorado, Paraguay 126 A4
Pozo del Dátil, Mexico 114 B2
Pozoblanco, Spain 31 G6
Pozuzo, Peru 124 C2
Pozzallo, Italy 35 F7
Pozzuoli, Italy 35 B7
Pra →, Ghana 79 D4
Prachin Buri, Thailand 58 E3
Prachuap Khiri Khan, Thailand 59 G2
Pradelles, France 26 D7
Pradera, Colombia 120 C2
Prades, France 26 F6
Prado, Brazil 123 E4
Prado del Rey, Spain 31 J5
Præstø, Denmark 11 J6
Pragersko, Slovenia 33 B12
Prague = Praha, Czech. 20 E4
Praha, Czech. 20 E4
Prahecq, France 26 B3
Prahova →, Romania 38 E8
Prahovo, Serbia, Yug. 21 L12
Praia, C. Verde Is. 71 E1
Praid, Romania 38 C8
Prainha, Amazonas, Brazil 125 B5
Prainha, Pará, Brazil 121 D7
Prairie, Australia 90 C3
Prairie →, U.S.A. 109 H5
Prairie City, U.S.A. 110 D4
Prairie du Chien, U.S.A. 108 D9
Prairies, Canada 96 C9
Pramánda, Greece 39 K4
Pran Buri, Thailand 58 F2
Prang, Ghana 79 D4
Prapat, Indonesia 56 D1
Prasonísi, Ákra, Greece 37 D9
Prata, Brazil 123 E2
Pratapgarh, India 62 G6
Prática di Mare, Italy 34 A5
Prätigau, Switz. 23 C9
Prato, Italy 32 E8
Prátola Peligna, Italy 33 F10
Pratovécchio, Italy 33 E8
Prats-de-Mollo-la-Preste, France 26 F6
Pratt, U.S.A. 109 G5
Pratteln, Switz. 22 A5
Prattville, U.S.A. 105 J2
Pravdinsk, Russia 42 B6
Pravia, Spain 30 B4
Praya, Indonesia 56 F5
Pré-en-Pail, France 24 D6
Pré-Saint-Didier, Italy 32 C4
Precordillera, Argentina 126 C2
Predáppio, Italy 33 D8
Predazzo, Italy 33 B8
Predejane, Serbia, Yug. 21 N12
Preeceville, Canada 101 C8
Préfailles, France 24 E4
Pregonero, Venezuela 120 B3
Pregrada, Croatia 33 B12
Preiļi, Latvia 9 H22
Preko, Croatia 33 D12
Prelate, Canada 101 C7
Prelog, Croatia 33 B13
Premier, Canada 100 B3
Premont, U.S.A. 109 M5
Premuda, Croatia 33 D11
Prenjasi, Albania 39 H3
Prentice, U.S.A. 108 C9
Prenzlau, Germany 18 B9
Preobrazheniye, Russia 48 C6
Preparis North Channel, Ind. Oc. 61 M18
Preparis South Channel, Ind. Oc. 61 M18
Přerov, Czech. 20 F7
Presanella, Italy 32 B7
Prescott, Canada 98 D4
Prescott, Ariz., U.S.A. 111 J7
Prescott, Ark., U.S.A. 109 J8
Preservation Inlet, N.Z. 87 M1
Preševo, Serbia, Yug. 21 N11
Presho, U.S.A. 108 D4
Presicce, Italy 35 C11
Presidencia de la Plaza, Argentina 126 B4
Presidencia Roque Saenz Peña, Argentina 126 B3
Presidente Epitácio, Brazil 123 F1
Presidente Hayes □, Paraguay 126 A4
Presidente Hermes, Brazil 125 C5
Presidente Prudente, Brazil 127 A5
Presidio, Mexico 114 B4
Presidio, U.S.A. 109 L2
Preslav, Bulgaria 38 F9
Prešov, Slovak Rep. 20 F11
Prespa, L. = Prespansko Jezero, Macedonia 39 J4
Prespansko Jezero, Macedonia 39 J4
Presque Isle, U.S.A. 99 C6
Prestbury, U.K. 13 F5
Prestea, Ghana 78 D4
Presteigne, U.K. 13 E5
Presto, Bolivia 125 D5
Preston, Canada 106 C4
Preston, U.K. 12 D5
Preston, Idaho, U.S.A. 110 E8
Preston, Minn., U.S.A. 108 D8
Preston, Nev., U.S.A. 110 G6
Preston, C., Australia 88 D2
Prestonpans, U.K. 14 F6
Prestwick, U.K. 14 F4
Prêto →, Amazonas, Brazil 121 D5
Prêto →, Bahia, Brazil 122 D3
Prêto do Igapó-Açu →, Brazil 121 D6
Pretoria, S. Africa 85 D4
Preuilly-sur-Claise, France 24 F7
Préveza, Greece 39 L3
Priazovskoye, Ukraine 41 J8
Pribilof Is., Bering S. 4 D17
Priboj, Serbia, Yug. 21 M9
Příbram, Czech. 20 F4
Price, U.S.A. 110 G8
Price I., Canada 100 C3
Prichard, U.S.A. 105 K1
Priego, Spain 28 E2
Priego de Córdoba, Spain 31 H6
Priekule, Latvia 9 H19
Prien, Germany 19 H8
Prienai, Lithuania 9 J20
Prieska, S. Africa 84 D3
Priest →, U.S.A. 110 B5
Priest L., U.S.A. 110 B5
Priest Valley, U.S.A. 112 J6
Priestly, Canada 100 C3
Prievidza, Slovak Rep. 20 G8
Prijedor, Bos.-H. 33 D13
Prikaspiyskaya Nizmennost = Caspian Depression, Eurasia 43 G9
Prikubanskaya Nizmennost, Russia 43 H4
Prilep, Macedonia 39 H4
Priluki = Pryluky, Ukraine 41 G7
Prime Seal I., Australia 90 G4
Primeira Cruz, Brazil 122 B3
Primorsk, Russia 40 B5
Primorsko-Akhtarsk, Russia 43 G4
Primorskoye, Ukraine 41 J9
Primrose L., Canada 101 C7
Prince Albert, Canada 101 C7
Prince Albert, S. Africa 84 E3
Prince Albert Mts., Antarctica 5 D11
Prince Albert Nat. Park, Canada 101 C7
Prince Albert Pen., Canada 96 A8
Prince Albert Sd., Canada 96 A8
Prince Alfred, C., Canada 4 B1
Prince Charles I., Canada 97 B12
Prince Charles Mts., Antarctica 5 D6
Prince Edward I. □, Canada 99 C7
Prince Edward Is., Ind. Oc. 3 G11
Prince George, Canada 100 C4
Prince of Wales, C., U.S.A. 94 C3
Prince of Wales I., Australia 90 A3
Prince of Wales I., Canada 96 A10
Prince of Wales I., U.S.A. 100 B2
Prince Patrick I., Canada 4 B2
Prince Regent Inlet, Canada 4 B3
Prince Rupert, Canada 100 C2
Princenhage, Neths. 17 F5
Princesa Isabel, Brazil 122 C4
Princess Charlotte B., Australia 90 A3
Princess May Ras., Australia 88 C4
Princess Royal I., Canada 100 C3
Princeton, Canada 100 D4
Princeton, Calif., U.S.A. 112 F4
Princeton, Ill., U.S.A. 108 E10
Princeton, Ind., U.S.A. 104 F2
Princeton, Ky., U.S.A. 104 G2
Princeton, Mo., U.S.A. 108 E8
Princeton, N.J., U.S.A. 107 F10
Princeton, W. Va., U.S.A. 104 G5
Principe, I. de, Atl. Oc. 70 F4
Principe Chan., Canada 100 C2
Principe da Beira, Brazil 125 C5
Prineville, U.S.A. 110 D3
Prins Harald Kyst, Antarctica 5 D4
Prinsesse Astrid Kyst, Antarctica 5 D3
Prinsesse Ragnhild Kyst, Antarctica 5 D4
Prinzapolca, Nic. 116 D3
Prior, C., Spain 30 B2
Priozersk, Russia 40 B6
Pripet → = Prypyat →, Europe 41 G6
Pripet Marshes, Europe 41 F5
Pripyat Marshes = Pripet Marshes, Europe 41 F5
Pripyats = Prypyat →, Europe 41 G6
Prislop, Pasul, Romania 38 B8
Pristen, Russia 42 E3
Priština, Serbia, Yug. 21 N11
Pritzwalk, Germany 18 B8
Privas, France 27 D8
Priverno, Italy 34 A6
Privolzhsk, Russia 42 B5
Privolzhskaya Vozvyshennost, Russia 42 E7
Privolzhskiy, Russia 42 E8
Privolzhye, Russia 42 D9
Priyutnoye, Russia 43 G6
Prizren, Serbia, Yug. 21 N10
Prizzi, Italy 34 E6
Prnjavor, Bos.-H. 21 L7
Probolinggo, Indonesia 57 G15
Procida, Italy 35 B7
Proddatur, India 60 M11
Prodhromos, Cyprus 37 E11
Proença-a-Nova, Portugal 31 F3
Prof. Van Blommestein Meer, Surinam 121 C6
Profítis Ilías, Greece 37 C9
Profondeville, Belgium 17 H5
Progreso, Mexico 115 C7
Prokhladnyy, Russia 43 J7
Prokletije, Albania 38 G2
Prokopyevsk, Russia 44 D9
Prokuplje, Serbia, Yug. 21 M11
Proletarsk, Russia 43 G5
Proletarskaya = Proletarsk, Russia 43 G5
Prome = Pyè, Burma 61 K19
Prophet →, Canada 100 B4
Propriá, Brazil 122 D4
Propriano, France 27 G12
Proserpine, Australia 90 C4
Prosser, U.S.A. 110 C4
Prostějov, Czech. 20 F7
Proston, Australia 91 D5
Protection, U.S.A. 109 G5
Próti, Greece 39 M4
Provadiya, Bulgaria 38 F10
Proven, Belgium 17 G1
Provence, France 27 E9
Providence, Ky., U.S.A. 104 G2
Providence, R.I., U.S.A. 107 E13
Providence Bay, Canada 98 C3
Providence Mts., U.S.A. 111 J6
Providencia, Ecuador 120 D2
Providencia, I. de, Colombia 116 D3
Provideniya, Russia 45 C19
Provins, France 25 D10
Provo, U.S.A. 110 F8
Provost, Canada 101 C6
Prozor, Bos.-H. 21 M7
Prudentópolis, Brazil 123 G1
Prud'homme, Canada 101 C7
Prudnik, Poland 20 E7
Prüm, Germany 19 E2
Pruszcz Gdański, Poland 20 A8
Pruszków, Poland 20 C10
Prut →, Romania 38 D11
Pruzhany, Belarus 41 F3
Prvič, Croatia 33 D11
Prydz B., Antarctica 5 C6
Pryluky, Ukraine 41 G7
Pryor, U.S.A. 109 G7
Prypyat →, Europe 41 G6
Przasnysz, Poland 20 B10
Przedbórz, Poland 20 D9
Przemyśl, Poland 20 F12
Przeworsk, Poland 20 E12
Przewóz, Poland 20 D4
Przhevalsk, Kyrgyzstan 44 E8
Przysuchla, Poland 20 D10
Psakhná, Greece 39 L6
Psará, Greece 39 L8
Psel →, Ukraine 41 H7
Pserimos, Greece 39 N10
Psíra, Greece 37 D7
Pskov, Russia 40 D5
Pskovskoye, Ozero, Russia 9 H22
Psunj, Croatia 21 K7
Pszczyna, Poland 20 F8
Pteleón, Greece 39 K5
Ptich = Ptsich →, Belarus 41 F5
Ptolemaís, Greece 39 J4
Ptsich →, Belarus 41 F5
Ptuj, Slovenia 33 B12
Ptujska Gora, Slovenia 33 B12
Pu Xian, China 50 F6
Pua, Thailand 58 C3
Puán, Argentina 126 D3
Pu'an, China 52 E5
Puan, S. Korea 51 G14
Pubei, China 52 F7
Pucacuro →, Peru 120 D3
Pucallpa, Peru 124 B3
Pucará, Bolivia 125 D5
Pucará, Peru 124 D3
Pucarani, Bolivia 124 D4
Pucheng, China 53 D12
Pučišće, Croatia 33 E13
Pucka, Zatoka, Poland 20 A8
Pudasjärvi, Finland 8 D22
Puding, China 52 D5
Pudozh, Russia 40 B9
Pudukkottai, India 60 P11
Puebla, Mexico 115 D5
Puebla □, Mexico 115 D5
Puebla de Alcocer, Spain 31 G5
Puebla de Don Fadrique, Spain 29 H2
Puebla de Don Rodrigo, Spain 31 F6
Puebla de Guzmán, Spain 31 H3
Puebla de Sanabria, Spain 30 C4
Puebla de Trives, Spain 30 C3
Puebla del Caramiñal, Spain 30 C2
Pueblo, U.S.A. 108 F2
Pueblo Hundido, Chile 126 B1
Pueblo Nuevo, Venezuela 120 B3
Puelches, Argentina 126 D2
Puelén, Argentina 126 D2
Puente Alto, Chile 126 C1
Puente del Arzobispo, Spain 30 F5
Puente-Genil, Spain 31 H6
Puente la Reina, Spain 28 C3
Puenteareas, Spain 30 C2
Puentedeume, Spain 30 B2
Puentes de Garcia Rodriguez, Spain 30 B3
Pu'er, China 52 F3
Puerco →, U.S.A. 111 J10
Puerto, Canary Is. 36 F2
Puerto Acosta, Bolivia 124 D4
Puerto Aisén, Chile 128 C2
Puerto Ángel, Mexico 115 D5
Puerto Arista, Mexico 115 D6
Puerto Armuelles, Panama 116 E3
Puerto Ayacucho, Venezuela 120 B4
Puerto Barrios, Guatemala 116 C2
Puerto Bermejo, Argentina 126 B4
Puerto Bermúdez, Peru 124 C3
Puerto Bolívar, Ecuador 120 D2
Puerto Cabello, Venezuela 120 A4
Puerto Cabezas, Nic. 116 D3
Puerto Cabo Gracias á Dios, Nic. 116 D3
Puerto Capaz = Jebba, Morocco 74 A4
Puerto Carreño, Colombia 120 B4
Puerto Castilla, Honduras 116 C2
Puerto Chicama, Peru 124 B2
Puerto Coig, Argentina 128 D3
Puerto Cortes, Costa Rica 116 E3
Puerto Cortés, Honduras 116 C2
Puerto Cumarebo, Venezuela 120 A4
Puerto de Alcudia, Spain 36 B10
Puerto de Andraitx, Spain 36 B9
Puerto de Cabrera, Spain 36 B9
Puerto de Gran Tarajal, Canary Is. 36 F5
Puerto de la Cruz, Canary Is. 36 F3
Puerto de Pozo Negro, Canary Is. 36 F6
Puerto de Sóller, Spain 36 B9
Puerto del Carmen, Canary Is. 36 F6
Puerto del Rosario, Canary Is. 36 F6
Puerto Deseado, Argentina 128 C3
Puerto Guaraní, Paraguay 125 E6
Puerto Heath, Bolivia 124 C4
Puerto Huitoto, Colombia 120 C3
Puerto Inca, Peru 124 B3
Puerto Juárez, Mexico 115 C7
Puerto La Cruz, Venezuela 121 A5
Puerto Leguízamo, Colombia 120 D3
Puerto Limón, Colombia 120 C3
Puerto Lobos, Argentina 128 B3
Puerto López, Colombia 120 C3
Puerto Lumbreras, Spain 29 H3
Puerto Madryn, Argentina 128 B3
Puerto Maldonado, Peru 124 C4
Puerto Manotí, Cuba 116 B4
Puerto Mazarrón, Spain 29 H3
Puerto Mercedes, Colombia 120 C3
Puerto Miraña, Colombia 120 D3
Puerto Montt, Chile 128 B2
Puerto Morelos, Mexico 115 C7
Puerto Nariño, Colombia 120 C4
Puerto Natales, Chile 128 D2
Puerto Nuevo, Colombia 120 B4
Puerto Nutrias, Venezuela 120 B4
Puerto Ordaz, Venezuela 121 B5
Puerto Padre, Cuba 116 B4
Puerto Páez, Venezuela 120 B4
Puerto Peñasco, Mexico 114 A2
Puerto Pinasco, Paraguay 126 A4
Puerto Pirámides, Argentina 128 B4
Puerto Plata, Dom. Rep. 117 C5
Puerto Pollensa, Spain 36 B10
Puerto Portillo, Peru 124 B3
Puerto Princesa, Phil. 55 G3
Puerto Quellón, Chile 128 B2
Puerto Quepos, Costa Rica 116 E3
Puerto Real, Spain 31 J4
Puerto Rico, Bolivia 124 C4
Puerto Rico, Canary Is. 36 G4
Puerto Rico ■, W. Indies 117 C6
Puerto Rico Trench, Atl. Oc. 117 C6
Puerto Saavedra, Chile 128 A2
Puerto Sastre, Paraguay 126 A4
Puerto Siles, Bolivia 125 C4
Puerto Suárez, Bolivia 125 D6
Puerto Tejada, Colombia 120 C2
Puerto Umbría, Colombia 120 C2
Puerto Vallarta, Mexico 114 C3
Puerto Varas, Chile 128 B2
Puerto Villazón, Bolivia 125 C5
Puerto Wilches, Colombia 120 B3
Puertollano, Spain 31 G6
Puertomarín, Spain 30 C3
Puesto Cunambo, Peru 120 D2
Pueyrredón, L., Argentina 128 C2
Pugachev, Russia 42 D9
Puge, China 52 D4
Puge, Tanzania 82 C3
Puget Sound, U.S.A. 110 C2
Puget-Théniers, France 27 E10
Púglia □, Italy 35 B9
Pugŏdong, N. Korea 51 C16
Pugu, Tanzania 82 D4
Pūgūnzī, Iran 65 E8
Pui, Romania 38 D6
Puica, Peru 124 C3
Puig Mayor, Spain 36 B9
Puigcerdá, Spain 28 C6
Puigmal, Spain 28 C7
Puigpuñent, Spain 36 B9
Puisaye, Collines de la, France 25 E10
Puiseaux, France 25 D9
Pujilí, Ecuador 120 D2
Pujon-chosuji, N. Korea 51 D14
Puka, Albania 38 G2
Pukaki L., N.Z. 87 L3
Pukapuka, Cook Is. 93 J11
Pukatawagan, Canada 101 B8
Pukchin, N. Korea 51 D13
Pukchŏng, N. Korea 51 D15
Pukekohe, N.Z. 87 G5
Pukou, China 53 A12
Pula, Croatia 33 D10
Pula, Italy 34 D2
Pulacayo, Bolivia 124 E4
Pulaski, N.Y., U.S.A. 107 C8
Pulaski, Tenn., U.S.A. 105 H2
Pulaski, Va., U.S.A. 104 G5
Puławy, Poland 20 D11
Pulga, U.S.A. 112 F5
Pulicat, L., India 60 N12
Pullman, U.S.A. 110 C5
Pulog, Phil. 55 C4
Pułtusk, Poland 20 C11
Pülümür, Turkey 67 C8
Pumlumon Fawr, U.K. 13 E4
Puna, Bolivia 125 D4
Puná, I., Ecuador 120 D1
Punakha, Bhutan 61 F16
Punasar, India 62 F5
Punata, Bolivia 125 D4
Punch, India 63 C6
Pune, India 60 K8
Pungsan, N. Korea 51 D15
Pungue, Ponte de, Mozam. 83 F3
Puning, China 53 F11
Punjab □, India 62 D6
Punjab □, Pakistan 62 E6
Puno, Peru 124 D3
Punta Alta, Argentina 128 A4
Punta Arenas, Chile 128 D2
Punta Cardón, Venezuela 120 A3
Punta Coles, Peru 124 D3
Punta de Bombón, Peru 124 D3
Punta de Díaz, Chile 126 B1
Punta Delgado, Argentina 128 B4
Punta Gorda, Belize 115 D7
Punta Gorda, U.S.A. 105 M5
Punta Prieta, Mexico 114 B2
Punta Prima, Spain 36 B11
Puntabie, Australia 91 E1
Puntarenas, Costa Rica 116 E3
Punto Fijo, Venezuela 120 A3
Punxsatawney, U.S.A. 106 F5
Puqi, China 53 C9
Puquio, Peru 124 C3
Pur →, Russia 44 C8
Purace, Vol., Colombia 120 C2
Puralia = Puruliya, India 63 H12
Purbeck, Isle of, U.K. 13 G5
Purcell, U.S.A. 109 H6
Purchena Tetica, Spain 29 H2
Puri, India 61 K14
Purificación, Colombia 120 C3
Purmerend, Neths. 16 C5
Purnia, India 63 G12
Purukcahu, Indonesia 56 E4
Puruliya, India 63 H12
Purus →, Brazil 121 D5
Puruvesi, Finland 40 B5
Pŭrvomay, Bulgaria 38 G8
Purwakarta, Indonesia 57 G12

Purwodadi, *Jawa, Indonesia* 57 G14
Purwodadi, *Jawa, Indonesia* 57 G13
Purwokerto, *Indonesia* 57 G13
Purworejo, *Indonesia* 57 G14
Puryŏng, *N. Korea* 51 C15
Pusan, *S. Korea* 51 G15
Pushchino, *Russia* 45 D16
Pushkin, *Russia* 40 C6
Pushkino, *Russia* 42 E8
Pushkino, *Russia* 42 B3
Püspökladány, *Hungary* 21 H11
Pustoshka, *Russia* 40 D5
Putahow L., *Canada* 101 B8
Putao, *Burma* 61 F20
Putaruru, *N.Z.* 87 H5
Putbus, *Germany* 18 A9
Puthein Myit →, *Burma* 61 M19
Putian, *China* 53 E12
Putignano, *Italy* 35 B10
Putina, *Peru* 124 C4
Puting, Tanjung, *Indonesia* 56 E4
Putlitz, *Germany* 18 B8
Putna →, *Romania* 38 D10
Putnam, *U.S.A.* 107 E13
Putorana, Gory, *Russia* 45 C10
Putre, *Chile* 124 D4
Puttalam, *Sri Lanka* 60 Q11
Putte, *Neths.* 17 F4
Putten, *Neths.* 16 D7
Puttgarden, *Germany* 18 A7
Putumayo →, *S. Amer.* 120 D4
Putuo, *China* 53 C14
Putussibau, *Indonesia* 56 D4
Puurs, *Belgium* 17 F4
Puy-de-Dôme, *France* 26 C6
Puy-de-Dôme □, *France* 26 C7
Puy-Guillaume, *France* 26 C7
Puy-l'Évêque, *France* 26 D5
Puyallup, *U.S.A.* 112 C4
Puyang, *China* 50 G8
Puyehue, *Chile* 128 B2
Puylaurens, *France* 26 E6
Puyo, *Ecuador* 120 D2
Pūzeh Rīg, *Iran* 65 E8
Pwani □, *Tanzania* 82 D4
Pweto, *Zaïre* 83 D2
Pwllheli, *U.K.* 12 E3
Pyana →, *Russia* 42 C8
Pyapon, *Burma* 61 L19
Pyasina →, *Russia* 45 B9
Pyatigorsk, *Russia* 43 H6
Pyatykhatky, *Ukraine* 41 H7
Pyè, *Burma* 61 K19
Pyetrikaw, *Belarus* 41 F5
Pyhäjoki, *Finland* 8 D21
Pyinmana, *Burma* 61 K20
Pyla, C., *Cyprus* 37 E12
Pyŏktong, *N. Korea* 51 D13
Pyŏnggang, *N. Korea* 51 E14
Pyŏngtaek, *S. Korea* 51 F14
P'yŏngyang, *N. Korea* 51 E13
Pyote, *U.S.A.* 109 K3
Pyramid L., *U.S.A.* 110 G4
Pyramid Pk., *U.S.A.* 113 J10
Pyramids, *Egypt* 76 J7
Pyrénées, *Europe* 26 F4
Pyrénées-Atlantiques □, *France* 26 E3
Pyrénées-Orientales □, *France* 26 F6
Pyryatyn, *Ukraine* 41 G7
Pyrzyce, *Poland* 20 B4
Pytalovo, *Russia* 40 D4
Pyttegga, *Norway* 10 B1
Pyu, *Burma* 61 K20

Q

Qaanaaq = Thule, *Greenland* 4 B4
Qabirri →, *Azerbaijan* 43 K8
Qachasnek, *S. Africa* 85 E4
Qādib, *Yemen* 68 E5
Qa'el Jafr, *Jordan* 69 E5
Qa'emābād, *Iran* 65 D9
Qā'emshahr, *Iran* 65 B7
Qagan Nur, *China* 50 C8
Qahar Youyi Zhongqi, *China* 50 D7
Qahremānshahr = Bākhtarān, *Iran* 67 E12
Qaidam Pendi, *China* 54 C4
Qajarīyeh, *Iran* 65 D6
Qala, Ras il, *Malta* 37 C1
Qala-i-Jadid, *Afghan.* 62 D2
Qala Yangi, *Afghan.* 62 B2
Qal'at al Akhḍar, *Si. Arabia* 64 E3
Qal'at Dīzah, *Iraq* 67 D11
Qal'at Sukkar, *Iraq* 67 G12
Qal'eh Darreh, *Iran* 64 B5
Qal'eh Shaharak, *Afghan.* 60 B4
Qalyûb, *Egypt* 76 H7
Qamar, Ghubbat al, *Yemen* 68 D5
Qamdo, *China* 52 B1
Qamruddin Karez, *Pakistan* 62 D3
Qandahār, *Afghan.* 60 D4
Qandahār □, *Afghan.* 60 D4
Qapān, *Iran* 65 B7
Qapshaghay, *Kazakstan* 44 E8
Qaqortoq = Julianehåb, *Greenland* 4 C5
Qâra, *Egypt* 76 B2
Qara Qash →, *India* 63 B8
Qarabutaq, *Kazakstan* 44 E7
Qaraçala, *Azerbaijan* 43 L9
Qaraghandy, *Kazakstan* 44 E8
Qārah, *Si. Arabia* 64 D4
Qarataū, *Kazakstan* 44 E8
Qardud, *Sudan* 77 E2
Qareh →, *Iran* 67 C12
Qareh Tekān, *Iran* 65 B6
Qarqan, *China* 54 C3
Qarqan He →, *China* 54 C3
Qarqaraly, *Kazakstan* 44 E8
Qarrasa, *Sudan* 77 E3
Qarshi, *Uzbekistan* 44 F7
Qartabā, *Lebanon* 69 A4
Qaryat al Gharab, *Iraq* 64 D5
Qaryat al 'Ulyā, *Si. Arabia* 64 E5
Qasr 'Amra, *Jordan* 64 D3
Qaṣr-e Qand, *Iran* 65 E9
Qasr Farâfra, *Egypt* 76 B2
Qatanā, *Syria* 69 B5
Qatar ■, *Asia* 65 E6
Qatlīsh, *Iran* 65 B8
Qattâra, *Egypt* 76 A2
Qattâra, Munkhafed el, *Egypt* 76 B2
Qattâra Depression = Qattâra, Munkhafed el, *Egypt* 76 B2
Qawām al Ḩamzah, *Iraq* 64 D5
Qāyen, *Iran* 65 C8
Qazaqstan = Kazakstan ■, *Asia* 44 E7
Qazimämmäd, *Azerbaijan* 43 K9
Qazvin, *Iran* 65 B6
Qena, *Egypt* 76 B3
Qena, W. →, *Egypt* 76 B3
Qeqertarsuaq = Disko, *Greenland* 4 C5
Qeqertarsuaq = Godhavn, *Greenland* 4 C5
Qeshlāq, *Iran* 67 E12
Qeshm, *Iran* 65 E8
Qezi'ot, *Israel* 69 E3
Qi Xian, *China* 50 G8
Qian Gorlos, *China* 51 B13
Qian Xian, *China* 50 G5
Qiancheng, *China* 52 D7
Qianjiang, *Guangxi Zhuangzu, China* 52 F7
Qianjiang, *Hubei, China* 53 B9
Qianjiang, *Sichuan, China* 52 C7
Qianshan, *China* 53 B11
Qianwei, *China* 52 C4
Qianxi, *China* 52 D6
Qianyang, *Hunan, China* 53 D8
Qianyang, *Shaanxi, China* 50 G4
Qianyang, *Zhejiang, China* 53 B12
Qiaojia, *China* 52 D4
Qibā', *Si. Arabia* 64 E5
Qichun, *China* 53 B10
Qidong, *Hunan, China* 53 D9
Qidong, *Jiangsu, China* 53 B13
Qijiang, *China* 52 C6
Qila Safed, *Pakistan* 60 E2
Qila Saifullāh, *Pakistan* 62 D3
Qilian Shan, *China* 54 C4
Qimen, *China* 53 C11
Qin He →, *China* 50 G7
Qin Jiang →, *China* 53 D10
Qin Ling = Qinling Shandi, *China* 50 H5
Qin'an, *China* 50 G3
Qing Xian, *China* 50 E9
Qingcheng, *China* 51 F9
Qingdao, *China* 51 F11
Qingfeng, *China* 50 G8
Qinghai □, *China* 54 C4
Qinghai Hu, *China* 54 C5
Qinghecheng, *China* 51 D13
Qinghemen, *China* 51 D11
Qingjian, *China* 50 F6
Qingjiang, *Jiangsu, China* 51 H10
Qingjiang, *Jiangxi, China* 53 C10
Qingliu, *China* 53 D11
Qinglong, *China* 52 E5
Qingping, *China* 52 D6
Qingpu, *China* 53 B13
Qingshui, *China* 50 G4
Qingshuihe, *China* 50 E6
Qingtian, *China* 53 C13
Qingtongxia Shuiku, *China* 50 F3
Qingxi, *China* 52 D7
Qingxu, *China* 50 F7
Qingyang, *Anhui, China* 53 B11
Qingyang, *Gansu, China* 50 F4
Qingyi Jiang →, *China* 52 C4
Qingyuan, *Guangdong, China* 53 F9
Qingyuan, *Liaoning, China* 51 C13
Qingyuan, *Zhejiang, China* 53 D12
Qingyun, *China* 51 F9
Qingzhen, *China* 52 D6
Qinhuangdao, *China* 51 E10
Qinling Shandi, *China* 50 H5
Qinshui, *China* 50 G7
Qinyang, *China* 50 G7
Qinyuan, *China* 50 F7
Qinzhou, *China* 52 G7
Qionghai, *China* 58 C8
Qionglai, *China* 52 B4
Qionglai Shan, *China* 52 B4
Qiongshan, *China* 58 C8
Qiongzhou Haixia, *China* 58 B8
Qiqihar, *China* 45 E13
Qirâiya, W. →, *Egypt* 69 E3
Qiryat Ata, *Israel* 69 C4
Qiryat Gat, *Israel* 69 D3
Qiryat Mal'akhi, *Israel* 69 D3
Qiryat Shemona, *Israel* 69 B4
Qiryat Yam, *Israel* 69 C4
Qishan, *China* 50 G4
Qitai, *China* 54 B3
Qiubei, *China* 52 E5
Qixia, *China* 51 F11
Qiyang, *China* 53 D8
Qızılağac Körfäzi, *Azerbaijan* 67 C13
Qojūr, *Iran* 64 B5
Qom, *Iran* 65 C6
Qomsheh, *Iran* 65 D6
Qorveh, *Iran* 67 E12
Qostanay, *Kazakstan* 44 D7
Qoṭūr, *Iran* 67 C11
Qu Jiang →, *China* 52 B6
Qu Xian, *Sichuan, China* 52 B6
Qu Xian, *Zhejiang, China* 53 C12
Quairading, *Australia* 89 F2
Quakenbrück, *Germany* 18 C3
Quakertown, *U.S.A.* 107 F9
Qualeup, *Australia* 89 F2
Quambatook, *Australia* 91 F3
Quambone, *Australia* 91 E4
Quamby, *Australia* 90 C3
Quan Long, *Vietnam* 59 H5
Quanah, *U.S.A.* 109 H5
Quandialla, *Australia* 91 E4
Quang Ngai, *Vietnam* 58 E7
Quang Yen, *Vietnam* 58 B6
Quannan, *China* 53 E10
Quantock Hills, *U.K.* 13 F4
Quanzhou, *Fujian, China* 53 E12
Quanzhou, *Guangxi Zhuangzu, China* 53 E8
Quaqtaq, *Canada* 97 B13
Quaraí, *Brazil* 126 C4
Quarré-les-Tombes, *France* 25 E10
Quartu Sant'Elena, *Italy* 34 C2
Quartzsite, *U.S.A.* 113 M12
Quatsino, *Canada* 100 C3
Quatsino Sd., *Canada* 100 C3
Quba, *Azerbaijan* 43 K9
Qūchān, *Iran* 65 B8
Queanbeyan, *Australia* 91 F4
Québec, *Canada* 99 C5
Québec □, *Canada* 99 B6
Quedlinburg, *Germany* 18 D7
Queen Alexandra Ra., *Antarctica* 5 E11
Queen Charlotte, *Canada* 100 C2
Queen Charlotte Bay, *Falk. Is.* 128 D4
Queen Charlotte Is., *Canada* 100 C2
Queen Charlotte Str., *Canada* 100 C3
Queen Elizabeth Is., *Canada* 94 B10
Queen Elizabeth Nat. Park, *Uganda* 82 C3
Queen Mary Land, *Antarctica* 5 D7
Queen Maud G., *Canada* 96 B9
Queen Maud Land, *Antarctica* 5 D3
Queen Maud Mts., *Antarctica* 5 E13
Queens Chan., *Australia* 88 C4
Queenscliff, *Australia* 91 F3
Queensland □, *Australia* 90 C3
Queenstown, *Australia* 90 G4
Queenstown, *N.Z.* 87 L2
Queenstown, *S. Africa* 84 E4
Queets, *U.S.A.* 112 C2
Queguay Grande →, *Uruguay* 126 C4
Queimadas, *Brazil* 122 D4
Quela, *Angola* 80 F3
Quelimane, *Mozam.* 83 F4
Quelpart = Cheju Do, *S. Korea* 51 H14
Quemado, *N. Mex., U.S.A.* 111 J9
Quemado, *Tex., U.S.A.* 109 L4
Quemoy = Chinmen, *Taiwan* 53 E13
Quemú-Quemú, *Argentina* 126 D3
Quequén, *Argentina* 126 D4
Querco, *Peru* 124 C3
Querétaro, *Mexico* 114 C4
Querétaro □, *Mexico* 114 C5
Querfurt, *Germany* 18 D7
Quesada, *Spain* 29 H1
Queshan, *China* 50 H8
Quesnel, *Canada* 100 C4
Quesnel →, *Canada* 100 C4
Quesnel L., *Canada* 100 C4
Questa, *U.S.A.* 111 H11
Questembert, *France* 24 E4
Quetena, *Bolivia* 124 E4
Quetico Prov. Park, *Canada* 98 C1
Quetrequile, *Argentina* 128 B3
Quetta, *Pakistan* 62 D2
Quevedo, *Ecuador* 120 D2
Quezaltenango, *Guatemala* 116 D1
Quezon City, *Phil.* 55 D4
Qufār, *Si. Arabia* 64 E4
Qui Nhon, *Vietnam* 58 F7
Quibaxe, *Angola* 80 F2
Quibdo, *Colombia* 120 B2
Quiberon, *France* 24 E3
Quíbor, *Venezuela* 120 B4
Quick, *Canada* 100 C3
Quickborn, *Germany* 18 B5
Quiet L., *Canada* 100 A2
Quiévrain, *Belgium* 17 H3
Quiindy, *Paraguay* 126 B4
Quila, *Mexico* 114 C3
Quilán, C., *Chile* 128 B2
Quilcene, *U.S.A.* 112 C4
Quilengues, *Angola* 81 G2
Quilimarí, *Chile* 126 C1
Quilino, *Argentina* 126 C3
Quillabamba, *Peru* 124 C3
Quillacollo, *Bolivia* 124 D4
Quillagua, *Chile* 126 A2
Quillaicillo, *Chile* 126 C1
Quillan, *France* 26 F6
Quillebeuf-sur-Seine, *France* 24 C7
Quillota, *Chile* 126 C1
Quilmes, *Argentina* 126 C4
Quilon, *India* 60 Q10
Quilpie, *Australia* 91 D3
Quilpué, *Chile* 126 C1
Quilua, *Mozam.* 83 F4
Quime, *Bolivia* 124 D4
Quimilí, *Argentina* 126 B3
Quimper, *France* 24 D2
Quimperlé, *France* 24 E3
Quinault →, *U.S.A.* 112 C2
Quincemil, *Peru* 124 C3
Quincy, *Calif., U.S.A.* 112 F6
Quincy, *Fla., U.S.A.* 105 K3
Quincy, *Ill., U.S.A.* 108 F9
Quincy, *Mass., U.S.A.* 107 D14
Quincy, *Wash., U.S.A.* 110 C4
Quines, *Argentina* 126 C2
Quinga, *Mozam.* 83 F5
Quingey, *France* 25 E12
Quintana de la Serena, *Spain* 31 G5
Quintana Roo □, *Mexico* 115 D7
Quintanar de la Orden, *Spain* 28 F1
Quintanar de la Sierra, *Spain* 28 D2
Quintanar del Rey, *Spain* 29 F3
Quintero, *Chile* 126 C1
Quintin, *France* 24 D4
Quinto, *Spain* 28 D4
Quinyambie, *Australia* 91 E3
Quípar →, *Spain* 29 G3
Quipungo, *Angola* 81 G2
Quirihue, *Chile* 126 D1
Quirindi, *Australia* 91 E5
Quiroga, *Spain* 30 C3
Quiruvilca, *Peru* 124 B2
Quissac, *France* 27 E8
Quissanga, *Mozam.* 83 E5
Quitilipi, *Argentina* 126 B3
Quitman, *Ga., U.S.A.* 105 K4
Quitman, *Miss., U.S.A.* 105 J1
Quitman, *Tex., U.S.A.* 109 J7
Quito, *Ecuador* 120 D2
Quixadá, *Brazil* 122 B4
Quixaxe, *Mozam.* 83 F5
Quixeramobim, *Brazil* 122 C4
Qujing, *China* 52 E4
Qul'ân, Jazâ'ir, *Egypt* 76 C4
Qumbu, *S. Africa* 85 E4
Quneitra, *Syria* 69 B4
Qŭnghirot, *Uzbekistan* 44 E6
Quoin I., *Australia* 88 B4
Quoin Pt., *S. Africa* 84 E2
Quondong, *Australia* 91 E3
Quorn, *Australia* 91 E2
Qŭqon, *Uzbekistan* 44 E8
Qurein, *Sudan* 77 E3
Qurnat as Sawdā', *Lebanon* 69 A5
Qûs, *Egypt* 76 B3
Qusar, *Azerbaijan* 43 K9
Qusaybah, *Iraq* 67 E9
Quseir, *Egypt* 76 B3
Qūshchī, *Iran* 67 D11
Quthing, *Lesotho* 85 E4
Qūṭīābād, *Iran* 67 E13
Quwo, *China* 50 G6
Quyang, *China* 50 E8
Quynh Nhai, *Vietnam* 58 B4
Quzi, *China* 50 F4
Qvareli, *Georgia* 43 K7
Qytet Stalin = Kuçova, *Albania* 39 J2
Qyzylorda, *Kazakstan* 44 E7

R

Ra, Ko, *Thailand* 59 H2
Råå, *Sweden* 11 J6
Raahe, *Finland* 8 D21
Raalte, *Neths.* 16 D8
Raamsdonksveer, *Neths.* 17 E5
Raasay, *U.K.* 14 D2
Raasay, Sd. of, *U.K.* 14 D2
Rab, *Croatia* 33 D11
Raba, *Indonesia* 57 F5
Rába →, *Hungary* 21 H7
Rabaçal →, *Portugal* 30 D3
Rabah, *Nigeria* 79 C6
Rabai, *Kenya* 82 C4
Rabastens, *France* 26 E5
Rabastens-de-Bigorre, *France* 26 E4
Rabat, *Malta* 37 D1
Rabat, *Morocco* 74 B3
Rabaul, *Papua N. G.* 92 H7
Rabbit →, *Canada* 100 B3
Rabbit Lake, *Canada* 101 C7
Rabbitskin →, *Canada* 100 A4
Rabka, *Poland* 20 F9
Rābor, *Iran* 65 D8
Răcale, *Italy* 35 C11
Racalmuto, *Italy* 34 E6
Racconigi, *Italy* 32 D4
Race, C., *Canada* 99 C9
Rach Gia, *Vietnam* 59 G5
Raciąż, *Poland* 20 C10
Racibórz, *Poland* 20 E8
Racine, *U.S.A.* 104 D2
Rackerby, *U.S.A.* 112 F5
Radama, Nosy, *Madag.* 85 A8
Radama, Saikanosy, *Madag.* 85 A8
Rădăuţi, *Romania* 38 B8
Radbuza →, *Czech.* 20 F3
Radeburg, *Germany* 18 D9
Radeče, *Slovenia* 33 B12
Radekhiv, *Ukraine* 41 G3
Radekhov = Radekhiv, *Ukraine* 41 G3
Radford, *U.S.A.* 104 G5
Radhanpur, *India* 62 H4
Radiska →, *Macedonia* 39 H3
Radisson, *Canada* 101 C7
Radium Hot Springs, *Canada* 100 C5
Radna, *Romania* 38 C4
Radnor Forest, *U.K.* 13 E4
Radolfzell, *Germany* 19 H4
Radom, *Poland* 20 D11
Radomir, *Bulgaria* 38 G6
Radomsko, *Poland* 20 D9
Radomyshl, *Ukraine* 41 G5
Radoviš, *Macedonia* 39 H5
Radovljica, *Slovenia* 33 B11
Radstock, *U.K.* 13 F5
Radstock, C., *Australia* 91 E1
Răducăneni, *Romania* 38 C10
Radviliškis, *Lithuania* 9 J20
Radville, *Canada* 101 D8
Rae, *Canada* 100 A5
Rae Bareli, *India* 63 F9
Rae Isthmus, *Canada* 97 B11
Raeren, *Belgium* 17 G8
Raeside, L., *Australia* 89 E3
Raetihi, *N.Z.* 87 H5
Rafaela, *Argentina* 126 C3
Rafah, *Gaza Strip* 69 D3
Rafai, *C.A.R.* 82 B1
Raffadali, *Italy* 34 E6
Rafḥā, *Si. Arabia* 64 D4
Rafsanjān, *Iran* 65 D8
Raft Pt., *Australia* 88 C3
Ragachow, *Belarus* 41 F6
Ragag, *Sudan* 77 E1
Ragama, *Sri Lanka* 60 R11
Ragged, Mt., *Australia* 89 F3
Raglan, *Australia* 90 C5
Raglan, *N.Z.* 87 G5
Ragunda, *Sweden* 10 A10
Ragusa, *Italy* 35 F7
Raha, *Indonesia* 57 E6
Rahad, Nahr ed →, *Sudan* 77 E3
Rahad al Bardī, *Sudan* 73 F9
Rahaeng = Tak, *Thailand* 58 D2
Rahden, *Germany* 18 C4
Raheita, *Eritrea* 77 E5
Raḥīmah, *Si. Arabia* 65 E6
Rahimyar Khan, *Pakistan* 62 E4
Rāhjerd, *Iran* 65 C6
Raichur, *India* 60 L10
Raiganj, *India* 63 G13
Raigarh, *India* 61 J13
Raijua, *Indonesia* 57 F6
Railton, *Australia* 90 G4
Rainbow Lake, *Canada* 100 B5
Rainier, *U.S.A.* 112 D4
Rainier, Mt., *U.S.A.* 112 D5
Rainy L., *Canada* 101 D10
Rainy River, *Canada* 101 D10
Raippaluoto, *Finland* 8 E19
Raipur, *India* 61 J12
Raisio, *Finland* 9 F20
Raj Nandgaon, *India* 61 J12
Raja, Ujung, *Indonesia* 56 D1
Raja Ampat, Kepulauan, *Indonesia* 57 E7
Rajahmundry, *India* 61 L12
Rajang →, *Malaysia* 56 D4
Rajapalaiyam, *India* 60 Q10
Rajasthan □, *India* 62 F5
Rajasthan Canal, *India* 62 E5
Rajauri, *India* 63 C6
Rajgarh, *Mad. P., India* 62 G7
Rajgarh, *Raj., India* 62 E6
Rajhenburg, *Slovenia* 33 B12
Rajkot, *India* 62 H4
Rajmahal Hills, *India* 63 G12
Rajpipla, *India* 60 J8
Rajpura, *India* 62 D7
Rajshahi, *Bangla.* 61 G16
Rajshahi □, *Bangla.* 63 G13
Rakaia, *N.Z.* 87 K4
Rakaia →, *N.Z.* 87 K4
Rakan, Ra's, *Qatar* 65 E6
Rakaposhi, *Pakistan* 63 A6
Rakata, Pulau, *Indonesia* 56 F3
Rakhiv, *Ukraine* 41 H3
Rakhni, *Pakistan* 62 D3
Rakitnoye, *Russia* 48 B7
Rakkestad, *Norway* 10 E5
Rakops, *Botswana* 84 C3
Rákospalota, *Hungary* 21 H9

Rakovica, *Croatia* 33 D12
Rakovník, *Czech.* 20 E3
Rakovski, *Bulgaria* 38 G7
Rakvere, *Estonia* 9 G22
Raleigh, *U.S.A.* 105 H6
Raleigh B., *U.S.A.* 105 H7
Ralja, *Serbia, Yug.* 21 L10
Ralls, *U.S.A.* 109 J4
Ram →, *Canada* 100 A4
Rām Allāh, *West Bank* 69 D4
Ram Hd., *Australia* 91 F4
Rama, *Nic.* 116 D3
Ramacca, *Italy* 35 E7
Ramales de la Victoria, *Spain* 28 B1
Ramalho, Serra do, *Brazil* 123 D3
Raman, *Thailand* 59 J3
Ramanathapuram, *India* 60 Q11
Ramanetaka, B. de, *Madag.* 85 A8
Ramat Gan, *Israel* 69 C3
Ramatlhabama, *S. Africa* 84 D4
Ramban, *India* 63 C6
Rambervillers, *France* 25 D13
Rambipuji, *Indonesia* 57 H15
Rambouillet, *France* 25 D8
Ramea, *Canada* 99 C8
Ramechhap, *Nepal* 63 F12
Ramelau, *Indonesia* 57 F7
Ramenskoye, *Russia* 42 C4
Ramgarh, *Bihar, India* 63 H11
Ramgarh, *Raj., India* 62 F6
Ramgarh, *Raj., India* 62 F4
Rāmhormoz, *Iran* 65 D6
Ramīān, *Iran* 65 B7
Ramingining, *Australia* 90 A2
Ramla, *Israel* 69 D3
Ramlu, *Eritrea* 77 E5
Ramme, *Denmark* 11 H2
Ramnad = Ramanathapuram, *India* 60 Q11
Ramnagar, *India* 63 C6
Ramnäs, *Sweden* 10 E10
Ramon, *Russia* 42 E4
Ramona, *U.S.A.* 113 M10
Ramore, *Canada* 98 C3
Ramotswa, *Botswana* 84 C4
Rampur, *H.P., India* 62 D7
Rampur, *Mad. P., India* 62 H5
Rampur, *Ut. P., India* 63 E8
Rampur Hat, *India* 63 G12
Rampura, *India* 62 G6
Ramree I. = Ramree Kyun, *Burma* 61 K18
Ramree Kyun, *Burma* 61 K18
Rāmsar, *Iran* 65 B6
Ramsel, *Belgium* 17 F5
Ramsey, *Canada* 98 C3
Ramsey, *U.K.* 12 C3
Ramsgate, *U.K.* 13 F9
Ramsjö, *Sweden* 10 B9
Ramtek, *India* 60 J11
Ramvik, *Sweden* 10 B11
Ranaghat, *India* 63 H13
Ranahu, *Pakistan* 62 G3
Ranau, *Malaysia* 56 C5
Rancagua, *Chile* 126 C1
Rance, *Belgium* 17 H4
Rance →, *France* 24 D5
Rance, Barrage de la, *France* 24 D4
Rancharia, *Brazil* 123 F1
Rancheria →, *Canada* 100 A3
Ranchester, *U.S.A.* 110 D10
Ranchi, *India* 63 H11
Rancho Cucamonga, *U.S.A.* 113 L9
Ranco, L., *Chile* 128 B2
Randan, *France* 26 B7
Randazzo, *Italy* 35 E7
Randers, *Denmark* 11 H4
Randers Fjord, *Denmark* 11 H4
Randfontein, *S. Africa* 85 D4
Randle, *U.S.A.* 112 D5
Randolph, *Mass., U.S.A.* 107 D13
Randolph, *N.Y., U.S.A.* 106 D6
Randolph, *Utah, U.S.A.* 110 F8
Randolph, *Vt., U.S.A.* 107 C12
Randsfjorden, *Norway* 10 D4
Råne älv →, *Sweden* 8 D20
Rangae, *Thailand* 59 J3
Rangaunu B., *N.Z.* 87 F4
Rångedala, *Sweden* 11 G7
Rangeley, *U.S.A.* 107 B14
Rangely, *U.S.A.* 110 F9
Ranger, *U.S.A.* 109 J5
Rangia, *India* 61 F17
Rangiora, *N.Z.* 87 K4
Rangitaiki →, *N.Z.* 87 G6
Rangitata →, *N.Z.* 87 K3
Rangkasbitung, *Indonesia* 57 G12
Rangon →, *Burma* 61 L20
Rangoon, *Burma* 61 L20
Rangpur, *Bangla.* 61 G16
Rangsit, *Thailand* 58 F3
Ranibennur, *India* 60 M9
Raniganj, *India* 63 H12
Raniwara, *India* 60 G8
Rāniyah, *Iraq* 64 B5
Ranken →, *Australia* 90 C2
Rankin, *U.S.A.* 109 K4
Rankin Inlet, *Canada* 96 B10
Rankins Springs, *Australia* 91 E4
Rannoch, L., *U.K.* 14 E4
Rannoch Moor, *U.K.* 14 E4
Ranobe, Helodranon' i, *Madag.* 85 C7
Ranohira, *Madag.* 85 C8
Ranomafana, *Toamasina, Madag.* 85 B8
Ranomafana, *Toliara, Madag.* 85 C8
Ranong, *Thailand* 59 H2
Rānsa, *Iran* 65 C6
Ransiki, *Indonesia* 57 E8
Rantau, *Indonesia* 56 E5
Rantauprapat, *Indonesia* 56 D1
Rantemario, *Indonesia* 57 E5
Rantoul, *U.S.A.* 104 E1
Ranum, *Denmark* 11 H3
Raon l'Étape, *France* 25 D13
Raoui, Erg er, *Algeria* 75 C4
Raoyang, *China* 50 E8
Rapa, *Pac. Oc.* 93 K13
Rapallo, *Italy* 32 D6
Rāpch, *Iran* 65 E8
Rapid →, *Canada* 100 B3
Rapid City, *U.S.A.* 108 D3
Rapid River, *U.S.A.* 104 C2
Rapides des Joachims, *Canada* 98 C4
Rapla, *Estonia* 9 G21
Rapperswil, *Switz.* 23 B7
Rapu Rapu I., *Phil.* 55 E6
Rarotonga, *Cook Is.* 93 K12
Ra's al 'Ayn, *Syria* 67 D9
Ra's al Khaymah, *U.A.E.* 65 E8
Ra's al-Unuf, *Libya* 73 B8
Ra's an Naqb, *Jordan* 69 F4
Ras Bânâs, *Egypt* 76 C4
Ras Dashen, *Ethiopia* 77 E4
Ras el Ma, *Algeria* 75 B4
Râs Ghârib, *Egypt* 76 J8
Ras Mallap, *Egypt* 76 J8
Râs Timirist, *Mauritania* 78 B1
Rasa, Punta, *Argentina* 128 B4
Rasca, Pta. de la, *Canary Is.* 36 G3
Raseiniai, *Lithuania* 9 J20
Rashad, *Sudan* 77 E3
Rashîd, *Egypt* 76 H7
Rashîd, Masabb, *Egypt* 76 H7
Rasht, *Iran* 67 D13
Rasi Salai, *Thailand* 58 E5
Raška, *Serbia, Yug.* 21 M10
Rason L., *Australia* 89 E3
Rașova, *Romania* 38 E10
Rasra, *India* 63 G10
Rass el Oued, *Algeria* 75 A6
Rasskazovo, *Russia* 42 D5
Rastatt, *Germany* 19 G4
Rat Buri, *Thailand* 58 F2
Rat Islands, *U.S.A.* 96 C1
Rat River, *Canada* 100 A6
Ratangarh, *India* 62 E6
Raṭāwī, *Iraq* 64 D5
Rath, *India* 63 G8
Rath Luirc, *Ireland* 15 D3
Rathdrum, *Ireland* 15 D5
Rathenow, *Germany* 18 C8
Rathkeale, *Ireland* 15 D3
Rathlin I., *U.K.* 15 A5
Rathlin O'Birne I., *Ireland* 15 B3
Ratibor = Racibórz, *Poland* 20 E8
Ratlam, *India* 62 H6
Ratnagiri, *India* 60 L8
Raton, *U.S.A.* 109 G2
Rattaphum, *Thailand* 59 J3
Rattray Hd., *U.K.* 14 D7
Ratz, Mt., *Canada* 100 B2
Ratzeburg, *Germany* 18 B6
Raub, *Malaysia* 59 L3
Rauch, *Argentina* 126 D4
Raufarhöfn, *Iceland* 8 C6
Raufoss, *Norway* 10 D4
Raukumara Ra., *N.Z.* 87 H6
Raul Soares, *Brazil* 123 F3
Rauland, *Norway* 10 E2
Rauma, *Finland* 9 F19
Rauma →, *Norway* 10 B1
Raurkela, *India* 63 H11
Rausu-Dake, *Japan* 48 B12
Rava-Ruska, *Ukraine* 41 G2
Rava Russkaya = Rava-Ruska, *Ukraine* 41 G2
Ravānsar, *Iran* 67 E12
Ravanusa, *Italy* 34 E6
Rāvar, *Iran* 65 D8
Ravels, *Belgium* 17 F6
Ravena, *U.S.A.* 107 D11
Ravenna, *Italy* 33 D9
Ravenna, *Nebr., U.S.A.* 108 E5
Ravenna, *Ohio, U.S.A.* 106 E3
Ravensburg, *Germany* 19 H5
Ravenshoe, *Australia* 90 B4
Ravenstein, *Neths.* 16 E7
Ravensthorpe, *Australia* 89 F3
Ravenswood, *Australia* 90 C4
Ravenswood, *U.S.A.* 104 F5
Ravi →, *Pakistan* 62 D4
Ravna Gora, *Croatia* 33 C11
Rawa Mazowiecka, *Poland* 20 D10
Rawalpindi, *Pakistan* 62 C5
Rawāndūz, *Iraq* 67 D11
Rawang, *Malaysia* 59 L3
Rawdon, *Canada* 98 C5
Rawene, *N.Z.* 87 F4
Rawicz, *Poland* 20 D6
Rawlinna, *Australia* 89 F4
Rawlins, *U.S.A.* 110 F10
Rawlinson Ra., *Australia* 89 D4
Rawson, *Argentina* 128 B3
Ray, *U.S.A.* 108 A3
Ray, C., *Canada* 99 C8
Rayadurg, *India* 60 M10
Rayagada, *India* 61 K13
Raychikhinsk, *Russia* 45 E13
Rāyen, *Iran* 65 D8
Raymond, *Canada* 100 D6
Raymond, *Calif., U.S.A.* 112 H7
Raymond, *Wash., U.S.A.* 112 D3
Raymondville, *U.S.A.* 109 M6
Raymore, *Canada* 101 C8
Rayne, *U.S.A.* 109 K8
Rayón, *Mexico* 114 B2
Rayong, *Thailand* 58 F3
Rayville, *U.S.A.* 109 J9
Raz, Pte. du, *France* 24 D2
Razan, *Iran* 67 E13
Ražana, *Serbia, Yug.* 21 L9
Ražanj, *Serbia, Yug.* 21 M11
Razdel'naya = Rozdilna, *Ukraine* 41 J6
Razdolnoye, *Russia* 48 C5
Razdolnoye, *Ukraine* 41 K7
Razeh, *Iran* 65 C6
Razelm, Lacul, *Romania* 38 E12
Razgrad, *Bulgaria* 38 F9
Razmak, *Pakistan* 62 C3
Ré, I. de, *France* 26 B2
Reading, *U.K.* 13 F7
Reading, *U.S.A.* 107 F9
Real, Cordillera, *Bolivia* 124 D4
Realicó, *Argentina* 126 D3
Réalmont, *France* 26 E6
Reata, *Mexico* 114 B4
Rebais, *France* 25 D10
Rebecca, L., *Australia* 89 F3
Rebi, *Indonesia* 57 F8
Rebiana, *Libya* 73 D9
Rebun-Tō, *Japan* 48 B10
Recanati, *Italy* 33 E10
Recaș, *Romania* 38 D4
Recherche, Arch. of the, *Australia* 89 F3
Recht, *Belgium* 17 H8
Rechytsa, *Belarus* 41 F6
Recife, *Brazil* 122 C5
Recklinghausen, *Germany* 17 E10
Reconquista, *Argentina* 126 B4
Recreio, *Brazil* 125 B6
Recreo, *Argentina* 126 B2
Recuay, *Peru* 124 B2
Red →, *La., U.S.A.* 109 K9
Red →, *N. Dak., U.S.A.* 108 A6
Red Bank, *U.S.A.* 107 F10
Red Bay, *Canada* 99 B8
Red Bluff, *U.S.A.* 110 F2
Red Bluff L., *U.S.A.* 109 K3
Red Cliffs, *Australia* 91 E3
Red Cloud, *U.S.A.* 108 E5
Red Deer, *Canada* 100 C6
Red Deer →, *Alta., Canada* 101 C6
Red Deer →, *Man., Canada* 101 C8
Red Deer L., *Canada* 101 C8
Red Indian L., *Canada* 99 C8
Red Lake, *Canada* 101 C10
Red Lake Falls, *U.S.A.* 108 B6
Red Lodge, *U.S.A.* 110 D9
Red Mountain, *U.S.A.* 113 K9
Red Oak, *U.S.A.* 108 E7
Red Rock, *Canada* 98 C2
Red Rock, L., *U.S.A.* 108 E8
Red Rocks Pt., *Australia* 89 F4
Red Sea, *Asia* 68 C2
Red Slate Mt., *U.S.A.* 112 H8
Red Sucker L., *Canada* 101 C10
Red Tower Pass = Turnu Roșu, P., *Romania* 38 D7
Red Wing, *U.S.A.* 108 C8
Rédange, *Lux.* 17 J7
Redbridge, *U.K.* 13 F8
Redcar, *U.K.* 12 C6
Redcar & Cleveland □, *U.K.* 12 C6
Redcliff, *Canada* 101 C6
Redcliffe, *Australia* 91 D5
Redcliffe, Mt., *Australia* 89 E3
Reddersburg, *S. Africa* 84 D4
Redding, *U.S.A.* 110 F2
Redditch, *U.K.* 13 E6
Redenção, *Brazil* 122 B4
Redfield, *U.S.A.* 108 C5
Redkino, *Russia* 42 B3
Redknife →, *Canada* 100 A5
Redlands, *U.S.A.* 113 M9
Redmond, *Australia* 89 F2
Redmond, *Oreg., U.S.A.* 110 D3
Redmond, *Wash., U.S.A.* 112 C4
Redon, *France* 24 E4
Redonda, *Antigua* 117 C7
Redondela, *Spain* 30 C2
Redondo, *Portugal* 31 G3
Redondo Beach, *U.S.A.* 113 M8
Redrock Pt., *Canada* 100 A5
Redruth, *U.K.* 13 G2
Redvers, *Canada* 101 D8
Redwater, *Canada* 100 C6
Redwood, *U.S.A.* 107 B9
Redwood City, *U.S.A.* 111 H2
Redwood Falls, *U.S.A.* 108 C7
Ree, L., *Ireland* 15 C4
Reed, L., *Canada* 101 C8
Reed City, *U.S.A.* 104 D3
Reeder, *U.S.A.* 108 B3
Reedley, *U.S.A.* 111 H4
Reedsburg, *U.S.A.* 108 D9
Reedsport, *U.S.A.* 110 E1
Reefton, *N.Z.* 87 K3
Refahiye, *Turkey* 67 C8
Refugio, *U.S.A.* 109 L6
Rega →, *Poland* 20 A5
Regalbuto, *Italy* 35 E7
Regen, *Germany* 19 G9
Regen →, *Germany* 19 F8
Regeneração, *Brazil* 122 C3
Regensburg, *Germany* 19 F8
Regensdorf, *Switz.* 23 B6
Réggio di Calábria, *Italy* 35 D8
Réggio nell'Emília, *Italy* 32 D7
Regina, *Canada* 101 C8
Régina, *Fr. Guiana* 121 C7
Registro, *Brazil* 127 A6
Reguengos de Monsaraz, *Portugal* 31 G3
Rehar →, *India* 63 H10
Rehoboth, *Namibia* 84 C2
Rehovot, *Israel* 69 D3
Rei-Bouba, *Cameroon* 73 G7
Reichenbach, *Germany* 18 E8
Reichenbach, *Switz.* 22 C5
Reid, *Australia* 89 F4
Reid River, *Australia* 90 B4
Reiden, *Switz.* 22 B5
Reidsville, *U.S.A.* 105 G6
Reigate, *U.K.* 13 F7
Reillo, *Spain* 28 F3
Reims, *France* 25 C11
Reina Adelaida, Arch., *Chile* 128 D2
Reinach, *Aargau, Switz.* 22 B6
Reinach, *Basel, Switz.* 22 B5
Reinbeck, *U.S.A.* 108 D8
Reindeer →, *Canada* 101 B8
Reindeer I., *Canada* 101 C9
Reindeer L., *Canada* 101 B8
Reinga, C., *N.Z.* 87 F4
Reinosa, *Spain* 30 B6
Reinosa, Paso, *Spain* 30 C6
Reitdiep, *Neths.* 16 B8
Reitz, *S. Africa* 85 D4
Reivilo, *S. Africa* 84 D3
Rejmyre, *Sweden* 11 F9
Reka →, *Slovenia* 33 C11
Rekinniki, *Russia* 45 C17
Reliance, *Canada* 101 A7
Remad, Oued →, *Algeria* 75 B4
Rémalard, *France* 24 D7
Remarkable, Mt., *Australia* 91 E2
Rembang, *Indonesia* 57 G14
Remchi, *Algeria* 75 A4
Remedios, *Colombia* 120 B3
Remedios, *Panama* 116 E3
Remeshk, *Iran* 65 E8
Remich, *Lux.* 17 J8
Rémire, *Fr. Guiana* 121 C7
Remiremont, *France* 25 D13
Remo, *Ethiopia* 77 F5
Remontnoye, *Russia* 43 G6
Remoulins, *France* 27 E8
Remscheid, *Germany* 18 D3
Ren Xian, *China* 50 F8
Renascença, *Brazil* 120 D4
Rende, *Italy* 35 C9
Rendeux, *Belgium* 17 H7
Rendína, *Greece* 39 K4
Rendsburg, *Germany* 18 A5
Rene, *Russia* 45 C19
Renfrew, *Canada* 98 C4
Renfrew, *U.K.* 14 F4
Renfrewshire □, *U.K.* 14 F4
Rengat, *Indonesia* 56 E2
Rengo, *Chile* 126 C1
Renhua, *China* 53 E9
Renhuai, *China* 52 D6
Reni, *Ukraine* 41 K5
Renk, *Sudan* 77 E3
Renkum, *Neths.* 16 E7
Renmark, *Australia* 91 E3
Rennell Sd., *Canada* 100 C2
Renner Springs T.O., *Australia* 90 B1
Rennes, *France* 24 D5
Rennes, Bassin de, *France* 24 E5
Reno, *U.S.A.* 112 F7
Reno →, *Italy* 33 D9
Renovo, *U.S.A.* 106 E7
Renqiu, *China* 50 E9
Rensselaer, *Ind., U.S.A.* 104 E2
Rensselaer, *N.Y., U.S.A.* 107 D11
Rentería, *Spain* 28 B3
Renton, *U.S.A.* 112 C4
Réo, *Burkina Faso* 78 C4
Reotipur, *India* 63 G10
Republic, *Mich., U.S.A.* 104 B2
Republic, *Wash., U.S.A.* 110 B4
Republican →, *U.S.A.* 108 F6
Republican City, *U.S.A.* 108 E5
Republiek, *Surinam* 121 B6
Repulse Bay, *Canada* 97 B11
Requena, *Peru* 124 B3
Requena, *Spain* 29 F3
Resadiye = Datça, *Turkey* 66 D2
Reşadiye, *Turkey* 66 B7
Resele, *Sweden* 10 A11
Reserve, *Canada* 101 C8
Reserve, *U.S.A.* 111 K9
Resht = Rasht, *Iran* 67 D13
Resistencia, *Argentina* 126 B4
Reşiţa, *Romania* 38 D4
Resolution I., *Canada* 97 B13
Resolution I., *N.Z.* 87 L1
Resplandes, *Brazil* 122 C2
Resplendor, *Brazil* 123 E3
Ressano Garcia, *Mozam.* 85 D5
Reston, *Canada* 101 D8
Retalhuleu, *Guatemala* 116 D1
Reteag, *Romania* 38 B7
Retenue, L. de, *Zaïre* 83 E2
Retford, *U.K.* 12 D7
Rethel, *France* 25 C11
Rethem, *Germany* 18 C5
Réthímnon, *Greece* 37 D6
Réthímnon □, *Greece* 37 D6
Retiche, Alpi, *Switz.* 23 D10
Retie, *Belgium* 17 F6
Retiers, *France* 24 E5
Retortillo, *Spain* 30 E4
Reuland, *Belgium* 17 H8
Réunion ■, *Ind. Oc.* 70 J9
Reus, *Spain* 28 D6
Reusel, *Neths.* 17 F6
Reuss →, *Switz.* 23 B6
Reutlingen, *Germany* 19 G5
Reutte, *Austria* 19 H6
Reuver, *Neths.* 17 F8
Reval = Tallinn, *Estonia* 9 G21
Revel, *France* 26 E6
Revelganj, *India* 63 G11
Revelstoke, *Canada* 100 C5
Reventazón, *Peru* 124 B1
Revigny-sur-Ornain, *France* 25 D11
Revilla Gigedo, Is., *Pac. Oc.* 94 H8
Revillagigedo I., *U.S.A.* 100 B2
Revin, *France* 25 C11
Revuè →, *Mozam.* 83 F3
Rewa, *India* 63 G9
Rewa →, *Guyana* 121 C6
Rewari, *India* 62 E7
Rexburg, *U.S.A.* 110 E8
Rey, *Iran* 65 C6
Rey, Rio del →, *Nigeria* 79 E6
Rey Malabo, *Eq. Guin.* 79 E6
Reyðarfjörður, *Iceland* 8 D6
Reyes, *Bolivia* 124 C4
Reyes, Pt., *U.S.A.* 112 H3
Reyhanlı, *Turkey* 66 D7
Reykjahlið, *Iceland* 8 D5
Reykjanes, *Iceland* 8 E2
Reykjavík, *Iceland* 8 D3
Reynolds, *Canada* 101 D9
Reynolds Ra., *Australia* 88 D5
Reynoldsville, *U.S.A.* 106 E6
Reynosa, *Mexico* 115 B5
Rēzekne, *Latvia* 9 H22
Rezvān, *Iran* 65 E8
Rharis, O. →, *Algeria* 75 C6
Rhayader, *U.K.* 13 E4
Rheden, *Neths.* 16 D8
Rhein, *Canada* 101 C8
Rhein →, *Europe* 16 E8
Rhein-Main-Donau-Kanal, *Germany* 19 F7
Rheinbach, *Germany* 18 E2
Rheine, *Germany* 18 C3
Rheineck, *Switz.* 23 B9
Rheinfelden, *Switz.* 22 A5
Rheinland-Pfalz □, *Germany* 19 E2
Rheinsberg, *Germany* 18 B8
Rheinwaldhorn, *Switz.* 23 D8
Rhenen, *Neths.* 16 E7
Rheriss, Oued →, *Morocco* 74 B4
Rheydt, *Germany* 18 D2
Rhin = Rhein →, *Europe* 16 E8
Rhinau, *France* 25 D14
Rhine = Rhein →, *Europe* 16 E8
Rhineland-Palatinate □ = Rheinland-Pfalz □, *Germany* 19 E2
Rhinelander, *U.S.A.* 108 C10
Rhino Camp, *Uganda* 82 B3
Rhir, Cap, *Morocco* 74 B3
Rhisnes, *Belgium* 17 G5
Rho, *Italy* 32 C6
Rhode Island □, *U.S.A.* 107 E13
Rhodes = Ródhos, *Greece* 37 C10
Rhodesia = Zimbabwe ■, *Africa* 83 F2
Rhodope Mts. = Rhodopi Planina, *Bulgaria* 39 H7
Rhodopi Planina, *Bulgaria* 39 H7
Rhön = Hohe Rhön, *Germany* 19 E5
Rhondda, *U.K.* 13 F4
Rhondda Cynon Taff □, *U.K.* 13 F4
Rhône □, *France* 27 C8
Rhône →, *France* 27 E8
Rhum, *U.K.* 14 E2
Rhyl, *U.K.* 12 D4
Rhymney, *U.K.* 13 F4
Ri-Aba, *Eq. Guin.* 79 E6
Riachão, *Brazil* 122 C2
Riacho de Santana, *Brazil* 123 D3
Rialma, *Brazil* 123 E2
Riaño, *Spain* 30 C5
Rians, *France* 27 E9
Riansares →, *Spain* 28 F1
Riasi, *India* 63 C6
Riau □, *Indonesia* 56 D2
Riau, Kepulauan, *Indonesia* 56 D2
Riau Arch. = Riau, Kepulauan, *Indonesia* 56 D2
Riaza, *Spain* 28 D1
Riaza →, *Spain* 28 D1
Riba de Saelices, *Spain* 28 E2
Ribadavia, *Spain* 30 C2
Ribadeo, *Spain* 30 B3
Ribadesella, *Spain* 30 B5

Ribamar, Brazil 122 B3
Ribas, Spain 28 C7
Ribas do Rio Pardo, Brazil 125 E7
Ribble →, U.K. 12 C5
Ribe, Denmark 11 J2
Ribeauvillé, France 25 D14
Ribécourt, France 25 C9
Ribeira, Spain 30 C2
Ribeira Brava, Madeira 36 D2
Ribeira do Pombal, Brazil 122 D4
Ribeirão Prêto, Brazil 127 A6
Ribeiro Gonçalves, Brazil 122 C2
Ribemont, France 25 C10
Ribera, Italy 34 E6
Ribérac, France 26 C4
Riberalta, Bolivia 125 C4
Ribnica, Slovenia 33 C11
Rîbniţa, Moldova 41 J5
Ribnitz-Damgarten, Germany 18 A8
Riccarton, N.Z. 87 K4
Riccia, Italy 35 A7
Riccione, Italy 33 D9
Rice, U.S.A. 113 L12
Rice L., Canada 106 B6
Rice Lake, U.S.A. 108 C9
Rich, Morocco 74 B4
Rich Hill, U.S.A. 109 F7
Richards Bay, S. Africa 85 D5
Richards L., Canada 101 B7
Richardson →, Canada 101 B6
Richardson Springs, U.S.A. 112 F5
Richardton, U.S.A. 108 B3
Riche, C., Australia 89 F2
Richelieu, France 24 E7
Richey, U.S.A. 108 B2
Richfield, Idaho, U.S.A. 110 E6
Richfield, Utah, U.S.A. 111 G8
Richford, U.S.A. 107 B12
Richibucto, Canada 99 C7
Richland, Ga., U.S.A. 105 J3
Richland, Oreg., U.S.A. 110 D5
Richland, Wash., U.S.A. 110 C4
Richland Center, U.S.A. 108 D9
Richlands, U.S.A. 104 G5
Richmond, N.S.W., Australia 91 E5
Richmond, Queens., Australia 90 C3
Richmond, N.Z. 87 J4
Richmond, U.K. 12 C6
Richmond, Calif., U.S.A. 112 H4
Richmond, Ind., U.S.A. 104 F3
Richmond, Ky., U.S.A. 104 G3
Richmond, Mich., U.S.A. 106 D2
Richmond, Mo., U.S.A. 108 F8
Richmond, Tex., U.S.A. 109 L7
Richmond, Utah, U.S.A. 110 F8
Richmond, Va., U.S.A. 104 G7
Richmond Ra., Australia 91 D5
Richmond-upon-Thames, U.K. 13 F7
Richterswil, Switz. 23 B7
Richton, U.S.A. 105 K1
Richwood, U.S.A. 104 F5
Ricla, Spain 28 D3
Ridder = Leninogorsk, Kazakstan 44 D9
Ridderkerk, Neths. 16 E5
Riddes, Switz. 22 D4
Ridgecrest, U.S.A. 113 K9
Ridgedale, Canada 101 C8
Ridgefield, U.S.A. 112 E4
Ridgeland, U.S.A. 105 J5
Ridgelands, Australia 90 C5
Ridgetown, Canada 98 D3
Ridgewood, U.S.A. 107 F10
Ridgway, U.S.A. 106 E6
Riding Mountain Nat. Park, Canada 101 C8
Ridley, Mt., Australia 89 F3
Ried, Austria 21 G3
Riedlingen, Germany 19 G5
Riel, Neths. 17 E6
Rienza →, Italy 33 B8
Riesa, Germany 18 D9
Riesco, I., Chile 128 D2
Riesi, Italy 35 E7
Riet →, S. Africa 84 D3
Rieti, Italy 33 F9
Rieupeyroux, France 26 D6
Riez, France 27 E10
Riffe L., U.S.A. 112 D4
Rifle, U.S.A. 110 G10
Rift Valley □, Kenya 82 B4
Rig Rig, Chad 73 F7
Rīga, Latvia 9 H21
Riga, G. of, Latvia 9 H20
Rīgān, Iran 65 D8
Rīgas Jūras Līcis = Riga, G. of, Latvia 9 H20
Rigaud, Canada 107 A10
Rigby, U.S.A. 110 E8
Rīgestān □, Afghan. 60 D4
Riggins, U.S.A. 110 D5
Rignac, France 26 D6
Rigolet, Canada 99 B8
Riihimäki, Finland 9 F21
Riiser-Larsen-halvøya, Antarctica 5 C4
Rijau, Nigeria 79 C6
Rijeka, Croatia 33 C11
Rijen, Neths. 17 E5
Rijkevorsel, Belgium 17 F5
Rijn →, Neths. 16 D4
Rijnsberg, Neths. 16 D4
Rijsbergen, Neths. 17 E5
Rijssen, Neths. 16 D9
Rijswijk, Neths. 16 D4
Rike, Ethiopia 77 E4
Rikuzentakada, Japan 48 E10
Rila Planina, Bulgaria 38 G6
Riley, U.S.A. 110 E4
Rima →, Nigeria 79 C6
Rimah, Wadi ar →, Si. Arabia 64 E4
Rimavská Sobota, Slovak Rep. 21 G10
Rimbey, Canada 100 C6
Rimbo, Sweden 10 E12
Rimi, Nigeria 79 C6
Rímini, Italy 33 D9
Rîmnicu Sărat, Romania 38 D10
Rîmnicu Vîlcea, Romania 38 D7
Rimouski, Canada 99 C6
Rimrock, U.S.A. 112 D5
Rinca, Indonesia 57 F5
Rincón de Romos, Mexico 114 C4
Rinconada, Argentina 126 A2
Ringarum, Sweden 11 F10
Ringe, Denmark 11 J4
Ringim, Nigeria 79 C6
Ringkøbing, Denmark 11 H2
Ringling, U.S.A. 110 C8
Ringsaker, Norway 10 D4
Ringsted, Denmark 11 J5
Ringvassøy, Norway 8 B18
Rinjani, Indonesia 56 F5
Rinteln, Germany 18 C5
Río, Punta del, Spain 29 J2
Rio Branco, Brazil 124 B4
Río Branco, Uruguay 127 C5
Rio Brilhante, Brazil 127 A5
Río Bueno, Chile 128 B2
Río Chico, Venezuela 120 A4
Rio Claro, Brazil 127 A6
Rio Claro, Trin. & Tob. 117 D7
Río Colorado, Argentina 128 A4
Río Cuarto, Argentina 126 C3
Rio das Pedras, Mozam. 85 C6
Rio de Contas, Brazil 123 D3
Rio de Janeiro, Brazil 123 F3
Rio de Janeiro □, Brazil 123 F3
Rio do Prado, Brazil 123 E3
Rio do Sul, Brazil 127 B6
Río Gallegos, Argentina 128 D3
Río Grande, Argentina 128 D3
Río Grande, Bolivia 124 E4
Rio Grande, Brazil 127 C5
Río Grande, Mexico 114 C4
Río Grande, Nic. 116 D3
Rio Grande →, U.S.A. 109 N6
Rio Grande City, U.S.A. 109 M5
Río Grande del Norte →, N. Amer. 103 E7
Rio Grande do Norte □, Brazil 122 C4
Rio Grande do Sul □, Brazil 127 C5
Río Hato, Panama 116 E3
Río Lagartos, Mexico 115 C7
Rio Largo, Brazil 122 C4
Rio Maior, Portugal 31 F2
Rio Marina, Italy 32 F7
Río Mayo, Argentina 128 C2
Río Mulatos, Bolivia 124 D4
Río Muni = Mbini □, Eq. Guin. 80 D2
Rio Negro, Brazil 127 B6
Río Negro, Chile 128 B2
Rio Negro, Pantanal do, Brazil 125 D6
Rio Pardo, Brazil 127 C5
Río Pico, Argentina 128 B2
Rio Real, Brazil 123 D4
Río Segundo, Argentina 126 C3
Río Tercero, Argentina 126 C3
Rio Tinto, Brazil 122 C4
Rio Tinto, Portugal 30 D2
Rio Verde, Brazil 123 E1
Río Verde, Mexico 115 C5
Rio Verde de Mato Grosso, Brazil 125 D7
Rio Vista, U.S.A. 112 G5
Ríobamba, Ecuador 120 D2
Ríohacha, Colombia 120 A3
Rioja, Peru 124 B2
Riom, France 26 C7
Riom-ès-Montagnes, France 26 C6
Rion-des-Landes, France 26 E3
Rionegro, Colombia 120 B2
Rionero in Vúlture, Italy 35 B8
Rioni →, Georgia 43 J5
Rios, Spain 30 D3
Ríosucio, Caldas, Colombia 120 B2
Ríosucio, Choco, Colombia 120 B2
Riou L., Canada 101 B7
Rioz, France 25 E13
Riozinho →, Brazil 120 D4
Riparia, Dora →, Italy 32 C4
Ripatransone, Italy 33 F10
Ripley, Canada 106 B3
Ripley, Calif., U.S.A. 113 M12
Ripley, N.Y., U.S.A. 106 D5
Ripley, Tenn., U.S.A. 109 H10
Ripoll, Spain 28 C7
Ripon, U.K. 12 C6
Ripon, Calif., U.S.A. 112 H5
Ripon, Wis., U.S.A. 104 D1
Riposto, Italy 35 E8
Risalpur, Pakistan 62 B4
Risan, Montenegro, Yug. 21 N8
Risaralda □, Colombia 120 B2
Riscle, France 26 E3
Rishā', W. ar →, Si. Arabia 64 E5
Rishiri-Tō, Japan 48 B10
Rishon le Ẕiyyon, Israel 69 D3
Risle →, France 24 C7
Rison, U.S.A. 109 J8
Risør, Norway 11 F3
Rissani, Morocco 74 B4
Riti, Nigeria 79 D6
Rittman, U.S.A. 106 F3
Ritzville, U.S.A. 110 C4
Riva Bella, France 24 C6
Riva del Garda, Italy 32 C7
Rivadavia, Buenos Aires, Argentina 126 D3
Rivadavia, Mendoza, Argentina 126 C2
Rivadavia, Salta, Argentina 126 A3
Rivadavia, Chile 126 B1
Rivarolo Canavese, Italy 32 C4
Rivas, Nic. 116 D2
Rive-de-Gier, France 27 C8
River Cess, Liberia 78 D3
Rivera, Uruguay 127 C4
Riverdale, U.S.A. 112 J7
Riverhead, U.S.A. 107 F12
Riverhurst, Canada 101 C7
Riverina, Australia 89 E3
Rivers, Canada 101 C8
Rivers □, Nigeria 79 E6
Rivers, L. of the, Canada 101 D7
Rivers Inlet, Canada 100 C3
Riversdale, S. Africa 84 E3
Riverside, Calif., U.S.A. 113 M9
Riverside, Wyo., U.S.A. 110 F10
Riversleigh, Australia 90 B2
Riverton, Australia 91 E2
Riverton, Canada 101 C9
Riverton, N.Z. 87 M1
Riverton, U.S.A. 110 E9
Riverton Heights, U.S.A. 112 C4
Rives, France 27 C9
Rivesaltes, France 26 F6
Riviera, Europe 32 E5
Riviera di Levante, Italy 32 D6
Riviera di Ponente, Italy 32 D5
Rivière-à-Pierre, Canada 99 C5
Rivière-au-Renard, Canada 99 C7
Rivière-du-Loup, Canada 99 C6
Rivière-Pentecôte, Canada 99 C6
Rivière-Pilote, Martinique 117 D7
Rivne, Ukraine 41 G4
Rívoli, Italy 32 C4
Rivoli B., Australia 91 F3
Rixensart, Belgium 17 G5
Riyadh = Ar Riyāḍ, Si. Arabia 64 E5
Rize, Turkey 67 B9
Rizhao, China 51 G10
Rizokarpaso, Cyprus 66 E6
Rizzuto, C., Italy 35 D10
Rjukan, Norway 10 E2
Roa, Norway 10 D4
Roa, Spain 30 D7
Road Town, Virgin Is. 117 C7
Roag, L., U.K. 14 C2
Roanne, France 27 B8
Roanoke, Ala., U.S.A. 105 J3
Roanoke, Va., U.S.A. 104 G6
Roanoke →, U.S.A. 105 H7
Roanoke I., U.S.A. 105 H8
Roanoke Rapids, U.S.A. 105 G7
Roatán, Honduras 116 C2
Robbins I., Australia 90 G4
Robe →, Australia 88 D2
Robe →, Ireland 15 C2
Röbel, Germany 18 B8
Robert Lee, U.S.A. 109 K4
Roberts, U.S.A. 110 E7
Robertsganj, India 63 G10
Robertson, S. Africa 84 E2
Robertson I., Antarctica 5 C18
Robertson Ra., Australia 88 D3
Robertsport, Liberia 78 D2
Robertstown, Australia 91 E2
Roberval, Canada 99 C5
Robeson Chan., Greenland 4 A4
Robinson →, Australia 90 B2
Robinson Ra., Australia 89 E2
Robinson River, Australia 90 B2
Robinvale, Australia 91 E3
Roblin, Canada 101 C8
Roboré, Bolivia 125 D6
Robson, Mt., Canada 100 C5
Robstown, U.S.A. 109 M6
Roca, C. da, Portugal 6 H4
Roca Partida, I., Mexico 114 D2
Rocas, I., Brazil 122 B5
Rocca d'Aspidé, Italy 35 B8
Rocca San Casciano, Italy 33 D8
Roccalbegna, Italy 33 F8
Roccastrada, Italy 33 F8
Roccella Iónica, Italy 35 D9
Rocha, Uruguay 127 C5
Rochdale, U.K. 12 D5
Rochechouart, France 26 C4
Rochedo, Brazil 125 D7
Rochefort, Belgium 17 H6
Rochefort, France 26 C3
Rochefort-en-Terre, France 24 E4
Rochelle, U.S.A. 108 E10
Rocher River, Canada 100 A6
Rocherath, Belgium 17 H8
Rocheservière, France 24 F5
Rochester, Canada 100 C6
Rochester, U.K. 13 F8
Rochester, Ind., U.S.A. 104 E2
Rochester, Minn., U.S.A. 108 C8
Rochester, N.H., U.S.A. 107 C14
Rochester, N.Y., U.S.A. 106 C7
Rociana, Spain 31 H4
Rociu, Romania 38 E8
Rock →, Canada 100 A3
Rock Hill, U.S.A. 105 H5
Rock Island, U.S.A. 108 E9
Rock Rapids, U.S.A. 108 D6
Rock River, U.S.A. 110 F11
Rock Sound, Bahamas 116 B4
Rock Springs, Mont., U.S.A. 110 C10
Rock Springs, Wyo., U.S.A. 110 F9
Rock Valley, U.S.A. 108 D6
Rockall, Atl. Oc. 6 D3
Rockanje, Neths. 16 E4
Rockdale, Tex., U.S.A. 109 K6
Rockdale, Wash., U.S.A. 112 C5
Rockefeller Plateau, Antarctica 5 E14
Rockford, U.S.A. 108 D10
Rockglen, Canada 101 D7
Rockhampton, Australia 90 C5
Rockhampton Downs, Australia 90 B2
Rockingham, Australia 89 F2
Rockingham B., Australia 90 B4
Rockingham Forest, U.K. 13 E7
Rocklake, U.S.A. 108 A5
Rockland, Canada 107 A9
Rockland, Idaho, U.S.A. 110 E7
Rockland, Maine, U.S.A. 99 D6
Rockland, Mich., U.S.A. 108 B10
Rocklin, U.S.A. 112 G5
Rockmart, U.S.A. 105 H3
Rockport, Mo., U.S.A. 108 E7
Rockport, Tex., U.S.A. 109 L6
Rocksprings, U.S.A. 109 K4
Rockville, Conn., U.S.A. 107 E12
Rockville, Md., U.S.A. 104 F7
Rockwall, U.S.A. 109 J6
Rockwell City, U.S.A. 108 D7
Rockwood, U.S.A. 105 H3
Rocky Ford, U.S.A. 108 F3
Rocky Gully, Australia 89 F2
Rocky Lane, Canada 100 B5
Rocky Mount, U.S.A. 105 H7
Rocky Mountain House, Canada 100 C6
Rocky Mts., N. Amer. 100 C4
Rockyford, Canada 100 C6
Rocroi, France 25 C11
Rod, Pakistan 60 E3
Rødberg, Norway 10 D2
Rødby, Denmark 11 K5
Rødbyhavn, Denmark 11 K5
Roddickton, Canada 99 B8
Rødding, Denmark 11 J3
Rødekro, Denmark 11 J3
Roden, Neths. 16 B8
Rødenes, Norway 10 E5
Rodenkirchen, Germany 18 B4
Roderick I., Canada 100 C3
Rodez, France 26 D6
Rodholívas, Greece 39 J6
Rodhopoú, Greece 37 D5
Ródhos, Greece 37 C10
Rodi Gargánico, Italy 35 A8
Rodna, Romania 38 B7
Rodney, Canada 106 D3
Rodney, C., N.Z. 87 G5
Rodniki, Russia 42 B5
Rodriguez, Ind. Oc. 3 E13
Roe →, U.K. 15 A5
Roebling, U.S.A. 107 F10
Roebourne, Australia 88 D2
Roebuck B., Australia 88 C3
Roebuck Plains, Australia 88 C3
Roer →, Neths. 17 F7
Roermond, Neths. 17 F7
Roes Welcome Sd., Canada 97 B11
Roeselare, Belgium 17 G2
Rœulx, Belgium 17 G4
Rogachev = Ragachow, Belarus 41 F6
Rogagua, L., Bolivia 124 C4
Rogaška Slatina, Slovenia 33 B12
Rogatec, Slovenia 33 B12
Rogatyn, Ukraine 41 H3
Rogdhia, Greece 37 D7
Rogers, U.S.A. 109 G7
Rogers City, U.S.A. 104 C4
Rogerson, U.S.A. 110 E6
Rogersville, U.S.A. 105 G4
Roggan River, Canada 98 B4
Roggel, Neths. 17 F7
Roggeveldberge, S. Africa 84 E3
Roggiano Gravina, Italy 35 C9
Rogliano, France 27 F13
Rogliano, Italy 35 C9
Rogoaguado, L., Bolivia 125 C4
Rogue →, U.S.A. 110 E1
Rohan, France 24 D4
Róhda, Greece 37 A3
Rohnert Park, U.S.A. 112 G4
Rohrbach-lès-Bitche, France 25 C14
Rohri, Pakistan 62 F3
Rohri Canal, Pakistan 62 F3
Rohtak, India 62 E7
Roi Et, Thailand 58 D4
Roisel, France 25 C10
Roja, Latvia 9 H20
Rojas, Argentina 126 C3
Rojo, C., Mexico 115 C5
Rokan →, Indonesia 56 D2
Rokeby, Australia 90 A3
Rokiškis, Lithuania 9 J21
Rokitno, Russia 42 E2
Rolândia, Brazil 127 A5
Rolde, Neths. 16 C9
Rolette, U.S.A. 108 A5
Rolla, Kans., U.S.A. 109 G4
Rolla, Mo., U.S.A. 109 G9
Rolla, N. Dak., U.S.A. 108 A5
Rollag, Norway 10 D3
Rolle, Switz. 22 D2
Rolleston, Australia 90 C4
Rollingstone, Australia 90 B4
Rom, Sudan 77 F3
Roma, Australia 91 D4
Roma, Italy 34 A5
Roma, Sweden 9 H18
Roman, Romania 38 C9
Roman, Russia 45 C12
Roman-Kosh, Gora, Ukraine 41 K8
Romanche →, France 27 C9
Romang, Indonesia 57 F7
Români, Egypt 69 E1
Romania ■, Europe 38 D8
Romano, Cayo, Cuba 116 B4
Romano di Lombárdia, Italy 32 C6
Romanovka = Basarabeasca, Moldova 41 J5
Romans-sur-Isère, France 27 C9
Romanshorn, Switz. 23 A8
Romblon, Phil. 55 E5
Rombo □, Tanzania 82 C4
Rome = Roma, Italy 34 A5
Rome, Ga., U.S.A. 105 H3
Rome, N.Y., U.S.A. 107 C9
Romeleåsen, Sweden 11 J7
Romenay, France 27 B9
Romerike, Norway 10 D5
Romilly-sur-Seine, France 25 D10
Romîni, Romania 38 E7
Rommani, Morocco 74 B3
Romney, U.S.A. 104 F6
Romney Marsh, U.K. 13 F8
Romny, Ukraine 41 G7
Rømø, Denmark 11 J2
Romodan, Ukraine 41 G7
Romodanovo, Russia 42 C7
Romont, Switz. 22 C3
Romorantin-Lanthenay, France 25 E8
Romsdalen, Norway 10 B2
Ron, Vietnam 58 D6
Rona, U.K. 14 D3
Ronan, U.S.A. 110 C6
Roncador, Cayos, Caribbean 116 D3
Roncador, Serra do, Brazil 123 D1
Roncesvalles, Paso, Spain 28 B3
Ronceverte, U.S.A. 104 G5
Ronciglione, Italy 33 F9
Ronco →, Italy 33 D9
Ronda, Spain 31 J5
Ronda, Serranía de, Spain 31 J5
Rondane, Norway 10 C3
Rondón, Colombia 120 B3
Rondônia, Brazil 125 C5
Rondônia □, Brazil 125 C5
Rondonópolis, Brazil 125 D7
Rong Jiang →, China 52 E7
Rong Xian, Guangxi Zhuangzu, China 53 F8
Rong Xian, Sichuan, China 52 C5
Rong'an, China 52 E7
Rongchang, China 52 C5
Ronge, L. la, Canada 101 B7
Rongjiang, China 52 E7
Rongshui, China 52 E7
Rønne, Denmark 9 J16
Ronne Ice Shelf, Antarctica 5 D18
Ronsard, C., Australia 89 D1
Ronse, Belgium 17 G3
Ronuro →, Brazil 125 C7
Roodepoort, S. Africa 85 D4
Roodeschool, Neths. 16 B9
Roof Butte, U.S.A. 111 H9
Roompot, Neths. 17 E3
Roorkee, India 62 E7
Roosendaal, Neths. 17 E4
Roosevelt, Minn., U.S.A. 108 A7
Roosevelt, Utah, U.S.A. 110 F8
Roosevelt →, Brazil 125 B5
Roosevelt, Mt., Canada 100 B3
Roosevelt I., Antarctica 5 D12
Roosevelt Res., U.S.A. 111 K8
Roper →, Australia 90 A2
Ropesville, U.S.A. 109 J3
Roque Pérez, Argentina 126 D4
Roquefort, France 26 D3
Roquemaure, France 27 D8
Roquetas, Spain 28 E5
Roquevaire, France 27 E9
Roraima □, Brazil 121 C5
Roraima, Mt., Venezuela 121 B5
Rorketon, Canada 101 C9
Røros, Norway 10 B5
Rorschach, Switz. 23 B8
Rosa, Zambia 83 D3
Rosa, C., Algeria 75 A6
Rosa, Monte, Europe 22 E5
Rosal, Spain 30 D2
Rosal de la Frontera, Spain 31 H3
Rosalia, U.S.A. 110 C5
Rosamond, U.S.A. 113 L8

Rosans, *France* 27 D9
Rosario, *Argentina* 126 C3
Rosário, *Brazil* 122 B3
Rosario, *Baja Calif., Mexico* 114 A1
Rosario, *Sinaloa, Mexico* 114 C3
Rosario, *Paraguay* 126 A4
Rosario, Villa del, *Venezuela* 120 A3
Rosario de la Frontera, *Argentina* 126 B3
Rosario de Lerma, *Argentina* 126 A2
Rosario del Tala, *Argentina* 126 C4
Rosário do Sul, *Brazil* 127 C5
Rosário Oeste, *Brazil* 125 C6
Rosarito, *Mexico* 113 N9
Rosarno, *Italy* 35 D8
Rosas, *Spain* 28 C8
Rosas, G. de, *Spain* 28 C8
Roscoe, *U.S.A.* 108 C5
Roscoff, *France* 24 D3
Roscommon, *Ireland* 15 C3
Roscommon, *U.S.A.* 104 C3
Roscommon □, *Ireland* 15 C3
Roscrea, *Ireland* 15 D4
Rose →, *Australia* 90 A2
Rose Blanche, *Canada* 99 C8
Rose Harbour, *Canada* 100 C2
Rose Pt., *Canada* 100 C2
Rose Valley, *Canada* 101 C8
Roseau, *Domin.* 117 C7
Roseau, *U.S.A.* 108 A7
Rosebery, *Australia* 90 G4
Rosebud, *U.S.A.* 109 K6
Roseburg, *U.S.A.* 110 E2
Rosedale, *Australia* 90 C5
Rosedale, *U.S.A.* 109 J9
Rosée, *Belgium* 17 H5
Roseland, *U.S.A.* 112 G4
Rosemary, *Canada* 100 C6
Rosenberg, *U.S.A.* 109 L7
Rosendaël, *France* 25 A9
Rosenheim, *Germany* 19 H8
Roseto degli Abruzzi, *Italy* 33 F11
Rosetown, *Canada* 101 C7
Rosetta = Rashîd, *Egypt* 76 H7
Roseville, *U.S.A.* 112 G5
Rosewood, *N. Terr., Australia* 88 C4
Rosewood, *Queens., Australia* 91 D5
Roshkhvār, *Iran* 65 C8
Rosières-en-Santerre, *France* 25 C9
Rosignano Maríttimo, *Italy* 32 E7
Rosignol, *Guyana* 121 B6
Roşiori de Vede, *Romania* 38 E8
Rositsa, *Bulgaria* 38 F10
Rositsa →, *Bulgaria* 38 F8
Roskilde, *Denmark* 11 J6
Roskilde Amtskommune □, *Denmark* 11 J6
Roskilde Fjord, *Denmark* 11 J6
Roslavl, *Russia* 40 F7
Roslyn, *Australia* 91 E4
Rosmaninhal, *Portugal* 31 F3
Rosmead, *S. Africa* 84 E4
Røsnæs, *Denmark* 11 J4
Rosolini, *Italy* 35 F7
Rosporden, *France* 24 E3
Ross, *Australia* 90 G4
Ross, *N.Z.* 87 K3
Ross I., *Antarctica* 5 D11
Ross Ice Shelf, *Antarctica* 5 E12
Ross L., *U.S.A.* 110 B3
Ross-on-Wye, *U.K.* 13 F5
Ross Sea, *Antarctica* 5 D11
Rossa, *Switz.* 23 D8
Rossan Pt., *Ireland* 15 B3
Rossano Cálabro, *Italy* 35 C9
Rossburn, *Canada* 101 C8
Rosseau, *Canada* 106 A5
Rossignol, L., *Canada* 98 B5
Rossignol Res., *Canada* 99 D6
Rossland, *Canada* 100 D5
Rosslare, *Ireland* 15 D5
Rosslau, *Germany* 18 D8
Rosso, *Mauritania* 78 B1
Rosso, C., *France* 27 F12
Rossosh, *Russia* 42 E4
Rossport, *Canada* 98 C2
Rossum, *Neths.* 16 E6
Røssvatnet, *Norway* 8 D16
Rossville, *Australia* 90 B4
Røst, *Norway* 8 C15
Rosthern, *Canada* 101 C7
Rostock, *Germany* 18 A8
Rostov, *Don, Russia* 43 G4
Rostov, *Yarosl., Russia* 42 B4
Rostrenen, *France* 24 D3
Roswell, *Ga., U.S.A.* 105 H3
Roswell, *N. Mex., U.S.A.* 109 J2
Rosyth, *U.K.* 14 E5
Rota, *Spain* 31 J4
Rotälven →, *Sweden* 10 C8
Rotan, *U.S.A.* 109 J4
Rotem, *Belgium* 17 F7
Rotenburg, *Germany* 18 B5
Roth, *Germany* 19 F7
Rothaargebirge, *Germany* 18 E4
Rothenburg, *Switz.* 23 B6
Rothenburg ob der Tauber, *Germany* 19 F6
Rother →, *U.K.* 13 G8
Rotherham, *U.K.* 12 D6
Rothes, *U.K.* 14 D5
Rothesay, *Canada* 99 C6
Rothesay, *U.K.* 14 F3
Rothrist, *Switz.* 22 B5
Roti, *Indonesia* 57 F6
Roto, *Australia* 91 E4
Rotondella, *Italy* 35 B9
Rotoroa, L., *N.Z.* 87 J4
Rotorua, *N.Z.* 87 H6
Rotorua, L., *N.Z.* 87 H6
Rotselaar, *Belgium* 17 G5
Rott →, *Germany* 19 G9
Rotten →, *Switz.* 22 D5
Rottenburg, *Germany* 19 G4
Rotterdam, *Neths.* 16 E5
Rottnest I., *Australia* 89 F2
Rottumeroog, *Neths.* 16 A9
Rottweil, *Germany* 19 G4
Rotuma, *Fiji* 92 J9
Roubaix, *France* 25 B10
Rouen, *France* 24 C8
Rouergue, *France* 26 D5
Rouillac, *France* 26 C3
Rouleau, *Canada* 101 C8
Round Mountain, *U.S.A.* 110 G5
Round Mt., *Australia* 91 E5
Roundup, *U.S.A.* 110 C9
Roura, *Fr. Guiana* 121 C7
Rousay, *U.K.* 14 B5
Rouses Point, *U.S.A.* 107 B11
Roussillon, *Isère, France* 27 C8
Roussillon, *Pyrénées-Or., France* 26 F6
Rouveen, *Neths.* 16 C8
Rouxville, *S. Africa* 84 E4
Rouyn, *Canada* 98 C4
Rovaniemi, *Finland* 8 C21
Rovato, *Italy* 32 C7
Rovenki, *Ukraine* 41 H10
Rovereto, *Italy* 32 C8
Rovigo, *Italy* 33 C8
Rovinari, *Romania* 38 E6
Rovinj, *Croatia* 33 C10
Rovira, *Colombia* 120 C2
Rovno = Rivne, *Ukraine* 41 G4
Rovnoye, *Russia* 42 E8
Rovuma →, *Tanzania* 83 E5
Row'ān, *Iran* 65 C6
Rowena, *Australia* 91 D4
Rowley Shoals, *Australia* 88 C2
Roxa, *Guinea-Biss.* 78 C1
Roxas, *Capiz, Phil.* 55 F5
Roxas, *Isabela, Phil.* 55 C4
Roxas, *Mindoro, Phil.* 55 E4
Roxboro, *U.S.A.* 105 G6
Roxborough Downs, *Australia* 90 C2
Roxburgh, *N.Z.* 87 L2
Roxen, *Sweden* 11 F9
Roy, *Mont., U.S.A.* 110 C9
Roy, *N. Mex., U.S.A.* 109 H2
Roy Hill, *Australia* 88 D2
Roya, Peña, *Spain* 28 E4
Royal Leamington Spa, *U.K.* 13 E6
Royal Tunbridge Wells, *U.K.* 13 F8
Royan, *France* 26 C2
Roye, *France* 25 C9
Røyken, *Norway* 10 E4
Rožaj, *Montenegro, Yug.* 21 N10
Rozay-en-Brie, *France* 25 D9
Rozdilna, *Ukraine* 41 J6
Rozhyshche, *Ukraine* 41 G3
Rožňava, *Slovak Rep.* 20 G10
Rozoy-sur-Serre, *France* 25 C11
Rtishchevo, *Russia* 42 D6
Rúa, *Spain* 30 C3
Ruacaná, *Angola* 84 B1
Ruahine Ra., *N.Z.* 87 H6
Ruapehu, *N.Z.* 87 H5
Ruapuke I., *N.Z.* 87 M2
Ruâq, W. →, *Egypt* 69 F2
Rub' al Khali, *Si. Arabia* 68 D4
Rubeho Mts., *Tanzania* 82 D4
Rubezhnoye = Rubizhne, *Ukraine* 41 H10
Rubh a' Mhail, *U.K.* 14 F2
Rubha Hunish, *U.K.* 14 D2
Rubha Robhanais = Lewis, Butt of, *U.K.* 14 C2
Rubiataba, *Brazil* 123 E2
Rubicon →, *U.S.A.* 112 G5
Rubicone →, *Italy* 33 D9
Rubinéia, *Brazil* 123 F1
Rubino, *Ivory C.* 78 D4
Rubio, *Venezuela* 120 B3
Rubizhne, *Ukraine* 41 H10
Rubtsovsk, *Russia* 44 D9
Ruby L., *U.S.A.* 110 F6
Ruby Mts., *U.S.A.* 110 F6
Rucheng, *China* 53 E9
Rud, *Norway* 10 D4
Rūd Sar, *Iran* 65 B6
Ruda Śląska, *Poland* 20 E8
Rudall, *Australia* 91 E2
Rudall →, *Australia* 88 D3
Ruden, *Germany* 18 A9
Rüdersdorf, *Germany* 18 C9
Rudewa, *Tanzania* 83 E3
Rudkøbing, *Denmark* 11 K4
Rudnik, *Serbia, Yug.* 21 L10
Rudnogorsk, *Russia* 45 D11
Rudnya, *Russia* 40 E6
Rudnyy, *Kazakstan* 44 D7
Rudolf, Ostrov, *Russia* 44 A6
Rudolstadt, *Germany* 18 E7
Rudong, *China* 53 A13
Rudozem, *Bulgaria* 39 H7
Rudyard, *U.S.A.* 104 B3
Rue, *France* 25 B8
Ruelle, *France* 26 C4
Rufa'a, *Sudan* 77 E3
Ruffec, *France* 26 B4
Rufiji □, *Tanzania* 82 D4
Rufiji →, *Tanzania* 82 D4
Rufino, *Argentina* 126 C3
Rufisque, *Senegal* 78 C1
Rufunsa, *Zambia* 83 F2
Rugao, *China* 53 A13
Rugby, *U.K.* 13 E6
Rugby, *U.S.A.* 108 A5
Rügen, *Germany* 18 A9
Rugles, *France* 24 D7
Ruhengeri, *Rwanda* 82 C2
Ruhla, *Germany* 18 E6
Ruhland, *Germany* 18 D9
Ruhnu saar, *Estonia* 9 H20
Ruhr →, *Germany* 18 D2
Ruhuhu →, *Tanzania* 83 E3
Rui Barbosa, *Brazil* 123 D3
Rui'an, *China* 53 D13
Ruichang, *China* 53 C10
Ruidosa, *U.S.A.* 109 L2
Ruidoso, *U.S.A.* 111 K11
Ruili, *China* 52 E1
Ruinen, *Neths.* 16 C8
Ruinerwold, *Neths.* 16 C8
Ruiten A Kanaal →, *Neths.* 16 C10
Ruivo, Pico, *Madeira* 36 D3
Rujm Tal'at al Jamā'ah, *Jordan* 69 E4
Ruk, *Pakistan* 62 F3
Rukwa □, *Tanzania* 82 D3
Rukwa L., *Tanzania* 82 D3
Rulhieres, C., *Australia* 88 B4
Rulles, *Belgium* 17 J7
Rum = Rhum, *U.K.* 14 E2
Rum Cay, *Bahamas* 117 B5
Rum Jungle, *Australia* 88 B5
Ruma, *Serbia, Yug.* 21 K9
Rumāḥ, *Si. Arabia* 64 E5
Rumania = Romania ■, *Europe* 38 D8
Rumaylah, *Iraq* 64 D5
Rumbalara, *Australia* 90 D1
Rumbêk, *Sudan* 77 F2
Rumbeke, *Belgium* 17 G2
Rumelange, *Lux.* 17 K8
Rumford, *U.S.A.* 107 B14
Rumilly, *France* 27 C9
Rumoi, *Japan* 48 C10
Rumonge, *Burundi* 82 C2
Rumsey, *Canada* 100 C6
Rumula, *Australia* 90 B4
Rumuruti, *Kenya* 82 B4
Runan, *China* 50 H8
Runanga, *N.Z.* 87 K3
Runaway, C., *N.Z.* 87 G6
Runcorn, *U.K.* 12 D5
Rungwa, *Tanzania* 82 D3
Rungwa →, *Tanzania* 82 D3
Rungwe, *Tanzania* 83 D3
Rungwe □, *Tanzania* 83 D3
Runka, *Nigeria* 79 C6
Runton Ra., *Australia* 88 D3
Ruokolahti, *Finland* 40 B5
Ruoqiang, *China* 54 C3
Rupa, *India* 61 F18
Rupar, *India* 62 D7
Rupat, *Indonesia* 56 D2
Rupert →, *Canada* 98 B4
Rupert House = Waskaganish, *Canada* 98 B4
Rupununi →, *Guyana* 121 C6
Rur →, *Germany* 18 E2
Rurrenabaque, *Bolivia* 124 C4
Rus →, *Spain* 29 F2
Rusambo, *Zimbabwe* 83 F3
Rusape, *Zimbabwe* 83 F3
Ruschuk = Ruse, *Bulgaria* 38 F8
Ruse, *Bulgaria* 38 F8
Ruşeţu, *Romania* 38 E10
Rushan, *China* 51 F11
Rushden, *U.K.* 13 E7
Rushford, *U.S.A.* 108 D9
Rushville, *Ill., U.S.A.* 108 E9
Rushville, *Ind., U.S.A.* 104 F3
Rushville, *Nebr., U.S.A.* 108 D3
Rushworth, *Australia* 91 F4
Russas, *Brazil* 122 B4
Russell, *Canada* 101 C8
Russell, *U.S.A.* 108 F5
Russell L., *Man., Canada* 101 B8
Russell L., *N.W.T., Canada* 100 A5
Russellkonda, *India* 61 K14
Russellville, *Ala., U.S.A.* 105 H2
Russellville, *Ark., U.S.A.* 109 H8
Russellville, *Ky., U.S.A.* 105 G2
Russi, *Italy* 33 D9
Russia ■, *Eurasia* 45 C11
Russian →, *U.S.A.* 112 G3
Russkaya Polyana, *Kazakstan* 44 D8
Russkoye Ustie, *Russia* 4 B15
Rustam, *Pakistan* 62 B5
Rustam Shahr, *Pakistan* 62 F2
Rustavi, *Georgia* 43 K7
Rustenburg, *S. Africa* 84 D4
Ruston, *U.S.A.* 109 J8
Ruswil, *Switz.* 22 B6
Rutana, *Burundi* 82 C2
Rute, *Spain* 31 H6
Ruteng, *Indonesia* 57 F6
Ruth, *Mich., U.S.A.* 106 C2
Ruth, *Nev., U.S.A.* 110 G6
Rutherford, *U.S.A.* 112 G4
Rutherglen, *U.K.* 14 F4
Rüti, *Switz.* 23 B7
Rutigliano, *Italy* 35 A10
Rutland Plains, *Australia* 90 B3
Rutledge →, *Canada* 101 A6
Rutledge L., *Canada* 101 A6
Rutqa, W. →, *Syria* 67 E9
Rutshuru, *Zaïre* 82 C2
Ruurlo, *Neths.* 16 D8
Ruvo di Púglia, *Italy* 35 A9
Ruvu, *Tanzania* 82 D4
Ruvu →, *Tanzania* 82 D4
Ruvuma □, *Tanzania* 83 E4
Ruwais, *U.A.E.* 65 E7
Ruwenzori, *Africa* 82 B2
Ruyigi, *Burundi* 82 C3
Ruyuan, *China* 53 E9
Ruzayevka, *Russia* 42 C7
Ružomberok, *Slovak Rep.* 20 F9
Rwanda ■, *Africa* 82 C3
Ry, *Denmark* 11 H3
Ryakhovo, *Bulgaria* 38 F9
Ryan, L., *U.K.* 14 G3
Ryazan, *Russia* 42 C4
Ryazhsk, *Russia* 42 D5
Rybache = Rybachye, *Kazakstan* 44 E9
Rybachye = Ysyk-Köl, *Kyrgyzstan* 46 E11
Rybachye, *Kazakstan* 44 E9
Rybinsk, *Russia* 42 A4
Rybinskoye Vdkhr., *Russia* 40 C10
Rybnik, *Poland* 20 E8
Rybnitsa = Rîbniţa, *Moldova* 41 J5
Rybnoye, *Russia* 42 C4
Rychwał, *Poland* 20 C8
Ryde, *U.K.* 13 G6
Ryderwood, *U.S.A.* 112 D3
Rydöbruk, *Sweden* 11 H7
Rydułtowy, *Poland* 20 E8
Rye, *U.K.* 13 G8
Rye →, *U.K.* 12 C7
Rye Patch Reservoir, *U.S.A.* 110 F4
Ryegate, *U.S.A.* 110 C9
Rylsk, *Russia* 42 E2
Rylstone, *Australia* 91 E4
Ryn Peski, *Kazakstan* 43 G9
Ryōthu, *Japan* 48 E9
Rypin, *Poland* 20 B9
Ryūgasaki, *Japan* 49 G10
Ryūkyū Is. = Ryūkyū-rettō, *Japan* 49 M2
Ryūkyū-rettō, *Japan* 49 M2
Rzeszów, *Poland* 20 E11
Rzhev, *Russia* 42 B2

S

Sa, *Thailand* 58 C3
Sa Dec, *Vietnam* 59 G5
Sa'ādatābād, *Fārs, Iran* 65 D7
Sa'ādatābād, *Kermān, Iran* 65 D7
Saale →, *Germany* 18 D7
Saaler Bodden, *Germany* 18 A8
Saalfeld, *Germany* 18 E7
Saane →, *Switz.* 22 B4
Saar →, *Europe* 25 C13
Saarbrücken, *Germany* 19 F2
Saarburg, *Germany* 19 F2
Saaremaa, *Estonia* 9 G20
Saarijärvi, *Finland* 9 E21
Saariselkä, *Finland* 8 B23
Saarland □, *Germany* 25 C13
Saarlouis, *Germany* 19 F2
Saas Fee, *Switz.* 22 D5
Sab 'Ābar, *Syria* 66 F7
Saba, *W. Indies* 117 C7
Šabac, *Serbia, Yug.* 21 L9
Sabadell, *Spain* 28 D7
Sabah □, *Malaysia* 56 C5
Sabak Bernam, *Malaysia* 59 L3
Sabalān, Kūhhā-ye, *Iran* 67 C12
Sábana de la Mar, *Dom. Rep.* 117 C6
Sábanalarga, *Colombia* 120 A3
Sabang, *Indonesia* 56 C1
Sabará, *Brazil* 123 E3
Sabattis, *U.S.A.* 107 B10
Sabáudia, *Italy* 34 A6
Sabaya, *Bolivia* 124 D4
Saberania, *Indonesia* 57 E9
Sabhah, *Libya* 73 C7
Sabie, *S. Africa* 85 D5
Sabinal, *Mexico* 114 A3
Sabinal, *U.S.A.* 109 L5
Sabinal, Punta del, *Spain* 29 J2
Sabinas, *Mexico* 114 B4
Sabinas →, *Mexico* 114 B4
Sabinas Hidalgo, *Mexico* 114 B4
Sabine →, *U.S.A.* 109 L8
Sabine L., *U.S.A.* 109 L8
Sabine Pass, *U.S.A.* 109 L8
Sabinópolis, *Brazil* 123 E3
Sabinov, *Slovak Rep.* 20 F11
Sabirabad, *Azerbaijan* 43 K9
Sabkhet el Bardawîl, *Egypt* 69 D2
Sablayan, *Phil.* 55 E4
Sable, C., *Canada* 99 D6
Sable, C., *U.S.A.* 103 E10
Sable I., *Canada* 99 D8
Sablé-sur-Sarthe, *France* 24 E6
Saboeiro, *Brazil* 122 C4
Sabor →, *Portugal* 30 D3
Sabou, *Burkina Faso* 78 C4
Sabrātah, *Libya* 75 B7
Sabria, *Tunisia* 75 B6
Sabrina Coast, *Antarctica* 5 C9
Sabugal, *Portugal* 30 E3
Sabulubek, *Indonesia* 56 E1
Sabzevār, *Iran* 65 B8
Sabzvārān, *Iran* 65 D8
Sac City, *U.S.A.* 108 D7
Sacedón, *Spain* 28 E2
Sachigo →, *Canada* 98 A2
Sachigo, L., *Canada* 98 B1
Sachkhere, *Georgia* 43 J6
Sachseln, *Switz.* 23 C6
Sachsen □, *Germany* 18 E9
Sachsen-Anhalt □, *Germany* 18 D8
Sacile, *Italy* 33 C9
Sackets Harbor, *U.S.A.* 107 C8
Saco, *Maine, U.S.A.* 105 D10
Saco, *Mont., U.S.A.* 110 B10
Sacramento, *Brazil* 123 E2
Sacramento, *U.S.A.* 112 G5
Sacramento →, *U.S.A.* 112 G5
Sacramento Mts., *U.S.A.* 111 K11
Sacramento Valley, *U.S.A.* 112 G5
Sacratif, C., *Spain* 29 J1
Săcueni, *Romania* 38 B5
Sada, *Spain* 30 B2
Sádaba, *Spain* 28 C3
Sadani, *Tanzania* 82 D4
Sadao, *Thailand* 59 J3
Sadd el Aali, *Egypt* 76 C3
Saddle Mt., *U.S.A.* 112 E3
Sade, *Nigeria* 79 C7
Sadimi, *Zaïre* 83 D1
Sa'dīyah, Hawr as, *Iraq* 67 F12
Sado, *Japan* 48 E9
Sado →, *Portugal* 31 G2
Sadon, *Burma* 61 G20
Sadon, *Russia* 43 J6
Sæby, *Denmark* 11 G4
Saegerstown, *U.S.A.* 106 E4
Saelices, *Spain* 28 F2
Safaga, *Egypt* 76 B3
Şafājah, *Si. Arabia* 64 E3
Säffle, *Sweden* 9 G15
Safford, *U.S.A.* 111 K9
Saffron Walden, *U.K.* 13 E8
Safi, *Morocco* 74 B3
Şafīābād, *Iran* 65 B8
Safīd Dasht, *Iran* 65 C6
Safīd Kūh, *Afghan.* 60 B3
Safonovo, *Russia* 40 E7
Safranbolu, *Turkey* 66 B5
Safwān, *Iraq* 64 D5
Sag Harbor, *U.S.A.* 107 F12
Saga, *Indonesia* 57 E8
Saga, *Japan* 49 H5
Saga □, *Japan* 49 H5
Sagae, *Japan* 48 E10
Sagala, *Mali* 78 C3
Sagar, *India* 60 M9
Sagara, L., *Tanzania* 82 D3
Sagay, *Phil.* 55 F5
Sagil, *Mongolia* 54 A4
Saginaw, *U.S.A.* 104 D4
Saginaw B., *U.S.A.* 104 D4
Şagīr, Zāb aş →, *Iraq* 67 E10
Sagleipie, *Liberia* 78 D3
Saglouc = Salluit, *Canada* 97 B12
Sagŏ-ri, *S. Korea* 51 G14
Sagone, *France* 27 F12
Sagone, G. de, *France* 27 F12
Sagres, *Portugal* 31 J2
Sagua la Grande, *Cuba* 116 B3
Saguache, *U.S.A.* 111 G10
Saguenay →, *Canada* 99 C5
Sagunto, *Spain* 28 F4
Sahaba, *Sudan* 76 D3
Sahagún, *Colombia* 120 B2
Sahagún, *Spain* 30 C5
Saḩam al Jawlān, *Syria* 69 C4
Sahand, Kūh-e, *Iran* 67 D12
Sahara, *Africa* 72 D5
Saharan Atlas = Saharien, Atlas, *Algeria* 75 B5
Saharanpur, *India* 62 E7
Saharien, Atlas, *Algeria* 75 B5
Sahasinaka, *Madag.* 85 C8
Sahaswan, *India* 63 E8
Sahel, Canal du, *Mali* 78 C3
Sahibganj, *India* 63 G12
Sāḩilīyah, *Iraq* 67 F10
Sahiwal, *Pakistan* 62 D5
Şaḩneh, *Iran* 67 E12
Sahtaneh →, *Canada* 100 B4
Sahuaripa, *Mexico* 114 B3
Sahuarita, *U.S.A.* 111 L8
Sahuayo, *Mexico* 114 C4
Sahy, *Slovak Rep.* 21 G8
Sai Buri, *Thailand* 59 J3
Sai-Cinza, *Brazil* 125 B6
Sa'id Bundas, *Sudan* 73 G9
Saïda, *Algeria* 75 B5
Sa'īdābād, *Kermān, Iran* 65 D7
Sa'īdābād, *Semnān, Iran* 65 B7
Saïdia, *Morocco* 75 A4
Sa'īdīyeh, *Iran* 65 B6
Saidpur, *Bangla.* 61 G16
Saidu, *Pakistan* 63 B5
Saignelégier, *Switz.* 22 B3

Saignes, *France* 26 C6
Saigon = Phanh Bho Ho Chi Minh, *Vietnam* 59 G6
Saijō, *Japan* 49 H6
Saikhoa Ghat, *India* 61 F19
Saiki, *Japan* 49 H5
Saillans, *France* 27 D9
Sailolof, *Indonesia* 57 E8
Saimaa, *Finland* 9 F23
Saimbeyli, *Turkey* 66 D7
Şa'in Dezh, *Iran* 67 D12
St. Abb's Head, *U.K.* 14 F6
St. Aegyd, *Austria* 21 H5
St.-Affrique, *France* 26 E6
St.-Agrève, *France* 27 C8
St.-Aignan, *France* 24 E8
St. Alban's, *Canada* 99 C8
St. Albans, *U.K.* 13 F7
St. Albans, *Vt., U.S.A.* 107 B11
St. Albans, *W. Va., U.S.A.* 104 F5
St. Alban's Head, *U.K.* 13 G5
St. Albert, *Canada* 100 C6
St.-Amand-en-Puisaye, *France* 25 E10
St.-Amand-les-Eaux, *France* 25 B10
St.-Amand-Mont-Rond, *France* 26 B6
St.-Amarin, *France* 25 E14
St.-Amour, *France* 27 B9
St.-André-de-Cubzac, *France* 26 D3
St.-André-de-l'Eure, *France* 24 D8
St.-André-les-Alpes, *France* 27 E10
St. Andrew's, *Canada* 99 C8
St. Andrews, *U.K.* 14 E6
St-Anicet, *Canada* 107 A10
St. Ann B., *Canada* 99 C7
St. Anne, *U.K.* 24 C4
St. Ann's Bay, *Jamaica* 116 C4
St. Anthony, *Canada* 99 B8
St. Anthony, *U.S.A.* 110 E8
St.-Antonin-Noble-Val, *France* 26 D5
St. Arnaud, *Australia* 91 F3
St. Arthur, *Canada* 99 C6
St. Asaph, *U.K.* 12 D4
St.-Astier, *France* 26 C4
St.-Aubin, *Switz.* 22 C3
St.-Aubin-du-Cormier, *France* 24 D5
St-Augustin-Saguenay, *Canada* 99 B8
St. Augustine, *U.S.A.* 105 L5
St. Austell, *U.K.* 13 G3
St.-Avold, *France* 25 C13
St.-Barthélemy, I., *W. Indies* 117 C7
St. Bees Hd., *U.K.* 12 C4
St.-Benoît-du-Sault, *France* 26 B5
St.-Bernard, Col du Grand, *Europe* 22 E4
St.-Bernard, Col du Petit, *France* 27 C10
St.-Blaise, *Switz.* 22 B3
St. Boniface, *Canada* 101 D9
St.-Bonnet, *France* 27 D10
St.-Brévin-les-Pins, *France* 24 E4
St.-Brice-en-Coglès, *France* 24 D5
St. Bride's, *Canada* 99 C9
St. Brides B., *U.K.* 13 F2
St.-Brieuc, *France* 24 D4
St.-Calais, *France* 24 E7
St.-Cast-le-Guildo, *France* 24 D4
St. Catharines, *Canada* 98 D4
St. Catherines I., *U.S.A.* 105 K5
St. Catherine's Pt., *U.K.* 13 G6
St.-Céré, *France* 26 D5
St.-Cergue, *Switz.* 22 D2
St.-Cernin, *France* 26 C6
St.-Chamond, *France* 27 C8
St. Charles, *Ill., U.S.A.* 104 E1
St. Charles, *Mo., U.S.A.* 108 F9
St.-Chély-d'Apcher, *France* 26 D7
St.-Chinian, *France* 26 E6
St. Christopher = St. Kitts, *W. Indies* 117 C7
St. Christopher-Nevis ■ = St. Kitts & Nevis ■, *W. Indies* 117 C7
St.-Ciers-sur-Gironde, *France* 26 C3
St. Clair, *Mich., U.S.A.* 106 D2
St. Clair, *Pa., U.S.A.* 107 F8
St. Clair, L., *Canada* 98 D3
St. Clairsville, *U.S.A.* 106 F4
St.-Claud, *France* 26 C4
St. Claude, *Canada* 101 D9
St.-Claude, *France* 27 B9
St. Cloud, *Fla., U.S.A.* 105 L5
St. Cloud, *Minn., U.S.A.* 108 C7
St-Coeur de Marie, *Canada* 99 C5
St. Cricq, C., *Australia* 89 E1
St. Croix, *Virgin Is.* 117 C7
St. Croix →, *U.S.A.* 108 C8
St. Croix Falls, *U.S.A.* 108 C8
St.-Cyr-sur-Mer, *France* 27 E9
St. David's, *Canada* 99 C8
St. David's, *U.K.* 13 F2
St. David's Head, *U.K.* 13 F2
St.-Denis, *France* 25 D9
St.-Denis-d'Orques, *France* 24 D6
St.-Dié, *France* 25 D13
St.-Dizier, *France* 25 D11
St.-Égrève, *France* 27 C9
St. Elias, Mt., *U.S.A.* 96 B5
St. Elias Mts., *Canada* 100 A1
St.-Élie, *Fr. Guiana* 121 C7
St.-Eloy-les-Mines, *France* 26 B6
St.-Émilion, *France* 26 D3
St.-Étienne, *France* 27 C8
St.-Étienne-de-Tinée, *France* 27 D10
St. Eugène, *Canada* 107 A10
St. Eustatius, *W. Indies* 117 C7
St-Félicien, *Canada* 98 C5
St.-Florent, *France* 27 F13
St.-Florent, G. de, *France* 27 F13
St.-Florent-sur-Cher, *France* 25 F9
St.-Florentin, *France* 25 D10
St.-Flour, *France* 26 C7
St.-Fons, *France* 27 C8
St. Francis, *U.S.A.* 108 F4
St. Francis →, *U.S.A.* 109 H9
St. Francis, C., *S. Africa* 84 E3
St. Francisville, *U.S.A.* 109 K9
St-François, L., *Canada* 107 A10
St.-Fulgent, *France* 24 F5
St-Gabriel-de-Brandon, *Canada* 98 C5
St. Gallen = Sankt Gallen, *Switz.* 23 B8
St.-Gaudens, *France* 26 E4
St.-Gengoux-le-National, *France* 27 B8
St.-Geniez-d'Olt, *France* 26 D6
St. George, *Australia* 91 D4
St. George, *Canada* 99 C6
St. George, *S.C., U.S.A.* 105 J5
St. George, *Utah, U.S.A.* 111 H7
St. George, C., *Canada* 99 C8
St. George, C., *U.S.A.* 105 L3
St. George Ra., *Australia* 88 C4
St-Georges, *Belgium* 17 G6
St. George's, *Canada* 99 C8
St-Georges, *Canada* 99 C5
St.-Georges, *Fr. Guiana* 121 C7
St. George's, *Grenada* 117 D7
St. George's B., *Canada* 99 C8
St. Georges Basin, *Australia* 88 C4
St. George's Channel, *Europe* 15 E6
St.-Georges-de-Didonne, *France* 26 C3
St. Georges Hd., *Australia* 91 F5
St.-Gérard, *Belgium* 17 H5
St.-Germain-de-Calberte, *France* 26 D7
St.-Germain-des-Fossés, *France* 26 B7
St.-Germain-du-Plain, *France* 25 F11
St.-Germain-en-Laye, *France* 25 D9
St.-Germain-Laval, *France* 27 C8
St.-Germain-Lembron, *France* 26 C7
St.-Gervais-d'Auvergne, *France* 26 B6
St.-Gervais-les-Bains, *France* 27 C10
St.-Gildas, Pte. de, *France* 24 E4
St.-Gilles, *France* 27 E8
St.-Gilles-Croix-de-Vie, *France* 26 B2
St.-Gingolph, *Switz.* 22 D3
St.-Girons, *France* 26 F5
St. Gotthard P. = San Gottardo, P. del, *Switz.* 23 C7
St.-Gualtier, *France* 24 F8
St.-Guénolé, *France* 24 E2
St. Helena, *U.S.A.* 110 G2
St. Helena ■, *Atl. Oc.* 71 H3
St. Helena, Mt., *U.S.A.* 112 G4
St. Helena B., *S. Africa* 84 E2
St. Helens, *Australia* 90 G4
St. Helens, *U.K.* 12 D5
St. Helens, *U.S.A.* 112 E4
St. Helens, Mt., *U.S.A.* 112 D4
St. Helier, *U.K.* 13 H5
St.-Hilaire-du-Harcouët, *France* 24 D5
St.-Hippolyte, *France* 25 E13
St.-Hippolyte-du-Fort, *France* 26 E7
St.-Honoré-les-Bains, *France* 25 F10
St-Hubert, *Belgium* 17 H6
St-Hyacinthe, *Canada* 98 C5
St. Ignace, *U.S.A.* 104 C3
St. Ignace I., *Canada* 98 C2
St. Ignatius, *U.S.A.* 110 C6
St-Imier, *Switz.* 22 B3
St. Ives, *Cambs., U.K.* 13 E7
St. Ives, *Corn., U.K.* 13 G2
St.-James, *France* 24 D5
St. James, *U.S.A.* 108 D7
St-Jean, *Canada* 98 C5
St-Jean →, *Canada* 99 B7
St-Jean, L., *Canada* 99 C5
St. Jean Baptiste, *Canada* 101 D9
St.-Jean-d'Angély, *France* 26 C3
St.-Jean-de-Bournay, *France* 27 C9
St.-Jean-de-Luz, *France* 26 E2
St.-Jean-de-Maurienne, *France* 27 C10
St.-Jean-de-Monts, *France* 24 F4
St.-Jean-du-Gard, *France* 26 D7
St.-Jean-en-Royans, *France* 27 C9
St-Jean-Port-Joli, *Canada* 99 C5
St-Jérôme, *Qué., Canada* 98 C5
St-Jérôme, *Qué., Canada* 99 C5
St. John, *Canada* 99 C6
St. John, *Kans., U.S.A.* 109 G5
St. John, *N. Dak., U.S.A.* 108 A5
St. John →, *U.S.A.* 99 C6
St. John, C., *Canada* 99 B8
St. John's, *Antigua* 117 C7
St. John's, *Canada* 99 C9
St. Johns, *Ariz., U.S.A.* 111 J9
St. Johns, *Mich., U.S.A.* 104 D3
St. Johns →, *U.S.A.* 105 K5
St. Johnsbury, *U.S.A.* 107 B12
St. Johnsville, *U.S.A.* 107 C10
St. Joseph, *La., U.S.A.* 109 K9
St. Joseph, *Mich., U.S.A.* 104 D2
St. Joseph, *Mo., U.S.A.* 108 F7
St. Joseph →, *U.S.A.* 104 D2
St. Joseph, I., *Canada* 98 C3
St. Joseph, L., *Canada* 98 B1
St-Jovite, *Canada* 98 C5
St.-Juéry, *France* 26 E6
St.-Julien-Chapteuil, *France* 27 C8
St.-Julien-du-Sault, *France* 25 D10
St.-Julien-en-Genevois, *France* 27 B10
St.-Junien, *France* 26 C4
St.-Just-en-Chaussée, *France* 25 C9
St.-Just-en-Chevalet, *France* 26 C7
St.-Justin, *France* 26 E3
St. Kilda, *N.Z.* 87 L3
St. Kitts, *W. Indies* 117 C7
St. Kitts & Nevis ■, *W. Indies* 117 C7
St. Laurent, *Canada* 101 C9
St.-Laurent, *Fr. Guiana* 121 B7
St.-Laurent-du-Pont, *France* 27 C9
St.-Laurent-en-Grandvaux, *France* 27 B9
St. Lawrence, *Australia* 90 C4
St. Lawrence, *Canada* 99 C8
St. Lawrence →, *Canada* 99 C6
St. Lawrence, Gulf of, *Canada* 99 C7
St. Lawrence I., *U.S.A.* 96 B3
St.-Léger, *Belgium* 17 J7
St. Leonard, *Canada* 99 C6
St.-Léonard-de-Noblat, *France* 26 C5
St. Lewis →, *Canada* 99 B8
St.-Lô, *France* 24 C5
St-Louis, *Senegal* 78 B1
St. Louis, *Mich., U.S.A.* 104 D3
St. Louis, *Mo., U.S.A.* 108 F9
St. Louis →, *U.S.A.* 108 B8
St.-Loup-sur-Semouse, *France* 25 E13
St. Lucia ■, *W. Indies* 117 D7
St. Lucia, L., *S. Africa* 85 D5
St. Lucia Channel, *W. Indies* 117 D7
St. Lunaire-Griquet, *Canada* 99 B8
St. Maarten, *W. Indies* 117 C7
St.-Maixent-l'École, *France* 26 B3
St.-Malo, *France* 24 D4
St.-Malo, G. de, *France* 24 D4
St.-Mandrier-sur-Mer, *France* 27 E9
St-Marc, *Haiti* 117 C5
St.-Marcellin, *France* 27 C9
St.-Marcouf, Is., *France* 24 C5
St. Maries, *U.S.A.* 110 C5
St-Martin, *W. Indies* 117 C7
St. Martin, L., *Canada* 101 C9
St.-Martin-de-Ré, *France* 26 B2
St.-Martin-Vésubie, *France* 27 D11
St. Martins, *Canada* 99 C6
St. Martinville, *U.S.A.* 109 K9
St.-Martory, *France* 26 E4
St. Mary Pk., *Australia* 91 E2
St. Marys, *Australia* 90 G4
St. Marys, *Canada* 106 C3
St. Mary's, *U.K.* 13 H1
St. Marys, *U.S.A.* 106 E6
St. Mary's, C., *Canada* 99 C9
St. Mary's B., *Canada* 99 C9
St. Marys Bay, *Canada* 99 D6
St.-Mathieu, Pte., *France* 24 D2
St. Matthews, I. = Zadetkyi Kyun, *Burma* 59 H2
St.-Maur-des-Fossés, *France* 25 D9
St. Maurice, *Switz.* 22 D4
St-Maurice →, *Canada* 98 C5
St.-Médard-de-Guizières, *France* 26 C3
St.-Méen-le-Grand, *France* 24 D4
St. Michael's Mount, *U.K.* 13 G2
St.-Michel-de-Maurienne, *France* 27 C10
St.-Mihiel, *France* 25 D12
St.-Nazaire, *France* 24 E4
St. Neots, *U.K.* 13 E7
St.-Nicolas-de-Port, *France* 25 D13
St. Niklass = Sint Niklaas, *Belgium* 17 F4
St. Niklaus, *Switz.* 22 D5
St.-Omer, *France* 25 B9
St-Pacome, *Canada* 99 C6
St.-Palais-sur-Mer, *France* 26 C2
St-Pamphile, *Canada* 99 C6
St.-Pardoux-la-Rivière, *France* 26 C4
St. Pascal, *Canada* 99 C6
St. Paul, *Canada* 100 C6
St. Paul, *Minn., U.S.A.* 108 C8
St. Paul, *Nebr., U.S.A.* 108 E5
St. Paul, I., *Ind. Oc.* 3 F13
St.-Paul-de-Fenouillet, *France* 26 F6
St. Paul I., *Canada* 99 C7
St.-Paul-lès-Dax, *France* 26 E2
St.-Péray, *France* 27 D8
St.-Père-en-Retz, *France* 24 E4
St. Peter, *U.S.A.* 108 C8
St-Peter-Ording, *Germany* 18 A4
St. Peter Port, *U.K.* 13 H5
St. Peters, *N.S., Canada* 99 C7
St. Peters, *P.E.I., Canada* 99 C7
St. Petersburg = Sankt-Peterburg, *Russia* 40 C6
St. Petersburg, *U.S.A.* 105 M4
St.-Philbert-de-Grand-Lieu, *France* 24 E5
St.-Pierre, *St- P. & M.* 99 C8
St-Pierre, L., *Canada* 98 C5
St.-Pierre-d'Oléron, *France* 26 C2
St.-Pierre-Église, *France* 24 C5
St.-Pierre-en-Port, *France* 24 C7
St.-Pierre et Miquelon □, *St- P. & M.* 99 C8
St.-Pierre-le-Moûtier, *France* 25 F10
St.-Pierre-sur-Dives, *France* 24 C6
St-Pieters Leew, *Belgium* 17 G4
St.-Pol-de-Léon, *France* 24 D2
St.-Pol-sur-Mer, *France* 25 A9
St.-Pol-sur-Ternoise, *France* 25 B9
St.-Pons, *France* 26 E6
St.-Pourçain-sur-Sioule, *France* 26 B7
St.-Quay-Portrieux, *France* 24 D4
St.-Quentin, *France* 25 C10
St.-Rambert-d'Albon, *France* 27 C8
St.-Raphaël, *France* 27 E10
St. Regis, *U.S.A.* 110 C6
St.-Rémy-de-Provence, *France* 27 E8
St.-Renan, *France* 24 D2
St.-Saëns, *France* 24 C8
St.-Sauveur-en-Puisaye, *France* 25 E10
St.-Sauveur-le-Vicomte, *France* 24 C5
St.-Savin, *France* 26 B4
St.-Savinien, *France* 26 C3
St. Sebastien, Tanjon' i, *Madag.* 85 A8
St.-Seine-l'Abbaye, *France* 25 E11
St.-Sernin-sur-Rance, *France* 26 E6
St.-Servan-sur-Mer, *France* 24 D4
St.-Sever, *France* 26 E3
St.-Sever-Calvados, *France* 24 D5
St-Siméon, *Canada* 99 C6
St. Stephen, *Canada* 99 C6
St.-Sulpice, *France* 26 E5
St.-Sulpice-Laurière, *France* 26 B5
St.-Syprien, *France* 26 F7
St.-Thégonnec, *France* 24 D3
St. Thomas, *Canada* 98 D3
St. Thomas I., *Virgin Is.* 117 C7
St-Tite, *Canada* 98 C5
St.-Tropez, *France* 27 E10
St. Troud = Sint Truiden, *Belgium* 17 G6
St.-Vaast-la-Hougue, *France* 24 C5
St.-Valéry-en-Caux, *France* 24 C7
St.-Valéry-sur-Somme, *France* 25 B8
St.-Vallier, *France* 27 C8
St.-Vallier-de-Thiey, *France* 27 E10
St.-Varent, *France* 24 F6
St. Vincent, *W. Indies* 117 D7
St. Vincent, G., *Australia* 91 F2
St. Vincent & the Grenadines ■, *W. Indies* 117 D7
St.-Vincent-de-Tyrosse, *France* 26 E2
St. Vincent Passage, *W. Indies* 117 D7
St-Vith, *Belgium* 17 H8
St.-Yrieix-la-Perche, *France* 26 C5
Ste.-Adresse, *France* 24 C7
Ste-Agathe-des-Monts, *Canada* 98 C5
Ste-Anne de Beaupré, *Canada* 99 C5
Ste-Anne-des-Monts, *Canada* 99 C6
Ste-Croix, *Switz.* 22 C3
Ste.-Enimie, *France* 26 D7
Ste.-Foy-la-Grande, *France* 26 D4
Ste. Genevieve, *U.S.A.* 108 G9
Ste.-Hermine, *France* 26 B2
Ste.-Livrade-sur-Lot, *France* 26 D4
Ste-Marguerite →, *Canada* 99 B6
Ste.-Marie, *Martinique* 117 D7
Ste.-Marie-aux-Mines, *France* 25 D14
Ste-Marie de la Madeleine, *Canada* 99 C5
Ste.-Maure-de-Touraine, *France* 24 E7
Ste.-Maxime, *France* 27 E10
Ste.-Menehould, *France* 25 C11
Ste.-Mère-Église, *France* 24 C5
Ste.-Rose, *Guadeloupe* 117 C7
Ste. Rose du Lac, *Canada* 101 C9
Saintes, *France* 26 C3
Saintes, I. des, *Guadeloupe* 117 C7
Stes.-Maries-de-la-Mer, *France* 27 E8
Saintonge, *France* 26 C3
Saipan, *Pac. Oc.* 92 F6
Sairang, *India* 61 H18
Sairecábur, Cerro, *Bolivia* 126 A2
Saitama □, *Japan* 49 F9
Sajama, *Bolivia* 124 D4
Sajum, *India* 63 C8
Sak →, *S. Africa* 84 E3
Sakai, *Japan* 49 G7
Sakaide, *Japan* 49 G6
Sakaiminato, *Japan* 49 G6
Sakākah, *Si. Arabia* 64 D4
Sakakawea, L., *U.S.A.* 108 B3
Sakami, L., *Canada* 98 B4
Sâkâne, 'Erg i-n, *Mali* 74 D4
Sakania, *Zaïre* 83 E2
Sakarya = Adapazarı, *Turkey* 66 B4
Sakarya →, *Turkey* 66 B4
Sakashima-Guntō, *Japan* 49 M2
Sakata, *Japan* 48 E9
Sakchu, *N. Korea* 51 D13
Sakeny →, *Madag.* 85 C8
Sakété, *Benin* 79 D5
Sakha □, *Russia* 45 C13
Sakhalin, *Russia* 45 D15
Sakhalinskiy Zaliv, *Russia* 45 D15
Şaki, *Azerbaijan* 43 K8
Šakiai, *Lithuania* 9 J20
Sakon Nakhon, *Thailand* 58 D5
Sakrand, *Pakistan* 62 F3
Sakrivier, *S. Africa* 84 E3
Sakskøbing, *Denmark* 11 K5
Sakuma, *Japan* 49 G8
Sakurai, *Japan* 49 G7
Saky, *Ukraine* 41 K7
Sal →, *Russia* 43 G5
Sala, *Sweden* 9 G17
Sala Consilina, *Italy* 35 B8
Sala-y-Gómez, *Pac. Oc.* 93 K17
Salaberry-de-Valleyfield, *Canada* 98 C5
Saladas, *Argentina* 126 B4
Saladillo, *Argentina* 126 D4
Salado →, *Buenos Aires, Argentina* 126 D4
Salado →, *La Pampa, Argentina* 128 A3
Salado →, *Río Negro, Argentina* 128 B3
Salado →, *Santa Fe, Argentina* 126 C3
Salado →, *Mexico* 114 B5
Salaga, *Ghana* 79 D4
Sālah, *Syria* 69 C5
Sálakhos, *Greece* 37 C9
Salala, *Liberia* 78 D2
Salala, *Sudan* 76 C4
Salālah, *Oman* 68 D5
Salamanca, *Chile* 126 C1
Salamanca, *Spain* 30 E5
Salamanca, *U.S.A.* 106 D6
Salamanca □, *Spain* 30 E5
Salāmatābād, *Iran* 64 C5
Salamina, *Colombia* 120 B2
Salamis, *Cyprus* 37 D12
Salamís, *Greece* 39 M6
Salar de Atacama, *Chile* 126 A2
Salar de Uyuni, *Bolivia* 124 E4
Sălard, *Romania* 38 B5
Salas, *Spain* 30 B4
Salas de los Infantes, *Spain* 28 C1
Salatiga, *Indonesia* 57 G14
Salaverry, *Peru* 124 B2
Salawati, *Indonesia* 57 E8
Salayar, *Indonesia* 57 F6
Salazar →, *Spain* 28 C3
Salbris, *France* 25 E9
Salcombe, *U.K.* 13 G4
Saldaña, *Spain* 30 C6
Saldanha, *S. Africa* 84 E2
Saldanha B., *S. Africa* 84 E2
Saldus, *Latvia* 9 H20
Sale, *Australia* 91 F4
Salé, *Morocco* 74 B3
Sale, *U.K.* 12 D5
Salekhard, *Russia* 44 C7
Salem, *India* 60 P11
Salem, *Ind., U.S.A.* 104 F2
Salem, *Mass., U.S.A.* 107 D14
Salem, *Mo., U.S.A.* 109 G9
Salem, *N.J., U.S.A.* 104 F8
Salem, *Ohio, U.S.A.* 106 F4
Salem, *Oreg., U.S.A.* 110 D2
Salem, *S. Dak., U.S.A.* 108 D6
Salem, *Va., U.S.A.* 104 G5
Salemi, *Italy* 34 E5
Salernes, *France* 27 E10
Salerno, *Italy* 35 B7
Salerno, G. di, *Italy* 35 B7
Salford, *U.K.* 12 D5
Salgir →, *Ukraine* 41 K8
Salgótarján, *Hungary* 21 G9
Salgueiro, *Brazil* 122 C4
Salida, *U.S.A.* 102 C5
Salies-de-Béarn, *France* 26 E3
Salihli, *Turkey* 66 C3
Salihorsk, *Belarus* 41 F4
Salima, *Malawi* 81 G6
Salina, *Italy* 35 D7
Salina, *U.S.A.* 108 F6
Salina Cruz, *Mexico* 115 D5
Salinas, *Brazil* 123 E3
Salinas, *Chile* 126 A2
Salinas, *Ecuador* 120 D1

Salinas, *U.S.A.* 111 H3
Salinas →, *Guatemala* 115 D6
Salinas →, *U.S.A.* 111 H3
Salinas, B. de, *Nic.* 116 D2
Salinas, C. de, *Spain* 36 B10
Salinas, Pampa de las, *Argentina* 126 C2
Salinas Ambargasta, *Argentina* 126 B3
Salinas de Hidalgo, *Mexico* 114 C4
Salinas Grandes, *Argentina* 126 B2
Saline →, *Ark., U.S.A.* 109 J8
Saline →, *Kans., U.S.A.* 108 F6
Salines, *Spain* 36 B10
Salinópolis, *Brazil* 122 B2
Salins-les-Bains, *France* 25 F12
Salir, *Portugal* 31 H2
Salisbury = Harare, *Zimbabwe* 83 F3
Salisbury, *Australia* 91 E2
Salisbury, *U.K.* 13 F6
Salisbury, *Md., U.S.A.* 104 F8
Salisbury, *N.C., U.S.A.* 105 H5
Salisbury Plain, *U.K.* 13 F6
Săliște, *Romania* 38 D6
Salitre →, *Brazil* 122 C3
Salka, *Nigeria* 79 C5
Şalkhad, *Syria* 69 C5
Salla, *Finland* 8 C23
Sallent, *Spain* 28 D6
Salles-Curan, *France* 26 D6
Salling, *Denmark* 11 H2
Sallisaw, *U.S.A.* 109 H7
Sallom Junction, *Sudan* 76 D4
Salluit, *Canada* 97 B12
Salmās, *Iran* 67 C11
Salmerón, *Spain* 28 E2
Salmo, *Canada* 100 D5
Salmon, *U.S.A.* 110 D7
Salmon →, *Canada* 100 C4
Salmon →, *U.S.A.* 110 D5
Salmon Arm, *Canada* 100 C5
Salmon Falls, *U.S.A.* 110 E6
Salmon Gums, *Australia* 89 F3
Salmon Res., *Canada* 99 C8
Salmon River Mts., *U.S.A.* 110 D6
Salo, *Finland* 9 F20
Salò, *Italy* 32 C7
Salobreña, *Spain* 31 J7
Salome, *U.S.A.* 113 M13
Salon-de-Provence, *France* 27 E9
Salonica = Thessaloníki, *Greece* 39 J5
Salonta, *Romania* 38 C4
Salor →, *Spain* 31 F3
Salou, C., *Spain* 28 D6
Salpausselkä, *Finland* 9 F22
Salsacate, *Argentina* 126 C2
Salses, *France* 26 F6
Salsk, *Russia* 43 G5
Salso →, *Italy* 34 E6
Salsomaggiore Terme, *Italy* 32 D6
Salt →, *Canada* 100 B6
Salt →, *U.S.A.* 111 K7
Salt Creek, *Australia* 91 F2
Salt Fork Arkansas →, *U.S.A.* 109 G6
Salt Lake City, *U.S.A.* 110 F8
Salt Range, *Pakistan* 62 C5
Salta, *Argentina* 126 A2
Salta □, *Argentina* 126 A2
Saltcoats, *U.K.* 14 F4
Saltee Is., *Ireland* 15 D5
Saltfjellet, *Norway* 8 C16
Saltfjorden, *Norway* 8 C16
Saltholm, *Denmark* 11 J6
Saltillo, *Mexico* 114 B4
Salto, *Argentina* 126 C3
Salto, *Uruguay* 126 C4
Salto da Divisa, *Brazil* 123 E4
Salton City, *U.S.A.* 113 M11
Salton Sea, *U.S.A.* 113 M11
Saltpond, *Ghana* 79 D4
Saltsjöbaden, *Sweden* 10 E12
Saltville, *U.S.A.* 104 G5
Saluda →, *U.S.A.* 105 H5
Salûm, *Egypt* 76 A2
Salûm, Khâlig el, *Egypt* 76 A2
Salur, *India* 61 K13
Salut, Is. du, *Fr. Guiana* 121 B7
Saluzzo, *Italy* 32 D4
Salvación, B., *Chile* 128 D1
Salvador, *Brazil* 123 D4
Salvador, *Canada* 101 C7
Salvador, L., *U.S.A.* 109 L9
Salvaterra, *Brazil* 122 B2
Salvaterra de Magos, *Portugal* 31 F2
Sálvora, I., *Spain* 30 C2
Salween →, *Burma* 61 L20
Salyan, *Azerbaijan* 67 C13
Salyersville, *U.S.A.* 104 G4
Salza →, *Austria* 21 H4
Salzach →, *Austria* 21 G2
Salzburg, *Austria* 21 H3
Salzgitter, *Germany* 18 C6
Salzwedel, *Germany* 18 C7
Sam Neua, *Laos* 58 B5
Sam Ngao, *Thailand* 58 D2
Sam Rayburn Reservoir, *U.S.A.* 109 K7
Sam Son, *Vietnam* 58 C5
Sam Teu, *Laos* 58 C5
Sama, *Russia* 44 C7
Sama de Langreo, *Spain* 30 B5
Samagaltay, *Russia* 45 D10
Samaipata, *Bolivia* 125 D5
Samales Group, *Phil.* 55 J4
Samâlût, *Egypt* 76 J7
Samana, *India* 62 D7
Samana Cay, *Bahamas* 117 B5
Samandağı, *Turkey* 66 D6
Samanga, *Tanzania* 83 D4
Samangwa, *Zaïre* 82 C1
Samani, *Japan* 48 C11
Samar, *Phil.* 55 F6
Samara, *Russia* 42 D10
Samara →, *Russia* 42 D10
Samara →, *Ukraine* 41 H8
Samaria = Shōmrōn, *West Bank* 69 C4
Samariá, *Greece* 37 D5
Samarinda, *Indonesia* 56 E5
Samarkand = Samarqand, *Uzbekistan* 44 F7
Samarqand, *Uzbekistan* 44 F7
Sāmarrā, *Iraq* 67 E10
Samastipur, *India* 63 G11
Samatan, *France* 26 E4
Samaúma, *Brazil* 125 B5
Şamaxi, *Azerbaijan* 43 K9
Samba, *India* 63 C6
Samba, *Zaïre* 82 C2
Sambaíba, *Brazil* 122 C2
Sambalpur, *India* 61 J14
Sambar, Tanjung, *Indonesia* 56 E4
Sambas, *Indonesia* 56 D3
Sambava, *Madag.* 85 A9
Sambawizi, *Zimbabwe* 83 F2
Sambhal, *India* 63 E8
Sambhar, *India* 62 F6
Sambiase, *Italy* 35 D9
Sambir, *Ukraine* 41 H2
Sambonifacio, *Italy* 32 C8
Sambor, *Cambodia* 58 F6
Sambre →, *Europe* 17 H5
Sambuca di Sicília, *Italy* 34 E6
Samburu □, *Kenya* 82 B4
Samchŏk, *S. Korea* 51 F15
Samchonpo, *S. Korea* 51 G15
Same, *Tanzania* 82 C4
Samedan, *Switz.* 23 C9
Samer, *France* 25 B8
Samfya, *Zambia* 83 E2
Sámi, *Greece* 39 L3
Şämkir, *Azerbaijan* 43 K8
Samnah, *Si. Arabia* 64 E3
Samnaun, *Switz.* 23 C10
Samo Alto, *Chile* 126 C1
Samobor, *Croatia* 33 C12
Samoëns, *France* 27 B10
Samokov, *Bulgaria* 38 G6
Samoorombón, B., *Argentina* 126 D4
Samorogouan, *Burkina Faso* 78 C4
Sámos, *Greece* 39 M9
Samoš, *Serbia, Yug.* 21 K10
Samos, *Spain* 30 C3
Samothráki, *Évros, Greece* 39 J8
Samothráki, *Kérkira, Greece* 37 A3
Samoylovka, *Russia* 42 E6
Sampa, *Ghana* 78 D4
Sampacho, *Argentina* 126 C3
Sampang, *Indonesia* 57 G15
Samper de Calanda, *Spain* 28 D4
Sampit, *Indonesia* 56 E4
Sampit, Teluk, *Indonesia* 56 E4
Samrée, *Belgium* 17 H7
Samrong, *Cambodia* 58 E4
Samrong, *Thailand* 58 E3
Samsø, *Denmark* 11 J4
Samsø Bælt, *Denmark* 11 J4
Samsun, *Turkey* 66 B7
Samtredia, *Georgia* 43 J6
Samui, Ko, *Thailand* 59 H3
Samur →, *Russia* 43 K9
Samurskiy Khrebet, *Russia* 43 K8
Samusole, *Zaïre* 83 E1
Samut Prakan, *Thailand* 58 F3
Samut Sakhon, *Thailand* 58 F3
Samut Songkhram →, *Thailand* 58 F3
Samwari, *Pakistan* 62 E2
San, *Mali* 78 C4
San →, *Cambodia* 58 F5
San →, *Poland* 20 E11
San Adrián, C. de, *Spain* 30 B2
San Agustín, *Colombia* 120 C2
San Agustin, C., *Phil.* 55 H7
San Agustín de Valle Fértil, *Argentina* 126 C2
San Ambrosio, *Pac. Oc.* 118 F3
San Andreas, *U.S.A.* 112 G6
San Andrés, I. de, *Caribbean* 116 D3
San Andres Mts., *U.S.A.* 111 K10
San Andrés Tuxtla, *Mexico* 115 D5
San Angelo, *U.S.A.* 109 K4
San Anselmo, *U.S.A.* 112 H4
San Antonio, *Belize* 115 D7
San Antonio, *Chile* 126 C1
San Antonio, *Phil.* 55 D4
San Antonio, *Spain* 36 C7
San Antonio, *N. Mex., U.S.A.* 111 K10
San Antonio, *Tex., U.S.A.* 109 L5
San Antonio, *Venezuela* 120 C4
San Antonio →, *U.S.A.* 109 L6
San Antonio, C., *Argentina* 126 D4
San Antonio, C., *Cuba* 116 B3
San Antonio, C. de, *Spain* 29 G5
San Antonio, Mt., *U.S.A.* 113 L9
San Antonio de los Baños, *Cuba* 116 B3
San Antonio de los Cobres, *Argentina* 126 A2
San Antonio Oeste, *Argentina* 128 B4
San Arcángelo, *Italy* 35 B9
San Ardo, *U.S.A.* 112 J6
San Augustín, *Canary Is.* 36 G4
San Augustine, *U.S.A.* 109 K7
San Bartolomé, *Canary Is.* 36 F6
San Bartolomé de Tirajana, *Canary Is.* 36 G4
San Bartolomeo in Galdo, *Italy* 35 A8
San Benedetto del Tronto, *Italy* 33 F10
San Benedetto Po, *Italy* 32 C7
San Benedicto, I., *Mexico* 114 D2
San Benito, *U.S.A.* 109 M6
San Benito →, *U.S.A.* 112 J5
San Benito Mt., *U.S.A.* 112 J6
San Bernardino, *U.S.A.* 113 L9
San Bernardino, Paso del, *Switz.* 23 D8
San Bernardino Mts., *U.S.A.* 113 L10
San Bernardino Str., *Phil.* 55 E6
San Bernardo, *Chile* 126 C1
San Bernardo, I. de, *Colombia* 120 B2
San Blas, *Mexico* 114 B3
San Blas, Arch. de, *Panama* 116 E4
San Blas, C., *U.S.A.* 105 L3
San Borja, *Bolivia* 124 C4
San Buenaventura, *Bolivia* 124 C4
San Buenaventura, *Mexico* 114 B4
San Carlos = Butuku-Luba, *Eq. Guin.* 79 E6
San Carlos, *Argentina* 126 C2
San Carlos, *Bolivia* 125 D5
San Carlos, *Chile* 126 D1
San Carlos, *Mexico* 114 B4
San Carlos, *Nic.* 116 D3
San Carlos, *Negros, Phil.* 55 F5
San Carlos, *Pangasinan, Phil.* 55 D4
San Carlos, *Spain* 36 B8
San Carlos, *Uruguay* 127 C5
San Carlos, *U.S.A.* 111 K8
San Carlos, *Amazonas, Venezuela* 120 C4
San Carlos, *Cojedes, Venezuela* 120 B4
San Carlos de Bariloche, *Argentina* 128 B2
San Carlos de la Rápita, *Spain* 28 E5
San Carlos del Zulia, *Venezuela* 120 B3
San Carlos L., *U.S.A.* 111 K8
San Cataldo, *Italy* 34 E6
San Celoni, *Spain* 28 D7
San Clemente, *Chile* 126 D1
San Clemente, *Spain* 29 F2
San Clemente, *U.S.A.* 113 M9
San Clemente I., *U.S.A.* 113 N8
San Costanzo, *Italy* 33 E10
San Cristóbal, *Argentina* 126 C3
San Cristóbal, *Colombia* 120 D3
San Cristóbal, *Dom. Rep.* 117 C5
San Cristóbal, *Mexico* 115 D6
San Cristóbal, *Spain* 36 B11
San Cristóbal, *Venezuela* 120 B3
San Damiano d'Asti, *Italy* 32 D5
San Daniele del Friuli, *Italy* 33 B10
San Demétrio Corone, *Italy* 35 C9
San Diego, *Calif., U.S.A.* 113 N9
San Diego, *Tex., U.S.A.* 109 M5
San Diego, C., *Argentina* 128 D3
San Diego de la Unión, *Mexico* 114 C4
San Dimitri, Ras, *Malta* 37 C1
San Doná di Piave, *Italy* 33 C9
San Elpídio a Mare, *Italy* 33 E10
San Estanislao, *Paraguay* 126 A4
San Esteban de Gormaz, *Spain* 28 D1
San Felice sul Panaro, *Italy* 32 D8
San Felipe, *Chile* 126 C1
San Felipe, *Colombia* 120 C4
San Felipe, *Mexico* 114 A2
San Felipe, *Venezuela* 120 A4
San Felipe →, *U.S.A.* 113 M11
San Felíu de Guíxols, *Spain* 28 D8
San Felíu de Llobregat, *Spain* 28 D7
San Félix, *Pac. Oc.* 118 F2
San Fernando, *Chile* 126 C1
San Fernando, *Mexico* 114 B1
San Fernando, *La Union, Phil.* 55 C4
San Fernando, *Pampanga, Phil.* 55 D4
San Fernando, *Baleares, Spain* 36 C7
San Fernando, *Cádiz, Spain* 31 J4
San Fernando, *Trin. & Tob.* 117 D7
San Fernando, *U.S.A.* 113 L8
San Fernando →, *Mexico* 114 C5
San Fernando de Apure, *Venezuela* 120 B4
San Fernando de Atabapo, *Venezuela* 120 C4
San Fernando di Púglia, *Italy* 35 A9
San Francisco, *Argentina* 126 C3
San Francisco, *Bolivia* 125 D4
San Francisco, *U.S.A.* 111 H2
San Francisco →, *U.S.A.* 111 K9
San Francisco, Paso de, *S. Amer.* 126 B2
San Francisco de Macorîs, *Dom. Rep.* 117 C5
San Francisco del Monte de Oro, *Argentina* 126 C2
San Francisco del Oro, *Mexico* 114 B3
San Francisco Javier, *Spain* 36 C7
San Francisco Solano, Pta., *Colombia* 120 B2
San Fratello, *Italy* 35 D7
San Gabriel, *Ecuador* 120 C2
San Gavino Monreale, *Italy* 34 C1
San Gil, *Colombia* 120 B3
San Gimignano, *Italy* 32 E8
San Giórgio di Nogaro, *Italy* 33 C10
San Giórgio Iónico, *Italy* 35 B10
San Giovanni Bianco, *Italy* 32 C6
San Giovanni in Fiore, *Italy* 35 C9
San Giovanni in Persiceto, *Italy* 33 D8
San Giovanni Rotondo, *Italy* 35 A8
San Giovanni Valdarno, *Italy* 33 E8
San Giuliano Terme, *Italy* 32 E7
San Gorgonio Mt., *U.S.A.* 113 L10
San Gottardo, P. del, *Switz.* 23 C7
San Gregorio, *Uruguay* 127 C4
San Gregorio, *U.S.A.* 112 H4
San Guiseppe Iato, *Italy* 34 E6
San Ignacio, *Belize* 115 D7
San Ignacio, *Bolivia* 125 D5
San Ignacio, *Mexico* 114 B2
San Ignacio, *Paraguay* 126 B4
San Ignacio, L., *Mexico* 114 B2
San Ildefonso, C., *Phil.* 55 C5
San Isidro, *Argentina* 126 C4
San Jacinto, *Colombia* 120 B2
San Jacinto, *U.S.A.* 113 M10
San Jaime, *Spain* 36 B11
San Javier, *Misiones, Argentina* 127 B4
San Javier, *Santa Fe, Argentina* 126 C4
San Javier, *Beni, Bolivia* 125 C5
San Javier, *Santa Cruz, Bolivia* 125 D5
San Javier, *Chile* 126 D1
San Javier, *Spain* 29 H4
San Jerónimo, Sa. de, *Colombia* 120 B2
San Jeronimo Taviche, *Mexico* 115 D5
San Joaquín, *Bolivia* 125 C5
San Joaquin, *U.S.A.* 112 J6
San Joaquín, *Venezuela* 120 A4
San Joaquín →, *Bolivia* 125 C5
San Joaquin →, *U.S.A.* 111 G3
San Joaquin Valley, *U.S.A.* 112 J6
San Jordi, *Spain* 36 B9
San Jorge, *Argentina* 126 C3
San Jorge, *Spain* 36 C7
San Jorge, B. de, *Mexico* 114 A2
San Jorge, G., *Argentina* 128 C3
San Jorge, G. de, *Spain* 28 E4
San Jorge, G. of, *Argentina* 118 H4
San José, *Bolivia* 125 D5
San José, *Costa Rica* 116 E3
San José, *Guatemala* 116 D1
San José, *Mexico* 114 C2
San Jose, *Phil.* 55 D4
San José, *Spain* 36 C7
San Jose, *U.S.A.* 111 H3
San Jose →, *U.S.A.* 111 J10
San Jose de Buenovista, *Phil.* 55 E4
San José de Feliciano, *Argentina* 126 C4
San José de Jáchal, *Argentina* 126 C2
San José de Mayo, *Uruguay* 126 C4
San José de Ocune, *Colombia* 120 C3
San José de Uchapiamonas, *Bolivia* 124 C4
San José del Cabo, *Mexico* 114 C3
San José del Guaviare, *Colombia* 120 C3
San José do Anauá, *Brazil* 121 C5
San Juan, *Argentina* 126 C2
San Juan, *Colombia* 120 B2
San Juan, *Mexico* 114 C4
San Juan, *Ica, Peru* 124 D2
San Juan, *Puno, Peru* 124 C4
San Juan, *Phil.* 55 G7
San Juan, *Puerto Rico* 117 C6
San Juan □, *Argentina* 126 C2
San Juan →, *Argentina* 126 C2
San Juan →, *Bolivia* 125 E4
San Juan →, *Colombia* 120 C2
San Juan →, *Nic.* 116 D3
San Juan →, *U.S.A.* 111 H8
San Juan →, *Venezuela* 121 A5
San Juan, C., *Eq. Guin.* 80 D1
San Juan Bautista, *Paraguay* 126 B4
San Juan Bautista, *Spain* 36 B8
San Juan Bautista, *U.S.A.* 111 H3
San Juan Bautista Valle Nacional, *Mexico* 115 D5
San Juan Capistrano, *U.S.A.* 113 M9
San Juan Cr. →, *U.S.A.* 112 J5
San Juan de Guadalupe, *Mexico* 114 C4
San Juan de los Morros, *Venezuela* 120 B4
San Juan del César, *Colombia* 120 A3
San Juan del Norte, *Nic.* 116 D3
San Juan del Norte, B. de, *Nic.* 116 D3
San Juan del Puerto, *Spain* 31 H4
San Juan del Río, *Mexico* 115 C5
San Juan del Sur, *Nic.* 116 D2
San Juan I., *U.S.A.* 112 B3
San Juan Mts., *U.S.A.* 111 H10
San Julián, *Argentina* 128 C3
San Just, Sierra de, *Spain* 28 E4
San Justo, *Argentina* 126 C3
San Kamphaeng, *Thailand* 58 C2
San Lázaro, C., *Mexico* 114 C2
San Lázaro, Sa., *Mexico* 114 C3
San Leandro, *U.S.A.* 111 H2
San Leonardo, *Spain* 28 D1
San Lorenzo, *Argentina* 126 C3
San Lorenzo, *Beni, Bolivia* 125 D4
San Lorenzo, *Tarija, Bolivia* 125 E5
San Lorenzo, *Ecuador* 120 C2
San Lorenzo, *Paraguay* 126 B4
San Lorenzo, *Spain* 36 B10
San Lorenzo, *Venezuela* 120 B3
San Lorenzo →, *Mexico* 114 C3
San Lorenzo, I., *Mexico* 114 B2
San Lorenzo, I., *Peru* 124 C2
San Lorenzo, Mt., *Argentina* 128 C2
San Lorenzo de la Parrilla, *Spain* 28 F2
San Lorenzo de Morunys, *Spain* 28 C6
San Lucas, *Bolivia* 125 E4
San Lucas, *Baja Calif. S., Mexico* 114 C3
San Lucas, *Baja Calif. S., Mexico* 114 B2
San Lucas, *U.S.A.* 112 J5
San Lucas, C., *Mexico* 114 C3
San Lúcido, *Italy* 35 C9
San Luis, *Argentina* 126 C2
San Luis, *Cuba* 116 B3
San Luis, *Guatemala* 116 C2
San Luis, *U.S.A.* 111 H11
San Luis □, *Argentina* 126 C2
San Luis, I., *Mexico* 114 B2
San Luis, L. de, *Bolivia* 125 C5
San Luis, Sierra de, *Argentina* 126 C2
San Luis de la Paz, *Mexico* 114 C4
San Luis Obispo, *U.S.A.* 113 K6
San Luis Potosí, *Mexico* 114 C4
San Luis Potosí □, *Mexico* 114 C4
San Luis Reservoir, *U.S.A.* 112 H5
San Luis Río Colorado, *Mexico* 114 A2
San Marco Argentano, *Italy* 35 C9
San Marco dei Cavoti, *Italy* 35 A7
San Marco in Lámis, *Italy* 35 A8
San Marcos, *Colombia* 120 B2
San Marcos, *Guatemala* 116 D1
San Marcos, *Mexico* 114 B2
San Marcos, *U.S.A.* 109 L6
San Marino ■, *Europe* 33 E9
San Martín, *Argentina* 126 C2
San Martín, *Colombia* 120 C3
San Martin →, *Bolivia* 125 C5
San Martín, L., *Argentina* 128 C2
San Martin de los Andes, *Argentina* 128 B2
San Martín de Valdeiglesias, *Spain* 30 E6
San Martino de Calvi, *Italy* 32 C6
San Mateo, *Phil.* 55 C4
San Mateo, *Baleares, Spain* 36 B7
San Mateo, *Valencia, Spain* 28 E5
San Mateo, *U.S.A.* 111 H2
San Matías, *Bolivia* 125 D6
San Matías, G., *Argentina* 128 B4
San Miguel, *El Salv.* 116 D2
San Miguel, *Panama* 116 E4
San Miguel, *Spain* 36 B7
San Miguel, *U.S.A.* 111 J3
San Miguel, *Venezuela* 120 B4
San Miguel →, *Bolivia* 125 C5
San Miguel →, *S. Amer.* 120 C2
San Miguel de Huachi, *Bolivia* 124 D4
San Miguel de Salinas, *Spain* 29 H4
San Miguel de Tucumán, *Argentina* 126 B2
San Miguel del Monte, *Argentina* 126 D4
San Miguel I., *U.S.A.* 113 L6
San Miniato, *Italy* 32 E7
San Narciso, *Phil.* 55 D4
San Nicolás, *Canary Is.* 36 G4
San Nicolas, *Phil.* 55 B4
San Nicolás de los Arroyas, *Argentina* 126 C3
San Nicolas I., *U.S.A.* 113 M7
San Onofre, *Colombia* 120 B2
San Onofre, *U.S.A.* 113 M9

San Pablo, *Bolivia* 126 A2
San Pablo, *Phil.* 55 D4
San Páolo di Civitate, *Italy* 35 A8
San Pedro, *Buenos Aires, Argentina* 127 B5
San Pedro, *Jujuy, Argentina* 126 A3
San Pedro, *Colombia* 120 C3
San-Pédro, *Ivory C.* 78 E3
San Pedro, *Mexico* 114 C2
San Pedro, *Peru* 124 C3
San Pedro □, *Paraguay* 126 A4
San Pedro →, *Chihuahua, Mexico* 114 B3
San Pedro →, *Michoacan, Mexico* 114 D4
San Pedro →, *Nayarit, Mexico* 114 C3
San Pedro →, *U.S.A.* 111 K8
San Pedro, Pta., *Chile* 126 B1
San Pedro, Sierra de, *Spain* 31 F4
San Pedro Channel, *U.S.A.* 113 M8
San Pedro de Arimena, *Colombia* 120 C3
San Pedro de Atacama, *Chile* 126 A2
San Pedro de Jujuy, *Argentina* 126 A3
San Pedro de las Colonias, *Mexico* 114 B4
San Pedro de Lloc, *Peru* 124 B2
San Pedro de Macorís, *Dom. Rep.* 117 C6
San Pedro del Norte, *Nic.* 116 D3
San Pedro del Paraná, *Paraguay* 126 B4
San Pedro del Pinatar, *Spain* 29 H4
San Pedro Mártir, Sierra, *Mexico* 114 A1
San Pedro Mixtepec, *Mexico* 115 D5
San Pedro Ocampo = Melchor Ocampo, *Mexico* 114 C4
San Pedro Sula, *Honduras* 116 C2
San Pieto, *Italy* 34 C1
San Pietro Vernótico, *Italy* 35 B11
San Quintín, *Mexico* 114 A1
San Rafael, *Argentina* 126 C2
San Rafael, *Calif., U.S.A.* 112 H4
San Rafael, *N. Mex., U.S.A.* 111 J10
San Rafael, *Venezuela* 120 A3
San Rafael Mt., *U.S.A.* 113 L7
San Rafael Mts., *U.S.A.* 113 L7
San Ramón, *Bolivia* 125 C5
San Ramón, *Peru* 124 C2
San Ramón de la Nueva Orán, *Argentina* 126 A3
San Remo, *Italy* 32 E4
San Román, C., *Venezuela* 120 A3
San Roque, *Argentina* 126 B4
San Roque, *Spain* 31 J5
San Rosendo, *Chile* 126 D1
San Saba, *U.S.A.* 109 K5
San Salvador, *Bahamas* 117 B5
San Salvador, *El Salv.* 116 D2
San Salvador, *Spain* 36 B10
San Salvador de Jujuy, *Argentina* 126 A3
San Salvador I., *Bahamas* 117 B5
San Sebastián, *Argentina* 128 D3
San Sebastián, *Spain* 28 B3
San Sebastián, *Venezuela* 120 B4
San Sebastian de la Gomera, *Canary Is.* 36 F2
San Serra, *Spain* 36 B10
San Serverino Marche, *Italy* 33 E10
San Simeon, *U.S.A.* 112 K5
San Simon, *U.S.A.* 111 K9
San Stéfano di Cadore, *Italy* 33 B9
San Telmo, *Mexico* 114 A1
San Telmo, *Spain* 36 B9
San Tiburcio, *Mexico* 114 C4
San Valentin, Mte., *Chile* 128 C2
San Vicente de Alcántara, *Spain* 31 F3
San Vicente de la Barquera, *Spain* 30 B6
San Vicente del Caguán, *Colombia* 120 C3
San Vincenzo, *Italy* 32 E7
San Vito, *Italy* 34 C2
San Vito, C., *Italy* 34 D5
San Vito al Tagliamento, *Italy* 33 C9
San Vito Chietino, *Italy* 33 F11
San Vito dei Normanni, *Italy* 35 B10
San Yanaro, *Colombia* 120 C4
San Ygnacio, *U.S.A.* 109 M5
Saña, *Peru* 124 B2
Sana', *Yemen* 68 D3
Sana →, *Bos.-H.* 33 C13
Sanaba, *Burkina Faso* 78 C4
Şanāfīr, *Si. Arabia* 76 B3
Sanaga →, *Cameroon* 79 E6
Sanaloa, Presa, *Mexico* 114 C3
Sanana, *Indonesia* 57 E7
Sanand, *India* 62 H5
Sanandaj, *Iran* 67 E12
Sanandita, *Bolivia* 126 A3
Sanary-sur-Mer, *France* 27 E9
Sanawad, *India* 62 H7
Sancellas, *Spain* 36 B9
Sancergues, *France* 25 E9
Sancerre, *France* 25 E9
Sancerrois, Collines du, *France* 25 E9
Sancha He →, *China* 52 D6
Sanchahe, *China* 51 B14
Sánchez, *Dom. Rep.* 117 C6
Sanchor, *India* 62 G4
Sanco Pt., *Phil.* 57 C7
Sancoins, *France* 25 F9
Sancti-Spíritus, *Cuba* 116 B4
Sancy, Puy de, *France* 26 C6
Sand →, *S. Africa* 85 C5
Sand Springs, *U.S.A.* 109 G6
Sanda, *Japan* 49 G7
Sandakan, *Malaysia* 56 C5
Sandan = Sambor, *Cambodia* 58 F6
Sandanski, *Bulgaria* 39 H6
Sandaré, *Mali* 78 C2
Sanday, *U.K.* 14 B6
Sandefjord, *Norway* 10 E4
Sanders, *U.S.A.* 111 J9
Sanderson, *U.S.A.* 109 K3
Sandfly L., *Canada* 101 B7
Sandgate, *Australia* 91 D5
Sandía, *Peru* 124 C4
Sandıklı, *Turkey* 66 C4
Sandnes, *Norway* 9 G11
Sandness, *U.K.* 14 A7
Sandnessjøen, *Norway* 8 C15
Sandoa, *Zaïre* 80 F4
Sandona, *Colombia* 120 C2
Sandover →, *Australia* 90 C2
Sandoway, *Burma* 61 K19
Sandoy, *Færoe Is.* 8 F9
Sandpoint, *U.S.A.* 110 B5
Sandringham, *U.K.* 12 E8
Sandslån, *Sweden* 10 A11
Sandspit, *Canada* 100 C2
Sandstone, *Australia* 89 E2
Sandu, *China* 52 E6
Sandusky, *Mich., U.S.A.* 98 D3
Sandusky, *Ohio, U.S.A.* 106 E2
Sandvig, *Sweden* 11 J8
Sandviken, *Sweden* 9 F17
Sandwich, C., *Australia* 90 B4
Sandwich B., *Canada* 99 B8
Sandwich B., *Namibia* 84 C1
Sandwip Chan., *Bangla.* 61 H17
Sandy, *Nev., U.S.A.* 113 K11
Sandy, *Oreg., U.S.A.* 112 E4
Sandy, *Utah, U.S.A.* 110 F8
Sandy Bight, *Australia* 89 F3
Sandy C., *Queens., Australia* 90 C5
Sandy C., *Tas., Australia* 90 G3
Sandy Cay, *Bahamas* 117 B4
Sandy Cr. →, *U.S.A.* 110 F9
Sandy L., *Canada* 98 B1
Sandy Lake, *Canada* 98 B1
Sandy Narrows, *Canada* 101 B8
Sanford, *Fla., U.S.A.* 105 L5
Sanford, *Maine, U.S.A.* 107 C14
Sanford, *N.C., U.S.A.* 105 H6
Sanford →, *Australia* 89 E2
Sanford, Mt., *U.S.A.* 96 B5
Sang-i-Masha, *Afghan.* 62 C2
Sanga, *Mozam.* 83 E4
Sanga →, *Congo* 80 E3
Sanga-Tolon, *Russia* 45 C15
Sangamner, *India* 60 K9
Sangar, *Afghan.* 62 C1
Sangar, *Russia* 45 C13
Sangar Sarai, *Afghan.* 62 B4
Sangasangadalam, *Indonesia* 56 E5
Sangatte, *France* 25 B8
Sangay, *Ecuador* 120 D2
Sange, *Zaïre* 82 D2
Sangeang, *Indonesia* 57 F5
Sanger, *U.S.A.* 111 H4
Sangerhausen, *Germany* 18 D7
Sanggan He →, *China* 50 E9
Sanggau, *Indonesia* 56 D4
Sangihe, Kepulauan, *Indonesia* 57 D7
Sangihe, P., *Indonesia* 57 D7
Sangju, *S. Korea* 51 F15
Sangkapura, *Indonesia* 56 F4
Sangkhla, *Thailand* 58 E2
Sangli, *India* 60 L9
Sangmélina, *Cameroon* 79 E7
Sangonera →, *Spain* 29 H3
Sangre de Cristo Mts., *U.S.A.* 109 G2
Sangro →, *Italy* 33 F11
Sangudo, *Canada* 100 C6
Sangue →, *Brazil* 125 C6
Sangüesa, *Spain* 28 C3
Sanguinaires, Is., *France* 27 G12
Sangzhi, *China* 53 C8
Sanhala, *Ivory C.* 78 C3
Sanje, *Uganda* 82 C3
Sanjiang, *China* 52 E7
Sanjo, *Japan* 48 F9
Sankt Antönien, *Switz.* 23 C9
Sankt Blasien, *Germany* 19 H4
Sankt Gallen, *Switz.* 23 B8
Sankt Gallen □, *Switz.* 23 B8
Sankt Goar, *Germany* 19 E3
Sankt Ingbert, *Germany* 19 F3
Sankt Margrethen, *Switz.* 23 B9
Sankt Moritz, *Switz.* 23 D9
Sankt-Peterburg, *Russia* 40 C6
Sankt Pölten, *Austria* 21 G5
Sankt Valentin, *Austria* 21 G4
Sankt Veit, *Austria* 21 J4
Sankt Wendel, *Germany* 19 F3
Sankuru →, *Zaïre* 80 E4
Sanliurfa, *Turkey* 67 D8
Sanlúcar de Barrameda, *Spain* 31 J4
Sanlúcar la Mayor, *Spain* 31 H4
Sanluri, *Italy* 34 C1
Sanmenxia, *China* 50 G6
Sanming, *China* 53 D11
Sannaspos, *S. Africa* 84 D4
Sannicandro Gargánico, *Italy* 35 A8
Sannidal, *Norway* 10 F3
Sannieshof, *S. Africa* 84 D4
Sannīn, J., *Lebanon* 69 B4
Sanok, *Poland* 20 F12
Sanquhar, *U.K.* 14 F5
Sansanding Dam, *Mali* 78 C3
Sansepolcro, *Italy* 33 E9
Sansha, *China* 53 D13
Sanshui, *China* 53 F9
Sanski Most, *Bos.-H.* 33 D13
Sansui, *China* 52 D7
Santa, *Peru* 124 B2
Sant' Ágata de Goti, *Italy* 35 A7
Sant' Ágata di Militello, *Italy* 35 D7
Santa Ana, *Beni, Bolivia* 125 C4
Santa Ana, *Santa Cruz, Bolivia* 125 D6
Santa Ana, *Santa Cruz, Bolivia* 125 D5
Santa Ana, *Ecuador* 120 D1
Santa Ana, *El Salv.* 116 D2
Santa Ana, *Mexico* 114 A2
Santa Ana, *U.S.A.* 113 M9
Santa Ana →, *Venezuela* 120 B3
Sant' Ángelo Lodigiano, *Italy* 32 C6
Sant' Antíoco, *Italy* 34 C1
Sant' Arcángelo di Romagna, *Italy* 33 D9
Santa Barbara, *Colombia* 120 B2
Santa Barbara, *Honduras* 116 D2
Santa Bárbara, *Mexico* 114 B3
Santa Bárbara, *Spain* 28 E5
Santa Barbara, *U.S.A.* 113 L7
Santa Bárbara, *Venezuela* 120 B3
Santa Bárbara, Mt., *Spain* 29 H2
Santa Barbara Channel, *U.S.A.* 113 L7
Santa Barbara I., *U.S.A.* 113 M7
Santa Catalina, *Colombia* 120 A2
Santa Catalina, *Mexico* 114 B2
Santa Catalina, Gulf of, *U.S.A.* 113 N9
Santa Catalina I., *U.S.A.* 113 M8
Santa Catarina □, *Brazil* 127 B6
Santa Catarina, I. de, *Brazil* 127 B6
Santa Caterina Villarmosa, *Italy* 35 E7
Santa Cecília, *Brazil* 127 B5
Santa Clara, *Cuba* 116 B4
Santa Clara, *Calif., U.S.A.* 111 H3
Santa Clara, *Utah, U.S.A.* 111 H7
Santa Clara de Olimar, *Uruguay* 127 C5
Santa Clotilde, *Peru* 120 D3
Santa Coloma de Farners, *Spain* 28 D7
Santa Coloma de Gramanet, *Spain* 28 D7
Santa Comba, *Spain* 30 B2
Santa Croce Camerina, *Italy* 35 F7
Santa Croce di Magliano, *Italy* 35 A7
Santa Cruz, *Argentina* 128 D3
Santa Cruz, *Bolivia* 125 D5
Santa Cruz, *Brazil* 122 C4
Santa Cruz, *Chile* 126 C1
Santa Cruz, *Costa Rica* 116 D2
Santa Cruz, *Madeira* 36 D3
Santa Cruz, *Peru* 124 B2
Santa Cruz, *Phil.* 55 D4
Santa Cruz, *U.S.A.* 111 H2
Santa Cruz, *Venezuela* 121 B5
Santa Cruz □, *Argentina* 128 C3
Santa Cruz □, *Bolivia* 125 D5
Santa Cruz →, *Argentina* 128 D3
Santa Cruz Cabrália, *Brazil* 123 E4
Santa Cruz de la Palma, *Canary Is.* 36 F2
Santa Cruz de Mudela, *Spain* 29 G1
Santa Cruz de Tenerife, *Canary Is.* 36 F3
Santa Cruz del Norte, *Cuba* 116 B3
Santa Cruz del Retamar, *Spain* 30 E6
Santa Cruz del Sur, *Cuba* 116 B4
Santa Cruz do Rio Pardo, *Brazil* 127 A6
Santa Cruz do Sul, *Brazil* 127 B5
Santa Cruz I., *Solomon Is.* 92 J8
Santa Cruz I., *U.S.A.* 113 M7
Santa Domingo, Cay, *Bahamas* 116 B4
Santa Elena, *Argentina* 126 C4
Santa Elena, *Ecuador* 120 D1
Santa Elena, C., *Costa Rica* 116 D2
Sant' Eufémia, G. di, *Italy* 35 D9
Santa Eugenia, Pta., *Mexico* 114 B1
Santa Eulalia, *Spain* 36 C8
Santa Fe, *Argentina* 126 C3
Santa Fe, *Spain* 31 H7
Santa Fe, *U.S.A.* 111 J11
Santa Fé □, *Argentina* 126 C3
Santa Filomena, *Brazil* 122 C2
Santa Galdana, *Spain* 36 B10
Santa Gertrudis, *Spain* 36 B7
Santa Helena, *Brazil* 122 B2
Santa Helena de Goiás, *Brazil* 123 E1
Santa Inês, *Brazil* 123 D4
Santa Inés, *Baleares, Spain* 36 B7
Santa Inés, *Extremadura, Spain* 31 G5
Santa Inés, I., *Chile* 128 D2
Santa Isabel = Rey Malabo, *Eq. Guin.* 79 E6
Santa Isabel, *Argentina* 126 D2
Santa Isabel, *Brazil* 123 D1
Santa Isabel, Pico, *Eq. Guin.* 79 E6
Santa Isabel do Araguaia, *Brazil* 122 C2
Santa Isabel do Morro, *Brazil* 123 D1
Santa Lucía, *Corrientes, Argentina* 126 B4
Santa Lucía, *San Juan, Argentina* 126 C2
Santa Lucía, *Spain* 29 H4
Santa Lucia, *Uruguay* 126 C4
Santa Lucia Range, *U.S.A.* 111 J3
Santa Magdalena, I., *Mexico* 114 C2
Santa Margarita, *Argentina* 126 D3
Santa Margarita, *Mexico* 114 C2
Santa Margarita, *Spain* 36 B10
Santa Margarita, *U.S.A.* 112 K6
Santa Margarita →, *U.S.A.* 113 M9
Santa Margherita, *Italy* 32 D6
Santa María, *Argentina* 126 B2
Santa Maria, *Brazil* 127 B5
Santa Maria, *Phil.* 55 C4
Santa Maria, *Spain* 36 B9
Santa Maria, *Switz.* 23 C10
Santa Maria, *U.S.A.* 113 L6
Santa María →, *Mexico* 114 A3
Santa María, B. de, *Mexico* 114 B3
Santa Maria, C. de, *Portugal* 31 J3
Santa Maria Cápua Vétere, *Italy* 35 A7
Santa Maria da Vitória, *Brazil* 123 D3
Santa María de Ipire, *Venezuela* 121 B4
Santa Maria di Leuca, C., *Italy* 35 C11
Santa Maria do Suaçuí, *Brazil* 123 E3
Santa Maria dos Marmelos, *Brazil* 125 B5
Santa María la Real de Nieva, *Spain* 30 D6
Santa Marta, *Colombia* 120 A3
Santa Marta, *Spain* 31 G4
Santa Marta, Ría de, *Spain* 30 B3
Santa Marta, Sierra Nevada de, *Colombia* 120 A3
Santa Marta Grande, C., *Brazil* 127 B6
Santa Maura = Levkás, *Greece* 39 L3
Santa Monica, *U.S.A.* 113 M8
Santa Olalla, *Huelva, Spain* 31 H4
Santa Olalla, *Toledo, Spain* 30 E6
Sant' Onofrio, *Italy* 35 D9
Santa Pola, *Spain* 29 G4
Santa Ponsa, *Spain* 36 B9
Santa Quitéria, *Brazil* 122 B3
Santa Rita, *U.S.A.* 111 K10
Santa Rita, *Guarico, Venezuela* 120 B4
Santa Rita, *Zulia, Venezuela* 120 A3
Santa Rita do Araquaia, *Brazil* 125 D7
Santa Rosa, *La Pampa, Argentina* 126 D3
Santa Rosa, *San Luis, Argentina* 126 C2
Santa Rosa, *Bolivia* 124 C4
Santa Rosa, *Brazil* 127 B5
Santa Rosa, *Colombia* 120 C4
Santa Rosa, *Ecuador* 120 D2
Santa Rosa, *Peru* 124 C3
Santa Rosa, *Calif., U.S.A.* 112 G4
Santa Rosa, *N. Mex., U.S.A.* 109 H2
Santa Rosa, *Venezuela* 120 C4
Santa Rosa de Cabal, *Colombia* 120 C2
Santa Rosa de Copán, *Honduras* 116 D2
Santa Rosa de Osos, *Colombia* 120 B2
Santa Rosa de Río Primero, *Argentina* 126 C3
Santa Rosa de Viterbo, *Colombia* 120 B3
Santa Rosa del Palmar, *Bolivia* 125 D5
Santa Rosa I., *Calif., U.S.A.* 113 M6
Santa Rosa I., *Fla., U.S.A.* 105 K2
Santa Rosa Range, *U.S.A.* 110 F5
Santa Rosalía, *Mexico* 114 B2
Santa Sofia, *Italy* 33 E8
Santa Sylvina, *Argentina* 126 B3
Santa Tecla = Nueva San Salvador, *El Salv.* 116 D2
Santa Teresa, *Argentina* 126 C3
Santa Teresa, *Brazil* 123 E3
Santa Teresa, *Mexico* 115 B5
Santa Teresa, *Venezuela* 121 C5
Santa Teresa di Riva, *Italy* 35 E8
Santa Teresa Gallura, *Italy* 34 A2
Santa Vitória, *Brazil* 123 E1
Santa Vitória do Palmar, *Brazil* 127 C5
Santa Ynez →, *U.S.A.* 113 L6
Santa Ynez Mts., *U.S.A.* 113 L6
Santa Ysabel, *U.S.A.* 113 M10
Santadi, *Italy* 34 C1
Santai, *China* 52 B5
Santaluz, *Brazil* 122 D4
Santana, *Brazil* 123 D3
Santana, *Madeira* 36 D3
Santana, Coxilha de, *Brazil* 127 C4
Santana do Ipanema, *Brazil* 122 C4
Santana do Livramento, *Brazil* 127 C4
Santanayi, *Spain* 36 B10
Santander, *Colombia* 120 C2
Santander, *Spain* 30 B7
Santander Jiménez, *Mexico* 115 C5
Santaquin, *U.S.A.* 110 G8
Santarém, *Brazil* 121 D7
Santarém, *Portugal* 31 F2
Santarém □, *Portugal* 31 F2
Santaren Channel, *W. Indies* 116 B4
Santee, *U.S.A.* 113 N10
Santéramo in Colle, *Italy* 35 B9
Santerno →, *Italy* 33 D8
Santhià, *Italy* 32 C5
Santiago, *Bolivia* 125 D6
Santiago, *Brazil* 127 B5
Santiago, *Chile* 126 C1
Santiago, *Panama* 116 E3
Santiago, *Peru* 124 C2
Santiago, *Phil.* 55 C4
Santiago □, *Chile* 126 C1
Santiago →, *Mexico* 94 G9
Santiago →, *Peru* 120 D2
Santiago, C., *Chile* 128 D1
Santiago, Punta de, *Eq. Guin.* 79 E6
Santiago, Serranía de, *Bolivia* 125 D6
Santiago de Chuco, *Peru* 124 B2
Santiago de Compostela, *Spain* 30 C2
Santiago de Cuba, *Cuba* 116 C4
Santiago de los Cabelleros, *Dom. Rep.* 117 C5
Santiago del Estero, *Argentina* 126 B3
Santiago del Estero □, *Argentina* 126 B3
Santiago del Teide, *Canary Is.* 36 F3
Santiago do Cacém, *Portugal* 31 G2
Santiago Ixcuintla, *Mexico* 114 C3
Santiago Papasquiaro, *Mexico* 114 B3
Santiaguillo, L. de, *Mexico* 114 C4
Santillana del Mar, *Spain* 30 B6
Säntis, *Switz.* 23 B8
Santisteban del Puerto, *Spain* 29 G1
Santo →, *Peru* 124 B2
Santo Amaro, *Brazil* 123 D4
Santo Anastácio, *Brazil* 127 A5
Santo André, *Brazil* 127 A6
Santo Ângelo, *Brazil* 127 B5
Santo Antonio, *Brazil* 125 D6
Santo Antônio de Jesus, *Brazil* 123 D4
Santo Antônio do Içá, *Brazil* 120 D4
Santo Antônio do Leverger, *Brazil* 125 D6
Santo Corazón, *Bolivia* 125 D6
Santo Domingo, *Dom. Rep.* 117 C6
Santo Domingo, *Baja Calif., Mexico* 114 A1
Santo Domingo, *Baja Calif. S., Mexico* 114 B2
Santo Domingo, *Nic.* 116 D3
Santo Domingo de la Calzada, *Spain* 28 C2
Santo Domingo de los Colorados, *Ecuador* 120 D2
Santo Stéfano di Camastro, *Italy* 35 D7
Santo Stino di Livenza, *Italy* 33 C9
Santo Tirso, *Portugal* 30 D2
Santo Tomás, *Mexico* 114 A1
Santo Tomás, *Peru* 124 C3
Santo Tomé, *Argentina* 127 B4
Santo Tomé de Guayana = Ciudad Guayana, *Venezuela* 121 B5
Santoña, *Spain* 30 B7
Santoríni = Thíra, *Greece* 39 N8
Santos, *Brazil* 127 A6
Santos, Sierra de los, *Spain* 31 G5
Santos Dumont, *Brazil* 123 F3
Santpoort, *Neths.* 16 D5
Sanvignes-les-Mines, *France* 25 F11

Sanyuan, China 50 G5
Sanza Pombo, Angola 80 F3
São Anastácio, Brazil 127 A5
São Bartolomeu de Messines, Portugal 31 H2
São Benedito, Brazil 122 B3
São Bento, Brazil 122 B3
São Bento do Norte, Brazil 122 C4
São Bernado de Campo, Brazil 123 F2
São Borja, Brazil 127 B4
São Bras d'Alportel, Portugal 31 H3
São Caitano, Brazil 122 C4
São Carlos, Brazil 127 A6
São Cristóvão, Brazil 122 D4
São Domingos, Brazil 123 D2
São Domingos do Maranhão, Brazil 122 C3
São Félix, Brazil 123 D1
São Francisco, Brazil 123 E3
São Francisco →, Brazil 122 D4
São Francisco do Maranhão, Brazil 122 C3
São Francisco do Sul, Brazil 127 B6
São Gabriel, Brazil 127 C5
São Gabriel da Palha, Brazil 123 E3
São Gonçalo, Brazil 123 F3
São Gotardo, Brazil 123 E2
Sao Hill, Tanzania 83 D4
São João da Boa Vista, Brazil 127 A6
São João da Pesqueira, Portugal 30 D3
São João da Ponte, Brazil 123 E3
São João del Rei, Brazil 123 F3
São João do Araguaia, Brazil 122 C2
São João do Paraíso, Brazil 123 E3
São João do Piauí, Brazil 122 C3
São João dos Patos, Brazil 122 C3
São Joaquim da Barra, Brazil 123 F2
São Jorge, Pta. de, Madeira 36 D3
São José, B. de, Brazil 122 B3
São José da Laje, Brazil 122 C4
São José de Mipibu, Brazil 122 C4
São José do Peixe, Brazil 122 C3
São José do Rio Prêto, Brazil 127 A6
São José dos Campos, Brazil 127 A6
São Leopoldo, Brazil 127 B5
São Lourenço, Brazil 123 F2
São Lourenço →, Brazil 125 D6
São Lourenço, Pantanal do, Brazil 125 D6
São Lourenço, Pta. de, Madeira 36 D3
São Luís, Brazil 122 B3
São Luís do Curu, Brazil 122 B4
São Luís Gonzaga, Brazil 127 B5
São Marcos →, Brazil 123 E2
São Marcos, B. de, Brazil 122 B3
São Martinho, Portugal 30 E2
São Mateus, Brazil 123 E4
São Mateus →, Brazil 123 E4
São Miguel do Araguaia, Brazil 123 D1
São Miguel dos Campos, Brazil 122 C4
São Nicolau →, Brazil 122 C3
São Paulo, Brazil 127 A6
São Paulo □, Brazil 127 A6
São Paulo, I., Atl. Oc. 2 D8
São Paulo de Olivença, Brazil 120 D4
São Pedro do Sul, Portugal 30 E2
São Rafael, Brazil 122 C4
São Raimundo das Mangabeiras, Brazil 122 C2
São Raimundo Nonato, Brazil 122 C3
São Romão, Brazil 123 E2
São Roque, Madeira 36 D3
São Roque, C. de, Brazil 122 C4
São Sebastião, I. de, Brazil 127 A6
São Sebastião do Paraíso, Brazil 127 A6
São Simão, Brazil 123 E1
São Teotónio, Portugal 31 H2
São Tomé, Atl. Oc. 70 F4
São Tomé, Brazil 122 C4
São Tomé, C. de, Brazil 123 F3
São Tomé & Principe ■, Africa 71 F4
São Vicente, Brazil 127 A6
São Vicente, Madeira 36 D2
São Vicente, C. de, Portugal 31 H2
Saona, I., Dom. Rep. 117 C6
Saône →, France 27 C8
Saône-et-Loire □, France 25 F11
Saonek, Indonesia 57 E8
Saoura, O. →, Algeria 75 C4
Sapanca, Turkey 66 B4
Sapão →, Brazil 122 D2
Saparua, Indonesia 57 E7
Sapé, Brazil 122 C4
Sapele, Nigeria 79 D6
Sapelo I., U.S.A. 105 K5
Sapiéntza, Greece 39 N4
Sapone, Burkina Faso 79 C4
Saposoa, Peru 124 B2
Sapozhok, Russia 42 D5
Sappemeer, Neths. 16 B9
Sappho, U.S.A. 112 B2
Sapporo, Japan 48 C10
Sapri, Italy 35 B8
Sapudi, Indonesia 57 G16
Sapulpa, U.S.A. 109 G7
Saqqez, Iran 67 D12
Sar Dasht, Iran 65 C6
Sar Gachīneh, Iran 65 D6
Sar Planina, Macedonia 38 G4
Sara, Burkina Faso 78 C4
Sara, Phil. 55 F5
Sara Buri, Thailand 58 E3
Sarāb, Iran 67 D12
Sarabadi, Iraq 64 C5
Sarada →, India 61 F12
Saragossa = Zaragoza, Spain 28 D4
Saraguro, Ecuador 120 D2
Sarajevo, Bos.-H. 21 M8
Saramacca □, Surinam 121 C6
Saramacca →, Surinam 121 B6
Saran, G., Indonesia 56 E4
Saranac Lake, U.S.A. 107 B10
Saranda, Tanzania 82 D3
Sarandí del Yi, Uruguay 127 C4
Sarandí Grande, Uruguay 126 C4
Sarangani B., Phil. 55 J6
Sarangani Is., Phil. 55 J6
Sarangarh, India 61 J13
Saransk, Russia 42 C7
Sarapul, Russia 44 D6
Sarasota, U.S.A. 105 M4
Saratoga, Calif., U.S.A. 112 H4
Saratoga, Wyo., U.S.A. 110 F10
Saratoga Springs, U.S.A. 107 C11
Saratov, Russia 42 E7
Saravane, Laos 58 E6
Sarawak □, Malaysia 56 D4
Saray, Tekirdağ, Turkey 66 B2
Saray, Van, Turkey 67 C11
Saraya, Senegal 78 C2
Sarayköy, Turkey 66 D3
Sarayönü, Turkey 66 C5
Sarbāz, Iran 65 E9
Sarbīsheh, Iran 65 C8
Sarca →, Italy 32 C7
Sarda → = Sarada →, India 61 F12
Sardalas, Libya 75 C7
Sardarshahr, India 62 E6
Sardegna □, Italy 34 B2
Sardhana, India 62 E7
Sardina, Pta., Canary Is. 36 F4
Sardinata, Colombia 120 B3
Sardinia = Sardegna □, Italy 34 B2
Sardis, Turkey 66 C2
Sārdūīyeh = Dar Mazār, Iran 65 D8
Saréyamou, Mali 78 B4
Sargent, U.S.A. 108 E5
Sargodha, Pakistan 62 C5
Sarh, Chad 73 G8
Sarhro, Djebel, Morocco 74 B3
Sārī, Iran 65 B7
Sária, Greece 39 P10
Sarıgöl, Turkey 66 C3
Sarikamiş, Turkey 67 B10
Sarıkaya, Turkey 66 C6
Sarikei, Malaysia 56 D4
Sarina, Australia 90 C4
Sariñena, Spain 28 D4
Sarita, U.S.A. 109 M6
Sariwŏn, N. Korea 51 E13
Sariyar Baraji, Turkey 66 B4
Sark, U.K. 13 H5
Sarkad, Hungary 21 J11
Şarkışla, Turkey 66 C7
Şarköy, Turkey 66 B2
Sarlat-la-Canéda, France 26 D5
Sarles, U.S.A. 108 A5
Sărmaşu, Romania 38 C7
Sarmi, Indonesia 57 E9
Sarmiento, Argentina 128 C3
Särna, Sweden 10 C7
Sarnano, Italy 33 E10
Sarnen, Switz. 22 C6
Sarnia, Canada 98 D3
Sarno, Italy 35 B7
Sarny, Ukraine 44 D3
Särö, Sweden 11 G5
Sarolangun, Indonesia 56 E2
Saronikós Kólpos, Greece 39 M6
Saronno, Italy 32 C6
Saros Körfezi, Turkey 66 B2
Sárospatak, Hungary 21 G11
Sarpsborg, Norway 10 E5
Sarracín, Spain 28 C1
Sarralbe, France 25 D14
Sarre = Saar →, Europe 25 C13
Sarre-Union, France 25 D14
Sarrebourg, France 25 D14
Sarreguemines, France 25 C14
Sarriá, Spain 30 C3
Sarrión, Spain 28 E4
Sarro, Mali 78 C3
Sarstedt, Germany 18 C5
Sartène, France 27 G12
Sarthe □, France 24 E7
Sarthe →, France 24 E6
Sartilly, France 24 D5
Sartynya, Russia 44 C7
Sárvár, Hungary 21 H6
Sarvestān, Iran 65 D7
Särvfjället, Sweden 10 B7
Sárviz →, Hungary 21 J8
Sary-Tash, Kyrgyzstan 44 F8
Sarych, Mys, Ukraine 41 K7
Saryshagan, Kazakstan 44 E8
Sarzana, Italy 32 D6
Sarzeau, France 24 E4
Sas van Gent, Neths. 17 F3
Sasabeneh, Ethiopia 68 F3
Sasaram, India 63 G11
Sasebo, Japan 49 H4
Saser, India 63 B7
Saskatchewan □, Canada 101 C7
Saskatchewan →, Canada 101 C8
Saskatoon, Canada 101 C7
Saskylakh, Russia 45 B12
Sasolburg, S. Africa 85 D4
Sasovo, Russia 42 C5
Sassandra, Ivory C. 78 E3
Sassandra →, Ivory C. 78 E3
Sássari, Italy 34 B1
Sassenheim, Neths. 16 D5
Sassnitz, Germany 18 A9
Sasso Marconi, Italy 33 D8
Sassocorvaro, Italy 33 E9
Sassoferrato, Italy 33 E9
Sassuolo, Italy 32 D7
Sástago, Spain 28 D4
Sastown, Liberia 78 E3
Sasumua Dam, Kenya 82 C4
Sasyk, Ozero, Ukraine 41 K5
Sata-Misaki, Japan 49 J5
Satadougou, Mali 78 C2
Satakunta, Finland 9 F20
Satanta, U.S.A. 109 G4
Satara, India 60 L8
Satilla →, U.S.A. 105 K5
Satipo, Peru 124 C3
Satmala Hills, India 60 J9
Satna, India 63 G9
Šator, Bos.-H. 33 D13
Sátoraljaújhely, Hungary 21 G11
Satpura Ra., India 62 J7
Satrup, Germany 18 A5
Satsuna-Shotō, Japan 49 K5
Sattahip, Thailand 58 F3
Satu Mare, Romania 38 B5
Satui, Indonesia 56 E5
Satun, Thailand 59 J3
Saturnina →, Brazil 125 C6
Sauce, Argentina 126 C4
Sauceda, Mexico 114 B4
Saucillo, Mexico 114 B3
Sauda, Norway 9 G12
Saúde, Brazil 122 D3
Sauðarkrókur, Iceland 8 D4
Saudi Arabia ■, Asia 68 B3
Sauer →, Germany 17 J9
Saugeen →, Canada 106 B3
Saugerties, U.S.A. 107 D11
Saugues, France 26 D7
Sauherad, Norway 10 E3
Saujon, France 26 C3
Sauk Centre, U.S.A. 108 C7
Sauk Rapids, U.S.A. 108 C7
Saül, Fr. Guiana 121 C7
Saulgau, Germany 19 G5
Saulieu, France 25 E11
Sault, France 27 D9
Sault Ste. Marie, Canada 98 C3
Sault Ste. Marie, U.S.A. 104 B3
Saumlaki, Indonesia 57 F8
Saumur, France 24 E6
Saunders C., N.Z. 87 L3
Saunders I., Antarctica 5 B1
Saunders Point, Australia 89 E4
Sauri, Nigeria 79 C6
Saurimo, Angola 80 F4
Sausalito, U.S.A. 112 H4
Sautatá, Colombia 120 B2
Sauveterre-de-Béarn, France 26 E3
Sauzé-Vaussais, France 26 B4
Savá, Honduras 116 C2
Sava →, Serbia, Yug. 21 L10
Savage, U.S.A. 108 B2
Savage I. = Niue, Cook Is. 93 J11
Savai'i, W. Samoa 87 A12
Savalou, Benin 79 D5
Savane, Mozam. 83 F4
Savanna, U.S.A. 108 D9
Savanna la Mar, Jamaica 116 C4
Savannah, Ga., U.S.A. 105 J5
Savannah, Mo., U.S.A. 108 F7
Savannah, Tenn., U.S.A. 105 H1
Savannah →, U.S.A. 105 J5
Savannakhet, Laos 58 D5
Savant L., Canada 98 B1
Savant Lake, Canada 98 B1
Savanur, India 60 M9
Savé, Benin 79 D5
Save →, France 26 E5
Save →, Mozam. 85 C5
Sāveh, Iran 65 C6
Savelugu, Ghana 79 D4
Savenay, France 24 E5
Saverdun, France 26 E5
Saverne, France 25 D14
Savièse, Switz. 22 D4
Savigliano, Italy 32 D4
Savigny-sur-Braye, France 24 E7
Saviñao, Spain 30 C3
Savio →, Italy 33 D9
Savo, Finland 8 E22
Savognin, Switz. 23 C9
Savoie □, France 27 C10
Savona, Italy 32 D5
Savonlinna, Finland 40 B5
Şavşat, Turkey 67 B10
Sawahlunto, Indonesia 56 E2
Sawai, Indonesia 57 E7
Sawai Madhopur, India 62 F7
Sawang Daen Din, Thailand 58 D4
Sawankhalok, Thailand 58 D2
Sawara, Japan 49 G10
Sawatch Mts., U.S.A. 111 G10
Sawel Mt., U.K. 15 B4
Sawi, Thailand 59 G2
Sawmills, Zimbabwe 83 F2
Sawu, Indonesia 57 F6
Sawu Sea, Indonesia 57 F6
Saxby →, Australia 90 B3
Saxon, Switz. 22 D4
Saxony, Lower = Niedersachsen □, Germany 18 C5
Saxton, U.S.A. 106 F6
Say, Niger 79 C5
Saya, Nigeria 79 D5
Sayabec, Canada 99 C6
Sayaboury, Laos 58 C3
Sayán, Peru 124 C2
Sayan, Vostochnyy, Russia 45 D10
Sayan, Zapadnyy, Russia 45 D10
Saydā, Lebanon 69 B4
Sayhan-Ovoo, Mongolia 50 B2
Sayhandulaan, Mongolia 50 B5
Sayḥut, Yemen 68 D5
Saykhin, Kazakstan 43 F8
Saynshand, Mongolia 50 B6
Sayre, Okla., U.S.A. 109 H5
Sayre, Pa., U.S.A. 107 E8
Sayula, Mexico 114 D4
Sazin, Pakistan 63 B5
Sazlika →, Bulgaria 39 H8
Sbeïtla, Tunisia 75 A6
Scaër, France 24 D3
Scafell Pike, U.K. 12 C4
Scalea, Italy 35 C8
Scalpay, U.K. 14 D2
Scandia, Canada 100 C6
Scandiano, Italy 32 D7
Scandinavia, Europe 6 C8
Scansano, Italy 33 F8
Scapa Flow, U.K. 14 C5
Scappoose, U.S.A. 112 E4
Scarborough, Trin. & Tob. 117 D7
Scarborough, U.K. 12 C7
Scebeli, Wabi →, Somali Rep. 68 G3
Šćedro, Croatia 33 E13
Scenic, U.S.A. 108 D3
Schaalsee, Germany 18 B6
Schaan, Liech. 23 B9
Schaesberg, Neths. 17 G8
Schaffen, Belgium 17 G6
Schaffhausen, Switz. 23 A7
Schaffhausen □, Switz. 23 A7
Schagen, Neths. 16 C5
Schaijk, Neths. 16 E7
Schalkhaar, Neths. 16 D8
Schalkwijk, Neths. 16 E6
Schangnau, Switz. 22 C5
Schänis, Switz. 23 B8
Schärding, Austria 20 G3
Scharhörn, Germany 18 B4
Scharnitz, Austria 19 H7
Scheessel, Germany 18 B5
Schefferville, Canada 99 B6
Schelde →, Belgium 17 F4
Schell Creek Ra., U.S.A. 110 G6
Schenectady, U.S.A. 107 D11
Scherfede, Germany 18 D5
Scherpenheuvel, Belgium 17 G5
Scherpenisse, Neths. 17 E4
Scherpenzeel, Neths. 16 D7
Schesaplana, Switz. 23 B9
Schesslitz, Germany 19 F7
Scheveningen, Neths. 16 D4
Schiedam, Neths. 16 E4
Schiermonnikoog, Neths. 16 B8
Schiers, Switz. 23 C9
Schifferstadt, Germany 19 F4
Schifflange, Lux. 17 K8
Schijndel, Neths. 17 E6
Schiltigheim, France 25 D14
Schio, Italy 33 C8
Schipbeek, Neths. 16 D8
Schipluiden, Neths. 16 E4
Schirmeck, France 25 D14
Schlanders = Silandro, Italy 32 B7
Schlei →, Germany 18 A5
Schleiden, Germany 18 E2
Schleiz, Germany 18 E7
Schleswig, Germany 18 A5
Schleswig-Holstein □, Germany 18 A5
Schlieren, Switz. 23 B6
Schlüchtern, Germany 19 E5
Schmalkalden, Germany 18 E6
Schmölln, Brandenburg, Germany 18 B10
Schmölln, Thüringen, Germany 18 E8
Schneeberg, Austria 21 H5
Schneeberg, Germany 18 E8
Schoenberg, Belgium 17 H8
Schofield, U.S.A. 108 C10
Scholls, U.S.A. 112 E4
Schönberg, Mecklenburg-Vorpommern, Germany 18 B6
Schönberg, Schleswig-Holstein, Germany 18 A6
Schönebeck, Germany 18 C7
Schönenwerd, Switz. 22 B5
Schongau, Germany 19 H6
Schöningen, Germany 18 C6
Schoondijke, Neths. 17 F3
Schoonebeek, Neths. 16 C9
Schoonhoven, Neths. 16 E5
Schoorl, Neths. 16 C5
Schortens, Germany 18 B3
Schoten, Belgium 17 F5
Schouten I., Australia 90 G4
Schouten Is. = Supiori, Indonesia 57 E9
Schouwen, Neths. 17 E3
Schramberg, Germany 19 G4
Schrankogl, Austria 19 H7
Schreckhorn, Switz. 22 C6
Schreiber, Canada 98 C2
Schrobenhausen, Germany 19 G7
Schruns, Austria 19 H5
Schuler, Canada 101 C6
Schuls, Switz. 23 C10
Schumacher, Canada 98 C3
Schüpfen, Switz. 22 B4
Schüpfheim, Switz. 22 C6
Schurz, U.S.A. 110 G4
Schuyler, U.S.A. 108 E6
Schuylkill Haven, U.S.A. 107 F8
Schwabach, Germany 19 F7
Schwäbisch Gmünd, Germany 19 G5
Schwäbisch Hall, Germany 19 F5
Schwäbische Alb, Germany 19 G5
Schwabmünchen, Germany 19 G6
Schwanden, Switz. 23 C8
Schwandorf, Germany 19 F8
Schwaner, Pegunungan, Indonesia 56 E4
Schwarmstedt, Germany 18 C5
Schwärze, Germany 18 C9
Schwarze Elster →, Germany 18 D8
Schwarzenberg, Germany 18 E8
Schwarzenburg, Switz. 22 C4
Schwarzwald, Germany 19 H4
Schwaz, Austria 19 H7
Schwedt, Germany 18 B10
Schweinfurt, Germany 19 E6
Schweizer Mittelland, Switz. 22 C4
Schweizer-Reneke, S. Africa 84 D4
Schwenningen = Villingen-Schwenningen, Germany 19 G4
Schwerin, Germany 18 B7
Schweriner See, Germany 18 B7
Schwetzingen, Germany 19 F4
Schwyz, Switz. 23 B7
Schwyz □, Switz. 23 B7
Sciacca, Italy 34 E6
Scicli, Italy 35 F7
Scilla, Italy 35 D8
Scilly, Isles of, U.K. 13 H1
Ścinawa, Poland 20 D6
Scioto →, U.S.A. 104 F4
Scobey, U.S.A. 108 A2
Scone, Australia 91 E5
Scórdia, Italy 35 E7
Scoresbysund, Greenland 4 B6
Scorno, Punta dello, Italy 34 A1
Scotia, Calif., U.S.A. 110 F1
Scotia, N.Y., U.S.A. 107 D11
Scotia Sea, Antarctica 5 B18
Scotland, U.S.A. 108 D6
Scotland □, U.K. 14 E5
Scotland Neck, U.S.A. 105 G7
Scott, C., Australia 88 B4
Scott City, U.S.A. 108 F4
Scott Glacier, Antarctica 5 C8
Scott I., Antarctica 5 C11
Scott Inlet, Canada 97 A12
Scott Is., Canada 100 C3
Scott L., Canada 101 B7
Scott Reef, Australia 88 B3
Scottburgh, S. Africa 85 E5
Scottdale, U.S.A. 106 F5
Scottsbluff, U.S.A. 108 E3
Scottsboro, U.S.A. 105 H2
Scottsburg, U.S.A. 104 F3
Scottsdale, Australia 90 G4
Scottsdale, U.S.A. 111 K7
Scottsville, Ky., U.S.A. 105 G2
Scottsville, N.Y., U.S.A. 106 C7
Scottville, U.S.A. 104 D2
Scranton, U.S.A. 107 E9
Scugog, L., Canada 106 B6
Scunthorpe, U.K. 12 D7
Scuol, Switz. 23 C10
Scusciuban, Somali Rep. 68 E5
Scutari = Üsküdar, Turkey 39 H11
Seabra, Brazil 123 D3
Seabrook, L., Australia 89 F2
Seaford, U.S.A. 104 F8
Seaforth, Canada 98 D3
Seagraves, U.S.A. 109 J3
Seal →, Canada 101 B10
Seal Cove, Canada 99 C8
Seal L., Canada 99 B7
Sealy, U.S.A. 109 L6
Searchlight, U.S.A. 113 K12
Searcy, U.S.A. 109 H9
Searles L., U.S.A. 113 K9
Seaside, Calif., U.S.A. 112 J5
Seaside, Oreg., U.S.A. 112 E3
Seaspray, Australia 91 F4
Seattle, U.S.A. 112 C4
Seaview Ra., Australia 90 B4

Sebastián Vizcaíno, B., *Mexico* 114 B2
Sebastopol = Sevastopol, *Ukraine* 41 K7
Sebastopol, *U.S.A.* 112 G4
Sebderat, *Eritrea* 77 D4
Sebdou, *Algeria* 75 B4
Seben, *Turkey* 66 B4
Sebewaing, *U.S.A.* 104 D4
Sebezh, *Russia* 40 D5
Sebha = Sabhah, *Libya* 73 C7
Sébi, *Mali* 78 B4
Şebinkarahisar, *Turkey* 67 B8
Sebiş, *Romania* 38 C5
Sebkhet Te-n-Dghâmcha, *Mauritania* 78 B1
Sebkra Azzel Mati, *Algeria* 75 C5
Sebkra Mekerghene, *Algeria* 75 C5
Sebnitz, *Germany* 18 E10
Sebou, Oued →, *Morocco* 74 B3
Sebring, *Fla., U.S.A.* 105 M5
Sebring, *Ohio, U.S.A.* 106 F3
Sebringville, *Canada* 106 C3
Sebta = Ceuta, *N. Afr.* 74 A3
Sebuku, *Indonesia* 56 E5
Sebuku, Teluk, *Malaysia* 56 D5
Secchia →, *Italy* 32 C8
Sechelt, *Canada* 100 D4
Sechura, *Peru* 124 B1
Sechura, Desierto de, *Peru* 124 B1
Seclin, *France* 25 B10
Secondigny, *France* 24 F6
Secretary I., *N.Z.* 87 L1
Secunderabad, *India* 60 L11
Sécure →, *Bolivia* 125 D5
Sedalia, *U.S.A.* 108 F8
Sedan, *Australia* 91 E2
Sedan, *France* 25 C11
Sedan, *U.S.A.* 109 G6
Sedano, *Spain* 28 C1
Seddon, *N.Z.* 87 J5
Seddonville, *N.Z.* 87 J4
Sedeh, *Fārs, Iran* 65 D7
Sedeh, *Khorāsān, Iran* 65 C8
Sederot, *Israel* 69 D3
Sedgewick, *Canada* 100 C6
Sedhiou, *Senegal* 78 C1
Sedičany, *Czech.* 20 F4
Sedico, *Italy* 33 B9
Sedley, *Canada* 101 C8
Sedova, Pik, *Russia* 44 B6
Sedrata, *Algeria* 75 A6
Sedro Woolley, *U.S.A.* 112 B4
Sedrun, *Switz.* 23 C7
Seebad Ahlbeck, *Germany* 18 B10
Seehausen, *Germany* 18 C7
Seeheim, *Namibia* 84 D2
Seekoei →, *S. Africa* 84 E4
Seelow, *Germany* 18 C10
Sées, *France* 24 D7
Seesen, *Germany* 18 D6
Sefadu, *S. Leone* 78 D2
Seferihisar, *Turkey* 66 C2
Séfeto, *Mali* 78 C3
Sefrou, *Morocco* 74 B4
Sefwi Bekwai, *Ghana* 78 D4
Segamat, *Malaysia* 59 L4
Segarcea, *Romania* 38 E6
Segbwema, *S. Leone* 78 D2
Seget, *Indonesia* 57 E8
Seggueur, O. →, *Algeria* 75 B5
Segonzac, *France* 26 C3
Segorbe, *Spain* 28 F4
Ségou, *Mali* 78 C3
Segovia = Coco →, *Cent. Amer.* 116 D3
Segovia, *Colombia* 120 B3
Segovia, *Spain* 30 E6
Segovia □, *Spain* 30 E6
Segré, *France* 24 E6
Segre →, *Spain* 28 D5
Séguéla, *Ivory C.* 78 D3
Seguin, *U.S.A.* 109 L6
Segundo →, *Argentina* 126 C3
Segura →, *Spain* 29 G4
Segura, Sierra de, *Spain* 29 G2
Seh Qal'eh, *Iran* 65 C8
Sehitwa, *Botswana* 84 C3
Sehore, *India* 62 H7
Sehwan, *Pakistan* 62 F2
Şeica Mare, *Romania* 38 C7
Seiland, *Norway* 8 A20
Seiling, *U.S.A.* 109 G5
Seille →, *Moselle, France* 25 C13
Seille →, *Saône-et-Loire, France* 27 B8
Seilles, *Belgium* 17 G6
Sein, I. de, *France* 24 D2
Seinäjoki, *Finland* 9 E20
Seine →, *France* 24 C7
Seine, B. de la, *France* 24 C6
Seine-et-Marne □, *France* 25 D9
Seine-Maritime □, *France* 24 C7
Seine-St.-Denis □, *France* 25 D9
Seistan, *Iran* 65 D9
Sejerø, *Denmark* 11 J5
Sejerø Bugt, *Denmark* 11 J5
Seka, *Ethiopia* 77 F4
Sekayu, *Indonesia* 56 E2
Seke, *Tanzania* 82 C3
Sekenke, *Tanzania* 82 C3
Sekondi-Takoradi, *Ghana* 78 E4
Seksna, *Russia* 40 C10
Sekuma, *Botswana* 84 C3
Selah, *U.S.A.* 110 C3
Selama, *Malaysia* 59 K3
Selárgius, *Italy* 34 C2
Selaru, *Indonesia* 57 F8
Selb, *Germany* 19 E8
Selby, *U.K.* 12 D6
Selby, *U.S.A.* 108 C4
Selca, *Croatia* 33 E13
Selçuk, *Turkey* 66 D2
Selden, *U.S.A.* 108 F4
Sele →, *Italy* 35 B7
Selemdzha →, *Russia* 45 D13
Selenga = Selenge Mörön →, *Asia* 54 A5
Selenge Mörön →, *Asia* 54 A5
Selenica, *Albania* 39 J2
Selenter See, *Germany* 18 A6
Sélestat, *France* 25 D14
Seletan, Tg., *Indonesia* 56 E4
Selfridge, *U.S.A.* 108 B4
Sélibabi, *Mauritania* 78 B2
Seliger, Ozero, *Russia* 42 B1
Seligman, *U.S.A.* 111 J7
Şelim, *Turkey* 67 B10
Selîma, El Wâhât el, *Sudan* 76 C2
Selinda Spillway, *Botswana* 84 B3
Selinoús, *Greece* 39 M4
Selizharovo, *Russia* 42 B1
Seljord, *Norway* 10 E2
Selkirk, *Canada* 101 C9
Selkirk, *U.K.* 14 F6
Selkirk I., *Canada* 101 C9
Selkirk Mts., *Canada* 100 C5
Selles-sur-Cher, *France* 25 E8
Selliá, *Greece* 37 D6
Sellières, *France* 25 F12
Sells, *U.S.A.* 111 L8
Sellye, *Hungary* 21 K7
Selma, *Ala., U.S.A.* 105 J2
Selma, *Calif., U.S.A.* 111 H4
Selma, *N.C., U.S.A.* 105 H6
Selmer, *U.S.A.* 105 H1
Selongey, *France* 25 E12
Selowandoma Falls, *Zimbabwe* 83 G3
Selpele, *Indonesia* 57 E8
Selsey Bill, *U.K.* 13 G7
Seltso, *Russia* 42 D2
Seltz, *France* 25 D15
Selu, *Indonesia* 57 F8
Sélune →, *France* 24 D5
Selva, *Argentina* 126 B3
Selva, *Italy* 33 B8
Selva, *Spain* 28 D6
Selvas, *Brazil* 124 B4
Selwyn, *Australia* 90 C3
Selwyn L., *Canada* 101 A8
Selwyn Ra., *Australia* 90 C3
Selyatyn, *Ukraine* 38 B8
Semani →, *Albania* 39 J2
Semara, *W. Sahara* 74 C2
Semarang, *Indonesia* 57 G14
Semau, *Indonesia* 57 F6
Sembabule, *Uganda* 82 C3
Şemdinli, *Turkey* 67 D11
Sémé, *Senegal* 78 B2
Semeih, *Sudan* 77 E3
Semenov, *Russia* 42 B7
Semenovka, *Ukraine* 41 H7
Semenovka, *Ukraine* 41 F7
Semeru, *Indonesia* 57 H15
Semey, *Kazakstan* 44 D9
Semikarakorskiy, *Russia* 43 G5
Semiluki, *Russia* 42 E4
Seminoe Reservoir, *U.S.A.* 110 E10
Seminole, *Okla., U.S.A.* 109 H6
Seminole, *Tex., U.S.A.* 109 J3
Semiozernoye, *Kazakstan* 44 D7
Semipalatinsk = Semey, *Kazakstan* 44 D9
Semirara Is., *Phil.* 55 F4
Semisopochnoi I., *U.S.A.* 96 C2
Semitau, *Indonesia* 56 D4
Semiyarka, *Kazakstan* 44 D8
Semiyarskoye = Semiyarka, *Kazakstan* 44 D8
Semmering P., *Austria* 21 H5
Semnān, *Iran* 65 C7
Semnān □, *Iran* 65 C7
Semois →, *Europe* 17 J5
Semporna, *Malaysia* 57 D5
Semuda, *Indonesia* 56 E4
Semur-en-Auxois, *France* 25 E11
Sena, *Bolivia* 124 C4
Senā, *Iran* 65 D6
Sena, *Mozam.* 83 F3
Sena →, *Bolivia* 124 C4
Sena Madureira, *Brazil* 124 B4
Senador Pompeu, *Brazil* 122 C4
Senaja, *Malaysia* 56 C5
Senaki, *Georgia* 43 J6
Senanga, *Zambia* 84 B3
Senatobia, *U.S.A.* 109 H10
Sendafa, *Ethiopia* 77 F4
Sendai, *Kagoshima, Japan* 49 J5
Sendai, *Miyagi, Japan* 48 E10
Sendai-Wan, *Japan* 48 E10
Sendenhorst, *Germany* 18 D3
Seneca, *Oreg., U.S.A.* 110 D4
Seneca, *S.C., U.S.A.* 105 H4
Seneca Falls, *U.S.A.* 107 D8
Seneca L., *U.S.A.* 106 D8
Seneffe, *Belgium* 17 G4
Senegal ■, *W. Afr.* 78 C2
Senegal →, *W. Afr.* 78 B1
Senegambia, *Africa* 70 E2
Senekal, *S. Africa* 85 D4
Senftenberg, *Germany* 18 D10
Senga Hill, *Zambia* 83 D3
Senge Khambab = Indus →, *Pakistan* 62 G2
Sengerema □, *Tanzania* 82 C3
Sengiley, *Russia* 42 D9
Sengkang, *Indonesia* 57 E6
Sengua →, *Zimbabwe* 83 F2
Senguerr →, *Argentina* 128 C3
Senhor-do-Bonfim, *Brazil* 122 D3
Senica, *Slovak Rep.* 20 G7
Senigállia, *Italy* 33 E10
Senio →, *Italy* 33 D9
Senirkent, *Turkey* 66 C4
Senise, *Italy* 35 B9
Senj, *Croatia* 33 D11
Senja, *Norway* 8 B17
Senlis, *France* 25 C9
Senmonorom, *Cambodia* 58 F6
Sennâr, *Sudan* 77 E3
Senne →, *Belgium* 17 G4
Senneterre, *Canada* 98 C4
Senniquelle, *Liberia* 78 D3
Senno, *Belarus* 40 E5
Sennori, *Italy* 34 B1
Seno, *Laos* 58 D5
Senonches, *France* 24 D8
Senorbì, *Italy* 34 C2
Senožeče, *Slovenia* 33 C11
Sens, *France* 25 D10
Senta, *Serbia, Yug.* 21 K10
Sentani, *Indonesia* 57 E10
Sentery, *Zaïre* 82 D2
Sentinel, *U.S.A.* 111 K7
Sentolo, *Indonesia* 57 G14
Senya Beraku, *Ghana* 79 D4
Seo de Urgel, *Spain* 28 C6
Seohara, *India* 63 E8
Seoni, *India* 63 H8
Seoul = Sŏul, *S. Korea* 51 F14
Separation Point, *Canada* 99 B8
Sepīdān, *Iran* 65 D7
Sepo-ri, *N. Korea* 51 E14
Sepone, *Laos* 58 D6
Sept-Îles, *Canada* 99 B6
Septemvri, *Bulgaria* 38 G7
Sepúlveda, *Spain* 30 D7
Sequeros, *Spain* 30 E4
Sequim, *U.S.A.* 112 B3
Sequoia National Park, *U.S.A.* 111 H4
Serafimovich, *Russia* 42 F6
Seraing, *Belgium* 17 G7
Seraja, *Indonesia* 59 L7
Serakhis →, *Cyprus* 37 D11
Seram, *Indonesia* 57 E7
Seram Laut, Kepulauan, *Indonesia* 57 E8
Seram Sea, *Indonesia* 57 E7
Serang, *Indonesia* 57 G12
Serasan, *Indonesia* 59 L7
Seravezza, *Italy* 32 E7
Serbia □, *Yugoslavia* 21 M11
Serdo, *Ethiopia* 77 E5
Serdobsk, *Russia* 42 D7
Seredka, *Russia* 40 C5
Şereflikoçhisar, *Turkey* 66 C5
Seregno, *Italy* 32 C6
Seremban, *Malaysia* 59 L3
Serengeti □, *Tanzania* 82 C3
Serengeti Plain, *Tanzania* 82 C3
Serenje, *Zambia* 83 E3
Sereth = Siret →, *Romania* 38 D11
Sergach, *Russia* 42 C7
Serge →, *Spain* 28 D5
Sergipe □, *Brazil* 122 D4
Sergiyev Posad, *Russia* 42 B4
Seria, *Brunei* 56 D4
Serian, *Malaysia* 56 D4
Seriate, *Italy* 32 C6
Seribu, Kepulauan, *Indonesia* 56 F3
Sérifontaine, *France* 25 C8
Sérifos, *Greece* 39 M7
Sérignan, *France* 26 E7
Serik, *Turkey* 66 D4
Seringapatam Reef, *Australia* 88 B3
Sermaize-les-Bains, *France* 25 D11
Sermata, *Indonesia* 57 F7
Sérmide, *Italy* 33 C8
Sernovodsk, *Russia* 42 D10
Sernur, *Russia* 42 B9
Serny Zavod, *Turkmenistan* 44 F6
Serón, *Spain* 29 H2
Serós, *Spain* 28 D5
Serov, *Russia* 44 D7
Serowe, *Botswana* 84 C4
Serpa, *Portugal* 31 H3
Serpeddi, Punta, *Italy* 34 C2
Serpentara, Isola, *Italy* 34 C2
Serpentine, *Australia* 89 F2
Serpentine Lakes, *Australia* 89 E4
Serpis →, *Spain* 29 G4
Serpukhov, *Russia* 42 C3
Serra do Navio, *Brazil* 121 C7
Serra San Bruno, *Italy* 35 D9
Serra Talhada, *Brazil* 122 C4
Serracapriola, *Italy* 35 A8
Serradilla, *Spain* 30 F4
Sérrai, *Greece* 39 H6
Serramanna, *Italy* 34 C1
Serrat, C., *Tunisia* 75 A6
Serre-Ponçon, L. de, *France* 27 D10
Serres, *France* 27 D9
Serrezuela, *Argentina* 126 C2
Serrinha, *Brazil* 123 D4
Serrita, *Brazil* 122 C4
Sersale, *Italy* 35 C9
Sertã, *Portugal* 30 F2
Sertânia, *Brazil* 122 C4
Sertanópolis, *Brazil* 127 A5
Sêrtar, *China* 52 A3
Sertig, *Switz.* 23 C9
Serua, *Indonesia* 57 F8
Serui, *Indonesia* 57 E9
Serule, *Botswana* 84 C4
Sérvia, *Greece* 39 J4
Sese Is., *Uganda* 82 C3
Sesepe, *Indonesia* 57 E7
Sesfontein, *Namibia* 84 B1
Sesheke, *Zambia* 84 B3
Sesia →, *Italy* 32 C5
Sesimbra, *Portugal* 31 G1
Sessa Aurunca, *Italy* 34 A6
S'estañol, *Spain* 36 B9
Sesto San Giovanni, *Italy* 32 C6
Sestri Levante, *Italy* 32 D6
Sestriere, *Italy* 32 D3
Sestroretsk, *Russia* 40 B6
Sestrunj, *Croatia* 33 D12
Sestu, *Italy* 34 C2
Sesvenna, *Switz.* 23 C10
Setana, *Japan* 48 C9
Sète, *France* 26 E7
Sete Lagôas, *Brazil* 123 E3
Sétif, *Algeria* 75 A6
Seto, *Japan* 49 G8
Setonaikai, *Japan* 49 G6
Settat, *Morocco* 74 B3
Setté-Cama, *Gabon* 80 E1
Séttimo Tor, *Italy* 32 C4
Setting L., *Canada* 101 B9
Settle, *U.K.* 12 C5
Settlement Pt., *Bahamas* 105 M6
Setto Calende, *Italy* 32 C5
Setúbal, *Portugal* 31 G2
Setúbal □, *Portugal* 31 G2
Setúbal, B. de, *Portugal* 31 G2
Seugne →, *France* 26 C3
Seulimeum, *Indonesia* 56 C1
Seuzach, *Switz.* 23 A7
Sevan, *Armenia* 43 K7
Sevan, Ozero = Sevana Lich, *Armenia* 43 K7
Sevana Lich, *Armenia* 43 K7
Sevastopol, *Ukraine* 41 K7
Sevelen, *Switz.* 23 B8
Seven Emu, *Australia* 90 B2
Seven Sisters, *Canada* 100 C3
Sevenum, *Neths.* 17 F8
Sever →, *Spain* 31 F3
Sévérac-le-Château, *France* 26 D7
Severn →, *Canada* 98 A2
Severn →, *U.K.* 13 F5
Severn L., *Canada* 98 B1
Severnaya Zemlya, *Russia* 45 B10
Severo-Kurilsk, *Russia* 45 D16
Severo-Yeniseyskiy, *Russia* 45 C10
Severodonetsk = Syeverodonetsk, *Ukraine* 41 H10
Severodvinsk, *Russia* 44 C4
Sevier, *U.S.A.* 111 G7
Sevier →, *U.S.A.* 111 G7
Sevier L., *U.S.A.* 110 G7
Sevilla, *Colombia* 120 C2
Sevilla, *Spain* 31 H5
Sevilla □, *Spain* 31 H5
Seville = Sevilla, *Spain* 31 H5
Sevnica, *Slovenia* 33 B12
Sèvre-Nantaise →, *France* 24 E5
Sèvre-Niortaise →, *France* 26 B3
Sevsk, *Russia* 42 D2
Seward, *Alaska, U.S.A.* 96 B5
Seward, *Nebr., U.S.A.* 108 E6
Seward Pen., *U.S.A.* 96 B3
Sewell, *Chile* 126 C1
Sewer, *Indonesia* 57 F8
Sewickley, *U.S.A.* 106 F4
Sexbierum, *Neths.* 16 B6
Sexsmith, *Canada* 100 B5
Seychelles ■, *Ind. Oc.* 71 G9
Seyðisfjörður, *Iceland* 8 D6
Seydişehir, *Turkey* 66 D4
Seydvān, *Iran* 67 C11
Seyhan Barajı, *Turkey* 66 D6
Seyitgazi, *Turkey* 66 C4
Seym →, *Ukraine* 41 G7
Seymchan, *Russia* 45 C16
Seymour, *Australia* 91 F4
Seymour, *S. Africa* 85 E4
Seymour, *Conn., U.S.A.* 107 E11
Seymour, *Ind., U.S.A.* 104 F3
Seymour, *Tex., U.S.A.* 109 J5
Seymour, *Wis., U.S.A.* 104 C1
Seyne, *France* 27 D10
Seyssel, *France* 27 C9
Sežana, *Slovenia* 33 C10
Sézanne, *France* 25 D10
Sezze, *Italy* 34 A6
Sfax, *Tunisia* 75 B7
Sfîntu Gheorghe, *Romania* 38 D8
Sfîntu Gheorghe, Braţul →, *Romania* 38 E12
Sha Xi →, *China* 53 D12
Sha Xian, *China* 53 D11
Shaanxi □, *China* 50 G5
Shaba □, *Zaïre* 82 D2
Shabunda, *Zaïre* 82 C2
Shache, *China* 54 C2
Shackleton Ice Shelf, *Antarctica* 5 C8
Shackleton Inlet, *Antarctica* 5 E11
Shādegān, *Iran* 65 D6
Shadi, *China* 53 D10
Shadi, *India* 63 C7
Shadrinsk, *Russia* 44 D7
Shaffa, *Nigeria* 79 C7
Shafter, *Calif., U.S.A.* 113 K7
Shafter, *Tex., U.S.A.* 109 L2
Shaftesbury, *U.K.* 13 F5
Shagamu, *Nigeria* 79 D5
Shagram, *Pakistan* 63 A5
Shah Bunder, *Pakistan* 62 G2
Shahabad, *Punjab, India* 62 D7
Shahabad, *Raj., India* 62 G7
Shahabad, *Ut. P., India* 63 F8
Shahadpur, *Pakistan* 62 G3
Shahba, *Syria* 69 C5
Shahdād, *Iran* 65 D8
Shahdadkot, *Pakistan* 62 F2
Shahe, *China* 50 F8
Shahganj, *India* 63 F10
Shahgarh, *India* 60 F6
Shaḩḩāt, *Libya* 73 B9
Shahjahanpur, *India* 63 F8
Shahpur, *India* 62 H7
Shahpur, *Pakistan* 62 E3
Shahpura, *India* 63 H9
Shahr Kord, *Iran* 65 C6
Shāhrakht, *Iran* 65 C9
Shahrig, *Pakistan* 62 D2
Shahukou, *China* 50 D7
Shaikhabad, *Afghan.* 62 B3
Shajapur, *India* 62 H7
Shakargarh, *Pakistan* 62 C6
Shakawe, *Botswana* 84 B3
Shaker Heights, *U.S.A.* 106 E3
Shakhty, *Russia* 43 G5
Shakhunya, *Russia* 42 B8
Shaki, *Nigeria* 79 D5
Shala, L., *Ethiopia* 77 F4
Shali, *Russia* 43 J7
Shallow Lake, *Canada* 106 B3
Shalqar, *Kazakstan* 44 E6
Shalskiy, *Russia* 40 B8
Shaluli Shan, *China* 52 B2
Shām, *Iran* 65 E8
Shamâl Dârfûr □, *Sudan* 77 D2
Shamâl Kordofân □, *Sudan* 77 D2
Shamanovo, *Russia* 45 C15
Shamattawa, *Canada* 101 B10
Shamattawa →, *Canada* 98 A2
Shambe, *Sudan* 77 F3
Shambu, *Ethiopia* 77 F4
Shamīl, *Iran* 65 E8
Shamkhor = Şämkir, *Azerbaijan* 43 K8
Shāmkūh, *Iran* 65 C8
Shamli, *India* 62 E7
Shamo = Gobi, *Asia* 50 C5
Shamo, L., *Ethiopia* 77 F4
Shamokin, *U.S.A.* 107 F8
Shamrock, *U.S.A.* 109 H4
Shamva, *Zimbabwe* 83 F3
Shan □, *Burma* 61 J21
Shan Xian, *China* 50 G9
Shanan →, *Ethiopia* 77 F5
Shanchengzhen, *China* 51 C13
Shāndak, *Iran* 65 D9
Shandon, *U.S.A.* 112 K6
Shandong □, *China* 51 F10
Shandong Bandao, *China* 51 F11
Shang Xian, *China* 50 H5
Shangalowe, *Zaïre* 83 E2
Shangani →, *Zimbabwe* 83 F2
Shangbancheng, *China* 51 D10
Shangcai, *China* 53 A10
Shangcheng, *China* 53 B10
Shangchuan Dao, *China* 53 G9
Shangdu, *China* 50 D7
Shanggao, *China* 53 C10
Shanghai, *China* 53 B13
Shanghang, *China* 53 E11
Shanghe, *China* 51 F9
Shangjin, *China* 53 A8
Shanglin, *China* 52 F7
Shangnan, *China* 50 H6
Shangqiu, *China* 50 G8
Shangrao, *China* 53 C11
Shangshui, *China* 50 H8
Shangsi, *China* 52 F6
Shangyou, *China* 53 E10
Shangzhi, *China* 51 B14
Shanhetun, *China* 51 B14
Shani, *Nigeria* 79 C7
Shaniko, *U.S.A.* 110 D3
Shannon, *N.Z.* 87 J5
Shannon →, *Ireland* 15 D2
Shansi = Shanxi □, *China* 50 F7
Shantar, Ostrov Bolshoy, *Russia* 45 D14
Shantipur, *India* 63 H13
Shantou, *China* 53 F11
Shantung = Shandong □, *China* 51 F10
Shanxi □, *China* 50 F7
Shanyang, *China* 50 H5
Shanyin, *China* 50 E7
Shaoguan, *China* 53 E9
Shaowu, *China* 53 D11
Shaoxing, *China* 53 C13
Shaoyang, *Hunan, China* 53 D8
Shaoyang, *Hunan, China* 53 D8
Shapinsay, *U.K.* 14 B6
Shaqra', *Si. Arabia* 64 E5
Shaqrā', *Yemen* 68 E4
Sharafa, *Sudan* 77 E2
Sharafkhāneh, *Iran* 67 C11
Sharbot Lake, *Canada* 107 B8
Shari, *Japan* 48 C12

Sharjah = Ash Shāriqah, *U.A.E.* 65 E7
Shark B., *Australia* 89 E1
Sharm el Sheikh, *Egypt* 76 B3
Sharon, *Mass., U.S.A.* 107 D13
Sharon, *Pa., U.S.A.* 106 E4
Sharon Springs, *U.S.A.* 108 F4
Sharp Pt., *Australia* 90 A3
Sharpe L., *Canada* 101 C10
Sharpsville, *U.S.A.* 106 E4
Sharq el Istiwa'iya □, *Sudan* 77 F3
Sharya, *Russia* 42 A7
Shasha, *Ethiopia* 77 F4
Shashemene, *Ethiopia* 77 F4
Shashi, *Botswana* 85 C4
Shashi, *China* 53 B9
Shashi →, *Africa* 83 G2
Shasta, Mt., *U.S.A.* 110 F2
Shasta L., *U.S.A.* 110 F2
Shatsk, *Russia* 42 C5
Shatt al'Arab →, *Iraq* 65 D6
Shattuck, *U.S.A.* 109 G5
Shatura, *Russia* 42 C4
Shaumyani = Shulaveri, *Georgia* 43 K7
Shaunavon, *Canada* 101 D7
Shaver L., *U.S.A.* 112 H7
Shaw →, *Australia* 88 D2
Shaw I., *Australia* 90 C4
Shawan, *China* 54 B3
Shawanaga, *Canada* 106 A4
Shawano, *U.S.A.* 104 C1
Shawinigan, *Canada* 98 C5
Shawnee, *U.S.A.* 109 H6
Shaybārā, *Si. Arabia* 64 E3
Shayib el Banat, Gebel, *Egypt* 76 B3
Shaykh Sa'īd, *Iraq* 67 F12
Shchekino, *Russia* 42 C3
Shcherbakov = Rybinsk, *Russia* 42 A4
Shchigry, *Russia* 42 E3
Shchors, *Ukraine* 41 G6
Shchuchinsk, *Kazakstan* 44 D8
She Xian, *Anhui, China* 53 C12
She Xian, *Hebei, China* 50 F7
Shea, *Guyana* 121 C6
Shebekino, *Russia* 42 E3
Shebele = Scebeli, Wabi →, *Somali Rep.* 68 G3
Sheboygan, *U.S.A.* 104 D2
Shediac, *Canada* 99 C7
Sheelin, L., *Ireland* 15 C4
Sheep Haven, *Ireland* 15 A4
Sheerness, *U.K.* 13 F8
Sheet Harbour, *Canada* 99 D7
Sheffield, *U.K.* 12 D6
Sheffield, *Ala., U.S.A.* 105 H2
Sheffield, *Mass., U.S.A.* 107 D11
Sheffield, *Pa., U.S.A.* 106 E5
Sheffield, *Tex., U.S.A.* 109 K4
Sheho, *Canada* 101 C8
Shehojele, *Ethiopia* 77 E4
Shehong, *China* 52 B5
Shehuen →, *Argentina* 128 C3
Sheikhpura, *India* 63 G11
Shek Hasan, *Ethiopia* 77 E4
Shekhupura, *Pakistan* 62 D5
Sheki = Şaki, *Azerbaijan* 43 K8
Shelburne, *N.S., Canada* 99 D6
Shelburne, *Ont., Canada* 98 D3
Shelburne, *U.S.A.* 107 B11
Shelburne B., *Australia* 90 A3
Shelburne Falls, *U.S.A.* 107 D12
Shelby, *Mich., U.S.A.* 104 D2
Shelby, *Mont., U.S.A.* 110 B8
Shelby, *N.C., U.S.A.* 105 H5
Shelby, *Ohio, U.S.A.* 106 F2
Shelbyville, *Ill., U.S.A.* 108 F10
Shelbyville, *Ind., U.S.A.* 104 F3
Shelbyville, *Tenn., U.S.A.* 105 H2
Sheldon, *U.S.A.* 108 D7
Sheldrake, *Canada* 99 B7
Shelikhova, Zaliv, *Russia* 45 D16
Shell Lake, *Canada* 101 C7
Shell Lakes, *Australia* 89 E4
Shellbrook, *Canada* 101 C7
Shellharbour, *Australia* 91 E5
Shelling Rocks, *Ireland* 15 E1
Shelon →, *Russia* 40 C6
Shelton, *Conn., U.S.A.* 107 E11
Shelton, *Wash., U.S.A.* 112 C3
Shemakha = Şamaxi, *Azerbaijan* 43 K9
Shen Xian, *China* 50 F8
Shenandoah, *Iowa, U.S.A.* 108 E7
Shenandoah, *Pa., U.S.A.* 107 F8
Shenandoah, *Va., U.S.A.* 104 F6
Shenandoah →, *U.S.A.* 104 F7
Shenchi, *China* 50 E7
Shendam, *Nigeria* 79 D6
Shendī, *Sudan* 77 D3
Sheng Xian, *China* 53 C13
Shengfang, *China* 50 E9
Shëngjergji, *Albania* 39 H3
Shëngjini, *Albania* 39 H2
Shenjingzi, *China* 51 B13
Shenmu, *China* 50 E6
Shennongjia, *China* 53 B8
Shenqiu, *China* 50 H8
Shenqiucheng, *China* 50 H8
Shensi = Shaanxi □, *China* 50 G5
Shenyang, *China* 51 D12
Shenzhen, *China* 53 F10
Sheopur Kalan, *India* 60 G10
Shepetivka, *Ukraine* 41 G4
Shepetovka = Shepetivka, *Ukraine* 41 G4
Shepparton, *Australia* 91 F4
Sheqi, *China* 50 H7
Sher Qila, *Pakistan* 63 A6
Sherborne, *U.K.* 13 G5
Sherbro I., *S. Leone* 78 D2
Sherbrooke, *Canada* 99 C5
Shereik, *Sudan* 76 D3
Sheridan, *Ark., U.S.A.* 109 H8
Sheridan, *Wyo., U.S.A.* 110 D10
Sherkot, *India* 63 E8
Sherman, *U.S.A.* 109 J6
Sherridon, *Canada* 101 B8
Sherwood, *N. Dak., U.S.A.* 108 A4
Sherwood, *Tex., U.S.A.* 109 K4
Sherwood Forest, *U.K.* 12 D6
Sheslay, *Canada* 100 B2
Sheslay →, *Canada* 100 B2
Shethanei L., *Canada* 101 B9
Shetland □, *U.K.* 14 A7
Shetland Is., *U.K.* 14 A7
Shewa □, *Ethiopia* 77 F4
Shewa Gimira, *Ethiopia* 77 F4
Sheyenne, *U.S.A.* 108 B5
Sheyenne →, *U.S.A.* 108 B6
Shibām, *Yemen* 68 D4
Shibata, *Japan* 48 F9
Shibecha, *Japan* 48 C12
Shibetsu, *Japan* 48 B11
Shibîn el Kôm, *Egypt* 76 H7
Shibîn el Qanâtir, *Egypt* 76 H7
Shibing, *China* 52 D7
Shibogama L., *Canada* 98 B2
Shibushi, *Japan* 49 J5
Shicheng, *China* 53 D11
Shickshock Mts. = Chic-Chocs, Mts., *Canada* 99 C6
Shidao, *China* 51 F12
Shidian, *China* 52 E2
Shido, *Japan* 49 G7
Shiel, L., *U.K.* 14 E3
Shield, C., *Australia* 90 A2
Shiga □, *Japan* 49 G8
Shigaib, *Sudan* 73 E9
Shigu, *China* 52 D2
Shiguaigou, *China* 50 D6
Shihchiachuangi = Shijiazhuang, *China* 50 E8
Shijiazhuang, *China* 50 E8
Shijiu Hu, *China* 53 B12
Shikarpur, *India* 62 E8
Shikarpur, *Pakistan* 62 F3
Shikoku □, *Japan* 49 H6
Shikoku-Sanchi, *Japan* 49 H6
Shilabo, *Ethiopia* 68 F3
Shiliguri, *India* 61 F16
Shilka, *Russia* 45 D12
Shilka →, *Russia* 45 D13
Shillelagh, *Ireland* 15 D5
Shillong, *India* 61 G17
Shilo, *West Bank* 69 C4
Shilong, *China* 53 F9
Shilou, *China* 50 F6
Shilovo, *Russia* 42 C5
Shimabara, *Japan* 49 H5
Shimada, *Japan* 49 G9
Shimane □, *Japan* 49 G6
Shimanovsk, *Russia* 45 D13
Shimen, *China* 53 C8
Shimenjie, *China* 53 C11
Shimian, *China* 52 C4
Shimizu, *Japan* 49 G9
Shimodate, *Japan* 49 F9
Shimoga, *India* 60 N9
Shimoni, *Kenya* 82 C4
Shimonoseki, *Japan* 49 H5
Shimpuru Rapids, *Angola* 84 B2
Shimsk, *Russia* 40 C6
Shin, L., *U.K.* 14 C4
Shin-Tone →, *Japan* 49 G10
Shinan, *China* 52 F7
Shinano →, *Japan* 49 F9
Shīndand, *Afghan.* 60 C3
Shingleton, *U.S.A.* 98 C2
Shingū, *Japan* 49 H7
Shinjō, *Japan* 48 E10
Shinkafe, *Nigeria* 79 C6
Shinshār, *Syria* 69 A5
Shinyanga, *Tanzania* 82 C3
Shinyanga □, *Tanzania* 82 C3
Shiogama, *Japan* 48 E10
Shiojiri, *Japan* 49 F8
Ship I., *U.S.A.* 109 K10
Shipehenski Prokhod, *Bulgaria* 38 G8
Shiping, *China* 52 F4
Shipki La, *India* 60 D11
Shippegan, *Canada* 99 C7
Shippensburg, *U.S.A.* 106 F7
Shiprock, *U.S.A.* 111 H9
Shiqian, *China* 52 D7
Shiqma, N. →, *Israel* 69 D3
Shiquan, *China* 50 H5
Shīr Kūh, *Iran* 65 D7
Shiragami-Misaki, *Japan* 48 D10
Shirakawa, *Fukushima, Japan* 49 F10
Shirakawa, *Gifu, Japan* 49 F8
Shirane-San, *Gumma, Japan* 49 F9
Shirane-San, *Yamanashi, Japan* 49 G9
Shiraoi, *Japan* 48 C10
Shīrāz, *Iran* 65 D7
Shirbīn, *Egypt* 76 H7
Shire →, *Africa* 83 F4
Shiretoko-Misaki, *Japan* 48 B12
Shirinab →, *Pakistan* 62 D2
Shiriya-Zaki, *Japan* 48 D10
Shiroishi, *Japan* 48 E10
Shīrvān, *Iran* 65 B8
Shirwa, L. = Chilwa, L., *Malawi* 83 F4
Shishou, *China* 53 C9
Shitai, *China* 53 B11
Shivpuri, *India* 62 G7
Shixian, *China* 51 C15
Shixing, *China* 53 E10
Shiyan, *China* 53 A8
Shiyata, *Egypt* 76 B2
Shizhu, *China* 52 C7
Shizong, *China* 52 E5
Shizuishan, *China* 50 E4
Shizuoka, *Japan* 49 G9
Shizuoka □, *Japan* 49 G9
Shklov = Shklow, *Belarus* 40 E6
Shklow, *Belarus* 40 E6
Shkoder = Shkodra, *Albania* 38 G2
Shkodra, *Albania* 38 G2
Shkumbini →, *Albania* 39 H2
Shmidta, O., *Russia* 45 A10
Shō-Gawa →, *Japan* 49 F8
Shoal Lake, *Canada* 101 C8
Shōdo-Shima, *Japan* 49 G7
Shoeburyness, *U.K.* 13 F8
Sholapur = Solapur, *India* 60 L9
Shologontsy, *Russia* 45 C12
Shōmrōn, *West Bank* 69 C4
Shoshone, *Calif., U.S.A.* 113 K10
Shoshone, *Idaho, U.S.A.* 110 E6
Shoshone L., *U.S.A.* 110 D8
Shoshone Mts., *U.S.A.* 110 G5
Shoshong, *Botswana* 84 C4
Shoshoni, *U.S.A.* 110 E9
Shostka, *Ukraine* 41 G7
Shou Xian, *China* 53 A11
Shouchang, *China* 53 C12
Shouguang, *China* 51 F10
Shouning, *China* 53 D12
Shouyang, *China* 50 F7
Show Low, *U.S.A.* 111 J9
Shpola, *Ukraine* 41 H6
Shreveport, *U.S.A.* 109 J8
Shrewsbury, *U.K.* 12 E5
Shrirampur, *India* 63 H13
Shropshire □, *U.K.* 13 E5
Shu, *Kazakstan* 44 E8
Shu →, *Kazakstan* 46 E10
Shuangbai, *China* 52 E3
Shuangcheng, *China* 51 B14
Shuangfeng, *China* 53 D9
Shuanggou, *China* 51 G9
Shuangjiang, *China* 52 F2
Shuangliao, *China* 51 C12
Shuangshanzi, *China* 51 D10
Shuangyang, *China* 51 C13
Shuangyashan, *China* 54 B8
Shucheng, *China* 53 B11
Shugozero, *Russia* 40 C8
Shuguri Falls, *Tanzania* 83 D4
Shuiji, *China* 53 D12
Shuiye, *China* 50 F8
Shujalpur, *India* 62 H7
Shukpa Kunzang, *India* 63 B8
Shulan, *China* 51 B14
Shulaveri, *Georgia* 43 K7
Shule, *China* 54 C2
Shumagin Is., *U.S.A.* 96 C4
Shumerlya, *Russia* 42 C8
Shumikha, *Russia* 44 D7
Shunchang, *China* 53 D11
Shunde, *China* 53 F9
Shungay, *Kazakstan* 43 F8
Shungnak, *U.S.A.* 96 B4
Shuo Xian, *China* 50 E7
Shūr →, *Iran* 65 D7
Shūr Āb, *Iran* 65 C6
Shūr Gaz, *Iran* 65 D8
Shūrāb, *Iran* 65 C8
Shūrjestān, *Iran* 65 D7
Shurugwi, *Zimbabwe* 83 F3
Shūsf, *Iran* 65 D9
Shūsh, *Iran* 67 F13
Shūshtar, *Iran* 65 D6
Shuswap L., *Canada* 100 C5
Shuya, *Russia* 42 B5
Shuyang, *China* 51 G10
Shūzū, *Iran* 65 D7
Shwebo, *Burma* 61 H19
Shwegu, *Burma* 61 G20
Shweli →, *Burma* 61 H20
Shymkent, *Kazakstan* 44 E7
Shyok, *India* 63 B8
Shyok →, *Pakistan* 63 B6
Si Chon, *Thailand* 59 H2
Si Kiang = Xi Jiang →, *China* 53 F9
Si-ngan = Xi'an, *China* 50 G5
Si Prachan, *Thailand* 58 E3
Si Racha, *Thailand* 58 F3
Si Xian, *China* 51 H9
Siahan Range, *Pakistan* 60 F4
Siaksriindrapura, *Indonesia* 56 D2
Sialkot, *Pakistan* 62 C6
Siam = Thailand ■, *Asia* 58 E4
Siantan, P., *Indonesia* 59 L6
Siàpo →, *Venezuela* 120 C4
Sīāreh, *Iran* 65 D9
Siargao, *Phil.* 55 G7
Siari, *Pakistan* 63 B7
Siasi, *Phil.* 57 C6
Siasi I., *Phil.* 55 J4
Siátista, *Greece* 39 J4
Siau, *Indonesia* 57 D7
Šiauliai, *Lithuania* 9 J20
Siaya □, *Kenya* 82 B3
Siazan = Siyäzän, *Azerbaijan* 43 K9
Sibâi, Gebel el, *Egypt* 76 B3
Sibari, *Italy* 35 C9
Sibayi, L., *S. Africa* 85 D5
Šibenik, *Croatia* 33 E12
Siberia, *Russia* 4 D13
Siberut, *Indonesia* 56 E1
Sibi, *Pakistan* 62 E2
Sibil, *Indonesia* 57 E10
Sibiti, *Congo* 80 E2
Sibiu, *Romania* 38 D7
Sibley, *Iowa, U.S.A.* 108 D7
Sibley, *La., U.S.A.* 109 J8
Sibolga, *Indonesia* 56 D1
Sibret, *Belgium* 17 J7
Sibsagar, *India* 61 F19
Sibu, *Malaysia* 56 D4
Sibuco, *Phil.* 55 H5
Sibuguey B., *Phil.* 55 H5
Sibut, *C.A.R.* 73 G8
Sibutu, *Phil.* 57 D5
Sibutu Group, *Phil.* 55 J3
Sibutu Passage, *E. Indies* 57 D5
Sibuyan, *Phil.* 55 E5
Sibuyan Sea, *Phil.* 55 E5
Sicamous, *Canada* 100 C5
Sichuan □, *China* 52 B5
Sicilia, *Italy* 35 E7
Sicilia □, *Italy* 35 E7
Sicilia, Canale di, *Italy* 34 E5
Sicilian Channel = Sicilia, Canale di, *Italy* 34 E5
Sicily = Sicilia, *Italy* 35 E7
Sicuani, *Peru* 124 C3
Siculiana, *Italy* 34 E6
Sidamo □, *Ethiopia* 77 G4
Sidaouet, *Niger* 79 B6
Sidári, *Greece* 37 A3
Siddeburen, *Neths.* 16 B9
Siddhapur, *India* 62 H5
Siddipet, *India* 60 K11
Sidéradougou, *Burkina Faso* 78 C4
Siderno, *Italy* 35 D9
Sídheros, Ákra, *Greece* 37 D8
Sidhirókastron, *Greece* 39 H6
Sîdi Abd el Rahmân, *Egypt* 76 H6
Sîdi Barrâni, *Egypt* 76 A2
Sidi-bel-Abbès, *Algeria* 75 A4
Sidi Bennour, *Morocco* 74 B3
Sidi Haneish, *Egypt* 76 A2
Sidi Kacem, *Morocco* 74 B3
Sidi Omar, *Egypt* 76 A1
Sidi Slimane, *Morocco* 74 B3
Sidi Smaïl, *Morocco* 74 B3
Sidlaw Hills, *U.K.* 14 E5
Sidley, Mt., *Antarctica* 5 D14
Sidmouth, *U.K.* 13 G4
Sidmouth, C., *Australia* 90 A3
Sidney, *Canada* 100 D4
Sidney, *Mont., U.S.A.* 108 B2
Sidney, *N.Y., U.S.A.* 107 D9
Sidney, *Nebr., U.S.A.* 108 E3
Sidney, *Ohio, U.S.A.* 104 E3
Sidoarjo, *Indonesia* 57 G15
Sidon = Saydā, *Lebanon* 69 B4
Sidra, G. of = Surt, Khalīj, *Libya* 73 B8
Sidra, G. of, *Libya* 70 C5
Siedlce, *Poland* 20 C12
Sieg →, *Germany* 18 E3
Siegburg, *Germany* 18 E3
Siegen, *Germany* 18 E4
Siem Pang, *Cambodia* 58 E6
Siem Reap, *Cambodia* 58 F4
Siena, *Italy* 33 E8
Sieradz, *Poland* 20 D8
Sierck-les-Bains, *France* 25 C13
Sierpc, *Poland* 20 C9
Sierpe, Bocas de la, *Venezuela* 121 B5
Sierra Blanca, *U.S.A.* 111 L11
Sierra Blanca Peak, *U.S.A.* 111 K11
Sierra City, *U.S.A.* 112 F6
Sierra Colorada, *Argentina* 128 B3
Sierra de Yeguas, *Spain* 31 H6
Sierra Gorda, *Chile* 126 A2
Sierra Grande, *Argentina* 128 B3
Sierra Leone ■, *W. Afr.* 78 D2
Sierra Madre, *Mexico* 115 D6
Sierra Mojada, *Mexico* 114 B4
Sierraville, *U.S.A.* 112 F6
Sierre, *Switz.* 22 D5
Sífnos, *Greece* 39 N7
Sifton, *Canada* 101 C8
Sifton Pass, *Canada* 100 B3
Sig, *Algeria* 75 A4
Sigdal, *Norway* 10 D3
Sigean, *France* 26 E6
Sighetu-Marmatiei, *Romania* 38 B6
Sighişoara, *Romania* 38 C7
Sigli, *Indonesia* 56 C1
Siglufjörður, *Iceland* 8 C4
Sigmaringen, *Germany* 19 G5
Signakhi = Tsnori, *Georgia* 43 K7
Signal, *U.S.A.* 113 L13
Signal Pk., *U.S.A.* 113 M12
Signau, *Switz.* 22 C5
Signy-l'Abbaye, *France* 25 C11
Sigsig, *Ecuador* 120 D2
Sigtuna, *Sweden* 10 E11
Sigüenza, *Spain* 28 D2
Siguiri, *Guinea* 78 C3
Sigulda, *Latvia* 9 H21
Sigurd, *U.S.A.* 111 G8
Sihanoukville = Kompong Som, *Cambodia* 59 G4
Sihaus, *Peru* 124 B2
Sihui, *China* 53 F9
Siikajoki →, *Finland* 8 D21
Siilinjärvi, *Finland* 8 E22
Siirt, *Turkey* 67 D9
Sijarira Ra., *Zimbabwe* 83 F2
Sikao, *Thailand* 59 J2
Sikar, *India* 62 F6
Sikasso, *Mali* 78 C3
Sikeston, *U.S.A.* 109 G10
Sikhote Alin, Khrebet, *Russia* 45 E14
Sikhote Alin Ra. = Sikhote Alin, Khrebet, *Russia* 45 E14
Sikiá., *Greece* 39 J6
Síkinos, *Greece* 39 N8
Sikkani Chief →, *Canada* 100 B4
Sikkim □, *India* 61 F16
Sikotu-Ko, *Japan* 48 C10
Sil →, *Spain* 30 C3
Silacayoapan, *Mexico* 115 D5
Silandro, *Italy* 32 B7
Silay, *Phil.* 55 F5
Silba, *Croatia* 33 D11
Silchar, *India* 61 G18
Silcox, *Canada* 101 B10
Şile, *Turkey* 66 B3
Silenrieux, *Belgium* 17 H4
Siler City, *U.S.A.* 105 H6
Silesia = Śląsk, *Poland* 20 E6
Silet, *Algeria* 75 D5
Silgarhi Doti, *Nepal* 63 E9
Silghat, *India* 61 F18
Silifke, *Turkey* 66 D5
Siliguri = Shiliguri, *India* 61 F16
Siling Co, *China* 54 C3
Silíqua, *Italy* 34 C1
Silistra, *Bulgaria* 38 E10
Silivri, *Turkey* 66 B3
Siljan, *Sweden* 9 F16
Silkeborg, *Denmark* 11 H3
Sillajhuay, Cordillera, *Chile* 124 D4
Sillamäe, *Estonia* 9 G22
Sillé-le-Guillaume, *France* 24 D6
Sillustani, *Peru* 124 D3
Siloam Springs, *U.S.A.* 109 G7
Silopi, *Turkey* 67 D10
Silsbee, *U.S.A.* 109 K7
Šilute, *Lithuania* 9 J19
Silva Porto = Kuito, *Angola* 81 G3
Silvan, *Turkey* 67 C9
Silvaplana, *Switz.* 23 D9
Silver City, *N. Mex., U.S.A.* 111 K9
Silver City, *Nev., U.S.A.* 110 G4
Silver Cr. →, *U.S.A.* 110 E4
Silver Creek, *U.S.A.* 106 D5
Silver L., *Calif., U.S.A.* 112 G6
Silver L., *Calif., U.S.A.* 113 K10
Silver Lake, *U.S.A.* 110 E3
Silver Streams, *S. Africa* 84 D3
Silverton, *Colo., U.S.A.* 111 H10
Silverton, *Tex., U.S.A.* 109 H4
Silves, *Portugal* 31 H2
Silvi Marina, *Italy* 33 F11
Silvia, *Colombia* 120 C2
Silvies →, *U.S.A.* 110 E4
Silvolde, *Neths.* 16 E8
Silvretta-Gruppe, *Switz.* 23 C10
Silwa Bahari, *Egypt* 76 C3
Silz, *Austria* 19 H6
Sim, C., *Morocco* 74 B3
Simanggang, *Malaysia* 56 D4
Simao, *China* 52 F3
Simão Dias, *Brazil* 122 D4
Simard, L., *Canada* 98 C4
Şimareh →, *Iran* 67 F12
Simav, *Turkey* 66 C3
Simba, *Tanzania* 82 C4
Simbach, *Germany* 19 G9
Simbirsk, *Russia* 42 C9
Simbo, *Tanzania* 82 C2
Simcoe, *Canada* 98 D3
Simcoe, L., *Canada* 98 D4
Simenga, *Russia* 45 C11
Simeto →, *Italy* 35 E8
Simeulue, *Indonesia* 56 D1
Simferopol, *Ukraine* 41 K8
Sími, *Greece* 66 D2
Simi Valley, *U.S.A.* 113 L8
Simikot, *Nepal* 63 E9
Simití, *Colombia* 120 B3
Simla, *India* 62 D7
Şimleu-Silvaniei, *Romania* 38 B5
Simme →, *Switz.* 22 C4
Simmern, *Germany* 19 F3
Simmie, *Canada* 101 D7
Simmler, *U.S.A.* 113 K7
Simões, *Brazil* 122 C3
Simojoki →, *Finland* 8 D21
Simojovel, *Mexico* 115 D6
Simonette →, *Canada* 100 B5
Simonstown, *S. Africa* 84 E2
Simplício Mendes, *Brazil* 122 C3
Simplon, *Switz.* 22 D6
Simplon P., *Switz.* 22 D6
Simplon Tunnel, *Switz.* 22 D6
Simpson Desert, *Australia* 90 D2
Simpungdong, *N. Korea* 51 D15
Simrishamn, *Sweden* 9 J16

Simunjan, *Malaysia* 56 D4
Simushir, Ostrov, *Russia* 45 E16
Sinabang, *Indonesia* 56 D1
Sinadogo, *Somali Rep.* 68 F4
Sinai = Es Sînâ', *Egypt* 76 J8
Sinai, Mt. = Mûsa, G., *Egypt* 76 J8
Sinai Peninsula, *Egypt* 69 F2
Sinaia, *Romania* 38 D8
Sinaloa □, *Mexico* 114 C3
Sinaloa de Levya, *Mexico* 114 B3
Sinalunga, *Italy* 33 E8
Sinan, *China* 52 D7
Sinarádhes, *Greece* 37 A3
Sīnāwan, *Libya* 75 B7
Sincan, *Turkey* 66 B5
Sincé, *Colombia* 120 B2
Sincelejo, *Colombia* 120 B2
Sinchang, *N. Korea* 51 D15
Sinchang-ni, *N. Korea* 51 E14
Sinclair, *U.S.A.* 110 F10
Sinclair Mills, *Canada* 100 C4
Sincorá, Serra do, *Brazil* 123 D3
Sind, *Pakistan* 62 G3
Sind □, *Pakistan* 62 F3
Sind →, *India* 63 B6
Sind Sagar Doab, *Pakistan* 62 D4
Sindal, *Denmark* 11 G4
Sindangan, *Phil.* 55 G5
Sindangbarang, *Indonesia* 57 G12
Sinde, *Zambia* 83 F2
Sinegorskiy, *Russia* 43 G5
Sinelnikovo = Synelnykove, *Ukraine* 41 H8
Sines, *Portugal* 31 H2
Sines, C. de, *Portugal* 31 H2
Sineu, *Spain* 36 B10
Sinfra, *Ivory C.* 78 D3
Sing Buri, *Thailand* 58 E3
Singa, *Sudan* 77 E3
Singapore ■, *Asia* 59 M4
Singapore, Straits of, *Asia* 59 M5
Singaraja, *Indonesia* 56 F5
Singen, *Germany* 19 H4
Singida, *Tanzania* 82 C3
Singida □, *Tanzania* 82 D3
Singitikós Kólpos, *Greece* 39 J6
Singkaling Hkamti, *Burma* 61 G19
Singkawang, *Indonesia* 56 D3
Singleton, *Australia* 91 E5
Singleton, Mt., *N. Terr., Australia* 88 D5
Singleton, Mt., *W. Austral., Australia* 89 E2
Singoli, *India* 62 G6
Singora = Songkhla, *Thailand* 59 J3
Singosan, *N. Korea* 51 E14
Sinhung, *N. Korea* 51 D14
Sînî □, *Egypt* 69 F2
Siniscóla, *Italy* 34 B2
Sinj, *Croatia* 33 E13
Sinjai, *Indonesia* 57 F6
Sinjār, *Iraq* 67 D9
Sinkat, *Sudan* 76 D4
Sinkiang Uighur = Xinjiang Uygur Zizhiqu □, *China* 54 B3
Sinmak, *N. Korea* 51 E14
Sinnai, *Italy* 34 C2
Sinni →, *Italy* 35 B9
Sinnuris, *Egypt* 76 J7
Sinoe, L., *Romania* 38 E11
Sinop, *Turkey* 66 A6
Sinpo, *N. Korea* 51 E15
Sins, *Switz.* 23 B6
Sinsk, *Russia* 45 C13
Sint-Amandsberg, *Belgium* 17 F3
Sint Annaland, *Neths.* 17 E4
Sint Annaparoch, *Neths.* 16 B7
Sint-Denijs, *Belgium* 17 G2
Sint Eustatius, I., *Neth. Ant.* 117 C7
Sint-Genesius-Rode, *Belgium* 17 G4
Sint-Gillis-Waas, *Belgium* 17 F4
Sint-Huibrechts-Lille, *Belgium* 17 F6
Sint-Katelinje-Waver, *Belgium* 17 F5
Sint-Kruis, *Belgium* 17 F2
Sint-Laureins, *Belgium* 17 F3
Sint Maarten, I., *W. Indies* 117 C7
Sint-Michiels, *Belgium* 17 F2
Sint Nicolaasga, *Neths.* 16 C7
Sint Niklaas, *Belgium* 17 F4
Sint Oedenrode, *Neths.* 17 E6
Sint Pancras, *Neths.* 16 C5
Sint Philipsland, *Neths.* 17 E4
Sint Truiden, *Belgium* 17 G6
Sint Willebrord, *Neths.* 17 E5
Sîntana, *Romania* 38 C4
Sintang, *Indonesia* 56 D4
Sintjohannesga, *Neths.* 16 C7
Sinton, *U.S.A.* 109 L6
Sintra, *Portugal* 31 G1
Sinŭiju, *N. Korea* 51 D13
Sinyukha →, *Ukraine* 41 H6
Siocon, *Phil.* 55 H5
Siófok, *Hungary* 21 J8
Sioma, *Zambia* 84 B3
Sion, *Switz.* 22 D4
Sioux City, *U.S.A.* 108 D6
Sioux Falls, *U.S.A.* 108 D6
Sioux Lookout, *Canada* 98 B1
Sipalay, *Phil.* 55 G5
Siping, *China* 51 C13
Sipiwesk L., *Canada* 101 B9
Sipura, *Indonesia* 56 E1
Siquia →, *Nic.* 116 D3
Siquijor, *Phil.* 55 G5
Siquirres, *Costa Rica* 116 D3
Siquisique, *Venezuela* 120 A4
Sir Edward Pellew Group, *Australia* 90 B2
Sir Graham Moore Is., *Australia* 88 B4
Sira →, *Norway* 9 G12
Siracusa, *Italy* 35 E8
Sirajganj, *Bangla.* 63 G13
Sirakoro, *Mali* 78 C3
Şiran, *Turkey* 67 B8
Sirasso, *Ivory C.* 78 D3
Sīrdān, *Iran* 67 D13
Sirdaryo = Syrdarya →, *Kazakstan* 44 E7
Sirer, *Spain* 36 C7
Siret, *Romania* 38 B9
Siret →, *Romania* 38 D11
Şiria, *Romania* 38 C4
Sirino, Mte., *Italy* 35 B8
Sírna, *Greece* 39 N9
Sirnach, *Switz.* 23 B7
Şirnak, *Turkey* 67 D10
Sirohi, *India* 62 G5
Sironj, *India* 62 G7
Síros, *Greece* 39 M7
Sirretta Pk., *U.S.A.* 113 K8
Sirsa, *India* 62 E6
Siruela, *Spain* 31 G5
Sisak, *Croatia* 33 C13
Sisaket, *Thailand* 58 E5
Sisante, *Spain* 29 F2
Sisargas, Is., *Spain* 30 B2
Sishen, *S. Africa* 84 D3
Sishui, *Henan, China* 50 G7
Sishui, *Shandong, China* 51 G9
Sisipuk L., *Canada* 101 B8
Sisophon, *Cambodia* 58 F4
Sissach, *Switz.* 22 B5
Sisseton, *U.S.A.* 108 C6
Sissonne, *France* 25 C10
Sīstān va Balūchestān □, *Iran* 65 E9
Sisteron, *France* 27 D9
Sisters, *U.S.A.* 110 D3
Sitamarhi, *India* 63 F11
Sitapur, *India* 63 F9
Siteki, *Swaziland* 85 D5
Sitges, *Spain* 28 D6
Sitía, *Greece* 37 D8
Sítio da Abadia, *Brazil* 123 D2
Sitka, *U.S.A.* 96 C6
Sitoti, *Botswana* 84 C3
Sitra, *Egypt* 76 B2
Sittang Myit →, *Burma* 61 L20
Sittard, *Neths.* 17 G7
Sittensen, *Germany* 18 B5
Sittona, *Eritrea* 77 E4
Sittwe, *Burma* 61 J18
Siuna, *Nic.* 116 D3
Siuri, *India* 63 H12
Sivana, *India* 62 E8
Sīvand, *Iran* 65 D7
Sivas, *Turkey* 66 C7
Siverek, *Turkey* 67 D8
Sivrihisar, *Turkey* 66 C4
Sivry, *Belgium* 17 H4
Sîwa, *Egypt* 76 B2
Sîwa, El Wâhât es, *Egypt* 76 B2
Siwa Oasis, *Egypt* 70 D6
Siwalik Range, *Nepal* 63 F10
Siwan, *India* 63 F11
Siyâl, Jazâ'ir, *Egypt* 76 C4
Siyäzän, *Azerbaijan* 43 K9
Sizewell, *U.K.* 13 E9
Siziwang Qi, *China* 50 D6
Sjælland, *Denmark* 11 J5
Sjællands Odde, *Denmark* 11 J5
Själevad, *Sweden* 10 A12
Sjenica, *Serbia, Yug.* 21 M10
Sjoa, *Norway* 10 C3
Sjöbo, *Sweden* 11 J7
Sjösa, *Sweden* 11 F11
Sjumen = Šumen, *Bulgaria* 38 F9
Skadovsk, *Ukraine* 41 J7
Skaftafell, *Iceland* 8 D5
Skagafjörður, *Iceland* 8 D4
Skagastølstindane, *Norway* 9 F12
Skagaströnd, *Iceland* 8 D3
Skagen, *Denmark* 11 G4
Skagerrak, *Denmark* 11 G3
Skagit →, *U.S.A.* 112 B4
Skagway, *U.S.A.* 100 B1
Skala-Podilska, *Ukraine* 41 H4
Skala Podolskaya = Skala-Podilska, *Ukraine* 41 H4
Skalat, *Ukraine* 41 H3
Skalni Dol = Kamenyak, *Bulgaria* 38 F9
Skals, *Denmark* 11 H3
Skanderborg, *Denmark* 11 H3
Skåne, *Sweden* 9 J15
Skanör, *Sweden* 11 J6
Skara, *Sweden* 9 G15
Skardu, *Pakistan* 63 B6
Skarrild, *Denmark* 11 J2
Skarzysko-Kamienna, *Poland* 20 D10
Skebokvarn, *Sweden* 10 E10
Skeena →, *Canada* 100 C2
Skeena Mts., *Canada* 100 B3
Skegness, *U.K.* 12 D8
Skeldon, *Guyana* 121 B6
Skellefte älv →, *Sweden* 8 D19
Skellefteå, *Sweden* 8 D19
Skelleftehamn, *Sweden* 8 D19
Skender Vakuf, *Bos.-H.* 21 L7
Skene, *Sweden* 11 G6
Skerries, The, *U.K.* 12 D3
Skhoinoúsa, *Greece* 39 N8
Ski, *Norway* 10 E4
Skíathos, *Greece* 39 K6
Skibbereen, *Ireland* 15 E2
Skiddaw, *U.K.* 12 C4
Skien, *Norway* 10 E3
Skierniewice, *Poland* 20 D10
Skikda, *Algeria* 75 A6
Skilloura, *Cyprus* 37 D12
Skinári, Ákra, *Greece* 39 M3
Skipton, *Australia* 91 F3
Skipton, *U.K.* 12 D5
Skirmish Pt., *Australia* 90 A1
Skíros, *Greece* 39 L7
Skivarp, *Sweden* 11 J7
Skive, *Denmark* 11 H3
Skjálfandafljót →, *Iceland* 8 D5
Skjálfandi, *Iceland* 8 C5
Skjeberg, *Norway* 10 E5
Skjern, *Denmark* 11 J2
Škofja Loka, *Slovenia* 33 B11
Skoghall, *Sweden* 9 G15
Skole, *Ukraine* 41 H2
Skópelos, *Greece* 39 K6
Skopí, *Greece* 37 D8
Skopin, *Russia* 42 D4
Skopje, *Macedonia* 39 G4
Skórcz, *Poland* 20 B8
Skövde, *Sweden* 9 G15
Skovorodino, *Russia* 45 D13
Skowhegan, *U.S.A.* 99 D6
Skownan, *Canada* 101 C9
Skradin, *Croatia* 33 E12
Skreanäs, *Sweden* 11 H6
Skull, *Ireland* 15 E2
Skultorp, *Sweden* 11 F7
Skunk →, *U.S.A.* 108 E9
Skuodas, *Lithuania* 9 H19
Skurup, *Sweden* 11 J7
Skutskär, *Sweden* 10 D11
Skvyra, *Ukraine* 41 H5
Skwierzyna, *Poland* 20 C5
Skye, *U.K.* 14 D2
Skykomish, *U.S.A.* 110 C3
Skyros = Skíros, *Greece* 39 L7
Slættaratindur, *Færoe Is.* 8 E9
Slagelse, *Denmark* 11 J5
Slagharen, *Neths.* 16 C9
Slamet, *Indonesia* 56 F3
Slaney →, *Ireland* 15 D5
Slangerup, *Denmark* 11 J6
Slano, *Croatia* 21 N7
Slantsy, *Russia* 40 C5
Śląsk, *Poland* 20 E6
Slate Is., *Canada* 98 C2
Slatina, *Romania* 38 E7
Slaton, *U.S.A.* 109 J4
Slave →, *Canada* 100 A6
Slave Coast, *W. Afr.* 79 D5
Slave Lake, *Canada* 100 B6
Slave Pt., *Canada* 100 A5
Slavgorod, *Russia* 44 D8
Slavonska Požega, *Croatia* 21 K7
Slavonski Brod, *Croatia* 21 K8
Slavuta, *Ukraine* 41 G4
Slavyanka, *Russia* 48 C5
Slavyansk = Slovyansk, *Ukraine* 41 H9
Slavyansk-na-Kubani, *Russia* 43 H4
Slawharad, *Belarus* 40 F6
Sławno, *Poland* 20 A6
Sławoborze, *Poland* 20 B5
Sleaford, *U.K.* 12 E7
Sleaford B., *Australia* 91 E2
Sleat, Sd. of, *U.K.* 14 D3
Sleeper Is., *Canada* 97 C11
Sleepy Eye, *U.S.A.* 108 C7
Sleidinge, *Belgium* 17 F3
Sleman, *Indonesia* 57 G14
Slemon L., *Canada* 100 A5
Slidell, *U.S.A.* 109 K10
Sliedrecht, *Neths.* 16 E5
Sliema, *Malta* 37 D2
Slieve Aughty, *Ireland* 15 C3
Slieve Bloom, *Ireland* 15 C4
Slieve Donard, *U.K.* 15 B6
Slieve Gullion, *U.K.* 15 B5
Slieve Mish, *Ireland* 15 D2
Slievenamon, *Ireland* 15 D4
Sligeach = Sligo, *Ireland* 15 B3
Sligo, *Ireland* 15 B3
Sligo □, *Ireland* 15 B3
Sligo B., *Ireland* 15 B3
Slijpe, *Belgium* 17 F1
Slikkerveer, *Neths.* 16 E5
Slite, *Sweden* 9 H18
Sliven, *Bulgaria* 38 G9
Slivnitsa, *Bulgaria* 38 G6
Sljeme, *Croatia* 33 C12
Sloan, *U.S.A.* 113 K11
Sloansville, *U.S.A.* 107 D10
Slobozia, *Romania* 38 E10
Slocan, *Canada* 100 D5
Slochteren, *Neths.* 16 B9
Slöinge, *Sweden* 11 H6
Slonim, *Belarus* 41 F3
Slotermeer, *Neths.* 16 C7
Slough, *U.K.* 13 F7
Sloughhouse, *U.S.A.* 112 G5
Slovak Rep. ■, *Europe* 20 G9
Slovakia = Slovak Rep. ■, *Europe* 20 G9
Slovakian Ore Mts. = Slovenské Rudohorie, *Slovak Rep.* 20 G9
Slovenia ■, *Europe* 33 C11
Slovenija = Slovenia ■, *Europe* 33 C11
Slovenj Gradec, *Slovenia* 33 B12
Slovenska Bistrica, *Slovenia* 33 B12
Slovenská Republika = Slovak Rep. ■, *Europe* 20 G9
Slovenské Rudohorie, *Slovak Rep.* 20 G9
Slovyansk, *Ukraine* 41 H9
Słubice, *Poland* 20 C4
Sluch →, *Ukraine* 41 G4
Sluis, *Neths.* 17 F2
Slunj, *Croatia* 33 C12
Słupca, *Poland* 20 C7
Słupsk, *Poland* 20 A7
Slurry, *S. Africa* 84 D4
Slutsk, *Belarus* 41 F4
Slyne Hd., *Ireland* 15 C1
Slyudyanka, *Russia* 45 D11
Småland, *Sweden* 9 H16
Smålandsfarvandet, *Denmark* 11 J5
Smålandsstenar, *Sweden* 11 G7
Smalltree L., *Canada* 101 A7
Smara, *Morocco* 72 B3
Smarhon, *Belarus* 40 E4
Smarje, *Slovenia* 33 B12
Smartt Syndicate Dam, *S. Africa* 84 E3
Smartville, *U.S.A.* 112 F5
Smeaton, *Canada* 101 C8
Smederevo, *Serbia, Yug.* 21 L10
Smederevska Palanka, *Serbia, Yug.* 21 L10
Smela = Smila, *Ukraine* 41 H6
Smethport, *U.S.A.* 106 E6
Smidovich, *Russia* 45 E14
Smila, *Ukraine* 41 H6
Smilde, *Neths.* 16 C8
Smiley, *Canada* 101 C7
Smith, *Canada* 100 B6
Smith →, *Canada* 100 B3
Smith Arm, *Canada* 96 B7
Smith Center, *U.S.A.* 108 F5
Smith Sund, *Greenland* 4 B4
Smithburne →, *Australia* 90 B3
Smithers, *Canada* 100 C3
Smithfield, *S. Africa* 85 E4
Smithfield, *N.C., U.S.A.* 105 H6
Smithfield, *Utah, U.S.A.* 110 F8
Smiths Falls, *Canada* 98 D4
Smithton, *Australia* 90 G4
Smithtown, *Australia* 91 E5
Smithville, *Canada* 106 C5
Smithville, *U.S.A.* 109 K6
Smoky →, *Canada* 100 B5
Smoky Bay, *Australia* 91 E1
Smoky Falls, *Canada* 98 B3
Smoky Hill →, *U.S.A.* 108 F6
Smoky Lake, *Canada* 100 C6
Smøla, *Norway* 10 A2
Smolensk, *Russia* 40 E7
Smolikas, Óros, *Greece* 39 J3
Smolník, *Slovak Rep.* 20 G10
Smolyan, *Bulgaria* 39 H7
Smooth Rock Falls, *Canada* 98 C3
Smoothstone L., *Canada* 101 C7
Smorgon = Smarhon, *Belarus* 40 E4
Smyadovo, *Bulgaria* 38 F10
Smyrna = İzmir, *Turkey* 66 C2
Snæfell, *Iceland* 8 D6
Snaefell, *U.K.* 12 C3
Snæfellsjökull, *Iceland* 8 D2
Snake →, *U.S.A.* 110 C4
Snake I., *Australia* 91 F4
Snake L., *Canada* 101 B7
Snake Range, *U.S.A.* 110 G6
Snake River Plain, *U.S.A.* 110 E7
Snarum, *Norway* 10 D3
Snåsavatnet, *Norway* 8 D14
Snedsted, *Denmark* 11 H2
Sneek, *Neths.* 16 B7
Sneeker-meer, *Neths.* 16 B7
Sneeuberge, *S. Africa* 84 E3
Snejbjerg, *Denmark* 11 H2
Snelling, *U.S.A.* 112 H6
Snezhnoye, *Ukraine* 41 J10
Snežnik, *Slovenia* 33 C11
Snigirevka = Snihurivka, *Ukraine* 41 J7
Snihurivka, *Ukraine* 41 J7
Snizort, L., *U.K.* 14 D2
Snøhetta, *Norway* 10 B3
Snohomish, *U.S.A.* 112 C4
Snoul, *Cambodia* 59 F6
Snow Hill, *U.S.A.* 104 F8
Snow Lake, *Canada* 101 C8
Snow Mt., *U.S.A.* 112 F4
Snowbird L., *Canada* 101 A8
Snowdon, *U.K.* 12 D3
Snowdrift →, *Canada* 101 A6
Snowflake, *U.S.A.* 111 J8
Snowshoe Pk., *U.S.A.* 110 B6
Snowtown, *Australia* 91 E2
Snowville, *U.S.A.* 110 F7
Snowy →, *Australia* 91 F4
Snowy Mts., *Australia* 91 F4
Snug Corner, *Bahamas* 117 B5
Snyatyn, *Ukraine* 41 H3
Snyder, *Okla., U.S.A.* 109 H5
Snyder, *Tex., U.S.A.* 109 J4
Soacha, *Colombia* 120 C3
Soahanina, *Madag.* 85 B7
Soalala, *Madag.* 85 B8
Soan →, *Pakistan* 62 C4
Soanierana-Ivongo, *Madag.* 85 B8
Soap Lake, *U.S.A.* 110 C4
Sobat, Nahr →, *Sudan* 77 F3
Sobhapur, *India* 62 H8
Sobinka, *Russia* 42 C5
Sobolevo, *Russia* 45 D16
Sobótka, *Poland* 20 E6
Sobradinho, Représa de, *Brazil* 122 C3
Sobrado, *Spain* 30 B2
Sobral, *Brazil* 122 B3
Sobreira Formosa, *Portugal* 31 F3
Soc Giang, *Vietnam* 58 A6
Soc Trang, *Vietnam* 59 H5
Soča →, *Europe* 33 B10
Sochaczew, *Poland* 20 C10
Soch'e = Shache, *China* 54 C2
Sochi, *Russia* 43 J4
Société, Is. de la, *Pac. Oc.* 93 J12
Society Is. = Société, Is. de la, *Pac. Oc.* 93 J12
Socompa, Portezuelo de, *Chile* 126 A2
Socorro, *Colombia* 120 B3
Socorro, *U.S.A.* 111 J10
Socorro, I., *Mexico* 114 D2
Socotra, *Ind. Oc.* 68 E5
Socúellmos, *Spain* 29 F2
Soda L., *U.S.A.* 111 J5
Soda Plains, *India* 63 B8
Soda Springs, *U.S.A.* 110 E8
Sodankylä, *Finland* 8 C22
Söderhamn, *Sweden* 9 F17
Söderköping, *Sweden* 9 G17
Södermanland, *Sweden* 9 G17
Södermanlands län □, *Sweden* 10 E10
Södertälje, *Sweden* 10 E11
Sodiri, *Sudan* 77 E2
Sodo, *Ethiopia* 77 F4
Sodražica, *Slovenia* 33 C11
Sodus, *U.S.A.* 106 C7
Soekmekaar, *S. Africa* 85 C4
Soest, *Germany* 18 D4
Soest, *Neths.* 16 D6
Soestdijk, *Neths.* 16 D6
Sofádhes, *Greece* 39 K5
Sofara, *Mali* 78 C4
Sofia = Sofiya, *Bulgaria* 38 G6
Sofia →, *Madag.* 85 B8
Sofievka, *Ukraine* 41 H7
Sofikón, *Greece* 39 M6
Sofiya, *Bulgaria* 38 G6
Sofiysk, *Russia* 45 D14
Sōfu-Gan, *Japan* 49 K10
Sogakofe, *Ghana* 79 D5
Sogamoso, *Colombia* 120 B3
Sogār, *Iran* 65 E8
Sögel, *Germany* 18 C3
Sogndalsfjøra, *Norway* 9 F12
Søgne, *Norway* 9 G12
Sognefjorden, *Norway* 9 F11
Söğüt, *Turkey* 66 B4
Sŏgwi-po, *S. Korea* 51 H14
Soh, *Iran* 65 C6
Sohâg, *Egypt* 76 B3
Sŏhori, *N. Korea* 51 D15
Soignies, *Belgium* 17 G4
Soira, *Eritrea* 77 E4
Soissons, *France* 25 C10
Sōja, *Japan* 49 G6
Sojat, *India* 62 G5
Sok →, *Russia* 42 D10
Sokal, *Ukraine* 41 G3
Söke, *Turkey* 66 D2
Sokelo, *Zaïre* 83 D1
Sokhumi, *Georgia* 43 J5
Sokki, Oued In →, *Algeria* 75 C5
Sokna, *Norway* 10 D3
Soknedal, *Norway* 10 B4
Soko Banja, *Serbia, Yug.* 21 M11
Sokodé, *Togo* 79 D5
Sokol, *Russia* 40 C11
Sokółka, *Poland* 20 B13
Sokolo, *Mali* 78 C3
Sokołów Małpolski, *Poland* 20 E12
Sokołów Podlaski, *Poland* 20 C12
Sokoto, *Nigeria* 79 C6
Sokoto □, *Nigeria* 79 C6
Sokoto →, *Nigeria* 79 C5
Sol Iletsk, *Russia* 44 D6
Solai, *Kenya* 82 B4
Solano, *Phil.* 55 C4
Solapur, *India* 60 L9
Solares, *Spain* 30 B7
Soléa □, *Cyprus* 37 D12
Solec Kujawski, *Poland* 20 B8
Soledad, *Colombia* 120 A3
Soledad, *U.S.A.* 111 H3
Soledad, *Venezuela* 121 B5
Solent, The, *U.K.* 13 G6
Solenzara, *France* 27 G13
Solesmes, *France* 25 B10
Solfonn, *Norway* 9 F12
Solhan, *Turkey* 67 C9
Soligorsk = Salihorsk, *Belarus* 41 F4
Solikamsk, *Russia* 44 D6
Solila, *Madag.* 85 C8
Solimões = Amazonas →, *S. Amer.* 121 D7
Solingen, *Germany* 17 F10

Sollebrunn, *Sweden* 11 F6
Sollefteå, *Sweden* 10 A11
Sollentuna, *Sweden* 10 E11
Sóller, *Spain* 36 B9
Solling, *Germany* 18 D5
Solna, *Sweden* 10 E12
Solnechnogorsk, *Russia* 42 B3
Sologne, *France* 25 E8
Solok, *Indonesia* 56 E2
Sololá, *Guatemala* 116 D1
Solomon, N. Fork →, *U.S.A.* 108 F5
Solomon, S. Fork →, *U.S.A.* 108 F5
Solomon Is. ■, *Pac. Oc.* 92 H7
Solon, *China* 54 B7
Solon Springs, *U.S.A.* 108 B9
Solonópole, *Brazil* 122 C4
Solor, *Indonesia* 57 F6
Solotcha, *Russia* 42 C4
Solothurn, *Switz.* 22 B5
Solothurn □, *Switz.* 22 B5
Solsona, *Spain* 28 D6
Šolta, *Croatia* 33 E13
Solṭānābād, *Khorāsān, Iran* 65 C8
Solṭānābād, *Khorāsān, Iran* 65 B8
Solṭānābād, *Markazī, Iran* 65 C6
Soltau, *Germany* 18 C5
Soltsy, *Russia* 40 C6
Solunska Glava, *Macedonia* 39 H4
Solvang, *U.S.A.* 113 L6
Solvay, *U.S.A.* 107 C8
Sölvesborg, *Sweden* 9 H16
Solway Firth, *U.K.* 12 C4
Solwezi, *Zambia* 83 E2
Sōma, *Japan* 48 F10
Soma, *Turkey* 66 C2
Somali Pen., *Africa* 70 F8
Somali Rep. ■, *Africa* 68 F4
Somalia = Somali Rep. ■, *Africa* 68 F4
Sombernon, *France* 25 E11
Sombor, *Serbia, Yug.* 21 K9
Sombra, *Canada* 106 D2
Sombrerete, *Mexico* 114 C4
Sombrero, *Anguilla* 117 C7
Someren, *Neths.* 17 F7
Somers, *U.S.A.* 110 B6
Somerset, *Canada* 101 D9
Somerset, *Colo., U.S.A.* 111 G10
Somerset, *Ky., U.S.A.* 104 G3
Somerset, *Mass., U.S.A.* 107 E13
Somerset, *Pa., U.S.A.* 106 F5
Somerset □, *U.K.* 13 F5
Somerset East, *S. Africa* 84 E4
Somerset I., *Canada* 96 A10
Somerset West, *S. Africa* 84 E2
Somerton, *U.S.A.* 111 K6
Somerville, *U.S.A.* 107 F10
Someş →, *Romania* 38 B5
Someşul Mare →, *Romania* 38 B7
Somma Lombardo, *Italy* 32 C5
Somma Vesuviana, *Italy* 35 B7
Sommariva, *Australia* 91 D4
Sommatino, *Italy* 34 E6
Somme □, *France* 25 C9
Somme →, *France* 25 B8
Somme, B. de la, *France* 24 B8
Sommelsdijk, *Neths.* 16 E4
Sommepy-Tahure, *France* 25 C11
Sömmerda, *Germany* 18 D7
Sommesous, *France* 25 D11
Sommières, *France* 27 E8
Somoto, *Nic.* 116 D2
Sompolno, *Poland* 20 C8
Somport, Paso, *Spain* 28 C4
Somport, Puerto de, *Spain* 28 C4
Somuncurá, Meseta de, *Argentina* 128 B3
Son, *Neths.* 17 E6
Son, *Norway* 10 E4
Son, *Spain* 30 C2
Son Ha, *Vietnam* 58 E7
Son Hoa, *Vietnam* 58 F7
Son La, *Vietnam* 58 B4
Son Tay, *Vietnam* 58 B5
Soná, *Panama* 116 E3
Sonamarg, *India* 63 B6
Sonamukhi, *India* 63 H12
Sŏnchŏn, *N. Korea* 51 E13
Soncino, *Italy* 32 C6
Sondags →, *S. Africa* 84 E4
Sóndalo, *Italy* 32 B7
Sondar, *India* 63 C6
Sønder Omme, *Denmark* 11 J2
Sønder Tornby, *Denmark* 11 G3
Sønderborg, *Denmark* 11 K3
Sønderjyllands Amtskommune □, *Denmark* 11 J3
Sondershausen, *Germany* 18 D6
Søndre Strømfjord, *Greenland* 97 B14
Sóndrio, *Italy* 32 B6
Sone, *Mozam.* 83 F3
Sonepur, *India* 61 J13
Song, *Thailand* 58 C3
Song Cau, *Vietnam* 58 F7
Song Xian, *China* 50 G7
Songchŏn, *N. Korea* 51 E14
Songea, *Tanzania* 83 E4
Songea □, *Tanzania* 83 E4
Songeons, *France* 25 C8
Songhua Hu, *China* 51 C14
Songhua Jiang →, *China* 54 B8
Songjiang, *China* 53 B13
Songjin, *N. Korea* 51 D15
Songjŏng-ni, *S. Korea* 51 G14
Songkan, *China* 52 C6
Songkhla, *Thailand* 59 J3
Songming, *China* 52 E4
Songnim, *N. Korea* 51 E13
Songpan, *China* 52 A4
Songtao, *China* 52 C7
Songwe, *Zaïre* 82 C2
Songwe →, *Africa* 83 D3
Songxi, *China* 53 D12
Songzi, *China* 53 B8
Sonid Youqi, *China* 50 C7
Sonipat, *India* 62 E7
Sonkovo, *Russia* 42 B3
Sonmiani, *Pakistan* 62 G2
Sonnino, *Italy* 34 A6
Sono →, *Minas Gerais, Brazil* 123 E2
Sono →, *Tocantins, Brazil* 122 C2
Sonogno, *Switz.* 23 D7
Sonora, *Calif., U.S.A.* 111 H3
Sonora, *Tex., U.S.A.* 109 K4
Sonora □, *Mexico* 114 B2
Sonora →, *Mexico* 114 B2
Sonora Desert, *U.S.A.* 113 L12
Sonoyta, *Mexico* 114 A2
Sonqor, *Iran* 67 E12
Sŏnsan, *S. Korea* 51 F15
Sonsonate, *El Salv.* 116 D2
Sonthofen, *Germany* 19 H6
Soochow = Suzhou, *China* 53 B13
Sop Hao, *Laos* 58 B5
Sop Prap, *Thailand* 58 D2
Sopachuy, *Bolivia* 125 D5
Sopi, *Indonesia* 57 D7
Sopo, Nahr →, *Sudan* 77 F2
Sopot, *Poland* 20 A8
Sopotnica, *Macedonia* 39 H4
Sopron, *Hungary* 21 H6
Sop's Arm, *Canada* 99 C8
Sopur, *India* 63 B6
Sør-Rondane, *Antarctica* 5 D4
Sør-Trøndelag fylke □, *Norway* 10 B3
Sora, *Italy* 34 A6
Sorah, *Pakistan* 62 F3
Söråker, *Sweden* 10 B11
Sorano, *Italy* 33 F8
Sorata, *Bolivia* 124 D4
Sorbas, *Spain* 29 H2
Sorel, *Canada* 98 C5
Sörenberg, *Switz.* 22 C6
Soreq, N. →, *Israel* 69 D3
Soresina, *Italy* 32 C6
Sorgono, *Italy* 34 B2
Sorgues, *France* 27 D8
Sorgun, *Turkey* 66 C6
Soria, *Spain* 28 D2
Soria □, *Spain* 28 D2
Soriano, *Uruguay* 126 C4
Soriano nel Cimino, *Italy* 33 F9
Sorkh, Kuh-e, *Iran* 65 C8
Sorø, *Denmark* 11 J5
Soro, *Guinea* 78 C3
Soroca, *Moldova* 41 H5
Sorocaba, *Brazil* 127 A6
Soroki = Soroca, *Moldova* 41 H5
Soron, *India* 63 F8
Sorong, *Indonesia* 57 E8
Soroní, *Greece* 37 C10
Soroti, *Uganda* 82 B3
Sørøya, *Norway* 8 A20
Sørøysundet, *Norway* 8 A20
Sorraia →, *Portugal* 31 G2
Sorrento, *Australia* 91 F3
Sorrento, *Italy* 35 B7
Sorsele, *Sweden* 8 D17
Sorso, *Italy* 34 B1
Sorsogon, *Phil.* 55 E6
Sortavala, *Russia* 40 B6
Sortino, *Italy* 35 E8
Sortland, *Norway* 8 B16
Sorvizhi, *Russia* 42 B9
Sos, *Spain* 28 C3
Sŏsan, *S. Korea* 51 F14
Soscumica, L., *Canada* 98 B4
Sosna →, *Russia* 42 D4
Sosnovka, *Russia* 42 B10
Sosnovka, *Russia* 42 D5
Sosnovka, *Russia* 45 D11
Sosnovyy Bor, *Russia* 40 C5
Sosnowiec, *Poland* 20 E9
Sospel, *France* 27 E11
Sostanj, *Slovenia* 33 B12
Sŏsura, *N. Korea* 51 C16
Sotkamo, *Finland* 8 D23
Soto la Marina →, *Mexico* 115 C5
Soto y Amío, *Spain* 30 C5
Sotteville-lès-Rouen, *France* 24 C8
Sotuta, *Mexico* 115 C7
Souanké, *Congo* 80 D2
Soúdha, *Greece* 37 D6
Soúdhas, Kólpos, *Greece* 37 D6
Sougne-Remouchamps, *Belgium* 17 H7
Souillac, *France* 26 D5
Souk-Ahras, *Algeria* 75 A6
Souk el Arba du Rharb, *Morocco* 74 B3
Soukhouma, *Laos* 58 E5
Sŏul, *S. Korea* 51 F14
Soulac-sur-Mer, *France* 26 C2
Soultz-sous-Forêts, *France* 25 D14
Soumagne, *Belgium* 17 G7
Sound, The = Øresund, *Europe* 11 J6
Sound, The, *U.K.* 13 G3
Soúnion, Ákra, *Greece* 39 M7
Sour el Ghozlane, *Algeria* 75 A5
Sources, Mt. aux, *Lesotho* 85 D4
Sourdeval, *France* 24 D6
Soure, *Brazil* 122 B2
Soure, *Portugal* 30 E2
Souris, *Man., Canada* 101 D8
Souris, *P.E.I., Canada* 99 C7
Souris →, *Canada* 108 A5
Sousa, *Brazil* 122 C4
Sousel, *Brazil* 122 B1
Sousel, *Portugal* 31 G3
Souss, O. →, *Morocco* 74 B3
Sousse, *Tunisia* 75 A7
Soustons, *France* 26 E2
South Africa ■, *Africa* 84 E3
South Atlantic Ocean 118 H7
South Aulatsivik I., *Canada* 99 A7
South Australia □, *Australia* 91 E2
South Ayrshire □, *U.K.* 14 F4
South Baldy, *U.S.A.* 111 J10
South Bend, *Ind., U.S.A.* 104 E2
South Bend, *Wash., U.S.A.* 112 D3
South Boston, *U.S.A.* 105 G6
South Branch, *Canada* 99 C8
South Brook, *Canada* 99 C8
South Carolina □, *U.S.A.* 105 J5
South Charleston, *U.S.A.* 104 F5
South China Sea, *Asia* 56 C4
South Dakota □, *U.S.A.* 108 C5
South Downs, *U.K.* 13 G7
South East C., *Australia* 90 G4
South East Is., *Australia* 89 F3
South Esk →, *U.K.* 14 E5
South Foreland, *U.K.* 13 F9
South Fork →, *U.S.A.* 110 C7
South Fork, American →, *U.S.A.* 112 G5
South Fork, Feather →, *U.S.A.* 112 F5
South Georgia, *Antarctica* 5 B1
South Gloucestershire □, *U.K.* 13 F5
South Haven, *U.S.A.* 104 D2
South Henik, L., *Canada* 101 A9
South Honshu Ridge, *Pac. Oc.* 92 E6
South Horr, *Kenya* 82 B4
South I., *Kenya* 82 B4
South I., *N.Z.* 87 L3
South Invercargill, *N.Z.* 87 M2
South Knife →, *Canada* 101 B10
South Korea ■, *Asia* 51 F15
South Lake Tahoe, *U.S.A.* 112 G6
South Lanarkshire □, *U.K.* 14 F5
South Loup →, *U.S.A.* 108 E5
South Magnetic Pole, *Antarctica* 5 C9
South Milwaukee, *U.S.A.* 104 D2
South Molton, *U.K.* 13 F4
South Nahanni →, *Canada* 100 A4
South Natuna Is. = Natuna Selatan, Kepulauan, *Indonesia* 59 L7
South Negril Pt., *Jamaica* 116 C4
South Orkney Is., *Antarctica* 5 C18
South Ossetia □, *Georgia* 43 J7
South Pagai, I. = Pagai Selatan, P., *Indonesia* 56 E2
South Pass, *U.S.A.* 110 E9
South Pittsburg, *U.S.A.* 105 H3
South Platte →, *U.S.A.* 108 E4
South Pole, *Antarctica* 5 E
South Porcupine, *Canada* 98 C3
South River, *Canada* 98 C4
South River, *U.S.A.* 107 F10
South Ronaldsay, *U.K.* 14 C6
South Sandwich Is., *Antarctica* 5 B1
South Saskatchewan →, *Canada* 101 C7
South Seal →, *Canada* 101 B9
South Shetland Is., *Antarctica* 5 C18
South Shields, *U.K.* 12 C6
South Sioux City, *U.S.A.* 108 D6
South Taranaki Bight, *N.Z.* 87 H5
South Thompson →, *Canada* 100 C4
South Twin I., *Canada* 98 B4
South Tyne →, *U.K.* 12 C5
South Uist, *U.K.* 14 D1
South West Africa = Namibia ■, *Africa* 84 C2
South West C., *Australia* 90 G4
South Yorkshire □, *U.K.* 12 D6
Southampton, *Canada* 98 D3
Southampton, *U.K.* 13 G6
Southampton, *U.S.A.* 107 F12
Southampton I., *Canada* 97 B11
Southbridge, *N.Z.* 87 K4
Southbridge, *U.S.A.* 107 D12
Southend, *Canada* 101 B8
Southend-on-Sea, *U.K.* 13 F8
Southern □, *Malawi* 83 F4
Southern □, *S. Leone* 78 D2
Southern □, *Uganda* 82 C3
Southern □, *Zambia* 83 F2
Southern Alps, *N.Z.* 87 K3
Southern Cross, *Australia* 89 F2
Southern Hills, *Australia* 89 F3
Southern Indian L., *Canada* 101 B9
Southern Ocean, *Antarctica* 5 C6
Southern Pines, *U.S.A.* 105 H6
Southern Uplands, *U.K.* 14 F5
Southington, *U.S.A.* 107 E12
Southold, *U.S.A.* 107 E12
Southport, *Australia* 91 D5
Southport, *U.K.* 12 D4
Southport, *U.S.A.* 105 J6
Southwest C., *N.Z.* 87 M1
Southwold, *U.K.* 13 E9
Soutpansberg, *S. Africa* 85 C4
Souvigny, *France* 26 B7
Sovetsk, *Kaliningd., Russia* 9 J19
Sovetsk, *Kirov, Russia* 42 B9
Sovetskaya Gavan, *Russia* 45 E15
Soviciile, *Italy* 33 E8
Sovra, *Croatia* 21 N7
Soweto, *S. Africa* 85 D4
Sōya-Kaikyō = La Perouse Str., *Asia* 48 B11
Sōya-Misaki, *Japan* 48 B10
Soyo, *Angola* 80 F2
Sozh →, *Belarus* 41 F6
Sozopol, *Bulgaria* 38 G10
Spa, *Belgium* 17 H7
Spain ■, *Europe* 7 H5
Spakenburg, *Neths.* 16 D6
Spalding, *Australia* 91 E2
Spalding, *U.K.* 12 E7
Spalding, *U.S.A.* 108 E5
Spangler, *U.S.A.* 106 F6
Spaniard's Bay, *Canada* 99 C9
Spanish, *Canada* 98 C3
Spanish Fork, *U.S.A.* 110 F8
Spanish Town, *Jamaica* 116 C4
Sparks, *U.S.A.* 112 F7
Sparta = Spárti, *Greece* 39 M5
Sparta, *Ga., U.S.A.* 105 J4
Sparta, *Wis., U.S.A.* 108 D9
Spartanburg, *U.S.A.* 105 H4
Spartansburg, *U.S.A.* 106 E5
Spartel, C., *Morocco* 74 A3
Spárti, *Greece* 39 M5
Spartivento, C., *Calabria, Italy* 35 E9
Spartivento, C., *Sard., Italy* 34 D1
Spas-Demensk, *Russia* 42 C2
Spas-Klepiki, *Russia* 42 C5
Spassk Dalniy, *Russia* 45 E14
Spassk-Ryazanskiy, *Russia* 42 C5
Spátha, Ákra, *Greece* 37 D5
Spatsizi →, *Canada* 100 B3
Spearfish, *U.S.A.* 108 C3
Spearman, *U.S.A.* 109 G4
Speer, *Switz.* 23 B8
Speers, *Canada* 101 C7
Speightstown, *Barbados* 117 D8
Speke Gulf, *Tanzania* 82 C3
Spekholzerheide, *Neths.* 17 G8
Spencer, *Idaho, U.S.A.* 110 D7
Spencer, *Iowa, U.S.A.* 108 D7
Spencer, *N.Y., U.S.A.* 107 D8
Spencer, *Nebr., U.S.A.* 108 D5
Spencer, *W. Va., U.S.A.* 104 F5
Spencer, C., *Australia* 91 F2
Spencer B., *Namibia* 84 D1
Spencer G., *Australia* 91 E2
Spencerville, *Canada* 107 B9
Spences Bridge, *Canada* 100 C4
Spenser Mts., *N.Z.* 87 K4
Sperkhiós →, *Greece* 39 L5
Sperrin Mts., *U.K.* 15 B5
Spessart, *Germany* 19 E5
Spétsai, *Greece* 39 M6
Spey →, *U.K.* 14 D5
Speyer, *Germany* 19 F4
Speyer →, *Germany* 19 F4
Spezzano Albanese, *Italy* 35 C9
Spiekeroog, *Germany* 18 B3
Spielfeld, *Austria* 33 B12
Spiez, *Switz.* 22 C5
Spijk, *Neths.* 16 B9
Spijkenisse, *Neths.* 16 E4
Spíli, *Greece* 37 D6
Spilimbergo, *Italy* 33 B9
Spin Baldak = Qala-i-Jadid, *Afghan.* 62 D2
Spinalónga, *Greece* 37 D7
Spinazzola, *Italy* 35 B9
Spirit Lake, *Idaho, U.S.A.* 110 C5
Spirit Lake, *Wash., U.S.A.* 112 D4
Spirit River, *Canada* 100 B5
Spiritwood, *Canada* 101 C7
Spišská Nová Ves, *Slovak Rep.* 20 G10
Spithead, *U.K.* 13 G6
Spittal, *Austria* 21 J3
Spitzbergen = Svalbard, *Arctic* 4 B8
Spjelkavik, *Norway* 9 E12
Split, *Croatia* 33 E13
Split L., *Canada* 101 B9
Splitski Kanal, *Croatia* 33 E13
Splügen, *Switz.* 23 C8
Splügenpass, *Switz.* 23 C8
Spofford, *U.S.A.* 109 L4
Spokane, *U.S.A.* 110 C5
Spoleto, *Italy* 33 F9
Spooner, *U.S.A.* 108 C9
Sporyy Navolok, Mys, *Russia* 44 B7
Spragge, *Canada* 98 C3
Sprague, *U.S.A.* 110 C5
Sprague River, *U.S.A.* 110 E3
Spratly Is., *S. China Sea* 56 C4
Spray, *U.S.A.* 110 D4
Spree →, *Germany* 18 C9
Spremberg, *Germany* 18 D10
Sprengisandur, *Iceland* 8 D5
Sprimont, *Belgium* 17 G7
Spring City, *U.S.A.* 110 G8
Spring Garden, *U.S.A.* 112 F6
Spring Mts., *U.S.A.* 111 H6
Spring Valley, *Calif., U.S.A.* 113 N10
Spring Valley, *Minn., U.S.A.* 108 D8
Springbok, *S. Africa* 84 D2
Springdale, *Canada* 99 C8
Springdale, *Ark., U.S.A.* 109 G7
Springdale, *Wash., U.S.A.* 110 B5
Springe, *Germany* 18 C5
Springer, *U.S.A.* 109 G2
Springerville, *U.S.A.* 111 J9
Springfield, *Canada* 106 D4
Springfield, *N.Z.* 87 K3
Springfield, *Colo., U.S.A.* 109 G3
Springfield, *Ill., U.S.A.* 108 F10
Springfield, *Mass., U.S.A.* 107 D12
Springfield, *Mo., U.S.A.* 109 G8
Springfield, *Ohio, U.S.A.* 104 F4
Springfield, *Oreg., U.S.A.* 110 D2
Springfield, *Tenn., U.S.A.* 105 G2
Springfield, *Vt., U.S.A.* 107 C12
Springfontein, *S. Africa* 84 E4
Springhill, *Canada* 99 C7
Springhouse, *Canada* 100 C4
Springhurst, *Australia* 91 F4
Springs, *S. Africa* 85 D4
Springsure, *Australia* 90 C4
Springvale, *Queens., Australia* 90 C3
Springvale, *W. Austral., Australia* 88 C4
Springvale, *U.S.A.* 107 C14
Springville, *Calif., U.S.A.* 112 J8
Springville, *N.Y., U.S.A.* 106 D6
Springville, *Utah, U.S.A.* 110 F8
Springwater, *Canada* 101 C7
Spruce-Creek, *U.S.A.* 106 F6
Spur, *U.S.A.* 109 J4
Spurn Hd., *U.K.* 12 D8
Spuž, *Montenegro, Yug.* 21 N9
Spuzzum, *Canada* 100 D4
Squam L., *U.S.A.* 107 C13
Squamish, *Canada* 100 D4
Square Islands, *Canada* 99 B8
Squillace, G. di, *Italy* 35 D9
Squinzano, *Italy* 35 B11
Squires, Mt., *Australia* 89 E4
Sragen, *Indonesia* 57 G14
Srbac, *Bos.-H.* 21 K7
Srbija = Serbia □, *Yugoslavia* 21 M11
Srbobran, *Serbia, Yug.* 21 K9
Sre Khtum, *Cambodia* 59 F6
Sre Umbell, *Cambodia* 59 G4
Srebrnica, *Bos.-H.* 21 L9
Sredinny Ra. = Sredinnyy Khrebet, *Russia* 45 D16
Sredinnyy Khrebet, *Russia* 45 D16
Središče, *Slovenia* 33 B13
Sredna Gora, *Bulgaria* 38 G7
Sredne Tambovskoye, *Russia* 45 D14
Srednekolymsk, *Russia* 45 C16
Srednevilyuysk, *Russia* 45 C13
Śrem, *Poland* 20 C7
Sremska Mitrovica, *Serbia, Yug.* 21 L9
Srepok →, *Cambodia* 58 F6
Sretensk, *Russia* 45 D12
Sri Lanka ■, *Asia* 60 R12
Srikakulam, *India* 61 K13
Srinagar, *India* 63 B6
Środa Wielkopolski, *Poland* 20 C7
Srpska Itabej, *Serbia, Yug.* 21 K10
Staaten →, *Australia* 90 B3
Staberhuk, *Germany* 18 A7
Stabroek, *Belgium* 17 F4
Stad Delden, *Neths.* 16 D9
Stade, *Germany* 18 B5
Staden, *Belgium* 17 G2
Städjan, *Sweden* 10 C6
Stadskanaal, *Neths.* 16 B9
Stadthagen, *Germany* 18 C5
Stadtlohn, *Germany* 18 D2
Stadtroda, *Germany* 18 E7
Stäfa, *Switz.* 23 B7
Staffa, *U.K.* 14 E2
Stafford, *U.K.* 12 E5
Stafford, *U.S.A.* 109 G5
Stafford Springs, *U.S.A.* 107 E12
Staffordshire □, *U.K.* 12 E5
Stagnone, Isole dello, *Italy* 34 E5
Staines, *U.K.* 13 F7
Stakhanov, *Ukraine* 41 H10
Stalden, *Switz.* 22 D5
Stalingrad = Volgograd, *Russia* 43 F7
Staliniri = Tskhinvali, *Georgia* 43 J7
Stalino = Donetsk, *Ukraine* 41 J9
Stalinogorsk = Novomoskovsk, *Russia* 42 C4
Stalis, *Greece* 37 D7
Stalowa Wola, *Poland* 20 E12
Stalybridge, *U.K.* 12 D5
Stamford, *Australia* 90 C3
Stamford, *U.K.* 13 E7
Stamford, *Conn., U.S.A.* 107 E11
Stamford, *Tex., U.S.A.* 109 J5
Stamps, *U.S.A.* 109 J8
Stanberry, *U.S.A.* 108 E7
Stančevo = Kalipetrovo, *Bulgaria* 38 E10

Standerton, *S. Africa* 85 D4
Standish, *U.S.A.* 104 D4
Stanford, *U.S.A.* 110 C8
Stange, *Norway* 10 D5
Stanger, *S. Africa* 85 D5
Stanislaus →, *U.S.A.* 112 H5
Stanislav = Ivano-Frankivsk, *Ukraine* 41 H3
Stanke Dimitrov, *Bulgaria* 38 G6
Stanley, *Australia* 90 G4
Stanley, *N.B., Canada* 99 C6
Stanley, *Sask., Canada* 101 B8
Stanley, *Falk. Is.* 128 D5
Stanley, *Idaho, U.S.A.* 110 D6
Stanley, *N. Dak., U.S.A.* 108 A3
Stanley, *N.Y., U.S.A.* 106 D7
Stanley, *Wis., U.S.A.* 108 C9
Stanovoy Khrebet, *Russia* 45 D13
Stanovoy Ra. = Stanovoy Khrebet, *Russia* 45 D13
Stans, *Switz.* 23 C6
Stansmore Ra., *Australia* 88 D4
Stanthorpe, *Australia* 91 D5
Stanton, *U.S.A.* 109 J4
Stanwood, *U.S.A.* 112 B4
Staphorst, *Neths.* 16 C8
Staples, *U.S.A.* 108 B7
Stapleton, *U.S.A.* 108 E4
Star City, *Canada* 101 C8
Stara Moravica, *Serbia, Yug.* 21 K9
Stara Planina, *Bulgaria* 38 F6
Stara Zagora, *Bulgaria* 38 G8
Starachowice, *Poland* 20 D11
Staraya Russa, *Russia* 40 D6
Starbuck I., *Kiribati* 93 H12
Stargard Szczeciński, *Poland* 20 B5
Stari Trg, *Slovenia* 33 C12
Staritsa, *Russia* 42 B2
Starke, *U.S.A.* 105 K4
Starkville, *Colo., U.S.A.* 109 G2
Starkville, *Miss., U.S.A.* 105 J1
Starnberg, *Germany* 19 G7
Starnberger See, *Germany* 19 H7
Starobilsk, *Ukraine* 41 H10
Starodub, *Russia* 41 F7
Starogard Gdański, *Poland* 20 B8
Starokonstantinov = Starokonstyantyniv, *Ukraine* 41 H4
Starokonstyantyniv, *Ukraine* 41 H4
Starominskaya, *Russia* 43 G4
Staroshcherbinovskaya, *Russia* 43 G4
Start Pt., *U.K.* 13 G4
Staryy Biryuzyak, *Russia* 43 H8
Staryy Chartoriysk, *Ukraine* 41 G3
Staryy Kheydzhan, *Russia* 45 C15
Staryy Krym, *Ukraine* 41 K8
Staryy Oskol, *Russia* 42 E3
Stassfurt, *Germany* 18 D7
State College, *U.S.A.* 106 F7
Stateline, *U.S.A.* 112 G7
Staten, I. = Estados, I. de Los, *Argentina* 128 D4
Staten, I., *Argentina* 118 J4
Staten I., *U.S.A.* 107 F10
Statesboro, *U.S.A.* 105 J5
Statesville, *U.S.A.* 105 H5
Stauffer, *U.S.A.* 113 L7
Staunton, *Ill., U.S.A.* 108 F10
Staunton, *Va., U.S.A.* 104 F6
Stavanger, *Norway* 9 G11
Staveley, *N.Z.* 87 K3
Stavelot, *Belgium* 17 H7
Stavenhagen, *Germany* 18 B8
Stavenisse, *Neths.* 17 E4
Staveren, *Neths.* 16 C6
Stavern, *Norway* 10 F4
Stavre, *Sweden* 10 B9
Stavropol, *Russia* 43 H6
Stavros, *Cyprus* 37 D11
Stavrós, *Greece* 37 D6
Stavros, Ákra, *Greece* 37 D6
Stavroúpolis, *Greece* 39 H7
Stawell, *Australia* 91 F3
Stawell →, *Australia* 90 C3
Stawiszyn, *Poland* 20 D8
Stayner, *Canada* 106 B4
Steamboat Springs, *U.S.A.* 110 F10
Steckborn, *Switz.* 23 A7
Steele, *U.S.A.* 108 B5
Steelton, *U.S.A.* 106 F8
Steelville, *U.S.A.* 109 G9
Steen River, *Canada* 100 B5
Steenbergen, *Neths.* 17 E4
Steenkool = Bintuni, *Indonesia* 57 E8
Steenvoorde, *France* 25 B9
Steenwijk, *Neths.* 16 C8
Steep Pt., *Australia* 89 E1
Steep Rock, *Canada* 101 C9
Ştefăneşti, *Romania* 38 B10
Stefanie L. = Chew Bahir, *Ethiopia* 77 G4
Stefansson Bay, *Antarctica* 5 C5
Steffisburg, *Switz.* 22 C5
Stege, *Denmark* 11 K6
Steiermark □, *Austria* 21 H5
Steigerwald, *Germany* 19 F6
Steilacoom, *U.S.A.* 112 C4
Stein, *Neths.* 17 G7
Steinbach, *Canada* 101 D9
Steinfort, *Lux.* 17 J7
Steinfurt, *Germany* 18 C3
Steinheim, *Germany* 18 D5
Steinhuder Meer, *Germany* 18 C5
Steinkjer, *Norway* 8 D14
Steinkopf, *S. Africa* 84 D2
Stekene, *Belgium* 17 F4
Stellarton, *Canada* 99 C7
Stellenbosch, *S. Africa* 84 E2
Stellendam, *Neths.* 16 E4
Stelvio, Paso dello, *Italy* 32 B7
Stemshaug, *Norway* 10 A2
Stendal, *Germany* 18 C7
Stene, *Belgium* 17 F1
Stenstorp, *Sweden* 11 F7
Steornabhaigh = Stornoway, *U.K.* 14 C2
Stepanakert = Xankändi, *Azerbaijan* 67 C12
Stepanavan, *Armenia* 43 K7
Stephen, *U.S.A.* 108 A6
Stephens Creek, *Australia* 91 E3
Stephens I., *Canada* 100 C2
Stephenville, *Canada* 99 C8
Stephenville, *U.S.A.* 109 J5
Stepnica, *Poland* 20 B4
Stepnoi = Elista, *Russia* 43 G7
Stepnyak, *Kazakstan* 44 D8
Steppe, *Asia* 46 D9
Sterkstroom, *S. Africa* 84 E4
Sterling, *Colo., U.S.A.* 108 E3
Sterling, *Ill., U.S.A.* 108 E10
Sterling, *Kans., U.S.A.* 108 F5
Sterling City, *U.S.A.* 109 K4
Sterling Run, *U.S.A.* 106 E6
Sterlitamak, *Russia* 44 D6
Šternberg, *Germany* 18 B7
Šternberk, *Czech.* 20 F7
Stérnes, *Greece* 37 D6
Sterzing = Vipiteno, *Italy* 33 B8
Stettin = Szczecin, *Poland* 20 B4
Stettiner Haff, *Germany* 18 B10
Stettler, *Canada* 100 C6
Steubenville, *U.S.A.* 106 F4
Stevens Point, *U.S.A.* 108 C10
Stevenson, *U.S.A.* 112 E5
Stevenson L., *Canada* 101 C9
Stevns Klint, *Denmark* 11 J6
Stewart, *B.C., Canada* 100 B3
Stewart, *N.W.T., Canada* 96 B6
Stewart, *U.S.A.* 112 F7
Stewart, C., *Australia* 90 A1
Stewart, I., *Chile* 128 D2
Stewart I., *N.Z.* 87 M1
Stewarts Point, *U.S.A.* 112 G3
Stewiacke, *Canada* 99 C7
Steynsburg, *S. Africa* 84 E4
Steyr, *Austria* 21 G4
Steytlerville, *S. Africa* 84 E3
Stia, *Italy* 33 E8
Stiens, *Neths.* 16 B7
Stigler, *U.S.A.* 109 H7
Stigliano, *Italy* 35 B9
Stigsnæs, *Denmark* 11 J5
Stigtomta, *Sweden* 11 F10
Stikine →, *Canada* 100 B2
Stilfontein, *S. Africa* 84 D4
Stilís, *Greece* 39 L5
Stillwater, *N.Z.* 87 K3
Stillwater, *Minn., U.S.A.* 108 C8
Stillwater, *N.Y., U.S.A.* 107 D11
Stillwater, *Okla., U.S.A.* 109 G6
Stillwater Range, *U.S.A.* 110 G4
Stilwell, *U.S.A.* 109 H7
Štip, *Macedonia* 39 H5
Stíra, *Greece* 39 L7
Stirling, *Australia* 90 B3
Stirling, *Canada* 100 D6
Stirling, *U.K.* 14 E5
Stirling □, *U.K.* 14 E4
Stirling Ra., *Australia* 89 F2
Stittsville, *Canada* 107 A9
Stjernøya, *Norway* 8 A20
Stjørdalshalsen, *Norway* 8 E14
Stockach, *Germany* 19 H5
Stockerau, *Austria* 21 G6
Stockett, *U.S.A.* 110 C8
Stockholm, *Sweden* 10 E12
Stockholms län □, *Sweden* 10 E12
Stockhorn, *Switz.* 22 C5
Stockport, *U.K.* 12 D5
Stockton, *Calif., U.S.A.* 111 H3
Stockton, *Kans., U.S.A.* 108 F5
Stockton, *Mo., U.S.A.* 109 G8
Stockton-on-Tees, *U.K.* 12 C6
Stockton-on-Tees □, *U.K.* 12 C6
Stockvik, *Sweden* 10 B11
Stöde, *Sweden* 10 B10
Stogovo, *Macedonia* 39 H3
Stoke on Trent, *U.K.* 12 D5
Stokes Bay, *Canada* 98 C3
Stokes Pt., *Australia* 90 G3
Stokes Ra., *Australia* 88 C5
Stokksnes, *Iceland* 8 D6
Stokmarknes, *Norway* 8 B16
Stolac, *Bos.-H.* 21 M7
Stolberg, *Germany* 18 E2
Stolbovaya, *Russia* 45 C16
Stolbovoy, Ostrov, *Russia* 45 D17
Stolbtsy = Stowbtsy, *Belarus* 40 F4
Stolin, *Belarus* 41 G4
Stolwijk, *Neths.* 16 E5
Stomíon, *Greece* 37 D5
Ston, *Croatia* 21 N7
Stonehaven, *U.K.* 14 E6
Stonehenge, *Australia* 90 C3
Stonewall, *Canada* 101 C9
Stony L., *Man., Canada* 101 B9
Stony L., *Ont., Canada* 106 B6
Stony Rapids, *Canada* 101 B7
Stony Tunguska = Podkamennaya Tunguska →, *Russia* 45 C10
Stonyford, *U.S.A.* 112 F4
Stopnica, *Poland* 20 E10
Stora Lulevatten, *Sweden* 8 C18
Storavan, *Sweden* 8 D18
Stord, *Norway* 9 G11
Store Bælt, *Denmark* 11 J5
Store Creek, *Australia* 91 E4
Store Heddinge, *Denmark* 11 J6
Støren, *Norway* 10 A4
Storm B., *Australia* 90 G4
Storm Lake, *U.S.A.* 108 D7
Stormberge, *S. Africa* 84 E4
Stormsrivier, *S. Africa* 84 E3
Stornoway, *U.K.* 14 C2
Storozhinets = Storozhynets, *Ukraine* 41 H3
Storozhynets, *Ukraine* 41 H3
Storsjö, *Sweden* 10 B7
Storsjøen, *Hedmark, Norway* 10 D5
Storsjøen, *Hedmark, Norway* 10 C5
Storsjön, *Sweden* 10 B7
Storstrøms Amtskommune □, *Denmark* 11 K5
Storuman, *Sweden* 8 D17
Storuman, sjö, *Sweden* 8 D17
Stoughton, *Canada* 101 D8
Stour →, *Dorset, U.K.* 13 G5
Stour →, *Here. & Worcs., U.K.* 13 E5
Stour →, *Kent, U.K.* 13 F9
Stour →, *Suffolk, U.K.* 13 F9
Stourbridge, *U.K.* 13 E5
Stout, L., *Canada* 101 C10
Stove Pipe Wells Village, *U.S.A.* 113 J9
Stowbtsy, *Belarus* 40 F4
Stowmarket, *U.K.* 13 E9
Strabane, *U.K.* 15 B4
Strabane □, *U.K.* 15 B4
Stracin, *Macedonia* 38 G5
Stradella, *Italy* 32 C6
Strahan, *Australia* 90 G4
Strakonice, *Czech.* 20 F3
Straldzha, *Bulgaria* 38 G9
Stralsund, *Germany* 18 A9
Strand, *S. Africa* 84 E2
Stranda, *Møre og Romsdal, Norway* 9 E12
Stranda, *Nord-Trøndelag, Norway* 8 E14
Strangford L., *U.K.* 15 B6
Strängnäs, *Sweden* 10 E11
Strangsville, *U.S.A.* 106 E3
Stranraer, *U.K.* 14 G3
Strasbourg, *Canada* 101 C8
Strasbourg, *France* 25 D14
Strasburg, *Germany* 18 B9
Strasburg, *U.S.A.* 108 B4
Strassen, *Lux.* 17 J8
Stratford, *Canada* 98 D3
Stratford, *N.Z.* 87 H5
Stratford, *Calif., U.S.A.* 111 H4
Stratford, *Conn., U.S.A.* 107 E11
Stratford, *Tex., U.S.A.* 109 G3
Stratford-upon-Avon, *U.K.* 13 E6
Strath Spey, *U.K.* 14 D5
Strathalbyn, *Australia* 91 F2
Strathcona Prov. Park, *Canada* 100 D3
Strathmore, *Australia* 90 B3
Strathmore, *Canada* 100 C6
Strathmore, *U.K.* 14 E5
Strathmore, *U.S.A.* 112 J7
Strathnaver, *Canada* 100 C4
Strathpeffer, *U.K.* 14 D4
Strathroy, *Canada* 98 D3
Strathy Pt., *U.K.* 14 C4
Stratton, *U.S.A.* 108 F3
Straubing, *Germany* 19 G8
Straumnes, *Iceland* 8 C2
Strausberg, *Germany* 18 C9
Strawberry Reservoir, *U.S.A.* 110 F8
Strawn, *U.S.A.* 109 J5
Strážnice, *Czech.* 20 G7
Streaky B., *Australia* 91 E1
Streaky Bay, *Australia* 91 E1
Streator, *U.S.A.* 108 E10
Streé, *Belgium* 17 H4
Streeter, *U.S.A.* 108 B5
Streetsville, *Canada* 106 C5
Strehaia, *Romania* 38 E6
Strelcha, *Bulgaria* 38 G7
Strelka, *Russia* 45 D10
Streng →, *Cambodia* 58 F4
Strésa, *Italy* 32 C5
Streymoy, *Færoe Is.* 8 E9
Strezhevoy, *Russia* 44 C8
Stříbro, *Czech.* 20 F3
Strijen, *Neths.* 16 E5
Strimón →, *Greece* 39 J6
Strimonikós Kólpos, *Greece* 39 J6
Stroeder, *Argentina* 128 B4
Strofádhes, *Greece* 39 M4
Strömbacka, *Sweden* 10 C10
Strómboli, *Italy* 35 D8
Stromeferry, *U.K.* 14 D3
Stromness, *U.K.* 14 C5
Stromsburg, *U.S.A.* 108 E6
Strömstad, *Sweden* 9 G14
Strömsund, *Sweden* 8 E16
Strόngoli, *Italy* 35 C10
Stronsay, *U.K.* 14 B6
Stroud, *U.K.* 13 F5
Stroud Road, *Australia* 91 E5
Stroudsburg, *U.S.A.* 107 F9
Stroumbi, *Cyprus* 37 E11
Struer, *Denmark* 11 H2
Struga, *Macedonia* 39 H3
Strugi Krasnyye, *Russia* 40 C5
Strumica, *Macedonia* 39 H5
Strumica →, *Europe* 39 H6
Struthers, *Canada* 98 C2
Struthers, *U.S.A.* 106 E4
Stryker, *U.S.A.* 110 B6
Stryy, *Ukraine* 41 H2
Strzegom, *Poland* 20 E6
Strzelce Krajeńskie, *Poland* 20 C5
Strzelecki Cr. →, *Australia* 91 D2
Strzelin, *Poland* 20 E7
Strzelno, *Poland* 20 C8
Strzyzów, *Poland* 20 F11
Stuart, *Fla., U.S.A.* 105 M5
Stuart, *Nebr., U.S.A.* 108 D5
Stuart →, *Canada* 100 C4
Stuart Bluff Ra., *Australia* 88 D5
Stuart L., *Canada* 100 C4
Stuart Ra., *Australia* 91 D1
Stubbekøbing, *Denmark* 11 K6
Stugun, *Sweden* 10 A9
Stull, L., *Canada* 98 B1
Stung Treng, *Cambodia* 58 F5
Stupart →, *Canada* 101 B10
Stupino, *Russia* 42 C4
Sturgeon B., *Canada* 101 C9
Sturgeon Bay, *U.S.A.* 104 C2
Sturgeon Falls, *Canada* 98 C4
Sturgeon L., *Alta., Canada* 100 B5
Sturgeon L., *Ont., Canada* 106 B6
Sturgeon L., *Ont., Canada* 98 B1
Sturgis, *Mich., U.S.A.* 104 E3
Sturgis, *S. Dak., U.S.A.* 108 C3
Sturt Cr. →, *Australia* 88 C4
Sturt Creek, *Australia* 88 C4
Stutterheim, *S. Africa* 84 E4
Stuttgart, *Germany* 19 G5
Stuttgart, *U.S.A.* 109 H9
Stuyvesant, *U.S.A.* 107 D11
Stykkishólmur, *Iceland* 8 D2
Styria = Steiermark □, *Austria* 21 H5
Su Xian, *China* 50 H9
Suakin, *Sudan* 76 D4
Suan, *N. Korea* 51 E14
Suapure →, *Venezuela* 120 B4
Suaqui, *Mexico* 114 B3
Suatá →, *Venezuela* 121 B4
Subang, *Indonesia* 57 G12
Subansiri →, *India* 61 F18
Subayhah, *Si. Arabia* 64 D3
Subi, *Indonesia* 59 L7
Subiaco, *Italy* 33 G10
Subotica, *Serbia, Yug.* 21 J9
Success, *Canada* 101 C7
Suceava, *Romania* 38 B9
Suceava →, *Romania* 38 B9
Sucha-Beskidzka, *Poland* 20 F9
Suchan, *Poland* 20 B5
Suchan, *Russia* 48 C6
Suchitoto, *El Salv.* 116 D2
Suchou = Suzhou, *China* 53 B13
Süchow = Xuzhou, *China* 51 G9
Suchowola, *Poland* 20 B13
Sucio →, *Colombia* 120 B2
Suck →, *Ireland* 15 C3
Sucre, *Bolivia* 125 D4
Sucre, *Colombia* 120 B3
Sucre □, *Colombia* 120 B2
Sucre □, *Venezuela* 121 A5
Sucuaro, *Colombia* 120 C4
Sućuraj, *Croatia* 33 E14
Sucuriju, *Brazil* 122 A2
Sucuriú →, *Brazil* 125 E7
Sud, Pte., *Canada* 99 C7
Sud-Ouest, Pte. du, *Canada* 99 C7
Suda →, *Russia* 40 C9
Sudak, *Ukraine* 41 K8
Sudan, *U.S.A.* 109 H3
Sudan ■, *Africa* 77 E3
Sudbury, *Canada* 98 C3
Sudbury, *U.K.* 13 E8
Sûdd, *Sudan* 77 F2
Suddie, *Guyana* 121 B6
Süderbrarup, *Germany* 18 A5
Süderlügum, *Germany* 18 A4
Süderoogsand, *Germany* 18 A4
Sudeten Mts. = Sudety, *Europe* 20 E6
Sudety, *Europe* 20 E6
Suðuroy, *Færoe Is.* 8 F9
Sudi, *Tanzania* 83 E4
Sudirman, Pegunungan, *Indonesia* 57 E9
Sudogda, *Russia* 42 C5
Sudr, *Egypt* 76 J8
Sudzha, *Russia* 42 E2
Sueca, *Spain* 29 F4
Suedala, *Sweden* 11 J7
Suez = El Suweis, *Egypt* 76 J8
Suez, G. of = Suweis, Khalîg el, *Egypt* 76 J8
Suez Canal = Suweis, Qanâ es, *Egypt* 76 H8
Suffield, *Canada* 101 C6
Suffolk, *U.S.A.* 104 G7
Suffolk □, *U.K.* 13 E9
Sugar City, *U.S.A.* 108 F3
Suğla Gölü, *Turkey* 66 D5
Sugluk = Salluit, *Canada* 97 B12
Sugny, *Belgium* 17 J5
Suhaia, L., *Romania* 38 F8
Suhār, *Oman* 65 E8
Suhbaatar, *Mongolia* 54 A5
Sühbaatar □, *Mongolia* 50 B8
Suhl, *Germany* 18 E6
Suhr, *Switz.* 22 B6
Şuhut, *Turkey* 66 C4
Sui Xian, *Henan, China* 50 G8
Sui Xian, *Henan, China* 53 B9
Suiá Missu →, *Brazil* 125 C7
Suichang, *China* 53 C12
Suichuan, *China* 53 D10
Suide, *China* 50 F6
Suifenhe, *China* 51 B16
Suihua, *China* 54 B7
Suijiang, *China* 52 C4
Suining, *Hunan, China* 53 D8
Suining, *Jiangsu, China* 51 H9
Suining, *Sichuan, China* 52 B5
Suiping, *China* 50 H7
Suippes, *France* 25 C11
Suir →, *Ireland* 15 D4
Suixi, *China* 53 G8
Suiyang, *Guizhou, China* 52 D6
Suiyang, *Heilongjiang, China* 51 B16
Suizhong, *China* 51 D11
Sujangarh, *India* 62 F6
Sukabumi, *Indonesia* 57 G12
Sukadana, *Kalimantan, Indonesia* 56 E3
Sukadana, *Sumatera, Indonesia* 56 F3
Sukagawa, *Japan* 49 F10
Sukaraja, *Indonesia* 56 E4
Sukarnapura = Jayapura, *Indonesia* 57 E10
Sukchŏn, *N. Korea* 51 E13
Sukhinichi, *Russia* 42 C2
Sukhona →, *Russia* 44 D4
Sukhothai, *Thailand* 58 D2
Sukhumi = Sokhumi, *Georgia* 43 J5
Sukkur, *Pakistan* 62 F3
Sukkur Barrage, *Pakistan* 62 F3
Sukumo, *Japan* 49 H6
Sukunka →, *Canada* 100 B4
Sul, Canal do, *Brazil* 122 B2
Sula →, *Ukraine* 41 H7
Sula, Kepulauan, *Indonesia* 57 E7
Sulaco →, *Honduras* 116 C2
Sulaiman Range, *Pakistan* 62 D3
Sulak →, *Russia* 43 J8
Sūlār, *Iran* 65 D6
Sulawesi □, *Indonesia* 57 E6
Sulawesi Sea = Celebes Sea, *Indonesia* 57 D6
Sulechów, *Poland* 20 C5
Sulejów, *Poland* 20 D9
Sulgen, *Switz.* 23 A8
Sulima, *S. Leone* 78 D2
Sulina, *Romania* 38 D12
Sulina, Braţul →, *Romania* 38 D12
Sulingen, *Germany* 18 C4
Sulitjelma, *Norway* 8 C17
Sullana, *Peru* 124 A1
Sullivan, *Ill., U.S.A.* 108 F10
Sullivan, *Ind., U.S.A.* 104 F2
Sullivan, *Mo., U.S.A.* 108 F9
Sullivan Bay, *Canada* 100 C3
Sully-sur-Loire, *France* 25 E9
Sulmona, *Italy* 33 F10
Sulphur, *La., U.S.A.* 109 K8
Sulphur, *Okla., U.S.A.* 109 H6
Sulphur Pt., *Canada* 100 A6
Sulphur Springs, *U.S.A.* 109 J7
Sulphur Springs Draw →, *U.S.A.* 109 J4
Sultan, *Canada* 98 C3
Sultan, *U.S.A.* 112 C5
Sultan Dağları, *Turkey* 66 C4
Sultanpur, *India* 63 F10
Sulu Arch., *Phil.* 55 J4
Sulu Sea, *E. Indies* 55 G4
Sülüklü, *Turkey* 66 C5
Sululta, *Ethiopia* 77 F4
Suluova, *Turkey* 66 B6
Suluq, *Libya* 73 B9
Sulzbach, *Germany* 19 F3
Sulzbach-Rosenberg, *Germany* 19 F7
Sulzberger Ice Shelf, *Antarctica* 5 D10
Sumalata, *Indonesia* 57 D6
Sumampa, *Argentina* 126 B3
Sumatera □, *Indonesia* 56 D2
Sumatra = Sumatera □, *Indonesia* 56 D2
Sumatra, *U.S.A.* 110 C10
Sumba, *Indonesia* 57 F5
Sumba, Selat, *Indonesia* 57 F5
Sumbawa, *Indonesia* 56 F5
Sumbawa Besar, *Indonesia* 56 F5
Sumbawanga □, *Tanzania* 82 D3
Sumbe, *Angola* 80 G2
Sumburgh Hd., *U.K.* 14 B7
Sumdo, *India* 63 B8
Sumé, *Brazil* 122 C4
Sumedang, *Indonesia* 57 G12
Šumen, *Bulgaria* 38 F9

Sumenep, *Indonesia* 57 G15
Sumgait = Sumqayıt, *Azerbaijan* 43 K9
Sumiswald, *Switz.* 22 B5
Summer L., *U.S.A.* 110 E3
Summerland, *Canada* 100 D5
Summerside, *Canada* 99 C7
Summerville, *Ga., U.S.A.* 105 H3
Summerville, *S.C., U.S.A.* 105 J5
Summit Lake, *Canada* 100 C4
Summit Peak, *U.S.A.* 111 H10
Sumner, *Iowa, U.S.A.* 108 D8
Sumner, *Wash., U.S.A.* 112 C4
Sumoto, *Japan* 49 G7
Sumqayıt, *Azerbaijan* 43 K9
Sumter, *U.S.A.* 105 J5
Sumy, *Ukraine* 41 G8
Sun City, *Ariz., U.S.A.* 111 K7
Sun City, *Calif., U.S.A.* 113 M9
Sunagawa, *Japan* 48 C10
Sunan, *N. Korea* 51 E13
Sunart, L., *U.K.* 14 E3
Sunburst, *U.S.A.* 110 B8
Sunbury, *Australia* 91 F3
Sunbury, *U.S.A.* 107 F8
Sunchales, *Argentina* 126 C3
Suncho Corral, *Argentina* 126 B3
Sunchon, *S. Korea* 51 G14
Suncook, *U.S.A.* 107 C13
Sunda, Selat, *Indonesia* 56 F3
Sunda Is., *Indonesia* 46 K14
Sunda Str. = Sunda, Selat, *Indonesia* 56 F3
Sundance, *U.S.A.* 108 C2
Sundarbans, The, *Asia* 61 J16
Sundargarh, *India* 61 H14
Sundays = Sondags →, *S. Africa* 84 E4
Sundbyberg, *Sweden* 10 E11
Sunderland, *Canada* 106 B5
Sunderland, *U.K.* 12 C6
Sundre, *Canada* 100 C6
Sundridge, *Canada* 98 C4
Sunds, *Denmark* 11 H3
Sundsjö, *Sweden* 10 B9
Sundsvall, *Sweden* 10 B11
Sung Hei, *Vietnam* 59 G6
Sungai Kolok, *Thailand* 59 J3
Sungai Lembing, *Malaysia* 59 L4
Sungai Patani, *Malaysia* 59 K3
Sungaigerong, *Indonesia* 56 E2
Sungailiat, *Indonesia* 56 E3
Sungaipakning, *Indonesia* 56 D2
Sungaipenuh, *Indonesia* 56 E2
Sungaitiram, *Indonesia* 56 E5
Sungari = Songhua Jiang →, *China* 54 B8
Sungguminasa, *Indonesia* 57 F5
Sunghua Chiang = Songhua Jiang →, *China* 54 B8
Sungikai, *Sudan* 77 E2
Sungurlu, *Turkey* 66 B6
Sunja, *Croatia* 33 C13
Sunndalsøra, *Norway* 9 E13
Sunnyside, *Utah, U.S.A.* 110 G8
Sunnyside, *Wash., U.S.A.* 110 C3
Sunnyvale, *U.S.A.* 111 H2
Sunray, *U.S.A.* 109 G4
Suntar, *Russia* 45 C12
Sunyani, *Ghana* 78 D4
Suomenselkä, *Finland* 8 E21
Suomussalmi, *Finland* 8 D23
Suoyarvi, *Russia* 40 A7
Supai, *U.S.A.* 111 H7
Supamo →, *Venezuela* 121 B5
Supaul, *India* 63 F12
Supe, *Peru* 124 C2
Superior, *Ariz., U.S.A.* 111 K8
Superior, *Mont., U.S.A.* 110 C6
Superior, *Nebr., U.S.A.* 108 E5
Superior, *Wis., U.S.A.* 108 B8
Superior, L., *U.S.A.* 98 C2
Supetar, *Croatia* 33 E13
Suphan Buri, *Thailand* 58 E3
Suphan Dağı, *Turkey* 67 C10
Supiori, *Indonesia* 57 E9
Supung Sk., *China* 51 D13
Sūq Suwayq, *Si. Arabia* 64 E3
Suqian, *China* 51 H10
Sūr, *Lebanon* 69 B4
Sur, Pt., *U.S.A.* 111 H3
Sura →, *Russia* 42 C8
Surab, *Pakistan* 62 E2
Surabaja = Surabaya, *Indonesia* 57 G15
Surabaya, *Indonesia* 57 G15
Suraia, *Romania* 38 D10
Surakarta, *Indonesia* 57 G14
Surakhany, *Azerbaijan* 43 K10
Surat, *Australia* 91 D4
Surat, *India* 60 J8
Surat Thani, *Thailand* 59 H2
Suratgarh, *India* 62 E5
Surazh, *Belarus* 40 E6
Surazh, *Russia* 41 F7
Surduc Pasul, *Romania* 38 D6
Surdulica, *Serbia, Yug.* 21 N12
Sûre = Sauer →, *Germany* 17 J9
Surendranagar, *India* 62 H4
Surf, *U.S.A.* 113 L6
Surgères, *France* 26 B3
Surgut, *Russia* 44 C8
Surhuisterveen, *Neths.* 16 B8
Suriapet, *India* 60 L11
Surigao, *Phil.* 55 G6
Surigao Strait, *Phil.* 55 F6
Surin, *Thailand* 58 E4
Surin Nua, Ko, *Thailand* 59 H1
Surinam ■, *S. Amer.* 121 C6
Suriname □, *Surinam* 121 B6
Suriname ■ = Surinam ■, *S. Amer.* 121 C6
Suriname →, *Surinam* 121 B6
Sūrmaq, *Iran* 65 D7
Sürmene, *Turkey* 67 B9
Surovikino, *Russia* 43 F6
Surprise L., *Canada* 100 B2
Surrey □, *U.K.* 13 F7
Sursee, *Switz.* 22 B6
Sursk, *Russia* 42 D7
Surskoye, *Russia* 42 C8
Surt, *Libya* 73 B8
Surt, Khalīj, *Libya* 73 B8
Surtsey, *Iceland* 8 E3
Surubim, *Brazil* 122 C4
Sürüç, *Turkey* 67 D8
Suruga-Wan, *Japan* 49 G9
Surumu →, *Brazil* 121 C5
Susa, *Italy* 32 C4
Suså →, *Denmark* 11 J5
Sušac, *Croatia* 33 F13
Susak, *Croatia* 33 D11
Susaki, *Japan* 49 H6
Sūsangerd, *Iran* 67 G13
Susanino, *Russia* 45 D15
Susanville, *U.S.A.* 110 F3
Susch, *Switz.* 23 C10
Suşehri, *Turkey* 67 B8
Susong, *China* 53 B11
Susquehanna →, *U.S.A.* 107 G8
Susquehanna Depot, *U.S.A.* 107 E9
Susques, *Argentina* 126 A2
Sussex, *Canada* 99 C6
Sussex, *U.S.A.* 107 E10
Sussex, E. □, *U.K.* 13 G8
Sussex, W. □, *U.K.* 13 G7
Susteren, *Neths.* 17 F7
Sustut →, *Canada* 100 B3
Susuman, *Russia* 45 C15
Susunu, *Indonesia* 57 E8
Susurluk, *Turkey* 66 C3
Susuz, *Turkey* 67 B10
Sütçüler, *Turkey* 66 D4
Sutherland, *S. Africa* 84 E3
Sutherland, *U.S.A.* 108 E4
Sutherland Falls, *N.Z.* 87 L1
Sutherlin, *U.S.A.* 110 E2
Sutivan, *Croatia* 33 E13
Sutlej →, *Pakistan* 62 E4
Sutter, *U.S.A.* 112 F5
Sutter Creek, *U.S.A.* 112 G6
Sutton, *Canada* 107 A12
Sutton, *U.S.A.* 108 E6
Sutton →, *Canada* 98 A3
Sutton in Ashfield, *U.K.* 12 D6
Suttor →, *Australia* 90 C4
Suttsu, *Japan* 48 C10
Suva, *Fiji* 87 D8
Suva Reka, *Serbia, Yug.* 21 N10
Suvo Rudište, *Serbia, Yug.* 21 M10
Suvorov, *Russia* 42 C3
Suvorov Is. = Suwarrow Is., *Cook Is.* 93 J11
Suwałki, *Poland* 20 A12
Suwannaphum, *Thailand* 58 E4
Suwannee →, *U.S.A.* 105 L4
Suwanose-Jima, *Japan* 49 K4
Suwarrow Is., *Cook Is.* 93 J11
Suwayq aş Şuqban, *Iraq* 64 D5
Suweis, Khalîg el, *Egypt* 76 J8
Suweis, Qanâ es, *Egypt* 76 H8
Suwŏn, *S. Korea* 51 F14
Suzdal, *Russia* 42 B5
Suzhou, *China* 53 B13
Suzu, *Japan* 49 F8
Suzu-Misaki, *Japan* 49 F8
Suzuka, *Japan* 49 G8
Suzzara, *Italy* 32 C7
Svalbard, *Arctic* 4 B8
Svalöv, *Sweden* 11 J7
Svappavaara, *Sweden* 8 C19
Svarstad, *Norway* 10 E3
Svartisen, *Norway* 8 C15
Svartvik, *Sweden* 10 B11
Svatove, *Ukraine* 41 H10
Svatovo = Svatove, *Ukraine* 41 H10
Svay Chek, *Cambodia* 58 F4
Svay Rieng, *Cambodia* 59 G5
Svealand □, *Sweden* 9 G16
Sveg, *Sweden* 9 E16
Svendborg, *Denmark* 11 J4
Svene, *Norway* 10 E3
Svenljunga, *Sweden* 11 G7
Svenstrup, *Denmark* 11 H3
Sverdlovsk = Yekaterinburg, *Russia* 44 D7
Sverdlovsk, *Ukraine* 41 H10
Sverdrup Is., *Canada* 4 B3
Svetac, *Croatia* 33 E12
Sveti Ivan Zelina, *Croatia* 33 C13
Sveti Jurij, *Slovenia* 33 B12
Sveti Lenart, *Slovenia* 33 B12
Sveti Nikole, *Macedonia* 39 H4
Sveti Trojica, *Slovenia* 33 B12
Svetlaya, *Russia* 48 A9
Svetlogorsk = Svyetlahorsk, *Belarus* 41 F5
Svetlograd, *Russia* 43 H6
Svetlovodsk = Svitlovodsk, *Ukraine* 41 H7
Svetozarevo, *Serbia, Yug.* 21 L11
Svidník, *Slovak Rep.* 20 F11
Svilaja Planina, *Croatia* 33 E13
Svilengrad, *Bulgaria* 39 H9
Svir →, *Russia* 40 B7
Sviritsa, *Russia* 40 B7
Svishtov, *Bulgaria* 38 F8
Svislach, *Belarus* 41 F3
Svitava →, *Czech.* 20 F6
Svitavy, *Czech.* 20 F6
Svitlovodsk, *Ukraine* 41 H7
Svobodnyy, *Russia* 45 D13
Svolvær, *Norway* 8 B16
Svratka →, *Czech.* 20 F6
Svrljig, *Serbia, Yug.* 21 M12
Svyetlahorsk, *Belarus* 41 F5
Swabian Alps = Schwäbische Alb, *Germany* 19 G5
Swainsboro, *U.S.A.* 105 J4
Swakopmund, *Namibia* 84 C1
Swale →, *U.K.* 12 C6
Swalmen, *Neths.* 17 F8
Swan Hill, *Australia* 91 F3
Swan Hills, *Canada* 100 C5
Swan Is., *W. Indies* 116 C3
Swan L., *Canada* 101 C8
Swan River, *Canada* 101 C8
Swanage, *U.K.* 13 G6
Swansea, *Australia* 91 E5
Swansea, *U.K.* 13 F4
Swansea □, *U.K.* 13 F3
Swar →, *Pakistan* 63 B5
Swartberge, *S. Africa* 84 E3
Swartmodder, *S. Africa* 84 D3
Swartruggens, *S. Africa* 84 D4
Swarzędz, *Poland* 20 C7
Swastika, *Canada* 98 C3
Swatow = Shantou, *China* 53 F11
Swaziland ■, *Africa* 85 D5
Sweden ■, *Europe* 9 G16
Swedru, *Ghana* 79 D4
Sweet Home, *U.S.A.* 110 D2
Sweetwater, *Nev., U.S.A.* 112 G7
Sweetwater, *Tex., U.S.A.* 109 J4
Sweetwater →, *U.S.A.* 110 E10
Swellendam, *S. Africa* 84 E3
Świdnica, *Poland* 20 E6
Świdnik, *Poland* 20 D12
Świdwin, *Poland* 20 B5
Świebodzin, *Poland* 20 C5
Świecie, *Poland* 20 B8
Świętokrzyskie, Góry, *Poland* 20 E10
Swift Current, *Canada* 101 C7
Swiftcurrent →, *Canada* 101 C7
Swilly, L., *Ireland* 15 A4
Swindle, I., *Canada* 100 C3
Swindon, *U.K.* 13 F6
Swinemünde = Świnoujście, *Poland* 20 B4
Świnoujście, *Poland* 20 B4
Switzerland ■, *Europe* 22 D6
Swords, *Ireland* 15 C5
Syasstroy, *Russia* 40 B7
Sychevka, *Russia* 42 C2
Sydney, *Australia* 91 E5
Sydney, *Canada* 99 C7
Sydney Mines, *Canada* 99 C7
Sydprøven, *Greenland* 4 C5
Sydra, G. of = Surt, Khalīj, *Libya* 73 B8
Syeverodonetsk, *Ukraine* 41 H10
Syke, *Germany* 18 C4
Syktyvkar, *Russia* 44 C6
Sylacauga, *U.S.A.* 105 J2
Sylarna, *Sweden* 8 E15
Sylhet, *Bangla.* 61 G17
Sylt, *Germany* 18 A4
Sylvan Lake, *Canada* 100 C6
Sylvania, *U.S.A.* 105 J5
Sylvester, *U.S.A.* 105 K4
Sym, *Russia* 44 C9
Symón, *Mexico* 114 C4
Synelnykove, *Ukraine* 41 H8
Synnott Ra., *Australia* 88 C4
Syracuse, *Kans., U.S.A.* 109 F4
Syracuse, *N.Y., U.S.A.* 107 C8
Syrdarya →, *Kazakstan* 44 E7
Syria ■, *Asia* 67 E8
Syrian Desert = Ash Shām, Bādiyat, *Asia* 46 F7
Syul'dzhyukyor, *Russia* 45 C12
Syzran, *Russia* 42 D9
Szaraz →, *Hungary* 21 J10
Szarvas, *Hungary* 21 J10
Szczebrzeszyn, *Poland* 20 E12
Szczecin, *Poland* 20 B4
Szczecinek, *Poland* 20 B6
Szczekocimy, *Poland* 20 E9
Szczytno, *Poland* 20 B11
Szechwan = Sichuan □, *China* 52 B5
Szeged, *Hungary* 21 J10
Szeghalom, *Hungary* 21 H11
Székesfehérvár, *Hungary* 21 H8
Szekszárd, *Hungary* 21 J8
Szendrö, *Hungary* 21 G10
Szentendre, *Hungary* 21 H9
Szentes, *Hungary* 21 J10
Szentgotthárd, *Hungary* 21 J6
Szentlörinc, *Hungary* 21 J8
Szigetvár, *Hungary* 21 J7
Szolnok, *Hungary* 21 H10
Szombathely, *Hungary* 21 H6
Szprotawa, *Poland* 20 D5
Szydłowiec, *Poland* 20 D10
Szypliszki, *Poland* 20 A13

T

't Harde, *Neths.* 16 D7
't Zandt, *Neths.* 16 B9
Ta Khli Khok, *Thailand* 58 E3
Ta Lai, *Vietnam* 59 G6
Tabacal, *Argentina* 126 A3
Tabaco, *Phil.* 55 E5
Tabagné, *Ivory C.* 78 D4
Ţābah, *Si. Arabia* 64 E4
Tabajara, *Brazil* 125 B5
Tabalos, *Peru* 124 B2
Tabarca, I. de, *Spain* 29 G4
Tabarka, *Tunisia* 75 A6
Ţabas, *Khorāsān, Iran* 65 C9
Ţabas, *Khorāsān, Iran* 65 C8
Tabasará, Serranía de, *Panama* 116 E3
Tabasco □, *Mexico* 115 D6
Tabatinga, Serra da, *Brazil* 122 D3
Tabāzīn, *Iran* 65 D8
Tabelbala, Kahal de, *Algeria* 75 C4
Taber, *Canada* 100 D6
Tabernas, *Spain* 29 H2
Tabernes de Valldigna, *Spain* 29 F4
Tabira, *Brazil* 122 C4
Tablas, *Phil.* 55 E5
Tablas Strait, *Phil.* 55 E4
Table B. = Tafelbaai, *S. Africa* 84 E2
Table B., *Canada* 99 B8
Table Mt., *S. Africa* 84 E2
Tableland, *Australia* 88 C4
Tabletop, Mt., *Australia* 90 C4
Tábor, *Czech.* 20 F4
Tabora, *Tanzania* 82 D3
Tabora □, *Tanzania* 82 D3
Tabou, *Ivory C.* 78 E3
Tabrīz, *Iran* 67 C12
Tabuaeran, *Pac. Oc.* 93 G12
Tabuelan, *Phil.* 55 F5
Tabuenca, *Spain* 28 D3
Tabūk, *Si. Arabia* 64 D3
Tacámbaro de Codallos, *Mexico* 114 D4
Tacheng, *China* 54 B3
Tachia, *Taiwan* 53 E13
Tach'ing Shan = Daqing Shan, *China* 50 D6
Táchira □, *Venezuela* 120 B3
Tácina →, *Italy* 35 D9
Tacloban, *Phil.* 55 F6
Tacna, *Peru* 124 D3
Tacna □, *Peru* 124 D3
Tacoma, *U.S.A.* 112 C4
Tacuarembó, *Uruguay* 127 C4
Tacutu →, *Brazil* 121 C5
Tademaït, Plateau du, *Algeria* 75 C5
Tadent, O. →, *Algeria* 75 D6
Tadjerdjeri, O. →, *Algeria* 75 C6
Tadjerouna, *Algeria* 75 B5
Tadjettaret, O. →, *Algeria* 75 D6
Tadjmout, *Oasis, Algeria* 75 B5
Tadjmout, *Saoura, Algeria* 75 C5
Tadjoura, *Djibouti* 68 E3
Tadjoura, Golfe de, *Djibouti* 77 E5
Tadmor, *N.Z.* 87 J4
Tadoule, L., *Canada* 101 B9
Tadoussac, *Canada* 99 C6
Tadzhikistan = Tajikistan ■, *Asia* 44 F8
Taechŏn-ni, *S. Korea* 51 F14
Taegu, *S. Korea* 51 G15
Taegwan, *N. Korea* 51 D13
Taejŏn, *S. Korea* 51 F14
Tafalla, *Spain* 28 C3
Tafar, *Sudan* 77 F2
Tafassasset, O. →, *Algeria* 75 D6
Tafelbaai, *S. Africa* 84 E2
Tafelney, C., *Morocco* 74 B3
Tafermaar, *Indonesia* 57 F8
Taffermit, *Morocco* 74 C3
Tafí Viejo, *Argentina* 126 B2
Tafīhān, *Iran* 65 D7
Tafiré, *Ivory C.* 78 D3
Tafnidilt, *Morocco* 74 C2
Tafraoute, *Morocco* 74 C3
Taft, *Iran* 65 D7
Taft, *Phil.* 55 F6
Taft, *Calif., U.S.A.* 113 K7
Taft, *Tex., U.S.A.* 109 M6
Taga Dzong, *Bhutan* 61 F16
Taganrog, *Russia* 43 G4
Taganrogskiy Zaliv, *Russia* 43 G4
Tagânt, *Mauritania* 78 B2
Tagatay, *Phil.* 55 D4
Tagbilaran, *Phil.* 55 G5
Tággia, *Italy* 32 E4
Taghzout, *Morocco* 74 B4
Tagish, *Canada* 100 A2
Tagish L., *Canada* 100 A2
Tagliacozzo, *Italy* 33 F10
Tagliamento →, *Italy* 33 C10
Táglio di Po, *Italy* 33 D9
Tagna, *Colombia* 120 D3
Tago, *Phil.* 55 G7
Tagomago, I. de, *Spain* 36 B8
Taguatinga, *Brazil* 123 D3
Tagudin, *Phil.* 55 C4
Tagum, *Phil.* 55 H6
Tagus = Tejo →, *Europe* 31 G1
Tahakopa, *N.Z.* 87 M2
Tahala, *Morocco* 74 B4
Tahan, Gunong, *Malaysia* 59 K4
Tahat, *Algeria* 75 D6
Tāherī, *Iran* 65 E7
Tahiti, *Pac. Oc.* 93 J13
Tahoe, L., *U.S.A.* 112 G6
Tahoe City, *U.S.A.* 112 F6
Taholah, *U.S.A.* 112 C2
Tahoua, *Niger* 79 C6
Tahta, *Egypt* 76 B3
Tahtalı Dağları, *Turkey* 66 C7
Tahuamanu →, *Bolivia* 124 C4
Tahulandang, *Indonesia* 57 D7
Tahuna, *Indonesia* 57 D7
Taï, *Ivory C.* 78 D3
Tai Hu, *China* 54 C7
Tai Shan, *China* 51 F9
Tai Xian, *China* 53 A13
Tai'an, *China* 51 F9
Taibei = T'aipei, *Taiwan* 53 E13
Taibique, *Canary Is.* 36 G2
Taibus Qi, *China* 50 D8
T'aichung, *Taiwan* 53 E13
Taieri →, *N.Z.* 87 M3
Taigu, *China* 50 F7
Taihang Shan, *China* 50 G7
Taihape, *N.Z.* 87 H5
Taihe, *Anhui, China* 50 H8
Taihe, *Jiangxi, China* 53 D10
Taihu, *China* 53 B11
Taijiang, *China* 52 D7
Taikang, *China* 50 G8
Tailem Bend, *Australia* 91 F2
Tailfingen, *Germany* 19 G5
Taimyr Peninsula = Taymyr, Poluostrov, *Russia* 45 B11
Tain, *U.K.* 14 D4
T'ainan, *Taiwan* 53 F13
Taínaron, Ákra, *Greece* 39 N5
Taining, *China* 53 D11
Taintignies, *Belgium* 17 G2
Taiobeiras, *Brazil* 123 E3
T'aipei, *Taiwan* 53 E13
Taiping, *China* 53 B12
Taiping, *Malaysia* 59 K3
Taipingzhen, *China* 50 H6
Taipu, *Brazil* 122 C4
Tairbeart = Tarbert, *U.K.* 14 D2
Taishan, *China* 53 F9
Taishun, *China* 53 D12
Taita □, *Kenya* 82 C4
Taita Hills, *Kenya* 82 C4
Taitao, C., *Chile* 128 C1
Taitao, Pen. de, *Chile* 128 C2
T'aitung, *Taiwan* 53 F13
Taivalkoski, *Finland* 8 D23
Taiwan ■, *Asia* 53 F13
Taixing, *China* 53 A13
Taïyetos Óros, *Greece* 39 N5
Taiyiba, *Israel* 69 C4
Taiyuan, *China* 50 F7
Taizhong = T'aichung, *Taiwan* 53 E13
Taizhou, *China* 53 A12
Taizhou Liedao, *China* 53 C13
Ta'izz, *Yemen* 68 E3
Tājābād, *Iran* 65 D7
Tajapuru, Furo do, *Brazil* 122 B1
Tajikistan ■, *Asia* 44 F8
Tajima, *Japan* 49 F9
Tajo = Tejo →, *Europe* 31 G1
Tajrīsh, *Iran* 65 C6
Tājūrā, *Libya* 73 B7
Tak, *Thailand* 58 D2
Takāb, *Iran* 67 D12
Takachiho, *Japan* 49 H5
Takada, *Japan* 49 F9
Takahagi, *Japan* 49 F10
Takaka, *N.Z.* 87 J4
Takamatsu, *Japan* 49 G7
Takaoka, *Japan* 49 F8
Takapuna, *N.Z.* 87 G5
Takasaki, *Japan* 49 F9
Takatsuki, *Japan* 49 G7
Takaungu, *Kenya* 82 C4
Takayama, *Japan* 49 F8
Take-Shima, *Japan* 49 J5
Takefu, *Japan* 49 G8
Takengon, *Indonesia* 56 D1
Takeo, *Cambodia* 59 G5
Takeo, *Japan* 49 H5
Tåkern, *Sweden* 11 F8
Tākestān, *Iran* 65 C6
Taketa, *Japan* 49 H5
Takh, *India* 63 C7
Takhman, *Cambodia* 59 G5
Takikawa, *Japan* 48 C10
Takla L., *Canada* 100 B3
Takla Landing, *Canada* 100 B3
Takla Makan = Taklamakan Shamo, *China* 46 F12
Taklamakan Shamo, *China* 46 F12
Taku →, *Canada* 100 B2
Takum, *Nigeria* 79 D6
Takutu →, *Guyana* 121 C5
Tal Halāl, *Iran* 65 D7
Tala, *Uruguay* 127 C4
Talachyn, *Belarus* 40 E5
Talacogan, *Phil.* 55 G6
Talagante, *Chile* 126 C1
Talaïnt, *Morocco* 74 C3
Talak, *Niger* 79 B6
Talamanca, Cordillera de, *Cent. Amer.* 116 E3
Talara, *Peru* 124 A1

Talas, *Kyrgyzstan* 44 E8
Talas, *Turkey* 66 C6
Talâta, *Egypt* 69 E1
Talata Mafara, *Nigeria* 79 C6
Talaud, Kepulauan, *Indonesia* 57 D7
Talaud Is. = Talaud, Kepulauan, *Indonesia* 57 D7
Talavera de la Reina, *Spain* 30 F6
Talawana, *Australia* 88 D3
Talayan, *Phil.* 55 H6
Talbert, Sillon de, *France* 24 D3
Talbot, C., *Australia* 88 B4
Talbragar →, *Australia* 91 E4
Talca, *Chile* 126 D1
Talca □, *Chile* 126 D1
Talcahuano, *Chile* 126 D1
Talcher, *India* 61 J14
Talcho, *Niger* 79 C5
Taldy Kurgan = Taldyqorghan, *Kazakstan* 44 E8
Taldyqorghan, *Kazakstan* 44 E8
Tālesh, *Iran* 67 D13
Tālesh, Kūhhā-ye, *Iran* 67 D13
Talguharai, *Sudan* 76 D4
Tali Post, *Sudan* 77 F3
Talibon, *Phil.* 57 B6
Talibong, Ko, *Thailand* 59 J2
Talihina, *U.S.A.* 109 H7
Talisayan, *Phil.* 55 G6
Taliwang, *Indonesia* 56 F5
Tall 'Afar, *Iraq* 67 D10
Tall 'Asūr, *West Bank* 69 D4
Tall Kalakh, *Syria* 69 A5
Talla, *Egypt* 76 J7
Talladega, *U.S.A.* 105 J2
Tallahassee, *U.S.A.* 105 K3
Tallangatta, *Australia* 91 F4
Tallarook, *Australia* 91 F4
Tallering Pk., *Australia* 89 E2
Tallinn, *Estonia* 9 G21
Tallulah, *U.S.A.* 109 J9
Talmest, *Morocco* 74 B3
Talmont, *France* 26 B2
Talne, *Ukraine* 41 H6
Talnoye = Talne, *Ukraine* 41 H6
Talodi, *Sudan* 77 E3
Talovaya, *Russia* 42 E5
Taloyoak, *Canada* 96 B10
Talpa de Allende, *Mexico* 114 C4
Talsi, *Latvia* 9 H20
Talsinnt, *Morocco* 75 B4
Taltal, *Chile* 126 B1
Taltson →, *Canada* 100 A6
Talwood, *Australia* 91 D4
Talyawalka Cr. →, *Australia* 91 E3
Tam Chau, *Vietnam* 59 G5
Tam Ky, *Vietnam* 58 E7
Tam Quan, *Vietnam* 58 E7
Tama, *U.S.A.* 108 E8
Tamala, *Australia* 89 E1
Tamalameque, *Colombia* 120 B3
Tamale, *Ghana* 79 D4
Taman, *Russia* 43 H3
Tamanar, *Morocco* 74 B3
Tamano, *Japan* 49 G6
Tamanrasset, *Algeria* 75 D6
Tamanrasset, O. →, *Algeria* 75 D5
Tamaqua, *U.S.A.* 107 F9
Tamar →, *U.K.* 13 G3
Támara, *Colombia* 120 B3
Tamarang, *Australia* 91 E5
Tamarinda, *Spain* 36 B10
Tamarite de Litera, *Spain* 28 D5
Tamashima, *Japan* 49 G6
Tamaské, *Niger* 79 C6
Tamaulipas □, *Mexico* 115 C5
Tamaulipas, Sierra de, *Mexico* 115 C5
Tamazula, *Mexico* 114 C3
Tamazunchale, *Mexico* 115 C5
Tamba-Dabatou, *Guinea* 78 C2
Tambacounda, *Senegal* 78 C2
Tambelan, Kepulauan, *Indonesia* 56 D3
Tambellup, *Australia* 89 F2
Tambo, *Australia* 90 C4
Tambo, *Peru* 124 C3
Tambo →, *Peru* 124 C3
Tambo de Mora, *Peru* 124 C2
Tambobamba, *Peru* 124 C3
Tambohorano, *Madag.* 85 B7
Tambopata →, *Peru* 124 C4
Tambora, *Indonesia* 56 F5
Tambov, *Russia* 42 D5
Tambre →, *Spain* 30 C2
Tambuku, *Indonesia* 57 G15
Tamburâ, *Sudan* 77 F2
Tâmchekket, *Mauritania* 78 B2
Tame, *Colombia* 120 B3
Tamega →, *Portugal* 30 D2
Tamelelt, *Morocco* 74 B3
Tamenglong, *India* 61 G18
Tamerza, *Tunisia* 75 B6
Tamgak, Mts., *Niger* 72 E6
Tamiahua, L. de, *Mexico* 115 C5
Tamil Nadu □, *India* 60 P10
Tamines, *Belgium* 17 H5
Tamis →, *Serbia, Yug.* 38 E3
Tamluk, *India* 63 H12
Tammerfors = Tampere, *Finland* 9 F20
Tammisaari, *Finland* 9 F20
Tamo Abu, Pegunungan, *Malaysia* 56 D5
Tampa, *U.S.A.* 105 M4
Tampa B., *U.S.A.* 105 M4
Tampere, *Finland* 9 F20
Tampico, *Mexico* 115 C5
Tampin, *Malaysia* 59 L4
Tamri, *Morocco* 74 B3
Tamrida = Qādib, *Yemen* 68 E5
Tamsagbulag, *Mongolia* 54 B6
Tamu, *Burma* 61 G19
Tamuja →, *Spain* 31 F4
Tamworth, *Australia* 91 E5
Tamworth, *U.K.* 13 E6
Tamyang, *S. Korea* 51 G14
Tan An, *Vietnam* 59 G6
Tan-tan, *Morocco* 74 C2
Tana →, *Kenya* 82 C5
Tana →, *Norway* 8 A23
Tana, L., *Ethiopia* 77 E4
Tana River, *Kenya* 82 C4
Tanabe, *Japan* 49 H7
Tanabi, *Brazil* 123 F2
Tanafjorden, *Norway* 8 A23
Tanaga, Pta., *Canary Is.* 36 G1
Tanagro →, *Italy* 35 B8
Tanahbala, *Indonesia* 56 E1
Tanahgrogot, *Indonesia* 56 E5
Tanahjampea, *Indonesia* 57 F6
Tanahmasa, *Indonesia* 56 E1
Tanahmerah, *Indonesia* 57 F10
Tanakura, *Japan* 49 F10
Tanami, *Australia* 88 C4
Tanami Desert, *Australia* 88 C5
Tanana, *U.S.A.* 96 B4
Tanana →, *U.S.A.* 96 B4
Tananarive = Antananarivo, *Madag.* 85 B8
Tanannt, *Morocco* 74 B3
Tánaro →, *Italy* 32 C5
Tanaunella, *Italy* 34 B2
Tanbar, *Australia* 90 D3
Tancarville, *France* 24 C7
Tancheng, *China* 51 G10
Tanchŏn, *N. Korea* 51 D15
Tanda, *Ut. P., India* 63 F10
Tanda, *Ut. P., India* 63 E8
Tanda, *Ivory C.* 78 D4
Tandag, *Phil.* 55 G7
Tandaia, *Tanzania* 83 D3
Tăndărei, *Romania* 38 E10
Tandaué, *Angola* 84 B2
Tandil, *Argentina* 126 D4
Tandil, Sa. del, *Argentina* 126 D4
Tandlianwala, *Pakistan* 62 D5
Tando Adam, *Pakistan* 62 G3
Tandou L., *Australia* 91 E3
Tandsbyn, *Sweden* 10 A8
Tane-ga-Shima, *Japan* 49 J5
Taneatua, *N.Z.* 87 H6
Tanen Tong Dan, *Burma* 58 D2
Tanezrouft, *Algeria* 75 D5
Tang, Koh, *Cambodia* 59 G4
Tang Krasang, *Cambodia* 58 F5
Tanga, *Tanzania* 82 D4
Tanga □, *Tanzania* 82 D4
Tanganyika, L., *Africa* 82 D2
Tanger = Tangier, *Morocco* 74 A3
Tangerang, *Indonesia* 57 G12
Tangerhütte, *Germany* 18 C7
Tangermünde, *Germany* 18 C7
Tanggu, *China* 51 E9
Tanggula Shan, *China* 54 C4
Tanghe, *China* 50 H7
Tangier, *Morocco* 74 A3
Tangorin P.O., *Australia* 90 C3
Tangshan, *China* 51 E10
Tangtou, *China* 51 G10
Tanguiéta, *Benin* 79 C5
Tangxi, *China* 53 C12
Tangyan He →, *China* 52 C7
Tanimbar, Kepulauan, *Indonesia* 57 F8
Tanimbar Is. = Tanimbar, Kepulauan, *Indonesia* 57 F8
Taninges, *France* 27 B10
Tanjay, *Phil.* 55 G5
Tanjong Malim, *Malaysia* 59 L3
Tanjore = Thanjavur, *India* 60 P11
Tanjung, *Indonesia* 56 E5
Tanjungbalai, *Indonesia* 56 D1
Tanjungbatu, *Indonesia* 56 D5
Tanjungkarang Telukbetung, *Indonesia* 56 F3
Tanjungpandan, *Indonesia* 56 E3
Tanjungpinang, *Indonesia* 56 D2
Tanjungpriok, *Indonesia* 57 G12
Tanjungredeb, *Indonesia* 56 D5
Tanjungselor, *Indonesia* 56 D5
Tank, *Pakistan* 62 C4
Tänndalen, *Sweden* 10 B6
Tannis Bugt, *Denmark* 11 G4
Tannu-Ola, *Russia* 45 D10
Tano →, *Ghana* 78 D4
Tanon Str., *Phil.* 55 F5
Tanout, *Niger* 79 C6
Tanquinho, *Brazil* 123 D4
Tanshui, *Taiwan* 53 E13
Tanta, *Egypt* 76 H7
Tantoyuca, *Mexico* 115 C5
Tantung = Dandong, *China* 51 D13
Tanumshede, *Sweden* 11 F5
Tanunda, *Australia* 91 E2
Tanus, *France* 26 D6
Tanzania ■, *Africa* 82 D3
Tanzilla →, *Canada* 100 B2
Tao Ko, *Thailand* 59 G2
Tao'an, *China* 51 B12
Tao'er He →, *China* 51 B13
Taohua Dao, *China* 53 C14
Taolanaro, *Madag.* 85 D8
Taole, *China* 50 E4
Taormina, *Italy* 35 E8
Taos, *U.S.A.* 111 H11
Taoudenni, *Mali* 74 D4
Taoudrart, Adrar, *Algeria* 75 D5
Taounate, *Morocco* 74 B4
Taourirt, *Algeria* 75 C5
Taourirt, *Morocco* 75 B4
Taouz, *Morocco* 74 B4
Taoyuan, *China* 53 C8
T'aoyüan, *Taiwan* 53 E13
Tapa, *Estonia* 9 G21
Tapa Shan = Daba Shan, *China* 52 B7
Tapachula, *Mexico* 115 E6
Tapah, *Malaysia* 59 K3
Tapajós →, *Brazil* 121 D7
Tapaktuan, *Indonesia* 56 D1
Tapanahoni →, *Surinam* 121 C7
Tapanui, *N.Z.* 87 L2
Tapauá, *Brazil* 125 B5
Tapauá →, *Brazil* 125 B5
Tapeta, *Liberia* 78 D3
Taphan Hin, *Thailand* 58 D3
Tapi →, *India* 60 J8
Tapia, *Spain* 30 B4
Tápiószele, *Hungary* 21 H9
Tapiraí, *Brazil* 123 E2
Tapirapé →, *Brazil* 122 D1
Tapirapecó, Serra, *Venezuela* 121 C5
Tapirapuã, *Brazil* 125 C6
Tapoeripa, *Surinam* 121 B6
Tapolca, *Hungary* 21 J7
Tappahannock, *U.S.A.* 104 G7
Tapuaenuku, Mt., *N.Z.* 87 J4
Tapul Group, *Phil.* 55 J4
Tapurucuará, *Brazil* 121 D4
Taqīābād, *Iran* 65 C8
Ṭaqṭaq, *Iraq* 67 E11
Taquara, *Brazil* 127 B5
Taquari →, *Brazil* 125 D6
Taquaritinga, *Brazil* 123 F2
Tara, *Australia* 91 D5
Tara, *Canada* 106 B3
Tara, *Russia* 44 D8
Tara, *Zambia* 83 F2
Tara →, *Russia* 44 D8
Taraba □, *Nigeria* 79 D7
Tarabagatay, Khrebet, *Kazakstan* 44 E9
Tarabuco, *Bolivia* 125 D5
Tarābulus, *Lebanon* 69 A4
Tarābulus, *Libya* 75 B7
Tarahouahout, *Algeria* 75 D6
Tarajalejo, *Canary Is.* 36 F5
Tarakan, *Indonesia* 56 D5
Tarakit, Mt., *Kenya* 82 B4
Taralga, *Australia* 91 E4
Tarama-Jima, *Japan* 49 M2
Taran, Mys, *Russia* 9 J18
Taranagar, *India* 62 E6
Taranaki □, *N.Z.* 87 H5
Tarancón, *Spain* 28 E1
Taranga, *India* 62 H5
Taranga Hill, *India* 62 H5
Táranto, *Italy* 35 B10
Táranto, G. di, *Italy* 35 B10
Tarapacá, *Colombia* 120 D4
Tarapacá □, *Chile* 126 A2
Tarapoto, *Peru* 124 B2
Taraquá, *Brazil* 120 C4
Tarare, *France* 27 C8
Tararua Ra., *N.Z.* 87 J5
Tarascon, *France* 27 E8
Tarascon-sur-Ariège, *France* 26 F5
Tarashcha, *Ukraine* 41 H6
Tarata, *Peru* 124 D3
Tarauacá, *Brazil* 124 B3
Tarauacá →, *Brazil* 124 B4
Taravo →, *France* 27 G12
Tarawera, *N.Z.* 87 H6
Tarawera L., *N.Z.* 87 H6
Tarazona, *Spain* 28 D3
Tarazona de la Mancha, *Spain* 29 F3
Tarbat Ness, *U.K.* 14 D5
Tarbela Dam, *Pakistan* 62 B5
Tarbert, *Arg. & Bute, U.K.* 14 F3
Tarbert, *W. Isles, U.K.* 14 D2
Tarbes, *France* 26 E4
Tarboro, *U.S.A.* 105 H7
Tarbrax, *Australia* 90 C3
Tarcento, *Italy* 33 B10
Tarcoola, *Australia* 91 E1
Tarcoon, *Australia* 91 E4
Tardets-Sorholus, *France* 26 E3
Tardoire →, *France* 26 C4
Taree, *Australia* 91 E5
Tarentaise, *France* 27 C10
Tarf, Ras, *Morocco* 74 A3
Tarfa, W. el →, *Egypt* 76 J7
Tarfaya, *Morocco* 74 C2
Targon, *France* 26 D3
Targuist, *Morocco* 74 B4
Tarhbalt, *Morocco* 74 B3
Tarhit, *Algeria* 75 B4
Táriba, *Venezuela* 120 B3
Tarifa, *Spain* 31 J5
Tarija, *Bolivia* 126 A3
Tarija □, *Bolivia* 126 A3
Tariku →, *Indonesia* 57 E9
Tarim Basin = Tarim Pendi, *China* 54 C3
Tarim He →, *China* 54 C3
Tarim Pendi, *China* 54 C3
Tarime □, *Tanzania* 82 C3
Taritatu →, *Indonesia* 57 E9
Tarka →, *S. Africa* 84 E4
Tarkastad, *S. Africa* 84 E4
Tarkhankut, Mys, *Ukraine* 41 K7
Tarko Sale, *Russia* 44 C8
Tarkwa, *Ghana* 78 D4
Tarlac, *Phil.* 55 D4
Tarlton Downs, *Australia* 90 C2
Tarm, *Denmark* 11 J2
Tarma, *Peru* 124 C2
Tarn □, *France* 26 E6
Tarn →, *France* 26 D5
Tarn-et-Garonne □, *France* 26 D5
Tarna →, *Hungary* 21 H9
Tårnby, *Denmark* 11 J6
Tarnobrzeg, *Poland* 20 E11
Tarnów, *Poland* 20 F11
Táro →, *Italy* 32 D7
Taroom, *Australia* 91 D4
Taroudannt, *Morocco* 74 B3
Tarp, *Germany* 18 A5
Tarpon Springs, *U.S.A.* 105 L4
Tarquínia, *Italy* 33 F8
Tarragona, *Spain* 28 D6
Tarragona □, *Spain* 28 D6
Tarrasa, *Spain* 28 D7
Tárrega, *Spain* 28 D6
Tarrytown, *U.S.A.* 107 E11
Tarshiha = Me'ona, *Israel* 69 B4
Tarso Emissi, *Chad* 73 D8
Tarsus, *Turkey* 66 D6
Tartagal, *Argentina* 126 A3
Tärtär, *Azerbaijan* 43 K8
Tärtär →, *Azerbaijan* 43 K8
Tartas, *France* 26 E3
Tartu, *Estonia* 9 G22
Ṭarṭūs, *Syria* 66 E6
Tarumirim, *Brazil* 123 E3
Tarumizu, *Japan* 49 J5
Tarussa, *Russia* 42 C3
Tarutao, Ko, *Thailand* 59 J2
Tarutung, *Indonesia* 56 D1
Tarvísio, *Italy* 33 B10
Tarz Ulli, *Libya* 75 C7
Tasāwah, *Libya* 73 C7
Taschereau, *Canada* 98 C4
Taseko →, *Canada* 100 C4
Tash-Kömür, *Kyrgyzstan* 44 E8
Tash-Kumyr = Tash-Kömür, *Kyrgyzstan* 44 E8
Tashauz = Dashhowuz, *Turkmenistan* 44 E6
Tashi Chho Dzong = Thimphu, *Bhutan* 61 F16
Tashkent = Toshkent, *Uzbekistan* 44 E7
Tashtagol, *Russia* 44 D9
Tasikmalaya, *Indonesia* 57 G13
Tåsjön, *Sweden* 8 D16
Taskan, *Russia* 45 C16
Taşköprü, *Turkey* 66 B6
Tasman B., *N.Z.* 87 J4
Tasman Mts., *N.Z.* 87 J4
Tasman Pen., *Australia* 90 G4
Tasman Sea, *Pac. Oc.* 92 L8
Tasmania □, *Australia* 90 G4
Tăşnad, *Romania* 38 B5
Tassil Tin-Rerhoh, *Algeria* 75 D5
Tassili n-Ajjer, *Algeria* 75 C6
Tassili-Oua-n-Ahaggar, *Algeria* 75 D6
Tasu Sd., *Canada* 100 C2
Tata, *Morocco* 74 C3
Tatabánya, *Hungary* 21 H8
Tatahouine, *Tunisia* 75 B7
Tatar Republic □ = Tatarstan □, *Russia* 42 C10
Tatarbunary, *Ukraine* 41 K5
Tatarsk, *Russia* 44 D8
Tatarstan □, *Russia* 42 C10
Tateyama, *Japan* 49 G9
Tathlina L., *Canada* 100 A5
Tathra, *Australia* 91 F4
Tatinnai L., *Canada* 101 A9
Tatnam, C., *Canada* 101 B10
Tatra = Tatry, *Slovak Rep.* 20 F9
Tatry, *Slovak Rep.* 20 F9
Tatsuno, *Japan* 49 G7
Tatta, *Pakistan* 62 G2
Tatuī, *Brazil* 127 A6
Tatum, *U.S.A.* 109 J3
Tat'ung = Datong, *China* 50 D7
Tatvan, *Turkey* 67 C10
Tauá, *Brazil* 122 C3
Taubaté, *Brazil* 127 A6
Tauberbischofsheim, *Germany* 19 F5
Taucha, *Germany* 18 D8
Taufikia, *Sudan* 77 F3
Taumarunui, *N.Z.* 87 H5
Taumaturgo, *Brazil* 124 B3
Taung, *S. Africa* 84 D3
Taungdwingyi, *Burma* 61 J19
Taunggyi, *Burma* 61 J20
Taungup, *Burma* 61 K19
Taungup Pass, *Burma* 61 K19
Taungup Taunggya, *Burma* 61 K18
Taunsa Barrage, *Pakistan* 62 D4
Taunton, *U.K.* 13 F4
Taunton, *U.S.A.* 107 E13
Taunus, *Germany* 19 E4
Taupo, *N.Z.* 87 H6
Taupo, L., *N.Z.* 87 H5
Tauragė, *Lithuania* 9 J20
Tauranga, *N.Z.* 87 G6
Tauranga Harb., *N.Z.* 87 G6
Taurianova, *Italy* 35 D9
Taurus Mts. = Toros Dağları, *Turkey* 66 D5
Tauste, *Spain* 28 D3
Tauz = Tovuz, *Azerbaijan* 43 K7
Tavannes, *Switz.* 22 B4
Tavas, *Turkey* 66 D3
Tavda, *Russia* 44 D7
Tavda →, *Russia* 44 D7
Taverny, *France* 25 C9
Taveta, *Tanzania* 82 C4
Taveuni, *Fiji* 87 C9
Tavignano →, *France* 27 F13
Tavira, *Portugal* 31 H3
Tavistock, *Canada* 106 C4
Tavistock, *U.K.* 13 G3
Tavolara, *Italy* 34 B2
Távora →, *Portugal* 30 D3
Tavoy, *Burma* 58 E2
Tavşanlı, *Turkey* 66 C3
Taw →, *U.K.* 13 F3
Tawas City, *U.S.A.* 104 C4
Tawau, *Malaysia* 56 D5
Tawitawi, *Phil.* 55 J4
Taxila, *Pakistan* 62 C5
Tay →, *U.K.* 14 E5
Tay, Firth of, *U.K.* 14 E5
Tay, L., *Australia* 89 F3
Tay, L., *U.K.* 14 E4
Tay Ninh, *Vietnam* 59 G6
Tayabamba, *Peru* 124 B2
Tayabas Bay, *Phil.* 55 E4
Taylakova, *Russia* 44 D8
Taylakovy = Taylakova, *Russia* 44 D8
Taylor, *Canada* 100 B4
Taylor, *Nebr., U.S.A.* 108 E5
Taylor, *Pa., U.S.A.* 107 E9
Taylor, *Tex., U.S.A.* 109 K6
Taylor, Mt., *U.S.A.* 111 J10
Taylorville, *U.S.A.* 108 F10
Taymā, *Si. Arabia* 64 E3
Taymyr, Oz., *Russia* 45 B11
Taymyr, Poluostrov, *Russia* 45 B11
Tayport, *U.K.* 14 E6
Tayshet, *Russia* 45 D10
Taytay, *Phil.* 55 F3
Taz →, *Russia* 44 C8
Taza, *Morocco* 74 B4
Tāzah Khurmātū, *Iraq* 67 E11
Tazawa-Ko, *Japan* 48 E10
Tazenakht, *Morocco* 74 B3
Tazin L., *Canada* 101 B7
Tazoult, *Algeria* 75 A6
Tazovskiy, *Russia* 44 C8
Tbilisi, *Georgia* 43 K7
Tchad = Chad ■, *Africa* 73 E8
Tchad, L., *Chad* 73 F7
Tchaourou, *Benin* 79 D5
Tch'eng-tou = Chengdu, *China* 52 B5
Tchentlo L., *Canada* 100 B4
Tchibanga, *Gabon* 80 E2
Tchien, *Liberia* 78 D3
Tchin Tabaraden, *Niger* 79 B6
Tch'ong-k'ing = Chongqing, *China* 52 C6
Tczew, *Poland* 20 A8
Te Anau, L., *N.Z.* 87 L1
Te Aroha, *N.Z.* 87 G5
Te Awamutu, *N.Z.* 87 H5
Te Kuiti, *N.Z.* 87 H5
Te Puke, *N.Z.* 87 G6
Te Waewae B., *N.Z.* 87 M1
Tea →, *Brazil* 120 D4
Tea Tree, *Australia* 90 C1
Teague, *U.S.A.* 109 K6
Teano, *Italy* 35 A7
Teapa, *Mexico* 115 D6
Teba, *Spain* 31 J6
Tebakang, *Malaysia* 56 D4
Teberda, *Russia* 43 J5
Tébessa, *Algeria* 75 A6
Tebicuary →, *Paraguay* 126 B4
Tebingtinggi, *Indonesia* 56 D1
Tébourba, *Tunisia* 75 A6
Téboursouk, *Tunisia* 75 A6
Tebulos, *Georgia* 43 J7
Tecate, *Mexico* 113 N10
Tecer Dağları, *Turkey* 66 C7
Tech →, *France* 26 F7
Techiman, *Ghana* 78 D4
Tecka, *Argentina* 128 B2
Tecomán, *Mexico* 114 D4
Tecopa, *U.S.A.* 113 K10
Tecoripa, *Mexico* 114 B3
Tecuala, *Mexico* 114 C3
Tecuci, *Romania* 38 D10
Tecumseh, *U.S.A.* 104 D4
Tedzhen = Tejen, *Turkmenistan* 44 F7
Tees →, *U.K.* 12 C6
Teesside, *U.K.* 12 C6
Teeswater, *Canada* 106 C3
Tefé, *Brazil* 121 D5
Tefé →, *Brazil* 121 D5
Tefenni, *Turkey* 66 D3
Tegal, *Indonesia* 57 G13
Tegelen, *Neths.* 17 F8
Tegernsee, *Germany* 19 H7
Teggiano, *Italy* 35 B8
Teghra, *India* 63 G11
Tegid, L. = Bala, L., *U.K.* 12 E4

Tegina, *Nigeria* 79 C6
Tegucigalpa, *Honduras* 116 D2
Tehachapi, *U.S.A.* 113 K8
Tehachapi Mts., *U.S.A.* 113 L8
Tehamiyam, *Sudan* 76 D4
Tehilla, *Sudan* 76 D4
Téhini, *Ivory C.* 78 D4
Tehrān, *Iran* 65 C6
Tehuacán, *Mexico* 115 D5
Tehuantepec, *Mexico* 115 D5
Tehuantepec, G. de, *Mexico* 115 D5
Tehuantepec, Istmo de, *Mexico* 115 D6
Teide, *Canary Is.* 36 F3
Teifi →, *U.K.* 13 E3
Teign →, *U.K.* 13 G4
Teignmouth, *U.K.* 13 G4
Teixeira, *Brazil* 122 C4
Teixeira Pinto, *Guinea-Biss.* 78 C1
Tejen, *Turkmenistan* 44 F7
Tejo →, *Europe* 31 G1
Tejon Pass, *U.S.A.* 113 L8
Tekamah, *U.S.A.* 108 E6
Tekapo, L., *N.Z.* 87 K3
Tekax, *Mexico* 115 C7
Tekeli, *Kazakstan* 44 E8
Tekeze →, *Ethiopia* 77 E4
Tekija, *Serbia, Yug.* 21 L12
Tekirdağ, *Turkey* 66 B2
Tekkali, *India* 61 K14
Tekke, *Turkey* 66 B7
Tekman, *Turkey* 67 C9
Tekoa, *U.S.A.* 110 C5
Tekouiât, O. →, *Algeria* 75 D5
Tel Aviv-Yafo, *Israel* 69 C3
Tel Lakhish, *Israel* 69 D3
Tel Megiddo, *Israel* 69 C4
Tela, *Honduras* 116 C2
Télagh, *Algeria* 75 B4
Telanaipura = Jambi, *Indonesia* 56 E2
Telavi, *Georgia* 43 J7
Telde, *Canary Is.* 36 G4
Telegraph Creek, *Canada* 100 B2
Telekhany = Tsyelyakhany, *Belarus* 41 F3
Telemark, *Norway* 9 G12
Telemark fylke □, *Norway* 10 E2
Telén, *Argentina* 126 D2
Teleng, *Iran* 65 E9
Teleño, *Spain* 30 C4
Teleorman →, *Romania* 38 E8
Teles Pires →, *Brazil* 125 B6
Telescope Pk., *U.S.A.* 113 J9
Teletaye, *Mali* 79 B5
Telford, *U.K.* 12 E5
Telfs, *Austria* 19 H7
Télimélé, *Guinea* 78 C2
Telkwa, *Canada* 100 C3
Tell City, *U.S.A.* 104 G2
Tellicherry, *India* 60 P9
Tellin, *Belgium* 17 H6
Telluride, *U.S.A.* 111 H10
Teloloapán, *Mexico* 115 D5
Telpos Iz, *Russia* 6 C17
Telsen, *Argentina* 128 B3
Telšiai, *Lithuania* 9 H20
Teltow, *Germany* 18 C9
Teluk Anson, *Malaysia* 59 K3
Teluk Betung = Tanjungkarang Telukbetung, *Indonesia* 56 F3
Teluk Intan = Teluk Anson, *Malaysia* 59 K3
Telukbutun, *Indonesia* 59 K7
Telukdalem, *Indonesia* 56 D1
Tema, *Ghana* 79 D5
Temanggung, *Indonesia* 57 G14
Temapache, *Mexico* 115 C5
Temax, *Mexico* 115 C7
Temba, *S. Africa* 85 D4
Tembe, *Zaïre* 82 C2
Temblador, *Venezuela* 121 B5
Tembleque, *Spain* 28 F1
Temblor Range, *U.S.A.* 113 K7
Teme →, *U.K.* 13 E5
Temecula, *U.S.A.* 113 M9
Temerloh, *Malaysia* 59 L4
Temir, *Kazakstan* 44 E6
Temirtau, *Kazakstan* 44 D8
Temirtau, *Russia* 44 D9
Témiscaming, *Canada* 98 C4
Temma, *Australia* 90 G3
Temnikov, *Russia* 42 C6
Temo →, *Italy* 34 B1
Temora, *Australia* 91 E4
Temosachic, *Mexico* 114 B3
Tempe, *U.S.A.* 111 K8
Tempe Downs, *Australia* 88 D5
Témpio Pausánia, *Italy* 34 B2
Tempiute, *U.S.A.* 112 H11
Temple, *U.S.A.* 109 K6
Temple B., *Australia* 90 A3
Templemore, *Ireland* 15 D4
Templeton, *U.S.A.* 112 K6
Templeton →, *Australia* 90 C2
Templeuve, *Belgium* 17 G2
Templin, *Germany* 18 B9
Tempoal, *Mexico* 115 C5
Temryuk, *Russia* 43 H3
Temse, *Belgium* 17 F4
Temska →, *Serbia, Yug.* 21 M12
Temuco, *Chile* 128 A2
Temuka, *N.Z.* 87 L3
Ten Boer, *Neths.* 16 B9
Tena, *Ecuador* 120 D2
Tenabo, *Mexico* 115 C6
Tenaha, *U.S.A.* 109 K7
Tenali, *India* 60 L12
Tenancingo, *Mexico* 115 D5
Tenango, *Mexico* 115 D5
Tenasserim, *Burma* 59 F2
Tenasserim □, *Burma* 58 F2
Tenay, *France* 27 C9
Tenby, *U.K.* 13 F3
Tenda, Col di, *France* 27 D11
Tendaho, *Ethiopia* 68 E3
Tende, *France* 27 D11
Tendelti, *Sudan* 77 E3
Tendjedi, Adrar, *Algeria* 75 D6
Tendrara, *Morocco* 75 B4
Tendre, Mt., *Switz.* 22 C2
Tendrovskaya Kosa, *Ukraine* 41 J6
Teneida, *Egypt* 76 B2
Tenente Marques →, *Brazil* 125 C6
Ténéré, *Niger* 79 B7
Tenerife, *Canary Is.* 36 F3
Tenerife, Pico, *Canary Is.* 36 G1
Ténès, *Algeria* 75 A5
Teng Xian, *Guangxi Zhuangzu, China* 53 F8
Teng Xian, *Shandong, China* 51 G9
Tengah □, *Indonesia* 57 E6
Tengah Kepulauan, *Indonesia* 56 F5
Tengchong, *China* 52 E2
Tengchowfu = Penglai, *China* 51 F11
Tenggara □, *Indonesia* 57 E6
Tenggarong, *Indonesia* 56 E5
Tenggol, P., *Malaysia* 59 K4
Tengiz, Ozero, *Kazakstan* 44 D7
Tenigerbad, *Switz.* 23 C7
Tenino, *U.S.A.* 112 D4
Tenkasi, *India* 60 Q10
Tenke, *Shaba, Zaïre* 83 E2
Tenke, *Shaba, Zaïre* 83 E2
Tenkodogo, *Burkina Faso* 79 C4
Tenna →, *Italy* 33 E10
Tennant Creek, *Australia* 90 B1
Tennessee □, *U.S.A.* 105 H2
Tennessee →, *U.S.A.* 104 G1
Tenneville, *Belgium* 17 H7
Tennille, *U.S.A.* 105 J4
Tennsift, Oued →, *Morocco* 74 B3
Teno, Pta. de, *Canary Is.* 36 F3
Tenom, *Malaysia* 56 C5
Tenosique, *Mexico* 115 D6
Tenryū-Gawa →, *Japan* 49 G8
Tent L., *Canada* 101 A7
Tenterfield, *Australia* 91 D5
Teófilo Otoni, *Brazil* 123 E3
Teotihuacán, *Mexico* 115 D5
Tepa, *Indonesia* 57 F7
Tepalcatepec →, *Mexico* 114 D4
Tepehuanes, *Mexico* 114 B3
Tepequem, Serra, *Brazil* 121 C5
Tepetongo, *Mexico* 114 C4
Tepic, *Mexico* 114 C4
Tepoca, C., *Mexico* 114 A2
Tequila, *Mexico* 114 C4
Ter →, *Spain* 28 C8
Ter Apel, *Neths.* 16 C10
Téra, *Niger* 79 C5
Tera →, *Spain* 30 D5
Teraina, *Kiribati* 93 G11
Téramo, *Italy* 33 F10
Terang, *Australia* 91 F3
Terborg, *Neths.* 16 E8
Tercan, *Turkey* 67 C9
Tercero →, *Argentina* 126 C3
Terebovlya, *Ukraine* 41 H3
Terek →, *Russia* 43 J8
Terenos, *Brazil* 125 E7
Tereshka →, *Russia* 42 E8
Teresina, *Brazil* 122 C3
Teresinha, *Brazil* 121 C7
Terewah, L., *Australia* 91 D4
Terges →, *Portugal* 31 H3
Tergnier, *France* 25 C10
Terhazza, *Mali* 74 D3
Terheijden, *Neths.* 17 E5
Teridgerie Cr. →, *Australia* 91 E4
Terlizzi, *Italy* 35 A9
Terme, *Turkey* 66 B7
Termez = Termiz, *Uzbekistan* 44 F7
Términi Imerese, *Italy* 34 E6
Términos, L. de, *Mexico* 115 D6
Termiz, *Uzbekistan* 44 F7
Térmoli, *Italy* 33 F12
Ternate, *Indonesia* 57 D7
Terneuzen, *Neths.* 17 F3
Terney, *Russia* 45 E14
Terni, *Italy* 33 F9
Ternitz, *Austria* 21 H6
Ternopil, *Ukraine* 41 H3
Ternopol = Ternopil, *Ukraine* 41 H3
Terowie, *N.S.W., Australia* 91 E4
Terowie, *S. Austral., Australia* 91 E2
Terra Bella, *U.S.A.* 113 K7
Terrace, *Canada* 100 C3
Terrace Bay, *Canada* 98 C2
Terracina, *Italy* 34 A6
Terralba, *Italy* 34 C1
Terranova = Ólbia, *Italy* 34 B2
Terranuova Bracciolini, *Italy* 33 E8
Terrasini Favarotta, *Italy* 34 D6
Terrassa = Tarrasa, *Spain* 28 D7
Terrasson-la-Villedieu, *France* 26 C5
Terre Haute, *U.S.A.* 104 F2
Terrebonne B., *U.S.A.* 109 L9
Terrecht, *Mali* 75 D4
Terrell, *U.S.A.* 109 J6
Terrenceville, *Canada* 99 C9
Terrick Terrick, *Australia* 90 C4
Terry, *U.S.A.* 108 B2
Terschelling, *Neths.* 16 B6
Tersko-Kumskiy Kanal →, *Russia* 43 H7
Terter → = Tärtär →, *Azerbaijan* 43 K8
Teruel, *Spain* 28 E3
Teruel □, *Spain* 28 E4
Tervel, *Bulgaria* 38 F10
Tervola, *Finland* 8 C21
Teryaweyna L., *Australia* 91 E3
Tešanj, *Bos.-H.* 21 L7
Teseney, *Eritrea* 77 D4
Tesha →, *Russia* 42 C6
Teshio, *Japan* 48 B10
Teshio-Gawa →, *Japan* 48 B10
Tesiyn Gol →, *Mongolia* 54 A4
Teslin, *Canada* 100 A2
Teslin →, *Canada* 100 A2
Teslin L., *Canada* 100 A2
Tesouro, *Brazil* 125 D7
Tessalit, *Mali* 79 A5
Tessaoua, *Niger* 79 C6
Tessenderlo, *Belgium* 17 F6
Tessin, *Germany* 18 A8
Tessit, *Mali* 79 B5
Test →, *U.K.* 13 F6
Testa del Gargano, *Italy* 35 A9
Têt →, *France* 26 F7
Tetachuck L., *Canada* 100 C3
Tetas, Pta., *Chile* 126 A1
Tete, *Mozam.* 83 F3
Tete □, *Mozam.* 83 F3
Teterev →, *Ukraine* 41 G6
Teteringen, *Neths.* 17 E5
Teterow, *Germany* 18 B8
Teteven, *Bulgaria* 38 G7
Tethul →, *Canada* 100 A6
Tetiyev, *Ukraine* 41 H5
Teton →, *U.S.A.* 110 C8
Tétouan, *Morocco* 74 A3
Tetovo, *Macedonia* 38 G4
Tetyukhe Pristan, *Russia* 48 B7
Tetyushi, *Russia* 42 C9
Teuco →, *Argentina* 126 B3
Teufen, *Switz.* 23 B8
Teulada, *Italy* 34 D1
Teulon, *Canada* 101 C9
Teun, *Indonesia* 57 F7
Teutoburger Wald, *Germany* 18 C4
Tévere →, *Italy* 33 G9
Teverya, *Israel* 69 C4
Teviot →, *U.K.* 14 F6
Tewantin, *Australia* 91 D5
Tewkesbury, *U.K.* 13 F5
Texada I., *Canada* 100 D4
Texarkana, *Ark., U.S.A.* 109 J8
Texarkana, *Tex., U.S.A.* 109 J7
Texas, *Australia* 91 D5
Texas □, *U.S.A.* 109 K5
Texas City, *U.S.A.* 109 L7
Texel, *Neths.* 16 B5
Texhoma, *U.S.A.* 109 G4
Texline, *U.S.A.* 109 G3
Texoma, L., *U.S.A.* 109 J6
Teykovo, *Russia* 42 B5
Teza →, *Russia* 42 B5
Tezin, *Afghan.* 62 B3
Teziutlán, *Mexico* 115 D5
Tezpur, *India* 61 F18
Tezzeron L., *Canada* 100 C4
Tha-anne →, *Canada* 101 A10
Tha Deua, *Laos* 58 D4
Tha Deua, *Laos* 58 C3
Tha Pla, *Thailand* 58 D3
Tha Rua, *Thailand* 58 E3
Tha Sala, *Thailand* 59 H2
Tha Song Yang, *Thailand* 58 D1
Thaba Putsoa, *Lesotho* 85 D4
Thabana Ntlenyana, *Lesotho* 85 D4
Thabazimbi, *S. Africa* 85 C4
Thai Binh, *Vietnam* 58 B6
Thai Hoa, *Vietnam* 58 C5
Thai Muang, *Thailand* 59 H2
Thai Nguyen, *Vietnam* 58 B5
Thailand ■, *Asia* 58 E4
Thailand, G. of, *Asia* 59 G3
Thakhek, *Laos* 58 D5
Thal, *Pakistan* 62 C4
Thal Desert, *Pakistan* 62 D4
Thala, *Tunisia* 75 A6
Thala La, *Burma* 61 E20
Thalabarivat, *Cambodia* 58 F5
Thalkirch, *Switz.* 23 C8
Thallon, *Australia* 91 D4
Thalwil, *Switz.* 23 B7
Thame →, *U.K.* 13 F6
Thames, *N.Z.* 87 G5
Thames →, *Canada* 98 D3
Thames →, *U.K.* 13 F8
Thames →, *U.S.A.* 107 E12
Thamesford, *Canada* 106 C3
Thamesville, *Canada* 106 D3
Than Uyen, *Vietnam* 58 B4
Thane, *India* 60 K8
Thanesar, *India* 62 D7
Thanet, I. of, *U.K.* 13 F9
Thangoo, *Australia* 88 C3
Thangool, *Australia* 90 C5
Thanh Hoa, *Vietnam* 58 C5
Thanh Hung, *Vietnam* 59 H5
Thanh Pho Ho Chi Minh = Phanh Bho Ho Chi Minh, *Vietnam* 59 G6
Thanh Thuy, *Vietnam* 58 A5
Thanjavur, *India* 60 P11
Thann, *France* 25 E14
Thaon-les-Vosges, *France* 25 D13
Thap Sakae, *Thailand* 59 G2
Thap Than, *Thailand* 58 E2
Thar Desert, *India* 62 F4
Tharad, *India* 62 G4
Thargomindah, *Australia* 91 D3
Tharrawaddy, *Burma* 61 L19
Tharthār, Mileh, *Iraq* 67 E10
Tharthār, W. ath →, *Iraq* 67 E10
Thásos, *Greece* 39 J7
That Khe, *Vietnam* 58 A6
Thatcher, *Ariz., U.S.A.* 111 K9
Thatcher, *Colo., U.S.A.* 109 G2
Thaton, *Burma* 61 L20
Thau, Bassin de, *France* 26 E7
Thaungdut, *Burma* 61 G19
Thayer, *U.S.A.* 109 G9
Thayetmyo, *Burma* 61 K19
Thayngen, *Switz.* 23 A7
Thazi, *Burma* 61 J20
The Alberga →, *Australia* 91 D2
The Bight, *Bahamas* 117 B4
The Coorong, *Australia* 91 F2
The Dalles, *U.S.A.* 110 D3
The English Company's Is., *Australia* 90 A2
The Frome →, *Australia* 91 D2
The Grampians, *Australia* 91 F3
The Great Divide = Great Dividing Ra., *Australia* 90 C4
The Hague = 's-Gravenhage, *Neths.* 16 D4
The Hamilton →, *Australia* 91 D2
The Macumba →, *Australia* 91 D2
The Neales →, *Australia* 91 D2
The Officer →, *Australia* 89 E5
The Pas, *Canada* 101 C8
The Range, *Zimbabwe* 83 F3
The Rock, *Australia* 91 F4
The Salt L., *Australia* 91 E3
The Stevenson →, *Australia* 91 D2
The Warburton →, *Australia* 91 D2
Thebes = Thívai, *Greece* 39 L6
Thebes, *Egypt* 76 B3
Thedford, *Canada* 106 C3
Thedford, *U.S.A.* 108 E4
Theebine, *Australia* 91 D5
Thekulthili L., *Canada* 101 A7
Thelon →, *Canada* 101 A8
Thénezay, *France* 24 F6
Thenia, *Algeria* 75 A5
Thenon, *France* 26 C5
Theodore, *Australia* 90 C5
Thepha, *Thailand* 59 J3
Thérain →, *France* 25 C9
Theresa, *U.S.A.* 107 B9
Thermaïkós Kólpos, *Greece* 39 J5
Thermopolis, *U.S.A.* 110 E9
Thermopylae P., *Greece* 39 L5
Thessalía □, *Greece* 39 L4
Thessalon, *Canada* 98 C3
Thessaloníki, *Greece* 39 J5
Thessaloniki, Gulf of = Thermaïkós Kólpos, *Greece* 39 J5
Thessaly = Thessalía □, *Greece* 39 L4
Thetford, *U.K.* 13 E8
Thetford Mines, *Canada* 99 C5
Theun →, *Laos* 58 C5
Theunissen, *S. Africa* 84 D4
Theux, *Belgium* 17 G7
Thevenard, *Australia* 91 E1
Thiámis →, *Greece* 39 K3
Thiberville, *France* 24 C7
Thibodaux, *U.S.A.* 109 L9
Thicket Portage, *Canada* 101 B9
Thief River Falls, *U.S.A.* 108 A6
Thiel Mts., *Antarctica* 5 E16
Thiene, *Italy* 33 C8
Thiérache, *France* 25 C10
Thiers, *France* 26 C7
Thies, *Senegal* 78 C1
Thiet, *Sudan* 77 F2
Thika, *Kenya* 82 C4
Thikombia, *Fiji* 87 B9
Thille-Boubacar, *Senegal* 78 B1
Thimphu, *Bhutan* 61 F16
þingvallavatn, *Iceland* 8 D3
Thionville, *France* 25 C13
Thíra, *Greece* 39 N8
Thirasía, *Greece* 39 N8
Thirsk, *U.K.* 12 C6
Thisted, *Denmark* 9 H13
Thistle I., *Australia* 91 F2
Thívai, *Greece* 39 L6
Thiviers, *France* 26 C4
Thizy, *France* 27 B8
þjórsá →, *Iceland* 8 E3
Thlewiaza →, *Man., Canada* 101 B8
Thlewiaza →, *N.W.T., Canada* 101 A10
Thmar Puok, *Cambodia* 58 F4
Tho Vinh, *Vietnam* 58 C5
Thoa →, *Canada* 101 A7
Thoen, *Thailand* 58 D2
Thoeng, *Thailand* 58 C3
Thoissey, *France* 27 B8
Tholdi, *Pakistan* 63 B7
Tholen, *Neths.* 17 E4
Thomas, *Okla., U.S.A.* 109 H5
Thomas, *W. Va., U.S.A.* 104 F6
Thomas, L., *Australia* 91 D2
Thomaston, *U.S.A.* 105 J3
Thomasville, *Ala., U.S.A.* 105 K2
Thomasville, *Ga., U.S.A.* 105 K3
Thomasville, *N.C., U.S.A.* 105 H5
Thommen, *Belgium* 17 H8
Thompson, *Canada* 101 B9
Thompson, *U.S.A.* 111 G9
Thompson →, *Canada* 100 C4
Thompson →, *U.S.A.* 108 F8
Thompson Falls, *U.S.A.* 110 C6
Thompson Landing, *Canada* 101 A6
Thompson Pk., *U.S.A.* 110 F2
Thomson's Falls = Nyahururu, *Kenya* 82 B4
Thon Buri, *Thailand* 59 F3
Thônes, *France* 27 C10
Thonon-les-Bains, *France* 27 B10
Thorez, *Ukraine* 41 H10
þórisvatn, *Iceland* 8 D4
Thornaby on Tees, *U.K.* 12 C6
Thornbury, *Canada* 106 B4
Thorold, *Canada* 106 C5
þórshöfn, *Iceland* 8 C6
Thouarcé, *France* 24 E6
Thouars, *France* 24 F6
Thouet →, *France* 24 E6
Thouin, C., *Australia* 88 D2
Thousand Oaks, *U.S.A.* 113 L8
Thrace, *Turkey* 66 B2
Thrakikón Pélagos, *Greece* 39 J8
Three Forks, *U.S.A.* 110 D8
Three Hills, *Canada* 100 C6
Three Hummock I., *Australia* 90 G3
Three Lakes, *U.S.A.* 108 C10
Three Points, C., *Ghana* 78 E4
Three Rivers, *Australia* 89 E2
Three Rivers, *Calif., U.S.A.* 112 J8
Three Rivers, *Tex., U.S.A.* 109 L5
Three Sisters, *U.S.A.* 110 D3
Throssell, L., *Australia* 89 E3
Throssell Ra., *Australia* 88 D3
Thuan Hoa, *Vietnam* 59 H5
Thubun Lakes, *Canada* 101 A6
Thueyts, *France* 27 D8
Thuillies, *Belgium* 17 H4
Thuin, *Belgium* 17 H4
Thuir, *France* 26 F6
Thule, *Greenland* 4 B4
Thun, *Switz.* 22 C5
Thundelarra, *Australia* 89 E2
Thunder B., *U.S.A.* 106 B1
Thunder Bay, *Canada* 98 C2
Thunersee, *Switz.* 22 C5
Thung Song, *Thailand* 59 H2
Thunkar, *Bhutan* 61 F17
Thuong Tra, *Vietnam* 58 D6
Thur →, *Switz.* 23 A8
Thurgau □, *Switz.* 23 A8
Thüringen □, *Germany* 18 E7
Thüringer Wald, *Germany* 18 E7
Thurles, *Ireland* 15 D4
Thurloo Downs, *Australia* 91 D3
Thurn P., *Austria* 19 H8
Thursday I., *Australia* 90 A3
Thurso, *Canada* 98 C4
Thurso, *U.K.* 14 C5
Thurston I., *Antarctica* 5 D16
Thury-Harcourt, *France* 24 D6
Thusis, *Switz.* 23 C8
Thutade L., *Canada* 100 B3
Thyborøn, *Denmark* 11 H2
Thylungra, *Australia* 91 D3
Thyolo, *Malawi* 83 F4
Thysville = Mbanza Ngungu, *Zaïre* 80 F2
Ti-n-Barraouene, O. →, *Africa* 79 B5
Ti-n-Medjerdam, O. →, *Algeria* 75 C5
Ti-n-Tarabine, O. →, *Algeria* 75 D6
Ti-n-Zaouaténe, *Algeria* 75 E5
Tia, *Australia* 91 E5
Tiahuanacu, *Bolivia* 124 D4
Tian Shan, *Asia* 54 B3
Tianchang, *China* 53 A12
Tiandong, *China* 52 F6
Tian'e, *China* 52 E6
Tianguá, *Brazil* 122 B3
Tianhe, *China* 52 E7
Tianjin, *China* 51 E9
Tiankoura, *Burkina Faso* 78 C4
Tianlin, *China* 52 E6
Tianmen, *China* 53 B9
Tianquan, *China* 52 B4
Tianshui, *China* 50 G3
Tiantai, *China* 53 C13
Tianyang, *China* 52 F6

Tianzhen, *China* 50 D8
Tianzhu, *China* 52 D7
Tianzhuangtai, *China* 51 D12
Tiaret, *Algeria* 75 A5
Tiassalé, *Ivory C.* 78 D4
Tibagi, *Brazil* 127 A5
Tibagi →, *Brazil* 127 A5
Tibati, *Cameroon* 79 D7
Tiber = Tévere →, *Italy* 33 G9
Tiber Reservoir, *U.S.A.* 110 B8
Tiberias = Teverya, *Israel* 69 C4
Tiberias, L. = Yam Kinneret, *Israel* 69 C4
Tibesti, *Chad* 73 D8
Tibet = Xizang □, *China* 54 C3
Tibet, Plateau of, *Asia* 46 F12
Tibiao, *Phil.* 55 F5
Tibiri, *Niger* 79 C6
Ţibleş, *Romania* 38 B7
Tibnī, *Syria* 67 E8
Tibooburra, *Australia* 91 D3
Tibro, *Sweden* 11 F8
Tibugá, G. de, *Colombia* 120 B2
Tiburón, *Mexico* 114 B2
Ticao I., *Phil.* 55 E5
Tîchît, *Mauritania* 78 B3
Tichla, *Mauritania* 74 D2
Ticho, *Ethiopia* 77 F4
Ticino □, *Switz.* 23 D7
Ticino →, *Italy* 32 C6
Ticonderoga, *U.S.A.* 107 C11
Ticul, *Mexico* 115 C7
Tidaholm, *Sweden* 11 F7
Tiddim, *Burma* 61 H18
Tideridjaouine, Adrar, *Algeria* 75 D5
Tidikelt, *Algeria* 75 C5
Tidjikja, *Mauritania* 78 B2
Tidore, *Indonesia* 57 D7
Tiébissou, *Ivory C.* 78 D3
Tiefencastel, *Switz.* 23 C9
Tiel, *Neths.* 16 E6
Tiel, *Senegal* 78 C1
Tieling, *China* 51 C12
Tielt, *Belgium* 17 F2
Tien Shan = Tian Shan, *Asia* 54 B3
Tien-tsin = Tianjin, *China* 51 E9
Tien Yen, *Vietnam* 58 B6
T'ienching = Tianjin, *China* 51 E9
Tienen, *Belgium* 17 G5
Tiénigbé, *Ivory C.* 78 D3
Tientsin = Tianjin, *China* 51 E9
Tierra Amarilla, *Chile* 126 B1
Tierra Amarilla, *U.S.A.* 111 H10
Tierra Colorada, *Mexico* 115 D5
Tierra de Barros, *Spain* 31 G4
Tierra de Campos, *Spain* 30 C6
Tierra del Fuego □, *Argentina* 128 D3
Tierra del Fuego, I. Gr. de, *Argentina* 128 D3
Tierralta, *Colombia* 120 B2
Tiétar →, *Spain* 30 F4
Tieté →, *Brazil* 127 A5
Tieyon, *Australia* 91 D1
Tifarati, *W. Sahara* 74 C2
Tiffin, *U.S.A.* 104 E4
Tiflèt, *Morocco* 74 B3
Tiflis = Tbilisi, *Georgia* 43 K7
Tifton, *U.S.A.* 105 K4
Tifu, *Indonesia* 57 E7
Tighina, *Moldova* 41 J5
Tigil, *Russia* 45 D16
Tignish, *Canada* 99 C7
Tigray □, *Ethiopia* 77 E4
Tigre →, *Peru* 120 D3
Tigre →, *Venezuela* 121 B5
Tigris = Dijlah, Nahr →, *Asia* 64 D5
Tiguentourine, *Algeria* 75 C6
Tigyaing, *Burma* 61 H20
Tigzerte, O. →, *Morocco* 74 C3
Tîh, Gebel el, *Egypt* 76 J8
Tihodaine, Dunes de, *Algeria* 75 C6
Tijesno, *Croatia* 33 E12
Tījī, *Libya* 75 B7
Tijuana, *Mexico* 113 N9
Tikal, *Guatemala* 116 C2
Tikamgarh, *India* 63 G8
Tikhoretsk, *Russia* 43 H5
Tikhvin, *Russia* 40 C7
Tikkadouine, Adrar, *Algeria* 75 D5
Tiko, *Cameroon* 79 E6
Tikrīt, *Iraq* 67 E10
Tiksi, *Russia* 45 B13
Tilamuta, *Indonesia* 57 D6
Tilburg, *Neths.* 17 E6
Tilbury, *Canada* 98 D3
Tilbury, *U.K.* 13 F8
Tilcara, *Argentina* 126 A2
Tilden, *Nebr., U.S.A.* 108 D6
Tilden, *Tex., U.S.A.* 109 L5
Tilemses, *Niger* 79 B5
Tilemsi, Vallée du, *Mali* 79 B5
Tilhar, *India* 63 F8
Tilia, O. →, *Algeria* 75 C5
Tilichiki, *Russia* 45 C17
Tililane, *Algeria* 75 C4
Tílissos, *Greece* 37 D7
Till →, *U.K.* 12 B5
Tillabéri, *Niger* 79 C5
Tillamook, *U.S.A.* 110 D2
Tillberga, *Sweden* 10 E10
Tillia, *Niger* 79 B5
Tillsonburg, *Canada* 98 D3
Tillyeria □, *Cyprus* 37 D11
Tílos, *Greece* 39 N10
Tilpa, *Australia* 91 E3
Tilrhemt, *Algeria* 75 B5
Tilsit = Sovetsk, *Russia* 9 J19
Tilt →, *U.K.* 14 E5
Tilton, *U.S.A.* 107 C13
Timagami L., *Canada* 98 C3
Timaru, *N.Z.* 87 L3
Timashevo, *Russia* 42 D10
Timashevsk, *Russia* 43 H4
Timau, *Italy* 33 B10
Timau, *Kenya* 82 B4
Timbákion, *Greece* 37 D6
Timbaúba, *Brazil* 122 C4
Timbedgha, *Mauritania* 78 B3
Timber Lake, *U.S.A.* 108 C4
Timber Mt., *U.S.A.* 112 H10
Timbío, *Colombia* 120 C2
Timbiquí, *Colombia* 120 C2
Timboon, *Australia* 91 F3
Timbuktu = Tombouctou, *Mali* 78 B4
Timellouline, *Algeria* 75 C6
Timétrine Montagnes, *Mali* 79 B4
Timfristós, Óros, *Greece* 39 L4
Timhadit, *Morocco* 74 B3
Timi, *Cyprus* 37 E11
Tìmia, *Niger* 79 B6
Timimoun, *Algeria* 75 C5
Timiş = Tamis →, *Serbia, Yug.* 38 E3
Timişoara, *Romania* 38 D4
Timmins, *Canada* 98 C3
Timok →, *Serbia, Yug.* 21 L12
Timon, *Brazil* 122 C3
Timor, *Indonesia* 57 F7
Timor □, *Indonesia* 57 F7
Timor Sea, *Ind. Oc.* 88 B4
Tin Alkoum, *Algeria* 75 D7
Tin Gornai, *Mali* 79 B4
Tin Mt., *U.S.A.* 112 J9
Tîna, Khalîg el, *Egypt* 76 H8
Tinaca Pt., *Phil.* 55 J6
Tinaco, *Venezuela* 120 B4
Tinafak, O. →, *Algeria* 75 C6
Tinajo, *Canary Is.* 36 E6
Tinaquillo, *Venezuela* 120 B4
Tinca, *Romania* 38 C4
Tinchebray, *France* 24 D6
Tindouf, *Algeria* 74 C3
Tinée →, *France* 27 E11
Tineo, *Spain* 30 B4
Tinerhir, *Morocco* 74 B3
Tinfouchi, *Algeria* 74 C3
Ting Jiang →, *China* 53 E11
Tinggi, Pulau, *Malaysia* 59 L5
Tinglev, *Denmark* 11 K3
Tingo Maria, *Peru* 124 B2
Tinh Bien, *Vietnam* 59 G5
Tinharé, I. de, *Brazil* 123 D4
Tinjoub, *Algeria* 72 C3
Tinkurrin, *Australia* 89 F2
Tinnevelly = Tirunelveli, *India* 60 Q10
Tinnoset, *Norway* 10 E3
Tinnsjø, *Norway* 10 E2
Tinogasta, *Argentina* 126 B2
Tínos, *Greece* 39 M8
Tiñoso, C., *Spain* 29 H3
Tinta, *Peru* 124 C3
Tintigny, *Belgium* 17 J7
Tintina, *Argentina* 126 B3
Tintinara, *Australia* 91 F3
Tinto →, *Spain* 31 H4
Tioga, *U.S.A.* 106 E7
Tioman, Pulau, *Malaysia* 59 L5
Tione di Trento, *Italy* 32 B7
Tionesta, *U.S.A.* 106 E5
Tior, *Sudan* 77 F3
Tioulilin, *Algeria* 75 C4
Tipongpani, *India* 61 F19
Tipperary, *Ireland* 15 D3
Tipperary □, *Ireland* 15 D4
Tipton, *U.K.* 13 E5
Tipton, *Calif., U.S.A.* 111 H4
Tipton, *Ind., U.S.A.* 104 E2
Tipton, *Iowa, U.S.A.* 108 E9
Tipton Mt., *U.S.A.* 113 K12
Tiptonville, *U.S.A.* 109 G10
Tiquié →, *Brazil* 120 C4
Tiracambu, Serra do, *Brazil* 122 B2
Tīrān, *Iran* 65 C6
Tīrān, *Si. Arabia* 76 B3
Tirana, *Albania* 39 H2
Tiranë = Tirana, *Albania* 39 H2
Tirano, *Italy* 32 B7
Tiraspol, *Moldova* 41 J5
Tirat Karmel, *Israel* 69 C3
Tiratimine, *Algeria* 75 C5
Tirdout, *Mali* 79 B4
Tire, *Turkey* 66 C2
Tirebolu, *Turkey* 67 B8
Tiree, *U.K.* 14 E2
Tîrgovişte, *Romania* 38 E8
Tîrgu Frumos, *Romania* 38 B10
Tîrgu-Jiu, *Romania* 38 D6
Tîrgu Mureş, *Romania* 38 C7
Tîrgu Neamţ, *Romania* 38 B9
Tîrgu Ocna, *Romania* 38 C9
Tîrgu Secuiesc, *Romania* 38 D9
Tirich Mir, *Pakistan* 60 A7
Tiriolo, *Italy* 35 D9
Tiririca, Serra da, *Brazil* 123 E2
Tiris, *W. Sahara* 74 D2
Tîrnava Mare →, *Romania* 38 C7
Tîrnava Mică →, *Romania* 38 C7
Tîrnăveni, *Romania* 38 C7
Tírnavos, *Greece* 39 K5
Tirodi, *India* 60 J11
Tiros, *Brazil* 123 E2
Tirschenreuth, *Germany* 19 F8
Tirso →, *Italy* 34 C1
Tirso, L. del, *Italy* 34 B1
Tiruchchirappalli, *India* 60 P11
Tirunelveli, *India* 60 Q10
Tirupati, *India* 60 N11
Tiruppur, *India* 60 P10
Tiruvannamalai, *India* 60 N11
Tisa →, *Serbia, Yug.* 21 J10
Tisdale, *Canada* 101 C8
Tishomingo, *U.S.A.* 109 H6
Tisnaren, *Sweden* 10 F9
Tisovec, *Slovak Rep.* 20 G9
Tissemsilt, *Algeria* 75 A5
Tissint, *Morocco* 74 C3
Tissø, *Denmark* 11 J5
Tisza = Tisa →, *Serbia, Yug.* 21 J10
Tiszafüred, *Hungary* 21 H10
Tiszavasvári, *Hungary* 21 H11
Tit, *Ahaggar, Algeria* 75 D6
Tit, *Tademait, Algeria* 75 C5
Tit-Ary, *Russia* 45 B13
Titaguas, *Spain* 28 F3
Titel, *Serbia, Yug.* 21 K10
Tithwal, *Pakistan* 63 B5
Titicaca, L., *S. Amer.* 124 D4
Titiwa, *Nigeria* 79 C7
Titlis, *Switz.* 23 C6
Titograd = Podgorica, *Montenegro, Yug.* 21 N9
Titov Veles, *Macedonia* 39 H4
Titova Korenica, *Croatia* 33 D12
Titova-Mitrovica, *Serbia, Yug.* 21 N10
Titovo Užice, *Serbia, Yug.* 21 M9
Titule, *Zaïre* 82 B2
Titumate, *Colombia* 120 B2
Titusville, *Fla., U.S.A.* 105 L5
Titusville, *Pa., U.S.A.* 106 E5
Tivaouane, *Senegal* 78 C1
Tiveden, *Sweden* 11 F8
Tiverton, *U.K.* 13 G4
Tívoli, *Italy* 33 G9
Tiyo, *Eritrea* 77 E5
Tizga, *Morocco* 74 B3
Ti'zi N'Isli, *Morocco* 74 B3
Tizi-Ouzou, *Algeria* 75 A5
Tizimín, *Mexico* 115 C7
Tiznados →, *Venezuela* 120 B4
Tiznit, *Morocco* 74 C3
Tjeggelvas, *Sweden* 8 C17
Tjeukemeer, *Neths.* 16 C7
Tjirebon = Cirebon, *Indonesia* 57 G13
Tjøme, *Norway* 10 E4
Tjonger Kanaal, *Neths.* 16 C7
Tjörn, *Sweden* 11 G5
Tkibuli = Tqibuli, *Georgia* 43 J6
Tkvarcheli = Tqvarcheli, *Georgia* 43 J5
Tlacotalpan, *Mexico* 115 D5
Tlahualilo, *Mexico* 114 B4
Tlaquepaque, *Mexico* 114 C4
Tlaxcala, *Mexico* 115 D5
Tlaxcala □, *Mexico* 115 D5
Tlaxiaco, *Mexico* 115 D5
Tlell, *Canada* 100 C2
Tlemcen, *Algeria* 75 B4
Tleta Sidi Bouguedra, *Morocco* 74 B3
Tlyarata, *Russia* 43 J8
Tmassah, *Libya* 73 C8
Tnine d'Anglou, *Morocco* 74 C3
To Bong, *Vietnam* 58 F7
Toad →, *Canada* 100 B4
Toamasina, *Madag.* 85 B8
Toamasina □, *Madag.* 85 B8
Toay, *Argentina* 126 D3
Toba, *Japan* 49 G8
Toba Kakar, *Pakistan* 62 D3
Toba Tek Singh, *Pakistan* 62 D5
Tobago, *W. Indies* 117 D7
Tobarra, *Spain* 29 G3
Tobelo, *Indonesia* 57 D7
Tobermorey, *Australia* 90 C2
Tobermory, *Canada* 98 C3
Tobermory, *U.K.* 14 E2
Tobin, *U.S.A.* 112 F5
Tobin, L., *Australia* 88 D4
Tobin L., *Canada* 101 C8
Toblach = Dobbiaco, *Italy* 33 B9
Toboali, *Indonesia* 56 E3
Tobol, *Kazakstan* 44 D7
Tobol →, *Russia* 44 D7
Toboli, *Indonesia* 57 E6
Tobolsk, *Russia* 44 D7
Tobruk = Tubruq, *Libya* 73 B9
Tobyhanna, *U.S.A.* 107 E9
Tobyl = Tobol →, *Russia* 44 D7
Tocache Nuevo, *Peru* 124 B2
Tocantínia, *Brazil* 122 C2
Tocantinópolis, *Brazil* 122 C2
Tocantins □, *Brazil* 122 D2
Tocantins →, *Brazil* 122 B2
Toccoa, *U.S.A.* 105 H4
Toce →, *Italy* 32 C5
Tochigi, *Japan* 49 F9
Tochigi □, *Japan* 49 F9
Tocina, *Spain* 31 H5
Tocopilla, *Chile* 126 A1
Tocumwal, *Australia* 91 F4
Tocuyo →, *Venezuela* 120 A4
Tocuyo de la Costa, *Venezuela* 120 A4
Todd →, *Australia* 90 C2
Todeli, *Indonesia* 57 E6
Todenyang, *Kenya* 82 B4
Todi, *Italy* 33 F9
Tödi, *Switz.* 23 C7
Todos os Santos, B. de, *Brazil* 123 D4
Todos Santos, *Mexico* 114 C2
Todtnau, *Germany* 19 H3
Toecé, *Burkina Faso* 79 C4
Tofield, *Canada* 100 C6
Tofino, *Canada* 100 D3
Töfsingdalens nationalpark, *Sweden* 10 B6
Toftlund, *Denmark* 11 J3
Tofua, *Tonga* 87 D11
Tōgane, *Japan* 49 G10
Togba, *Mauritania* 78 B2
Toggenburg, *Switz.* 23 B8
Togian, Kepulauan, *Indonesia* 57 E6
Togliatti, *Russia* 42 D9
Togo ■, *W. Afr.* 79 D5
Togtoh, *China* 50 D6
Tohma →, *Turkey* 66 C7
Tōhoku □, *Japan* 48 E10
Toinya, *Sudan* 77 F2
Tojikiston = Tajikistan ■, *Asia* 44 F8
Tojo, *Indonesia* 57 E6
Tōjō, *Japan* 49 G6
Toka, *Guyana* 121 C6
Tokachi-Dake, *Japan* 48 C11
Tokachi-Gawa →, *Japan* 48 C11
Tokaj, *Hungary* 21 G11
Tokala, *Indonesia* 57 E6
Tōkamachi, *Japan* 49 F9
Tokanui, *N.Z.* 87 M2
Tokar, *Sudan* 76 D4
Tokara-Rettō, *Japan* 49 K4
Tokarahi, *N.Z.* 87 L3
Tokashiki-Shima, *Japan* 49 L3
Tokat, *Turkey* 66 B7
Tŏkchŏn, *N. Korea* 51 E14
Tokeland, *U.S.A.* 112 D3
Tokelau Is., *Pac. Oc.* 92 H10
Tokmak, *Kyrgyzstan* 44 E8
Tokmak, *Ukraine* 41 J8
Toko Ra., *Australia* 90 C2
Tokoro-Gawa →, *Japan* 48 B12
Tokuno-Shima, *Japan* 49 L4
Tokushima, *Japan* 49 G7
Tokushima □, *Japan* 49 H7
Tokuyama, *Japan* 49 G5
Tōkyō, *Japan* 49 G9
Tolaga Bay, *N.Z.* 87 H7
Tolbukhin = Dobrich, *Bulgaria* 38 F10
Toledo, *Spain* 30 F6
Toledo, *Ohio, U.S.A.* 104 E4
Toledo, *Oreg., U.S.A.* 110 D2
Toledo, *Wash., U.S.A.* 110 C2
Toledo, Montes de, *Spain* 31 F6
Tolentino, *Italy* 33 E10
Tolga, *Algeria* 75 B6
Tolga, *Norway* 10 B5
Toliara, *Madag.* 85 C7
Toliara □, *Madag.* 85 C8
Tolima, *Colombia* 120 C2
Tolima □, *Colombia* 120 C2
Tolitoli, *Indonesia* 57 D6
Tolkamer, *Neths.* 16 E8
Tollhouse, *U.S.A.* 112 H7
Tolmachevo, *Russia* 40 C5
Tolmezzo, *Italy* 33 B10
Tolmin, *Slovenia* 33 B10
Tolo, *Zaïre* 80 E3
Tolo, Teluk, *Indonesia* 57 E6
Tolochin = Talachyn, *Belarus* 40 E5
Tolosa, *Spain* 28 B2
Tolox, *Spain* 31 J6
Toltén, *Chile* 128 A2
Toluca, *Mexico* 115 D5
Tom Burke, *S. Africa* 85 C4
Tom Price, *Australia* 88 D2
Tomah, *U.S.A.* 108 D9
Tomahawk, *U.S.A.* 108 C10
Tomakomai, *Japan* 48 C10
Tomales, *U.S.A.* 112 G4
Tomales B., *U.S.A.* 112 G3
Tomar, *Portugal* 31 F2
Tomarza, *Turkey* 66 C6
Tomás Barrón, *Bolivia* 124 D4
Tomaszów Mazowiecki, *Poland* 20 D9
Tomatlán, *Mexico* 114 D3
Tombador, Serra do, *Brazil* 125 C6
Tombé, *Sudan* 77 F3
Tombigbee →, *U.S.A.* 105 K2
Tombouctou, *Mali* 78 B4
Tombstone, *U.S.A.* 111 L8
Tombua, *Angola* 84 B1
Tomé, *Chile* 126 D1
Tomé-Açu, *Brazil* 122 B2
Tomelilla, *Sweden* 11 J7
Tomelloso, *Spain* 29 F1
Tomingley, *Australia* 91 E4
Tomini, *Indonesia* 57 D6
Tomini, Teluk, *Indonesia* 57 E6
Tominian, *Mali* 78 C4
Tomiño, *Spain* 30 D2
Tomkinson Ras., *Australia* 89 E4
Tommot, *Russia* 45 D13
Tomnavoulin, *U.K.* 14 D5
Tomnop Ta Suos, *Cambodia* 59 G5
Tomo, *Colombia* 120 C4
Tomo →, *Colombia* 120 B4
Tomorit, *Albania* 39 J3
Toms Place, *U.S.A.* 112 H8
Toms River, *U.S.A.* 107 G10
Tomsk, *Russia* 44 D9
Tonalá, *Mexico* 115 D6
Tonale, Passo del, *Italy* 32 B7
Tonalea, *U.S.A.* 111 H8
Tonantins, *Brazil* 120 D4
Tonasket, *U.S.A.* 110 B4
Tonate, *Fr. Guiana* 121 C7
Tonawanda, *U.S.A.* 106 D6
Tonbridge, *U.K.* 13 F8
Tondano, *Indonesia* 57 D6
Tondela, *Portugal* 30 E2
Tønder, *Denmark* 11 K2
Tondi Kiwindi, *Niger* 79 C5
Tondibi, *Mali* 79 B4
Tonekābon, *Iran* 65 B6
Tong Xian, *China* 50 E9
Tonga ■, *Pac. Oc.* 87 D11
Tonga Trench, *Pac. Oc.* 92 J10
Tongaat, *S. Africa* 85 D5
Tong'an, *China* 53 E12
Tongareva, *Cook Is* 93 H12
Tongatapu, *Tonga* 87 E11
Tongbai, *China* 53 A9
Tongcheng, *Anhui, China* 53 B11
Tongcheng, *Hubei, China* 53 C9
Tongchŏn-ni, *N. Korea* 51 E14
Tongchuan, *China* 50 G5
Tongdao, *China* 52 D7
Tongeren, *Belgium* 17 G6
Tonggu, *China* 53 C10
Tongguan, *China* 50 G6
Tonghai, *China* 52 E4
Tonghua, *China* 51 D13
Tongjiang, *Heilongjiang, China* 54 B8
Tongjiang, *Sichuan, China* 52 B6
Tongjosŏn Man, *N. Korea* 51 E14
Tongking, G. of = Tonkin, G. of, *Asia* 58 B7
Tongliang, *China* 52 C6
Tongliao, *China* 51 C12
Tongling, *China* 53 B11
Tonglu, *China* 53 C12
Tongnae, *S. Korea* 51 G15
Tongnan, *China* 52 B5
Tongobory, *Madag.* 85 C7
Tongoy, *Chile* 126 C1
Tongren, *China* 52 D7
Tongres = Tongeren, *Belgium* 17 G6
Tongsa Dzong, *Bhutan* 61 F17
Tongue, *U.K.* 14 C4
Tongue →, *U.S.A.* 108 B2
Tongwei, *China* 50 G3
Tongxin, *China* 50 F3
Tongyang, *N. Korea* 51 E14
Tongyu, *China* 51 B12
Tongzi, *China* 52 C6
Tonj, *Sudan* 77 F2
Tonk, *India* 62 F6
Tonkawa, *U.S.A.* 109 G6
Tonkin = Bac Phan, *Vietnam* 58 B5
Tonkin, G. of, *Asia* 58 B7
Tonlé Sap, *Cambodia* 58 F4
Tonnay-Charente, *France* 26 C3
Tonneins, *France* 26 D4
Tonnerre, *France* 25 E10
Tönning, *Germany* 18 A4
Tono, *Japan* 48 E10
Tonopah, *U.S.A.* 111 G5
Tonosí, *Panama* 116 E3
Tønsberg, *Norway* 10 E4
Tonya, *Turkey* 67 B8
Tooele, *U.S.A.* 110 F7
Toompine, *Australia* 91 D3
Toonpan, *Australia* 90 B4
Toora, *Australia* 91 F4
Toora-Khem, *Russia* 45 D10
Toowoomba, *Australia* 91 D5
Topalu, *Romania* 38 E11
Topaz, *U.S.A.* 112 G7
Topeka, *U.S.A.* 108 F7
Topki, *Russia* 44 D9
Topl'a →, *Slovak Rep.* 20 G11
Topley, *Canada* 100 C3
Toplica →, *Serbia, Yug.* 21 M11
Topliţa, *Romania* 38 C8
Topocalma, Pta., *Chile* 126 C1
Topock, *U.S.A.* 113 L12
Topola, *Serbia, Yug.* 21 L10
Topol'čany, *Slovak Rep.* 20 G8
Topolnitsa →, *Bulgaria* 38 G7
Topolobampo, *Mexico* 114 B3
Topolovgrad, *Bulgaria* 38 G9
Toppenish, *U.S.A.* 110 C3
Topusko, *Croatia* 33 C12
Toquepala, *Peru* 124 D3
Torá, *Spain* 28 D6
Tora Kit, *Sudan* 77 E3
Toraka Vestale, *Madag.* 85 B7
Torata, *Peru* 124 D3
Torbalı, *Turkey* 66 C2
Torbay, *Canada* 99 C9
Torbay, *U.K.* 13 G4
Tørdal, *Norway* 10 E2
Tordesillas, *Spain* 30 D6
Tordoya, *Spain* 30 B2
Töreboda, *Sweden* 11 F8

Torfaen □, U.K. 13 F4
Torgau, Germany 18 D8
Torgelow, Germany 18 B9
Torhout, Belgium 17 F2
Tori, Ethiopia 77 F3
Tori-Shima, Japan 49 J10
Torigni-sur-Vire, France 24 C6
Torija, Spain 28 E1
Torin, Mexico 114 B2
Toriñana, C., Spain 30 B1
Torino, Italy 32 C4
Torit, Sudan 77 G3
Torkamān, Iran 67 D12
Torkovichi, Russia 40 C6
Tormes →, Spain 30 D4
Tornado Mt., Canada 100 D6
Torne älv →, Sweden 8 D21
Torneå = Tornio, Finland 8 D21
Torneträsk, Sweden 8 B18
Tornio, Finland 8 D21
Tornionjoki →, Finland 8 D21
Tornquist, Argentina 126 D3
Toro, Baleares, Spain 36 B11
Toro, Zamora, Spain 30 D5
Torö, Sweden 11 F11
Toro, Cerro del, Chile 126 B2
Toro Pk., U.S.A. 113 M10
Törökszentmiklós, Hungary 21 H10
Toroníios Kólpos, Greece 39 J6
Toronto, Australia 91 E5
Toronto, Canada 98 D4
Toronto, U.S.A. 106 F4
Toropets, Russia 40 D6
Tororo, Uganda 82 B3
Toros Dağları, Turkey 66 D5
Torotoro, Bolivia 125 D4
Torpshammar, Sweden 10 B10
Torquay, Canada 101 D8
Torquay, U.K. 13 G4
Torquemada, Spain 30 C6
Torralba de Calatrava, Spain 31 F7
Torrance, U.S.A. 113 M8
Torrão, Portugal 31 G2
Torre Annunziata, Italy 35 B7
Tôrre de Moncorvo, Portugal 30 D3
Torre del Greco, Italy 35 B7
Torre del Mar, Spain 31 J6
Torre-Pacheco, Spain 29 H4
Torre Péllice, Italy 32 D4
Torreblanca, Spain 28 E5
Torrecampo, Spain 31 G6
Torrecilla en Cameros, Spain 28 C2
Torredembarra, Spain 28 D6
Torredonjimeno, Spain 31 H7
Torrejoncillo, Spain 30 F4
Torrelaguna, Spain 28 E1
Torrelavega, Spain 30 B6
Torremaggiore, Italy 35 A8
Torremolinos, Spain 31 J6
Torrens, L., Australia 91 E2
Torrens Cr. →, Australia 90 C4
Torrens Creek, Australia 90 C4
Torrente, Spain 29 F4
Torrenueva, Spain 29 G1
Torreón, Mexico 114 B4
Torreperogil, Spain 29 G1
Torres, Mexico 114 B2
Torres Novas, Portugal 31 F2
Torres Strait, Australia 92 H6
Torres Vedras, Portugal 31 F1
Torrevieja, Spain 29 H4
Torrey, U.S.A. 111 G8
Torridge →, U.K. 13 G3
Torridon, L., U.K. 14 D3
Torrijos, Spain 30 F6
Torrington, Conn., U.S.A. 107 E11
Torrington, Wyo., U.S.A. 108 D2
Torroella de Montgrí, Spain 28 C8
Torrox, Spain 31 J7
Tórshavn, Færoe Is. 8 E9
Torsö, Sweden 11 F7
Tortola, Virgin Is. 117 C7
Tórtoles de Esgueva, Spain 30 D6
Tortona, Italy 32 D5
Tortoreto, Italy 33 F10
Tortorici, Italy 35 D7
Tortosa, Spain 28 E5
Tortosa, C. de, Spain 28 E5
Tortosendo, Portugal 30 E3
Tortue, I. de la, Haiti 117 B5
Tortum, Turkey 67 B9
Ţorūd, Iran 65 C7
Torul, Turkey 67 B8
Toruń, Poland 20 B8
Torup, Sweden 11 H7
Tory I., Ireland 15 A3
Torysa →, Slovak Rep. 20 G11
Torzhok, Russia 42 B2
Tosa, Japan 49 H6
Tosa-Shimizu, Japan 49 H6
Tosa-Wan, Japan 49 H6
Toscana □, Italy 32 E8
Toscano, Arcipelago, Italy 32 F7
Toshkent, Uzbekistan 44 E7
Tosno, Russia 40 C6
Tossa, Spain 28 D7
Tostado, Argentina 126 B3
Tostedt, Germany 18 B5
Tostón, Pta. de, Canary Is. 36 F5
Tosu, Japan 49 H5
Tosya, Turkey 66 B6
Totana, Spain 29 H3
Toten, Norway 10 D4
Toteng, Botswana 84 C3
Tôtes, France 24 C8
Tótkomlós, Hungary 21 J10
Totma, Russia 44 C5
Totnes, U.K. 13 G4
Totness, Surinam 121 B6
Totonicapán, Guatemala 116 D1
Totora, Bolivia 125 D4
Totten Glacier, Antarctica 5 C8
Tottenham, Australia 91 E4
Tottenham, Canada 106 B5
Tottori, Japan 49 G7
Tottori □, Japan 49 G7
Touat, Algeria 75 C5
Touba, Ivory C. 78 D3
Toubkal, Djebel, Morocco 74 B3
Toucy, France 25 E10
Tougan, Burkina Faso 78 C4
Touggourt, Algeria 75 B6
Tougué, Guinea 78 C2
Toukmatine, Algeria 75 D6
Toul, France 25 D12
Toulepleu, Ivory C. 78 D3
Toulon, France 27 E9
Toulouse, France 26 E5
Toummo, Niger 73 D7
Toumodi, Ivory C. 78 D3
Tounan, Taiwan 53 F13
Tounassine, Hamada, Algeria 74 C3
Toungoo, Burma 61 K20
Touques →, France 24 C7
Touraine, France 24 E7
Tourane = Da Nang, Vietnam 58 D7
Tourcoing, France 25 B10
Tourine, Mauritania 74 D2
Tournai, Belgium 17 G2
Tournan-en-Brie, France 25 D9
Tournay, France 26 E4
Tournon, France 27 C8
Tournon-St.-Martin, France 24 F7
Tournus, France 27 B8
Touros, Brazil 122 C4
Tours, France 24 E7
Touwsrivier, S. Africa 84 E3
Tovar, Venezuela 120 B3
Tovarkovskiy, Russia 42 D4
Tovdal, Norway 11 F2
Tovdalselva →, Norway 11 F2
Tovuz, Azerbaijan 43 K7
Towada, Japan 48 D10
Towada-Ko, Japan 48 D10
Towamba, Australia 91 F4
Towanda, U.S.A. 107 E8
Towang, India 61 F17
Tower, U.S.A. 108 B8
Towerhill Cr. →, Australia 90 C3
Towner, U.S.A. 108 A4
Townsend, U.S.A. 110 C8
Townshend I., Australia 90 C5
Townsville, Australia 90 B4
Towson, U.S.A. 104 F7
Toya-Ko, Japan 48 C10
Toyah, U.S.A. 109 K3
Toyahvale, U.S.A. 109 K3
Toyama, Japan 49 F8
Toyama □, Japan 49 F8
Toyama-Wan, Japan 49 F8
Toyohashi, Japan 49 G8
Toyokawa, Japan 49 G8
Toyonaka, Japan 49 G7
Toyooka, Japan 49 G7
Toyota, Japan 49 G8
Tozeur, Tunisia 75 B6
Tqibuli, Georgia 43 J6
Tqvarcheli, Georgia 43 J5
Trá Li = Tralee, Ireland 15 D2
Tra On, Vietnam 59 H5
Trabancos →, Spain 30 D5
Traben-Trarbach, Germany 19 F3
Trabzon, Turkey 67 B8
Tracadie, Canada 99 C7
Tracy, Calif., U.S.A. 111 H3
Tracy, Minn., U.S.A. 108 C7
Tradate, Italy 32 C5
Trafalgar, C., Spain 31 J4
Traiguén, Chile 128 A2
Trail, Canada 100 D5
Trainor L., Canada 100 A4
Traíra →, Brazil 120 D4
Trákhonas, Cyprus 37 D12
Tralee, Ireland 15 D2
Tralee B., Ireland 15 D2
Tramelan, Switz. 22 B4
Tramore, Ireland 15 D4
Tran Ninh, Cao Nguyen, Laos 58 C4
Tranås, Sweden 9 G16
Trancas, Argentina 126 B2
Trancoso, Portugal 30 E3
Tranebjerg, Denmark 11 J4
Tranemo, Sweden 11 G7
Trang, Thailand 59 J2
Trangahy, Madag. 85 B7
Trangan, Indonesia 57 F8
Trangie, Australia 91 E4
Trångsviken, Sweden 10 A8
Trani, Italy 35 A9
Tranoroa, Madag. 85 C8
Tranqueras, Uruguay 127 C4
Trans Nzoia □, Kenya 82 B3
Transantarctic Mts., Antarctica 5 E12
Transcona, Canada 101 D9
Transilvania, Romania 38 D8
Transilvanian Alps = Carpaţii Meridionali, Romania 38 D8
Transylvania = Transilvania, Romania 38 D8
Trápani, Italy 34 D5
Trapper Pk., U.S.A. 110 D6
Traralgon, Australia 91 F4
Trarza, Mauritania 78 B2
Trasacco, Italy 33 G10
Trăscău, Munţii, Romania 38 C6
Trasimeno, L., Italy 33 E9
Trat, Thailand 59 F4
Traun, Austria 21 G4
Traunstein, Germany 19 H8
Trâvad, Sweden 11 F7
Traveller's L., Australia 91 E3
Travemünde, Germany 18 B6
Travers, Mt., N.Z. 87 K4
Traverse City, U.S.A. 104 C3
Travnik, Bos.-H. 21 L7
Trayning, Australia 89 F2
Trazo, Spain 30 B2
Trbovlje, Slovenia 33 B12
Trébbia →, Italy 32 C6
Trebel →, Germany 18 B9
Trebinje, Bos.-H. 21 N8
Trebisacce, Italy 35 C9
Trebišnica →, Bos.-H. 21 N8
Trebišov, Slovak Rep. 20 G11
Trebižat →, Bos.-H. 21 M7
Trebnje, Slovenia 33 C12
Třeboň, Czech. 20 G4
Trebujena, Spain 31 J4
Trecate, Italy 32 C5
Trece Martires, Phil. 55 D4
Tredegar, U.K. 13 F4
Tregaron, U.K. 13 E4
Trégastel-Plage, France 24 D3
Tregnago, Italy 33 C8
Tregrosse Is., Australia 90 B5
Tréguier, France 24 D3
Trégunc, France 24 E3
Treherne, Canada 101 D9
Tréia, Italy 33 E10
Treignac, France 26 C5
Treinta y Tres, Uruguay 127 C5
Treis, Germany 19 E3
Trelde Næs, Denmark 11 J3
Trelew, Argentina 128 B3
Trélissac, France 26 C4
Trelleborg, Sweden 11 J7
Trélon, France 25 B11
Tremiti, Italy 33 F12
Tremonton, U.S.A. 110 F7
Tremp, Spain 28 C5
Trenche →, Canada 98 C5
Trenčín, Slovak Rep. 20 G8
Trenggalek, Indonesia 57 H14
Trenque Lauquen, Argentina 126 D3
Trent →, U.K. 12 D7
Trentino-Alto Adige □, Italy 32 B8
Trento, Italy 32 B8
Trenton, Canada 98 D4
Trenton, Mo., U.S.A. 108 E8
Trenton, N.J., U.S.A. 107 F10
Trenton, Nebr., U.S.A. 108 E4
Trenton, Tenn., U.S.A. 109 H10
Trepassey, Canada 99 C9
Trepuzzi, Italy 35 B11
Tres Arroyos, Argentina 126 D3
Três Corações, Brazil 123 F2
Três Lagoas, Brazil 123 F1
Tres Lagos →, Argentina 128 C2
Tres Marías, Mexico 114 C3
Três Marias, Reprêsa, Brazil 123 E2
Tres Montes, C., Chile 128 C1
Tres Pinos, U.S.A. 112 J5
Três Pontas, Brazil 123 F2
Tres Puentes, Chile 126 B1
Tres Puntas, C., Argentina 128 C3
Três Rios, Brazil 123 F3
Tres Valles, Mexico 115 D5
Treska →, Macedonia 39 H4
Trespaderne, Spain 28 C1
Trets, France 27 E9
Treuchtlingen, Germany 19 G6
Treuenbrietzen, Germany 18 C8
Trevíglio, Italy 32 C6
Trevinca, Peña, Spain 30 C4
Treviso, Italy 33 C9
Trévoux, France 27 C8
Treysa, Germany 18 E5
Trgovište, Serbia, Yug. 21 N12
Triabunna, Australia 90 G4
Triánda, Greece 37 C10
Triang, Malaysia 59 L4
Triaucourt-en-Argonne, France 25 D12
Tribsees, Germany 18 A8
Tribulation, C., Australia 90 B4
Tribune, U.S.A. 108 F4
Tricárico, Italy 35 B9
Tricase, Italy 35 C11
Trichinopoly = Tiruchchirappalli, India 60 P11
Trichur, India 60 P10
Trida, Australia 91 E4
Trier, Germany 19 F2
Trieste, Italy 33 C10
Trieste, G. di, Italy 33 C10
Trieux →, France 24 D3
Triggiano, Italy 35 A9
Triglav, Slovenia 33 B10
Trigno →, Italy 33 F11
Trigueros, Spain 31 H4
Trikhonis, Límni, Greece 39 L4
Tríkkala, Greece 39 K4
Trikomo, Cyprus 37 D12
Trikora, Puncak, Indonesia 57 E9
Trilj, Croatia 33 E13
Trillo, Spain 28 E2
Trim, Ireland 15 C5
Trincomalee, Sri Lanka 60 Q12
Trindade, Brazil 123 E2
Trindade, I., Atl. Oc. 2 F8
Trinidad, Bolivia 125 C5
Trinidad, Colombia 120 B3
Trinidad, Cuba 116 B3
Trinidad, Uruguay 126 C4
Trinidad, U.S.A. 109 G2
Trinidad, W. Indies 117 D7
Trinidad →, Mexico 115 D5
Trinidad, G., Chile 128 C1
Trinidad, I., Argentina 128 A4
Trinidad & Tobago ■, W. Indies 117 D7
Trinitápoli, Italy 35 A9
Trinity, Canada 99 C9
Trinity, U.S.A. 109 K7
Trinity →, Calif., U.S.A. 110 F2
Trinity →, Tex., U.S.A. 109 L7
Trinity B., Canada 99 C9
Trinity Range, U.S.A. 110 F4
Trinkitat, Sudan 76 D4
Trino, Italy 32 C5
Trion, U.S.A. 105 H3
Trionto, C., Italy 35 C9
Triora, Italy 32 E4
Tripoli = Tarābulus, Lebanon 69 A4
Tripoli = Tarābulus, Libya 75 B7
Tripolitania, N. Afr. 70 C5
Tripp, U.S.A. 108 D6
Tripura □, India 61 H17
Tripylos, Cyprus 37 E11
Trischen, Germany 18 A4
Tristan da Cunha, Atl. Oc. 71 K2
Trivandrum, India 60 Q10
Trivento, Italy 35 A7
Trnava, Slovak Rep. 21 G7
Trochu, Canada 100 C6
Trodely I., Canada 98 B4
Trogir, Croatia 33 E13
Troglav, Croatia 33 E13
Trøgstad, Norway 10 E5
Tróia, Italy 35 A8
Troilus, L., Canada 98 B5
Troina, Italy 35 E7
Trois Fourches, Cap des, Morocco 75 A4
Trois-Pistoles, Canada 99 C6
Trois-Rivières, Canada 98 C5
Troisvierges, Belgium 17 H8
Troitsk, Russia 44 D7
Troitsko Pechorsk, Russia 44 C6
Trölladyngja, Iceland 8 D5
Trollhättan, Sweden 11 F6
Trollheimen, Norway 10 B3
Trombetas →, Brazil 121 D6
Tromsø, Norway 8 B18
Trona, U.S.A. 113 K9
Tronador, Argentina 128 B2
Trøndelag, Norway 8 D14
Trondheim, Norway 10 A4
Trondheimsfjorden, Norway 8 E14
Trönninge, Sweden 11 H6
Trönö, Sweden 10 C10
Tronto →, Italy 33 F10
Troodos, Cyprus 66 E5
Troon, U.K. 14 F4
Tropea, Italy 35 D8
Tropic, U.S.A. 111 H7
Tropoja, Albania 38 G3
Trossachs, The, U.K. 14 E4
Trostan, U.K. 15 A5
Trostberg, Germany 19 G8
Trostyanets, Ukraine 41 G8
Trotternish, U.K. 14 D2
Troup, U.S.A. 109 J7
Trout →, Canada 100 A5
Trout L., N.W.T., Canada 100 A4
Trout L., Ont., Canada 101 C10
Trout Lake, Mich., U.S.A. 98 C2
Trout Lake, Wash., U.S.A. 112 E5
Trout River, Canada 99 C8
Trouville-sur-Mer, France 24 C7
Trowbridge, U.K. 13 F5
Troy, Turkey 66 C2
Troy, Ala., U.S.A. 105 K3
Troy, Idaho, U.S.A. 110 C5
Troy, Kans., U.S.A. 108 F7
Troy, Mo., U.S.A. 108 F9
Troy, Mont., U.S.A. 110 B6
Troy, N.Y., U.S.A. 107 D11
Troy, Ohio, U.S.A. 104 E3
Troyan, Bulgaria 38 G7
Troyes, France 25 D11
Trpanj, Croatia 21 M7
Trstena, Slovak Rep. 20 F9
Trstenik, Serbia, Yug. 21 M10
Trubchevsk, Russia 41 F7
Trucial States = United Arab Emirates ■, Asia 65 F7
Truckee, U.S.A. 112 F6
Trudfront, Russia 43 H8
Trudovoye, Russia 48 C6
Trujillo, Colombia 120 C2
Trujillo, Honduras 116 C2
Trujillo, Peru 124 B2
Trujillo, Spain 31 F5
Trujillo, U.S.A. 109 H2
Trujillo, Venezuela 120 B3
Trujillo □, Venezuela 120 B3
Truk, Pac. Oc. 92 G7
Trumann, U.S.A. 109 H9
Trumbull, Mt., U.S.A. 111 H7
Trun, France 24 D7
Trun, Switz. 23 C7
Trundle, Australia 91 E4
Trung-Phan, Vietnam 58 E7
Truro, Canada 99 C7
Truro, U.K. 13 G2
Truskavets, Ukraine 41 H2
Truslove, Australia 89 F3
Trustrup, Denmark 11 H4
Truth or Consequences, U.S.A. 111 K10
Trutnov, Czech. 20 E5
Truyère →, France 26 D6
Tryavna, Bulgaria 38 G8
Tryon, U.S.A. 105 H4
Tryonville, U.S.A. 106 E5
Trzcianka, Poland 20 B6
Trzebiatów, Poland 20 A5
Trzebiez, Poland 20 B4
Trzebinia-Siersza, Poland 20 E9
Trzebnica, Poland 20 D7
Tržič, Slovenia 33 B11
Tsagan Aman, Russia 43 G8
Tsaratanana, Madag. 85 B8
Tsaratanana, Mt. de, Madag. 85 A8
Tsarevo = Michurin, Bulgaria 38 G10
Tsau, Botswana 84 C3
Tsebrykove, Ukraine 41 J6
Tselinograd = Aqmola, Kazakstan 44 D8
Tsetserleg, Mongolia 54 B5
Tshabong, Botswana 84 D3
Tshane, Botswana 84 C3
Tshela, Zaïre 80 E2
Tshesebe, Botswana 85 C4
Tshibeke, Zaïre 82 C2
Tshibinda, Zaïre 82 C2
Tshikapa, Zaïre 80 F4
Tshilenge, Zaïre 82 D1
Tshinsenda, Zaïre 83 E2
Tshofa, Zaïre 82 D2
Tshwane, Botswana 84 C3
Tsigara, Botswana 84 C4
Tsihombe, Madag. 85 D8
Tsimlyansk, Russia 43 G6
Tsimlyansk Res. = Tsimlyanskoye Vdkhr., Russia 43 F6
Tsimlyanskoye Vdkhr., Russia 43 F6
Tsinan = Jinan, China 50 F9
Tsineng, S. Africa 84 D3
Tsinghai = Qinghai □, China 54 C4
Tsingtao = Qingdao, China 51 F11
Tsinjomitondraka, Madag. 85 B8
Tsiroanomandidy, Madag. 85 B8
Tsiteli-Tsqaro, Georgia 43 K8
Tsivilsk, Russia 42 C8
Tsivory, Madag. 85 C8
Tskhinvali, Georgia 43 J7
Tsna →, Russia 42 C6
Tsnori, Georgia 43 K7
Tso Moriri, L., India 63 C8
Tsodilo Hill, Botswana 84 B3
Tsogttsetsiy, Mongolia 50 C3
Tsolo, S. Africa 85 E4
Tsomo, S. Africa 85 E4
Tsu, Japan 49 G8
Tsu L., Canada 100 A6
Tsuchiura, Japan 49 F10
Tsugaru-Kaikyō, Japan 48 D10
Tsumeb, Namibia 84 B2
Tsumis, Namibia 84 C2
Tsuruga, Japan 49 G8
Tsurugi-San, Japan 49 H7
Tsuruoka, Japan 48 E9
Tsushima, Gifu, Japan 49 G8
Tsushima, Nagasaki, Japan 49 G4
Tsvetkovo, Ukraine 41 H6
Tsyelyakhany, Belarus 41 F3
Tua →, Portugal 30 D3
Tual, Indonesia 57 F8
Tuam, Ireland 15 C3
Tuamotu Arch. = Tuamotu Is., Pac. Oc. 93 J13
Tuamotu Is., Pac. Oc. 93 J13
Tuamotu Ridge, Pac. Oc. 93 K14
Tuanfeng, China 53 B10
Tuanxi, China 52 D6
Tuao, Phil. 55 C4
Tuapse, Russia 43 H4
Tuatapere, N.Z. 87 M1
Tuba City, U.S.A. 111 H8
Tuban, Indonesia 57 G15
Tubarão, Brazil 127 B6
Tūbās, West Bank 69 C4
Tubau, Malaysia 56 D4
Tubbergen, Neths. 16 D9
Tübingen, Germany 19 G5
Tubize, Belgium 17 G4
Tubruq, Libya 73 B9
Tubuai Is., Pac. Oc. 93 K12
Tuc Trung, Vietnam 59 G6
Tucacas, Venezuela 120 A4
Tucano, Brazil 122 D4
T'uch'ang, Taiwan 53 E13
Tuchodi →, Canada 100 B4

Tuchola, *Poland* 20 B7
Tucson, *U.S.A.* 111 K8
Tucumán □, *Argentina* 126 B2
Tucumcari, *U.S.A.* 109 H3
Tucunaré, *Brazil* 125 B6
Tucupido, *Venezuela* 120 B4
Tucupita, *Venezuela* 121 B5
Tucuruí, *Brazil* 122 B2
Tucuruí, Représa de, *Brazil* 122 B2
Tudela, *Spain* 28 C3
Tudela de Duero, *Spain* 30 D6
Tudmur, *Syria* 67 E8
Tudor, L., *Canada* 99 A6
Tudora, *Romania* 38 B9
Tuella →, *Portugal* 30 D3
Tuen, *Australia* 91 D4
Tueré →, *Brazil* 122 B1
Tugela →, *S. Africa* 85 D5
Tuguegarao, *Phil.* 55 C4
Tugur, *Russia* 45 D14
Tuineje, *Canary Is.* 36 F5
Tukangbesi, Kepulauan, *Indonesia* 57 F6
Tukarak I., *Canada* 98 A4
Tukayyid, *Iraq* 64 D5
Tûkh, *Egypt* 76 H7
Tukobo, *Ghana* 78 D4
Tūkrah, *Libya* 73 B9
Tuktoyaktuk, *Canada* 96 B6
Tukums, *Latvia* 9 H20
Tukuyu, *Tanzania* 83 D3
Tula, *Hidalgo, Mexico* 115 C5
Tula, *Tamaulipas, Mexico* 115 C5
Tula, *Nigeria* 79 D7
Tula, *Russia* 42 C3
Tulancingo, *Mexico* 115 C5
Tulare, *U.S.A.* 111 H4
Tulare Lake Bed, *U.S.A.* 111 J4
Tularosa, *U.S.A.* 111 K10
Tulbagh, *S. Africa* 84 E2
Tulcán, *Ecuador* 120 C2
Tulcea, *Romania* 38 D11
Tulchyn, *Ukraine* 41 H5
Tüleh, *Iran* 65 C7
Tulemalu L., *Canada* 101 A9
Tuli, *Indonesia* 57 E6
Tuli, *Zimbabwe* 83 G2
Tulia, *U.S.A.* 109 H4
Tulita, *Canada* 96 B7
Ţūlkarm, *West Bank* 69 C4
Tullahoma, *U.S.A.* 105 H2
Tullamore, *Australia* 91 E4
Tullamore, *Ireland* 15 C4
Tulle, *France* 26 C5
Tullibigeal, *Australia* 91 E4
Tullins, *France* 27 C9
Tulln, *Austria* 21 G6
Tullow, *Ireland* 15 D4
Tullus, *Sudan* 77 E1
Tully, *Australia* 90 B4
Ţulmaythah, *Libya* 73 B9
Tulmur, *Australia* 90 C3
Tulnici, *Romania* 38 D9
Tulovo, *Bulgaria* 38 G8
Tulsa, *U.S.A.* 109 G7
Tulsequah, *Canada* 100 B2
Tulu Milki, *Ethiopia* 77 F4
Tulu Welel, *Ethiopia* 77 F3
Tulua, *Colombia* 120 C2
Tulun, *Russia* 45 D11
Tulungagung, *Indonesia* 56 F4
Tum, *Indonesia* 57 E8
Tuma, *Russia* 42 C5
Tuma →, *Nic.* 116 D3
Tumaco, *Colombia* 120 C2
Tumaco, Ensenada, *Colombia* 120 C2
Tumatumari, *Guyana* 121 B6
Tumba, *Sweden* 10 E11
Tumba, L., *Zaïre* 80 E3
Tumbarumba, *Australia* 91 F4
Tumbaya, *Argentina* 126 A2
Túmbes, *Peru* 124 A1
Tumbes □, *Peru* 124 A1
Tumbwe, *Zaïre* 83 E2
Tumby Bay, *Australia* 91 E2
Tumd Youqi, *China* 50 D6
Tumen, *China* 51 C15
Tumen Jiang →, *China* 51 C16
Tumeremo, *Venezuela* 121 B5
Tumiritinga, *Brazil* 123 E3
Tumkur, *India* 60 N10
Tummel, L., *U.K.* 14 E5
Tump, *Pakistan* 60 F3
Tumpat, *Malaysia* 59 J4
Tumu, *Ghana* 78 C4
Tumucumaque, Serra, *Brazil* 121 C7
Tumupasa, *Bolivia* 124 C4
Tumut, *Australia* 91 F4
Tumwater, *U.S.A.* 110 C2
Tunas de Zaza, *Cuba* 116 B4
Tunbridge Wells = Royal Tunbridge Wells, *U.K.* 13 F8
Tunceli, *Turkey* 67 C8
Tuncurry, *Australia* 91 E5
Tunduru, *Tanzania* 83 E4
Tunduru □, *Tanzania* 83 E4
Tundzha →, *Bulgaria* 39 H9
Tunga Pass, *India* 61 E19
Tungabhadra →, *India* 60 M11
Tungaru, *Sudan* 77 E3
Tungla, *Nic.* 116 D3
Tungshih, *Taiwan* 53 E13
Tungsten, *Canada* 100 A3
Tungurahua □, *Ecuador* 120 D2
Tunguska, Nizhnyaya →, *Russia* 45 C9
Tunia, *Colombia* 120 C2
Tunica, *U.S.A.* 109 H9
Tunis, *Tunisia* 75 A7
Tunis, Golfe de, *Tunisia* 75 A7
Tunisia ■, *Africa* 75 B6
Tunja, *Colombia* 120 B3
Tunkhannock, *U.S.A.* 107 E9
Tunliu, *China* 50 F7
Tunnsjøen, *Norway* 8 D15
Tunungayualok I., *Canada* 99 A7
Tunuyán, *Argentina* 126 C2
Tunuyán →, *Argentina* 126 C2
Tunxi, *China* 53 C12
Tuo Jiang →, *China* 52 C5
Tuolumne, *U.S.A.* 111 H3
Tuolumne →, *U.S.A.* 112 H5
Tuoy-Khaya, *Russia* 45 C12
Tūp Āghāj, *Iran* 67 D12
Tupã, *Brazil* 127 A5
Tupaciguara, *Brazil* 123 E2
Tupelo, *U.S.A.* 105 H1
Tupik, *Russia* 42 C1
Tupik, *Russia* 45 D12
Tupinambaranas, *Brazil* 121 D6
Tupirama, *Brazil* 122 C2
Tupiratins, *Brazil* 122 C2
Tupiza, *Bolivia* 126 A2
Tupman, *U.S.A.* 113 K7
Tupper, *Canada* 100 B4
Tupper Lake, *U.S.A.* 107 B10
Tupungato, Cerro, *S. Amer.* 126 C2
Tuquan, *China* 51 B11
Túquerres, *Colombia* 120 C2
Tura, *Russia* 45 C11
Turabah, *Si. Arabia* 64 D4
Turagua, Serranía, *Venezuela* 121 B5
Turān, *Iran* 65 C8
Turan, *Russia* 45 D10
Turayf, *Si. Arabia* 64 D3
Turbenthal, *Switz.* 23 B7
Turégano, *Spain* 30 D6
Turek, *Poland* 20 C8
Turen, *Venezuela* 120 B4
Turfan = Turpan, *China* 54 B3
Turfan Depression = Turpan Hami, *China* 54 B3
Tŭrgovishte, *Bulgaria* 38 F9
Turgutlu, *Turkey* 66 C2
Turhal, *Turkey* 66 B7
Turia →, *Spain* 29 F4
Turiaçu, *Brazil* 122 B2
Turiaçu →, *Brazil* 122 B2
Turin = Torino, *Italy* 32 C4
Turin, *Canada* 100 D6
Turkana □, *Kenya* 82 B4
Turkana, L., *Africa* 82 B4
Turkestan = Türkistan, *Kazakstan* 44 E7
Túrkeve, *Hungary* 21 H10
Turkey ■, *Eurasia* 66 C7
Turkey Creek, *Australia* 88 C4
Turki, *Russia* 42 D6
Türkistan, *Kazakstan* 44 E7
Türkmenbashi, *Turkmenistan* 44 E6
Turkmenistan ■, *Asia* 44 F6
Türkoğlu, *Turkey* 66 D7
Turks & Caicos Is. ■, *W. Indies* 117 B5
Turks Island Passage, *W. Indies* 117 B5
Turku, *Finland* 9 F20
Turkwe →, *Kenya* 82 B4
Turlock, *U.S.A.* 111 H3
Turnagain →, *Canada* 100 B3
Turnagain, C., *N.Z.* 87 J6
Turneffe Is., *Belize* 115 D7
Turner, *Australia* 88 C4
Turner, *U.S.A.* 110 B9
Turner Pt., *Australia* 90 A1
Turner Valley, *Canada* 100 C6
Turners Falls, *U.S.A.* 107 D12
Turnhout, *Belgium* 17 F5
Turnor L., *Canada* 101 B7
Tŭrnovo = Veliko Tŭrnovo, *Bulgaria* 38 F8
Turnu Măgurele, *Romania* 38 F7
Turnu Roşu, P., *Romania* 38 D7
Turon, *U.S.A.* 109 G5
Turpan, *China* 54 B3
Turpan Hami, *China* 54 B3
Turriff, *U.K.* 14 D6
Tursāq, *Iraq* 67 F11
Tursi, *Italy* 35 B9
Turtle Head I., *Australia* 90 A3
Turtle L., *Canada* 101 C7
Turtle Lake, *N. Dak., U.S.A.* 108 B4
Turtle Lake, *Wis., U.S.A.* 108 C8
Turtleford, *Canada* 101 C7
Turukhansk, *Russia* 45 C9
Turzovka, *Slovak Rep.* 20 F8
Tuscaloosa, *U.S.A.* 105 J2
Tuscánia, *Italy* 33 F8
Tuscany = Toscana □, *Italy* 32 E8
Tuscola, *Ill., U.S.A.* 104 F1
Tuscola, *Tex., U.S.A.* 109 J5
Tuscumbia, *U.S.A.* 105 H2
Tuskar Rock, *Ireland* 15 D5
Tuskegee, *U.S.A.* 105 J3
Tustin, *U.S.A.* 113 M9
Tustna, *Norway* 10 A2
Tutak, *Turkey* 67 C10
Tutayev, *Russia* 42 B4
Tuticorin, *India* 60 Q11
Tutin, *Serbia, Yug.* 21 N10
Tutóia, *Brazil* 122 B3
Tutong, *Brunei* 56 D4
Tutova →, *Romania* 38 C10
Tutrakan, *Bulgaria* 38 E9
Tutshi L., *Canada* 100 B2
Tuttle, *U.S.A.* 108 B5
Tuttlingen, *Germany* 19 H4
Tutuala, *Indonesia* 57 F7
Tutuila, *Amer. Samoa* 87 B13
Tututepec, *Mexico* 115 D5
Tuva □, *Russia* 45 D10
Tuvalu ■, *Pac. Oc.* 92 H9
Tuxpan, *Mexico* 115 C5
Tuxtla Gutiérrez, *Mexico* 115 D6
Tuy, *Spain* 30 C2
Tuy An, *Vietnam* 58 F7
Tuy Duc, *Vietnam* 59 F6
Tuy Hoa, *Vietnam* 58 F7
Tuy Phong, *Vietnam* 59 G7
Tuya L., *Canada* 100 B2
Tuyen Hoa, *Vietnam* 58 D6
Tuyen Quang, *Vietnam* 58 B5
Tūysarkān, *Iran* 67 E13
Tuz Gölü, *Turkey* 66 C5
Ţūz Khurmātū, *Iraq* 67 E11
Tuzla, *Bos.-H.* 21 L8
Tuzlov →, *Russia* 43 G4
Tuzluca, *Turkey* 67 B10
Tvååker, *Sweden* 11 G6
Tvedestrand, *Norway* 11 F2
Tver, *Russia* 42 B2
Tvŭrditsa, *Bulgaria* 38 G8
Twain, *U.S.A.* 112 E5
Twain Harte, *U.S.A.* 112 G6
Tweed, *Canada* 106 B7
Tweed →, *U.K.* 14 F7
Tweed Heads, *Australia* 91 D5
Tweedsmuir Prov. Park, *Canada* 100 C3
Twello, *Neths.* 16 D8
Twentynine Palms, *U.S.A.* 113 L10
Twillingate, *Canada* 99 C9
Twin Bridges, *U.S.A.* 110 D7
Twin Falls, *U.S.A.* 110 E6
Twin Valley, *U.S.A.* 108 B6
Twisp, *U.S.A.* 110 B3
Twistringen, *Germany* 18 C4
Two Harbors, *U.S.A.* 108 B9
Two Hills, *Canada* 100 C6
Two Rivers, *U.S.A.* 104 C2
Twofold B., *Australia* 91 F4
Tyachiv, *Ukraine* 41 H2
Tychy, *Poland* 20 E8
Tykocin, *Poland* 20 B12
Tyler, *U.S.A.* 103 D7
Tyler, *Minn., U.S.A.* 108 C6
Tyler, *Tex., U.S.A.* 109 J7
Tyligul →, *Ukraine* 41 J6
Tylldal, *Norway* 10 B4
Týn nad Vltavou, *Czech.* 20 F4
Tynda, *Russia* 45 D13
Tyne →, *U.K.* 12 C6
Tyne & Wear □, *U.K.* 12 C6
Tynemouth, *U.K.* 12 B6
Tynset, *Norway* 10 B4
Tyre = Sūr, *Lebanon* 69 B4
Tyrifjorden, *Norway* 10 D4
Tyringe, *Sweden* 11 H7
Tyristrand, *Norway* 10 D4
Tyrnyauz, *Russia* 43 J6
Tyrone, *U.S.A.* 106 F6
Tyrrell →, *Australia* 91 F3
Tyrrell, L., *Australia* 91 F3
Tyrrell Arm, *Canada* 101 A9
Tyrrell L., *Canada* 101 A7
Tyrrhenian Sea, *Medit. S.* 34 B5
Tysfjorden, *Norway* 8 B17
Tystberga, *Sweden* 11 F11
Tyub Karagan, Mys, *Kazakstan* 43 H10
Tyuleni, Ostrova, *Kazakstan* 43 H10
Tyuleniy, *Russia* 43 H8
Tyuleniy, Mys, *Azerbaijan* 43 K10
Tyumen, *Russia* 44 D7
Tywi →, *U.K.* 13 F3
Tywyn, *U.K.* 13 E3
Tzaneen, *S. Africa* 85 C5
Tzermiádhes, *Greece* 37 D7
Tzermiádhes Neápolis, *Greece* 39 P8
Tzoumérka, Óros, *Greece* 39 K4
Tzukong = Zigong, *China* 52 C5
Tzummarum, *Neths.* 16 B7

U

U Taphao, *Thailand* 58 F3
U.S.A. = United States of America ■, *N. Amer.* 102 C7
Uachadi, Sierra, *Venezuela* 121 C4
Uainambi, *Colombia* 120 C4
Uanda, *Australia* 90 C3
Uarsciek, *Somali Rep.* 68 G4
Uasin □, *Kenya* 82 B4
Uato-Udo, *Indonesia* 57 F7
Uatumã →, *Brazil* 121 D6
Uauá, *Brazil* 122 C4
Uaupés, *Brazil* 120 D4
Uaupés →, *Brazil* 120 C4
Uaxactún, *Guatemala* 116 C2
Ubá, *Brazil* 123 F3
Ubaitaba, *Brazil* 123 D4
Ubangi = Oubangi →, *Zaïre* 80 E3
Ubaté, *Colombia* 120 B3
Ubauro, *Pakistan* 62 E3
Ubaye →, *France* 27 D10
Ubayyiḑ, W. al →, *Iraq* 67 F10
Ube, *Japan* 49 H5
Ubeda, *Spain* 29 G1
Uberaba, *Brazil* 123 E2
Uberaba, L., *Brazil* 125 D6
Uberlândia, *Brazil* 123 E2
Überlingen, *Germany* 19 H5
Ubiaja, *Nigeria* 79 D6
Ubolratna Res., *Thailand* 58 D4
Ubombo, *S. Africa* 85 D5
Ubon Ratchathani, *Thailand* 58 E5
Ubondo, *Zaïre* 82 C2
Ubort →, *Belarus* 41 F5
Ubrique, *Spain* 31 J5
Ubundu, *Zaïre* 82 C2
Ucayali →, *Peru* 124 A3
Uccle, *Belgium* 17 G4
Uchi Lake, *Canada* 101 C10
Uchiura-Wan, *Japan* 48 C10
Uchiza, *Peru* 124 B2
Uchte, *Germany* 18 C4
Uchur →, *Russia* 45 D14
Ucluelet, *Canada* 100 D3
Ucuriş, *Romania* 38 C4
Uda →, *Russia* 45 D14
Udaipur, *India* 62 G5
Udaipur Garhi, *Nepal* 63 F12
Udbina, *Croatia* 33 D12
Uddel, *Neths.* 16 D7
Uddevalla, *Sweden* 11 F5
Uddjaur, *Sweden* 8 D17
Uden, *Neths.* 17 E7
Udgir, *India* 60 K10
Udhampur, *India* 63 C6
Udi, *Nigeria* 79 D6
Údine, *Italy* 33 B10
Udmurtia □, *Russia* 44 D6
Udon Thani, *Thailand* 58 D4
Udupi, *India* 60 N9
Udvoy Balkan, *Bulgaria* 38 G9
Udzungwa Range, *Tanzania* 83 D4
Ueckermünde, *Germany* 18 B10
Ueda, *Japan* 49 F9
Uedineniya, Os., *Russia* 4 B12
Uele →, *Zaïre* 80 D4
Uelen, *Russia* 45 C19
Uelzen, *Germany* 18 C6
Uetendorf, *Switz.* 22 C5
Ufa, *Russia* 44 D6
Uffenheim, *Germany* 19 F6
Ugab →, *Namibia* 84 C1
Ugalla →, *Tanzania* 82 D3
Uganda ■, *Africa* 82 B3
Ugchelen, *Neths.* 16 D7
Ugento, *Italy* 35 C11
Ugep, *Nigeria* 79 D6
Ugie, *S. Africa* 85 E4
Ugijar, *Spain* 29 J1
Ugine, *France* 27 C10
Uglegorsk, *Russia* 45 E15
Uglich, *Russia* 42 B4
Ugljane, *Croatia* 33 E13
Ugolyak, *Russia* 45 C13
Ugra →, *Russia* 42 C3
Ugûn Mûsa, *Egypt* 69 F1
Ugŭrchin, *Bulgaria* 38 F7
Uh →, *Slovak Rep.* 21 G11
Uherske Hradiště, *Czech.* 20 F7
Uhrichsville, *U.S.A.* 106 F3
Uibhist a Deas = South Uist, *U.K.* 14 D1
Uibhist a Tuath = North Uist, *U.K.* 14 D1
Uíge, *Angola* 80 F2
Uijŏngbu, *S. Korea* 51 F14
Ŭiju, *N. Korea* 51 D13
Uinta Mts., *U.S.A.* 110 F8
Uitenhage, *S. Africa* 84 E4
Uitgeest, *Neths.* 16 C5
Uithoorn, *Neths.* 16 D5
Uithuizen, *Neths.* 16 B9
Uitkerke, *Belgium* 17 F2
Újfehértó, *Hungary* 21 H11
Ujhani, *India* 63 F8
Uji-guntō, *Japan* 49 J4
Ujjain, *India* 62 H6
Újpest, *Hungary* 21 H9
Újszász, *Hungary* 21 H10
Ujung Pandang, *Indonesia* 57 F5
Uka, *Russia* 45 D17
Ukara I., *Tanzania* 82 C3
Uke-Shima, *Japan* 49 K4
Ukerewe □, *Tanzania* 82 C3
Ukerewe I., *Tanzania* 82 C3
Ukholovo, *Russia* 42 D5
Ukhrul, *India* 61 G19
Ukhta, *Russia* 44 C6
Ukiah, *U.S.A.* 112 F3
Ukki Fort, *India* 63 C7
Ukmerge, *Lithuania* 9 J21
Ukraine ■, *Europe* 41 H7
Ukwi, *Botswana* 84 C3
Ulaanbaatar, *Mongolia* 45 E11
Ulaangom, *Mongolia* 54 A4
Ulamba, *Zaïre* 83 D1
Ulan Bator = Ulaanbaatar, *Mongolia* 45 E11
Ulan Erge, *Russia* 43 G7
Ulan Khol, *Russia* 43 H8
Ulan Ude, *Russia* 45 D11
Ulanga □, *Tanzania* 83 D4
Ulanów, *Poland* 20 E12
Ulaş, *Turkey* 66 C7
Ulaya, *Morogoro, Tanzania* 82 D4
Ulaya, *Tabora, Tanzania* 82 C3
Ulcinj, *Montenegro, Yug.* 39 H2
Ulco, *S. Africa* 84 D3
Ulefoss, *Norway* 9 G13
Ulfborg, *Denmark* 11 H2
Ulft, *Neths.* 16 E8
Ulhasnagar, *India* 60 K8
Uljma, *Serbia, Yug.* 21 K11
Ulla →, *Spain* 30 C2
Ulladulla, *Australia* 91 F5
Ullånger, *Sweden* 10 B12
Ullapool, *U.K.* 14 D3
Ullared, *Sweden* 11 G6
Ulldecona, *Spain* 28 E5
Ullswater, *U.K.* 12 C5
Ullung-do, *S. Korea* 51 F16
Ulm, *Germany* 19 G5
Ulmarra, *Australia* 91 D5
Ulmeni, *Romania* 38 D9
Ulonguè, *Mozam.* 83 E3
Ulricehamn, *Sweden* 9 H15
Ulrum, *Neths.* 16 B8
Ulsan, *S. Korea* 51 G15
Ulsberg, *Norway* 10 B3
Ulster □, *U.K.* 15 B5
Ulubaria, *India* 63 H13
Ulubat Gölü, *Turkey* 66 B3
Ulubey, *Turkey* 66 C3
Uluborlu, *Turkey* 66 C4
Uluçinar, *Turkey* 66 D6
Uludağ, *Turkey* 66 B3
Uludere, *Turkey* 67 D10
Uluguru Mts., *Tanzania* 82 D4
Ulukışla, *Turkey* 66 D6
Ulungur He →, *China* 54 B3
Uluru = Ayers Rock, *Australia* 89 E5
Ulutau, *Kazakstan* 44 E7
Ulvenhout, *Neths.* 17 E5
Ulverston, *U.K.* 12 C4
Ulverstone, *Australia* 90 G4
Ulya, *Russia* 45 D15
Ulyanovsk = Simbirsk, *Russia* 42 C9
Ulyasutay, *Mongolia* 54 B4
Ulysses, *U.S.A.* 109 G4
Umag, *Croatia* 33 C10
Umala, *Bolivia* 124 D4
Uman, *Ukraine* 41 H6
Umaria, *India* 61 H12
Umarkot, *Pakistan* 60 G6
Umatilla, *U.S.A.* 110 D4
Umba, *Russia* 44 C4
Umbértide, *Italy* 33 E9
Umbrella Mts., *N.Z.* 87 L2
Umbria □, *Italy* 33 F9
Ume älv →, *Sweden* 8 E19
Umeå, *Sweden* 8 E19
Umera, *Indonesia* 57 E7
Umfuli →, *Zimbabwe* 83 F2
Umgusa, *Zimbabwe* 83 F2
Umka, *Serbia, Yug.* 21 L10
Umkomaas, *S. Africa* 85 E5
Umm ad Daraj, J., *Jordan* 69 C4
Umm al Qaywayn, *U.A.E.* 65 E7
Umm al Qittayn, *Jordan* 69 C5
Umm Arda, *Sudan* 77 D3
Umm Bāb, *Qatar* 65 E6
Umm Bel, *Sudan* 77 E2
Umm Dubban, *Sudan* 77 D3
Umm el Fahm, *Israel* 69 C4
Umm Koweika, *Sudan* 77 E3
Umm Lajj, *Si. Arabia* 64 E3
Umm Merwa, *Sudan* 76 D3
Umm Ruwaba, *Sudan* 77 E3
Umm Sidr, *Sudan* 77 E2
Ummanz, *Germany* 18 A9
Umnak I., *U.S.A.* 96 C3
Umniati →, *Zimbabwe* 83 F2
Umpqua →, *U.S.A.* 110 E1
Umreth, *India* 62 H5
Umtata, *S. Africa* 85 E4
Umuahia, *Nigeria* 79 D6
Umuarama, *Brazil* 127 A5
Umvukwe Ra., *Zimbabwe* 83 F3
Umzimvubu = Port St. Johns, *S. Africa* 85 E4
Umzingwane →, *Zimbabwe* 83 G2
Umzinto, *S. Africa* 85 E5
Una, *India* 62 J4
Una →, *Bos.-H.* 33 C13
Unac →, *Bos.-H.* 33 D13
Unadilla, *U.S.A.* 107 D9
Unalaska, *U.S.A.* 96 C3
'Unāzah, J., *Asia* 67 F8
Uncastillo, *Spain* 28 C3
Uncía, *Bolivia* 124 D4
Uncompahgre Peak, *U.S.A.* 111 G10
Unden, *Sweden* 11 F8
Underbool, *Australia* 91 F3
Undersaker, *Sweden* 10 A7
Undersvik, *Sweden* 10 C10
Unecha, *Russia* 41 F7
Uneiuxi →, *Brazil* 120 D4
Ungarie, *Australia* 91 E4
Ungarra, *Australia* 91 E2
Ungava B., *Canada* 97 C13
Ungava Pen., *Canada* 97 C12
Ungeny = Ungheni, *Moldova* 41 J4

Unggi, *N. Korea* 51 C16
Ungheni, *Moldova* 41 J4
Ungwatiri, *Sudan* 77 D4
Uni, *Russia* 42 B10
União da Vitória, *Brazil* 127 B5
União dos Palmares, *Brazil* 122 C4
Unije, *Croatia* 33 D11
Unimak I., *U.S.A.* 96 C3
Unini →, *Brazil* 121 D5
Union, *Miss., U.S.A.* 109 J10
Union, *Mo., U.S.A.* 108 F9
Union, *S.C., U.S.A.* 105 H5
Union, Mt., *U.S.A.* 111 J7
Union City, *Calif., U.S.A.* 112 H4
Union City, *N.J., U.S.A.* 107 F10
Union City, *Pa., U.S.A.* 106 E5
Union City, *Tenn., U.S.A.* 109 G10
Union Gap, *U.S.A.* 110 C3
Union Springs, *U.S.A.* 105 J3
Uniondale, *S. Africa* 84 E3
Uniontown, *U.S.A.* 104 F6
Unionville, *U.S.A.* 108 E8
United Arab Emirates ■, *Asia* 65 F7
United Kingdom ■, *Europe* 7 E5
United States of America ■, *N. Amer.* 102 C7
Unity, *Canada* 101 C7
Universales, Mtes., *Spain* 28 E3
Unjha, *India* 62 H5
Unnao, *India* 63 F9
Uno, Ilha, *Guinea-Biss.* 78 C1
Unst, *U.K.* 14 A8
Unstrut →, *Germany* 18 D7
Unter-engadin, *Switz.* 23 C10
Unterägeri, *Switz.* 23 B7
Unterkulm, *Switz.* 22 B6
Unterseen, *Switz.* 22 C5
Unterwaldner Alpen, *Switz.* 23 C6
Unuk →, *Canada* 100 B2
Ünye, *Turkey* 66 B7
Unzha, *Russia* 42 A7
Unzha →, *Russia* 42 B6
Uors, *Switz.* 23 C8
Uozu, *Japan* 49 F8
Upa →, *Czech.* 20 E6
Upata, *Venezuela* 121 B5
Upemba, L., *Zaïre* 83 D2
Upernavik, *Greenland* 4 B5
Upington, *S. Africa* 84 D3
Upleta, *India* 62 J4
Upolu, *W. Samoa* 87 A13
Upper Alkali Lake, *U.S.A.* 110 F3
Upper Arrow L., *Canada* 100 C5
Upper Foster L., *Canada* 101 B7
Upper Hutt, *N.Z.* 87 J5
Upper Klamath L., *U.S.A.* 110 E3
Upper Lake, *U.S.A.* 112 F4
Upper Musquodoboit, *Canada* 99 C7
Upper Red L., *U.S.A.* 108 A7
Upper Sandusky, *U.S.A.* 104 E4
Upper Volta = Burkina Faso ■, *Africa* 78 C4
Upphärad, *Sweden* 11 F6
Uppland, *Sweden* 9 F17
Uppsala, *Sweden* 10 E11
Upshi, *India* 63 C7
Upstart, C., *Australia* 90 B4
Upton, *U.S.A.* 108 C2
Ur, *Iraq* 64 D5
Urabá, G. de, *Colombia* 120 B2
Uracara, *Brazil* 121 D6
Urad Qianqi, *China* 50 D5
Urakawa, *Japan* 48 C11
Ural = Zhayyq →, *Kazakstan* 44 E6
Ural, *Australia* 91 E4
Ural Mts. = Uralskie Gory, *Eurasia* 44 D6
Uralla, *Australia* 91 E5
Uralsk = Oral, *Kazakstan* 42 E10
Uralskie Gory, *Eurasia* 44 D6
Urambo, *Tanzania* 82 D3
Urambo □, *Tanzania* 82 D3
Urandangi, *Australia* 90 C2
Uranium City, *Canada* 101 B7
Uranquinty, *Australia* 91 F4
Uraricaá →, *Brazil* 121 C5
Uraricoera →, *Brazil* 121 C5
Urawa, *Japan* 49 G9
Uray, *Russia* 44 C7
'Uray'irah, *Si. Arabia* 65 E6
Urbana, *Ill., U.S.A.* 104 E1
Urbana, *Ohio, U.S.A.* 104 E4
Urbánia, *Italy* 33 E9
Urbano Santos, *Brazil* 122 B3
Urbel →, *Spain* 28 C1
Urbino, *Italy* 33 E9
Urbión, Picos de, *Spain* 28 C2
Urcos, *Peru* 124 C3
Urda, *Spain* 31 F7
Urdinarrain, *Argentina* 126 C4
Urdos, *France* 26 F3
Urdzhar, *Kazakstan* 44 E9
Ure →, *U.K.* 12 C6
Uren, *Russia* 42 B7
Ures, *Mexico* 114 B2
Urfa = Sanliurfa, *Turkey* 67 D8
Urfahr, *Austria* 21 G4
Urganch, *Uzbekistan* 44 E7
Urgench = Urganch, *Uzbekistan* 44 E7
Uri, *India* 63 B6
Uri □, *Switz.* 23 C7
Uribante →, *Venezuela* 120 B3
Uribe, *Colombia* 120 C3
Uribia, *Colombia* 120 A3
Uriondo, *Bolivia* 126 A3
Urique, *Mexico* 114 B3
Urique →, *Mexico* 114 B3
Urirotstock, *Switz.* 23 C7
Urk, *Neths.* 16 C7
Urla, *Turkey* 66 C2
Urlati, *Romania* 38 E9
Urmia = Orūmīyeh, *Iran* 67 D11
Urmia, L. = Orūmīyeh, Daryācheh-ye, *Iran* 67 D11
Urner Alpen, *Switz.* 23 C7
Uroševac, *Serbia, Yug.* 21 N11
Urrao, *Colombia* 120 B2
Ursus, *Poland* 20 C10
Uruaçu, *Brazil* 123 D2
Uruana, *Brazil* 123 E2
Uruapan, *Mexico* 114 D4
Uruará →, *Brazil* 121 D7
Urubamba, *Peru* 124 C3
Urubamba →, *Peru* 124 C3
Urubaxi →, *Brazil* 121 D5
Urubu →, *Brazil* 121 D6
Uruçara, *Brazil* 121 D6
Uruçuí, *Brazil* 122 C3
Uruçuí, Serra do, *Brazil* 122 C3
Uruçuí Prêto →, *Brazil* 122 C3
Urucuia →, *Brazil* 123 E2
Urucurituba, *Brazil* 121 D6
Uruguai →, *Brazil* 127 B5
Uruguaiana, *Brazil* 126 B4
Uruguay ■, *S. Amer.* 126 C4
Uruguay →, *S. Amer.* 126 C4
Urumchi = Ürümqi, *China* 44 E9
Ürümqi, *China* 44 E9
Urup →, *Russia* 43 H5
Urup, Os., *Russia* 45 E16
Urutaí, *Brazil* 123 E2
Uryupinsk, *Russia* 42 E5
Urzhum, *Russia* 42 B9
Urziceni, *Romania* 38 E9
Uşak, *Turkey* 66 C3
Usakos, *Namibia* 84 C2
Usborne, Mt., *Falk. Is.* 128 D5
Ušće, *Serbia, Yug.* 21 M10
Usedom, *Germany* 18 B9
'Usfān, *Si. Arabia* 76 C4
Ush-Tobe, *Kazakstan* 44 E8
Ushakova, Os., *Russia* 4 A12
Ushant = Ouessant, I. d', *France* 24 D1
Ushashi, *Tanzania* 82 C3
Ushat, *Sudan* 77 F2
Ushibuka, *Japan* 49 H5
Ushuaia, *Argentina* 128 D3
Ushumun, *Russia* 45 D13
Usk →, *U.K.* 13 F5
Üsküdar, *Turkey* 39 H11
Uslar, *Germany* 18 D5
Usman, *Russia* 42 D4
Usoke, *Tanzania* 82 D3
Usolye Sibirskoye, *Russia* 45 D11
Usoro, *Nigeria* 79 D6
Uspallata, P. de, *Argentina* 126 C2
Uspenskiy, *Kazakstan* 44 E8
Usquert, *Neths.* 16 B9
Ussel, *France* 26 C6
Ussuri →, *Asia* 48 A7
Ussuriysk, *Russia* 45 E14
Ussurka, *Russia* 48 B6
Ust-Aldan = Batamay, *Russia* 45 C13
Ust Amginskoye = Khandyga, *Russia* 45 C14
Ust-Bolsheretsk, *Russia* 45 D16
Ust Buzulukskaya, *Russia* 42 E6
Ust Chaun, *Russia* 45 C18
Ust-Donetskiy, *Russia* 43 G5
Ust'-Ilga, *Russia* 45 D11
Ust Ilimpeya = Yukti, *Russia* 45 C11
Ust-Ilimsk, *Russia* 45 D11
Ust Ishim, *Russia* 44 D8
Ust-Kamchatsk, *Russia* 45 D17
Ust-Kamenogorsk = Öskemen, *Kazakstan* 44 E9
Ust-Karenga, *Russia* 45 D12
Ust Khayryuzovo, *Russia* 45 D16
Ust-Kut, *Russia* 45 D11
Ust Kuyga, *Russia* 45 B14
Ust-Labinsk, *Russia* 43 H4
Ust Luga, *Russia* 40 C5
Ust Maya, *Russia* 45 C14
Ust-Mil, *Russia* 45 D14
Ust Muya, *Russia* 45 D12
Ust-Nera, *Russia* 45 C15
Ust-Nyukzha, *Russia* 45 D13
Ust Olenek, *Russia* 45 B12
Ust-Omchug, *Russia* 45 C15
Ust Port, *Russia* 44 C9
Ust Tsilma, *Russia* 44 C6
Ust-Tungir, *Russia* 45 D13
Ust Urt = Ustyurt, Plateau, *Asia* 44 E6
Ust Vorkuta, *Russia* 44 C7
Ustaoset, *Norway* 10 D2
Ustaritz, *France* 26 E2
Uster, *Switz.* 23 B7
Ústí nad Labem, *Czech.* 20 E4
Ústí nad Orlicí, *Czech.* 20 F6
Ustica, *Italy* 34 D6
Ustinov = Izhevsk, *Russia* 44 D6
Ustka, *Poland* 20 A6
Ustrzyki Dolne, *Poland* 20 F12
Ustye, *Russia* 45 D10
Ustyurt, Plateau, *Asia* 44 E6
Ustyuzhna, *Russia* 40 C9
Usu, *China* 54 B3
Usuki, *Japan* 49 H5
Usulután, *El Salv.* 116 D2
Usumacinta →, *Mexico* 115 D6
Usumbura = Bujumbura, *Burundi* 82 C2
Usure, *Tanzania* 82 C3
Uta, *Indonesia* 57 E9
Utah □, *U.S.A.* 110 G8
Utah, L., *U.S.A.* 110 F8
Ute Creek →, *U.S.A.* 109 H3
Utena, *Lithuania* 9 J21
Ütersen, *Germany* 18 B5
Utete, *Tanzania* 82 D4
Uthai Thani, *Thailand* 58 E3
Uthal, *Pakistan* 62 G2
Utiariti, *Brazil* 125 C6
Utica, *N.Y., U.S.A.* 107 C9
Utica, *Ohio, U.S.A.* 106 F2
Utiel, *Spain* 28 F3
Utik L., *Canada* 101 B9
Utikuma L., *Canada* 100 B5
Utinga, *Brazil* 123 D3
Utrecht, *Neths.* 16 D6
Utrecht, *S. Africa* 85 D5
Utrecht □, *Neths.* 16 D6
Utrera, *Spain* 31 H5
Utsjoki, *Finland* 8 B22
Utsunomiya, *Japan* 49 F9
Uttar Pradesh □, *India* 63 F9
Uttaradit, *Thailand* 58 D3
Uttoxeter, *U.K.* 12 E6
Ütze, *Germany* 18 C6
Uummannarsuaq = Farvel, Kap, *Greenland* 4 D5
Uusikaarlepyy, *Finland* 8 E20
Uusikaupunki, *Finland* 9 F19
Uva, *Russia* 42 B11
Uvá →, *Colombia* 120 C3
Uvalde, *U.S.A.* 109 L5
Uvarovo, *Russia* 42 E6
Uvat, *Russia* 44 D7
Uvinza, *Tanzania* 82 D3
Uvira, *Zaïre* 82 C2
Uvs Nuur, *Mongolia* 54 A4
Uwajima, *Japan* 49 H6
Uweinat, Jebel, *Sudan* 76 C1
Uxbridge, *Canada* 106 B5
Uxin Qi, *China* 50 E5
Uxmal, *Mexico* 115 C7
Uyandi, *Russia* 45 C15
Uyo, *Nigeria* 79 D6
Uyuni, *Bolivia* 124 E4
Uzbekistan ■, *Asia* 44 E7
Uzen, Bolshoi →, *Kazakstan* 43 F9
Uzen, Mal →, *Kazakstan* 43 F9
Uzerche, *France* 26 C5
Uzès, *France* 27 D8
Uzh →, *Ukraine* 41 G6
Uzhgorod = Uzhhorod, *Ukraine* 41 H2
Uzhhorod, *Ukraine* 41 H2
Uzlovaya, *Russia* 42 D4
Uzunköprü, *Turkey* 66 B2
Uzwil, *Switz.* 23 B8

V

Vaal →, *S. Africa* 84 D3
Vaal Dam, *S. Africa* 85 D4
Vaals, *Neths.* 17 G8
Vaalwater, *S. Africa* 85 C4
Vaasa, *Finland* 8 E19
Vaassen, *Neths.* 16 D7
Vabre, *France* 26 E6
Vác, *Hungary* 21 H9
Vacaria, *Brazil* 127 B5
Vacaville, *U.S.A.* 112 G5
Vaccarès, Étang de, *France* 27 E8
Vach → = Vakh →, *Russia* 44 C8
Vache, Î.-à-, *Haiti* 117 C5
Vadnagar, *India* 62 H5
Vado Lígure, *Italy* 32 D5
Vadodara, *India* 62 H5
Vadsø, *Norway* 8 A23
Vadstena, *Sweden* 11 F8
Vaduz, *Liech.* 23 B9
Værøy, *Norway* 8 C15
Vágar, *Færoe Is.* 8 E9
Vagney, *France* 25 E13
Vagnhärad, *Sweden* 10 F11
Vagos, *Portugal* 30 E2
Vågsfjorden, *Norway* 8 B17
Váh →, *Slovak Rep.* 21 H8
Vahsel B., *Antarctica* 5 D1
Váï, *Greece* 37 D8
Vaigach, *Russia* 44 B6
Vaiges, *France* 24 D6
Vaihingen, *Germany* 19 G4
Vailly-sur-Aisne, *France* 25 C10
Vaison-la-Romaine, *France* 27 D9
Vakfikebir, *Turkey* 67 B8
Vakh →, *Russia* 44 C8
Vakhtan, *Russia* 42 B8
Val-de-Marne □, *France* 25 D9
Val-d'Oise □, *France* 25 C9
Val d'Or, *Canada* 98 C4
Val Marie, *Canada* 101 D7
Valaam, *Russia* 40 B6
Valadares, *Portugal* 30 D2
Valahia, *Romania* 38 E8
Valais □, *Switz.* 22 D5
Valais, Alpes du, *Switz.* 22 D5
Valandovo, *Macedonia* 39 H5
Valcheta, *Argentina* 128 B3
Valdagno, *Italy* 33 C8
Valdahon, *France* 25 E13
Valday, *Russia* 42 B1
Valdayskaya Vozvyshennost, *Russia* 42 B1
Valdeazogues →, *Spain* 31 G6
Valdemarsvik, *Sweden* 11 F10
Valdepeñas, *Ciudad Real, Spain* 31 G7
Valdepeñas, *Jaén, Spain* 31 H7
Valderaduey →, *Spain* 30 D5
Valderrobres, *Spain* 28 E5
Valdés, Pen., *Argentina* 128 B4
Valdez, *Ecuador* 120 C2
Valdez, *U.S.A.* 96 B5
Valdivia, *Chile* 128 A2
Valdivia, *Colombia* 120 B2
Valdivia □, *Chile* 128 B2
Valdobbiádene, *Italy* 33 C9
Valdosta, *U.S.A.* 105 K4
Valdoviño, *Spain* 30 B2
Valdres, *Norway* 10 D3
Vale, *Georgia* 43 K6
Vale, *U.S.A.* 110 E5
Vale of Glamorgan □, *U.K.* 13 F4
Valea lui Mihai, *Romania* 38 B5
Valença, *Brazil* 123 D4
Valença, *Portugal* 30 C2
Valença do Piauí, *Brazil* 122 C3
Valençay, *France* 25 E8
Valence, *Drôme, France* 27 D8
Valence, *Tarn-et-Garonne, France* 26 D4
Valencia, *Spain* 29 F4
Valencia, *Venezuela* 120 A4
Valencia □, *Spain* 29 F4
Valencia, G. de, *Spain* 29 F5
Valencia de Alcántara, *Spain* 31 F3
Valencia de Don Juan, *Spain* 30 C5
Valencia del Ventoso, *Spain* 31 G4
Valencia Harbour, *Ireland* 15 E1
Valencia I., *Ireland* 15 E1
Valenciennes, *France* 25 B10
Valensole, *France* 27 E9
Valentim, Sa. do, *Brazil* 122 C3
Valentin, *Russia* 48 C7
Valentine, *Nebr., U.S.A.* 108 D4
Valentine, *Tex., U.S.A.* 109 K2
Valenza, *Italy* 32 C5
Valera, *Venezuela* 120 B3
Valga, *Estonia* 9 H22
Valguarnera Caropepe, *Italy* 35 E7
Valier, *U.S.A.* 110 B7
Valinco, G. de, *France* 27 G12
Valjevo, *Serbia, Yug.* 21 L9
Valka, *Latvia* 9 H21
Valkeakoski, *Finland* 9 F20
Valkenburg, *Neths.* 17 G7
Valkenswaard, *Neths.* 17 F6
Vall de Uxó, *Spain* 28 F4
Valla, *Sweden* 10 E10
Valladolid, *Mexico* 115 C7
Valladolid, *Spain* 30 D6
Valladolid □, *Spain* 30 D6
Vallata, *Italy* 35 A8
Valldemosa, *Spain* 36 B9
Valle d'Aosta □, *Italy* 32 C4
Valle de Arán, *Spain* 28 C5
Valle de Cabuérniga, *Spain* 30 B6
Valle de la Pascua, *Venezuela* 120 B4
Valle de las Palmas, *Mexico* 113 N10
Valle de Santiago, *Mexico* 114 C4
Valle de Suchil, *Mexico* 114 C4
Valle de Zaragoza, *Mexico* 114 B3
Valle del Cauca □, *Colombia* 120 C2
Valle Fértil, Sierra del, *Argentina* 126 C2
Valle Hermoso, *Mexico* 115 B5
Vallecas, *Spain* 30 E7
Valledupar, *Colombia* 120 A3
Vallehermoso, *Canary Is.* 36 F2
Vallejo, *U.S.A.* 112 G4
Vallenar, *Chile* 126 B1
Valleraugue, *France* 26 D7
Vallet, *France* 24 E5
Valletta, *Malta* 37 D2
Valley Center, *U.S.A.* 113 M9
Valley City, *U.S.A.* 108 B6
Valley Falls, *U.S.A.* 110 E3
Valley Springs, *U.S.A.* 112 G6
Valley Wells, *U.S.A.* 113 K11
Valleyview, *Canada* 100 B5
Valli di Comácchio, *Italy* 33 D9
Vallimanca, Arroyo, *Argentina* 126 D4
Vallo della Lucánia, *Italy* 35 B8
Vallon-Pont-d'Arc, *France* 27 D8
Vallorbe, *Switz.* 22 C2
Valls, *Spain* 28 D6
Vallsta, *Sweden* 10 C10
Valmaseda, *Spain* 28 B1
Valmiera, *Latvia* 9 H21
Valmont, *France* 24 C7
Valmontone, *Italy* 34 A5
Valmy, *France* 25 C11
Valnera, Mte., *Spain* 28 B1
Valognes, *France* 24 C5
Valona = Vlóra, *Albania* 39 J2
Valongo, *Portugal* 30 D2
Valozhyn, *Belarus* 40 E4
Valpaços, *Portugal* 30 D3
Valparaíso, *Chile* 126 C1
Valparaíso, *Mexico* 114 C4
Valparaiso, *U.S.A.* 104 E2
Valparaíso □, *Chile* 126 C1
Valpovo, *Croatia* 21 K8
Valréas, *France* 27 D8
Vals, *Switz.* 23 C8
Vals →, *S. Africa* 84 D4
Vals, Tanjung, *Indonesia* 57 F9
Vals-les-Bains, *France* 27 D8
Valsad, *India* 60 J8
Valskog, *Sweden* 10 E9
Válta, *Greece* 39 J6
Valtellina, *Italy* 32 B6
Valuyki, *Russia* 42 E4
Valverde, *Canary Is.* 36 G2
Valverde del Camino, *Spain* 31 H4
Valverde del Fresno, *Spain* 30 E4
Vama, *Romania* 38 B8
Vammala, *Finland* 9 F20
Vámos, *Greece* 37 D6
Van, *Turkey* 67 C10
Van, L. = Van Gölü, *Turkey* 67 C10
Van Alstyne, *U.S.A.* 109 J6
Van Bruyssel, *Canada* 99 C5
Van Buren, *Canada* 99 C6
Van Buren, *Ark., U.S.A.* 109 H7
Van Buren, *Maine, U.S.A.* 105 B11
Van Buren, *Mo., U.S.A.* 109 G9
Van Canh, *Vietnam* 58 F7
Van Diemen, C., *N. Terr., Australia* 88 B5
Van Diemen, C., *Queens., Australia* 90 B2
Van Diemen G., *Australia* 88 B5
Van Gölü, *Turkey* 67 C10
Van Horn, *U.S.A.* 109 K2
Van Ninh, *Vietnam* 58 F7
Van Rees, Pegunungan, *Indonesia* 57 E9
Van Tassell, *U.S.A.* 108 D2
Van Wert, *U.S.A.* 104 E3
Van Yen, *Vietnam* 58 B5
Vanadzor, *Armenia* 43 K7
Vanavara, *Russia* 45 C11
Vancouver, *Canada* 100 D4
Vancouver, *U.S.A.* 112 E4
Vancouver, C., *Australia* 89 G2
Vancouver I., *Canada* 100 D3
Vandalia, *Ill., U.S.A.* 108 F10
Vandalia, *Mo., U.S.A.* 108 F9
Vandenburg, *U.S.A.* 113 L6
Vanderbijlpark, *S. Africa* 85 D4
Vandergrift, *U.S.A.* 106 F5
Vanderhoof, *Canada* 100 C4
Vanderkloof Dam, *S. Africa* 84 E3
Vanderlin I., *Australia* 90 B2
Vandyke, *Australia* 90 C4
Vänern, *Sweden* 11 F7
Vänersborg, *Sweden* 11 F6
Vang Vieng, *Laos* 58 C4
Vanga, *Kenya* 82 C4
Vangaindrano, *Madag.* 85 C8
Vanguard, *Canada* 101 D7
Vanier, *Canada* 98 C4
Vankleek Hill, *Canada* 98 C5
Vanna, *Norway* 8 A18
Vännäs, *Sweden* 8 E18
Vannes, *France* 24 E4
Vanoise, Massif de la, *France* 27 C10
Vanrhynsdorp, *S. Africa* 84 E2
Vanrook, *Australia* 90 B3
Vansbro, *Sweden* 9 F16
Vansittart B., *Australia* 88 B4
Vantaa, *Finland* 9 F21
Vanthli, *India* 62 J4
Vanua Levu, *Fiji* 87 C8
Vanua Mbalavu, *Fiji* 87 C9
Vanuatu ■, *Pac. Oc.* 92 J8
Vanwyksvlei, *S. Africa* 84 E3
Vanzylsrus, *S. Africa* 84 D3
Vapnyarka, *Ukraine* 41 H5
Var □, *France* 27 E10
Var →, *France* 27 E11
Vara, *Sweden* 11 F6
Varades, *France* 24 E5
Varáita →, *Italy* 32 D4
Varallo, *Italy* 32 C5
Varanasi, *India* 63 G10
Varanger-halvøya, *Norway* 8 A23
Varangerfjorden, *Norway* 8 A23
Varaždin, *Croatia* 33 B13
Varazze, *Italy* 32 D5
Varberg, *Sweden* 11 G6
Vardar = Axiós →, *Greece* 39 J5
Varde, *Denmark* 11 J2
Varde Å →, *Denmark* 11 J2
Vardø, *Norway* 8 A24
Varel, *Germany* 18 B4
Varella, Mui, *Vietnam* 58 F7
Varėna, *Lithuania* 9 J21
Varennes-sur-Allier, *France* 26 B7
Vareš, *Bos.-H.* 21 L8
Varese, *Italy* 32 C5
Varese Lígure, *Italy* 32 D6
Vårgårda, *Sweden* 11 F6
Vargem Bonita, *Brazil* 123 F2
Vargem Grande, *Brazil* 122 B3
Varginha, *Brazil* 127 A6

Vargön, *Sweden* 11 F6
Variadero, *U.S.A.* 109 H2
Varillas, *Chile* 126 A1
Väring, *Sweden* 11 F8
Varkaus, *Finland* 9 E22
Varna, *Bulgaria* 38 F10
Värnamo, *Sweden* 9 H16
Värö, *Sweden* 11 G6
Vars, *Canada* 107 A9
Varsseveld, *Neths.* 16 E8
Varto, *Turkey* 67 C9
Varvarin, *Serbia, Yug.* 21 M11
Varzaneh, *Iran* 65 C7
Várzea Alegre, *Brazil* 122 C4
Várzea da Palma, *Brazil* 123 E3
Várzea Grande, *Brazil* 125 D6
Varzi, *Italy* 32 D6
Varzo, *Italy* 32 B5
Varzy, *France* 25 E10
Vasa Barris →, *Brazil* 122 D4
Vascão →, *Portugal* 31 H3
Vaşcău, *Romania* 38 C5
Vascongadas = País Vasco □, *Spain* 28 C2
Vasht = Khāsh, *Iran* 60 E2
Vasilevichi, *Belarus* 41 F5
Vasilikón, *Greece* 39 L6
Vasilkov = Vasylkiv, *Ukraine* 41 G6
Vaslui, *Romania* 38 C10
Vassar, *Canada* 101 D9
Vassar, *U.S.A.* 104 D4
Västerås, *Sweden* 10 E10
Västerbotten, *Sweden* 8 D18
Västerdalälven →, *Sweden* 9 F16
Västernorrlands län □, *Sweden* 10 A11
Västervik, *Sweden* 9 H17
Västmanland, *Sweden* 9 G16
Vasto, *Italy* 33 F11
Vasvár, *Hungary* 21 H6
Vasylkiv, *Ukraine* 41 G6
Vatan, *France* 25 E8
Vathí, *Greece* 39 M10
Váthia, *Greece* 39 N5
Vatican City ■, *Europe* 33 G9
Vaticano, C., *Italy* 35 D8
Vatili, *Cyprus* 37 D12
Vatnajökull, *Iceland* 8 D5
Vatnås, *Norway* 10 E3
Vatoa, *Fiji* 87 D9
Vatólakkos, *Greece* 37 D5
Vatoloha, *Madag.* 85 B8
Vatomandry, *Madag.* 85 B8
Vatra-Dornei, *Romania* 38 B8
Vättern, *Sweden* 11 F8
Vättis, *Switz.* 23 C8
Vaucluse □, *France* 27 E9
Vaucouleurs, *France* 25 D12
Vaud □, *Switz.* 22 C2
Vaughn, *Mont., U.S.A.* 110 C8
Vaughn, *N. Mex., U.S.A.* 111 J11
Vaulruz, *Switz.* 22 C3
Vaupés = Uaupés →, *Brazil* 120 C4
Vaupes □, *Colombia* 120 C3
Vauvert, *France* 27 E8
Vauxhall, *Canada* 100 C6
Vava'u, *Tonga* 87 D11
Vavoua, *Ivory C.* 78 D3
Vawkavysk, *Belarus* 41 F3
Vaxholm, *Sweden* 10 E12
Växjö, *Sweden* 9 H16
Vaygach, Ostrov, *Russia* 44 C6
Váyia, Ákra, *Greece* 37 C10
Veadeiros, *Brazil* 123 D2
Vechta, *Germany* 18 C4
Vechte →, *Neths.* 16 C8
Vecsés, *Hungary* 21 H9
Veddige, *Sweden* 11 G6
Vedea →, *Romania* 38 F8
Vedia, *Argentina* 126 C3
Vedra, I. del, *Spain* 36 C7
Vedrin, *Belgium* 17 G5
Veendam, *Neths.* 16 B9
Veenendaal, *Neths.* 16 D7
Veerle, *Belgium* 17 F5
Vefsna →, *Norway* 8 D15
Vega, *Norway* 8 D14
Vega, *U.S.A.* 109 H3
Vegadeo, *Spain* 30 B3
Veghel, *Neths.* 17 E7
Vegorritis, Límni, *Greece* 39 J4
Vegreville, *Canada* 100 C6
Vegusdal, *Norway* 11 F2
Veii, *Italy* 33 F9
Vejen, *Denmark* 11 J3
Vejer de la Frontera, *Spain* 31 J5
Vejle, *Denmark* 11 J3
Vejle Fjord, *Denmark* 11 J3
Vela Luka, *Croatia* 33 F13
Velas, C., *Costa Rica* 116 D2
Velasco, Sierra de, *Argentina* 126 B2
Velay, Mts. du, *France* 26 D7
Velddrif, *S. Africa* 84 E2
Veldegem, *Belgium* 17 F2
Velden, *Neths.* 17 F8
Veldhoven, *Neths.* 17 F6
Velebit Planina, *Croatia* 33 D12
Velebitski Kanal, *Croatia* 33 D11
Veleka →, *Bulgaria* 38 G10
Velenje, *Slovenia* 33 B12
Velestínon, *Greece* 39 K5
Vélez, *Colombia* 120 B3
Vélez Blanco, *Spain* 29 H2
Vélez Málaga, *Spain* 31 J6
Vélez Rubio, *Spain* 29 H2
Velhas →, *Brazil* 123 E3
Velika, *Croatia* 21 K7
Velika Gorica, *Croatia* 33 C13
Velika Kapela, *Croatia* 33 C12
Velika Kladuša, *Bos.-H.* 33 C12
Velika Morava →, *Serbia, Yug.* 21 L11
Velikaya →, *Russia* 40 D5
Velikaya Kema, *Russia* 48 B8
Velikaya Lepetikha, *Ukraine* 41 J7
Velike Lašče, *Slovenia* 33 C11
Velikiye Luki, *Russia* 40 D6
Veliko Tŭrnovo, *Bulgaria* 38 F8
Velikonda Range, *India* 60 M11
Velingrad, *Bulgaria* 39 G6
Velino, Mte., *Italy* 33 F10
Velizh, *Russia* 40 E6
Velke Meziřici, *Czech.* 20 F6
Velletri, *Italy* 34 A5
Vellinge, *Sweden* 11 J7
Vellore, *India* 60 N11
Velp, *Neths.* 16 D7
Velsen-Noord, *Neths.* 16 D5
Velsk, *Russia* 40 B11
Velten, *Germany* 18 C9
Veluwe Meer, *Neths.* 16 D7
Velva, *U.S.A.* 108 A4
Veme, *Norway* 10 D4
Ven, *Sweden* 11 J6
Venaco, *France* 27 F13
Venado Tuerto, *Argentina* 126 C3
Venafro, *Italy* 35 A7
Venarey-les-Laumes, *France* 25 E11
Venaria, *Italy* 32 C4
Venčane, *Serbia, Yug.* 21 L10
Vence, *France* 27 E11
Vendas Novas, *Portugal* 31 G2
Vendée □, *France* 24 F5
Vendée →, *France* 24 F5
Vendéen, Bocage, *France* 26 B2
Vendeuvre-sur-Barse, *France* 25 D11
Vendôme, *France* 24 E8
Vendrell, *Spain* 28 D6
Vendsyssel, *Denmark* 11 G4
Véneta, L., *Italy* 33 C9
Véneto □, *Italy* 33 C8
Venev, *Russia* 42 C4
Venézia, *Italy* 33 C9
Venézia, G. di, *Italy* 33 C10
Venezuela ■, *S. Amer.* 120 B4
Venezuela, G. de, *Venezuela* 120 A3
Vengurla, *India* 60 M8
Venice = Venézia, *Italy* 33 C9
Venkatapuram, *India* 61 K12
Venlo, *Neths.* 17 F8
Vennesla, *Norway* 9 G12
Venraij, *Neths.* 17 E7
Venta de Cardeña, *Spain* 31 G6
Venta de San Rafael, *Spain* 30 E6
Ventana, Punta de la, *Mexico* 114 C3
Ventana, Sa. de la, *Argentina* 126 D3
Ventersburg, *S. Africa* 84 D4
Venterstad, *S. Africa* 84 E4
Ventimíglia, *Italy* 32 E4
Ventnor, *U.K.* 13 G6
Ventotene, *Italy* 34 B6
Ventoux, Mt., *France* 27 D9
Ventspils, *Latvia* 9 H19
Ventuarí →, *Venezuela* 120 C4
Ventucopa, *U.S.A.* 113 L7
Ventura, *U.S.A.* 113 L7
Venus B., *Australia* 91 F4
Veøy, *Norway* 10 B1
Vera, *Argentina* 126 B3
Vera, *Spain* 29 H3
Veracruz, *Mexico* 115 D5
Veracruz □, *Mexico* 115 D5
Veraval, *India* 62 J4
Verbánia, *Italy* 32 C5
Verbicaro, *Italy* 35 C8
Verbier, *Switz.* 22 D4
Vercelli, *Italy* 32 C5
Verchovchevo, *Ukraine* 41 H8
Verdalsøra, *Norway* 8 E14
Verde →, *Argentina* 128 B3
Verde →, *Goiás, Brazil* 123 E1
Verde →, *Goiás, Brazil* 123 E1
Verde →, *Mato Grosso, Brazil* 125 C6
Verde →, *Mato Grosso do Sul, Brazil* 125 E7
Verde →, *Chihuahua, Mexico* 114 B3
Verde →, *Oaxaca, Mexico* 115 D5
Verde →, *Veracruz, Mexico* 114 C4
Verde →, *Paraguay* 126 A4
Verde, Cay, *Bahamas* 116 B4
Verde Grande →, *Brazil* 123 E3
Verde Island Pass, *Phil.* 55 E4
Verde Pequeno →, *Brazil* 123 D3
Verden, *Germany* 18 C5
Verdi, *U.S.A.* 112 F7
Verdigre, *U.S.A.* 108 D5
Verdon →, *France* 27 E9
Verdun, *France* 25 C12
Verdun-sur-le-Doubs, *France* 25 F12
Vereeniging, *S. Africa* 85 D4
Vérendrye, Parc Prov. de la, *Canada* 98 C4
Verga, C., *Guinea* 78 C2
Vergato, *Italy* 32 D8
Vergemont, *Australia* 90 C3
Vergemont Cr. →, *Australia* 90 C3
Vergennes, *U.S.A.* 107 B11
Vergt, *France* 26 C4
Verín, *Spain* 30 D3
Veriña, *Spain* 30 B5
Verkhnedvinsk = Vyerkhnyadzvinsk, *Belarus* 40 E4
Verkhnevilyuysk, *Russia* 45 C13
Verkhneye Kalinino, *Russia* 45 D11
Verkhniy Baskunchak, *Russia* 43 F8
Verkhnyaya Amga, *Russia* 45 D13
Verkhovye, *Russia* 42 D3
Verkhoyansk, *Russia* 45 C14
Verkhoyansk Ra. = Verkhoyanskiy Khrebet, *Russia* 45 C13
Verkhoyanskiy Khrebet, *Russia* 45 C13
Verlo, *Canada* 101 C7
Verma, *Norway* 10 B2
Vermenton, *France* 25 E10
Vermilion, *Canada* 101 C6
Vermilion →, *Alta., Canada* 101 C6
Vermilion →, *Qué., Canada* 98 C5
Vermilion, B., *U.S.A.* 109 L9
Vermilion Bay, *Canada* 101 D10
Vermilion Chutes, *Canada* 100 B6
Vermilion L., *U.S.A.* 108 B8
Vermillion, *U.S.A.* 108 D6
Vermont □, *U.S.A.* 107 C12
Vernal, *U.S.A.* 110 F9
Vernalis, *U.S.A.* 112 H5
Vernayaz, *Switz.* 22 D4
Verner, *Canada* 98 C3
Verneuil-sur-Avre, *France* 24 D7
Verneukpan, *S. Africa* 84 D3
Vernier, *Switz.* 22 D2
Vernon, *Canada* 100 C5
Vernon, *France* 24 C8
Vernon, *U.S.A.* 109 H5
Vernonia, *U.S.A.* 112 E3
Vero Beach, *U.S.A.* 105 M5
Véroia, *Greece* 39 J5
Verolanuova, *Italy* 32 C7
Véroli, *Italy* 34 A6
Verona, *Italy* 32 C8
Versailles, *France* 25 D9
Versalles, *Bolivia* 125 C5
Versoix, *Switz.* 22 D2
Vert, C., *Senegal* 78 C1
Vertou, *France* 24 E5
Vertus, *France* 25 D11
Verulam, *S. Africa* 85 D5
Verviers, *Belgium* 17 G7
Vervins, *France* 25 C10
Verzej, *Slovenia* 33 B13
Vescavoto, *France* 27 F13
Vesdre →, *Belgium* 17 G7
Veselí nad Lužnicí, *Czech.* 20 F4
Veselovskoye Vdkhr., *Russia* 43 G5
Veshenskaya, *Russia* 42 F5
Vesle →, *France* 25 C10
Vesoul, *France* 25 E13
Vessigebro, *Sweden* 11 H6
Vester Torup, *Denmark* 11 G3
Vesterålen, *Norway* 8 B16
Vestersche Veld, *Neths.* 16 C8
Vestfjorden, *Norway* 8 C15
Vestmannaeyjar, *Iceland* 8 E3
Vestmarka, *Norway* 10 E5
Vestone, *Italy* 32 C7
Vestsjællands Amtskommune □, *Denmark* 11 J5
Vestspitsbergen, *Svalbard* 4 B8
Vestvågøy, *Norway* 8 B15
Vesuvio, *Italy* 35 B7
Vesuvius, Mt. = Vesuvio, *Italy* 35 B7
Vesyegonsk, *Russia* 40 C9
Veszprém, *Hungary* 21 H7
Vésztő, *Hungary* 21 J11
Vetlanda, *Sweden* 9 H16
Vetluga, *Russia* 42 B7
Vetlugu →, *Russia* 42 B8
Vetluzhskiy, *Russia* 42 B7
Vetluzhskiy, *Russia* 42 A7
Vetovo, *Bulgaria* 38 F9
Vetralia, *Italy* 33 F9
Vettore, Mte., *Italy* 33 F10
Veurne, *Belgium* 17 F1
Vevey, *Switz.* 22 D3
Veynes, *France* 27 D9
Veys, *Iran* 65 D6
Vézelise, *France* 25 D13
Vézère →, *France* 26 D4
Vezirköprü, *Turkey* 66 B6
Vi Thanh, *Vietnam* 59 H5
Viacha, *Bolivia* 124 D4
Viadana, *Italy* 32 D7
Viamão, *Brazil* 127 C5
Viana, *Brazil* 122 B3
Viana, *Spain* 28 C2
Viana del Bollo, *Spain* 30 C3
Viana do Alentejo, *Portugal* 31 G3
Viana do Castelo, *Portugal* 30 D2
Vianden, *Belgium* 17 J8
Vianen, *Neths.* 16 E6
Vianna do Castelo □, *Portugal* 30 D2
Vianópolis, *Brazil* 123 E2
Viar →, *Spain* 31 H5
Viaréggio, *Italy* 32 E7
Viaur →, *France* 26 D5
Vibank, *Canada* 101 C8
Vibo Valéntia, *Italy* 35 D9
Viborg, *Denmark* 11 H3
Vibraye, *France* 24 D7
Vic, Étang de, *France* 26 E7
Vic-en-Bigorre, *France* 26 E4
Vic-Fézensac, *France* 26 E4
Vic-sur-Cère, *France* 26 D6
Vicenza, *Italy* 33 C8
Vich, *Spain* 28 D7
Vichada □, *Colombia* 120 C4
Vichada →, *Colombia* 120 C4
Vichuga, *Russia* 42 B5
Vichy, *France* 26 B7
Vicksburg, *Ariz., U.S.A.* 113 M13
Vicksburg, *Mich., U.S.A.* 104 D3
Vicksburg, *Miss., U.S.A.* 109 J9
Vico, L. di, *Italy* 33 F9
Vico del Gargano, *Italy* 35 A8
Viçosa, *Brazil* 122 C4
Viçosa do Ceará, *Brazil* 122 B3
Vicosoprano, *Switz.* 23 D9
Victor, *India* 62 J4
Victor, *Colo., U.S.A.* 108 F2
Victor, *N.Y., U.S.A.* 106 D7
Victor Harbor, *Australia* 91 F2
Victoria, *Argentina* 126 C3
Victoria, *Canada* 100 D4
Victoria, *Chile* 128 A2
Victoria, *Guinea* 78 C2
Victoria, *Malaysia* 56 C5
Victoria, *Malta* 37 C1
Victoria, *Phil.* 55 D4
Victoria, *Kans., U.S.A.* 108 F5
Victoria, *Tex., U.S.A.* 109 L6
Victoria □, *Australia* 91 F3
Victoria →, *Australia* 88 C4
Victoria, Grand L., *Canada* 98 C4
Victoria, L., *Africa* 82 C3
Victoria, L., *Australia* 91 E3
Victoria Beach, *Canada* 101 C9
Victoria de Durango, *Mexico* 114 C4
Victoria de las Tunas, *Cuba* 116 B4
Victoria Falls, *Zimbabwe* 83 F2
Victoria Harbour, *Canada* 98 D4
Victoria I., *Canada* 96 A8
Victoria Ld., *Antarctica* 5 D11
Victoria Nile →, *Uganda* 82 B3
Victoria Res., *Canada* 99 C8
Victoria River Downs, *Australia* 88 C5
Victoria Taungdeik, *Burma* 61 J18
Victoria West, *S. Africa* 84 E3
Victorias, *Phil.* 55 F5
Victoriaville, *Canada* 99 C5
Victorica, *Argentina* 126 D2
Victorville, *U.S.A.* 113 L9
Vicuña, *Chile* 126 C1
Vicuña Mackenna, *Argentina* 126 C3
Vidal, *U.S.A.* 113 L12
Vidal Junction, *U.S.A.* 113 L12
Vidalia, *U.S.A.* 105 J4
Vidauban, *France* 27 E10
Vídho, *Greece* 37 A3
Vidigueira, *Portugal* 31 G3
Vidin, *Bulgaria* 38 F5
Vidio, C., *Spain* 30 B4
Vidisha, *India* 62 H7
Vidzy, *Belarus* 9 J22
Viechtach, *Germany* 19 F8
Viedma, *Argentina* 128 B4
Viedma, L., *Argentina* 128 C2
Vieira, *Portugal* 30 D2
Viella, *Spain* 28 C5
Vielsalm, *Belgium* 17 H7
Vienenburg, *Germany* 18 D6
Vieng Pou Kha, *Laos* 58 B3
Vienna = Wien, *Austria* 21 G6
Vienna, *U.S.A.* 109 G10
Vienne, *France* 27 C8
Vienne □, *France* 26 B4
Vienne →, *France* 24 E7
Vientiane, *Laos* 58 D4
Vientos, Paso de los, *Caribbean* 117 C5
Vierlingsbeek, *Neths.* 17 E8
Viersen, *Germany* 18 D2
Vierwaldstättersee, *Switz.* 23 C7
Vierzon, *France* 25 E9
Vieste, *Italy* 35 A9
Vietnam ■, *Asia* 58 C5
Vieux-Boucau-les-Bains, *France* 26 E2
Vif, *France* 27 C9
Vigan, *Phil.* 55 C4
Vigévano, *Italy* 32 C5
Vigia, *Brazil* 122 B2
Vigía Chico, *Mexico* 115 D7
Víglas, Ákra, *Greece* 37 D9
Vignemale, Pic du, *France* 26 F3
Vigneulles-lès-Hattonchâtel, *France* 25 D12
Vignola, *Italy* 32 D8
Vigo, *Spain* 30 C2
Vigo, Ría de, *Spain* 30 C2
Vihiers, *France* 24 E6
Vijayawada, *India* 61 L12
Vijfhuizen, *Neths.* 16 D5
Vík, *Iceland* 8 E4
Vikeke, *Indonesia* 57 F7
Viken, *Sweden* 11 F8
Viking, *Canada* 100 C6
Vikna, *Norway* 8 D14
Viksjö, *Sweden* 10 B11
Vikulovo, *Russia* 44 D8
Vila da Maganja, *Mozam.* 83 F4
Vila de João Belo = Xai-Xai, *Mozam.* 85 D5
Vila de Rei, *Portugal* 31 F2
Vila do Bispo, *Portugal* 31 H2
Vila do Chibuto, *Mozam.* 85 C5
Vila do Conde, *Portugal* 30 D2
Vila Franca de Xira, *Portugal* 31 G2
Vila Gamito, *Mozam.* 83 E3
Vila Gomes da Costa, *Mozam.* 85 C5
Vila Machado, *Mozam.* 83 F3
Vila Mouzinho, *Mozam.* 83 E3
Vila Nova de Foscôa, *Portugal* 30 D3
Vila Nova de Ourém, *Portugal* 31 F2
Vila Novo de Gaia, *Portugal* 30 D2
Vila Pouca de Aguiar, *Portugal* 30 D3
Vila Real, *Portugal* 30 D3
Vila Real de Santo António, *Portugal* 31 H3
Vila Vasco da Gama, *Mozam.* 83 E3
Vila Velha, *Amapá, Brazil* 121 C7
Vila Velha, *Espírito Santo, Brazil* 123 F3
Vila Viçosa, *Portugal* 31 G3
Vilaboa, *Spain* 30 C2
Vilaine →, *France* 24 E4
Vilanandro, Tanjona, *Madag.* 85 B7
Vilanculos, *Mozam.* 85 C6
Vilar Formosa, *Portugal* 30 E4
Vilareal □, *Portugal* 30 D3
Vilaseca-Salou, *Spain* 28 D6
Vilcabamba, Cordillera, *Peru* 124 C3
Vilcanchos, *Peru* 124 C3
Vileyka, *Belarus* 40 E4
Vilhelmina, *Sweden* 8 D17
Vilhena, *Brazil* 125 C5
Viliga, *Russia* 45 C16
Viliya →, *Lithuania* 9 J21
Viljandi, *Estonia* 9 G21
Vilkitskogo, Proliv, *Russia* 45 B11
Vilkovo = Vylkove, *Ukraine* 41 K5
Villa Abecia, *Bolivia* 126 A2
Villa Ahumada, *Mexico* 114 A3
Villa Ana, *Argentina* 126 B4
Villa Ángela, *Argentina* 126 B3
Villa Bella, *Bolivia* 125 C4
Villa Bens = Tarfaya, *Morocco* 74 C2
Villa Cañás, *Argentina* 126 C3
Villa Carlos, *Spain* 36 B11
Villa Cisneros = Dakhla, *W. Sahara* 74 D1
Villa Colón, *Argentina* 126 C2
Villa Constitución, *Argentina* 126 C3
Villa de Cura, *Venezuela* 120 A4
Villa de María, *Argentina* 126 B3
Villa del Rosario, *Venezuela* 120 A3
Villa Dolores, *Argentina* 126 C2
Villa Frontera, *Mexico* 114 B4
Villa Guillermina, *Argentina* 126 B4
Villa Hayes, *Paraguay* 126 B4
Villa Iris, *Argentina* 126 D3
Villa Juárez, *Mexico* 114 B4
Villa María, *Argentina* 126 C3
Villa Mazán, *Argentina* 126 B2
Villa Minozzo, *Italy* 32 D7
Villa Montes, *Bolivia* 126 A3
Villa Ocampo, *Argentina* 126 B4
Villa Ocampo, *Mexico* 114 B3
Villa Ojo de Agua, *Argentina* 126 B3
Villa San Giovanni, *Italy* 35 D8
Villa San José, *Argentina* 126 C4
Villa San Martín, *Argentina* 126 B3
Villa Santina, *Italy* 33 B9
Villa Unión, *Mexico* 114 C3
Villablino, *Spain* 30 C4
Villacañas, *Spain* 28 F1
Villacarriedo, *Spain* 28 B1
Villacarrillo, *Spain* 29 G1
Villacastín, *Spain* 30 E6
Villach, *Austria* 21 J3
Villacidro, *Italy* 34 C1
Villada, *Spain* 30 C6
Villadiego, *Spain* 30 C6
Villadóssola, *Italy* 32 B5
Villafeliche, *Spain* 28 D3
Villafranca, *Spain* 28 C3
Villafranca de los Barros, *Spain* 31 G4
Villafranca de los Caballeros, *Baleares, Spain* 36 B10
Villafranca de los Caballeros, *Toledo, Spain* 29 F1

Villafranca del Bierzo, *Spain* 30 C4
Villafranca del Cid, *Spain* 28 E4
Villafranca del Panadés, *Spain* 28 D6
Villafranca di Verona, *Italy* 32 C7
Villagarcía de Arosa, *Spain* 30 C2
Villagrán, *Mexico* 115 C5
Villaguay, *Argentina* 126 C4
Villaharta, *Spain* 31 G6
Villahermosa, *Mexico* 115 D6
Villahermosa, *Spain* 29 G2
Villaines-la-Juhel, *France* 24 D6
Villajoyosa, *Spain* 29 G4
Villalba, *Spain* 30 B3
Villalba de Guardo, *Spain* 30 C6
Villalcampo, Pantano de, *Spain* 30 D4
Villalón de Campos, *Spain* 30 C5
Villalpando, *Spain* 30 D5
Villaluenga, *Spain* 30 E7
Villamanán, *Spain* 30 C5
Villamartín, *Spain* 31 J5
Villamayor, *Spain* 28 F2
Villamblard, *France* 26 C4
Villanova Monteleone, *Italy* 34 B1
Villanueva, *Colombia* 120 A3
Villanueva, *U.S.A.* 111 J11
Villanueva de Castellón, *Spain* 29 F4
Villanueva de Córdoba, *Spain* 31 G6
Villanueva de la Fuente, *Spain* 29 G2
Villanueva de la Serena, *Spain* 31 G5
Villanueva de la Sierra, *Spain* 30 E4
Villanueva de los Castillejos, *Spain* 31 H3
Villanueva del Arzobispo, *Spain* 29 G1
Villanueva del Duque, *Spain* 31 G5
Villanueva del Fresno, *Spain* 31 G3
Villanueva y Geltrú, *Spain* 28 D6
Villaodrid, *Spain* 30 B3
Villaputzu, *Italy* 34 C2
Villar del Arzobispo, *Spain* 28 F4
Villar del Rey, *Spain* 31 F4
Villarcayo, *Spain* 28 C1
Villard-Bonnot, *France* 27 C9
Villard-de-Lans, *France* 27 C9
Villarino de los Aires, *Spain* 30 D4
Villarosa, *Italy* 35 E7
Villarramiel, *Spain* 30 C6
Villarreal, *Spain* 28 F4
Villarrica, *Chile* 128 A2
Villarrica, *Paraguay* 126 B4
Villarrobledo, *Spain* 29 F2
Villarroya de la Sierra, *Spain* 28 D3
Villarrubia de los Ojos, *Spain* 29 F1
Villars-les-Dombes, *France* 27 B9
Villarta de San Juan, *Spain* 29 F1
Villasayas, *Spain* 28 D2
Villaseca de los Gamitos, *Spain* 30 D4
Villastar, *Spain* 28 E3
Villatobas, *Spain* 28 F1
Villavicencio, *Argentina* 126 C2
Villavicencio, *Colombia* 120 C3
Villaviciosa, *Spain* 30 B5
Villazón, *Bolivia* 126 A2
Ville-Marie, *Canada* 98 C4
Ville Platte, *U.S.A.* 109 K8
Villedieu-les-Poêlles, *France* 24 D5
Villefort, *France* 26 D7
Villefranche-de-Lauragais, *France* 26 E5
Villefranche-de-Rouergue, *France* 26 D6
Villefranche-du-Périgord, *France* 26 D5
Villefranche-sur-Cher, *France* 25 E8
Villefranche-sur-Saône, *France* 27 C8
Villegrande, *Bolivia* 125 D5
Villel, *Spain* 28 E3
Villemaur-sur-Vanne, *France* 25 D10
Villemur-sur-Tarn, *France* 26 E5
Villena, *Spain* 29 G4
Villenauxe-la-Grande, *France* 25 D10
Villenave-d'Ornon, *France* 26 D3
Villeneuve, *Italy* 32 C4
Villeneuve, *Switz.* 22 D3
Villeneuve-l'Archevêque, *France* 25 D10
Villeneuve-lès-Avignon, *France* 27 E8
Villeneuve-St.-Georges, *France* 25 D9
Villeneuve-sur-Allier, *France* 26 B7
Villeneuve-sur-Lot, *France* 26 D4
Villeréal, *France* 26 D4
Villers-Bocage, *France* 24 C6
Villers-Bretonneux, *France* 25 C9
Villers-Cotterêts, *France* 25 C10
Villers-le-Bouillet, *Belgium* 17 G6
Villers-le-Gambon, *Belgium* 17 H5
Villers-sur-Mer, *France* 24 C6
Villersexel, *France* 25 E13
Villerupt, *France* 25 C12
Villerville, *France* 24 C7
Villiers, *S. Africa* 85 D4
Villingen-Schwenningen, *Germany* 19 G4
Villisca, *U.S.A.* 108 E7
Vilna, *Canada* 100 C6
Vilnius, *Lithuania* 9 J21
Vils →, *Germany* 19 G9
Vilsbiburg, *Germany* 19 G8
Vilshofen, *Germany* 19 G9
Vilusi, *Montenegro, Yug.* 21 N8
Vilvoorde, *Belgium* 17 G4
Vilyuy →, *Russia* 45 C13
Vilyuysk, *Russia* 45 C13
Vimercate, *Italy* 32 C6
Vimiosa, *Portugal* 30 D4
Vimoutiers, *France* 24 D7
Vimperk, *Czech.* 20 F3
Viña del Mar, *Chile* 126 C1
Vinaroz, *Spain* 28 E5
Vincennes, *U.S.A.* 104 F2
Vincent, *U.S.A.* 113 L8
Vinces, *Ecuador* 120 D2
Vinchina, *Argentina* 126 B2
Vindelälven →, *Sweden* 8 E18
Vindeln, *Sweden* 8 D18
Vinderup, *Denmark* 11 H2
Vindhya Ra., *India* 62 H7
Vineland, *U.S.A.* 104 F8
Vinga, *Romania* 38 D4
Vingnes, *Norway* 10 C4
Vinh, *Vietnam* 58 C5
Vinh Linh, *Vietnam* 58 D6
Vinh Long, *Vietnam* 59 G5
Vinh Yen, *Vietnam* 58 B5
Vinhais, *Portugal* 30 D3
Vinica, *Croatia* 33 B13
Vinica, *Slovenia* 33 C12
Vinita, *U.S.A.* 109 G7
Vinkeveen, *Neths.* 16 D5
Vinkovci, *Croatia* 21 K8
Vinnitsa = Vinnytsya, *Ukraine* 41 H5
Vinnytsya, *Ukraine* 41 H5
Vinstra, *Norway* 10 C3
Vinton, *Calif., U.S.A.* 112 F6
Vinton, *Iowa, U.S.A.* 108 D8
Vinton, *La., U.S.A.* 109 K8
Vinţu de Jos, *Romania* 38 D6
Viöl, *Germany* 18 A5
Vipava, *Slovenia* 33 C10
Vipiteno, *Italy* 33 B8
Vir, *Croatia* 33 D12
Virac, *Phil.* 55 E6
Virachei, *Cambodia* 58 F6
Virago Sd., *Canada* 100 C2
Viramgam, *India* 62 H5
Viranşehir, *Turkey* 67 D8
Virden, *Canada* 101 D8
Vire, *France* 24 D6
Vire →, *France* 24 C5
Virgem da Lapa, *Brazil* 123 E3
Vírgenes, C., *Argentina* 128 D3
Virgin →, *Canada* 101 B7
Virgin →, *U.S.A.* 111 H6
Virgin Gorda, *Virgin Is.* 117 C7
Virgin Is. (British) ■, *W. Indies* 117 C7
Virgin Is. (U.S.) ■, *W. Indies* 117 C7
Virginia, *S. Africa* 84 D4
Virginia, *U.S.A.* 108 B8
Virginia □, *U.S.A.* 104 G7
Virginia Beach, *U.S.A.* 104 G8
Virginia City, *Mont., U.S.A.* 110 D8
Virginia City, *Nev., U.S.A.* 112 F7
Virginia Falls, *Canada* 100 A3
Virginiatown, *Canada* 98 C4
Virieu-le-Grand, *France* 27 C9
Viroqua, *U.S.A.* 108 D9
Virovitica, *Croatia* 21 K7
Virton, *Belgium* 17 J7
Virú, *Peru* 124 B2
Virudunagar, *India* 60 Q10
Vis, *Croatia* 33 E13
Vis Kanal, *Croatia* 33 E13
Visalia, *U.S.A.* 111 H4
Visayan Sea, *Phil.* 55 F5
Visby, *Sweden* 9 H18
Viscount Melville Sd., *Canada* 4 B2
Visé, *Belgium* 17 G7
Višegrad, *Bos.-H.* 21 M9
Viseu, *Brazil* 122 B2
Viseu, *Portugal* 30 E3
Viseu □, *Portugal* 30 E3
Vişeu de Sus, *Romania* 38 B7
Vishakhapatnam, *India* 61 L13
Viskafors, *Sweden* 11 G6
Visnagar, *India* 62 H5
Višnja Gora, *Slovenia* 33 C11
Viso, Mte., *Italy* 32 D4
Viso del Marqués, *Spain* 29 G1
Visoko, *Bos.-H.* 21 M8
Visokoi I., *Antarctica* 5 B1
Visp, *Switz.* 22 D5
Vispa →, *Switz.* 22 D5
Visselhövede, *Germany* 18 C5
Vissoie, *Switz.* 22 D5
Vista, *U.S.A.* 113 M9
Vistula = Wisła →, *Poland* 20 A8
Vit →, *Bulgaria* 38 F7
Vitanje, *Slovenia* 33 B12
Vitebsk = Vitsyebsk, *Belarus* 40 E6
Viterbo, *Italy* 33 F9
Viti Levu, *Fiji* 87 C7
Vitigudino, *Spain* 30 D4
Vitim, *Russia* 45 D12
Vitim →, *Russia* 45 D12
Vitória, *Brazil* 123 F3
Vitoria, *Spain* 28 C2
Vitória da Conquista, *Brazil* 123 D3
Vitória de São Antão, *Brazil* 122 C4
Vitorino Friere, *Brazil* 122 B2
Vitré, *France* 24 D5
Vitry-le-François, *France* 25 D11
Vitsi, Óros, *Greece* 39 J4
Vitsyebsk, *Belarus* 40 E6
Vitteaux, *France* 25 E11
Vittel, *France* 25 D12
Vittória, *Italy* 35 F7
Vittório Véneto, *Italy* 33 C9
Vivario, *France* 27 F13
Vivegnis, *Belgium* 17 G7
Viver, *Spain* 28 F4
Vivero, *Spain* 30 B3
Viviers, *France* 27 D8
Vivonne, *France* 26 B4
Vizcaíno, Desierto de, *Mexico* 114 B2
Vizcaíno, Sierra, *Mexico* 114 B2
Vizcaya □, *Spain* 28 B2
Vize, *Turkey* 66 B2
Vizianagaram, *India* 61 K13
Vizille, *France* 27 C9
Viziñada, *Croatia* 33 C10
Viziru, *Romania* 38 E10
Vizovice, *Czech.* 20 F7
Vizzini, *Italy* 35 E7
Vlaardingen, *Neths.* 16 E4
Vlădeasa, *Romania* 38 C5
Vladikavkaz, *Russia* 43 J7
Vladimir, *Russia* 42 B5
Vladimir Volynskiy = Volodymyr-Volynskyy, *Ukraine* 41 G3
Vladimirovac, *Serbia, Yug.* 21 K10
Vladimirovka, *Russia* 43 F8
Vladimirovka, *Kazakstan* 42 E10
Vladislavovka, *Ukraine* 41 K8
Vladivostok, *Russia* 45 E14
Vlamertinge, *Belgium* 17 G1
Vlasenica, *Bos.-H.* 21 L8
Vlasinsko Jezero, *Serbia, Yug.* 21 N12
Vleuten, *Neths.* 16 D6
Vlieland, *Neths.* 16 B5
Vliestroom, *Neths.* 16 B6
Vlijmen, *Neths.* 17 E6
Vlissingen, *Neths.* 17 F3
Vlóra, *Albania* 39 J2
Vlorës, Gjiri i, *Albania* 39 J2
Vltava →, *Czech.* 20 E4
Vo Dat, *Vietnam* 59 G6
Vobarno, *Italy* 32 C7
Voćin, *Croatia* 21 K7
Vodice, *Croatia* 33 E12
Vodnjan, *Croatia* 33 D10
Vogelkop = Doberai, Jazirah, *Indonesia* 57 E8
Vogelsberg, *Germany* 18 E5
Voghera, *Italy* 32 D6
Vohibinany, *Madag.* 85 B8
Vohimarina, *Madag.* 85 A9
Vohimena, Tanjon' i, *Madag.* 85 D8
Vohipeno, *Madag.* 85 C8
Voi, *Kenya* 82 C4
Void, *France* 25 D12
Voiron, *France* 27 C9
Voisey B., *Canada* 99 A7
Voitsberg, *Austria* 21 H5
Voiviïs Límni, *Greece* 39 K5
Vojens, *Denmark* 11 J3
Vojmsjön, *Sweden* 8 D17
Vojnić, *Croatia* 33 C12
Vojnik, *Italy* 33 B12
Vokhtoga, *Russia* 40 C11
Volborg, *U.S.A.* 108 C2
Volcano Is. = Kazan-Rettō, *Pac. Oc.* 92 E6
Volchansk = Vovchansk, *Ukraine* 41 G9
Volchayevka, *Russia* 45 E14
Volchya →, *Ukraine* 41 H8
Volda, *Norway* 9 E12
Volendam, *Neths.* 16 D6
Volga, *Russia* 42 A4
Volga →, *Russia* 43 G9
Volga Hts. = Privolzhskaya Vozvyshennost, *Russia* 42 E7
Volgo-Baltiyskiy Kanal, *Russia* 40 B9
Volgo-Donskoy Kanal, *Russia* 43 F7
Volgodonsk, *Russia* 43 G6
Volgograd, *Russia* 43 F7
Volgogradskoye Vdkhr., *Russia* 42 E8
Volgorechensk, *Russia* 42 B5
Volkach, *Germany* 19 F6
Volkerak, *Neths.* 17 E4
Volkhov, *Russia* 40 C7
Volkhov →, *Russia* 40 B7
Völklingen, *Germany* 19 F2
Volkovysk = Vawkavysk, *Belarus* 41 F3
Volksrust, *S. Africa* 85 D4
Vollenhove, *Neths.* 16 C7
Volnansk, *Ukraine* 41 H8
Volnovakha, *Ukraine* 41 J9
Volochanka, *Russia* 45 B10
Volodarsk, *Russia* 42 B6
Volodymyr-Volynskyy, *Ukraine* 41 G3
Vologda, *Russia* 40 C10
Volokolamsk, *Russia* 42 B2
Volokonovka, *Russia* 42 E3
Vólos, *Greece* 39 K5
Volosovo, *Russia* 40 C5
Volovets, *Ukraine* 41 H2
Volovo, *Russia* 42 D4
Volozhin = Valozhyn, *Belarus* 40 E4
Volsk, *Russia* 42 D8
Volta →, *Ghana* 79 D5
Volta, L., *Ghana* 79 D5
Volta Blanche = White Volta →, *Ghana* 79 D4
Volta Redonda, *Brazil* 123 F3
Voltaire, C., *Australia* 88 B4
Volterra, *Italy* 32 E7
Voltri, *Italy* 32 D5
Volturara Appula, *Italy* 35 A8
Volturno →, *Italy* 34 A6
Volubilis, *Morocco* 74 B3
Volvo, *Australia* 91 E3
Volzhsk, *Russia* 42 C9
Volzhskiy, *Russia* 43 F7
Vondrozo, *Madag.* 85 C8
Voorburg, *Neths.* 16 D4
Voorne Putten, *Neths.* 16 E4
Voorst, *Neths.* 16 D8
Voorthuizen, *Neths.* 16 D7
Vopnafjörður, *Iceland* 8 D6
Vóras Óros, *Greece* 39 J4
Vorbasse, *Denmark* 11 J3
Vorden, *Neths.* 16 D8
Vorderrhein →, *Switz.* 23 C8
Vordingborg, *Denmark* 11 K5
Voreppe, *France* 27 C9
Voríai Sporádhes, *Greece* 39 K6
Vórios Evvoïkos Kólpos, *Greece* 39 L6
Vorkuta, *Russia* 44 C7
Vorma →, *Norway* 10 D5
Vormsi, *Estonia* 9 G20
Vorona →, *Russia* 42 E6
Voronezh, *Russia* 42 E4
Voronezh, *Ukraine* 41 G7
Voronezh →, *Russia* 42 E4
Vorontsovo-Aleksandrovskoye = Zelenokumsk, *Russia* 43 H6
Voroshilovgrad = Luhansk, *Ukraine* 41 H10
Voroshilovsk = Alchevsk, *Ukraine* 41 H10
Vorovskoye, *Russia* 45 D16
Vorselaar, *Belgium* 17 F5
Vorskla →, *Ukraine* 41 H8
Võrts Järv, *Estonia* 9 G22
Võru, *Estonia* 9 H22
Vosges, *France* 25 D14
Vosges □, *France* 25 D13
Voskopoja, *Albania* 39 J3
Voskresensk, *Russia* 42 C4
Voskresenskoye, *Russia* 42 B7
Voss, *Norway* 9 F12
Vosselaar, *Belgium* 17 F5
Vostok I., *Kiribati* 93 J12
Vouga →, *Portugal* 30 E2
Vouillé, *France* 24 F7
Vouvray, *France* 24 E7
Vouvry, *Switz.* 22 D3
Voúxa, Ákra, *Greece* 37 D5
Vouzela, *Portugal* 30 E2
Vouziers, *France* 25 C11
Vovchansk, *Ukraine* 41 G9
Voves, *France* 25 D8
Voxna, *Sweden* 10 C9
Vozhe Ozero, *Russia* 40 B10
Vozhega, *Russia* 40 B11
Voznesenka, *Russia* 45 D10
Voznesensk, *Ukraine* 41 J6
Voznesenye, *Russia* 40 B8
Vrådal, *Norway* 10 E2
Vrakhnéïka, *Greece* 39 L4
Vrancei, Munţii, *Romania* 38 D9
Vrangelya, Ostrov, *Russia* 45 B19
Vranica, *Bos.-H.* 21 M7
Vranje, *Serbia, Yug.* 21 N11
Vransko, *Slovenia* 33 B11
Vratsa, *Bulgaria* 38 F6
Vrbas, *Serbia, Yug.* 21 K9
Vrbas →, *Bos.-H.* 21 K7
Vrbnik, *Croatia* 33 C11
Vrbovec, *Croatia* 33 C13
Vrbovsko, *Croatia* 33 C12
Vrchlabí, *Czech.* 20 E5
Vrede, *S. Africa* 85 D4
Vredefort, *S. Africa* 84 D4
Vredenburg, *S. Africa* 84 E2
Vredendal, *S. Africa* 84 E2
Vreeswijk, *Neths.* 16 D6
Vrena, *Sweden* 11 F10
Vrgorac, *Croatia* 21 M7
Vrhnika, *Slovenia* 33 C11
Vridi, *Ivory C.* 78 D4
Vries, *Neths.* 16 B9
Vriezenveen, *Neths.* 16 D9
Vrindavan, *India* 62 F7
Vríses, *Greece* 37 D6
Vrnograč, *Bos.-H.* 33 C12
Vroomshoop, *Neths.* 16 D9
Vršac, *Serbia, Yug.* 21 K11
Vrsacki Kanal, *Serbia, Yug.* 21 K11
Vryburg, *S. Africa* 84 D3
Vryheid, *S. Africa* 85 D5
Vsetín, *Czech.* 20 F8
Vu Liet, *Vietnam* 58 C5
Vucha →, *Bulgaria* 39 G7
Vught, *Neths.* 17 E6
Vukovar, *Croatia* 21 K8
Vulcan, *Canada* 100 C6
Vulcan, *U.S.A.* 104 C2
Vulcaneşti, *Moldova* 41 K5
Vulcano, *Italy* 35 D7
Vŭlchedruma, *Bulgaria* 38 F6
Vulci, *Italy* 33 F8
Vulkaneshty = Vulcaneşti, *Moldova* 41 K5
Vunduzi →, *Mozam.* 83 F3
Vung Tau, *Vietnam* 59 G6
Vŭrbitsa, *Bulgaria* 38 G9
Vyartsilya, *Russia* 40 A6
Vyatka = Kirov, *Russia* 44 D5
Vyatka →, *Russia* 42 C10
Vyatskiye Polyany, *Russia* 42 B10
Vyazemskiy, *Russia* 45 E14
Vyazma, *Russia* 42 C2
Vyazniki, *Russia* 42 B6
Vyborg, *Russia* 40 B5
Vychegda →, *Russia* 44 C5
Vychodné Beskydy, *Europe* 41 H2
Vyerkhnyadzvinsk, *Belarus* 40 E4
Vyksa, *Russia* 42 C6
Vylkove, *Ukraine* 41 K5
Vynohradiv, *Ukraine* 41 H2
Vyrnwy, L., *U.K.* 12 E4
Vyshniy Volochek, *Russia* 42 B2
Vyškov, *Czech.* 20 F6
Vysoké Mýto, *Czech.* 20 F6
Vysokovsk, *Russia* 42 B3
Vytegra, *Russia* 40 B9

W

W.A.C. Bennett Dam, *Canada* 100 B4
Wa, *Ghana* 78 C4
Waal →, *Neths.* 16 E6
Waalwijk, *Neths.* 17 E6
Waarschoot, *Belgium* 17 F3
Waasmunster, *Belgium* 17 F4
Wabakimi L., *Canada* 98 B2
Wabana, *Canada* 99 C9
Wabasca, *Canada* 100 B6
Wabash, *U.S.A.* 104 E3
Wabash →, *U.S.A.* 104 G1
Wabeno, *U.S.A.* 104 C1
Wabi →, *Ethiopia* 77 F5
Wabigoon L., *Canada* 101 D10
Wabowden, *Canada* 101 C9
Wąbrzeźno, *Poland* 20 B8
Wabu Hu, *China* 53 A11
Wabuk Pt., *Canada* 98 A2
Wabush, *Canada* 99 B6
Wabuska, *U.S.A.* 110 G4
Wachtebeke, *Belgium* 17 F3
Wächtersbach, *Germany* 19 E5
Waco, *U.S.A.* 109 K6
Waconichi, L., *Canada* 98 B5
Wad Ban Naqa, *Sudan* 77 D3
Wad Banda, *Sudan* 77 E2
Wad el Haddad, *Sudan* 77 E3
Wad en Nau, *Sudan* 77 E3
Wad Hamid, *Sudan* 77 D3
Wâd Medanî, *Sudan* 77 E3
Wad Thana, *Pakistan* 62 F2
Wadai, *Africa* 70 E5
Wadayama, *Japan* 49 G7
Waddeneilanden, *Neths.* 16 B6
Waddenzee, *Neths.* 16 B6
Wadderin Hill, *Australia* 89 F2
Waddington, *U.S.A.* 107 B9
Waddington, Mt., *Canada* 100 C3
Waddinxveen, *Neths.* 16 D5
Waddy Pt., *Australia* 91 C5
Wadena, *Canada* 101 C8
Wadena, *U.S.A.* 108 B7
Wädenswil, *Switz.* 23 B7
Wadesboro, *U.S.A.* 105 H5
Wadhams, *Canada* 100 C3
Wādī as Sīr, *Jordan* 69 D4
Wadi Gemâl, *Egypt* 76 C4
Wadi Halfa, *Sudan* 76 C3
Wadian, *China* 53 A9
Wadowice, *Poland* 20 F9
Wadsworth, *U.S.A.* 110 G4
Waegwan, *S. Korea* 51 G15
Wafrah, *Si. Arabia* 64 D5
Wagenberg, *Neths.* 17 E5
Wageningen, *Neths.* 16 E7
Wageningen, *Surinam* 121 B6
Wager B., *Canada* 97 B11
Wager Bay, *Canada* 97 B10
Wagga Wagga, *Australia* 91 F4
Waghete, *Indonesia* 57 E9
Wagin, *Australia* 89 F2
Wagon Mound, *U.S.A.* 109 G2
Wagoner, *U.S.A.* 109 G7
Wagrowiec, *Poland* 20 C7
Wah, *Pakistan* 62 C5
Wahai, *Indonesia* 57 E7
Wahiawa, *U.S.A.* 102 H15

Wâḫid, *Egypt* 69 E1
Wahnai, *Afghan.* 62 C1
Wahoo, *U.S.A.* 108 E6
Wahpeton, *U.S.A.* 108 B6
Wai, Koh, *Cambodia* 59 H4
Waiau →, *N.Z.* 87 K4
Waibeem, *Indonesia* 57 E8
Waiblingen, *Germany* 19 G5
Waidhofen, *Niederösterreich, Austria* 20 G5
Waidhofen, *Niederösterreich, Austria* 21 H4
Waigeo, *Indonesia* 57 E8
Waihi, *N.Z.* 87 G5
Waihou →, *N.Z.* 87 G5
Waika, *Zaïre* 82 C2
Waikabubak, *Indonesia* 57 F5
Waikari, *N.Z.* 87 K4
Waikato →, *N.Z.* 87 G5
Waikerie, *Australia* 91 E2
Waikokopu, *N.Z.* 87 H6
Waikouaiti, *N.Z.* 87 L3
Waimakariri →, *N.Z.* 87 K4
Waimate, *N.Z.* 87 L3
Waimes, *Belgium* 17 H8
Wainganga →, *India* 60 K11
Waingapu, *Indonesia* 57 F6
Waini →, *Guyana* 121 B6
Wainwright, *Canada* 101 C6
Wainwright, *U.S.A.* 96 A3
Waiouru, *N.Z.* 87 H5
Waipara, *N.Z.* 87 K4
Waipawa, *N.Z.* 87 H6
Waipiro, *N.Z.* 87 H7
Waipu, *N.Z.* 87 F5
Waipukurau, *N.Z.* 87 J6
Wairakei, *N.Z.* 87 H6
Wairarapa, L., *N.Z.* 87 J5
Wairoa, *N.Z.* 87 H6
Waitaki →, *N.Z.* 87 L3
Waitara, *N.Z.* 87 H5
Waitsburg, *U.S.A.* 110 C5
Waiuku, *N.Z.* 87 G5
Wajima, *Japan* 49 F8
Wajir, *Kenya* 82 B5
Wajir □, *Kenya* 82 B5
Wakasa, *Japan* 49 G7
Wakasa-Wan, *Japan* 49 G7
Wakatipu, L., *N.Z.* 87 L2
Wakaw, *Canada* 101 C7
Wakayama, *Japan* 49 G7
Wakayama-ken □, *Japan* 49 H7
Wake Forest, *U.S.A.* 105 H6
Wake I., *Pac. Oc.* 92 F8
Wakefield, *N.Z.* 87 J4
Wakefield, *U.K.* 12 D6
Wakefield, *Mass., U.S.A.* 107 D13
Wakefield, *Mich., U.S.A.* 108 B10
Wakeham Bay = Maricourt, *Canada* 97 C12
Wakema, *Burma* 61 L19
Wakkanai, *Japan* 48 B10
Wakkerstroom, *S. Africa* 85 D5
Wakool, *Australia* 91 F3
Wakool →, *Australia* 91 F3
Wakre, *Indonesia* 57 E8
Wakuach L., *Canada* 99 A6
Walamba, *Zambia* 83 E2
Wałbrzych, *Poland* 20 E6
Walbury Hill, *U.K.* 13 F6
Walcha, *Australia* 91 E5
Walcheren, *Neths.* 17 E3
Walcott, *U.S.A.* 110 F10
Wałcz, *Poland* 20 B6
Wald, *Switz.* 23 B7
Waldbröl, *Germany* 18 E3
Waldburg Ra., *Australia* 88 D2
Waldeck, *Germany* 18 D5
Walden, *Colo., U.S.A.* 110 F10
Walden, *N.Y., U.S.A.* 107 E10
Waldenburg, *Switz.* 22 B5
Waldport, *U.S.A.* 110 D1
Waldron, *U.S.A.* 109 H7
Waldshut, *Germany* 19 H4
Walembele, *Ghana* 78 C4
Walensee, *Switz.* 23 B8
Walenstadt, *Switz.* 23 B8
Wales □, *U.K.* 13 E4
Walewale, *Ghana* 79 C4
Walgett, *Australia* 91 E4
Walgreen Coast, *Antarctica* 5 D15
Walhalla, *Australia* 91 F4
Walhalla, *U.S.A.* 101 D9
Walker, *U.S.A.* 108 B7
Walker L., *Man., Canada* 101 C9
Walker L., *Qué., Canada* 99 B6
Walker L., *U.S.A.* 110 G4
Walkerston, *Australia* 90 C4
Walkerton, *Canada* 106 B3
Wall, *U.S.A.* 108 C3
Walla Walla, *U.S.A.* 110 C4
Wallabadah, *Australia* 90 B3
Wallace, *Idaho, U.S.A.* 110 C6
Wallace, *N.C., U.S.A.* 105 H7
Wallace, *Nebr., U.S.A.* 108 E4
Wallaceburg, *Canada* 98 D3
Wallachia = Valahia, *Romania* 38 E8
Wallal, *Australia* 91 D4
Wallal Downs, *Australia* 88 C3
Wallambin, L., *Australia* 89 F2
Wallaroo, *Australia* 91 E2
Wallasey, *U.K.* 12 D4
Walldürn, *Germany* 19 F5
Wallerawang, *Australia* 91 E5
Wallhallow, *Australia* 90 B2
Wallingford, *U.S.A.* 107 E12
Wallis & Futuna, Is., *Pac. Oc.* 92 J10
Wallisellen, *Switz.* 23 B7
Wallowa, *U.S.A.* 110 D5
Wallowa Mts., *U.S.A.* 110 D5
Wallsend, *Australia* 91 E5
Wallsend, *U.K.* 12 C6
Wallula, *U.S.A.* 110 C4
Wallumbilla, *Australia* 91 D4
Walmsley, L., *Canada* 101 A7
Walney, I. of, *U.K.* 12 C4
Walnut Creek, *U.S.A.* 112 H4
Walnut Ridge, *U.S.A.* 109 G9
Walsall, *U.K.* 13 E6
Walsenburg, *U.S.A.* 109 G2
Walsh, *U.S.A.* 109 G3
Walsh →, *Australia* 90 B3
Walsh P.O., *Australia* 90 B3
Walshoutem, *Belgium* 17 G6
Walsrode, *Germany* 18 C5
Walterboro, *U.S.A.* 105 J5
Walters, *U.S.A.* 109 H5
Waltershausen, *Germany* 18 E6
Waltham, *U.S.A.* 107 D13
Waltham Station, *Canada* 98 C4
Waltman, *U.S.A.* 110 E10
Walton, *U.S.A.* 107 D9
Walvisbaai, *Namibia* 84 C1
Wamba, *Kenya* 82 B4
Wamba, *Zaïre* 82 B2
Wamego, *U.S.A.* 108 F6
Wamena, *Indonesia* 57 E9
Wamulan, *Indonesia* 57 E7
Wan Xian, *China* 50 E8
Wana, *Pakistan* 62 C3
Wanaaring, *Australia* 91 D3
Wanaka, *N.Z.* 87 L2
Wanaka L., *N.Z.* 87 L2
Wan'an, *China* 53 D10
Wanapiri, *Indonesia* 57 E9
Wanapitei L., *Canada* 98 C3
Wanbi, *Australia* 91 E3
Wandaik, *Guyana* 121 C6
Wandarrie, *Australia* 89 E2
Wandel Sea = McKinley Sea, *Arctic* 4 A7
Wanderer, *Zimbabwe* 83 F3
Wandoan, *Australia* 91 D4
Wandre, *Belgium* 17 G7
Wanfercée-Baulet, *Belgium* 17 H5
Wanfu, *China* 51 D12
Wang →, *Thailand* 58 D2
Wang Kai, *Sudan* 77 F2
Wang Noi, *Thailand* 58 E3
Wang Saphung, *Thailand* 58 D3
Wang Thong, *Thailand* 58 D3
Wanga, *Zaïre* 82 B2
Wangal, *Indonesia* 57 F8
Wanganella, *Australia* 91 F3
Wanganui, *N.Z.* 87 H5
Wangaratta, *Australia* 91 F4
Wangary, *Australia* 91 E2
Wangcang, *China* 52 A6
Wangdu, *China* 50 E8
Wangerooge, *Germany* 18 B3
Wangi, *Kenya* 82 C5
Wangiwangi, *Indonesia* 57 F6
Wangjiang, *China* 53 B11
Wangmo, *China* 52 E6
Wangqing, *China* 51 C15
Wankaner, *India* 62 H4
Wanless, *Canada* 101 C8
Wannian, *China* 53 C11
Wanon Niwat, *Thailand* 58 D4
Wanquan, *China* 50 D8
Wanrong, *China* 50 G6
Wanshan, *China* 52 D7
Wanshengchang, *China* 52 C6
Wanssum, *Neths.* 17 E8
Wanxian, *China* 52 B7
Wanyuan, *China* 52 A7
Wanzai, *China* 53 C10
Wanze, *Belgium* 17 G6
Wapakoneta, *U.S.A.* 104 E3
Wapato, *U.S.A.* 110 C3
Wapawekka L., *Canada* 101 C8
Wapikopa L., *Canada* 98 B2
Wappingers Falls, *U.S.A.* 107 E11
Wapsipinicon →, *U.S.A.* 108 E9
Warangal, *India* 60 L11
Waratah, *Australia* 90 G4
Waratah B., *Australia* 91 F4
Warburg, *Germany* 18 D5
Warburton, *Vic., Australia* 91 F4
Warburton, *W. Austral., Australia* 89 E4
Warburton Ra., *Australia* 89 E4
Ward, *N.Z.* 87 J5
Ward →, *Australia* 91 D4
Ward Cove, *U.S.A.* 100 B2
Ward Mt., *U.S.A.* 112 H8
Warden, *S. Africa* 85 D4
Wardha, *India* 60 J11
Wardha →, *India* 60 K11
Wardlow, *Canada* 100 C6
Ware, *Canada* 100 B3
Ware, *U.S.A.* 107 D12
Waregem, *Belgium* 17 G2
Wareham, *U.S.A.* 107 E14
Waremme, *Belgium* 17 G6
Waren, *Germany* 18 B8
Warendorf, *Germany* 18 D3
Warialda, *Australia* 91 D5
Wariap, *Indonesia* 57 E8
Warin Chamrap, *Thailand* 58 E5
Warkopi, *Indonesia* 57 E8
Warley, *U.K.* 13 E6
Warm Springs, *U.S.A.* 111 G5
Warman, *Canada* 101 C7
Warmbad, *Namibia* 84 D2
Warmbad, *S. Africa* 85 C4
Warmenhuizen, *Neths.* 16 C5
Warmeriville, *France* 25 C11
Warmond, *Neths.* 16 D5
Warnambool Downs, *Australia* 90 C3
Warnemünde, *Germany* 18 A8
Warner, *Canada* 100 D6
Warner Mts., *U.S.A.* 110 F3
Warner Robins, *U.S.A.* 105 J4
Warnes, *Bolivia* 125 D5
Warneton, *Belgium* 17 G1
Warnow →, *Germany* 18 A8
Warnsveld, *Neths.* 16 D8
Waroona, *Australia* 89 F2
Warracknabeal, *Australia* 91 F3
Warragul, *Australia* 91 F4
Warrawagine, *Australia* 88 D3
Warrego →, *Australia* 91 E4
Warrego Ra., *Australia* 90 C4
Warren, *Australia* 91 E4
Warren, *Ark., U.S.A.* 109 J8
Warren, *Mich., U.S.A.* 104 D4
Warren, *Minn., U.S.A.* 108 A6
Warren, *Ohio, U.S.A.* 106 E4
Warren, *Pa., U.S.A.* 106 E5
Warrenpoint, *U.K.* 15 B5
Warrensburg, *U.S.A.* 108 F8
Warrenton, *S. Africa* 84 D3
Warrenton, *U.S.A.* 112 D3
Warrenville, *Australia* 91 D4
Warri, *Nigeria* 79 D6
Warrina, *Australia* 91 D2
Warrington, *U.K.* 12 D5
Warrington, *U.S.A.* 105 K2
Warrnambool, *Australia* 91 F3
Warroad, *U.S.A.* 108 A7
Warsa, *Indonesia* 57 E9
Warsaw = Warszawa, *Poland* 20 C11
Warsaw, *Ind., U.S.A.* 104 E3
Warsaw, *N.Y., U.S.A.* 106 D6
Warsaw, *Ohio, U.S.A.* 106 F2
Warstein, *Germany* 18 D4
Warszawa, *Poland* 20 C11
Warta →, *Poland* 20 C4
Warthe = Warta →, *Poland* 20 C4
Waru, *Indonesia* 57 E8
Warwick, *Australia* 91 D5
Warwick, *U.K.* 13 E6
Warwick, *U.S.A.* 107 E13
Warwickshire □, *U.K.* 13 E6
Wasaga Beach, *Canada* 106 B4
Wasatch Ra., *U.S.A.* 110 F8
Wasbank, *S. Africa* 85 D5
Wasco, *Calif., U.S.A.* 113 K7
Wasco, *Oreg., U.S.A.* 110 D3
Waseca, *U.S.A.* 108 C8
Wasekamio L., *Canada* 101 B7
Wash, The, *U.K.* 12 E8
Washago, *Canada* 106 B5
Washburn, *N. Dak., U.S.A.* 108 B4
Washburn, *Wis., U.S.A.* 108 B9
Washim, *India* 60 J10
Washington, *D.C., U.S.A.* 104 F7
Washington, *Ga., U.S.A.* 105 J4
Washington, *Ind., U.S.A.* 104 F2
Washington, *Iowa, U.S.A.* 108 E9
Washington, *Mo., U.S.A.* 108 F9
Washington, *N.C., U.S.A.* 105 H7
Washington, *N.J., U.S.A.* 107 F10
Washington, *Pa., U.S.A.* 106 F4
Washington, *Utah, U.S.A.* 111 H7
Washington □, *U.S.A.* 110 C3
Washington, Mt., *U.S.A.* 107 B13
Washington I., *U.S.A.* 104 C2
Washougal, *U.S.A.* 112 E4
Wasian, *Indonesia* 57 E8
Wasior, *Indonesia* 57 E8
Waskaganish, *Canada* 98 B4
Waskaiowaka, L., *Canada* 101 B9
Waskesiu Lake, *Canada* 101 C7
Wasmes, *Belgium* 17 H3
Waspik, *Neths.* 17 E5
Wassen, *Switz.* 23 C7
Wassenaar, *Neths.* 16 D4
Wasserburg, *Germany* 19 G8
Wasserkuppe, *Germany* 18 E5
Wassy, *France* 25 D11
Waswanipi, *Canada* 98 C4
Waswanipi, L., *Canada* 98 C4
Watangpone, *Indonesia* 57 E6
Water Park Pt., *Australia* 90 C5
Water Valley, *U.S.A.* 109 H10
Waterberge, *S. Africa* 85 C4
Waterbury, *Conn., U.S.A.* 107 E11
Waterbury, *Vt., U.S.A.* 107 B12
Waterbury L., *Canada* 101 B8
Waterdown, *Canada* 106 C5
Waterford, *Canada* 106 D4
Waterford, *Ireland* 15 D4
Waterford, *U.S.A.* 112 H6
Waterford □, *Ireland* 15 D4
Waterford Harbour, *Ireland* 15 D5
Waterhen L., *Man., Canada* 101 C9
Waterhen L., *Sask., Canada* 101 C7
Wateringen, *Neths.* 16 D4
Waterloo, *Belgium* 17 G4
Waterloo, *Ont., Canada* 98 D3
Waterloo, *Qué., Canada* 107 A12
Waterloo, *S. Leone* 78 D2
Waterloo, *Ill., U.S.A.* 108 F9
Waterloo, *Iowa, U.S.A.* 108 D8
Waterloo, *N.Y., U.S.A.* 106 D8
Watermeal-Boitsford, *Belgium* 17 G4
Watersmeet, *U.S.A.* 108 B10
Waterton-Glacier International Peace Park, *U.S.A.* 110 B7
Watertown, *Conn., U.S.A.* 107 E11
Watertown, *N.Y., U.S.A.* 107 C9
Watertown, *S. Dak., U.S.A.* 108 C6
Watertown, *Wis., U.S.A.* 108 D10
Waterval-Boven, *S. Africa* 85 D5
Waterville, *Canada* 107 A13
Waterville, *Maine, U.S.A.* 99 D6
Waterville, *N.Y., U.S.A.* 107 D9
Waterville, *Pa., U.S.A.* 106 E7
Waterville, *Wash., U.S.A.* 110 C3
Watervliet, *Belgium* 17 F3
Watervliet, *U.S.A.* 107 D11
Wates, *Indonesia* 57 G14
Watford, *Canada* 106 D3
Watford, *U.K.* 13 F7
Watford City, *U.S.A.* 108 B3
Wathaman →, *Canada* 101 B8
Watheroo, *Australia* 89 F2
Wating, *China* 50 G4
Watkins Glen, *U.S.A.* 106 D8
Watling I. = San Salvador, *Bahamas* 117 B5
Watonga, *U.S.A.* 109 H5
Watou, *Belgium* 17 G1
Watrous, *Canada* 101 C7
Watrous, *U.S.A.* 109 H2
Watsa, *Zaïre* 82 B2
Watseka, *U.S.A.* 104 E2
Watson, *Australia* 89 F5
Watson, *Canada* 101 C8
Watson Lake, *Canada* 100 A3
Watsonville, *U.S.A.* 111 H3
Wattenwil, *Switz.* 22 C5
Wattiwarriganna Cr. →, *Australia* 91 D2
Wattwil, *Switz.* 23 B8
Watuata = Batuata, *Indonesia* 57 F6
Watubela, Kepulauan, *Indonesia* 57 E8
Watubela Is. = Watubela, Kepulauan, *Indonesia* 57 E8
Wau, *Sudan* 71 F6
Waubach, *Neths.* 17 G8
Waubamik, *Canada* 106 A4
Waubay, *U.S.A.* 108 C6
Waubra, *Australia* 91 F3
Wauchope, *Australia* 91 E5
Wauchula, *U.S.A.* 105 M5
Waugh, *Canada* 101 D9
Waukarlycarly, L., *Australia* 88 D3
Waukegan, *U.S.A.* 104 D2
Waukesha, *U.S.A.* 104 D1
Waukon, *U.S.A.* 108 D9
Wauneta, *U.S.A.* 108 E4
Waupaca, *U.S.A.* 108 C10
Waupun, *U.S.A.* 108 D10
Waurika, *U.S.A.* 109 H6
Wausau, *U.S.A.* 108 C10
Wautoma, *U.S.A.* 108 C10
Wauwatosa, *U.S.A.* 104 D2
Wave Hill, *Australia* 88 C5
Waveney →, *U.K.* 13 E9
Waverley, *N.Z.* 87 H5
Waverly, *Iowa, U.S.A.* 108 D8
Waverly, *N.Y., U.S.A.* 107 D8
Wavre, *Belgium* 17 G5
Wavreille, *Belgium* 17 H6
Wâw, *Sudan* 77 F2
Wāw al Kabīr, *Libya* 73 C8
Wawa, *Canada* 98 C3
Wawa, *Nigeria* 79 D5
Wawa, *Sudan* 76 C3
Wawanesa, *Canada* 101 D9
Wawona, *U.S.A.* 112 H7
Waxahachie, *U.S.A.* 109 J6
Way, L., *Australia* 89 E3
Wayabula Rau, *Indonesia* 57 D7
Wayatinah, *Australia* 90 G4
Waycross, *U.S.A.* 105 K4
Wayi, *Sudan* 77 F3
Wayne, *Nebr., U.S.A.* 108 D6
Wayne, *W. Va., U.S.A.* 104 F4
Waynesboro, *Ga., U.S.A.* 105 J4
Waynesboro, *Miss., U.S.A.* 105 K1
Waynesboro, *Pa., U.S.A.* 104 F7
Waynesboro, *Va., U.S.A.* 104 F6
Waynesburg, *U.S.A.* 104 F5
Waynesville, *U.S.A.* 105 H4
Waynoka, *U.S.A.* 109 G5
Wāzin, *Libya* 75 B7
Wazirabad, *Pakistan* 62 C6
We, *Indonesia* 56 C1
Weald, The, *U.K.* 13 F8
Wear →, *U.K.* 12 C6
Weatherford, *Okla., U.S.A.* 109 H5
Weatherford, *Tex., U.S.A.* 109 J6
Weaverville, *U.S.A.* 110 F2
Webb City, *U.S.A.* 109 G7
Webo = Nyaake, *Liberia* 78 E3
Webster, *Mass., U.S.A.* 107 D13
Webster, *N.Y., U.S.A.* 106 C7
Webster, *S. Dak., U.S.A.* 108 C6
Webster, *Wis., U.S.A.* 108 C8
Webster City, *U.S.A.* 108 D8
Webster Green, *U.S.A.* 108 F9
Webster Springs, *U.S.A.* 104 F5
Weda, *Indonesia* 57 D7
Weda, Teluk, *Indonesia* 57 D7
Weddell I., *Falk. Is.* 128 D4
Weddell Sea, *Antarctica* 5 D1
Wedderburn, *Australia* 91 F3
Wedel, *Germany* 18 B5
Wedgeport, *Canada* 99 D6
Wedza, *Zimbabwe* 83 F3
Wee Waa, *Australia* 91 E4
Weed, *U.S.A.* 110 F2
Weed Heights, *U.S.A.* 112 G7
Weedsport, *U.S.A.* 107 C8
Weedville, *U.S.A.* 106 E6
Weemelah, *Australia* 91 D4
Weenen, *S. Africa* 85 D5
Weener, *Germany* 18 B3
Weert, *Neths.* 17 F7
Weesp, *Neths.* 16 D6
Weggis, *Switz.* 23 B6
Wegliniec, *Poland* 20 D5
Węgorzewo, *Poland* 20 A11
Węgrów, *Poland* 20 C12
Wehl, *Neths.* 16 E8
Wei He →, *Hebei, China* 50 F8
Wei He →, *Shaanxi, China* 50 G6
Weichang, *China* 51 D9
Weichuan, *China* 50 G7
Weida, *Germany* 18 E8
Weiden, *Germany* 19 F8
Weifang, *China* 51 F10
Weihai, *China* 51 F12
Weilburg, *Germany* 18 E4
Weilheim, *Germany* 19 H7
Weimar, *Germany* 18 E7
Weinan, *China* 50 G5
Weinfelden, *Switz.* 23 A8
Weingarten, *Germany* 19 H5
Weinheim, *Germany* 19 F4
Weining, *China* 52 D5
Weipa, *Australia* 90 A3
Weir →, *Australia* 91 D4
Weir →, *Canada* 101 B10
Weir River, *Canada* 101 B10
Weirton, *U.S.A.* 106 F4
Weisen, *Switz.* 23 C9
Weiser, *U.S.A.* 110 D5
Weishan, *Shandong, China* 51 G9
Weishan, *Yunnan, China* 52 E3
Weissenburg, *Germany* 19 F6
Weissenfels, *Germany* 18 D8
Weisshorn, *Switz.* 22 D5
Weissmies, *Switz.* 22 D6
Weisstannen, *Switz.* 23 C8
Weisswasser, *Germany* 18 D10
Weiswampach, *Belgium* 17 H8
Weixi, *China* 52 D2
Weixin, *China* 52 D5
Weiyuan, *China* 50 G3
Weiz, *Austria* 21 H5
Weizhou Dao, *China* 52 G7
Wejherowo, *Poland* 20 A8
Wekusko L., *Canada* 101 C9
Welbourn Hill, *Australia* 91 D1
Welch, *U.S.A.* 104 G5
Weldya, *Ethiopia* 77 E4
Welega □, *Ethiopia* 77 F3
Welkenraedt, *Belgium* 17 G7
Welkite, *Ethiopia* 77 F4
Welkom, *S. Africa* 84 D4
Welland, *Canada* 98 D4
Welland →, *U.K.* 12 E7
Wellen, *Belgium* 17 G6
Wellesley Is., *Australia* 90 B2
Wellin, *Belgium* 17 H6
Wellingborough, *U.K.* 13 E7
Wellington, *Australia* 91 E4
Wellington, *Canada* 98 D4
Wellington, *N.Z.* 87 J5
Wellington, *S. Africa* 84 E2
Wellington, *Shrops., U.K.* 12 E5
Wellington, *Somst., U.K.* 13 G4
Wellington, *Colo., U.S.A.* 108 E2
Wellington, *Kans., U.S.A.* 109 G6
Wellington, *Nev., U.S.A.* 112 G7
Wellington, *Ohio, U.S.A.* 106 E2
Wellington, *Tex., U.S.A.* 109 H4
Wellington, I., *Chile* 128 C2
Wellington, L., *Australia* 91 F4
Wells, *U.K.* 13 F5
Wells, *Maine, U.S.A.* 107 C14
Wells, *Minn., U.S.A.* 108 D8
Wells, *Nev., U.S.A.* 110 F6
Wells, L., *Australia* 89 E3
Wells Gray Prov. Park, *Canada* 100 C4
Wells-next-the-Sea, *U.K.* 12 E8
Wells River, *U.S.A.* 107 B12
Wellsboro, *U.S.A.* 106 E7
Wellsburg, *U.S.A.* 106 F4
Wellsville, *Mo., U.S.A.* 108 F9
Wellsville, *N.Y., U.S.A.* 106 D7
Wellsville, *Ohio, U.S.A.* 106 F4
Wellsville, *Utah, U.S.A.* 110 F8
Wellton, *U.S.A.* 111 K6
Welmel, Wabi →, *Ethiopia* 77 F5
Welo □, *Ethiopia* 77 E4
Wels, *Austria* 21 G4
Welshpool, *U.K.* 13 E4
Wem, *U.K.* 12 E5
Wembere →, *Tanzania* 82 C3
Wemindji, *Canada* 98 B4
Wemmel, *Belgium* 17 G4
Wen Xian, *Gansu, China* 50 H3
Wen Xian, *Henan, China* 50 G7

Wenatchee, *U.S.A.* 110 C3
Wenchang, *China* 58 C8
Wencheng, *China* 53 D13
Wenchi, *Ghana* 78 D4
Wenchow = Wenzhou, *China* 53 C13
Wenchuan, *China* 52 B4
Wendell, *U.S.A.* 110 E6
Wenden, *U.S.A.* 113 M13
Wendeng, *China* 51 F12
Wendesi, *Indonesia* 57 E8
Wendo, *Ethiopia* 77 F4
Wendover, *U.S.A.* 110 F6
Wenduine, *Belgium* 17 F2
Weng'an, *China* 52 D6
Wengcheng, *China* 53 E9
Wengen, *Switz.* 22 C5
Wengyuan, *China* 53 E10
Wenjiang, *China* 52 B4
Wenling, *China* 53 C13
Wenlock →, *Australia* 90 A3
Wenshan, *China* 52 F5
Wenshang, *China* 50 G9
Wenshui, *Guizhou, China* 52 C6
Wenshui, *Shanxi, China* 50 F7
Wensu, *China* 54 B3
Wentworth, *Australia* 91 E3
Wenut, *Indonesia* 57 E8
Wenxi, *China* 50 G6
Wenzhou, *China* 53 C13
Weott, *U.S.A.* 110 F2
Wepener, *S. Africa* 84 D4
Werbomont, *Belgium* 17 H7
Werda, *Botswana* 84 D3
Werdau, *Germany* 18 E8
Werder, *Ethiopia* 68 F4
Werder, *Germany* 18 C8
Werdohl, *Germany* 18 D3
Wereilu, *Ethiopia* 77 E4
Weri, *Indonesia* 57 E8
Werkendam, *Neths.* 16 E5
Werne, *Germany* 18 D3
Werneck, *Germany* 19 F6
Wernigerode, *Germany* 18 D6
Werra →, *Germany* 18 D5
Werribee, *Australia* 91 F3
Werrimull, *Australia* 91 E3
Werris Creek, *Australia* 91 E5
Wersar, *Indonesia* 57 E8
Wertach →, *Germany* 19 G6
Wertheim, *Germany* 19 F5
Wertingen, *Germany* 19 G6
Wervershoof, *Neths.* 16 C6
Wervik, *Belgium* 17 G2
Wesel, *Germany* 18 D2
Weser →, *Germany* 18 B4
Wesiri, *Indonesia* 57 F7
Wesley Vale, *U.S.A.* 111 J10
Wesleyville, *Canada* 99 C9
Wesleyville, *U.S.A.* 106 D4
Wessel, C., *Australia* 90 A2
Wessel Is., *Australia* 90 A2
Wesselburen, *Germany* 18 A4
Wessem, *Neths.* 17 F7
Wessington, *U.S.A.* 108 C5
Wessington Springs, *U.S.A.* 108 C5
West, *U.S.A.* 109 K6
West Allis, *U.S.A.* 104 D1
West B., *U.S.A.* 109 L10
West Baines →, *Australia* 88 C4
West Bank □, *Asia* 69 C4
West Bend, *U.S.A.* 104 D1
West Bengal □, *India* 63 H12
West Beskids = Západné Beskydy, *Europe* 20 F9
West Branch, *U.S.A.* 104 C3
West Bromwich, *U.K.* 13 E5
West Cape Howe, *Australia* 89 G2
West Chazy, *U.S.A.* 107 B11
West Chester, *U.S.A.* 104 F8
West Columbia, *U.S.A.* 109 L7
West Covina, *U.S.A.* 113 L9
West Des Moines, *U.S.A.* 108 E8
West Dunbartonshire □, *U.K.* 14 F4
West End, *Bahamas* 116 A4
West Falkland, *Falk. Is.* 128 D4
West Fjord = Vestfjorden, *Norway* 8 C15
West Frankfort, *U.S.A.* 108 G10
West Hartford, *U.S.A.* 107 E12
West Haven, *U.S.A.* 107 E12
West Helena, *U.S.A.* 109 H9
West Ice Shelf, *Antarctica* 5 C7
West Indies, *Cent. Amer.* 117 C7
West Lorne, *Canada* 106 D3
West Lothian □, *U.K.* 14 F5
West Lunga →, *Zambia* 83 E1
West Memphis, *U.S.A.* 109 H9
West Midlands □, *U.K.* 13 E6
West Mifflin, *U.S.A.* 106 F5
West Monroe, *U.S.A.* 109 J8
West Newton, *U.S.A.* 106 F5
West Nicholson, *Zimbabwe* 83 G2
West Palm Beach, *U.S.A.* 105 M5
West Plains, *U.S.A.* 109 G9
West Point, *Ga., U.S.A.* 105 J3
West Point, *Miss., U.S.A.* 105 J1
West Point, *Nebr., U.S.A.* 108 E6
West Point, *Va., U.S.A.* 104 G7
West Pokot □, *Kenya* 82 B4
West Pt. = Ouest, Pte., *Canada* 99 C7
West Pt., *Australia* 91 F2
West Road →, *Canada* 100 C4
West Rutland, *U.S.A.* 107 C11
West Schelde = Westerschelde →, *Neths.* 17 F2
West Seneca, *U.S.A.* 106 D6
West Siberian Plain, *Russia* 46 C11
West Sussex □, *U.K.* 13 G7
West-Terschelling, *Neths.* 16 B6
West Valley City, *U.S.A.* 110 F8
West Virginia □, *U.S.A.* 104 F5
West-Vlaanderen □, *Belgium* 17 G2
West Walker →, *U.S.A.* 112 G7
West Wyalong, *Australia* 91 E4
West Yellowstone, *U.S.A.* 110 D8
West Yorkshire □, *U.K.* 12 D6
Westall Pt., *Australia* 91 E1
Westbrook, *Maine, U.S.A.* 105 D10
Westbrook, *Tex., U.S.A.* 109 J4
Westbury, *Australia* 90 G4
Westby, *U.S.A.* 108 A2
Westend, *U.S.A.* 113 K9
Westerbork, *Neths.* 16 C9
Westerland, *Germany* 9 J13
Western □, *Kenya* 82 B3
Western □, *Uganda* 82 B3
Western □, *Zambia* 83 F1
Western Australia □, *Australia* 89 E2
Western Cape □, *S. Africa* 84 E3
Western Dvina = Daugava →, *Latvia* 9 H21
Western Ghats, *India* 60 N9
Western Isles □, *U.K.* 14 D1
Western Sahara ■, *Africa* 74 D2
Western Samoa ■, *Pac. Oc.* 87 A13
Westernport, *U.S.A.* 104 F6
Westerschelde →, *Neths.* 17 F2
Westerstede, *Germany* 18 B3
Westervoort, *Neths.* 16 E7
Westerwald, *Germany* 18 E4
Westfield, *Mass., U.S.A.* 107 D12
Westfield, *N.Y., U.S.A.* 106 D5
Westfield, *Pa., U.S.A.* 106 E7
Westgat, *Neths.* 17 E3
Westhope, *U.S.A.* 108 A4
Westkapelle, *Belgium* 17 F2
Westkapelle, *Neths.* 17 E2
Westland Bight, *N.Z.* 87 K3
Westlock, *Canada* 100 C6
Westmalle, *Belgium* 17 F5
Westmeath □, *Ireland* 15 C4
Westminster, *U.S.A.* 104 F7
Westmorland, *U.S.A.* 111 K6
Weston, *Malaysia* 56 C5
Weston, *Oreg., U.S.A.* 110 D4
Weston, *W. Va., U.S.A.* 104 F5
Weston I., *Canada* 98 B4
Weston-super-Mare, *U.K.* 13 F5
Westport, *Canada* 107 B8
Westport, *Ireland* 15 C2
Westport, *N.Z.* 87 J3
Westport, *Oreg., U.S.A.* 112 D3
Westport, *Wash., U.S.A.* 110 C1
Westray, *Canada* 101 C8
Westray, *U.K.* 14 B6
Westree, *Canada* 98 C3
Westville, *Calif., U.S.A.* 112 F6
Westville, *Ill., U.S.A.* 104 E2
Westville, *Okla., U.S.A.* 109 G7
Westwood, *U.S.A.* 110 F3
Wetar, *Indonesia* 57 F7
Wetaskiwin, *Canada* 100 C6
Wethersfield, *U.S.A.* 107 E12
Wetteren, *Belgium* 17 G3
Wettingen, *Switz.* 23 B6
Wetzikon, *Switz.* 23 B7
Wetzlar, *Germany* 18 E4
Wevelgem, *Belgium* 17 G2
Wewoka, *U.S.A.* 109 H6
Wexford, *Ireland* 15 D5
Wexford □, *Ireland* 15 D5
Wexford Harbour, *Ireland* 15 D5
Weyburn, *Canada* 101 D8
Weyburn L., *Canada* 100 A5
Weyer, *Austria* 21 H4
Weyib →, *Ethiopia* 77 F5
Weymouth, *Canada* 99 D6
Weymouth, *U.K.* 13 G5
Weymouth, *U.S.A.* 107 D14
Weymouth, C., *Australia* 90 A3
Wezemaal, *Belgium* 17 G5
Wezep, *Neths.* 16 D7
Wha Ti, *Canada* 96 B8
Whakatane, *N.Z.* 87 G6
Whale →, *Canada* 99 A6
Whale Cove, *Canada* 101 A10
Whales, B. of, *Antarctica* 5 D12
Whalsay, *U.K.* 14 A7
Whangamomona, *N.Z.* 87 H5
Whangarei, *N.Z.* 87 F5
Whangarei Harb., *N.Z.* 87 F5
Wharfe →, *U.K.* 12 D6
Wharfedale, *U.K.* 12 C5
Wharton, *N.J., U.S.A.* 107 F10
Wharton, *Pa., U.S.A.* 106 E6
Wharton, *Tex., U.S.A.* 109 L6
Wheatland, *Calif., U.S.A.* 112 F5
Wheatland, *Wyo., U.S.A.* 108 D2
Wheatley, *Canada* 106 D2
Wheaton, *U.S.A.* 108 C6
Wheelbarrow Pk., *U.S.A.* 112 H10
Wheeler, *Oreg., U.S.A.* 110 D2
Wheeler, *Tex., U.S.A.* 109 H4
Wheeler →, *Canada* 101 B7
Wheeler Pk., *N. Mex., U.S.A.* 111 H11
Wheeler Pk., *Nev., U.S.A.* 111 G6
Wheeler Ridge, *U.S.A.* 113 L8
Wheeling, *U.S.A.* 106 F4
Whernside, *U.K.* 12 C5
Whidbey I., *U.S.A.* 100 D4
Whiskey Gap, *Canada* 100 D6
Whiskey Jack L., *Canada* 101 B8
Whistleduck Cr. →, *Australia* 90 C2
Whitby, *Canada* 106 C6
Whitby, *U.K.* 12 C7
White →, *Ark., U.S.A.* 109 J9
White →, *Ind., U.S.A.* 104 F2
White →, *S. Dak., U.S.A.* 108 D5
White →, *Utah, U.S.A.* 110 F9
White →, *Wash., U.S.A.* 112 C4
White, L., *Australia* 88 D4
White B., *Canada* 99 B8
White Bear Res., *Canada* 99 C8
White Bird, *U.S.A.* 110 D5
White Butte, *U.S.A.* 108 B3
White City, *U.S.A.* 108 F6
White Cliffs, *Australia* 91 E3
White Deer, *U.S.A.* 109 H4
White Hall, *U.S.A.* 108 F9
White Haven, *U.S.A.* 107 E9
White Horse, Vale of, *U.K.* 13 F6
White I., *N.Z.* 87 G6
White L., *Canada* 107 A8
White L., *U.S.A.* 109 L8
White Mts., *Calif., U.S.A.* 111 H4
White Mts., *N.H., U.S.A.* 107 B13
White Nile = Nîl el Abyad →, *Sudan* 77 D3
White Nile Dam = Khazzân Jabal el Awliyâ, *Sudan* 77 D3
White Otter L., *Canada* 98 C1
White Pass, *Canada* 100 B1
White Pass, *U.S.A.* 112 D5
White Plains, *U.S.A.* 107 E11
White River, *Canada* 98 C2
White River, *S. Africa* 85 D5
White River, *U.S.A.* 108 D4
White Russia = Belarus ■, *Europe* 40 F4
White Sea = Beloye More, *Russia* 44 C4
White Sulphur Springs, *Mont., U.S.A.* 110 C8
White Sulphur Springs, *W. Va., U.S.A.* 104 G5
White Swan, *U.S.A.* 112 D6
White Volta →, *Ghana* 79 D4
Whitecliffs, *N.Z.* 87 K3
Whitecourt, *Canada* 100 C5
Whiteface, *U.S.A.* 109 J3
Whitefield, *U.S.A.* 107 B13
Whitefish, *U.S.A.* 110 B6
Whitefish L., *Canada* 101 A7
Whitefish Point, *U.S.A.* 104 B3
Whitegull, L., *Canada* 99 A7
Whitehall, *Mich., U.S.A.* 104 D2
Whitehall, *Mont., U.S.A.* 110 D7
Whitehall, *N.Y., U.S.A.* 107 C11
Whitehall, *Wis., U.S.A.* 108 C9
Whitehaven, *U.K.* 12 C4
Whitehorse, *Canada* 100 A1
Whitemark, *Australia* 90 G4
Whitemouth, *Canada* 101 D9
Whiteplains, *Liberia* 78 D2
Whitesboro, *N.Y., U.S.A.* 107 C9
Whitesboro, *Tex., U.S.A.* 109 J6
Whiteshell Prov. Park, *Canada* 101 C9
Whiteside, Canal, *Chile* 128 D2
Whitetail, *U.S.A.* 108 A2
Whiteville, *U.S.A.* 105 H6
Whitewater, *U.S.A.* 104 D1
Whitewater Baldy, *U.S.A.* 111 K9
Whitewater L., *Canada* 98 B2
Whitewood, *Australia* 90 C3
Whitewood, *Canada* 101 C8
Whitfield, *Australia* 91 F4
Whithorn, *U.K.* 14 G4
Whitianga, *N.Z.* 87 G5
Whitman, *U.S.A.* 107 D14
Whitmire, *U.S.A.* 105 H5
Whitney, *Canada* 98 C4
Whitney, Mt., *U.S.A.* 111 H4
Whitney Point, *U.S.A.* 107 D9
Whitstable, *U.K.* 13 F9
Whitsunday I., *Australia* 90 C4
Whittier, *U.S.A.* 113 M8
Whittlesea, *Australia* 91 F4
Whitwell, *U.S.A.* 105 H3
Wholdaia L., *Canada* 101 A8
Whyalla, *Australia* 91 E2
Whyjonta, *Australia* 91 D3
Wiarton, *Canada* 98 D3
Wiawso, *Ghana* 78 D4
Wibaux, *U.S.A.* 108 B2
Wichabai, *Guyana* 121 C6
Wichian Buri, *Thailand* 58 E3
Wichita, *U.S.A.* 109 G6
Wichita Falls, *U.S.A.* 109 J5
Wick, *U.K.* 14 C5
Wickenburg, *U.S.A.* 111 K7
Wickepin, *Australia* 89 F2
Wickham, C., *Australia* 90 F3
Wickliffe, *U.S.A.* 106 E3
Wicklow, *Ireland* 15 D5
Wicklow □, *Ireland* 15 D5
Wicklow Hd., *Ireland* 15 D5
Widgiemooltha, *Australia* 89 F3
Widnes, *U.K.* 12 D5
Wiedenbrück, *Germany* 18 D4
Wiehl, *Germany* 18 E3
Wiek, *Germany* 18 A9
Wielbark, *Poland* 20 B10
Wieliczka, *Poland* 20 F10
Wieluń, *Poland* 20 D8
Wien, *Austria* 21 G6
Wiener Neustadt, *Austria* 21 H6
Wieprz →, *Koszalin, Poland* 20 A6
Wieprz →, *Lublin, Poland* 20 D11
Wierden, *Neths.* 16 D9
Wiers, *Belgium* 17 H3
Wiesbaden, *Germany* 19 E4
Wiesental, *Germany* 19 F4
Wigan, *U.K.* 12 D5
Wiggins, *Colo., U.S.A.* 108 E2
Wiggins, *Miss., U.S.A.* 109 K10
Wight, I. of □, *U.K.* 13 G6
Wigtown, *U.K.* 14 G4
Wigtown B., *U.K.* 14 G4
Wijchen, *Neths.* 16 E7
Wijhe, *Neths.* 16 D8
Wijk bij Duurstede, *Neths.* 16 E6
Wil, *Switz.* 23 B8
Wilber, *U.S.A.* 108 E6
Wilberforce, *Canada* 106 A6
Wilberforce, C., *Australia* 90 A2
Wilburton, *U.S.A.* 109 H7
Wilcannia, *Australia* 91 E3
Wilcox, *U.S.A.* 106 E6
Wildbad, *Germany* 19 G4
Wildervank, *Neths.* 16 B9
Wildeshausen, *Germany* 18 C4
Wildhorn, *Switz.* 22 D4
Wildrose, *Calif., U.S.A.* 113 J9
Wildrose, *N. Dak., U.S.A.* 108 A3
Wildspitze, *Austria* 19 J6
Wildstrubel, *Switz.* 22 D5
Wildwood, *U.S.A.* 104 F8
Wilge →, *S. Africa* 85 D4
Wilhelm II Coast, *Antarctica* 5 C7
Wilhelm-Pieck-Stadt-Guben, *Germany* 18 D10
Wilhelmina, Geb., *Surinam* 121 C6
Wilhelmina Kanaal, *Neths.* 17 E6
Wilhelmsburg, *Austria* 21 G5
Wilhelmshaven, *Germany* 18 B4
Wilhelmstal, *Namibia* 84 C2
Wilkes-Barre, *U.S.A.* 107 E9
Wilkesboro, *U.S.A.* 105 G5
Wilkie, *Canada* 101 C7
Wilkinsburg, *U.S.A.* 106 F5
Wilkinson Lakes, *Australia* 89 E5
Willamina, *U.S.A.* 110 D2
Willandra Billabong Creek →, *Australia* 91 E4
Willapa B., *U.S.A.* 110 C2
Willapa Hills, *U.S.A.* 112 D3
Willard, *N. Mex., U.S.A.* 111 J10
Willard, *Utah, U.S.A.* 110 F7
Willcox, *U.S.A.* 111 K9
Willebroek, *Belgium* 17 F4
Willemstad, *Neth. Ant.* 117 D6
Willeroo, *Australia* 88 C5
William →, *Canada* 101 B7
William Creek, *Australia* 91 D2
Williambury, *Australia* 89 D2
Williams, *Australia* 89 F2
Williams, *Ariz., U.S.A.* 111 J7
Williams, *Calif., U.S.A.* 112 F4
Williams Lake, *Canada* 100 C4
Williamsburg, *Ky., U.S.A.* 105 G3
Williamsburg, *Pa., U.S.A.* 106 F6
Williamsburg, *Va., U.S.A.* 104 G7
Williamson, *N.Y., U.S.A.* 106 C7
Williamson, *W. Va., U.S.A.* 104 G4
Williamsport, *U.S.A.* 106 E7
Williamston, *U.S.A.* 105 H7
Williamstown, *Australia* 91 F3
Williamstown, *Mass., U.S.A.* 107 D11
Williamstown, *N.Y., U.S.A.* 107 C9
Williamsville, *U.S.A.* 109 G9
Willimantic, *U.S.A.* 107 E12
Willis Group, *Australia* 90 B5
Willisau, *Switz.* 22 B6
Williston, *S. Africa* 84 E3
Williston, *Fla., U.S.A.* 105 L4
Williston, *N. Dak., U.S.A.* 108 A3
Williston L., *Canada* 100 B4
Willits, *U.S.A.* 110 G2
Willmar, *U.S.A.* 108 C7
Willoughby, *U.S.A.* 106 E3
Willow Bunch, *Canada* 101 D7
Willow L., *Canada* 100 A5
Willow Lake, *U.S.A.* 108 C6
Willow Springs, *U.S.A.* 109 G8
Willow Wall, The, *China* 51 C12
Willowlake →, *Canada* 100 A4
Willowmore, *S. Africa* 84 E3
Willows, *Australia* 90 C4
Willows, *U.S.A.* 112 F4
Willowvale = Gatyana, *S. Africa* 85 E4
Wills, L., *Australia* 88 D4
Wills Cr. →, *Australia* 90 C3
Wills Point, *U.S.A.* 109 J7
Willunga, *Australia* 91 F2
Wilmette, *U.S.A.* 104 D2
Wilmington, *Australia* 91 E2
Wilmington, *Del., U.S.A.* 104 F8
Wilmington, *Ill., U.S.A.* 104 E1
Wilmington, *N.C., U.S.A.* 105 H7
Wilmington, *Ohio, U.S.A.* 104 F4
Wilpena Cr. →, *Australia* 91 E2
Wilrijk, *Belgium* 17 F4
Wilsall, *U.S.A.* 110 D8
Wilson, *U.S.A.* 105 H7
Wilson →, *Queens., Australia* 91 D3
Wilson →, *W. Austral., Australia* 88 C4
Wilson Bluff, *Australia* 89 F4
Wilsons Promontory, *Australia* 91 F4
Wilster, *Germany* 18 B5
Wilton, *U.K.* 13 F6
Wilton, *U.S.A.* 108 B4
Wilton →, *Australia* 90 A1
Wiltshire □, *U.K.* 13 F6
Wiltz, *Lux.* 17 J7
Wiluna, *Australia* 89 E3
Wimereux, *France* 25 B8
Wimmera →, *Australia* 91 F3
Winam G., *Kenya* 82 C3
Winburg, *S. Africa* 84 D4
Winchendon, *U.S.A.* 107 D12
Winchester, *U.K.* 13 F6
Winchester, *Conn., U.S.A.* 107 E11
Winchester, *Idaho, U.S.A.* 110 C5
Winchester, *Ind., U.S.A.* 104 E3
Winchester, *Ky., U.S.A.* 104 G3
Winchester, *N.H., U.S.A.* 107 D12
Winchester, *Nev., U.S.A.* 113 J11
Winchester, *Tenn., U.S.A.* 105 H2
Winchester, *Va., U.S.A.* 104 F6
Wind →, *U.S.A.* 110 E9
Wind River Range, *U.S.A.* 110 E9
Windau = Ventspils, *Latvia* 9 H19
Windber, *U.S.A.* 106 F6
Windermere, L., *U.K.* 12 C5
Windfall, *Canada* 100 C5
Windflower L., *Canada* 100 A5
Windhoek, *Namibia* 84 C2
Windom, *U.S.A.* 108 D7
Windorah, *Australia* 90 D3
Window Rock, *U.S.A.* 111 J9
Windrush →, *U.K.* 13 F6
Windsor, *Australia* 91 E5
Windsor, *N.S., Canada* 99 D7
Windsor, *Nfld., Canada* 99 C8
Windsor, *Ont., Canada* 98 D3
Windsor, *U.K.* 13 F7
Windsor, *Colo., U.S.A.* 108 E2
Windsor, *Conn., U.S.A.* 107 E12
Windsor, *Mo., U.S.A.* 108 F8
Windsor, *N.Y., U.S.A.* 107 D9
Windsor, *Vt., U.S.A.* 107 C12
Windsorton, *S. Africa* 84 D3
Windward Is., *W. Indies* 117 D7
Windward Passage = Vientos, Paso de los, *Caribbean* 117 C5
Windy L., *Canada* 101 A8
Winefred L., *Canada* 101 B6
Winejok, *Sudan* 77 F2
Winfield, *U.S.A.* 109 G6
Wingate Mts., *Australia* 88 B5
Wingen, *Australia* 91 E5
Wingene, *Belgium* 17 F2
Wingham, *Australia* 91 E5
Wingham, *Canada* 98 D3
Winifred, *U.S.A.* 110 C9
Winisk, *Canada* 98 A2
Winisk →, *Canada* 98 A2
Winisk L., *Canada* 98 B2
Wink, *U.S.A.* 109 K3
Winkler, *Canada* 101 D9
Winlock, *U.S.A.* 112 D4
Winneba, *Ghana* 79 D4
Winnebago, *U.S.A.* 108 D7
Winnebago, L., *U.S.A.* 104 D1
Winnecke Cr. →, *Australia* 88 C5
Winnemucca, *U.S.A.* 110 F5
Winnemucca L., *U.S.A.* 110 F4
Winner, *U.S.A.* 108 D5
Winnett, *U.S.A.* 110 C9
Winnfield, *U.S.A.* 109 K8
Winnibigoshish, L., *U.S.A.* 108 B7
Winning, *Australia* 88 D1
Winnipeg, *Canada* 101 D9
Winnipeg →, *Canada* 101 C9
Winnipeg, L., *Canada* 101 C9
Winnipeg Beach, *Canada* 101 C9
Winnipegosis, *Canada* 101 C9
Winnipegosis L., *Canada* 101 C9
Winnipesaukee, L., *U.S.A.* 107 C13
Winnsboro, *La., U.S.A.* 109 J9
Winnsboro, *S.C., U.S.A.* 105 H5
Winnsboro, *Tex., U.S.A.* 109 J7
Winokapau, L., *Canada* 99 B7
Winona, *Minn., U.S.A.* 108 C9
Winona, *Miss., U.S.A.* 109 J10
Winooski, *U.S.A.* 107 B11
Winschoten, *Neths.* 16 B10
Winsen, *Germany* 18 B6
Winslow, *Ariz., U.S.A.* 111 J8
Winslow, *Wash., U.S.A.* 112 C4
Winsted, *U.S.A.* 107 E11
Winston-Salem, *U.S.A.* 105 G5
Winsum, *Neths.* 16 B9
Winter Garden, *U.S.A.* 105 L5
Winter Haven, *U.S.A.* 105 M5
Winter Park, *U.S.A.* 105 L5
Winterberg, *Germany* 18 D4
Winterhaven, *U.S.A.* 113 N12
Winters, *Calif., U.S.A.* 112 G5
Winters, *Tex., U.S.A.* 109 K5
Winterset, *U.S.A.* 108 E7
Wintersville, *U.S.A.* 106 F4
Winterswijk, *Neths.* 16 E9
Winterthur, *Switz.* 23 B7

Winthrop, *Minn., U.S.A.* 108 C7
Winthrop, *Wash., U.S.A.* 110 B3
Winton, *Australia* 90 C3
Winton, *N.Z.* 87 M2
Winton, *U.S.A.* 105 G7
Wintzenheim, *France* 25 D14
Wipper →, *Germany* 18 D7
Wirral, *U.K.* 12 D4
Wirrulla, *Australia* 91 E1
Wisbech, *U.K.* 12 E8
Wisconsin □, *U.S.A.* 108 C10
Wisconsin →, *U.S.A.* 108 D9
Wisconsin Dells, *U.S.A.* 108 D10
Wisconsin Rapids, *U.S.A.* 108 C10
Wisdom, *U.S.A.* 110 D7
Wishaw, *U.K.* 14 F5
Wishek, *U.S.A.* 108 B5
Wisła, *Poland* 20 F8
Wisła →, *Poland* 20 A8
Wisłok →, *Poland* 20 E12
Wisłoka →, *Poland* 20 E11
Wismar, *Germany* 18 B7
Wismar, *Guyana* 121 B6
Wisner, *U.S.A.* 108 E6
Wissant, *France* 25 B8
Wissembourg, *France* 25 C14
Wissenkerke, *Neths.* 17 E3
Witbank, *S. Africa* 85 D4
Witdraai, *S. Africa* 84 D3
Witham →, *U.K.* 12 D7
Withernsea, *U.K.* 12 D8
Witmarsum, *Neths.* 16 B6
Witney, *U.K.* 13 F6
Witnossob →, *Namibia* 84 D3
Wittdün, *Germany* 18 A4
Witten, *Germany* 17 F10
Wittenberg, *Germany* 18 D8
Wittenberge, *Germany* 18 B7
Wittenburg, *Germany* 18 B7
Wittenoom, *Australia* 88 D2
Wittingen, *Germany* 18 C6
Wittlich, *Germany* 19 F2
Wittmund, *Germany* 18 B3
Wittow, *Germany* 18 A9
Wittstock, *Germany* 18 B8
Witzenhausen, *Germany* 18 D5
Wlingi, *Indonesia* 57 H15
Włocławek, *Poland* 20 C9
Włodawa, *Poland* 20 D13
Włoszczowa, *Poland* 20 E9
Woburn, *U.S.A.* 107 D13
Wodian, *China* 50 H7
Wodonga, *Australia* 91 F4
Woerden, *Neths.* 16 D5
Woerth, *France* 25 D14
Woëvre, *France* 25 C12
Wognum, *Neths.* 16 C6
Wohlen, *Switz.* 23 B6
Woinbogoin, *China* 52 A2
Wokam, *Indonesia* 57 F8
Wolbrom, *Poland* 20 E9
Woldegk, *Germany* 18 B9
Wolf →, *Canada* 100 A2
Wolf Creek, *U.S.A.* 110 C7
Wolf L., *Canada* 100 A2
Wolf Point, *U.S.A.* 108 A2
Wolfe I., *Canada* 98 D4
Wolfenbüttel, *Germany* 18 C6
Wolfheze, *Neths.* 16 D7
Wolfsberg, *Austria* 21 J4
Wolfsburg, *Germany* 18 C6
Wolgast, *Germany* 18 A9
Wolhusen, *Switz.* 22 B6
Wolin, *Poland* 20 B4
Wollaston, Is., *Chile* 128 E3
Wollaston L., *Canada* 101 B8
Wollaston Pen., *Canada* 96 B8
Wollogorang, *Australia* 90 B2
Wollongong, *Australia* 91 E5
Wolmaransstad, *S. Africa* 84 D4
Wolmirstedt, *Germany* 18 C7
Wolseley, *Australia* 91 F3
Wolseley, *Canada* 101 C8
Wolseley, *S. Africa* 84 E2
Wolstenholme, C., *Canada* 94 C12
Wolsztyn, *Poland* 20 C6
Wolvega, *Neths.* 16 C7
Wolverhampton, *U.K.* 13 E5
Wommels, *Neths.* 16 B7
Wonarah, *Australia* 90 B2
Wonck, *Belgium* 17 G7
Wondai, *Australia* 91 D5
Wondelgem, *Belgium* 17 F3
Wongalarroo L., *Australia* 91 E3
Wongan Hills, *Australia* 89 F2
Wongawol, *Australia* 89 E3
Wŏnju, *S. Korea* 51 F14
Wonosari, *Indonesia* 57 G14
Wŏnsan, *N. Korea* 51 E14
Wonthaggi, *Australia* 91 F4
Woocalla, *Australia* 91 E2
Wood Buffalo Nat. Park, *Canada* 100 B6
Wood Is., *Australia* 88 C3
Wood L., *Canada* 101 B8
Wood Lake, *U.S.A.* 108 D4
Woodah I., *Australia* 90 A2
Woodanilling, *Australia* 89 F2
Woodbridge, *Canada* 106 C5
Woodburn, *Australia* 91 D5
Woodenbong, *Australia* 91 D5
Woodend, *Australia* 91 F3
Woodfords, *U.S.A.* 112 G7
Woodgreen, *Australia* 90 C1
Woodlake, *U.S.A.* 112 J7
Woodland, *U.S.A.* 112 G5
Woodlands, *Australia* 88 D2
Woodpecker, *Canada* 100 C4
Woodridge, *Canada* 101 D9
Woodroffe, Mt., *Australia* 89 E5
Woodruff, *Ariz., U.S.A.* 111 J8
Woodruff, *Utah, U.S.A.* 110 F8
Woods, L., *Australia* 90 B1
Woods, L., *Canada* 99 B6
Woods, L. of the, *Canada* 101 D10
Woodstock, *Queens., Australia* 90 B4
Woodstock, *W. Austral., Australia* 88 D2
Woodstock, *N.B., Canada* 99 C6
Woodstock, *Ont., Canada* 98 D3
Woodstock, *U.K.* 13 F6
Woodstock, *Ill., U.S.A.* 108 D10
Woodstock, *Vt., U.S.A.* 107 C12
Woodsville, *U.S.A.* 107 B13
Woodville, *N.Z.* 87 J5
Woodville, *U.S.A.* 109 K7
Woodward, *U.S.A.* 109 G5
Woody, *U.S.A.* 113 K8
Woolamai, C., *Australia* 91 F4
Woolgoolga, *Australia* 91 E5
Woombye, *Australia* 91 D5
Woomera, *Australia* 91 E2
Woonsocket, *R.I., U.S.A.* 107 D13
Woonsocket, *S. Dak., U.S.A.* 108 C5
Wooramel, *Australia* 89 E1
Wooramel →, *Australia* 89 E1
Wooroloo, *Australia* 89 F2
Wooster, *U.S.A.* 106 F3
Worb, *Switz.* 22 C5
Worcester, *S. Africa* 84 E2
Worcester, *U.K.* 13 E5
Worcester, *Mass., U.S.A.* 107 D13
Worcester, *N.Y., U.S.A.* 107 D10
Wörgl, *Austria* 19 H8
Workington, *U.K.* 12 C4
Worksop, *U.K.* 12 D6
Workum, *Neths.* 16 C6
Worland, *U.S.A.* 110 D10
Wormerveer, *Neths.* 16 D5
Wormhoudt, *France* 25 B9
Worms, *Germany* 19 F4
Wörth, *Germany* 19 F8
Wortham, *U.S.A.* 109 K6
Wörther See, *Austria* 21 J4
Worthing, *U.K.* 13 G7
Worthington, *U.S.A.* 108 D7
Wosi, *Indonesia* 57 E7
Wou-han = Wuhan, *China* 53 B10
Woubrugge, *Neths.* 16 D5
Woudenberg, *Neths.* 16 D6
Woudsend, *Neths.* 16 C7
Wour, *Chad* 73 D8
Wousi = Wuxi, *China* 53 B13
Wouw, *Neths.* 17 E4
Wowoni, *Indonesia* 57 E6
Woy Woy, *Australia* 91 E5
Wrangel I. = Vrangelya, Ostrov, *Russia* 45 B19
Wrangell, *U.S.A.* 96 C6
Wrangell I., *U.S.A.* 100 B2
Wrangell Mts., *U.S.A.* 96 B5
Wrath, C., *U.K.* 14 C3
Wray, *U.S.A.* 108 E3
Wrekin, The, *U.K.* 12 E5
Wrens, *U.S.A.* 105 J4
Wrexham, *U.K.* 12 D4
Wrexham □, *U.K.* 12 D5
Wriezen, *Germany* 18 C10
Wright, *Canada* 100 C4
Wright, *Phil.* 55 F6
Wrightson Mt., *U.S.A.* 111 L8
Wrightwood, *U.S.A.* 113 L9
Wrigley, *Canada* 96 B7
Wrocław, *Poland* 20 D7
Września, *Poland* 20 C7
Wschowa, *Poland* 20 D6
Wu Jiang →, *China* 52 C6
Wu'an, *China* 50 F8
Wubin, *Australia* 89 F2
Wubu, *China* 50 F6
Wuchang, *China* 51 B14
Wucheng, *China* 50 F9
Wuchuan, *Guangdong, China* 53 G8
Wuchuan, *Guizhou, China* 52 C7
Wuchuan, *Nei Mongol Zizhiqu, China* 50 D6
Wudi, *China* 51 F9
Wuding, *China* 52 E4
Wuding He →, *China* 50 F6
Wudu, *China* 50 H3
Wufeng, *China* 53 B8
Wugang, *China* 53 D8
Wugong Shan, *China* 53 D9
Wuhan, *China* 53 B10
Wuhe, *China* 51 H9
Wuhsi = Wuxi, *China* 53 B13
Wuhu, *China* 53 B12
Wujiang, *China* 53 B13
Wukari, *Nigeria* 79 D6
Wulajie, *China* 51 B14
Wulanbulang, *China* 50 D6
Wulehe, *Ghana* 79 D5
Wulian, *China* 51 G10
Wuliang Shan, *China* 52 E3
Wuliaru, *Indonesia* 57 F8
Wulumuchi = Ürümqi, *China* 44 E9
Wum, *Cameroon* 79 D7
Wuming, *China* 52 F7
Wuning, *China* 53 C10
Wunnummin L., *Canada* 98 B2
Wunsiedel, *Germany* 19 E8
Wunstorf, *Germany* 18 C5
Wuntho, *Burma* 61 H19
Wuping, *China* 53 E11
Wuppertal, *Germany* 18 D3
Wuppertal, *S. Africa* 84 E2
Wuqing, *China* 51 E9
Würenlingen, *Switz.* 23 A6
Wurung, *Australia* 90 B3
Würzburg, *Germany* 19 F5
Wurzen, *Germany* 18 D8
Wushan, *Gansu, China* 50 G3
Wushan, *Sichuan, China* 52 B7
Wusuli Jiang = Ussuri →, *Asia* 48 A7
Wutach →, *Germany* 19 H4
Wutai, *China* 50 E7
Wuting = Huimin, *China* 51 F9
Wutong, *China* 53 E8
Wutonghaolai, *China* 51 C11
Wutongqiao, *China* 52 C4
Wuustwezel, *Belgium* 17 F5
Wuwei, *Anhui, China* 53 B11
Wuwei, *Gansu, China* 54 C5
Wuxi, *Jiangsu, China* 53 B13
Wuxi, *Sichuan, China* 52 B7
Wuxiang, *China* 50 F7
Wuxing, *China* 53 B13
Wuxuan, *China* 52 F7
Wuyang, *China* 50 H7
Wuyi, *Hebei, China* 50 F8
Wuyi, *Zhejiang, China* 53 C12
Wuyi Shan, *China* 53 D11
Wuyo, *Nigeria* 79 C7
Wuyuan, *Jiangxi, China* 53 C11
Wuyuan, *Nei Mongol Zizhiqu, China* 50 D5
Wuzhai, *China* 50 E6
Wuzhi Shan, *China* 54 E5
Wuzhong, *China* 50 E4
Wuzhou, *China* 53 F8
Wyaaba Cr. →, *Australia* 90 B3
Wyalkatchem, *Australia* 89 F2
Wyalusing, *U.S.A.* 107 E8
Wyandotte, *U.S.A.* 104 D4
Wyandra, *Australia* 91 D4
Wyangala Res., *Australia* 91 E4
Wyara, L., *Australia* 91 D3
Wycheproof, *Australia* 91 F3
Wye →, *U.K.* 13 F5
Wyemandoo, *Australia* 89 E2
Wyk, *Germany* 18 A4
Wymondham, *U.K.* 13 E7
Wymore, *U.S.A.* 108 E6
Wynbring, *Australia* 91 E1
Wyndham, *Australia* 88 C4
Wyndham, *N.Z.* 87 M2
Wyndmere, *U.S.A.* 108 B6
Wynne, *U.S.A.* 109 H9
Wynnum, *Australia* 91 D5
Wynyard, *Australia* 90 G4
Wynyard, *Canada* 101 C8
Wyola, L., *Australia* 89 E5
Wyoming □, *U.S.A.* 110 E10
Wyong, *Australia* 91 E5
Wyszków, *Poland* 20 C11
Wyszogród, *Poland* 20 C10
Wytheville, *U.S.A.* 104 G5

X

Xaçmaz, *Azerbaijan* 43 K9
Xai-Xai, *Mozam.* 85 D5
Xainza, *China* 54 C3
Xambioá, *Brazil* 122 C2
Xangongo, *Angola* 84 B2
Xankändi, *Azerbaijan* 67 C12
Xanlar, *Azerbaijan* 43 K8
Xanten, *Germany* 18 D2
Xánthi, *Greece* 39 H7
Xanthos, *Turkey* 66 D3
Xapuri, *Brazil* 124 C4
Xar Moron He →, *China* 51 C11
Xau, L., *Botswana* 84 C3
Xavantina, *Brazil* 127 A5
Xenia, *U.S.A.* 104 F4
Xeropotamos →, *Cyprus* 37 E11
Xhora, *S. Africa* 85 E4
Xhumo, *Botswana* 84 C3
Xi Jiang →, *China* 53 F9
Xi Xian, *Henan, China* 53 A10
Xi Xian, *Shanxi, China* 50 F6
Xia Xian, *China* 50 G6
Xiachengzi, *China* 51 B16
Xiachuan Dao, *China* 53 G9
Xiaguan, *China* 52 E3
Xiajiang, *China* 53 D10
Xiajin, *China* 50 F8
Xiamen, *China* 53 E12
Xi'an, *China* 50 G5
Xian Xian, *China* 50 E9
Xianfeng, *China* 52 C7
Xiang Jiang →, *China* 53 C9
Xiangcheng, *Henan, China* 50 H8
Xiangcheng, *Henan, China* 50 H7
Xiangcheng, *Sichuan, China* 52 C2
Xiangdu, *China* 52 F6
Xiangfan, *China* 53 A9
Xianghuang Qi, *China* 50 C7
Xiangning, *China* 50 G6
Xiangquan, *China* 50 F7
Xiangshan, *China* 53 C13
Xiangshui, *China* 51 G10
Xiangtan, *China* 53 D9
Xiangxiang, *China* 53 D9
Xiangyin, *China* 53 C9
Xiangyun, *China* 52 E3
Xiangzhou, *China* 52 F7
Xianju, *China* 53 C13
Xianning, *China* 53 C10
Xianshui He →, *China* 52 B3
Xianyang, *China* 50 G5
Xianyou, *China* 53 E12
Xiao Hinggan Ling, *China* 54 B7
Xiao Xian, *China* 50 G9
Xiaofeng, *China* 53 B12
Xiaogan, *China* 53 B9
Xiaojin, *China* 52 B4
Xiaolan, *China* 53 F9
Xiaoshan, *China* 53 B13
Xiaoyi, *China* 50 F6
Xiapu, *China* 53 D12
Xiawa, *China* 51 C11
Xiayi, *China* 50 G9
Xichang, *China* 52 D4
Xichong, *China* 52 B5
Xichuan, *China* 50 H6
Xiemahe, *China* 53 B8
Xieng Khouang, *Laos* 58 C4
Xifei He →, *China* 50 H9
Xifeng, *Guizhou, China* 52 D6
Xifeng, *Liaoning, China* 51 C13
Xifengzhen, *China* 50 G4
Xigazê, *China* 54 D3
Xihe, *China* 50 G3
Xihua, *China* 50 H8
Xiliao He →, *China* 51 C12
Xilin, *China* 52 E5
Xilókastron, *Greece* 39 L5
Xin Jiang →, *China* 53 C11
Xin Xian, *China* 50 E7
Xinavane, *Mozam.* 85 D5
Xinbin, *China* 51 D13
Xincai, *China* 53 A10
Xinchang, *China* 53 C13
Xincheng, *Guangxi Zhuangzu, China* 52 E7
Xincheng, *Jiangxi, China* 53 D10
Xinfeng, *Guangdong, China* 53 E10
Xinfeng, *Jiangxi, China* 53 D11
Xinfeng, *Jiangxi, China* 53 E10
Xing Xian, *China* 50 E6
Xing'an, *Guangxi Zhuangzu, China* 53 E8
Xingan, *Jiangxi, China* 53 D10
Xingcheng, *China* 51 D11
Xingguo, *China* 53 D10
Xinghe, *China* 50 D7
Xinghua, *China* 51 H10
Xinghua Wan, *China* 53 E12
Xinglong, *China* 51 D9
Xingning, *China* 53 E10
Xingping, *China* 50 G5
Xingren, *China* 52 E5
Xingshan, *China* 53 B8
Xingtai, *China* 50 F8
Xingu →, *Brazil* 121 D7
Xingyang, *China* 50 G7
Xinhe, *China* 50 F8
Xinhua, *China* 53 D8
Xinhuang, *China* 52 D7
Xinhui, *China* 53 F9
Xining, *China* 54 C5
Xinjiang, *China* 50 G6
Xinjiang Uygur Zizhiqu □, *China* 54 B3
Xinjie, *China* 52 D3
Xinjin, *Liaoning, China* 51 E11
Xinjin, *Sichuan, China* 52 B4
Xinkai He →, *China* 51 C12
Xinle, *China* 50 E8
Xinlitun, *China* 51 D12
Xinlong, *China* 52 B3
Xinmin, *China* 51 D12
Xinning, *China* 53 D8
Xinping, *China* 52 E3
Xinshao, *China* 53 D8
Xintai, *China* 51 G9
Xintian, *China* 53 E9
Xinxiang, *China* 50 G7
Xinxing, *China* 53 F9
Xinyang, *China* 53 A10
Xinye, *China* 53 A9
Xinyi, *China* 53 F8
Xinyu, *China* 53 D10
Xinzhan, *China* 51 C14
Xinzheng, *China* 50 G7
Xinzhou, *China* 53 B10
Xiong Xian, *China* 50 E9
Xiongyuecheng, *China* 51 D12
Xiping, *Henan, China* 50 H8
Xiping, *Henan, China* 50 H6
Xiping, *Zhejiang, China* 53 C12
Xique-Xique, *Brazil* 122 D3
Xiruá →, *Brazil* 124 B4
Xisha Qundao = Paracel Is., *S. China Sea* 56 A4
Xishui, *China* 53 B10
Xituozhen, *China* 52 B7
Xiuning, *China* 53 C12
Xiuren, *China* 53 E8
Xiushan, *China* 52 C7
Xiushui, *China* 53 C10
Xiuwen, *China* 52 D6
Xiuyan, *China* 51 D12
Xixabangma Feng, *China* 61 E14
Xixia, *China* 50 H6
Xixiang, *China* 50 H4
Xiyang, *China* 50 F7
Xizang □, *China* 54 C3
Xlendi, *Malta* 37 C1
Xu Jiang →, *China* 53 D11
Xuan Loc, *Vietnam* 59 G6
Xuancheng, *China* 53 B12
Xuan'en, *China* 52 C7
Xuanhan, *China* 52 B6
Xuanhua, *China* 50 D8
Xuchang, *China* 50 G7
Xudat, *Azerbaijan* 43 K9
Xuefeng Shan, *China* 53 D8
Xuejiaping, *China* 53 B8
Xun Jiang →, *China* 53 F8
Xun Xian, *China* 50 G8
Xundian, *China* 52 E4
Xunwu, *China* 53 E10
Xunyang, *China* 50 H5
Xunyi, *China* 50 G5
Xupu, *China* 53 D8
Xushui, *China* 50 E8
Xuwen, *China* 53 G8
Xuyen Moc, *Vietnam* 59 G6
Xuyong, *China* 52 C5
Xuzhou, *China* 51 G9
Xylophagou, *Cyprus* 37 E12

Y

Ya Xian, *China* 58 C7
Yaamba, *Australia* 90 C5
Ya'an, *China* 52 C4
Yaapeet, *Australia* 91 F3
Yabassi, *Cameroon* 79 E6
Yabelo, *Ethiopia* 77 G4
Yablonovy Ra. = Yablonovyy Khrebet, *Russia* 45 D12
Yablonovyy Khrebet, *Russia* 45 D12
Yabrai Shan, *China* 50 E2
Yabrūd, *Syria* 69 B5
Yacuiba, *Bolivia* 126 A3
Yacuma →, *Bolivia* 125 C4
Yadgir, *India* 60 L10
Yadkin →, *U.S.A.* 105 H5
Yadrin, *Russia* 42 C8
Yagaba, *Ghana* 79 C4
Yagodnoye, *Russia* 45 C15
Yagoua, *Cameroon* 80 B3
Yaguas →, *Peru* 120 D3
Yaha, *Thailand* 59 J3
Yahila, *Zaïre* 82 B1
Yahk, *Canada* 100 D5
Yahotyn, *Ukraine* 41 G6
Yahuma, *Zaïre* 80 D4
Yahyalı, *Turkey* 66 C6
Yaita, *Japan* 49 F9
Yaiza, *Canary Is.* 36 F6
Yajiang, *China* 52 B3
Yajua, *Nigeria* 79 C7
Yakima, *U.S.A.* 110 C3
Yakima →, *U.S.A.* 110 C3
Yako, *Burkina Faso* 78 C4
Yakoruda, *Bulgaria* 39 G6
Yakovlevka, *Russia* 48 B6
Yaku-Shima, *Japan* 49 J5
Yakutat, *U.S.A.* 96 C6
Yakutia = Sakha □, *Russia* 45 C13
Yakutsk, *Russia* 45 C13
Yala, *Thailand* 59 J3
Yalbalgo, *Australia* 89 E1
Yalboroo, *Australia* 90 C4
Yale, *U.S.A.* 106 C2
Yalgoo, *Australia* 89 E2
Yalinga, *C.A.R.* 73 G9
Yalkubul, Punta, *Mexico* 115 C7
Yalleroi, *Australia* 90 C4
Yalobusha →, *U.S.A.* 109 J9
Yalong Jiang →, *China* 52 D3
Yalova, *Turkey* 66 B3
Yalpuh, Ozero, *Ukraine* 38 D11
Yalta, *Ukraine* 41 K8
Yalu Jiang →, *China* 51 E13
Yalutorovsk, *Russia* 44 D7
Yalvaç, *Turkey* 66 C4
Yam Ha Melah = Dead Sea, *Asia* 69 D4
Yam Kinneret, *Israel* 69 C4
Yamada, *Japan* 49 H5
Yamagata, *Japan* 48 E10
Yamagata □, *Japan* 48 E10
Yamaguchi, *Japan* 49 G5
Yamaguchi □, *Japan* 49 G5
Yamal, Poluostrov, *Russia* 44 B8
Yamal Pen. = Yamal, Poluostrov, *Russia* 44 B8
Yamanashi □, *Japan* 49 G9
Yamantau, Gora, *Russia* 44 D6
Yamba, *N.S.W., Australia* 91 D5
Yamba, *S. Austral., Australia* 91 E3
Yambah, *Australia* 90 C1
Yambarran Ra., *Australia* 88 C5
Yâmbiô, *Sudan* 77 G2
Yambol, *Bulgaria* 38 G9
Yamdena, *Indonesia* 57 F8
Yame, *Japan* 49 H5
Yamethin, *Burma* 61 J20
Yamil, *Nigeria* 79 C6
Yamma-Yamma, L., *Australia* 91 D3
Yamoussoukro, *Ivory C.* 78 D3

Yampa →, *U.S.A.* 110 F9
Yampi Sd., *Australia* 88 C3
Yampil, *Moldova* 41 H5
Yampol = Yampil, *Moldova* 41 H5
Yamrat, *Nigeria* 79 C6
Yamrukchal, *Bulgaria* 38 G7
Yamuna →, *India* 63 G9
Yamzho Yumco, *China* 54 D4
Yan, *Nigeria* 79 C7
Yana →, *Russia* 45 B14
Yanac, *Australia* 91 F3
Yanagawa, *Japan* 49 H5
Yanai, *Japan* 49 H6
Yan'an, *China* 50 F5
Yanbian, *China* 52 D3
Yanbu 'al Baḥr, *Si. Arabia* 64 F3
Yancannia, *Australia* 91 E3
Yanchang, *China* 50 F6
Yancheng, *Henan, China* 50 H7
Yancheng, *Jiangsu, China* 51 H11
Yanchi, *China* 50 F4
Yanchuan, *China* 50 F6
Yanco Cr. →, *Australia* 91 F4
Yandal, *Australia* 89 E3
Yandanooka, *Australia* 89 E2
Yandaran, *Australia* 90 C5
Yandoon, *Burma* 61 L19
Yanfeng, *China* 52 E3
Yanfolila, *Mali* 78 C3
Yang Xian, *China* 50 H4
Yangambi, *Zaïre* 82 B1
Yangbi, *China* 52 E2
Yangcheng, *China* 50 G7
Yangch'ü = Taiyuan, *China* 50 F7
Yangchun, *China* 53 F8
Yanggao, *China* 50 D7
Yanggu, *China* 50 F8
Yangjiang, *China* 53 G8
Yangliuqing, *China* 51 E9
Yangon = Rangoon, *Burma* 61 L20
Yangping, *China* 53 B8
Yangpingguan, *China* 50 H4
Yangquan, *China* 50 F7
Yangshan, *China* 53 E9
Yangshuo, *China* 53 E8
Yangtze Kiang = Chang Jiang →, *China* 53 B13
Yangxin, *China* 53 C10
Yangyang, *S. Korea* 51 E15
Yangyuan, *China* 50 D8
Yangzhou, *China* 53 A12
Yanhe, *China* 52 C7
Yanji, *China* 51 C15
Yanjin, *China* 52 C5
Yanjing, *China* 52 C2
Yankton, *U.S.A.* 108 D6
Yanna, *Australia* 91 D4
Yanonge, *Zaïre* 82 B1
Yanqi, *China* 54 B3
Yanqing, *China* 50 D8
Yanshan, *Hebei, China* 51 E9
Yanshan, *Jiangxi, China* 53 C11
Yanshan, *Yunnan, China* 52 F5
Yanshou, *China* 51 B15
Yantabulla, *Australia* 91 D4
Yantai, *China* 51 F11
Yanting, *China* 52 B5
Yantra →, *Bulgaria* 38 F8
Yanwa, *China* 52 D2
Yanykurgan, *Kazakstan* 44 E7
Yanyuan, *China* 52 D3
Yanzhou, *China* 50 G9
Yao, *Chad* 73 F8
Yao Xian, *China* 50 G5
Yao Yai, Ko, *Thailand* 59 J2
Yao'an, *China* 52 E3
Yaodu, *China* 52 A5
Yaoundé, *Cameroon* 79 E7
Yaowan, *China* 51 G10
Yap I., *Pac. Oc.* 92 G5
Yapen, *Indonesia* 57 E9
Yapen, Selat, *Indonesia* 57 E9
Yappar →, *Australia* 90 B3
Yaqui →, *Mexico* 114 B2
Yar-Sale, *Russia* 44 C8
Yaracuy □, *Venezuela* 120 A4
Yaracuy →, *Venezuela* 120 A4
Yaraka, *Australia* 90 C3
Yaransk, *Russia* 42 B8
Yardea P.O., *Australia* 91 E2
Yare →, *U.K.* 13 E9
Yaremcha, *Ukraine* 41 H3
Yarensk, *Russia* 44 C5
Yarí →, *Colombia* 120 D3
Yaritagua, *Venezuela* 120 A4
Yarkand = Shache, *China* 54 C2
Yarker, *Canada* 107 B8
Yarkhun →, *Pakistan* 63 A5
Yarmouth, *Canada* 99 D6
Yarmūk →, *Syria* 69 C4
Yaroslavl, *Russia* 42 B4
Yarqa, W. →, *Egypt* 69 F2
Yarra Yarra Lakes, *Australia* 89 E2
Yarraden, *Australia* 90 A3
Yarraloola, *Australia* 88 D2
Yarram, *Australia* 91 F4
Yarraman, *Australia* 91 D5
Yarranvale, *Australia* 91 D4
Yarras, *Australia* 91 E5
Yarrowmere, *Australia* 90 C4
Yartsevo, *Russia* 40 E7
Yartsevo, *Russia* 45 C10
Yarumal, *Colombia* 120 B2
Yasawa Group, *Fiji* 87 C7
Yaselda, *Belarus* 41 F4
Yashi, *Nigeria* 79 C6
Yashkul, *Russia* 43 G7
Yasin, *Pakistan* 63 A5
Yasinovataya, *Ukraine* 41 H9
Yasinski, L., *Canada* 98 B4
Yasinya, *Ukraine* 41 H3
Yasothon, *Thailand* 58 E5
Yass, *Australia* 91 E4
Yata →, *Bolivia* 125 C4
Yatağan, *Turkey* 66 D3
Yates Center, *U.S.A.* 109 G7
Yathkyed L., *Canada* 101 A9
Yatsushiro, *Japan* 49 H5
Yatta Plateau, *Kenya* 82 C4
Yauca, *Peru* 124 D3
Yauya, *Peru* 124 B2
Yauyos, *Peru* 124 C2
Yavari →, *Peru* 124 A3
Yavatmal, *India* 60 J11
Yavne, *Israel* 69 D3
Yavoriv, *Ukraine* 41 H2
Yavorov = Yavoriv, *Ukraine* 41 H2
Yavuzeli, *Turkey* 66 D7
Yawatahama, *Japan* 49 H6
Yawri B., *S. Leone* 78 D2
Yaxi, *China* 52 D6
Yayama-Rettō, *Japan* 49 M1
Yazd, *Iran* 65 D7
Yazd □, *Iran* 65 D7
Yazoo →, *U.S.A.* 109 J9
Yazoo City, *U.S.A.* 109 J9
Yding Skovhøj, *Denmark* 9 J13
Ye Xian, *Henan, China* 50 H7
Ye Xian, *Shandong, China* 51 F10
Yealering, *Australia* 89 F2
Yebyu, *Burma* 61 M21
Yechŏn, *S. Korea* 51 F15
Yecla, *Spain* 29 G3
Yécora, *Mexico* 114 B3
Yedintsy = Edinița, *Moldova* 41 H4
Yeeda, *Australia* 88 C3
Yeelanna, *Australia* 91 E2
Yefremov, *Russia* 42 D4
Yeghegnadzor, *Armenia* 67 C11
Yegorlyk →, *Russia* 43 G6
Yegorlykskaya, *Russia* 43 G5
Yegoryevsk, *Russia* 42 C4
Yegros, *Paraguay* 126 B4
Yehuda, Midbar, *Israel* 69 D4
Yei, *Sudan* 77 G3
Yei, Nahr →, *Sudan* 77 F3
Yejmiadzin, *Armenia* 43 K7
Yekaterinburg, *Russia* 44 D7
Yekaterinodar = Krasnodar, *Russia* 43 H4
Yelabuga, *Russia* 42 C11
Yelan, *Russia* 42 E6
Yelanskoye, *Russia* 45 C13
Yelarbon, *Australia* 91 D5
Yelatma, *Russia* 42 C5
Yelcho, L., *Chile* 128 B2
Yelets, *Russia* 42 D4
Yélimané, *Mali* 78 B2
Yelizavetgrad = Kirovohrad, *Ukraine* 41 H7
Yell, *U.K.* 14 A7
Yell Sd., *U.K.* 14 A7
Yellow Sea, *China* 51 G12
Yellowhead Pass, *Canada* 100 C5
Yellowknife, *Canada* 100 A6
Yellowknife →, *Canada* 100 A6
Yellowstone →, *U.S.A.* 108 B3
Yellowstone L., *U.S.A.* 110 D8
Yellowstone National Park, *U.S.A.* 110 D8
Yellowtail Res., *U.S.A.* 110 D9
Yelnya, *Russia* 40 E7
Yelsk, *Belarus* 41 G5
Yelvertoft, *Australia* 90 C2
Yelwa, *Nigeria* 79 C5
Yemen ■, *Asia* 68 E3
Yen Bai, *Vietnam* 58 B5
Yenakiyeve, *Ukraine* 41 H10
Yenakiyevo = Yenakiyeve, *Ukraine* 41 H10
Yenangyaung, *Burma* 61 J19
Yenbo = Yanbu 'al Baḥr, *Si. Arabia* 64 F3
Yenda, *Australia* 91 E4
Yendéré, *Ivory C.* 78 C4
Yendi, *Ghana* 79 D4
Yenice, *Ankara, Turkey* 66 C5
Yenice, *Çanakkale, Turkey* 66 C2
Yenice →, *Turkey* 66 D6
Yenisaía, *Greece* 39 H7
Yenişehir, *Turkey* 66 B3
Yenisey →, *Russia* 44 B9
Yeniseysk, *Russia* 45 D10
Yeniseyskiy Zaliv, *Russia* 44 B9
Yennádhi, *Greece* 37 C9
Yenne, *France* 27 C9
Yenotayevka, *Russia* 43 G8
Yenyuka, *Russia* 45 D13
Yeo, L., *Australia* 89 E3
Yeola, *India* 60 J9
Yeoryioúpolis, *Greece* 37 D6
Yeovil, *U.K.* 13 G5
Yepes, *Spain* 28 F1
Yeppoon, *Australia* 90 C5
Yeráki, *Greece* 39 N4
Yerbent, *Turkmenistan* 44 F6
Yerbogachen, *Russia* 45 C11
Yerevan, *Armenia* 43 K7
Yerilla, *Australia* 89 E3
Yerköy, *Turkey* 66 C6
Yermak, *Kazakstan* 44 D8
Yermakovo, *Russia* 45 D13
Yermo, *U.S.A.* 113 L10
Yerofey Pavlovich, *Russia* 45 D13
Yerólakkos, *Cyprus* 37 D12
Yeropol, *Russia* 45 C17
Yeropótamos →, *Greece* 37 D6
Yeroskipos, *Cyprus* 37 E11
Yerseke, *Neths.* 17 F4
Yershov, *Russia* 42 E9
Yerunaja, Cerro, *Peru* 124 C2
Yerushalayim = Jerusalem, *Israel* 69 D4
Yerville, *France* 24 C7
Yes Tor, *U.K.* 13 G4
Yesan, *S. Korea* 51 F14
Yeşilhisar, *Turkey* 66 C6
Yeşilırmak →, *Turkey* 66 B7
Yeşilkent, *Turkey* 66 D7
Yesnogorsk, *Russia* 42 C3
Yeso, *U.S.A.* 109 H2
Yessentuki, *Russia* 43 H6
Yessey, *Russia* 45 C11
Yeste, *Spain* 29 G2
Yeu, I. d', *France* 24 F4
Yevlakh = Yevlax, *Azerbaijan* 43 K8
Yevlax, *Azerbaijan* 43 K8
Yevpatoriya, *Ukraine* 41 K7
Yeya →, *Russia* 43 G4
Yeysk, *Russia* 43 G4
Yezd = Yazd, *Iran* 65 D7
Yezerishche, *Belarus* 40 E5
Yhati, *Paraguay* 126 B4
Yhú, *Paraguay* 127 B4
Yi →, *Uruguay* 126 C4
Yi 'Allaq, G., *Egypt* 69 E2
Yi He →, *China* 51 G10
Yi Xian, *Anhui, China* 53 C11
Yi Xian, *Hebei, China* 50 E8
Yi Xian, *Liaoning, China* 51 D11
Yialí, *Greece* 39 N10
Yialiás →, *Cyprus* 37 D12
Yi'allaq, G., *Egypt* 76 H8
Yialousa, *Cyprus* 37 D13
Yiáltra, *Greece* 39 L5
Yianisádhes, *Greece* 37 D8
Yiannitsa, *Greece* 39 J5
Yibin, *China* 52 C5
Yichang, *China* 53 B8
Yicheng, *Henan, China* 53 B9
Yicheng, *Shanxi, China* 50 G6
Yichuan, *China* 50 F6
Yichun, *Heilongjiang, China* 54 B7
Yichun, *Jiangxi, China* 53 D10
Yidu, *Hubei, China* 53 B8
Yidu, *Shandong, China* 51 F10
Yidun, *China* 52 B2
Yihuang, *China* 53 D11
Yijun, *China* 50 G5
Yıldızeli, *Turkey* 66 C7
Yiliang, *Yunnan, China* 52 D5
Yiliang, *Yunnan, China* 52 E4
Yilong, *China* 52 B6
Yimen, *China* 52 E4
Yimianpo, *China* 51 B15
Yinchuan, *China* 50 E4
Yindarlgooda, L., *Australia* 89 F3
Ying He →, *China* 50 H9
Ying Xian, *China* 50 E7
Yingcheng, *China* 53 B9
Yingde, *China* 53 E9
Yingjiang, *China* 52 E1
Yingjing, *China* 52 C4
Yingkou, *China* 51 D12
Yingshan, *Henan, China* 53 B9
Yingshan, *Hubei, China* 53 B10
Yingshan, *Sichuan, China* 52 B6
Yingshang, *China* 53 A11
Yingtan, *China* 54 D6
Yining, *China* 44 E9
Yinjiang, *China* 52 C7
Yinmabin, *Burma* 61 H19
Yinnietharra, *Australia* 88 D2
Yiofiros →, *Greece* 37 D7
Yioúra, *Greece* 39 K7
Yipinglang, *China* 52 E3
Yirga Alem, *Ethiopia* 77 F4
Yishan, *China* 52 E7
Yishui, *China* 51 G10
Yíthion, *Greece* 39 N5
Yitiaoshan, *China* 50 F3
Yitong, *China* 51 C13
Yiwu, *China* 53 C13
Yixing, *China* 53 B12
Yiyang, *Henan, China* 50 G7
Yiyang, *Hunan, China* 53 C9
Yiyang, *Jiangxi, China* 53 C11
Yizhang, *China* 53 E9
Yizheng, *China* 53 A12
Yli-Kitka, *Finland* 8 C23
Ylitornio, *Finland* 8 C20
Ylivieska, *Finland* 8 D21
Yngaren, *Sweden* 11 F10
Ynykchanskiy, *Russia* 45 C14
Yoakum, *U.S.A.* 109 L6
Yobe □, *Nigeria* 79 C7
Yog Pt., *Phil.* 57 B6
Yogan, *Togo* 79 D5
Yogyakarta, *Indonesia* 57 G14
Yoho Nat. Park, *Canada* 100 C5
Yojoa, L. de, *Honduras* 116 D2
Yŏju, *S. Korea* 51 F14
Yokadouma, *Cameroon* 80 D2
Yokkaichi, *Japan* 49 G8
Yoko, *Cameroon* 79 D7
Yokohama, *Japan* 49 G9
Yokosuka, *Japan* 49 G9
Yokote, *Japan* 48 E10
Yola, *Nigeria* 79 D7
Yolaina, Cordillera de, *Nic.* 116 D3
Yonago, *Japan* 49 G6
Yonaguni-Jima, *Japan* 49 M1
Yŏnan, *N. Korea* 51 F14
Yonezawa, *Japan* 48 F10
Yong Peng, *Malaysia* 59 L4
Yong Sata, *Thailand* 59 J2
Yongampo, *N. Korea* 51 E13
Yong'an, *China* 53 E11
Yongcheng, *China* 50 H9
Yŏngchŏn, *S. Korea* 51 G15
Yongchuan, *China* 52 C5
Yongchun, *China* 53 E12
Yongdeng, *China* 50 F2
Yongding, *China* 53 E11
Yŏngdŏk, *S. Korea* 51 F15
Yŏngdŭngpo, *S. Korea* 51 F14
Yongfeng, *China* 53 D10
Yongfu, *China* 52 E7
Yonghe, *China* 50 F6
Yŏnghŭng, *N. Korea* 51 E14
Yongji, *China* 50 G6
Yŏngju, *S. Korea* 51 F15
Yongkang, *Yunnan, China* 52 E2
Yongkang, *Zhejiang, China* 53 C13
Yongnian, *China* 50 F8
Yongning, *Guangxi Zhuangzu, China* 52 F7
Yongning, *Ningxia Huizu, China* 50 E4
Yongping, *China* 52 E2
Yongqing, *China* 50 E9
Yongren, *China* 52 D3
Yongshan, *China* 52 C4
Yongsheng, *China* 52 D3
Yongshun, *China* 52 C7
Yongtai, *China* 53 E12
Yŏngwŏl, *S. Korea* 51 F15
Yongxin, *China* 53 D10
Yongxing, *China* 53 D9
Yongxiu, *China* 53 C10
Yonibana, *S. Leone* 78 D2
Yonkers, *U.S.A.* 107 F11
Yonne □, *France* 25 E10
Yonne →, *France* 25 D9
York, *Australia* 89 F2
York, *U.K.* 12 D6
York, *Ala., U.S.A.* 105 J1
York, *Nebr., U.S.A.* 108 E6
York, *Pa., U.S.A.* 104 F7
York □, *U.K.* 12 D6
York, C., *Australia* 90 A3
York, Kap, *Greenland* 4 B4
York Sd., *Australia* 88 B4
Yorke Pen., *Australia* 91 E2
Yorkshire Wolds, *U.K.* 12 D7
Yorkton, *Canada* 101 C8
Yorktown, *U.S.A.* 109 L6
Yorkville, *U.S.A.* 112 G3
Yornup, *Australia* 89 F2
Yoro, *Honduras* 116 C2
Yoron-Jima, *Japan* 49 L4
Yos Sudarso, Pulau, *Indonesia* 57 F9
Yosemite National Park, *U.S.A.* 111 H4
Yosemite Village, *U.S.A.* 112 H7
Yoshkar Ola, *Russia* 42 B8
Yŏsu, *S. Korea* 51 G14
Yotala, *Bolivia* 125 D4
Yotvata, *Israel* 69 F4
You Xian, *China* 53 D9
Youbou, *Canada* 100 D4
Youghal, *Ireland* 15 E4
Youghal B., *Ireland* 15 E4
Youkounkoun, *Guinea* 78 C2
Young, *Australia* 91 E4
Young, *Canada* 101 C7
Young, *Uruguay* 126 C4
Younghusband, L., *Australia* 91 E2
Younghusband Pen., *Australia* 91 F2
Youngstown, *Canada* 101 C6
Youngstown, *N.Y., U.S.A.* 106 C5
Youngstown, *Ohio, U.S.A.* 106 E4
Youngsville, *U.S.A.* 106 E5
Youssoufia, *Morocco* 74 B3
Youxi, *China* 53 D12
Youyang, *China* 52 C7
Youyu, *China* 50 D7
Yowerabgabbie, *Australia* 89 E2
Yozgat, *Turkey* 66 C6
Ypané →, *Paraguay* 126 A4
Yport, *France* 24 C7
Ypres = Ieper, *Belgium* 17 G1
Ypsilanti, *U.S.A.* 104 D4
Yreka, *U.S.A.* 110 F2
Ysleta, *U.S.A.* 111 L10
Yssingeaux, *France* 27 C8
Ystad, *Sweden* 11 J7
Ysyk-Köl, *Kyrgyzstan* 46 E11
Ysyk-Köl, Ozero, *Kyrgyzstan* 44 E8
Ythan →, *U.K.* 14 D7
Ytterhogdal, *Sweden* 10 B8
Ytyk Kyuyel, *Russia* 45 C14
Yu Jiang →, *China* 54 D6
Yu Xian, *Hebei, China* 50 E8
Yu Xian, *Henan, China* 50 G7
Yu Xian, *Shanxi, China* 50 E7
Yuan Jiang →, *Hunan, China* 53 C8
Yuan Jiang →, *Yunnan, China* 52 F4
Yuan'an, *China* 53 B8
Yuanjiang, *Hunan, China* 53 C9
Yuanjiang, *Yunnan, China* 52 F4
Yüanli, *Taiwan* 53 E13
Yüanlin, *Taiwan* 53 F13
Yuanlin, *Taiwan* 53 F13
Yuanling, *China* 53 C8
Yuanmou, *China* 52 E3
Yuanqu, *China* 50 G6
Yuanyang, *Henan, China* 50 G7
Yuanyang, *Yunnan, China* 52 F4
Yuba →, *U.S.A.* 112 F5
Yuba City, *U.S.A.* 112 F5
Yūbari, *Japan* 48 C10
Yūbetsu, *Japan* 48 B11
Yucatán □, *Mexico* 115 C7
Yucatán, Canal de, *Caribbean* 116 B2
Yucatán, Península de, *Mexico* 94 H11
Yucatán Basin, *Cent. Amer.* 94 H11
Yucatan Str. = Yucatán, Canal de, *Caribbean* 116 B2
Yucca, *U.S.A.* 113 L12
Yucca Valley, *U.S.A.* 113 L10
Yucheng, *China* 50 F9
Yuci, *China* 50 F7
Yudino, *Russia* 44 D7
Yudu, *China* 53 E10
Yuendumu, *Australia* 88 D5
Yueqing, *China* 53 C13
Yueqing Wan, *China* 53 C13
Yuexi, *Anhui, China* 53 B11
Yuexi, *Sichuan, China* 52 C4
Yueyang, *China* 53 C9
Yugan, *China* 53 C11
Yugoslavia ■, *Europe* 21 M10
Yuhuan, *China* 53 C13
Yujiang, *China* 53 C11
Yukhnov, *Russia* 42 C2
Yukon →, *U.S.A.* 96 B3
Yukon Territory □, *Canada* 96 B6
Yüksekova, *Turkey* 67 D11
Yukti, *Russia* 45 C11
Yukuhashi, *Japan* 49 H5
Yule →, *Australia* 88 D2
Yuli, *Nigeria* 79 D7
Yulin, *Guangxi Zhuangzu, China* 53 F8
Yulin, *Shaanxi, China* 50 E5
Yuma, *Ariz., U.S.A.* 113 N12
Yuma, *Colo., U.S.A.* 108 E3
Yuma, B. de, *Dom. Rep.* 117 C6
Yumbe, *Uganda* 82 B3
Yumbi, *Zaïre* 82 C2
Yumbo, *Colombia* 120 C2
Yumen, *China* 54 C4
Yumurtalık, *Turkey* 66 D6
Yun Ho →, *China* 51 E9
Yun Xian, *Hubei, China* 53 A8
Yun Xian, *Yunnan, China* 52 E3
Yunak, *Turkey* 66 C4
Yunan, *China* 53 F8
Yuncheng, *Henan, China* 50 G8
Yuncheng, *Shanxi, China* 50 G6
Yundamindra, *Australia* 89 E3
Yunfu, *China* 53 F9
Yungas, *Bolivia* 125 D4
Yungay, *Chile* 126 D1
Yungay, *Peru* 124 B2
Yunhe, *China* 53 C12
Yunlin, *Taiwan* 53 F13
Yunling, *China* 52 D2
Yunlong, *China* 52 E2
Yunmeng, *China* 53 B9
Yunnan □, *China* 52 E4
Yunquera de Henares, *Spain* 28 E1
Yunta, *Australia* 91 E2
Yunxi, *China* 50 H6
Yunxiao, *China* 53 F11
Yunyang, *China* 52 B7
Yuping, *China* 52 D7
Yupukarri, *Guyana* 121 C6
Yupyongdong, *N. Korea* 51 D15
Yuqing, *China* 52 D6
Yur, *Russia* 45 D14
Yurgao, *Russia* 44 D9
Yuribei, *Russia* 44 B8
Yurimaguas, *Peru* 124 B2
Yuryev-Polskiy, *Russia* 42 B4
Yuryevets, *Russia* 42 B6
Yuryung Kaya, *Russia* 45 B12
Yuscarán, *Honduras* 116 D2
Yushanzhen, *China* 52 C7
Yushe, *China* 50 F7
Yushu, *Jilin, China* 51 B14
Yushu, *Qinghai, China* 54 C4
Yusufeli, *Turkey* 67 B9
Yutai, *China* 50 G9
Yutian, *China* 51 E9
Yuxarı Qarabağ = Nagorno-Karabakh, *Azerbaijan* 67 C12
Yuxi, *China* 52 E4
Yuyao, *China* 53 B13
Yuzawa, *Japan* 48 E10
Yuzha, *Russia* 42 B6
Yuzhno-Sakhalinsk, *Russia* 45 E15
Yvelines □, *France* 25 D8
Yverdon, *Switz.* 22 C3
Yvetot, *France* 24 C7
Yvonand, *Switz.* 22 C3

Z

Zaamslag, *Neths.* 17 F3
Zaan →, *Neths.* 16 D5
Zaandam, *Neths.* 16 D5
Zab, Monts du, *Algeria* 75 B6
Žabalj, *Serbia, Yug.* 21 K10
Žabari, *Serbia, Yug.* 21 L11
Zabarjad, *Egypt* 76 C4
Zabaykalsk, *Russia* 45 E12
Zabid, *Yemen* 68 E3
Ząbkowice Śląskie, *Poland* 20 E6
Zabłudów, *Poland* 20 B13
Zābol, *Iran* 65 D9
Zābolī, *Iran* 65 E9
Zabré, *Burkina Faso* 79 C4
Zabrze, *Poland* 20 E8
Zacapa, *Guatemala* 116 D2
Zacapu, *Mexico* 114 D4
Zacatecas, *Mexico* 114 C4
Zacatecas □, *Mexico* 114 C4
Zacatecoluca, *El Salv.* 116 D2
Zacoalco, *Mexico* 114 C4
Zacualtipán, *Mexico* 115 C5
Zadar, *Croatia* 33 D12
Zadawa, *Nigeria* 79 C7
Zadetkyi Kyun, *Burma* 59 H2
Zadonsk, *Russia* 42 D4
Zafarqand, *Iran* 65 C7
Zafra, *Spain* 31 G4
Żagań, *Poland* 20 D5
Zagazig, *Egypt* 76 H7
Zāgheh, *Iran* 65 C6
Zaghouan, *Tunisia* 75 A7
Zaglivérion, *Greece* 39 J6
Zaglou, *Algeria* 75 C4
Zagnanado, *Benin* 79 D5
Zagorá, *Greece* 39 K6
Zagora, *Morocco* 74 B3
Zagorsk = Sergiyev Posad, *Russia* 42 B4
Zagreb, *Croatia* 33 C12
Zāgros, Kūhhā-ye, *Iran* 65 C6
Zagros Mts. = Zāgros, Kūhhā-ye, *Iran* 65 C6
Zaguinaso, *Ivory C.* 78 C3
Zāhedān, *Fārs, Iran* 65 D7
Zāhedān, *Sīstān va Balūchestān, Iran* 65 D9
Zahlah, *Lebanon* 69 B4
Zahna, *Germany* 18 D8
Zahrez Chergui, *Algeria* 75 A5
Zahrez Rharbi, *Algeria* 75 B5
Zainsk, *Russia* 42 C11
Zaïre ■, *Africa* 80 E4
Zaïre →, *Africa* 80 F2
Zaječar, *Serbia, Yug.* 21 M12
Zakamensk, *Russia* 45 D11
Zakataly = Zaqatala, *Azerbaijan* 43 K8
Zakhodnaya Dzvina = Daugava →, *Latvia* 9 H21
Zākhū, *Iraq* 67 D10
Zákinthos, *Greece* 39 M3
Zakopane, *Poland* 20 F9
Zákros, *Greece* 37 D8
Zala →, *Hungary* 21 J7
Zalaegerszeg, *Hungary* 21 J6
Zalalövö, *Hungary* 21 J6
Zalamea de la Serena, *Spain* 31 G5
Zalamea la Real, *Spain* 31 H4
Žalec, *Slovenia* 33 B12
Zaleshchiki = Zalishchyky, *Ukraine* 41 H3
Zalingei, *Sudan* 73 F9
Zalishchyky, *Ukraine* 41 H3
Zaltbommel, *Neths.* 16 E6
Zambeke, *Zaïre* 82 B2
Zambeze →, *Africa* 83 F4
Zambezi = Zambeze →, *Africa* 83 F4
Zambezi, *Zambia* 81 G4
Zambezia □, *Mozam.* 83 F4
Zambia ■, *Africa* 83 E2
Zamboanga, *Phil.* 55 H5
Zamboanguita, *Phil.* 55 G5
Zambrano, *Colombia* 120 B3
Zambrów, *Poland* 20 C12
Zametchino, *Russia* 42 D6
Zamora, *Ecuador* 120 D2
Zamora, *Mexico* 114 C4
Zamora, *Spain* 30 D5
Zamora □, *Spain* 30 D5
Zamora-Chinchipe □, *Ecuador* 120 D2
Zamość, *Poland* 20 E13
Zamuro, Sierra del, *Venezuela* 121 C5
Zan, *Ghana* 79 D4
Zanaga, *Congo* 80 E2
Záncara →, *Spain* 29 F1
Zandijk, *Neths.* 16 D5
Zandvoort, *Neths.* 16 D5
Zanesville, *U.S.A.* 106 G2
Zangābād, *Iran* 64 B5
Zangue →, *Mozam.* 83 F4
Zanjān, *Iran* 67 D13
Zanjān □, *Iran* 65 B6
Zannone, *Italy* 34 B6
Zante = Zákinthos, *Greece* 39 M3
Zanthus, *Australia* 89 F3
Zanzibar, *Tanzania* 82 D4
Zanzūr, *Libya* 75 B7
Zaouiet El-Kala = Bordj Omar Driss, *Algeria* 75 C6
Zaouiet Reggane, *Algeria* 75 C5
Zaoyang, *China* 53 A9
Zaozhuang, *China* 51 G9
Zap Suyu = Kabīr, Zab al →, *Iraq* 67 D10
Zapadna Morava →, *Serbia, Yug.* 21 M11
Zapadnaya Dvina, *Russia* 40 D7
Zapadnaya Dvina → = Daugava →, *Latvia* 9 H21
Západné Beskydy, *Europe* 20 F9
Zapala, *Argentina* 128 A2
Zapaleri, Cerro, *Bolivia* 126 A2
Zapata, *U.S.A.* 109 M5
Zapatón →, *Spain* 31 G4
Zapiga, *Chile* 124 D4
Zaporizhzhya, *Ukraine* 41 J8
Zaporozhye = Zaporizhzhya, *Ukraine* 41 J8
Zapponeta, *Italy* 35 A8
Zaqatala, *Azerbaijan* 43 K8
Zara, *Turkey* 66 C7
Zaragoza, *Colombia* 120 B3
Zaragoza, *Coahuila, Mexico* 114 B4
Zaragoza, *Nuevo León, Mexico* 115 C5
Zaragoza, *Spain* 28 D4
Zaragoza □, *Spain* 28 D4
Zarand, *Kermān, Iran* 65 D8
Zarand, *Markazī, Iran* 65 C6
Zărandului, Munţii, *Romania* 38 C5
Zaranj, *Afghan.* 60 D2
Zarasai, *Lithuania* 9 J22
Zárate, *Argentina* 126 C4
Zaraysk, *Russia* 42 C4
Zaraza, *Venezuela* 121 B4
Zāreh, *Iran* 65 C6
Zarembo I., *U.S.A.* 100 B2
Zaria, *Nigeria* 79 C6
Zarneh, *Iran* 64 C5
Zarós, *Greece* 37 D6
Zarqā' →, *Jordan* 69 C4
Zarrīn, *Iran* 65 C7
Zaruma, *Ecuador* 120 D2
Żary, *Poland* 20 D5
Zarza de Alange, *Spain* 31 G4
Zarza de Granadilla, *Spain* 30 E4
Zarzaïtine, *Algeria* 75 C6
Zarzal, *Colombia* 120 C2
Zarzis, *Tunisia* 75 B7
Zas, *Spain* 30 B2
Zashiversk, *Russia* 45 C15
Zaskar →, *India* 63 B7
Zaskar Mts., *India* 63 C7
Zastron, *S. Africa* 84 E4
Zaterechnyy, *Russia* 43 H7
Zavāreh, *Iran* 65 C7
Zaventem, *Belgium* 17 G4
Zavetnoye, *Russia* 43 G6
Zavidovići, *Bos.-H.* 21 L8
Zavitinsk, *Russia* 45 D13
Zavodovski, I., *Antarctica* 5 B1
Zavolzhsk, *Russia* 42 B6
Zavolzhye, *Russia* 42 B6
Zawiercie, *Poland* 20 E9
Zawyet Shammâs, *Egypt* 76 A2
Zâwyet Um el Rakham, *Egypt* 76 A2
Zâwyet Ungeîla, *Egypt* 76 A2
Zāyā, *Iraq* 64 C5
Zayarsk, *Russia* 45 D11
Zaysan, *Kazakstan* 44 E9
Zaysan, Oz., *Kazakstan* 44 E9
Zayü, *China* 52 C1
Zazir, O. →, *Algeria* 75 D6
Zbarazh, *Ukraine* 41 H3
Zbąszyń, *Poland* 20 C5
Zblewo, *Poland* 20 B8
Zdolbuniv, *Ukraine* 41 G4
Ždrelo, *Serbia, Yug.* 21 L11
Zduńska Wola, *Poland* 20 D8
Zeballos, *Canada* 100 D3
Zebediela, *S. Africa* 85 C4
Zedelgem, *Belgium* 17 F2
Zeebrugge, *Belgium* 17 F2
Zeehan, *Australia* 90 G4
Zeeland, *Neths.* 17 E7
Zeeland □, *Neths.* 17 F3
Zeelst, *Neths.* 17 F6
Zeerust, *S. Africa* 84 D4
Zefat, *Israel* 69 C4
Zegdou, *Algeria* 74 C4
Zege, *Ethiopia* 77 E4
Zegelsem, *Belgium* 17 G3
Zégoua, *Mali* 78 C3
Zehdenick, *Germany* 18 C9
Zeil, Mt., *Australia* 88 D5
Zeila, *Somali Rep.* 68 E3
Zeist, *Neths.* 16 D6
Zeitz, *Germany* 18 D8
Zele, *Belgium* 17 F4
Zelenodolsk, *Russia* 42 C9
Zelenogorsk, *Russia* 40 B5
Zelenograd, *Russia* 42 B3
Zelenogradsk, *Russia* 9 J19
Zelenokumsk, *Russia* 43 H6
Zelhem, *Neths.* 16 D8
Zell, *Baden-W., Germany* 19 H3
Zell, *Rhld-Pfz., Germany* 19 E3
Zell am See, *Austria* 21 H2
Zella-Mehlis, *Germany* 18 E6
Zelzate, *Belgium* 17 F3
Zembra, I., *Tunisia* 75 A7
Zémio, *C.A.R.* 82 A2
Zemmora, *Algeria* 75 A5
Zemmur, *W. Sahara* 74 C2
Zemoul, O. →, *Algeria* 74 C3
Zemst, *Belgium* 17 G4
Zemun, *Serbia, Yug.* 21 L10
Zengbe, *Cameroon* 79 D7
Zengcheng, *China* 53 F9
Zenica, *Bos.-H.* 21 L7
Žepce, *Bos.-H.* 21 L8
Zeraf, Bahr ez →, *Sudan* 77 F3
Zerbst, *Germany* 18 D8
Zermatt, *Switz.* 22 D5
Zernez, *Switz.* 23 C10
Zernograd, *Russia* 43 G5
Zerqani, *Albania* 39 H3
Zestaponi, *Georgia* 43 J6
Zetel, *Germany* 18 B3
Zetten, *Neths.* 16 E7
Zeulenroda, *Germany* 18 E7
Zeven, *Germany* 18 B5
Zevenaar, *Neths.* 16 E8
Zevenbergen, *Neths.* 17 E5
Zévio, *Italy* 32 C8
Zeya, *Russia* 45 D13
Zeya →, *Russia* 45 D13
Zêzere →, *Portugal* 31 F2
Zghartā, *Lebanon* 69 A4
Zgierz, *Poland* 20 D9
Zgorzelec, *Poland* 20 D5
Zhabinka, *Belarus* 41 F3
Zhailma, *Kazakstan* 44 D7
Zhambyl, *Kazakstan* 44 E8
Zhangaly, *Kazakstan* 43 G10
Zhangaqazaly, *Kazakstan* 44 E7
Zhangbei, *China* 50 D8
Zhangguangcai Ling, *China* 51 B15
Zhangjiakou, *China* 50 D8
Zhangping, *China* 53 E11
Zhangpu, *China* 53 E11
Zhangwu, *China* 51 C12
Zhangye, *China* 54 C5
Zhangzhou, *China* 53 E11
Zhanhua, *China* 51 F10
Zhanjiang, *China* 53 G8
Zhanyi, *China* 52 E4
Zhanyu, *China* 51 B12
Zhao Xian, *China* 50 F8
Zhao'an, *China* 53 F11
Zhaocheng, *China* 50 F6
Zhaojue, *China* 52 C4
Zhaoping, *China* 53 E8
Zhaoqing, *China* 53 F9
Zhaotong, *China* 52 D4
Zhaoyuan, *Heilongjiang, China* 51 B13
Zhaoyuan, *Shandong, China* 51 F11
Zharkovskiy, *Russia* 40 E7
Zhashkiv, *Ukraine* 41 H6
Zhashui, *China* 50 H5
Zhayyq →, *Kazakstan* 44 E6
Zhdanov = Mariupol, *Ukraine* 41 J9
Zhecheng, *China* 50 G8
Zhegao, *China* 53 B11
Zhejiang □, *China* 53 C13
Zheleznogorsk, *Russia* 42 D2
Zheleznogorsk-Ilimskiy, *Russia* 45 D11
Zheltyye Vody = Zhovti Vody, *Ukraine* 41 H7
Zhen'an, *China* 50 H5
Zhenfeng, *China* 52 E5
Zheng'an, *China* 52 C6
Zhengding, *China* 50 E8
Zhenghe, *China* 53 D12
Zhengyang, *China* 53 A10
Zhengyangguan, *China* 53 A11
Zhengzhou, *China* 50 G7
Zhenhai, *China* 53 C13
Zhenjiang, *China* 53 A12
Zhenlai, *China* 51 B12
Zhenning, *China* 52 D5
Zhenping, *Henan, China* 50 H7
Zhenping, *Shaanxi, China* 52 B7
Zhenxiong, *China* 52 D5
Zhenyuan, *Gansu, China* 50 G4
Zhenyuan, *Guizhou, China* 52 D7
Zherdevka, *Russia* 42 E5
Zherong, *China* 53 D12
Zhetiqara, *Kazakstan* 44 D7
Zhezqazghan, *Kazakstan* 44 E7
Zhidan, *China* 50 F5
Zhigansk, *Russia* 45 C13
Zhigulevsk, *Russia* 42 D9
Zhijiang, *Hubei, China* 53 B8
Zhijiang, *Hunan, China* 52 D7
Zhijin, *China* 52 D5
Zhilinda, *Russia* 45 C12
Zhirnovsk, *Russia* 42 E7
Zhitomir = Zhytomyr, *Ukraine* 41 G5
Zhizdra, *Russia* 42 D2
Zhlobin, *Belarus* 41 F6
Zhmerinka = Zhmerynka, *Ukraine* 41 H5
Zhmerynka, *Ukraine* 41 H5
Zhodino = Zhodzina, *Belarus* 40 E5
Zhodzina, *Belarus* 40 E5
Zhokhova, Ostrov, *Russia* 45 B16
Zhong Xian, *China* 52 B7
Zhongdian, *China* 52 D2
Zhongdong, *China* 52 F6
Zhongdu, *China* 52 E7
Zhongning, *China* 50 F3
Zhongshan, *Guangdong, China* 53 F9
Zhongshan, *Guangxi Zhuangzu, China* 53 E8
Zhongtiao Shan, *China* 50 G6
Zhongwei, *China* 50 F3
Zhongxiang, *China* 53 B9
Zhongyang, *China* 50 F6
Zhoucun, *China* 51 F9
Zhouning, *China* 53 D12
Zhoushan Dao, *China* 53 C14
Zhouzhi, *China* 50 G5
Zhovti Vody, *Ukraine* 41 H7
Zhovtneve, *Ukraine* 41 J7
Zhovtnevoye = Zhovtneve, *Ukraine* 41 J7
Zhuanghe, *China* 51 E12
Zhucheng, *China* 51 G10
Zhugqu, *China* 50 H3
Zhuhai, *China* 53 F9
Zhuji, *China* 53 C13
Zhukovka, *Russia* 42 D1
Zhumadian, *China* 50 H8
Zhuo Xian, *China* 50 E8
Zhuolu, *China* 50 D8
Zhuozi, *China* 50 D7
Zhupanovo, *Russia* 45 D16
Zhushan, *China* 53 A8
Zhuxi, *China* 52 A7
Zhuzhou, *China* 53 D9
Zhytomyr, *Ukraine* 41 G5
Zi Shui →, *China* 53 C9
Zīārān, *Iran* 65 B6
Ziarat, *Pakistan* 62 D2
Zibo, *China* 51 F10
Zichang, *China* 50 F5
Zichem, *Belgium* 17 F5
Zielona Góra, *Poland* 20 D5
Zierikzee, *Neths.* 17 E3
Ziesar, *Germany* 18 C8
Zifta, *Egypt* 76 H7
Zigey, *Chad* 73 F8
Zigong, *China* 52 C5
Zigui, *China* 53 B8
Ziguinchor, *Senegal* 78 C1
Zihuatanejo, *Mexico* 114 D4
Zijin, *China* 53 F10
Zile, *Turkey* 66 B6
Žilina, *Slovak Rep.* 20 F8
Zillah, *Libya* 73 C8
Zillertaler Alpen, *Austria* 19 H7
Zima, *Russia* 45 D11
Zimane, Adrar in, *Algeria* 75 D5
Zimapán, *Mexico* 115 C5
Zimba, *Zambia* 83 F2
Zimbabwe, *Zimbabwe* 83 G3
Zimbabwe ■, *Africa* 83 F2
Zimovniki, *Russia* 43 G6
Zinal, *Switz.* 22 D5
Zinder, *Niger* 79 C6
Zinga, *Tanzania* 83 D4
Zingem, *Belgium* 17 G3
Zingst, *Germany* 18 A8
Ziniaré, *Burkina Faso* 79 C4
Zinkgruvan, *Sweden* 11 F9
Zinnowitz, *Germany* 18 A9
Zion National Park, *U.S.A.* 111 H7
Zipaquirá, *Colombia* 120 C3
Zirc, *Hungary* 21 H7
Žiri, *Slovenia* 33 B11
Žirje, *Croatia* 33 E12
Zirl, *Austria* 19 H7
Ziros, *Greece* 37 D8
Zitácuaro, *Mexico* 114 D4
Zitava →, *Slovak Rep.* 21 G8
Zittau, *Germany* 18 E10
Zitundo, *Mozam.* 85 D5
Živinice, *Bos.-H.* 21 L8
Ziway, L., *Ethiopia* 77 F4
Zixi, *China* 53 D11
Zixing, *China* 53 E9
Ziyang, *Shaanxi, China* 50 H5
Ziyang, *Sichuan, China* 52 B5
Ziyun, *China* 52 E6
Ziz, Oued →, *Morocco* 74 B4
Zizhixian, *China* 53 E8
Zizhong, *China* 52 C5
Zlarin, *Croatia* 33 E12
Zlatar, *Croatia* 33 B13
Zlataritsa, *Bulgaria* 38 F8
Zlatitsa, *Bulgaria* 38 G7
Zlatograd, *Bulgaria* 39 H8
Zlatoust, *Russia* 44 D6
Zletovo, *Macedonia* 39 H5
Zlin, *Czech.* 20 F7
Zlītan, *Libya* 73 B7
Złocieniec, *Poland* 20 B6
Złoczew, *Poland* 20 D8
Złotoryja, *Poland* 20 D5
Złotów, *Poland* 20 B7
Zmeinogorsk, *Kazakstan* 44 D9
Żmigród, *Poland* 20 D6
Zmiyev, *Ukraine* 41 H9
Znamenka = Znamyanka, *Ukraine* 41 H7
Znamyanka, *Ukraine* 41 H7
Żnin, *Poland* 20 C7
Znojmo, *Czech.* 20 G6
Zobeyrī, *Iran* 64 C5
Zobia, *Zaïre* 82 B2
Zoetermeer, *Neths.* 16 D5
Zofingen, *Switz.* 22 B5
Zogang, *China* 52 C1
Zogno, *Italy* 32 C6
Zogqên, *China* 52 A2
Zolder, *Belgium* 17 F6
Zollikofen, *Switz.* 22 C4
Zollikon, *Switz.* 23 B7
Zolochev = Zolochiv, *Ukraine* 41 H3
Zolochiv, *Ukraine* 41 H3
Zolotonosha, *Ukraine* 41 H7
Zomba, *Malawi* 83 F4
Zomergem, *Belgium* 17 F3
Zongo, *Zaïre* 80 D3
Zonguldak, *Turkey* 66 B4
Zonhoven, *Belgium* 17 G6
Zonqor Pt., *Malta* 37 D2
Zonza, *France* 27 G13
Zorgo, *Burkina Faso* 79 C4
Zorita, *Spain* 31 F5
Zorritos, *Peru* 124 A1
Zorzor, *Liberia* 78 D3
Zossen, *Germany* 18 C9
Zottegem, *Belgium* 17 G3
Zou Xiang, *China* 50 G9
Zouar, *Chad* 73 D8
Zouérate, *Mauritania* 74 D2
Zousfana, O. →, *Algeria* 75 B4
Zoushan Dao, *China* 53 B14
Zoutkamp, *Neths.* 16 B8
Zrenjanin, *Serbia, Yug.* 21 K10
Zuarungu, *Ghana* 79 C4
Zuba, *Nigeria* 79 D6
Zubayr, *Yemen* 77 D5
Zubia, *Spain* 31 H7
Zubtsov, *Russia* 42 B2
Zudáñez, *Bolivia* 125 D5
Zuénoula, *Ivory C.* 78 D3
Zuera, *Spain* 28 D4
Zuetina = Az Zuwaytīnah, *Libya* 73 B9
Zufar, *Oman* 68 D5
Zug, *Switz.* 23 B7
Zug □, *Switz.* 23 B7
Zugdidi, *Georgia* 43 J5
Zugersee, *Switz.* 23 B7
Zugspitze, *Germany* 19 H6
Zuid-Holland □, *Neths.* 16 E5
Zuidbeveland, *Neths.* 17 F3
Zuidbroek, *Neths.* 16 B9
Zuidelijk-Flevoland, *Neths.* 16 D6
Zuidhorn, *Neths.* 16 B8
Zuidlaarder meer, *Neths.* 16 B9
Zuidlaren, *Neths.* 16 B9
Zuidwolde, *Neths.* 16 C8
Zújar, *Spain* 29 H2
Zújar →, *Spain* 31 F5
Zújar, Pantano del, *Spain* 31 G5
Zula, *Eritrea* 77 D4
Zulia □, *Venezuela* 120 B3
Zülpich, *Germany* 18 E2
Zumaya, *Spain* 28 B2
Zumbo, *Mozam.* 83 F3
Zummo, *Nigeria* 79 D7
Zumpango, *Mexico* 115 D5
Zundert, *Neths.* 17 F5
Zungeru, *Nigeria* 79 D6
Zunhua, *China* 51 D9
Zuni, *U.S.A.* 111 J9
Zunyi, *China* 52 D6
Zuoquan, *China* 50 F7
Zuozhou, *China* 52 F6
Županja, *Croatia* 21 K8
Zurbātīyah, *Iraq* 67 F12
Zürich, *Switz.* 23 B7
Zürich □, *Switz.* 23 B7
Zürichsee, *Switz.* 23 B7
Żuromin, *Poland* 20 B9
Zuru, *Nigeria* 79 C6
Zurzach, *Switz.* 23 A6
Žut, *Croatia* 33 E12
Zutendaal, *Belgium* 17 G7
Zutphen, *Neths.* 16 D8
Zuwārah, *Libya* 75 B7
Zūzan, *Iran* 65 C8
Žužemberk, *Slovenia* 33 C11
Zvenigorodka = Zvenyhorodka, *Ukraine* 41 H6
Zvenyhorodka, *Ukraine* 41 H6
Zverinogolovskoye, *Russia* 44 D7
Zvezdets, *Bulgaria* 38 G10
Zvishavane, *Zimbabwe* 83 G3
Zvolen, *Slovak Rep.* 20 G9
Zvonce, *Serbia, Yug.* 21 N12
Zvornik, *Bos.-H.* 21 L9
Zwaag, *Neths.* 16 C6
Zwanenburg, *Neths.* 16 D5
Zwarte Meer, *Neths.* 16 C7
Zwarte Waler, *Neths.* 16 C8
Zwartemeer, *Neths.* 16 C10
Zwartsluis, *Neths.* 16 C8
Zwedru = Tchien, *Liberia* 78 D3
Zweibrücken, *Germany* 19 F3
Zwenkau, *Germany* 18 D8
Zwevegem, *Belgium* 17 G2
Zwickau, *Germany* 18 E8
Zwiesel, *Germany* 19 F9
Zwijnaarde, *Belgium* 17 F3
Zwijndrecht, *Belgium* 17 F4
Zwijndrecht, *Neths.* 16 E5
Zwischenahn, *Germany* 18 B4
Zwolle, *Neths.* 16 C8
Zwolle, *U.S.A.* 109 K8
Zymoetz →, *Canada* 100 C3
Żyrardów, *Poland* 20 C10
Zyryan, *Kazakstan* 44 E9
Zyryanka, *Russia* 45 C16
Zyryanovsk = Zyryan, *Kazakstan* 44 E9
Zyyi, *Cyprus* 37 E12

KEY TO WORLD MAP PAGES

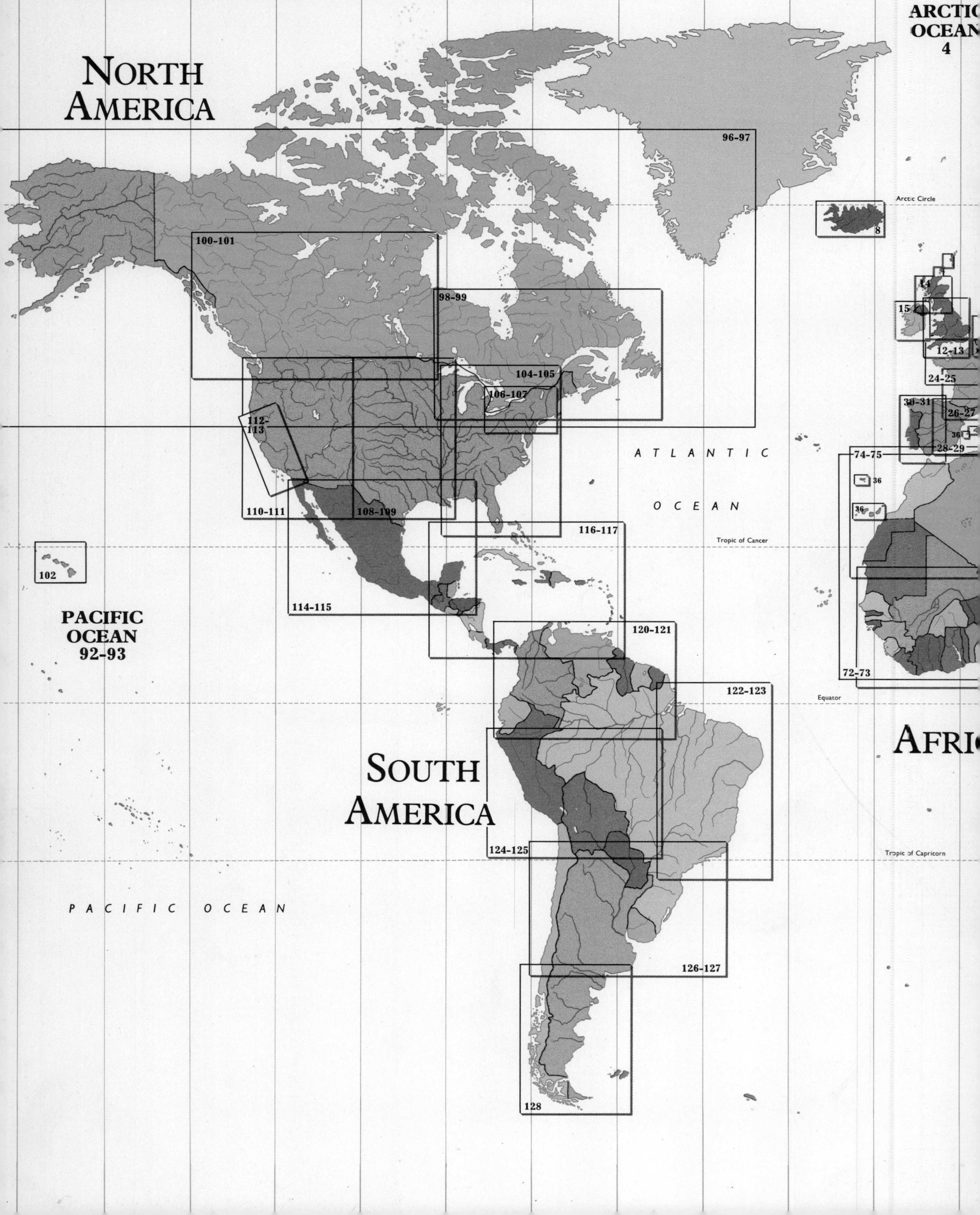
NORTH AMERICA
ARCTIC OCEAN 4
96-97
Arctic Circle
8
100-101
98-99
14
15
12-13
104-105
106-107
24-25
30-31
26-27
112-113
36
28-29
ATLANTIC
74-75
36
36
OCEAN
110-111
108-109
116-117
Tropic of Cancer
102
114-115
PACIFIC OCEAN 92-93
120-121
122-123
72-73
Equator
AFRI
SOUTH AMERICA
124-125
Tropic of Capricorn
PACIFIC OCEAN
126-127
128